T0395942

The Oxford Handbook of Child Protection Systems

OXFORD LIBRARY OF
INTERNATIONAL SOCIAL POLICY

EDITORS-IN-CHIEF

Douglas Besharov and Neil Gilbert
In collaboration with the International Network
for Social Policy Teaching and Research

The Oxford Handbook of Governance and Management for Social Policy
Edited by Karen J. Baehler

The Oxford Handbook of Family Policy Over the Life Course
Edited by Mary Daly, Birgit Pfau-Effinger, Neil Gilbert, and Douglas Besharov

The Oxford Handbook of Child Protection Systems
Edited by Jill Duerr Berrick, Neil Gilbert, and Marit Skivenes

OXFORD LIBRARY OF
INTERNATIONAL SOCIAL POLICY

The Oxford Handbook of Child Protection Systems

Edited by

Jill Duerr Berrick

Neil Gilbert

Marit Skivenes

OXFORD
UNIVERSITY PRESS

OXFORD
UNIVERSITY PRESS

Oxford University Press is a department of the University of Oxford. It furthers
the University's objective of excellence in research, scholarship, and education
by publishing worldwide. Oxford is a registered trade mark of Oxford University
Press in the UK and certain other countries.

Published in the United States of America by Oxford University Press
198 Madison Avenue, New York, NY 10016, United States of America.

© Oxford University Press 2023

Library of Congress Control Number: 2022046972
ISBN 978–0–19–750354–6

DOI: 10.1093/oxfordhb/9780197503546.001.0001

9 8 7 6 5 4 3 2 1

Printed by Marquis, Canada

CONTENTS

Acknowledgments   ix
List of Contributors   xi

1. Child Protection Systems Across the World   1
   Jill Duerr Berrick, Neil Gilbert, and Marit Skivenes

Part I · Institutionalized
2. Child Protection in Australia and New Zealand: An Overview
   of Systems   25
   Judith Cashmore and Nicola Taylor
3. The Austrian Child Welfare System: Moving Towards
   Professionalization and Participation   47
   Katrin Križ, Jenny Krutzinna, and Peter Pantuček-Eisenbacher
4. Child Protection in Belgium: An Overview of the Systems   67
   Johan Vanderfaeillie, Erik Van Dooren, and Jessica Segers
5. Child Welfare in Canada   90
   *Nico Trocmé, Melanie Doucet, Barbara Fallon, Jennifer Nutton, and
   Tonino Esposito*
6. The Child Protection Systems in Denmark and Norway   112
   *Anne-Dorthe Hestbæk, Marit Skivenes, Asgeir Falch-Eriksen, Idamarie
   Leth Svendsen, and Elisabeth Backe-Hansen*
7. Child Welfare and Child Protection Services in England   135
   June Thoburn
8. Child Protection in Finland and Sweden   156
   Ingrid Höjer and Tarja Pösö
9. Child Protection and Welfare in France   173
   Flora Bolter
10. Child Protection and Welfare in Germany   195
    Kay Biesel and Heinz Kindler
11. Child Protection and Welfare on the Island of Ireland: Irish Themes,
    Global Relevance   216
    Kenneth Burns, John Devaney, Stephanie Holt, and Gerry Marshall

12. Child Protection in Israel   239
    Daphna Gross-Manos, Eran Melkman, and Aya Almog-Zaken
13. Child Protection in Mediterranean Countries: Italy and Greece   261
    Teresa Bertotti, Roberta T. Di Rosa, and Charis Asimopoulos
14. A New Era for Child Protection in Japan   287
    Shoko Tokunaga, Mitsuru Fukui, Misa Saigo, and Saki Nagano
15. The Child Protection System in the Netherlands: Characteristics, Trends, and Evidence   294
    Erik J. Knorth, Helen Bouma, Hans Grietens, and Mónica López López
16. The Development of the Korean Child Protection System: Cultural Influences, Unique Challenges, and Policy Strategies   316
    Yiyoon Chung and T. J. Lah
17. Child Protection Systems in Spain   332
    Sagrario Segado
18. Child Protection and Children's Services in Switzerland   356
    Stefan Schnurr and Joel Gautschi
19. Child Protection in the United States   381
    Jennifer Lawson and Jill Duerr Berrick

Part II · Emerging

20. The Chilean Child Protection System   399
    Carolina Muñoz-Guzman, Miguel Cillero Bruñol, and Mariana Bernasconi
21. Czech Child Protection after 1989: Between Socialist Legacy and the European Call for Democratic Legitimacy   423
    Victoria Shmidt
22. Child Protection Systems in Estonia and Latvia   444
    Merle Linno and Judit Strömpl
23. Child Protection in Lithuania   467
    Ilona Tamutienė and Dalija Snieškienė
24. Child Protection in Poland   486
    Violetta Tanaś
25. Child Protection in Portugal   506
    Jorge Ferreira
26. The Child Protection System in the Slovak Republic   527
    Lenka Kvašňáková and Beáta Balogová
27. Child Protection in South Africa   544
    Julia Sloth-Nielsen
28. The Child Protection System in Uruguay   564
    María del Luján González Tornaría and Delfina Miller

Part III · Nascent

29. Building the Child Protection System in Argentina   587
    Carla Villalta and Valeria Llobet

30. Child Protection Systems in Brazil   608
    Diene Monique Carlos, Ailton de Souza Aragão, Eliana Mendes de Souza Teixeira Roque, and Lygia Maria Pereira da Silva

31. Child Protection Policy and Service in China   625
    Fang Zhao and Yanfeng Xu

32. The Colombian Child Protection System   648
    María Cristina Torrado P. and Ernesto Duran Strauch

33. Child and Adolescent Protection Systems in Ecuador   666
    Verónica Jiménez Borja, Micaela Jiménez-Borja, and Teresita Borja-Álvarez

34. Child Protection in Egypt   683
    Hmoud S. Olimat and Amal A. ElGamal

35. Child Protection Systems in Ghana   706
    Mavis Dako-Gyeke, Abigail Adubea Mills, and Doris Akyere Boateng

36. The Child Protection System in India: An Overview   724
    Sanjai Bhatt and Subhashree Sanyal

37. The Social Construction and Development of an Integrated Child Protection System: In Search of Core Templates in a Diversified and Decentralized Indonesia   747
    Erna Dinata

38. Child Protection in Iran   771
    Marzieh Takaffoli, Meroe Vameghi, Maliheh Arshi, and Leila Ostadhashemi

39. Child Protection in Lebanon   794
    Hoda Rizk

40. Children at Risk in Mexico: Issues, Policies, and Interventions   814
    Martha Frías-Armenta

41. The Child Protection System in Nigeria   832
    Chimezie L. Elekwachi and Peter O. Ebigbo

42. Protecting Children in the Philippines: A System-focused Overview of Policy and Practice   851
    Steven Roche and Florence Flores-Pasos

43. Reforming Russia's Child Protection System: From Residential to Family Care   877
    Meri Kulmala, Maija Jäppinen, and Zhanna Chernova

44. Child Protection Systems in Uganda   900
    Deogratias Yiga

45. Making Child Protection Systems Work for Children: Lessons from Zimbabwe   922
   Mildred T. Mushunje

Conclusion

46. Child Protection Systems: A Global Typology   943
   Jill Duerr Berrick, Neil Gilbert, and Marit Skivenes

Index   971

ACKNOWLEDGMENTS

A body of work of this size requires the generosity of many. We offer our thanks to the chapter authors from across the globe who patiently responded to multiple requests for clarification, edits, and adjustments over many months. For their critical review of the introductory and concluding chapters, we are indebted to Kenneth Burns, Katrin Kriz, Tarja Pösö, and June Thoburn. And for assistance with editing, organizing, and providing a range of general assistance tasks, we extend our sincere gratitude to the following individuals associated with the University of Bergen: Siri Hansen Pedersen, Barbara Ruiken, Trond Helland, Amy McEwan-Strand, and Florian Wingens. With financial support from the Zellerbach Family Foundation Chair and the Chernin Chair in Social Welfare at UC Berkeley we extend our appreciation to Joe Roscoe, Angie Wooton, and Kelly Ziemer. This project has also received funding from the European Research Council (ERC) under the European Union's Horizon 2020 research and innovation programme (grant agreement no. 724460) and from the Research Council of Norway under the Independent Projects—Humanities and Social Science program (grant no. 262773). Finally, we would like to thank the members of the International Network for Social Policy Teaching and Research Advisory Board for their thoughtful review and constructive recommendations.

LIST OF CONTRIBUTORS

Aya Almog-Zaken
  Brookdale Institute, Israel.
Teresita Borja-Álvarez
  Universidad San Francisco de Quito
  USFQ, Ecuador.
Ailton de Souza Aragão
  Triângulo Mineiro Federal University,
  Uberaba, MG, Brazil.
Maliheh Arshi
  Department of Social Work,
  University of Social Welfare and
  Rehabilitation Sciences, Iran.
Charis Asimopoulos
  Department of Social Work,
  University of West Attika, Greece.
Elisabeth Backe-Hansen
  Oslo Metropolitan University, Norway.
Beáta Balogová
  Institute of Educology and Social
  Work, Faculty of Arts, University of
  Presov, Slovakia.
Mariana Bernasconi
  Psicóloga Clínica, Red de
  Apoyo Psicológico Feminista
  RedPsicoFem, Chile.
Jill Duerr Berrick
  School of Social Welfare, U.C.
  Berkeley, USA.
Teresa Bertotti
  Department of Sociology and Social
  Research, University of Trento, Italy.
Sanjai Bhatt
  Department of Social Work,
  University of Delhi, India.

Kay Biesel
  School of Social Work, Institute
  for Studies in Children and Youth
  Services, University of Applied
  Sciences and Arts North Western
  Switzerland FHNW, Switzerland.
Doris Akyere Boateng
  Department of Social Work,
  University of Ghana, Legon, Ghana.
Flora Bolter
  Association Française de Science
  Politique, France.
Verónica Jiménez Borja
  Universidad San Francisco de Quito
  USFQ, Ecuador.
Micaela Jiménez-Borja
  Universidad San Francisco de Quito
  USFQ, Ecuador.
Helen Bouma
  Expertise and Treatment Center for
  Child Protection and Family Welfare,
  Fier, The Netherlands.
Miguel Cillero Bruñol
  Law School Universidad Diego
  Portales, Chile.
Kenneth Burns
  School of Applied Social Studies,
  Social Work, University College
  Cork, Ireland.
Diene Monique Carlos
  Federal University of São Carlos,
  São Paolo, Brazil.
Judith Cashmore
  Research Centre for Children and
  Families and Sydney Law School,
  University of Sydney, Australia.

Zhanna Chernova
Smolny College of Liberal Arts and Sciences and Sociological Institute of the Ras, Russia.

Yiyoon Chung
Konkuk University, South Korea.

Mavis Dako-Gyeke
Department of Social Work, Centre for Ageing Studies, University of Ghana, Legon, Ghana.

John Devaney
School of Social and Political Science, University of Edinburgh, UK.

Roberta T. Di Rosa
Department Culture and Society, University of Palermo, Italy.

Erna Dinata
Department of Social Work, University of South Dakota, USA.

Melanie Doucet
School of Social Work, McGill University, Canada.

Peter O. Ebigbo
University of Nigeria, Nsukka, (emeritus), Nigeria.

Chimezie L. Elekwachi
African Network for the Prevention and Protection Against Child Abuse and Neglect, ANPPCAN, Nigeria Chapter.

Amal A. ElGamal
Social Work Program, Department of Social Sciences, Qatar University.

Tonino Esposito
School of Social Work, University of Montreal, Canada.

Asgeir Falch-Eriksen
Department of Social Work, Child Welfare and Social Policy, Oslo Metropolitan University, Norway.

Barbara Fallon
Factor-Inwentash Faculty of Social Work, University of Toronto, Canada.

Jorge Ferreira
ISCTE – University Institute of Lisbon, Portugal.

Florence Flores-Pasos
College of Social Work and Community Development (CSWCD), University of the Philippines, Philippines.

Martha Frías-Armenta
Law Department, University of Sonora, Mexico.

Mitsuru Fukui
Family Services Development Division, Fukuoka City Children's Bureau, Japan.

Joel Gautschi
Institute of Childhood, Youth and Family, ZHAW Zurich University of Applied Sciences, Switzerland.

Neil Gilbert
School of Social Welfare, U.C. Berkeley, USA.

Hans Grietens
Department of Parenting and Special Education, Faculty of Psychology and Educational Sciences, University of Leuven, Belgium.

Daphna Gross-Manos
Social Work Department, Tel Hai University, Israel.

Anne-Dorthe Hestbæk
The Danish National Centre for Social Research, Denmark.

Ingrid Höjer
Department of Social Work, University of Gothenburg, Sweden.

Stephanie Holt
School of Social Work and Social Policy, Trinity College Dublin, Ireland.

Maija Jäppinen
Social Work, University of Helsinki, Finland.

Heinz Kindler
DIJ German Youth Institute, Munich, Germany.

Erik J. Knorth
Department of Child and Family Welfare, Faculty of Behavioral and Social Sciences, University of Groningen, The Netherlands.

Katrin Križ
Department of Sociology, Emmanuel College, USA.

Jenny Krutzinna
Department of Media and Communication (IMK), University of Oslo, Norway.

Meri Kulmala
Faculty of Social Sciences, University of Helsinki, Finland.

Lenka Kvašňáková
Institute of Educology and Social Work, Faculty of Arts, University of Presov, Slovak Republic.

T. J. Lah
Yonsei University, South Korea.

Jennifer Lawson
Texas Alliance of Child and Family Services, and Texas Center for Child and Family Studies, USA.

Merle Linno
Institute of Social Studies, University of Tartu, Estonia.

Valeria Llobet
Laboratorio de Ciencias Humanas – CONICET-UNSAM, Argentina.

Mónica López López
Department of Child and Family Welfare, Faculty of Behavioral and Social Sciences, University of Groningen, The Netherlands.

Gerry Marshall
School of Social Sciences, Education and Social Work, Queen's University Belfast, Northern Ireland.

Eran Melkman
Department of Education, Tel Aviv University, Israel.

Delfina Miller
Universidad Católica del Uruguay, Uruguay.

Abigail Adubea Mills
Department of Social Work, University of Ghana, Legon, Ghana.

Carolina Muñoz-Guzman
School of Social Work, Pontificia Universidad Católica de Chile, Chile.

Mildred T. Mushunje
School of Social Work, Midlands State University, Zimbabwe.

Saki Nagano
Department of Social Welfare, Faculty of Human Sciences, Musashino University, Japan.

Jennifer Nutton
University of Victoria, Canada.

Hmoud S. Olimat
Social Work Program, Doha Institute for Graduate Studies, Doha, Qatar.

Leila Ostadhashemi
Department of Social Work, University of Social Welfare and Rehabilitation Sciences, Iran.

Peter Pantuček-Eisenbacher
Bertha von Suttner Private University, St. Pölten, Austria.

Tarja Pösö
Faculty of Social Sciences, Tampere University, Finland.

Hoda Rizk
Institute of Social Science, Lebanese University, Lebanon.

Steven Roche
College of Health and Human Sciences, Charles Darwin University, Australia.

Eliana Mendes de Souza Teixeira Roque
Ribeirão Preto University (retired),
Brazil.

Misa Saigo
HITOTOWA INC./Research
Institute for Children's Social Care,
Waseda University, Japan.

Subhashree Sanyal
Department of Social Work, Visva
Bharati University Sriniketan, India.

Stefan Schnurr
School of Social Work, Institute
for Studies in Children and Youth
Services, University of Applied
Sciences and Arts North Western
Switzerland FHNW, Switzerland.

Sagrario Segado
Department of Social Work,
Distance Education National
University, and European Research
Center for Policies and Actions on
Minors and Migration, Spain.

Jessica Segers
SOS Children Agency of the Office
of Birth and Childhood, Belgium.

Victoria Shmidt
Center of Southeastern European
History and Anthropology,
University of Graz, Austria.

Lygia Maria Pereira da Silva
Nossa Senhora das Graças Nursing
School, University of Pernambuco,
Recife, PE, Brazil.

Marit Skivenes
Centre for Research on Discretion
and Paternalism, Department of
Government, University of Bergen,
Norway.

Julia Sloth-Nielsen
School of Law, University of
Huddersfield, UK.

Dalija Snieškienė
Vytautas Magnus University,
Lithuania.

Ernesto Duran Strauch
Centro de Estudios Sociales,
Universidad Nacional de Colombia.

Judit Strömpl
Institute of Social Studies, University
of Tartu, Estonia.

Idamarie Leth Svendsen
Department of Social Work,
University College Copenhagen,
Denmark.

Marzieh Takaffoli
Social Welfare Management Research
Center, University of Social Welfare
and Rehabilitation Sciences, Iran.

Ilona Tamutienė
Department of Public
Administration, Vytautas Magnus
University, Lithuania.

Violetta Tanaś
Department of Social Sciences,
Academy of Business and Health
Sciences, University of Lodz, Poland.

Nicola Taylor
Faculty of Law, University of
Otago; Children's Issues Centre,
New Zealand.

June Thoburn
Department of Social Work,
University of East Anglia, England.

Shoko Tokunaga
Ritsumeikan University,
Kyoto, Japan.

María del Luján González Tornaría
Universidad Católica del Uruguay,
Uruguay.

María Cristina Torrado P.
Centro de Estudios Sociales.
Universidad Nacional de, Colombia.

Nico Trocmé
    School of Social Work, McGill
    University, Canada.
Meroe Vameghi
    Social Welfare Management Research
    Center, University of Social Welfare
    and Rehabilitation Sciences, Iran.
Erik Van Dooren
    Brussels Confidential Center of
    Child Abuse and Neglect, Belgium.
Johan Vanderfaeillie
    Faculty of Psychology and
    Educational Sciences, Vrije
    Universiteit Brussel, Belgium.

Carla Villalta
    Instituto de Ciencias Antropológicas,
    Facultad de Filosofía y Letras,
    Universidad de Buenos Aires,
    Argentina.
Yanfeng Xu
    College of Social Work, University of
    South Carolina, USA.
Deogratias Yiga
    Development Links Consult,
    Uganda.
Fang Zhao
    Department of Social Work, School
    of Social Development and Public
    Policy, Fudan University, China.

Child Protection Systems Across the World

Jill Duerr Berrick, Neil Gilbert, *and* Marit Skivenes

Abstract

This introductory chapter presents a landscape view of the vast range of demographic, social, and cultural differences among the 50 countries throughout the world, which are included in the Handbook's case studies of child protection systems. The differences in, for example, standards of living, children's rights and their levels of well-being, types and levels of state intervention, and degree of confidence in government have a bearing on the alternative developmental stages of child protection systems among the 50 countries. This chapter also reviews the comparative analytic framework that focuses on four fundamental dimensions of choice employed to provide systematic information on the design of each country's child protection system and its policies. The chapter closes with a discussion of how this comparative lens will be used to develop a new global typology that is elaborated in the Handbook's concluding chapter.

Key Words: child protection, children, parents, society, modernization, UNCRC, human rights

Introduction

Across the spectrum of political ideologies there is, in principle, widespread agreement that the state has a legitimate role in protecting children from harm. Even the Nobel Prize winning economist Milton Friedman (1962), among the most ardent liberal supporters of the laissez-faire philosophy, recognized this "paternalistic" function of government. At the same time, the traditional view of children, that they are the property of the father (pater) or the parents, is under pressure (Zelizer, 1994; James & Prout, 1997; Archard, 2004). Societies are at an intersection when it comes to how children are treated and how their rights are respected, which creates tensions in the traditional relationship between the family and the state. Children are a focus of government responsibility under certain state-defined norms relating to harm and need. And parents are sometimes constrained by the state from exercising their (familial or property) rights under state-defined criteria of harm and need.

The process of modernization in the 20th century has resulted in new sensitivities about human rights across the globe, with increased recognition of marginalized groups in society. Among these developments, the rights of children have increasingly become a direct concern of the state (Archard 2004; Shapiro 1999). These considerations about children's rights and the growing role of the state are codified in the United Nations Convention on the Rights of the Child (UNCRC) of 1989. The UN Convention advances four core principles related to children's rights (Sutherland and Macfarlane, 2016). According to these principles:

1. The state is obliged to protect children's rights and to shield them from discrimination (Article 2).
2. The state is expected to ensure children's survival and development (Article 6).
3. Children should be afforded the opportunity to participate in decisions concerning them (Article 12).
4. A "best interests" standard should be applied in all state actions concerning children (Article 3).

Impressive gains have been made in some areas pertaining to children's rights in the 30 years since the CRC was ratified by the United Nations Assembly. In the areas of health, immunization, and mortality, children are better off today than they were prior to the Convention. Educational advances have also occurred; today many more children attend primary school, and disparities in educational access for girls has diminished markedly (UNICEF, 2019a). In other areas germane to the topic of this book, progress in securing children's rights to an adequate standard of care, safety, and protection has been less pronounced. Child maltreatment, in all its forms, is a serious issue on a global scale (Stoltenborgh et al., 2015). This is recognized in Article 19 of the UNCRC, which highlights children's right to protection from all types of maltreatment along with the state's responsibility to implement social programs and a system to protect against abuse and neglect within a judicial frame of due process:

1. State Parties shall take all appropriate legislative, administrative, social and educational measures to protect the child from all forms of physical or mental violence, injury or abuse, neglect or negligent treatment, maltreatment or exploitation, including sexual abuse, while in the care of parent(s), legal guardian(s) or any other person who has the care of the child.
2. Such protective measures should, as appropriate, include effective procedures for the establishment of social programs to provide necessary support for the child and for those who have the care of the child, as well as for other forms of prevention and for identification, reporting, referral, investigation, treatment and follow-up of instances of child maltreatment described heretofore, and, as appropriate, for judicial involvement (Article 19).

This Handbook describes and analyzes the ways in which 50 countries from every continent, except Antarctica, have devised measures for child protection emphasized in the UNCRC. In 2019, there were about 2.5 billion children in the world. The countries represented in this Handbook account for more than one-half of the world's child population. The UNCRC was rapidly adopted by dozens of countries in the early 1990s. Today, all of the countries in the world except the United States have ratified the Convention. The United States signed the UN Convention, thereby endorsing its principles,[1] and most American laws are already consistent with the UNCRC (Alderson, 2000; S.C. 2013).

The worldwide affirmation of the UNCRC commits nations to design measures for the protection and advancement of child welfare and child well-being. Article 19, section 2, outlines the procedural and system requirements that states must ensure are in place, in addition to supportive services to prevent and treat child maltreatment. Additional articles in the Convention specifically address risk for children, such as Articles 34, 35, and 36, on the right to be free from sexual and other forms of exploitation, and Article 37 on the right not to experience torture and ill treatment. In response, many countries have formulated legislation, implemented policies, and developed networks of public and private services to safeguard children against many forms of maltreatment.

But government bodies across the world vary dramatically in their understandings of maltreatment. What does "protection against physical violence" mean when corporal punishment is outlawed in one country, but in another, the large majority of children experience harsh physical discipline at the hands of parents? What does "protection from sexual abuse" mean when one country prohibits sexual contact between adults and children under age 18, and another country allows child marriage for girls under the age of 10? The common characteristic is the state's interest in protection from maltreatment, but the central problem of concern is not defined the same way by all countries.

This Handbook discusses the legislative responses, public administrative systems, and social service networks that governments have put in place to secure the protection of children against maltreatment and exploitation. Our focus is on the *systems* that are established for protecting children "while in the care of parent(s), legal guardian(s) or any other person who has the care of the child" (Article 19). Such systems may be labeled child protection systems or child welfare systems (or other country-specific labels). In this volume we use the term child protection system. Although the OECD (2011), WHO (Sethi et al., 2014) and the Committee on Social Affairs, Health and Sustainable Development (World Health Organization, 2015, para 8.6) have all requested systematic knowledge and reliable data about child protection systems, uniformity and accuracy have not yet

---

[1] However, the USA did not formally ratify, which requires approval by a two-thirds majority of the US Senate. Hence, while the US endorses the UN Convention, it is not legally bound by the treaty. The USA's reluctance to ratify the UNCRC was based on concerns that the social and economic rights established by the treaty could undermine parental authority and usurp American sovereignty.

been realized. While this Handbook cannot fully resolve the problematic lack of data, it provides a detailed survey of the varied landscape of child protection arrangements in 50 countries throughout the world (as shown in Figure 1.1). In spite of the wealth of information presented here, we recognize that significant knowledge gaps remain in terms of the functioning and workings of child protection systems.

To describe a child protection system, we must start with a definition of the child. Even this is contested and open to interpretation in the literature and among states. Children are defined by UNICEF as persons below the age of 18 years. Most countries align with the UNICEF definition, but a handful of states in this volume (for example Lebanese Republic and Slovak Republic) primarily aim to protect children below age 13 or 14, and others include young adults up to 21 and 25 years (Sweden and Finland, respectively). The definition of children is also of relevance for the administrative data available; for some countries the child population includes those from ages 0–19 (for example, Sweden) and for others it is the ages 0–14 (Czech Republic) or 0–15 (Argentina).

The child protection arrangements in many of these countries are in different stages of development (Gilbert 1997; Hetherington, Cooper, Smith, & Wilford, 1997; Gilbert et al., 2011; Burns et al., 2017). They vary on a number of dimensions such as: the definition of risks, how state responses are regulated and organized, decision-making processes for determining eligibility, the level of professionalization, the degree of service integration, and the availability of administrative data to keep track of operations. In some countries, child protection systems are well developed, embedded in law, professionally enacted, and administratively well documented. Elsewhere, these systems are still

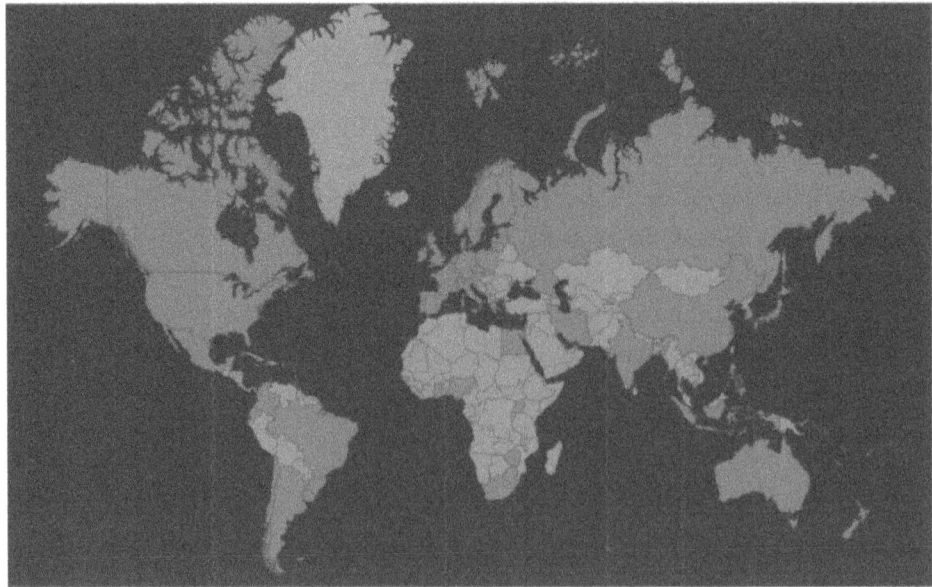

Figure 1.1 Overview of countries included in the Handbook

in an early phase of development, are loosely organized, and largely reflect local interests and efforts. This Handbook discusses the *child protection systems* that are established for protecting children "while in the care of parent(s), legal guardian(s) or any other person who has the care of the child" (Article 19). Thus, this Handbook is about each country government's responsibility to establish a system that has the authority to intervene into the family to support, restrict and even terminate parental rights if parents or caregivers are unable or unwilling to protect the child. This Handbook shows that some children are living in exceptionally difficult conditions everywhere, facing life-threatening violence, abuse, and deprivation. The magnitude of problems and the number of children affected by such difficulties are, however, very different across societies. The developmental stage of the child protection system within a state appears to be correlated with the developmental stage of the overall welfare state and the governmental institutions in a country. Protecting children's rights, of course, is more difficult in low-income countries where living standards pose general risks for families and the welfare state does not have sufficient resources to respond to family needs and assist parents and the family to provide for their children.

Living Standards, Child Well-being, and Child Protection

Living conditions such as the degree of poverty, access to health services, and availability of education are related to the types of risks children face and the types of protection they require. In India, for example, a country with one-fifth of the world's population, a large proportion of children live in extreme situations of deprivation. Many children live on the streets, they lack access to educational opportunities, they are forced into labor, and some are involved in armed conflict. In contrast, none of these circumstances apply to children in many of the western countries. In Denmark or Norway, for example, children enjoy a high level of well-being, little poverty, and generous services to meet their needs. Respective protection of children against neglect, abuse, and maltreatment is bound to be very different in India and the Nordic countries, just on these grounds. And even within the OECD countries there are large differences in children's living standards and levels of well-being (UNICEF 2013).

Indeed, the context of need and care varies widely across the globe. Many children in low-income countries are separated temporarily from their parents due to work-related migration or permanently due to death. In high-income countries, however, parent–child separation is much more likely due to intrusive interventions by the state.[2] Parents' expression of care toward their children varies widely as well. In some sub-Saharan African nations, the prevalence of severe corporal punishment is high (Nkuba et al., 2018); 90% of children in Ghana, for example, report experiencing physical violence at home or at school (Dako-Gyeke et al., this volume). Family life for children in Ghana poses a stark

---

[2] Not including divorce in which the state functions as arbitrator (Scott & Karberg, 2016), a qualitatively different phenomenon.

contrast to the experiences of children in the 63 countries that have outlawed corporal punishment.[3] Violence, in general, is more prevalent in some countries than others, either within the family due to high rates of domestic violence (e.g., Mexico and Poland), or in the community due to crime (e.g., Venezuela[4]) or due to war and terrorism (e.g., Nigeria and India).

Of course, the context of poverty significantly influences child and family well-being. According to UNICEF, almost 20% of children throughout the world live on less than $2 a day (UNICEF, 2019b), which has implications for malnutrition, stunted growth, limited education, and early death (Pemberton et al., 2007). Parents' capacities to effectively care for their children under conditions of extreme deprivation must be considered as a powerful factor shaping the definitional frame and the public response to child protection. In many high-income countries, the correlation between family poverty and child maltreatment is high. Bywaters and colleagues make the case forcefully: "There is a strong association between families' socio-economic circumstances and the chances that their children will experience CAN [child abuse and neglect]. This association exists across developed countries, types of abuse, definitions, measures and research approaches to both poverty and CAN, and different child protection systems" (2016, p. 21). As an example of the severe impact of poverty, UNICEF points out that "children from the poorest households are, on average twice as likely to die before they reach their fifth birthday than children from the most affluent households" (UNICEF 2019a, p. 3).

Rates of parental violence against children, and the injury and death of children are all more prevalent in low-income countries (Krug et al., 2002). The 2019 UNICEF report marking the 30th year of the CRC identifies the many achievements reached in improving children's health, opportunities for education, empowerment, and recognition across the world. However, the most vulnerable children, especially those in low-income countries, too often do not experience these positive developments. One such problem area is child marriage, for example, which has shown an overall decline globally, but with slow progress in the poorest countries. In some countries, "children may even be at a somewhat higher risk of child marriage today than children were three decades ago" (UNICEF 2019a, p. 3). Challenges such as these accentuate the need to examine thoroughly how governments are protecting children being exploited, mistreated or neglected.

---

[3] This handbook covers 25 countries of the 63 countries that have outlawed corporeal punishment. Specifically, Argentina, Austria, Brazil, Colombia, Denmark, Estonia, Finland, France, Germany, Greece, Ireland, Israel, Japan, Korea, Latvia, Lithuania, Netherlands, New Zealand, Norway, Poland, Portugal, South Africa, Spain, Sweden, and Uruguay. https://endcorporalpunishment.org/reports-on-every-state-and-territory/, retrieved June 24, 2022.

[4] Due to Venezuela's significant political instability, it is currently ranked as the country with the highest crime rate in the world. See http://worldpopulationreview.com/countries/crime-rate-by-country/, retrieved June 24, 2022.

The 50 countries in this book represent a vast range of living standards using a conventional measure of Gross Domestic Product (GDP) per capita (Figure 1.2). Switzerland, Ireland, and Norway enjoy very high rates of GDP at or near 80,000 USD per capita. Nigeria, India, and Uganda, in contrast, are at or near the bottom, with 1,000 USD or less per capita. This measure offers some indication of family living standards, though the data do not speak directly to children's need for protection.

In addition to GDP per capita, there are various measures employed to characterize children's well-being globally. The Kids Rights Index (KRI) is an annual global index that ranks countries based on several composite measures, to indicate the degree to which

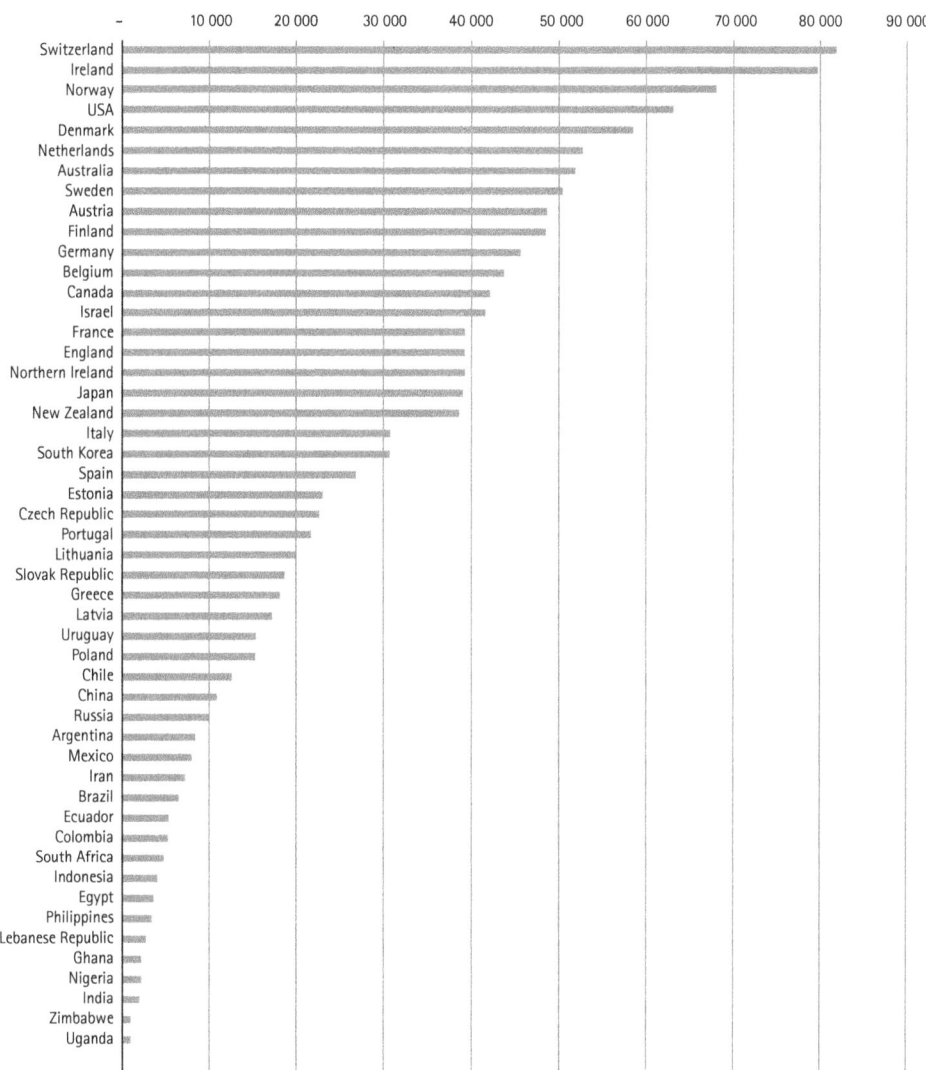

Figure 1.2 Rankings of GDP per capita (2020)

countries attend to children's rights. There are five domains included in the assessment: (1) Right to Life; (2) Right to Health; (3) Right to Education; (4) Right to Protection (defined according to measures of child labor, the adolescent birth rate, and birth registration); and (5) Enabling Environment for Child Rights. The measure is a rough approximation of children's rights, although there are concerns about the accuracy of the data available in some countries and the extent to which the measures included offer an appropriate definition of children's "rights."[5] Moreover, the difference between countries that are numerically close may be less meaningful than grouping countries in wide bands of similarity. With these caveats, the KRI, along with measures of GDP per capita, provides ballpark estimates for comparing children's circumstances from a global perspective. We return to this later in the chapter.

A majority of the countries in this Handbook score relatively high on the KRI (see Figure 1.3).[6] Most country scores have been relatively stable since 2013, so we report data from the most recent report (2019). The countries appear to cluster into three general groups, shown here as high (scores of 0.8–1.0), medium (0.7–0.8), and low (below 0.7).

Whether we assess children's circumstances by means of GDP or KRI, some general patterns emerge (with some exceptions). Of the 18 richest countries included in this Handbook (Switzerland to France in Figure 1.2), all are rated highly on the KRI. Countries in the mid-range on GDP (Japan to Lithuania) typically have somewhat lower KRI scores. And countries with relatively low GDPs also struggle to provide for a robust children's rights context. These variations in living standards and in the promotion of children's rights have implications for child protection needs as well as for the level of development of the systems established in response to these needs.

In the WHO-UNICEF Lancet commission report (Clark et al., 2020) a total of 180 countries are measured and ranked on fundamental conditions for children to survive and thrive (Child Flourishing Index). In Figure 1.4 the rankings of those counties in the Handbook are presented, and here the correlation between the general living conditions in a society and children's opportunities in life is also clearly evident.

Child Protection Systems in Action

Almost all of the countries in the Handbook firmly express their responsibility for children in legislation. Some have included child protection matters in one law that separately regulates the child protection system, such as Estonia's *Family Law Act 2015*, regulating

---

[5] The UK and New Zealand's low rankings are attributed to discrimination against children from minority groups such as refugees or migrants as well as concerns that the views of children, especially children from poorer social backgrounds, are systematically unheard in policymaking on issues that affect them. https://www.kidsrightsindex.org/News/ArticleID/20/KidsRights-Index-2019-Economic-growth-doesnt-lead-to-improved-childrens-rights). An objection to including the CRC committees' country report as a source is that its information may not have been checked for accuracy (see Sætre, 2017; Helland, 2019).

[6] The United States is not included in the KRI.

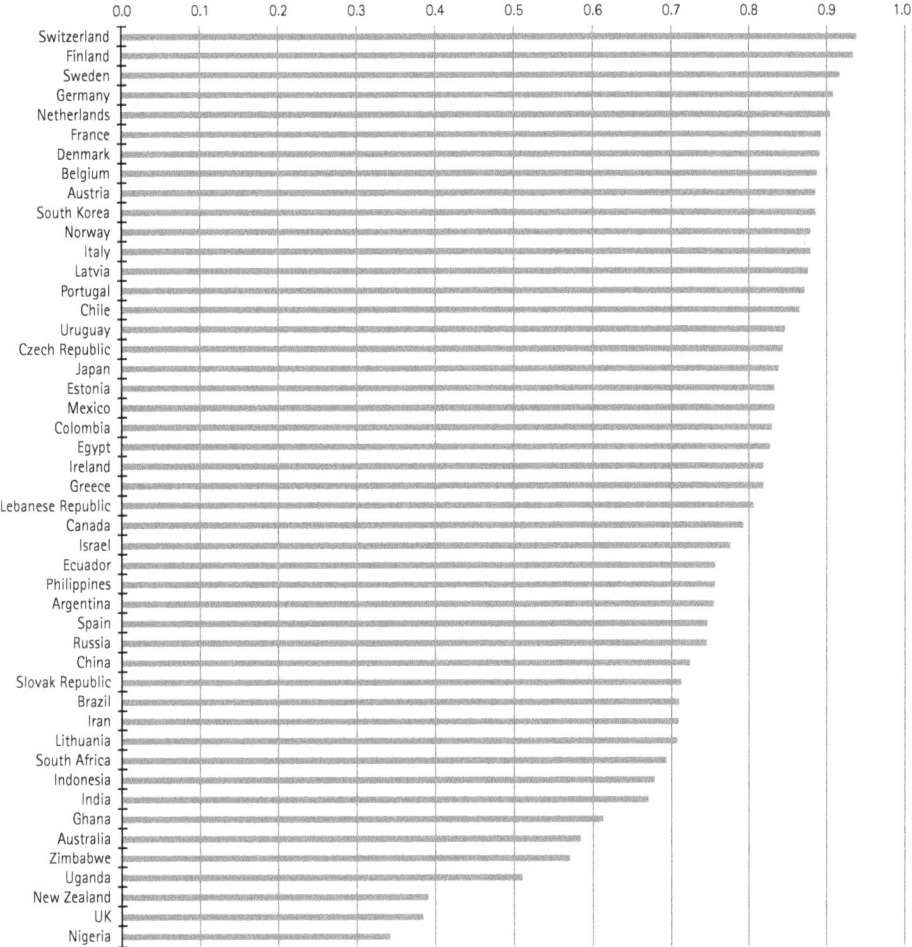

Figure 1.3 Handbook countries ranking on Kids Right Index (KRI) (2020) Note: Poland is not included due to lack of data. USA has not ratified the CRC and is thus not included.

the rights and obligations of parents and the grounds for removal and adoption of children. Similarly, South Korea's relatively recent *Special Act on the Punishment of Child Abuse 2013* outlines procedures for child maltreatment reporting, investigation, and response. Other countries have a series of laws regulating various areas of child abuse and neglect, such as the Slovak Republic, regulating child protection in the *Constitution*, in a *Family Act*, a *Social Protection of Children Act*, and a *Social Work Act*. Uganda also has a range of laws regulating the rights of children and prohibition of child marriage, the *Prohibition of Female Genital Mutilation Act*, the *Trafficking in Persons Act*, and others. Some countries have combined child protection with protection for other groups. For example, Denmark and Sweden have general social services acts (*Consolidation Act of Social Services* and *Social Services Act*, respectively), covering children, the elderly, the disabled, and other groups in need of public support.

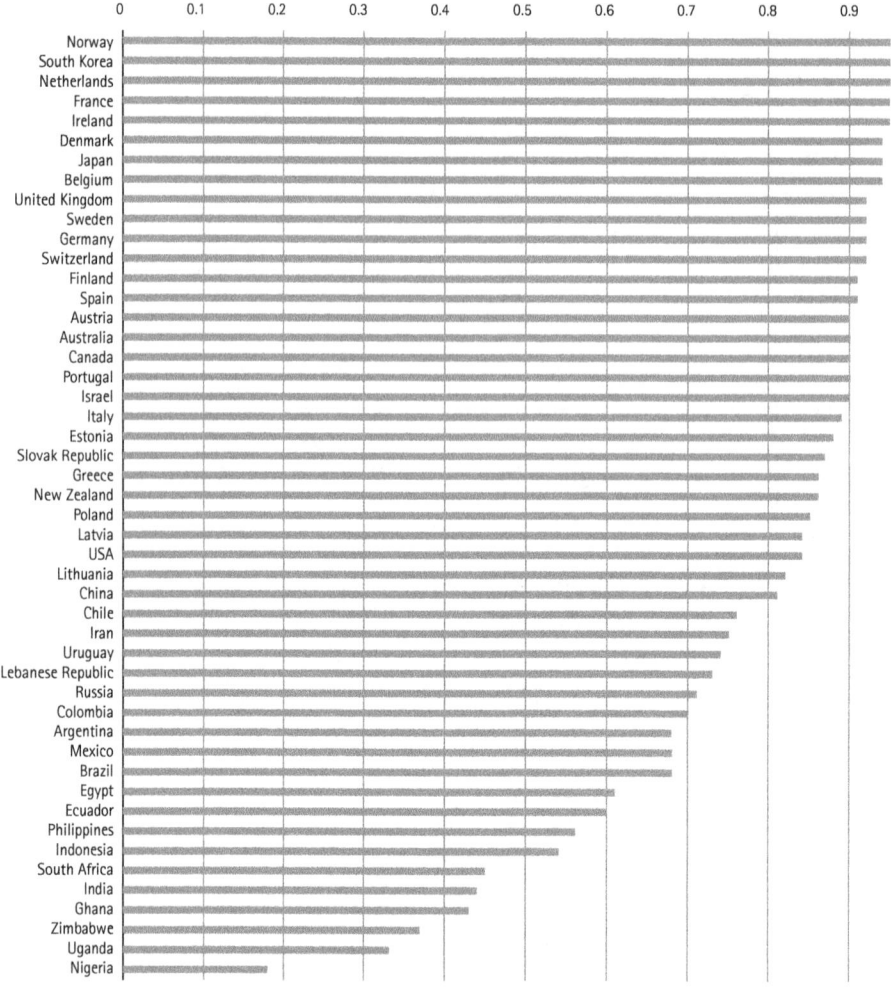

Figure 1.4 Child flourishing index (2020) Note: N = 48; Czech Republic not included; for England and Ireland, data for UK is used. For full overview, see Clark et al. (2020).

The way child protection is regulated involves deliberate choices—as to whether it is a criminal matter or a social problem—which reflect a country's legal traditions and governmental culture about how problems are treated. For example, Norway was the first country with a child protection act (*Guardian Council Act* (Vergerådsloven), 1896). The dual motivation for the law was to protect society against criminal and unwanted behavior, as well as to protect and raise children in need (Dahl, 1978). However, the law leaned towards a child perspective as the age for being criminally responsible was set at age 14 (today it is 15). By way of contrast, India has a criminally responsible age of 7, and England and Wales have set it at age 10.

The state's authority to undertake intrusive interventions into the family by restricting, sometimes even terminating, parental rights, is a controversial aspect of child protection systems. To secure due process and the rule of law, the courts have the authority to make decisions about involuntary and/or intrusive interventions in the large majority of the countries included in this volume. There are a variety of court types. Some use the ordinary court systems with decision making in district courts; others rely on specialized courts such as family courts, juvenile courts, orphan's courts, and so on. In the remaining countries there are established decision-making bodies that are interdisciplinary and have the character of a board or committee.

Whatever the type of decision-making body, any state removal of a child is consequential. All nations include procedures for separating children from their parents. The United Nations has also developed guidelines to support quality care environments for children (see: Better Care Network Guidelines on Alternative Care, 2019). Nonetheless, there is considerable variation in the frequency with which governments remove children for child protection purposes. The data in Table 1.1 offer an overview of national out-of-home placement rates, which range from lows of 0.4 and 0.6 per 1,000 children in Ecuador and Columbia, respectively, to highs of 14.3 per 1,000 children in the Czech Republic and 21.4 per 1,000 children in South Africa (see Table 1.1, column 4). These numerical summaries, however, are based on metrics that are not entirely equivalent. The high placement rates for Russia and Finland, for example, include the total number of children who experienced a removal at any time during the year (flow), and children may be counted twice. This metric typically yields a larger rate than a point-in-time (stock), which provides a snapshot of the number of children being cared for on a particular date each year. Neither figure tells us how many children entered care that year or how long they remained in care. There are no reliable data available on out-of-home placement for many of the poorest and least developed countries, reflecting both the lack of resources required to provide out-of-home placements and the early stages in the institutionalization of a mature public administrative system to collect empirical information on child protection services. In many of these countries, informal kinship care is the primary source of care for children who cannot live with their parents (Leinaweaver, 2014).

Adoption from care is a permanency measure that is allowed in many countries, but practice varies significantly and knowledge about these governmental interventions and proceedings are often scarce (Burns et al., 2019). For example, a study of eight European countries tellingly titled "*The Hidden Proceedings*," revealed a lack of accountability and oversight relating to the practice of adoption from care (Burns et al., 2019). Based on the country chapters in this volume and the spare information about adoption from care from other sources, we conclude that this is a highly understudied area. Given the information available, we find that some countries actively use adoption as a measure, such as Russia (4.6 per 1,000 children) and USA (0.8 per 1,000 children). Other countries hardly use it, such as Finland (0.005 per 1,000 children), Norway (0.05 per 1,000 children) or Iran (0.07 per 1,000 children) (see Table 1.1, column 6).

Table 1.1 Overview of children placed out of home by the child protection system (based on court order and/or parental agreement or abandonment) and adoptions from care or due to abandonment. N and per 1,000 children # = stock stat/^ = flow/ND = no data

1	2	3	4	5	6
Country	Child population total (0–17) (year)	Children placed out-of-home in total (year)	Out-of-home placements per 1,000 children	Adopted from care in total	Adopted from care per 1,000 children
Argentina	10,222,317 (0–15 years) (2010)	9,219 (2014) #	0.9 #	ND	ND
Australia	5,440,000 (2020)	44,906 (2020) #	8.0 #	147 (2020) ^	0.03
Austria	1,535,958 (2018)	13,325 (2018) ^	8.7 ^	110 (2018) ^	0.07
Belgium	2,301,495 (2018)	22,132 (2012) ^	9.6 ^	ND (few)	ND (few)
Brazil	59,700,000 (0–18) (2015)	ND	ND	ND	ND
Canada	7,006,303 (2015)	62,428 (2015) #	8.9 #	1,633	0.23
Chile	4,250,155 (2017)	14,233 (2017) #	3.3 #	428 (2017) ^	0.1
China	282,260,000 (2016)	ND	ND	ND	ND
Colombia	14,144,000 (2015)	8,691	0.6	1,200	0.008
Czech Republic	1,671,000 (0–14) (2016)	26,372 (2018) #	15.8 #	377	0.23
Denmark	1,168,222 (2016)	11,916 (2016) #	10.2 #	10 (2016) ^	0.009
Ecuador	5,588,000 (2015)	2,462 (2018) ^	0.4 ^	82 (2018) ^	0.015
Egypt	33,400,000 (2017)	ND	ND	ND	ND
England	11,785,311 (2016)	78,150 (2018–19) #	6.5 #	3,570 (2018–19) ^	0.3
Estonia	252,117 (2018)	2,599 (2016) #	10 #	49 (2016)	0.19
Finland	1,071,905 (2016)	17,689 (2015) ^	16.5 ^	5 (2016)	0.005
France	14,420,000 (2020)	146,322 (2015) #	9.9 #	982 (2016)	0.068
Germany	13,470,300 (2016)	145,949 (2016) #	10.8 #	661 (2016)	0.51
Ghana	10,467,808 (2015)	ND	ND	ND	ND
Greece	1,889,916 (2011)	3,000 (2015) #	1.6 #	ND	ND
India	451,990,000 (2016)	ND	ND	ND	ND
Indonesia	79,500,000 (2018)	ND	ND	ND	ND
Iran	22,149,000 (2017)	26,285 # (2016)	1.2 #	1,594 (2016)	0.07
Ireland	1,190,478 (2017)	5,916 (2019) #	5.0 #	21 ^ (2019)	0.02
Israel	2,768,700 (2015)	10,842 (2016) ^	3.9 ^	131 (2016)	0.05
Italy	10,008,033 (2017)	26,420 (2014) #	2.6 #	2,286 (2015)	0.2
Japan	18,900,000 (2018)	45,000 (2017) #	2.4 #	495	0.03
Latvia	358,762 (2018)	5805 (2016) #	15.7 #	246 (2016)	0.69

Table 1.1 *Continued*

1	2	3	4	5	6
Country	Child population total (0–17) (year)	Children placed out-of-home in total (year)	Out-of-home placements per 1,000 children	Adopted from care in total	Adopted from care per 1,000 children
Lebanese Republic	1,380,000 (0–14) (2019)	ND	ND	ND	ND
Lithuania	503,015 (2017)	8,752 (2017) #	17.4 (2017) #	139 (2017)	0.28
Mexico	39,200,000 (2015)	ND	ND	ND	ND
Netherlands	3,404,098 (2017)	31,000 # (2017)	9.1 #	ND	ND
New Zealand	1,124,000 (2018)	4,716 ^ (2016/17)	4.2 ^	ND	ND
Nigeria	91,854,928 (0–14) (2018)	ND	ND	ND	ND
Northern Ireland	436,403 (2017)	3,281 (2019) #	7.48 #	79 (2019)	0.18
Norway	1,131,051 (2016)	11,994 (2016) #	10.6 #	59 (2016)	0.05
Philippines	36,600,000 (2015)	ND	ND	ND	ND
Poland	6,920,800 (2017)	73,393 # (2016)	10.6 #	2,354 (0–14) (2018)	0.4
Portugal	1,781,663 (2015)	8,673 (2018) #	4.9 #	456 (2018)	0.25
Russia	26,652,174 (2014)	613,000 ^ (2014)	23 ^	122,600 (2014)	4.6
Slovak Republic	840,228 (0–14) (2016)	8,739 ^ (2017)	10.4 ^	ND	ND
South Africa	19,600,000 (2018)	420,000 # (2017)	21.4 #	1,651 (2014–15)	0.08
South Korea	8,255,490 (2018)	4,307 (2018) ^	0.5 ^	ND	ND
Spain	8,119,000 (2015)	34,644 # (2017)	4.3 #	588 (2016)	0.72
Sweden	2,239,615 (0–19) (2015)	29,473 ^ (2015) 21,051 #	13.2 ^	56 (2015)	0.023
Switzerland (*3 cantons*)	1,500,000 (2017) 251,721 (2016)	- 2665 # (2016)	10.6 #	ND	ND
Uganda	21,200,000 (2019)	ND	ND	ND	ND
Uruguay	982,860 (2016)	4,517 (2019) ^	4.6 ^	171 (2017)	0.17
USA	73,600,000 (2016)	424,000 # (2019)	5.8 #	57,238 (2016)	0.78
Zimbabwe	7,504,000 (0–14) (2012)	ND	ND	ND	ND

Note: Statistics are overall based on the chapters in this volume, but some information is from official statistics or research publications. The numbers are reliability tested up against official sources on child protection statistics and national statistics. In cases of discrepancy in the material, the editors have consulted authors and authorized official sources. Some information has only been available for regions or larger cities.

Comparative Analyses: Interpreting the Data

Generally, the highest rates of out-of-home care are found in both the Eastern European countries, which are moderately developed but among the least wealthy in Europe, and some of the Scandinavian and western European countries, which are highly developed and among the most affluent in the world. Beyond consideration of the different ways to count child protection measures, many factors related to diverse social contexts contribute to our knowledge of how the child protection systems in these 50 countries function. These factors include available resources, cultural norms and values concerning family life, the objectives of public intervention, and the general level of child well-being. Comparisons based on administrative data from different countries require cautious interpretation. Statistics are not uniform across nations in terms of type of risk categories, age used to define children, and the range of variables reported.

Administrative data tend to be available in the wealthy, developed countries, where net social welfare expenditures are high enough to support the kind of institutionalized welfare bureaucracy needed for data collection. Although improving, there are still many countries across the world that do not have adequate information about the life-circumstances of their children (UNICEF, 2019). Among a sample of countries where data are available, it is evident that out-of-home placement rates have increased in recent times. As illustrated in Table 1.2, with the exception of the United States and Italy, all of

Table 1.2 Changing out-of-home placement rates per 1,000 children 0–17 years—selected countries # = stock stat/^ = flow/– = no data

	Time A	Time B	Time C	Time D
Austria	-	-	8.1 (2011) ^	8.7 (2018) ^
Belgium	7.9 (2004) ^	8.6 (2008) ^	-	9.6 (2012) ^
Canada	4 (1991) NM	9.7 (2007) #	-	8.9 (2015) #
Denmark	9.5 (1993) #	10.2 (2007) #	-	10.2 (2016) #
England	4.5 (1994) #	5.5 (2009) #	5.6 (2013) #	6.5 (2018–19) #
Finland	8 (1994) ^	12 (2007) ^	14 (2011) ^	16.5 (2015) ^
Germany	9.5 (1995) NM	9.9 (2005) NM	9.5 (2012) #	10.8 (2016) #
Ireland	-	-	5.6 (2014) #	5.0 (2019) #
Italy	-	-	3 (2010) #	2.6 (2014) #
Netherlands	-	-	9.3 (2010) #	9.1 (2017) #
Norway	5.9 (1994) #	8.2 (2008) #	10.1 (2013) #	10.6 (2016) #
Spain	-	-	-	4.3 (2017) #
Sweden	8 (2000) #	9 (2005) #	8.5 (2013) #	13.2 (2015) #[a]
Switzerland	-	-	10.4 (2013) #	10.6 (2016) #
USA	7 (1997) #	6 (2007) #	5.5 (2013) #	5.8 (2019) #

Source: Data Time A and B from Gilbert, Parton, Skivenes (2011). Time C from Skivenes et al (2015) or Burns, Pösö, Skivenes (2017). Time D from Handbook, Berrick, Gilbert, Skivenes (2023).

[a] 0–19 year olds.

the countries in this sample experienced an increasing rate of out-of-home placements since the 1990s.

The case studies in this Handbook provide insights into the diverse factors that shape the efforts and accomplishments of child-protection systems around the world. Thus, for example, in comparing the foster care placement data in Table 1.1 it is important to know that the high rates of out-of-home placements in Russia and South Africa are influenced by a very different set of circumstances than the rates of placement in, for example, Germany and France. In South Africa, a significant proportion of children placed in foster care represent not so much a disruption of parental custody based on assessments of child maltreatment as the fact that government policies made foster care grants available to relatives in an effort to address the orphan crisis caused by the HIV/AIDS pandemic. In family service-oriented child protection systems (Gilbert et al., 2011) such as Austria, Finland, Netherlands and Denmark, foster care placements are based on assessments of need including whether the child's health and development are seriously at risk following an exhaustive provision of in-home services. In most child protection systems, the ultimate goal of intervention is to reunify the parents and children whenever possible; whereas in a country such as South Africa, children's parents may not be available (Schmid, 2006).

Shifts in policy also provide insights into trends over time. Among the countries in Table 1.2, the United States had one of the lowest out-of-home care rates, which registered a decline since the 1990s. What do the low and declining rates signify? To what extent have the rates of serious maltreatment declined? On the most serious measure, the rate of fatalities related to maltreatment increased from 1.7 per 100,000 in 1997 to 2.32 per 100,000 in 2017; yet the victimization rate (subjects of allegations of maltreatment that have been substantiated or indicated) declined from 13.9 per 1,000 in 1997 to 9.1 per 1,000 in 2016 (US Dept. of HHS, 1999; US Dept. HHS, 2018). Although these factors may partially account for the out-of-home care rate, at the same time a shift in policy also entered the picture. The 1997 Adoption and Safe Families Act (PL 105-89) encouraged states to increase the adoption rates of children in care (when they were unable to realize timely reunification with birth parents). The number of children adopted from the public foster care system increased by almost 50% from 36,000 in 1998 to 53,000 in 2007—which alone accounts for about one-third of the difference in the out-of-home care rate (Adoption Statistics, 1999; US DHHS, 2010). In addition, there was a growing emphasis on finding relatives to care for maltreated children, which opened a path of "voluntary" kinship care that diverted children from the formal child welfare system. An examination of placement rates alone tells only a partial story about a country's child protection system; the details provided in each of the chapters herein give greater insight into the demographic, cultural, historical, and political factors shaping country responses to children's needs.

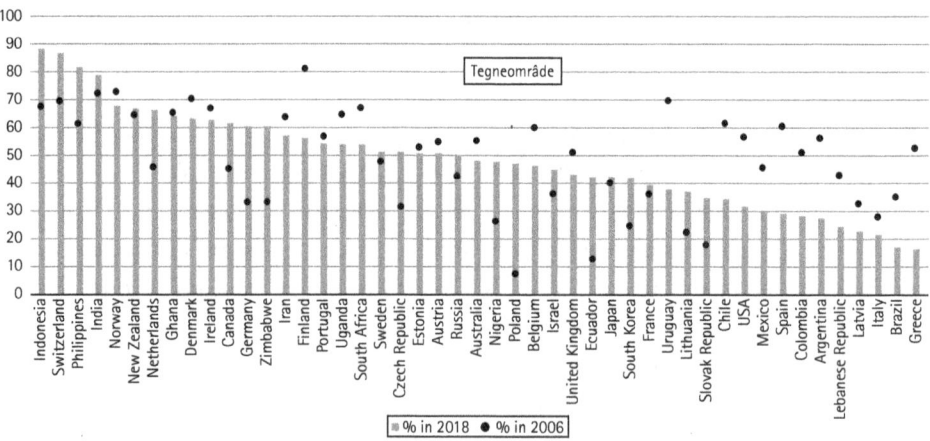

Figure 1.5 Confidence in National Government in 2018 and its change since 2006 (Gallup data) Note: Data from two countries, China and Egypt, are not available and for England and Northern Ireland, data for UK is used.

Social-Cultural Differences and Public Confidence in Governments

Protecting children by means of family separation is an extreme intervention that creates social friction between the exercise of the state's power and parental rights. In these cases, the degree of social friction varies among countries according to cultural differences, particularly those regarding citizens' trust in their government and the family's responsibility for its members. Figure 1.5 offers an illustration of public confidence in government in the countries included in this Handbook.

As the data suggest, public confidence varies dramatically by country, with Indonesia and Switzerland on the high end, and Greece and Brazil on the low end. Some countries have experienced huge drops in confidence levels during the last 10 years (e.g., Greece), others have experienced huge increases (e.g., Poland), and some remained stable (e.g., Norway, New Zealand, Ghana). These cultural differences may influence some degree of variation in processes and rates of out-of-home placements. In Sweden, for example, citizens have historically referred to the welfare state as the "people's home": social welfare expenditures as a percentage of GDP are much higher than the OECD average, paying for benefits that are universally available to all citizens, and the degree of trust in the government is higher than the OECD average. The Nordic countries, with social democratic welfare state models, provide universal benefits and generous welfare services to their citizens. They all score consistently high on trust in government (although Finland has a marked drop from 2006), and may be seen as supporting the process of what Esping-Andersen (1999) described as "de-familialisation," which promotes shifting responsibility for family care to the state. By providing a range of social benefits for care and support, the welfare state reduces the individual's dependence on kinship. In this sociocultural context the majority of out-of-home placements in the Nordic countries are formally voluntary, with the exception of Norway (Skivenes & Søvig, 2017; Skivenes 2020). (Some also question, however, whether a degree of coercion might be operating informally in these countries; see Höjer & Pösö, this volume.)

To the degree that a state embraces the ethos that children have individual rights, separate from their parents, additional tensions between the state, the parent, and the child are likely to emerge. Just as states may be considered along a continuum in the degree to which their welfare state is familialized or de-familialized (or re-familialized, as per Hantrais, 2004), states have incorporated the core ideology of the UN Convention on the Rights of the Child to varying degrees. In terms of child protection, this child-oriented approach has been characterized by Gilbert and colleagues (2011) as child-centric. This approach is expressed through legislation framing children's rights, to procedures that are responsive to children's unique needs, and to the promotion of children's authentic participation in decisions that affect their lives.

Sociocultural factors in Nordic countries offer a distinct contrast to those in, for example, South Korea where the level of social welfare expenditures as a percentage of GDP is well below the OECD average. More importantly, perhaps, traditional cultural norms in South Korea have long considered children the property of their parents and child-rearing a family responsibility (Kim, 2003). While corporal punishment is against the law in Sweden, it is seen as an expression of care by many South Koreans (Chung & Lah, this volume)—though we note that the country recently joined 62 other nations that have prohibited corporal punishment. The Confucian emphasis on strong family relationships, altruistic paternalism, and family harmony comprises a set of cultural attributes that influence the definition and responses to maltreatment. In contrast to the out-of-home care rate of about 10 children per 1,000 in some European and Nordic countries, a 2017 study in South Korea found only 4,307 (0.4 per 1,000 children) were placed out of home (Chung & Lah, this volume). Among all the children who were separated from their homes in South Korea, about one quarter were returned home within the year.

Sociocultural factors are also at play when we examine the role of religion or traditional cultural practices, and how states accommodate these influences. Thus, in Lebanon, the law makes accommodations for different religious values allowing, for example, adoption for children whose families follow the Christian religion, but banning the practice for Muslims (Rizk, this volume). In Indonesia, recent legislative debates concerning the age of marriage for girls highlighted the conflict between religious factions in the country, international pressure relating to children's rights, and questions of local governance (Dinata, this volume). And in Ghana, where some cultural enclaves continue to engage in practices that can be harmful to children (e.g., "baby farming," or infanticide), the state child protection apparatus is insufficiently strong to respond (Dako-Gyeke et al., this volume).

The data on out-of-home placements and adoption rates in Tables 1.1 and 1.2 reflect, in part, the influences of different political, familial, and sociocultural factors at play across countries. But the exact impact of these differences is not self-evident. Out-of-home care and adoption rates provide a rough comparison of child welfare services that involve a profound disruption in parent–child relationships—the transfer or restriction of parental custody of children—in efforts to protect children from the risk of serious harm. The state's approach to protecting children and engaging with family life involves much more, of course, than only out-of-home care.

Child Protection Systems: Child Rights, Child Well-being, Child Maltreatment, Child Deprivation, and Child Exploitation

The case studies in this Handbook shed light on the contextual factors and policy developments that are fundamental to an in-depth understanding of child protection systems at various stages of development in many countries with diverse cultures. Although some of this diversity is captured in established typologies of child protection systems that distinguish among alternative models, these classifications tend to focus on the institutionalized arrangements for child welfare in relatively high-income countries with mature welfare states. Previous work by Gilbert, Parton, and Skivenes (2011), for example, has characterized three primary orientations to child welfare systems in western industrialized nations: the child risk approach, the family service approach and the child-centric focus. According to this classification, a risk-oriented child protection system is distinguished by a relatively high threshold for intervention, which is designed to prevent or stop serious risk and harm. The general orientation is based on an ideology that the state should not interfere in the private sphere of family life; there are thus few preventive services or provisions for in-home services. In a family service-oriented system, the state provides services to the child and the family prior to, or at the early onset of risk, aimed to strengthen the family's protective factors and thereby prevent intrusive interventions. The third orientation is labeled child centrism and focuses on children as individual right-bearers. This orientation is, to a varying degree, present in many countries, though Norway and Finland are often identified as exemplars (Gilbert et al., 2011; Pösö et al., 2015). The child-centric orientation accentuates tensions between the state and the family because the traditional two-party relationship between the family and the state has become a three-party relationship. The state has an independent responsibility to protect children's rights. When this responsibility involves protecting children from maltreatment by their parents, the state has an obligation to prioritize the child's interests over the parents' rights. This emphasis on children's rights creates a seedbed for conflicts and tensions between parents and the state, which may help to explain current criticisms of the Norwegian child protection system in international mass media (see, for example, Whewell, 2018).

This Handbook seeks to extend the analytic purview beyond the three orientations developed from the study of 11 OECD countries (Gilbert et al., 2011). The Handbook includes a wide range of countries across the globe, from Eastern Europe, Asia and South Asia, Africa, Latin America, and the Middle East. These countries represent diverse cultural, sociopolitical, economic, religious, and demographic contexts. Some countries have not yet produced the economic surplus necessary to finance significant social welfare expenditures nor a comprehensive child protection system; other countries have elaborate policies, procedures, and professional bureaucracies. Given the comparative nature of this Handbook and the variation among countries, each chapter provides systematic information on a country's or on several countries' child protection systems. The ambition is that chapters address four fundamental dimensions of choice that shape the design and implementation of a child protection system and its policies. The first involves the bases of social allocations, which are the operational definitions of eligibility criteria. Here the analysis examines the processes and standards used to identify who is considered a child, how children and their needs are identified, and what risks need protection. The second focuses on choices regarding the nature of social provisions allocated to protect children. That is, what are the services or benefits allocated to children or families identified by the state? The third theme concerns the methods for the delivery of child protection measures and provisions. These might include delivery by public or by private agencies, the provisions might be centralized or de-centralized, and various public and private actors may be involved in service delivery. The final choice involves how child protection services are financed. Based on these case studies, our goal is to identify some of the critical dimensions around which different types of child protection systems cluster. We recognize that COVID-19 interrupted state systems of every kind, including child protection. This Handbook does not address the unique and disruptive circumstances of COVID as we anticipate that the policies and structures underlying child protection are—in essence—likely to persist through and following the pandemic.

We conclude the Handbook with an analysis of these dimensions across 50 countries and suggest a strategy to conceptualize a new, global typology of child protection systems. Drawing on data from 50 countries, this typology is based on a conceptualization of cumulative hierarchies of childhood risk and typify the focal strategies for protecting children, which correspond to five types of child protection systems—each system imbedding the previous risk orientation(s):

- child exploitation-protective systems,
- child deprivation-protective systems,
- child maltreatment-protective systems,
- child well-being-protective systems, and
- child rights-protective systems.

This typology offers a comparative lens that advances our understanding of alternative child protection practices and policies throughout the world, and will be explained in full in the concluding chapter.

The diversity of child protection arrangements poses a challenge to organizing the chapters in this book. In the absence of a ready-made classification or an established typology to distinguish among the range of child protection systems represented by the 50 countries, we have divided the countries by an overall estimate of the public administrative stages of institutional development, from the most to the least fully developed capacity to safeguard children's rights in a wide sense: *Institutionalized*, *Emerging*, and *Nascent*. This initial classification is based on the degree to which governments are able to provide family and children's services that are systematically organized and professionally functioning. The dividing line between these stages is porous; the division is strongly influenced by a country's wealth. The metric of GDP per capita (shown in Figure 1.2) offers a practical estimate of the generosity of family and welfare provisions and the governmental capacity to finance well-organized, professionally staffed child protection agencies.

Governmental systems in the *institutionalized* stage have family policies and possess the legal framework, financial resources, and professionally trained practitioners to report, assess, and intervene in family situations where children are harmed or are at risk of harm. These include many western industrialized countries frequently referred to as high-income nations. The *emerging* governmental systems are not as well financed or professionally staffed as institutionalized systems, the administrative operations are not fully integrated, and the role of public intervention in private life is still being formulated. Governmental systems in the *nascent* stage of development involve countries that have legislation to support the objectives of the United Nations Convention on the Rights of the Child, but either do not have the financial and/or organizational resources to initiate the systematic implementation of programs to directly address these objectives, or they are in the very early stages of implementation.

The Handbook is organized into three parts according to these divisions: I Institutionalized, II Emerging, and III Nascent. Within each section, the country case studies are arranged alphabetically by country. Part I includes Australia and New Zealand, Austria, Belgium, Canada, Denmark and Norway, England, Finland and Sweden, France, Germany, Ireland and Northern Ireland, Israel, Italy and Greece, Japan, Netherlands, South Korea, Spain, Switzerland, and the United States. Part II includes Chile, Czech Republic, Estonia and Latvia, Lithuania, Poland, Portugal, Slovak Republic, South Africa, and Uruguay. Part III includes Argentina, Brazil, China, Colombia, Ecuador, Egypt, Ghana, India, Indonesia, Iran, Lebanon, Mexico, Nigeria, Philippines, Russia, Uganda, and Zimbabwe. This division is based on our approximation of capacity and there are borderline cases in each group. For example, Russia's position in the nascent category reflects its relatively low GDP per capita and ranking on the Child Flourishing Index, though it could also be seen in the emerging category.

International comparisons about the nature and scope of child protection offer opportunities to understand global similarities and differences; they also shed light on the underlying values, mechanisms, and institutions across states. As such, they serve an aspirational purpose as residents and legislators of individual nations develop and strengthen their approach to supporting children and families. The questions at the heart of child protection are thorny; finding the appropriate balance between the child, the parents, and the state has no absolute answer. The relative differences in state approaches across the globe, however, offer important insights to learn from others.

References

Alderson, P. (2000). UN Convention on the Rights of the Child: Some common criticisms and suggested responses. *Child Abuse Review*, 9(6), 439–443.

Archard, D. (2004). *Children, rights and childhood* (2nd ed.). Routledge.

Better Care Network. (2019). Guidelines on alternative care. Available at: https://bettercarenetwork.org/intern ational-framework/guidelines-on-alternative-care. Retrieved January 5, 2020.

Bywaters, P., Bunting, L., Davidson, G., Hanratty, J., Mason, W., McCartatn, C., and Steils, N. (2016). *The relationship between poverty, child abuse and neglect: An evidence review.* Joseph Rowntree Foundation.

Burns, K., Pösö, T., and Skivenes, M. (2017). *Child welfare removals by the state.* Oxford University Press.

Burns, K., Križ, K., Krutzinna, J., Luhamaa, K., Meysen, T., Pösö, T., and Thoburn, J. (2019). The hidden proceedings–an analysis of accountability of child protection adoption proceedings in eight European juris-dictions. *European Journal of Comparative Law and Governance*, 6(4), 339–371.

Clark, H., Coll-Seck, A.M., Banerjee, A., Peterson, S., Dalglish, S. L., Ameratunga, S., Balabanova, D., Bhan, M. K., Bhutta, Z. A., Borrazzo, J., Claeson, M., Doherty, T., El-Jardali, F., George, A. S., Gichaga, A., Gram, L., Hipgrave, D. B., Kwamie, A., Meng, O., Mercer, R., Narain, S., Nsungwa-Sabiiti, J., Olumide, A. O., Osrin, D., Powell-Jackson, T., Rasanathan, K., Rasul, I., Reid, P., Requejo, J., Rohde, S. S., Rollins, N., Romedenne, M., Sachdev, H. S., Saleh, R., Shawar, Y. R., Shiffman, J., Simon, J., Sly, P. D., Stenberg, K., Tomlinson, M., Ved, R. R., and Costello, A. (2020). A future for the world's children? A WHO-UNICEF-*Lancet* Commission. *The Lancet*, 395(10224), 605–658.

Dahl, T. (1978). *Barnevern og samfunnsvern. Om stat, vitenskap og profesjoner under barnevernets oppkomst i Norge.* Pax Forlag A/S.

End Corporal Punishment. (2019). *Reports on every state and territory.* Available at: https://endcorporalpun ishment.org/reports-on-every-state-and-territory/. Retrieved November 19, 2019.

Esping-Andersen, G. (1990). *The three worlds of welfare capitalism.* Princeton University Press.

Friedman, M. (1962). *Capitalism and freedom.* University of Chicago Press.

Gilbert, N. (1997). *Combatting child abuse: International perspectives and trends.* Oxford University Press.

Gilbert, N., Parton, N., and Skivenes, M. (Eds.) (2011). *Child protection systems: International trends and emerg-ing orientations.* Oxford University Press.

Hantrais, L. (2004). *Family policy matters: Responding to family change in Europe.* Policy Press.

Hetherington, R., Cooper, A., Smith, P., and Wilford, G. (1997). *Protecting children: Messages from Europe.* Russel House.

James, A. and Prout, A. (1997). *Constructing and reconstructing childhood: contemporary issues in the sociological study of childhood.* Routledge Falmer.

KidsRights Foundation (2019). *The KidsRights Index.* Available at: https://www.kidsrightsindex.org. Retrieved November 19, 2019.

Kim, Y. H. (2003). Productive welfare: Korea's third way? *International Journal of Social Welfare*, 12(1), 61–67.

Krug, E. G., Dahlberg, L. L., Mercy, J. A., Zwi, A. B., and Lozano, R. (Eds.) (2002). *World report on violence and health.* World Health Organization.

Leinaweaver, J. (2014). Informal kinship-based fostering around the world: Anthropological findings. *Child Development Perspectives*, 8(3), 131–136.

OECD. (2017). *Government at a Glance 2017.* OECD Publishing. Available at: https://doi.org/10.1787/gov _glance-2017-en.

Nkuba, M., Hermenau, K., and Hecker, T. (2018). Violence and maltreatment in Tanzanian families: Findings from a nationally representative sample of secondary school students and their parents. *Child Abuse and Neglect*, 77, 110–120.

Pemberton, S., Gordon, D., Nandy, S., Pantazis, C., and Townsend, P. (2007). Child Rights and Child Poverty: Can the International Framework of Children's Rights Be Used to Improve Child Survival Rates? *PLoS Med*, 4(10), Article e307. https://doi.org/10.1371/journal.pmed.0040307.

Schmid, J. (2006). Responding to the South African child welfare crisis. *Canadian Social Work Review*, 23(1), 111–127.

Schmid, J. (2007). 'Quo vadis? Trends in South African child welfare policies. *International Social Work*, 50(4), 500–514.

Scott, M. E. and Karberg, E. (2016). Measuring children's care arrangements and their educational and health outcomes internationally. *Global Social Welfare*, 3(2 SI), 75–89.

Sethi, D., Bellis, M., Hughes, K., Gilbert, R., Mitis, F., and Galea, G. (2014). *European report on preventing child maltreatment*. WHO Regional Office for Europe.

Shapiro, I. (1999). *Democratic justice*. Yale University Press.

Skivenes, M. (2020). *Consensual Removals in Child Protection Cases*. Available at: https://www.discretion.uib.no/consensual-removals-in-child-protection-cases/. Retrieved January 25, 2020.

Stoltenborgh, M., Bakersmans-Kranenburg, M. J., Alink, L. R. A., and van Izendoorn, M. H. (2015). The prevalence of child maltreatment across the globe: Review of a series of meta-analyses. *Child Abuse Review*, 24, 37–50.

Sutherland, E. (2016). Introduction. In E.E. Sutherland and L.A. Macfarlane (Eds.), *Implementing Article 3 of the United Nations Convention of the Rights of the Child: Best interests, welfare and well-being*. Cambridge University Press, pp. 1–17.

S.C. (2013). *Why won't America ratify the UN convention on children's rights? The Economist*. Available at: https://www.economist.com/the-economist-explains/2013/10/06/why-wont-america-ratify-the-un-convention-on-childrens-rights. Retrieved November 19, 2019.

UNICEF. (2013). *Child well-being in rich countries: A comparative overview*. UNICEF Office of Research.

UNICEF. (2019a). *For every child, every right: The convention on the rights of the child at a crossroads*. UNICEF.

UNICEF. (2019b). *The state of the world's children 2019. Children, Food and Nutrition: Growing well in a changing world*. UNICEF.

US Dept. of HHS, 1999; US Dept. HHS. (2018). *The 1997 Adoption and Safe Families Act (P.L. 105-89)*.

Whewell, T. (2018). *Norway's hidden scandal*. Available at: https://www.bbc.co.uk/news/resources/idt-sh/norways_hidden_scandal. Retrieved December 26, 2019.

World Health Organization. (2015). *Health in 2015: From MDGs to SDGs*. World Health Organization.

World Population Review. (2019). *Crime rate by country*. Available at: http://worldpopulationreview.com/countries/crime-rate-by-country/. Retrieved November 19, 2019.

Zelitzer, V. (1994). *Pricing the priceless child: The changing social value of children*. Princeton University Press.

PART I

Institutionalized

Child Protection in Australia and New Zealand: An Overview of Systems

Judith Cashmore *and* Nicola Taylor

Abstract

This chapter delivers an overview of child protection services in Australia and New Zealand. Both nations' main concern primarily revolves around numerous reports of children at risk and the overrepresentation of Aboriginal and Torres Strait Islander (ATSI) children in Australia and Māori children in New Zealand. In Australia, child protection legislation, policy and practice processes are mostly similar across states and territories and differ in terms of reporting, investigation, and interventions for a child in either risk or need of protection and care. On the other hand, New Zealand's *whangai* system was eroded due to state intervention to protect children and westernized laws governing adoption and welfare. The over-representation of Indigenous children living away from their *whanau* sparked major reform of the country's child protection system.

Key Words: child protection services, Australia, New Zealand, ATSI, Maori, Indigenous children, risk, intervention, whangai

Introduction

Australia and New Zealand, separated by the Tasman Sea, are very similar South Pacific countries in many respects with parallel common law English-based legal systems and comparable child protection systems. In both countries, the main concerns in the child protection field relate to the high number of reports of children at risk and the over-representation of Indigenous children—Aboriginal and Torres Strait Islander (ATSI) children in Australia and Māori children in New Zealand.

There are, however, some significant differences in terms of history, size, population, and culture. Australia has a population of 25.7 million,[1] 5.67 million (22.0%) of whom are children aged 0–17 years (Australian Bureau of Statistics, 2022). Nearly 800,000 (3.3% of the overall population) are ATSI people, but a much higher proportion (40.3%) of ATSI people are under the age of 18 than in the non-Indigenous population (21.9%).

---

[1] As of June 30, 2021, the Australian population was estimated to be 25,738, 142 (Australian Bureau of Statistics: https://www.abs.gov.au/statistics/people/population/national-state-and-territory-population/latest-release#data-download).

New Zealand's much smaller population of 5.12 million is about the same size as that of Australia's largest city, Sydney (Stats NZ, 2022).[2] The majority of the New Zealand population is of European descent (74%), with Indigenous Māori being the largest minority (15%), followed by Asians (12%) and Pacifika people (7%). There are 1,124,000 children aged 0–17 years, comprising 23% of the total population (Office of the Children's Commissioner, 2018). Most children are European (71%), with Māori (26%), Asian (15%), and Pacifika (14%) being the other major ethnicities.[3] About 23% of children born in New Zealand identify with more than one ethnicity (Stats NZ, 2015).[4] New Zealand's aging population has meant that the proportion who are children has fallen over time but, like Australia, the Indigenous (Māori) population has a younger age-structure than that of Europeans (Families Commission, 2012).[5]

Australia and New Zealand have quite different Indigenous histories, with Australia being settled from Indonesia or New Guinea around 50,000 years ago, and New Zealand from islands in the tropical Pacific around 750 years ago (Mein Smith, 2012). Both were mapped by the British explorer, James Cook, in 1769–1770, leading to their colonization by Britain from the 18th century. Constitutionally New Zealand began as an extension of the Australian colony of New South Wales, but became a separate colony in 1841 after the Treaty of Waitangi 1840 was signed between the British Crown and Māori Chiefs. Indigenous rights stemming from this Treaty, which value Māori *tamariki* (children) as *taonga* (treasures), are central to New Zealand's contemporary social, cultural, and economic development, and have significantly influenced care and protection reforms over the past 40 years. Australia, however, took a quite different path and the Federation of Australian States formed the Commonwealth of Australia in 1901.

In Australia, child protection legislation, policy, and practice are the jurisdiction of the six states and two territories. There is, however, increasing recognition of the need to provide some national direction and greater consistency across jurisdictions, reflected in the *National Frameworks for Protecting Australia's Children* 2009–2020 and 2021–2031 (Council of Australian Governments, 2009, 2021). Broader aspects of social welfare and family law come under the jurisdiction of the Commonwealth government. Public law child "at risk" concerns are dealt with by the state statutory departments and in Children's Court proceedings, separate from private family law matters in the Family Courts, though there is increasing similarity in the child risk factors of the families involved with both courts (Kaspiew et al., 2015). In contrast, New Zealand does not have any state governments but a central single-chamber Parliament (the House of Representatives) with jurisdiction over all aspects of social welfare, child protection, and family law nationally.

---

[2] As of March 31, 2022. www.stats.govt.nz/information-releases/national-population-estimates-at-31-march-2022/.

[3] Ethnicities add to over 100% because some children have more than one ethnicity.

[4] Based on 2013 Census data, compared with 11% of the population overall.

[5] This is true for the Pacifika and Asian populations as well.

The *Children, Young Persons and Their Families Act 1989*, renowned for its introduction of family group conferences, addresses both care and protection and youth justice issues. In July 2017 it was renamed as the *Oranga Tamariki Act 1989*, with an accompanying title of the *Children's and Young People's Well-being Act 1989*, to signal changes in the purposes, principles, and provisions of the Act as part of a major overhaul transforming New Zealand's care and protection system to better meet the needs of vulnerable children.

Australia

Bases of Social Allocations

Child protection legislation, policy, and practice processes are broadly similar across Australian state and territory jurisdictions, but there are some noteworthy differences. The legislation in all jurisdictions specifies the basis for reporting, investigation, and possible intervention when a child is variously defined as being "in need of care and protection," "in need of protection," or "at risk."[6] This generally applies when children have been or are at risk of being abused or neglected or when their parents are unable or unwilling to care for them, which includes circumstances in which the only available parent/s have died or been imprisoned. In two states, there is also provision for reports to be made about an unborn child to facilitate pre-natal care and assistance for the mother (particularly in relation to substance abuse problems and housing) and as an alert that the child may be at risk when born.

The threshold for reporting and investigation differs across jurisdictions in that it may refer to a child being "at risk of harm" or to "significant harm." The threshold is also justifiably higher for taking court action, particularly if it results in the child's removal from their home. Mandatory reporting operates in all states and territories and requires people in specified occupations, whose work brings them into contact with children or who supervise those who have contact with children, to report a reasonable belief or suspicion that a child has been or is being abused or neglected, or is likely to be abused or neglected.[7] Police are the most common source of reports which result in a statutory investigation (21.1%), followed by schools (19.7%), social workers, and health personnel (12.3%); family members, friends, and neighbours contribute about 12% (Australian Institute of Health and Welfare 2020, Table S3.2).

---

[6] For example, "in need of care and protection" in New South Wales, Victoria and the Northern Territory: *Children and Young Persons (Care and Protection) Act* 1998 (NSW) s 34(1) and *Care and Protection of Children Act* (NT) s 20; "in need of protection" in *Children Youth and Families Act* 2005 (Vic) s 162; *Children and Community Services Act* 2004 (WA), s 28(1); Child Protection Act 1999 (Qld) s 10, 14; or "at risk" in South Australia and Tasmania, *Children's Protection Act* 1993 (SA) s 19(1); *Children, Young Persons and Their Families Act* 1997 (Tas) ss 4(1), 18(1).

[7] The list and inclusion of occupations differs by state and is generally more inclusive for sexual abuse than for other forms of abuse or neglect: see "Mandatory reporting of child abuse and neglect," *CFCA Resource Sheet*, September 2017. Available at: https://aifs.gov.au/cfca/publications/mandatory-reporting-child-abuse-and-neglect.

The definitions of abuse and neglect vary to some extent across jurisdictions, but the federal government agency which collects and reports on child protection statistics, the Australian Institute of Health and Welfare (AIHW), uses an agreed general definition of reported abuse and neglect to take account of the differences in legislation, policy and practice.[8] In the year 2020–21, 117,940 children across Australia (a rate of 21 per 1,000 children aged 0–17 years) were the subject of a finalized child protection investigation. The concerns were substantiated for 48,886 children (41.4% of those children where an investigation occurred), meaning that the statutory department concluded that the child had been, is being, or is likely to be, abused, neglected, or otherwise harmed. The most common type of substantiated maltreatment was emotional abuse (54%), followed by neglect (22%), physical abuse (14%) and sexual abuse (9%). These are the figures for the primary type of maltreatment but there was significant co-occurrence (AIHW, 2022, pp. 21–22). One reason for the high incidence of emotional abuse is the relatively recent extension of the definition of abuse to include the exposure of children to family violence, in recognition of the emotional harm caused to them by witnessing such violence whether or not they are physically harmed (Shonkoff et al., 2009).

Child Protection Processes

The overall approach in all jurisdictions tends to be forensic, based on "risk-focused paradigms that concentrate on identifying parental failings" (Connolly, 2013, p. 191). This is in line with other English speaking common law countries and the United States, with parental compliance and change encouraged or coerced by the powers that statutory child protection workers hold (Bilson, Cant, Harries, & Thorpe, 2015; Harris, 2011).

Reports to the statutory government departments, to centralized helplines in some states, are assessed and screened by caseworkers; in some states, reports by police, teachers, and health workers are first screened within those government agencies. The reports are triaged depending upon the urgency and need for further information and/or services. A substantial proportion of children have been reported to child protection statutory departments.[9] Some will be "screened out" and referred to other services, on a voluntary basis, for various forms of family support, including drug and alcohol services, housing or counselling. There is no guarantee that they will actually go to, or be able to obtain, these services. Others will be "screened in" for further information from agencies and persons involved with the child—including family members, schools or health services—and for more formal investigation. This may involve caseworkers interviewing parents and an

---

[8] https://www.aihw.gov.au/getmedia/9f0fe22e-67fa-43bb-be11-3f5b12f0c89a/aihw-cws-63-appendixes-c-to-e.pdf.aspx.

[9] In New South Wales, 26.5% of children born in the period 2003–2005 were reported at least once before the age of 13 (Green et al., 2018). Similarly, one in four children born in South Australia between 1999 and 2005 were notified to child protection by the age of 10, and 76.2% born between 1999 and 2009 who were notified before age two were re-notified by the time they were five years old: https://dhs.sa.gov.au/__data/assets/pdf_file/0004/78871/Research-Report-Summary-of-Research-Findings-March-2019.pdf.

assessment of the risk to the child and the parents' capacity to provide safe and adequate care for the child. It may involve medical examination of the child and police investigation in relation to sexual and severe physical abuse or neglect.

If the concerns are substantiated and the child deemed to be at risk or to have been abused or neglected, typically the next step is for the statutory agency or government department to engage with the parents and the family to try to work out arrangements and provide supports and referrals to keep the child safe. This may occur in case planning meetings or family group conferences, following the New Zealand approach. Parents and children who are considered old enough may be involved in these meetings.

Where the statutory agency considers that children cannot remain safely with their parent/s, an application is made to the Children's Court for a supervision or related order or for a care application. The paramount consideration is the best interests of the child (Cashmore, 2016). Children's Courts operate with less formality than other Australian courts, but the processes remain largely adversarial in contested matters and family participants are often intimidated and confused by these. The level of proof in child protection matters is "on the balance of probabilities" (Sheehan, 2001). Children's Court Magistrates "play a more active role in proceedings, directly question witnesses, professionals and lawyers, and call for further information and advice" in both types of matters (Sheehan & Borowski, 2013, p. 125). As part of this process, the court in some states may refer the matter to a dispute resolution conference to narrow the issues that are in dispute between the department and the parents or birth family and "provide the parties with an opportunity to agree on the action that should be taken in the best interests of the child." Where there is no agreement, the matter is referred back to court for "child protection decisions that are better informed and more responsive" (Morgan et al., 2012, p. xiv). Children are generally legally represented in these proceedings but do not appear at court.

When Aboriginal children have been determined to be at risk, Care Circles can provide an alternative dispute resolution process using culturally appropriate decision making that involves respected Aboriginal Elders and community members to determine appropriate care plans.[10] Evaluation of these ADR processes has been positive, with families and legal professionals and caseworkers expressing satisfaction with the process and the outcomes in a relatively cost efficient and effective manner (Morgan et al., 2012, p. xix).

Nature of Social Provisions Allocated to Protect Children

Family income in Australia is underpinned by several forms of welfare type payments—almost universal family support payments for families with children, and targeted income

---

[10] For the Alternative Dispute Resolution (ADR) procedures in care and protection cases in the NSW Children's Court, see https://www.childrenscourt.nsw.gov.au/childrens-court/care-and-protection/alternative-dispute-resolution.html.

and housing support payments for unemployed and very low-income families. As Howlett, Gray and Hunter (2016) point out:

> Australia's welfare system is one of the most targeted systems in the Organisation for Economic Cooperation and Development, and these transfer payments tend to provide support to those most in need—recipients who are out of work temporarily, or permanently in the case of those with a disability or long-term illness . . . Government payments are particularly important as a source of income for Indigenous persons, because they are more likely to be unemployed and more likely to be out of work for longer, and have very little non-wage income to support them. (p. 68)

Recently, Child Protection Income Management was introduced in various regions to ensure welfare payments are used to buy food and other necessities for children, and to prevent their use on gambling and alcohol, in families where children are "receiving child protection services due to neglect and where this neglect is related to money." This has been contentious because it was first differentially applied to Aboriginal families and communities and it is difficult to assess whether it has been effective in contributing to improved outcomes for children, particularly when it has been imposed on unwilling parents and other family services are not accessible (Hand et al., 2016). With the 2022 change of government in Australia, this scheme is likely to be ended.

Family Support Services

While a range of voluntary services are available to support families in meeting the needs of their children, the extent to which these are accessible varies markedly according to location, with some regional rural areas and particularly remote areas and Aboriginal communities being poorly serviced. These family support services include linking families to family violence prevention and treatment services, physical and mental health services, disability services and parenting programs, and counselling and substance abuse services. These services are funded by the federal and state governments but can be delivered by either a relevant government department or a non-government agency; they tend to be short-term with little longer-term monitoring.

Families and children with "more complex needs" may be referred to more intensive family support services and specialist therapeutic services with in-home support and/or supported accommodation for children and parents. This may involve care and protection orders that require parents to engage with these services, to be supervised, and to allow monitoring of the child's safety and wellbeing. If concerns about the child continue and cannot be resolved, this is likely to lead to further statutory intervention and the removal of the child from the parents, resulting in guardianship or custody orders or third party parental responsibility orders. In 2020–2021, 10.8 children per 1,000 across Australia were on some type of care and protection orders.

Out-of-home Care

Removing children from their families and placing them in out-of-home care is "a measure of last resort," and the aim is to return children to their families as soon as and whenever it is considered safe to do so. Across Australia, 46,200 children were in out-of-home care as of June 30, 2021, at a rate of 8.1 per 1,000 children.[11] Infants under 12 months of age are the most likely to enter care. Indigenous children are heavily over-represented, at 11 times the rate of non-Indigenous children (57.6 children per 1,000 in care compared with 5.0 per 1,000; AIHW, 2022, Table S5.9).

The two most common placements for children in Australia who enter out-of-home care are relative or kinship care (53.7%) and foster care (36.1%) (AIHW, 2022).[12] Only 7.6% of children are in residential care, which is mainly used for children and adolescents with difficult and challenging behaviors, and also in some cases to keep large sibling groups together.

The use of kinship care has increased substantially over the last 10–15 years because it fits with notions of family preservation and the importance of children maintaining connections with their families. It is also cost-effective and practical because of the shortage of foster carers and the difficulty of finding suitable placements for children in need of care. There are, however, some concerns about the lack of support and proper assessment for relative carers, many of whom are grandmothers with minimal economic resources, called on to care for young children with little financial and practical support.

Kinship care has particular advantages for Indigenous children and is consistent with traditional practices of caring for children within kinship groups. All states and territories have adopted the Aboriginal and Torres Strait Islander Child Placement Principle in both legislation and policy, specifying that Indigenous children should be placed with their Indigenous relatives or extended family members or with family-based carers within their community. The Aboriginal and Torres Strait Islander Child Placement Principle (the ATSICPP) aims to keep children connected to their families, communities, cultures and country, and to ensure the participation of Aboriginal and Torres Strait Islander people in decisions about their children's care and protection. However, the over-representation of Indigenous children in out-of-home care is increasing with a substantial proportion of Indigenous children in placements outside their culturally appropriate group due to lack of attention to the five key elements of the ATSICPP: prevention, partnership,

---

[11] Out-of-home care is overnight care for children aged under 18 who are unable to live with their families due to child safety concerns. This includes placements approved by the department responsible for child protection for which there is ongoing case management and financial payment (including where a financial payment has been offered but has been declined by the carer). Out-of-home care includes legal (court-ordered) and voluntary placements, as well as placements made for the purpose of providing respite for parents and/or carers (AIHW, 2022, Table 5.1).

[12] Nationally as at June 30, 2021, 91.1% of children in care were in home-based care (AIHW, 2022, p. 51; Supplementary Table 5.3).

participation, placement and connection. Recent reports have outlined the failures in relation to prevention, support for reunification, poor identification and assessment of carers and kin, and inadequate involvement of Indigenous people and organizations in decision-making (Davis, 2019; SNAICC, 2018, 2021).

Adoption by carers in Australia is much less common than in the USA and UK, with only 171 children adopted from care in 2019–20, and 100 in 2020–21, with almost all in one state, New South Wales (eg 169 of 171 in 2019–20), reflecting this state's hierarchy of placement priorities (AIHW, 2021; Conley-Wright et al., 2021; Ross & Cashmore, 2016). Adoption is very rare for Indigenous children, regarded as culturally inappropriate, particularly with the legacy of the harm done to the "Stolen Generations" by the earlier large-scale removals of Aboriginal children (Human Rights and Equal Opportunity Commission, 1997). In other states, and increasingly too in New South Wales, an increasing number of children in out-of-home care are being placed on legal orders called third-party permanency orders (permanent care and guardianship orders) to provide legal permanency. These orders transfer parental authority from the state (represented by the executive of a statutory department or Minister) to a carer other than the child's parents until the child reaches 18 years of age. This type of legal order transfers parental responsibility to the carer and these children are not counted as being in care. There is little or no data on these children or research to indicate whether these orders result in long-term relationships of care, continuity, and cultural connection for the child.

Methods for the Delivery of These Provisions

Funding for child protection services in Australia is provided by state and territory governments. This includes the statutory departments which accept, assess, and investigate reports concerning children believed to be at risk of harm as well as the range of other government services that may be involved in providing services to vulnerable children and their families. These services include physical and mental health services, housing, education, and child care services, as well as police investigations of serious allegations of child abuse and neglect which constitute criminal matters. According to the Productivity Commission (2022), 60.3% of the total national recurrent expenditure on family support services, intensive family support services, protective intervention services, and out-of-home care services ($7.5 billion nationally in 2020–21) was expended on out-of-home care services ($4.5 billion). The focus is still very much on tertiary services rather than on primary prevention and early intervention services.

Non-government organizations (NGOs) of varying sizes, including church-related agencies and other private charities, have historically played an important role in the provision of family support, out-of-home care, and other social programs. These agencies derive some funding from state and federal governments and public donations, and they also involve some fee-for-service arrangements. Increasingly, state governments have contracted NGOs to provide early intervention and out-of-home care services for children in competitive tendering processes which have the unfortunate effect of discouraging collaboration between agencies.

Some of these NGOs have engaged in innovative early intervention programs and family support for parents and children (Arney & Scott, 2013). One of the notable successful programs is Newpin, initially based on an English model. Newpin, in different locations across several states, includes therapeutic clinical practice and peer support services for mothers and fathers seeking the return of their children from care and long-term post-restoration support to help parents provide a safe and nurturing environment for their children. The New South Wales state government has invested in an innovative funding model via a Social Benefit Bond with a non-government agency and a financial intermediary that returns funds to investors based on the proportion of children returned safely to their families and the related cost saving to government.[13]

A relatively recent initiative of the coalition of Australian Governments at federal and state levels, in collaboration with the NGO sector, the *National Framework for Protecting Australia's Children* spells out the joint responsibility across different levels of government for a long-term national public health approach to protect the safety and well-being of Australia's children. The *National Frameworks* clearly argued for a focus on prevention and early intervention, and outlined three-year action plans that identify key outcome areas, strategies, actions, responsibilities, and timeframes for implementation. While the framework provides direction, it is still aspirational in many respects. Shifting the loading from the tertiary statutory crisis response of the child protection system to early intervention and family support with services at each level—child, parent, family, and community—continues to be a major challenge (Russ et al., 2022). Driving the associated research agenda and evidence-based policy and practice, with a skilled workforce, has also been challenging.

Evidence-based Practice

Evidence-based practice is the mantra in Australia for child protection services, and the *National Framework* is intended to promote a national research agenda and a solid basis for practice. There have been some significant developments in providing national data based on consistent definitions—as far as that is possible given the differences in legislation, policy, and practice across jurisdictions. There are still, however, some major limitations in access to unit record data and in providing good measures in various areas, as the Productivity Commission (2022) points out. For example, the Commission could not report on some key indicators such as the "percentage of children and young people in the child protection system with improved wellbeing."

---

[13] The model and the evaluation report is available at https://www.osii.nsw.gov.au/tools-and-resources/evaluation-of-the-social-impact-investment/.

Research in relation to child protection and out-of-home care is relatively sparse in Australia, and the national research agenda developed as part of the *National Framework* has so far done little to remedy this. Several useful studies, and particularly the focus on intensive family support services for ATSI children, have filled an important gap. There has also been some useful research and reporting of the experience of children and young people in care by Create, the non-government advocacy organization involving children and young people (McDowall, 2018). There is only a relatively small number of researchers in this field and more rigorous studies evaluating programs are needed, mostly beyond the capacity of small non-government agencies to conduct. Adequate government funding and philanthropic funding of research centers of the type found in the United States is rare. There have been several small scale longitudinal studies of children in care and of children restored home in several states (Fernandez, 2009, 2013; Delfabbro et al., 2013). More recently, the Victorian government has funded a study of young people leaving care (*Beyond 18*) and the New South Wales government has funded an important large-scale longitudinal study of children who entered care over an 18-month period on court orders for the first time (*Pathways of Care*).[14] The Pathways study has completed five waves of data collection and will provide significant insights into children's pathways into, through and out of care, and the factors that make a difference.[15] Another large scale national longitudinal study, *Growing Up in Australia*, provides a useful backdrop and comparison of 10,000 children and families in the general population across Australia.[16]

New Zealand

Bases of Social Allocations

Prior to colonization, Māori children were not considered the property of their parents, but belonged to their *whānau* (family) and had close connections with their *hapu* (subtribe) and *iwi* (tribe). The *whangai* system enabled children to be raised by adults other than their biological parents in open arrangements that strengthened kinship ties and *whakapapa* (genealogy) within the extended family group (Atwool, 2006). However, these Indigenous practices gradually eroded as state intervention to protect children became increasingly common and westernized laws governing adoption (e.g., *Adoption of Children Act* 1881; *Adoption Act* 1955) and welfare (e.g., *Infants Act* 1908; *Child Welfare Act* 1925; *Children and Young Persons Act* 1974) took effect. Over time, this led to the significant over-representation of Māori children living away from their *whānau*, *hapu*, and *iwi* in out-of-home care, which ultimately drove major reform of New Zealand's child protection system in the 1980s (Connolly, 2013).

---

[14] https://www.facs.nsw.gov.au/resources/research/pathways-of-care.

[15] See www.community.nsw.gov.au/research-centre/pathways-of-care-longitudinal-study.

[16] The Longitudinal Study of Australian Children: https://growingupinaustralia.gov.au/.

Statutory child protection services were, by this time, provided by the Department of Social Welfare (DSW) and new initiatives were emerging to respond to child abuse and neglect. Joint protocols enabled co-ordination of the investigation and prosecution of child sexual abuse cases by social workers and the Police. Multidisciplinary child protection teams were established across the country, but thwarted by their lack of a statutory mandate (Tapp & Taylor, 2013). Draft Bills to replace the *Children and Young Persons Act 1974* aimed to remedy this, but arguments ensued between DSW social workers and child protection teams about who should be involved in making care and protection decisions and what the process should be (Atwool, 2006). Against this backdrop, there "was acute interest in the cultural sensitivity of any piece of legislation and its adherence to the principles of the Treaty of Waitangi" (Tapp & Taylor, 2013, p. 99). A significant report, *Puao-Te-Ata-Tu* (Daybreak), by the Ministerial Advisory Committee on a Māori Perspective for the Department of Social Welfare (1988) identified the harm done to Māori and their culture by British colonization and its detrimental impact on their well-being and socioeconomic status. Māori also felt very disempowered about the severing of cultural identity and heritage that occurred when their children were placed in institutional and foster care (Connolly, 2013).

A combination of cultural, financial, philosophical, and social work influences thus led to a decisive shift away from a professionalized team approach, dominated by medical and legal practitioners, to a new more family- and *whānau*-oriented response in the *Children, Young Persons and Their Families Act 1989* (Tapp & Taylor, 2013). This statute introduced Family Group Conferences (FGCs) as the primary mechanism for care and protection decision-making. Following a notification and its investigation, the FGC coordinator works with the family to identify which extended family members should be invited to the FGC in order to mobilize support for the family to keep the child safe. Other FGC participants include the statutory social worker responsible for the case and the staff of other services involved with the child and family (including school, health, and social service agencies). The FGC has three phases: (1) information sharing with the family by all those invited to attend; (2) a family-only discussion during which the family members develop a plan to keep the child safe; and (3) sharing of the plan with all the FGC participants and negotiated agreement to implement it. If the family's plan is not sufficiently protective or realistic the matter is referred back to the CYF social worker for further action, which may include an application to the Family Court. Enthusiasm for the FGC as the vehicle for family empowerment and decision-making quickly spread beyond New Zealand and FGCs are now incorporated in the child protection systems of several countries including Australia, Canada, UK, and USA.

Concerns about the FGC process emerged within a relatively short time, particularly regarding the quality of the decision making and its impact on children's best interests. Inadequate funding also affected family member participation in FGCs and the resourcing of FGC plans (Atwool, 2008). The statutory response by the new government department,

Child Youth and Family (CYF), also came under frequent scrutiny as it struggled to demonstrate it was "making a sufficiently positive difference in the lives of the children and young people" it served (Modernising Child, Youth and Family Expert Panel, 2015a, p. 6). CYF was reviewed almost continuously from 1988 to 2016 (see, for example, Mason, 1992; Brown, 2000; Smith, 2011), including 14 restructures during one decade from 1998 to 2008. Fatal case reviews undertaken by the Commissioner for Children identified failings within CYF including glaring weaknesses in social worker training, an unwillingness to upset *whānau* by properly focusing on the harm suffered by an abused child (Hassall, 1993), and fragmented service delivery, lack of a coherent cross-sectoral approach to child protection (Commissioner for Children, 2000), and failure to recognize the risk to children exposed to domestic violence in their home (Kiro, 2003). CYF was also struggling with a substantial increase in the number of notifications throughout the 1990s, "and by 222 per cent from 2002 to 2014" (Modernising Child, Youth and Family Expert Panel, 2015a, p. 22). The Office of the Children's Commissioner, which independently monitors CYF annually, found CYF's performance "concerning" (2015, p. 2) and pointed to inconsistent practice, the failure to place children at the center of its work, and the high degree of variability among the sites and residences visited (Office of the Children's Commissioner, 2015).

The Government launched a discussion paper in 2011 to give people and communities a say on how New Zealand can better protect abused, neglected and disadvantaged children (Ministry of Social Development, 2011). Nearly 10,000 submissions were received, leading to the White Paper for Vulnerable Children (Ministry of Social Development, 2012) that set out how to keep vulnerable children safe from harm. The Children's Action Plan, released in 2012, now provides the framework around the action to be taken to protect children. The *Vulnerable Children Act* 2014 was enacted and amendments made to the *Children, Young Persons and Their Families Act* 1989.

In 2015 the Minister for Social Development appointed an Expert Panel to modernize CYF and transform the lives of vulnerable children once and for all. While there were pockets of good practice and a committed frontline workforce, the panel's interim report concluded that CYF lacked clarity of purpose and accountability within the wider sector, was reactive and incident-focused, and was not sufficiently responsive to increasing demand and the complexity of current need: "Our overall observation is that the care and protection system in New Zealand requires significant improvement in order to fulfil its purpose" (Modernising Child, Youth and Family Expert Panel, 2015a, p. 79).

The Modernising Child, Youth and Family Expert Panel (2015b) then developed an ambitious reform program to significantly extend the range of services provided to vulnerable children and young people, and to take a proactive and life outcomes-focused approach to meeting their needs. Their proposed operating model was focused on prevention, early intervention and development of a child-centered system prioritizing children and young people's voices and needs.

The Government agreed with the Expert Panel that a bold and urgent overhaul of the care and protection system was required. The *Investing in Children Programme*, launched in response in 2016, is a long-term transformation program underpinned by six foundation building blocks, including a child-centered system, high aspirations for Māori children, an investment approach, strategic partnerships, a professional practice framework, and engagement with all New Zealanders. CYF was replaced in 2017 by *Oranga Tamariki—Ministry for Children*, which now focuses on five core services: prevention, intensive intervention, care support, youth justice, and transition support. Its broader remit also signals a whole of sector approach and a single point of accountability. The *Children's Act 2014* has also enhanced the responsibilites of the Chief Executives of the Ministries of Education, Health, Justice, and Social Development to improve the wellbeing of vulnerable children and to ensure that child protection policies are in place for government agency staff who work with children. A national *Child and Youth Wellbeing Strategy* was launched in 2019.

Child Protection Processes

In New Zealand child maltreatment ranges from fatal injuries to physical abuse, sexual abuse, and emotional abuse, including exposure to family violence and long-term chronic neglect. Nearly one in five children will come into contact with Oranga Tamariki by age 17 because of care and protection concerns (Modernising Child, Youth and Family Expert Panel, 2015a). The Expert Panel (2015b) estimated that:

> there are about 230,000 children and young people currently under age 18 who might experience vulnerability at some point during their childhood. Around six out of 10 of this group are likely to be Māori. Based on what currently occurs, it is estimated that one quarter of this group will require intensive support and a statutory response at some point in their childhood. (p. 41)

Using CYF data, 8% of all children born in 1993 were found to have suffered abuse or neglect, and around 3% to have spent time in state care, at some stage during their childhood (Modernising Child, Youth and Family Expert Panel, 2015b). Most children referred to Oranga Tamariki are living in families with multiple and complex needs and disadvantage including "the combined impacts of long-term unemployment, low income, unaddressed physical and mental health needs, parental alcohol and drug addiction, and family violence" (Modernising Child, Youth and Family Expert Panel, 2015b, p. 42).

Māori children and young people are twice as likely to be referred to the statutory agency compared to the total population:

> Although Māori children make up 30% of all children in New Zealand under five years, 57% of children seen by CYF by aged five are Māori. This over-representation is likely to be a

consequence of the disproportionate number of Māori children and young people in families with high levels of need and disadvantage. For example, Māori children born between 2003 and 2007 were four times more likely to have a mother who had been dependent on a benefit than non-Māori children born in the same period. Importantly, the over-representation of Māori children and young people increases with the extent of involvement with CYF. About five out of every 10 referrals to CYF are for Māori children and young people, yet Māori make up six out of every 10 children and young people in care. (Modernising Child, Youth and Family Expert Panel, 2015b, p. 43)

In contrast to the trends in Australia, the overall number of children coming to the attention of CYF/Oranga Tamariki has been decreasing in recent years from a 2009 peak, but there is an increasing proportion of children being referred who are already known to the agency (Modernising Child, Youth and Family Expert Panel, 2015a). "In 2014, six out of ten notifications made to CYF for protection were for children the agency already knew about, and many had extensive history with the agency" (Modernising Child, Youth and Family Expert Panel, 2015a, p. 7). National data for the year July 2020–June 2021 showed that there were 77,953 reports of concern to Oranga Tamariki, of which 42,250 were referred for assessment or investigation (Oranga Tamariki, 2021). There were 8,909 FGCs convened. Children and young people in the custody of the Chief Executive totaled 5,250. There is a concerning level of revictimization, with three out of every 10 care leavers in 2010 being renotified to CYF within 18 months of exiting care (Modernising Child, Youth and Family Expert Panel, 2015a). On average, 10 children are killed each year as a result of family-related violence and most of these are aged under 5 years, with the largest group less than a year old (Connolly & Doolan, 2007; Duncanson et al., 2009).

The *Oranga Tamariki Act 1989* aims to promote the well-being of children, young persons, and their families and family groups. Part Two of the Act sets out the principles governing the care and protection of children (under the age of 14 years) and young people (of or over the age of 14 years, but under the age of 18 years). This Part also includes the definition of a child or young person in need of care and protection, the reporting of child abuse, FGCs, medical examinations, powers to remove, Family Court proceedings, counselling, access, the range of orders (services, support, custody, guardianship) and agreements that can be made, and the making and reviewing of plans.

Mandatory reporting by professionals has been considered several times in New Zealand.[17] Various professional groups did, at times, support mandatory reporting, but it was ultimately rejected each time by the Government in favor of improved public and professional awareness of child abuse and neglect and the development of voluntary

---

[17] The Child Protection Bill 1982 and the Mason Report (1992) recommended its introduction, and the Brown Report (2000) considered the matter.

reporting protocols (Tapp & Taylor, 2013). Notifications about a child's safety and well-being are therefore made voluntarily to a national contact center within Oranga Tamariki, where an initial safety and risk screen is undertaken using an evidence-based intake decision response tool. The intake social worker decides whether the notification meets the threshold for statutory action and, if so, determines the timeframe for response by the appropriate Oranga Tamariki site office. Local staff then review the initial decision, either confirm or amend it, and move into the assessment stage, where two options are possible—an assessment by an Oranga Tamariki social worker alone or a joint assessment/investigation with the Police where there is the possibility of criminal charges being laid (known as a Child Protection Protocol Investigation). Each child or young person referred for assessment must have their Safety and Risk Screen completed within 24 or 48 hours where there is high risk and no immediate protection is available, or within seven days, or 20 working days, for all other cases. These statutory investigations and assessments are designed to ensure the child is kept safe and that an understanding of needs, strengths and risk is obtained. Where there is immediate risk to the child's safety or well-being, the child will be removed from home and placed in a temporary living arrangement pending a further decision.

If the assessment identifies the need for further statutory intervention then, where there are enough safety factors present, a family/*whānau* agreement may be entered into. This is a voluntary written contract between the family/*whānau* and Oranga Tamariki intended to provide the minimum necessary level of intervention required to address the safety and protection concerns for the child or young person. Alternatively, when the child or young person is in need of care and/or protection under the *Oranga Tamariki Act 1989*, then an FGC will be convened and a plan developed. This may result in the state providing care for the child in the custody of the Chief Executive via a mix of options including family-*whānau*/kinship care, foster care, supervised family-like (small group) settings, or residential care. "Caregiving in New Zealand predominantly relies on volunteers, the majority of whom are related to the children" (Modernising Child, Youth and Family Expert Panel, 2015a, p. 60).

Nature of Social Provisions Allocated to Protect Children

FAMILY SUPPORT SERVICES

Notifications to Oranga Tamariki that do not require statutory intervention may be referred through the *Partnered Response* pathway to a non-governmental social service provider in the family support sector. This is a less intrusive intervention for lower risk cases and, because the pathway is voluntary, the family can decide whether or not to engage with the agency.

The Children's Action Plan is also "focused on prevention and early intervention services working with at risk families so that they do not require a statutory response" (Office of the Children's Commissioner, 2015, p. 11). To help achieve this, Children's Teams were progressively established across much of New Zealand from 2013 to support vulnerable children with multiple needs who were below the statutory intervention threshold. Children's Teams support local practitioners and professionals (including paediatricians, social workers, teachers, government agencies, *iwi*, and non-governmental organizations) to coordinate existing services for vulnerable children into one personalized plan for each child and their family/*whānau*. Each Children's Team approves the referral of a child to the Team and assigns a Lead Professional to undertake an assessment and plan of action for that child. The Lead Professional regularly reports back to their Children's Team on progress against that plan, which the Children's Team monitors and reviews until the child's needs are met.

Numerous non-government church-based, *iwi*, and charitable agencies provide child and family support services across New Zealand, some through contractual partnerships with Oranga Tamariki. Key programs include *Strengthening Families, Early Start, The Incredible Years*, and *Triple P*. Eleven government agencies, together with community-based services, are actively involved with the free *Strengthening Families*[18] program. This assists family/*whānau* requiring help with a child or young person's education, health, or behavior, budgeting, or finding a suitable home when more than one community support organization or government service is, or could be, required. *Early Start*[19] is an intensive home visiting support service for families/*whānau* with new-born babies where social and family circumstances may challenge the health and well-being of their children. *The Incredible Years*[20] program involves parents attending fun interactive weekly group sessions over one to two school terms to discuss and practice new ways of managing children's challenging behavior, learn how to develop positive social skills in children and enhance relationships in families. *Triple P*[21] provides a range of positive parenting programs to provide parents with a choice of simple strategies to build better relationships and manage children's behavior. These integrated social services are increasingly being seen as key to addressing service fragmentation and poor outcomes with vulnerable children, young people, families, and *whānau* who have multiple needs. However, there are few rigorous quantitative outcome evaluations of integrated services, and none in New Zealand, so evidence regarding their effectiveness for vulnerable groups is emerging and mixed (Social Policy Evaluation and Research Unit, 2015).

OUT-OF-HOME CARE

Prior to 1989, children were placed with family when the opportunity arose, but foster care with strangers was the primary means of caring for children who could not live at

---

[18] http://www.strengtheningfamilies.govt.nz/index.html.

[19] https://www.earlystart.co.nz/.

[20] http://incredibleyearsnz.co.nz/parents.

[21] https://www.triplep-parenting.net.nz/nz-uken/find-help/the-triple-p-centre/.

home (Connolly, 2013). This changed when kinship care assumed increased significance with passage of the 1989 Act and social workers were required to seek family/*whānau* placements in the first instance. Oranga Tamariki aims to return children to their own parents and caregivers when it is safe to do so. However, those who need to remain in permanent out-of-home care are placed with family/*whānau* carers where possible, or live in a variety of other situations including foster placements, residential care,[22] other supported accommodation, or live independently (only a small number).

Once a child has been placed in the custody of the Chief Executive as their legal guardian, social workers are required to prepare plans (semi-annually for children under seven years of age, and annually for children over seven) and gain agreement from relevant parties at planning meetings. The Family Court reviews these plans.

When it is not possible to return the child or young person to the care of their parents, an approved Home for Life placement is sought (Centre for Social Research and Evaluation, 2012). The custody orders in favor of the Chief Executive are then discharged and the caregivers obtain legal orders to secure the placement. The Home for Life package provides support for three years, including the payment of reasonable legal costs, an upfront payment to set the home up for the child, access to support, advocacy with other agencies, respite care, and review.

Until recently, a young person aged-out of state care on their 17th birthday, but was often ill-prepared for this transition to independence and struggled with the lack of support and enduring legacy of their care journey (Atwool, 2010, 2016; Modernising Child, Youth and Family Expert Panel, 2015a). Amongst New Zealand's most vulnerable young people, care-leavers had adverse childhood events, experienced highly disrupted childhoods, and faced poor long-term life outcomes (Modernising Child, Youth and Family Expert Panel, 2015b). The age of leaving state care was therefore raised, in 2017, from 17 to 18 years. *VOYCE—Whakarongo Mai*[23] was also established in 2017 as an independent youth connect and advocacy service to give children and young people in care a voice. Adoption has been steadily declining in New Zealand since the 1960s and is now a very rare, culturally inappropriate, option for children in out-of-home care.

An attempt by Oranga Tamariki to remove a week-old baby from his Māori mother in hospital in 2019 sparked public outrage and dramatically highlighted the competing tensions involved in the state uplifting Māori newborn babies from their families and *whānau*. Formal reviews ensued (by Oranga Tamariki, the Children's Commissioner, the Chief Ombudsman), as well as Māori-led reviews (by the Whânau Ora Commissioning Agency and the Waitangi Tribunal), which urged the Government to either improve their

---

[22] Large residential facilities started closing in the 1980s, but Oranga Tamariki still operates four secure Care and Protection residences for children at serious risk of harm who cannot be placed in the community and need to be cared for and protected.

[23] VOYCE (Voice of the Young and Care Experienced): https://voyce.org.nz/.

partnership model with Māori or to transfer power and resources to enable *by Māori, for Māori* approaches (Taylor & Ballantyne, 2020). This issue is dominating current debates about how best to deliver care and protection services and reduce the disparities for Māori children and young people.

How Are Child Protection Services Financed?

Child abuse costs New Zealand around $2 billion each year (Infometrics Ltd., 2008). Statutory services are funded by the Government and the 2018 Budget provided an additional $269.9m over four years for Oranga Tamariki to expand its services. This is part of the Government's plan to better assist low- and middle-income families with children and to reduce child poverty.

Evidence-based Practice

Small-scale research undertaken in New Zealand has shown how FGCs have contributed positively to family empowerment and participation in decision making (see, for example, Gilling et al., 1995; Morris & Connolly, 2012). However, unlike other countries that have adopted the FGC model, New Zealand has never invested in rigorous evaluative research, "making it difficult to prove by evidence-based practice that the FGC does provide safety and well-being for children by protecting them from abuse and neglect" (Kayni, 2013, p. 40). Rather, a proliferation of commentaries, descriptive or analytical reports, and small-scale qualitative studies on aspects of the care and protection system have been authored by Government departments, commissioned researchers, the Office of the Children's Commissioner, academics, and postgraduate university students (Atwool, 2008; Tapp & Taylor, 2013; Smith, 2016).

The University of Otago hosts two of the world's most significant longitudinal studies: the *Dunedin Multidisciplinary Health and Development Study*, documenting the lives of around 1,000 children born in 1972–73[24]; and the *Christchurch Health and Development Study*, following the lives of 1,265 children born during mid-1977.[25] A more contemporary cohort of nearly 7,000 children, born in 2009–10 in Auckland and Waikato, are also being tracked by the University of Auckland through the newer *Growing Up in New Zealand* longitudinal study.[26] These studies have identified the link between disadvantaged and dysfunctional upbringings, including exposure to child abuse, poverty and impaired parenting capacity, and adverse child and adult outcomes (Fergusson & Lynskey, 1997; Morton et al., 2017). With respect to the care and protection system specifically, New Zealand does not yet "have enough information to say conclusively whether children are better off as a result of state intervention, but the limited data we do have about health,

---

[24] https://www.otago.ac.nz/profiles/otago045632.html.
[25] https://www.otago.ac.nz/christchurch/research/healthdevelopment/.
[26] http://www.growingup.co.nz/en.html.

education and justice outcomes is concerning" (Office of the Children's Commissioner, 2015, p. 5).

Research ascertaining the perspectives of children and young people with direct experience of New Zealand's care and protection system has been an important influence on reform processes, particularly for those children living in out-of-home care (Smith et al., 1999; Atwool, 2010; Smith, 2016). A Youth Advisory Panel made up of young people with experience of CYF services informed the recommendations of the Modernising Child, Youth and Family Expert Panel (2015a, 2015b) and in-depth research undertaken with 19 young people in state care (Modernising Child, Youth and Family Expert Panel, 2015a) helped achieve the raising of the care-leaving age from 17 to 18 years. To help inform the *Child and Youth Wellbeing Strategy*, extensive consultations were undertaken with over 6,000 children and young people who shared their views on what wellbeing means to them (Office of the Children's Commissioner and Oranga Tamariki, 2019).

Conclusion

The presence of mandatory reporting in Australia, and its absence in New Zealand, is a key difference between the child protection policies of these two jurisdictions. However, in most other respects, these two countries are very similar in their statutory response to the notification, investigation, assessment, and decision-making processes for child abuse and neglect. Both demonstrate a preference for the placement of children in family contexts and have emphasized kinship care in recent times. Australia and New Zealand have both endeavored to reduce the number of children in out-of-home care, and continue to struggle with substantial over-representation of Indigenous and minority children and young people in their child protection systems (Social Policy Evaluation and Research Unit, 2016).

In the face of mounting evidence of the poor outcomes experienced by vulnerable and particularly Indigenous children, both countries have embarked upon modernization and reform programs to improve the quality of their statutory response and to provide increased support to abused and neglected children and their families, and to care-leavers through into adulthood (Fernandez & Atwool, 2013). Australia is struggling to move the focus to prevention, early intervention, and family support to provide services to families in need rather than removing their children. Children's rights to participate in the care and protection decisions that affect them are articulated in the legislation in both Australian and New Zealand, but barely realized in practice (Connolly, 2013; Fernandez & Atwool, 2013; Smith, 2016). Finally, Australia and New Zealand face the challenge of transforming their child protection responses to children and families from a deficit approach to more collaborative ways of providing support for families that involve working out solutions in the best interests of children and families for both their immediate and longer-term outcomes.

References

Arney, F. and Scott, D. (Eds). (2013). *Working with vulnerable families: A partnership approach*. Cambridge University Press.

Atwool, N. (2006). Participation in decision-making: The experience of New Zealand children in care. *Child Care in Practice*, 12(3), 259–267.

Atwool, N. (2008). *Who cares? The role of attachment assessments in decision-making for children in care* [Unpublished doctoral dissertation]. University of Otago.

Atwool, N. (2010). *Children in care: A report into the quality of services provided to children in care*. Office of the Children's Commissioner.

Atwool, N. (2016). Journeys of exclusion: Unpacking the experience of adolescent care leavers in New Zealand. In P. Mendes and P. Snow (Eds.), *Young people transitioning from out-of-home care: International research, policy and practice* (pp. 309–328). Palgrave Macmillan.

Australian Institute of Health and Welfare. (2021). *Adoptions Australia 2020–21*. Child welfare series no. 76. Cat. no. CWS 85. AIHW.

Australian Institute of Health and Welfare. (2020). *Child protection Australia 2018–19*. Child welfare series no. 72. Cat. no. CWS 74. AIHW.

Australian Institute of Health and Welfare. (2022). *Child protection Australia 2020–21*. Child welfare series no. 72. Cat. no. CWS 87. AIHW.

Brown, M. J. A. (2000). *Care and protection is about adult behaviour: The Ministerial Review of the Department of Child, Youth and Family Services*. Report to the Minister of Social Services and Employment, New Zealand. Available at: https://www.msd.govt.nz/documents/about-msd-and-our-work/publications-resources/arch ive/2000-care-and-protection-is-about-adult-behaviour.pdf.

Cashmore, J. (2016). "Best interests" in care proceedings: Law, policy and practice. In E. E. Sutherland and L.-A. Barnes Macfarlane (Eds.), *Implementing Article 3 of the United Nations Convention on the Rights of the Child: Best interests, welfare and well-being* (pp. 326–340). Cambridge University Press.

Centre for Social Research and Evaluation. (2012). *Home for Life evaluation findings*. Ministry of Social Development.

Commissioner for Children. (2000). *Final report on the investigation into the death of James Whakaruru, 1994–1999*. Office of the Commissioner for Children.

Conley-Wright, A., Luu, B., and Cashmore, J. (2021). Adoption in Australia: Past, present and considerations for the future. *Australian Law Journal*, 95, 67–80.

Connolly, M. (2013). Care and protection: Australia and the international context. In R. Sheehan and A. Borowski (Eds.), *Australia's Children's Courts today and tomorrow* (pp. 187–196). Springer Science and Business Media.

Connolly, M. and Doolan, M. (2007). *Lives cut short: Child death by maltreatment*. Dunmore Press.

Council of Australian Governments. (2009). *Protecting children is everyone's business: National Framework for Protecting Australia's Children*. Commonwealth of Australia.

Davis, M. (2019). *Family is culture: independent review of Aboriginal children in out-of-home care*. Sydney, University of New South Wales.

Delfabbro, P. H., Fernandez, E., and McCormick, J. (2013). Reunification in a complete entry cohort: A longitudinal study of children entering out-of-home care in Tasmania, Australia. *Children and Youth Services Review*, 35, 1592–1600.

Duncanson, M., Smith, D., and Davies, E. (2009). *Death and serious injury from assault of children under 5 years in Aotearoa New Zealand: A review of international literature and recent findings*. Office of the Children's Commissioner.

Families Commission. (2012). *New Zealand families today: A brief demographic profile*. Families Commission.

Fergusson, D. M. and Lynskey, M. T. (1997). Physical punishment/maltreatment during childhood and adjustment in young adulthood. *Child Abuse & Neglect*, 21(7), 617–630.

Fernandez, E. A. (2009). Children's wellbeing in care: Evidence from a longitudinal study of outcomes. *Children and Youth Services Review*, 31, 1092–1100.

Fernandez, E. A. (2013). *Accomplishing permanency: Reunification pathways and outcomes for foster care children*. Springer.

Fernandez, E. and Atwool, N. (2013). Child protection and out of home care: Policy, practice, and research connections Australia and New Zealand. *Psychosocial Intervention*, 22(3), 175–184.

Gilling, M., Paterson, L., and Walker, B. (1995). *Family members' experiences of the child and protection family group conference.* Social Policy Agency.

Green, M. J., Harris, F., Laurens, K. R., Tzoumakis, S., Dean, K., Brinkman, S., Chilvers, M., Sprague, T., Stevens, R. and Carr, V. J. (2018). The New South Wales Child Development Study (NSW-CDS) – Wave 2 (Child age 13 years). *International Journal of Epidemiology*, 45(5), 1396–1397k. doi:10.1093/ije/dyy115.

Hand, K., Katz, I., Gray, M., and Bray, R. (2016). Welfare conditionality as a child protection tool. *Family Matters*, 97, 16–29.

Harris, N. (2011). Does responsive regulation offer an alternative? Questioning the role of formalistic assessment in child protection investigations. *British Journal of Social Work*, 41, 1383–1403.

Hassall, I. B. (1993). *Report to the Minister of Social Welfare on the NZ Children and Young Persons Service's Review of Practice in relation to Craig Manukau and his family.* Office of the Commissioner for Children.

Howlett, M., Gray, M., and Hunter, B. (2016). Wages, government payments and other income of Indigenous and non-Indigenous Australians. *Australian Journal of Labour Economics*, 19, 53–76.

Human Rights and Equal Opportunity Commission. (1997). *Bringing them home: National Inquiry into the Separation of Aboriginal and Torres Strait Islander Children from Their Families.* Human Rights and Equal Opportunity Commission NSW.

Infometrics Ltd. (2008). *The nature of economic costs from child abuse and neglect in New Zealand.* Every Child Counts.

Kanyi, T. (2013). Lack of outcome research on New Zealand care and protection family group conference. *Aotearoa New Zealand Social Work Journal*, 25(1), 35–42.

Kaspiew, R., Carson, R., Dunstan, J. Qu, L. Horsfall, B., De Maio, J., Moore, S., Moloney, L., Coulson M., and Tayton, S. (2015). *Evaluation of the 2012 family violence amendments: Synthesis report.* Australian Institute of Family Studies.

Kiro, C. (2003). *Report of the investigation into the deaths of Saliel Jalessa Aplin and Olympia Marisa Aplin.* Office of the Commissioner for Children.

McDowall, J. J. (2018). *Out-of-home care in Australia: Children and young people's views after five years of National Standards.* Sydney: CREATE Foundation.

Mason, K. (1992). *Report of the Ministerial Review Team to the Minister of Social Welfare.* Ministerial Review Team.

Mein Smith, P. (2012). *Australia and New Zealand—Shared colonial history.* Te Ara—The Encyclopedia of New Zealand, Ministry for Culture and Heritage, New Zealand. Available at: https://teara.govt.nz/en/australia-and-new-zealand/page-1.

Ministerial Advisory Committee on a Māori Perspective for the Department of Social Welfare. (1988). *Puao-Te-Ata-Tu.* Department of Social Welfare.

Ministry of Social Development. (2011). *Every child thrives, belongs, achieves—Ka whai orange, ka whai wahi, ka whai taumata ia tamaiti: The Green Paper for vulnerable children.* Ministry of Social Development.

Ministry of Social Development. (2012). *The White Paper for Vulnerable Children.* Ministry of Social Development.

Modernising Child, Youth, and Family Expert Panel. (2015a). *Expert Panel Interim Report: Investing in New Zealand's children and their families.* Ministry of Social Development.

Modernising Child, Youth, and Family Expert Panel. (2015b). *Expert Panel Final Report: Investing in New Zealand's children and their families.* Ministry of Social Development.

Morgan, A., Boxall, H., Terer, K., and Harris, N. (2012). *Evaluation of alternative dispute resolution initiatives in the care and protection jurisdiction of the NSW Children's Court.* Research and public policy series No. 118. Australian Institute of Criminology. Available at: https://www.aic.gov.au/publications/rpp/rpp118.

Morris, K. and Connolly, M. (2012). Family decision making in child welfare: Challenges in developing a knowledge base for practice. *Child Abuse Review*, 21, 41–52.

Morton, S. M. B., Grant, C. C., Berry, S. D., Walker, C. G., Corkin, M., Ly, K., de Castro, T. G., Atatoa Carr, P. E., Bandara, D. K., Mohal, J., Bird, A., Underwood, L., and Fa'alili-Fidow, J. (2017). *Growing Up in New Zealand: A longitudinal study of New Zealand children and their families. Now we are four: Describing the preschool years.* Growing Up in New Zealand, University of Auckland, New Zealand. Available at: https://cdn.auckland.ac.nz/assets/growingup/research-findings-impact/GUiNZ_Now%20we%20are%20four%20report.pdf.

Office of the Children's Commissioner. (2015). *State of Care 2015.* Office of the Children's Commissioner.

Office of the Children's Commissioner. (2018). *Population, ages and ethnicities of children.* Office of the Children's Commissioner.

Office of the Children's Commissioner and Oranga Tamariki—Ministry for Children. (2019). *What makes a good life? Children and young people's views on wellbeing.* Office of the Children's Commissioner and Oranga Tamariki.

Oranga Tamariki—Ministry for Children. (2021). *Annual Report 2021.* Wellington: Oranga Tamariki.

Productivity Commission. (2022). *Report on Government Services* Part F Section 16. Australian Government Productivity Commission. https://www.pc.gov.au/research/ongoing/report-on-government-services/2022/community-services/child-protection

Ross, N. and Cashmore, J. (2016). Adoption reforms New South Wales style: A comparative look. *Australian Journal of Family Law*, 30(1), 51–75.

Russ, E., Morley, L., Driver, M., Lonne, B., Harries, M., and Higgins, D. (2022). *Trends and needs in the Australian child welfare workforce: an exploratory study.* ACU Institute of Child Protection Studies. https://doi.org/10.24268/acu.8x396.

Sheehan, R. (2001). *Magistrates' decision-making in child protection cases.* Ashgate.

Sheehan, R. and Borowski, A. (Eds.) (2013). *Australia's Children's Courts today and tomorrow.* Springer.

Shonkoff, J. P., Boyce, W. T., and McEwen, B. S. (2009). Neuroscience, molecular biology, and the childhood roots of health disparities: Building a new framework for health promotion and disease prevention. *The Journal of the American Medical Association*, 301, 2252–2259.

Smith, A. B. (2016). Children's rights in child protection systems. In A. B. Smith (Ed.), *Children's rights: Towards social justice* (pp. 91–112). Momentum Press.

Smith, A. B., Gollop, M., Taylor, N. J., and Atwool, N. (1999). Children's voices in foster or kinship care: Knowledge, understanding and participation. *Journal of Child Centred Practice*, 6(1), 9–37.

Smith, M. (2011). *Report to Hon Paula Bennett, Minister for Social Development and Employment following an inquiry into the serious abuse of a nine year old girl and other matters relating to the welfare, safety and protection of children in New Zealand.* Ministry of Social Development and Employment, New Zealand. Available at: https://www.beehive.govt.nz/sites/default/files/Smith_report.pdf. Retrieved February 21, 2013.

Secretariat of National Aboriginal and Islander Child Care (SNAICC). (2018). *The Aboriginal and Torres Strait Islander Child Placement Principle: A guide to implementation,* Melbourne, SNAICC. Retrieved from https://www.snaicc.org.au/wp-content/uploads/2019/06/928_SNAICC-ATSICPP-resource-June2019.pdf.

Secretariat of National Aboriginal and Islander Child Care (SNAICC). (2021). *The Family Matters report 2021,* Melbourne: SNAICC. Retrieved from https://www.familymatters.org.au/the-family-matters-report-2021/

Social Policy Evaluation and Research Unit. (2015). *What works: Integrated social services for vulnerable people.* Superu.

Social Policy Evaluation and Research Unit. (2016). *Modernising child protection in New Zealand: Learning from system reforms in other jurisdictions.* In Focus Series. Superu.

Stats NZ. (2015). *National ethnic population projections: 2013 (base)—2038.* Stats NZ.

Stats NZ. (2022). *National population estimates: At 31 December 2021.* Stats NZ.

Tapp, P. F. and Taylor, N. J. (2013). Protecting the family. In R. M. Henaghan and B. Atkin (Eds.), *Family law policy in New Zealand* (4th ed.) (pp. 99–161). LexisNexis NZ Ltd.

Taylor, N. J. and Ballantyne, R. (2020). Protecting children, families and whānau from family violence. In R.M. Henaghan and B. Atkin (Eds.), *Family law policy in New Zealand* (5th ed.) (pp. 99–147). LexisNexis NZ Ltd.

The Austrian Child Welfare System: Moving Towards Professionalization and Participation

Katrin Križ, Jenny Krutzinna, *and* Peter Pantuček-Eisenbacher

Abstract

This chapter expounds on the shift to professionalization and participation of the child welfare system in Austria. It clarifies how Austrian states have lesser autonomy compared to Germany or the USA. Child welfare is ultimately under the responsibility of Austrian states. Child welfare services (CWS) have a legal obligation to intervene when a child's well-being is at risk under the purview of the provincial states, while the wider preventive CWS is under the care of local communities. Additionally, national laws have been drafted and interpreted in accordance with the principles of the UN Convention on the Rights of the Child.

Key Words: child welfare services, professionalization, UNCRC, Austria, states, local communities, national laws

Introduction

Austria is a federal republic, consisting of nine states (*Länder*), with a total population of 8,858,775 and a child population of 1,535,958 (Statistik Austria, 2019, as of January 1, 2019). The City of Vienna serves a dual role as capital city and state (the most populous of the nine states). The states have their own elected legislatures, a state government and a governor as well as a state constitution. In practice, Austrian federalism is limited, as very few legislative powers remain with the states— child and youth protection being one of them. Many key areas, such as healthcare and education, are regulated by federal laws. In line with the Austrian constitution, the judiciary is an exclusively federal matter. Thus, Austrian states have a much smaller degree of autonomy than their equivalents in Germany or the USA. The domain of child welfare falls under the responsibility of the states. Although the federal 1989 Youth Welfare Law (Jugendwohlfahrtsgesetz, 1989) constitutes the basis of the Child Welfare Services (CWS) in Austria, the nine states all have their own applicable laws. While the states' legal provisions do not significantly differ from one another, there is large variation in the approaches to child welfare practice and outcomes.

Child welfare in the wider sense, including child welfare and preventive and support services, such as centers for children and young people or other social support services for disadvantaged children and young people, is organized in two parallel systems. The CWS, which falls within the purview of the provincial state and the district bureaucracies, has a legal obligation to intervene only when the child's well-being is at risk. The wider, preventive child welfare services fall within the purview of the local communities, by way of their elected representatives and bureaucracies (Pantuček-Eisenbacher, 2014b).

We will first discuss child welfare laws and policies before explaining the system responses to child endangerment and providing statistics about these responses. Subsequently, we will describe the methods of service delivery and discuss recent reforms. We will close the chapter by highlighting the public debate about the Austrian child welfare system.

Child Welfare Laws and Policies

Austria's Legal System

The Republic of Austria is grounded in a federal constitution, which is the body of all constitutional legislation at the federal level, while the nine states have their own written constitutions. Practically, all matters of importance, including criminal law, foreign policy, defense, and most aspects of education, welfare, and the health system lie with the federation, giving the states very little autonomy. There are also no state courts, as the judicial system is an exclusively federal matter in Austria. Cases are predominantly tried in the district courts, with regional courts serving as courts of appeal. The Supreme Court is the court of last resort and as Austria's legal system recognizes a statutory right to appeal, higher courts cannot simply refuse to review a decision reached by a lower court. Matters of child welfare fall within the responsibility of the states. Each state drafts its own child welfare legislation, guided by the federal 1989 Youth Welfare Law (Jugendwohlfahrtsgesetz, 1989). While the states' legal provisions do not significantly differ, the child welfare responses do.

Status of the UN Convention on the Rights of the Child (CRC)

Austria has ratified the CRC, which entered into force in Austria in 1992. Since then, national laws must be drafted and interpreted in accordance with the principles laid down by the CRC, but the direct applicability of the Convention is explicitly excluded in Austria (Neudorfer and Wernig, 2010). Following pressures by advocacy groups, including the child and youth representatives from the nine states, the National Council in 2011 decided to incorporate some of the main provisions of the CRC into the federal constitution— albeit in limited form (Kinder- und Jugendanwaltschaft Österreichs, 2011). For instance, the rights of children with disabilities to equal treatment and the right to violence-free upbringing now have constitutional protection (Bundesgesetzblatt, 2011).

Article 5 of the 2011 Constitutional Law and Article 137 of the Austrian Civil Code forbids any type of violence and bodily or emotional suffering. It stipulates:

(1) Every child has the right to a violence-free upbringing. Physical punishments, the infliction of emotional suffering, sexual abuse and other types of abuse are prohibited. Every child has the right to protection from economic and sexual exploitation.

(2) Every child who has been the victim of violence or exploitation has the right to appropriate compensation and rehabilitation. The laws determine the details. (Bundeskanzleramt, 2018)

The prohibition of violence against children encompasses treatment of the child that is averse to the child's well-being. This definition includes bodily harm as well as the infliction of physical pain ("the healthy blow to the ear"), as well as every other treatment that violates the human dignity of the child, even when the child does not concretely experience the treatment as "suffering." Child-rearing practices such as hitting a child's behind with a soup spoon, putting soap water into a child's mouth, and depriving a child of food justify the withdrawal of parental custody except for when these are incidents that happen once (Beck, 2013, p. 355).

Child Welfare Legislation

The Austrian child welfare system is a family support service-oriented child welfare system, embodied in the guiding principle of "protecting children and supporting families" (Hausegger, 2015). The system has a dual responsibility towards the prevention of child maltreatment through support services and protection centered on the idea of a child's well-being. The legal basis for child welfare interventions in Austria is the protection of the welfare of the child, which was established in the Austrian constitution in Article 1 of the 2011 Constitutional Law on the Rights of Children (Bundesverfassungsgesetz über die Rechte von Kindern, 2011):

Every child has the right to the protection and the care that are necessary for their well-being, to the best-possible development and growth and the maintenance of their interests, also under the perspective of justice between the generations. The well-being of the child must be a primary consideration in measures of public and private institutions concerning all children. (http://www.kinderrechte.gv.at/kinderrechte-in-osterreich/)

The principle of the child's well-being has most recently been defined in the Austrian Civil Code (ABGB) in Article 138:

The well-being of the child should be used as the guiding principle in all matters concerning the minor child and be guaranteed in the best manner possible, especially in matters regarding parental custody and personal contacts.

Article 138 further provides a non-exhaustive list of criteria to be included in the assessment of the child's well-being, which is multidimensional and includes aspects of physical and psychological/mental/emotional well-being. The three Ps—provision, protection, and participation—are further substantiated in 12 criteria, which are to be given special consideration in any child welfare assessment. These criteria are:

(1) suitable provisions, in particular of food, medical care, hygiene, living space, and a thorough education for the child;

(2) care, security, and the protection of the child's physical and mental integrity;

(3) parental appreciation and acceptance of the child;

(4) fostering the child's talents, skills, interests, and opportunities to grow;

(5) considering the child's opinion in accordance with her or his understanding and ability to form an opinion;

(6) preventing adverse impact on the child because of the implementation of a measure against the child's will;

(7) removing the danger that the child may suffer assault or violence or see it happen to important caregivers;

(8) removing the danger that the child may be illegally removed or retained or otherwise come to any harm;

(9) reliable contacts of the child to both parents and important caregivers and secure relationships with these individuals;

(10) preventing loyalty conflicts and feelings of guilt on the part of the child;

(11) protecting the child's rights, claims, and interests; and

(12) the living conditions of the child, her or his parents, and other environment.

In 2013, a new federal law was passed to regulate the public child welfare services in Austria. According to Hausegger (2015), the 2013 law aimed at improving the protection of children from family violence and strengthening preventive measures, providing incentives to unify child welfare standards, improving the collaboration between different types of support systems available to families, and enhancing data protection. Although the recent devolution of child welfare services from the federal to the regional level might eventually lead to great legislative variation between the states, at present, the states' laws continue to follow the now-obsolete part 1 of the 2013 Child Welfare Services Law (B-KJHG). In Articles 2 and 3, the law states that the CWS is responsible for "the promotion of the development of children through informational and support services in the areas of care and upbringing and children's protection through the implementation of protective measures" (Beck, 2013, p. 367). The system is guided by five basic principles: the child's well-being, family reunification, family autonomy, subsidiarity (the family, not the state, is the primary institution carrying out child welfare-related functions), and the principle of the least possible means of intervention into family life by the state.

According to Article 24 of the 2013 child welfare legislation, clients (children, youth, parents, or other caregivers) must be able to participate in risk assessments and in decisions about support services by the CWS and the impact of changes in the kinds and scope of these services on the child or youth's development. The wishes of children, youth, and parents must be heeded as long as they do not negatively affect the children and youth, or the child's participation endangers the child's well-being. The law has introduced a change in practice approach in some of the states. Before the 2013 law, child welfare agencies did little to systematically implement procedures to enable client participation. (This does not mean that individual social workers did not try and/or manage to involve their clients; Pantuček-Eisenbacher, 2014b.) However, the CWS practice of client participation has changed since the 2013 law in some of the states, including Lower Austria, Styria, Upper Austria, and the Carinthia (*Kärnten*). The practice of family group conferencing, which allows the participation of children, youth and families, is not systematically practiced in Austria, even though CWS agencies in some states (Lower Austria and Styria) have adopted similar approaches.

Criticism of the 2013 Law

The language used in the 2013 child welfare law has been met with some criticism on part of the scholarly community in Austria. For example, Fenninger-Buchner (2017) argued that the law's language obfuscates the proven correlation between poverty and risk of child neglect and other types of child maltreatment. The law uses the vague term "supports for the child's upbringing" to describe CWS responsibilities. This term separates the CWS from the responsibility to provide the economic conditions for parents to raise their children, which falls within the purview of other organizations (Fenninger-Bucher, 2017). In Austria, social services aimed at material support for families are organizationally separated from the CWS,[1] and the possibilities for the CWS to organize emergency material supports for families are limited. As poverty is strongly correlated with child maltreatment, this separation makes the CWS less effective. A case management approach that includes material supports for families would be useful in bridging this schism (Pantuček-Eisenbacher, 2014b).

---

[1] In addition, there is a disproportionally lower accessibility to public (and therefore affordable) daycare in rural areas (addendum.org, 2018).

Fenninger-Buchner (2017) calls this linguistic obfuscation "the definitional power(lessness) of the CWS in Austria." She argues that the concept of "supports for the child's upbringing" in the law obfuscates structural violence and denies children the status of agents by defining them as objects of caregivers' upbringing. Further, the law does not reflect the demand for material support as stipulated in the definition of the child's well-being in Article 138 of the Austrian Civil Code. Since 2016, she argues, Austrian society has experienced controlling, stigmatizing, and disciplining approaches to governance in neo-liberal politics and the law that exclude certain social groups, including refugees and recipients of social transfers. In Austria, this can be seen in the recent reduction of the minimal income and the political discussions preceding it (Fenninger-Bucher, 2017). Fenninger-Bucher addresses one of the main challenges of the Austrian CWS with a rhetorical question:

> In the pathway of welfare state retrenchment, the CWS social work is confronting the consequences of rising social inequality and social exclusion. Which space for agency can the tools supporting the child's upbringing offer or open up in light of the challenge of an increasing group of economically disadvantaged children and young people? (2017, p. 12, translation ours).

Risks to Children and System Responses

Children growing up with one or more of the following risk factors are especially at risk of poverty and social exclusion: single parent household, low education level, migration background, more than two siblings and a socially disadvantaged place of residence (Fenninger-Bucher, 2017, citing Holz & Puhlmann, 2005). According to the most recent statistical report by the Child Welfare Services (CWS) agency of the City of Vienna from 2018, neglect was the most prominent risk determined in child welfare investigations (57%), followed by emotional abuse (26%), physical abuse (15%), and sexual abuse (2%) (MAG ELF, 2019).[2] Similarly to other child welfare systems, one of the challenges of Austrian CWS agencies is to remain involved with families who are difficult to reach because they do not attend scheduled meetings, hide family problems, do not comply with CWS supports or move residence (Pantuček-Eisenbacher, 2014b).

Mandated reporting
When a child welfare-related report reaches the CWS agency, the CWS investigates and determines the risk to the child. The process is guided by the principles of the child's well-being, the

---

[2] The 2013 federal Child Welfare Law stipulates the collection of data about the types and scope of child endangerment by the Child Welfare Services (CWS) agencies. However, we could only find public information about the character and scopes of risks in the report of the Child Protective Services agency of Vienna (MAG ELF, 2019).

least intrusive measure, and participation (Hausegger, 2015; Jugendwohlfahrt Oberösterreich, 2018). According to Article 37 of the 2013 Child Welfare Law, reporting of potential child welfare concerns is mandatory for a range of institutions: courts, public authorities, care and educational institutions for children and adolescents, psychosocial counselling facilities, private institutions of child and youth welfare, hospitals and medical institutions, and nursing homes (Article 37 B-KJHG). In addition, such a reporting duty falls on any person charged with the care or education of children or youths, individuals who provide services for the child and youth welfare service in a freelance capacity, or self-employed professionals in regulated health care professions (Hausegger, 2015; Jugendwohlfahrt Oberösterreich, 2018). For example, in Vienna in 2018, most of the reports were made by others (25%), followed by the police (24%), schools and after-school programs (24%), internal reports by the CWS (9%), anonymous sources (8%), doctors or hospitals (5%) and self-reported maltreatment (5%) (MAG ELF, 2019). The law requires written notification, which must contain full details of the suspected child endangerment as well as the names and addresses of the concerned children or youths, and the person subject to the obligation to report. Professional regulations on confidentiality do not preclude compliance with the duty to report. Beyond a statutory reporting duty, any person concerned about the welfare of a child is entitled to notify the CWS. A form is available.[3] The CWS agencies are obliged to investigate all notifications, whether oral, written, or electronically submitted, except where a family already under investigation or assistance by the CWS is concerned.

Child Endangerment Investigation

Where there is reasonable suspicion and a notification has been received which outlines relevant observations and the conclusions drawn from them, the CWS will investigate the situation to establish whether there has in fact been a child endangerment. An investigation can be undertaken without the consent of the parents, as child safety takes precedence. The focus of the investigation is to determine the level of risk or endangerment to the child. The investigating caseworker discusses the report with their manager and determines subsequent steps, depending on the child's age and the type and extent of the endangerment (MAG ELF, 2015). An assessment will entail an evaluation of both risks and any potential protective factors. This risk evaluation thus consists of four assessment phases: emergency/urgency, safety, risk, and need for support. Since the legal reform of 2013, child endangerment assessments have become a standardized, fully documented procedure. This includes a four-eyes-approach, the involvement of the child or adolescent through an informal hearing, a hearing of the parents, a home visitation, and, where required for safety reasons, an emergency placement of the child or adolescent (Article 211 AGBG, MAG ELF 2015). Where an emergency placement becomes necessary, three

---

[3] See https://www.gewaltinfo.at/recht/mitteilungspflicht/.

alternatives are available: crisis center placements, placements with emergency foster carers, or placements with close relatives. In Vienna, approximately three out of 1,000 children were cared for by crisis centers (n = 883) and 0.5 out of 1,000 children were in the care of emergency foster carers (n = 174) in 2018 (MAG ELF, 2019; Statistik Austria, 2019b).[4] Where parents do not consent to such placements, the CWS can apply to the guardianship court for an interim care order within eight days (§ 211 AGBG). The goal of these measures is to ensure the child's safety while providing an opportunity to resolve the current issues in the family and find sustainable solutions for the problems with all parties involved. Where this cannot be achieved, and a return home is not possible, the child will be placed in out-of-home care (Article 181 AGBG, Article 26 B-KJHG).

Support Measures

There is a two-tiered approach to child welfare in Austria. At the first level, voluntary social service offerings are in place to support families in raising their children.[5] This includes crisis counselling, for instance where a family is going through a difficult period due to illness or other reasons, or parenting classes so parents can better understand children's needs. Since these are offered on an entirely voluntary basis, parents are free to enroll in or leave such measures at any time. According to the handbook for social work with families of the City of Vienna (2015), this wider social work with families in the regional offices, parent–child centers, and birthing units of hospitals is constituted of "short-term, problem-oriented and preventive counseling services that serve the development of the child and the child's family's promotion and violence-free child-rearing" (p. 34). Their goal is to strengthen the child's caregivers' caregiving ability through direct counseling services and supports for pregnant women, fathers-to-be, single parents and families. Children and young people and their caregivers can access these services free of charge. These services include counseling about parenting, financial problems, and after separation or divorce; provision of financial supports; and prevention of eviction and housing services (MAG ELF, 2015).

Beyond this, support measures are offered that can be voluntary or involuntary. The precondition is always an endangerment of the child. Following the assessment and agreement with the parents, voluntary measures can be agreed in a support measures plan. Alternatively, involuntary support measures can be ordered, which may include counselling, coaching or in-house family support services. If these are not deemed effective or safe for the child, an out-of-home placement is possible (Rille-Pfeiffer & Kapella, 2017). The specific measures offered depend on the individual states' regulations. Most services are provided by the CWS of the states, but some tasks are outsourced to private institutions. In

---

[4] According to Statistik Austria (2019a), the child population (0–18 years) in Vienna was 327,931 as of January 1, 2019.

[5] Unlike in Germany, parents in Austria do not have the legal right to support services for raising their children—a relic from the Austro-Hungarian monarchy (Pantuček-Eisenbacher, 2014b).

Table 3.1 Statistics on the child welfare system in Austria (2018)

Child welfare in Austria	Statistics	Per 1,000 children
Population of Austria (2019)[1]	8,858,775	
Number of children (under 18)[2]	1,535,958	
Number of investigations into child endangerment[2]	38,347	25.0
Number of children receiving CWS services, including care support services and full care provision[2]	49,580	32.3
Number of children receiving care support measures[2]	36,255	23.6
Number of children receiving full care provision	13,325	8.7
Number of children in residential care[2a]	8,110	5.3
Number of children in foster homes[2a]	5,325	3.5
Number of court-ordered measures [2]	5,413	3.5
—as out-of-home care[2]	4,784	
—as other support services[2]	629	

Sources:

[1] Statistik Austria (2019a).

[2] Bundeskanzleramt (2019).

[a] These numbers are only partially adjusted for those cases where a child received support under both categories.

Vienna, 3,040 support measures began in 2018, in addition to 3,755 continuing support measures, and only 2% of all support measures were court-ordered (MAG ELF, 2019).

Statistics

In 2018, the most recent year for which statistical data on child welfare have been published, 38,347 investigations into potential child welfare endangerment were undertaken, as Table 3.1 shows (Bundeskanzleramt, 2019). Austrian law and statistics differentiate between two types of support measures[6] through the Child Welfare Services (CWS)

---

[6] Support measures are called "Erziehungshilfen" in Austria; care support is "Unterstützung der Erziehung," and cull care provision is "Volle Erziehung." Any support measures will begin with the family, including the involvement of the children, as well as any relevant third parties. The aims are to ensure the safety of the child, secure the child's social, psychological and physical development, and protect the welfare and rights of the child. The drafting of a support plan involves three main tasks: to determine the specific risks to the child, to specify concrete goals for the future, and to decide on specific support measures. Any support measures always require a written agreement with the parents (or custodian, where the parents do not have custody of the child), or a court order. Cooperation between the family members and the CWS is considered crucial in achieving the best outcome for the child. However, where parents do not agree to the support measures, the CWS must apply to the family court for a court order. This applies to out-of-home care, which can be the result of an agreement between the parents and the CWS, or they can be court-ordered (Bundeskanzleramt, 2019).

available once child endangerment has been determined: (1) *care support measures*, where CWS provides support measures to the family to ensure that the child can remain safely in the family; and (2) *full care provision*, in cases in which the child is removed from home and care is provided outside the home in foster care, by kin or in residential care.[7] Ninety percent of the total of support measures (including care support measures and full care provision measures) were based on an agreement between the CWS and the parents; 10% followed a court order (Bundeskanzleramt, 2019). Care support measures include services such as counselling, parenting support and family support through a social worker. In Vienna, for example, families can seek advice and support in eight public family centers (Gaigg & Hagen, 2018).

As Table 3.1 shows, a total of 49,580 children received support services through the CWS in Austria in 2018: care support measures were granted to 36,255 children and 13,325 children received full care provision services, either following a written agreement with the parents, or, in cases where no agreement with the parents could be reached, based on an order by the court (sought by the CWS) (Bundeskanzleramt, 2019). Almost all of the 39,916 care support measures (98.4% or 39,287) were based on an agreement between the CWS and families.[8] This contrasts with full care provision measures (out-of-home care): two thirds of a total of 14,245 full care provision measures (66.4% or 9,461) were full care provisions based on an agreement between the parent(s) and the CWS; one third (33.6% or 4,784) were the result of a court order[9] (Bundeskanzleramt, 2019).

Generally, the majority of children is placed in residential care institutions (60.4%, n = 8,110), but there are significant differences between age groups (see Table 3.2). Younger children are more frequently placed in foster homes than teenagers (Bundeskanzleramt, 2019).

Adoptions

There are several pathways into adoption from care in Austria: children are adopted because their parents decided that adoption was the best course of action given the parent's or family's circumstances; children are adopted because their mothers gave birth anonymously or their parent dropped them off at a so-called baby chute at a hospital (Land Salzburg, 2019); or children in foster care are adopted by their foster carers. Adoptions of children who were placed in foster care are relatively rare: according to the authors' own research, there were only a couple of adoptions by their foster parents per state in 2016 and 2017.

---

[7] In 2018, there were 1,019 care institutions and 6,229 foster carers, most of them (25%) in Vienna, followed by Lower Austria (*Niederösterreich*) (22%) (Bundeskanzleramt, 2019).

[8] The statistical report (Bundeskanzleramt, 2019) does not provide the exact number of children whose care support services were based on an agreement versus a court order. The percentage of support measures based on an agreement versus a court order refers to the number of services provided, not the number of children. If a child receives a support measure more than once a year, then this receipt of support measures would count more than once (Bundeskanzleramt, 2019).

[9] The statistical report (Bundeskanzleramt, 2019) does not provide the exact number of children whose full care provision was based on an agreement versus a court order.

Table 3.2 Out-of-home placements by type and age group in 2018

Type of placement	Number of children	Percentage
Out-of-home placement	**13,325**	**100**
Residential care institutions, of which . . .	**8,110**	**60.4**
0–6 years	543	7
6–14 years	3,283	40
14–18 years	4,284	53
Foster homes, of which . . .	**5,325**	**39.6**
0–6 years	1,568	29
6–14 years	2,544	48
14–18 years	1,213	23

Source: Bundeskanzleramt (2019).

Some of the states had no such adoptions at all. There were 36 anonymous births in Austria in 2018 (20 of them in Styria, seven in Vienna, and five in Upper Austria), and five children were placed in baby chutes (Bundeskanzleramt, 2019). The CWS participated in adoptions of 110 children in 2018, that is 0.07 per 1,000 children in Austria overall. Vienna and Styria were the states with the highest proportion of adoptions—24% and 20%, respectively. The vast majority of adoptions (90%) were domestic adoptions (Bundeskanzleramt, 2019).

Section 1 of Article 194 of the Austrian Civil Code[10] (ABGB) stipulates the condition for an adoption: "The adoption of a minor child shall be granted if it serves the child's well-being, and if a relationship [between the child and her or his adoptive parents] has been established or should be established." The court can only approve an adoption of a minor child if the parents of the adopted child, the spouse or domestic partner of the adoptive parent, and the legal representative of the adoptive child consent to the adoption (Bundeskanzleramt, 2019). An adoption in Austria can only occur with the parents' consent unless the parents are permanently incapable of stating their opinion or they cannot be located for six months (Article 195 of the Austrian Civil Code). The children who are placed for adoption must stay with their future adoptive parents for at least six months before the CWS can apply for the adoption with the local district court. The Child Welfare Services will have a meeting with the parents, in which they explain the legal consequences of the adoption. The child and adoptive parents will sign an adoption contract, with the help of a notary public, lawyer or the CWS (Land Salzburg, 2019), which they send to the local district court for approval. The application for approval

---

[10] *Allgemeines bürgerliches Gesetzbuch für die gesammten deutschen Erbländer der Österreichischen Monarchie* (Austrian Civil Code), Consolidated version from January 17, 2019, StF: JGS Nr. 946/1811, available at: https://www.ris.bka.gv.at/GeltendeFassung.wxe?Abfrage=Bundesnormen&Gesetzesnummer=10001622.

of the adoption contract includes a report about the foster carers and the rationale for the application. The court has to ensure that the conditions for the adoption are met (Bundeskanzleramt, 2019).

Local and Regional Variation

There is significant regional variation in the rate of care support (Dachverband Öster-reichischer Kinder- und Jugendhilfeeinrichtungen, 2015), full care provision, and adoption measures because of differences in demographics, the distribution of support services between the state and private institutions, cultures, and laws. For example, the states of Burgenland and Styria (*Steiermark*) offered care support measures to a significantly higher proportion of children than the other states—33.9 and 33.2 out of 1,000 children, respectively, in contrast to, for example, Upper Austria (*Oberösterreich*), which provided care supportive measures to 17.1 out of 1,000 children. There was considerable variation regarding full care provision measures as well: Vienna had a comparatively high rate of full care provisions (12.3 out of 1,000 children), whereas Tirol had a comparatively low rate (6.0 per 1,000 children). This was a big enough issue for the previous government for the Family Ministry to start assessing the child welfare law to balance out the differences across states in terms of children in full care provisions and funds spent per child on care support measures (Egyed & Mittelstaedt, 2017).

The quantitative differences in the provision of child and youth welfare benefits are found not only between states, but also more significantly between different administrative districts *within* states. Heimgartner and Scheipl (2013, p. 22) found no evidence of variation in families' sociocultural differences across districts in their study of Styria. This suggests that there are different organizational and decision-making cultures that account for the variation in support services. The district administrative authorities within the states (except for the districts within Vienna) enjoy relatively large autonomy and the control possibilities of the public administration are weak. Thus, decision-making cultures differ greatly from state to state, and within states from district to district.

The annual statistical report about the Austrian child welfare system captures variations in the system's response by a child's gender and states but not, for example, by a child's migrant background, ability, sexuality, or the educational background or income of a child's parents—measures used by social scientists to gauge socioeconomic status. Therefore, we do not have evidence about the relevance of intersectionality (of gender, age, migrant background, ability, etc.), or the proportions of different groups of children in the child welfare system. The ages of children receiving support services are lumped together in ranges of four, five or eight years (0–5 years, 6–13 years, 15–18), which makes it difficult to discern which ages receive the most attention from the child welfare agencies and may be most at risk of ending up in public care. These more nuanced statistics would be important given that we know that in the Carinthia, for example, the serious mistreatment of infants (under 1 year old) increased significantly between 2012 and 2015 (Höllmüller & Schmid, 2017). We do not learn how long children receive services and how long they remain in out-of-home care. (Some of this information is available in other countries.) Austrian law, specifically *BGBl. I Nr. 69/2013: Bundesgesetz über die Grundsätze für Hilfen für Familien und Erziehungshilfen für Kinder und Jugendliche* (Bundes-Kinder- und Jugendhilfegesetz, 2013; B-KJHG, 2013), does not require the capture of these important data. It is interesting that the Austria-wide statistical report does not contain any information about the risks to the child determined in the investigations. We believe that these types of data would be salient for policymakers and the Austrian public to determine risks and responses and affect change for children and their families. Public funding for research on the CWS is necessary to increase transparency by gauging the impacts of reforms and develop organizational cultures that allow for innovation and further development based on research evidence (Gharwal & Pantuček-Eisenbacher, 2016; Höllmüller & Schmid, 2017). Pantuček-Eisenbacher et al. (2007) and Pantuček-Eisenbacher (2014b) recommend the creation of an independent think tank that conducts research and promotes the development of the child welfare sector independently of the CWS organizations.

Methods of Delivery of Service Provisions

The federal child welfare law is implemented at various levels: the legal level of the nine states based on decisions by the state parliaments, the state-level bureaucracy responsible for child welfare that then implements legal changes, and the district bureaucracies. The autonomy of the latter is a relic of the Austro-Hungarian monarchy and their governance is not based on elective representatives but appointed bureaucrats (Pantuček-Eisenbacher, 2014b). Since 1989, some states have focused CWS work on child welfare investigations and reduced their involvement in counseling services, thus raising the threshold of CWS interventions to only those cases that needed an investigation into child endangerment and providing support measures for children determined to be at risk. Counseling services were outsourced to private agencies. This led to higher caseloads for social workers (in the context of decreasing positions for social workers in CWS) and increased costs resulting from the use of private support services. The outsourcing of informational and counseling support services to private agencies has not led to more effective and timelier CWS interventions (Pantuček-Eisenbacher, 2014b).

With regard to family support measures, the City of Vienna reports on different offerings depending on the location of the child. Where a child remains with the family, in-home support and parent training courses are offered. In 2018, these were provided to 630 families with 1,197 children (approximately 3.7 out of 1,000 children in Vienna) and 53 parents with 27 children (0.1 out of 1,000 children), respectively (MAG ELF, 2019; Statistik Austria, 2019a). Where a child had to be removed (temporarily) from the family home due to an endangerment situation, the CWS in Vienna currently offers family coaching and residential socio-pedagogical support with the goal of reunification. In 2018, 116 children from 60 families were in receipt of family coaching and 57 children/youths from crisis centres (33), residential units (23), and mother-child-units (1) were reunified with their families (MAG ELF, 2019). The City of Vienna outsources the provision of residential socio-pedagogical support to the private agency, ProSoz Wien, which focuses on the reunification of children and youth from crisis centers and residential units and provides intensive preventative services to ensure children can remain with their families. In 2018, this type of support was provided to 54 families with 154 children (MAG ELF, 2019).

Sources of Financing

Child and youth welfare is financed by the states. In addition to official social work (youth welfare offices), the financing of outpatient and inpatient support services, which are primarily provided by private and civil society institutions, plays a major role. Commissioning and billing are case-related in most states. In some states, costs rose rapidly and significantly faster than other expenditures by the states. This has led to considerations that could curb cost development.

In some regions, the so-called SRO-approach ("Sozialraumorientierung" or the re-orientation of social services spaces) was attempted by CWS agencies. This organizational approach subsumed a diverse array of organizations and institutions that provided child welfare services under the CWS or a private umbrella organization. This amounts to the privatization of public organizations—a loss in democratic practice, which is anchored in a diversity of civil society institutions and organizations. The City of Graz adopted this approach based on similar organizational reforms in German cities; however, it has not been unequivocally empirically proven that this organizational reform has improved the challenges faced by the CWS (Pantuček-Eisenbacher, 2014b). This approach was particularly attractive for policymakers because of its promise of better control of cost development. However, the pilot project in Graz, which had already been started before the legal reforms in 2013, had no successors. In the discussions about the project, negative effects were criticized. These included an intensified turnover of staff in the youth welfare offices, the restriction of the professionals' decision-making authority, and a loss of diversity of the support offers through civil society (Höllmüller, 2014; Zach, 2014). Attempts to extend the approach of Graz to the whole of Styria failed because of the resistance of the district administration authorities, which consistently opted for an alternative approach based on social work case management (Pantuček-Eisenbacher, 2014b). This approach included the creation of a holistic consortium with the guarantee of support measures. The other states have not made any such far-reaching changes to the organization and forms of financing of child and youth services. Independent studies on the effects of these reforms have not been conducted or published.

Expenditures and Per Capita Spending

The net expenses for child welfare-related measures (support services and out-of-home care for children and young adults by CWS) for Austria for 2018 amounted to €615.8million. €43.8 million was income from parties responsible to pay for children's financial support. The gross expenses were €659.6 million. Of this, 76% was used for out-of-home care and 24% for in-home support services. Most of the funds spent on out-of-home care went towards institutional care (87%), while 13% of the costs of out-of-home care was used for foster carers. (These data were derived from the provincial states, towns with their own statutes and public welfare organizations; Bundeskanzleramt, 2019.)

Criticisms, Reforms, and Future Outlook

The Austrian child welfare system has undergone significant changes in recent decades. The 1989 Youth Welfare Law emphasized the role of private or civil society institutions in providing family support measures for the first time. This led to a substantial withdrawal of state facilities in some states, including housing, while the public agencies remained dominant in other states, such as Vienna or Lower Austria. Starting in 2001, the former social work academies stopped running—social work education was transferred to Universities of Applied Sciences and was integrated into the tertiary education system. The first graduates of these programs started practicing in 2005. Since then, the proportion of graduates in Child Welfare Services has grown steadily, which has promoted the professionalization process. The ratification of the UN Convention on the Rights of the Child in 1992 was followed by the far-reaching adoption of this legal status in 2011 into the constitution by the Federal Constitutional Law on the Rights of Children. As a result, the Federal Children and Youth Welfare Act (B-KJHG, 2013) created a new basis for the activities of child and youth welfare services, which was interpreted and clarified by corresponding state laws. The most important changes were the definition of criteria for the "welfare of the child"; the establishment of the dual-control principle in the assessment of risks of harm; an extended disclosure obligation for child endangerment; the obligation to draw up a care plan; and the mandatory participation of parents and children and youth during the risk assessment process and the creation of a support plan. Thus, for the first time in the field of child and youth welfare, professional standards were incorporated into basic law.

At the same time as the discussion that preceded this legislative act took place, and similarly to some other European countries, serious grievances and human rights violations were discovered in residential institutions for children and youth in the second half of the 20th century (see, for example, Sieder & Smioski, 2012 and Helige et al., 2013). Since 2012, the Ombudsperson's Office has been responsible for the review of institutions where children's freedom might be restricted, including child and youth welfare institutions. While the situation was either largely ignored in relation to discussing historical human rights violations or adopting a fundamentally child law-compliant practice, a special report by the Austrian Ombudsman's Office (2017) revealed serious shortcomings in child and youth welfare institutions. However, this report was not significantly highlighted in the media or discussed in the scientific debate. Unlike in other countries, where CWS failures are subject to independent investigations (such as, for example, the Laming report into the death of Victoria Climbié and the Munroe report in Britain, or similar reports by independent experts in Germany), the Austrian system has failed to systematically investigate other system failures, especially in cases of the CWS failing to recognize children's risk early enough or not at all. The lack of such expert investigations precludes the opportunity for casting light on the structural failures of the CWS (see Pantuček-Eisenbacher, 2014a).

In 2015, the Austrian Institute for Family Research of the University of Vienna was entrusted with conducting an evaluation of B-KJHG 2013 by the Federal Ministry for Families and Youth. The evaluation report, based on extensive surveys of case-managing social workers, other professionals, parents and youth, was published in December 2018 (Kapella et al., 2018). The nationwide negotiation process in the reform of the basic legislation was evaluated favorably. The evaluation report showed an overall positive image of the public child and youth welfare services. It is particularly noteworthy that a clear majority of the parents surveyed rated the supports as effective and were satisfied with their participation in decision-making. On the other hand, the study demonstrated a need for improvement, in particular with regard to the inclusion of children and youth. The effects of the reform were viewed as positive, mainly because the reform incorporates professional standards into the law.

These were the evaluators' recommendations:

- The caseloads of social workers in the youth welfare offices are too high; an increase in human resources is needed.
- The four-eye-principle in the sense of a joint assessment of the child's and family's situation needs to be uniformly applied.
- In the area of prevention, social services need to be expanded— thus, those support measures which are also granted without the existence of an acute danger. (This is in accordance with the child welfare law.)
- The participation of children and young people must be promoted. This could be achieved primarily by improving the quality of the relationships between the case-managing social workers in the youth welfare office and the children and youth.
- Austria-wide uniform standards need to be developed and implemented, especially with regard to risk assessment.
- Continuing training opportunities for professionals must be expanded and improved in terms of content.

- The case-related and case-independent communication with partners of the child welfare system has to be improved.

Changes underway in the Austrian child welfare system today reflect recent paradigm shifts towards restructuring the Austrian public bureaucracy to make it more efficient and financially sustainable. In fall 2017, a right-wing government came into power which promoted the devolution of the child welfare agenda from the federal level to the level of the nine regional states as of June 2018 (Die Presse, 2018). Article 12 of the Austrian Constitution regulates combined responsibilities of the federal and provincial governments, including child welfare. Professionals working in the field of child welfare criticized the proposed changes, arguing that they would fragment the statutory requirements of the current (2013) child welfare law. They predicted that the planned reform would exacerbate variation in the implementation of the law across provincial states, which has been a problem for years. Critics fear that the minimum standards guiding child welfare that are now provided by federal law would be watered down, that individual states would decrease the child welfare budgets, and that the service standards would plummet. The federal association of social workers expressed that "the elimination of the child welfare competency by the federal state threatens to decrease professional standards related to the standardized processes used [by child welfare agencies] during assessments of endangerment, would lead to a limitation of the four-eye-principle and a lack of cooperation across provincial states in emergency cases where a child's life is at stake" (Die Presse, 2018). Notwithstanding these criticisms, the proposed changes came into effect on January 1, 2020. The first part of the B-KJHG has been repealed and responsibility for child welfare services and child protection now rests with the regional states. It is too early to determine the effects of these recent changes, but it can only be hoped that the existing inter-state differences do not increase and prevent effective child protection services from becoming a "postcode lottery" (Hagen, 2019).

As in other countries, the Austrian child welfare system has been the target of intense debate and criticism in the media in recent years. The debate about improvements of the Austrian CWS includes suggestions to increase participation-oriented methods; support care leavers; strengthen the role of child and adolescent psychiatry; expand school social work and develop regional cooperation, such as the so-called "Industrieviertel" (industrial zone) alliance. Problems result from a lack of data and the poor quality of the data that are collected, which can be partially explained by differences in data collection practices across states. Data collection needs to take into account the increasing diversity of the Austrian population.

The debate reflects the system's inherent challenge of child welfare agencies protecting children as representatives of the state while safeguarding the rights of parents and children. Parents, attorneys working in the field of family law, and politicians have criticized the child welfare agencies for lack of consistency and transparency in situations when children are removed into out-of-home care (Gaigg & Hagen, 2018; Melzer & Gasteiger, 2018). They believe that the child welfare agencies do not admit mistakes; that judges too often agree with the removal decisions made by the child welfare agency, and that there could be improvements in the legal representation of parents (Gaigg & Hagen, 2018; Melzer & Gasteiger, 2018). The public has questioned whether children from economically disadvantaged families and families with a migration background are removed from home at a higher rate (Gaigg & Hagen, 2018). It has been debated in the media whether single mother-households, very young mothers, families with a migration background, and families in poverty have been disproportionately affected by sudden, disproportionate interventions by the child welfare agency in situations when support services should be provided instead. Barbara Beclin, a legal scholar and politician, thinks that these groups are affected by premature removals as a result of a lack of resources to provide support measures (Melzer & Gasteiger, 2018). These questions are difficult to answer empirically given the lack of the kind of data that would allow to highlight the intersection of social class and ethnicity or migrant background in Austria. The introduction of family court aides has been noted as an improvement (Gaigg & Hagen, 2018).

Systematic research would be of critical importance in assessing CWS policies and programs, especially in the event of a devolved CWS. To our knowledge, there are no scholarly studies assessing which child welfare policies appear to be most effective. Austria does not have a federal research agency focused on child welfare services or a research center that assesses child welfare services in particular. We have discussed the problems with the official statistics in more detail above. The states are supposed to conduct research, but do not publish studies on their findings.

Conclusion

To conclude, the Austrian child welfare services have undergone a largely positive development in recent decades, characterized by a strengthening of the rights and participation of parents and children and youth, and by professionalization and at least partial establishment of professional standards. Potential for improvement is particularly evident in the staffing of the public specialist services; in the support of the professional development of the social work staff through further education and supervision; in the establishment of cooperation with neighboring systems (education, health care, etc.); and in the compulsory establishment of professional standards. The lack of nationwide fora for technical discussions and systematic research and scientific monitoring slows this development. The recent decision of the federal government to remove the general competency of the federal state for the CWS raises concerns about a further slowdown of reform processes. However, the regional states might also start collaborating to establish a joint research and development agency. This could create the platform for continuing and reinforcing positive developments beyond discussions about organizational reforms.

References

Addendum.org. (2018). Project 037: Kinderbetreung. https://www.addendum.org/kinderbetreuung/gemeinde/.

Beck, S. (2013). *Kindschaftsrecht.* (2nd ed.). Manz.

Bundeskanzleramt. (2019). Ablauf der Adoption. https://www.help.gv.at/Portal.Node/hlpd/public/content/72/Seite.720003.html.

Bundeskanzleramt. (2018). *Kinderrechte in Österreich.* https://www.kinderrechte.gv.at/kinderrechte-in-ost erreich/.

Dachverband österreichischer Kinder- und Jugendhilfeeinrichtungen. (2015). *Eklatante Unterschiede: Das Kindeswohl ist den Bundesländern unterschiedlich viel wert!* http://doej.at/index.php/aktuelles/pressea ussendungen/31-aktuelles/presseaussendungen/86-kindeswohl-ist-den-bundeslaendern-unterschiedl ich-viel-wert.

Die Presse. (2018). *Breiter Widerstand gegen "Verländerung" der Kinder- und Jugendhilfe.* June 21. https://diepre sse.com/home/innenpolitik/5450874/Breiter-Widerstand-gegen-Verlaenderung-der-Kinder-und-Juge ndhilfe.

Egyed, M.-T. and Mittelstaedt, K. (2017). Jugendhilfe variiert von Bregenz bis Wien. *Der Standard.* March 1. https://derstandard.at/2000053319417/Jugendhilfe-variiert-von-Bregenz-bis-Wien.

Fenninger-Bucher, D. (2017). Die Definitions[ohn]macht der Kinder-und Jugendhilfe in Österreich oder "es ist alles eine Frage der Erziehung." *Soziales_kapital,* 18, 3–17.

Gaigg, V. and Hagen, L. (2018). *Sechs Baustellen der Wiener Kinder- und Jugendhilfe: Ein Überblick.* Available at: https://derstandard.at/2000078280212/Sechs-Baustellen-der-Wiener-Kinder-und-Jugendhilfe-Ein-Ueb erblick.

Gharwal, D. and Pantuček-Eisenbacher, P. (2016). Worin besteht die Krise? *Soziales_kapital,* 15, 3–8.

Hagen, L. (2019). Notlösung Für Ungleichbehandlung in Kinder- Und Jugendhilfe. *Der Standard.* May 7. https://www.derstandard.at/story/2000102668887/notloesung-fuer-ungleichbehandlung-in-kinder-und-jugendhilfe-praesentiert.

Hausegger, M. (2015). *Kindeswohlgefährdung und Hilfeplanung: Kinderschutz in der Praxis der Kinder- und Jugendhilfe.* Presentation, TAGUNG: TREFFPUNKT FAMILIE KINDESWOHLGEFÄHRDUNG und HILFEPLANUNG. MAG Elf.

Heimgartner, A. and Scheipl, J. (2013). *Kinder-, Jugend- und Familienwohlfahrt in der Steiermark.* Sozialpädagogik, Institut für Erziehungs- und Bildungswissenschaft.

Helige, B., John, M., Schmucker, H., and Wörgötter, G. (2013). *Endbericht der Kommission Wilhelminenberg.* Available at: http://www.kommission-wilhelminenberg.at/presse/jun2013/Bericht-Wilhelminenberg-web_code.pdf.

Holz, G. and Puhlmann, A. (2005). *Alles schon entschieden? Wege und Lebenssituationen armer und nicht-armer Kinder zwischen Kindergarten und weiterführender Schule. Zwischenbericht zur AWO-ISS Längsschnittstudie.* Institut für Sozialarbeit und Sozialpädagogik.

Höllmüller, H. (2014). Modell Graz. Organisationstheoretische und entscheidungstheoretische Aspekte einer top-down Reform des Jugendamtes Graz. *Soziales_kapital,* 11, 1–16.

Höllmüller, H. and Schmid, R. (2017). Forschung in der Kinder-und Jugendhilfe Österreich. Der weite Weg zur Profession. *Soziales_kapital,* 18, 57–74.

Kapella, O., Rille-Pfeiffer, C., and Schmidt, E. (2018). *Evaluierung des Bundes- Kinder- und Jugendhilfegesetzes (B-KJG) 2013. Zusammenfassender Bericht aller Module und Beurteilung.* Österreichisches Institut für Familienforschung.

Jugendwohlfahrt Oberösterreich. (2018). *Handbuch.* Soziale Diagnose. Methoden zur Standortbestimmung von Kindern-und Jugendlichen. Land Oberösterreich. Available at: https://docplayer.org/9294797-Soziale-diagnose-methoden-zur-standort-bestimmung-von-kindern-und-jugendlichen-oberoesterreich-handbuch.html.

Kinder- und Jugendanwaltschaften Österreichs. (2011). *Bericht der Kinder- und Jugendanwaltschaften Österreichs an die Vereinten Nationen zum Übereinkommen über die Rechte des Kindes.* Available at: https://www.kija.at/files/KIJA-Bericht-2011.pdf.

Land Salzburg. (2019). *Adoption.* Available at: https://www.salzburg.gv.at/themen/soziales/kinder-und-juge ndliche/kinder-adoptionen.

MAG ELF. (2019). *Jahresbericht 2018.* Stadt Wien.

Melzer, A. and Gasteiger, A. (2018). Jugendamt: als sie das Kind abholten. News. March 28. https://www.news.at/a/kindesabnahme-jugendamt-9564579.

MAG ELF. (2015). *Qualitätshandbuch—Soziale Arbeit mit Familien*. Stadt Wien.

Neudorfer, S. and Wernig, C. (2010). Implementation of International Treaties into National Legal Orders: The Protection of the Rights of the Child within the Austrian Legal System. *Max Planck YBUNL*, 14, 409.

Pantuček-Eisenbacher, P., Pfleger, J., Viertelmayr, A., and Zottel, C. (2007). *Leitlinien zur Organisation der Fremdunterbringung und zur Vergabe von Aufträgen. Ein Vorschlag zur Weiterentwicklung des Systems der Jugendwohlfahrt*.

Pantuček-Eisenbacher, P. (2014a). *Entwurf für ein Fachkonzept der Kinder- und Jugendhilfe*. Available at: http://www.pantucek.com/texte/201401fachkonzept.pdf.

Pantuček-Eisenbacher, P. (2014b). *Was machen aus dem neuen KJHG?* aAvailable at: b.

Rille-Pfeiffer, C. and Kapella, O. (2017). *Familienpolitik in Österreich: Wirkungsanalyse familienpolitischer Maßnahmen des Bundes* (Vol. 27). Verlag Barbara Budrich.

Sieder, R. and Smioski, A. (2012). *Gewalt gegen Kinder in Erziehungsheimen der Stadt Wien. Endbericht.* Available at: https://digital.wienbibliothek.at/wbrup/content/titleinfo/3043096.

Statistik Austria. (2019a). *Bevölkerung am 1.1.2019 nach Alter und Bundesland—Insgesamt.* Available at: https://www.statistik.at/web_de/statistiken/menschen_und_gesellschaft/bevoelkerung/bevoelkerungsstruktur/bevoelkerung_nach_alter_geschlecht/index.html. Retrieved October 16, 2019.

Statistik Austria. (2019b). *Kinder-und Jugendhilfestatistik 2018*. Vienna: Bundesanstalt Statistik Österreich.

Zach, B. (2014). *Sozialraumorientierung in Graz. Eine Gegenüberstellung von Programmatik und Praxis. Soziales_kapital. Soziales_kapital* 12, 131–147.

Legislation

Allgemeines bürgerliches Gesetzbuch für die gesammten deutschen Erbländer der Oesterreichischen Monarchie (2019). Consolidated version from January 17, 2019, StF: JGS Nr. 946/1811. Available at: https://www.ris.bka.gv.at/GeltendeFassung.wxe?Abfrage=Bundesnormen&Gesetzesnummer=10001622.

Bundesgesetzblatt für die Republik Österreich. (2011). Teil I. Ausgegeben am 15. Februar 2011. Available at: https://www.kija.at/images/entwurf_bundesverfassungsgesetz_kinderrechtskonvention.pdf.

Bundes-Kinder- und Jugendhilfegesetz 2013—B-KJHG 2013. (2013). Available at: https://www.ris.bka.gv.at.

Bundesverfassungsgesetz über die Rechte von Kindern. (2011). Available at: https://www.ris.bka.gv.at.

Jugendwohlfahrtsgesetz 1989—B-JWG 1989. (1989). Available at: https://www.ris.bka.gv.at.

Child Protection in Belgium: An Overview of the Systems

Johan Vanderfaeillie, Erik Van Dooren, *and* Jessica Segers

Abstract

This chapter explores the child protection systems in Belgium. The complex structure of Belgium's three communities has implications for the child protection system, most of which are related to child maltreatment. The regulation and legislation addressing help for child maltreatment differ between the Flemish Community, the German Community, and the Walloon Community. Additionally, child abuse and neglect (CAN) are treated as a criminal act at a federal level. The Belgian child protection systems emphasize the protective function of the government with a more social democratic approach of defamiliarization policies. The characterization of CAN depends on social structures, attitudes, values, norms, and laws.

Key Words: child protection systems, child abuse, neglect, Belgium, Flemish Community, German Community, Walloon Community

Introduction

Belgium is a rather small country of only 35,528 km² with, as of January 2018, 11,376,070 inhabitants across three regions: 6,552,967 residents live in Flanders, 3,624,377 in Wallonia, and 1,198,726 in the Brussels-Capital Region (Statbel, n.d.). About 2,301,495 persons (20.2%) of the total population are minors younger than 18 years. Belgium is a federal state composed of communities and regions. Regions have powers largely relating to the economy. The term "community" refers to a linguistic and cultural entity and concerns personal matters. Belgium has three communities: the Flemish Community, the German Community, and the Walloon Community (Wallonia-Brussels Federation, WBF). A community is authorized in culture, education, use of languages, and matters relating to the individual which concern health policy and assistance to individuals (protection of youth, social welfare, support to families, immigrant assistance services, etc.). Besides the federal government and the federal parliament, each of the three communities and each of the three regions have their own separate governments and parliaments. These parliaments are legally equal, and they exercise their authority independently within their domains.

The complex structure of Belgium has implications for the child protection system. As child maltreatment is a matter relating to the individual, the organization of (child welfare) services providing help in cases of child maltreatment is mainly addressed at the community level and consequently regulated by community legislation. As regulations differ between communities, the organization of services offering help and the support offered differ between communities.

Child abuse and neglect (CAN) is also a criminal act dealt with at the federal level. Federal laws, such as the penal code, are enforced throughout the country. However, the concrete measures a juvenile judge can impose are determined by the communities, as child protection, including social and judicial protection, is defined as a personal matter in the constitution (Pas, 2007). This implies that judicial measures imposed by a juvenile judge differ according to the community to which the youngster belongs (see below for the different measures). Related to cases of child maltreatment, the federal powers are, among others, the deprivation of parental rights.

The Belgian child protection systems can probably best be characterized as "family service oriented" on the continuum from a more neo-liberal approach emphasizing the protective function of the government and the more social democratic approach that advances defamiliarization policies (Gilbert et al., 2011). As will become clear below, child abuse is considered a health, welfare, and familial problem of the child that is solved best with help and support (Desair & Adriaenssens, 2011). Parents who have engaged in child abuse receive services and voluntary youth care is preferred over judicial measures (De Craim & Traets, 2010). Furthermore, if multiple options for help are available, all guaranteeing equivalent protection of the child, the least radical alternative is chosen.

Defining Child Maltreatment in Belgium

What precisely constitutes CAN is determined by the social meaning given to specific behavior at a particular time and in a particular culture. Consequently, the behaviors labeled as CAN change according to social structures, attitudes, values, norms, and laws. CAN closely correlates with views of the child's place in a particular society or culture, with acceptable ways of enforcing parental authority, and with who has the power to enforce a definition at a given point in time (Herrenkohl, 2005). This implies that there is much discussion and ambiguity about what exactly constitutes child maltreatment and what are the definitive signs of evidence of CAN (O'Toole et al., 1999). Moreover, there is a lack of agreement over whether child maltreatment should be defined based on the actions of the perpetrator, the effects on the child, or both. In addition, the question of whether parental intent should be considered in determining maltreatment has also been debated (Cicchetti & Manly, 2001). Several factors contribute to the lack of clarity about the concept of CAN: definitions differ between and within professional groups such as child welfare social workers and judicial authorities; different professional groups use definitions in a different way; and definitions evolve over time (Cicchetti & Manly, 2001;

Egu & Weiss, 2003; Webster et al., 2005). The aforementioned problems not only apply to Belgium, but are possibly aggravated by the complex structure of the Belgian state. The definition of child maltreatment is provided in the following sections for the federal level, Flanders, and Wallonia-Brussels Federation.

Federal: Penal Code

In Belgium, several definitions of child maltreatment are used depending on the context in which the problem is addressed. At the federal level, judicial authorities use separate definitions regarding intrafamilial and extrafamilial violence. Intrafamilial violence is defined as "any form of physical, sexual, emotional and economical violence between members of the same family irrespective of their age"; extrafamilial violence as "any form of physical, sexual, emotional and economical violence on the person of a child by someone not belonging to his/her family." Violence comprises all criminal offenses causing damage to a victim actively (due to an act) or passively (due to an omission). Violence can be physical (e.g., intentional battery and assault), sexual (e.g., rape), psychological (e.g., insulting, defamation, stalking), or economical (e.g., abandoning of children). Also, all acts that are reported to judicial authorities and that are usually described as "family dispute" or "child in danger", are deemed as violence, even though they do not seem to be a criminal offense. A family is defined broadly as all persons related to each other, including spouses or persons who cohabit(ed) and who have/had an affective or sexual relation, and relatives of the partners who live(d) together (Parket Generaal, 2006).

Notwithstanding the existence of these definitions at the federal level, child maltreatment does not exist as a separate offense in the Belgian penal code. Different forms of CAN are taken up in different articles throughout the penal code. The penal code determines what actions are criminal offenses irrespective of the age of the offender (minor or adult). However, in cases of a minor offender, the juvenile judge will determine the necessary measures. In cases of adult offenders, the penal code determines the sentence. Physical child abuse is categorized as the deliberate beating and inflicting of physical injury, sexual abuse as an indecent assault and/or rape of minors. Neglect is categorized as abandonment or leaving behind in a needy state minors or incompetent persons or withholding food and care to minors or incompetent persons. Psychological abuse of minors is categorized as "untruthfully and intentionally misusing someone's physical or psychological weakness to make him or her do things or omit things and this affects the physical or psychological integrity of the person." However, the latter description is not specific for minors and was created to penalize suggestion and intrusiveness. In addition to the above mentioned forms, in the Belgian penal code, the following are discerned: female genital mutilation, child murder or manslaughter of a child at birth or short after birth, poisoning, moral decay of youth, juvenile prostitution, child pornography, exploitation of the mendicancy of minors, trade of children, torture, inhumane treatment, disgraceful treatment, and forced marriage (De Craim, 2013). However, confusion exists regarding emotional abuse and neglect. Although, the definitions used by judicial authorities clearly include intrafamilial and extrafamilial emotional abuse and neglect, no specific article of the penal code explicitly targets these forms of child maltreatment (Desair & Adriaenssens, 2011; De Craim, 2013; Vinck et al., 2016).

Flanders: The Decree on Integral Youth Care (Decreet betreffende Integrale Jeugdhulp)
In the Decree on Integral Youth Care (IYC), CAN is defined as "any form of physical, psychological or sexual violence against minors, either actively by harmful acting, or passively by serious neglect by parents or by any other people to whom the minor has a dependency relationship with" (Vlaamse Gemeenschap, 2013, Article 2 §1 32°). According to lawmakers, this definition is based on the definition of Article 19 of the Convention on the Rights of the Child (CRC). Although the definition used in the Decree on IYC is rather wide, the fact that CAN is linked to parents and other people to whom the child has a dependency relationship, suggests that the lawmakers had in mind mainly intrafamilial CAN and situations where the victim is dependent on the offender. The latter observation is in line with the Flemish Protocol Child Maltreatment. The protocol states that intrafamilial CAN is preferably dealt with by child welfare services, and in the case of extrafamilial child abuse, the prosecution of the offender is appropriate (De Clerck & Vandeurzen, 2010). Notwithstanding the fact that the Decree on IYC seems to limit CAN to intrafamilial child maltreatment or abuse by educators, this does not imply that Flemish lawmakers limit the appropriateness of youth care to intrafamilial CAN. On the contrary, youth care is indicated in *alarming situations* or can be imposed by a juvenile judge to a minor and his/her parents in cases of *societal exigency* (maatschappelijke noodzaak). Nevertheless, some authors regret the aforementioned limitation in the Decree on IYC and question its added value (De Craim, 2013).

Although the Flemish Confidential Centers of Child Abuse and Neglect (CCCAN) are covered by the IYC decree (see below), these centers use the definition of Article 19 of the CRC. According to CCCAN, this CRC-definition is clinically workable and comprises all kinds of abuse: physical, emotional, and sexual. The definition focuses on the minor and not on the offender or his/her intentions. This is important as, according to CCCAN, child maltreatment is possible in any relationship and is not limited to families. The determination of whether specific behavior can be labeled as CAN does not relate to the intentions of the offender. The most important is the effect on the development of the child (Van Dooren, 2016).

Wallonia-Brussels Federation: Decree on Assistance to Victims of Child Maltreatment in the Wallonia-Brussels Federation (Décret relatif à l'Aide aux Enfants Victimes de Maltraitance en Fédération Wallonie-Bruxelles)
In WBF, a decree in 2004 on the assistance to victims of child maltreatment defines a situation of abuse as "any situation of physical violence, physical abuse, sexual abuse,

psychological violence or neglect that endangers the physical, mental or emotional development of the child. An abusive attitude or behavior may be intentional or unintentional" (Communauté Française, 2004, Article 1 4°). As in WBF, child welfare workers are very aware of the aforementioned difficulty of finding a common definition of CAN and professionals are asked not to assess situations of CAN singlehanded. Concepts such as urgency, suffering, or well-being are indeed partly based on personal beliefs. What is considered abusive by one person may not be equally judged by someone else. Therefore, it is considered important to compare and confront one's impressions, emotions, and feelings about the "abusive" situation with a third party, if possible someone from another professional setting. In addition, attention is paid to feelings of discomfort experienced in a situation, even if there is no evidence of injury or harm to the child.

Recently, the Directorate for Equal Opportunities of the Ministry of the Wallonia-Brussels Federation (Direction de l'Egalité des Chances, 2013) published a report entitled "A Child Exposed to Domestic Violence Is an Abused Child." This report aims at making professionals aware of domestic violence and the need to develop interventions for children and for the parents. Next, the report seeks to help professionals in identifying cases of domestic violence, expanding the insight of professionals in domestic violence, and understanding the impact of domestic violence on children and the way children function in these situations. With the publication of this report, it becomes clear that in WBF serious marital conflict and domestic violence are considered CAN and that professionals also in these situations are expected to intervene and protect the child.

Reporting Child Maltreatment in Belgium

In order to adequately protect children from CAN, an effective reporting system combining a maximal detection of CAN with a minimum of unnecessary reports of child maltreatment is indispensable. In spite of this, it is likely that a considerable number of cases of CAN are not detected, and the identification of (potential) CAN does not always result in reporting.

In Belgium, it is not mandatory to report suspected or observed situations of CAN to the judicial authorities. Yet every member of society has the moral obligation to ensure the well-being of children and to act accordingly. That means that the decision to report depends on the professionals' discretion: they have to decide (1) whether the situation should be reported in order to come forth to the obligation by law to provide help to a person in need (Article 422[bis] of the Penal Code: failure to render assistance to a person in danger) or (2) whether the situation can be adequately addressed by subsidiary services within a reasonable time frame and/or reporting does not serve the best interest of the child. With regards to the subsidiarity: in Belgium, (intrafamilial) CAN is framed as a health and welfare problem of the child and his/her family (Desair & Adriaenssens, 2011), and therapeutic interventions and help from the extrajudicial system are preferred.

A partnership with the parents is sought over a more adversarial relationship between the parents and the state.

Extent of the Problem

Since there is no national registration of CAN-cases nor any studies on the incidence or prevalence of CAN in Belgium, the extent of the problem in Belgium is unknown (Vinck et al., 2016). At all levels, a uniform registration of CAN is lacking. Nevertheless, some surveys and administrative databases may reveal the scale of the problem.

Flanders

In 2011, the Flemish Office of the Children's Rights Commissioner asked 2,000 Flemish children (10–11 years old) and adolescents (12–18 years old) using a self-report web survey to report on their experiences with violence at home, school, and during leisure time. In all settings, all forms of violence (physical, psychological, and sexual) were found. About 5% of the pupils reported they were sometimes or often a victim of sexual violence and 60% reported they were sometimes or often victim of humiliation at *school*. Regarding experiences of violence at *home*, about 38% of the pupils reported that they were sometimes or often victim of verbal violence, 25% of physical violence, and 20% of emotional violence. Moreover, about 5% of the interviewees reported that sometimes or often they were victim of extreme physical abuse (threatened with a knife, beaten with an object, forced to stay in the same position) and 2% were the victim of sexual violence (De Rycke et al., 2011).

In 2016, the Flemish CCCAN received 6,904 reports regarding CAN of at least one minor (as a report can concern several children). The reports to Flemish CCCAN stabilized over the past 6 years to around 7,000 reports a year with a slight decreasing trend (see Table 4.1). A possible explanation for this decline is the effect of the hotline "1712"

Table 4.1 Number of reports to Flemish CCCAN or to WBF's team SOS-children

		2010	2011	2012	2013	2014	2015	2016
Flanders	Number of unique reports concerning (at least) one minor	7,144	7,605	7,244	7,477	7,311	6,787	6,904
WBF	Number of reported children	5,226	5,260	5,398	5,402	5,609	6,044	5,911
Total reports/ children in Flanders and WBF		12,370	12,865	12,642	12,879	12,920	12,831	12,815

Source: Kind en Gezin (2017) and Office de la Naissance et de l'Enfance (ONE)—Service SOS Enfants (2018).

Note: In Flanders, a report can concern several children. In WBF, each child is registered even if they are reported at the same time in the same report.

(see below). Since 2012, the hotline "1712" has dealt with less severe and less urgent cases while more serious cases are referred to CCCAN or a Support Center Youth Care (SCYC; see below). As reports cover allegations of CAN, data consist of suspected as well as confirmed abuse. These 6,904 reports on at least one minor concerned 9,133 unique children or 66.6 per 10,000 children (see Table 4.2). Of these 9,133 reported children, 0.8% were unborn, 13.4% were younger than 3 years, and 31.4% were younger than 6 years old. Children aged between 6 and 11 years were most frequently reported (36.1%) followed by youngsters between 12 and 18 years old (29.8%). Age was missing for about 2.6% of the reported children (see Table 4.3) (Kind en Gezin, 2017).

About 10% of the 9,133 unique children were reported more than once, resulting in 9,835 reported children. For each reported child, the child welfare worker had to indicate the most important form of CAN. For about 21% of the reported children, the most important form of CAN was physical abuse, 18% neglect, 15% sexual abuse, 11% psychological abuse and 9% of children were exposed to serious marital conflict or domestic violence (Kind en Gezin, 2017) (see Table 4.4).

Wallonia-Brussels Federation (WBF)

In the WBF, 55.8 children per 10,000 were reported to the SOS Children teams (SOS-CT) in 2016. In comparison to the Flemish community, the number of reports registered by the

Table 4.2 Numbers of children per 10,000 reported to a Flemish CCCAN or to WBF's team SOS-children

Number/10,000	2010	2011	2012	2013	2014	2015	2016
Flanders	75.5	77.1	75.2	74.5	70.7	64.0	66.6
WBF	51.2	51.2	51.9	51.3	52.9	57.2	55.8

Source: Kind en Gezin (2017) and Office de la naissance et de l'enfance (ONE)—Service SOS Enfants (2018).

Table 4.3 Age of reported victims reported to a Flemish CCCAN or to WBF's team SOS-children

Age	Flanders	Flanders	WBF	WBF
	N	%	n	%
Unborn	73	0.8	154	2.6
0–3	1,224	13.4	583	9.9
3–6	1,571	17.2	946	16.0
6–11	3,297	36.1	1,976	33.43
12–18	2,722	29.8	1,251	21.2
Extended minority	9	0.1	-	-
Missing	237	2.6	1,001	16.9
Total	9,133	100	5,911	100

Source: Kind en Gezin (2017) and ONE—Service SOS Enfants (2018).

Table 4.4 Reported forms of abuse

Form of abuse	Flanders		WBF	
	N	%	N	%
Physical abuse	2,017	21	1,282	21.6
Emotional abuse	1,035	11	787	13.3
Neglect	1,799	18	493	8.3
Sexual abuse	1,466	15	1,393	23.6
Institutional abuse	Not available	Not available	6	0.1
Domestic violence	901	9	386	6.5
At risk	1,341	14	1,961	33.2
Others (unclear problem, unacceptable behavior of minors)	1,276	13	479	8.1
Total	9,835	100	5,911	114.8

Source: Kind en Gezin (2017) and ONE—Service SOS Enfants (2018).

Note: In Flanders the most important problem/form of CAN is registered by the CCCAN-worker. In WBF no distinction is made between the most important form and comorbid problems. All forms of suspected CAN are registered, therefore, the percentages do not add up to 100% because a child can be a victim of more than one form of CAN.

SOS-CT in WBF increased gradually until 2015 (Office de la naissance et de l'enfance, 2017). In 2016, 5,911 cases concerning 5,742 children (sometimes the same child was reported several times) were reported to the SOS-CT. Of these 5,911 reports, 33% of the cases were concerns related to minors at risk, 59% regarded allegations of CAN, and 8% had other content such as requests for information and so on. Only 3,505 cases were assessed. Reasons for not assessing the case included anonymous reports and immediate re-orientation to other services because the problems reported were not CAN. Among 1,591 cases, the allegations of CAN were substantiated and a diagnosis of the type of abuse was available: 32% of children were exposed to serious marital conflict or domestic violence, 28% were victims of emotional abuse, 27% of neglect, 25% of sexual abuse, 16% of physical abuse, and 1% of institutional abuse (see Table 4.5). In 10% of the cases, the allegations of abuse were not confirmed, and in 28%, the living conditions of the child were putting the child at risk for abuse.

Federal Level: Dealing with Child Abuse and Neglect by the Judicial Authorities

At the federal level, judicial authorities can prosecute the offender and impose mandatory help to protect the minor. Below, we describe the trajectory starting with a notification to the public prosecutor eventually resulting in the prosecution of the offender and/or protection of the child.

Several parties can report a case to the public prosecutor's office: the police after a complaint or own findings with a police report, a Support Center Youth Care (SCYC, in Dutch "Ondersteuningscentrum Jeugdhulp"), a CCCAN, a SOS-CT, a Child and Family

Table 4.5 Forms of abuse after assessment

Form of diagnosed abuse	Flanders		WBF
Physical abuse	Not available	261	16.4
Emotional abuse	Not available	452	28.4
Neglect	Not available	429	27.0
Sexual abuse	Not available	400	25.1
Institutional abuse	Not available	18	1.1
Domestic violence	Not available	512	32.2
None (no or previous abuse)	Not available	164	10.3
At risk	Not available	438	27.5
Total	-	1,591	168

Source: ONE—Service SOS Enfants (2018).

Note: The percentages do not add up to 100% because more than one form of CAN be diagnosed.

service (CFS, in French "Service de l'Aide à la Jeunesse") or a care provider in accordance with Article 458bis of the penal code[1] or in cases of an emergency situation (in Dutch, "noodtoestand"). The victim and other persons involved can also inform the public prosecutor of a CAN situation. When informed of (suspected) child maltreatment, the public prosecutor's office has three possibilities: (1) protect the child by referring to voluntary care, investigating the case or referring to a juvenile court when necessary, (2) prosecute the presumed offender, or (3) both (De Craim, 2013). Only the public prosecutor's office can refer cases to a juvenile judge, if the prosecutor regards this appropriate and when two cumulative conditions are met: (1) it is not possible to install voluntary youth care and every effort to install voluntary care has been made and (2) a judicial measure is urgently needed because there is sufficient evidence that the minor has to be protected immediately (Communauté Française, 1991, Article 38 §1 and §2, and Article 39; Vlaamse Gemeenschap, 2013). That both conditions must be met before a case can be referred to juvenile court emphasizes subsidiarity of the referral to judiciary services and prioritization of voluntary care (Communauté Française, 1991; Communauté Française, 2004; Vlaamse Gemeenschap, 2013).

In cases of intrafamilial child maltreatment, the option of protection of the child is frequently chosen. In cases of extrafamilial child maltreatment, mostly the prosecution of the offender is chosen. Indeed, in cases of extrafamilial child maltreatment, no protection measures for the child are needed and no security plan with the necessary guarantees can be set up. On the contrary, the prosecution of the offender is necessary in order to prevent

---

[1] Holders of a duty of confidentiality who are aware of the abuse of a minor or vulnerable persons can inform the public prosecutor, on condition that a serious and threatening danger exists for the psychological or physical integrity of the person concerned and that the integrity cannot be protected by the person or with the help of others.

future victims (De Craim, 2013; Van Dooren, 2016). However, as extrafamilial CAN be the result of intrafamilial neglect, in these cases additional protection measures are taken. Victim support services are also provided.

In Flanders, a juvenile judge can impose the following measures (Vlaamse Gemeenschap, 2013):

- Offer the parents or guardians educational guidelines;
- Put the minor under the supervision of the social service of the juvenile court for up to one year;
- Impose contextual counseling for a maximum of one year;
- Impose an educational project to the minor, eventually together with the parents or guardians for maximally six months;
- Impose on the minor counseling from an ambulatory service for up to of one year;
- Let minors live independently for a maximum of one year when having a minimum age of 17 and having sufficient income;
- Let minors live in lodgings under permanent supervision when having a minimum age of 17;
- Place the minor in an admission and orientation center for a maximum of 30 days;
- Place the minor in an observation center for a maximum of 60 days;
- Place the minor in a foster family for a maximum of three years;
- Exceptionally, consign the minor to an "open service" for a maximum of one year;
- Exceptionally, consign the minor who has reached a minimum age of 14 to a "closed facility" for a maximum of three months. This is only possible when the previous two measures have been rejected and a closed facility is necessary to protect the integrity of the child;
- Consign the minor to a child psychiatric unit, if this is deemed necessary according to psychiatric expertise for a maximum of one year.

Although most measures are limited in time, they can be prolonged.

In WBF, a juvenile judge can impose the following measures (Communauté Française, 1991):

- Educational measures;
- Supervision by a social service and if necessary accompanied with conditions such as going to school;
- Psychosocial, educational, or therapeutic counseling of the family and/ or child;

- Educational project;
- Counseling for the minor from a semi-residential service;
- Autonomous or supervised independent living to the minor;
- Out-of-home care.

In case of a crisis, the youngster can only be placed in an emergency shelter, an emergency and observation center, a foster home, with a trustworthy person, or in exceptional circumstances in an open group home. This placement can last for 30 days in Brussels and 14 days in the Walloon region; in both settings the placement can be renewed once. In the meantime, this service will try to organize voluntary help. If this is successful, then the crisis measure of the juvenile court is removed. If not, the juvenile judge continues the imposed help.

Although the concrete measures a juvenile judge can impose differ between communities, there are similarities in their authority. Juvenile judges can impose three kinds of measures: educational support and guidance for the child and his/her parents while the child stays (safely) at home; place the child in out-of-home care in order to protect the child when safety cannot be guaranteed; or help the youngster live independently when out-of-home care is not appropriate given the wishes and age of the youngster.

Collaboration Between Judicial Authorities at the Federal level and Care Providers at the Community Level

As child maltreatment is a complex problem that must be addressed in a comprehensive way, measures need to be taken across several domains. This implies that all actors should work together to take into account the rights of the child and all others involved. Particularly, judicial authorities and child welfare services need to collaborate. However, it must be considered that stakeholders come from different fields of expertise with specific missions and different goals (e.g., offering support, prosecuting offenders) related to their profession. As a consequence of the subsidiarity of judicial measures and the prioritization of voluntary youth care, it is preferred that help is first offered by child welfare services (De Craim & Traets, 2010). To promote collaboration and subsidiarity, partnership agreements between the Minister of Justice and the Minister of Welfare were signed in both Flanders (Protocol Kindermishandeling Justitie—Welzijn) and in WBF (Protocol d'intervention entre le secteur medico-psycho-social et le secteur judiciaire), in 2010 and 2007, respectively. Below we present a non-exhaustive list of initiatives included in the previously mentioned protocols.

Coordination Commissions on Assistance to Victims of Child Abuse

In WBF, with Article 4 of the decree of 2004 on the assistance to victims of child abuse, in each judicial district (of WBF and Brussels), Coordination Commissions on assistance to victims of child abuse were installed. In 2010, similar commissions (*arrondissementele raden voor slachtofferbeleid*) were installed in Flanders as a result of the Protocol Kindermishandeling Justitie—Welzijn. These commissions bring together, in one place, local actors involved in situations of abuse. The actors are representatives from child welfare services, psychosocial services, judicial authorities/police and school-based services. The interest of these commissions lies in their advisory task and their mission, which is to "ensure the improvement of procedures to appropriately handle situations of child abuse" (Communauté Française, 2004; De Clerck & Vandeurzen, 2010). These commissions only treat anonymous cases aimed at promoting the expertise of all actors participating, promoting mutual greater knowledge of the activities of each participant, and (at least for the Flemish district commissions) signaling structural problems to the Flemish Forum of Child Abuse.

The Flemish Forum of Child Abuse

In the Flemish Forum of Child Abuse, structural problems of child abuse are discussed and recommendations regarding the approach of child abuse are formulated to the proper authorities. The discussion points are brought up by the aforementioned commissions. The Flemish Forum advises the federal Minister of Justice and the Flemish Minister of Welfare regarding their policy in preventing and treating CAN. The Forum also supervises the implementation of the Protocol for Child Maltreatment. Furthermore, the Forum monitors and evaluates local initiatives regarding the treatment of CAN (Van Dooren, 2016).

Permanent Conference on Child Abuse (in WBF)

At the end of 1998, a task force consisting of representatives of the Ministry of Justice, the judicial authorities, and the Communities was formed in response to the implementation of decisions taken by the Interministerial Conference on the protection of the rights of the child in 1997. The aim of the task force was to develop guidelines to improve the approach to cases of CAN by the appropriate services. In WBF, this task force is still active, and it consists of representatives of the police, judicial services, CFS and child welfare services, ensuring a smooth cooperation between the aforementioned services.

The Flemish Step-by-step Plan to Address Child Maltreatment

The step-by-step plan to address child maltreatment describes a stepwise approach and ethical code for all actors involved. The protocol states that every intervention concerning CAN should include five steps: information, advice, reporting, assessment and diagnosis, and care plan (in child welfare) or prosecution (in the judicial system). Each of the steps mentioned above are elucidated for child welfare services and for judiciary services.

The Courage Protocol (Protocol van Moed)

The Courage Protocol started in January 2012 in Antwerp and ran for one and a half years. It offered an experimental framework for collaboration between child welfare and judiciary services in cases of CAN. Such a direct collaboration was often hindered by the current legal framework regarding professional secrecy. The aim of the collaboration was to find the best solution for each individual case. The protocol foresaw case-based deliberation for chronic or unclear situations of CAN between child welfare workers, medical professionals, and judiciary officials to explore whether a case could stay in voluntary child welfare care or should be referred to judiciary services in order to secure the child (Op de Beeck & Put, 2017).

Family Justice Centers

In Flanders, a regional *case coordination* was installed (Van Mulders, 2017). This originated from both the positive experiences with the above-mentioned experiments and the growing insight in Flanders that collaboration and information sharing between all actors involved is crucial in order to deal appropriately with situations of child maltreatment. The primary aim of case coordination is to end intrafamilial violence (one family, one plan). In case coordination, a chain approach is used: intake, analysis, and design of the plan; appointment of a coordinator; implementation; and evaluation. Collaboration of services is based on agreements between the mandated services of CCCAN and SCYC (see below), social service of the juvenile court, centers of general social welfare, mental health services, the local police, and the public prosecutor.

Community Level: Dealing with Child Maltreatment by Child Welfare Services

As CAN is a matter relating to the individual, the organization of (child welfare) services providing help in cases of child maltreatment is mainly handled at the community level and organized by community legislation. As regulations differ between communities, the organization of services offering help and the support offered differs between communities.

In Flanders

IN FLEMISH YOUTH CARE

Since March 1, 2014, the landscape of Flemish youth care has been determined by the Decree on IYC. The objectives of the Decree are: (1) the socialization of youth care by, amongst others, activating the social network and the extended family, (2) facilitating access to youth welfare services, (3) guaranteeing the continuity of care, (4) acting appropriately in alarming situations such as CAN, (5) ensuring that during crisis the most appropriate help is offered in order to ensure de-escalation and restore safety, (6) maximizing participation of children/adolescents and their family, and (7) realizing an integral approach (child welfare services of different subsectors working together and the help is coordinated from the client's perspective) (Vlaamse Gemeenschap, 2013). The objective of the socialization of youth care implies that, even in cases of CAN, formal and informal help needs to be integrated, an influx in youth care is prevented, and participation in care and empowerment of the client/family is maximized (Vlaamse Gemeenschap, 2013). Socialization of youth care also means that every Flemish care provider should be able to act appropriately in cases of CAN (Vlaamse Gemeenschap, 2013). When care providers report a case of child maltreatment to a mandated service (see below), care providers have to document their own actions and the help offered to the family. Instead of referring cases of (intrafamilial) CAN immediately to highly specialized services such as CCCAN, CAN is considered a matter for the whole society (Louwagie & Gevaert, 2012; Germeijs, 2015). The same applies to the hotline 1712. Any civilian can call the hotline 1712 for advice, information, and referral in cases of violence, including child maltreatment. If the 1712 staff decides, based on a risk assessment, that notwithstanding the (low) risk of CAN, there is no immediate danger but help is necessary, the case will be referred to a low threshold service. If, however, an investigation is necessary, the case is referred to CCCAN for diagnosis and care provision.

MANAGEMENT BY MANDATED SERVICES

Minors, their parents, and (low threshold) care providers can contact a *mandated service* when the integrity of a minor and/or his/her family can no longer be guaranteed or when the situation is *alarming* (see above for a definition) (Vlaamse Gemeenschap, 2013). CCCAN and SCYCs are categorized as mandated services in the Decree on IYC. As already mentioned above, referrals can also come from the public prosecutor's office. When a case is reported to a mandated service, the service assesses whether there is a notion of *social exigency* (in Dutch, "maatschappelijke noodzaak") to start youth care (Vlaamse Gemeenschap, 2013). The notion of social exigency and the necessity of the youth care need to be motivated. If youth care appears to be socially exigent and the ongoing care sufficiently guarantees the development and the safety of the minor, help offered will be continued and followed up by a mandated service. If youth care is not yet installed, the ongoing help is ineffective, or appropriate youth care is not immediately available, the mandated service organizes youth care in agreement with the minor and his/her family (Vlaamse Gemeenschap, 2013). If voluntary care is not accepted or if the minor or his/her parents refuse to collaborate during the assessment of social exigency, the case is referred to the public prosecutor's office. Before official referral, the youngster and the parents are invited to a meeting (Vlaamse Gemeenschap, 2013).

As stated above, the Decree on IYC recognizes two kinds of mandated services: CCCAN and SCYCs. Basically, both services have the same competences and tasks, but they differ from each other in terms of expertise. CCCAN are more specialized in the management of cases of CAN, while SCYCs are mostly contacted for problematic life or problematic educational situations in general, such as difficult family relationships or behavioral problems. CCCAN and SCYCs can refer cases to one another.

To handle reports of (intra-familial) child maltreatment, the Flemish government created CCCAN in 1987. Nowadays CCCAN have the following tasks (Vlaamse Gemeenschap, 2013):

- Assess reports of suspicion of CAN from any person or organization;
- Provide adequate care to victims of CAN and their family;
- Provide advice to persons and youth care providers who offer youth care in alarming situations with a suspicion of social exigency;
- Assess and follow-up alarming situations reported by the victim, his/her parents, his/her confidential advisor, other persons, and youth care providers;
- Guarantee the juvenile public prosecutor that alarming situations will be assessed and monitored. The duration of the assessment may not exceed 65 days;
- Refer the minor to the public prosecutor in the event of social exigency.

CCCAN assess the seriousness and the aspects of the problem in several ways. The first is to contact other social workers, such as a center for student assistance or services that earlier provided help, in order to gather information on the victim and his/her family. The second is by means of psychological assessments of the victim, his/her parents, or other directly involved persons. In the efforts of CCCAN to point out the direction for change, the best interest of the child is the guiding principle. CCCAN have a unique position in the care landscape. They work with criminal offenses without the obligation to report these crimes. Indeed, the information gathered during the assessment is bound by professional secrecy. This ensures that CCCAN can offer help in a non-judicial context (Van Dooren, 2016). The underlying assumption is that the best results are achieved when parents can name and face the violence in their family. This involves the encouragement of self-reporting by the victims and the perpetrators and providing help in a confidential setting of accountable care (Desair & Adriaenssens, 2011). Psychological assessment is considered supportive rather than leading. The assessment aims at an analysis of the vulnerabilities and strengths of the child, the parents, and the family, in order to lay a foundation for care and support. CCCAN work, if possible, with the whole family in a systemic way (Desair & Adriaenssens, 2011).

CCCAN offer help to the whole family in cases of intra-familial CAN. In cases of extra-familial abuse, CCCAN focus on victim support (Van Dooren, 2016). All services offered are voluntary and provided through collaboration and dialogue with everyone involved (victim, offender, parents, etc.). The CCCAN model combines an interventionist approach with an empowering one. On the one hand, children need protection because they are vulnerable. On the other hand, the competencies of children and families need to be recognized and treated respectfully. An appreciative and questioning model is used to motivate and move families towards change in favor of the best interest of the child (Desair & Adriaenssens, 2011). As already mentioned, when the child's safety cannot be guaranteed, other steps are considered, such as reporting to the office of the public prosecutor in juvenile affairs. The latter possibility of referral raises the question of the voluntary nature of the help offered. Voluntary help is often not voluntary but conditional: aiming at preventing more formal (judicial) interventions.

Wallonia-Brussels Federation

According to the principle of assistance to persons in danger and Article 3 §1 of the 2004 Decree on assistance to victims of child abuse, anyone who is aware of a situation of violence must try to end it. This order refers to the obligation to be active and act positively but does not imply an obligation to achieve results (Office de la naissance et de l'enfance, 2014). Acting in situations of violence can, however, be difficult. Social workers *can* report these situations to services such as: psycho-medico-social centers (PMS), school health promotion services (PSE), SOS-CT, social workers of CFS, or any other appropriate specialized professional (Communauté Française, 2004). Next, civilians are encouraged not to singlehandedly assess a situation but instead are urged to call upon specific authorities or services that support them.

As mentioned, an intervention protocol between welfare services and the judicial sector was signed by the respective Ministers in 2007. Its aim is to help stakeholders recognize the most appropriate services to which they can refer, to be aware of their limits, and to identify the actors who can take over when necessary. This protocol stresses that cases of CAN are preferably dealt with by child welfare services and situates each actor, their limits, and their duties.

SOS CHILDREN TEAMS (SOS-CT)

The SOS-CT have a major role in the management of children at risk and victims of CAN. These multidisciplinary teams are mandated to prevent and treat situations of CAN (Communauté Française, 2004). They intervene on their own initiative or on the request of (1) any person, institution or service, (2) a social worker of CFS, or (3) the head of a CFS following a judicial decision (Communauté Française, 1991). In case of the notification of suspected CAN, the situation is assessed in terms of severity and size of the problem by a multidisciplinary group.

Possible SOS-CT interventions include mobilizing the capacities of the reporter and collaborating with the child and his/her family. The best interest of the child is the guiding principle. If the team cannot ensure the safety of a child, it may request the intervention of the social worker from a CFS or, in the case of serious and imminent danger, and if it is not possible to protect the child otherwise, call on other child welfare actors, even the public prosecutor. When the prosecutor is called in, a social worker of the CFS is simultaneously informed. The teams offer their services free of charge throughout the French Community.

CHILD AND FAMILY SERVICES (LES SERVICES DE L'AIDE À LA JEUNESSE)

The services offered by Child and Family Services (CFS) are free. CFS can be called upon by the victim, his/her family or a professional in the context of voluntary help. Social workers of CFS do not intervene on the basis of anonymous information. They act based on concrete, objective and written information which can be consulted by all parties involved, except for judicial documents, and medical and psychological reports. In addition to the content, the origin of the information can be consulted. The help offered by CFS is specialized and subsidiary. It is only provided when low threshold services (SOS-CT, psycho-medico-social service, etc.) regard their support to be insufficient. When CFS intervene, the help offered by the low threshold service is continued. After assessment of a request for help, CFS can:

- Reorient the management of the case towards actors from low threshold services or ask for the intervention of a SOS-CT;
- Ensure a (medical, psycho-social and educational) follow-up of the child and his/her family;
- Place the child in out-of-home care;
- Coordinate the services if more services are involved, organizing specialized and exceptional assistance if necessary (Communauté Française, 1991).

If the proposal of help is accepted by the parents, CFS ask the appropriate service to offer the help to the youngster and his/her parents. The duration of the help offered is one year. However, if in the meantime the situation changes, this period may be shortened. The proposal can be renegotiated and new proposals can be implemented. All proposals from the CFS need to be accepted by the parents. If the refusal of a proposal for help results in an endangerment of the minor, the social worker will refer the case to the public prosecutor. The latter will assess the necessity for court ordered help and support.

REFERRAL TO JUDICIARY SERVICES AND THE PUBLIC PROSECUTOR

If a child or adolescent is in danger, if his/her well-being or safety is threatened, or if s/he or his/her parents do not accept the help offered, then the intervention of the Juvenile Court may be necessary. The measures that can be ordered by judicial authorities and juvenile courts are regulated in the Walloon Region a decree on youth care and in the Brussels-Capital Region by an Ordonnance on the assistance to victims of child abuse. Although the principles underpinning both regulations and the criteria used for referral to judicial authorities are similar, the measures imposed by a juvenile judge differ depending on the place of residence of the youngster and his/her family.

Out-of-home Placement

Figures on out-of-home placements can be seen as an indicator of the response of a society to CAN. However, since a variety of problems can result in out-of-home care, these figures must be handled carefully. Some placements are voluntary; others are court-ordered. Out-of-home care is also used as a parenting support measure in addition to being a protection and/or curative measure. Reasons for out-of-home care are diverse and include parenting problems as well as care due to a disabled child. Additionally, it is very difficult to obtain figures for Belgium regarding out-of-home placements rates as out-of-home care is organized in both communities by different administrations and is mostly provided by private subsidized organizations. Very few institutions are state run. Finally, although the term out-of-home care is used frequently, a clear operational definition is lacking, leading to the difficulties in determining how many children are in out-of-home care (Swaluë, 2013). In Belgium, it is very unusual to adopt children in out-of-home care (foster care or residential care). This implies that child protection measures such as out-of-home care are always temporary measures in contrast to adoption, which is not temporary and cannot be undone.

In Table 4.6, figures are presented of children in out-of-home care most likely because of issues, such as parenting problems and CAN. The number does not consider children in residential facilities for children with disabilities, child psychiatric units, and so on. As shown in the table, almost one third of the children in stay in family foster care. Two thirds of the children, however, stay in residential care. Around 10 per 1,000 children live

Table 4.6 Total number of children in out-of-home care by foster care and residential care

		2011		2012	
		N	% foster/resid care	N	% foster/resid care
Flanders	Foster care	4,817	37.6	4,845	37.7
	Residential care	8,007	62.4	8,016	62.3
	Total out-of-home care	12,824	100	12,816	100
	Number/1,000		10.41		10.40
WBF	Foster care	4,907	41.9	2,503	27.0
	Residential care	6,793	58.1	6,768	73.0
	Total out-of-home care	11,700	100	9,271	100
	Number/1,000		11.71		9.20
Belgium	Foster care	9,724	39.7	7,348	33.2
	Residential care	14,800	60.3	14,784	66.8
	Total out-of-home care	24,524	100	22,132	100
	Number/1,000		10.99		9.86

Source: Flanders: Agentschap Jongerenwelzijn (2012, 2013); WBF: L'aide à la jeunesse (2013, 2014).

in out-of-home care. Although the number of children in out-of-home care seems quite large, increasingly more subsidiary policy efforts are made towards ambulatory provision in comparison to residential care. Another remarkable finding is that in WBF in 2012 only one child in four was placed in foster care. This is a decrease of 15% compared to the previous year, while in international data (e.g., Brown, 2009) and policy (cf. CRC), foster care is favored over residential care.

Discussion and Conclusion

In this chapter, the child protection systems in Belgium were presented. Emblematic of the complexity of the Belgian child protection system, we started with an introduction into the Belgian political system. To add to this complexity, we turned to the problem of defining CAN. In addition to the difficulty of defining what constitutes child maltreatment, different governing levels (federal and communities) and communities (Flemish and WBF) use different definitions of CAN. However, when studying these definitions in detail, the differences are rather small and to a considerable extent the definition of Article 19 of the CRC can be recognized. In spite of the similarities, some differences deserve attention. First, the definition used in the Decree on Integral Youth Care of the Flemish community implies a relationship of dependency between the victim and perpetrator, restricting child maltreatment to very specific situations and excluding many situations of extrafamilial abuse. This is not the case in the definitions used by the judicial authorities and by child welfare workers in WBF. Second, aligned with scientific research, judicial authorities at the federal level, the SOS-CT, and CFS in WBF recognize the deleterious effects of domestic violence on children. Indeed, children are often present during domestic altercations and children who witness marital violence are at higher risk for a whole range of emotional and behavioral problems, including anxiety, poor school performance, low self-esteem, nightmares, and physical health problems. In addition, research even shows that marital violence directly and indirectly affects child mortality (Krug et al., 2002). Consequently, children affected by domestic violence are at risk of increased exposure to other adversities in their lives. Domestic violence is associated with child abuse, parental substance abuse and mental health difficulties, homelessness, social isolation and involvement in crime (Osofsky, 2003; Holt et al., 2008). This kind of violence is, strictly speaking, not embodied in the definition used in the Flemish community. The latter does not imply that domestic violence is considered harmless in Flanders. Rather, these situations will be considered *alarming* situations in which help and support can even be imposed if necessary.

Comparison of numbers of forms of CAN reported to the Flemish CCCAN or the SOS-CT in WBF reveal important differences between Flanders and WBF. These differences are the most salient regarding neglect, sexual abuse, and situations at risk. Several explications are possible. A first and maybe the most important explanation is that the numbers are calculated in a different way. A second explanation could be that the same behavior is labeled differently by professionals of different communities. A possible third explanation is that professionals referring to the Flemish CCCAN or the SOS-CT in WBF differ in the extent of their collaboration efforts with judicial authorities, which consequently impacts reporting to a CCCAN or SOS-CT. This hypothesis is in line with international research that found that different professional groups focus on different forms of CAN. For example, Tonmyr and colleagues (2010) found that non-health professionals reported more domestic violence while health professionals reported more neglect and emotional abuse. In line with the aforementioned explanation, it can be hypothesized that differences regarding the organization of care result in differences concerning the CAN reported most frequently to the Flemish CCCAN or the WBF SOS-CT. For example, the existence of the hotline 1712 in Flanders and the absence of such a hotline in WBF can be an explanation for differences regarding the number of children "at risk." It can be hypothesized that cases of children "at risk" concern less severe and less urgent cases that are referred to a low threshold service by the hotline in Flanders, while these cases will be referred to SOS-CT in WBF. More profound, thorough analysis of these differences would be interesting. Finally, Flanders and WBF differ in socioeconomic profile. Walloon families have lower income and depend more on social benefits than Flemish families (Cantillon et al., 1994). Although poverty does not cause maltreatment, evidence suggests that CAN and the associated risks occur disproportionally among families living in poverty (Freisthler et al., 2007; Drake et al., 2009). In addition, impoverished families are more likely to come to the attention of child welfare services because of the risk factors associated with poverty (Font et al., 2012). Consequently, differences in socioeconomic status may be accountable for the observed differences.

Both communities differ in their collaboration with judicial authorities. As mentioned above, in Flanders child welfare services and judicial authorities are more involved. Collaboration and information sharing of child welfare services and judicial services is almost the norm. Moreover, these initiatives are not based on individual networks of professionals, but they are structurally organized and enshrined in decrees and circulars. Flanders' efforts to have child and welfare services collaborate with judicial authorities originates from the view that cases of CAN need to be treated in a comprehensive way. This view also implies that professional secrecy is not an aim in itself but a condition facilitating a therapeutic relationship with the offender aiming at ensuring the protection and security of the child (Van Dooren, 2016). In WBF, however, child welfare professionals are more reluctant to share information with judicial authorities. The safeguarding of professional secrecy and the therapeutic relationship as a guiding principle for the support offered are emphasized much more. Confidentiality is experienced as an obstacle in collaborating with judicial authorities.

Regarding the responses to CAN, ambulatory support and out-of-home placements are used. The number of children in out-of-home care in both communities and therefore in Belgium, approaches the European mean (around 1%) (Eurochild, 2010). Compared to other countries such as the UK, Sweden, Ireland, and even France, the number of children in residential care compared to the number in foster care is high, despite research that growing up in institutions has detrimental psychological, emotional, and physical implications, such as attachment disorders, cognitive and developmental delays, and a lack of social and life skills leading to multiple disadvantages during adulthood (Brown, 2009). Not only scientific evidence but also the CRC states that children should be placed preferably in family-like settings and that placement in residential facilities should only happen when necessary. Particularly in WBF, as shown in Table 4.6, the number of children placed in foster care has declined in recent years while the number of children placed in institutions has stayed stable.

Related to the topic above, the question remains about the use of evidence-based methods and instruments in assessment and treatment. As far as we know, insufficient attention is paid by the SCYC, CCCAN, and SOS-CT to use validated and reliable questionnaires during CAN assessment. Counseling is rarely guided by evidence-based practices and empirically supported treatments. However, to offset the prejudices and distortions of the individual assessor, team decision-making procedures are installed. The question remains if a team is sufficient to protect against false positives and negatives.

In conclusion, Belgium is a complex country, as is its child protection system. In this chapter, we showed that both parts of Belgium differ in definition and treatment of CAN. As a consequence of future political evolutions, it can be expected that differences will become greater. This should not be a problem, if structures (including differences within structures) are transparent, fair, and efficient.

References

Agentschap Jongerenwelzijn. (2012). *Jaarverslag 2011*. Van Mulders, Stefaan.

Agentschap Jongerenwelzijn. (2013). *Jaarverslag 2012*. Van Mulders, Stefaan.

Brown, K. (2009). *The risk of harm to young children in institutional care*. Save the Children.

Cantillon, B., Marx, I., and Van Dam, R. (1994). *Intercommunautaire verschillen inzake uitkeringen en bijdragen in de sociale zekerheid*. Centrum voor sociaal beleid, Ufsia—Universiteit Antwerpen.

Cicchetti, D. and Manly, J. T. (2001). Editorial: Operationalizing child maltreatment: Developmental processes and outcomes. *Development and Psychopathology*, 13, 755–757.

Communauté Française. (1991). Décret du 4 mars 1991 relatif à l'Aide à la Jeunesse. *Belgisch Staatsblad*, 161, 13028–13039.

Communauté Française. (2004). Décret du 12 mai 2004 relatif à l'Aide aux enfants victimes de maltraitance. *Belgisch Staatsblad*, 174, 44260–44265.

Communauté Française. (2013). *Un enfant exposé aux violences conjugales est un enfant maltraité*. Delcor Frédéric

De Clerck, S. and Vandeurzen, J. (2010). *Protocol Kindermishandeling Justitie-Welzijn*. Authors.

De Craim, C. (2013). Kindermishandeling: De wetgevende aspecten en de aanpak door de gerechtelijke overheden. In H. Blow (Ed.). *Handboek Familiaal geweld* (pp. 1–26). Politeia.

De Craim, C. and Traets, E. (2010). Protocol kindermishandeling. Naar een intensere samenwerking tussen justitie en hulpverlening. *Tijdschrift Jeugd- en kinderrechten*, 71, 177–183.

De Rycke, L., Vanobbergen, B., Van den Akker, D., and Cnudde, H. (2011). *Geweld, gemeld en geteld. Aanbevelingen in de aanpak van geweld tegen kinderen en jongeren*. Kinderrechtencommissariaat.

Desair, K. and Adriaenssens, P. (2011). Policy toward child abuse and neglect in Belgium: shared responsibility, differentiated response. In N. Gilbert, N. Parton, and M. Skivenes (Eds.). *Child protection systems. International trends and orientations* (pp. 204–222). Oxford University Press.

Direction de l'Egalité des Chances. (2013). *Un enfant exposé aux violences conjugales est un enfant maltraité.* Fédération Wallonie-Bruxelles.

Drake, B., Lee, S. M., and Jonson-Reid, M. (2009). Race and child maltreatment reporting: Are Blacks overrepresented? *Children and Youth Services Review*, 31, 309–316.

Egu, C. L. and Weiss, D. J. (2003). The role of race and severity of abuse in teachers' recognition or reporting of child abuse. *Journal of Child and Family Studies*, 12, 465–474.

Eurochild. (2010). *Children in alternative care: National surveys.* Eurochild.

Font, S. A., Berger, L. M., and Slack, K. S. (2012). Examining racial disproportionality in child protective services case decisions. *Children and Youth Services Review*, 34, 2188–2200.

Freisthler, B., Bruce, E., and Needell, B. (2007). Understanding the geospatial relationship of neighborhood characteristics and rates of maltreatment for Black, Hispanic, and White Children. *Social Work*, 52, 7–16.

Germeijs, V. (2015). Het decreet integrale jeugdhulp voor dummies. *Caleidoscoop*, 25, 6–19.

Gilbert, N., Parton, N., and Skivenes, M. (2011). Changing patterns of response and emerging orientations. In N. Gilbert, N. Parton, and M. Skivenes (Eds.). *Child protection systems: International trends and orientations* (pp. 243–257). Oxford University Press.

Herrenkohl, R. C. (2005). The definition of child maltreatment: from case study to construct. *Child Abuse and Neglect*, 29, 413–424.

Holt, S., Buckley, H., and Whelan, S. (2008). The impact of exposure to domestic violence on children and young people: A review of the literature. *Child Abuse and Neglect*, 32, 797–810.

Kind en Gezin. (2017). *Het Kind in Vlaanderen 2016.* Kind en Gezin.

Krug, E. G. Dahlberg, L. L., Mercy, J. A., Zwi, A. B., and Lozano, R. (2002). *World report on violence and health.* World Health Organization.

L'aide à la jeunesse. (2013). *Rapport de l'aide à la jeunesse Année 2011.* Baudart, Liliane.

L'aide à la jeunesse. (2014). *Rapport de l'aide à la jeunesse Année 2012.* Baudart, Liliane.

Louwagie, J. and Gevaert, K. (2012). Verontrusting: een zaak van iedereen. *Tijdschrift voor Welzijnswerk*, 36, 22–27.

Op de Beeck, H. and Put, J. (2017). Case-based deliberation in cases of child abuse: An innovative way to cooperate between justice and care. *European Journal on Criminal Policy and Research*, 23, 353–370.

O'Toole, R., Webster, S. W., O'Toole, A. W., and Lucal, B. (1999). Teachers' recognition and reporting of child abuse: A factorial survey. *Child Abuse and Neglect*, 23, 1083–1101.

Office de la naissance et de l'enfance. (2014). *Les équipes SOS. A l'attention des professionnels.* Office de la naissance et de l'enfance.

Office de la naissance et de l'enfance. (2017). *L'ONE en chiffres 2016.* Fédération Wallonie-Bruxelles.

Office de la naissance et de l'enfance—Service SOS Enfants. (2018). *Recueil des données statistiques sur la maltraitance infantile en Fédération Wallonie-Bruxelles (IMISOS).* Office de la naissance et de l'enfance.

Osofsky, J. D. (2003). Prevalence of children's exposure to domestic violence and child maltreatment: Implications for prevention and intervention. *Clinical Child and Family Psychology Review*, 6, 161–170.

Parket Generaal. (2006). *Omzendbrief COL 3 d.d. 01.03.2006: Definitie van het intrafamiliaal geweld en de extrafamiliale kindermishandeling, de identificatie en de registratie van de dossiers door de politiediensten van de parketten.* Author

Pas, W. (2007). Bevoegdheidsvraagstukken. In J. Put and M. Rom (Eds.). *Het nieuwe jeugdrecht* (pp. 15–43). De Boeck & Larcier.

Statbel. (n.d.). *Structure of the population.* Available at: https://statbel.fgov.be/en/themes/population/structure-population. Retrieved February 15, 2019.

Swaluë, A. (2013). *Du placement d'enfants: définir et quantifier pour réaliser le droits des enfants placés.* OEJAJ.

Tonmyr, L. Li, Y. A., Williams, G., Scott, D., and Jack, S. M. (2010). Patterns of reporting by health care and nonhealth care professionals to child protection services in Canada. *Paediatrics and Child Health*, 15, 25–32.

Van Dooren, E. (2016). De werking van de Vertrouwenscentra Kindermishandeling in Vlaanderen: In evolutie met het belang van het kind als centrale bekommernis. *Cahiers Politiestudies*, 3, 133–148.

Van Mulders, S. (2017). *Omzendbrief in het kader van het realiseren van gebiedsdekkende casuscoördinatie in Vlaanderen m.b.t. intrafamiliaal geweld en kindermishandeling.* Author.

Vinck, I., Christiaens, W., Jonckheer, P., and Veereman, G. (2016). *How to improve the detection of child abuse in Belgium?*. Belgian Health Care Knowledge Centre.

Vlaamse Gemeenschap. (2013). Decreet van 12 juli 2013 betreffende de integrale jeugdhulp. *Belgisch Staatsblad*, 183, 65154–65173.

Webster, S. W., O'Toole, R., O'Toole, A. W., and Lucal, B. (2005). Overreporting and underreporting of child abuse: Teachers' use of professional discretion. *Child Abuse and Neglect*, 29, 1281–1296.

Child Welfare in Canada

Nico Trocmé, Melanie Doucet, Barbara Fallon, Jennifer Nutton, *and* Tonino Esposito

Abstract

This chapter looks into the child welfare system in Canada, which is focused on the child's safety instead of the welfare of the family and child. Child protection systems have characteristics of mandatory reporting of suspected cases, service eligibility depending on maltreatment investigations, the option of using court orders, and out-of-home care settings. Indigenous children are significantly overrepresented in the child welfare system and children being placed in out-of-home care. The chapter also notes the rise of child welfare services in response to industrialism, capitalism, and urbanization as it sparked social issues like child labor, poverty, and the destitution of families.

Key Words: Canada, child welfare system, industrialism, Indigenous children, out-of-home care, maltreatment, child labor, poverty, welfare

Introduction

In comparison to several other jurisdictions, the Canadian child welfare system is usually described as focused on safety of the child as opposed to a focus on child and family welfare (Fallon et al., 2012). Child welfare services—including child protection legislation, maltreatment investigations, family support services, and out-of-home placements—primarily fall under jurisdiction of the 13 Canadian provinces and territories, with the Federal government having the responsibility to fund child welfare services for Indigenous children living in First Nation communities. Several provinces and territories are attempting to broaden to a child and family welfare approach with the introduction of differential or alternate response models (Waldfogel, 2009), a shift that is also stressed in emerging Indigenous service delivery models.

Over 299,000 child maltreatment investigations (48.22 per 1,000 children) are conducted every year across Canada, and on any given day, almost 60,000 children are in out-of-home care (8.8 per 1,000 children) (Fallon et al., 2022; Saint-Girons et al., 2020).

While there is significant variation across provinces in the structure and organization of services and in the statutes defining investigation procedures and intervention

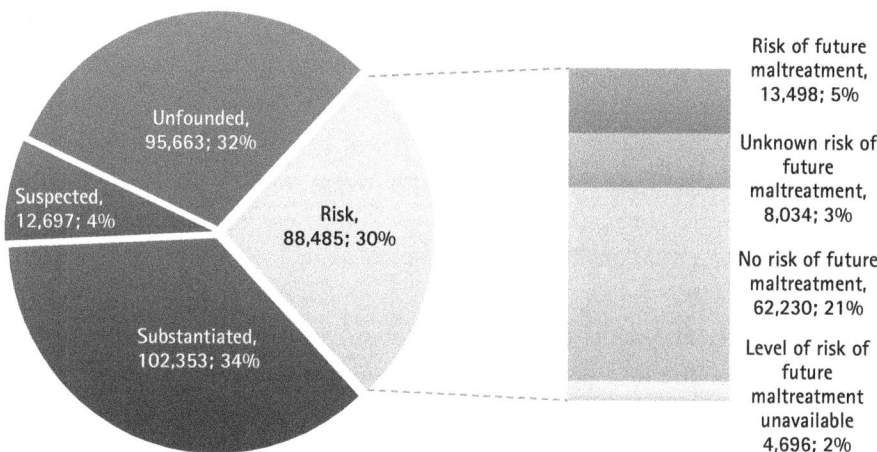

Figure 5.1 Type of child maltreatment investigations and level of substantiation in Canada in 2008 *Source*: Trocmé et al. (2010), Figure 3-11, p. 24.

mandates, these systems nevertheless share many common characteristics. These characteristics include:

- Mandatory reporting of suspected child abuse and neglect;
- Child maltreatment investigations and risk and safety assessments as a primary framework for determining service eligibility;
- The option to use court orders to enforce services; and
- The placement of children and youth in a range of out-of-home care settings, from kinship care to foster homes to group homes to residential treatment facilities.

Key Characteristics and Trends in Investigated Maltreatment

The Canadian Incidence Study of Reported Child Abuse and Neglect (CIS), a periodic survey of Canadian child welfare investigations, is the only national source of data on child maltreatment investigations. The most recent full national survey was conducted in 2019 and found that, of an estimated 299,171 child-maltreatment-related investigations, 210,713 (70%, or 33.97 per 1,000 children) focused on possible incidents of abuse or neglect that may have already occurred and 88,458 (30%, or 14.26 per 1,000 children) were concerns about risk of future maltreatment (see Figure 5.1; Fallon et al., 2022). Thirty-four percent of the investigations were substantiated. In a further 4% of investigations, there was insufficient evidence to substantiate maltreatment, but maltreatment remained suspected by the worker at the completion of the intake investigation. Thirty-two percent of investigations were deemed unfounded (Fallon et al., 2022).

The inclusion of investigations for risk of future maltreatment in the CIS 2008 and CIS 2019 reflects a general expansion across the country in the scope of child protection mandates (Fallon et al., 2022; Fallon, Trocmé, & MacLaurin, 2011; Fallon, Trocmé, MacLaurin, Sinha, & Black, 2011). Of the 30% of risk-only investigations, 5% were judged to involve significant risk of future maltreatment, while 21% were judged to not involve significant risk. In another 3%, the level of future risk was not determined and in 2% of investigations from Quebec, the information about level of future risk of maltreatment was not available (Fallon et al., 2022).

The four national cycles of the CIS conducted in 1998, 2003, 2008, and 2019 document the expansion in the scope of child protection mandates across Canada that occurred in the early 2000s, with the total number of child investigations increasing from an estimated 135,261 in 1998 (21.47 per 1,000 children), to 235,315 in 2003 (38.33 per 1,000 children) (see Figure 5.2). While increases have been reported across most jurisdictions, the extent of this expansion varies by province. In Ontario, Canada's largest province, Ontario Incidence Studies (OIS) have been conducted since 1993 on a five-year cycle through to 2018. Rates of investigation increased from an estimated 21.32 investigations per 1,000 children in 1993 to 62.89 in 2018, with the sharpest increase occurring between 1998 and 2003 (Fallon et al., 2020). In Quebec, Canada's second largest province, Quebec Incidence Studies (QIS) have been conducted since 1998; investigations have increased at a slower rate, going from 15.44 per thousand in 1998, to 23.6 in 2019 (Hélie et al., 2022). The QIS data represents children in Quebec, excluding Métis and Inuit children, who were investigated because of maltreatment related concerns or for serious behavior problems (Hélie et al., 2022).

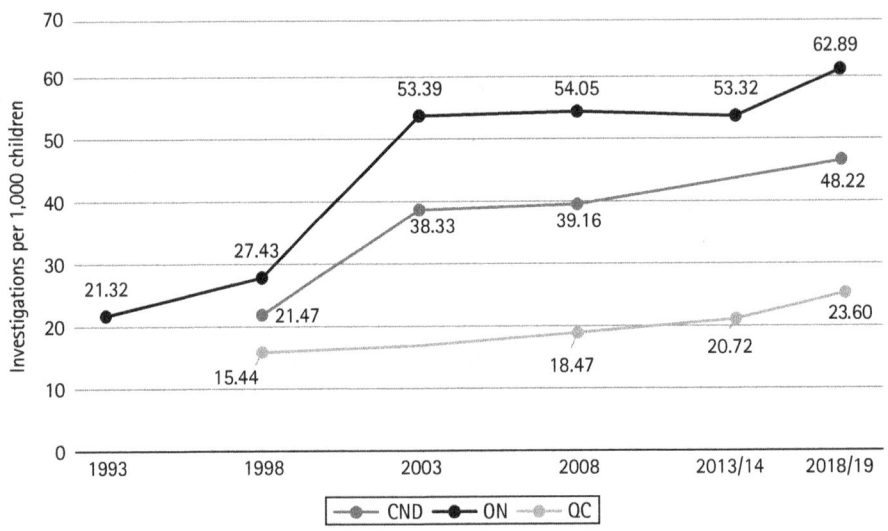

Figure 5.2 Child maltreatment-related investigations in Canada, Ontario, and Quebec, 1993–2014 *Source*: Data for investigation rate in Canada adapted from Trocmé et al. (2010), Table 3-1, p. 23. Data for investigation rate in Ontario adapted from Fallon et al. (2015), Figure 3-1, p. 41, Data for investigation rate in Quebec adapted from Hélie et al. (2017), Tableau 3-2, p. 47.

These increases have been primarily driven by investigations involving concerns about exposure to intimate partner violence, emotional maltreatment and risk of maltreatment, while there has been little change over time in those involving serious injuries or child sexual abuse (Fallon, Trocmé, & MacLaurin, 2011; Trocmé et al., 2011). Analysis of investigations re-classified as urgent or chronic on the basis of injury, child age, and severity of maltreatment from all CIS cycles shows urgent protection cases have dropped from 28% in 1998, to 19% in 2003, to 15% in 2008. In 2008, 7% of cases involved neglect of a child under 4, 4% sexual abuse, 2% physical abuse of a child under 4, and 1% children who had sustained severe enough physical harm that medical treatment was required. The other 85% of maltreatment investigations involved situations where concerns appear to focus less on immediate safety and more on the long-term effects of a range of family-related problems. These findings underscore the importance of considering the dual mandate of Canadian child welfare authorities: protecting children from imminent harm and supporting the development and well-being of children living in difficult circumstances (Trocmé et al., 2014).

Children in Out-of-home Care

There are limited Canada-wide data on the number and characteristics of children in out-of-home care. The CIS tracks placement of children in out-of-home care during the investigation period, typically the first 30 to 60 days of involvement with child welfare services. At that initial point of contact, 5% of children investigated by child welfare services are formally placed in out-of-home care (Fallon et al., 2022). Previous analysis of placements in the CIS 2008 found that over 85% are in relative or non-relative foster care, and less than 15% (11,000, or 1.8 placements per 1,000 children) involve group homes or residential treatment facilities, a rate that has not changed over the three cycles of the CIS (Trocmé et al., 2010). The CIS estimates significantly underestimate the placement rate, however, since many children in care are placed after the initial investigation. Because provincial statutes require that, wherever possible, in-home services be provided prior to considering out-of-home placement, more than half of all placements occur after initial investigation (Esposito et al., 2013).

A second source of estimation is a compilation of the number of children in care reported by each provincial and territorial jurisdiction. In a recent analysis of CIS-2019, Saint-Girons and colleagues found that the number of children in out-of-home care in Canada 2019 at year end is 54,139 when informal kinship services are excluded and 59,283 when reported informal kinship services are included in the final count (2020). As such, the rate of children in care per 1,000 children is of 7.46 or of 8.16 in Canada depending on whether reported informal kinship care services are excluded or included (Saint-Girons et al., 2020).One of the challenges with using cross-sectional counts is that they confound two very different populations: children placed in short-term care because of a short-term family crisis, and children who end up in long-term care. While there are no national longitudinal data tracking different types of placement trajectories, analysis of administrative placement data from Quebec describes the range of these different trajectories in Canada's second largest province. Following a cohort of 127,181 children investigated for maltreatment-related concerns between 2002 and 2010, Esposito et al. (2013) found that 22.8% experience at least one out-of-home placement lasting more than 72 hours. Further analysis of the children who experienced at least one placement shows that over 80% were reunified with their family, half of these within 175 days of their initial placement (Esposito et al., 2014). At the population level, a study from Manitoba, the province with one of the highest rates of out-of-home placement, found that by age 12, 9.4% of all children born between 1998 and 2001 had been placed in out-of-home care at least once (O'Donnell et al., 2016).

Overrepresentation of Indigenous Children in Care

Indigenous children are significantly overrepresented in the child welfare system. In Canada, the Indigenous population is comprised of First Nations, Métis, and Inuit;[1] it is important to note that the CIS data includes First Nations populations. Using data from the 2019 CIS, Fallon and colleagues (2021) show that, in the population served by sampled agencies, the rate of investigations for First Nations children was 3.6 times that of non-Indigenous children, at a rate of 151.00/1000 versus 42.11/1000 for non-Indigenous children. Overrepresentation increases even further when comparing children who are placed in out-of-home care following investigation, with rates close to 13 times higher for First Nations children placed in formal and informal care (20.20 per 1,000 First Nations children versus 1.56 per 1,000 non-Indigenous children; Fallon et al., 2021).

In a recent analysis of the 2016 Canadian Census, Black, Fallon and Trocmé (2022) examined disparities between the rates of First Nations and Non-Indigenous foster children and found that, even though First Nations children aged 0–15 make up only 5% of the child population in Canada, they represent 42.3% of children in foster care. By Indigenous identity group, the Canadian Census data indicate that the rate of children in foster care was 42.46 per 1,000 First Nations children compared to only 2.55 per 1,000 non-Indigenous children (Black et al., 2022). The Census data also show that over-representation was particularly marked for First Nations children in Western Canada, where the rate was between 15.3 and 32.2 times the rate of non-Indigenous foster children.

---

[1] As defined by the Government of Canada, "First Nations are those peoples who historically lived in North America, from the Atlantic to the Pacific, below the Arctic. Inuit historically lived along the coastal edge and on the islands of Canada's far north. The Métis descend from the historical joining of First Nations members and Europeans" (INAC, 2011). These three broad categories of Indigenous peoples have different histories with respect to negotiation and recognition of their rights, and each includes different communities. There are, for instance, over 600 First Nations across Canada speaking more than 50 distinct languages.

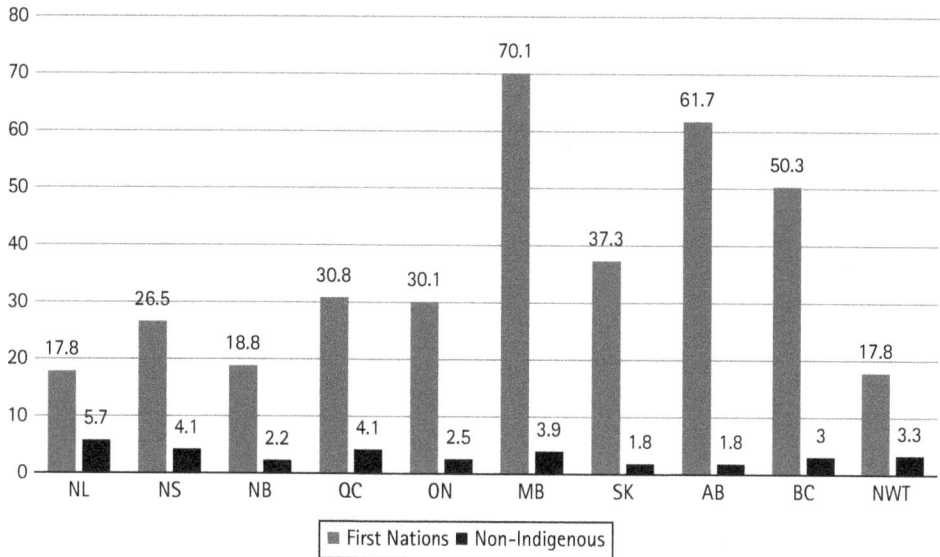

Figure 5.3 Rates of First Nations and Non-Indigenous Children per 1,000 children, by Province/Territory (Statistics Canada, 2011) *Source*: Adapted from Sinha & Wray (2015).

The extent of the overrepresentation of Indigenous children in out-of-home care is a key indicator being tracked by a growing number of jurisdictions. Alberta and British Columbia (BC), the two provinces with the most comprehensive reports tracking child welfare outcomes, break down most of their statistics by comparing outcomes for Indigenous and non-Indigenous children. In Alberta, in 2016, 69% of children in care were Indigenous; this rate has been increasing over time (Alberta Human Services, n.d). The British Columbia Ministry of Children and Family Development (MCFD, 2016) reports that while the number of Indigenous children in care has declined from a rate of 63.6 per thousand in 2002 to 55.4 per thousand in 2016, the number of non-Indigenous children in care has been decreasing at a faster rate; as a result, by 2016 61% of children in care were Indigenous. Consistent nation-wide monitoring of the placement of Indigenous children in out-of-home care is one of the key recommendations from the Truth and Reconciliation Commission of Canada (TRCC) report (2015).

Historical Context of Canada's Child Welfare Systems: The "Child Saving" Movement and Colonialism

The rise of industrialism, capitalism and urbanization in the 18th and 19th centuries brought forward social issues such as child labor, poverty, and destitution of families. In response to increasing child abuse concerns, a philanthropic movement emerged in North America, under which church-run orphanages were reorganized and "child saving" societies for the prevention of cruelty to children were established. Canada's child welfare system emerged at the end of the 19th century and was largely influenced by the U.S. "child saving" movement.

The Toronto Humane Society, founded in 1887 for the protection of women, children, and animals, was the first child protection organization in Canada. It was subsequently renamed the Children's Aid Society (CAS) in 1891, and Canada's first child protection act—an *Act for the Prevention of Cruelty to and Better Protection of Children*—was passed in Ontario in 1893. The Act promoted foster care and gave CAS guardianship power over children taken into their care. Similar societies developed in many municipalities across Canada, and a rapid expansion of child welfare services occurred in most provinces over the next 20 years, with provinces eventually seeking legal mandates that gave them the power to remove children who were victims of abuse or neglect from their homes (Bala et al., 2004).

In the 1950s and 1960s, as part of the establishment of the Canadian welfare state after World War I, a comprehensive network of provincially regulated or run child welfare agencies was developed by establishing the legislative, regulatory, and financial frameworks required to transform these organizations from voluntary community-based societies to professionally organized bureaucracies. The various child protection statutes that shaped these frameworks maintained much of the late 19th-century child-saving language and moral values. For instance, Quebec's 1951 *Youth Protection Schools Act* was established to protect children "exposed to moral or physical dangers" (Article 15). Similarly, Ontario's 1970 *Child Welfare Act* included in its definition of a child in need of protection situations where: "a child [was] found associating with an unfit or improper person" (section 20 [1] [b] [v]) or "a child [was] found begging or receiving alms in a public place" (section 20 [1] [b] [vi]).

In the 1970s and 1980s, provinces sought to modernize their child welfare statutes by replacing explicit reference to morality with terminology reflecting the emerging focus on research and practice in child maltreatment, including physical and sexual abuse and neglect (Trocmé, 1991; Bala et al., 2004). The new statutes also included more specific procedures to protect parent and child rights, and shifted the onus onto child welfare authorities to ensure that in-home family support services were provided as an alternative to placement whenever possible. Ontario's 1984 *Child and Family Services Act*, which served as a model for other provinces, required that agencies demonstrate they were employing the "least disruptive course of action that is available and is appropriate" (section 1 [2]). This period also marked a dramatic shift in child welfare practice. For example, in Ontario, the number of children placed in out-of-home care significantly dropped from 17,807 in 1977 to 9,712 in 1988, while the number of families receiving services dramatically increased from 28,323 to 74,116 during the same timeframe (Trocmé, 1991).

The shift to a less intrusive approach came under fire following a series of inquests in BC, Manitoba, Ontario, Quebec, and New Brunswick. In 1995, the Gove (1995) Inquiry into Child Protection in BC, examining the death of five-year-old Matthew Vaudreuil at the hands of his mother, provided detailed documentation of a disorganized health and social service system. Dozens of professionals failed to report their concerns on Matthew's case and appeared more concerned about minimizing intrusion than responding to alarming signs of serious neglect and abuse. The inquiry led to a complete restructuring of the province's child welfare system. Similar concerns were raised in Ontario, leading to a "rebalancing" of the legislation to ensure that child protection and well-being were clearly identified as the primary consideration over parental rights (Bala, 1999).

To underscore the primary importance of child safety, several jurisdictions also adopted risk assessment tools, specific service eligibility criteria, and triage guidelines. This shift towards a lower threshold for intervention was compounded by a significant expansion in child welfare mandates in response to the growing body of research on the effects of child neglect and emotional maltreatment—especially in the context of children's exposure to intimate partner violence (Wolfe et al., 2003). The increase in child abuse and neglect investigations, and in the number of children placed in out-of-home care between 1998 and 2003, can be largely attributed to these changes (Fallon, Trocmé, MacLaurin, Sinha, et al., 2011; Trocmé et al., 2011).

The sharp increase in investigations and out-of-home placements that occurred in the late 90s and early 2000s led to calls across Canada to once again find the right balance between protection and over-intervention (Trocmé et al., 2014). Reviews and inquests focusing on the conditions for children placed in care have led to calls for developing family support services that can provide less intrusive alternatives to removal (MCFD, 2011; Government of New Brunswick, 2015; Gharabaghi et al., 2016; Milward, 2016). The call for more family and community-based alternatives has gained even more momentum in the face of growing evidence that Indigenous children are dramatically over-represented in the Canadian child welfare system.

The History of Child Welfare Services for First Nation, Métis, and Inuit Communities

The development of child welfare services for Indigenous (First Nations, Inuit, and Métis) communities in Canada has followed a very different trajectory, shaped by the history of colonization and cultural genocide of Indigenous peoples in North America. The history of colonialist child welfare practices in Canada began in the 19th century with the introduction of the residential school system, one of many colonial policies implemented to eradicate Indigenous culture by assimilating Indigenous peoples into Canadian culture and Christianity (Indigenous and Northern Affairs Canada (INAC), 1996; Miller, 1996). Beginning in 1876, the Canadian government began systematically removing Indigenous children from their families and communities and forcefully placing them into residential boarding schools, which were run by Christian churches (INAC, 1996; Sinha & Kozlowski, 2013). Residential schools served not only assimilative and indoctrination functions, but also as state-imposed child protection for Indigenous children living on reserves who were suspected of being abused and/or neglected based on Eurocentric notions of appropriate parenting (Milloy & McCallum, 2017).

Residential schools were chronically underfunded, which often led to failure to provide students with necessities such as medical care, clothing, and food (Hamilton & Sinclair, 1991; Sinha et al., 2011); demands by parents to return their children home to live in better conditions went unanswered. Many children died of disease and neglect or were physically, emotionally, and sexually abused (Hamilton & Sinclair, 1991; Sinha et al., 2011; Milloy & McCallum, 2017), and were disciplined harshly for using their language (Johnston, 1983). In some schools, children tried to escape and many died from drowning or freezing in remote or water-locked areas (INAC, 1996; Milloy & McCallum, 2017). Estimates indicate that nearly 50% of Indigenous children attending residential schools in the early 20th century died because of poor conditions (Miller, 1996).

By the time the last residential school closed in 1996 in Saskatchewan, over 150,000 Indigenous children in Canada had attended (INAC, 1996; Milloy & McCallum, 2017). The mass removal of Indigenous children over several generations meant that, when Indigenous children returned to their communities as young adults, many were confused about their identities—belonging neither to their community nor white society (Kirmayer et al., 2003).

In 1951, the *Indian Act* was amended to include language under Section 88, which stated that "all laws of general application from time to time in force in any province are applicable to and in respect of Indians in the province." This section has been interpreted to mean, in the absence of any explicit mention of child protection, that provincial child welfare laws and services be extended to Indigenous children on reserve (Hamilton & Sinclair, 1991; Auditor General of Canada, 2008). Following this amendment and federal and provincial governments coming to agreement over time on funding issues, provincial child welfare services expanded onto reserves (Bennett et al., 2005). This led to the next period of mass removal of Indigenous children from the 1960s to late 1980s, commonly referred to as the 'Sixties Scoop' (Sinclair, 2007). This term originated from an interview Patrick Johnston (1983) had with an employee from the Ministry of Human Resources in BC, who commented that "provincial social workers would, quite literally, scoop children from reserves on the slightest pretext" (p. 23).

For many Indigenous children, removal from their families and communities was made permanent—with over 11,000 put up for adoption between 1960 and 1990 (Ontario Ministry of Children and Youth Services, 2016). Once placed in foster care or adopted out, few would ever return home, and most were sent to live with non-Indigenous families, often in other provinces and (less frequently) in the United States (Johnston, 1983; Bennett et al., 2005). By the 1970s, foster care placement and adoption had replaced residential schools as the primary child protection system for Indigenous children (Libesman, 2014). Today, the impacts of the Sixties Scoop continue to be experienced. In October 2017, the federal government agreed to settle a class action lawsuit led by survivors, and announced that it would award up to $750 million to claimants plus $50 million donated to a Foundation for healing services (Tasker, 2017). However, this settlement has been criticized by advocates and survivor groups, due to the significant payment awarded to the lawyers representing the claimants to the amount of $75 million to be divided between four law firms (Pauls, 2018). While certain provinces, such as Manitoba and Alberta, have issued official apologies to the survivors of the Sixties Scoop, many provinces have yet to do so.

The history of child welfare services for Indigenous peoples in Canada is complex. The beginning of colonial Indigenous child welfare policy was influenced by countless treaties and agreements between hundreds of Indigenous communities and successive Canadian governments across the provinces and territories over several hundred years. Many political, economic, social, and cultural factors have impacted the ways in which Indigenous child welfare has been shaped over time. Although the Canadian government may no longer explicitly engage in deliberate acts of assimilation that would be considered cultural genocide, this history of explicitly racist colonial policies continues to have an impact on Canadian child welfare systems and Indigenous peoples. The mass removal of Indigenous children from their families and communities is not only a tragic period of history but also persists today with the overrepresentation of Indigenous children in the child welfare system. Conceding that it is likely that some of these placements are appropriate to keep children safe from harm, there are certainly structural problems and cultural conflicts that play a part in the overrepresentation of Indigenous children in care, the cycle of intergenerational foster care and trauma, and the continued colonization and systemic discrimination of Indigenous peoples.

Legislative and Administrative Structure of Child Welfare Services across Canada

The responsibility to protect children in Canada is delegated to the provinces and territories. Except for funding services to First Nations children and families living on reserves, the Canadian federal government has no direct funding nor policymaking jurisdiction in child welfare.

Structure of Child Welfare Service Delivery Systems

Canada's decentralized child welfare system has led to a range of child welfare service delivery models across the country. In some provinces, most notably Ontario where child welfare services are provided by 48 delegated community-run agencies (Wegner-Lohin et al., 2014), child welfare agencies provide a broad spectrum of services, ranging from the core investigative function to providing on-going supervision, counselling, and some out-of-home care services. In some communities, these were historically faith-based organizations that continue to maintain service on a religious basis, notably agencies serving the Catholic and Jewish communities. In Ontario, CAS manage all child welfare services including investigations, family support services, case-management and many foster homes. Group and residential care services are, however, mostly provided by a range of private for-profit and not-for-profit organizations (Gharabaghi et al., 2016).

In most other provinces and territories, services are provided through government offices with varying levels of regional and local independence and services contracted with non-government organizations. In Quebec, a significant reform was implemented in 2015 through Bill 10, *An Act to Modify the Organization and Governance of the Health and Social Services Network, in Particular by Abolishing the Regional Agencies*; this restructure had significant impacts on the provision of child welfare services by centralizing health and social services under regional authorities. Quebec is also the first province in Canada to have a union representing all foster parents, and unlike most jurisdictions, child welfare agencies also provide services for young offenders. In Alberta, investigation and case-management functions are also provided through regional government-run offices; however, many ongoing treatment, family support, and out-of-home placement services are contracted out to a mix of private for-profit and not-for profit organizations (Kyte & Wegner-Lohin, 2014).

Several jurisdictions are moving towards differential response models emphasizing more collaborative and community-based approaches in situations where forensically focused maltreatment investigations are not required (Kyte et al., 2013). In jurisdictions like Quebec and Ontario, the shift away from an investigation-driven approach has been primarily developed in the form of a statement of principles of collaboration and flexibility (Wegner-Lohin et al., 2014). Other jurisdictions have developed more formal separations between child protection and family support streams. The Alberta Response Model has two legislated streams of activity: family enhancement services and child protection services (Kyte & Wegner-Lohin, 2014), with three quarters of investigations being streamed to child protection (Alberta Human Services, n.d.). In BC, low-risk cases are diverted to a Family Development Response (FDR) that provides community-based resources (Kozlowski et al., 2014). The MCFD (2016) found that reports streamed to the FDR track have steadily increased, with over 75% referred in 2015.

Legislation

Child welfare interventions are governed through provincial and territorial legislative frameworks. However, these child welfare statutes share a common legislative history and, as a result, share many features. All statutes, for instance, identify both child safety and well-being as the paramount principles of their legislation (Trocmé et al., 2014). All include some type of mandatory reporting requirement which, at a minimum, apply to professionals working with children—and often extend to all members of the public (Gough et al., 2009). All statutes define child maltreatment in relatively broad terms, including physical abuse, sexual abuse, neglect, and emotional maltreatment. Many also include exposure to intimate partner violence, and Quebec includes situations where a child has serious behavior problems (Hélie et al., 2017). These definitions apply when children have been harmed or are at risk of harm, and the majority of investigations involve situations in which demonstrable harm has not yet occurred. These broad intervention mandates are usually balanced by the principle of providing the least intrusive or disruptive services.

The age range covered by each jurisdiction varies, with some jurisdictions limiting child protection mandates to children and youth under 16 (e.g., Saskatchewan and Newfoundland), others under 18 (e.g., Quebec and Alberta), and under 19 in BC (Gough et al., 2009). Ontario's mandate was revised from age 16 to 18 in January 2018 (MCYS, 2018); similar revisions were made in recent years to the *New Brunswick Family Services Act.*

In addition to provincial and territorial child welfare statutes, the federal *Criminal Code* (1985) covers a range of criminal activities, such as physical assault, sexual assault, abduction, exploitation, and trafficking. Unlike child welfare statutes that follow the balance of probability family court evidentiary rules, the *Criminal Code* requires a much higher level of evidence beyond a reasonable doubt, and does not cover services to children (Bala et al., 2004). In cases of physical abuse involving an injury, sexual abuse, some cases of serious neglect, and situations involving domestic violence, child welfare and criminal proceedings may proceed concurrently, usually through joint protocols between child welfare and the police. In 2008, 22% of child maltreatment-related investigations were referred by the police, most involving intimate partner violence; 14% of maltreatment investigations involved some type of joint police investigation (Fallon et al., 2013).

Section 43 of the *Criminal Code* provides explicit permission to schoolteachers, parents or persons standing in the place of the parent to use "force by way of correction . . . if the force does not exceed what is reasonable under the circumstances." This section applies to the physical punishment of children younger than 2, and older than 12, after the Supreme Court of Canada found that it was not appropriate to use disciplinary force on a young child or a teenager (*Canadian Foundation for Children, Youth and the Law v. Canada*, 2004). Section 43 has come under criticism because it is inconsistent with provincial child welfare statutes and violates the Canadian Charter of Rights and Freedoms and the United Nations Convention on the Rights of the Child (Durrant et al., 2009). The confusion created by *Criminal Code* is reflected in the rates of cases investigated and substantiated by Canadian child welfare authorities. In 2008, 74% of cases of physical abuse were considered by the investigating worker to have occurred in a context of punishment, an estimated rate of 2.3 cases of substantiated punitive physical abuse per 1,000 children in Canada (Jud & Trocmé, 2012). There is also emerging peer-reviewed research on the negative impacts of corporal punishment on children, showcasing outcomes such as depression, aggression, anti-social behavior and decreased quality of the parent–child relationship (Smith, 2012).

Research in the last 20 years in North America has shown that young people in the general population are progressively taking longer periods of time to transition to adulthood (Beaujot & Kerr, 2007; Arnett, 2015). This phenomenon, termed by Arnett (2015) as *emerging adulthood*, is associated with young people transitioning to adulthood between the ages of 25 and 29. In Canada, census data illustrates that 42% of young people between the ages of 20 and 29 are still living with their parents (Statistics Canada, 2011). In contrast, youth in long-term government care are expected to transition to adulthood and become self-sufficient quite rapidly due to provincial legislation mandating child welfare services to release youth from their care at the age of majority. Age and conditions for provision of ongoing services for youth in long-term care varies considerably across Canada, with extended care and maintenance supports conditionally provided up to the ages of 18 to 21 depending on the province (Mulcahy & Trocmé, 2010). Unlike the U.S., which has specific federal legislation pertaining to extended care up to age 21 (The *Fostering Connections to Success and Increasing Adoptions Act*, 2008), extended care is not typically mandated by the provinces, and is often based on political will and the availability of resources in the youth's service delivery region.

First Nations Federally Funded Services

In September 2019 there was a landmark compensation decision at the Canadian Human Rights Tribunal (CHRT) (First Nations Child and Family Caring Society and Assembly of First Nations v. Attorney General of Canada, 2019). It issued a series of orders to redress the systematic discrimination experienced by First Nations children and families through compensation of claimants and reform of services. Two class action lawsuits (Moushoom, Meawasige, Meawasige v. The Attorney General of Canada, 2019; Assembly of First Nations, Trout v. The Attorney General of Canada, 2020) also sought compensation for individuals who were part of the compensation decision. On December 31, 2021, after over 14 years of legal procedures, two agreements-in-principle (AIP) were reached among the parties.

Current Structure of First Nations Child Welfare in Canada

Child welfare in Canada is administered at the federal, provincial, territorial, and band level, resulting in a complex web of policies, structures and services that vary across these jurisdictions. First Nations children involved with child welfare are subject to different child welfare mandates and funding based on their place of residence. First Nations children ordinarily resident on-reserve may interact with a locally run First Nations child welfare agency or one run by the province, while First Nations children living off-reserve who have contact with child welfare are likely to interact with the provincial designate that serves the area where they live. A small number of urban Indigenous child and family services agencies serve First Nations children off-reserve in urban settings.

Canada's child welfare system consists of over 400 child welfare agencies, operating both federally and under the jurisdiction of 13 provinces and territories (Trocmé et al., 2010). In 2016, the First Nations Child and Family Caring Society of Canada estimated that there were over 140 First Nations agencies delivering services to First Nations peoples and eight Métis agencies delivering culturally relevant services to Métis families (National Collaborating Centre for Aboriginal Health, 2017; Sinha & Kozlowski, 2013). Indigenous child welfare agencies typically sign agreements with either the federal or provincial governments—or both governments—authorizing them to provide a range of child protection services to Indigenous children (Canadian Child Welfare Research Portal, 2019; Bennett, n.d.; Sinha & Kozlowski, 2013). Variations in child welfare practice are also found within jurisdictions.

Until recently, both First Nations and mainstream agencies had to apply the child welfare legislation of their province or territory when providing services to families. In Canada, most provinces and territories have incorporated provisions within their child welfare legislation for Indigenous children, families and communities, such as: band notification of court or placement; Indigenous involvement in case management; Indigenous involvement in service planning or delivery; prioritization of kinship care; submission of cultural connection plan; and connection to Indigenous culture in the best interest of the child (Sinha & Kozlowski, 2013).

On January 1, 2020, *An Act Respecting First Nations, Inuit and Métis Children, Youth and Families* came into force, allowing Indigenous communities to have control over child and family services. Although the Act is the first to recognize Indigenous jurisdiction over child welfare, the law has been critiqued because of its lack of commitment to core funding and the limits it imposes on Indigenous jurisdiction (e.g., Metallic et al., 2019). In July 2020, the first coordination agreement under the Act was signed by the Cowessess First Nation with Government of Canada and the Government of Saskatchewan, focusing on prevention, and ensuring that families are provided with the necessary resources to heal from intergenerational trauma (Indigenous Services Canada, 2022, n.p.).

While the legislative mandate for child welfare has rested with provinces and territories, funding for child welfare services for First Nations families living on-reserve lies with the federal government, through the First Nations Child and Family Services (FNCFS) program at Indigenous Services Canada. Funding for children living off-reserve lies with the province/territory. In fiscal year 2018–2019, there were 153 FNCFS-funded bodies in Canada, including both delegated First Nations agencies (105 agencies) and provincial ministries serving First Nations communities.

Jordan's Principle

On December 12, 2007, the House of Commons voted with unanimous support to adopt Jordan's Principle. In 2007, the federal government approved a fund of $11 million over 4 years for the implementation of Jordan's Principle. The implementation focused on "jurisdictional disputes involving First Nation children living on reserve with multiple disabilities requiring services from multiple service providers" (Indigenous Services Canada, n.d.).

By 2016, no Jordan's Principle cases were identified and all requests were siloed through existing federal programs. In January 2016, the CHRT found that Canada had failed to implement the full meaning of Jordan's Principle, which resulted in service gaps, delays, and denials for First Nations children (Indigenous Services Canada, n.d.).

As a response the CHRT finding, in July 2016, Canada committed to provide $382 million in funding and to "broaden the scope of Jordan's Principle and deliver service coordination services for First Nations families" (Sangster et al., 2019, p. 7). Between 2016 and 2018, Health Canada and INAC shared the responsibility for processing requests for health, and social/education services respectively.

In May 2017 (2017 CHRT 14) and November 2017 (2017 CHRT 35), the CHRT ruled that the definition of Jordan's Principle be expanded to include First Nations children living on and off reserve. The rulings also ensured that the government department of first contact would incur the costs of the service requested, with case conferencing happening after the service had been provided.

Child Welfare Service Outcomes

With over 299,000 children investigated by child welfare authorities every year in Canada, over 59,283 children in out-of-home care (Fallon et al., 2022; Saint-Girons et al., 2020), and over $5 billion[2] spent on child welfare services, surprisingly little is known about the outcomes of these services. A 2005 review of Canadian experimental and quasi-experimental evaluations of program impact in child welfare found only 10 published evaluations using comparison groups, four of which used a randomized design (Flynn & Bouchard, 2005). More recently, a Royal Society of Canada panel concluded that "despite consistent evidence of the severe and long-lasting effects of child maltreatment, research on how best to intervene to prevent maltreatment and its recurrence is surprisingly limited" (Boivin & Hertzman, 2012, pp. 102–103). When rigorous evaluation designs have been implemented, the results have been disappointing. A randomized controlled trial of an intensive home visitation program in Hamilton, Ontario for children receiving child welfare services due to abuse or neglect found no statistically significant differences in maltreatment recurrence rates (MacMillan et al., 2005).

Beyond outcome studies specifically designed to evaluate intervention efficacy, a growing number of jurisdictions are reporting on outcomes of child welfare services. Using the National Outcomes Matrix (NOM) framework, several jurisdictions are reporting on the recurrence of maltreatment, which is measured as the proportion of child protection cases that are reopened because of a substantiated incident of maltreatment within 12 months

---

[2] Expenditure estimates extracted by the authors from provincial budget statements.

of case closure (Trocmé et al., 2009). The reported rate of recurrence for Quebec was 9.3% for cases closed during the fiscal year 2012–13, 11.2% in BC for protection investigations and 3.6% of Family Development Response (FDR) cases in 2014–15, and 19% in Ontario for protection cases closed in 2014–15 (MCFD, 2016; Esposito et al., 2017; MCYS, 2017).

Two key outcome indicators reported for children and youth in out-of-home care are placement stability and permanency. Unfortunately, because of differences in definitions of placement, permanence, and follow-up, timeframes comparisons between jurisdictions are difficult to make. However, placement stability can be measured by the number of significant placement changes. For example, using data from Quebec, Esposito and colleagues (2017) report that, tracked over a period of up to 36 months, children who came into care in 2010 and 2011 moved an average of 1.87 times, with 31% of children experiencing no changes within 36 months, 25% having one change in placement, 27% having two to three changes, and 18% with four or more changes. Tracking placement changes during a 12-month period, the Ministry of Children and Family Development report from British Columbia (MCFD, 2016) reported that 68.7% of children did not move, 22.7% moved once, and 8.6% moved two or more times. Permanency is measured by tracking the proportion of children who end up returning home, are adopted, or are in a placement considered to be permanent. Reported rates of permanency range from a low of 21.8% in BC (MCFD, 2016), measured as the proportion of all children in care who exit care to a permanent arrangement, to between 60 and 70% in Quebec (Esposito et al., 2017).

Educational outcomes, which provide a more direct measure of success, are tracked in some jurisdictions. The Government of BC MCFD report (2016) provides the most extensive annually reported indicators, showing that 86% of children and youth in out-of-home care who are at school are in an age-appropriate grade; however, only 52.7% of youth in care who turn 19 have high school credentials. Analysis from Manitoba provides the most comprehensive portrait of the educational challenges faced by children and youth in child welfare: while 85% of youth in the general population tested in Grade 8 were competent in reading and writing, only 66% of youth who had received family support services through child welfare tested as competent, while only 49% of youth in out-of-home care met the Grade 8 reading and writing level of competency (Houden, 2015). Emerging findings from a longitudinal study in Quebec illustrate that by age 17, four out of five youth in care report a significant delay in education level attainment (Gagnon, 2018).

According to national estimates, approximately 10% of the youth in care population transitions out ("ages out") of the Canadian child welfare system every year (Flynn, 2003). The numbers of youth leaving care across the provinces vary; for example, 1,000 youth "aging out" of care in BC on a yearly basis (Vancouver Foundation, 2016), while approximately 2,000 youth exit the child protection system in Quebec each year (Gagnon, 2018).

Evidence to date demonstrates that youth exiting care in Canada are at a much higher risk of facing multiple challenges than their peers who are not in care, such as high rates of homelessness, under-education, unemployment or under-employment, poverty, mental health issues and post-traumatic stress, substance abuse, and early pregnancy or parenthood (Rutman et al., 2007; Ontario Provincial Advocate for Children & Youth, 2012; Tessier, 2015).

Emerging and Promising Practices in Canadian Child Welfare

While the Canadian child welfare systems have gaps in supports and areas for improvement, some emerging and promising practices have been implemented in various provinces in recent years. Regarding extended supports for youth in care, BC implemented a province-wide Tuition Waiver program in 2017 for youth up to age 26 pursuing their education at all post-secondary schools in the province (Government of BC, 2017). In June 2018, the government announced an expansion to the program to include construction trades training (CBC News, 2018). MCFD also has an Agreements with Youth Adults (AYA) program, which is available for former youth in care attending school or a rehabilitation program, and covers costs such as living expenses, child care and health care (Government of BC, 2018). In 2016, MCFD announced that it would expand to program from 2 to 4 years, continue to provide funding during school breaks, and raise the age limit from age 24 to 26 (Culbert, 2016). New Brunswick also has similar supports for youth exiting care who are pursuing post-secondary under their Free Tuition Program, which provides a non-repayable bursary for college and undergraduate degrees up to a maximum of four years (Government of New Brunswick, n.d.).

Another promising practice is New Brunswick's Integrated Service Delivery (ISD) framework for children and youth, initially piloted in two demonstration sites in 2011 and recently incrementally implemented province-wide (Education and Early Childhood Development, 2018). The framework aims to eliminate the silos between the various ministries and agencies providing services to children and youth, and adopts a more holistic, multidisciplinary, team-based, and preventative service delivery approach. The demonstration sites evaluation showcased a significant reduction in wait times for mental health services (86 to 100%), as well as a decrease of mental health issues and an increase in classroom adaptation in children and youth. In contrast to Canadian mental health services statistics where only one in five youth receive the services they require, three out of five youth in need received treatment during the two-year evaluation period. A pre- and post-pilot phase costing analysis demonstrated that recurring costs associated with the project would be balanced in less than three years, with subsequent cost savings to be achieved thereafter (B. Eckstein, personal communication, January 16, 2015). These findings demonstrate that the considerable benefits of implemented integrated service delivery approaches via multidisciplinary service delivery teams, both on a systems efficiency and a child and youth outcomes level.

There are also promising practices related to child welfare services for Indigenous children and youth. For instance, BC has recently committed to preventing Indigenous children from going into care, and placing an increased focus on family preservation, kinship, and culturally appropriate placements, with an emphasis on keeping Indigenous children and youth in their communities of origin. In support of this commitment, MCFD announced Bill 26, amending existing BC child protection law in April 2018 to include Indigenous communities and their leaders as decision makers in all Indigenous child welfare investigation and placement decisions. The ministry is also working on agreements with several First Nations communities in the province to allow them to take jurisdiction over their own child welfare services (Sherlock, 2018). Similar movement towards Indigenous self-governance of child welfare services is happening on the east coast: a new First Nations child welfare agency was established in early 2018 in New Brunswick, representing the seven Mi'kmaq First Nations in the province (Donkin, 2018).

Conclusions

Canada's provincially organized child welfare system has been profoundly shaped by its origins in the late 19th century's morally driven child-saving movements and policies designed to assimilate Indigenous peoples. Although legislative and policy reforms have attempted to reorient services towards family and community centered approaches, expanding definitions of child maltreatment and emphasis on risk and safety assessments have curtailed efforts to move away from an investigatory protection model. The rate of investigation nearly doubled from 2003 to 2008, and the number of children in out-of-home care has grown, including staggeringly high rates of Indigenous children in care. This approach stands in contrast to many European jurisdictions, which offer family support services and conduct far fewer child maltreatment investigations. Several jurisdictions are placing a renewed emphasis of shifting towards a more diverse array of service options, most notably for children and families from Indigenous communities. Monitoring of investigation and placement trends are key to understanding the extent to which Canadian child welfare systems can shift towards a child and family support orientation.

References

Alberta Human Services. (n.d.). *Child intervention information and statistics summary 2017/18, First Quarter (June) Update*. Alberta, Canada. http://www.humanservices.alberta.ca/documents/child-intervention-info-stats-summary-2017-18-q1.pdf.

Arnett, J. J. (2015). *Emerging adulthood: The winding road from the late teens through the twenties* (2nd ed.). Oxford University Press.

Assembly of First Nations and Trout v. The Attorney General of Canada, 2020. Court File No. T-141-20. https://www.aptnnews.ca/wp-content/uploads/2021/06/T-402-19-ZACHEUS-JOSEPH-TROUT-STATEMENT-OFCLAIM.pdf.

Auditor General of Canada. (2008). *First Nations child and family services program—Indian and Northern Affairs Canada*. Auditor General of Canada, Ch. 4.

Bala, N. (1999). Reforming Ontario's *Child and Family Services Act*: Is the pendulum swinging back too far? *Canadian Family Law Quarterly*, 17, 121–172.

Bala, N., Zapf, M. K., Williams, R. J., Vogl, R., and Hornick, J. P. (Eds.) (2004). *Canadian child welfare law: Children, families and the state* (2nd ed.). Thompson Educational Publishing.

Barrera, J. (2018, February 1). Ottawa to increase funding for First Nations child welfare services. *CBC News Indigenous*. https://www.cbc.ca/news/indigenous/ottawa-fnchildwelfare-tribunal-1.4513951.

Beaujot R. and Kerr, J. (2007). Emerging youth transition patterns in Canada: Opportunities and risks. *PSC Discussion Papers Series*, 21(5), Article 1, 1–40.

Bennett, M. (n.d.). *A general profile of First Nations child welfare in Canada*. First Nations Child and Family Caring Society of Canada. https://fncaringsociety.com/sites/default/files/FirstNationsFS1.pdf.

Bennett, M., Blackstock, C., and De La Ronde, R. (2005). *A literature review and annotated bibliography on aspects of Aboriginal child welfare in Canada*. First Nations Child and Family Caring Society of Canada.

Black, T., Fallon, B., and Trocmé, N. (2022). *First Nations children in foster care in Canada in 2016*. Unpublished manuscript.

Blackstock, C. (2011). The Canadian Human Rights Tribunal on First Nations child welfare: Why if Canada wins, equality and justice lose. *Children and Youth Services Review*, 33(1), 187–194.

Blackstock, C. and Trocmé, N. (2005). Community-based child welfare for Aboriginal children: Supporting resilience through structural change. *Social Policy Journal of New Zealand*, 24, 12–33.

Boivin, M. and Hertzman, C. (Eds.) (2012). *Early childhood development: Adverse experiences and developmental health*. Royal Society of Canada.

Canadian Child Welfare Research Portal. (2019). *Indigenous Child Welfare*. https://cwrp.ca/indigenous-child-welfare.

CBC News. (2018, June 4). Youth-in-care tuition waver program expands to include trades training. *CBC News British Columbia*.

Culbert, L. (2016, October 17). B.C. expands Agreements with Youth Adults program. *Vancouver Sun*.

Donkin, K. (2018, April 13). New First Nations child welfare agency aims to reverse decades of children being seized. *CBC News New Brunswick*.

Durrant, J. E., Trocmé, N., Fallon, B., Milne, C., and Black, T. (2009). Protection of children from physical maltreatment in Canada: An evaluation of the Supreme Court's definition of reasonable force. *Journal of Aggression, Maltreatment & Trauma*, 18(1), 64–87.

Education and Early Childhood Development. (2018). *Integrated Service Delivery (ISD) for children and youth with emotional, behavioural, and mental health issues*. Government of New Brunswick.

Esposito, T., Trocmé, N., Chabot, M., Collin-Vézina, D., Shlonsky, A., and Sinha, V. (2014). Family reunification for placed children in Québec, Canada: A longitudinal study. *Children and Youth Services Review*, 44, 278–287.

Esposito, T., Trocmé, N., Chabot, M., Robichaud, M.-J., Léveillé, S., Desmarais, S., . . . Sirois, M.-C. (2017). *Gestion fondée sur les indicateurs de suivi clinique (GFISC) en protection de la jeunesse: Rapport synthèse*. Centre for Research on Children and Families (CRCF).

Esposito, T., Trocmé, N., Chabot, M., Shlonsky, A., Collin-Vézina, D., and Sinha, V. (2013). Placement of children in out-of-home care in Québec, Canada: When and for whom initial out-of-home placement is most likely to occur. *Children and Youth Services Review*, 35(12), 2031–2039.

Fallon, B., Joh-Carnella, N., Trocmé, N., Esposito, T., Hélie, S., and Lefebvre R. (2022). Major findings from the Canadian Incidence Study of reported child abuse and neglect 2019. *International Journal on Child Maltreatment*, 5, 1–17 (2022). https://doi.org/10.1007/s42448-021-00110-9.

Fallon, B., Lefebvre, R., Seto, M., and Van Wert, M. (2013). *Cases involving multiple sectors of the justice system: Information from the 2008 Canadian Incidence Study of Reported Child Abuse and Neglect*. Internal Report for the Department of Justice Canada.

Fallon, B., Trocmé, N., Fluke, J., Van Wert, M., MacLaurin, B., Sinha, V., . . . Turcotte, D. (2012). Responding to child maltreatment in Canada: Context for international comparisons. *Advances in Mental Health*, 11(1), 76–86.

Fallon, B., Trocmé, N., and MacLaurin, B. (2011). Should child protection services respond differently to maltreatment, risk of maltreatment, and risk of harm? *Child Abuse & Neglect*, 35(4), 236–239.

Fallon, B., Trocmé, N., MacLaurin, B., Sinha, V., and Black, T. (2011). Untangling risk of maltreatment from events of maltreatment: An analysis of the 2008 Canadian Incidence Study of Reported Child Abuse and Neglect (CIS-2008). *International Journal of Mental Health and Addiction, 9*(5), 460–479.

Fallon, B., Van Wert, M., Trocmé, N., MacLaurin, B., Sinha, V., Lefebvre, R., . . . Goel, S. (2015). *Ontario Incidence Study of Reported Child Abuse and Neglect-2013 (OIS-2013)*. Child Welfare Research Portal.

First Nations Child and Family Caring Society and Assembly of First Nations v. Attorney General of Canada, 2019 CHRT 39. https://fncaringsociety.com/sites/default/files/2019_chrt_39.pdf.

First Nations Child and Family Caring Society. (2017). *Jordan's Principle*. First Nations Child and Family Caring Society.

Flynn, R. (2003). *Resilience in transitions from out-of-home care in Canada: A prospective longitudinal study*. Unpublished research proposal.

Flynn, R. and Bouchard, D. (2005). Randomized and quasi-experimental evaluations of program impact in child welfare in Canada: A review. *Canadian Journal of Program Evaluation, 20*, 65–100.

Gagnon, K. (2018). Quatre jeunes de la DPJ sur cinq accusent un retard scolaire. *La Presse*. December 3.

Gharabaghi, K., Trocmé, N., and Newman, D. (2016). *Because Young People Matter: Report of the Residential Services Review Panel*. Ontario Ministry of Children and Youth Services.

Gough, P., Shlonsky, A., and Dudding, P. (2009). An overview of the child welfare systems in Canada. *International Journal of Child Health & Human Development, 2*(3), 357–371.

Gove, T. J. (1995). *Executive summary: Report of the Gove Inquiry into child protection in British Columbia*. Victoria: Government of BC.

Government of British Columbia. (2017). *Premier Horgan expands tuition waiver for former youth in care*. Office of the Premier. September 1.

Government of British Columbia. (2018). *Agreements with Youth Adults*. Government of BC.

Government of Canada. (2018). *Jordan's Principle*. Government of Canada.

Government of New Brunswick. (n.d.). *Free Tuition Program*. Fredericton: Government of N.B.

Government of New Brunswick. (2015). *Keeping children and youth safe from harm in New Brunswick: A five-year strategy by New Brunswickers*. Province of New Brunswick.

Hamilton, A. C. and Sinclair, C. M. (1991). *The justice system and Aboriginal people: Report of the Aboriginal Justice Inquiry of Manitoba* (Vol. 1). The Queen's Printer.

Hélie, S., Collin-Vézina, D., Turcotte, D., Trocmé, N., and Girouard, N. (2017). *Étude d'incidence québécoise sur les situations évaluées en protection de la jeunesse en 2014 (ÉIQ-2014)*. Quebec, Canada.

Hélie, S., Trocmé, S., Collin-Vézina, D., Esposito, T., Morin, S., and Saint-Girons, M. (2022). *Volet Premières Nations de l'Étude d'incidence québécoise sur les situations évaluées en protection de la jeunesse en 2019*. Rapport EIQ/PN-2019. Institut universitaire Jeunes en difficulté. Quebec, Canada.

Houden, M. (2015). *Manitoba can do better for kids in care*. University of Manitoba, Faculty of Health Sciences.

Indigenous and Northern Affairs Canada. (1996). *Highlights from the Report of the Royal Commission on Aboriginal Peoples: People to people, nation to nation* (Catalogue no. Z1-1991/1-6E). Minister of Supply and Services Canada.

Indigenous and Northern Affairs Canada. (2011). *Frequently asked questions*. Government of Canada.

Indigenous Services Canada. (n.d.). *Timeline: Jordan's Principle and First Nations child and family services*. https://www.sac-isc.gc.ca/eng/1500661556435/1533316366163.

Johnston, P. (1983). *Native children and the child welfare system*. Canadian Council on Social Development.

Jones, A., Sinha, V., and Trocmé, N. (2015). *Children and youth in out-of-home care in the Canadian provinces* (CWRP Information Sheet #167E). CRCF.

Jud, A. and Trocmé, N. (2012). *Physical abuse and physical punishment in Canada* (CWRP Information Sheet #122E). CRCF.

Kirmayer, L., Simpson, C., and Cargo, M. (2003). Healing traditions: Culture, community and mental health promotion with Canadian Aboriginal peoples. *Australasian Psychiatry*, 11, 2–9.

Kozlowski, A., Milne, L., and Sinha, V. (2014). *British Columbia's child welfare system* (CWRP Information Sheet #139E). CRCF.

Kozlowski, A., Sinha, V., Hartsook, G., Thomas Prokop, S., and Montgomery, H. M. (2011). *First Nations child welfare in Saskatchewan* (CWRP Information Sheet #99E). CRCF.

Kozlowski, A., Sinha, V., Petti, T., and Flette, E. (2011). *First Nations child welfare in Manitoba* (CWRP Information Sheet #97E). CRCF.

Kyte, A., Trocmé, N., and Chamberland, C. (2013). Evaluating where we're at with differential response. *Child Abuse & Neglect*, 37(2), 125–132.

Kyte, A. and Wegner-Lohin, J. (2014). *Alberta's child welfare system* (CWRP Information Sheet #137E). CRCF.

Libesman, T. (2014). *Decolonising Indigenous child welfare*. Routledge.

MacMillan, H. L., Thomas, B. H., Jamieson, E., Walsh, C. A., Boyle, M. H., Shannon, H. S., and Gafni, A. (2005). Effectiveness of home visitation by public-health nurses in prevention of the recurrence of child physical abuse and neglect: A randomized controlled trial. *The Lancet*, 365(9473), 1786–1793.

MCFD. (2011). *Residential Review Project: Phase One—Findings Report*. MCFD.

MCFD. (2016). *Performance Management Report* (Vol. 8). Ministry of Children and Family Development. https://www2.gov.bc.ca/assets/gov/family-and-social-supports/services-supports-for-parents-with-young-children/reporting-monitoring/00-public-ministry-reports/volume_8_draftv7.pdf.

Metallic, N., Friedland, H., & Morales, S. (2019). The Promise and Pitfalls of C-92: An Act Respecting First Nations, Inuit and Métis Children, Youth and Families. *Articles, Book Chapters, & Popular Press*. https://digitalcommons.schulichlaw.dal.ca/scholarly_works/13.

Miller, J. R. (1996). *Shingwauk's vision: A history of native residential schools*. University of Toronto Press.

Milloy, J. S. and McCallum, M. J. (2017). *A national crime: The Canadian government and the residential school system, 1879 to 1986*. University of Manitoba Press.

Milward, D. (2016). *Children need families, not courtrooms: Alternatives to adversarial litigation in child welfare*. Office of the Children's Advocate.

Moushoom, Meawasige, Meawasige v. The Attorney General of Canada, 2019 Court File No. T-402-19. https://sotosclassactions.com/wp-content/uploads/2019/06/FN-Amended-Statement-of-Claim.pdf.

Mulcahy, M. and Trocmé, N. (2010). *Children and Youth in Out-of-Home Care in Canada. CECW Information Sheet #78*. CRCF.

National Collaborating Centre for Aboriginal Health. (2011). *The Aboriginal health legislation and policy framework in Canada. National Collaborating Centre for Aboriginal Health*. https://www.nccih.ca/docs/context/FSHealthLegislationPolicy-Lavoie-Gervais-Toner-Bergeron-Thomas-EN.pdf.

O'Donnell, M., Maclean, M., Sims, S., Brownell, M., Ekuma, O., and Gilbert, R. (2016). Entering out-of-home care during childhood: Cumulative incidence study in Canada and Australia. *Child Abuse & Neglect*, 59, 78–87.

Ontario Ministry of Children and Youth Services. (2016). *The Aboriginal Advisor's Report on the status of Aboriginal child welfare in Ontario*. Queen's Printer for Ontario.

Ontario Ministry of Children and Youth Services. (2017). *Safety*. Queen's Printer for Ontario.

Ontario Ministry of Children and Youth Services. (2018). *Ontario strengthens legislation for child, youth and family services*. Queen's Printer for Ontario.

Ontario Provincial Advocate for Children and Youth. (2012). *25 is the new 21: The cost and benefits of providing care & maintenance to Ontario youth until the age of 25*. Ontario Provincial Advocate for Children and Youth.

Pauls, K. (2018). Sixties Scoop adoptees want to scuttle $800M settlement, saying it's just not enough. *CBC News*. February 15. Manitoba, Canada. https://www.cbc.ca/news/canada/manitoba/sixties-scoop-settlement-1.4536735.

Rutman, D., Hubberstey, C., Feduniw, A., and Brown, E. (2007). *When Youth Age out of care where to from there. Final report based on a three-year longitudinal study*. University of Victoria.

Saint-Girons, M., Trocmé, N., Esposito, T., and Fallon, B. (2020). *Children in Out-of-Home Care in Canada in 2019*. CWRP Information Sheet #211E. Canadian Child Welfare Research Portal.

Sangster, M., Vives, L., Chadwick, K., Gerlach, A., and Sinha, V. (2019). *Advancing Jordan's Principle by realizing Enhanced Service Coordination in the Alberta Region*. First Nations Health Consortium.

Sherlock, T. (2018). B.C. working on big changes for Indigenous child welfare. *National Observer*. February 6.

Sinclair, R. (2007). Identity lost and found: Lessons from the sixties scoop. *The First Peoples Child & Family Review*, 3(1), 65–82.

Sinha, V. and Kozlowski, A. (2013). The structure of Aboriginal child welfare in Canada. *The International Indigenous Policy Journal*, 4(2), 1–21.

Sinha, V., Trocmé, N., Fallon, B., MacLaurin, B., Fast, E., Thomas Prokop, S., . . . Richard, K. (2011). *Kiskisik Awasisak: Remember the children. Understanding the overrepresentation of First Nations children in the child welfare system*. Assembly of First Nations.

Sinha, V. and Wray, M. (2015). *Foster care disparity for Aboriginal children in 2011* (CWRP Information Sheet #165E). CRCF.

Smith, B. L. (2012). The case against spanking: Physical discipline is slowly declining as some studies reveal lasting harms for children. *American Psychological Association Monitor on Psychology*, 43(4), 60.

Statistics Canada. (2011). *Living arrangements of young adults aged 20 to 29.* Census in Brief No.3: Families, households and marital status, 2011 Census of Population. Catalogue no. 98-312-X2011003. Ottawa, Canada.

Strega, S. and Esquao, S. A. (Carrière, J.) (Eds.). (2009). *Walking this path together: Antiracist and anti-oppressive child welfare practice.* Fernwood.

Tasker, J. P. (2017, October 5). Ottawa announces $800M settlement with Indigenous survivors of Sixties Scoop. *CBC News.*

Tessier, N. G. (2015). *Three Studies of Transitions of Young People in Public Care: A Focus on Educational Outcomes.* Doctoral Thesis, Clinical Psychology. University of Ottawa.

Trocmé, N. (1991). Child welfare services. In D. Barnhorst & L. Johnson (Eds.), *State of the child in Ontario* (pp. 63–91). Oxford University Press.

Trocmé, N., Fallon, B., Maclaurin, B., Chamberland, C., Chabot, M., and Esposito, T. (2011). Shifting definitions of emotional maltreatment: An analysis child welfare investigation laws and practices in Canada. *Child Abuse & Neglect,* 35(10), 831–840.

Trocmé, N., Fallon, B., MacLaurin, B., Sinha, V., Black, T., Fast, E., . . . Holroyd, J. (2010). *Canadian incidence study of reported child abuse and neglect—2008: Major findings.* Public Health Agency of Canada.

Trocmé, N., Kyte, A., Sinha, V., and Fallon, B. (2014). Urgent protection versus chronic need: Clarifying the dual mandate of child welfare services across Canada. *Social Sciences,* 3(3), 483–498.

Trocmé, N., MacLaurin, B., Fallon, B., Shlonsky, A., Mulcahy, M., and Esposito, T. (2009). *National child welfare outcomes indicator matrix (NOM).* CRCF.

Truth and Reconciliation Commission of Canada. (2015). *Calls to action.* TRCC.

Vancouver Foundation. (2016). *Opportunities in transition: An economic analysis of investing in youth aging out of foster care (summary report).* Fostering Change.

Waldfogel, J. (2009). Differential response. In K. A. Dodge and D. L. Coleman (Eds.), *Preventing child maltreatment: Community approaches* (pp. 139–155). Guilford Press.

Wegner-Lohin, J., Kyte, A., and Trocmé, N. (2014). *Ontario's child welfare system* (CWRP Information Sheet #138E). CRCF.

Wolfe, D. A., Crooks, C. V., Lee, V., McIntyre-Smith, A., and Jaffe, P. G. (2003). The effects of children's exposure to domestic violence: A meta-analysis and critique. *Clinical Child and Family Psychology Review,* 6(3), 171–187.

Legislation

An Act respecting First Nations, Inuit and Métis children, youth and families, S.C. 2019. c. 24, s. 22.

Canadian Foundation for Children, Youth and the Law v. Canada (Attorney General). 2004. 1 S.C.R. 76, 2004 SCC 4.

Child and Family Services Act, R.S.O. 1990, c. 11 (CanLII).

Child Welfare Act, R.S.O. 1970, c. 64.

Criminal Code of Canada, R.S.C. 1985, c. 46, s. 231(6).

Indian Act, R.S.C. 1985, c. I-5 (CanLII).

The Child Protection Systems in Denmark and Norway

Anne-Dorthe Hestbæk, Marit Skivenes, Asgeir Falch-Eriksen, Idamarie Leth Svendsen, and Elisabeth Backe-Hansen

Abstract

This chapter expounds on Denmark and Norway's child protection systems being developed parallel to the development of the social democratic welfare state. Both countries' child protection systems have family-service-oriented systems that are centered around children's rights and needs. In line with the UN Convention on the Rights of the Child, European Council and Court of Human Rights, the basic principle of child protection systems consists of birth parents raising children or state intervention if risks are apparent. Out-of-home care will be taken if in-home services are inappropriate. Additionally, Denmark and Norway's assessment of children's welfare range between material well-being, health, safety, education, behaviour, risks, housing, and environment.

Key Words: Denmark, Norway, child protection systems, welfare, UNCRC, European Council, out-of-home care, social democratic

Introduction

Historically, the child protection systems of Norway and Denmark have developed in parallel to the broader and more comprehensive development of the welfare state.[1] The two countries in the north of Europe with populations of 5.4 million and 5.8 million, respectively, fall into the type of welfare state that has been categorized as "social democratic" (Esping-Andersen, 1999). Broadly, it can be argued that citizens across Nordic countries[2] share basic ideas toward having a higher fraction of public social expenditures

---

[1] This chapter was written in 2019 and with some updates in 2021 and 2022. Thus, statistics and the latest reforms are not discussed in detail. The project has received funding from the European Research Council (ERC) under the European Union's Horizon 2020 research and innovation program (grant agreement no. 724460), and from the Research Council of Norway under the Independent Projects – Humanities and Social Science program (grant no. 262773). The term *child protection* characterizes public systems that are responsible for children who are at risk of harm or neglect from their caregivers or who may be at risk of harm to themselves or others. This system may also be referred to as *child welfare* systems.

[2] The Nordic countries consist of Denmark, Finland, Iceland, Norway, and Sweden (but also include Greenland as an autonomous constitutional state, and the Føroyar Islands and Åland Islands as autonomous areas).

of GDP than other welfare-state models. Many benefits are distributed universally according to individual rights. To finance a high level of welfare, both Norway and Denmark have a comparatively high tax level, something that calls for specific solidarity to maintain the state construct. Although it has not been common to analyze child protection systems according to specific welfare-state models, the responsibility to protect children does not exist in a vacuum outside of the welfare state nor of the rule of law. A child protection system is closely connected to the welfarist norms governing society in general (Forsberg & Kröger, 2010; Blomberg et al., 2013; Pösö et al., 2014). The social democratic welfare-state model, the economic capability of the state, the political and economic investments in children and families as well as social norms reflected in civil society all contribute to influencing children's exposure to risk and social problems, and their chance of receiving services and help when in need thereof.

Norway and Denmark are ranked high in international comparisons measuring child well-being in society, implementation of children's rights and handling of poverty (Falch-Eriksen & Skivenes, 2019). An essential characteristic of both countries is that intrusive child protection services run parallel to a broader interventionist welfare-state system that intervenes universally at early stages to prevent a multitude of serious harms from occurring across the lifespan. From this perspective, child protection services actively contribute to upholding the right to family life, borne by both parents and children.

In this chapter, we delineate the core features of the Danish and Norwegian[3] child protection legislation, policy and programs. Although there are many similarities, there are also differences that must be addressed. The chapter has 10 sections. The next presents the types of child protection systems that are in place, and the relevant legislation and principles. This is followed by a section on mandatory reporting. The role of service provision in the local municipalities and child protection in numbers are discussed in the next two sections, followed by an outline of the removal of children and then a section on placement alternatives. The last three sections delineate the topics of children's rights in an international setting, policy trends and a concluding section.

Family-service-oriented Child Protection Systems in the Nordic Welfare States

Child protection systems in both Denmark and Norway have been referred to in the literature as family-service-oriented systems, in contrast to risk-oriented (protection) systems (Gilbert, 1997; Gilbert et al., 2011). Although recent developments show that child protection systems, either family-service- or risk-oriented, are increasingly incorporating elements from each other (Gilbert et al., 2011), the underlying ideologies of the two types

---

[3] For an in-depth overview of the Norwegian system, please see Skivenes (2011), Skivenes and Søvig (2017), and Falch-Eriksen and Skivenes (2019). For an in-depth overview of the Danish system, see Hestbæk (2011) and Bryderup et al. (2017).

of systems are still different. The most significant differences between risk-oriented and family-service-oriented systems lie in the ways in which they provide services for children at risk. Risk-oriented systems rely more on sanctions, legalistic interventions and an adversarial relationship with parents (Gilbert et al., 2011).

Family-service-oriented systems such as the Danish and Norwegian have an increasingly child-centric approach, highlighting the needs and rights of the individual child (Hestbæk, 2011; Skivenes, 2011). They set as a premise to cooperate with the families by providing family-based services, often from a therapeutic view of rehabilitation, believing that it is possible to change and improve people's life circumstances, preferences, and behaviors. From this perspective, child protection services can actively contribute to upholding the right to family life for both parents and children. Consequently, the systems are arranged to prevent out-of-home placements actively, although at least in Denmark, the legislation has become less engineered in this direction over recent years by emphasizing the children's independent rights (described later in this chapter).

Common ground seems to exist between the family-service system and the social democratic model characteristic of the welfare states of Denmark and Norway (Kronborg, 2016). The type of child protection system, its underlying premises, and the type of welfare-state model in place are critical contextual components for understanding the challenges that at-risk families and children face, and the type of social structure the child protection services operate within. The overall standards of living conditions for families and children, reflected in international comparisons, are likely to influence the thresholds for intervention and the conception of risk and needs for a child. Thus, compared with the risk-oriented system, it has a higher number of children being involved in the child protection system because the threshold for providing services is low.

Law and Principles

Norway and Denmark have integrated the principles from the UN Convention of the Rights of the Child (CRC) of 1989 and also the European Convention on Human Rights (1953) and later protocols into national law. The CRC was fully annexed in the Norwegian *Human Rights Act* in 2003, and with only a few amendments it led to a presumption of harmony with current law. This implies that the legislators held that current law does not need amendments as it upheld the principal norms of human rights. More significantly, though, was the incorporation of the CRC into the Norwegian Constitution in 2014 (Section 104).

In Denmark, unlike the European Convention of Human Rights—which was *en bloc* incorporated into Danish law by a specific statute in 1992—the CRC, which was ratified by Denmark in 1991, has been implemented into Danish law by a presumption of harmonization and single amendments (Schultz et al., 2020). The latter is also the case of the Convention on the Rights of Persons with Disabilities, which holds important rights to protection for children with disabilities. This convention was ratified by Denmark in 2009 and by Norway in 2013. For example, the principle of the best interests of the child is now integrated into the *Consolidation Act on Social Services* (CASS), in the Danish *Act on Parental Responsibility*, and in other parts of the social and welfare legislation, while in Norway it is incorporated into the Constitution, in the *Human Rights Act* and in the *Child Protection Act*.[4]

The constitutions of Denmark and Norway are different in relation to children's rights. In Norway, a section on the status of children (Section 104), included in 2014, provides children with rights and status on an equal footing with other citizens. In Denmark, children are mentioned specifically in the Danish Constitution (Section 76) regarding the right to free education and the duty of parents to ensure their children's education (Hartoft, 2019). Children in both countries are protected by the rights of the Constitution broadly targeting citizens, such as the right to personal freedom and freedom of speech—albeit within the limitations that the state's responsibility is dominantly secondary to the parental responsibility. In Denmark, child protection is embedded into the legislation more broadly targeting several groups in need, that is, the CASS, which came into effect in 1998 after an extensive legal reform of the child protection legislation in 1993 and with numerous later amendments (Svendsen, 2016). Norway has a separate *Child Protection Act* of 1992 (CPA) that came into effect in 1993. A new *Child Protection Act* will be implemented in 2023.

The basic principle of the child protection systems in both countries is that children are raised by their birth parents (principle of biology), and only if there are dangers or risks of harm for the child may the state intervene (objectivity and proportionality principles), and only so far as the law allows (legality principle). These principles are interpreted in both countries in accordance with the principles of the best interests of the child, non-discrimination, the right to be heard, and the right to protection as stated by the CRC, European Council, and Court of Human Rights.

In Norway, the principle of least intrusion is a core principle, as setting aside the rights of parents for family life and privacy cannot be done without proper justification. This principle is explicitly reflected in the legal criteria for interventions. The principle was formerly part of the Danish CASS as well but has been somewhat downplayed during recent years to emphasize that the authorities shall as a first solution choose the intervention that is in the best interests of the child (CASS Sections 46 and 52). It follows from the legislative history that if out-of-home placement is the best option for the child, it is not required by law that other measures must have been tried out first.

---

[4] As a member of the European Union, Danish authorities are obliged by the European Charter of Fundamental Rights of the European Union, including Article 24 on children's rights. This is relevant in relation in EU-regulated areas such as data sharing—both as regards welfare services and protection against abuse.

Both systems are premised on consent, so that the child protection system is providing help and services to families and children who freely accept support. The majority of services in Denmark and Norway are in-home services with parental consent, although the children's views are supposed to be heard as well, and taken into consideration according to their age and maturity. Thus, services provided to families and children in the child protection system are often similar to welfare services that are provided to families in need of support, such as economic support for holidays and/or subsidized daycare.

The responsibility of the child protection system is to provide help and services when a child needs it, and in both countries the threshold for service provision is low. In Norway this is formulated in CPA Section 4-4: "The child protection agency shall, when the child is in need of it due to the circumstances of the home or other reasons, arrange for assistance for the child and the family." Similarly, in Denmark, the municipal council shall choose the measure or measures that are best suited to resolve the problems and needs. There is a wide array of services that can be provided, and a child can also be placed out of the home, in a foster home or a residential unit, as a voluntary service. An action plan with measurable short- and long-term goals is obligatory in all cases of special support.

Although the basic principle for the systems is consent, and most in-home services are provided in collaboration with families, in-home services—for example supervision, counseling, or mandatory day care—may be put in place as an involuntary measure, (cf. CASS Sections 56 and 57a, and CPA Section 4-4(3)). In Norway, these decisions or legal orders can only be made by the County Board for Child Protection and Social Affairs (County Board). In contrast, the local municipal child protection agency in Denmark has the authority to decide on such nonconsensual orders to be implemented in-home (CASS Section 57a), and parents can temporarily lose their child benefits if they do not comply with the specific demands for action stated in the municipal order. This option is only used very rarely, however.

The systems in both countries are based on the premise that only if in-home services do not help the child, or if in-home services are inappropriate (in a situation of maltreatment or abuse), out-of-home placement may be undertaken. At that point, an obvious risk of severe harm to the child's health or development must have been documented, due to neglect, abuse (on the part of the parents), or criminality or destructive behavior from the young person (CPA Sections 4-12, 4-24; CASS Section 58). Placement must be considered to be necessary based on an overall assessment of the child's best interests. In both Norway and Denmark, a newborn can be placed directly from the hospital (CPA Section 4-8 (2).

Furthermore, even a child placed voluntarily by the parents can be retained in public care if deemed necessary (CPA Section 4-8) due to, for example, attachment to the caregiver. In Denmark, strong attachment to the caregiver is obligatory, and it is also a criterion that the child has been placed for more than three years (CASS Section 68a). We will describe the organization of decision-making bodies and the court system below.

Mandatory Notification

Both Norway and Denmark have strict legislation on mandatory notification. In Denmark, all citizens are subject to mandatory notification in case of potential child abuse and neglect: "Any person who learns or becomes aware that a child or young person under the age of 18 is being neglected or abused . . . shall notify the municipal authorities" (CASS Section 154). This responsibility for private persons is rather unique globally. Professionals who hold public office or who provide public services to children have a strengthened *mandatory notification obligation* when a child or young person is assumed to need special support.[5] In Norway, the notification obligation is narrower and professionals must refer to the CPA when there are reasons to believe a child is exposed to misconduct or serious neglect, including children who display behavioral problems or are exploited in human trafficking (CPA Section 6-4).

The differences in types of obligations are mirrored in the number of notifications. In 2018, Danish municipalities received circa 127,000 notifications—an immense number to examine. When calculated by the child population it amounts to 10% of all children. The equivalent numbers in Norway were 58,580 notifications, which amounts to 5.2% of all children.[6]

In Denmark, all notifications must be registered in a national database and screened by the municipality within 24 hours to assess whether there is a reason for immediate action (CASS Section 155.2). The child or young person in question can be interviewed without the consent and presence of parents. This is obligatory if abuse is suspected, in which case the Children's House (a specialized entity, integrating police, health, and social services) must participate in the further assessment.

In Norway, the child protection agency has one week to assess the notification. Norway is about to change legislation in this area, and especially duties of disclosure are put upon different conjoining services like kindergartens, schools, and family services, as well as a duty of being attentive to children potentially receiving detrimental care (NOU 2016: 16; Prop 169 L (2016-2017)).

Child Protection Based in Local Municipalities

In both Denmark and Norway, the responsibility for child protection is delegated to the local authorities, which mainly correspond to municipalities, albeit within the auspices of the

---

[5] Specific criteria for mandatory notification—abuse, violence, and absence from school—have been made explicit in CASS. The professional's duty to try to solve the problem first is no longer explicit, although it is still stated in the administrative guidelines and the preparatory works that problems that can reasonably be expected to be solved in other sectors, for instance the school, should be solved there. The provisions on notification in Denmark have been extended to encompass all parents-to-be, where the child is assumed to be in need of support after birth. In 2005, Denmark had its first court case in which a professional (a teacher) was convicted for not reporting a girl who had disclosed that she was being abused by her 19-year-old boyfriend (Appeal Court Decision, 2005). As yet, no private persons have been sentenced.

[6] We calculate per 100 children to compare, although the same child may have several notifications.

state. While Denmark is a small country of 43,000 square kilometers with 98 municipalities, Norway has an immense 385,000 square kilometers with 356 municipalities. Historically, the importance of municipalities has always been justified from the point of view of *subsidiarity and local democracy*. That is, local problems are best solved through local democratic solutions, and in Denmark, the right for the municipalities to govern under the supervision of the state follows from the Constitution. Even though child protection is locally organized in different ways due to the municipal autonomy and local budget conditions, the overall municipal responsibilities remain the same in both countries. Services to children and families can be provided by the municipal child protection agency itself. However, the municipalities may decide to buy or arrange for services delivered by, for example, other municipalities, NGOs, or private for-profit companies, often in the form of private welfare foundations, which have dominated the private field offering services in the child protection area for many years. Nowadays, we find an increasing number of private, for-profit companies offering "soft" services (treatment, care) for children and youth in need of support.

In Denmark, the municipalities are entirely responsible for enforcing services to protect children as well as other regulations locally, albeit within the auspices of the state. Likewise, the economic responsibility of child protection and other services is to a considerable extent delegated to the local level. A fundamental principle is the so-called sector-responsibility principle, according to which the sector responsible for a specific area such as the school system or health system is responsible for all services within the sector, also in relation to children with special needs. This calls for a high degree of cooperation between sector authorities and may present serious challenges for children and families. For instance, services to children with learning disabilities or health issues are particularly challenging to establish and coordinate with the child protection system, resulting in sub-optimization (Villumsen, 2018). In Norway, the municipalities are responsible for most of the child protection work, but responsibility for some tasks, mainly connected with finding suitable out-of-home placement alternatives, has so far been shared between the state and the municipalities. A recent political–legal development will change the Norwegian system to become more like the current Danish system, granting municipalities almost all responsibilities except for specialized foster homes and residential units (Prop 95 L (2013–2014)).

Child Protection in Numbers

The number of children with child protection services in both Denmark and Norway, as for many high-income countries (Burns et al., 2017), is increasing[7]. A likely cause for this is an increased awareness about children's rights and their enhanced position in society. In Table 6.1, we present numbers for essential child protection measures from 2012, 2014, 2016, and 2018[8].

---

[7] During the years following 2018, the number of children has stopped increasing and even been reduced slightly in Norway.

[8] As for Denmark, some numbers are publicly accessible at Statistics Denmark. Other numbers derive from own calculations based on data. from Statistics Denmark. https://dst.dk/en#.

Table 6.1 Children 0–17 years old, child protection services in Norway (No) and Denmark (Dk), 2012–2018

	2012		2014		2016		2018	
	No	Dk	No	Dk	No	Dk	No	Dk[a]
Child population 0–17 years measured on 1 January the following year. N = children	1,122,897	1,190,301	1,0125,604	1,169,894	1,127,400	1,168,222	1,122,508	1,160,384
Referrals investigated, total Referrals per 1,000 children, 0–17 years	30.1		36.3		39.7	105,020 55.6	39.1	127,182 64.7
No. of children 0–17 years with child protection services (all types), end of year Per 1,000 children 0–17 years	30.6	-	29.6		30.7	42.719[1] 50.2	30.3	43.960 52.1
New cases with child protection services. N = children 0–17 years	13,583[2]	3,161	13,746[2]	2,927	15,257[2]	E	14,588	2,844
In-home measures, end of year, per 1,000 children 0–17 years	23.7	21.6	22	24	22.7	25	22.4	26.1
Out-of-home placements, total end of year, per 1,000 children 0–17 years	8.1	10.7	8.7	10.3	10.3	10.2	10	10.1
Out-of-home placements, voluntary, end of year, per 1,000 children 0–17 years	2.7	8.5	2.8	7.7	3.1	7.5	2	7.3
Care orders, end of year, per 1,000 children	5.4	2.2	5.9	2.6	7.2	2.7	8	2.8
Average age at placement, years		11.2		11.1		11.3		11.3

(*continued*)

Table 6.1 Continued

	2012		2014		2016		2018	
	No	Dk	No	Dk	No	Dk	No	Dk[a]
Emergency placements during the year, per 100 children, 0–17 years	1.4	0.1	1.3	0.1	1.3	0.1	0.3	0.1
Young adults in aftercare 18–22 years old (aftercare placements included)	6,638	4,791	6,830	5,806	6,852	5,798	7,469	7,103
Young adults in aftercare 18–22 years old during the year per 1,000 (aftercare placements included)	22.9	14.4	23.3	16.8	23.3	17.0	22.3	19.3
Adoptions from care, N = children	31	4	63	0	59	0	65	9
Child protection expenditures[3]	1.8 billion US$	2.4 billion US$	2.0 billion US$	2.4 billion US$	2.3 billion US$	2.4 billion US$	2.4 billion US$	2.5 billion US$

Notes:

[a] As for Denmark, some numbers are publicly accessible at Statistics Denmark. Other numbers derive from own calculations based on data. From Statistics Denmark. https://dst.dk/en#.

1. Services include in-home as well as out-of-home care, and child-targeted interventions as well as family-oriented interventions targeted at the challenges of the child. One child may have more than one type of service in a given year.

2. For Norway, these numbers may include a few young adults. Sources: Norway: Statistics Norway (2018); Skivenes (2011, 2015), Skivenes and Søvig (2017; 2016), Falch-Eriksen & Skivenes (2019); Central Unit of the County Boards in Norway. Sources: Denmark: KL (2016, 2020); www.statistikbanken.dk.

3. For Norway, expenditure it is net, in billion NOK. For municipality level: 7.7 (2012), 9 (2014), 10.1 (2016). For state level: 8.1 (2012), 8.7 (2014), 10 (2016). Exchange rates: 1 US$ = 6,67DKK; 1 US$ = 8,76 NOK (May 15, 2019).

Decision-making Bodies and Involuntary Interventions

In both countries, a separate decision-making body makes decisions about care orders or adoption from care. In Norway, all interventions that are considered intrusive are decided by a court-like decision-making body, the County Board, constituted with a judge, a child expert, and one layperson. In cases of acute risk of harm, the municipal manager makes a call to intervene and remove a child immediately, but this decision must be verified within 48 hours by the County Board chair on a preliminary basis—the board will in six weeks reach a final decision (see Skivenes & Søvig (2016) for details of child protection removals in the Norwegian system). In Denmark, an equivalent to the Norwegian County Board is the municipal Child and Youth Committee (CY-Committee).

Decisions to remove a child from the home without consent—of the parents and the child who has reached the age of 15 years—can be reached by the CY-Committee if this is necessary because the child's health or development is at obvious risk of serious harm (see above). The CY-Committee consists of five persons: one judge, two child experts, and two laypersons. Cases are prepared and put before the Committee by the municipal child protection and family-service department. In these, as in all cases of family service and child protection, the decision must refer to the assessment, including, if possible, an account of earlier interventions in the family and their effect, an action plan with realistic and measurable short- and long-term goals, and the estimated duration of care. In case of need for emergency action, the chair of the committee, who is always a local politician, has the authority to decide on a preliminary emergency placement, which must be confirmed by the Child and Youth Committee within seven days, and is valid for one month. Within this month, a normal, comprehensive placement decision process must be executed. The decisions of the Committee can be appealed to the National Social Appeals Board,[9] which is an administrative body with the authority to handle complaints in a broad spectrum of social welfare cases, to supervise the local authorities' practice, to offer guidance, and to carry out surveys and practice studies. The National Appeals Board's decisions can be further appealed within the court system.

When children are taken into public care, for example, foster care, residential care, or group care, this is meant to be temporary. Therefore, in both countries, the County Board/CY-Committee must set a timetable, generally of one or two years, for a reassessment of the decision on placement without consent. In both countries, an out-of-home placement of a child cannot be terminated before a certain waiting period—stipulated by the municipality. Notwithstanding the voluntary or involuntary character of interventions, they must be overseen and reassessed by the municipal authority every six months with the participation of the child or young person and

---

[9] National Social Appeals Board webpage: https://ast.dk/.

parents. The care plan forms the basis of the follow-up sessions. When the child or young person is in an out-of-home placement, an interview at the facility without the presence of personnel or without out the presence of foster parents must be carried out unless the child refuses.

In Denmark, all decisions on intervention can be appealed by the parents and by the child from the age of 12 to the National Social Appeals Board. Placement and contact decisions without consent may in the next instance be appealed to the district court. Both the Appeals Board and the courts are supported by child experts in these cases and carry out a full assessment. In Norway, all County Board decisions can be appealed to the district court, which conducts a full assessment of the case, and thereafter one can appeal to the appeal court and supreme court, but then only on selective grounds (cf. Skivenes & Søvig, 2017).

Out-of-home Placements

In Norway in 2017, 90% of all out-of-home placements were in foster homes, and 10% in residential units/family group homes. In Denmark 66% are in foster homes and 30% in residential units and group homes (and the remaining 4% in other types of 24-hour care). However, there are differences between municipalities, as the amount of cared for children in foster care spans from 34% to 80% (KL, 2019). In relation to out-of-home placement, the Danish municipalities have, through an amendment of CASS, become obliged to consider traditional foster care, kinship care and network care (i.e., care with a friend of the family, a teacher of the child, or other person in the family's network) before any other form of placement. Since this amendment, Denmark has witnessed a doubling in the number of children in all types of kinship and network care from around 4% in 2009, to 8% of all placements in 2018. During the last few years, political negotiations on an amendment to the legislation have been taking place in Denmark, and suggestions to recognize the child's right to remain with the foster family, if close attachment has developed, are being debated. In Norway, the possibility of kinship or network placements has had to be investigated as the first option for placement since 2004. Foster care is also used for "permanent placements" in that they last throughout childhood, although the placement formally is temporary.

In both countries, when a child is taken into care involuntarily, the parents keep their legal parental rights but share custody with the child protection service (CPS) (and the foster home or residential unit). The "shared care" between three parties (four parties when a young person gets his or her rights as an independent party at age 15 years) necessitates collaboration between caseworkers, parents, and those who are responsible for the daily care of a child on behalf of CPS, including consulting the child. As part of the process of long-term planning for a child in care, the CPS is obliged to follow up with the parents, offer services, or refer them to other service providers. In both countries, a core task is to ensure the right of the child to have contact with family, siblings, and other network during placement. The legal code presupposes that a child returns to his or her parents as soon as they can offer adequate care, but this may be denied if it is in the child's best interest to remain in care. In Norway, it is relatively rare for children and young people to return home once they have been in care a few years, unless they themselves insist strongly. A move will more frequently take place to another foster home or another residential unit (Jessen & Backe-Hansen, 2017). The same is true for Denmark, however with a changing mindset, increasingly focusing on the possibilities of moving the child from institutional care to foster care, and on long-term care.

For the parents to lose all legal rights, parental rights must be terminated by court order, with adoption as the objective. In Denmark, the decision is made by an administrative authority, the National Social Appeals Board, on the recommendation of the local Child and Youth Committee, with the right to appeal to the courts. In both Denmark and Norway, adoption from care without parental consent is rarely used, on average about 50 children a year in Norway and until 2018 about 4–10 children a year in Denmark. In Norway, policy discussions were initiated in 2005 to increase the use of adoptions to secure permanence for the child, and in 2010 it was allowed for so-called open adoption so that contact between birth parents and the child could occur (Tefre, 2020). In 2019, there was a renewal of the discussion about the use of adoption in the Norwegian child protection system (Helland & Skivenes, 2019).

In Denmark, adoption has since 2009 been emphasized in the Danish CASS as a desired outcome in cases where parents permanently lack parental capacities and are not able to develop those. The Danish Parliament changed CASS in 2015 by clarifying that the child protection system has a responsibility to consider adoption for children who cannot be reunified with their birth parents. Similar to Norway, important criteria for reunification are a consideration of the parents' situation and capabilities to care for the child, and/or the child's situation. The Danish legislation now states that "where it is assumed that the child or the young person will be placed for a long period of time, the municipal council must consider whether the consideration of continuity and stability in the child's upbringing justify that the child be adopted instead" (CASS, Section 68d, cf. L 121 2014–15). Previously, the practice has been that the child who had been in care for at least seven years, and had not had contact with the parents for six to eight years, could be considered for adoption. This no longer applies. The new rules make it clear that children in care on a long-term basis should be considered for adoption, and it is understood that "long-term placement" may include children under 1 year old, and children who have been placed for at least three years may be adopted without consent. Detailed guidelines to instruct and advise the frontline staff have been issued (Socialstyrelsen, 2015). The expected increase in adoption decisions has been realized only slowly, probably due to both local reluctance and legal barrierers. Thus, the legal procedure has been eased recently,[10] and decisions on adoption have been confirmed by the Danish Supreme Court (2019a, 2019b), weighing among other things the significance of a possibility of post-adoption contact. However, case law on post-adoption contact is very limited.

Involvement of Children and Families

Children and parents have strong and unambiguous rights to be involved in child protection cases. The systems are based on consent and the provision of services and help to ensure that the needs of the child and the family are met. The significance of parental participation is recognized in the legislation where the demands for informed, explicit consent, disclosure of information, right to be heard, representation rights,[11] cooperation on planning, and follow-up procedures are emphasized in both CASS and CPA Chapter 6, and in corresponding administration acts. More substantially, the focus on preventive measures, counseling, in-home services, practical assistance, and so on is also considered to strengthen the position of the parents. Particularly in placement cases, parents' right to a support person and an individual support plan during placement is stipulated in the Danish CASS, Section 54. In Norway, every service across municipalities has a duty to provide counsel and follow-up, and if the parents want it, child protection services must arrange other types of support from other services, such as, for example, family services (CPA Section 4-16). These rights have been emphasized in administrative practices, too. However, the emphasis on children's rights has led to an increasingly greater acceptance of measures without parental consent, even in the case of assessment and in-home services, as described above.

Children's right to be heard is a constitutional right in Norway, Article 104, and the CPA was recently amended and now clearly states children's right to participate in cases that concern themselves (cf. Section 1-6):

> All children who are able to form their own views are entitled to participate in all matters relating to the child under this Act. The child shall receive adequate and adapted information and shall be free to express his or her views. The child shall be listened to and the views of the child given due weight in accordance with the age and maturity of the child.

Similar provisions are found in CASS Sections 46 and 48. In both countries, children at all ages must be heard in cases they are involved with, but the Norwegian CPA still uses an age limit of 7 years as a rule of thumb for which children should be heard and have a spokesperson (Section 6-3). Although children under the age of 7 years also are supposed to be heard, practice suggests that in care order cases children under the age of 7 years are rarely involved or have a spokesperson (Magnussen & Skivenes, 2015; County Boards,

---

[10] L105 (2008-2009), L 121 (2014–2015), L155 (2018–2019).

[11] The right to legal aid only encompasses the coercive measures mentioned above.

2017, 2016). In Denmark, there is no age limit for involving children in child protection cases, and when children reach age 12 they have full rights in cases of placement and contact without parental consent, and individual complaint rights in other support cases (CASS Sections 167 and 168). In both countries, at age 15 children become a party to the case and have similar right as adults. In Norway, in cases that concern the behavior of the child, the child is always a party to the case (CPS Article 6-3).

In Denmark, a new act on *youth crime prevention* entered into force in January 2019. It involves among other initiatives, the establishment of local Youth Crime Prevention Boards, consisting of police, a judge and the municipality with the authority to assess individual cases from the age of 10, to decide on interventions to prevent further delinquency.

All children involved in support cases have a right to a layperson, other than the parents, who can participate in meetings, and so on, without them being a legal representative in the strict sense of the word (CASS Section 48a, CPO Section 1-6). A Danish longitudinal study interviewing young people in out-of-home care found that around half of the young people interviewed (11–17 years old) did not feel involved in the decision on out-of-home care—even when only young people placed in care within the previous year were analyzed (Hestbæk, 2018).

The extent to which children have such rights to representation or support independent of parental consent is subject to debate in Denmark with reference to CRC in relation to other sectors (health, education, family law, data protection, etc.). An important organization in this respect is the Danish NGO Børns Vilkår (Child Helpline), which during recent years has received public funding to offer children neutral support persons and legal support in complaint cases.

Policy Development in Denmark and Norway

In both Denmark and Norway, the child protection sector is permeated by policy activity, but the most important policies can be gathered under two main headings: (1) practice improvement through legal and organizational means, and (2) practice improvement through other initiatives. Public policies with significant impact are usually initiated, developed, and implemented directly through parliamentary policies or by the central government in both Denmark and Norway. Central policies of this kind attempt to guide activities that are either mandated through spending bills, administrative directives, white papers, or law, and are thereby approved as valuable courses of development (Selznick, 1985).

An important international monitoring instrument is the observations and recommendations by the UN Committee on the Rights of the Child. In overview, Norway and Denmark face rather similar challenges (CRC/C/NOR/CO/5-6-2018; CRC/C/DNK/CO/5-2017). In its latest reports, the Committee points at a need for action in both countries as regards children with disabilities and psychiatric diagnoses, bullying, conditions for children deprived of a family environment, sexual abuse and exploitation, rights of asylum-seeking minors and immigrant children, and the placement of children in detention and adult prisons.

Practice Improvement through Legal and Organizational Means

These policies include the constant policy efforts to change regular law and lower-level regulation and the organization of services on a large scale, and typically have a significant impact as they change the entire sector on a national level. The essential policy movement here is the continued implementation and improvement of how the rights of the child are practiced and understood. For instance, in Norway, the 1992-CPA has been through four significant amendments where the lead focus has been to ensure services are practiced according to the rights of the child.[12] In addition, through annual spending bills, a unique section is dedicated to "working with human rights." In Denmark, a similar number of smaller and larger reforms have been carried out over the last decades aiming at ensuring the rights of children and parents as well as the efficiency of the administration by adding new provisions on assessment, prevention, interventions and sanctions, continuity of interventions, abuse, specialization of authorities, and so on.[13]

Different policies arise from the effort to secure the rights of the child. Most notable are efforts to secure Article 12 of the CRC, that is, hearing the voice of the child and taking the child's views into account according to maturity and age. Furthermore, as a matter of routine, having children participate in policymaking as so-called "experts by experience" has led to a significant shift in how legislation and policy development are oriented towards children. In Norway, the organization called the Change Factory (*Forandringsfabrikken*) has influenced legislation in a significant manner, both concerning the legislative purpose of child protection itself (i.e., CPA Section 1), but also how practitioners should listen to the child and know how the child is affected by decision making. Another influential organization is "The National association for child welfare children" (*Landsforeningen for barneverns-barn)* which has lobbied successfully for raising the maximum age limit for aftercare service.

In Denmark, a central rights mechanism is the children's independent right to legal recourse. As opposed to Norway, Denmark has ratified the third optional protocol to the CRC on an individual complaint's procedure (2011). Reports from the Parliamentary Ombudsman's Children's Office (The Danish Parliamentary Ombudsman. http://en.ombudsmanden.dk) and the National Social Appeals Board, as well as new ground-breaking judgments from The Eastern High Court referring to the case law of the European Court of Human Rights and the CRC, have recently been important drivers

---

[12] Ot.prp.nr. 45 (2002–2003), Ot.prp.nr.76 (2005–2006), Prop 106 L (2012–2013), and Prop 169 L (2016–2017).

[13] See, for example, the following bills: L 8 (2004–2005), L 105 (2008–2009), L 116 (2008–2009), L 178 (2009–2010), L 107 (2011–2012), L 141 (2011–2012), L 188 (2011–2012), L 205 (2011–2012), L 181 (2012–2013), L 168 (2013–2014), L 121 (2014–2015), and L 155 (2018–2019).

of development in child protection. Thus, The Eastern High Court in 2017 sentenced a Danish municipality to pay compensation due to insufficient child protection according to Article 3 of the European Convention on Human Rights (Appeal Court Decision, 2017). Following an amendment in 2018 of the Danish Act on the expiration of legal action, removing all time limits to sue municipal authorities in cases of abuse, more municipalities have been sentenced (Appeal Court Decision, 2018). In addition, in relation to the protection of children against sexual exploitation on the Internet, the Danish Courts—and the State Attorney—have been active drivers in public child protection, by sentencing, according to the criminal law provisions on child pornography, a large number of young persons who had shared illegally recorded videos—of youngsters—with a sexual and abusive content.

Children and youth also influence policies and legislation through children's rights organizations (see, for instance, www.deanbragtesvilkar.dk, www.tabuka.dk, www.boern svilkar.dk, and www.boerneraadet.dk), which host panels of children (children in out-of-home care included) that are heard in specific matters.

Although both Denmark and Norway have become better at including children in decision making and policy development, both countries are still subjected to both internal as well as external criticism stipulating a long way to go—especially in municipality practices (.Vis & Fossum, 2013; Magnussen & Skivenes, 2015; Falch-Eriksen & Skivenes, 2019).

In neither Denmark nor Norway are there clear-cut design principles for how protection services are going to be organized. How practices are implemented will therefore vary according to how services are organized. Although not demanded by the law itself, in Norway there have been massive efforts in creating larger service units with a greater degree of specialization. Intermunicipal cooperation is the most broadly used tool to achieve this goal. Denmark has merged municipalities through a nationwide reform in 2007, hence creating larger administrative units. Norway has also reduced the number of municipalities through mergers. A lead motivation for creating larger units with a more specialized design is that traditionally service offices have been too small, and thus contained inadequate competence. However, the Norwegian Board of Health Supervision (Helsetilsynet, 2019) states in a recent report that several summaries of nationwide audits with municipal child protection services have not been able to find a correlation between quality of services and municipality size (p. 122).

Practice Improvement through Other Initiatives

In both Denmark and Norway, key policy efforts are made to improve street-level practice. Denmark has a National Board of Social Services (established in 2001), with the responsibility to develop guidelines and new practices, and to test evidence-based programs in close collaboration with local governments. The Department has specialized units aiming at improving practice in various areas of child protection such as a Task Force that the municipalities can call (established in cooperation with the National Social Appeals Board), a unit that gathers and disseminates information on knowledge-based or innovative treatment or evaluation methods, specialized supervision and education offers, case management tools, and so on. Units also specialize in particular target groups or problem areas such as children with disabilities, diagnoses, abuse and exploitation, children in out-of-home care, and immigrant children. In Norway, the Directorate for Child, Youth, and Family Affairs was established in 2013 as a dedicated directorate to develop practice guidelines, routines, and professional advice. In addition, the directorate aims to influence how education can become more relevant to the field of practice. The policy work to improve practice is, however, driven by the Directorate with little to no democratic oversight (NOU, 2016, p. 16).

Another large-scale Norwegian effort has been the annual funding, from 2002 to the present, of the Norwegian Center for Child Behavioral Development (NUBU). The center is dedicated to implement two practice guidelines depicting evidence-based practices, focusing on Multi-Systemic Treatment and Parent Management Training–Oregon Model. These are two dominating evidence-based practices in Norway with significant financial support (in 2019 about 6 million USD). Denmark lags behind Norway concerning public investment in building evidence-based capacity, and a rough estimate is that for most services in child protection there is only poor documentation of effects and thereby a minor part of current practices.

Multiple policy efforts have been made across sectors to improve practices in child protection, especially regarding school, health, and social services. In Norway, a large-scale policy effort is called the "0–24 cooperation," which stipulates a clear effort across sectors to allocate correct service resources to children and families in need. In child protection, there has been an emphasis primarily on the need for psychiatric treatment of children subjected to detrimental care, and on alleviating or compensating the negative psychological consequences of growing up with child abuse and neglect. Out-of-home care is not a health-care service, but a majority of the children are found to have one or more health-related challenges, not least mental health issues (Lehmann & Kayed, 2018). Hence, significant efforts have been initiated in Norway to create more seamless cooperation with the health sector to provide better services for children. In Denmark, such policy initiatives have taken the form of reforms of the school system, new legislation, and funding to ease holistic planning and data sharing on children between sectors, and projects on an experimental level in selected municipalities. Recently, the Danish government has launched a policy initiative to reconstruct the welfare sector fundamentally in a more holistic direction, and a large-scale initiative has been taken to enhance early intervention for children. Digitalization of welfare services is a core policy value across the political spectrum, as is a strong focus on the quality of services and administration. Thus, a reform of the foster care system has recently been launched, and new administrative entities focusing on compliance and accountability have been introduced in the form of Children's Houses (cases of abuse), supervision and authorization of private placement facilities and service providers (the regional Social Audit authorities), and a new family law system (the Family Law House and Court). Many of the new policies and reforms mentioned in this chapter are heavily and increasingly influenced by a political focus on immigration and integration, to some extent challenging the family-service approach by a stronger focus on protection and security. However, securing the rights of children with an immigrant background remains a serious challenge (Adolphsen, 2016), as does also the question of children's right to protection on an increasingly wild-growing Internet.

All in all, the policy map is much more complex than what we can put forth here. Both local municipalities and private actors also have policies they work by, but predominantly within the child protection in-home practice field. Finally, the governments have a multitude of specialized policies (e.g., early intervention, digitalization of new administrative systems, automation of decision making, countering in-home violence, more professional foster care, specific education programs, and aftercare).

Denmark and Norway in an International Context

Children's rights operations and countries' ranking on different welfare indicators are broadly used to map children's well-being across countries (see Table 6.2 for an overview). Most of these international measurements are developed for countries to set goals and raise the quality regarding how children are treated. From an overall perspective, Denmark and Norway are doing well regarding children's living conditions and rights compliance. In the newly published WHO-UNICEF Lancet commission report (Clark et al., 2020), 180 countries are measured and ranked on fundamental conditions for children to survive and thrive. Here, Norway and Denmark are ranked 1 and 6. Norway and Denmark are also ranked as 16 and 10, respectively, out of 182 countries on the KidsRights Index (KidsRights, 2019). The specific measure of child protection in the KidsRights Index ranks Denmark and Norway as numbers 3 and 7, respectively. However, the indicators used do not separate the top 10 countries to any significant extent as regards child labor, adolescent birth rate, and birth registrations. An important measure of how welfare

Table 6.2 Denmark and Norway's ranking in international league tables		
	Denmark	Norway
WHO, UNICEF – Lancet commission (2020)	6	1
KidsRights (2019)	10	16
UNICEF Sustainable Development Goals (2017)	3	1
UNICEF (2016) Child inequality	1	3
CRIN (2016) Children's rights	46	13
UNICEF (2014) Poverty	24	6
UNICEF (2013) Well-being	11	2

states provide for children is measured in the UNICEF well-being index for high-income countries (UNICEF Office of Research, 2013). The situation for children is measured along five dimensions: Material well-being, health and safety, education, behavior and risks, and housing and environment. Norway and Denmark's average rank score across all five dimensions were 2 and 11, respectively, of 28 European countries and the United States. UNICEF (UNICEF Office of Research, 2014) studied how the economic recession impacted the living conditions of children, measuring child poverty before 2008 and then in 2012[14] in 41 high- and middle-income countries from the EU and OECD. For Denmark, ranked 24, child poverty increased to 10.2% in 2012. Norway, ranked 6, had a significant reduction in child poverty to 5.3% in 2012. In 2016, UNICEF ranked child inequality across 41 high- and middle-income countries from the EU and OECD (UNICEF Office of Research, 2016). On average, the two countries were ranked favorably on the four parameters on child inequality: economic welfare, education, health, and children's life satisfaction (Denmark no. 1 and Norway no. 3). Despite an international top rank, new studies on Denmark point to a polarization process, where the rich get richer, and both the income as well as the societal inclusion among the small group of poorest families decline (Hestbæk & Andreasen, 2018).

UNICEF also ranks sustainable development goals (SDGs) from children's point of view in 41 high- and middle-income countries from the EU and OECD on, for example, poverty, hunger and food security, healthy lives, education, gender equality, employment, inequality reduction, inclusive cities, sustainable production, and peaceful societies. Denmark and Norway are ranked as number 3 and 1, respectively (UNICEF, 2017). Children in the child protection system may be involved in court proceedings, and thus access to justice and support become relevant to measure. The Child Rights International Network (CRIN) collected information on 197 country jurisdictions, and developed an index based on the CRC on the legal status of the child within each country and the legal means available to challenge violations of the rights of the child. CRIN ranked Denmark as number 46 and Norway as number 13 in their "Global Report on Access to Justice for Children" of 2016.

Conclusion

From an overall perspective, based on the above description of the family-service-oriented child protection systems in Norway and Denmark, we can conclude that these two Nordic welfare states contain quite a few similarities in their legal structure and organization and how child protection unfolds on a practical level. Both countries put great political weight on prevention and early intervention and the following social investment philosophy, heavily enhanced by the "Heckmanization" of the understanding of societal costs related

---

[14] Computing child poverty in 2008 using a poverty line fixed at 60% of median income, and then using the same poverty line in 2012, adjusted for inflation.

to child abuse and neglect. However, from a research point of view, it seems that the states succeed more in establishing a political agenda on prevention rather than documenting the positive results of early intervention. Both countries have protection from structural inequality, for example, poverty, as one of the important drivers for child protection. Both Denmark and Norway have faced an ideological shift, where the child is considered to be a citizen in their own right with specific rights throughout the child protection processes. In addition, Norway and Denmark are inspired by the ecological framework for understanding the holistic needs of a vulnerable child and its family, requiring cross-sectorial social work, and resulting in systems that cover a wide range of problems, and a correspondingly large number of measures targeting different groups.

From a child perspective, the organization of the system means that local child protection services and its caseworkers who serve within the same national legal framework may have different preferences as to types of measures, qualifications of professionals, the extent to which they look to extramunicipal measures or only locally based measures, the extent to which they use measures with and without consent, and the extent to which children are put into out-of-home care and so on. The fact that certain basic life conditions for children with special needs vary between municipalities is interesting in the context of highly regulated welfare states with heavy documentation obligations for local professionals—such heavy bureaucratic burdens that many consider this as a major barrier to a smooth, flexible, and professional child protection system (Munro, 2011; Benbenishty et al., 2015; Svendsen, 2016; Andersen & Bengtsson, 2018; Falch-Eriksen & Backe-Hansen, 2018; Falch-Eriksen & Skivenes, 2019).

Both countries face regular amendments of the legal bases, it being the CPA in Norway and the CASS in Denmark. Thus, both countries exhibit an incremental approach to the legal development of child protection, regularly supplemented by more overall reforms focused on, for example, involvement and continuity. The child protection systems of Denmark and Norway are in international comparisons labeled as "family-service oriented," signaling an ambition for collaboration with, and involvement of, the family and the child at an early stage.

In international comparisons, both countries are ranked in the absolute top as concerns, for example, child poverty, health, and schooling, with Norway often one step ahead of Denmark. At the same time, when comparing child protection systems, Denmark and Norway (along with Finland and Sweden) demonstrate fairly high levels of children with social interventions, preventive in-home measures, and different types of out-of-home placements. The billion-dollar question is: why still a high level of intervention, when these welfare states simultaneously host far-reaching social security networks?

One explanation is that welfare states perform better when it comes to setting an agenda focusing on early intervention, underpinned by the latest research focusing on, for example, "the first 1,000 days" in a child's life, and on studies on the return on investment in early preventive measures. However, they perform worse when it comes to social reality—the actual outcomes of preventive strategies. Thus, even in the Nordic welfare states, many of the classic social problems stand out, such as abuse of alcohol or drugs and mental health problems. Unemployment and poverty are comparatively low, and often relatively well compensated through welfare schemes. However, in both countries, a small group of families suffer from life conditions influenced by poverty and most often combined with other social problems.

Another explanation for the relatively large number of children receiving child protection measures might rest on the cultural-normative condition as both countries are comprehensive welfare states. Therefore, while Norway and Denmark in an international context have a high level of children with child protection services, this is partly due to culturally customized norms for when a child is in need, and when the state must intervene and on which level. In addition, both countries search for how to balance the requests for adequate documentation on one hand, for example, to uphold a high level of justice, and on the other hand to develop rules and guidance that fit with the practical conditions of the local child protection administration.

As concerns the evidence base for interventions and their expected outcomes, both Danish and Norwegian social policies have displayed a great interest in increasing the level of evidence-based practices in child protection. However, only a small proportion of interventions are evidence based in the classical understanding of evidence-based practices, and, further, the policy discussion hereon is now slowly turning toward the concept of knowledge-based rather than evidence-based in a strict sense.

References

Adolphsen, C. (2016). Rights of children seeking asylum: A Danish perspective. *Nordic Journal on Human Rights*, 34(3), 178–188.

Andersen, D. and Bengtsson, T. T. (2018). Timely care: Rhythms of bureaucracy and everyday life in cases involving youths with complex needs. *Time and Society*, 28(4), 1509–1531.

Appeal Court Decision. (2005). U2005.822Ø (Case no. S3246-04). Available at: https://domstol.fe1.tangora.com/S%C3%B8geside---H%C3%B8jesteretten.31488.aspx.

Appeal Court Decision. (2017). U2017.3272Ø (Case no. B-2952-15 & B-2081-16). Available at: https://domstol.fe1.tangora.com/S%C3%B8geside---H%C3%B8jesteretten.31488.aspx.

Appeal Court Decision. (2018). U2018.3631Ø (Case no. B-2973-15). Available at: https://domstol.fe1.tangora.com/S%C3%B8geside---H%C3%B8jesteretten.31488.aspx.

Benbenishty, R., Davidson-Arad, B., López, M., Devaney, J., Spratt, T., Koopmans, C., Knorth, E.J., Witteman, C. L. M., Del Valle, J. F., and Hayes, D. (2015). Decision making in child protection: An international comparative study on maltreatment substantiation, risk assessment and interventions recommendations, and the role of professionals' child welfare attitudes. *Child Abuse & Neglect*, 49(11), 63–75.

Blomberg, H., Kroll, C., and Meeuwisse, A. (2013). Nordic social workers' assessments of child welfare problems and interventions: a common model in child welfare? *European Journal of Social Work*, 16(3), 311–326.

Burns, K., Pösö, T., and Skivenes, M. (Eds.). (2017). *When the state takes children from their home*. Oxford University Press.

Bryderup, I., Enge, M., and Kring, S. (2017). *Familiepleje i Danmark*. KLIM.

Central Unit of the County Boards in Norway. https://www.fylkesnemndene.no/en/.

Clark, H., Coll-Seck, A. M., Banerjee, A., Peterson, S., Dalglish, S. L., Ameratunga, S., Balabanova, D., . . . Costello, A. (2020). A future for the world's children? A WHO-UNICEF-*Lancet* Commission. *The Lancet*, 395(10224), 605–658.

County Boards. (2016). *County Boards year report 2016.* County Boards. Available at: https://www.fylkesn emndene.no/globalassets/pdfer/arsrapport-2016.pdf.

Danish Supreme Court. (2019a). U2019.1721H (Case no. 106/218). Available at: https://domstol.fe1.tang ora.com/S%C3%B8geside---H%C3%B8jesteretten.31488.aspx.

Danish Supreme Court. (2019b). U2019.1565H, (Case nr. 140/2018 & 144/2018). Available at: https://doms tol.fe1.tangora.com/S%C3%B8geside---H%C3%B8jesteretten.31488.aspx.

Esping-Andersen, G. (1999). *Social foundations of postindustrial economies.* Oxford University Press.

Falch-Eriksen, A. and Backe-Hansen, E. (2018). Child protection and human rights: A call for professional practice and policy. In A. Falch-Eriksen and E. Backe-Hansen (Eds.), *Human rights in child protection: Implications for professional practice and policy* (pp. 1–14). Palgrave.

Falch-Eriksen, A. and Skivenes, M. (2019). The Child's Right to Protection. In M. Langford, M. Skivenes, and K. H. Søvig (Eds.), *Child rights in Norway: An implementation paradox* (pp. 107–134). Universitetsforlaget.

Forlag. Vis, S. A. and Fossum, S. (2013). Representation of children's views in court hearings about custody and parental visitations: A comparison between what children wanted and what the courts ruled. *Children and Youth Services Review*, 35(12): 2101–2109.

Forsberg, H. and Kröger, T. (2010). Introduction: Social work within 'a welfare paradise'. In H. Forsberg and T. Kröger (Eds.), *Social work and child welfare politics: Through Nordic lenses* (pp. 1–9). The Policy Press.

Gilbert, N. (1997). *Combatting child abuse: International perspectives and trends.* Oxford University Press.

Gilbert, N., Parton, N., and Skivenes, M. (Eds.) (2011). *Child protection systems: International trends and orientations.* Oxford University Press.

Hartoft, H. (2019). The rights of children to participation according to Danish law. In T. Haugli, A. Nylund, R. Sigurdsen, and L. Bendiksen (Eds.), *Children's constitutional rights in the Nordic countries* (pp. 295–314). Brill Nijhoff.

Helland, H. and Skivenes, M. (2019). *Adopsjon som barneverntiltak.* Centre for Research on Discretion and Paternalism: Universitetet i Bergen.

Helsetilsynet (Norwegian Board of Health Supervision). (2019). *Marit og co - her må I ændre.* Helsetilsynet.

Hestbæk, A.-D. (2011). Denmark: A child welfare system under reframing. In N. Gilbert, N. Parton, and M. Skivenes (Eds.). *Child protection systems: International trends and orientations* (pp. 131–153). Oxford University Press.

Hestbæk, A.-D. (2018). The rights of children placed in out-of-home care. In A. Falch-Eriksen and E. Backe-Hansen (Eds.), *Human rights in child protection: Implications for professional practice and policy* (pp. 129–146). Palgrave Macmillan.

Hestbæk, A.-D. and Andreasen, A. G. (2018). Materiel velfærd. In M. H. Ottosen, A. G. Andreasen, K. M. Dahl, A.-D. Hestbæk, M. Lausten, and S. B. Rayce (Eds.), *Børn og unge i Danmark Velfærd og trivsel 2018* (pp. 28–45). Det nationale forsknings- og analysecenter for velfærd.

Jessen, J. T. and Backe-Hansen, E. (2017). *Samvær, samarbeid og støtte. Familiens mulighet for å hjelpe unge voksne etter plassering utenfor hjemmet (Report No. 2/2017).* Norwegian Institute of Social Research / NOVA.

KidsRights. (2019). *The KidsRights Index 2019.* Available at: https://kidsrights.org/research/kidsrights-index/reports-and-publications/.

KL. (2016). *De udsatte børn—nøgletal.* Kommuneforlaget.

KL. (2019). *Udsatte børn—nøgletal.* Kommuneforlaget.

Kronborg, A. (2016). Family formation in Scandinavia: A comparative study in family law. *Utrecht Law Review*, 12(2), 81–97.

Lehmann, S. and Kayed, N. S. (2018). Children placed in alternate care in Norway: A review of mental health needs and current official measures to meet them. *International Journal of Social Welfare*, 27(4), 364–371.

Magnussen, A.-M. and Skivenes, M. (2015). The child's opinion and position in care order proceedings. *The International Journal of Children's Rights*, 23(4), 705–723.

Munro, E. (2011). *Munro Review of Child Protection, Final Report: A child-centred system.* Department for Education.

NOU (2016): 16. *Ny barnevernlov. Sikring av barns rett til omsorg og beskyttelse [New Child Protection Act: Securing the child's right to care and protection].* Barne- og likestillingsdepartementet.

Ot.prp.nr.45. (2002–2003). *Om lov om endring i menneskerettsloven mv. (innarbeiding av barnekonvensjonen i norsk lov).* Justis- og politidepartementet.

Ot.prp.nr.76. (2005–2006). *Om lov om endringer I barnevernloven og sosialtjenesteloven—saksbehandlingsregler for fylkesnemndene for barnevern og sosiale saker.* barne- og familiedepartementet.

Pösö, T., Skivenes, M., and Hestbæk, A.-D. (2014). Child protection systems within the Danish, Finnish and Norwegian welfare states: Time for a child centric approach? *European Journal of Social Work*, 17(4), 475–490.

Prop 95 L. (2013–2014). *Kommuneproposisjonen 2015*. Kommunal- og moderniseringsdepartementet.

Prop 106 L. (2012–2013). *Endringer i tresholdnevernloven*. Tresholdne-, likestillings- og inkluderingsdepartementet

Prop 169 L. (2016–2017). *Endringer barne*. Tresholdne-, likestillings- og inkluderingsdepartementet.

Prop 169 L. (2016–2017). *Endringer i tresholdnevernloven mv. (bedre rettssikkerhet for tresholdn og foreldre) [Amendment to the Child Protection Act etc. (better legal protections for children and parents]*. Tresholdne-, likestillings- og inkluderingsdepartementet.Pösö, T., Skivenes, M., and Hestbæk, A.-D. (2014). Child protection systems within the Danish, Finnish and Norwegian welfare states: Time for a child centric approach? *European Journal of Social Work*, 17(4), 475–490.

Schultz, T., Mørk, A., and Hartoft, H. (Eds.). (2020). *Children's rights. The Convention on the Rights of the Child in Danish law*. DJØF Forlag.

Selznick, P. (1985). Focusing organizational research on regulation. *Regulatory policy and the social sciences*, 1, 363–367.

Skivenes, M. (2011). Norway: Toward a child-centric perspective. In N. Gilbert, N. Parton, and M. Skivenes (Eds.), *Child protection systems: International trends and orientations* (pp. 154–180). Oxford University Press.

Skivenes, M. (2015). How the Norwegian child welfare system address immigrant children and families. In M. Skivenes, R. Barn, K. Kriz, and, and T. Pösö (Eds.), *Child welfare systems and migrant children: A cross country study of policies and practice* (pp. 39–61). Oxford University Press.

Skivenes, M. and Søvig, K. H. (2017). Norway – Child welfare decision-making in cases of removals of children. In K. Burns, T. Pösö, and M. Skivenes (Eds.), *Child welfare removals by the state: a cross-country analysis of decision-making systems*, 3 (pp. 40–64). Oxford University Press.

Skivenes, M. and Søvig, K. H. (2016). Judicial discretion and the child's best interests: The European Court of Human Rights on adoptions in child protection cases. In E. E. Sutherland and L.-A. Macfarlane (Eds.), *Implementing Article 3 of the United Nations Convention on the Rights of the Child* (pp. 341–357). Cambridge University Press.

Socialstyrelsen (2015). *Adoption uden samtykke – et vejlednings- og inspirationsmateriale til sagsbehandlere* (1st ed.) [Adoption without consent – a guideline- and inspirational material for caseworkers]. Available at: https://socialstyrelsen.dk.

Statistics Denmark. *Data on placements, notifications etc. in Denmark*. Available at: https://dst.dk/en#.

Statistics Norway (2018). *Child protection*. Available at: https://www.ssb.no/en/statbank/list/barneverng/.

Svendsen, I. L. (2016). Managing complex child law: Social workers' decision making under Danish legal regulation. *Social Work and Society*, 14(2), 1–12.

Tefre, Ø. (2020). The child's best interests and the politics of adoptions from care in Norway. *The International Journal of Children's Rights*, 28(2), 288–321.

The Danish Parliamentary Ombudsman. Available at: http://en.ombud smanden.dk.

UN Committee on the Rights of the Child. Convention, optional protocol, concluding Observations. Available at: https://www.ohchr.org/EN/HRBodies/CRC/Pages/CRCIndex.aspx.

UNICEF Office of Research. (2013). *Child well-being in rich countries: A comparative overview*. Innocenti Report Card 11. UNICEF Office of Research.

UNICEF Office of Research. (2014). *Children of the recession: The impact of the economic crisis on child well-being in rich countries*. Innocenti Report Card 12. UNICEF Office of Research.

UNICEF Office for Research. (2016). *Fairness for children: A league table of inequality in child well-being in rich countries*. UNICEF Office of Research.

UNICEF Office of Research. (2017). *Building the future: Children and the sustainable development goals in rich countries*. Innocenti Report Card 14. UNICEF Office of Research – Innocenti, Florence.

Villumsen, A. M. (Ed.). (2018). *Helhedsorienteret social arbejde med udsatte familier*. Akademisk.

Child Welfare and Child Protection Services in England

June Thoburn

Abstract

This chapter explores the child welfare and child protection services in England. The child protection system refers to the multi-agency and inter-professional arrangements following specific government guidelines on the assessment and service concerning child maltreatment. Suspected maltreatment reports are directed to the police or children's social services. Data on rates of abuse cannot be quantified easily due to the lack of a formal system of reporting and substantiation of abuse allegations. However, England does have a robust administrative data collection to understand the demands on the child welfare system. Tension is growing between policy-makers, social workers, and advocacy groups with regards to enforcing a rights-based and participatory approach to child welfare.

Key Words: child welfare, child protection services, England, data, reporting, maltreatment, government, social services, police

Context and Discourse

Before turning in detail to an exploration of the character and scope of the child protection systems and services in England,[1] it is important to start by unpacking the discourse and language of "child protection." The terms "child protection" and "child protection system" are usually understood as referring to the multi-agency and inter-professional arrangements that follow very specific government guidelines for assessment and service provision if there are concerns about child maltreatment. In England, since the implementation in 1991 of the 1989 England and Wales Children Act (still the substantive legislation governing child welfare services in England), successive versions of *Working Together* (Home Office et al., 1991; DfE, 2018 have broadened the guidance from specifically referring to maltreatment to the present one, which uses the term "safeguarding" and

---

[1] The child welfare services of the four UK nations have much in common but also important differences in legislation and aspects of practice. Legislation and guidance and some additional funding is provided by the national and three devolved governments but the service itself is delegated to democratically elected Local Authorities who are accountable for the services provided by the professionals they employ. Since data are reported separately, this chapter focuses on England.

provides guidance on collaborative practice with all vulnerable children who need an additional service. However, several sections still specifically mandate the identification and formal response to actual or likely child abuse or neglect. In terms of service provision and professional practice, formal child protection services, as in protecting children from, and working towards recovery from in-family or extra-familial abuse, are part of the broader child and family welfare services. Although in some texts making international comparisons of child welfare systems, the UK nations are referred to as a "child protection" as opposed to a "family welfare" system, the legal mandate is one which requires the public services to respond to all children "in need" of additional services, and closely adheres to the requirements of the UNCRC (United Nations, 1989). The categorization, in some texts making international comparisons of the UK/England as being a "child protection" system (Parton & Berridge in Gilbert et al., 2011) may have occurred because of *de jure* and *de facto* differences. In law, the UK child welfare/broader child protection services have much in common with other western European child welfare systems, requiring a child welfare and family support approach to families experiencing difficulties that require a targeted response over and above universally available provision. However, because of a combination of cuts in resources, and the predominance of a practice approach that has been characterized as "risk averse," the resultant high thresholds for provision of a child and family welfare service have in practice meant that, since the mid-1990s, professionals spend most time and resources on "heavy end" "child protection" cases. In this chapter I refer to "the formal child protection system" when referring to more coercive interventions with cases of actual or likely significant harm, and "child and family social work" or "child and family social services" when referring to the full range of Local Authority social services for children and their families assessed as in need of "targeted" services, additional to those available to all families. These include, for example, services to disabled children and unaccompanied asylum-seeking children as well as those where there are concerns about abuse or neglect. The term "child welfare services" is sometimes used to include universal as well as targeted services.[2] The chapter first summarizes the legal mandate for the provision of child protection and support services for vulnerable children and families and locates them within the context of policy changes between 1991 and 2021. It then outlines the governance and service delivery arrangements in 2021 and provides data on referrals and service responses, noting main changes after 2010. There are separate sections on services to children in the community and those needing out-of-home care or adoption, which include brief information on rights-based and other approaches to service delivery.

---

[2] The term "statutory powers" is sometimes erroneously used to refer only to child protection powers and compulsory interventions. This is inaccurate since any power or duty conveyed by statute, including family support powers and duties with respect to children assessed as "in need" is "statutory" in the sense that, having been referred to a local authority for assessment of additional needs, there is a statutory duty to respond appropriately.

The Legal Mandate for Child Protection and Family Support Services

The main legislation governing service provision for vulnerable children and their families, including children in need of protection from maltreatment, remains the Children Act 1989. This covers the provision of family support under collaborative arrangements with family members as well as provision for compulsory measures where necessary. There has been amending legislation, mainly with respect to children in out-of-home care and adoption (to be referred to later) but these have not resulted in fundamental shifts. Changes have also been made to arrangements for the governance of service provision and the mandate for all agencies to work collaboratively has been strengthened.

The relevant sections of the 1989 Act governing referral and assessment as a "child in need" of additional services (Children Act, 1989, Section 17) has three parts. A child is "in need" of additional services if he or she:

- Is unlikely to achieve a reasonable standard of health or development without the provision of a [additional social care] service;
- [His or her] health or development [mental, physical or cognitive] is likely to be significantly impaired without the provision of a [additional social care] service;
- Is disabled [but disability is tightly defined—although a child with a moderate impairment may be assessed as "in need" under the first two provisions];
- Is aged 16 or 17 and his or her health or development is likely to be seriously harmed unless provided with [out-of-home] accommodation.

If a referral is made, the local authority is required to assess whether or not this is a "child in need." This duty is usually interpreted (a practice reinforced in statutory guidance and inspection reports) as requiring allocation of a registered social worker. Note the term "referral" not "report" is used and referrals may be made by family members seeking assistance as well as professionals who know them and others who have a concern about possible maltreatment. The guidance to the legislation states that these definitions are deliberately broad, and may not be changed, but that local authorities have discretion to decide what services (if any) are to be provided. If a child is assessed as "in need" a service can be provided to any member of that child's family, provided that the child assessed as "in need" can gain some direct or indirect benefit. As a result of the breadth of this legal definition, most local authorities have their own "threshold criteria" for the provision of services. Specifically relevant to inter-agency and inter-professional collaboration is Section 10 of the 2004 Children Act (sometimes referred to as "the duty to cooperate"), which requires providers of universal services (including health, education, police) to collaborate with the local authority in the provision of services to children in need.

However, the over-arching accountability for the co-ordination and delivery of these services remains with the local authority.

The threshold for compulsory investigation of suspected maltreatment is a child being referred to the police or children's social services because of concerns about actual or likely abuse or neglect. Part 5 of the 1989 Act specifies that a referral should take place when there is evidence that a child "is suffering or is likely to suffer significant harm" (Children Act, 1989, Section 47). "Harm" is defined as "ill-treatment or the impairment of development." The 1933 Children and Young Persons Act and guidance, under which a parent or carer may be prosecuted for harming or failing to protect a child from harm has been amended over the years to make it clear that those suspected of willfully causing or exposing a child to emotional and psychological abuse may be subject to criminal prosecution. In recognition of the fact that criminal proceedings can take longer to get under way, but that a care plan for a vulnerable child should be arrived at as soon as possible, in some cases where a criminal prosecution is being considered a Family Court Judge will start the care proceedings by hearing the details or the allegation and making a "finding of fact" as to whether, "on the balance of probabilities," the alleged maltreatment has taken place. The case can then be heard in the Family Court to decide on future plans for the child, and if necessary, separately in the criminal court. In all cases where an application for a Care or Supervision Order has been made (a Public Law application) the family court judge or magistrates will hear witnesses and receive reports as to whether a child has suffered or is likely to suffer significant harm, whether the harm is due to the action or inaction of a parent or other person with parental responsibility, and whether in the light of all the facts, including a consideration of the Local Authority's proposed care plan, a care order, a supervision order, or a private law order (Residence, Special Guardianship, or Child Arrangements Order) is necessary, or whether to make no order.

The Policy Context 1991–2020

1991–2010: The Implementation of the 1989 Children Act and "Every Child Matters"
Parton and Berridge (2011) reviewed the policy context during this period up to the end of the New Labour government, a period characterized by the *Every Child Matters* Green Paper (DH, 2004). This followed the murder of Victoria Climbie and the Laming Report (2003), which made recommendations beyond those that were relevant to that specific case. The resultant policy direction sought to both tighten up formal child protection processes and practice on the one hand and strengthen the services available to support all children and families who may be living in stressful circumstances. This included providing not only funding for children assessed as "in need" but also community support services more broadly, most notably by the establishment and funding of multidisciplinary and inter-agency "Sure Start" family centers. These were open access for any child under

5 and his or her parents living in a defined geographical neighborhood, which also aimed to be available to families who were more vulnerable and possibly already receiving "child in need" or "child protection" services. A key policy aim was to encourage parents of young children to become members of these centers, both helping to design a range of multidisciplinary services as well as using them. By identifying neighborhoods that might benefit from additional services rather than specific "at risk" families, a key aim was to reduce stigma for those families most in need, and to increase service take-up, including take-up of social work services. A substantial program of independent evaluations and research demonstrated that the open access approach did indeed succeed in encouraging families with more complex difficulties, including some already identified as needing a formal child protection plan, to make use of the center-based and outreach parenting and therapeutic services as well as practical assistance in claiming financial benefits, finding employment, and additional family support during school holidays (Tunstill et al., 2005; Tunstill & Blewett, 2009). Also encouraged following the publication of *Every Child Matters* (Department for Education and Skills, 2004) by the provision of government funding was the expansion of voluntary association (NGO) community provision for children in the 5 to 11 age group (Morris, 2012). During this period the numbers of children in poverty, and the numbers of families with children in homeless families' accommodation declined, whilst the number of families with formal child protection plans stabilized at around 30,000.

In parallel, the government tightened the child protection policies and guidance, issuing new versions of *Working Together* in 2006 and 2010. The second of these, issued after a second Laming Review (Laming, 2009) following the death of Peter Connolly, continued a trend towards very detailed guidance about social work practice and the introduction of recording and monitoring systems, which, as has been shown over time and was particularly regretted by the *Munro Review of Child Protection*, led to the increased bureaucratization of social work processes and practice (Department for Education, 2011). Many if not most local councillors, social work managers, and practitioners, pushed by the media criticism of their work and anxiety about potential consequences to their family as well as their working lives of being found at fault, adopted a "risk-averse" stance and either went along with or welcomed a service model that appeared to offer more certainty about how to manage cases of potential harm (Jones, 2015).

By the time the coalition government came into power in 2010, there had been a swing back towards an emphasis—in funding decisions as well as in practice—on "heavier end" child abuse cases and away from providing support to families of children in need. The majority of local authority social workers were employed in "child protection teams" or teams working with children in care rather than in neighborhood-based child and family social work teams. An unintended consequence of the post-Laming Report attempts to improve and monitor practice was a big increase in form filling and social workers complaining that they had insufficient time to spend with parents and children (Laming,

2009; DfE, 2011). In 2009–10, over 600,000 children were referred for assessment as children in need of a family support or formal child protection service. However only 390,000 (65%) of these were fully assessed. These included 87,700 (14% of those referred) assessed under formal child protection procedures and 44,300 (11% of those assessed as potentially in need of a service) who became the subject of a formal child protection plan. At year end in 2010 there were 375,900 children receiving a child in need or child protection service (a rate of 341.3 per 10,000 children) and 39,100 of these were subjects of a formal child protection plan. At the end of 2009 66,000 children were in out-of-home care (referred to in the legislation as "Looked After Children") (a rate of 55 per 10,000 children[3]). One response of the Blair government to rising numbers in care was to call for the increased use of adoptions from care, if necessary without parental consent (Cabinet Office, 2000).

2010–2020: The Years of Austerity and Increasing Pressures on Families and Services
The first four years of the Conservative and Liberal Democrat coalition are important largely because of the impact of Tim Loughton MP, Children's Minister from 2010–2012, who, as Conservative Shadow Children's Minister, convened a working party of policymakers, practitioners, and researchers to consider what might be done to respond positively to the declining morale, and growing vacancy rates amongst social workers. The recommendations, published as *No More Blame Game*, informed a very busy first phase of the new government's activity in the sphere of child welfare and protection (Conservative Party Commission on Social Workers, 2007). The new Minister immediately commissioned Professor Eileen Munro and a team of practitioners and researchers to make recommendations on improving child and family social work specifically and child protection services more broadly. The Munro report recommendations (DfE, 2011) were followed by the setting up of a cross-sector Social Work Task Force and then a Reform Board to inform how the recommendations could be implemented. Amongst other recommendations that were planned to improve the status of the social work profession was the setting up of The College of Social Work and the appointment of a Chief Social Worker—a social work-qualified civil servant who would both support the implementation of the proposed improvements and also act as an advisor to the Minister. In the end, under a new Children's Minister, and contrary to the majority professional view, a Chief Social Work for Children and Families and a Chief Social Worker for Adults were appointed. The Munro review, the Task Force, and subsequently the Reform Board chaired by a very experienced social worker and senior manager Dame Moira Gibb (Social Work Reform Board, 2012), made detailed recommendations for changes in social work practice and

---

[3] The term (sometimes shortened to LAC) is used for all children in public care, whether they are the subject of a Court Order or "accommodated" (Children Act 1989 Sec 20) with the agreement of parents or youth aged 16 or 17.

to strengthen social work education. The recommendations aimed at reducing the time spent on administrative tasks not directly relevant to practice were widely welcomed.

The Department for Education published in 2013 and updated in 2015 and 2018 new and much shortened versions of the official Guidance *Working Together to Safeguard Children* to encourage the moves recommended by all these reports (DfE, 2015a, 2018). However, changes in practice on the ground have been slow, not least because local authorities had invested heavily in cumbersome case management and recording systems and also because, though welcoming the recommendations, social workers and their managers had become used to following the guidelines as a way of protecting themselves and their agencies from criticism in the event of a high-profile child death or serious injury case.

The second period of the Coalition and the post-2015 Conservative government saw changes of policy priorities as austerity began to bite on local authority budgets and resources for child protection and social work services diminished. The reforms proposed by the Munro Report and Social Work Reform Board were given little chance to achieve the desired moves towards earlier help and a more family-centered service, as thresholds for the receipt of a social work service continued to tighten. These were exacerbated by increased stresses on families resulting from cuts in public services more generally, including changes in the social security system (mainly involving cuts in income level for the poorest families) and a rapidly deteriorating housing situation, increasing homelessness. Major changes to the funding mechanisms and delivery of preventive, acute, and chronic health services (especially the delivery of health visiting services and mental health and addictions services) caused confusion and made collaborative practice more difficult. The local authority role in education and an emphasis, encouraged by the *Every Child Matters* reforms, on schools working closely with other professionals within (especially high deprivation) neighborhoods was weakened by an emphasis on academy chains and Free Schools,[4] which were outside the "duty to collaborate" legislation. An emphasis on testing and published performance measures led to more children experiencing difficulties being excluded from school and becoming more vulnerable to abuse and exploitation within and outside the family.

In the light of new reports of child deaths or serious injury, as well as inspection reports by OFSTED (Office for Standards in Education, Children's Services and Skills) concluding that almost a third of the 150 local authority children's social services were "inadequate" and detailing high social worker turnover and vacancy rates, the central government has taken an increasingly interventionist role. Funding has been held back from local government allocation for "services as usual" and allocated by the Department

---

[4] There has been a move from the majority of schools being provided by school governing bodies directly responsible to the local authorities who also provided children's social welfare services, to the majority of schools being provided by national government-funded chains of academies or "free schools." These are free to set most of their own policies on admissions and behavioral sanction or exclusion policies. Admissions are less likely to be neighborhood-based, making collaborative practice within neighborhoods more difficult.

for Education (via an Innovations fund and competitive tendering process) to fund "new ways of working" and new approaches to service delivery. Though introduced with the aim of improving the quality of services, these policy moves have been controversial since they have resulted in inequality of available funding between those parts of the country with "innovations money" and those without, and arguably a more unequal service to children and families (Jones, 2015; National Audit Office, 2016; Tunstill & Thoburn, 2019; Purcell, 2020).

Government spokespeople have continued throughout this period to assert a commitment to early intervention in order to avoid the need for children to be brought before the Court because of child protection concerns. The *Troubled Families Programme* (Casey, 2015) following on from the *Family Intervention Projects* was introduced towards the end of the Labour period of office to use a "tough love," "carrot and stick," intensive but short-term whole family approach to "turn troubled families around" (Thoburn et al., 2013; Casey, 2015). The dedicated government funding used a payment by results approach to target identified families whose difficulties were likely to increase if intensive help was not provided. As Thoburn (2013) points out, there was ambiguity about whether the families to receive help were families where there were child welfare concerns (often with younger children) or families and especially teenagers who were seen as troublesome to their neighbors and schools. Although intended to be an "early help" service, not requiring qualified social workers, a substantial minority of the children had a protection plan and there was scope for confusion about accountability between children's services social workers and the Troubled Families workers and managers (Brandon et al., 2015; Davies, 2015). The "payment by results" element was confusing and quickly dropped in most areas, although dedicated, though ring-fenced, government funding continued into the 2020s.

However, increases in the numbers in poverty and the numbers of families in temporary and insecure accommodation saw larger numbers referred because of child protection concerns, associated as these are with stress-related family problems including addiction, mental ill-health, and inter-partner violence. Resources that the local authorities were able to invest in early help diminished, resulting in the closure in many areas of youth services and Sure Start family centers and neighborhood youth facilities. Tables 7.1 and 7.2 show that referrals for assistance as a child in need diminished, as local authorities increased the thresholds of need and risk required before a service was provided and colleagues in other agencies opted against referring if assistance failed to result. Despite the worsening economic climate, there was only a slight rise in the numbers receiving early help. However, a risk-averse climate amongst referrers and social workers, heightened following media reports of child deaths, resulted in a rise in the numbers accepted for a service where there were elements of risk. This showed up in the increased rates being the subject of a formal child protection enquiry and having a child protection plan and placed in out-of-home care. For most local authorities (though some have bucked the trend), aspirations to reduce these numbers by providing help at an early stage are failing because the more

Table 7.1 Numbers and rates per 1,000 of children receiving a formal child welfare service

Service	Year 2020–21		Year 2009–10	
	Total number	Rate per 1,000 children	Total number	Rate per 1,000 children
"Child in need" (new referrals)	597,760	47.9	607,500	55.1
Receiving any child in need service	388,490	32.4	382,300	33.9
Children subject to a Section 47 child protection inquiry during year	198,790	16.4	87,700	8.0
Children with a child protection plan at year end	50,010	4.0	35,700	3.2
Children in out-of-home care	80,850	6.7	64,400	5.8
Children starting a care episode during the year	28,440	2.3	27,800	2.5

Table 7.2 Primary reason for needing a formal child protection plan 2009 and March 2021

Category of maltreatment	Number 2021	% 2021	% with CP plan in this category 2009
Neglect	24,120	48%	45%
Physical abuse	3,650	7%	15%
Sexual abuse	1,930	4%	6%
Emotional abuse	18,840	38%	25%
Multiple	1,480	3%	9%
Total	50,020	100%	N=37,000

expensive services to children in care or with a formal child protection plan continue to require the largest budget allocation. Bywaters and colleagues (CWIP, 2017) have provided data to show that even in wealthier local authorities the rate entering care is higher amongst those living in the most deprived areas.

Another major change over this period (following the general policy direction of the Conservative government to encourage competition in provision of public services) is the growth of outsourcing of service provision to the third sector. In some areas such as the provision of community resources like children's and youth centers, the charitable, not-for-profit, sector has grown by tendering for local authority contracts. In other sectors (especially residential care and foster care) the role of the charitable (NGO) sector has declined and private for-profit agencies have become the major providers. Although legislation was introduced to encourage small groups of social workers to leave local authority employment and set themselves up as not-for-profit social enterprises contracting with local authorities to undertake aspects of child and family social work, an early pilot petered out (Stanley et al., 2014). However, legislation permitting third sector organizations to take over the provision of children's social services (including child protection services) was introduced and new ways of local authorities contracting out the provision of social work services are being introduced, although as yet in a very small way (Jones, 2014, 2015)[5].

Child and Family Welfare Services in 2020: Accountability and Governance

Central government (principally the Department for Education but linking in with the Justice Ministry, the Home Office, the Department of Health and the Department for Communities and Local Government) decides on the legislation to bring forward and also consults on and publishes statutory guidance—notably *Working Together* and Statutory Guidance on the multidisciplinary service to be provided to children in care and leaving care (DfE, 2015a). The Children and Family Court Advisory and Support Service (Cafcass), which provides the family courts with an independent social work service on behalf of the child (probably the largest employer of qualified social workers in Europe) is an arms-length public sector agency accountable to the Ministry of Justice. OFSTED (an independent but central government funded body responsible for inspecting both schools and children's social services) provides regular reports on children's social services and (as already noted) has played an increasingly important role in policy development.

These services apart, accountability for ensuring the provision of services required by statute is delegated from the central government Department for Education to elected local authority councillors who in turn delegate overall responsibility to a Director of Children's Services (DCS). Although this person is also responsible for ensuring that children have access to education and appropriate leisure and youth services, because of a system of local management of schools, the main role of the DCS is to ensure the provision of services to vulnerable children and families who may need additional services. He or she is also given the lead role in coordinating the other services needed to safeguard the welfare of children. As noted above, this role was shared with the Local Safeguarding Children Board, whose members and Chairperson were appointed by the Council and senior officers of the Local Authority but which works closely with the DCS. Until the

---

[5] As this Chapter is being finalised, another government -commissioned review of child and family services is about to report: the Independent Review of Children's Social Care, https://childrenssocialcare.inde pendent-review.uk/.

Interim reports are confirming that the concerns referred to in this section continue. Wide-ranging reforms are likely to be recommended but proposed changes (subject to much debate across the legal and care professions) will depend on considerable increases in government funding. No substantial change to the legislation and service provision as described in this chapter is likely for some time.

1980s it was the norm for the DCS to be a qualified social worker. This is no longer a requirement but around half still have social work qualifications and experience though others take on this role after a career in the school system. The Police Service, now headed by a directly elected Police and Crime Commissioner, leads in the detection and prosecution of offences against children and vulnerable adults.

Throughout the period under discussion in this chapter it has been a requirement for each local authority and their statutory partners in the Health and Police services to fund and be accountable for a Local Safeguarding Children Board. The main roles of these continue to be to ensure inter-agency collaboration, including the provision of multidisciplinary child protection training at different levels to all who have unsupervised access to children; and to decide, in the event of a death or serious injury, whether there should be a serious case review. Although originally usually headed by the Director of Children's Services, for the last ten years or so they have had independent chairs, usually contracted by and answerable to the chief executive and council of the local authority. At the start of this period, the Children's Minister decided that serious case review reports should be made public (appropriately redacted as necessary to protect confidentiality). These arrangements have been changed under the 2017 Children and Social Work Act, which narrows the accountable professionals at the local government level to the Local Authority Children's Service Department, the Police Service, and the local commissioners of National Health Services. These may then decide which other agency representatives should be invited onto the co-ordinating body and it is left open to local authorities as to whether they will continue to appoint an independent chair of any co-ordinating bodies they set up. The legislation also centralized and tightened the arrangements for commissioning and responding to serious case reviews following a child death or serious injury.

Funding Arrangements

A large majority of child and family social services, including almost all social work assessment and coordinating of community-based social work services, are funded and provided by local authorities. However, to discharge their responsibilities they may contract out and monitor some services to the third sector. Nationally there are five large voluntary sector child welfare organizations—Action for Children, Barnardo's, The Children's Society, Family Action, and the National Society for Prevention of Cruelty to Children (NSPCC)—as well as many more smaller, more specialist, or locally based agencies. These provide services at national as well as local levels, although their direct services are unevenly spread. Although they raise charitable funds, their direct service provision is mainly funded under contract to local authorities. Local authority commissioners are responsible for the tendering and procurement processes. There has also been a growth of "sole trader" or small groups of "independent social workers" who contract with local authorities for specific tasks such as providing reports on potential kinship carers or providing a specialist service to a particular family or group of families. Because of shortages of social workers, and poor rates of retention, some local authorities contract with private for-profit agencies to supply "agency social workers." However, once engaged, these are directly employed by and accountable to the local authority.

As noted above, local authorities also increasingly contract with private for-profit companies to provide residential care and foster homes for children in their care. (In 2016 around 67% of the 12% of children in group care were in private for-profit children's homes (Narey, 2016) and around a third of all fostering households were in the private for-profit sector (OFSTED, 2016).) Finally, following legislative changes to permit this, a small number of local authorities have delegated the provision of services to specially formed not-for-profit "trusts" or public interest companies, although the locally elected councillors remain accountable for the service provided. Central government reserves the power to intervene if a local authority is not fulfilling its statutory duties to an adequate level (usually defined following an OFSTED inspection) and initially these new arrangements were imposed on "inadequate" local authorities. However, since 2015, some adequately functioning local authorities have decided to manage their services in these new ways and government policy encourages this diversification of service management and delivery arrangements (DfE, 2014). Early evaluations are included amongst the reports of a range of DfE-funded "innovations" (Sebba et al., 2017), though as yet it is too early to reach conclusions on these differently scaled and funded initiatives. Jones (2015, 2018) has critiqued the legislation that made this outsourcing by local authorities of statutorily-required children in need and child protection services possible and subsequent developments. As yet, services must be not-for-profit but these new bodies are not precluded from commissioning services from their "for-profit" arms.

What Are the Processes for Referring and Assisting Children Who May Need Protection?

England, along with the other UK nations, has not legislated for a system of mandatory reporting of child abuse (except for the specific area of female genital mutilation[6]). The various amended versions of *Working Together* set out in detail the requirements and processes for the different professions in statutory and third sector organizations to refer children who may be suffering significant harm or likely to do so to the Children's Services Department and/or the police service. A member of a statutorily registered profession (including doctors, nurses, psychologists, and social workers) may be disciplined and "struck off" if they fail to follow the guidance. Other professions including teachers, therapists, counsellors, and police officers have their own disciplinary procedures in such circumstances. Although in legislation the NSPCC is an agency to which referrals of child maltreatment can be made, in practice referrals are made to the police service or local authority. However, the NSPCC receives government funding for *Childline,* a

---

[6] Female Genital Mutilation Act, 2015.

confidential phone and web-based help line providing a skilled and knowledgeable listening ear mainly to children but also to parents, carers, and others who have concerns about possible harm to children and will. Call-takers also advise any caller who wishes to report a child protection concern to the local authority children's services or the police on how to do so, and will make the referral on behalf of any caller who gives their consent and provides contact details. The responsibility for assessing and deciding whether to take the case further, either as a "child in need" or to start a formal child protection inquiry, rests with the local authority, in consultation with the police service if it appears that a crime may have been committed. However, most authorities have multidisciplinary arrangements (sometimes referred to as Multi-Agency Safeguarding Hubs (MASH). In 2016–17 the largest proportion of referrals to children's services (27.5%) was from the police, followed by schools (17.7%) and health services (14.4%). This has been a consistent pattern over the last few years (Department for Education, 2022). The range of services provided to children and families is discussed below. If the assessing social work team, having consulted with other professionals who have knowledge of family members, concludes that there should be a formal child protection investigation, procedures are clearly laid out in the *Working Together* guidelines. A strategy discussion (usually but not necessarily a meeting and usually involving an allocated social worker and a senior police officer and any health or school staff involved) decides whether the referral should be proceeded with as a child protection case, the timing of a Child Protection Conference, and the steps to be taken by each agency prior to the conference.

Multidisciplinary and inter-agency child protection conferences are a feature of the child protection services of most jurisdictions, but the degree of formality varies. The extent of involvement in the decision making of parents and older children varies, with some systems being more "paternalistic" in their approach (professionals meeting away from family members) and others holding meetings such as Family Group Conferences that include family members. The UK nations' practice of routinely inviting parents to child protection conferences at which decisions are taken about whether formal intervention is necessary is shared with a few other jurisdictions but is not common practice in all jurisdictions. In part, this difference has opened up because of the greater potential consequences to family integrity of UK legislation (see section below on care orders and adoption), and the stronger imperative to observe principles of natural justice with such serious potential irreversible consequences from the decisions taken at such meetings. However, it also follows from the provisions and guidance on the 1989 Act, which requires social workers to seek to involve family members as fully as possible in the services that are provided. (See section below on services.)

The conference has specific tasks: to decide whether the child has suffered or is likely to suffer significant harm, the nature of the maltreatment that has led to the harm or likely harm, whether a formal child protection plan is necessary, and, if not, whether a child in need service will be provided. The components of the Child Protection (CP) plan or in need plan will be decided in outline. A lead professional/key worker (usually the case accountable social worker) is named as well as members of a core group to work as a team around the family and to agree, with family members, the details of the work to be carried out. If a formal plan is agreed, the date of the review meeting will be set. The decision as to whether there is no longer a need for a formal protection plan has to be taken by a Review Child Protection Conference.

Child Welfare and Child Protection in Numbers

Because there is no formal system of reporting and substantiation of abuse allegations, data specifically on rates of abuse cannot be easily compared with other countries. National level data specifically on the known incidence of maltreatment are only available on those cases where a formally constituted multidisciplinary conference, convened following a formal child protection inquiry, concludes that maltreatment has occurred or is likely to occur, and for which there is need for a formally agreed child protection plan (usually cases of more serious abuse, or where an element of (administrative or judicial) coercion to ensure parental compliance is considered necessary.

Having said which, England has a robust administrative data collection system, using a unique identifier for each child. There are two sets of government provided data that are relevant to understanding the demands on the child welfare system: the children in need census (2022a) and the children looked after census (2022b). A minimum data set is published annually (see Table 7.1) on:

- Children referred as possibly "in need" of additional children's social care services (in 1920–21, 6% were considered to need no further action and 30% of those assessed were assessed as not needing a social care service). More detail is known about those assessed as and receiving a "child in need" service on a specified date (this includes those receiving a formal child protection service and/or placed in out-of-home care; the primary assessed need for over half of these was recorded as "abuse or neglect. See Table 7.2 for main reason for referral);
- Children who were assessed as possibly being in need of a formal child protection plan (Section 47 assessment) in the course of the year and at year end (this is the nearest equivalent in the English system to a report of abuse or neglect in a child abuse reporting system);
- Children assessed during the year and at year end as needing a formal child protection plan (the nearest equivalent available in the data for substantiated cases of child abuse or neglect);
- Children entering public out-of-home care during the year and in care at year's end. During the year 2020–21, 28,440 started an episode of being "looked after."

The largest proportion of children receiving a service as a child in care, in need, or in need of protection were aged 1–9 (34%), followed by children aged 10–15 (31%). However numbers aged 16+ (nearly 25% in 2021) increased by 6% since 2015. An increasing proportion (just under 6% of open cases in 2021) concerned unborn children or those under 1. Fifty-two percent were boys and 43% girls, with a small proportion where there was no information (mainly not-yet born).

If figures for 2020–21 are compared with those for 2009–10 it can be seen that, despite the increased pressures on families due to cuts in social security payments and especially increased family homelessness (CWIP, 2017), the rate of referrals has risen only slightly. A broadly similar rate per 1,000 children actually received a service (32 per 1,000 in 2021), but for a larger proportion than in 2009 this was under formal child protection provisions (child protection inquiry or child protection plan) or an "in care" service than under "children in need"/family support provisions.

Table 7.2 shows that the primary reason for needing a formal child protection plan in 2020–21 for 48% of the children was neglect, a slight increase on the 45% in 2009. The proportions for whom physical abuse or sexual abuse was the main category of concern had gone down over this period. The biggest change has been the rise in cases in which emotional abuse is the main category of concern (25% in 2009 and 38% in 2021), though it should be noted that there is a lack of clarity about whether concerns about emotional well-being should be categorized as (emotional) neglect, or emotional abuse. But the striking figure is that for 86% of the children with a child protection plan, the principal cause for concern was neglect or emotional maltreatment. This rise reflects a growing awareness of the long-term consequences of neglect and of the negative consequences of being exposed to inter-partner violence and parental substance abuse and mental ill health. Although not yet showing up in the child welfare statistics, three more recently recognized forms of maltreatment have been subjects of concern to the child protection agencies and government guidance. Grooming and sexual exploitation (increasingly via social media sites) of children and adolescents by mainly unrelated men, often alongside the provision of alcohol and drugs, has been a particular challenge to police, social workers, and health workers. Radicalization by religious or political extremists has also resulted in collaborative action and government guidance. Though still proportionately small in the child welfare statistics, there has recently been a substantial increase in reports to the police of suspected criminal offences in these two areas. The third relatively recent area for concern is female genital mutilation and the enforced marriage of children, which are particular issues for children of minority ethnic heritage (Bernard & Harris, 2016).

Out-of-home Care Services

Even when there is evidence of significant harm and the harm is attributable to a person with parental responsibility, the court can only make a care or (home) supervision order if it concludes that such an order is necessary. Just over half of the children who started to be looked after in 2020–21 did so under voluntary arrangements. This is a large drop from the average of over 60% in preceding years, which appears to show a change in policy and practice to a greater use of compulsory orders. However, if it appears that they may be unable to return quickly to parental care, and there is not a clear plan that can be agreed with the parents (most likely to happen if a longer term or episodic shared care arrangement for a child with a long-term disability), the local authority is likely to apply to the court for a care order. Eighty-two percent of those looked after at year end 2021 were the subject of a court order. There is provision for children to be cared for via a series of short-term placements (intended to be with the same kin or non-kin foster family or residential home). This is usually used for children with disabilities but can be used when parents have disabilities or are living in particularly stressful circumstances. These numbers are left out of the official looked-after children statistics. The main category of need at the time the child was placed in care for 66% was recorded as "abuse or neglect." Other categories were family stresses and relationship difficulties (23%), disability of child or parent (6%), child's difficult behavior (1%), and no parent to care for the child (5%—mainly made up of unaccompanied asylum-seeking children). However, since the data collection form asks only for the main reason, it is possible that other contributory factors played as important a part as maltreatment in the need for out-of-home care.

Children of black African and Caribbean heritage and those of dual heritage continue to be over-represented amongst care entrants, though to a lesser extent than in earlier periods. However, those of South and East Asian descent are less likely to come into care than are white British children (Barnard & Harris, 2016).

As can be seen from Table 7.3, during the past decade numbers and rates of children entering care and in care at year end have increased substantially. Over three

Table 7.3 Children in public out-of-home care in 2008–9 and 2020-21 (DfE, 2022b)		
	2008–9	2020–21
All looked-after children	60,900	80,850
Unaccompanied asylum-seeking children	3,900 (6%)	4,070 (5%)
Looked-after children as Rate per 1,000 children	5.5	6.7
All starting to be looked-after during year	24,400	28,440
Number in care (%) in kinship foster care	6,800 (11%)	12,430 (16%)
Number in care (%) in non-kin foster care	37,400 (62%)	57,340 (60%)
Number (%) in residential care	7,920 (13%)	11,540 (14%)
Number leaving care during year via an adoption order (% of all leavers)	3,200 (12%)	2,870 (10%)
Number leaving care during year via a Guardianship or Residence Order	2,170 (9%)	3,800 (13%)

quarters (76%) live in foster families (including around 16% in kinship foster care), and these proportions have changed very little. Within these figures, as noted above, the proportion of children placed with foster carers in the private for-profit sector has increased in the last few years from 18% in 2009 to over 50% in 2021. Not included in the table are 2% in "independent living" in the community, 7% still in care but placed with parents, 3% placed with adopters prior to legal adoption, and a small number in hospital care or in parent and child placements. Numbers placed in regulated children's homes, including hostels and secure units, remain fairly constant at around 14% but there is growing concern about the numbers (around 10%) living in "unregulated accommodation". Other changes of note are that the proportion placed with adopters and leaving care via adoption have gone down in the last few years from a peak of over 5,000 in 2016, whereas the proportions leaving care via a special guardianship or other private law order, mainly to a relative or friend, have gone up (13% of those who left care in 2020–21 did so via this route compared with 9% in 2008–9). An important and at times heated debate is around the placement for adoption of very young children without parental consent (referred to in the media as "coerced adoption") and government encouragement of a foster for adoption service based on the US "concurrent planning" model (Tickle, 2016; Featherstone, Gupta, & Mills, 2018). Appeal court judges have emphasized the requirement that adoption orders without parental consent can only be made "if nothing else will do" (FRG, 2017). In particular, questions have been raised by Members of the European Parliament and its rights sub-committees over the use of non-consensual adoption for non-UK children of nationalities where adoption from care is rarely used (Fenton-Glynn, 2015). Research on outcomes of kinship care and adoption as well as the accounts of family members (Thoburn & Featherstone, 2019; Thoburn, 2021) has demonstrated that a large minority of children placed with substitute families from care display seriously challenging behavior as adolescents, or even younger, and government has recognized the need of the children and parents for both financial and therapeutic support by setting up a fund on which adopters and guardians can draw. It should be said that, amongst the government-recognized "permanence options" (DfE, 2015b), the poor relation in terms of funding is support and services for children who return to a parent from care that extends beyond the early months after return. Yet outcome research has shown that this is the least successful "permanence" option (Thoburn et al., 2012; Farmer & Patsios, 2016; Neil et al., 2020).

Another important change has been the recognition of a long-term foster family placement as a permanence option and a change of regulations to provide a greater sense of stability to foster carers and children (DfE, 2015b). In 2013 legislation was implemented to encourage young people who are well settled with their foster family to "stay put" after 18, and for funding to the foster family to continue.

What Services and Supports Are Provided in the Family Home and Community?

The actual roles and tasks undertaken by a child and family social worker and other professionals will vary in breadth and depth depending on the setting in which he or she works. The main responsibility for coordinating and leading multi-agency teams providing services to children and families with additional needs (including child protection conferences, review and planning meetings) lies with local authority social workers (Taylor & Thoburn, 2016). In collaboration with children, their parents, carers, and professionals from other disciplines, they assess needs and risks to well-being and either provide directly or commission a range of practical and emotional support services, parenting training, and therapy. As noted above, the service may include short or longer term out-of-home care with or without applying for a court order. Social workers also have the main responsibility for recruiting, assessing, supervising, and supporting foster carers and prospective adopters. The emphasis is on providing a relationship-based creative and purposive casework service to children, parents, carers, or whole families. Within this, a broad range of approaches and methods may be used to fit the particular circumstances, but strengths-based and systemic approaches are widely used. Some methods used by social workers are shared with other professionals (e.g., basic counselling skills, family therapy, cognitive behavioral work, psycho-social history taking and life story work with children, welfare rights advocacy, marital counselling, and mediation). Some specific approaches and methods that are currently in fairly wide usage include motivational interviewing, restorative practice, and family group meetings. Manualized programs incorporated into practice in some areas include Signs of Safety (Turnell & Edwards, 1999) and Multi Systemic Practice (National Implementation Service website; Sebba et al., 2017).

Conclusions

Although there is clarity in England about the legal mandate for providing services to children and their families who need additional services, including formal child protection services, and systems are in place for providing reliable data, political and professional opinion is divided about the way forward in terms of priorities and management systems (Parton & Williams, 2017). Time limits for decision making, restrictions to service duration, and especially the closure of neighborhood-based family centers are militating against stated government policy for more resources to be deployed earlier to avoid problems escalating. Alarm is expressed by national and local politicians and service managers about the rising numbers being the subject of child protection plans and entering out-of-home care. There is tension between policymakers, practitioners, social work researchers, and theorists that can broadly be expressed as pitting a rights-based and participatory approach against one which favors greater use of short-term evidence-based interventions and interpretations of permanence policies that emphasize speedy decision making and placement with substitute families if parenting does not improve within these tight time frames (Featherstone et al., 2014; Jones, 2015; Featherstone, Gupta, Morris, et al., 2018). The Department for Education has introduced a Knowledge and Skills statement against which all social workers undertaking statutory work must be assessed and is providing funding for pilots of evidence-based methods to encourage new ways of working with those who need statutory social work services (DfE, 2013; Chamberlain & Little, 2017; Forrester, 2017). Some consider this narrows the focus of child and family social work and reduces the part that family members can play in determining the characteristics of the service to be provided (Featherstone et al., 2014; Featherstone, Gupta, Morris, et al., 2018 and see note 5 on the government-commissioned review of children's social care). Underlying these debates is the continuing decline in funding available to meet the increase in referrals for service as neoliberal policies shrink universally available public services. Whilst some policymakers and senior managers see outsourcing and commissioning from the independent sector as a way of confronting the current pressures, other local politicians and senior professionals—as with the Leeds local authority—have shown an interest in the New York approach, which has succeeded in cutting the numbers entering care (Tobis, 2016), and are following a more community-based approach (Mason et al., 2017).

References

Barnard, C. A. and P. Harris, P. (Eds.). (2016). *Safeguarding black children: Good practice in child protection.* Jessica Kingsley.

Brandon, M., Sorensen, P., Thoburn, J., Bailey, S., and Connolly, S. (2015). Turning points or turning around: Family coach work with "troubled families." *International Journal of Child and Family Welfare*, 16, 57–77.

Cabinet Office. (2000). *The Prime Minister's review of adoption.* Performance and Innovations Unit.

Casey, L. (2015). The national troubled families programme. *Social Work and Social Sciences Review*, 17(2), 57–62.

Chamberlain, C. and Little, M. (2017). Supporting practice: Reflections on a career in children's social work. *Journal of Children's Services*, 12(2–3), 122–126.

Child Welfare Inequalities Project. (2017). *Identifying and understanding inequalities in child welfare intervention rates.* CWIP.

Conservative Party Commission on Social Workers. (2007). *No more blame game: The future of children's social workers.* The Conservative Party.

Davies, K. (Eds.). (2015). *Social work with troubled families.* Jessica Kingsley.

Department for Education and Skills. (2004). *Every child matters.* DfES.

Department for Education. (2011). *The Munro review of child protection.* DfE.

Department for Education. (2014). *Rethinking children's social work.* DfE.

Department for Education. (2015a). *Working together to safeguard children.* DfE.

Department for Education. (2015b). *Permanence, long-term foster placements and ceasing to look after a child: Statutory guidance for local authorities.* DfE.

Department for Education. (2018). *Working together to safeguard children.* DfE.

Department for Education. (2022a). *Characteristics of Children in Need.* GOV.UK.

Department for Education. (2022b). *Children looked after in England including placed for adoption.* GOV.UK.

Family Rights Group. (2017). *Holding the risk: The balance between child protection and the right to family life.* FRG.

Farmer, E. and Patsios, D. (2016). *Evaluation report on implementing the reunification practice framework.* University of Bristol.

Featherstone, B., White, S., and Morris K. (2014). *Re-Imaging Child Protection: Towards humane social work with families.* Policy Press.

Gupta, A. and Mills, S. (2018). *The role of the social worker in adoption: Ethics and human rights.* BASW.

Featherstone, B., Gupta, A., Morris, K., and White, S. (2018). *Protecting children: A social model*. Policy Press.

Fenton-Glynn, C. (2015). *Adoption without consent: Study for the Petit Committee*. Citizens' Rights and Constitutional Affairs European Parliament.

Forrester, D. (2017). Outcomes in children's social care. *Journal of Children's Services*, 12(2–3), 144–157.

Home Office, Department of Health, DFES, Welsh Office. (1991). *Working together under the Children Act 1989*. HMSO.

Jones, R. (2014). *The Story of Baby P*. Policy Press.

Jones, R. (2015). The end game: The marketisation and privatisation of children's social work and child protection. *Critical Social Policy*, 35(4), 447–469.

Jones, R. (2018). *In whose interests? The privatisation of child protection social work*. Policy Press.

Laming Report. (2003). *The Victoria Climbié inquiry*. TSO.

Laming Report. (2009). *The protection of children in England: A progress report*. TSO.

Mason, P., Ferguson, H., Morris, K., Munton, T., and Sen, R. (2017). *Leeds family values evaluation report*. DfE.

Morris, K. (2012). Thinking family? The complexities for family engagement in care and protection. *British Journal of Social Work*, 42(5), 906–920.

Narey, M. (2016). *Residential care in England*. DfE.

National Audit Office. (2016). *Children in need of help and protection*. NAO.

Neil, E., Gitsels, L., and Thoburn, J. (2020). Returning children home from care: What can be learned from local authority data? *Child & Family Social Work*, 25(3), 548–556.

OFSTED. (2016). *Fostering in England*. OFSTED/National Statistics.

Parton, N. and Berridge, D. (2011). Child protection in England. In N. Gilbert, N. Parton, and M. Skivenes (Eds.), *Child protection systems: International trends and orientations* (pp. 85–96). Oxford University Press.

Parton, N. and Williams, S. (2017). The contemporary refocussing of children's services in England. *Journal of Children's Services*, 12(2–3), 85–96.

Purcell, C. (2020). *The politics of children's services reform: Re-examining two decades of policy change*. Policy Press.

Social Work Reform Board. (2012). *Building a safe and confident future*. DfE. Available at: https://www.gov.uk/government/uploads/system/uploads/attachment_data/file/175947/SWRB_progress_report_-_June_2012.pdf. Retrieved February 2, 2018.

Sebba, J., Luke, N., McNeish, D., and Rees, A. (2017). *Children's social care innovation programme final evaluation report*. DfE.

Stanley, N., Austerberry, H., Bilson, A., Farelly, N., Hargreaves, K., Hussein, S., Ingold, A., Manthorpe, J., Ridley, J., and Strange, V. (2014). Establishing social work practices in England: The early evidence. *The British Journal of Social Work*, 44(2), 367–383.

Thoburn, J. (2013). "Troubled families," "troublesome families" and the trouble with payment by results. *Families, Relationships and Societies*, 2(3), 471–475.

Thoburn, J. (2016). Achieving good outcomes in foster care: a personal perspective on research across contexts and cultures. *Social Work and Society*, 14(2). https://ejournals.bib.uni-wuppertal.de/index.php/sws/article/view/478. Accessed July 20, 2022.

Thoburn, J. (2021). Adoption from care in England: learning from experience. In T. Poso, M. Skivenes, and J. Thoburn (Eds.), *Adoption from care: International perspectives on children's rights, family preservation and state intervention* (pp. 17–32). Policy Press.

Thoburn, J., Cooper, N., Brandon, M., and Connolly, S. (2013). The place of "Think Family" approaches in child and family social work: Messages from a process evaluation of an English pathfinder service. *Children and Youth Services Review*, 35(2), 228–236.

Thoburn, J., Robinson, J., and Anderson, B. (2012). *Returning children from public care*. Social Care Institute for Excellence Research Briefing 42. Available at: http://www.scie.org.uk/publications/briefings/briefing42/.

Thoburn, J. and Taylor, J. (2016). *Collaborative practice with vulnerable children and their families*. CRC Press.

Thoburn, J. and Featherstone, B. (2019). Adoption, child rescue, maltreatment and poverty. In S. Webb (Ed.), *Routledge Handbook of Critical Social Work* (pp. 401–411). Routledge.

Tickle, L. (2016). "I saw his fluffy little head going out of the door": One woman's fight to keep her baby. *The Guardian*, February 20.

Tobis, D. (2016). How New York City's parents took on the welfare system—and changed it. *The Guardian*, February 24.

Turnell, A. and Edwards, S. (1999). *Signs of safety: A solution and safety oriented approach to child protection casework*. Norton.

Tunstill, J., Allnock, D., Akhurst, S., and Garbers, C. (2005). Sure Start local programmes: Implications of case study data from the National Evaluation of Sure Start. *Children and Society*, 19(2), 158–117.

Tunstill, J. and Blewett, J. (2009). *The delivery of targeted family support in a universal setting.* Action for Children.

Tunstill, J. and Thoburn, J. (2019). The 1989 England and Wales Children Act: The high-water mark of progressive reform? In T. Bamford and K. Bilton (Eds.), *Social work: Past, present and future* (pp. 157–172). Policy Press.

United Nations. (1989). *Convention on the Rights of the Child.* United Nations.

Child Protection in Finland and Sweden

Ingrid Höjer *and* Tarja Pösö

Abstract

This chapter discusses Finland and Sweden's child protection which is based on the principle that children's overall well-being need a wide range of universal services and benefits. Child protection measures are only evoked when the children and families' universal services and needs are insufficient to ensure children's well-being. However, vulnerability related to socio-economic factors is often overlooked when child protection issues are at hand. The chapter notes the differences between the Swedish and Finnish systems with regards to legislation, organisation, decision-making, and practice of child protection.

Key Words: Finland, Sweden, legislation, organisation, decision-making, child protection, socio-economic factors, children, families, universal services

Introduction

In international comparisons, Finland and Sweden are typically described (e.g., Gilbert et al., 2011) as belonging to the Nordic or Social Democratic Welfare State models and family-service orientated child protection systems. Indeed, child protection in Finland and Sweden rests on the principle that children's overall well-being requires a wide array of universal services and benefits. Every child—or family with children—is entitled to receive social welfare, health care, and education services and benefits. Some services, such as maternity health care, child clinics, and education, are free of charge and others charge fees on a sliding scale subsidized by public funds. Child protection measures only come into play when these universal services are insufficient to assure children's well-being. These measures are based on the assessment of children's and families' needs rather than on that of the risks. Children and families who receive child protection services often have complex needs which have not been met by other services and other forms of support. The needs typically relate to parents' mental health problems, severe substance abuse, and family conflicts, including violence within the family and child abuse, and teenagers' conflicts with social norms. Additionally, parents who receive services from child protection units often have difficulties financially supporting themselves and their children—in many cases due to the above-described problems. The vulnerability connected to socioeconomic factors is often overlooked when child protection matters are discussed (Lundström & Sallnäs, 2003; Socialstyrelsen, 2006b).

With the emergence of the universal welfare state services in the 1940s and 1950s, placements in out-of-home care gradually decreased in both countries. Parents—in this case (poor) single mothers—had better opportunities to care for their children and, consequently, there was less need to take children into care. The development of publicly financed daycare for children was an important factor for single mothers to be able to support themselves and their children. However, it is difficult to identify established connections concerning the number of children in care and the welfare state as the interaction between the life situation of families, the welfare state, and the child protection system are complicated (Lundström & Sallnäs, 2014; Pösö et al., 2014). Despite the variety of services and support given to families, children are still maltreated in both countries and taken into care. Even progressive legislation has not abolished the need for child protection removals. For example, Sweden and Finland were among the first countries in the world to forbid corporal punishment; yet children are still exposed to violence in their homes (Ellonen et al., 2017). A recent study on the self-reported use of violence revealed that the use of violence against children was related to the mothers' (based on Finnish data only) and fathers' (based on both Swedish and Finnish data) own experiences of corporal punishment during their childhood. Socioeconomic factors did not play any significant role whereas, among the mothers especially, the risk of severe violent acts was higher among those who felt that they had not received adequate help in dealing with problematic situations with the child (Peltonen et al., 2014). The latter finding is a fundamentally critical remark about the availability, focus, and quality of services.

Despite several similarities between these countries and their approaches to child protection, a closer look reveals some fundamental differences between the Swedish and Finnish systems regarding legislation, organization, decision making, and the practice of child protection (e.g., Blomberg et al., 2010; Blomberg et al., 2012; Höjer et al., 2017).[1] Therefore, the chapter is organized so that enough attention is given to the differences. Its aim is to examine the organization of the child protection systems in Finland and Sweden on a fairly descriptive level while the implementation and the effects of the systems are given lesser attention.

Child Protection Services: The Main Principles and Eligibility Criteria

Parents are expected to look after and bring up their children in both countries; the role of the public services is to assist parents in their task through universal services and measures, as well as through specific needs-based services provided by separate legislation. In Finland, the Child Welfare Act (417/2007) sets the frame for child protection measures.

---

[1] The Finnish analysis was written as part of the project funded by the Academy of Finland (decision 308 402).

Sweden does not have specific legislation for child protection. Voluntary measures concerning child protection cases are employed according to the Social Services Act (SSA) and mandatory measures—when children and young people are taken into care without the parent's consent—according to the Care of Young People Act (CYPA). In both countries, it is the social services in the municipalities that have the responsibility to protect and support children and young people according to the national legislation.

The Finnish child protection legislation covers children aged 0–17, but aftercare services can be given until the age of 25. Child protection services are available for everyone registered as a resident in Finland. Those in Finland without registered residence are entitled to emergency child protection measures under the Child Welfare Act. In Sweden, the SSA defines a "child" as any person under the age of 18. Following the CYPA, mandatory measures can be used until the age of 21. According to the SSA, municipalities are responsible for all those who reside in their area whether they have a residence permit or not. In this chapter, when we refer to "child" or "children," we include all individuals 0–18 years of age in Finland and those 0–20 years of age in Sweden.

The Child's Best Interest Principle

Both countries have ratified the UN Convention on the Rights of the Child. The principle of the child's best interest is the overarching principle which should influence the assessment of eligibility criteria and all services and decisions made in child protection cases in Finland and Sweden. The principle presented in the Finnish Child Welfare Act reflects the Convention on the Rights of the Child (Child Welfare Act 417/2007, § 4). Likewise, in Sweden, the principle of child's best interest should always be the first priority according to the SSA, Chapter 1, § 2. This principle has been reinforced in a recent amendment of the SSA. There is an understanding that the assessment of the child's best interest is a process which should be grounded in scientific knowledge and information from those who know the child and from the child herself or himself (Socialstyrelsen, 2013b).

Mandatory Reporting and Parents' and Children's Requests for Services

Both countries have mandatory reporting systems. A variety of authorities and professionals working with children and families are obliged to notify child protection services: in Finland, if they have a reason to think that the child's needs for child protection services should be assessed due to her or his needs for care, conditions which might threaten her or his development or her or his behavior (Child Welfare Act 417/2007, § 25) and in Sweden, if children and young people are at risk and private persons should report if they have knowledge about children being exposed to risk (SSA, Chapter 14, § 1). All people have the right to notify child protection services. In addition, parents and children can apply for support and help. Upon notification of a possible problem, the social services have to start an assessment concerning the child/young person's situation and the need for support.

In addition, in Finland, an anticipatory notification can be given in the case of a pregnant woman if there is a reason to think that the child might need child protection immediately after birth. In that case, services should be given to the pregnant woman, and the child's needs for child protection services would be assessed at the moment of birth.

The Eligibility Criteria

In Finland, once a child becomes known to social services, the first step is to make "the assessment of the needs for services" (*palvelutarvearvio*). This term is important as it emphasizes "assessment" instead of "investigation." The key focus is on evaluating the conditions in which the child lives and the prospects of parents—or other carers—taking care of the child and her or his upbringing. This assessment should be done within certain time limits: it should start within seven days and be finalized within three months unless an immediate response is needed. The child will be registered as a client in the child protection system (Child Welfare Act 417/2007, § 27) if the outcome of this assessment is that:

1) the circumstances in which the child is being brought up are endangering or failing to safeguard her or his health and development; or
2) that the child's behavior is endangering her or his health and development; and
3) that the child needs services given according to the Child Welfare Act.

As a result of the assessment, the child may receive in-home services. If the child is in immediate danger, an emergency placement will be initiated. If the child is in need of some services but the above criteria are not met, the family, based on their agreement, will be given services according to the Social Welfare Act (2014). These services, family work, home help, therapeutic guidance, and family support, for example, are needs-based and differ from universal services.

If it turns out that the in-home services are not sufficient to support the family and to alleviate the problems, a care order may be issued. The criteria for a care order are:

1) the health or development of the child are at serious risk of being endangered by a lack of care or by other circumstances in which the child is being brought up; or
2) the child's health or development are seriously endangered by the child's abuse of intoxicants, by the child committing an illegal act other than a minor offence or by any other comparable behavior;
3) the in-home measures are not suitable for providing care in the interests of the child or if the measures make this impossible; and

4) substitute care, following the care order decision, is judged to be in the child's interest. (Child Welfare Act 417/2007, § 40)

In Sweden, the eligibility criteria differ depending on whether the services are given by the SSA or by the CYPA. As in Finland, the general aim of the child protection system is to identify parents' and children's problems and to find ways to help and support families (Wiklund, 2008). This is emphasized in the SSA, which regulates the responsibilities of the social welfare committees and the access to social support for citizens. Once contact is established between the child/young person, his or her family, and social services, either by an application or a notification, the aim is to find the relevant type of support that will meet the particular needs of the child/young person. When possible, the assessment is supposed to be done through discussions with the child/young person, the parents and the child protection social workers. Measures could be directed towards the child/young person or towards the parents/custodians. The latter type of support is more frequent when it comes to younger children (Socialstyrelsen, 2016).

If voluntary measures are not possible, the CYPA will be used in Sweden. As in Finland, there has to be serious problems in relation to the home environment or to the parent's and/or the young person's behavior. There also has to be a tangible risk of damage to the child's or young person's health, well-being and development. Furthermore, it must be shown that the necessary care cannot be provided on a voluntary basis. An emergency placement can be ordered if there is an imminent risk to the child's/young person's health or development, or problems that bar a timely completion of the investigation.

The criteria for involuntary care measures include serious endangerment, which makes a fundamental difference between the in-home services and care orders. The definition of "serious endangerment" is not elaborated in either the Finnish or Swedish legislation. There are also very little other instructions to guide social workers in assessing the seriousness of the risk. As a result of a care order, the child will be placed into foster care or residential care. Here, the child moves from private care into public care. In both countries, parents retain their custodial rights, but their rights as parents are considerably restricted as the most important decisions concerning the child will be made by the child protection authorities while the child is in care. Care order decisions are only valid "for the time being" and the needs for a care order are assessed, together with children and parents, at least once a year in Finland and every sixth months in Sweden. In both countries, the explicit aim is to reunify the parents and children. Thus, contact between the child and his or her parents and other networks is kept up during the placement. Adoption is not a placement option in out-of-home care provided by child protection.

The Trends of Children in Out-of-home Care
The number of children in out-of-home care in both countries includes children placed for voluntary purposes, emergency care, and care orders. It is important to note that one

Table 8.1 The number of children in out-of-home care (during the year)

	Finland: the number of children (per 100 children 0–17 years) (Flow)	Sweden: the number of children 0–20 (per 100 children 0–19 years) (Flow)	Sweden: Number of children 0–19 (stock)	Gender (Sweden)	Gender (Finland)
1995	10,739 (0.9)	* (0.8)	*	*	5,559 boys, 5,180 girls
2000	12,673 (1.1)	17,698 (0.8)	14,000 (0.7)	9,472 boys, 8,226 girls	6,741 boys, 5,932 girls
2005	15,716 (1.4)	19,939 (0.9)	15,200 (0.7)	10,373 boys, 9,566 girls	8,007 boys, 7,249 girls
2010	17,204 (1.5)	24,365 (1.1)	17,200 (0.8)	13,764 boys, 10,601 girls	9,122 boys, 8,082 girls
2015	17,689 (1.7)	29,473 (1.3)	21,051 (0.9)	17,648 boys, 11,825 girls	9,325 boys, 8,364 girls

Notes: * = exact data is lacking.

Sources: Sources in Finland: Lastensuojelu (2017), Liitetaulukko 8; Sotkanet (2018). Population numbers from www.stat.fi. Sources in Sweden: Socialstyrelsen (2001, 2006, 2011, 2017). Population numbers from www.scb.se.

child may be placed in out-of-home care several times during the course of care (and during one year): first as part of voluntary, supportive services, then by an emergency care decision, and finally, by a care order decision. The data in Table 8.1 show that the number of children in care has continually increased in both countries over the last two decades.

Some Reflections on the Eligibility Criteria

In Sweden, the relationship between the eligibility criteria of the SSA and the CYPA is worth reflecting upon. When the SSA was introduced in 1982, it noticeably echoed a new perspective in social work that focused explicitly on equality, participation, and consent. Voluntary measures should be used with the consent of parents and children. Mandatory measures were only to be used when all efforts to create voluntary consent had failed. The legislation clearly stated that the first priority for social workers is to find a way to cooperate with parents—and children—if possible (Leviner & Lundström, 2017). Leviner (2017) questions this and argues that the foundation for this construction of consent is problematic as it presupposes that social welfare clients are always able to make decisions, plan, and cooperate with social services, even in very stressful situations. Leviner claims that there is an obvious risk that "coercion is hidden in voluntary measures and that coercion is used where voluntary measures could have been chosen" (Leviner, 2017, p. 143, author's translation). This criticism is well known in Finnish child protection as well, although the voluntary and involuntary services are organized differently from Sweden (Pösö et al., 2018).

Furthermore, the SSA implied a more restrictive attitude towards out-of-home placements—whether voluntary or mandatory. Family problems should be prevented by early interventions in families, and such interventions should be based on voluntary participation and consent. The intention was to focus on preventive measures and thus avoid out-of-home placements. If such placements were deemed to be necessary, children should stay in touch with their parents and be reunified with them as soon as this was possible (Lundström & Sallnäs, 2014).

The emphasis on voluntary services has been equally employed in Finnish child protection since the change in child protection legislation in 1983. When the present Child Welfare Act was introduced in 2007, the processes for assessing needs and making decisions were specified, but the eligibility criteria remained the same (Valjakka, 2016). The threshold for emergency removals has, however, been specified: when the child is in immediate danger, the criteria for an emergency placement should be the same as for a care order. In addition, the new Social Welfare Act (1301/2014) has a lower threshold of need to provide services to children and families with children, aiming to prevent the need for child protection through early support.

Child Protection Services: Voluntary Support and Coercive Removals

The assessment of children's needs after a child protection notification or request for services may itself, if done thoroughly and in cooperation with the family, generate momentum for a change in the family's life (Hietamäki, 2015). As an outcome of the assessment, the family may be directed to the family and child services provided based on the Social Welfare Act or to those provided by the Child Welfare Act in Finland. In Sweden, the assessment takes the child and family either to the voluntary services provided by SSA or to the compulsory measures provided by the CYPA. Regardless of the legislation, the measures will be tailored, together with the child, family, and social workers, and the parents and the child should be involved in the planning processes. The priority is always to give voluntary in-home services.

In-home Services

In Sweden, in-home services by the SSA include structured non-institutional care programs (for example, summer camps, support, systematized contact with a social worker) and a contact family/contact person. The Finnish child protection system also provides family work, care and therapy services to the family and the child and other support services. Family work—assistance provided to the homes of families—is one of the most common, but also one of the contested, forms of in-home service (Heino, 2008). It is not clear, for example, how family work provided by the Social Welfare Act differs in practice from family work provided by the Child Welfare Act. It is also possible to place the child out-of-home as part of these services. The placement should be short-term and only for assessment, support or rehabilitation purposes. Unfortunately, the availability of services influences the plans made with the family. There is, for example, a shortage of support person/families in many parts of the country and the waiting lists for child and youth psychiatric care are long. Nevertheless, the in-home services appear to make adequate changes in families' and children's lives as only a fraction of the children receiving in-home services are taken further into public care.

Needs-tested non-institutional measures have increased by 20% since 2001 in Sweden. This goes particularly for the structured non-institutional care programs: 57 municipalities out of 290 used manual-based support for parents with children with problematic behavior, 32 municipalities used manual-based psycho-social treatment for young people with norm-breaking behavior, and 42 municipalities used manual-based support groups for children and young people from families with psycho-social problems (Socialstyrelsen, 2013a). No similar information is available for Finland. Nevertheless, the number of children receiving in-home services has increased since the 1990s in Finland: 3.1% of all children under the age of 18 received in-home services in 1998 compared to 7.5% in 2014 (Sotkanet, 2018). In 2016, the figure decreased to 4.6% as the new Social Welfare Act had been introduced and similar services were provided by that act, resulting in the decline of in-home services given by the Child Welfare Act.

A contact/support family is expected to be an "ordinary family with the qualification of having an extra capacity for others" (National Board of Health and Welfare, 1985, p. 7), where a child/young person can stay for a limited amount of time, usually one or two weekends per month. The contact family/person was introduced as a measure in 1982 in Sweden, following the focus within the SSA on voluntariness and self-determination. The idea was to give relief and support to the child's parents—in most cases single mothers (Regnér & Johnsson, 2007). For many years the contact family/person was the most used non-institutional measure in social work with children and families, but over the last decade, the use of this measure has decreased (Socialstyrelsen, 2013b). One reason for this decrease might be the results from a performed register study. The researchers found that no positive effects could be observed for those who received the measure of a "contact family" and that there was a higher prevalence for being taken into out-of-home care for this group (Vinnerljung et al., 2011).

Care Orders and Out-of-home Placements

When non-institutional measures are not sufficient for attending to the child or young person's needs, the alternative will be out-of-home placements and care orders. In both countries placements in foster care are preferred to placements in residential care. Swedish authorities have explicitly announced that residential care should only be used for emergency placements or for children and young people with severe behavioral problems. Thus, the majority of out-of-home placements are in foster care. The Finnish legislation emphasizes the principle of the child's best interest: residential care is only considered as a placement option if it serves the child's interest better than a foster care placement.

In both countries, placement with kin needs to be considered as an option in every case. If kin placement is not possible, other ways to support contacts between the child and the family are important. The Swedish legislation, for example, explicitly states that a placement in out-of-home care should be located as close to the child's home as possible and the care provided should promote the child's connection to her or his parents and other relatives, and also promote contact with the home environment (SSA Chapter 6 § 1; CYPA § 14).

Emergency Placements

When a child is in immediate danger, it is possible to place them into emergency care. In Finland, the emergency placement may last up to 30 days, to be continued for another 30 days if necessary. In Sweden, the length of the emergency placement is four weeks.

Aftercare Services

In Finland, aftercare services are available for children who have been taken into care and, under some circumstances, for those children who have been in out-of-home care as part of in-home services. The eligibility criteria include a requirement that the child (or young adult) gives his or her consent to receive these services. If he or she does, the obligation of the municipality is to provide the services according to the plan made by the child and the social worker. The right to receive aftercare services expires at the age of 25.

In Sweden, the law states that social services shall provide support to those who leave a placement in out-of-home care (Socialtjänstlagen, Chapter 5 §1). However, this provision is rather vague. There is no specification about the nature of this support nor the length of time a young person is entitled to receive it. As a consequence of this weak and general legislation, there is a lack of policies and processes concerning how to work with young people leaving out-of-home care (Höjer & Sjöblom, 2011).

Decision Making

In both countries, social workers are the key practitioners receiving notifications, making assessments and working with children and families. They make many decisions as well. Indeed, in Finland licensed social workers are the people responsible for decision making about the services children are entitled to receive under the Child Welfare Act. Since July 1, 2014, according to the SSA, Chapter 3, § 3, social workers in Sweden who are in charge of child protection assessments have to be qualified social workers (i.e., have a BA in social work or comparable credentials). It is also of importance that they have experience in child protection work; thus, the employing municipalities have to provide a relevant introduction and mentoring to newly employed social workers.

When it comes to decisions about child removals, however, the decision-making systems are very different. The CYPA regulates the placing of children and young people into care without the parents' or children's consent in Sweden. In such cases, social workers' assessments are presented to local the Social Welfare Committee and then forwarded to the County Administrative Court that makes the formal decision for placements in care. In cases where parents and children give their consent, the placement decision is made by the Social Welfare Committee. The difference between these two types of placement is that the child taken into care as a coercive measure may experience more restrictions of contact and movement (including placements in secure institutions) than the child in voluntary care. In addition, the child and parents can decide when to exit care if the decision was consent based. In 2019, 31,100 children and young people were placed in out-of-home care some time during the year: 78% were placed in care using voluntary measures from SSA (Chapter 4 1§), and 22% were placed in care using coercive measures from the CYPA (§§ 2, 3, and 6) (Socialstyrelsen, 2020).

One element is, as Leviner (2017) points out, that the foundation for consent is problematic, as mentioned in the text above. The possible misuse of consent is an especially delicate issue regarding the parents (mothers especially) of newborns who may be in a vulnerable situation after the birth, psychologically as well as physically.

Swedish law requires that every municipality has a board—a social welfare board— which deals with issues connected to the SSA and the CYPA. Political parties nominate the members of these boards. The members are all laypersons, with no requirements to have specific knowledge of child protection (Svensson & Höjer, 2017). The use of laypersons in this decision-making capacity is debated. Critics observe that laypersons lack specific knowledge of children's needs and thus will not be able to fully understand the consequences of their decisions. There are concerns that the system might lead to a de-professionalization of social work in the municipalities and that financial matters in the municipalities will be prioritized over children's and young person's needs. Others consider the public control of involuntary measures to be a positive feature of this local system, which can keep politicians informed about the situation for children and young people in the municipality (SOU, 2015, p. 71; Sveriges kommuner och landsting (SKL), 2017).

Discussing the decision-making role of laymen, Lundström (2017) notes that if the organization of Swedish child protection was invented today, it is unlikely that this system would be in place wherein important decisions concerning the lives of children are made by politicians and not professionals. However, the professional social workers' assessments are seldom questioned or refused by the laymen on the Social Welfare Boards (Höjer et al., 2017).

The Finnish decision-making system of care orders operates on two levels, based on the parents' or the child's (12 years or older) consent and objection (Pösö & Huhtanen, 2017). If the child (at least 12 years old) and his or her parents (guardians) give their consent to the care order proposal and to the proposed substitute home, the care order decision will be made by the leading social work authority in the municipality. These are designated "voluntary care orders." If there is any objection, the decision will be made by the administrative court. It has a panel of three—two judges and one expert member—to make the decision regarding "involuntary care orders." Although the decision-making body is different for voluntary care orders (where it is the local social welfare authority) and involuntary care orders (where it is the administrative courts), the consequences are similar in both cases in Finland. When the child is placed in care based on a care order decision, parental rights are restricted and the child is under the supervision of the public authorities. Certain restrictive measures may be imposed, but only under certain conditions, based on separate formal decisions. Most restrictive measures require that the child is placed in residential care; if she or he is placed in a foster home, only a decision about a restriction of contact can be made (Huhtanen & Pösö, 2018).

In both countries, the decision-making processes are supposed to involve children, parents, and other close people who receive relevant information and whose views are considered in different parts of the process. All children, regardless of age, should be heard. However, when children are aged 12 or older, their views have the same procedural impact on the decision-making process as that of their parents in Finland (as described above). In Sweden, a young person over 15 is entitled to plead his or her case, and voluntary measures can be taken against the will of the parents.

The Organization and Financing of Service Provision

The measures to support children and families are provided by the tax-financed social services in each of the 290 municipalities in Sweden and in 311 municipalities in Finland. The municipal service provision is guided by local governments, which are primarily steered by politically chosen local councils and boards, according to the local elections. The diversity among municipalities and their social and political profiles are reflected in different bundles of service provision in Finland (Harrikari, 2014). The right to make any decisions on the individual level—for example, the provision of in-home services—belongs to those who are employed by the municipality in Finland, whereas in Sweden the local social welfare bodies make decisions about individual child protection matters.

The task for the municipalities to provide services does not necessarily mean that they need to produce the services. At the moment, the municipalities finance the services but the production and delivery of services may be performed by other bodies, such as coalitions of municipalities, NGOs, and private enterprises. The contracts between the municipality and service providers are based on competitive bidding in which the quality of services and the efficiency and costs of the services are examined. Typically, the criteria and measurements for good quality are shaped by each municipality. The provision of residential care services by private profit-making agencies has been strong for the last 10 years or so, resulting in a situation in which 80% of all the residential services are provided by private agencies in Finland, suggesting that the municipalities have very few children's homes or youth's homes of their own (Porko et al., 2018). In addition, a variety of in-home services, such as family work and family rehabilitation, are purchased from companies. There are some hints that municipalities are considering re-introducing the provision of services produced by them themselves. Nevertheless, the trend towards privatization is likely to remain strong in the future in Finland.

The situation is similar in Sweden: over the last decades, there has been a huge increase of the private provision of child protection services (Meagher et al., 2016). This goes for both foster and residential care. The implication for foster care has been that private agencies provide foster care to social services in the municipalities. Foster carers recruited by such private organizations are supposed to get more support and supervision than other carers, recruited by the municipalities, and consequently the cost for placements are higher. The idea is that these foster parents should be able to care for children with more complicated problems, such as behavior difficulties and/or neuropsychiatric diagnoses. In 2015, 96% of the Swedish municipalities had used such private foster care (*kunsulentstödd familjehemsvård*), and about one third of the collected days in care (*vårddygn*) were provided by private foster care (Myndigheten för vård- och omsorgsanalys, 2016). For residential care, there has been a great increase of residential homes where care is provided by a for-profit organization. In 1980, less than 10% of residential care was in the private sector—which at that time meant only non-profit organizations. In 2014, if homes for unaccompanied asylum-seeking children were excluded, 70% of residential homes were operated by for-profit organizations (Meagher et al., 2016). As out-of-home placements are financed through public taxation, this has been a debated issue in Sweden. There is substantial criticism towards for-profit companies in the care sector.

The costs for child protection services are entirely financed through public taxation in the municipalities in both countries. The municipalities are responsible for all the connected costs—both when it comes to non-institutional measures and out-of-home placements. The budgets are made annually on the national level (to transfer the funds to the municipalities based on the population, its age structure, and other such factors) and on the local level (to transform the funds into different types of public services). Due to the independence of the decision making of the municipalities, influenced by local elections and related political views, the budgets available for child protection services may vary considerably from one municipality to another and from one year to another, as has been pointed out in Finland (National Audit Office of Finland, 2012, pp. 168–172).

There is a growing interest in estimating the costs of child protection in Finland. However, the expenditures on child protection services are not clearly separated from other services given to children and families in the national and local budgets. In addition, the wide array of in-home services (e.g., support families) is also very difficult to put a price on, and children may have a very diverse collection of services while in the child protection system (Heinonen et al., 2012). Consequently, there are no reliable estimates of expenditures on child protection services to cover the whole country. The six largest Finnish towns do, however, estimate that they spent more than 349 million euros in 2017 on child protection services,[2] the average costs varying between 11,976 euros and 22,073 euros per child under the age of 20. The majority of their expenditure is targeted on out-of-home care (Hiekkavuo & Forsell, 2018). In Sweden, the average cost for a placement in foster care, including both the remuneration to foster parents and the cost for board and lodging, is 120,000–140,000 SEK per year (Sveriges kommuner och landsting, 2019).

How Does It Work?

Although both Finland and Sweden rank highly in different international comparisons of children's well-being (see, e.g., UNICEF Office of Research, 2013) and their child protection systems are defined as being orientated towards family services, the countries still draw a lot of criticism about the quality, adequacy, and efficiency of their child protection services.

Finnish child protection has been the topic of several policy programs, reviews, and debates since the number of children in the child protection system has increased since the mid-1990s. The concerns have been about the expenditure on child protection, the quality and timing of services and the outcomes of the interventions, among other topics (see, e.g., Tuloksellisuuskertomus, 2012; Sosiaali- ja terveysministeriö, 2013), and most recently, the moral distress among social workers due to heavy workloads and the shortages of resources (see, e.g., Alhanen, 2014; Mänttäri-van der Kuipp, 2016). In a survey of 817 social workers in public social welfare, 11% reported experiencing moral distress which influenced their willingness to continue in their post (Mänttäri-van der Kuipp, 2016). The Social Welfare Act, introduced in 2014, aimed to provide services to families with children with a low problem-threshold (early intervention) and now the government programs intend to increase multi-agency responses to families as early as possible and with a low threshold. Although evidence-based methods (EBP) and interventions are increasingly employed to help families to bring up children, they are rarely introduced to child protection services in Finland, whereas evidence-based social work, in general, has become more established in Sweden than in Finland (Hübner, 2016). The reasons for this difference are speculated to be related to a campaign in Sweden in which contacts between representatives of the Swedish authorities and proponents of a radical EBP version in the United States have played an important role, but such proponents seem to be absent in Finland. The length of the education of social workers in Finland and the focus on academic skills in the education are also seen as

---

[2] GDP per capita in 2016 was 43,737 US dollars in Finland and 49,084 in Sweden (OECD data 2018).

contributing factors as education makes them more independent of external demands (Hübner, 2016). This is reflected in the child protection arena, where there are more studies aiming to explore "what works" in Sweden than there are in Finland. In addition, the systematic use of research knowledge has not yet taken root in child protection services in Finland (Pekkarinen, 2011).

There are a few issues which are recognized, but not sufficiently addressed, by the present child protection systems. In Sweden, mental health problems among children and young people, and the availability of treatment, in particular children's and young people's access to mental health care, are often recognized in current debates about child protection and public health. This problem is well known in Finland as well; in order to address these needs of children and young people, better cooperation between child protection and health care is required. Sweden has included undocumented children as receivers of child protection services, which is different from Finland. Here the issues with children who have migrated to Finland—the first or second generation of migrants—present a relatively new challenge to Finnish child protection services.

Conclusions

We started our chapter by saying that Finland and Sweden share many similarities in their approaches to child protection, but they also differ. Indeed, the overall philosophy of the Nordic welfare state and the role of the municipalities shape child protection in both countries. However, the very notion of "child protection" is rather different in these two countries as Sweden separates voluntary and involuntary measures by two different pieces of legislation, the first one being more about "social welfare" and the latter being more about "child protection." Finland only has one act—the Child Welfare Act—which covers all measures taken for child protection purposes. Yet the introduction of the new Social Welfare Act in 2014 makes the border between "child protection" and "social welfare" more blurred in Finland than before. Consequently, both countries seem to struggle with how to position child protection services among other services for children and families. In addition, both countries seem to struggle to find good ways to help children in need. Despite all the efforts given to support children and families, there are still concerns about the welfare of children both in and outside of the child protection system.

References

Alhanen, K. (2014). *Vaarantunut suojeluvalta—Tutkimus lastensuojelujärjestelmän uhkatekijöistä* [Compromised power of protection—a study of threats to the child welfare service system]. Report 24. Terveyden ja hyvinvoinnin laitos.

Blomberg, H., Corander C., Kroll, C., Meeuwisse, A., Scaramuzzino, R., and Swärd, H. (2010). A Nordic model in child welfare? In H. Forsberg and T. Kröger (Eds.), *Social work and child welfare politics: Through Nordic lenses* (pp. 29–46). Policy Press.

Blomberg, H., Kroll, C., and Meeuwisse, A. (2012). Nordic social workers' assessments of child welfare problems and interventions: A common model in child welfare. *European Journal of Social Work*, 16(3), 311–326.

Child Welfare Act 417/2007. Available at: http://finlex.fi/fi/laki/kaannokset/2007/en20070417_20131292. pdf. Retrieved May 30, 2018.

Ellonen, N., Peltonen, K., Pösö, T., and Janson, S. (2017). A multifaceted risk analysis of fathers' self-reported physical violence toward their children. *Aggressive Behavior*, 43(4), 315–418.

Gilbert, N., Parton, N., and Skivenes, M. (Eds.). (2011). *Child protection systems: International trends and orientations*. Oxford University Press.

Harrikari, T. (2014). Social disorganization and the profile of child welfare: Explaining child welfare activity by the community-level factors. *Child Abuse and Neglect*, 38(10), 1671–1682.

Heino, T. (2008). *Lastensuojelun avohuolto ja perhetyö: kehitys, nykytila, haasteet ja kehittämisehdotukset* [In-home services and family work in child protection: development, present situations, challenges and proposals for further development]. Working papers 9. Stakes.

Heinonen, H., Väisänen, A., and Hipp, T. (2012). *Miten lastensuojelun kustannukset kertyvät?* [What do the costs in child protection consist of?] Lastensuojelun Keskusliitto, Terveyden ja hyvinvoinnin laitos. Available at: https://www.lskl.fi/materiaali/lastensuojelun-keskusliitto/Miten_lastensuojelun_kustannuks et_kertyvat.pdf. Retrieved May 30, 2018.

Hiekkavuo, A. and Forsell, M. (2018). *Kuuden suurimman kaupungin lastensuojelun palvelujen ja kustannusten vertailu vuonna 2017* [The comparison of child protection services and expenditure in six largest towns in 2017]. Kuusikko—työryhmä. Available at: https://www.hel.fi/hel2/tietokeskus/julkaisut/pdf/18_06_ 20_Lastensuojelu_raportti_2017.pdf. Retrieved January 9, 2019.

Hietamäki, J. (2015). *Lastensuojelun alkuarvioinnin vaikutukset vanhempien näkökulmasta* [The outcomes of the assessment in child welfare from the parents' perspective]. Jyväskylän yliopisto.

Huhtanen, R. and Pösö, T. (2018). Restriktiva åtgärder i det finska barnskyddet—ett stöd för barns rättigheter, eller enbart att spärra in barn? [Restrictive measures in Finnish child protection: Supporting children's rights or just locking children up?]. In S. Enell and S. Gruber (Eds.), *Kontrollerade unga: Tvångspraktiker på institution* [Young people in control: Coercive practices in institutions] (pp. 213–234). Studentlitteratur.

Hübner, L. (2016). Reflections on knowledge management and evidence-based practice in the personal social services of Finland and Sweden. *Nordic Social Work Research*, 6(2), 114–125.

Höjer, I. and Sjöblom, Y. (2011). Procedures when young people leave care: Views of 111 Swedish social services managers. *Children and Youth Services Review*, 33, 2452–2460.

Höjer, S., Forkby, T., and Hultman, E. (2017). *Mot bättre beslut* [Towards better decisions]. Sveriges Kommuner och Landsting.

Lastensuojelu 2017 [Child Welfare 2017]. *Statistical report 17*. Terveyden ja hyvinvoinnin laitos, Suomen virallinen tilasto. Available at: http://www.julkari.fi/bitstream/handle/10024/136409/Tr17_18_LASU. pdf?sequence=5&isAllowed=y. Retrieved January 9, 2019.

Leviner, P. and Lundström, T. (Eds.). (2017). *Tvångsvård av barn och unga* [Coercive care of children and young people]. Wolters Kluwer.

Leviner, P. (2017). *Samtyckeskonstruktionen i LVU: En analys av gränsdragningen mellan frivillighet och tvång, grundantaganden om människans autonomi samt barns begränsade självbestämmanderätt* [Consent construction in LVU: An analysis of the boundary between voluntary and compulsory measures, basic assumptions about human autonomy and children's limited self-determination]. In P. Leviner and T. Lundström (Eds.), *Tvångsvård av barn och unga*. (Coercive care of children and young people). Wolters Kluwer.

Leviner, P. and Lundström, T. (Eds.) (2017). *Tvångsvård av barn och unga*. Wolters Kluwer.

Lundström, T. and Sallnäs, M. (2003). "Klass, kön och etnicitet i den sociala barnavården" [Class, gender and ethnicity in child protection]. *Socialvetenskaplig tidskrift*, 10(2), 193–213.

Lundström, T. and Sallnäs, M. (2014). "Social barnavård under 30 år – mer av samma eller något nytt?" (Child welfare during 30 years – more of the same or something new?). In U. Pettersson (Ed.), "Tre decennier med Socialtjänstlagen – utopi, vision, verklighet" (Three decades with the Social Services Act – utopia, vision, reality). Gleerups Utbildning AB.

Lundström, T. (2017). Från sedlig försummelse till brister i omsorgen, om barnvårdslagstiftningens historia (From moral deficiencies to neglect – the history of Child Welfare legislation) In P. Leviner and T. Lundström (Eds.), *Tvångsvård av barn och unga* (Coercive care of children and young people). Wolters Kluwer.

Meagher, G., Lundström, T., Sallnäs, M., and Wiklund, S. (2016). Big business in a thin market: understanding the privatization of residential care for childrenand youth in Sweden. *Social Policy and Administration*, 50(7), 805–823.

Mänttäri-van der Kuip, M. (2016). Moral distress among social workers: The role of insufficient resources. *International Journal of Social Welfare*, 25(1), 86–97.

Myndigheten för vård- och omsorgsanalys [Agency for Care and Care Analysis]. (2016). *Hittar vi hem? En kartläggning och analys av den sociala dygnsvården för barn och unga* [How can we find a home? A survey and an analysis of placements in out of home care for children and young people]. Myndigheten för vård- och omsorgsanalys. Rapport 2016:5.

National Audit Office of Finland. (2012). *Tuloksellisuuskertomus: Astensuojelu* [Performance management report: Child welfare]. Report 6, National Audit Office of Finland.

OECD Data. (2018). Gross domestic product. Available at: https://data.oecd.org/gdp/gross-domestic-product-gdp.htm. Retrieved January 23, 2019.

Pekkarinen, E. (2011). Lastensuojelun tieto ja tutkimus: Asiantuntijoiden näkökulma [Knowledge and research in child welfare: The view of experts]. Nuorisotutkimusverkosto & Nuorisotutkimusseura & Lapsuudentutkimuksen seura & Lastensuojelun Keskusliitto & Terveyden ja hyvinvoinnin laitos. Available at: http://www.nuorisotutkimusseura.fi/julkaisuja/lastensuojeluntieto.pdf. Retrieved January 9, 2019.

Peltonen, K., Ellonen, N. Pösö, T., and Lucas, S. (2014). Mothers' self-reported violence toward their children: a multifaceted risk analysis. *Child Abuse Neglect*, 38(12), 1923–1933.

Porko, P., Heino, T., and Eriksson, P. (2018). *Selvitys yksityisistä lastensuojelun yksiköistä* [Report about the private child protection units]. Working paper 28. THL. Available at: http://urn.fi/URN:ISBN:978-952-343-131-7. Retrieved June 8, 2018.

Pösö, T., Skivenes, M., and Hestbaeck, A. (2014). Child protection systems within the Danish, Finnish and Norwegian welfare states: Time for a child centric approach? *European Journal of Social Work*, 17(4), 475–490.

Pösö, T. and Huhtanen, R. (2017). Removals of children in Finland: A mix of voluntary and involuntary decisions. In K. Burns, T. Pösö, and M. Skivenes (Eds), *Child welfare removals by the state: A cross-country analysis of decision-making systems* (pp. 18–39). Oxford University Press.

Pösö, T., Pekkarinen, E., Helavirta, S., and Laakso, R. (2018). "Voluntary" and "involuntary" child welfare: Challenging the distinction. *Journal of Social Work*, 18(3), 253–272.

Regnér, M. and Johnsson, L. (2007). The "ordinary" family as a resource for single parents: On the Swedish contact family service. *European Journal of Social Work*, 10(3), 319–336.

Socialstyrelsen [National Board of Health and Welfare] (1985). *En vanlig människa. Om kontaktpersoner/kontaktfamiljer i socialt arbete* [An ordinary man: On contact persons/contact families in social services]. Socialstyrelsen redovisar.

Socialstyrelsen. (2001). *Barn och unga- insatser år 2000* [Measures concerning children and young people during 2000]. Socialstyrelsen.

Socialstyrelsen. (2006a). *Barn och unga- insatser år 2005* [Measures concerning children and young people during 2005]. Socialstyrelsen.

Socialstyrelsen. (2006b). *Social Rapport* [Social notifications]. Socialstyrelsen.

Socialstyrelsen. (2011). *Barn och unga- insatser år 2010* [Measures concerning children and young people during 2010]. Socialstyrelsen.

Socialstyrelsen. (2013a). *Nya bestämmelse för den sociala barn- och ungdomsvården: Uppföljning av 2013 års ändringar av Sol och LVU* [New regulations for child protection: A follow up of changes from 2013 in SSA and CYPA]. Socialstyrelsen.

Socialstyrelsen. (2013b). *Barns och ungas hälsa, vård och omsorg 2013* [Health, care and welfare of children and young people]. Socialstyrelsen.

Socialstyrelsen. (2016). *Utreda barn och unga. Handbok för socialtjänstens arbete enligt Socialtjänstlagen.* (Assessing children and young people. Handbook for social services according to the Social Services Act). Stockholm: Socialstyrelsen.

Socialstyrelsen. (2020). *Barn och unga- insatser år 2019* [Measures concerning children and young people during 2019]. Socialstyrelsen.

Sotkanet. (2018). *Tilastotietoja suomalaisten terveydestä ja hyvinvoinnista* [Statistical information on welfare and health in Finland]. Available at: from https://www.sotkanet.fi/sotkanet/fi/haku?g=354. Retrieved May 30, 2018.

SOU. (2015):71. *Barns och ungas rätt vid tvångsvård: Förslag till ny LVU* [Children and adolescents right in compulsory care: Proposal for new LVU]. Socialdepartementet.

Sosiaali- ja terveysministeriö [Ministry of Social Affairs and Health]. (2013). *Toimiva lastensuojelu* [Functioning child welfare]. Report 19. Sosiaali- ja terveysministeriö.

Svensson, G. and Höjer, S. (2017). Placing children in state care in Sweden: Decision-making bodies, laypersons and legal framework. In K. Burns, T. Pösö, and M. Skivenes (Eds.), *Child Welfare Removals by the State* (pp. 65–88). Oxford University Press.

Sveriges kommuner och landsting (SKL) [Swedish Municipalities and County Councils]. (2017). *Ersättningar och villkor vid familjehemsvård av barn, unga och vuxna, vårdnads överflyttningar m.m. för år 2018* [Remunerations and regulations for foster care and removals of custody]. Cirkulär 17(5).

UNICEF Office of Research. (2013). *Child well-being in rich countries: A comparative overview.* Innocenti Report Card 11. UNICEF Office of Research. Available at: https://www.unicef-irc.org/publications/pdf/rc11_eng.pdf. Retrieved May 30, 2018.

Valjakka, E. (2016). *Vain lakiko suojelee lasta?* [Is it only law to protect the child?]. Turun yliopisto.

Vinnerljung, B., Brännström, L., and Hjern, A. (2011). *Kontaktfamilj/person för barn—uppföljning och utvärdering med registerdata* [Contact families/persons for children- a follow up and an evaluation using register data]. University of Stockholm: Rapport 138 i Socialt Arbete. (Report 138 in Social Work).

Wiklund, S. (2008). Individ och familjeomsorgens barnavårdsarbete. (Social services work with children and families). In Å. Bergmark, T. Lundström, R. Minas, and S. Wiklund (Eds.), *Soialtjänsten i blickfånget. Organisation, resurser och insatser. Exempel från arbete med barn och ungdom, försörjningsstöd och missbruk.* (Focus on Social Services. Organisation, resources and measures. Examples from social work with children and young people, social assistance and drug and alcohol abuse). Natur och Kultur.

Child Protection and Welfare in France

Flora Bolter

Abstract

This chapter explicates child protection and welfare in France. The overall structure of France's child protection system relies on collaboration between the justice system and social services, the latter implementing virtually all care orders through the *département*-based *Aide sociale à l'enfance*. The main sources of funding for social action are fiscal after it devolved to *départements* as a consequence of the decentralization of state competencies. The chapter also notes the types of danger, local disparities, and principles of intervention. It looks into how the French child protection and welfare system is based on national solidarity and profoundly territorialized since most issues are connected to a lack of data and consistency over the territory.

Key Words: France, child protection, welfare, social action, territory, national solidarity, ASE, départements, decentralization

France is one of the major economies of the European Union and, with an estimated 67.06 million inhabitants, all territories combined (64.9 million of whom live in metropolitan France, and of whom 14.42 million are below the age of 18, or 21.5% of the French population; INSEE [Institut national de la statistique et des études économiques], 2020a, 2020b), also one of its demographic heavyweights. The macroeconomic context, as it is summarized by the French government's 2019 National Reform Program, points to a number of broad realities that have an impact on children and young people: massive structural unemployment despite a very slow downward trend (around 8.8% of the active population in 2019; the unemployment level of young people in particular has never descended below 15% in thirty years), slow economic growth (1.5% in 2019) and the ambivalent consequences of important public expenditure and deficit on the economy.

However, the broad realities that can be understood at the national level are misleading when it comes to describing the situations faced by children in practical terms, because the territories that comprise France are very diverse and their evolutions divergent. The average population density, for instance, is 106 inhabitants per square kilometer overall; but the Île-de-France region has 1,022 while Corsica has 40 and the overseas region of Guyane only 3 (INSEE, 2020c). While an estimated 32% of children in France are born to one or more parent(s) not born in France, they are 52% in Île-de-France, the Paris region (INSEE, 2020d). These are just a few indicators of the diverse social and economic realities across France.

In this context, France's very centralized administration has since the 1980s initiated a shift towards a necessary decentralization of social services in general. The *département*, a territorial and administrative level inherited from the French revolution, has been given more and more responsibility in terms of managing local services and defining priorities. For child welfare and protection, Law No 2007-293, passed on March 5, 2007, has formalized this new logic and acknowledged the local leadership of the *départements*, marking a new step in the devolution of this policy. It should be noted, however, that the flurry of new legislation voted in 2022 marks a limited shift toward more involvement by the state, with child protection being presented as a "shared policy" between state and *département* and the multiplication of "contracts" to incentivize *département* adherence to government priorities.

Other evolutions are still taking shape in child protection and welfare in France, and they concern the principles behind interventions. A major paradigm shift has been marked by Law No 2016-297 (2016): from an initial definition connected to preventing and identifying situations of danger within the family, as defined by the Civil code, article L 112-3 of the Code for social affairs and families now clearly proposes a definition that references the child (and the child's rights) as the focus of intervention and emphasizes the notion of developmental needs. Child protection now aims to "ensure that the child's fundamental rights are taken into account, their physical, affective, intellectual and social development supported, and their health, security, morality and education safeguarded with due regard to their rights."

Départements and their services are, in practice, still adapting to these various changes. Making sense of the commonalities and differences within the child welfare and protection system is a challenging endeavor, particularly in a time of rapid evolution. This chapter will focus on the superstructure of the system at national and *département* level before highlighting the main realities in practice. Finally, it will describe the main challenges that are currently emerging, as well as the attempts to tackle them.

The Child Protection and Welfare System in Context: An Outline

National Solidarity: Funding and Legislation

FRANCE'S WELFARE SYSTEM

The social dimension of the French state is strongly emphasized as one of its key components. This is even affirmed in Article 1 of the 1958 Constitution: "France is an indivisible, secular, democratic and social Republic." Paragraphs 10 and 11 of the preamble to the 1946 French constitution (which is one of the elements forming the current body of constitutional rules and principles in France) state that national solidarity shall ensure the "health, material security, rest and leisure" of all, including children, mothers, and the elderly.

This universalist dimension is, however, based on a work-related funding model relying on contributions by employers and employees: Esping-Andersen (1990) lists the French welfare system within the state-corporatist "bismarckian" models, though it has been "upgraded to cater to the new 'post-industrial class structure" (p. 27). Indeed, since 1999, all persons living in France can have access to some health insurance, even if they don't work or cannot contribute to work-related funding schemes. But the resulting system depends on an intricate network of various employment-related structures inspired by the mutualist model, though all of it is state-related.

Indeed, France's social expenditure is predominantly public: in 2018 (latest accessible data for OECD, 2021), public social expenditure was 733,627.8 million euros, while mandatory and voluntary private social expenditure barely reached 84,360.2 million euros (the proportion of all social expenditure represented by the private sector has, however, been steadily rising since the 1980s). The centralized, public nature of the welfare system is one of the reasons France's aggregated social expenditure reaches 31% of GDP in 2019, the highest rate of all OECD countries.

Despite the competitive disadvantage and public deficit issues that are the flip side of a heavily public system, the health and public interest services thus provided are generally well regarded, especially when it comes to health. "Public financing of health care expenditure is among the highest in Europe and out-of-pocket spending among the lowest" according to WHO, which also stresses that, "The French population has a good level of health, with the second highest life expectancy in the world for women. It has a high level of choice of providers, and a high level of satisfaction with the health system," despite the system's structural shortcomings in terms of prevention and integration of services, and despite important social and territorial health inequalities (Chevreul et al., 2015).

The public school system is another public system of note when it comes to examining the situation of children and families. In 2018, some 2-year-olds (11.5%) and virtually all 3-year-olds (97.0%) attended school (INSEE, 2020f).

The universal-access social transfer system is also a fairly important asset when considering the situation of families in France. In 2017, the monetary poverty rate in France is 14.1% with poverty intensity at 19.6%. "These two indicators would respectively reach 22.1% and 40.9% of the population without the existence of social and fiscal transfers" (DREES [Direction de la recherche, des études, de l'évaluation et des statistiques], 2020a, p. 37).

Universal-access social services, under the purview of the *département*, are also readily available across the territory, along with child-and-mother health protection services called PMI (for *protection maternelle et infantile*) that provide free healthcare for young children.

Although this is an indication of the resources available to parents and children, it should be noted that the French system, while very effective in ensuring minimal living standards, health, and access to education, has three main weakness points that should be mentioned when detailing the general context for children and families.

The first weakness point is that the system is very complex and difficult to navigate: non-take-up is a very real issue that most NGOs and local actors are concerned with, and that crops up time and again in France's National reform plan (see, for instance, Direction générale du Trésor, 2019, p. 51). Eighty-four percent of patients seen by NGO Doctors of the World in their France consultations in 2016 had no health coverage, while 79% of them were eligible for it (Observatoire de l'accès aux droits et aux soins de la mission France, 2018). Thirty-one percent of legally resident families with two children or more seen by the NGO Secours catholique in 2017 did not receive family benefits (Activity Report for the year 2017, quoted in Observatoire du non-recours aux droits et services, 2018). For many families, especially those who do not speak French very well or aren't familiar with the system's intricacies, many services are de facto unreachable.

The second weakness is the importance of social and territorial inequalities. What is accessible in each *département* in terms of healthcare, education and social action is vastly different, a fact that the World Health Organization has underlined in its analysis of the French healthcare system (Chevreul et al., 2015). When it comes to social inequalities all over the country and their effects, it should be noted that the school system, although it is accessible to all and is traditionally considered the epitome of "meritocracy" tasked with guaranteeing social mobility (Brown et al., 2010), is currently failing students of disadvantaged areas. Their educational results have been deteriorating steadily while their peers' in more affluent areas have been improving (Mattei & Aguilar, 2016). This is true across different types of results (Bruckauf & Chzhen, 2016). The OECD Programme for International Student Assessment (PISA) 2018 report underlines this tendency to reinforce inequalities rather than counter them, across all subject matters.

Finally, a more general concern in terms of public policies should be made explicit: the overall system relies on an important level of public expenditure, which as a macroeconomic issue can have consequences on the perennial nature of the existing system. Indeed, France's National Reform Program for 2019, as in 2017, makes reducing public spending one of its core strategic goals. The way the system is funded and organized, in other words, has been in crisis for some time and is the object of much political debate and speculation.

CHILD PROTECTION: AN INTER-SECTORAL COLLABORATION

In this general framework, child welfare and protection services are referred to as *Aide sociale à l'enfance* or ASE (literally: "social help for children") and have been gradually devolved to the *départements* since 1982. All *départements* combined, ASE represents an 8.3 billion euro public expenditure in France in 2018, which corresponds to 20.79% of all *département* spending for social action. Over three quarters

(79.37%) of this sum corresponds to placement in foster care or residential institutions (DREES, 2020b).

In terms of population, there were an estimated 306,800 children receiving one or more ASE interventions or service in 2018, or 21 per thousand of all under-18s in France (Mayotte excepted). In-home ASE interventions represent 49.6% of the total number of interventions, and out-of-home placement 50.4% (this was the first time since 2003 that out-of-home decisions outnumbered in-home interventions). For children, the overwhelming majority of out-of-home placement decisions are made by the judicial system. Young adults (from 18 to 21 years of age) receiving one or more ASE intervention or service are an additional 21,400, or 9.1 per thousand of the general population of 18-to-21-year-olds at the same time (ONPE, 2020a).

For young adults, the overwhelming majority of interventions (in all but eight *départements*) are placement/housing-related (ONPE, 2020b).

The overall structure of the French child protection system relies, as in many countries, on a collaboration between the justice system and social services (ONPE, 2016a). Virtually all services and interventions are carried out by *département* social services (ASE), either directly or indirectly through accredited third-sector associations funded by and closely associated with the *département*. An additional service, *Protection judiciaire de la jeunesse* or PJJ (literally: "judicial protection of youth"), is a branch of the ministry of Justice and carries out some welfare and protection interventions for children or young adults in conflict with the law, but this is a very small percentage of the total.

However, not all decisions are *département*-based. In 2015, 89.3% of all placements and 69.9% of all in-home interventions and services were initiated as a result of a decision by the justice system. The main distinction between the judicial track and the ASE track lies in how receptive the parents are or can be to an intervention: judicial decisions are warranted for situations where the child is "in danger" according to article 375 of the Civil code, but ASE is only required to refer a situation to the justice system when one (or more) of three additional conditions is present:

1) The child has already undergone one or more interventions in the framework of Article L 222-3 and L 222-4-2 and Article L 222-5 (1), and these interventions have not remedied the situation;

2) Even if no previous intervention mentioned in section 1 has taken place, such interventions cannot take place because the family refuses to accept the help offered by ASE services or because there is no possibility to initiate a collaboration between the service and this family;

3) The danger in question is severe and immediate, particularly in situations of ill-treatment (*maltraitance*).

(Article L 226-4 of the Code for social action and families, author's translation)

In other words, a judicial decision is theoretically only necessary when there are no parents available, or when they refuse the intervention or service proposed by ASE, or when multiple interventions have already failed, or when there is an element of emergency such as when child abuse is suspected. In all other situations, the idea is to obtain the parents' consent and if possible, support. The overall desire to maintain family ties, which is an overarching principle for social workers, also translates into a drive for more social service-based interventions as opposed to judicial orders. Since 2007, one of the driving principles of public intervention for child welfare and protection has been to put an emphasis on social services, and hence to the *départements* that are in charge of them. But reporting patterns and the harsh realities of many situations encountered by services make this very difficult, and judicial decisions still remain the majority of all decisions.

Adapting to Local Realities: The Département as a Driving Force
LOCAL PROCEDURES AND PRIORITIES

Départements have gradually been tasked with social action, including child protection, since the 1980s. As a consequence, they have become the main operational level in that field and have been recognized as such in legislation by Law No 2007-293 (2007). The president of the *département* council is now considered the local leader (*tête de file*) of child protection and welfare and this has led to the creation of a new triage system to determine whether a situation requires judicial intervention or not: the CRIP, for *Cellule de recueil des informations préoccupantes* (unit for the collection of all information giving rise to concern).

Organized at *département* level by ASE services, this unit involves professionals from all relevant sectors and aims to fluidify the exchange of information between judicial and social branches of child protection. All information reported to the *département* regarding a suspected situation of child(ren) in danger—either by social workers or by any person fulfilling their obligation to report—is centralized and analyzed by this intersectoral team to determine the best course of action and transfer the relevant elements to social services for assessment or to the specialized branch of the justice system to take action when it seems necessary. Much information is, however, not sent to this unit but rather to the justice system or to a national child helpline (119—Allô enfance en danger) either because the person giving the information doesn't know how/that they can contact the CRIP or because they feel there is an emergency. When this is the case, the information is sent to the CRIP, with information as to what emergency actions, if any, have been taken.

The CRIP is therefore in possession, inasmuch as possible, of all information "giving rise to concern" (*information préoccupante*), an expression used to clarify that the information does not need to be fully substantiated or immediately life-threatening before being given, and that therefore one should not hesitate to share one's concerns, even when not completely certain. This means that the *département*, in charge of the CRIP, is uniquely equipped to identify the local necessities and priorities.

In addition to CRIP, the *schéma départemental* (literally "local diagram") is a priority and procedure document drafted periodically by the *département* to list its priorities and objectives, and to clarify the existing structures and services that are involved in child welfare and protection at the local level. This involves ASE and the justice system, but also various services according to the local context: the local school board is usually represented in CRIP and/or the *schéma départemental*, as well as hospitals, health professionals, and the civil sector. A thorough examination conducted by ONPE in 2011 of the local protocols signed by the various *départements* gives an idea of the diversity of partnerships involved and highlights the discrepancies in how the law is interpreted and situations approached between territories.

Finally, one last tool has been created by the 2007 Law to help monitor and draft policy at the local level: the local observatory of child protection (*Observatoire départemental de la protection de l'enfance*, ODPE). This entity is mirrored at the national level by ONPE (*Observatoire nationale de la protection de l'enfance*), which provides quantitative estimates and qualitative studies to better understand child protection and promote best practices. However, a November 2020 report by the Court of Auditors on the French child protection system underlines that all recent reforms of child protection have been incompletely and differently implemented from one *département* to the next, and that the data collection system operated by ONPE, which has been set up over the past 12 years, is not likely to yield sufficient and/or comparable data in the near future: although the overall theoretical framework for the child protection system is set up by law—as well as the tools for piloting at local and national level—insufficient and inconsistent follow-through at implementation level prevent the system from being effective or manageable.

All in all, as a result of devolution and this inconsistent implementation, it is very difficult to give a unified description of the French child protection system and its priorities. There are 101 *départements* in France, and 101 ways to orchestrate the collaboration of services that is the child welfare and protection system, despite the common legislation.

FUNDING SERVICES AT THE LOCAL LEVEL

Since *départements* are very different in socioeconomic terms, an obvious difficulty raised by this highly decentralized system is that those *départements* whose population is less affluent are also those who will need to compensate more in terms of social action.

And indeed, the main sources of funding for social action are fiscal in nature and have been devolved to the *départements* as a consequence of the decentralization of state competences in terms of social action. Indirect taxation is the main source of funding for social action in France, representing 40% of all revenue devoted to social action (all in all, *départements* raised 61.3 billion euros and spent 69.7 billion euros for social action in 2018; indirect taxation represented a 28.1 billion revenue). This includes transfer rights, taxes on insurance contracts, and part of the consumption of energy tax. Direct taxation by the *département* is another major source of revenue, accounting for 22.4 billion euros in 2018 or 32.1% of all social-action funding. This includes various housing and property taxes, as well the added-value contribution for companies. Finally, direct state funding, of 16.4 billion euros, contributed 23.5% of all *département* revenue for social action, mainly through a general operating grant *(dotation globale de fonctionnement*, DGF). This operating grant has been on a constant downward spiral since 2013 (DREES, 2020b).

The relative importance of *département*-based direct taxation as opposed to the national solidarity principle represented by the operating grant points to a situation of risk for the least wealthy *départements*: as the social needs increase so too can local taxation, which results in a comparatively higher tax burden. In some *départements* in mainland France, where mobility is a factor, this can be a challenge.

A new process introduced by the October 14, 2019 National Strategy for Child Protection has introduced an additional funding mechanism from the state to the *départements* for local child protection policies, without increasing the overall operating grant: this takes the form of contracts whereby willing *départements* take on projects and schemes that correspond to national priorities for child protection, and receive additional funding. Eighty million euros were provisioned for the year 2020 for these contracts. While this additional funding is needed, it is conditional and significantly reframes the state/*département* relationship.

Policies and Programs at the Practice Level

Children in Care and Types of Intervention
TYPES OF DANGER AND PRINCIPLES OF INTERVENTION

As we have previously seen, 306,800 children and 21,400 young adults receive some form of intervention or service from the child welfare and protection system, with a majority of these interventions and services being decided by the justice system and almost all of them being carried out by ASE services, directly or through an accredited NGO.

Why have these children and young adults entered the child protection system? Understanding the various realities that they face is a long-term endeavor for which OLINPE, the longitudinal and national observation system for child protection *(Observation longitudinale et nationale en protection de l'enfance)*, has been set up by law in 2007 under the responsibility of ONPE. No consolidated figures exist at the national level yet, but more and more *départements* have been sending data that can give a general idea of the trajectories of children in care. The reasons why they are in care remain, however, difficult to grasp at a national level.

As previously described, the operational concept behind child protection and welfare intervention in France is not child maltreatment per se, but rather the notion of danger for the "health, security, morality, and education" of children and their development. This idea, introduced in Article 375 of the Civil Code and still the basis for judicial intervention, used to be the reference for ASE as well: the rationale was for social services to intervene in situations of risk, that is, before the situation of danger as defined by a judge could develop. This notion is still sometimes used in practice despite the very recent legal shift to a more positive definition of child protection intervention in terms of meeting the child's developmental needs with regard to their rights. In practical terms, the assessment of the situation the child is in (and its potential to become dangerous) is articulated to the capacity parents have to be a protective force for their children: the subsidiarity principle is operative. In other words, not all maltreated children are in ASE care (if their parent(s) are able to protect them effectively in cases where the maltreatment is not their doing, for instance), and not all children in ASE care are maltreated (failure to meet the child's needs is not necessarily understood as abuse or neglect), so the population in care cannot be equated to the population of maltreated children (regardless of the issue of unreported cases or "dark figure" of maltreatment). OLINPE and child protection data should therefore not be considered child maltreatment data, but they do underline important facts about the child protection and welfare system.

It should be mentioned here that estimating the scope and realities of child abuse and neglect is one of the ongoing problems faced by children's rights advocates in France. In 2016, the UN Committee on the Rights of the Child, not for the first time, commented that it was "deeply concerned about the absence of official statistics and the existence of reports that in the State party an estimated two children die each day, potentially as a result of domestic violence" (United Nations Committee on the Rights of the Child [UNCRC], 2016, concluding observations, para. 27).

The justice-related data collection system does not currently have capacity to give consolidated data on child abuse and neglect, though some data are accessible through the open portal data.gouv.fr, for instance on homicides of children under the age of 15. Using law enforcement data from the SSMSI (*Service statistique ministériel de la sécurité intérieur*) database, ONPE has published since 2017 a yearly estimate of homicides and manslaughters of under-18s. It thus estimates that 122 children died in 2018, 80 of whom from violence in the family. Two-thirds of these 80 victims were under the age of 5, and a slight majority were girls (44; ONPE, 2020a).

Victimization studies, by which the prevalence of different types of violent incidents is usually estimated, are numerous in France, but they don't specifically focus on violence or adversity experienced during childhood. *Événements de vie et santé*, a survey conducted by DREES in 2006 (DREES, 2010) on 10,000 respondents aged 18–75, is perhaps the most detailed source of information so far on self-reported experiences of child abuse and neglect among respondents aged 20–75. It highlights that 15% of men and 8.4% of women (11.6% total) report having experienced sustained physical violence in childhood/adolescence (only 6.1% of those men and 12.3% of those women received help from child protection services—8.5% total); that 0.2% of men and 2.5% of women (1.4% total) report having experienced repeated sexual violence in childhood/adolescence (only 7.8% of those men and 19.7% of those women received help from child protection services— 18.8% total); and that 11.6% of men and 16.7% of women (14.2% total) report having experienced a severe lack of affection in childhood/adolescence (only 12.5% of those men and 12.7% of those women received help from child protection services—12.6% total).

Other large-scale surveys give different insights on life experiences. The ongoing survey ELFE (https://www.elfe-france.fr), conducted by the French demographic institute INED, is expected to shed much-needed light on these events and others when completed. VIRAGE, a large-scale survey on experiences of violence by women and men, already gives a few elements, and estimates thus that 18% of female respondents and 13% of male respondents have experienced violence inside their family before the age of 18.

Finally, the child helpline 119—Allô enfance en danger publishes a yearly statistical analysis on the basis of calls it has received, and more specifically on those calls that have led to a report of information giving rise to concern being sent to a local unit. The definitions used by this statistical analysis are very close to the WHO nomenclature of child abuse and neglect. Categories include psychological violence toward child(ren), physical violence, severe neglect, sexual violence/sexual abuse, compromised education conditions without severe neglect, and behavior that endangers their security or morality as the different types of danger in any given situation. The same given situation can and frequently does involve more than one type of danger: on average, for the period 2010– 2014 examined by ONPE (2016b), 1.4 types of danger are mentioned for one situation. Psychological violence, on the same period, is the most frequently mentioned, being present in 35.5% of cases. Physical violence (22.9%) and severe neglect (20.6%) come next, followed by compromised education conditions (14.1%), then behavior of the child(ren) (3.6%), and sexual violence (3.4%). Although these data cannot be extrapolated because they cannot be considered representative of all child protection situations, they do include situations from all areas of France over a significant period of time and they give some indication regarding the range and prevalence of dangers by type.

TYPES OF INTERVENTION AND LOCAL DISPARITIES

To respond to these situations, the decision taken by the judge or by ASE services in cooperation with families (and under the nominal authority of the *département* council's president) can take many different forms. The overall diagram of child welfare and protection presented by ONPE (2016a) lists the main types of interventions found all over the territory.

If the main problems the family faces are socioeconomic in nature, the service or intervention provided can take the form of simple financial help, or of a social worker providing support in family budget management (*mesure d'accompagnement en économie sociale et familiale*) or in everyday tasks when there are short-term problems (*technicien.ne d'action sociale et familiale*, TISF).

If the problems faced by the family are more complex, and typically require educative or relational help, then a specialized social worker, an educator, can take action in a more durable way with the child and the family. This is called "educative assistance" (*assistance educative*).

For young adults with little to no parental protection (primarily those who were in care as children), a specific type of service exists, called *contrat jeune majeur*, which allows for some intervention and financial help to reach autonomy after the age of 18.

All the types of services and interventions we just mentioned keep parents and children together. They are therefore referred to as "open settings" (*milieu ouvert*) interventions. They represent roughly half of all interventions. This does not mean they are necessarily requested by the family or initiated with the agreement of the parents. In fact, 69.6% of all open-settings interventions and services are judicially mandated at the national level (ONPE, 2017a).

The other type of ASE interventions and services involve taking primary care of the child(ren). They fall into the category of placement. For some very specific situations, the parent(s) can be with the baby/child: this is the case with *centre parentaux*, that provide services and help for parents-to-be and new parents who are particularly vulnerable around the birth of their first child, and *accueil mère-enfant* services which provide shelter and care for mothers with children under the age of 3 who need temporary help.

The majority of placements, however, are for children who are deprived of parental care or need to be temporarily separated from their parents. A growing majority of placement interventions (around 58% on average) are in foster care (ONED [Observatoire national de l'enfance en dange]/ONPE, 2015a), although France still has small-scale residential institutions as well as alternative/innovative types of placement. Kinship care, whereby a child is placed with a member of the extended family, is still limited in France, with *tiers dignes de confiance* (literally: "trusted third-party persons"), the official title for a relative to whom a child is entrusted as opposed to a professional foster carer, being the small minority. As Tillard and Mosca (2016, p. 9) note: "In 2013, of 154,691 children in placement in metropolitan France, only 10,452 are entrusted to a relative, corresponding to 6.8% of all placements outside the parent(s)' home." This may change in the next few years, however, as articles 1 through 18 of Law No 2022-140, passed on February 7, 2022, prioritize placement within the extended family when possible.

Placement of a child is always temporary in nature, with pluri-disciplinary reviews being made at least once every year, or every six months for a child under the age of 2 (Article L. 223-1 and 5 of the Code for social action and families).

A specific form of placement concerns children who are definitively deprived of parental care and whose care is therefore completely entrusted to ASE: this refers to children who are declared wards of the state (*pupilles de l'Etat*). This can happen (in 37% of cases in 2018) because the child has no known parents, such as in cases of abandonment at birth or childbirth under secrecy (550 children in 2018). The latter is a system by which a woman can give birth without her name being recorded as the child's parent and directly entrust the child to ASE—the child then only becomes a full ward of the state after a two month's waiting period in which the birth parent(s) can claim parenthood (Bolter et al., 2018). Becoming a ward of the state can also happen as the result of being orphaned (for 10% of instances in 2015). Or it can be the result of a decision by a judge stripping parents of their rights (less than 7.2% of all wards of the state) or acknowledging that the parent(s) has/have not tried to contact the child in over a year, despite having had the possibility to do so (45% of all wards of the state): this is called *délaissement* and has been following new definitions and procedures since the 2016-297 Law. This data comes from the 2020 yearly report published by ONPE on the number and situation of these children; there were in all 3,010 wards of the state at the end of 2018 (ONPE, 2020a, 2020c).

Finally, there is a specific type of placement for young adults. This is the only case in which placement decisions are overwhelmingly consensual; these are de facto housing decisions for care leavers still struggling for autonomy. There were 21,400 such decisions for young adults in 2018 (ONPE, 2020a). Following years of under-funding by the central government, considerable attention has been devoted in recent years to the transition to adulthood of care leavers following the 2016 publication of the ELAP survey (*Etude sur l'autonomie des jeunes placés*, https://elap.site.ined.fr), which revealed that 40% of homeless persons aged 18–25 were care leavers. In February 2020, the government published a circular outlining a contract-based experiment with 30 *départements* to improve the situation of care leavers (Ministère des solidarités et de la santé, 2020).

There is enormous variation between *départements* when it comes to practices in care. The first major variation regards the overall population of children in the *département* who receive at least one ASE intervention or service. Their share of the general population of children in the *département* ranges from 10.9 per thousand to 44.8 per thousand, with a median of 26.5 per thousand in 2018 (ONPE, 2020b).

There is also an important variation in terms of what type of intervention is predominant, between open settings and placement. In 2018, for the first time in 15 years, children in out-of-home placement outnumber those receiving in-home interventions (11.4 per thousand of all children in France are receiving in-home interventions with their origin family compared to 11.6 per thousand of all children who have been placed outside of their family). However, the rate of all children receiving in-home interventions varies significantly from 5.1 per thousand in the Yvelines to 24.1 per thousand in Haute-Saône. The median value is around 12.1 per thousand of children in a given *département*.

The rise of placement decisions is observed across all *départements*, particularly since 2015. This is largely due to the number of unaccompanied children in care, who number 35,800 in 2018 as opposed to 14,800 in 2015. In 2018, 11.6% of all children in France were placed out-of-home. The rate within each *département*'s total child population ranges from 5.7 per thousand in Yvelines to 24.2 per thousand in Nièvre. The median value is 12.3 per thousand.

When it comes to the placement of children, there is also an important variation in terms of type of placement. In 2018, children and young adults combined, 44.2% of young persons in care are placed with foster families, 38% in residential care, 7.3% in autonomous housing, and 10.5% in alternative living arrangements. The proportion of children and young adults in care living with foster families ranges from 16% to 81.7% of the *département*'s population of under-21s in care, with a median value of 36% (ONPE, 2020b). Living arrangements that aren't in foster or residential care account range from 0% (in two *départements*) to 40.6% of all placement decisions (in Seine-Saint-Denis),with a median value of 14.4% (ONPE, 2020b).

Evaluating Situations and Intervention

ASSESSING THE SITUATION OF CHILDREN AND THEIR PROGRESS IN CARE

Assessment is a critical approach in child protection that is operative at three key moments: assessing the situation that is reported to be problematic, to see which intervention, if any, is warranted; assessing the child's progress over time to ensure that the interventions that have been decided are appropriate; and, more generally, to help inform service evaluation. These should be linked because children's progress should be the prime measure of a service's activity, and progress cannot be properly assessed without an appropriate understanding of the initial situation.

Law No 2007-293, for France, has initiated a tool that tries to articulate initial assessment of the situation and criteria for evolution inside a personal care plan that is meant to take into account the child's views and that of the family. This dynamic tool is called *Projet pour l'enfant* (PPE), or project for the child, and is a requirement of article L 223-1 of the Code for social action and families, which stresses that the assessment of the situation should take into account "the condition of the child, the situation if the family and the help they can find within their environment."

No unified assessment tool has, however, been defined by the lawmaker, as this would infringe on the *département*'s prerogatives. In practical terms, therefore, setting up procedures and criteria for PPE at the local level has been long and is indeed not complete in every *département* (ONPE, 2016b). While many *départements* use their own variation on the concept, two assessment approaches have gained momentum and are used in a variety of *départements*: the Alföldi method and the method developed by CREAI ARA with ONPE (ONPE, 2015b).

The Alföldi method relies on the concept of "meaningful assessment" that helps make sense of the situation in a multidimensional way so as to impact its future. The aim is to grasp "a process, a system, an organization, an action, a person" (Alföldi, 2010).

The ONPE/CREAI ARA method relies on a review of existing literature and identifies a number of characteristics of the situation that can have an impact according to various approaches. It is inspired by the Steinhauer method (1983) and has been amended and evaluated by a panel of professionals and researchers (ONPE, 2015b).

These methods are patented and are used by social workers for the assessment of situations both inside the CRIP (initial assessment) and in the framework of the annual reviews of situations. They are very qualitative and clinical in nature, following the French tradition of evaluation. Indicators of well-being and similar assessment tools are so far not very common in French usage (Gorza & Bolter, 2012).

It is therefore extremely complicated to try and assess the progress of children in a unified and/or aggregated fashion that would allow for more child-centric evaluations of child protection interventions at the policy level, although much quality work is done at the practice level to understand and help children on an individual basis.

PROMOTING BEST PRACTICES: ODPE AND ONPE

Because there is no agreed-upon common assessment tool and no standardized evaluation across *départements*, the identification of best practices is a challenge that is best tackled at the local level.

One of the institutions set up by Law No 2007-293 is specifically meant to make sense of practice at the local level and to provide guidance for the *département*: the local observatory of child protection or ODPE.

Set up by the *département*, the ODPE can take multiple forms. The ODPE in Gironde is very connected to the local universities and presided over by an academic; it organizes conferences for professionals and researchers alike. The ODPE in Finistère is very focused on participation and organizes programs that gather families and social workers to exchange ideas and opinions about local priorities. In other *départements*, the ODPE can take the form of annual inter-service meetings.

In all cases, the ODPE is tasked with local observation and the identification of practices at the local level, each active ODPE (not all *départements* have set up their ODPE yet) uses the assessment and evaluation methods that are accepted locally. At the local level, they help decision makers draft policy plans.

ONPE, the national observatory created in 2004, is in contact with the local ODPEs and is therefore aware of the different emerging practices. Part of the mission of ONPE is to assess the practices that are judged effective at the local level, which it does through evaluation missions with descriptive assessments of structures that are available on its website, and through its reports on specific topics and challenges.

The governance of ONPE includes the *départements* and the state, on an equal basis, and involves the participation of the main NGOs of the field. Although ONPE is not an inspectorate, and perhaps because it is not, it is able to interact with structures and *départements* alike to identify and promote good practices in the field.

As types of danger evolve and methods get refined, this role is particularly important for the emerging challenges professionals are faced with.

Emerging Trends and Challenges

The French system of child protection and welfare is based on national solidarity and is profoundly territorialized. It depends on a strong net of services collaborating on situations and focuses very strongly on maintaining family ties. In 2020, the main challenges that this system faces are precisely those that question territorial divisions and/or where the parent/child dyad is not the focal point of intervention: first among those is the question of unaccompanied children.

Tackling the Challenge of Unaccompanied Children
RISING NUMBERS AND PROCEDURAL ADJUSTMENTS

Contrary to what happens for some social benefits, legal residency status is not a prerequisite for children to receive ASE help; non-French children do not need residence permits until the age of 18. Any unaccompanied child is therefore first and foremost a child in need of care, and their nationality is, in principle, irrelevant. This explains why children with no primary caretaker were taken into care regardless of nationality even when there were no any legal text specifically outlining definitions and procedures for this situation.

But since the middle of the 1990s, because of rising numbers of foreign children with no adult caregiver(s) entering care (Duvivier, 2009), the need for guidance has been expressed by professionals and decision-makers in child protection.

The legal category of unaccompanied children (*mineurs non-accompagnés*, MNA), or "isolated foreign children" as they used to be referred to (*mineurs isolés étrangers*, MIE), has emerged over time in French legislation and practice and its rationale only officially entered the Code for social action and families in 2016, although they already qualified for child protection through European directive 2011/95/UE.

Although this legal change only happened in 2016, unaccompanied children had already been the focus of much debate and many practical arrangements inside the *départements* and at the national level.

In 2002, the secretary of state in charge of social inclusion created the first national-level program for unaccompanied children. It relied on the activity of five different NGOS active in the field of child protection and migration and organized a network of patrols and shelters in the Paris region. But by 2011, unaccompanied children were a reality all over France, and the main issue wasn't identifying them: it was caring for them in decent conditions despite the massive local inequalities between *départements*.

Départements are far from equal before migration flows: between rural, landlocked *départements* with no international point of entry, to major population areas in the Paris region, the number of unaccompanied children identified in a given year is in no way similar. In 2011, the two *départements* with the most unaccompanied children in care were

Paris (1,637) and Seine-Saint-Denis (1,000), totaling more than two-thirds of all unaccompanied children in care for that year in France. Seine-Saint-Denis is also the poorest in metropolitan France and has worrying levels of fiscal pressure (Cour des comptes, 2015). This all helps explain why, in 2011, the President of the *département* council of Seine-Saint-Denis, having just passed a deficit budget, wrote a memorandum for ASE services saying that unaccompanied children would temporarily not be accepted, due to the "lack of adequate national solidarity" (Capelier, 2015).

The crisis that followed allowed all different *départements* that were challenged by unaccompanied children to air their grievances. A tentative solution was brought forth in 2013 through the creation of *Cellule nationale MIE* (now *Cellule nationale MNA*), a specialized task force at the national level in charge of dispatching all unaccompanied children identified by social services throughout the territory using a distribution key now defined in article R221-13 of the Code for social action and families.

Following this first step, the procedure for the care of unaccompanied children has been refined, and now consists of two main stages:

1) A person reported as being an unaccompanied child is immediately taken into care for a five-day evaluation period that aims to assess that person's age and effective isolation. This evaluation is mainly done by social workers; additional investigations on identity documents may be requested in addition. Only in extreme cases will bone development be taken into account, and only if requested by a judge in agreement with the person (art. 388 of the Civil code). During this period, the person is under the care of/being assessed by the *département* (social) services where they were first identified (the state funds this evaluation period for five days). If needed, the president of the *département* council can request an emergency placement procedure (OPP).

2) At the end of the evaluation period, if the person is recognized as an unaccompanied child, Cellule MNA determines which *département* should look after the child and organizes the trip. Upon arrival in the final *département*, a care plan will be defined according to the child's need, typically following a second, different type of assessment that does not focus on the same elements.

The assessment that is conducted in the five-day period follows criteria set out by Article L 221-2-2 of the Code for social action and families and focuses on the child's "declarations of identity, age, origin family, nationality and state of isolation." The initial assessment that forms the basis of the personal care plan, and that for them is conducted after the five-day period, focuses instead on the child's "fundamental rights and

basic needs, health, education, development, well-being and potential signs of suffering"
(Article L 226-3 of the Code for social action and families).

REMAINING CHALLENGES

The system for unaccompanied children as it was in 2018 seemed to be fairly stable and accepted by social workers and political decision makers alike, but a number of issues remain.

One of these is the fact that the criteria that need to be taken into consideration for children in child protection in general on the one hand, and for unaccompanied children on the other, are conspicuously different. Not only does this raise a number of questions in terms of equality of treatment and respect for children's rights, it also means that efforts are being partially duplicated, to the detriment of children and social workers. Since different *départements* use different assessment tools and criteria, this also means that the same situation is routinely understood differently between the initial social workers in *département* A and the team in *département* B. More uniformity and common criteria would be necessary for this crucial stage (ONPE, 2017b). In part due to this complexity, the assessment period usually goes well beyond five days, which adds costs for the *département* and delays before children can be taken into care.

Furthermore, the continued usage of questionable age assessment methods using radiation needs to be addressed, as do the structural problems of unequal funding, delays, and sheer complexity of the system for potential users. The Council of Europe's European Committee of Social Rights (2018), in the decision of merits regarding the case of the *European Committee for Home-Based Priority Action for the Child and the Family (EUROCEF) v. France*, has unanimously found France in violation of Article 17 of the Charter (on the right of children and young persons to social, legal and economic protection), due to:

- shortcomings identified in the national shelter, assessment and allocation system of unaccompanied foreign minors;
- the delays in appointing an ad hoc guardian for unaccompanied foreign minors;
- the detention of unaccompanied foreign minors in waiting areas and in hotels;
- the use of bone testing to determine the age of unaccompanied foreign minors considered as inappropriate and unreliable;
- a lack of clarity to access an effective remedy for unaccompanied foreign minors.

Finally, there are huge challenges, as in many countries, regarding the tools and methods of intervention. Language is an issue in many cases, though NGOs like Inter-service Migrants (ISM) offer specialized translation services. Asylum and migration law is not necessarily well known by social workers, since children do not need permits before the age of 18, and this is a problem in cases where a knowledge of this legislation would help act in the best interests of the child, particularly when they want to go to a third country—especially since children, as minors, cannot initiate proceedings on their own in French law and require guardians. The protection of unaccompanied children is an "institutional metonymy" (Demailly, 2008), a policy within a policy, in which social workers have no control over or information about asylum and migration proceedings; training and information would help bridge this gap. More profoundly, the realities faced by these children create specific developmental needs compared to other children, and social workers are not necessarily always equipped to face them. Kohli (2016) calls these children "liquid" children: moving "within and across communities of experience." What resources can social workers find when there is no family, and not a lot of community, to work with? Centre Georges Devereux and Centre Babel, for instance, are developing new methods and tools to help children in these situations (ONPE, 2017b), but these tools are not widely disseminated and are still considered innovative.

As the number of children in care shows no sign of decreasing significantly, reaching 35,800 in 2018 (ONPE, 2020b), these challenges need to be taken seriously. They require a concerted effort by both *départements* and the state to reach a better compromise, in the interests of children.

Terra incognita: The Data We Don't Have

Unaccompanied children represent a "new" population in care, for which procedures and legislation have appeared relatively recently. As a result, this area of childcare and protection is still in flux, and actors are still adapting to new realities. But this does not mean that other populations and other types of care are without challenge. Indeed, the very fact that the child protection and welfare system is so developed and rich makes it very difficult to grasp, which can be a problem for policymakers.

WHAT YOU SEE AND WHAT YOU DON'T: OBSERVATIONAL BLIND SPOTS

Other blind spots in observation correspond to limitations of practice, and these limitations are particular challenges when they correspond to the fundamental rights of children.

The first and obvious such blind spot has already been mentioned: there are as of 2020 no robust data on child maltreatment that could give an idea of the scope of the problem. France has signed and ratified the United Nations Convention on the Rights of the Child (UNCRC); in the framework of its reporting obligations, this lack of data has been mentioned time and again. Law-enforcement or justice-based observation systems do not propose categories that could be compiled. Health-related data on child maltreatment and so far mostly related to the analysis of child death reports (Tursz et al., 2008). And child protection reports, in the framework of the assessment practices used by social workers with an emphasis on maintaining family ties, underplay maltreatment and do not systematically record suspicions even when they are there (Corbet et al., 2015). An ongoing initiative by Gilard-Pioc and colleagues (2017) has initiated an in-depth analysis of hospitalization data recorded by the healthcare system and should propose very robust data indeed in the coming years.

But some specific types of maltreatment will still remain elusive, most particularly those that correspond to exploitation and cannot be grasped by physical or mental health data alone. Although France has signed and ratified the UN Palermo Convention against Transnational Organized Crime, as well as the Council of Europe Lanzarote Convention on Protection of Children against Sexual Exploitation and Sexual Abuse, its action in that regard focuses mostly on transnational cooperation. In France itself, very few data are available and the action of police and justice services remains quite separate from child protection: there is no specific protocol for children entering care as the result of having been removed from a situation of exploitation.

The *Commission nationale consultative des droits de l'homme* (CNCDH) monitors the efforts made by the French government against trafficking. It published a first report on that question in 2016 in which it raises this question, highlighting that "trafficking and exploitation of human beings are not explicitly mentioned in the field of child protection and are not statistical entry points" (CNCDH, 2016, p. 210, author's translation), which makes it impossible to know how many children are victims and how many have received help.

This is particularly true and problematic for child sexual exploitation, a service need that currently goes undetected and underserved, as underlined by the Central Inspectorate for Social Action (*Inspection générale de l'action sociale*, IGAS) in 2012.

This does not necessarily mean that children who are victims of trafficking and sexual exploitation do not receive help, or that these issues are not taken seriously by social workers. On the contrary, the question of child sexual exploitation is an emerging concern, as are all questions related to sexual violence (in 2016, police services identified 19,700 child victims of sexual violence in France—ONPE, 2017b). But there is a clear gap between law enforcement and social work, and addressing situations of exploitation in themselves is still not something for which a clear process exists overall—social intervention is not always tailored to take into account the specificities of children who are victims of or exposed to sexual exploitation.

Conclusion

Many of the issues that face the French child protection and welfare system are connected to a lack of data and consistency over the territory, and this is not just a theoretical question. For policymakers, this lack of information on the types of situations faced by children, on what types of innovative interventions are attempted and with what results, is a navigational problem. Although the services at the *département* level are usually well informed on what happens in their *département*, this creates a problem when it comes to going beyond ASE services themselves, or when it comes to creating legislation and funding programs. Guesswork is not a viable policy option, even if every single situation is indeed unique, and even if the culture of evaluation in social services does not rely on quantified or standardized tools. Absence of data is a risk for this policy and for all services involved in it, since it represents a significant public expenditure; and it is a challenge when it comes to monitoring the effective implementation of children's rights. French services are aware of this and the system as a whole is slowly addressing the issue, but it is a frustratingly slow process.

The 2016 reform of child protection and welfare, moving from a danger perspective to an approach in terms of children's needs, paves the way for reframing child protection and the monitoring of this policy as a question of children's rights, a paradigm shift that should result in a positive development at the practice level as well.

References

Alföldi, A. (2010). *Évaluer en protection de l'enfance: Théorie et méthode* (4th ed.). Dunod.

Bolter, F., Keravel, E., Momic, M., and Séraphin, G. (2018). Protecting the children, protecting the gravidae: The dual imperative of childbirth under secrecy in France. *The Chronicle*, January.

Bordin, D. (2008). France Terre d'Asile et le dispositif parisien face aux mineurs isolés en transit. *Journal du droit des jeunes*, 7(277), 28–32.

Brown, P., Duru-Bellat, M., and Van Zanten, A. (2010). La méritocratie scolaire: Un modèle de justice à l'épreuve du marché. *Sociologies*, 1, 161–175.

Bruckauf, Z. and Chzhen, Y. (2016). *Education for all? Measuring inequality of educational outcomes among 15-year-olds across 39 industrialized nations*. Innocenti Working Paper No.2016-08. UNICEF Office of Research.

Capelier, F. (2015). *Comprendre la protection de l'enfance: L'enfant en danger face au droit*. Dunod.

Chevreul, K., Berg Brigham, K, Durand-Zaleski, I., and Hernandez-Quevedo, C. (2015). France: Health system review. *Health Systems in Transition*, 17(3), 1–218.

CNCDH. (2016). *Rapport sur la lutte contre la traite et l'exploitation des êtres humains*. La Documentation française.

Corbet, E., Séverac, N., and Le Duff, R. (2015). *Maltraitances en 2013: Comprendre les évolutions pour mieux y répondre. Appréciation des situations de maltraitance(s) intrafamiliale(s)*. Final report. Available at: https://www.onpe.gouv.fr/system/files/ao/aot2013.corbet_rf.pdf.

Cour des comptes. (2020, November). *La protection de l'enfance: une politique inadaptée au temps de l'enfant*. Rapport public thématique . Available at: https://www.ccomptes.fr/system/files/2020-11/20201130-rapport-protection-enfance_0.pdf.

Cour des comptes, Chambre régionale des comptes d'île-de-France. (2015, May 26). *Rapport d'observations définitives et sa réponse. Département de la Seine-Saint-Denis (93). Exercices 2010 et suivants*. Available at: https://www.ccomptes.fr/sites/default/files/EzPublish/Rapport-d-observation-d--finitives-et-sa-r--ponse_1.pdf.

Demailly, L. (2008). *Politiques de la relation: Approche sociologique des métiers et activités professionnelles relationnelles*. Presses universitaires du Septentrion.

DREES. (2010). *Violence et santé en France: État des lieux*. Ed. F. Beck, C. Cavalin, and F. Maillochon. La documentation française, Études et statistiques.

DREES. (2020a). *Minima sociaux et prestations sociales : Edition 2020*. Available at: https://drees.solidarites-sante.gouv.fr/IMG/pdf/drees_-_pano_-_minima_sociaux_-_assemblage_-_bat_-_210920.pdf.

DREES. (2020b). *L'aide et l'action sociales en France: Perte d'autonomie, handicap, protection de l'enfance et insertion. Edition 2020*. Available at: https://drees.solidarites-sante.gouv.fr/IMG/pdf/aas20.pdf.

Direction générale du Trésor. (2019). *Programme national de réforme 2019*. Available at: https://www.tresor.economie.gouv.fr/Articles/8793891e-4d59-4b58-a61f-126dbc5b3d19/files/175afe5d-f2dd-4011-8f3e-a27143628780.

Duvivier, É. (2009). Quand ils sont devenus visibles . . . Essai de mise en perspective des logiques de construction de la catégorie de "mineur étranger isolé". *Pensée plurielle*, 2(21), 65–79.

Esping-Andersen, G. (1990). *The Three Worlds of Welfare Capitalism*. Princeton University Press.

European Committee on Social Rights. (2018, June 15). *Decision on merits. European Committee for Home-Based Priority Action for the Child and the Family (EUROCEF) v. France, Complaint No. 114/2015*. Available at: https://rm.coe.int/cc-114-2015-dmerits-en/16808b372e.

Gilard-Pioc, S., Cottenet, J., Françoise-Pursell, I., and Quantin, C. (2017). Proposition d'une méthode d'exploitation d'une base de données nationales: le PMSI, pour estimer la fréquence, repérer les situations à risques et les conséquences, des maltraitances physiques à enfants en France. *Revue d'Épidémiologie et de Santé Publique*, 65, S16.

Gorza, M. and Bolter, F. (2012). Indicateurs de bien-être de l'enfant, une déclinaison en protection de l'enfance est-elle possible?. *Journal du droit des jeunes*, 3, 26–36.

Guillaume, P. (2001). L'état-providence en question. *Vingtième siècle*, 1(69), 43–50.

Guinot, H. (2012). *Cartographie des mineurs isolés étrangers en France. Rapport 2012*. Observatoire Méditerranéen de l'Enfance en Situation Précaire. Available at: https://www.infomie.net/IMG/pdf/cartographie_des_mineurs_isoles_etrangers_en_france_-_rapport_2012_-_omesp.pdf.

Inspection générale des affaires sociales. (2012). *Prostitution: Les enjeux sanitaires. Rapport RM2012-146P*. Available at: http://www.ladocumentationfrancaise.fr/var/storage/rapports-publics/124000667.pdf.

Institut national d'études démographiques. (2020). *Virage: Violences au cours de la vie*. Available at:https://virage.site.ined.fr/fichier/s_rubrique/29712/plaquette2.result.virage.2020_violences.vie.entiere.fr.pdf.

INSEE. (2020a). *Bilan démographique 2019. Chiffres détaillés* [Data set]. Available at: https://www.insee.fr/fr/statistiques/4281618?sommaire=1912926.

INSEE. (2020b). *Population totale par sexe et par âge. au 1er janvier 2020, France métropolitaine. Bilan démographique 2017. Chiffres détaillés* [Data set]. Available at:https://www.insee.fr/fr/statistiques/1892088?sommaire=1912926.

INSEE. (2020c). *Population totale par sexe et âge au 1er janvier 2020, France. Bilan démographique 2017. Chiffres détaillés* [Data set]. Available at: https://www.insee.fr/fr/statistiques/1892086?sommaire=1912926.

INSEE. (2020d). *Les naissances en 2019. Tableaux de comparaisons régionales et départementales* [Data set]. Available at: https://www.insee.fr/fr/statistiques/4647545?sommaire=4647557.

INSEE. (2020e). *Régions—Départements. Insee références* [Data set]. Available at: https://www.insee.fr/fr/statistiques/4277596?sommaire=4318291.

INSEE. (2020f). *Taux de scolarisation par âge en 2018. Chiffres-clés.* [Graph]. Retrieved from https://www.insee.fr/fr/statistiques/2383587.

Kohli, R. (2016, April 20). *Liquid children: Reflections on the movements forced migrant children make towards their "best interests"*. [Conference presentation]. Nottingham University. Available at: https://www.nottingham.ac.uk/cas/documents/ravi-kohli-liquid-children-20-04-16.pdf..

Mattei, P. and Aguilar, A. S. (2016). *Secular institutions, Islam and education policy: France and the U.S. in comparative perspective*. London.

Ministère des solidarités et de la santé. (2020). *Circulaire n° DGCS/SD2B/DGS/SP1/2020/34 du 20 fevrier relative à la contractualisation préfet/ARS/département pour la prévention et la protection de l'enfance*. Available at: https://solidarites-sante.gouv.fr/IMG/pdf/cir34.pdf.

Naves, P., Cathala, B., and Deparis J.-M. (2000). *Accueils provisoires et placements d'enfants et d'adolescents: des décisions qui mettent à l'épreuve le système français de protection de l'enfance et de la famille*. Ministère de l'emploi et de la solidarité. Available at: Retrieved from http://www.ladocumentationfrancaise.fr/rapports-publics/004001642/index.shtml.

Observatoire de l'accès aux droits et aux soins de la mission France de Médecins du Monde. (2017). *Rapport 2016*. Available at: https://www.medecinsdumonde.org/fr/actualites/publications/2017/10/13/rapport-de-lobservatoire-de-lacces-aux-droits-et-aux-soins-de-la-mission-france-2016.

Observatoire du non-recours aux droits et services. (2018). *Des chiffres du non-recours*. Available at: https://odenore.msh-alpes.fr/actualites/Des_chiffres_du_non_recours.

OECD. (2017). General government spending (indicator). doi:10.1787/a31cbf4d-en. Accessed on 28 June 28, 2022.

OECD. (2021). *Social expenditure—aggregated data: Public and private social expenditure by country* [Data set]. Available at: https://stats.oecd.org/Index.aspx?DataSetCode=SOCX_AGG#.

ONED/ONPE. (2011). *Enquête nationale informations préoccupantes.* Available at: https://www.onpe.gouv.fr/system/files/publication/enquete_ip_201110_5.pdf.

ONED/ONPE. (2015a). *L'accueil familial: quell travail d'équipe?* La documentation française. Available at: https://www.onpe.gouv.fr/system/files/publication/20150710_af_web_0.pdf.

ONED/ONPE. (2015b). *Journée d'étude ONED- CREAI Rhône-Alpes. Des référentiels pour évaluer en protection de l'enfance. Quelles démarches, Quelles methodes?* La documentation française. Available at: https://www.onpe.gouv.fr/system/files/publication/je120515_referentielsevalpe.pdf.

ONPE. (2016a). *Affiche sur le dispositif de protection de l'enfance.* [Diagram]. Available at: https://www.onpe.gouv.fr/ressources/affiche-format-a3.

ONPE. (2016b). *Le PPE: État des lieux, enjeux organisationnels et pratiques.* La documentation française. Available at: https://www.onpe.gouv.fr/system/files/publication/rapport_ppe_2016.pdf.

ONPE. (2017a). *Mineurs non accompagnés: quels besoins et quelles réponses?* Paris: La documentation française. Available at: https://www.onpe.gouv.fr/system/files/publication/dossier_mna_web2.pdf.

ONPE. (2017b). *Douzième rapport au gouvernement et au parlement.* La documentation française. Available at: https://www.onpe.gouv.fr/system/files/publication/ragp_2017_web_complet.pdf.

ONPE. (2018). *Synthèse du rapport sur la situation des pupilles de l'état au 31 décembre 2016.* Available at: https://www.onpe.gouv.fr/system/files/publication/synthese_enquete_pupilles_31dec2016_2018.pdf.

ONPE. (2020a). *Chiffres clés en protection de l'enfance au 31 décembre 2018.* Available at:https://www.onpe.gouv.fr/system/files/publication/note_chiffres_cles_annee2018_ok_0.pdf.

ONPE. (2020b). *La population des enfants suivis en protection de l'enfance au 31/12/2018: Les disparités départementales.* Available at: https://www.onpe.gouv.fr/system/files/publication/note_disparites_2018_dec20_b.pdf.

ONPE. (2020c). *La situation des pupilles de l'État. Situation au 31 décembre 2018.* Available at:https://onpe.gouv.fr/system/files/publication/rapport_pupilles_31dec2018_juin2020_1.pdf.

Steinhauer, P. (1983). Assessing for parenting capacity. *American Journal of Orthopsychiatry*, 53(3), 468–481.

Tillard, B. and Mosca, S. (2016). *Enfants confiés à un proche dansle cadre de la Protection de l'Enfance. Rapport final.* Available at:ttps://www.onpe.gouv.fr/system/files/ao/aoo2014.tillardrf.pdf.

Tursz, A., Crost, M., Gerbouin-Rérolle, P., and Beauté, J. (2008, January 22). Étude épidémiologique des morts suspectes de nourrissons en France: Quelle est la part des homicides? *Bulletin Épidémiologique Hebdomadaire thématique*, 3–4, 25–28. Available at: http://opac.invs.sante.fr/doc_num.php?explnum_id=1517.

United Nations Committee on the Rights of the Child. (2016). *Concluding observations on the fifth periodic report of France.* Available at: http://www.refworld.org/docid/56c17fb64.html.

Child Protection and Welfare in Germany

Kay Biesel *and* Heinz Kindler

Abstract

This chapter outlines Germany's child protection and welfare systems. Data on the prevalence of different types of Germanic child maltreatment are not well integrated into the international literature. Child and youth welfare offices are key institutions in enforcing child protection which is a communal task. Moreover, the health system plays a key role in some child protection cases, especially if child maltreatment is found by health professionals. Security, criminal prosecution, and victim support are the three primary responsibilities of police handling child endangerment. On the other hand, school laws require schools to cooperate with child and youth welfare offices to enact child protection measures.

Key Words: Germany, child protection, welfare, child maltreatment, health system, school, police, security, criminal prosecution, victim support

Introduction

This chapter outlines how child protection and welfare in Germany is structured and organized. Based on data on the prevalence of different types of child maltreatment the legal framework and responsible institutions are described. The roles of child and youth welfare offices and family courts in particular are clarified. Further, responsibilities of the health system, prosecuting authorities, and the school system in child protection are exemplified. Thereafter, core procedures and standards for handling endangerments of children's welfare and types and developments of interventions and measures to protect children are explained. Finally, trends and forthcoming issues are highlighted.

Prevalence and Types of Maltreatment

Germany has about 83 million inhabitants, including 13.5 million children (11.2%) under the age of 18 years. Around 19.3 million (16%) have a migration background; 10.9 million (9%) do not have German citizenship (Statistisches Bundesamt, 2019).

Data on the prevalence of different types of child maltreatment in Germany are not well integrated in the international literature. For example, a recent meta-analysis by Stoltenborgh (2012) on the prevalence of child maltreatment in different parts of the world was able to include only one study from Germany. One possible reason is that the number of studies using representative population samples is only slowly growing in Germany. Another reason may be that official data on the incidence of child maltreatment notifications as well as some of the prevalence studies have not as yet been published in English.

At the moment, there are three large population surveys on the prevalence of more than one form of child maltreatment in Germany. A pioneer study by Wetzels (1997) using random sampling included more than 3,000 German-speaking, non-institutionalized adults between the ages of 16 and 59. Using items from the Conflict Tactics Scale (CTS) for physical child abuse and self-developed items for child sexual abuse, 9.9% of all women and 11.8% of all men described physical abuse during their childhood (e.g., being kicked, bitten, or hit with a fist), while 9.6% of all females and 3.2% of all males reported sexual abuse with body contact before their 18th birthday. Häuser et al. (2011) and Witt et al. (2017) both used the Childhood Trauma Questionnaire (CTQ) with random samples of 2,000 (age range: 14–90 years) and 2,510 (age range: 14–94 years) non-institutionalized participants with sufficient German language skills. Severe to extreme physical neglect was reported by 9.0 and 10.8% in both samples. Comparable rates for emotional neglect were 6.5 and 7.1%, for physical abuse 2.7 and 3.3%, for psychological abuse 1.6 and 2.6%, and for sexual abuse 1.9 and 2.3%. Prevalence rates for severe to extreme forms of child maltreatment are highlighted because they may be closest to state intervention thresholds.

Up to now, only very few scientists from Germany have been part of international comparative research projects using similar methods of recruitment, data collection and analysis in different countries. A study comparing parental self-report on physical violence in child rearing from five western countries found the second highest rate of reported severe beatings in parents from Germany (9.0%) with lower rates in Spain (4.4%), Austria (5.6%), and Sweden (1.5%), and a higher rate in France (11.6%) (Bussmann et al., 2011). Krahé and Berger (2013) examined the prevalence of sexual victimization during adolescence and young adulthood using convenience samples of university students from different European countries. Rates of reported violent sexual victimization were 13.1% for females in Germany compared to an average of 19.5% for all female subsamples from participating European countries, and 5.4% for males in Germany compared to an average of 15.8% for all male subsamples.

Questions on child maltreatment related contacts to child protection services have not been part of questionnaires in prevalence studies in Germany until now. Despite these knowledge gaps there is a broad consensus including government, child and human rights organizations and researchers from social work, public health, and human resource fields, that child maltreatment constitutes a serious social problem in Germany.

The German System of Child Protection and Welfare

Legal Regulations Regarding State Interference with Parental Rights

For the protection of maltreated children, the constitution (Grundgesetz—GG) sets the rights and obligations of the state. Article 6 of the GG states that "care and upbringing of children is the natural right of parents and a duty primarily incumbent upon them. The state shall watch over them in the performance of this duty." Based on this "safeguard clause," the state has to support parents in need, but there is a right and a duty to interfere with parental rights as a last resort. The constitution itself goes on to state, that children may be separated from their families against the will of their parents only pursuant to law and only if parents or guardians fail in their duties or children are otherwise in danger of serious neglect (Article 6 Para. 3). The threshold for such child protection inference with parental rights is specified in section 1666 of the German civil code (BGB). In this section, "child endangerment" (*Kindeswohlgefährdung*) and parental unwillingness or unfitness to avert this danger are defined as two preconditions that have to be present. Also, involuntary measures assert that the state is entitled to intervene for the protection of endangered children if suitable and proportionate. According to section 1666, para 1 of the BGB, child endangerment encompasses significant harm to children's "physical, mental or emotional welfare or his/her property." Therefore, different aspects of children's welfare have to be considered and child protective measures are not restricted to dangers to life and limb. A more detailed definition of the legal term "child endangerment" has been given by the Federal Court of Justice (*Bundesgerichtshof—*BGH) and the Federal Constitutional Court (*Bundesverfassungsgericht—*BVerfG). Both have defined it as a current danger that will most certainly cause significant harm to the child in the future (BGH Judgment of July 14, 1956, IV ZB 32/56). As a result, the decision as to whether there is child endangerment or not is a prognostic one. In recent years, the Federal Constitutional Court and the Federal Court of Justice have made some clarifications regarding the threshold for child protection interventions. The Federal Court of Justice has ruled that the vulnerability of a child and his or her abilities to seek help have to be taken into account resulting in a somewhat lower threshold for very young children (BGH Judgment of November 23, 2016, XII ZB 149/16). It also has been decided that possible negative effects of state interventions (e.g., attachment disruption due to parent–child separation) have to be considered and an overall positive effect for a child has to be expected (e.g., BVerfG Judgment of March 24, 2014, 1 BvR 160/14). What has remained unchanged is, based on the principle of proportionality, an obligation of courts to select the least intrusive measure that seems to be suitable to avert existing dangers. Therefore, there is an ongoing, sometimes polemical debate between judges, lawyers, guardians ad litem, children and youth welfare offices, and court experts on case characteristics that justify the placement of children after some form of maltreatment (e.g., Tsokos & Guddat, 2014; Biesel et al., 2019).

A final termination of parental rights does not exist in German child protection law. The principle of proportionality and the regulations in the constitution have resulted in a strong tendency to avoid involuntary state interventions and court involvements in favor of more cooperative arrangements with parents. Child and youth welfare offices are involved in all child protection court proceedings. In child protection cases that stay below the level of court involvement their role is paramount.

Child and Youth Welfare Offices: Key Institutions for Child Protection

Germany includes 16 federal states and is constituted as a democratic and social constitutional state. Child protection is a communal task. The Federal Government and the federal states provide only the framework for child protection. For this purpose, they enact laws and implement regulations. The most important laws for child protection are the Civil Code, the social code book 8 (SGB VIII), and the Act on Cooperation and Information in Child Protection (KKG).

Child protection in Germany most often is understood as a broad task (Kindler, 2013, p. 16), which can be explained by the principal of a "family service orientation" (Gilbert et al., 2011, p. 255; Wolff et al., 2011). Within this approach, the core idea is to support parents and families in order to avoid or end child endangerment. As a result, there is no narrow focus on the identification and handling of cases of child endangerment, but a broader legislative program outlined in SGB VIII with two key elements. One key element is a legal entitlement of parents to receive parenting support well below the threshold of child endangerment. The second key element is participation of parents and children. Based on this general understanding of child protection, about 580 local children and youth welfare offices (*Jugendämter*) in municipalities are accountable for planning, funding, coordination, and delivery of early support services, parenting support, and other child and youth welfare services. However, most of the time they do not provide these services by themselves. Due to the principle of subsidiarity, state-financed, but independent non-governmental organizations (*Freie Träger*) are preferred over state organizations in providing such services. Consequently, different organizations with a range of various worldviews and values have emerged (for the history of the subsidiarity principle in the German welfare system, see Witte et al., 2016).

The SGB VIII emphasizes prevention and collaboration between families and social workers and is established on the idea that service user involvement and social pedagogical approaches together contribute to a democratic and effective social support system for parents and children in need. Hämäläinen (2013) has described essentials of social pedagogical thought for readers from the Anglo-Saxon world. The range of services includes general parenting support (cf. § 16 SGB VIII), counselling for parents in certain situations, for example divorce (cf. §§ 17, 18 SGB VIII), day care and kindergarten (cf. §§ 22–25 SGB VIII), and specific child welfare services (cf. § 27–35 SGB VIII) including social-pedagogical in-home child and family services, foster care, and residential care (Witte et al., 2016, p. 1). In addition to these services, the SGB VIII also includes two central child protection responsibilities for children and youth welfare offices and, partly, all children and youth welfare workers:

- Carrying out assessments regarding the presence of child endangerment and necessary measures to end such endangerment if there has been a child maltreatment notification or there are other grounds to suspect child endangerment. All children and youth welfare workers have an obligation to carry out such an assessment if they come across weighty grounds to suspect child endangerment and to inform the children and youth welfare office if necessary.

- Children and youth welfare offices can decide on crisis interventions such as emergency placements of children and adolescents (§ 42 SGB VIII). An emergency placement has to take place if there is an urgent danger for a child or an adolescent to be harmed in the family, if a minor asks for protection or if a foreign child or a foreign adolescent comes to Germany unaccompanied and his or her parents do not stay inland.

In an influential model, Schone (2008, p. 59) has divided services and measures of the children and youth welfare system in Germany along a need continuum. Incorporation of the endangerment threshold resulted in three areas: (1) promotion of child well-being

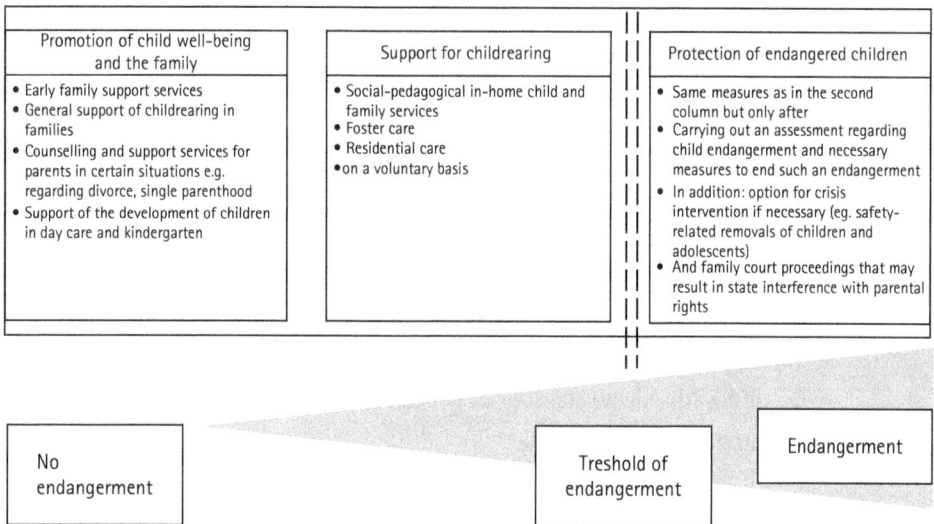

Figure 10.1 Services and measures of the children and youth welfare system including child protection based on a model by Schone (2008)

and the family, (2) support for childrearing, and (3) protection of endangered children (see also Wolff et al., 2011, p. 199 and Figure 10.1).

To understand the difference between the second and the third column in the model, it is important to mention that in Germany a legal distinction is made between a family situation in which the welfare of a child is not guaranteed and the endangerment of the welfare of a child. In the former case, parents are entitled to receive children and youth welfare services (cf. § 27 (1) SGB VIII), but they are not obliged to do so. In the case of child endangerment, however, the situation of the child has to be improved in substantial ways, preferably in cooperation with the parents. Nevertheless, if they are unable or unwilling, the state is entitled and obliged to interfere with parental rights (cf. § 1666 BGB) in order to protect the child.

The following case scenarios below and above the endangerment threshold occur (Schone, 2008, p. 39ff.):

- *Scenario 1*: The welfare of the child is not guaranteed, but there is (as yet) no child endangerment. Moreover, parents want and accept support for childrearing. In this case, voluntary child and family services are provided. Shared goals will be negotiated, noted in a service plan, and case conferences with parents and children will be held on a regular basis (§ 36 SGB VIII).
- *Scenario 2*: The welfare of the child is not guaranteed. Parents do not want or accept support for childrearing, but there is no child endangerment. In this case, no services will be provided, although there may be repeated attempts to offer support.
- *Scenario 3*: The welfare of a child is endangered, but parents want and accept support and control measures that seem reasonable to prevent (further) child maltreatment. If parents decide to work with the children and youth welfare office and agree with a proper protection and service concept, there is no justification for state interference with parental rights and no family court procedure will be initiated.
- *Scenario 4:* There is child endangerment, but parents refuse to agree with measures to protect the child from (further) maltreatment and services to re-establish parenting capacities. In this situation, the family court must be informed, most often by the child and youth welfare office. In addition, the children and youth welfare office may initiate a temporary emergency placement and health care institutions or police may be involved in order to avert the endangerment.

Regarding these scenarios, only in the event that the welfare of a child is endangered and parents are not willing or able to avert the endangerment state interference with parental rights does become an option. Even if custody or parts of it are removed from the parents a return to a voluntary and more collaborative pathway of the case is possible because an irrevocable termination of parental rights is unknown in German family law. If it seems necessary to remove custody or parts of it from the parents, a family court procedure is necessary, because the family court is the only authority that can do so (sec.1666 para. 2 BGB).

Family Courts: The Only Authority with Powers to Interfere with Parental Rights in Order to Protect Children

There are three routes to family court involvement. First, children and youth welfare offices can ask for a court hearing, even though a case is still below the endangerment threshold if a problem escalation seems to be likely. In such a case of potential child endangerment, the goal of the hearing is not to decide on involuntary state intervention but to use the authority of the court to talk to the parents about prevention and voluntary support measures that might help them to avoid involuntary measures in the future (sec. 157 family court procedures law—FamFG). The possibility of such hearings indicates that family courts in Germany go beyond making decisions on legal matters but have incorporated some preventive and educational functions into their role. Second, if children and youth welfare offices receive a child maltreatment notification but are unable to investigate the case because parents refuse to participate in necessary steps towards clarification the court has to be informed (sec 8a para 2 SGB VIII). Finally, there may be an appeal to the court declaring that a child is endangered and in need of protection. On the second and third routes, the family court has to investigate whether relevant conditions for state intervention are met. Four conditions are most important for such an intervention: (1) the welfare of a child has to be endangered (as defined above), (2) the court has to be convinced that the parents are not able or unwilling to avert existing dangers, (3) there has to be a child protection measure that is both suitable to avert the danger and proportionate, and (4) even if potential negative effects of an involuntary state intervention are taken into consideration, it has to be expected that the intervention will lead, at least in the medium-term, to an improvement for the child. If the court decides to interfere with parental rights it has to build its opinion on evidence.

If several measures seem suitable to end child endangerment, family courts must respect the principle of proportionality and select the least intrusive measure. Measures interfering with parental rights have to be reviewed by the family court periodically (sec. 166 para. 2 FamFG). If a court denies a necessity to intervene in a case it has to review this decision at least once, usually after three months (sec. 166 para. 3 FamFG).

The Health System and Its Responsibilities for Child Protection

The health system may play a key role in some child protection cases. This is especially true if child maltreatment is detected by health professionals or if medical expert knowledge is needed to document and diagnose maltreatment-related injuries or health problems. Moreover, the health system is called upon to provide treatment for health consequences of child maltreatment and, in a collaborative effort with children and youth welfare offices, to provide early preventive services. If health professionals detect signs of child maltreatment or serious risks for child maltreatment, they are authorized to report the case to children and youth welfare offices despite professional confidentiality (cf. sec. 4 para. 3 Act on Cooperation and Information in Child Protection—KKG, for more details see subchapter 3). There is, however, no mandatory reporting for health professionals in Germany. In addition to a small number of university-based institutes for forensic medicine the number of hospital-based child protection units specialized in medical diagnostics of suspected child maltreatment has risen in recent years (Herrmann et al., 2016), however hospitals are not obliged to organize such a unit. Therapeutic services for child maltreatment victims are provided by clinics for child and adolescent psychiatry, outpatient trauma clinics or therapists in private practice. If there is a medical indication, therapeutic treatment is financed by health insurance, which covers nearly all children and adolescents in Germany.

The Prosecuting Authorities and Their Responsibility for Child Protection

Child endangerment as a future-oriented category in the German child protection system includes cases where child maltreatment has already happened (and may happen again). Because physical child maltreatment (e.g., sec. 225 criminal code—StGB), child neglect (sec. 171 criminal code—StGB) and child sexual abuse (e.g., sec. 176 criminal code—StGB) are listed as criminal offenses in the criminal code, prosecuting authorities may become involved in these cases. However, due to the dominance of a "family service orientation" approach to child protection in Germany child maltreatment is mostly seen as a social problem. As a consequence, prosecuting authorities become involved most often in sexual abuse cases in contrast to child physical abuse or child neglect cases. If the police learn about a possible case, they have three primary responsibilities (Gerber, 2006, p. 1).

1) *Security*: Police can take emergency measures, for example, arrest an offender or issue a protective order in order to protect a victim from further maltreatment.

2) *Criminal prosecution*: Police has to pursue criminal prosecution, under certain circumstances, even if the victim does not want the case to be investigated.

3) *Victim support:* During criminal investigations and penal court procedures there are rules for reducing stress for child witnesses (e.g., only judges are allowed to ask questions of a child victim testifying in front of the court). Moreover, child victims have a right to receive psychosocial support by a

trained professional before, during and after a trial (sec. 406g German Code of Criminal Procedure).

Schools and the Responsibilities of Teachers in Child Protection

As home schooling is not permitted in Germany nearly all children between 6 and 16 years of age are to be seen by teachers on a day-to-day basis (for a description of the educational system in Germany, see Eckhardt, 2017). Moreover, social workers are present in a large number of schools (Pötter, 2018). As children and young people spend large parts of their daily lives in school, teachers and school social workers may become aware of signs of maltreatment shown by a pupil. Some pupils may also disclose maltreatment to school personnel.

If there are indications of child endangerment, the school laws of the 16 federal states and federal child protection law apply simultaneously. School laws require schools to cooperate with child and youth welfare offices and to take action if there are "weighty grounds" to suspect endangerment of a pupil. Federal law addresses teachers explicitly in the Act on Cooperation and Information in Child Protection (KKG), section 4 paragraph 3. Confronted with weighty grounds to suspect child endangerment, teachers ought to encourage pupils and their parents to seek support on a voluntary basis. If there are safety reasons not to talk to the parents or a discussion has no positive result, there is an authorization to inform the local child and youth welfare office about the case (for more details, see the following section).

After detecting a case of possible child endangerment schools might get involved in a protection and service concept formulated by the child and youth welfare office and the parents together (e.g., monitoring absence from school more closely). Yet schools have no obligation to do so and they have no right to be informed or involved if there is a protection and service concept regarding a pupil.

Core Child Protection Procedures and Standards

Central standards and specific procedures for handling cases of possible endangerment are specified in SGB VIII and in the Act on Cooperation and Information in Child Protection (KKG). Most regulations apply for case workers in the local child and youth welfare offices because of their central role in processing cases of possible child endangerment. Child and youth welfare offices are the institutions in Germany to which everybody can report endangerment about the welfare of a child.

Child and youth welfare offices are not obliged to accept every child endangerment notification for investigation. The decisions of case workers on whether to screen in or screen out a referral depend on the presence of "weighty grounds" to assume the endangerment of a child. Legal commentaries (e.g., Münder et al., 2013) have explained that "weighty grounds" have to include concrete facts or plausible conjectures pointing in the direction of a situation leading to significant harm for a child with a high degree of certainty. In principle, with the concept of "weighty grounds" for an endangerment of the welfare of a child (sec. 8a, para 1, social code book VIII—SGB VIII) the legislature has established an initial threshold to protect families from disproportionate interventions into their privacy. In practice, however, most referrals are accepted for investigation and the intake decision is much less formalized than in some other child protection systems (e.g., many states in the USA), where a high number of referrals are screened out without further investigation. The low degree of formalization of the intake decision in Germany has, inter alia, the consequence that no statistical data are collected on the number of reports that are screened out.

If workers take "weighty grounds" to be given in a case, the local child and youth welfare office is obliged to carry out an assessment. The goals of this assessment are not explicitly stated in the law, but commentaries agree that case workers have to determine whether a case is above or below the endangerment threshold, what dangers are present, how these dangers can be averted and whether the parents are willing and able to work with the child and youth welfare office on averting existing dangers. During the assessment, the professionals of the local child and youth welfare office—regularly social workers—must comply with the following procedure (8a, para. 1, social code book VIII—SGB VIII):

1) *Involving family members*: Caseworkers must involve parents and the child or adolescent in the endangerment assessment, if this does not undermine the effective protection of the child or adolescent.

2) *Home Visit*: As a rule, caseworkers should obtain an immediate impression of the child and his or her personal environment.

3) *Cooperative professional decision-making*: At least two professionals have to work together in making the assessment.

4) *Offer support measures (for childrearing)*: Appropriate support measures for averting an existing child endangerment have to be offered to the family.

5) *Appeal to the family court*: If considered necessary, caseworkers have to appeal to the family court. They also have to involve the court, if parents are unwilling or unable to cooperate in assessing the possible endangerment of the welfare of a child.

6) *Emergency measures*: If there is an urgent danger and the decision of the family court cannot be awaited, the professionals from the child and youth welfare office are obliged to organize emergency measures to ensure the safety of the child or young person.

7) *Involvement of other services providers*: If other service providers (e.g., healthcare institutions) are needed in order to avert endangerment, caseworkers must encourage parents to get them involved. In emergencies caseworkers themselves can involve other service providers.

Child protection law in Germany does not contain any provisions regarding quality criteria for safety and risk assessment instruments. Nor does the law include any obligation or suggestion to prefer support measures with supporting scientific evidence over measures without such evidence. In general, there is a heavy emphasis on social worker's professional discretion in assessment and service panning (Bode & Turba, 2014). However, some municipalities (e.g., Stuttgart, Düsseldorf, Hamburg, and Berlin) have determined that their caseworkers have to use risk assessment tools with a least some evidence on validity.

Employees in non-governmental child and youth welfare service organizations have to follow slightly different procedures compared to case workers in child and youth welfare offices (cf. sec. 8a, para. 2, social code book VIII—SGB VIII). They also have to do an assessment and make a decision regarding endangerment, when becoming aware of weighty grounds for the endangerment of a child or adolescent under their care. However, in this context they have to consult at least once with an experienced expert in child protection. Parallel to child and youth welfare offices, professionals from child and youth welfare service organizations must involve parents as well as the child or adolescent in the endangerment assessment, if this does not undermine effective protection. If professionals consider support measures necessary, they have to encourage parents to seek out such services. The rationale behind this point is that the success rate of support measures is higher, if parents themselves ask for them. Accordingly, it becomes less likely that children have to experience involuntary state intervention. If a case is seen above the endangerment threshold, there is an obligation to inform the child and youth welfare office if parents do not seek out necessary support measures on their own. That means that there is some form of mandatory reporting within the organizational field of child and youth welfare services in Germany. A form, however, that prioritizes voluntary help-seeking by maltreating parents or parents at risk for maltreatment.

For professionals outside child and youth welfare services, procedures for dealing with weighty grounds to suspect child endangerment are laid down in section 4 of the law on cooperation and information in child protection (KKG). Professionals (e.g., physicians, psychologists) are required to take protective action if they come across weighty grounds to suspect child endangerment in a case. Professionals should try to talk to the child or adolescent and the parents about the situation and encourage them to seek out support measures. If professionals think a child is endangered but are unable (for whatever reason) to find a way to get in contact with parents about the suspicion or cannot encourage them to use support measures on a voluntary basis, the law contains an explicit authorization to inform the local child and youth welfare office about the case. Again, there is a heavy emphasis in German child protection law to build upon already existing relationships of trust between family members and professionals and a decision against a quick and mandatory referral to a centralized and specialized child protection authority.

There are no national statistics on the number of cases where professionals according to section 4 of the law on cooperation and information in child protection (KKG) come across weighty grounds to suspect child endangerment. Not even the number of child endangerment assessments done by employees in independent non-governmental child and youth welfare service organizations is known. However, since 2012 there have been national official statistics on the number of child endangerment assessments done by professionals in child and youth welfare offices. As the child and youth welfare office has to make its own assessment after every child endangerment notification and every assessment has to be recorded by law, this statistic can be seen as a rough indicator of the number of child endangerment cases that become known to child protection authorities in Germany each year. It is only a rough indicator because there are families or children with two or more endangerment assessments per year. Moreover, there is hardly any information on the quality of these statistical data especially regional disparities in counting procedures (Mühlmann et al., 2015, p. 107). There are four categories for possible results of the endangerment assessment: (1) acute endangerment (child has already been maltreated or there are clear indicators for a situation in which significant harm in the near future is highly likely), (2) latent endangerment (the situation is more ambiguous, it is not possible to rule out or confirm child endangerment), (3) no endangerment but support needs, and (4) no endangerment and no support needs (false alarm). Excluding the first year of the

Table 10.1 Endangerment assessments according to sec. 8a para.1 SGB VIII by professionals of child and youth welfare offices between 2013 and 2016 (Statistisches Bundesamt, 2017). Percent of total in a given year noted. Data on the rate of assessments per 100,000 minors have been calculated by Pothmann and Kaufhold (2018).

Years	2013 (n=)	2013 (in %)	2014 (n=)	2014 (in %)	2015 (n=)	2015 (in %)	2016 (n=)	2016 (in %)
Assessments with the result: acute endangerment of the welfare of the child	17,211	15	18,630	15	20,806	16	21,571	16
Assessments with the result: latent endangerment to the welfare of the child	21,411	19	22,419	18	24,188	19	24,206	18
Assessments with the result: no endangerment but need for support	37,848	33	41,543	33	43,185	33	46,623	34
Assessments with the result: no endangerment and no (further) need for support	39,217	34	41,621	34	41,306	32	44,525	33
Assessments of endangerment done by child and youth welfare agencies (overall)	115,687	100	124,213	100	129,485	100	136,925	100
Rate of assessments of endangerment per 100,000 minors	88.5	-	94.7	-	97.2	-	101.6	-

statistical survey due to possibly invalid data Table 10.1 shows the figures for the years 2013 to 2016.

Table 10.1 illustrates that there has been a continual rise in the number of endangerment assessments since 2013. The table further points out that in about one-third of all assessments no danger and no need for support could be identified by the professionals (2013: 33.90%; 2014: 33.51%; 2015: 31.90%; 2016: 32.53%). With about 13 million minors in Germany, it can be estimated that a maximum of 1% of all children and adolescents experience an endangerment assessment per year. In England, Australia, and the United States, three to five times higher referral rates have been reported (Munro & Manful, 2012, p. 33). Data on the cumulative referral rate during childhood, published for some countries (e.g., Rouland & Vaithianathan, 2018), are not available for Germany.

The statistic on endangerment assessments done by professionals of child and youth welfare offices can also be analyzed regarding referral source. The main sources in 2016 were police (2016: 22.08%), schools, the education system, and child and youth welfare service organizations, including day care (17.9%), followed by acquaintances/neighbours (11.58%), anonymous reporters (10.44%), and the health sector (6.6%) (Statistisches Bundesamt, 2017). Most of the referrals from police were due to incidents of intimate partner violence involving parents (cf. Kaufhold & Pothmann, 2017, p. 2). The proportions of different referral sources remained almost stable between 2012 and 2016. Comparing these data to international figures it may be noteworthy that the health system seems to be badly integrated into the child protection systems in Germany because countries such as England, Australia, and the United States report many more notifications from this sector (Fry & Casey, 2017, p. 32). In contrast, self-referrals and referrals from child and youth welfare service organizations may be more prevalent in Germany.

Actions taken by the child and youth welfare office after the assessment are as follows. If a case was categorized as acute endangerment in 2016, in 29.4% of these cases, an emergency placement took place; in 28.1% a family court procedure was initiated. Both actions are not mutually exclusive but in fact highly correlated. As family courts are the only institution that can interfere with parental rights, it is clear that in most cases some kind of agreement between parents and the child protection authority was reached. In most cases (59.9%) some kind of support measure was delivered. For assessments with the result of a latent endangerment, 73.7% of these families received some kind of support measure with 11.5% appealing to the family court. This was even more true for emergency placements (4.4%) (Kaufhold & Pothmann, 2017, p. 5). The data demonstrate that involuntary state intervention in Germany is most likely in cases of acute endangerment, but even within this case category only a minority of families is confronted with some kind of compulsory measure. Although the distinction between voluntary and involuntary is gradual (Pösö et al., 2018), compulsory child protection measures seem to be much more likely in countries like England or the United States (Burns et al., 2017). Regarding the comparison between England, the Netherlands, and Germany, this has also been illustrated in a recent study comparing 400 child protection referrals accepted for investigation in each country with four sites in each country. On average, a decision was reached within 23 days in Germany, 38 days in England and 72 days in the Netherlands. If the case was categorized to be above the endangerment or significant harm threshold, involuntary measures were applied in 29% of the German cases, 46% of the cases from the Netherlands, and 90% of the cases from England (Witte & Kindler, 2018).

Types and Developments of Interventions and Measures to Protect Children

Under the heading of *Frühe Hilfen* (early support services), primary preventive interventions for families with young children have gained momentum in Germany during the last 10 years. For example, in about 90% of all municipalities early preventive home-visiting services are available (Sann & Küster, 2013, p. 40) and in a national study more than 40% of at-risk families reported receiving such services at least once (Eickhorst et al., 2016). In Germany, it has been difficult to demonstrate positive effects of early preventive home-visiting services (Taubner et al., 2015), although some programs with positive long-term effects in the United States were implemented in Germany with fidelity controlled (e.g., family-nurse partnership program: Sandner et al., 2017). A reason may be that services as usual have a high standard in Germany compared to the United States, making it more difficult for preventive programs to demonstrate strong effects in Germany. Nevertheless, at least for attachment-based prevention concepts working with high risk mothers, some effects have been demonstrated (e.g., Suess et al., 2016). Moreover, in general user feedback has been positive for preventive home-visiting services in Germany.

Family counseling (*Erziehungsberatung*) as a second type of service has a long tradition in Germany and high utilization rates. Parents of as many as 270 to 290 minors per 10,000 frequent counselling centers (Fendrich et al., 2018a), mostly seeking advice for child behavioral problems, parenting difficulties, or conflicts after parental separation. In about half of the cases there are counseling sessions not only with parents but also with children. Many different methods are used in the context of family counseling and follow-up studies have shown positive change in most of the cases (e.g., Macsenaere et al., 2018). After child maltreatment or in at-risk cases for child maltreatment, however, family counseling is rarely the sole form of intervention. Nevertheless, in about 5% of all cases in family counseling centers child protection concerns are a main reason for counseling (Menne, 2014, p. 242) and because so many families are served, this amounts to a substantial number of cases. However, in a recent evaluation study, family counseling was found to be not effective in ameliorating maltreatment risks (Macsenaere et al., 2018). Nevertheless, family counseling may be part of a larger service concept or useful as a bridge into other services.

Social-pedagogical in-home child and family service (*sozialpädagogische Familienhilfe*) is a common ambulant family support measure in the German child and youth welfare system. In a given year 140 per 10,000 children and young people receive such a service (Fendrich et al., 2016, p. 70). Most of these cases are below the endangerment threshold, but after an endangerment assessment, this service is the second most common ambulant support measure (Menne, 2014, p. 242). In a national sample of child protection court cases nearly a third of all families had received social-pedagogical in-home child and family service in the past and, if the children were not placed, it was the most common support measure afterwards (Bindel-Kögel & Seidenstücker, 2017). Social-pedagogical in-home child and family service is not like an intervention program (e.g., SafeCare), but a flexible support measure based on a loose set of principles developed since the 1970s (Schattner, 1997). One of the main principles is called lifeworld-orientation (*Lebensweltorientierung*) (Kraus, 2015). This principle includes support for families to access social welfare benefits and empowerment to improve family living conditions. The main focus, however, is on counseling based on an understanding of the everyday experiences, conflicts, and needs of family members. A systemic approach towards family problems can be considered to constitute a second principle, which includes a focus on relationships between family members and the functioning of the whole family in meeting children's needs. Among others, Wolf (2012) and Rothe (2017) have described the concept of social-pedagogical in-home child and family service in more detail. Despite its widespread use, effectiveness data are sparse and restricted to weak designs such as single case studies or pre-post studies without control groups (Macsenaere, 2014). This is especially true for cases of child endangerment. None of the studies until now has focused on effects for this group of families.

Out-of-home placement in a foster family or a residential care facility may be a third option in child protection cases. In a sample of 400 child protection cases from child and youth welfare offices from four sites a placement was planned in 26% of the cases after an endangerment assessment, and at a six-month follow-up 11% of the children were placed (Witte, 2017). In a sample of more than 200 child protection cases that went to court, placement rates were higher. After the court decision about 36% of the children lived in a foster family, kinship care, or residential care (Bindel-Kögel & Seidenstücker, 2017). Longitudinal studies with endangered children on placement trajectories and cumulative time in care are non-existent. But it is known that maltreatment or being at-risk for maltreatment is the main reason for the placement in a substantial minority of the cases (in 2012: 34.7% of the children in foster care and 21.7% of the children in residential care; Menne, 2014). Moreover, a majority of all children in placement have experienced one or more forms of maltreatment although this may not have been the reason for the placement (Kindler et al., 2011, p. 183; Rau et al., 2018). In general, placements in Germany tend to be long-term (in 2016 the average duration of foster care was 42 months; of residential care, 17 months; Fendrich et al., 2018b). Although adoption is not an exit option for children in placement in Germany and only in a small minority of cases parental rights have been withdrawn, permanency can be achieved for many foster children. For example, in a sample of adolescent foster children from different sites, 75% had experienced no more than two separations including the placement during their lifetime (Kindler et al., 2011, p. 347). Residential care as a type of out-of-home care is quite prevalent in Germany (Ainsworth & Thoburn, 2014). About half of all children in out-of-home placement live in a residential care facility. There are few longitudinal studies on the development of children in care in Germany and hardly any study has examined maltreated children as a separate group. Small-scale, cross-sectional studies suggest that maltreatment experiences as well as quality of care experienced during placement impact attachment development and mental health of children (e.g., Bovenschen et al., 2016; Kavemann et al., 2018). Because the number of maltreated children in care with chronic behavioral problems is quite high (see, e.g., Fischer et al., 2016; Ehrenberg et al., 2018), improvements in service are needed but have rarely been examined empirically (Besier et al., 2009). As in other countries, there have been horrific cases of historical institutional abuse in Germany since World War II (Kröger & Schrapper, 2009). Studies have also examined the current situation finding a substantial amount of (sexual) violence in residential care and to a lesser degree in foster care (e.g., Allroggen et al., 2017; van Santen et al., 2018) with children placed due to endangerment being especially vulnerable (Kavemann et al., 2018). To reduce sexual violence prevention concepts have been established in most residential care facilities (Pooch & Kappler, 2017) and first studies show positive effects on the incidence of sexual violence (Derr et al., 2017).

If a child seems to be in acute and urgent danger, the child and youth welfare office can take an emergency measure (*Inobhutnahme*) and place the child during an investigation phase. During this time, it has to be clarified whether there really is child endangerment, which measures are suitable to avert dangers, and whether the parents are willing to work with the child and youth welfare office. About 31,000 children (2.4 minors in a thousand) have experienced such an emergency measure in 2017 (Mühlmann, 2018) and numbers have increased by about 50% since 2005. Most of the measures end within one month, but being a massive intervention into the lives of children and families there is a discussion on negative effects (Petermann et al., 2014). Some studies have shown that children in emergency measures as a group are very stressed and some feel completely excluded from decisions regarding their own lives (Rücker et al., 2018).

If a child protection case goes to family court, a decision in the first instance is reached within six months in two thirds of the cases (Bindel-Kögel & Seidenstücker, 2017). In addition, there is a provisional order in about a third of the cases, which is a matter of days not months. Due to rulings of the Federal Constitutional Court, judges were required to hear children over the age of 3 since 2006. But in a large study with more than 200 cases from different sites this was done in only 54% of the cases (Bindel-Kögel & Seidenstücker, 2017), which suggests that many judges feel ill-prepared for this task. Therefore, in 2021 the law was changed and an obligation to hear the child and get a personal impression was introduced (sec. 159 family court procedures law—FamFG). During the court procedure a "guardian ad litem" has to be appointed and in about 40% of the cases an additional psychological or medical expert is appointed (Bindel-Kögel & Seidenstücker, 2017). Both have to support the court via information on children's thoughts and wishes (guardian ad litem) or the results of psychological or medical examinations of the child and the parents. The effects of such support on the decisions reached and effects on children or families have not been researched. But a recent study has reconstructed expert recommendations in child protection cases (Zumbach et al., 2018). Placement of the child was more likely to be recommended if developmental delays and/or disorganized attachment relationships were found. During recent years (2012–2015), family courts in Germany have made decisions regarding 14,000 to 17,000 child protection cases per year. The exact number of children affected is not known, but it has been estimated that between 110 and 130 minors per 100,000 go through such a proceeding each year (Seidenstücker & Weymann, 2017). Table 10.2 gives an overview of measures ordered by Family Courts in the years 2012–2015 for the protection of endangered children in Germany.

Because there may be several measures per case the number of cases heard is much lower than the number of measures taken. Over ten years (2006–2015) the number of child protection court cases has risen by 60% (9,572 to 15,403) (Münder, 2017, p. 109f.). But still only a tiny fraction of all child protection notifications received by child and youth welfare offices (129,485 in 2015) goes on to court.

At the moment, it is mostly unclear to what extent working together with parents or intervening in families leads to safety and a positive developmental pathway for children. Early studies have examined child maltreatment recurrence rates (e.g., Bae & Kindler,

Table 10.2 Measures of the family court because of an endangerment of the well-being of a child between 2012 and 2015 (Münder, 2017, p. 111)

Measures of the family court because of an endangerment of the well-being of a child	2012 (n=)	2013 (n=)	2014 (n=)	2015 (n=)
Obligations to use support such as child and youth welfare and health care services (1666 Abs. 3 No. 1 BGB)	8,970	8,360	8,446	8,730
Obligations to ensure that compulsory school attendance is respected; Prohibitions to use the family flat or another apartment temporarily or indefinitely, to stay in a certain area of the flat or to visit other places to be determined where the child regularly stays; Prohibitions to contact or arrange a meeting with the child (1666 Abs. 3 No. 2 - 4 BGB)	3,355	3,337	3,678	3,637
The replacement of declarations made by the holder of parental rights (1666 Abs. 3 No. 5 BGB)	2,102	1,534	1,598	1,635
Partial withdrawal of parental custody (1666 Abs. 3 No.6 BGB)	7,605	7,996	8,532	7,818
Total withdrawal of parental custody (1666 Abs. 3 No.6 BGB)	6,795	7,071	8,497	7,585
Measures of the family court because of an endangerment of the well-being of a child (overall)	28,797	28,298	30,751	29,405

2017; Witte & Kindler, 2018). During a six month follow-up with 400 cases from four sites, the recurrence rate for child neglect was especially high (17%) compared to physical abuse (11%) and psychological abuse (6%) (Witte & Kindler, 2018). As in other child protection systems, more research on outcomes of the child protection system is needed.

Trends and Forthcoming Issues

Since the mid-1990s, child protection issues have increasingly arisen in Germany. Discourses on failed child protection cases and on sexual abuse in institutions were main factors (Biesel, 2011; Wolff et al., 2011; Brandhorst, 2015). This led to several legal reforms since 2005, culminating in a federal child protection act (*Bundeskinderschutzgesetz*) in 2012 (Meysen & Eschelbach, 2012). Since then, child protection has been conceived as a state-regulated system that requires coordination and control at the federal level. The Federal Child Protection Act aims, for example, to improve cooperation between child and youth welfare and the health system and to strengthen the quality of child protection on the municipal level.

Traditionally, in Germany, the protection of endangered children is considered an integral responsibility of child and youth welfare. This view has not changed, but child protection is now also regarded as a duty of the federal government, which in recent years has not only been regulated by law, but also supported by special federal programs (e.g., on errors and mistakes in child protection or early services in municipalities).

However, child and youth welfare in Germany is no longer seen as the only field that can guarantee the protection of endangered children. Child protection is now considered to be a system whose quality and effectiveness is the responsibility of various professionals and organizations operating in different areas, mainly in child and youth welfare and in the health system. A result of that development is the adoption of a new child and youth welfare act in 2021 (*Kinder- und Jugendstärkungsgesetz—KJSG*). It aims to improve child protection through more supervision and control elements and to make child and youth services more accessible to children and young people with disabilities. Finally, the scientific debate acknowledges that child protection can only be successful in cooperation between children, parents and professionals. Therefore, what is required on the one hand is to establish a democratic child protection practice in which principles of participation and of dialog have space to emerge (see, e.g., Gedik & Wolff, 2021). On the other hand, it is important that rights of children attract attention without negation of the needs and rights of parents and the importance of the autonomy of families as warm and safe places where children should grow up, if possible.

References

Ainsworth, F. and Thoburn, J. (2014). An exploration of the differential usage of residential childcare across national boundaries. *International Journal of Social Welfare*, 23(1), 16–24.

Allroggen, M., Rau, T., Ohlert, J., and Fegert, J. M. (2017). Lifetime prevalence and incidence of sexual victimization of adolescents in institutional care. *Child Abuse and Neglect*, 66, 23–30.

Bae, H.-O. and Kindler, H. (2017). Child maltreatment re-notifications in Germany: Analysis of local case files. *Children and Youth Services Review*, 75, 42–49.

Besier, T., Fegert, J. M., and Goldbeck, L. (2009). Evaluation of psychiatric liaison services for adolescents in residential group homes. *European Psychiatry*, 24(7), 483–489.

Biesel, K. (2011). *Wenn Jugendämter scheitern: Zum Umgang mit Fehlern im Kinderschutz*. Transcript Verlag.

Biesel, K., Brandhorst, F., Rätz, R., and Krause, H.-U. (2019). *Deutschland schützt seine Kinder*. Transcript Verlag.

Bindel-Kögel, G. and Seidenstücker, B. (2017). Ergebnisse der Fallerhebung in den beteiligten Jugendämtern. In J. Münder (Ed.), *Kindeswohl zwischen Jugendhilfe und Justiz* (pp. 123–188). BeltzJuventa.

Bode, I. and Turba, H. (2014). *Organisierter Kinderschutz in Deutschland*. Springer.

Bovenschen, I., Lang, K., Zimmermann, J., Förthner, J., et al. (2016). Foster children's attachment behavior and representation: influence of children's pre-placement experiences and foster caregiver's sensitivity. *Child Abuse and Neglect*, 51, 323–335.

Brandhorst, F. (2015). *Kinderschutz und Öffentlichkeit: Der "Fall Kevin" als Sensation und Politikum*. Springer.

Burns, K., Pösö, T., and Skivenes, M. (Eds.). 2017. *Child welfare removals by the state: A cross-country analysis of decision-making systems*. Oxford University Press.

Bussman, K.-D., Erthal, C., and Schroth, A. (2011). Effects of banning corporal punishment in europe: a five-nation comparison. In J. Durrant and A. Smith (Eds.), *Global pathways to abolishing physical punishment* (pp. 299–322). New York: Routledge.

Derr, R., Hartl, J., Mosser, P., et al. (2017). *Kultur des Hinhörens. Sprechen über sexuelle Gewalt, Organisationsklima und Prävention in stationären Einrichtungen der Jugendhilfe*. DJI. .

Eckhardt, T. (2017). *The education system in the Federal Republic of Germany 2014/2015*. KMK.

Ehrenberg, D., Lohaus, A., Konrad, K., and Heinrichs, N. (2018). Kindesmisshandlung bei Pflegekindern. *Zeitschrift für klinische Psychologie und Psychotherapie*, 47(2), 77–88.

Eickhorst, A., Schreier, A., Brand, C., Lang, K., et al. (2016). Inanspruchnahme von Angeboten der Frühen Hilfen und darüber hinaus durch psychosozial belastete Eltern. *Bundesgesundheitsblatt*, 59(10), 1271–1280.

Fendrich, S., Pothmann, J., and Tabel, A. (2016). *Monitor Hilfen zur Erziehung 2016*. Technical University and German Youth Institute.

Fendrich, S., Pothmann, J., and Tabel, A. (2018a). Erziehungsberatung in Zahlen. In S. Rietmann and M. Sawatzki (Eds.), *Zukunft der Beratung* (pp. 159–164). Springer.

Fendrich, S., Pothmann, J., and Tabel, A. (2018b). *Monitor Hilfen zur Erziehung 2018*. Technical University and German Youth Institute.

Fischer, S., Dölitzsch, C., Schmeck, K., Fegert, J. M., et al. (2016). Interpersonal trauma and associated psychopathology in girls and boys living in residential care. Children and Youth Services Review, 67, 203–211.

Fry, D. and Casey, T. (2017). *Bringing the global to the local: Review of global trends in the prevalence and services for child maltreatment in order to inform research, policy and practice in England*. NSPCC.

Gedik, K. and Wolfff, R. (2021). Kinderschutz in der Demokratie - Eckpfeiler guter Fachpraxis. Ein Handbuch. Barbara Budrich.

Gerber, C. (2006). Was ist bei einer Kindeswohlgefährdung in Abgrenzung zum ASD der Aufgabenbereich der Polizei? In H. Kindler, S. Lilllig, H. Blüml, T. Meysen, and A. Werner (Eds.), *Handbuch Kindeswohlgefährdung nach § 1666 BGB und Allgemeiner Sozialer Dienst (ASD)* (pp. 229–231). Deutsches Jugendinstitut.

Gilbert, N., Parton, and Skivenes, M. (2011). Changing Patterns of Response and Emerging Orientations. In N. Gilbert, N. Parton, and M. Skivenes (Eds.), *Child protection systems: International trends and orientations* (pp. 243–257). Oxford University Press.

Hämäläinen, J. (2013). Defining social pedagogy: Historical, theoretical and practical considerations. *The British Journal of Social Work*, 45(3), 1022–1038.

Häuser, W., Schmutzer, G., Brähler, E., and Glaesmer, H. (2011). Maltreatment in childhood and adolescence: results from a survey of a representative sample of the German population. *Deutsches Ärzteblatt international*, 108(17), 287–294.

Herrmann, B., Dettmeyer, R., Banaschak, S., and Thyen, U. (2016). Spezielle Einrichtungen des Kinderschutzes. In B. Herrmann, R. Dettmeyer, S. Banaschak, and U. Thyen (Eds.), *Kindesmisshandlung* (pp. 377–386). Springer.

Kaufhold, G. and Pothmann, J. (2017). Knapp 45.800 Kindeswohlgefährdungen im Jahr 2016—jedes dritte 8a-Verfahren durch Jugendämter bestätigt Gefährdungsverdacht. *KomDat—kommentierte Daten der Kinder- und Jugendhilfe*, (2&3/2017), 1–5.

Kavemann, B., Helfferich, C., Kindler, H., and Nagel, B. (2018). Sexual re-victimisation of adolescent girls in institutional care with a history of sexual violence in childhood. *Journal of Gender-based Violence*, 2(1), 9–24.

Kindler, H. (2013). *Qualitätsindikatoren für den Kinderschutz in Deutschland. Analyse der nationalen und internationalen Diskussion*. Nationales Zentrum Frühe Hilfen.

Kindler, H., Helming, E., Meysen, T., and Jurczyk, K. (2011). *Handbuch Pflegekinderhilfe*. Deutsches Jugendinstitut.

Krahé, B. and Berger, A. (2013). Men and women as perpetrators and victims of sexual aggression in heterosexual and same-sex encounters: A study of first-year college students in Germany. *Aggressive Behavior*, 39(5), 391–404.

Kraus, B. (2015). The life we live and the life we experience: Introducing the epistemological difference between "Lifeworld"(Lebenswelt) and "Life Conditions" (Lebenslage). *Social Work and Society*, 13(2).

Kröger, R. and Schrapper, C. (2009). *Fürsorgeerziehung der 1950er und 1960er Jahre*. Universität Koblenz-Landau.

Macsenaere, M. (2014). Wirkungsforschung und ihre Ergebnisse. In M. Macsenaere, K. Esser, E. Knab, and S. Hiller (Eds.), *Handbuch der Hilfen zur Erziehung* (pp. 592–598). Lambertus.

Macsenaere, M., Arnold, J., and Hiller, S. (2018). *Wirksamkeit der Erziehungsberatung. Ergebnisse der bundesweiten Studie Wir.EB*. Lambertus.

Menne, K. (2014). Erziehungsberatung im Kontext der Hilfen zur Erziehung. In H. Scheuerer-Englisch, A. Hundsalz, and K. Andreas (Eds.), *Jahrbuch für Erziehungsberatung*. Band 10 (pp. 224–254). BeltzJuventa.

Meysen, T. and Eschelbach, D. (2012). *Das neue Bundeskinderschutzgesetz*. Nomos.

Mühlmann, T. (2018, August 28). *Inobhutnahmen zum Schutz von Kindern und Jugendlichen bleiben auf hohem Niveau* [Press release]. German Youth Institute.

Mühlmann, T., Pothmann, J., and Kopp, K. (2015). *Wissenschaftliche Grundlagen für die Evaluation des Budeskinderschutzgesetzes*. Technical University Dortmund and German Youth Institute.

Münder, J. (Ed.). (2017). *Kindeswohl zwischen Jugendhilfe und Justiz: Zur Entwicklung von Entscheidungsgrundlagen und Verfahren zur Sicherung des Kindeswohls zwischen Jugendämtern und Familiengerichten*. BeltzJuventa.

Münder, J., Meysen, T., and Trenczk, T. (2013). *Frankfurter Kommentar zum SGB VIII* (7th ed.). Nomos.

Munro, E. and Manful, E. (2012). *Safeguarding children: A comparison of England's data with that of Australia, Norway and the United States*. Department for Education.

Petermann, F., Besier, T., Büttner, P., Rücker, S., et al. (2014). Vorläufige Schutzmaßnahmen für gefährdete Kinder und Jugendliche. *Kindheit und Entwicklung*, 23(2), 124–133.

Pösö, T., Pekkarinen, E., Helavirta, S., and Laakso, R. (2018). "Voluntary" and "involuntary" child welfare: Challenging the distinction. *Journal of Social Work*, 18(3), 253–272.

Pötter, N. (2018). *Schulsozialarbeit*. Lambertus.

Pooch, M.-T. and Kappler, S. (2017). *Datenreport zum Stand der Prävention sexualisierter Gewalt an Kindern und Jugendlichen in Deutschland zu den Handlungsfeldern Kindertageseinrichtungen, Heime, Kliniken und Einrichtungen des ambulanten Gesundheitsbereichs*. UBSKM.

Pothmann, J. and Kaufhold, G. (2018). Mehr "8a-Verfahren," aber keine Zunahme der Kindeswohlgefährdungen. *KomDat—kommentierte Daten der Kinder- und Jugendhilfe*, (2), 5–8.

Rau, T., Ohlert, J., Fegert, J. M., Andresen, S., et al. (2018). Kindheitserlebnisse von Jugendlichen in Internaten: Ein Vergleich mit Jugendlichen aus Jugendhilfeeinrichtungen und der Allgemeinbevölkerung. *Praxis der Kinderpsychologie und Kinderpsychiatrie*, 67(1), 31–47.

Rothe, M. (2017). *Sozialpädagogische Familien-und Erziehungshilfe: eine Handlungsanleitung*. Kohlhammer.

Rouland, B. and Vaithianathan, R. (2018). Cumulative prevalence of maltreatment among New Zealand children, 1998–2015. *American Journal of Public Health*, 108(4), 511–513.

Rücker, S., Büttner, P., Karpinski, N., Petermann, F., et al. (2018). Geschlechtsspezifische Unterschiede im Belastungsausmaß bei in Obhut genommenen Kindern und Jugendlichen. *Praxis der Kinderpsychologie und Kinderpsychiatrie, 67*(1), 48–62.

Sandner, M., Jungmann, T., Cornelissen, T., and Herrmann, P. (2017). *Evaluating the Effects of a Targeted Home Visiting Program on Maternal and Child Health Outcomes.* Discussion Paper No. 10715. IZA Institute of Labor Economics.

Sann, A. and Küster, E.-U. (2013). Zum Stand des Ausbaus Früher Hilfen in den Kommunen. In NZFH (Ed.), *Datenreport Frühe Hilfen 2013* (pp. 36–45). NZFH.

Schattner, H. (1997). Sozialpädagogische Familienhilfe. In J. Eccarius (Ed.), *Handbuch Familie* (pp. 593–613). VS Verlag für Sozialwissenschaften.

Schone, R. (2008). *Kontrolle als Element von Fachlichkeit in den sozialpädagogischen Diensten der Kinder- und Jugendhilfe: Expertise im Auftrag der Arbeitsgemeinschaft für Kinder- und Jugendhilfe.* Berlin.

Seidenstücker, B. and Weymann, M. (2017). Entwicklungen im Kinderschutz: einesekundärstatistische Analyse. In J. Münder (Ed.), *Kindeswohl zwischen Jugendhilfe und Justiz* (pp. 108–122). BeltzJuventa.

Statistisches Bundesamt. (2019). *Bevölkerung und Erwerbstätigkeit. Bevölkerungsfortschreibung auf Grundlage des Zensus 2011.* Wiesbaden.

Statistisches Bundesamt. (2017). *Statistiken der Kinder- und Jugendhilfe. Gefährdungsein schätzungen nach § 8a Absatz 1 SGB VIII 2016.* Wiesbaden.

Stoltenborgh, M. (2012). *It should not hurt to be a child: Prevalence of child maltreatment across the globe* [Unpublished doctoral dissertation]. Universiteit Leiden.

Suess, G., Bohlen, U., Carlson, E., Spangler, G., and Frumentia Maier, M. (2016). Effectiveness of attachment based STEEP™ intervention in a German high-risk sample. *Attachment and Human Development, 18*(5), 443–460.

Taubner, S., Wolter, S., and Rabung, S. (2015). Effectiveness of early-intervention programs in German-speaking countries—a meta-analysis. *Mental Health and Prevention, 3,* 69–78.

Tsokos, M. and Guddat, S. (2014). *Deutschland misshandelt seine Kinder.* Droemer.

van Santen, E., Pluto, L., and Peuker, C. (2018). *Pflegekinderhilfe—Situation und Perspektiven.* BeltzJuventa.

Wetzels, P. (1997). Gewalterfahrungen in der Kindheit. Nomos.

Witt, A., Brown, R., Plener, P., Brähler, E., et al. (2017). Child maltreatment in Germany: prevalence rates in the general population. *Child and Adolescent Psychiatry and Mental Health, 11*(1), 47.

Witte, S. (2017). *Hestia project. Comparative case file analysis. Study design und descriptive statistics.* German Youth Institute.

Witte, S. and Kindler, H. (2018). *Decisions at the end of child protection investigations: Results from the Hestia Study.* Presentation of the Norface Welfare State Futures Conference, Florence, 25.05.2018.

Witte, S., Miehlbradt, L., van Santen, E., and Kindler, H. (2016). *Briefing on the German child protection system: HESTIA—an international research project on child protection policy and practice.* Available at: http://www.projecthestia.com/wp-content/uploads/2015/03/POLICY-BRIEFING-GERMANY.pdf.

Wolf, K. (2012). *Sozialpädagogische Interventionen in Familien.* BeltzJuventa.

Wolff, R., Biesel, K., and Heinitz, S. (2011). Child protection in an age of uncertainty: Germany's response. In N. Gilbert, N. Parton, and M. Skivenes (Ed.), *Child protection systems: International trends and orientations* (pp. 183–203). Oxford University Press.

Zumbach, J, Wetzels, P., and Koglin, U. (2018). Predictors of psychological recommendations in child protection evaluation. *Child Abuse and Neglect, 84,* 196–204.

CHAPTER

11

Child Protection and Welfare on the Island of Ireland: Irish Themes, Global Relevance

Kenneth Burns, John Devaney, Stephanie Holt, *and* Gerry Marshall

Abstract

This chapter explores the issues and global relevance of child protection and welfare in Ireland. It expounds on the evolving political context on the Island of Ireland being the reason behind the nation having two different and independent child protection systems. The chapter also focuses on the impact of Brexit, technologies, and migration while highlighting the importance of neighbouring jurisdictions working together. Technology and social media platforms have also enabled social workers to communicate, monitor, and analyze data on adults who might be a risk to children. On the other hand, migrants are at an increased risk of poverty and social exclusion as children from ethnic minority groups are over-represented in the Irish childcare system.

Key Words: child protection systems, welfare, Ireland, Brexit, technologies, migration, poverty, social exclusion, social media

Introduction

It could be argued at points in history that there was little focus on the welfare and needs of children and young people, and this was particularly true on the island of Ireland. In contemporary times, nation states have evolved from episodic bouts of attention and investment in child protection and welfare, mostly roused by crises and moral panics, to a more consistent model of planning, investment, and resourcing. How have these changes come about and how are the child protection systems on the island of Ireland organized and resourced? Are children and young people safer? Are models of practice with families more relationship-based, caring, responsive and available in a timely-fashion, when required? The child welfare and protection systems in Ireland and Northern Ireland are dynamic systems, evolving at pace, which means that it is difficult to write a definitive account. However, what is clear is that these child protection systems are unrecognizable from that which existed one, let alone two decades ago.

This chapter begins with a brief explanation of the political context on the island of Ireland, to explain why there are two different and independent child protection systems on the island. It is our contention that these two systems are worth comparing as little work has been done on examining their commonalities and differences. Much has been written about the English child protection system, and while Northern Ireland, like England, is a part of the United Kingdom, Northern Ireland's system is somewhat different to the English system (Stafford et al., 2010). This chapter charts the evolving political, legal, policy, and practice frameworks for both systems, and critically analyzes the key developmental changes since the early 1990s. Rather than addressing all of the changes in a superficial way, we have chosen to look in depth at three contemporary themes of particular relevance: Brexit, the impact of technologies on children and child protection systems, and migration. Furthermore, this chapter does not seek to repeat analyses undertaken elsewhere (see, for example, Devaney et al., 2010; Buckley & Burns, 2015; Devaney & McConville, 2016; Burns & McGregor, 2019), and the reader will be referred to these sources for additional commentary throughout the chapter. A limitation of this chapter is that it does not address the impact of COVID-19 on child protection and welfare systems on the island of Ireland. The core arguments of this chapter are as follows. First, countries that share borders need to work closely with one another given the ability of families and perpetrators to move between jurisdictions across open borders. Second, in an increasingly globalized world, countries need to be able to cooperate to deal with child protection issues that transcend physical borders such as the impact of technologies on children's welfare. Third, the three core themes examined in this chapter are not unique to our countries and the learning from our experiences is of wider relevance to other child protection systems.

The Island of Ireland: Two Countries and Two Separate Child Protection Systems

Comprised of two separate countries, the island of Ireland is linked by geography, history, and culture, but with very little written about how children are protected from abuse and neglect across the whole of the island of Ireland, and how services in these separate legal jurisdictions compare in their organization and response (Devaney & Reid, 2012).

The relationship between Ireland and Great Britain is a long and complicated one. The signing of the Anglo-Irish Treaty in 1921 ended 400 years of a contentious political union between both countries, although it also resulted in the partition of Ireland, with six of the 32 Irish counties remaining part of the United Kingdom, becoming the country of Northern Ireland. In 1931 the British Parliament relinquished its remaining authority to legislate over Irish affairs in the 26 counties in Ireland, and the basis for the fully independent Irish state solidified with the publication of the Irish Constitution in 1937, and Ireland officially became a republic in 1949. This settlement was not unproblematic: there has been extensive political conflict, instability, and paramilitary activity in Northern Ireland, the ripples of which extended across Ireland, Great Britain, and even into Europe, particularly from 1968 to 1998. The signing of the Good Friday Agreement in 1998, underwritten by the governments in Dublin and London, and with the support of the European Union and the United States, marked the beginning of the end of this protracted period of conflict, even though the peace is an uneasy one at times.

The countries of Ireland and Northern Ireland share populations of 4.76 million and 1.86 million, respectively, and a land border of 310 miles. This border brings its own challenges in the opportunities it presents for families and perpetrators to move from one jurisdiction to another in order to avoid child welfare or criminal justice interventions. The border reinforces the need for cross-border cooperation, an issue we return to later in the chapter. In both countries, the relationship between the state and the family has evolved in separate ways since the Anglo-Irish Treaty of 1921. This has been shaped by broader economic and social drivers, but has, essentially, seen welfare services which are largely provided by the State in Northern Ireland draw heavily on the broader British experience (Pinkerton & Campbell, 2002), whilst in Ireland, a broader European influence can be seen with a more diverse range of providers of services, including a larger role for the non-governmental sector (Buckley & Burns, 2015). In both jurisdictions there is a belief that the child protection system should be the responsibility of the State, exercised through public bodies being directly accountable to government for the exercise of their functions, as laid down in statute. In Northern Ireland, these statutory responsibilities are discharged through five sub-regional Health and Social Care Trusts. These Trusts are arms-length government bodies, which alongside responsibility for child protection services also deliver a wide range of health and social care services.

In Ireland, Tusla, the Child and Family Agency, also an arms-length government body, was established in 2014 as a new organization with responsibility for improving the wellbeing and outcomes for children across a range of services, including child protection. Prior to the establishment of Tusla, child protection was part of the remit of the Health Services Executive, the main statutory body for health and social care services in Ireland. Following a series of child abuse inquiries and a view that child protection and welfare was not prioritized in what was a predominately health-focused service, it was felt necessary to establish a separate dedicated agency with responsibility for child protection and welfare (Department of Public Expenditure and Reform, 2017). In both jurisdictions the police also have a significant child protection role in relation to investigating criminal acts of abuse and neglect, and in the arrangements for dealing with individuals who present a risk of harm to children and young people.

Internationally, child protection systems have suffered from regular crises, as the general public and politicians, usually whipped into a maelstrom of outrage by the media, have questioned the effectiveness of the system, typically on the back of the latest child death or high-profile case (Warner, 2015). Both Ireland and Northern Ireland have had their fair share of such cases and subsequent soul-searching. As such, the formal arrangements for child protection in both countries have been subject to what Pollitt and Bouckaert (2017, p. 2) define as a new public reform: "Deliberate attempts to change the structures, processes, and/or culture of public sector organizations with the objective of getting them (in some sense) to run better." This has resulted in the development of elaborate systems of governance that surround the child protection system and child protection work more specifically in order to achieve two outcomes: first, to ensure that the policy imperatives of central government are enacted, and second, to ensure that the system is operating as intended.

There is an inherent conundrum in seeking to have such bodies at arms-length from government, while also exercising significant ability to direct and control those same organizations. This is addressed in both jurisdictions through a series of mechanisms, including: the setting of the strategic direction for child protection through policies developed at government Departmental level with aligned budgets and targets; the commissioning of services based on these strategic priorities; an elaborate system for the regular reporting on activity, financial spending, and outcomes between the delivery bodies and central government; and periodic inspections of services by a separate governmental body, the Regulatory and Quality Improvement Authority (RQIA) in Northern Ireland, and the Health Information and Quality Authority (HIQA) in Ireland. These inspections are underpinned by the *National Standards for the Protection and Welfare of Children* (Health Information Quality Authority, 2012) and related standards on out of home care, and the implementation of *Children First: National Guidance for the Protection and Welfare of Children* (Department of Children and Youth Affairs, 2017) in Ireland, and by *Co-operating to Safeguard Children and Young People* (Department of Health, 2017) and the *Standards for Child Protection Services* (Department of Health, 2008) in Northern Ireland. With a view to highlighting both the commonalities and differences in the two systems that operate on one island—yet across two jurisdictions—this chapter will now consider some key comparative data and trends.

Profile of Child Protection in Northern Ireland and Ireland

In this section, we provide data from multiple sources to compare key trends in referrals, populations of children, and child protection in the two jurisdictions. As the data is drawn from multiple sources, where possible, we provide data from the same year for each category when providing comparisons, but this was not always possible, and we have focused our attention upon the years 2015–2019. The year-end for datasets in Northern Ireland is March 31 and the source for this data is the Department of Health statistics branch, whereas the year-end for Ireland is December 31 and all of the data for Ireland comes from the Tusla Performance Data and "Adequacy" reports (Tusla/Health Service Executive, 2007–2020; Tusla, 2014–2020).

Ireland has a population of 4,757,976, of which 1,190,478 (25%) are under 18. Northern Ireland has a population of 1,862,137, of which 436,403 (23%) are under 18. Despite a smaller population, there are proportionately a significantly higher number of children referred to social services in Northern Ireland than in Ireland. During the

Table 11.1 Breakdown of referrals

	1. Child sexual abuse	2. Physical abuse	3. Neglect	4. Emotional abuse	Child protection (1–4) sub-totals	Child welfare referrals	Total referrals
Northern Ireland (March 31, 2019)	Unavailable	Unavailable	Unavailable	Unavailable	*3,139*	*31,439*	**34,578**
Ireland (December 31, 2019)	3,909 (15%)	6,488 (26%)	4,308 (17)	10,722 (42%)	*25,427*	*31,134*	**56,561**

12 months to March 31, 2019, 34,578 referrals were made to children's social care in the five Health and Social Care Trusts in Northern Ireland, with 3,139 of these referrals in respect of child protection concerns (a rate of 7.2 children per 1,000 child population under 18 years) (Department of Health, 2019). This compares to 56,561 referrals to the Child and Family Agency (2020) during the 12 months to the end of December 2019, of whom 25,427 (45%) were referred for a child protection concern (a rate of 21.35 children per 1,000 child population under 18 years). A further breakdown of referrals by referral type is provided in Table 11.1.

One of the noticeable differences between the two jurisdictions is the proportions of referrals that relate to child protection concerns. In Northern Ireland this is proportionally smaller and reflects the division in the primary legislation between the state providing support to children in need and their families for a wide range of reasons (including the disability of a child), and the need to provide services to protect children from experiencing maltreatment. While the nature of the child protection concerns resulting in referral is not published in Northern Ireland, in Ireland the main reason for referral relates to emotional abuse. In both countries, referrals for child welfare concerns outweigh referrals for child protection reasons, reflecting a concern with providing earlier help to families.

On March 31, 2019, 3,281 children (7.5 per 1,000) were in the care of the state in Northern Ireland compared to 5,916 children (5 per 1,000) on December 31, 2019 in Ireland (Department of Health, 2019; Tusla, Child and Family Agency, 2020). A rate of 7.5 children in care per 1,000 children is the highest rate since the introduction of the Children (Northern Ireland) Order 1995 (for example, in 2000 the rate was 5.6 per 1,000), whereas the Irish rate has been declining steadily over the last decade. Both of these rates are significantly lower than rates in the Nordic countries, Germany, Switzerland, and the Netherlands, but are comparable with rates in England and the United States (see Burns et al., 2017). For the year 2018/19 for Northern Ireland there were 884 admissions to care, with 677 discharges. In Ireland, there were 945 admissions to care for 2019, which is a significant year-on-year reduction over the last nine years

Table 11.2 Children in state care by placement type

	General foster care	Relative foster care	General residential care	Special (secure care)	In care of parents under a legal order	Other placements	Total children in care
Northern Ireland (March 31, 2019)	1,336 (41%)	1,251 (38%)	203 (6%)	N/A	366 (11%)	125 (4%)	3,281 (100%)
Ireland (December 31, 2019)	3,895 (66%)	1,550 (26%)	363 (6.1%)	14 (<1%)	N/A	94 (1.6%)	5,916 (100%)

from a peak of 2,372 admissions in 2009. Three quarters of the children in state care in Northern Ireland and Ireland are subject to a legal [care] order from the courts. The remaining children—23% in NI and 25.9% in Ireland—were accommodated in the care of the state in a voluntary agreement with their parents. However, when one examines the care pathways for new admissions into care, the picture is somewhat different. In Northern Ireland 70% of children initially enter care on a voluntary basis in agreement with their parents, compared to 54% in Ireland in 2019 (see Brennan et al., 2020; O'Mahony et al., 2020). Admission to care through a legal [care] order (approved by a court) is 46% in Ireland and 16% in Northern Ireland. Table 11.2 presents data on the placement type for children in state care.

Both countries have made significant strides in reducing the use of residential care, which was the dominant care model in both jurisdictions in the 1980s and 1990s, in favor of foster care as the preferred placement type. Northern Ireland has a unique option to facilitate children to be in the care of their parents at home under a legal order: this is used in instances whenever a child is being rehabilitated into the care of their parents, or in situations where parents can provide day-to-day care for their child but require ongoing support by the state, which shares parental responsibility for the child. This option is not available in Ireland.

In March 2019, close to a third of children in the care population in Northern Ireland had been in state care for five years or longer, with 23% in care for less than a year, and 31% in care for five years or longer (Department of Health, 2019). At the end of 2019 in Ireland, 40% of children had been in care for between one to five years, 11% in care for less than one year, and 49% were in care for greater than five years (Tusla, Child and Family Agency, 2020). Table 11.3 presents data on the age ranges of children in care.

Of the children in care in Northern Ireland, 13% have a disability as confirmed by a pediatrician, of whom 41% have a learning disability and a further 41% have

Table 11.3 Children in state care by age and per 1,000 child population

	Under 1	1–4	5–11	12–15	16–17	Totals
Northern Ireland (March 31, 2019)	3.5% (N=116; 0.26 per 1,000)	19% (N=622; 1.42 per 1,000)	35.5% (N=1,165; 2.66 per 1,000)	26% (N=851; 1.94 per 1,000)	16% (N=527; 1.20 per 1,000)	100% (N=3,281; 7.48 per 1,000)
Ireland (December 31, 2019)	1.5% (N=90; 0.08 per 1,000)	12% (N=702; 0.59 per 1,000)	40.7% (N=2,411; 2.02 per 1,000)	28.2% (N=1,669; 1.4 per 1,000)	17.6% (N=1,044; 0.88 per 1,000)	100% (N=5,916; 5 per 1,000)

a diagnosis of autism. These children are most likely to be in state care for a series of short breaks to provide respite for their carers, rather than as a result of maltreatment. Similar data is not available in Ireland, but children with disabilities in need of respite or in need of full-time care in Ireland would be provided with services and respite through the Health Service Executive and civil society organizations, and these children would not be on care orders or be part of Tusla's systems. While Ireland has a new dedicated Child and Family Agency, children with disabilities, child and adolescent mental health (CAHMS), and public health nursing are illustrative examples of how all children's services were not fully centralized in the new Child and Family Agency.

In summary, in Northern Ireland at March 31, 2019 there were 7.2 child protection referrals per 1,000 of the child population; 5 children per 1,000 of the child population subject to a child protection plan; 7.5 children per 1,000 of the child population in the care system of whom 77% (5.5 per 1,000 children) were subject to a legal order; and 9% of children in care were discharged due to adoption (0.14 per 1,000 children) (Department of Health, 2019). In Ireland, on December 31, 2019, there were 24,827 cases open to the child protection department (20.85 per 1,000) and 47.5 referrals per 1,000 children; 876 children (0.7 per 1,000) were subject to a child protection plan; 4,384 (3.7 per 1,000) children were in care on a legal order at year-end and 1,532 (1.28 per 1,000) on a voluntary care agreement and 179 children (0.15 per 1,000) in foster care were referred for adoption in 2019 (Tusla, Child and Family Agency, 2020). There were 79 domestic adoptions in 2019, of which were 21 children were adopted from long-term foster care (Adoption Authority of Ireland, 2020).

Policy, Legislation, and Practice in Both Jurisdictions: Recent Developments, Forthcoming Reforms, and Key Drivers

In this section we take a critical look at the primary child welfare policies and programs that exemplify the child protection systems in both jurisdictions, illuminating trends in policy development over time, and providing evidence, where available, regarding what policies are deemed to be effective.

Ireland

The evolution of the child protection and welfare system and the reform of child care services in Ireland, largely in response to child abuse inquiries and crises, has been written about extensively elsewhere (see, for example, Buckley & O'Nolan, 2013; Buckley & Burns, 2015; McGregor & Quinn, 2015; Burns & McGregor, 2019). Reports such as the *Kilkenny Incest Investigation* (McGuinness, 1993); *Kelly—A Child is Dead* (Joint Committee on the Family, 1996); *The West of Ireland Farmer Case* (Bruton, 1998), the *Roscommon Child Care Case* (Gibbons, 2010), and the newly published *Final Report of the Commission of Investigation into Mother and Baby Homes* (Murphy, 2020), all highlight the influence that inadequate resources, poor professional practices, weak and ineffectual managerial systems, poor inter-professional communication, lack of inter-agency working, and inadequate training have contributed to child abuse and child death outcomes (Buckley & O' Nolan, 2013). These inquiries subsequently led to considerable reform of the child protection and welfare system. The *Kilkenny Incest Investigation* (McGuinness, 1993), for example, is considered to have acted as a "watershed" or "catalyst" for significant legislative reform, with the Child Care Act (1991) implemented in its wake. Responding to the concerns about poor inter-agency communication and cooperation, a new comprehensive national policy for child protection and welfare called *Children First: National Guidelines for the Protection and Welfare of Children* was introduced (Department of Health, 1999), which placed considerable emphasis on inter-agency working as the road map towards best practice in the protection and welfare of children. Revised in 2011 and 2017, *Children First* was recently placed on a statutory footing through the Children First Act 2015.

Reforms at an organizational level have included the establishment in 2011 of The Department of Children and Youth Affairs (recently renamed as the Department of Children, Equality, Disability, Integration and Youth), a dedicated government Department whose aim is to consolidate a range of functions previously discharged by various Government Ministers whilst simultaneously driving an ambitions reform agenda for children and family services. One such area of policy and provision within the remit of this Department is Tusla, the Child and Family Agency. Tusla received €786 million as an operating budget from the Department for 2019, which is an increase of 26% on its first operating budget in 2014. This budget will pay for child welfare and protection services, school completion, family and community supports (family centers and voluntary organizations providing counseling and support services), and Parenting, Prevention and Family Support (PPFS)/Meitheal. While the need for a standalone agency to promote an effective child protection and welfare system is not new, having first been raised in the 1980 *Task Force on Child Care Services* (Buckley & Burns, 2015), the rollout of Tusla has not been without challenge and criticism.

Much has been written, for example, in Ireland and elsewhere, about the impact of bureaucracy and standardized approaches to practice. Reflecting on the Victoria Climbié case in the United Kingdom, Featherstone and colleagues (2012) highlight the dangers associated with standardized practice responses as opposed to individualized needs-based responses. Munro (2011) similarly concluded in her review of children's services in the UK that standardized services cannot respond to a broad variation of need that families present. Since its inception in January 2014, Tusla has operated according to a set of standard processes called the "Standard Business Process," which Buckley and Burns (2015) suggest has reinforced a culture that does not necessarily have the capacity to meet the complex needs of children and families. Buckley (2017) further cautioned against standardized approaches undermining the potential for relationship-based practice, which research has established is at the core of effective interventions and outcomes for families (Ruch et al., 2010). Recent years have also witnessed a significant reduction (38%) in cases awaiting the allocation to a social worker. While this is an important improvement, Buckley and Burns (2015, p. 59), however, question if this reduction is to some degree a result of high thresholds filtering out referrals, concluding that "social work time appears to be invested in investigation at the expense of intervention," perhaps an unintended consequence of the bureaucratic drive towards standardization. These latter concerns would appear to have some resonance with families, with the *Tusla Research Needs Analysis Report* highlighting how parents experienced organizational bureaucracy obstructing interventions, rather than a service which is responsive and supportive of children and families (Crosse & Canavan, 2016). McGregor and colleagues' recent (2020) research highlighted ongoing ambiguity about what family support is, and a general lack of awareness amongst families in the community of the support structures and services available to them. However, as it matures, Tusla is working to actively address such issues with the rollout and mainstreaming of Parenting, Prevention and Family Support (PPFS)/Meitheal, Signs of Safety and Meitheal services.

Arising from a review of Tusla's responsibilities under a number of pieces of childcare legislation, the *Child Protection and Welfare Strategy 2017–2022* was launched in May 2017. As reflected in a recognition that the risk adverse culture needed to change, a significant drive within the strategy is the adoption of "Signs of Safety" (SoS) as the national approach to practice, described by the former CEO of Tusla as an "innovative, strengths based, safety organized approach to child protection casework, grounded in partnership and collaboration with children, families and their wider networks of support" (McBride, 2017, p. 4). While SoS brings with it renewed optimism for a return to relationship-based practice as recommended by experts in the field (Munro, 2011), the challenge facing Tusla concerns how harmoniously SOS will sit alongside the Standard Business Process. The success or failure of this unlikely relationship perhaps depends on how well Tusla can drive towards practice based on the paramountcy principle in child welfare, a return to focusing on parental and family strengths—while not ignoring risk—and a valuing of relationship-based practice, rather than a priority on bureaucracy and standardization. The right of children to have their voice heard alongside the need to promote a child's welfare through early intervention and support, are clearly articulated as key principles of best practice.

Indeed, while the initial concerns about children's rights, Buckley and O'Nolan (2013) observe, emerged in the 1980s, these concerns gathered impetus in the 1990s, primarily with Ireland's ratification of the United Nations Convention on the Rights of the Child in 1992 (UNCRC, 1989). While Article 3 States that "the best interest of the child shall be the primary consideration," the core ethos of Article 12 explicitly calls for children to be granted the opportunity to have their views heard and the right of participation in decisions that affect them. This reflects an empirically grounded awareness not only that this involvement is a right, but also that such participation can improve children's skills and self-esteem, inform decision making, and, as such, promote children's safety and welfare (Powell & Smith, 2009; Ewing et al., 2015). Interestingly, the historically weak and vulnerable position children occupied in the Irish Constitution, relative to their parents, was raised in both the Kilkenny Incest Case (McGuinness, 1993) and the Roscommon Child Care Inquiry (Gibbons, 2010). In response to these concerns and a growing international appreciation of children as competent sentient actors, the Children's Referendum was passed in 2012 and adopted in 2015, enshrining children's rights within the Constitution and paving the way for significant legislative reform and policy development, not least the Children and Family Relationships Act 2015 and the Children First Act 2015. Notwithstanding the accepted acumen underpinning children's rights within both of these pieces of legislation, reform can also bring unintended consequences.

A key issue for child protection and welfare services in Ireland concerns the implementation of the Children First Act 2015, which places the Children First policy and guidance on a statutory footing. In particular, mandatory reporting for certain professional groups commenced in December 2017. Informed by the international research evidence (Lonne et al., 2009; Gilbert et al., 2011), mandatory reporting is likely to result in a sharp increase in the volume of reports to child protection services, potentially diverting resources away from preventative services and more towards initial assessments and filtering of cases. This is of particular concern for a number of reasons. Burns and McGregor (2019) argue that the most significant element of the Parenting, Prevention and Family Support (PPFS) program introduced by Tusla is Meitheal, a new practice model grounded in the principles of early intervention and prevention. Designed to meet the needs of families and children who do not meet the threshold for child protection intervention, Meitheal represents a focused attempt to intervene not only early in a child's life, but also early in the origins of a problem (Devaney et al., 2017). While it is still too early to report on the impact of the introduction of mandatory reporting (see Tusla, Child and Family Agency, 2020, p. 23), the potential for diversion of resources following its introduction may undermine the valuable effort towards "refocusing" interventions towards parenting, prevention and family support. Indeed, Buckley (2017, p. 86) cautions that refocusing efforts to promote relationship-based practice, community-based prevention, and early intervention are at risk of being "blind-sided by increasing bureaucracy and legalism including mandatory reporting."

Returning briefly to the critical issue of children's rights, positive opportunities for the Child and Family Agency to embrace "a children's rights ethos across the whole service to shift Ireland from a family-centric model to one where children's as well as parental rights are operationalized" were identified by Burns and Buckley (2015, p. 63). The Meitheal model, referenced earlier, is grounded in an ethos of child and parental participation. Notwithstanding that the principle of participation can be difficult to operationalize in practice (see Rodriguez et al., 2018), Tusla's *Child and Youth Participation Strategy, 2019–2023* clearly outlines its strategy for the development of participatory practice within Tusla and its funded agencies (Tusla, Child and Family Agency, 2019). This is a welcome and timely development, but just one example of the many new and progressive initiatives being pursued as the Agency matures.

Northern Ireland

The political conflict in Northern Ireland ran from 1968 to the signing of the Good Friday Agreement in 1998, with more than 3,600 individuals dying as a result of the political unrest and community violence, and many tens of thousands of children and adults physically and psychologically traumatized by the experience (Eames & Bradley, 2009). It may seem that matters relating to the welfare of children might attract less attention from the public, politicians, and professionals than could be the case elsewhere. Conversely, children's issues have remained a central worry within civil society and political circles, while the issue of protection from child abuse and neglect has remained at the forefront of public and professional concerns (Devaney & McConville, 2016).

The child welfare and protection system in Northern Ireland has closely followed developments in England (Devaney et al., 2010). Recent research indicates that the outcomes, in terms of the numbers of children deemed in need of child protection measures, and subsequently admitted to care, are noticeably lower than the other parts of the United Kingdom (Bunting et al., 2018). While the overarching strategy for children and young people in Northern Ireland identifies "living in safety and with stability" as one of the six high-level outcomes to be achieved for children across society (Office of the First Minister and Deputy First Minister, 2020), the primary responsibility for developing and implementing policy rests with the Department of Health. The state has had responsibility for protecting children from maltreatment stretching back to the early part of the 20th century. However, in the 1970s and 1980s, a government inquiry into the sexual and physical abuse of boys in a children's residential home brought a sharper focus to the need for government in Northern Ireland to undertake these responsibilities more comprehensively (Department of Health, Social Services, and Public Safety, 2003).

The enactment of The Children (Northern Ireland) Order 1995 in November 1996 was hailed as "one of the most significant pieces of social legislation of the 20th century" in Northern Ireland (Department of Health, Social Services, and Public Safety, 2003, p. 13). Modeled on The Children Act 1989 (in operation in England and Wales) and reflecting many of the principles underpinning the United Nations Convention on the Rights of the Child, the Order sought to strike a better balance between supporting parents to enact their parental responsibilities, and greater judicial oversight of social workers' powers whenever parents were felt to be unable or unwilling to fulfil their responsibilities towards their children. The new legislation strengthened the position of childcare authorities by "imposing a duty to investigate whether to take action to safeguard a child rather than solely to bring a child before a court if they were in need of care, protection or control" (Department of Health, Social Services, and Public Safety, 2003, p. 168).

Under the Order, Article 66 places a duty on Health and Social Care Trusts to investigate when there is reasonable cause to suspect that a child who lives, or is found, in the authority's area is suffering, or is likely to suffer, significant harm. These duties were underpinned by a framework for planning children's services on an inter-agency basis in order to develop universal and preventative services to support children and their families before significant harm has occurred (McTernan & Godfrey, 2006). It is estimated that just under £230 million is spent on services to children and families by the five Health and Social Care Trusts in Northern Ireland (Department of Health, 2019). This is in comparison to the anticipated annual short-run cost to the public sector of late intervention in Northern Ireland. This is estimated at £536 million per year, or equivalent to £288 for every Northern Ireland resident, or £1,166 per child (Fitzsimons & Teager, 2018).

Since the enactment of the Children (Northern Ireland) Order 1995, a series of inspection reports (Department of Health, Social Services, and Public Safety, 2006; The Regulation and Quality Improvement Authority, 2011) and research studies (for example, Hayes & Spratt, 2012; Devaney et al., 2013; Hayes & Bunting, 2013; Devaney et al., 2017) on the operation of the child welfare and child protection system in Northern Ireland have been published. These publications report a series of key findings. Firstly, there is an understandable concern within the child welfare system to protect children from harm and manage the risk posed to children from carers or others. Hayes and Spratt (2012) noted this has often focused on the immediate risk to children, rather than focusing on the longer-term sequela of harm, especially neglect and emotional abuse. This has resulted in a debate about recognizing the impact across the life course of a range of adversities experienced in childhood, and the need to see harm as being attributable to abuse and neglect, but also other factors such as parental loss, poverty, and poor physical and mental health (Davidson et al., 2010). This focus on the immediate and longer-term outcomes of both maltreatment and interventions has fitted with a wider reform of public services in Northern Ireland, heralding the adoption of outcomes-based approaches to public governance (Northern Ireland Assembly, 2016).

A second emerging theme is the need to intervene earlier when families are experiencing difficulties. This could prevent children from experiencing serious harm, and before problems become entrenched and less amenable to remedy (Devaney & McConville, 2016). Similar to the PPFS and Meitheal in Ireland, funding has supported the development and trial of a range of interventions under the Early Intervention Transformation Programme (EITP) in Northern Ireland. This program has been designed to support children and families at an early stage in terms of their health development and education, and the support to families experiencing stress (Children and Young People's Strategic Partnership, 2014). The innovative aspect of this development has been the pooling of budgets across six different government departments to create a single budget to fund these initiatives. This has been supplemented by funding from Atlantic Philanthropies, a private philanthropic body committed to providing effective support to children and young people.

The third theme arising from inspections and research has been the need to improve integration of the work of different professionals and services in addressing child maltreatment. In 2012, the Northern Ireland Assembly Government established the Safeguarding Board for Northern Ireland. The Board is made up of senior representatives from key public, voluntary, and community organizations, and is charged through the Safeguarding Board Act (Northern Ireland) 2011 with primary responsibility for coordinating the activities of agencies in preventing and responding to child maltreatment. This includes developing policies and procedures to coordinate interagency child protection practice and undertaking reviews into the deaths of children through maltreatment. The Board is therefore the fulcrum upon which the professional and societal response to children's safety and well-being rests.

As this section has highlighted, there are many similarities in the historical development and trajectory of child protection services in both jurisdictions on the island of Ireland, not least the legislative and organizational responses to the child abuse inquiries in both countries. Acknowledging the complexity facing 21st-century child protection and welfare practice, there are further commonalties that will challenge best practice that unite both countries. The next sections address three themes which are Irish issues, but also ones of global relevance: Brexit, technology, and child migration.

Borders, Brexit, and Child Protection on the Island of Ireland: What Does Brexit Mean for Child Safety?

The departure of the United Kingdom from the European Union on January 1, 2021, has been a landmark event that will dominate the national zeitgeist for decades to come. On both sides of the Irish border there has been endless discussion and anticipation about the social, political, and economic repercussions of this seismic parting of the ways, especially given the never-ending missed deadlines and uncertainty about what the final Brexit deal will look like. In a somewhat unanticipated manner, the possibility of Ireland's landscape being dominated by a "hard" or "soft" border is a critical point of divergence between the EU and UK negotiators: the Irish border is the only land border between the

United Kingdom and the European Union. As such, it occupies a unique status within the broader Brexit discussion and is symbolic of the labyrinthine challenge involved in decoupling the UK from the rest of Europe. In short, the dispute about the Irish border was the moment when the high rhetoric of the referendum ended and the hard realities of the new order began in earnest.

At present, child protection matters are dealt with through a standing committee of the North South Ministerial Council, an inter-governmental meeting set up under the Belfast Agreement in 1998 that seeks to develop consultation, cooperation, and action within the island of Ireland on economic and social matters. In 2008, cross-border child protection matters became part of the agenda of this body, including for example, the movement of individuals convicted of sexual offences between the two jurisdictions (Devaney & Reid, 2012). The impact of Brexit on such local mechanisms is undetermined and is therefore uncertain. This uncertainty unfolds yet further with the potential diminution of the effectiveness of the UK's child protection systems being highlighted with a growing sense of unease (Stalford, 2017). Of concern was the UK withdrawing from a series of European protection mechanisms such as EUROPOL—the European Law Enforcement Agency; EUROJUST—the cross European judicial cooperation body; and ECRIS—the European Criminal Records Information System which exchanges information on individuals with criminal records between member states. Similar concerns were identified by the University of Liverpool, which noted significant EU structural developments since the 1990s from which the UK will no longer benefit. These included the European Cybercrime Centre, the European Framework for Safer Mobile Use by Teenagers and Children, and the Missing Children Hotline (Stalford, 2017).

The European Network of Ombudspersons for Children (European Network of Ombudspersons for Children, 2017) has also raised concerns about the "significant number of legal instruments" enacted by the EU that give entitlements and rights to children with respect to migration, asylum, and health care. Whilst UK law may have absorbed much of the relevant EU statute, this does not apply to the European Arrest Warrant, which facilitates a fast-track extradition process between European member States. In a post-Brexit landscape, it is unclear how child protection and police services can respond to a situation where an adult perpetrator of child abuse moves, for example, between the counties of Monaghan (Ireland, within EU) and Armagh (Northern Ireland, outside of the EU from January 2021), locations that are separated by a 30-minute car journey. The multitude of small weaving roads that crisscross the Irish border may represent a logistical headache to civil servants in London; however, to a child abuser they become a potential legal loophole which may help them avoid justice. Lengthy and protracted extradition court cases do not serve the best interests of vulnerable children on this island. As it turns out, however, such court cases have not been the only lengthy and protracted element to this Brexit discussion. With the enactment of Brexit from January 1, 2021,

Northern Ireland is now the front line of the new relationship between the UK and the EU. Some aspects of EU regulation relating to trade and the movement of people still apply to Northern Ireland, but Northern Ireland remains outside of most of the social protections afforded to citizens within the EU, creating both political tensions and practical difficulties.

Yet within this chaos the statutory mandate to protect children remains extant and unchanged. It is within this context that we conclude that the island of Ireland ultimately requires a border that is neither hard nor soft. What is required is legal and systemic congruence across and between the child protection structures within respective jurisdictions. Mechanisms are required that are simultaneously flexible and robust. Robust enough to prevent, disrupt, and prosecute adults who commit crimes against children, but sufficiently malleable and flexible to enhance and promote cross-jurisdictional cooperation between child protection agencies in Northern Ireland and Ireland. Ireland will remain in the EU and be party to all the laws, treaties, and cross-country agreements that will evolve. Northern Ireland's future position outside of the EU due to Brexit, something that a minority of its population voted for, is likely to lead to extensive confusion not only between the UK and the EU, but also between both countries on the island of Ireland. All landmark events cast a long shadow and Brexit likewise brings much uncertainty. Brexit will challenge European countries with a land border or those in close proximity with the United Kingdom. Irrespective of the final Brexit deal, its fraught implementation and attempts to renegotiate the Northern Ireland Protocol, politicians and institutions will need to ensure that the respective child protection services are responsive and flexible. There is a need to safeguard against political expediency; children should not be exposed to additional harm due to the collaborative capacity of child protection systems across nation states being weakened.

Technology and Child Welfare

The ubiquity of smart phones, social media platforms, and internet technologies in both countries has rapidly reshaped the landscape of child welfare practice. In the field of child welfare, there are an increasing number of reports examining how technologies such as big data, social media, mobile technologies, machine learning, and artificial intelligence are affecting the field of child welfare, children, and families, and those working within this field of practice.

There are few big data sources in Ireland and Northern Ireland and most of the administrative databases are not linked. However, new databases are continually under development. For example, in Ireland, the Child and Family Agency has created a new national child protection electronic record system called NCCIS to modernize its child protection record-keeping. The assembling and analysis of "big" datasets may provide more accurate models to assess parent, community, and societal risks, thereby supporting more accurate assessments by practitioners. However, there are also risks that such big datasets, when linked to machine learning, may also enable states to engage in "dataveillance" of perceived "at risk" groups (see Eubanks, 2017).

In the realm of child protection, social media platforms have also enabled groups to communicate, monitor, and analyze data on adults who may pose a risk to children. High profile cases of child sexual exploitation and grooming of children by adults through the misuse of social media apps in Ireland and Northern Ireland have profiled how technology is challenging child welfare bodies, police, and policymakers to fulfill their statutory duties in our highly connected, globalized world. Cases where vigilante groups in Ireland, Northern Ireland, and Great Britain are setting up fake social media profiles ("honey traps") to entrap adults whom they allege were attempting to groom a "child" for sex and other high-profile media coverage of cyberbullying and the shaming of children online, have sparked debates on the impact of technology on children's welfare. Key emerging themes include the "right" age at which children should be allowed access to smart phones and social media platforms, and what the digital age of consent should be. These cases have highlighted the knowledge and skill gap between children and their parents on digital and social media technologies, and focused attention on the degree of responsibility companies have to actively moderate content on their apps/platforms to protect their users. This is challenging when such material is posted publicly online, but even more challenging to moderate and intervene when images and videos are shared through less visible peer-to-peer technologies and the "dark" web.

The use of social media by social workers in their child protection practice has become the focus of academic research, commentary in the courts, and the grist for complaints against social workers to professional regulatory bodies (see, for example, Irish Association of Social Workers, 2017). Social media has made child protection practice and practitioners' private lives more "visible" to the public, with the boundaries between the personal and professional becoming more porous. Examples include: parents video recording practice in action and posting these videos on YouTube; practitioners using social media posts from service users as another component of their child welfare assessments; adoption social workers using social media in tracing or family members using Facebook to do their own adoption tracing work; and social workers' and social work students' personal lives and opinions posted on blogs/social media being reckonable for professional fitness to practice processes (see, e.g., *Ngole v. University of Sheffield*, 2019; Spencer-Lane, 2019); and practitioners being subject to abuse and harassment through social media and online platforms.

What is clear is that ethical, legal, research, policy frameworks, and societal norms are some paces behind these technologies. In the liberal, lightly regulated domain of the internet governed by principles of free market capitalism, have governments left it too late to regulate the internet and technology companies to protect children and young people? Government departments in Ireland and Northern Ireland have been proactive in seeking to modernize laws to take account of new technologies, for example in the areas of child pornography, online harassment, the distribution of intimate images without consent, child sexual exploitation, and domestic abuse. The Minister for Children and Youth Affairs in Ireland, in a submission to the Joint Oireachtas Committee on Children and Youth Affairs special hearing on cyber security for children and young adults, called on technology companies to collaborate with government to address their child protection responsibilities and to work proactively to minimize risks to children while using their platforms (Zappone, 2018). Similar debates have taken place in Northern Ireland. A UK study by the NSPCC (2017) noted an increase in reported incidents by young people of both cyber bullying and online child sexual exploitation. The Safeguarding Board for Northern Ireland was tasked with developing and implementing an e-safety strategy across the country in response to concerns about reports of an increase in both cyber-bullying and online child sexual exploitation (NSPCC, 2017).

Migration of Children and Child Protection

From a child protection and welfare perspective, migrants are identified as being at increased risk of poverty and social exclusion (Health Service Executive, 2008) and are twice as likely as Irish nationals to be in consistent poverty. Furthermore, children from ethnic minority backgrounds are over-represented in the Irish childcare system (Health Service Executive, 2011). The Child Care Law Reporting Project (Corbett and Coulter, 2021) highlighted a disproportionate number of families involved in childcare proceedings with at least one parent from an ethnic minority.

For those involved in child protection and welfare north and south of the border, issues of migration, immigration, ethnicity, and integration/inclusion are complex, intertwined, and multi-faceted. Similar to adults, children migrate for diverse and complex reasons, traveling within "mixed migratory flows" (Mannion, 2016), with complex population movements that include refugees, asylum seekers, and economic migrants amongst other migrants (IOM, 2019). The triggers for migration are equally complex, with international evidence asserting that children are displaced by war and other violent conflicts (IOM, 2019). They are also increasingly being trafficked or coerced to move for exploitation either into the sex trade or the unregulated economic market (United Nations, 2014). The challenges they have experienced pre-migration can often be compounded by their experiences post-migration, having to navigate a new language, culture, religious context, and educational system. Some of those challenges are common amongst many migrant groups, such as language difficulties and the need for interpreters.

Other challenges are more specific to particular migrant groups, for example asylum seekers and the controversial use of direct provision (Ní Raghallaigh et al., 2016; Foreman, 2018), sparking debates on issues of social justice, equality, and human rights, arguably principles considered to be at the heart of practice with vulnerable families. Other challenges are gender-specific, impacting directly on females only, including gender-based violence, honor killing, and the controversial practice of female genital mutilation (Foreman, 2018). Ireland has committed to ending direct provision by 2024.

While these experiences and challenges have received considered attention across policy, practice, and academic discourse, the experiences of particular ethnic minorities such as Roma (Jacob & Kirwan, 2016), and the practice of racial profiling (Logan, 2014; Shannon, 2017) hate speech (Townsend, 2014), ethnic profiling, or racial violence and attacks (Stewart, 2012), and the challenge to culturally competent practice have been subjects of more recent concern, both in Ireland and Northern Ireland. These resonate with challenging societal changes, both internationally and across the European Union, including the rise in fundamentalism and populism, the rise of extreme right-wing politics, civil and proxy wars, racism and xenophobia, and global issues such as climate change and the significant numbers of children fleeing from the war in Ukraine.

While these complexities challenge those practitioners, policymakers, and institutions who are charged with responsibility for responding to the diverse needs of this diverse population, they also offer opportunities for reflection and intervention. At the point of engagement with migrant families, and as articulated by Chand and Thoburn (2006), it is critical that practitioners and policymakers understand the particular issues for the minority ethnic families, in order to prevent those children and families being needlessly and inappropriately drawn into the child protection system. While the provision of culturally competent interventions for children from diverse ethnic backgrounds is an obvious starting point, practitioners also need to reflect on their assumptions and stereotypes about working with minority ethnic families with a view to challenging those beliefs and practices that lead to discrimination. To this end, Sawrikar and Katz (2017) argue for the application of a multicultural framework if we are to make a serious and unwavering commitment to respect cultural differences.

Concluding Comments

The partition of the island of Ireland occurred just over 100 years ago and social and economic policy has evolved in different ways between Ireland and Northern Ireland, within a wider set of European obligations. It has only been since the signing of the Good Friday Agreement in 1998 that formal mechanisms have developed to share good practice and coordinate policy across these two coterminous jurisdictions.

Key themes arising from recent inspections and reviews of the systems in both jurisdictions have included: a preoccupation with identifying and responding to the immediate risk to children (from physical and sexual abuse), without sufficient concern for the long-term negative impact of other types of maltreatment, such as neglect and emotional abuse (Hayes & Spratt, 2012); an increase in the thresholds being applied by statutory services for children and families to gain access to services, resulting in some children's needs going unmet, or becoming more significant and entrenched (Devaney, 2018); ongoing challenges with cooperation and coordination between services, such as children's services and adult mental health services in Northern Ireland (Grant et al., 2018), and children's services and the police in Ireland (An Garda Síochána Inspectorate, 2017); and an underestimation of the need for children to be protected from harm and also to have support in their recovery (Devaney et al., 2012).

A tension over the past decade has been the increase in demand for services at a time of significant financial retrenchment due to the global economic crisis that started in 2008 (Department of Education, 2017), resulting in significant public spending cuts in both countries. This will be exacerbated by the financial impact of responding to the COVID-19 pandemic. While services in both countries have sought to develop mechanisms to determine the thresholds for access to ever more scarce resources, in reality, staff are engaged in the process of rationing services based on a combination of assessed need, policy directives for services, and the exigencies of local services.

However, it is always easier to write about what is not working and what is yet to be achieved. In both countries, government departments, child protection agencies and services, professional bodies, civil society groups, along with the European Union and supranational bodies have undertaken phenomenal work since the 1980s. Significant resources have been invested to modernize policy, legislation, interventions, and procedures, and to improve the knowledge base in this field of practice. It is crucial for public confidence and trust in these services to acknowledge the tireless ongoing work by professionals and agencies in child protection to keep children safe. This is complex work addressing issues that are hard to 'solve', work that is often "hidden," little-understood, and rarely praised. In particular, at times of scrutiny, "simple" solutions and answers, particularly those retrospectively proffered when better quality information is available with time to process this information, should not be used to undermine the work in the sector. Nor should perceived "failings" be individualized or generalized to reflect the quality of work and endeavor across the sector. Service providers and Government departments in both jurisdictions need to improve their communication strategies to publicize positive stories and successes to increase the public's awareness and understanding of the necessary work being undertaken. Such initiatives could help develop professional morale by changing the narrative of how child protection is reported and increasing professionals' sense of self-efficacy.

In conclusion, this chapter has sought to highlight the importance of neighboring jurisdictions both working with each other, while also adapting to the increasing impact of globalization upon the form and nature of child maltreatment, and the professional response. No longer can nation states act in isolation of each other, given the movement of peoples, and the growth and ubiquity of digital technologies. Moving forward, our individual child protection systems need to be aligned to better meet the needs of children, and the realities of the social and economic context that countries find themselves facing.

References

Adoption Authority of Ireland. (2020). *Domestic adoption statistics 2015–2019*. Available at: https://aai.gov.ie/images/2020/Domestic_Adoption_Key_Statistics.pdf. Retrieved February 8, 2021.

An Garda Síochána Inspectorate. (2017). *Responding to child sexual abuse: A follow up review*. An Garda Síochána Inspectorate.

Brennan, R., Burns, K., and O'Mahony, C. (2020). The voluntary care in Ireland study: Key findings and recommendations for law reform and social work practice in Ireland. *Irish Social Worker*, December, 7–16.

Bruton, M. (1998, July). *West of Ireland farmer case: Report of review group, presented to North Western Health Board*. North Western Health Board.

Buckley, H. (2017). Service users as receivers of risk-dominated practice. In M. Connolly (Ed.), *Beyond the Risk Paradigm in Child Protection: Current Debates and New Directions* (pp. 77–90). Palgrave.

Buckley, H. and Burns, K. (2015). Child welfare and protection in Ireland: Déjà vu all over again. In A. Christie, B. Featherstone, S. Quin, and T. Walsh (Eds.), *Social work in Ireland: Continuities and changes* (pp. 51–70). Palgrave Macmillan.

Buckley, H. and O'Nolan, C. (2013). *An examination of recommendations from inquiries into the events in families and their interactions with state services, and their impact on policy and practice*. Department of Children and Youth Affairs.

Bunting, L., McCartan, C., McGhee, J., Bywaters, P., Daniel, B., Featherstone, B., and Slater, T. (2018). Trends in child protection across the UK: A comparative analysis. *The British Journal of Social Work*, 48(5), 1154–1175.

Burns, K. and McGregor, C. (2019). Child protection and welfare systems in Ireland: Continuities and discontinuities of the present. In L. Merkel-Holguin, K. Fluke, and R. D. Krugman (Eds.), *National systems of child protection: Understanding the international variability and context for developing policy and practice* (pp. 115–138). Springer International Publishing.

Burns, K., Pösö, T., and Skivenes, M. (Eds.). (2017). *Child welfare removals by the state: A cross-country analysis of decision-making systems*. Oxford University Press.

Chand, A. and Thoburn, J. (2006). Research review: Child protection referrals and minority ethnic children and families. *Child and Family Social Work*, 11, 368–377.

Children and Young People's Strategic Partnership. (2014). *Northern Ireland children and young people's plan 2014–17*. Health & Social Care Board.

Corbett, M. and Coulter, C. (2021). *Ripe for reform: an analytical review of three years of court reporting on child care proceedings*. Dublin: Child Care Law Reporting Project. Available at: www.childlawproject.ie. Retrieved June 21, 2022.

Crosse, R. and Canavan, J. (2016). *Tusla–child and family agency research needs analysis report*. Department of Children and Youth Affairs.

Davidson, G., Devaney, J., and Spratt, T. (2010). The impact of adversity in childhood on outcomes in adulthood: Research lessons and limitations. *Journal of Social Work*, 10(4), 369–390.

Department of Children and Youth Affairs. (2011). *Children first: National guidance for the protection and welfare of children*. Government Publications.

Department of Children and Youth Affairs. (2017). *Children first: National guidance for the protection and welfare of children*. Government Publications.

Department of Children and Youth Affairs. (2017). *Review of the child care act 1991*. Department of Children and Youth Affairs. Available at: http://childrensdatabase.ie/viewdoc.asp?fn=%2Fdocuments%2Flegislation%2F20171205ReviewofChildCareAct1991.htm&mn=legp8e&nID=2. Retrieved March 29, 2018.

Department for Education. (2017). *Children's services: Spending, 2010–11 to 2015–16*. Department for Education (London).

Department of Health. (2008). *Standards for child protection services*. Department for Health (Belfast).

Department of Health. (2017). *Co-operating to safeguard children and young people*. Department of Health (Belfast).

Department of Health. (2019). *Children's social care statistics for Northern Ireland 2018/19*. Department of Health (Belfast).

Department of Health and Children. (1999). *Children first: National guidelines for the protection and welfare of children*. Stationery Office (Dublin).

Department of Health and Social Security. (1982). *Child abuse: A study of inquiry reports 1973–1981*. HMSO.

Department of Health, Social Services, and Public Safety. (2003). *A better future—50 years of child care in Northern Ireland 1950–2000*. Department of Health, Social Services and Public Safety (Belfast).

Department of Health, Social Services and Public Safety. (2006). *Our children and young people—Our shared responsibility: Inspection of child protection services in Northern Ireland*. DHSSPS.

Department of Public Expenditure and Reform. (2017). *Case study on Tusla: The child and family agency. Case studies on innovation and reform in the Irish public sector*. Available at: http://www.per.gov.ie/wp-content/uploads/Tusla-IPA-Final-Print-Version-26-Sep-2017-002.pdf.

Devaney, J. (2019). The trouble with thresholds: Rationing as a rational choice in child and family social work. *Child & Family Social Work*, 24, 458–466.

Devaney, J., Bunting, L., Davidson, G., Hayes, D., Lazenbatt, A., and Spratt, T. (2012). *The impact of early childhood experiences on adolescent suicide and accidental death*. Northern Ireland Commissioner for Children and Young People.

Devaney, J., Bunting, L., Hayes, D., and Lazenbatt, A. (2013). *Translating learning into action: An overview of learning arising from Case Management Reviews in Northern Ireland 2003–2008*. Department of Health, Social Services, and Public Safety.

Devaney, J., Hayes, D., and Spratt, T. (2017). The influences of training and experience in removal and reunification decisions involving children at risk of maltreatment: Detecting a "Beginner Dip." *British Journal of Social Work*, 47(8), 2364–2383.

Devaney, J., McAndrew, F., and Rodgers, T. (2010). *Our children and young people—Our shared responsibility: The reform implementation process in child protection services in Northern Ireland*. In A. Stafford, S. Vincent, and N. Parton (Eds.), *Child protection reform across the United Kingdom* (pp. 37–53). Dunedin Academic Press.

Devaney, J. and McConville, P. (2016). Childhood neglect: The Northern Ireland experience. *The Journal of the Social Services Research Group*, 32(1), 53–64.

Devaney, J. and Reid, C. (2012). Two countries, one border: The challenges and opportunities for protecting children on an all island basis—a critical turning point. In K. Burns and D. Lynch (Eds.), *Children's Rights and Child Protection: Critical Times, Critical Issues in Ireland* (pp. 168–185). Manchester University Press.

Eames, R. and Bradley, D. (2009). *Report of the consultative group on the past*. Available at: http://cain.ulst.ac.uk/victims/docs/consultative_group/cgp_230109_report.pdf. Retrieved December 2017.

Eubanks, V. (2017). *Automating inequality: How high tech tools profile, police, and punish the poor*. St. Martin's Press.

European Network of Ombudspersons for Children. (2017, October). *Communication from the European network of ombudspersons for children regarding the potential impact of Brexit on children's rights*. European Network of Ombudspersons for Children.

Ewing, J., Hunter, R., Barlow, A., and Smithson, J. (2015). Children's voices: Centre-stage or side-lined in out-of-court dispute resolution in England and Wales? *Child and Family Law Quarterly*, 27, 43–62.

Featherstone, B., White, S., and Wastell, D. (2012). Ireland's opportunity to learn from England's difficulties? Auditing uncertainty in child protection. *Irish Journal of Applied Social Studies*, 12, 28–42.

Fitzsimons, P. and Teager, W. (2018). *The cost of late intervention in Northern Ireland*. Early Intervention Foundation.

Foreman, M. (2018). *Support services for victims of violence in asylum and migration: Comments paper Ireland*. European Commission on Justice.

Gibbons, N. (2010, October 27). *Roscommon child care case: Report of the inquiry team to the health service executive*. Health Service Executive. Available at: https://www.hse.ie/eng/services/publications/children/roscommonchildcarecase.pdf.

Gilbert, N., Parton, N., and Skivenes, M. (2011). *Child protection systems: International trends and orientations*. Oxford University Press.

Grant, A., Lagdon, S., Devaney, J., Davidson, G., Duffy, J., Perra, O., Galway, K., Leavey, G., and Monds-Watson, A. (2018). *A study of health and social care professionals' family focused practice with parents who have mental illness, their children and families in Northern Ireland: Final report*. Queen's University Belfast.

Hayes, D. and Bunting, L. (2013). "Just be brave": The experiences of young witnesses in criminal proceedings in Northern Ireland. *Child Abuse Review*, 22(6), 419–431.

Hayes, D. and Spratt, T. (2012). Child welfare as child protection then and now: What social workers did and continue to do. *British Journal of Social Work*, 44(3), 615–635.

Health Information and Quality Authority. (2012). *National standards for the protection and welfare of children*. HQIA (Dublin).

Health Service Executive. (2008). *National intercultural health strategy*. Health Service Executive (Dublin).

Health Service Executive. (2009). *Child welfare and protection social work departments' business processes*. Report of the NCCIS Business Process Standardisation Project. Health Service Executive (Dublin).

Health Service Executive. (2011). *Review of adequacy for HSE children and family Services 2011*. Health Service Executive (Dublin).

Irish Association of Social Workers. (2017, November). *Correspondence to members on social media element of new CORU fitness to practice allegations against social workers in Ireland*. Irish Association of Social Workers.

IOM. (2019). *International Migration Law – Glossary on Migration N° 34*. Geneva. Available at: https://www.iom.int/glossary-migration-2019.

Jacob, D. and Kirwan, G. (2016). *The Tallaght Roma integration project: Working for inclusion in health care through a community development model*. Health Services Executive (Dublin).

Joint Committee on the Family. (1996, April). *Kelly – A Child is Dead. Report of a Committee of Inquiry*. Interim Report. Government Publications. Available at: http://www.lenus.ie/hse/handle/10147/50273.

Lonne, B., Parton, N., Thomson, J., and Harries, M. (2009). *Reforming child protection*. Routledge.

Mannion, K. (2016). *Child migration matters: Child and young people's experience of migration*. Immigrant Council of Ireland.

McBride, F. (2017). *Cited in Tusla Child and Family Agency: Child protection and welfare strategy 2017–2022*. Department of Children and Youth Affairs (Dublin).

Mc Gregor, C. (2014). The Child and Family Agency 2014: Initial views and experiences of social work and social care practitioners. *The Irish Social Worker*, Spring/Summer, 2–8.

Mc Gregor, C. and Quin, S. (2015). Revisiting our history post "Celtic Tiger": So, what's new? In A. Christie, B. Featherstone, S. Quin, and T. Walsh (Eds.), *Social Work in Ireland* (pp. 1–17). Palgrave.

McGregor, C., Canavan, J., and Nic Gabhainn, S. (2020). A critical consideration of the relationship between professional and public understandings of family support: Towards greater public awareness and discursive coherence in concept and delivery. *Children and Youth Services Review*, 113, 1–12.

Mc Guinness, C. (1993). *Report of the Kilkenny Incest Investigation*. Stationery Office.

McTernan, E. and Godfrey, A. (2006). Children's services planning in Northern Ireland: Developing a planning model to address rights and needs. *Child Care in Practice*, 12(3), 219–240.

Munro, E. (2011). *The Munro Review of Child Protection: Final report, a child-centred system*. Department of Education (London).

Murphy, Y. (2020). *Final report of the Commission of Investigation into Mother and Baby Homes*. Department of Children, Equality, Disability, Integration and Youth.

Ngole, R. v. University of Sheffield. (2019, July 3). *EWCA Civ 1127*. Available at: https://www.judiciary.uk/wp-content/uploads/2019/07/ngole-v-sheffield-university-judgment.pdf.

Ní Raghallaigh, M., Foreman, M., and Feeley, M. (2016). *Transition from direct provision to life in the community*. Irish Research Council.

Northern Ireland Assembly. (2016). *Outcomes based government*. Research and information service briefing paper 41/16. Northern Ireland Assembly.

NSPCC. (2017). *How safe are our children?* Northern Ireland Briefing Paper. NSPCC.

Office of the First Minister and Deputy First Minister. (2020). *Children and Young People's Strategy: 2020–2030*. Office of the First Minister and Deputy First Minister.

O'Mahony, C., Brennan, R., and Burns, K. (2020). Informed consent and parental rights in voluntary care agreements. *Child and Family Law Quarterly*, 32(4), 373–396.

Pinkerton, J. and Campbell, J. (2002). Social work and social justice in Northern Ireland: Towards a new occupational space. *British Journal of Social Work*, 32, 723–737.

Pollitt, C. and Bouckaert, G. (2017). *Public management reform*. Oxford University Press.

Powell, M. A. and Smith, A. B. (2009). Children's participation rights in research. *Childhood*, 16, 124–142.

Rodriguez, L., Cassidy, A., and Devaney, C. (2018). *Meitheal and child and family support networks final report: Tusla's programme for prevention, partnership and family support*. UNESCO Child and Family Research Centre, National University of Ireland Galway.

Ruch, G., Turney, D., and Ward, A. (Eds.). (2010). *Relationship-based social worker: Getting to the heart of practice*. Jessica Kingsley.

Sawrikar, P. and Katz, I. (2017). The treatment needs of victims/survivors of child sexual abuse (CSA) from ethnic minority communities: A literature review and suggestions for practice. *Children and Youth Services Review*, 79, 166–179.

Stafford, A., Vincent, S., and Parton, N. (Eds.). (2010). *Child protection reform across the United Kingdom*. Dunedin Academic Press Ltd.

Stalford, H. (2017). *Making Brexit work for children: The impact of Brexit on children and young people*. The Children's Society.

Spencer-Lane, T. (2019). *Legitimate free speech or views incompatible with social work: An analysis of the Felix Ngole Case*. Community Care. Available at: https://www.communitycare.co.uk/2019/07/11/legitimate-free-speech-views-incompatible-social-work-analysis-felix-ngole-case/. Retrieved February 10, 2021.

Stewart, M. (2012). New forms of anti-Gypsy politics: A challenge for Europe. In M. Stewart (Ed.), *The Gypsy "menace": Populism and the new anti-Gypsy politics*. Hurst Publishers.

The Regulation and Quality Improvement Authority. (2011). *A review of child protection arrangements in Northern Ireland*. RQIA (Belfast).

Townsend, E. (2014). Hate speech or genocidal discourse? An examination of anti-Roma sentiment in contemporary Europe. *Journal of Multidisciplinary Studies*, 11(1), 1–24.

Tusla, Child and Family Agency. (2015). *"Measuring the Pressure." A Framework for the Analysis of Service Pressures, Performance and Reporting Social Work Intake, Assessment and Allocation Activity*. Tusla, Child and Family Agency.

Tusla, Child and Family Agency. (2017). *Child Protection and Welfare Strategy 2017–2022*. Available at: http://www.tusla.ie/uploads/content/Tusla_Child_Protection_and_Welfare_Strategy.pdf. Retrieved November 6, 2017.

Tusla, Child and Family Agency/Health Service Executive. (2008–2020). *Review of Adequacy Reports 2007–2019*. Available at: http://www.tusla.ie/publications/review-of-adequacy-reports/. Retrieved February 8, 2021.

Tusla, Child and Family Agency. (2014–2020). *Performance data*. Available at: https://data.tusla.ie/. Retrieved February 8, 2021.

Tusla, Child and Family Agency. (2019). *Child and youth participation strategy 2019–2023*. Child and Family Agency.

United Nations Offices on Drugs and Crime. (2014). *Global Report on Trafficking in Persons*. Available at: http://www.unodc.org/documents/data-and-analysis/glotip/GLOTIP_2014_full_report.pdf.

Warner, J. (2015). *The emotional politics of social work and child protection*. Policy Press.

Zappone, C. (2018, February 21). *Submission to the joint Oireachtas committee on children and youth affairs*. Houses of the Oireachtas.

Child Protection in Israel

Daphna Gross-Manos, Eran Melkman, *and* Aya Almog-Zaken

Abstract

This chapter explains child protection in Israel. Child protection policies, services, and practices are forced to adjust rapidly to the needs of the growing young population as Israel is still a relatively young state. Data collection is also another challenge within the Israeli child protection system. The chapter notes that neglect, physical abuse, sexual abuse, and emotional abuse are mostly referred in Israel's official reports of maltreatment cases to social services. It highlights the investigation, substantiation, and decision-making processes of Child Protection Officers regarding children in need of protection and its resemblance to the European welfare system model. Israeli child intervention and prevention services consist of out-of-home care and community-based services.

Key Words: Israel, child protection, CPOs, data collection, investigation, substantiation, decision-making, maltreatment, social services

This chapter is one of the first writings to review the child protection system in Israel. The Israeli context continues to have a critical impact on the way that child welfare policies have developed. It is beyond our scope to describe in detail all the aspects of this context or their possible implications. We will simply indicate highlights. It is important to remember that, at 70, Israel is a relatively young state, with a current population about 10 times that at its founding. This steep growth has forced child protection policy and practice to adjust rapidly to the needs of the growing population of children. At the end of 2015, 2,768,700 children aged 0–17 years were living in Israel—33.6% of the total population according to the Israel council for the Child [INCC] (2020), making Israel one of the youngest countries in the OECD (OECD, 2022b, with one of the highest fertility rates (OECD, 2022a). At the same time, and not unrelatedly, Israeli children are among the poorest in OECD countries (OECD, 2022b), with 31.7% of the children living below the poverty threshold (INCC, 2022).

Another important related feature is the broad ethnic and religious diversity characterizing Israel. Seventy percent of children are Jewish, 23% Muslim, 1.5% Christian, and 1.6% Druze (INCC, 2018). During its early decades, when socialist ideology prevailed, immigrants poured into the country from all over the world; this was followed in the 1990s by two large immigration waves from the former Soviet Union (FSU) and Ethiopia. Today, about 8.9% of the population of children are immigrants (born abroad or whose parents immigrated after 1990) (INCC, 2019). Furthermore, the Jewish population is divided by the level of religiosity into secular, religious, and ultra-Orthodox groups, which are characterized, in general, by major political, socioeconomic, and cultural differences (e.g., over-representation of Arab and ultra-Orthodox children among those living below the poverty threshold; 66% and 62%, respectively). These differences impact on rates of child maltreatment, service provision and response in each of the cultural groups (INCC, 2018).

The regulations governing child protection in Israel are stipulated in the Juvenile (Care and Supervision) Law 1960, which remains the foundation for child protection procedures. Although the law has been at the heart of the discourse around child protection over the years, its actual implementation was initially quite limited. It was only in the late 1980s, when child maltreatment was first perceived as a national health concern and more direct legal action was taken to protect children (Kadman, 1992), that child protection policy in Israel underwent a major development. This change was prompted by major public debates over several high-profile abuse cases and followed by a rapid development of services. New legislation included specific laws regarding child maltreatment and mandatory reporting, though, until now there is still no unified law system for children (Morag, 2010). Furthermore, research in this field is in its infancy and scientific interest in the processes of decision-making pertaining to the work of child protection professionals developed only in the early 2000s (e.g., Davidson-Arad & Benbenishty, 2010, 2016; Gold et al., 2001).

According to Gilbert and colleagues' three-dimensional framework (Gilbert et al., 2011), the Israeli child protection system originally had a child-protection orientation, adhering to the Israeli welfare system's original Anglo-American tradition (Gottfriend & Ben-Arieh, 2019). However, core parts of the "traditional" child protection services are currently undergoing a major reform, following the recommendations of several public committees. As will be shown, there is clear evidence that since the early 2000s, there have been policy efforts to make the system more family-service oriented. This is an ongoing process, reflected in an increased number of community- and home-based services, as well as a much higher budget allocation for the broader category of "children at risk," in many cases including prevention services. Concurrently, the beginning of a more child-focused orientation is evident in policy efforts to involve children at different stages of the protection system.

This chapter opens with general information on maltreatment rates in Israel followed by a description of the main legislation on which Israel's child protection system is based, referring to main developments over the years. We then describe the process of reporting and investigating suspected cases of child abuse and deciding on the appropriate intervention and service needed. Next, we discuss the main services provided by the child protection system, referring to main trends in out-of-home and community-based services. The following section will describe the methods of service delivery and funding models.

We conclude by discussing several challenges facing the Israeli child protection system. Note that this chapter focuses on child protection in the specific context of child abuse and neglect; additional risk contexts (e.g., mental health problems, juvenile offending or substance abuse) are beyond the scope of this review.

Child Maltreatment in Israel

Official reports indicate that in 2016, 32,955 (1.2% of Israel's child population) maltreatment cases were reported to social services according to the Israel Ministry of Labor, Social Affairs, and Social Services [IMLSASS] (2017b). Most salient were allegations of neglect (42%), followed by physical abuse (33.8%), sexual abuse (16.3%) and emotional abuse (7.7%) (Table 12.1); 92.7% of investigated reports were substantiated. These rates remained stable in the past decade, as shown in a comparison to 2007 data (Table 12.1)

Table 12.1 Child maltreatment rates and services provision in Israel for the years 2007 and 2016

	2007		2016	
	Number of children	Rate per 1,000	Number of children	Rate per 1,000
Overall number and rate of child maltreatment reports	34,071	14.4	32,955*	12.2
Number and rate of child physical abuse reports	12,165	5.1	11,150	4.1
Number and rate of sexual abuse reports	4,515	1.9	5,375	2.0
Number and rate of emotional abuse reports	4,982	2.1	2,539	0.9
Number and rate of neglect reports	12,409	5.2	13,891	5.2
Number and rate of child victims investigated by child investigator	6,765	2.9	9,550	3.6
Number and rate of children receiving community-based services (including prevention)	40,183	17.0	63,468	22.7
Number and rate of children in out-of-home care	10,293	4.4	10,842	3.9
Number and rate of children in residential care	7,678	3.2	7,168	2.6
Number and rate of children in foster-home (including emergency)	1,922	0.8	2,382	0.9

Note: Since 2014, the data refer to maltreatment reports rather the number of reported minors (each report might refer to more than one minor in the family).

Sources: Social Services Review, IMWSA (2017a); CPOs' annual report, IMWSA (2017a): this report refers to 97% of Israel localities; The State of the Child in Israel, INCC (2008).

and analysis of the rates in those years (Ben-Arieh et al., 2013). The slight drop between 2013 and 2016 should be interpreted with caution due to a change in the data analysis method. No published data on maltreatment rates among ethnic and minority groups are currently available. There is no clear figure of the number of children in the child protection system; a very rough calculation can cloud the number of reports adding the number of children in out-of-home care, but in this figure there might be some overlap of children their case have been reported and they have been placed out-of-home during the same year.

Note that the above official maltreatment rates differ substantially from self-reports of life-time maltreatment reported by Eizikovitz and Lev-Visel (2013), which assessed abuse and neglect from a different perspective. Their study of a representative sample of adolescents found that in the Jewish population, 14.3% reported physical neglect, 14.1% physical abuse, 17.6% sexual abuse, and 27.8% emotional abuse. Substantially higher rates of maltreatment across all types were indicated among the Arab population (for current attempts to construct a more reliable multi-informant national index of child maltreatment, see Arazi et al., 2017).

The Basis for Social Allocation: Main Legislation in the Area of Child Protection

Note that there is no systematic way of verifying the statistics of child maltreatment in Israel and there are concerns as to the accuracy and comprehensiveness of the available data. This section covers the main legislation for Israel's child protection system since the establishment of the State, and in more detail since 1990.

In the first decade of statehood, British mandate law provided much of the legal framework concerning at-risk children, with little attention paid to maltreatment. The system developed over the years largely in response to pressing social needs and public opinion, leading to inconsistent, "patchwork" regulations (Shnit, 1998; Morag, 2010).

In 1960, the Juvenile (Care and Supervision) Law provided the first legal definition of a "minor in need" and outlined the responsibilities of Child Protection Officers (CPOs) vis-à-vis these children (Faver, 2009). The law defines "minor in need" as a minor (under age 18) in situations where: (1) there is no responsible caregiver; (2) the caregiver is unable to care for, look after, or supervise the child, or is otherwise neglecting the child; (3) the minor committed a felony but was not prosecuted; (4) the minor was found wandering, loitering, or begging; (5) the minor's home environment exposes her or him to negative influences or is a place of regular law violation; (6) the minor's physical or mental well-being is or may be endangered by any other reason; and/or (7) the minor was born with Neonatal Abstinence Syndrome.

The law authorizes juvenile courts to issue any orders necessary for the care and protection of a minor in need, such as temporary removal from home (Faver & Slusky, 2007). The law also authorizes CPOs, who are social workers by training with a therapeutic orientation, to act as legal agents with extensive authority. They are thus authorized to implement emergency measures in extreme situations, such as the immediate temporary removal of a child from her/his home, even without the consent of the caregivers or court approval.

It is important to note that by law, minors are entitled to express their feelings prior to a decision on matters that affect them, while the weight to their wishes depends on age and maturity. To encourage the participation of minors, the law stipulates that information should be provided in a manner that is comprehensible to them (Faver, 2009). While being innovative for its time, the law's reference to child maltreatment was nevertheless quite broad and allowed flexible interpretation of the definition of child abuse (Ronen & Gilat, 2016). Until 1989, there was no separate legislation addressing child abuse and neglect, as the legislation covered various risk situations. The turning point, which triggered lengthy public debate and proposed legislation, was a case that caught public attention involving the sexual and physical abuse of a 3-year-old girl by her uncle, which eventually led to her death. The tragedy was exacerbated by the fact that family members, teachers, and friends knew about the abuse but failed to report it (Kadan, 1992). These events brought about the inclusion of maltreatment in the Israeli criminal code under the Penal (Harm to a Minor or a Helpless Person) Law—1989 (Faver & Slusky, 2007), explicitly acknowledging maltreatment as a major public health concern. The law stipulates the parents' responsibility to meet their children's needs and protect them from harm or abuse. The law recognized assault of a child, including sexual and emotional assault, as a felony per se, which had not previously been defined by law, and attributed greater severity to assaults perpetrated by caretakers or family members (extending the previous penalty of seven years of incarceration to nine years). This legislation put an end to the courts' tendency to treat felonies within the family more lightly, and acknowledged the severe consequences of intra-familial assault (Kadman, 1992; Faver, 2009).

A central feature of this law was the requirement of mandatory reporting by every adult citizen having reasonable suspicion of child abuse, prescribing three months of incarceration for those not doing so. Professionals, such as police officers, doctors, teachers, and social workers, have a particular obligation to report suspected abuse, and are liable for lengthier imprisonment (six months) when failing to do so. It is important to note that after the law came into effect, there was a very significant increase in reports of child maltreatment.

Another important law is the Domestic Violence Prevention Law 1991, which allows the court to issue a restraining order against an offender who is the parent or another family member. The order may avoid the child's removal from home and prevent unnecessary further suffering (Faver, 2009).

Another key influence on child-related legislation was the 1989 Convention on the Rights of the Child (UNCRC), ratified by Israel in 1991. Central to this is the work of the Rotlevi Committee (1997–2003), which examined the fundamental principles characterizing children's rights in Israel in various life domains in light of the UNCRC, prompting the need for new legislation (Morag, 2010; Rotlevi, 2004). In particular, an attempt was made to consolidate all of Israel's laws regarding children, which Morag (2010) described as a collection of Ottoman, British, and Israeli laws. Unfortunately, only a small proportion of the proposed legislation was enacted. Furthermore, while the committee played a very important role in changing court rhetoric, promoting the importance of children's views and their rights to participate, a review of verdicts has shown a less dramatic change (Morag, 2010; Ronen & Gilat, 2016).

While currently there is still no consolidated base for the various laws regarding children in Israel (Ronen & Gilat, 2016), the legal system has nevertheless gone through a dramatic growth process in the past three decades that forms the foundations of the work of the child protection services and CPOs in Israel. The next section describes the structure of the Israeli social services, and how they respond when a child is suspected to be in need of protection.

Investigation, Substantiation, and Decision-Making Processes

In Israel, children in need of protection are the responsibility of the municipal departments of Social Services (DSS) (Welfare Law 1955). There are 257 DSSs in Israel's 255 municipalities, each responsible for providing social services within the locality. Resembling the European model of the welfare system, the Israeli Ministry of Labor and Social Affairs and Services (IMLSASS) is in charge of setting the policy and supervising its implementation as well as providing 75% of the DSSs' budgets (though DSS social workers are employed by the municipality).

The DSSs predominantly comprise generalist social workers who deal with a range of community needs, as well as CPOs, specially trained social workers appointed by the IMLSASS to carry out all procedures relating to minors in need. Another important child protection role in some DSSs is that of child investigator: specially trained social workers who under the Evidence Amendment Law 1955 are responsible for the investigation and testimony in court of children under age 14, who are direct victims, witnesses, or alleged offenders.

Maltreatment reports from any source—private or professional—are referred to CPOs for evaluation, either directly or by the police, who have a duty to refer them to the CPOs. While initial screening often lies in the hands of CPOs, several large municipalities have emergency call centers operated by non-professional workers, who receive referrals and carry out initial screening (Szabo-Lael & Shevat, 2012). Cases lacking substantial evidence are closed without any formal requirement for registration or referral to the police, though they are often referred to generalist social workers for further treatment. When there is a high likelihood of maltreatment, the police are involved immediately. However, in cases where legal procedures may endanger the child or impede the potential for rehabilitation within the family, reports can be brought before an exemption committee (under the Mandatory Reporting Law), comprising the district attorney (chairman), a high ranking police officer and the district CPO (Nahmani-Rot, 2010).

As noted, after legal proceedings have been initiated, a child investigator assumes responsibility for gathering evidence, documenting the process, and supporting the child. The child investigator also evaluates the reliability of the child and recommends whether or not he or she should testify in court. The law stipulates that a minor who has been abused by an adult caretaker does not have to testify in court, but can give testimony to the child investigator who will testify on his or her behalf, which can lead to a conviction (Kadman, 1992). The number of children investigated by child investigators has risen in the last decade (see Table 12.1). In 2016, 29% of the reported abuse cases were investigated by child investigators (IMLSASS, 2016). In an effort to minimize secondary trauma caused by the proceedings, prevent unnecessary bureaucracy and save time, an initial investigative response for child abuse victims may be conducted by Israel's eight Child Protection Centers (Cohen, 2005; Rivkin & Szabo-Lael, 2009). The centers' multidisciplinary teams, which include CPOs, doctors, and child investigators, provide on-site protection, diagnosis, investigation, and decision making under one roof (IMLSASS, 2017b).

In situations involving immediate risk, cases may also be initially handled through an emergency order, which under the Juvenile Law 1960 can be issued by the CPO for up to seven days, pending authorization of the district CPO. A request for a court order is submitted retroactively following the immediate removal of the child from his or her home (Faver & Slutzky, 2007). This is quite rare (2.8% of abuse reports; IMLSASS, 2017b). Alternatively, an interim order, issued by the juvenile court per a CPO request, may be used in high-risk cases, to ensure the child's immediate safety while her/his situation is being assessed. The order is given for thirty days and can be extended for up to three months (Faver & Slutzky, 2007).

Most commonly, however, following assessment of alleged maltreatment, the CPOs will initiate an investigation. They are authorized to summon any relevant party and obligated to present their conclusions to the juvenile court (Faver & Slutzky, 2007). This often involves creating a treatment plan, including therapy and the assignment of authority, drawn up together by the minor, the family, and social services. Defined as "care in light of the law," this stage lasts three months. The majority of maltreatment reports are handled thus (IMLSASS, 2017b). Subsequently, the CPO can decide whether: (1) the goals of authoritative care have been accomplished, and the care plan should continue with a family social worker; (2) a therapeutic alliance has been formed and the care in light of the law should be extended; or (3) the minor is still considered legally "in need" and other forms of action should be considered, such as issuing a supervision order, whereby the Juvenile Court assumes responsibility over the child until age 18, or until circumstances change

(Faver & Slutzky, 2007). In 2016, the rate of children for whom a supervision order was issued or extended was 1.2 per 1,000.

Concurrently or subsequently, cases are brought before a planning, intervention, and evaluation committee (PIEC) for longer-term intervention decisions (Oppenheim-Weller et al., 2017). PIECs are interdisciplinary bodies of professionals (from the social, education, and health services) and family members that operate within the DSS, and are responsible for assessment and decision-making concerning children in need of intensive intervention (Dolev et al., 2001; Alfandari, 2017). The committee's chair (a senior social worker) and family social workers are responsible for preparing cases for the PIECs, implementing decisions, and monitoring outcomes (Alfandari, 2017). PIECs operate not only in cases of child abuse and neglect, but also in the broader context of children at risk and children with disabilities. The committees build an intervention plan for the child and the family to facilitate the child's development and prevent or reduce current risks (Angel-Rdai, 2014). The committees decide whether the child should be referred to services within the community (see below) or to out-of-home care, in high-risk cases. Decisions to place a child out-of-home are usually made with the parents' consent, although in its absence, when deemed necessary, the court may issue a custody order, transferring custodial rights to the DSS. In 2016, the rate of children for whom custody orders were issued or extended was 2.5 per 1,000 (IMLSASS, 2017b).

The PIECs' work has undergone a reform in the past two decades, following evaluation in 2001 (Dolev et al., 2001), and two subsequent ministerial committees that set new standards for their operation (Gilat Committee in 2002) and guidance for implementing the changes (Goldberg Committee in 2004). The change was also heavily influenced by the work of the Rotlevi Committee, which strongly encouraged children's participation in the PIECs (Angel-Rdai, 2014).

The changes were introduced as a pilot (in 11 DSSs), and subsequently implemented nationally. The main principles of the reform were: (1) the committees should be part of the treatment process and not a legal process; (2) professional, objective, and transparent standards should be determined, with a stable representation from the ministries of education and health and systematic record-keeping; and (3) culturally sensitive partnerships should be established with the parents and children, encouraging them (when appropriate) and preparing them to participate in committees (Angel-Rdai, 2014). The reform was officially implemented in 2017 and a new protocol for the PIECs was established. Note that further changes to the PIECs' work were recommended by another public committee, the Silman Committee in 2013, recommending separate committees for children at risk and children in need (Silman, 2014), however, evidently the change was not implemented (State Comptroller, 2017).

Intervention and Prevention Services in the Israeli Child Protection System

Out-of-home Care

The IMLSASS offers several interventions for children living in circumstances that endanger their safety and well-being, including residential, foster, and kinship care as well as emergency centers. In contrast to most western countries, where children placed out-of-home for their protection and well-being are mainly referred to foster care, in Israel, residential care is preferred and caters to 75% of children placed out of home by the IMLSASS (Table 12.1). IMLSASS-supervised residential settings are on a continuum of intensity of care according to the child's needs, including educational, rehabilitative, therapeutic, post-psychiatric hospitalization residential care, or residential care as an alternative to psychiatric hospitalization (Dolev et al., 2009). Relatedly, at-risk children from the social or geographical periphery of Israel may be placed in residential care on a voluntary basis, for example in "youth villages" supervised by the Israeli Ministry of Education (Kashti et al., 2008). Twenty-five percent of children in out-of-home care are placed in foster and kinship care provided by the Foster Care Families' Service. The service is supervised by the IMLSASS and operates through non-profit and private organizations, which are responsible for recruiting the families, preparing them for the child's arrival, and providing support to them (Sorek et al., 2014; IMLSASS, 2018). While there are no national data about children receiving foster, rather than kinship care in this rapidly changing area, sample findings show that about 37% of the children in foster-care families are in kinship care (Sorek et al., 2014). Additionally, children suffering from severe trauma with an indication of mental abuse requiring psychiatric treatment are referred to therapeutic foster care, which is often a long-term placement offering intensive daily support to the families (IMLSASS, 2018).

The predominance of residential over foster care in Israel has to do with the country's unique historical and ideological development, going back to the Zionist ideology on which the State was founded (Zeira, 2004; Maron, 2012). When Israel was dealing with mass immigration, during the 1950s and 1960s, residential care was the preferred option for immigrant children's optimal development (Kashti et al., 2000). Thus, for many years (and to some degree even today) it provided a service not only for children needing protection, but also for a broader population of children at risk, children living in the social and geographical peripheries, and children with educational difficulties. Over the years, the original policy preference for residential care has been strongly criticized as a deliberate attempt to remove children from their origins and place them in a "greenhouse" that would impose the early pioneers' values and ideology (Ronen & Gilat, 2016).

The policy was discontinued long ago, and today out-of-home care is decreasing, the IMLSASS preferring care in the community (see following section). However, it has left a large footprint on the structure of the system and the relative dominance of this kind of placement. An example of this is reflected in a recent finding that Israeli CPOs view residential care more favorably than CPOs in other countries, and as a slightly more favorable option than foster care (Benbenishty et al., 2015).

Moreover, current IMLSASS policy is to increase foster family care instead of residential care, especially for young children. This policy is emphasized in the recent enactment of the Foster Families Law 2016 as well as in the Silman Committee report (Silman, 2014), which called for a better balance between the out-of-home solutions, strengthening foster families in general, and relative foster families in particular. In line with this policy, the number of children in foster family care rose by 12.7% during 2000–2012 (Sorek et al., 2014). Furthermore, as shown in Table 12.1, from 2007 to 2016, the number of children placed with foster families rose (from 0.8 to 0.9 per 1,000), while the number of children in residential care dropped slightly (from 4.1 to 3.5 per 1,000 children). However, in 2016, out of all children in out-of-home care, the percentage of children in foster placements was still lower than may be expected (at 25%) (IMLSASS, 2017a). This is partially attributable to difficulties recruiting foster families and to the objection biological families in Israel have to foster family placements (Silman, 2014). It should be further noted that the division between foster families and residential care is very age-related, with foster care considered a more fitting placement for early childhood (Sorek et al., 2014). In 2016, 43% of the children below age 11 were placed in foster-families, while only 23% of the children between 12 and 17 years old were in foster care and the remainder in residential care (IMLSASS, 2017a).

As noted, emergency centers are another form of specialized out-of-home care established following the enactment of the Penal (Harm to a Minor or a Helpless Person) Law 1989 to provide protection, assessment, treatment, and support services for children in immediate danger for whom a treatment plan has not been yet determined. These are short-term small residential facilities, each catering to approximately 15 children up to age 14. They are managed by an interdisciplinary team of professionals responsible for diagnosing and treating the children and advising regarding the longer-term care plan once out of the center (Frid et al., 2010). Emphasis is placed on involving the abusive parents in the treatment process in an effort to maintain the parent–child relationship despite the past trauma (Cohen, 2005).

The centers provide an immediate and short-term solution for up to three months, though in reality children stay an average of 7–9 months (Frid et al., 2010), mainly due to time needed to evaluate the parenting abilities (as required by the court) or find a suitable out-of-home placement (INCC, 2016). In addition to the residential unit, most centers have an external unit that provides similar diagnostic and treatment services to maltreated children living at home and those reunited with their parents following initial treatment in the internal unit (Faver, 2005; Faver & Slutzky, 2007). There are currently 11 emergency centers throughout Israel, some providing specialized services for specific minority groups (e.g., the Arab population, the Jewish ultra-Orthodox population; IMLSASS, 2018). During 2015, a total number of 578 children were treated in the emergency centers; 21.5% of them eventually returned home (INCC, 2016).

Finally, adoption is yet another service, although one implemented so rarely that it cannot be truly regarded as an out-of-home service. A national service is authorized by the Child Adoption Law 1981 to act under the DSS in the IMLSASS. The service is provided in extreme cases when children cannot live with their biological families and the state is required to place them with a permanent alternative family. This service is engaged when the courts rule that a child should be adopted and is charged with finding and supporting an adoptive family (IMLSASS, 2018). In 2016, 55 children were adopted by relatives and 76 were adopted by families unknown to the child. The majority of the children (61%) were adopted by the foster family they had been living with, creating a stronger connection between the foster care services and the adoption services (IMLSASS, 2017a).

Community-based Services

While the foregoing section describes out-of-home services that fall within the main, original child-protection orientation of the Israeli system, there are a growing number of prevention and care programs supported by the IMLSASS within the community. They reflect a major policy shift introduced by the IMLSASS in 2004 in its Towards the Community policy. Two of its basic elements are: (1) restricting out-of-home care to three or four years; and (2) encouraging DSSs to refrain from out-of-home placements by allowing them to convert any unused out-of-home budget to programs within the community. The new policy intends to strengthen care options within the community thereby also providing the PIECs extended alternatives for addressing problems faced by children and families (IMLSASS, 2006). An evaluation study found the policy generally well implemented; it had a positive effect on collaboration among the DSSs and other community services, there was a substantial increase in the amount of community services for at-risk children, and a significant rise in the number of children reunified with their biological parents (Dolev et al., 2008).

Following the recommendations of the Schmidt Committee, appointed to review the issue of children at risk, adopted by the government in 2006, further steps were taken to promote family-oriented services and the development of more preventive services. The committee standardized the definition for children at risk based on the UNCRC, replacing the inconsistent assortment of definitions utilized until then (Szabo-Lael, 2017). Children at risk are defined as those in families and/or environments that endanger them, and whose rights—physical existence, health and development, family belonging, learning and acquiring skills, emotional well-being, social belonging and participation, and protection from others and from self-endangering behaviors—have been undermined.

Following the committee's recommendations, the government also established the inter-ministerial 360°—the National Program for Children and Youth at Risk (hereafter, 360°), a national conceptual framework to produce a thorough change in the way Israeli society deals with children and youth at risk and a decrease in the risk rates (IMLSASS, 2017c). Since 2008, the program has allocated budgets to a growing number of municipalities, mainly those with a low socioeconomic rating, for various programs that meet the munici-palities' needs and characteristics (Szabo-Lael, 2017). The municipalities can choose from a long list of community-based interventions targeting a range of life domains, popula-tions, and age groups. Some programs address similar needs in different ways, enabling the municipality to choose the most appropriate program to its needs. Most of the pro-grams were already in use in some areas but the national program helps their dissemina-tion. Examples include mothers' support groups, parent–child reading interventions, and substance-abuse prevention groups for immigrant youth and their parents (IMLSASS, 2017c). To date, the program has been implemented in 180 municipalities. The goal is to reach 250 of the 255 municipalities in Israel. Initially, municipalities need to map the status of children at risk and gather data to decide on the appropriate programs. This process has produced the first-ever database of children and youth at risk, showing 16% of them can be considered at risk (Szabo-Lael, 2017). The government and the district are responsible for policy and activity planning and supervise planning, implementation, and output in a structured process (IMLSASS, 2017c).

These policy changes have led to a dramatic rise (58%) in the number of children receiving community-based services in the last ten years (Figure 12.1). In 2016, 86.6% of the children in need for protection received them from the DSS and only 14.7% received out-of-home services. Provision of community-based services was exceptionally high among children aged 0–11 (94.3%), while among ages 12–17 it was only 58.8% (IMSLASS, 2017a). The rates of out-of-home placement seem to remain quite stable (Table 12.1). Earlier findings, though, show that between 2000 and 2012, there was an 8.2% decline in the number of children directed to out-of-home care (Sorek et al., 2014).

Most of the community-based services are provided mainly by the DSS, as described in the following section. The main service is occasional or ongoing social workers' care for children and their parents via casework and/or individual or group therapy, the latter provided by additional professionals (e.g., psychologist, psychiatrist) as necessary. Note there are also many universal services that support families with child-rearing and may be involved in identifying children at risk for abuse and neglect, and helping preven-tion efforts, notably the Tipat Halav mother and child healthcare clinics operated by the Health Ministry, as well as clinics and hospitals, including hospital-based child protec-tion teams.

Child-parent centers are a community service for children at risk (aged 5–12) and their parents. They are run by the DSSs and NGOs such as JDC-Ashalim, and employ an interdisciplinary team working in a home-like setting. They provide therapy for children

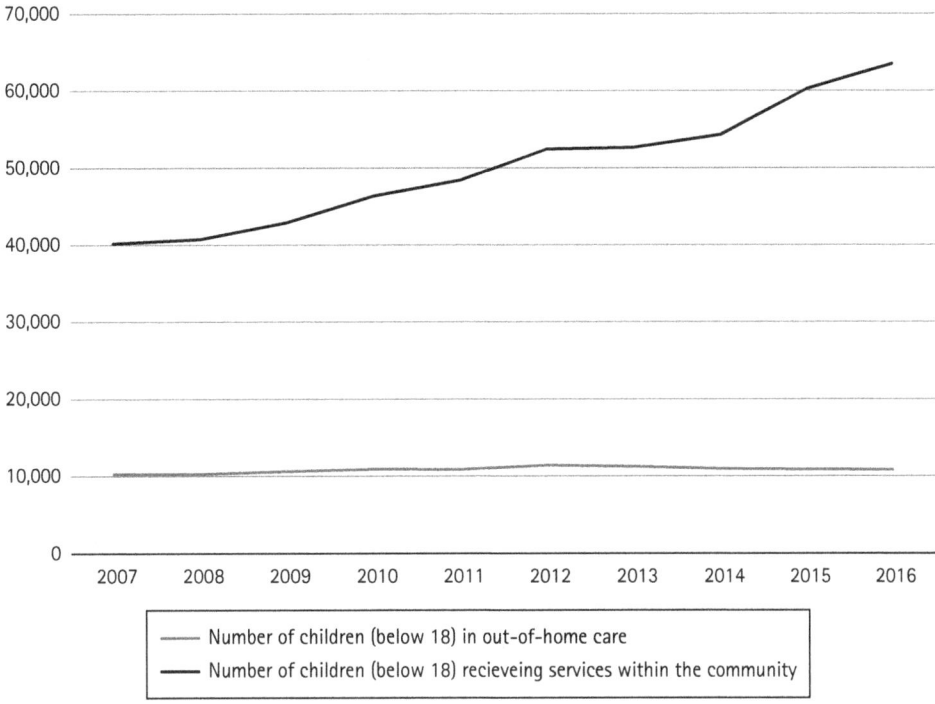

Figure 12.1 Number of children receiving out of home/within the community service between 2007 and 2016*

*It is estimated that several hundred children received services from both systems, e.g., 983 children in 2016 (IMSLASS, 2017a).

with emotional and behavioral problems due to poor parenting, and to their parents, either separately or together with the rest of the family. The main goal is to improve parenting and the child–parent relationship so as to facilitate a treatment plan enabling children to remain in their natural home (Rivkin et al., 2009).

Supervised visitation centers for parents and children provide a supervised safe place for children aged 0–18 and their non-custodial parents, who are referred by the courts, CPOs, or PIECs, due to situations such as divorce, violence, or child risk. The main goal of this service is to rebuild and strengthen relationships between parents and children, leading eventually to an independent and unsupervised relationship. To this end, the centers provide an intensive treatment program for a limited time, usually in the parents' home.

The DSS also subsidizes various daycare programs in the community such as:

1) Daycare services for children at risk operated under the terms of the Endangered Toddlers (the Right to Daycare) Law 2000. They serve children aged six months to three years from families with problems caring for them that might affect their development. The children are referred to daycare by the DSS as

part of a general support plan for the family, which requires the approval of the committee for toddlers at risk at the DSS (IMLSASS, 2014, 2018).

2) Multipurpose daycare offering a more intensive program with a multidisciplinary staff from 7 a.m. through 7 p.m. for children aged six months to six years for families needing more intensive support (IMLSASS, 2014).

3) Child home support for families in crisis, giving individual care for children in the family setting for a limited period of six months (IMLSASS 2014, 2018).

4) After-school programs for children at risk aged 3–12 implemented by the DSS, which provide free lunch, help with homework, enrichment classes, and emotional therapy if needed (Peretz et al., 2005; IMLSASS, 2017a).

5) "Residential" daycare (for school children who receive care at a residential facility, but come home at the end of the day) (IMLSASS, 2015) as a means of supporting the parent-child relationship (Ben-Rabi & Hasin, 2006).

Finally, important initiatives and services in the area of child protection are provided by NGOs (some of which work closely with the government): the Israel National Council for the Child [INCC]—an advocacy and lobby organization for children's rights and well-being that since 1992 has published an annual report on the status of children in Israel; the Haruv Institute—a leading training and research center in the field of child abuse and neglect; the Myers-JDC-Brookdale Institute—a partnership between the American Jewish Joint Distribution Committee and the government of Israel that conducts research to improve the effectiveness of social services in Israel; the Organization for Child Protection (ALI)—the first NGO to place the issue of child maltreatment on the public agenda and support abused children; the Rape Crisis Centers—nine centers throughout the country that provide treatment for victims (including a specially adapted service for children), training for parents, and activities for raising awareness in the community, the centers are NGOs funded today by the IMLSASS; and JDC-Ashalim, a partnership between the JDC-Israel, the Israeli government and the UJA-Federation of New York, which addresses the challenges of developing services for children and youth at risk.

Methods of Provision and Funding Model

A large proportion of the child protection services are partly privatized, following the gradual adoption of the mixed model for social services delivery over the past three decades. This policy was introduced by the government and is supported by the Ministry of Finance and IMLSASS (Katan, 2007). All services were originally provided by the national and local governments, but since the 1980s, NGOs and private companies have been responsible for providing many of the services, while government agencies remain responsible for defining and approving eligibility, as well as for funding and regulating the provision of services. Accordingly, a large portion of the government and municipal budgets for social services goes to non-government providers (Gal, 1994). The process of privatization has continued to grow over the past decade, with NGOs receiving a budget that increases incrementally every year both in absolute terms and proportionally to the general budget (Madhala-Brik & Gal, 2016). Note that in the case of social services, the main considerations for privatizing were not only organizational and financial, but also the growing preference for care in the community, based on the assumption that NGOs might have a more firm footing in the local community (Mandelkarn & Sherman, 2012).

Thus, many of the services for children, especially those not provided directly by DSS social workers, are provided by NGOs (residential care, foster-care organizations, emergency centers, etc.). The local DSS is mainly responsible for the work of CPOs, especially within the legal system; individual and group counseling and therapy for children and parents; supervision of community services for children; and initiating new community programs that will eventually be provided by NGOs (Katan, 2007).

Unfortunately, there are no published data specifically on child protection budgets. However, something can be learned from the trends in the IMLSASS budget for the Service for Children and Youth (SCY), which is responsible for most child protection services. The general budget of IMLSASS has grown in the last decade, reaching NIS 6 billion in 2017 (an increase of 44% since 2012). Twenty-one percent of this budget was allocated to the SCY (IMLSASS, 2018).

In 2016, 62% of the SCY budget was directed to out-of-home placement services and the remainder to services in the community (IMLSASS, 2015)—a decrease in expenditure on out-of-home care, which was about 70% of the budget in the 1990s (IMLSASS, 2015). Within the budget for out-of-home services, only 12.5% was allocated to foster-care organizations and the remainder to residential care (IMLSASS, 2017a). Note, too, that municipal social service budgets are added to that of IMLSASS following an agreement between the IMLSASS and the municipalities that 25% of every welfare activity must be funded by the municipality in order for the IMLSASS to match with the remaining 75%. This arrangement creates great inequality between the municipalities, since low socioeconomic municipalities are sometimes unable to provide their share (Gal et al., 2017).

The budget in the contracts is based on the standards developed for the different types of service. While these organizations receive government funding, in many cases they are dependent on philanthropy (Ben Shalom & Tzur, 2004). The proportion of donations in each organization's budget varies. Specific data are not available, but in 2014, 37% of the NGOs' welfare budgets were from donations, the rest coming mainly from government (ICBS, 2017b).

The Ministry has no published data indicating how much of the budget is allocated to governmental providers, private organizations or NGOs. A study by Madhala-Brik and Gal (2016) found that in 2015, 80% of the IMLSASS budget was earmarked for outsourced services, divided equally between private organizations and NGOs. The authors also found that generally, more NGOs than private companies had been allocated budgets since 2000, particularly in the Division for Personal and Social Services in charge of the SCY in the IMLSASS. Their analysis noted dominance of "veteran" services (those that had previously provided services to the ministry) in this department, which received 91% of the outsourcing budget, suggesting the provider market is very stable. This trend is associated with other findings that show that the social services market is quite centralized. Specifically, in the Division for Personal and Social Services, three organizations received 52% of the 2015 budget. The authors conclude that competition in the social service market is limited. However, while competition was one of the main general reasons for privatization, it seems in this specific market that organizations are actually chosen based on their experience in providing the services (as it is considered important for the state of the clients), making it harder for new organizations to enter (Madhala-Brik & Gal, 2016).

In the privatization process, the government is in charge of three main areas: (1) setting policy standards for the services; (2) funding; and (3) monitoring and supervising (Katan, 2007). This regulatory role, especially in the social service context, is complex. Lahat and Talit (2012) claim that in many cases in the Israeli social services, the supervisor's role is not clearly defined in the ministry's regulations and contracts. Furthermore, due to the high dependence of the clients on the providers, supervisors tend not to use sanctions against the contractors. Moreover, in many cases the supervisor is also the advisor for the program, which might create a conflict of interest. Another crucial "side effect" of the privatization process is that many social workers (though not CPOs) are no longer employed by the government, but by NGOs and private organizations, meaning that their employment conditions have deteriorated and the number of unionized social workers has declined (Maron, 2012).

One clear example of the privatization of child protection services is foster-care reform (Maron, 2012). An evaluation of the partial privatization in the service (Sorek et al., 2014) found that generally the representatives of both the Ministry and the organizations were satisfied with the current service provision. They considered that partial privatization has improved the service provided to the children and their families and contributed to professional knowledge. These improvements stem from the fact that the service was previously provided by family social workers who had many other responsibilities. Now that only four organizations, rather than over 200 municipalities, are responsible for recruiting families, cooperation is possible at the national level, and the pool of foster families has grown. Another benefit of the change is that the DSSs can focus on the care of the biological families. Moreover, the separation between the regulatory authority and the service is also viewed positively. The study mentions some limitations in the current services, such as gaps between regulations and actual service, and communication problems between the organizations and the DSSs.

The IMLSASS supervises and monitors the quality of service the many contractors provide (especially in residential care) using a method known as RAF (Regulation, Assessment, and Follow-up), which was developed by the Myers-JDC-Brookdale Institute.

The RAF method was first implemented in the late 1980s in out-of-home care, and since 2006 has also been used in community-based programs (Shapiro & Promer, 2008). The RAF method is based on a quality assurance model and includes a cycle of inspections to collect data, giving feedback to the organizations, monitoring inadequate findings, and implementing the necessary changes. This process takes place generally every year, though in some programs the inspections take place only every two or three years.

Summary: Main Trends and Challenges

The child protection system in Israel has developed extensively since the end of the 1990s, with major advances in both legislation and services. Originally, the system was child protection-oriented (Gilbert et al., 2011), in keeping with the British origins of the system in Israel. The orientation has gradually shifted to a more family-based orientation, since the early 2000s, though a greater focus on child protection is still pronounced. Indeed, the legislative and public discourse in Israel has been criticized for focusing on protecting children from people in their immediate environment, without looking at the broader context of the child in terms of social rights (nutrition, respect, education, etc.) (Ronen & Gilat, 2016). The discrepancy, however, may have to do with the lack of consistency in legislation for children (such as a comprehensive Children Act) that might standardize social policy for children, despite the efforts of the Rotlevy Committee (Morag, 2010; Ronen & Gilat, 2016).

The growth in community-based services, however, has led to only a slight drop in the number of children in out-of-home services, which have remained stable in the last decade. Moreover, despite the policy preference of foster-care over residential care, these changes have also been very slow, with a small decline in the number of children in residential care and an even smaller rise in the number of children in foster care. The slow change, despite policy, should be seen in the context of the historical preference for residential care in Israel (Benbenishty et al., 2015). Note also that organizational change is a slow process requiring a conceptual change in the system, especially the CPOs; the challenges of working in the child protection services also must be taken into account.

Alongside the growing family-focused orientation, policy attempts to promote children's participation in parts of the system reflect a nascent child-focused orientation, dating back to the Juvenile Law 1960, which encouraged the participation of children in court hearings relating to them. In 2004, the Rotlevi Committee report presented a very progressive and supportive position, noting many of the benefits of involving children, such as hearing the child's view and strengthening the child's autonomy. The recommendations led to changes in the regulations regarding the PIECs, which now stipulate that children should be prepared for the discussion in the committee and their opinion should be presented to the committee—either directly or by the social worker or third party—and recorded in the minutes. The reform also stressed that the child's physical participation is important, as it makes a direct impression on the committee members (Angel-Rdai, 2014).

Despite the Rotlevi Committee's progressive approach to children's participation, which has been largely adopted as policy, not all of the recommendations have been put into practice. According to Alfandari (2016), 40% of the children involved participated in PIEC hearings in 2014 and a survey of 80 PIEC coordinators showed 90% of them reported that in almost all of the cases, children had been prepared to participate in hearing. Nevertheless, doubts remain as to the extent of actual participation, especially as the new guidelines were not based on legislation and the child's involvement was at the coordinator's discretion (Oppenheim-Weller et al., 2017). A qualitative study of 21 children who were brought to PIECs found that only seven actually participated, and they had minimal impact on the outcome. The authors note that when children actually participated, the environment was unfriendly and the questioning was investigative. In cases where the child did not participate, only rarely did the social worker present the child's views or wishes by proxy. In general, the social workers did not support the participation of children, particularly those below age 12 (Alfandari, 2016). In other words, although strongly backed as policy, child participation remains rare and still presents a major challenge.

Many of the above shortcomings are due to major challenges the system has to contend with. Firstly, the CPOs have very heavy caseloads of up to 200 children (Szabo-Lael & Shevat, 2012); in Arab municipalities and those with a high proportion of ultra-Orthodox Jews these tend to be higher (Ben-Arieh et al., 2013). Heavy caseloads have been found to lead to poorer service quality, smaller numbers of service recipients, deficient reporting, less time for professional supervision, and staff burnout (Szabo-Lael & Shevat, 2012).

A related issue is the limited implementation of evidence-based practice (EBP) in Israel, perhaps because it is not required by child welfare organizations or offered to their staff, or perhaps because of the dominance of psychodynamic theories among professionals in Israel, which impede dissemination of manualized interventions (David & Shiff, 2015). Only two EBP programs focused on child maltreatment have been implemented in Israel: SafeCare®, a home-based support intervention for parents of children up to age 5 (Oppenheim-Weller & Zeira, 2018), and Child–Parent Psychotherapy (CPP) for treating early childhood trauma (David & Shiff, 2015). While implementation of these programs seems to be generally positive, evaluations have revealed some of the complexities in adopting such programs in Israel. These include the need for translation of all materials, and cultural adaptation and adjustment of the intervention to the context of the Israeli social services (Oppenheim-Weller & Zeira, 2018). Moreover, it is difficult to remain faithful to a program (as usually expected in EBP) in a country where professionals are not necessarily informed about the practice (David & Schiff, 2015). Also, international EBPs are rarely imported and implemented.

It should be noted that there have been efforts to collect evidence for practices in Israel and many of the programs implemented by IMLSASS are routinely evaluated. However, the evaluations do not usually include longitudinal study or systematic data collection using standardized, reliable study tools.

Yet another challenge in the Israeli child protection system is data collection. The 2016 State Comptroller's Report noted the lack of organized data collection on the status of children in out-of-home facilities, which if present could help evaluate effective programs (State Comptroller, 2017). Finally, many of the data are gathered in a very general way and there are limited data on specific populations of children. Thus, for example, no clear data have been published on types of foster care (such as kinship care). Much of the information about reports to the CPOs refer not only to abused and neglected children, but also to other client populations of the CPOs, for example, juvenile offenders, addicts, and so on. There are no data for various ethnic and minority populations, making it hard to evaluate trends in communities such as the ultra-Orthodox and the Arabs, who have been known to refrain from reporting child maltreatment, due to strong family values (Goldstein & Laor, 2007).

Finally, another major shift in the Israeli system over the years is the privatization process, with a large proportion of child protection services now provided in a mixed model. Under this model, NGOs and private organizations provide many of the services and the IMLSASS is responsible for defining and approving eligibility and funding, and for regulating the services provided. While this has been found beneficial in terms of efficient service provision, better connection to the local context and professionalization, it also presents some challenges. The IMLSASS supervisory role was found to be problematic (State Comptroller, 2017), partly due to conflict of interest when the supervisor also serves as the program's advisor, as well as dependence on the current providers (Lahat & Talit, 2012). Yet another challenge created by the mixed model is maintaining continuity among the services (Navot et al., 2017), for example, the combined efforts of out-of-home services and family social workers at the DSS result in limited preparation for the child's return home (State Comptroller, 2017).

Evidently, despite a series of attempts made in the past two decades to scrutinize and reform child protection policy in Israel, the child protection system faces complex challenges. The extent to which the Israeli child protection system manages to address these challenges in the years to come, will undoubtedly determine its ability to implement desired changes and provide for vulnerable children in need of its care and protection.

Acknowledgments

We would like to thank Naomi Halsted, from the Myers-JDC-Brookdale Institute for helping to edit this chapter.

References

Alfandari, R. (2017). An evaluation of a national reform in the Israeli child protection practice designed to improve children's participation in decision-making. *Child and Family Social Work*, 22, 54–62.

Angel-Rdai, A. (2014). *Planning, intervention and evaluation committees.* Israel Ministry of Labor and Social Affairs and Services (Hebrew).

Arazi, T., Szabo-Lael, R., and Ben Simon, B. (2017). *National index of child maltreatment in Israel: Process of development.* Myers-JDC-Brookdale Institute (Hebrew).

Avgar, I. (2016). *Budgeting student accommodation in residential care.* The Knesset Research and Information Center (Hebrew).

Ben Shalom, Y. and Bar-Tzuri, R. (2004). *Welfare policy for children.* Taub Center for Social Policy Studies in Israel (Hebrew).

Ben-Arieh, A., Zeira, A., Slusky, H., Levi, H., and Admon, K. (2013). *Reports to CPOs: Annual report for 2012.* Haruv Institute (Hebrew).

Benbenishty, R., Davidson-Arad, B., López, M., Devaney, J., Spratt, T., Koopmans, C., Knorth, E. J., Witteman, C. L., Del Valle, J. F., and Hayes, D. (2015). Decision making in child protection: An international comparative study on maltreatment substantiation, risk assessment and interventions recommendations, and the role of professionals' child welfare attitudes. *Child Abuse & Neglect*, 49, 63–75.

Ben-Rabi, D. and Hasin, T. (2006). *Community-based and day residential facilities: Intervention strategies and the status of the children and their parents: Summary of three years of study.* Myers-JDC-Brookdale Institute (Hebrew).

Berkovitz, M. (2007). Aspects of police investigations of child maltreatment. In D. Horowitz, Y. Ben-Yehuda, and M. Hovav (Eds.), *Abuse and neglect of children in Israel: Victims, law enforcement and justice, health, education and welfare* (pp. 209–269). JDC-Ashalim (Hebrew).

Cohen, S. (2005). *A house with a window: Advocacy centers for children and their families.* Ministry of Social Affairs and Social Services, the Schusterman Family Foundation and JDC-Ashalim (Hebrew).

David, P. and Schiff, M. (2015). Learning from bottom-up dissemination: Importing an evidence-based trauma intervention for infants and young children to Israel. *Evaluation and Program Planning*, 53, 18–24.

Davidson-Arad, B. and Benbenishty, R. (2010). Contribution of child protection workers' attitudes to their risk assessments and intervention recommendations: A study in Israel. *Health and Social Care in the Community*, 18(1), 1–9.

Davidson-Arad, B. and Benbenishty, R. (2016). Child welfare attitudes, risk assessments and intervention recommendations: The role of professional expertise. *British Journal of Social Work*, 46(1), 186–203.

Dolev, T., Benbenishty, R., and Timar, A. (2001). *Decision Committees in Israel: Their Organization, Work Processes, and Outcomes: A Summary Report.* Myers-JDC-Brookdale Institute (Hebrew).

Dolev, T., Ben Rabi, D., and Zemach-Marom, T. (2009). Residential care for children "at risk" in Israel: Current situation and future challenges. In M. E. Courtney M.E. and D. Iwaniec (Eds.), *Residential care of children: Comparative perspectives* (pp. 72–88). Oxford University Press.

Dolev, T., Szabo-Lael, R., Schmid, H., and Bar-Nir, D. (2008). *Policy of "facing the community": Research and evaluation.* Myers-JDC-Brookdale Institute (Hebrew).

Faver, M. (2009). *Child abuse: Acknowledging the phenomenon, legislative progress and development of treatment and protection.* The Haruv Institute (Hebrew).

Faver, M. and Slusky, H. (2007). Between protection and treatment of at risk minors: The role of child protective service workers. In D. Horowitz, Y. Ben-Yehuda, M. Hovav (Eds.), *Abuse and neglect of children in Israel: Victims, law enforcement and justice, health, education and welfare* (pp. 951–994). JJDC-Ashalim (Hebrew).

Frid, B., Pegelson, P., and Slusky, H. (2010). *Emergency centers: Information for professionals.* Ministry of Social Affairs and Services and Haruv Institute.

Gal, J. (1994). Commodification and privatization of the welfare state, consequences for Israel. *Sociality and Welfare*, 15(1), 7–24 (Hebrew).

Gal, G., Madhala, S., and Bleikh, H. (2017). *Social service budgeting in Israeli local authorities.* Taub Center for Social Policy Studies in Israel.

Gilbert, N., Parton, N., and Skivenes, M. (2011). *Child protection systems: International trends and orientations.* Oxford University Press.

Gold, N., Benbenishty, R., and Osmo, R. (2001). A comparative study of risk assessments and recommended interventions in Canada and Israel. *Child Abuse and Neglect*, 25(5), 607–622.

Goldstein, S. and Laor, R. (2007). Intercultural aspects of the obligation to report and locate children who are victims of abuse and neglect. In D. Horowitz, Y. Ben-Yehuda, and M. Hovav (Eds.), *Abuse and neglect of children in Israel: Victims, law enforcement and justice, health, education and welfare* (pp. 858–888). JDC-Ashalim (Hebrew).

Gottfriend, R. and Ben-Arieh, A. (2019). *The Israeli Child Protection System*. In *National systems of child protection* (pp. 139–171). Springer, Cham.

Hovav, M. (2007). Preface to the law, justice and enforcement section. In D. Horowitz, Y. Ben-Yehuda, and M. and Hovav (Eds.), *Abuse and neglect of children in Israel: Victims, law enforcement and justice, health, education and welfare* (pp. 673–680). Jerusalem: JDC-Ashalim (Hebrew).

ICBS. (2017a). *Employment and salary*. Israel Central Bureau of Statistics.

ICBS. (2017b). *Income and expenses of non-profit institutions 2014–2016*. Israel Central Bureau of Statistics.

IMLSASS. (2006). *Towards the community policy: Project book*. Ministry of Social Affairs and Services.

IMLSASS. (2015). *Social services review 2014*. Israel Ministry of Labor, Social Affairs, and Social Services.

IMLSASS. (2016). *Social services review 2015*. Israel Ministry of Labor, Social Affairs, and Social Services.

IMLSASS. (2017a). *Social services review 2016*. Israel Ministry of Labor, Social Affairs, and Social Services.

IMLSASS. (2017b). *Report to CPOs: Annual report for 2016*. Israel Ministry of Labor, Social Affairs, and Social Services.

IMLSASS. (2017c). *The national plan for children and youth at risk 360°*. Available at: http://www.molsa.gov.il/ProjectShmid/Pages/ProjectHome.aspx.

IMLSASS. (2018). *The service for children and youth: Israel Ministry of Labor, Social Affairs, and Social Services*. Available at: http://www.molsa.gov.il/Units/Wings/AgSherutim/Pages/ShirutEledNoar.aspx.

INCC. (2008). *The State of the Child in Israel 2007*. Israel National Council for the Child. (Hebrew)

INCC. (2016). *The State of the Child in Israel 2015*. Israel National Council for the Child. (Hebrew)

INCC. (2018). *The State of the Child in Israel 2017*. Israel National Council for the Child. (Hebrew)

INCC. (2019). *Immigrant children on Israel*, 7th edition. Israel National Council for the Child and the Ministry of Aliyah and integration. (Hebrew)

INCC. (2020). *The State of the Child in Israel 2019*. Israel National Council for the Child. (Hebrew)

Kadman, Y. (1992). The law preventing maltreatment of minors and helpless persons: A turning point in Israeli society in relation to child abuse. *Social Security*, 38, 137–146 (Hebrew).

Kashti, Y., Shlesky, S., and Arieli, S. (2000). *Youth communities*. Ramot Publication.

Kashti, Y., Gruper, E. N., and Shlasky, S. (2008). *Residential care towards the next century: Planning and developing educational facilities (committee report)*. Ministry of Education (Hebrew).

Katan, Y. (2007). *Partial Privatization of Personal Welfare Services in Israel*. The Ministry of Social Affairs and Social Services.

Lahat, L. and Talit, G. (2012). The regulation challenges in personal welfare services in Israel. *Social Policy*, 90, 81–120 (Hebrew).

Lev-Viesel, R., Eisikovits, Z., First, M., Gottfried, R., and Mehlhausen, D. (2016). Prevalence of child maltreatment in Israel: A national epidemiological study. *Journal of Child and Adolescent Trauma*, 11, 141–150.

Madhala-Brik, S. and Gal, J. (2016). *Out-sourcing of welfare services: Trends and changes*. Taub Center for Social Policy Studies in Israel.

Mandelkarn, R. and Sherman, A. (2012). The privatization of operation: Providing social services using outsourcing. In I. Galnnor, A. Paz-Fuchs, and N. Zion (Eds.), *Privatization policy in Israel: State responsibility and the boundaries between the public and the private* (pp. 265–319). The Van Leer Jerusalem Institute and Hakibbutz Hameuchad. (Hebrew).

Maron, A. (2012). Trend and process in privatization of social services in Israel. In I. Galnnor, A. Paz-Fuchs, N. and Zion (Eds.), *Privatization policy in Israel: State responsibility and the boundaries between the public and the private* (pp. 136–187). The Van Leer Jerusalem Institute and Hakibbutz Hameuchad. (Hebrew).

Morag. T. (2010). The influence of the evaluation committee of the basic rules in the area of child and law on conceptualization in Israel ruling. *Family in Law*, 3–4, 67–86.

Nahmani-Rot, D. (2010). The conditions by which child protection officers receive exemption from reporting offences committed towards children to the police. *Family Law*, 3-4, 379–399 (Hebrew).

Navot, M., Sorek, Y., Szabo-Lael, R., and Ben Rabi, D. (2017). *Achievements and challenges of the service system for at-risk children and their families: Two decades of MJB research*. Myers-JDC-Brookdale Institute (Hebrew).

Navot, M., Fass, H., and Zadka, H. (2014). *Supervised visitation centers for parents and children in Israel: National evaluation study*. Myers-JDC-Brookdale Institute (Hebrew).

OECD. (2022a). *Fertility rates (indicator)*. https://doi.org/10.1787/8272fb01-en.

OECD. (2022b). *Young population (indicator)*. https://doi.org/10.1787/3d774f19-en.

Oppenheim-Weller, S. and Zeira, A. (2018). Safe care in Israel: The challenges of implementing an evidence-based program. *Children and Youth Services Review*, 85, 187–193.

Oppenheim-Weller, S., Schwartz, E., and Ben-Arieh, A. (2017). Child involvement in treatment planning and assessment in Israel. *Child and Family Social Work*, 22, 1302–1312.

Peretz, R., Zemach-Marom, T., and Abutbul N. (2005). *Survey of welfare-education after-school programs of the children and youth service at the Ministry of Social Affairs: Situation before the implementation of the RAF method, according to staff reports.* Myers-JDC-Brookdale Institute.

Rivkin, D. with Shmaia-Yadgar, S., Shemesh, M., Szabo-Lael, R., and Sorek, Y. (2009). *Evaluation of child-parent centers.* Myers-JDC-Brookdale Institute.

Ronen. Y. and Gilat, Y. Z. (2016). Is child protection common in the Israeli law? *Law and Business*, 19, 1234–1143. (Hebrew).

Rotlevi, S. (2004). *Committee for the review of basic principles regarding the child and the law and their legal implementation in Israel.* Ministry of Justice (Hebrew).

Shapiro. S. and Promer, S. (2008). *The implementation of the standard technique in the ministry of social affairs and services residential care.* Ministry of Social Affairs and Services.

Shnit, D. (1998). The law and social work practice in Israel. In F. Loewenberg (Ed.), *Meeting the challenges of a changing society: Fifty years of social work in Israel* (pp. 383–388). Magnes Press.

Silman, Y. (2014). *Ministerial committee examining the policy regarding out-of-home placement and custody agreements: Interim report.* Israel Ministry of Labor and Social Affairs and Services.

Sorek, Y., Szabo-Lael, R., and Ben Simon, B. (2014). *Foster-care services in Israel: National study.* Myers-JDC-Brookdale Institute.

State Comptroller. (2017). *The Ministry of Labor and Social Affairs and Services, Annual report for 2017.* The State Comptroller and Ombudsman of Israel.

Szabo-Lael, R. (2017). *Children and youth at risk in Israel.* Myers-JDC-Brookdale Institute.

Szabo-Lael, R. and Shevat, M. (2012). *Magen ("Shield"): A program to upgrade the child protection system: evaluation study.* Myers-JDC-Brookdale Institute.

Zeira, A. (2004). New initiatives in out-of-home placements in Israel. *Child and Family Social Work*, 9(3), 305–307.

Child Protection in Mediterranean Countries: Italy and Greece

Teresa Bertotti, Roberta T. Di Rosa, *and* Charis Asimopoulos

Abstract

This chapter explores the child protection systems in Italy and Greece. Both countries have to deal with immigrant children due to the conflict between the rights of minors and immigration laws on control and defense. In Italy, the child protection system is the result of a patchwork of norms and regulations addressing different societal demands and pressures. Family and cash-transfers are fundamental factors in Italy's child welfare system. Greece, on the other hand, has adopted fragmented measures and policies connected with financial benefits, income support, social security, social care for disabled people, and rehabilitation for children at risk. The chapter also notes how the 2010 financial crisis affected the Greek child protection system.

Key Words: Italy, Greece, immigrant children, immigration laws, child protection system, disabled people, financial crisis, family, cash-transfers

This chapter includes analysis of child protection systems in two Mediterranean countries which share several relevant similarities: Italy and Greece. Their welfare systems have both been included in the Southern Europe and Mediterranean (SE/M) cluster, proposed as a fourth cluster where the family plays a pivotal role (among others, Ferrrera, 1996; Gal, 2010). Both countries have been hit hard by the post-2008 economic crisis, with increasing levels of poverty and unemployment; both have been subjected to austerity measures, albeit at different levels. Both countries lack a structured child protection system. They also have many differences. In order to better understand differences and similarities and the key future challenges they are facing, the first two sections of this chapter will outline how these countries have constructed their policies and practices on child protection. We also include a third section dedicated to immigrant children, since Italy and Greece are a first arrival country in Europe for many immigrants and refugees. Both countries have had to deal with the tension between minors' rights to be protected, and immigration laws focusing on principles of control and defense. Numbers, methods, and strategies adopted in the two countries will be briefly presented.[1]

---

[1] This chapter has been written before the Covid-19 pandemic. Data regarding the impact of the pandemic on children and families as well as on policies might be not reported in this chapter.

Italy: Blurring Responsibilities in Familial Welfare

The Italian child protection system is the result of a patchwork of norms and regulations which, over the years, have sought to address the different demands and pressures emerging from society. This section presents basic contextual elements regarding how the child protection system is structured, the legal framework, procedures and main protection measures, and the organizations and resources supporting the system, and closes with some general comments about main trends.

Background Context: Social-demographic Data

According to Istat, in 2019, the Italian population counted 60,350,000 persons, among whom 10,008,033 are children under 18 (16,6% of the whole population). Italy is an ageing country, with 21.7% over 65, and a steadily declining birth-rate since 2008, with less than 500,000 births in 2019. In an increasing trend, there are more than 5 million (8.3%) foreign citizens, 20.2% being children.

Families are getting smaller and "longer," decreasing in number (now 2.3 per family instead of 3 during the 1990s) and getting older. Single parents are also on the increase, counting 15.8% in 2016, compared to 5.5% in 1983. There is also more instability, with a steady increase in separations and divorces (around 63%, from 1996 to 2015) involving almost 65,000 children. Family models are also changing, with the emergence of a voluntary choice of single motherhood and an increase in same-gender parents.

The economic crisis has had a strong impact on increasing levels of poverty and social exclusion, especially affecting families and children. In 2013, the worst year of the recession, 2 million families (9.7% of households) and 1,434,000 (14.3%) children lived in absolute poverty. Youth levels of unemployment reached a peak of 40.3% in 2015, one of the highest rates in Europe (third after Greece (47.3%) and Spain (44.4%)). In 2019 the situation was improved, with a decrease of household in absolute poverty (6.4%) but still with a significant problem of child poverty. The gender gap is also relevant with high differences in employment rates and a low level of gender equality, being ranked 14th among European countries by the Gender Equality Index (EIGE, 2020).

Together with the shortcomings in policies supporting families, these features explain why Italy has been classified among countries with the lowest level of defamilialization (Cho, 2014). In a study comparing the impact of the economic crisis in 41 rich countries in the world, Italian children suffered the largest increase in poverty, with long standing effects on children's lives, and an evident connection to educational performance (UNICEF, 2014). Moreover, Italy is ranked 22nd in a study on the well-being of children in 29 rich countries in the world (UNICEF, 2013).

The incidence of children as victims of violence is difficult to ascertain, since Italy lacks a national monitoring system. However, a survey, carried out in 2015 with a representative sample of local municipalities estimated that 9.5 out of 1,000 minors are victims of ill-treatment, neglect, or abuse (AGIA et al., 2015).

The System of Child Welfare and Child Protection in Italy

Child welfare has to be regarded as part of a welfare system where the family is a fundamental player, with the main responsibility in supporting and protecting individuals from socioeconomic risks. Other features of Italian welfare are a preference for cash-transfers instead of investment in services, provisions available only to groups of guaranteed workers and a great and continuing disparity between the north and the south (Ascoli & Pavolini, 2015). During the 1980s, Italy laid down the bases for its universal welfare-system, which partially still remains. In 1978, the National Health Service (NHS) was established and fundamental services, which still constitute the backbone of the present welfare state, were created cross-nationally, including family counsel ing center s and mental health and drug addiction services. During the 1990s, the healthcare system underwent a radical transformation, with the introduction of managerial and neo liberal principles, and market competition (Maino & Neri, 2011).

Social welfare was regulated at the national level in 2000 (Law 328/2000), with a long-awaited reform, aimed at creating an integrated system of social services, based on the principle of selective universalism and the principle of subsidiarity. Accordingly, local governments are called upon to plan their own social policies and to make decisions on resource allocation. In 2001, the decentralization process brought additional autonomy to the regions in managing health, education and social services, thus increasing the already heterogeneous and geographically unequal system. Child welfare and protection policies should be considered within this system of multiple levels of governance, and with a focus on territories and marketization.

The Italian child protection system, as the result of the interplay of norms from different sources and national policies, only started to pay ample attention to children in the late 1990s, with adherence to the UN Convention on the Rights of the Child (UNCRC) and passage of the landmark bill (no. 285/1997) significantly called "Promotion of the Rights and Opportunities in Childhood and Adolescence." This law requests national and local authorities to draw a "plan of action for children and adolescents" every three years and supported the modernization of services for children and families. The National Observatory and the National Documentation Centre on Childhood and Adolescence were also established in 1997, followed by the institution of the National Ombudsman for Childhood and Adolescence in 2011.

Locally, child protection systems are developed according to regional policies and, although local authorities should guarantee equal minimum levels of assistance throughout the country, the level of heterogeneity is very high, especially between the north and south of Italy. This is a major criticism that has been repeatedly denounced and was the object of a specific recommendation from the UN Committee on the Rights of the Child (CRC, 2019).

The Basis for Social Allocation

Children in need receive help through the health and social system based on the notion that the municipality is the public administration's closest point of contact to local people, governed by a democratically elected body. In the field of child welfare, municipalities have the duty to "promote and support family responsibilities, to support children in distress, at risk, or in danger, and to actively promote the rights of children" (Article 16, Law 328/2000).

There are two main scenarios in which children in need are supported. The first is within the frame of general services provided by the municipalities—or the healthcare agencies—and is based on a deliberate request, or acceptance of help, coming from the parents. The second is mandatory, based on an obligation from the judiciary, following the assessment of need for protection and inability of the parents to provide.

Being linked to the municipality, social services are connected with the community and may include social support and counsel ing, pedagogical support, housing and education resources, and income and employment support. Provision is normally made for free (or for a small fee), varying according to family income and local regulation. Municipalities determine which services and resources they will provide and criteria for eligibility, within the minimum level of assistance that should be guaranteed nationally.

Municipalities also have the responsibility of implementing the measures as laid down by the Court, hence managing statutory services. Child protection can be therefore distinguished as administrative and judicial.

THE LEGAL FRAMEWORK OF CHILD PROTECTION

As for the legal framework, the Italian Constitution recognizes the rights of the family as a "natural society," and the duty (and right) of spouses to support, maintain and educate their children, even if born outside marriage. It also establishes the duty of the state to provide measures to "remove obstacles and support the family in the fulfilment of its duties" (Article 30 Cost). Parents have the "duty to support, train and educate their children, considering their capabilities, natural inclinations and aspirations" (Civil Code, Article 147). When this doesn't happen and the child is found to be in danger, the state is allowed to enter into the private life of families. According to the Civil Code, a threshold is determined where parental behavio r leads to "serious injuries" or is "detrimental" to the child (Article 330). In these cases, the Juvenile Court (JC) intervenes, ordering various measures. The JC can remove or limit parental responsibilities, establishing obligations on the parents, therapeutic treatments for the child, and assigning the support and control of these obligations to the local authority. It may also order the child's placement outside the family, being the only body entitled to do so. These measures aim to help overcome parental difficulties.

According to the Laws on Adoption and Foster Care (Law 184/1983 and Law 149/2001), however, if parental difficulties are not overcome, the court may declare the child to be in a "state of moral or material abandonment," a condition for initiating procedures for the adoption of the child, even against the parents' will. The same laws provide the obligation for all professionals in charge of a public service, including social workers, to report all situations in which children are found in a "state of moral or material abandonment."

A second area of legal protection is related to separation and divorce, which is regulated by the Civil Code. Since 2006, the law established shared custody of children (Law 54/2006). This Court makes its decisions considering the paramount interests of the child and may involve social services, in carrying out investigations and supervising parental contacts.

The third area of intersection is under criminal law, when specific acts toward the child are listed as crimes, such as sexual abuse and exploitation; or "abuse of the means of correction or discipline," "maltreatment in the family or towards children," "abduction of minors," "violation of care and family assistance obligations," and "domestic violence." In these cases, the laws adopted in the late 1990s provide special attention for the hearing and support of the child, also attributed to local child protection services (CPS).

Therefore, three courts might be involved in child protection: the Juvenile Court (staffed by two professional and two lay judges), the Civil Ordinary Court, and the Criminal Ordinary Court. Each of these courts may involve local CPS.

The need to change the judiciary system, to merge the civil and juvenile courts into a single one devoted to family matters, as well as the role of the juvenile and family judges, has been repeatedly discussed. Before that, following a wider debate at the national level regarding the right of defence, in the beginning of the 2000s elements of the adversarial proceedings and cross-examination were introduced to juvenile proceedings, based on allegations of partiality and abuse of powers by juvenile judges and the reduction of the rights of parents (Bertotti & Campanini, 2013).

HOW IT WORKS IN PRACTICE: THE PROCEDURE FOR CHILD PROTECTION

The Italian protection system stems from the link-up between the welfare system and the judiciary system with the absence of a law that connects the two domains; in practice, the child protection route follows the stages summarized in Figure 13.1. This process is not explicitly provided for by the law, and have differences at local level. The spaces for discretion are quite broad; many areas of the relations between the family, the Court and Child Protection Services remain unclear, creating doubts and uncertainties about different responsibilities.

Overall, the dual role of municipal social services, where social workers are ordinarily engaged in voluntary yet supportive relationships, may clash with the duty to report and to work with the Court. This dual role has been one of the key features of the Italian system, but is now showing strains at several levels, mainly, but not only, because of

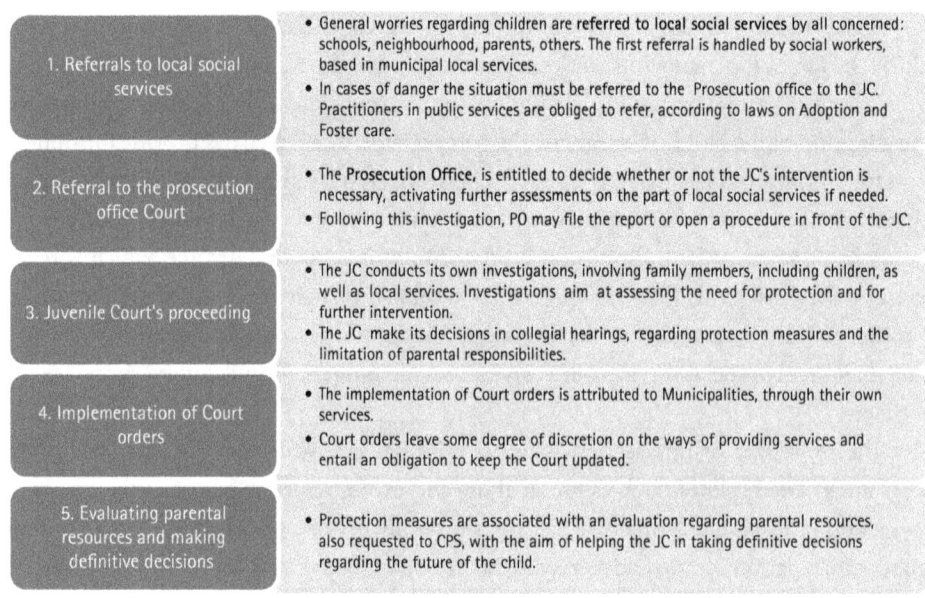

1. Referrals to local social services	• General worries regarding children are referred to local social services by all concerned: schools, neighbourhood, parents, others. The first referral is handled by social workers, based in municipal local services. • In cases of danger the situation must be referred to the Prosecution office to the JC. Practitioners in public services are obliged to refer, according to laws on Adoption and Foster care.
2. Referral to the prosecution office Court	• The Prosecution Office, is entitled to decide whether or not the JC's intervention is necessary, activating further assessments on the part of local social services if needed. • Following this investigation, PO may file the report or open a procedure in front of the JC.
3. Juvenile Court's proceeding	• The JC conducts its own investigations, involving family members, including children, as well as local services. Investigations aim at assessing the need for protection and for further intervention. • The JC make its decisions in collegial hearings, regarding protection measures and the limitation of parental responsibilities.
4. Implementation of Court orders	• The implementation of Court orders is attributed to Municipalities, through their own services. • Court orders leave some degree of discretion on the ways of providing services and entail an obligation to keep the Court updated.
5. Evaluating parental resources and making definitive decisions	• Protection measures are associated with an evaluation regarding parental resources, also requested to CPS, with the aim of helping the JC in taking definitive decisions regarding the future of the child.

Figure 13.1 Steps in the child protection system (untill 2022)

restrictions in resources. As a witness to this rising tension, recent research into violence on social workers shows that 64.2% of aggression from service users was related to child protection matters (Sicora et al., 2022).

Child Protection Measures

The main child protection measures fall within two broad categories: interventions regarding children who live with their family and interventions regarding children placed out-of-home.

The former may include psychological and counseling support, family therapy, and social mentoring for parents, carers, and children. Educational support can also be initiated, as well as intervention in the school context or other networks relevant for the child and the family. The family is supported in establishing positive relationships with social networks, and is provided with economic help or other assistance, for example, for accommodation or employment. A trend is spreading in encouraging the community to support families and children, that is, for "day foster care," or other initiatives, such as self-help and mutual support groups (Maurizio et al., 2015; Fazzi, 2018).

For the latter, in 2001, the already mentioned law on adoption and foster care (Law 149/2001) established the closure of all large institutions for children and the right of the child to be reared in a family. As alternative care, this law establishes that the priority for out-of-home care is family foster care (*affido familiare*) and only as a second choice, placement in family-like residential care units (*comunitá di accoglienza*).

Family foster-care can be either "judicial," when established by the court, or "consensual," when there is an agreement between the two families, validated by a guardianship judge. Foster families are assessed, monitored and supported by a specific foster-care team and receive a small contribution for the child's subsistence costs. Foster care is time-limited (two years) and conceived as a form of family co-operation, which foresees the child returning to the birth family. However, data shows that many placements last longer, envisaging masked forms of adoption, especially for adolescents (Del valle et al., 2013; Belotti, 2014). Various forms of foster care have developed in response to diverse needs, such as same-culture foster-care for foreign children, joint mother and child foster-care, and "professional family foster-care" (including specific training and remuneration).

Small residential care units are variously called *Comunità educative, comunità di tipo familiare*, or *case famiglia*, and were created in the 1980s as alternatives to large institutions. They are small, locally embedded, residential establishments, hosting not more than 10 children, run by professional educators (or by a family) fulfilling parental functions. These are primarily managed by third sector organiz ations, following accreditation by local public authorities.

THE NUMBERS IN CHILD PROTECTION

In 2014, 26,420 children were living in out-of-home care, almost equally divided between family-based foster care (14,020) and residential structures (12,400). The rate is 2.6 per 1,000 children, one of the lowest in Europe, with a decreasing trend since 2007 (32,400 minors). Around 2,000 children are adopted every year, which means a rate of 0.2 per 1,000 children. The number of children who may be adopted, such as those declared to be in a state of abandonment, is 1,340, with an almost stable trend over the years (CRC, 2018).

Beyond these data, it is not easy to know how many children are involved in child protection interventions because Italy still lacks a national system for registration and monitoring. It is estimated that 457,453 children (47.7 minors out of 1,000 residents) are assisted by local social services. Among them, an estimated 91,272 children are receiving services for problems of abuse or neglect: 47.1% for material and/or emotional negligence, 19.4% for witnessing violence, 13.7% for psychological maltreatment, 6.9% for physical maltreatment, and 4.2% for sexual violence (AGIA et al., 2015). See Table 13.1 for a summary of numbers describing child protection in Italy.

THE CHILD PROTECTION INFRASTRUCTURE: ORGANIZATIONAL SETTINGS

As mentioned, the infrastructure of the child protection system is administrated by the m unicipality in accordance with regional policies. The main organizational choice is whether child protection services should be a special ized service, with a dedicated team able to work in mandatory contexts, or a generalist service, dealing with both mandatory

Table 13.1 Numbers in child protection in Italy

		Total	Proportion of population (indicative)
1.	Children assisted by child and family social services - f or problems related to child neglect and abuse	457,453 91, 272	47.7 out of 1,000 9.5 out of 1,000
2.	Out of home children (2019) - in residential structures - family foster care	27.608 *14.053* *13.555*	2.7 out of 1,000
3.	Adoption (2019) - no. of children in domestic adoption - no. of children declared as adoptable and waiting to be adopted	2,804	0.2 out of 1,000
	- no. of children in domestic adoption	1,566	
	- no. of children declared as adoptable and waiting to be adopted	1,238	

Source: Adapted from V° report on the implementation of the law 149/2001 (MPLS, 2022) and AGIA et al. (2015)

and voluntary access. During the 1990s, the prevailing trend was to create specialized child protection teams, attached to the Health System. Later these teams were dismantled, since the health sector rejected the opportunity to work with social matters. Now the picture is varied. Still the trend is to have special ized teams, but they are attached to the social sector or result from collaboration between the two.

Child protection teams are composed of professional social workers, mostly employed by municipalities, sometimes paired with psychologists or social educators. Psychologists are hired from private agencies or "borrowed" from the health system.

Other services, such as social and educational services, residential care communities, home and school support, and innovative projects are mainly managed by non-profit organizations, connected with the municipalities. Hence, in Italy, child protection interventions are "network interventions," with significant work, usually carried out by social workers, dedicated to building and maintaining fruitful collaboration in "loosely coupled" organizations (Weick, 1976). Tensions and strained negotiations in these networks are frequently reported (Bertotti, 2016).

FINANCES AND RESOURCES AND THE IMPACT OF AUSTERITY

Finances are a hot issue and difficult to track because different funding comes from different sources, as was highlighted by the UNCRC Committee (CRC, 2019). Italian social policies include direct money transfers to individuals, supporting pensions, tax relief and other deductions (the majority of funding), and funding of services. In total, Italian social expenditures are slightly above the European average: in 2013 the total amounted to 461.8 billion euros (30% of Italian GDP) compared to the European 29.5%. Similarly, the annual per capita expenditure of 7.972 euros is above the EU average, but lower than other similar welfare systems (such as France, with a per capita of 10.621 euros). National public expenditures for childhood amount to approximately 100 billion euros per year (6% of GDP), mainly allocated in the three areas of social assistance (25 billion euros), education (45.6 billion euros) and healthcare (16/18 billion euros) as estimated in 2014.

Resources are distributed nationally, as direct expenses of the ministries, and locally, as state transfers to the regions and municipalities. In 2008, the economic crisis had a dramatic impact on public expenditures and the FNPS (Fondo Nazionale Politiche Sociali/ National Fund for Social Policies) was almost cancel ed, passing from 1.23 billion euros in 2008 to its lowest level of 71 million e uros in 2012, then slightly increasing, reaching 300 million in 2015 as guaranteed and stable funding for the following years.[2] Beyond national transfers, municipalities also have their own funding, made up of local taxation, users' contributions, and other forms of private funding.

To resist and overcome the austerity measures, municipalities adopted different strategies. Many started a policy of outsourcing social services and involved organ izations from the third sector as well as other private subjects, such as bank foundations and private companies in a comprehensive redesigning of new forms of a mixed welfare system (Bifulco, 2017). This strategy induced growth of the third sector's economy, with growth in the number of employees by 39% from 2001 to 2011 (Ferrera & Maino, 2015).

Whilst this trend enabled services for the population to be partially maintained, it also increased the precarious nature of the workforce and services with contested impacts on working and organizational conditions. It created a disengaged and compliant "austerity social worker" according to Garrett and Bertotti (2017) or increased the professional sense of self-fulfillment for workers involved in innovative services, according to Fazzi (2012).

Eligibility criteria were also adopted, reducing the number of provisions regardless of need. In the field of child protection this meant fewer resources for professional teams, increased workload and reduced supports for children and families. Tensions between professionals and service managers were also found, in relation to resources available for protecting children, with pressure on social workers to limit referrals made to the JC in order to reduce the use of out-of-home placements (Bertotti, 2016).

Best Practices and Key Challenges: Back to the Community in a Vanishing State?

Some local authorities reacted to the crisis and reduced funding by cutting back on excessive expenses and redesigning policies and interventions. With many ambiguities, and frequently associated with neoliberal rhetoric, innovations spread widely in the field of child and family support, providing Italy with a sort of creative "open-air laboratory" (Bifulco, 2017). Often with the support of bank foundations, hundreds of projects were implemented. These projects were geared towards wider involvement of families and

---

[2] With the pandemic, a vast number of resources have been put in social support for families, although with little attention to children (Gruppo CRC, 2020).

children in decision-making processes and co-planning, in child advocacy, and in support for young care leavers. Other projects aim at greater involvement of the community in building up new forms of solidarity, in supporting vulnerable families, and in strengthening neighborhood networks, with the creation of self-help groups and self-funded initiatives.

The spread of these innovations is not free from pitfalls, however. As Bifulco (2017) underlines, apart from creativity, this trend is characterized by fragmentation and tokenism with a risk of increasing the already existing inequalities between the north and south. Moreover, the lack of evaluation and the lack of the capacity to include single projects in a more general design affects the process of upscaling them to public policies.

Many of these projects are inscribed in a call for a "change of paradigm," toward a more family-oriented system (Serbati & Milani, 2013). Accordingly, the need to support parental care, and the "development and requalification of the integrated system of services, residential accommodation and foster care" is quoted as one of the four key priorities of the IV National Plan on Childhood and Adolescence in 2016.

FROM CHILD PROTECTION TO FAMILY SUPPORT: A REAL MOVE?

One wonders whether this call is a real move or is driven by other reasons, either ideological, moral, or political, related to lack of resources and the deficiencies of the state. For instance, the national program aimed at preventing the institutional ization of children, called PIPPI (2015), was very successful in disseminating new practices for working collaboratively with families and children but did not acknowledge that Italy enjoys the lowest rate of out-of-home placement among similar western countries.

Rethinking the system of child protection will undoubtedly bring to the fore the debate between child protection and family support orientations (Gilbert, 2012; Spratt et al., 2015). Hitherto, the Italian debate has never explicitly juxtaposed the two polarities. Instead, child protection has always been related to the need to consider the family, in a systemic framework (Bertotti & Campanini, 2013; Fargion, 2014). Until the early 2000s, the prevailing discourse regarded the protection of children, accepting the possibility that maltreatment and abuse may occur within the family. Nowadays, as compared to the 1990s, attention to child abuse and protection has a peripheral position; it is taken for granted, without worrying too much about the impact of cuts in resources and curtailment of specialized services.

In public discourse, the family is now more central, considered in its vulnerability and in light of the increased levels of poverty, and the needs for social protection. This might indicate the Italian move from the child protection approach to the family orientation approach. Further, the new attention given to children, and their right to be heard might indicate that a child focus approach is also spreading (Gilbert et al., 2011). However, it is questionable whether support for family and children is apparent or real. As Saraceno (2002) has often pointed out, emphasizing the centrality of the family (or the child) is not accompanied by the necessary resources and policies to provide the required services, as the Italian low degree of defamil ialization demonstrates. Moreover, the value given to communities and the increasing presence of the private sector may sound like a shift towards communitarianism, where the state withdraws from the regulation of child protection altogether. A similar attention to the family in a fragmented picture of the welfare system is present in Greece.

Greece: Struggling in the Years of Austerity

Charis Asimoupolous

Greece had a population of 10,815,197 in 2011, 1,889,916 of whom were children up to 18 years of age (17.5% of the total population).[3] Children are represented equally in the various regions of the country, with 44.6% of the child population living in the large urban centers of Athens and Thessaloniki. The country exhibits a low fertility rate, as well as a general decline in the number of births (Hellenic Statistical Authority, 2011).

The Socio economic Framework

Greece has not developed a structured and complete national system for child protection, but has instead adopted fragmented measures and policies connected with financial benefits, income support, social security, social care for specific groups with disabilities, and specific prevention and rehabilitation programs for children at risk, as well as care for infants and pre-school children. This is a result of the chronic weakness in the development of the welfare state, due to the dynamic interaction of various historical, social, economic, and political factors, as well as particular characteristics of Greek society (Asimopoulos, 1998). Greece has developed a welfare model similar to other southern Europe countries, with the prevalence of social transfers, unjustified social insurance privileges, delayed development of universal welfare policies, underdevelopment of social services, poor protection of the unemployed, distributional imbalance, administrative inefficiency, and a non-existent family policy, relying on the family as the main (and often only) basic care provider (Venieris, 2003; Petmesidou, 2006; Athanasiou, 2016). In Greece, the family plays a key role in constructing the individual's social identity and is a vital component of the country's social organization model. Greece is characterized by strong family ties, a highly developed element of social and emotional solidarity among family members, its child-centered orientation, and long-term protection/over-protection and cohabitation with children even into adulthood (Kallinikaki, 2015).

The needs of children's social care are growing dramatically due to demographic changes, transformations in the traditional family's character, increased awareness about children's rights, and the economic crisis and austerity policies that the country has been facing since 2010. Based on EUROSTAT data for Greece, the GDP ratio has decreased

---

[3] The data reported in this part of the chapter refer to 2018.

by a quarter since 2008, unemployment has risen dramatically to 27% (and 50% among the young) and one in five residents is living in conditions of serious material deprivation (UNICEF, 2016). During the years of the crisis, along with financial cuts for health care, mental health care, and social protection, there was a sharp increase in poverty, social exclusion, and adverse changes in lifestyle (Asimopoulos & Teloni, 2017). Socio economic problems acted as stress factors that brought about numerous and severe implications in the psychosocial health of the population, with increases in mental impairment, depression, alcohol abuse, and suicide (Giotakos, 2010; Bourasetal, 2011). Unemployment seriously affected not only adults but also the psychosocial conditions of children (Solantaus et al., 2004). The extent of these problems, as regards children's rights, child poverty, and social exclusion, demands wide-scale re designing of an effective child protection system in the country.

The Child Protection System in Greece

Until the early 1990s, the child protection system in Greece was focused mainly on poverty relief of unprotected children, children from large families, children with disabilities and in residential care (exclusively in traditional institutions). In 1998, the National System for Social Solidarity (Act 2646) was established in order to provide protection to individuals or groups with preventive and rehabilitation programs through the primary, secondary, and tertiary services of the public sector, the local government, and non-profit organizations (NGO'S).

During the same period, a process—which has not yet been completed—of decentralization of social welfare responsibilities was begun. While some skills might be transferred to regional services, the required human and financial resources were not (Athanasiou, 2016). As Skamnakis (2005) points out, transferring the responsibility for the implementation of social protection policies without the necessary eligibilities has resulted in additional weak links in social policy, with a deterioration in the efficiency of the social care system.

In this framework, a number of new, modern services covering a wider population of children with different needs has fragmentarily been developed (Smile of Children, 2009). Telephone lines for child social assistance have been installed (such as the Greek Ombudsman—Cycle of Children's Rights and the Observatory for Children's Rights), as well as institutions for the protection of children's rights. First-level social and counseling services for child and family support have been developed in urban areas, as well as social services for the coordination of local social care activities. In nearly all regions, Centers for Rehabilitation of Children with Disabilities have been established. Standard, but few, specialized care structures and residential care units also have been created for psychosocial problems (e.g., child abuse, children with mentally ill parents that are at risk). The National Center for Social Solidarity was created, a public organization with a coordinating and supervisory role in child protection and emergency social assistance for children in crisis. There has been a great increase in NGO s developing child support programs for children with disabilities, community residential care and rehabilitation structures for children and adolescents, and actions for prevention and early tracking of risk.

The organization of the child protection system is based on the cooperation of the juvenile prosecutor and the court with social services, and child psychiatry and health services. Responsibility for the protection of the child at risk lies with the juvenile prosecutor, while social services and child psychiatry services evaluate the psychosocial issues and the needs of the child.

An allowance policy continues to be exercised with targeted benefits that aim to support the most vulnerable families and children (poor families, single parent families, large families, disabled children, etc.). These welfare benefits are valid for an extended period of time, but fixed at unacceptably low levels and by no means serving their purpose (Greek Ombudsman, 2012). Indicatively, the allowance for an unprotected child amounts to 44 euros a month, provided only to mothers (not to fathers) with a monthly income that does not exceed the sum of 235 euros.

Since 2000, the child protection system has been abetted more effectively by the remarkable growth of mental health services for children and adolescents, which has taken place in the framework of national psychiatric reform. Overcoming huge past deficiencies, new mental health services for children and adolescents have been gradually developed in the public health system, which in 2010 had risen to over 60 in number throughout the country. These include child psychiatric clinics in p ediatric hospitals and psychiatric child diagnostic, treatment, and rehabilitation services in the community. Despite improvements, the situation remains inadequate (Kolaitisetal, 2010). Services are concentrated in Athens and in urban centers, with no child psychiatric service in 20 of the 52 prefectures around the country, thus leaving a large part of the population uncovered (Thornicroftetal, 2010). The main shortcomings concern: a shortage of places for children, especially adolescents; absence of specialized psycho social rehabilitation structures for children and adolescents with mental disorders; and an inadequacy of specialized programs and structures for children and adolescents with autism (Greek Ombudsman, 2012).

As regards the quantitative and qualitative characteristics of the child protection system in Greece, a chronic shortcoming is the fact that official data are not kept. The most recent mapping was made in 2009 by Smile of the Child (Hamogelotou Paidiou), one of the largest child protection NGOs in the country. According to this survey, out of 531 services that were recorded, 24% are governmental, 22.6% from the municipalities, 49% NGOs, and the remaining 4.5% are ecclesiastical.

The most populated service categories (25.4%) are those that promote activities of awareness, information, prevention, and social care programs; the second (11.5%) are those that provide primary social care services; and the third (10%) are protected childcare and rehabilitation services. Centers of physical and social rehabilitation for children with disabilities follow (7.9%).

There is no data collection mechanism and no national central database for children with indicators compatible with the UNCRC. No data are collected regarding violence, trafficking, and sexual exploitation of children, according to their age, gender, ethnic, and socio economic origin, or by groups of children in need of special protection. In addition, methodological tools have not been adopted and no quality control, evaluation, or quality assurance procedures are applicable.

Finally, there are no officially available financial data concerning the policies applied for child protection in total. There is no provision for a Child Budget law that captures the expenditure of the national budget, which aims to implement children's rights.

To sum up, despite the development of new services and programs, the system of child protection continues to remain inadequate in relation to the modern social care needs of children. The services have not been developed according to a plan according to the needs of each geographical area: they do not cover all the regions of the country, they are concentrated in the urban centers, and they display numerous quality problems in terms of operation and management needs. The main problems relate to difficulty in accessing care services, limited development of prevention, an institutional orientation of residential care, limited development of networking and cooperation mechanisms, lack of protocols, and common methodologies.

The Impact of the Financial Crisis on the Child Protection System

The need for child protection services has increased dramatically since the beginning of the financial crisis in Greece in 2010. Meanwhile, due to the implementation of the extreme neo liberal fiscal economic adjustment policies imposed on the country, human and material resources of the child protection services have been reduced. This situation has seriously damaged the already limited effectiveness of the child protection system and has amplified its chronic weaknesses and gaps in growth.

According to UNICEF's report, in 2016, 25.4% of children in Greece experienced poverty or social exclusion (UNICEF, 2017). Approximately one- third of children grow up with deprivation of material goods, while one in eight children grows up with both parents unemployed. Housing proves to be a major problem for one out of six households that have children. In parallel, other factors associated with increased child victimization rates are increasing, such as alcohol and substance use, increased mental disorders, delinquency, and social marginalization.

Within this context, an increase has been observed in requests for children to be admitted to institutions, as a result of their parents' inability to meet their basic needs (Kallinikaki, 2015; Asimopoulos & Teloni, 2017). Data from 2015 by two of the most representative agencies and the police show a worrying increase in child abuse and neglect cases. The "SOS Children's Villages" received requests to provide hospitality for children from 70 families in 2011, and from 400 in 2012. The number of children hosted by the "Hatzikosta Foundation" increased from 50 in 2011 to 100 children in 2012, while in the Ark of the World (Kivotostou Kosmou) organization the number of hosted children increased from 100 children in 2011 to 400 in 2012. In 2012, Smile of the Child registered an increase of 144% of children with serious welfare problems compared to 2011. Moreover, indicative of the material deprivation is the re-emergence in some regions of common municipal meals and free groceries, as well as children's meals in schools. In parallel, an increase was observed in the demand for child psychiatric services, as well as a qualitative change in everyday clinical practice in the gravity of childhood and adolescent psychopathology. The findings from the survey by Anagnostopoulos and Soumaki (2013) of children and adolescents, indicate increases between 2010 and 2012 of 40% in psychosocial problems, 28% in behavioral disorders, 20% in suicide attempts, 25% in school leaving, 22% in bullying, 19% in illicit addictive substances, and 51% in cases of family disputes (due to parental unemployment, serious financial problems, and excessive debts).

Child protection services were called upon to address these growing problems, though there were cuts in staffing, increases in burnout, increases in bureaucratization of services in order to respond to the new process of control-evaluation, and decreasing support for training costs and research (Greek Ombudsman, 2015; Kallinikaki, 2015). Similarly, regional and local social services were weakened; these are primary and urgent social care services, responsible for the coordination and management of most of the child protection requests, as well as managing the needs of children at risk following a court order. An indicative example is the 50% reduction in staffing of social workers (Hellenic Federation of Social Workers, 2014). Furthermore, there were also ramifications on the mental health system. The plan for the development of child psychiatric services was abolished and the operation of community mental health centers for children, the psycho-social rehabilitation units and specialized programs were interrupted or reduced. The impact was particularly serious for units dealing with special categories of disorders, such as autism (Anagnostopoulos & Soumaki, 2013).

The inability of the formal child protection system to respond to the effects of the crisis was covered by the mobilization of self-organized social solidarity. A large number of new supportive structures have been created in the community, such as free access to social grocery stores, social clinics, social pharmacies, rationing, and social solidarity networks functioning as a safety net against the adverse effects of the economic crisis.

The shrinking of social protection spending in the context of the crisis and austerity policies has weakened the already weak child protection system in the country. The result is a low response in the effective handling of children's poverty and deprivation, which disproportionately affects those children with accompanying problems, having a serious impact on their psychosocial development (Rukstele, 2011).

Specific Basic Problems of the Child Protection System

Within this context, specific problems that have been arising for years require immediate attention within the child protection system. These problems concern: 1) the institutional character of residential care, 2) the limited development of community care, particularly foster care, 3) the deficiencies in addressing child abuse, and 4) management schemes for the needs of unaccompanied minors. The latter will be presented together with the Italian situation in the last section of this chapter.

RESIDENTIAL CARE

In Greece, the residential care of children and adolescents with social problems, or with chronic diseases and disabilities, is provided exclusively by institutions from the public and private non-profit sector and the church. The number of children housed approaches 3,000, of whom 1,000 are in public and 2,000 in private and ecclesiastical institutions. Considering the number of children in Greece, this means that 1.6 children out of 1,000 are living in large institutions.

Most institutions operate on an anachronistic " asylum" model. The absence of national operating standards and a code of conduct, with uniform practice standards, combined with chronic staff shortages and infrastructure, leads to multiple violations of children's rights (Greek Ombudsman, 2015). In these institutions, there is no specialized care for children's various problems and disabilities, or for their particular needs. Specialized scientific staffing is almost non-existent. The ratio between care staff and children is the lowest possible, staff having neither support nor supervision, but frequently experiencing burnout. In many cases, the practice of binding is adopted for children with mental disabilities or developmental disorders, thus leading to possible institutional abuse and neglect (Asimopoulos et al., 2009).

The uncompromising situation of children in institutions in Greece has prompted national agencies, such as the Greek Ombudsman, as well as international organizations such as Eurochild, to press for the adoption of strong deinstitutionalization measures (Eurochild, 2015; Greek Ombudsman, 2015). In particular, Eurochild (2015), in the context of the "Opening Doors" campaign on ending institutional care in Europe, has called for the Greek government to take action, regarding three main goals: 1) elimination of old-type institutions for children, 2) increasing effectiveness and efficiency of prevention services to avoid institutionalization, and 3) provision of support to young people leaving the child protection system, in accordance with individual needs (including help in social housing and employment).

As a result of these pressures, a two-year program was launched in 2018 for the de-institutionalization of seven public institutions for children and adolescents with disabilities. In this context, a total of 305 children and adolescents with disabilities are to be rehabilitated in community-based hostels.

FOSTER CARE

Foster care in Greece has improved little, despite its widely recognized significant advantages over institutional care. It is used in a very small number of cases.

Moreover, there are very few child protection agencies able to implement foster care (Greek Ombudsman, 2012). According to the Greek Ombudsman (2012), the three main public foster care institutions carried out 22 placements during 2011 and 2012.

The reasons for this are the exclusively anachronistic institutional orientation of the country's residential care system, the lack of resources and know-how of the social services and child protection teams and the lack of a structured system for selecting, supporting and training foster families. In recent years however, a large network of child protection bodies and scientific associations have started a process of renewed attention and pressure for the promotion and development of foster care.

In May 2018, a new law on foster care and adoption was passed to bolster foster care. The new law provides for the implementation of a nation wide register of foster families, the introduction of professional fostering, and short-term fostering for children with disabilities. Foster care applicants may also be LGBTQ people. The law also provides for the registration of all children in institutional care, accelerating procedures that will assure that placement is beneficial and safeguard the child's rights.

CHILD ABUSE: LEGAL FRAMEWORK AND PRACTICE

Greece has an adequate legal framework for the protection of children's rights, having recently adapted its legislation to the requirements as laid down by the UNCRC, regarding children as victims of violence. The legislation demands that child victimization be reported to the Prosecutor's Office. The Public Prosecutor will then order an assessment report from Social Services and, if necessary, the child's separation from its parents, the transfer of the child to a health service for an examination, and finally possible admission to residential care.

Despite the improvement of the legislative framework, there are significant shortcomings in the process and the services they receive and the way they handle relevant complaints, with significant implications for immediate measures to protect child victims. According to the Greek Ombudsman (2012), there are no official figures regarding maltreatment or neglect of minors and no National Reference Center has been set up to monitor child abuse or neglect.

Prosecutors' offices are not run by social workers, the burden of abuse cases brought to the p rosecution offices of large urban centers is high, the number of minor prosecutors is small, and there are no prosecutors of minors in the rural areas. Social workers of the communities' social services often do not have time to visit families, there is confusion regarding their responsibilities, and common protocols to the investigative process are not applied. Neither protocols nor a common methodology for handling incidents have been adopted or implemented. Referrals are mainly presented to the police, who in the rural areas do not have specialized personnel for investigation activities with minors and do not have protective shelters. No specific preventive measures are being developed for children who are more likely to be victims of abuse, such as children living in institutions and unaccompanied minors.

CHILD PROTECTION GOOD PRACTICES

In the second decade of the 2000s, several new projects and good practices were developed. In 2015, the Protocol for the Management of Child Abuse and Neglect Cases was developed by the Department of Mental Health and Social Welfare, Institute of Child Health, in the context of the project "Integrated approach for the investigation, diagnosis and management of child abuse and neglect cases." The aim of this protocol was to promote the implementation of a common methodology in the process of investigating and handling child abuse and neglect cases for all professionals involved. The instructions referred to professionals working in the following sectors: health and mental health, social welfare, education, justice, and public order. The piloting of this protocol took place in Attica and the 25 professionals who participated in it were mostly social workers, child psychiatrists, psychologists, teachers, and pediatricians. The pilot-scheme only lasted three months and led to a few minor changes. Subsequently, 400 professionals working in the services and organizations of the above sectors were trained to implement the protocol in the capital cities of the 13 prefectures of Greece.

Two programs on the prevention of child abuse have also been launched. One refers to prevention of sexual abuse of children between the ages of 5 and 9 years. It is called "Safe Touches" and is based on a program initially implemented in the USA, with evidence-based results. The primary goal of this program is to teach children by using puppets as props to convey sensitive information about sexual abuse and body safety. With the assistance of expert psychologists and collaborators, basic safety concepts are taught, including differences between "safe" and "not safe" touching. The program also offers complementary information/training for parents and educators for the detection of signs and symptoms, as well as the handling of sexual abuse incidents.

The second program, "Stop Bullying: Intervention P rogram for Elementary Schools," aims to prevent and tackle school bullying. It includes a student awareness program, created in classroom workshops. In 2012, it was implemented in 50 Greek schools, with positive results and proven efficacy (Tsiantis et al., 2013). Consequently, the first anti-bullying network in the country was created, with the participation of many educational and child protection bodies and organizations.

A third important resource is the SOS Baby Home by the Greek SOS Children's Village association. The SOS Baby Home is a residential care facility hosting very young victims of abuse aged 18 months to 5 years. It accommodates up to 20 infants and it aims to protect the child, offering a stable living space and providing therapeutic intervention for both children and families, with the objective of mitigating risk factors. It is perhaps the only program for the care and treatment of abused babies and infants in the country.

Unaccompanied Minors: A Challenge for Mediterranean Countries

Roberta T. Di Rosa

Unaccompanied minors have presented a dramatic challenge for both Italy and Greece.[4] The vast majority enter Europe irregularly, through the two main gateways to the continent: Italy, via the central Mediterranean Sea route, or Greece, transiting through the eastern Mediterranean route from Turkey, mostly by sea. In the last decade both countries have had to deal with a twofold problem. On the one hand, unaccompanied foreign minors (UAM) have the right to social protection, but on the other, they are illegal immigrants, who ought to be repatriated and treated according to immigration law. In the following section, their profiles, the features of the system and the challenges faced by both countries will be jointly presented.

Profile of Migrant Minors in Italy and Greece: A Relevant Difference

The profiles of children traveling the central Mediterranean route and children traveling the eastern Mediterranean route are different, though they share Italy's and Greece's proximity to North Africa and the Middle East. Minors arriving in Italy are mostly unaccompanied (91%), they are mainly boys, aged 16 to 17, coming from countries in the West and the Horn of Africa. In 2017, Italy received 15,731 UAMs, with a strong decrease since 2016 (down 39%) (SPRAR, 2017). On December 31, 2017, there were 18,303 UAMs within the Italian protection system, from 40 nationalities (Ministry for Labour and Social Policy, 2018).

In Greece, 91% of minors arrive with their family, almost equally divided between boys and girls, and from all age groups. They arrive in Greece primarily from Syria (54%), Iraq (27%), and Afghanistan (13%) (REACH & UNICEF, 2017, p. 2). In 2015, according to the UNHCR, more than 1 million migrant refugees arrived or passed through the country. In December 2016, the number of refugees remaining in the country stood at 62,784. Of these, 21,000 were children and adolescents, of whom 2,300 were UAMs. As for the families, the vast majority of UAMs come from the same countries, experiencing conflicts, oppression or abuses of human rights, or the collapse of social structures. Most of them are boys between 15 and 18 years of age (UNICEF et al., 2017). In 2017, 2,290 children were waiting to be placed in dedicated shelters due to shortages, as the network of shelters managed by the National Center for Social Solidarity (EKKA) had a maximum capacity of 1,101 places at that time.

The Protection System for UAM in Italy and Greece

UAMs entering the system for protection in Italy, as in Greece, register at the frontier on arrival in the country, or are subsequently reported to the local authorities. In Italy, UAM are entitled to protection and placement in a safe place (community or foster

---

[4] The data reported in this part of the chapter refers to 2018.

family) by the local authority. They cannot be expelled or rejected, they can only be repatriated after careful analysis of their social situation and opportunities in their country of origin, and verification that repatriation does not pose a serious threat to the minor.

Local social services and the judicial authorities are responsible for minors' safeguarding, together with the national authorities (Ministry for Labour and Social Policy, and Children's Ombudsman). Until 2016, their accommodation was the responsibility of local bodies or SPRAR centers; later it was enhanced by the opening of the Ministry of the Interior's CAS (centers for extraordinary welcoming) and governmental refugee reception centers, with funding from the FAMI (EU Funds for Asylum, Migration and Integration).

The legislation (Law 47/2017) provides for three levels of reception: 1) in governmental structures in ports of arrival, equipped for initial reception (48 hours); 2) in primary reception centers (maximum 30 days), for intermediate transition, identification, and provision of all necessary information (regarding the minor's rights, including requests for international protection and family reunification); and 3) in secondary reception centers, aimed at guaranteeing not only hospitality, but also social integration and access to education and work opportunities, or voluntary repatriation.

In both Italy and Greece, minors have a right to safeguarding. In Greece, the care of UAM asylum seekers is managed by the National Office for the Management of Requests for Housing for Asylum Seekers and Unaccompanied Minors (in the EKKA), which includes: 1) the management of the requests from asylum seekers and unaccompanied minors; 2) the recording, management, and monitoring system of housing requests; and 3) the coordination of the network of authorized bodies for the necessary transfers of UAMs in hospitality centers.

The Greek system of protection is wanting in dealing with minors, who do not receive differentiated treatment as there is no specialized state infrastructure for receiving children and no staff professionally qualified to examine their claims. Furthermore, there are generally no guarantees for their accommodation. This often leads to "protective custody," which in practice means detention, pending their referral to a dedicated reception facility (Fili & Xythali, 2017). In addition, under the EU–Turkey Joint Statement (European Council, 2016), minors, like all new arrivals in the Greek islands, are immediately to be detained in order to be individually assessed by the Greek authorities.

In Italy, numerous organizations have made a contribution to tackling emergency situations of UAM such as Médecins sans Frontières, Terre des Hommes, Save the Children, and UNHCR. In Greece, it is also possible to find some good practices regulated by the NGO METAdrasi: the Guardianship Network for Unaccompanied Minors, started in 2014 and the program of Foster Care for Unaccompanied and Separated Children, implemented in accordance with the ICRC, in cooperation with local juvenile judges.

The Protection System in Practice

In practice, there are three main issues that should be considered: the claim for legal status, the concrete reception conditions, and minors dropping out of the system.

Claim for Legal Status: Permits, Family Reunification, Relocation

All minors arriving in Italy or Greece face great challenges due to the legal difficulties and time required to obtain documentation (including asylum and residence permits), to be reunited with their family or to be admitted to schools or work opportunities.

Minors who ask to stay in Italy or Greece may wait for months or even years to receive legal status. In Italy, between 2014 and 2016, the procedure lasted between 15 and 24 months (Italian Parliamentary Commission, 2016); in Greece in 2016, out of 6,718 asylum claims only 963 claims were considered (Greek Asylum Service, 2017). In both countries there is particular concern for children aged 16 to 17, as they fear they will reach adulthood before their case is determined, losing the chance to obtain a minor's temporary permit. In Greece, uncertainty has contributed to children suffering from anxiety and depression, as they feel caught in limbo; in Italy, the risk of becoming increasingly marginalized and isolated in reception facilities is reported.

Family reunification may also take a long time. In Italy in 2016, often it took more than one year and, in the same year, only 61 people out of 14,229 requests were reunited (AIDA, February 2017). In Greece, out of the 5,000 requests for family reunification in 2016 (of which 700 were by UAM), only 1,107 successful applicants reached their destination (European Commission, 2017).

Regarding relocation, during the two years in which the program was in force, only one in three migrants in the program were relocated from Italy and Greece (European Commission, 2017). In Greece, many children have been waiting to be relocated or reunified with their families since the closure of the Western Balkan route in spring 2016. Almost four months after the EU relocation program was interrupted, 384 unaccompanied minors registered in the program were still waiting to be transferred (Save the Children, 2017b).

RECEPTION CONDITIONS

There are also difficulties in securing adequate reception both in Italy and Greece, and the plight of UAM deprived of adequate care in both countries is being examined by the European Court of Human Rights.

In Greece, despite the limited capabilities of the country due to the economic crisis, programs of refugee hosting have been arranged in organized camp facilities and in apartments, and since 2016 the integration of refugee children into the education system has begun. The UAMs are housed in 48 hostels, with a capacity of 1,256 places. However, there are many cases of UAMs, living in the streets and non-approved camps: according to an estimate by the EKKA about 670 UAMs remain in the country without shelter, with 55% of them under the age of 14.

Minors inside reception centers in Italy and Greece also risk physical abuse. Refugee and migrant children in Greece reported frequent fights in the camps, with fear of theft and physical violence. In Italy, reports show that children's mental health may deteriorate in reception facilities which are not sufficiently tailored to their needs, when they are left with little to do for prolonged periods of time.

In Italy, access to education for UAMs is only obligatory for children hosted in secondary reception centers. However, on average, minors remain in primary reception centers for six months, meaning that children do not go to school for extended periods of time. When children go to school, schooling is not always sufficient, as it often only takes place a few days each week (Di Rosa, 2015; Di Rosa et al., 2019).

In Greece, while refugee and migrant children are by law entitled to go to school, many UAMs feel that the education available is not tailored to their needs, often due to the use of Greek as the language of education, a language that minors tend to perceive as of little use for their migratory project. As a result, children often do not attend school and miss out further on their education (Barn et al., 2020).

VOLUNTARY DROP-OUTS

In both Italy and Greece, children lack access to information in a language that they understand (REACH & UNICEF, 2017), which often leads to minors dropping out of reception shelters and making important decisions on the basis of rumors and hearsay.

A significant number of UAM in Italy and Greece drop out of the Italian and Greek reception shelters (UNICEF, 2017). In Italy the numbers are rising constantly (Mordeglia et al., 2018, p. 58): in 2017, 5,838 minors (31.7% of the total) dropped out of the protection system. In Greece, the number of UAM who have left the country irregularly since the closure of the western Balkan route is unknown. Yet the significant decrease in the number of refugees and migrant populations since the closure of the western Balkan route suggests that many, including minors, have left the country irregularly.

Outside the reception systems minors are at particular risk of abuse and exploitation, living in insecure shelter arrangements, without regular access to food, or engaging in transactional sex to finance their journey to other parts in Europe.

Summing up, the protection of UAMs is a challenge for both Italy and Greece and, despite concerted efforts, many urgent issues remain[5]. In particular, these concern the identification and registration of children with regard to access to international

---

[5] The situation described has undergone profound changes during 2018, due to changes in migration policies in both Italy and Greece. But even more importantly, the reception and protection procedures of unaccompanied migrant minors have been impacted by the covid 19 pandemic (Barn et al. 2021; Di Rosa, 2021).

protection procedures, the need to institutionalize the guardianship of UAMs and the commissioner's role, the absence of procedural protocols considering their specific conditions and their access to international protection procedures, the failure to establish binding and unified operational standards of hostels, along with the quality of practitioners' training.

Conclusion

Both Italy and Greece face severe difficulties largely brought on by the financial crisis and the adoption of austerity measures. Albeit with relevant differences, both countries are facing a process of reconfiguration of the welfare system based on neoliberal policies, a different (reduced) role of the state, and a rhetorical call for innovation with stronger involvement of civil society, communities and private companies; both countries suffer from an uneven distribution of welfare provisions throughout the country, and a considerable fragmentation of policies dedicated to children and families. They also rely on a strong role of the family, with a low degree of defamilialization and one of the lowest rates of children being placed out of home in Europe.

Driven by the urgency of combating high levels of poverty and pressured by the reduction of resources, in both countries the issue of child protection seems to have disappeared from public debate. The main future challenges are, therefore, related to establishing more equal levels of welfare provision throughout the country and to recomposing the fragmentation of family and child welfare policies, considering family support as part of child protection and not as an alternative.

The migrant crisis has brought an additional challenge to this picture. From 2015 to 2018 Italy and Greece faced the challenge of welcoming and hosting thousands of immigrants, becoming a unique observatory of policies and practices, especially regarding unaccompanied minors. This was possible thanks to a clear political will and to the involvement of local communities. However, especially for Italy, the concomitant factors of the continuing economic recession and the lack of European support have brought about a radical political shift towards a populist closure to immigrants, the long-term impact of which is still to be seen.

References

Adam, S. and Teloni, D. D. (2015). *Solidarity clinics in crisis-ridden Greece: The experience of health care provision when public health care is in retreat, Research Report.* Observatory of Social and Economic Developments. General Confederation of Greek Labour.

AGIA (Autorità Garante Infanzia Adolescenza), CISMAI, and Terres des Hommes. (2015). *Indagine nazionale sul maltrattamento dei bambini e degli adolescenti in Italia* (National survey on child maltreatment in Italy). Available at: https://terredeshommes.it/dnload/Indagine-Maltrattamento-bambini-TDH-Cismai-Garante.pdf.

AIDA (Asylum Information Database) (2017). *Country Report: Italy.* Bruxelles: European Council on Refugees and Exiles (ECRE).

Anagnostopoulos, D. C. and Soumaki, E. (2013). Financial crisis and adolescent mental health services in Greece during the crisis: A brief report. *European Child and Adolescent Psychiatry*, 22, 131–134.

Ascoli, U. and Pavolini, E. (2015). *The Italian welfare state in a European perspective.* Policy Press.

Asimopoulos, C., Margaritidou, M., Mavromati, A., Parashaki, M. E., and Psara, I. (2009). Children with disabilities in institutions in Greece: The phenomenon of institutional abuse and neglect, *Social Work (KinonikiErgasia)*, 94, 105–121.

Asimopoulos, C. and Teloni, D. D. (2017). Social work and the psychosocial effects of the economic crisis in Greece: Challenges for new radical directions in services, theory and values. *Comunitania: International Journal of Social Work and Social Sciences*, 13, 9–22.

Assimopoulos, H. (1998). Reform, developments and prevailing trends in mental health care in Greece. *Social Work in Europe*, 5(1), 41–48.

Athanasiou, H. (2016). *Working together to protect children: A case study of policy implementsion in Greece* [Unpublished doctoral thesis]. Department of Social Policy, London School of Economics and Political Sciences.

Barn, R., Di Rosa, R. T., and Argento, G. (2020). *Unaccompanied minors in Sicily: promoting conceptualization of child-wellbeing through children's own subjective realities.* In L. Gaitan, Y. Pechtelidis, C. Tomas, and N. Fernandes (Eds.), *Children's lives in Southern Europe. Contemporary challenges and risks* (pp. 181–195). Aranzadi: Social and Political Science.

Barn, R., Di Rosa R. T., and Kallinikaki, T. (2021). Unaccompanied minors in Greece and Italy: An exploration of the challenges for social work within tighter immigration and resource constraints in pandemic times. *Social Sciences*, 10, 134. https://doi.org/10.3390/socsci10040134.

Belotti V. (Ed.). (2014). *Bambine e bambini temporaneamente fuori dalla famiglia di origine.* Quaderni del Centro nazionale di documentazione per l'infanzia e l'adolescenza, 55. Istituto degli Innocenti.

Bertotti, T. (2016). Resources reduction and welfare changes: Tensions between social workers and organisations. The Italian case in child protection services. *European Journal of Social Work*, 19(6), 963–976.

Bertotti T. and Campanini, A. (2013). Italy. In P. Welbourne and J. Dixon (Eds.), *Child protection and child welfare: A global appraisal of cultures, policy and practice* (pp. 67–83). Jessica Kingsley.

Bifulco L. (2017). *Social policies and public action.* Routledge.

Bouras, G. and Lykouras, L. (2001). The economic crisis and its impact on mental health. *Engephalos*, 48, 54–61.

Cho, E. Y.-N. (2014). Defamilization typology re-examined: Re-measuring the economic independence of women in welfare states. *Journal of European Social Policy*, 24(5), 442–454.

CRC. (2018). *V and VI Combined Italian Report on Child Right Convention.* CRC/C/ITA/5-6. United Nations.

CRC. (2019). *Concluding observations on the combined V and VI periodic reports of Italy.* CRC/C/ITA/CO/5-6. United Nations.

Del Valle, J. F., Canali, C., Bravo, A., and Vecchiato, T. (2013). Child protection in Italy and Spain: Influence of the family supported society. *Psychosocial Intervention*, 22(3), 227–237.

Di Rosa, R. T., Gucciardo, G., Argento, G., and Leonforte, S. (2019). *Leggere, scrivere, esserci. Minori stranieri non accompagnati: bisogni formativi e processi di inclusione.* Franco Angeli.

Di Rosa, R. T. (2015). Public Services and Migrant Minors in Italy. Redefining skill for social work. In R. Barn, K. Kritz, T. Poso, and M. Skivenes (Eds.), *Child welfare systems and migrant children. A cross country study of policies and practices* (pp. 134–154). Oxford University Press.

Di Rosa, R. T. (2021). Servizio sociale e Covid-19 in accoglienza: strategie di prossimità e di cura. In S. Greco and G. Tumminelli (Eds.), *Migrazioni in Sicilia 2020* (pp. 281–291). Mimesis edizioni.

EIGE. (2020). Gender Equality Index. Available at: *https://eige.europa.eu/publications/gender-equality-index-2020-italy.*

Fargion, S. (2014). Synergies and tensions in child protection and parent support: Policy lines and practitioners cultures. *Child & Family Social Work*, 19(1), 24–33.

Fazzi, L. (2012). Social work in the public and non profit sector in Italy: What are the differences? *European Journal of Social Work*, 15, 629–644.

Fazzi, L. (2018). Involvement of the community in child protection: Is it enough to be competent practitioners? *Child and Family Social Work*, 24(1), 1–18. https://onlinelibrary.wiley.com/doi/10.1111/cfs.12472.

Ferrera, M. (1996). The "southern model" of welfare in social Europe. *Journal of European Social Policy*, 6(1), 17–37.

Ferrera, M. and Maino, F. (2015). *Conclusioni: bilancio e prospettive.* In F. Maino and M. Ferrera (Eds.), *Secondo Rapporto sul secondo welfare in Italia 2015* (pp. 365–382). Centro di Ricerca e Documentazione Luigi Einaudi, Turin.

Fili, A. and Xythali, V. (2017). The Continuum of Neglect: Unaccompanied Minors in Greece. *Social Work & Society*, 15(2), 1– 14. http://nbn-resolving.de/urn:nbn:de:hbz:464-sws-1264.

Gal, J. (2010). Is there an extended family of Mediterranean welfare states? *Journal of European Social Policy*, 20(4), 283–300.

Garrett P. and Bertotti T. (2017). Social work and the politics of "austerity ": Ireland and Italy. *European Journal of Social Work*, 20(1), 29–41.

Gilbert, N. (2012). A comparative study of child welfare systems: Abstract orientations and concrete results. *Children and Youth Services Review*, 34(3), 532–536.

Gilbert, N., Parton, N., and Skiveness, M. (Eds.). (2011). *Child protection systems: International trends and orientations*. Oxford University Press.

Giotakos, O. (2010). Financial crisis and mental health. *Psychiatriki*, 21, 195–204.

Greek Helsinki Monitor/Minority Rights Group-Greece. (2001). *Parallel report on Greece's compliance with the UN Convention on the Rights of the Child*.

Greek Ombudsman. (2012). *Report to the Committee on the Rights of the Child*. Hellenic Ombudsman.

Greek Ombudsman. (2015). *The rights of children living in institutions: Findings and proposals of the Ombudsman on the functioning of child protection institutions*. Special report. Hellenic Ombudsman.

Greek SOS Villages. (2014). *Our own actions*. Available at: http://www.sosvillages.gr/.

Gruppo CRC. (2020). XIrapporto di aggiornamento convenzione diritti infanzia. Available at: https://gruppo crc.net/wp-content/uploads/2020/11/XIrapportoCRC2020_compressed.pdf.

Hellenic Association of Social Workers. (2014). *Report on psychosocial effects of economic crisis and the social services in Greece*. Hellenic Association of Social Workers.

Istat. (2016/2019). Annual reports: IV Piano Nazionale Infanzia. Ministero del Lavoro e politiche sociali.

Kallinikaki, T. (2015). Child protection in times of crisis in Greece. *International Journal of Social Pedagogy*, 4(1), 177–189.

Kolaitis, G., Fissas, K., Christogiorgos, S., Asimopoulos, H., and Tsiantis, J. (2010). Patterns of child and adolescent mental health care in Greece. *The International Journal of Mental Health Promotion*, 12(4), 58–64.

Maino, F. and Neri, S. (2011). Explaining welfare reforms in Italy between economy and politics: External constraints and endogenous dynamics. *Social Policy and Administration*, 45(4), 445–464.

Maurizio, R., Perotto, N., and Salvadori, G. (2015). *L'affiancamento familiare*. Carocci.

Ministero del Lavoro e delle Politiche sociali. (2018). *Minori Stranieri non accompagnati (MSNA) in Italia*. National report. https://www.lavoro.gov.it/temi-e-priorita/immigrazione/focus-on/minori-stranieri/Pag ine/Dati-MSNA-2018.aspx.

Mordeglia, S., Storaci, M., and Di Rosa, R. T. (2018). Modelli eprassi innovative per l'accoglienza e la tutela dei minori stranieri non accompagnati: Il progetto PUERI. In A. Traverso (Ed.), *Infanzie movimentate* (pp. 53–61). Milano.

MPLS. (2022). "Ministero del lavoro e delle politiche sociali. V° relazione su stato di attuazione della legge 149/2001. periodo 2017–2020." Quaderni della ricerca sociale n. 50. [Ministery of Labours and Social Policies . V report on the implementation of the law 149/2001. period 2017–2020.] https://www.lavoro. gov.it/documenti-e-norme/studi-e-statistiche/Documents.

Petmesidou, M. (2006). Tracking social protection: Origins, path peculiarity, impasses and prospects. In M. Petmesidou and E. Mossialos (Eds.), *Social Policy Developments in Greece* (pp. 24–53). Ashgate.

PIPPI. (2015). Programma d'Intervento Perla Prevenzione dell'Istitituzionalizzazione. *Quaderni della ricerca sociale*, 24, 34 (pp. 4–41). MPLS.

REACH and UNICEF. (2017, June). *Children on the move in Italy and Greece*. https://www.unicef.org/eca/ sites/unicef.org.eca/files/2017-10/REACH_ITA_GRC_Report_Children_on_the_Move_in_Italy_and_G reece_June_2017.pdf.

Rukstele, R. (2011). Treatment of infants and their families. In J. R. Brandel (Ed.), *Theory and practice in clinical social work*. London.

Saraceno, C. (Ed.) (2002). *Social assistance dynamics in Europe: National and local poverty regimes*. Policy Press.

Save the Children. (2017a). *Atlante dei minori stranierin on accompagnati*. Available at: https://www.savethec hildren.it/sites/default/files/AtlanteMinoriMigranti2017.pdf.

Save the Children. (2017b). Futuro in partenza? L'impatto delle povertà educative sull'infanzia in Italia. Available at: https://www.savethechildren.it.

Sicora, A., Nothdurfter, U., Rosina, B., and Sanfelici, M. (2022). Service user violence against social workers in Italy: Prevalence and characteristics of the phenomenon. *Journal of Social Work*, 22(1), 255–274. doi:10.1177/14680173211009188.

Skamanakis, C. (2005). The sub-national parameter, the future or the weak link of welfare regimes. In J. Zaimakis and A. Kandylaki (Eds.), *Social protection network: Forms of intervention in vulnerable and multicultural communities*. Kritiki.

Smile of Children. (2009). *Action plan on horizontal networking and coordination of social solidarity services and institutions for the child*. Hamogelotou Paidiou.

Solantaus, T., Leinonen, J., and Punamaki, R. L. (2004). Children's mental health in times of economic recession: Replication and extension of the family economic stress model in Finland. *Developmental Psychology*, 40, 412–429.

Solidarity for All. (2014). *Four years of resistance and solidarity: Report*. Athens. Available at: https://issuu.com/solidarityforall/docs/report_2014.

Spratt, T., Nett, J., Bromfield, L., Hietamäki, J., Kindler, H., and Ponnert, L. (2015). Child protection in Europe: Development of an international cross- comparison model to inform national policies and practices. *British Journal of Social Work*, 45, 1508–1525.

Thornicroft, G., Craig, T., and Power, T. (2010). *Ex post evaluation of the National Action Plan Psychargos 2000–2009: Executive Summary*. Hellenic Ministry of Health and Social Solidarity.

Tsiantis, A. C., Syngelaki, E. M., Beratis, I. N., Asimopoulos, Ch., Dimitropoulou, E., and Tsiantis, J. (2013). Antibullying programs for primary and secondary education in Greece. *European Child and Adolescent Psychiatry*, 22(Suppl. 2), 135–136.

UNICEF. (2013). *Child well-being in rich countries: A comparative review*. Innocenti Report Card 11. UNICEF Office of Research.

UNICEF. (2016). *The state of the children in Greece: Report 2016*. UNICEF.

UNICEF. (2017). *The state of the children in Greece: Report 2017*. UNICEF.

UNICEF Office of Research. (2014). *Children of the recession: The impact of the economic crisis*. Innocenti Report Card 12. UNICEF Office of Research.

UNICEF, UNHCR, and IOM. (2017, April). *Refugee and migrant children—including unaccompanied and separated children—in Europe*.

Venieris, D. (2003). Social policy in Greece: Rhetoric versus reform. *Social Policy and Administration*, 37(2), 133–147.

Weick, K. E. (1976). Educational organizations as loosely coupled systems. *Administrative Science Quarterly*, 21(1), 1–19.

A New Era for Child Protection in Japan

Shoko Tokunaga, Mitsuru Fukui, Misa Saigo, *and* Saki Nagano

Abstract

This chapter expounds on the challenges of Japan in terms of serving children who cannot live with their biological parents due to maltreatment issues. The Child Welfare Act (1947) determines the roles of local child welfare authorities and their funding, while the Child Abuse Prevention Act (2000) codifies the definition of child abuse and establishes guidelines for early intervention and child protection and services. Additionally, the Child Guidance Centres are the frontline in child protection work with social workers at the core. The chapter also discusses institutional care and family-based care for looked after children. It mentions how Japan fronted the challenge of encouraging youth participation in policy-making.

Key Words: Japan, Child Welfare Act, Child Abuse Prevention Act, Child Guidance Centres, child protection work, social workers, youth, policy-making, maltreatment, parents

Introduction

In 2022, Japan is home to a population of 125.1 million people, 14.6 million of whom are children (11.7% under 18) and is often described as an economically developed country. Despite this, the country faces challenges serving children who, due to issues of maltreatment, cannot live with their biological parents. This chapter summarizes Japan's child welfare policy, appraises the status of placement programs for "looked-after children," and discusses possible ways of negotiating future challenges faced by the country's child welfare system.

The Core System and Legislation

Japan has seen a substantial increase in child abuse cases over the past decades. In comparison to 2,722 child abuse cases in 1995, the country saw 204,055 cases in 2020. Psychological abuse is the most common (59.2%), followed by physical abuse (24.4%), neglect (15.3%), and sexual abuse (1.1%). The increase is attributable to growing public awareness of child abuse, and also an increase in reporting of domestic violence incidents by the police (Ministry of Health, Labor, and Welfare, 2016).

Legislation for Child Welfare, Prevention, and Protection

In Japan, the Child Welfare Act (CWA 1947) and the Child Abuse Prevention Act (CAPA 2000) are the two main laws that inform policies and interventions involving children. The CWA determines the roles of local child welfare authorities and their funding, whereas CAPA codifies the definition of child abuse and establishes guidelines for early intervention and child protection and services. In addition to these two laws, several other sources provide guidance on child protection policy and practice; these include the Civil Code, the Adoption Agencies Regulation Act, the Maternal and Child Health Act, and guidelines established by the Ministry of Health, Labor, and Welfare (MHLW).

CAPA defines four kinds of child abuse: physical, sexual, psychological abuse, and neglect. It requires the central and local governments to intervene on child abuse in the form of prevention, early intervention, and protection programs. Regarding sexual abuse cases, the Ministry of Health, Labor, and Welfare has set independent guidelines as it is a hidden type of abuse. It also introduced forensic interviews and information about how to support the non-abusive parent.

Child Maltreatment Referral and Investigation Process

Frontline child protection work is carried out by Child Guidance Centers (CGCs), which oversee investigations of abuse allegations, interim child protection, and child placement decisions. Operational guidelines standardize the CGC's role, structure, and procedures, meaning that all 219 (in 2020) CGCs in Japan must adhere to the same standards in providing their services. The law requires that schools, child welfare institutions, and hospitals endeavor to detect child abuse and neglect and report children who are likely to have been abused or neglected to CGCs using an emergency call line called "189." According to guidelines, the CGCs are required to meet children within 48 hours from the call even at night or on weekends. The majority of these reports come from police and community members. Other reporters include members of the family, schools, community welfare office, and hospitals.

After receiving an emergency 189 call, a team of CGC employees assesses the needs of the child and family, if necessary conducting meetings to decide the level of action and/or support needed to ensure child safety. No laws or guidelines mandate that parents or children must be present in these meetings, however; often only professionals are invited. Many argue that making significant child welfare decisions without input from the child and family is unfair and unethical. If the team decides that the children and parents can receive support while the child remains at home, the case may be passed on to the town social welfare office in the community (lower than the local authority level). If a decision is made to separate the child from the parent, and the parent objects, the CGC has to apply for the section 28 of CWA to the Family Court. There were only 481 cases which required section 28 of CWA out of 9,061 new placements overall in Japan in 2020, indicating that the large majority of placements were voluntary.

Child Guidance Centres: Structure and Function

Now we look at the structure of the CGC. A director and supervising social worker oversee a team of social workers, a psychologist, and a doctor. There is usually an interim protection unit staffed by care workers where children live temporarily when they are removed from their families. The Child Welfare Law amended in 2016 requires all CGCs to employ lawyers to deal with complex legal issues.

Social workers are the core of the CGC team. The CWA requires one CGC social worker for every 30,000 people. There are about 5,000 CGC social workers in Japan. The CWA codifies no specific training requirements for CGC social workers, however. Although some social workers have a national social work qualification, others have studied either psychology, pedagogy, or sociology at university and have worked in a helping profession for one year. Still others have no relevant educational background, but become CGC social workers after attending some trainings. Social worker qualifications vary among local authorities. In one sample of 69 local authorities, 33 reported that 70% of the social work staff were qualified, whereas 14 reported only 30% of staff were.

CGC social workers provide a variety of services, including therapeutic intervention for children and parents while the child is placed outside the home, reunification services, and maintaining correspondence with the family by phone and/or mail. In addition to child abuse, which makes up about 40% of their work, CGC social workers assist with other issues as well. They intervene in the event of caregiver incapacitation, abandonment, or death (40%), consult with the parents of children with disabilities (41%) or delinquency problems (3%), and provide services around parenting (10%). Although it occupies a substantial proportion of the CGC workload, disability consultation is generally the obligation of a psychologist, who performs necessary testing and approves a "disability note." (The child and the family can obtain some financial support if they have this note.) Therefore it can be said that the social worker's main work still remains child protection and child care issues. Also in some cases, the Family Court can permit the social worker to go into houses and search for the child if the parents strongly and persistently refuse to cooperate with the assessment process (CAPA, Ch. 9-3).

Psychologists conduct developmental testing and observation of children and parents. They can also offer psychotherapy and counseling. Doctors assess the effects of trauma and abuse on the children. Care workers at interim units observe the children while they live there for a few weeks to months. The assessments and observations from each team member are all considered when making a final decision about services for the child and family.

Placement for Looked-after Children

The Number of Looked-after Children

In 2020, approximately 37,000 children were looked after in Japan. 79% of them live in institutions. The Ministry of Health, Labor, and Welfare has announced an overhauling of the foster care system, including the production of standardized foster care guidelines.

Child Placement Types

Japan has six types of institutional care for children.

INFANT INSTITUTIONS

These institutions are designed for care of children aged 0 to 3; 30% of them leave the institution within six months. Those who age out of infant institutions are likely to be placed in child care institutions or foster care.

CHILDCARE INSTITUTION

Childcare institutions are intended for children aged 3 to 18, though if necessary children can stay until age 20. 65% of children are placed in childcare institutions because of a history of abuse, whereas about 30% of children have some disabilities. In 2017, about 80% of childcare institutions have 40 or more children. In an effort to create a family-like institutional setting more similar to a family placement, some institutions are building smaller homes within the facility or in the surrounding community. Most children who live in childcare institutions go to school in the community.

CHILDREN'S PSYCHOLOGICAL TREATMENT FACILITY

Children's psychological treatment facilities offer medical and psychological treatment for children experiencing psychological difficulties. Children attend school within the facility. Placement in such facilities is typically short-term, on average about two years.

RESIDENTIAL SCHOOL

Residential school is an appropriate placement option for children, especially teenagers, who exhibit anti-social behavior, and/or troubles at school or at home. Some children are referred because of behavior problems in other institutions, whereas others are placed with a court order. As the name indicates, there is a school within the facility. Unlike other institutions, most residential schools are run by local authorities or the central government, whereas most of the other institutions are run by the private sector.

MATERNAL AND CHILD LIVING SUPPORT FACILITY

These facilities offer placements for mothers and their children. More than half of those placed are victims of domestic violence. Some mothers have mental health issues and/or learning disabilities, and their child may have similar issues.

GROUP HOME FOR TEENAGERS

After they finish compulsory education at age 15, children may live in Group Homes for teenagers until age 20. Teenagers typically pay about 300 USD per month to live in these facilities. Most teens receive some financial support for independent living, which helps defray this cost.

Types of Family-based Care

FOSTER CARE

Foster care placements provide a family home environment for looked-after children in Japan. Foster carers must register with the local authority and attend a series of trainings and home visits; these requirements often vary by local authority. Each foster carer can look after a maximum of four children (or six including biological children). Foster carers can receive an allowance which is about 900 USD per child in addition to a living cost of about 500 USD.

SPECIAL FOSTER CARE

Special foster carers look after a maximum of two children who have been abused or have delinquency problems or disabilities. These carers are required to attend special trainings and to obtain a license which must be renewed every two years. They receive an allowance of about 1,400 USD in addition to the 500 USD living costs that are ordinarily reimbursed to foster carers.

KINSHIP CARE

Kinship carers may look after a child within three degrees of kinship if the child's biological parents are deceased or missing. These carers are paid for living expenses of the child in common with other types but do not receive allowance and are not required to attend trainings, register with local authorities, or obtain licensure.

FAMILY HOME

With the assistance of two staff, foster carers may look after up to six children in their homes, a placement option known as family home foster care.

Adoption

In Japan, only children under age 15 are eligible for adoption. Only married couples may apply for adoption (provided one individuals is age 25 or older), and the biological parents must consent to the adoption. There is a trial period of six months, during which the adoptive parents look after the child. At the end of this trial period, the Family Court decides whether to approve the adoption. In 2019, 711 adoption cases were approved, and another 693 cases were approved in 2020. Half of these cases were supported by local authority CGCs and the other half were handled by non-government organizations.

Issues, Challenges, and the Future

New Law and New Vision

The major pressing issue in Japan involves the debate between institutional versus foster care. In 2016, the Child Welfare Act was amended, which declared that family preservation was the first principle and clearly stated the importance of family-based care rather than the institutionalization of looked-after children.

In 2017, MHLW announced the "New Vision for Children's Social Care" in order to shift practice along with policy. It clearly advocates a shift from institutional care to care in family-based environments such as parental care, adoption, kinship, foster, and family home care. Especially in the case of infants, such placement options are thought to offer a higher level of safety and quality of life. Furthermore, in 2019, Parliament passed the amendments of the Civil Code and the relevant laws to promote the use of adoption, which expands the age limit for adoption to under fifteen and separates the court procedures for judging whether the child should be placed for adoption by CGC from judging whether the child should be adopted by the adopter.

Challenge of Fukuoka City to Improve Child Protection Practices

Prior to this law and new vision came in force, Fukuoka city shifted their system for placing looked-after children from institutions to family-based environments and permanent solutions after conducting their research.

In 2015, Fukuoka city CGC conducted a study of child welfare placements and found that 75% of children who are reunified from institutional care do so within three years after placement; children who do not reunify within three years tend to stay in care until age 18. They also found that many of these children who stay in institutions for a long time tend to loose contact with their birth family (Fukui, 2021).

This finding highlights the first three years of placement as a critical period of time when social workers have to work hard to return the children to their birth home. If that is not possible, then the social workers try to place the children in kinship, adoption, or fostering rather than move them from an infant institution to a childcare institution, so that permanency can be achieved or the child can experience family life. As a result, the number of children in kinship care increased, and at the end of financial year 2021, the rate of fostering placement rose from 33.3% of financial year 2015 to 59.3% of looked-after children in the area.

Following the publication of these findings, the Fukuoka city officials collaborated with private fostering agencies and with CGC to improve fostering care quality and capacity. For instance, Key Assets Japan, a private organization that specializes in child welfare services and resources, has worked with Fukuoka since 2016 to recruit foster families for younger children. Fukuoka has also introduced new programs for foster families such as Fostering Change and PC-CARE. The Signs of Safety program and Family Group Conference are used as part of the program of reunification as well. They also employed a full time lawyer within the CGC so that the social workers can easily access support when facing the complex needs of parents and the child.

Other Issues

There are other issues when implementing new changes to practice.

First, little research has examined the outcomes of look-after children. Especially lacking are longitudinal studies and randomized control trials (RCTs). Although officials have collected administrative data on the budgetary decisions of the ministry and departments, these data have not yet been examined with any scientific rigor. To carry out a longitudinal study of child welfare services, Japan must surmount substantial ethical and financial obstacles, including obtaining access to confidential child and carer information. Lack of scientific evidence often leads to policies based on opinion, which by today's global standards needs to be improved. These data and researches are necessary when we propose to shift the care system from institutions to family/family like care, as mentioned. As they are essential to consider what care and supports are effective for the child's outcomes. Moreover it is very important to learn the core elements needed to improve outcomes for looked-after children, which includes not only the types of care, such as institutions or fostering, but also details on which meet the needs of children.

Japan also faces the issue of how to help children who leave care. As shown in a recent study, young people who left care received a public assistance 18 times more than the same age group as a result of lack of social networks and poor educational achievement, and a third of young people cannot be found within three years of leaving an institution (Nagano & Arimura, 2014). Although institutions are required to support children who leave their care, few services are available for children who leave care at age 18. Recently, the central government instituted a program that offers social skills training, counseling, support for daily living, and job support. Some grants are also available for these children to attend university. Although policy has improved, Japan may need to explore other ways to support children who have left care as well as those currently in care.

Finally, Japan faces the task of encouraging the participation of children and young people in policymaking. Currently, there are 10 such youth action groups in Japan; however, in order for youth voices to be taken into account, systems must be instituted that put them in dialogue with policy makers.

As this chapter has shown, Japan's current child welfare system is complex, and the country faces a number of issues critical to the well-being of its children. Because these issues are interrelated, we must develop new ways of addressing them simultaneously. Doing so will help us move forward with the objective of improving the health and well-being of Japan's vulnerable children including looked-after children.

References

Fukui, M. (2021). A review of the results of CGC's practice to achieve permanency; Achievements and challenges in the changes in the support process and discharge statistics. *Journal of Japanese Society for the Study of Social Work*, 43, 15–27. https://doi.org/10.20824/jjsssw.43.0_15.

Ministry of Health, Labor, and Welfare. (2022). *Welfare administration report example*.

Nagano, S., and Arimura, T. (2014). Deprivation of former youth in care; the hypothesis generated by the secondary analysis and suggested from the original dates. *Japanese Journal of Social Welfare*, 54(4), 28–40. doi https://doi.org/10.24469/jssw.54.4_28.

The Child Protection System in the Netherlands: Characteristics, Trends, and Evidence

Erik J. Knorth, Helen Bouma, Hans Grietens, *and* Mónica López López

Abstract

This chapter notes the characteristics, trends, and evidence of the child protection system in the Netherlands. It also expounds on the identification and processing of reports on child maltreatment such as physical, emotional, and sexual abuse and neglect. The basic principles of child protection and youth care are prevention, de-medicalization and normalization, parenting skills improvement, the safety of the child-rearing environment, and family group plans. Prevention and early intervention through parenting support, which is offered on a municipal level, have higher priority to deterring more expensive and specialized care. However, the research found that solutions for psychosocial and maltreatment issues for children and families are difficult to achieve.

Key Words: Netherlands, child protection system, maltreatment, prevention, specialized care, families, de-medicalization, family

Introduction

The NPM-2017 study showed that an estimated 108,175 children and youth in the Netherlands have experienced maltreatment in 2017[1] (Alink et al., 2018).[2] This amounts to 3.18% of children.[3] A distinction was made between five main types of maltreatment: emotional neglect (including educational neglect), physical neglect, emotional abuse,

---

[1] In the Youth Act 2015 child maltreatment is defined as "every form of violent or threatening behaviour towards children of physical, psychological or sexual nature. This behaviour is forced on children (actively or passively) by their parents or others to which these children are in a relationship of dependency and lack of freedom. This behaviour (threatens to) cause serious physical or psychological harm to the child" (cf. Bonnet, 2016, p. 63). Baartman (2009) suggests a definition which uses less "unnecessary" terminology: "Child maltreatment refers to all actions by parents (or by others who have the same kind of relationship towards the child as parents) which form a serious harmful effect or threat for the child's safety or wellbeing." Witnessing domestic violence is also seen as a form of child maltreatment, usually categorized under emotional abuse or neglect.

[2] NPM refers to the National Prevalence Study on Maltreatment of Children and Youth. Based on a confidence interval of 95%, the number of maltreated children and youth lies between 89,160 and 127,190. This corresponds to a range of 26 to 37 per 1,000 children in the Netherlands.

[3] By way of comparison, in the USA a percentage of 3.95 was estimated (Sedlak et al., 2010).

Table 15.1 Estimated prevalence of child maltreatment per type of maltreatment, based on information provided by sentinels (professional informants), and by Advice and Reporting Centers on Domestic Violence and Child Maltreatment (AMHK)

Type of child maltreatment	Percentage
Educational/emotional neglect	51.4
Physical neglect	26.9
Physical abuse	7.9
Emotional abuse	10.5
Sexual abuse	2.0
Other types of abuse or neglect	1.4
Total	100

Source: Alink et al. (2018, p. 35).

physical abuse, and sexual abuse. Table 15.1 shows the distribution on the different types of maltreatment. It is clear that educational/emotional neglect is the most prevalent (51.4%) and sexual abuse relatively the least (2%) observed type of maltreatment.

The research is based on 1) experiences with maltreatment of children put forward by professionals working in the youth sector (so-called sentinels or informants) and 2) reports by people concerned (family members, neighbors, teachers, etc.) offered to the Advice and Reporting Centers on Domestic Violence and Child Maltreatment (in Dutch: Advies- en Meldpunten Huiselijk geweld en Kindermishandeling, AMHK—see below). Compared with the first NPM-study conducted in 2005, which resulted in an estimated child maltreatment prevalence of 3% (Euser et al., 2010), and the second NPM-study conducted in 2010 and resulting in an estimated prevalence of 3.4% (Euser et al., 2013), the current 3.18% estimation hardly indicates a decline in numbers of maltreated children the child welfare policy is striving for.

Research based on self-reports by children gives a somewhat different picture. Vink and colleagues (2016) ascertained that more than a quarter (26.7%) of the older students in primary education (11–12 years of age) by their own account have faced *once in their lives* one or more instances of child maltreatment, inside or outside their family. With young adolescents (13–16 years of age) the percentage is a little bit lower (24.7%) (Schellingerhout & Ramakers, 2017). If a stricter NPM-norm[4] is applied, the latter percentage drops to 6.5%. These figures show that only some of the children and young people who have experienced child maltreatment seem to be in the sights of professionals in child welfare and child protection.

---

[4] This norm refers to child maltreatment that happened *only* in the child's own family and *only* during the last year.

The last point possibly applies still more to children who have to deal with human trafficking/forced labor, including prostitution and pornography. In 2015 the number was computed as 2,500,[5] a figure that matches 38% of all persons—children and adults—who were estimated to be a victim (Cruyff et al., 2017). Almost 64% of all the cases ($n =$ 6,600) concern sexual exploitation (see also Paganini, 2018). Women/girls are, compared with men/boys, strongly overrepresented in the numbers (ratio 5:1).

Child protection also partly concerns children and youth who come into contact with judicial authorities because of criminal offenses. These authorities (Public Prosecution Department, Juvenile Court, Examining Magistrate) always have to be informed and advised by the Child Care and Protection Board (*Raad voor de Kinderbescherming*; RvdK) what kind of settlement or punishment is considered most adequate according to pedagogical standards (RvdK, 2016). The number of children who came in contact with judicial authorities in 2014 as a (registered) suspect of violation of law, amounted to 19 per 1,000 juveniles (12–18 years of age)[6] (Van der Laan & Beerthuizen, 2018, p. 140). The number of offenders—the ones who actually are being punished—equated 7.3 per 1,000 juveniles (ibid., p. 147). In most cases (93%) a pedagogically motivated community service or training order was imposed or the delict was settled with a financial penalty (ibid., p. 78).

In the rest of this chapter we will focus on situations of (or threat of) child maltreatment. Thereby we will pay attention consecutively to the identification of and processing of reports on child maltreatment, the services for these children and families, arrangements for service delivery, and the evidence base on outcomes of interventions being applied. We conclude with some take-home messages.

Identifying Child Maltreatment and Investigating Reports

Principles

Article 2.1 of the Dutch Youth Act 2015 (Simons et al., 2015) presents the basic principles on which child protection and youth care have to be based. These are: 1) prevention, early identification, and intervention regarding parenting problems, psychical problems, and disorders; 2) de-medicalization and normalization by strengthening the child-rearing environment; 3) improvement of parenting skills and the social network; 4) using, redressing, and strengthening the problem-solving abilities of youth, parents, and their social environment; 5) promoting the safety of the child-rearing environment; 6) integral support for families according to the principle "one family, one plan, one director" to realize better cooperation around families; and 7) arranging and executing of

---

[5] This corresponds with 0.07% of all children in 2015.

[6] The juvenile justice system only applies to children who—during the commission of an offense—are 12 years or older. Below the age of 12 no criminal prosecution is possible. If a child younger than 12 years of age commits a serious crime or reoffends, according to Civil Law the Child Care and Protection Board will be involved to contact with the child and his/her parents or caretakers (cf. RvdK, 2016, p. 5).

family group plans and arranging support according to these plans (Ministry of Health, Welfare, and Sport et al., 2014).

The principles regarding early detection of problems (1) and promoting the safety of the child (5) are very important in the context of child protection. In accordance with the United Nations Convention on the Rights of the Child (UNCRC), the government, and therefore the municipalities (which are responsible for the provision of services and the outcome of help), have an important task in providing safety if parents are not able to do this appropriately.

Prevention, Child and Youth Care, Child Protection, and Juvenile Rehabilitation

The child welfare system consists of many institutions covering different layers of care, such as prevention, voluntary support, and compulsory measures. Within the Youth Act 2015, the child welfare system is divided into prevention and child and youth care. Besides these two types of care, child protection measures and juvenile rehabilitation are responsibilities of the municipalities (Simons et al., 2015).

Prevention and early intervention through parenting support have high priority in order to prevent the need for a more expensive and specialized care (like, for instance, child protection measures) (EM [Explanatory Memorandum] Youth Act, 2013, ch. 3.2). This support is offered on a municipal level by, for example, so-called Youth and Family Centers, local teams (*wijkteams*), healthcare and welfare agencies, child daycare centers, and schools. Examples of parenting support are informal exchange of knowledge within the social network, the provision of information by media, home visits, and parenting courses.

In cases in which prevention is not enough, municipalities have to offer child and youth care. This includes light, primary support which is freely accessible, as well as more intensive, specialized support which is not freely accessible. The primary support includes at-home support, light ambulant treatment, and advice regarding the not freely accessible, more intensive child and youth care. The provision of information and advice by the *Child Helpline* (*Kindertelefoon*) is another example of this primary support. Specialized child and youth care includes, among other, intensive ambulant care and residential services. The municipalities have to decide on the thresholds between the freely accessible and not freely accessible types of child and youth care, so this can differ by municipality (Meima & Van Yperen, 2013).

Furthermore, municipalities are responsible for child protection measures and rehabilitation of juveniles. In case a child protection measure is enforced, a municipality has to look after a sufficient supply of certified agencies regarding guardianship (see below), which have to execute the child protection measures (Youth Act, Article 2.4). Cooperation between municipalities, that is, the local authorities, is possible, for example to guarantee the supply of certified agencies and the provision of specialized care and treatment (EM Youth Act, 2013, ch. 3.8).

Assessment and Referral

The Dutch child protection system is part of the broader youth care system, which recently changed under the Youth Act 2015. In cases of child maltreatment, the municipalities are responsible for identifying, investigating, treating, and monitoring these cases. The Act "Compulsory Reporting Code Domestic Violence and Child Maltreatment" (briefly: Reporting Code) aims to improve the identification of child maltreatment. After reporting, the AMHK plays an important role in investigating maltreatment and referring children to voluntary care. The Child Care and Protection Board (CCPB) and Juvenile Court become involved in investigating and deciding whether involuntary, compulsory child protection measures are necessary, which fall under Civil Law. Moreover, within Criminal Law, the police and Public Prosecution Service can be involved in prosecution of perpetrators.[7]

REPORTING CODE

Although there is no mandatory reporting in the Netherlands, the Reporting Code obliges professionals working in healthcare, education, daycare, social support, child and youth care, and justice (e.g., residential care and the Central Agency for the reception of asylum seekers) to implement a reporting code in their organizations (cf. Rijskamp et al., 2013; Rijksoverheid, 2019). The Dutch government offers a conceptual model with five basic steps: 1) clarify the signals, 2) consult a colleague and, if necessary, consult the AMHK or an expert on injury interpretation, 3) talk with the client, 4) assess violence or child maltreatment, and 5) decide whether to provide support or report to the AMHK. The Reporting Code is not only applicable for professionals working with children, it also includes the "child check" for professionals working with adult clients. This implies that professionals have to examine whether their clients have children and whether the physical or mental well-being of their clients could be a risk for the safety or development of the children.

AMHK

Everyone who has concerns about child maltreatment, for example neighbors, teachers, parents, or professionals, can contact the AMHK. Someone can call for advice or report a case of child maltreatment. When someone calls for advice, the AMHK makes recommendations to the caller; this can be a single advice or follow-up advice. When the caller reports a case to the AMHK, the personal details of the reported family will be registered; this is only the case for a report. However, when someone calls to ask for advice, but the professional of the AMHK has serious concerns about the case, the professional can ask the caller to report the case. To undertake action, an official report is necessary. When the caller does not want to report the case, the AMHK can decide to report the case

---

[7] This paragraph is mainly based on Bouma et al. (2016).

themselves. The opposite is also possible: a report can be registered as an advice when there are insufficient indicators for suspicions of child maltreatment and/or when the reporter did not use all the resources to change the situation (Baeten, 2014).

The AMHK discusses each report in the triage: a peer consultation or multidisciplinary consultation in which the professionals decide on the priority of the report, the required next steps, and who will have the responsibility for these. The three main decisions that are made after a report are: 1) to refer the case to social care services already being accessed, 2) to arrange new social care services, or 3) to start an investigation by the AMHK. The criteria used by the AMHK to decide on the next steps are presented in Figure 15.1, a translation of the guidelines set up by the VNG (Association of Netherlands Municipalities). The investigation aims to examine if child maltreatment is present and which next steps are required. The AMHK can decide that no (further) support is needed, that the family should be referred to social care services, or that an investigation by the CCPB is needed (Baeten, 2014).

CHILD CARE AND PROTECTION BOARD

The CCPB is nationally organized and falls within the Ministry of Justice and Safety. Executing the child protection investigation is one of the several tasks of the CCPB: it is also involved in investigations regarding custody, juvenile justice, and adoption (RvdK, 2015a). Here, the focus will be on the child protection investigations of the CCPB.

Whereas everybody can report to the AMHK, this is not the case for the CCPB. As already mentioned, the AMHK can request that the CCPB starts a child protection investigation. Besides the AMHK, certified agencies and local authorities are authorized to request that the CCPB investigates a case. Also, the CCPB itself can decide to start a child protection investigation for cases in which they are involved for other types of investigations, such as a custody investigation (see Figure 15.2). Only in exceptional cases, in acute and serious threatening situations, can anyone report cases to the CCPB (Youth Act, Article 3.1; RvdK, 2015a). These requests need to be substantiated with documents in which previous voluntary support is described and why this voluntary support did not have enough impact or did not work. Furthermore, the social network of the family and its support must be described in the request (RvdK, 2015b).

The incoming requests are assessed by the Advice Teams of the CCPB, which have existed since 2015. These teams decide if the CCPB should start an investigation. Furthermore, the parties mentioned above can discuss a case with the Advice Team if they are considering whether to request a child protection investigation. Involving the CCPB as an advisor in an earlier stage aims to prevent the necessity of involuntary child protection measures (RvdK, 2015b).

When the CCPB starts an investigation, this should be executed according to the principles and guidelines as described in their Quality Framework and their Protocol for

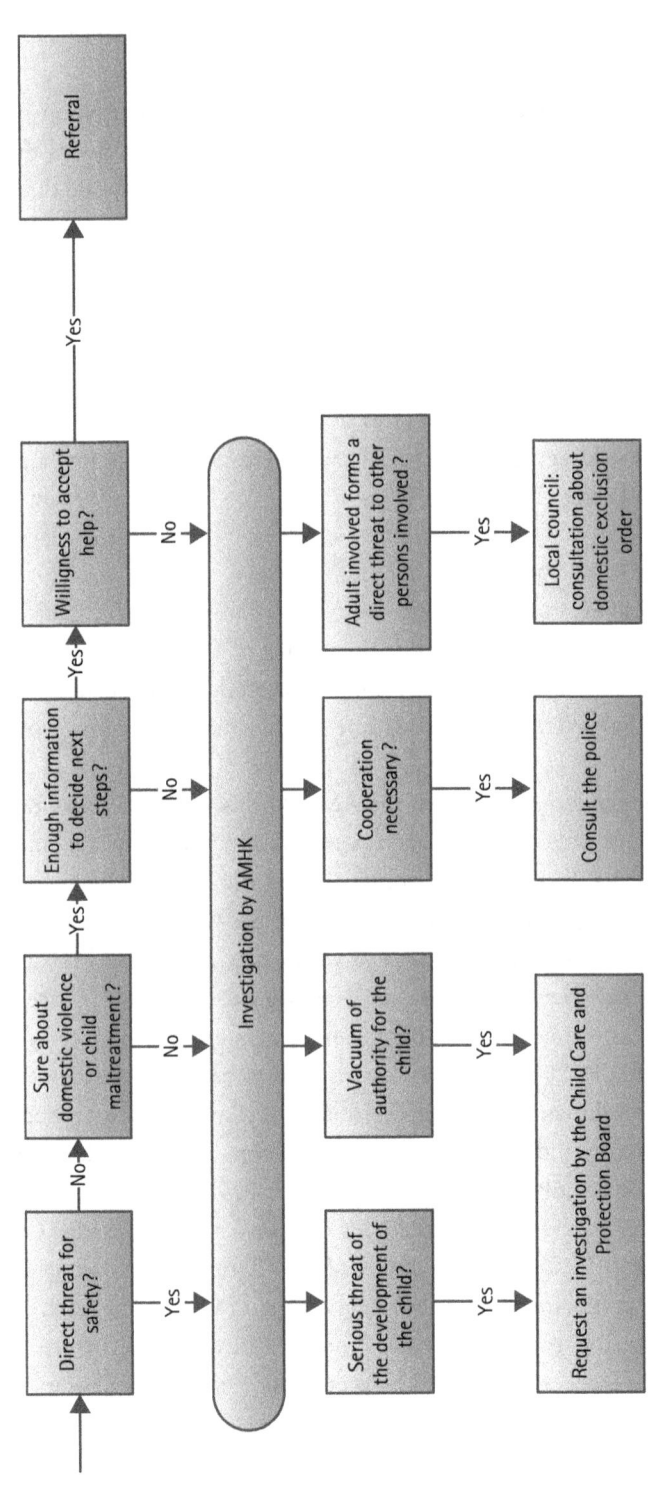

Figure 15.1 Criteria used by the AMHK to decide on the need for and processing of an investigation in a case of suspected or reported child maltreatment (Baeten, 2014, p. 21)

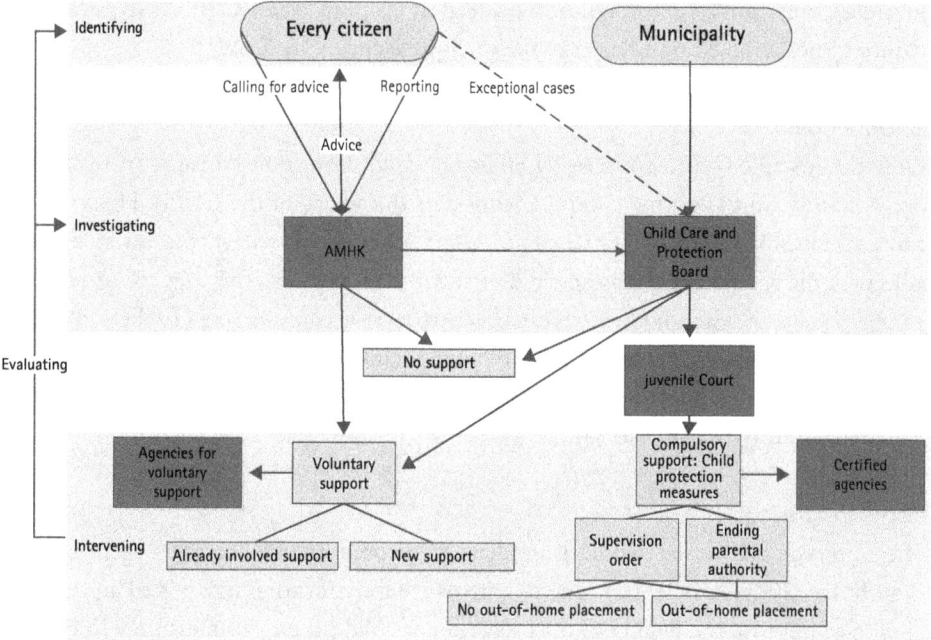

Figure 15.2 Derived from the HESTIA international research program on child welfare states (Hestia, 2016), provides a schematic overview of the Dutch child protection system

Protection Cases. An important issue is that the best interest of the child should form the basic principle in a child protection investigation; the investigation needs to focus on the (physical) safety and the development of the child. During the investigation, the family situation of the child is examined through conversations with the child, parents, and other persons involved in the family. The investigation is concluded with a report including information on the development of the child, the child rearing situation, the (child rearing) situation of other children in the family, risk factors and protective factors relating to the child and the family, and relevant information from other persons, such as teachers or social workers working with the family (RvdK, 2015a, 2015b).

Based on this investigation, the CCPB decides whether an involuntary child protection measure is necessary. When the CCPB decides that no child protection measure is needed, they refer the family to a local authority without interference of the Juvenile Court. However, when the local authority still has serious concerns and thinks a child protection measure is necessary, the burgomaster can request that the Juvenile Court enforces a child protection measure (RvdK, 2014). When the CCPB believes that a child protection measure is needed, the CCPB advises the Juvenile Court to enforce this (RvdK, n.d.).

Besides their advising and investigating role, the CCPB has an assessing and supervising role. When the Juvenile Court enforces a child protection measure, the certified agencies are responsible for the delivery of these measures. These agencies can request that the

Juvenile Court ends or extends a child protection measure. The CCPB has to assess these requests, substantiated by a report of the certified agency (RvdK, 2015b).

JUVENILE COURT

Only the Juvenile Court can actually enforce a child protection measure. In making its decision, the court uses the report and considers the advice of the CCPB. However, the court is not obliged to follow the advice given. Besides this report, the Juvenile Court talks with the parents involved and children older than 12 years. They can call up children younger than 12 years or these children can request a consultation (Topberaad Jeugd, 2014). The Juvenile Court can enforce two main child protection measures: enforcing a supervision order, with or without an out-of-home placement of a child, and overruling parental authority (RvdK, 2015a).

CERTIFIED AGENCY

The enforced child protection measures have to be performed by certified agencies (CA) (Youth Act, 2014, Article 3.2). The requirement of certification has existed since 2015, aiming to improve the quality of the execution of child protection measures. To become certified, an agency has to meet several legal requirements, related to expertise, methods, interventions, organization and processes, and cooperation with other agencies. Following the decision of the Juvenile Court, the CCPB transfers the case to the CA. Within the CA, a (family) guardian is appointed. This guardian gives the family and the social network of the family the opportunity to set up a plan to ensure and to improve the safety and development of the child. After this, a strategy will be determined in a multidisciplinary meeting. During the execution of this plan and strategy, progress will be constantly monitored (Simons et al., 2015). Furthermore, the guardian decides which type of youth care is necessary. However, the CAs are not allowed to offer regular youth care themselves; this support has to be delivered by other agencies or organizations. Guardians of CAs are mainly case directors instead of social care providers; they can decide which type of youth care is needed and they can, in cooperation with the municipality, arrange this (EM Youth Act, 2013, Articles 3.2 and 3.4).

POLICE AND PUBLIC PROSECUTION DEPARTMENT

The police and the Public Prosecution Department (*Openbaar Ministerie*; OM) can be involved in cases of child maltreatment in several ways. Guidelines have been drawn up regarding cooperation between the AMHK and the police, aiming to improve safety (Topberaad Jeugd, 2014; Pattje, 2015). The AMHK always requests information from the police about the persons involved in a report (Pattje, 2015). The police can also get involved during the triage and investigation, to improve the safety of the child. This is mainly done in cases of severe child maltreatment (i.e., physical abuse or neglect, sexual abuse, honor-related violence, circumcision of girls, forced marriages). Another reason to involve the police is when the AMHK has serious suspicions about the criminal behavior of one of the persons involved (Baeten, 2014).

Besides this, the police can report cases to the AMHK. The police often encounter cases in which children live in alarming circumstances. This can include directly threatening situations in which the child is a victim of child maltreatment, children witnessing domestic violence, children who have run away, or cases of prostitution. Furthermore, the police have a method for detecting risky child rearing situations for children younger than 12 years old (ProKid) (Topberaad Jeugd, 2014). Using this method, the police report cases of witnessing domestic violence or criminal behavior of children younger than 12 years old (Pattje, 2015).

Besides the police, the Public Prosecution Department has a role in the chain of child protection. First, they can ask the Juvenile Court to enforce a child protection measure; for example, in addition to a punishment regarding juvenile rehabilitation or when parents are detained (Topberaad Jeugd, 2014). Furthermore, the Public Prosecution Department is involved in the criminal justice aspect of child maltreatment. They search for a way in which Criminal Law can contribute to long-lasting improvements and a safer life for the child (OM, n.d.). In considering the use of criminal law, they cooperate with several agencies, such as the CCPB. In determining the sanction, the protection of the child forms the basic principle. Furthermore, support for the family and possible other civil decisions are considered (OM, 2016).

Child Protection Measures

In the Netherlands, the Juvenile Court is the institution that can enforce compulsory child protection measures. For this purpose, the Court uses the investigation report and the advice formulated by the CCPB (see above). Yet, the Court is not obliged to follow this advice. The following two main measures can be imposed: 1) a (temporary) supervision order, with or without an out-of-home placement of the child, and 2) the suspension or ending of the parental authority.[8]

Supervision order/family guardianship. In the case of a supervision order, the authority of the parents is restricted and partly taken over by an official family guardian from a certified agency; the parents remain responsible for the care of their child, but they are obliged to follow the advice of the guardian. In addition, an out-of-home placement is possible during a supervision order (EM Youth Act, 2013, ch. 5.2). The court can enforce a supervision order when a minor's development is threatened, when the required support to take away this threat is not accepted sufficiently, and when it is expected that the (authorized) parents are able to accept the full responsibility of child-rearing again in a longer term (BW [*Burgerlijk Wetboek*; Civil Code], book 1, Article 255). The maximum length of a supervision order is one year. However, until the child is 18 years old, this can

---

[8] This section is partly based on López López et al. (2019, p.186 ff.).

be prolonged by the court every year (BW, book 1, Articles 258, 260). In cases of real and immediate danger and where there are substantial grounds for a supervision order, a temporary supervision order and a temporary out-of-home placement can be enforced. This measure makes immediate action possible and can last at most three months (BW, book 1, Article 257).

Ending parental authority/guardianship. Besides enforcing a supervision order, the Juvenile Court can end parental authority. This can be done when parents make improper use of their authority or when the development of the child is seriously threatened and parents cannot be responsible for raising and caring for their child (BW, book 1, Article 266). When this measure is enforced, a guardian is appointed and the child is placed out-of-home (EM Youth Act, 2013; ch. 5.2). This measure is also applied if unaccompanied migrant children enter the Netherlands (Zijlstra et al., 2017). Besides a definitive over-ruling of parental authority, it is possible to *temporarily* suspend the parental authority, partially or totally, for a certain period of time, no longer than three months. This measure is used, for instance, when a parent does not give permission for the child to receive necessary health treatment, as is the case for some orthodox religious groups in the Netherlands (BW, book 1, article 268).

Table 15.2 shows the types and numbers of child protection measures that have been mapped, covering the most recent information (CBS [Central Bureau of Statistics], 2018a). The total number of supervision orders as of December 31, 2017 was 20,600. This number includes temporary supervision orders which form only a small part (1.6%) of the total. Compared to 2016 the number of "regular" family guardianships hardly changed (decrease 0.1%). The number of cases whereby the parental authority was ended as of December 31, 2017 amounts to 10,075. This number includes also temporary guardianships, which represents 130 children or 1.3% of the total number. Compared to

Table 15.2 Number of applicable child protection measures at the end of 2016 and 2017

Type of child protection measure	2016 (December 31)		2017 (December 31)	
	Number	Percentage	Number	Percentage
Supervision order (family guardianship)	*20,460*	*100*	*20,600*	*100*
Regular	20,145	98.5	20,270	98.4
Temporary	315	1.5	330	1.6
Ending parental authority (guardianship)	*9,895*	*100*	*10,075*	*100*
Regular	9,740	98.4	9,945	98.7
Temporary	155	1.6	130	1.3
Total number of child protection measures	*30,355*	*100*	*30,675*	*100*

Source: CBS (2018b, p. 6).

2016 the number of "regular" guardianships hardly changed (increase 0.3%). Taking both types of measures together, Table 15.2 shows that 30,675 children had to do with compulsory child protection measures at the end of 2017, corresponding with approximately 0.91% of all children at that point in time (CBS, 2018c). Of these children 64% were (temporarily) placed out of home, that is, they stayed in family foster care (41%) and/or residential child care (33%) (CBS, 2018b, p. 10).

Looking at a longer period of time (2007–2017) the number of supervision orders has substantially decreased: at the end of 2007 still some 30,000 family guardianships (supervision orders) were in force. However, during the same period the number of guardianships rose; in 2007 "only" a bit more than 5,000 cases were registered (CBS, 2018b, p. 7). A main reason for both trends has to do with the implementation of the so-called "Delta methodology" (*Delta-methode*). According to this methodology, a supervision order should be seen as a temporary, short-lived measure that needs to be substituted by the more permanent measure of guardianship if parents do not show changes in their behavior in the short term (Bakker, 2018, p. 11; see also Smit et al., 2015). Another reason for the second trend has to do with the rising number of unaccompanied migrant children—in need of a guardian—entering the Netherlands the last ten years (Zijlstra et al., 2017).

Services for Maltreated Children and Their Families

Support after an AMHK Investigation

In 2017, a total of 77,500 cases were registered by the AMHKs calling for advice (CBS, 2018a, p. 22ff).[9] In roughly three-quarters of these cases the concerns related to children. The number of finalized investigations in that year amounted to 14,700 cases. More than a third (35%) of investigated cases were referred to local services like social work, Child and Family Centers, or local teams. In 11.4% of the cases there was already support for the family. Other organizations that were engaged were certified agencies for guardianship (8.9%), child and youth care providers (7.7%), the Child Care and Protection Board (7.4%), general practitioners (6.8%), and child and adolescent mental healthcare providers (3.7%). In 11.1% no support seemed needed.

Support after a Child Protection Measure

During the year 2017, for 39,410 children a child protection measure was applied.[10] In addition to protection services, about 80% received a form of child and youth care (CBS, 2018b, p. 10). Table 15.3 presents the numbers of children related to the different types

---

[9] Because the monitoring by the AMHKs is not yet 100% reliable, numbers in this sub-section are only estimates.

[10] This number differs from the number presented in Table 15.2. The table refers to one specific moment in time (December 31, 2017), while here the number refers to all cases under protection during the whole of 2017.

Table 15.3 Number of children (0–17 years) with a child protection measure during 2017, who also receive a form of child and youth care

Type of care	Number of children	
	Frequency	Percentage
Child and youth care (total)	*31,515*	*100*
Child and youth care—without out-of-home placement	*21,930*	*69.6*
Ambulatory or outpatient services	14,730	46.7
Family/home-based services	8,075	25.6
Services by local teams in neighborhood	4,960	15.7
Day treatment services	1,990	6.3
Child and youth care—with out-of-home placement	*20,135*	*63.9*
Family foster care	13,285	42.2
Open residential group care	6,430	20.4
Open residential family-like care	2,375	7.5
Closed residential care	1,630	5.2

Note: Because children can be served by more than one type of provision at the same time and/or consecutively during the year, numbers do not sum up to 100%.

Source: CBS (2018b, p. 10).

of support and care they received. What can be seen is that almost two-thirds of the children (63.9%) experienced an out-of-home placement; a bit more often in family foster care than in residential care. Still more children (69.6%) received a form of ambulatory or home-based services—mostly provided by social or mental healthcare organizations, less often by local teams or day treatment services.

Considering a policy to avoid out-of-home placements as much as possible (Knijn & Van Nijnatten, 2011; López López et al., 2019), with more than 20,000 placements (which corresponds to 6 per 1,000 children) the Netherlands is not exactly the champion of family preservation in a western European context. Actually, the number rises to a bit over 9 per 1,000 children if voluntary placements are also counted (Knorth et al., 2016, p. 198). Compared with the European range—with Italy on the lower end (almost 4 per 1,000), and Denmark and France at the upper (more than 10 per 1,000) (cf. Thoburn, 2010, p. 36)—the Dutch placement rate lies somewhere between the middle and upper ranges.

The policy under the Youth Act 2015 is not only directed towards reducing the number of out-of-home placements but also—thereby underlining the need for normalization of the lives of children and families in care (Raad voor Maatschappelijke Ontwikkeling, 2012)—towards decreasing the use of specialized psychosocial services. Instead of those more expensive services clients should primarily be served on the level of their neighborhood or (small) municipality by "local teams," mainly staffed by social workers. However, Table 15.3 shows that specialized services are still much more popular compared with local teams for compulsory child protection cases.

In recent research by Friele and colleagues (2018, p. 267), roughly 80% of the interviewed parents (*n* = 239) would *not* contact a local team in case of concerns about the upbringing of their children. Instead, more than two thirds would consult a general practitioner; a discipline known as the main referrer of clients to specialized mental healthcare services (Nanninga et al., 2018). So the "normalization policy" of the government is not as successful as hoped for.

Arrangements for Delivery of Services

Responsibilities

Assessment, support, and treatment services are most often provided to children and families by local or regional agencies such as AMHKs, certified agencies, local teams, social and mental healthcare organizations, or individually operating professionals—actors that receive their funding from the municipality where the client is registered. For cases that may require more intrusive interventions like an out-of-home placement, the Child Care and Protection Board is the responsible national authority. Fluke and Merkel-Holguin (2018, p. 2) characterize this organization model as hybrid, because it combines nationally centralized functions with localized services.

Within the Child Care and Protection Board an Advice Team decides whether a child protection investigation by the board is necessary. Since 2015, such Advice Teams have been established in each region (*n* = 16). In these teams, selection is done, advice is given, and decisions are made as to whether a CCPB-investigation seems to be necessary. In this way, the Board is available for consultation by municipalities, agencies offering voluntary care, certified agencies, and AMHKs. They can consult the Advice Teams when they consider the necessity of involuntary child protection measures. This aims, when possible, to prevent the necessity of forced care (Topberaad Jeugd, 2014; RvdK, 2015a, 2015b).

Access and Finances

Municipalities have the responsibility to organize access to care for children and youth. In every municipality there is a primary point of contact or a "counter," often linked to a local social team, which has the mandate to advise and/or support children and families seeking help. In case of more complex concerns (like most protection cases), the municipalities can optionally involve regionally organized, multidisciplinary teams of experts to get additional advice.

The municipalities can decide themselves what part of the yearly budget goes to child/youth care and protection services; the lump sum payment[11] they receive from the central government—based on demographic criteria (like number of children and youth in the

---

[11] The budget available for child/youth care and protection services in all 355 Dutch municipalities jointly amounted in 2017 to 3.5 billion euros (Friele et al., 2019). This corresponds to 4.6% of the budgeted care expenses by the government for that year (*Miljoenennota 2017*).

municipality, number of single-parent households)—is not earmarked and can partially be used for other purposes (like, for instance, the maintenance of a swimming pool). The idea is that in this way "custom-made services" can be delivered (Simons et al., 2015). In reality, the sharing model creates legal inequality because the number and quality of services available depends on the priority that is being attributed to child/youth care and protection by the local administration. Research shows that substantial financial gaps have developed; many municipalities do not offer enough services considering the number and needs of clients (Friele et al., 2019; Kinderombudsman, 2015; Knorth, 2017). As a result, children and parents do not receive the professional support they need in due time.

Role of Clients

Policymakers in the Netherlands are increasingly focusing on the participation of children in the child protection system. Embedding children's participation in legislation and policy documents is an important prerequisite for achieving meaningful participation in child protection practice. In a recent study (Bouma et al., 2018), the participation of children in the Dutch CPS under the new Youth Act 2015 was critically analyzed. National legislation and policy documents were studied using a model of "meaningful participation" based on Article 12 of the UNCRC. Results show that the idea of children's participation is deeply embedded in the current Dutch CPS. However, Dutch policy documents do not fully cover the three dimensions of what is considered to be meaningful participation for children: informing, hearing, and involving them. Furthermore, children's participation differs among the organizations included in the child protection chain. A clear overall policy concerning the participation of children in the Dutch CPS is lacking.

Some recent studies were performed in the Netherlands on experiences with the actual participation of children in decision making in child protection and child welfare cases (Van Bijleveld et al., 2014) and in out-of-home care provisions (Ten Brummelaar et al., 2018; Zeijlmans et al., 2019). One consistent finding is that children's participation in decision making is far from a matter of course. A second finding is that the role of the practitioners, especially their attitudes on child participation, is pivotal. This was also seen in an international comparative vignette study wherein the Netherlands was one of the four participating countries (Benbenishty et al., 2015). According to that study, in comparison with the other three countries, child protection and welfare professionals in the Netherlands appeared to attach the least importance to child and parent participation in decision making in a case of suspected child abuse.

Considering the role of parents, a qualitative interview study ($n = 20$) revealed that serving the best interests of their child is most important to parents involved in the child protection system. To realize this, parents agree professionals should "not let it all happen" but do something by being decisive, making concrete agreements, and assuring collaboration between all agencies involved. In addition, professionals should get a clear picture of the situation by determining the truth and looking further than their first ideas. They should also take parents seriously by acting on what they tell, providing empathy and support, and being clear and honest towards them. Parents emphasize that a system providing sufficient resources is needed to enable professionals to ensure this. They have mixed experiences (positive and negative) with the system and their experiences seem to influence their trust in the system and their attitude towards it (Bouma et al., 2020). Comparable results can be found in other studies (see, for instance, Healy et al., 2011; Arbeiter & Toros, 2017; Smithson & Gibson, 2017).

Evidence on Outcomes

In one of the few studies available in the Netherlands on outcomes of child protection measures and interventions, especially by measuring the concerns regarding children and families after two years support with a supervision order ($n = 103$), it was found that in 28% of the cases the concerns had declined substantially (i.e., were more or less solved), in 38% concerns were still the same, and in 33% the situation got worse (Slot et al., 2001). Support consisted of ambulatory or family/home-based services (68%) and/or placement of a child in residential (39%) or family foster care (27%). By way of comparison, a more recent study which covered not only protection cases but tackled the broader field of child and youth care (CYC) and child and adolescent mental healthcare (CAMH) in the northern part of our country ($n = 1,378$) showed that problems in the domain of parenting were solved after one year of support in 38.5% (CYC) and 44.5% (CAMH), respectively, of the cases, while family problems were solved in 40.5% (CYC) and 42.3% (CAMH), respectively, of the cases (Nanninga et al., 2018). While the "problem solution rate" in child and adolescent social and mental healthcare lies at around 40% after one year, in child protection it lies at around 30% after two years. Both numbers, although not precisely comparable, give an indication that finding durable solutions for the psychosocial and maltreatment problems of all vulnerable children and families is quite difficult to achieve (see also Knorth, 2016).

The dominant type of professional support provided is ambulatory and family/home-based services (cf. Table 15.3; see also Van Rooijen et al., 2013). With respect to these types of professional support, a recently published review on the effects of interventions for families with multiple and complex problems seems relevant. This study by Jansen and colleagues (2019) reveals that from 2005 to 2018, 11 family-focused interventions have been empirically evaluated quite thoroughly in a Dutch context—some of them developed outside,[12] some of them inside the Netherlands.[13] Effect-sizes for children's

---

[12] It concerns: Parent Management Training Oregon (PMTO), Multisystemic Therapy (MST), Multidimensional Family Therapy (MDFT), Families First (FF), Functional Family Therapy (FFT), Triple P level 4-5 (TP4-5), and Stepping Stones Triple P (SSTP).

[13] It concerns: Intensief Ambulante Gezinsbegeleiding (IAG), Gezin Centraal (GC), Tien voor Toekomst (TvT), and Praktische Pedagogische Gezinsbegeleiding (PPG).

behavioral problems and perceived levels of stress in parents varied, from small (< .20) to large (> .80), with the best and most consistent outcomes for "Multisystemic Therapy" (see also Asscher et al., 2014) and "Families First" (see also Veerman & De Meyer, 2015). The latter intervention especially has been applied very frequently, not least while its main aim corresponds well with a policy of avoiding out-of-home placement of children.

Another (international) systematic review specifically addressed child outcomes, including continued child maltreatment and out-of-home placement after a period of intensive home-based family intervention (Van Assen et al., 2019a). Child maltreatment relapse rates vary between 6.5% and 40% (p. 342). The number of out-of-home placements amounts to 24.2% one year after termination of professional family support. By way of comparison, in the USA this number is 20.8% (ibid., p. 343). As a general finding, Van Assen and colleagues conclude that many children still show substantial emotional and behavioral problems after the intervention has stopped. They stress that more focused attention should be paid to children in addition to the attention already paid to the parents. Research on a Dutch program (called "Child and Youth Coaching"), specifically addressing this goal, is currently ongoing (Van Assen et al., 2019b).

Conclusions and Discussion

Summarizing some main findings we conclude that:

- The rate of child maltreatment hardly changed since 2005 and most recently was estimated by sentinels and AMHKs to be 3.18% of Dutch children—prevalence rates based on self-reports seem to be quite a bit higher.
- The number of supervision orders has substantially decreased between 2007 and 2017, the number of guardianships however rose in the same period of time.
- More than a third of the families—after an AMHK investigation—were referred to local services like social work, Child and Family Centers, or local teams.
- In contrast with national policy over many years, the number of compulsory child protection cases referred to specialized social and mental health-care services did not decrease, rather they increased.
- Compared with other western European countries the Dutch rate of out-of-home placements of children seems to lie somewhere between the middle and the upper ranges.
- As a result of financial gaps at the level of responsible municipalities children and parents do not always receive the professional support they need in due time.
- Although promoted in official policy documents the meaningful participation of children and parents in decision making on maltreatment

investigations and planning of/implementing professional support is not fully realized.

- Research shows that finding durable solutions for psychosocial and maltreatment problems for *all* vulnerable children and families is quite difficult to achieve.
- There are indications that one reason for enduring psychosocial problems of children is that home-based family interventions—mostly applied in the Netherlands—do not pay so much attention to the children involved.

With respect to these findings, two main topics for reflection arise: 1) the prevalence of child maltreatment, including assessing and deciding on it, and 2) the quality and outcomes achieved with eligible interventions.

Given the fact that the number of identified maltreatment cases seems relatively constant and furthermore a lot of cases stay hidden for professionals working in child welfare, healthcare, and educational settings, questions can be raised regarding the quality of arrangements that aim for early detection of children at risk of maltreatment. As described, the *Reporting Code* obliges professionals to act according to a clear-cut protocol. The Code is not only applicable for professionals working with children, but it also includes the "child check" for professionals working with adult clients. How well this is implemented in daily practice and what potential obstacles for valid identification of maltreatment (risks) are in order is under-researched (Van Rooijen et al., 2013). Illustrative is a study in daycare centers in Amsterdam. It showed that in 82% of the 56 participating locations workers had concerns about children, but did *not* as a matter of routine link this to the possibility of child maltreatment (Leyen et al., 2015). In contrast with this example of "underdiagnosis," a study by Schouten (2017) on the use of a screening questionnaire in the context of out-of-hours primary care for children showed big numbers of cases of suspected child abuse which proved unjustified. At the same time a lot of, as it turned out, "real" maltreatment cases were missed. Thus, the identification and assessment of children's maltreatment seriously needs ongoing attention in practice and research. This includes the quality of decision making by professionals in such cases (Bartelink et al., 2018, 2021).

We found that some 30–40% of children in child welfare and protection seem to benefit—measured one to two years after termination of support—from the intervention they received. This means that for others, the situation is stable or gets worse.[14] However, for this group it might take longer to measure progress. Results like these remind us of the

---

[14] Interestingly, a study by Thoburn et al. (2013) on new team approaches to families with multiple and complex problems in the UK (*n* = 33) also showed a success rate of 30%. However, it also noticed that 33–45% of the families were partly successful and—considering the continued professional support they received—the prognoses were positive.

pivotal question about the effectiveness of interventions. We already noticed that paying attention to the child in family interventions is not a case by default (Van Assen et al., 2019a, 2019b). Generally speaking, the evidence on family- and child-oriented interventions looks a bit like patchwork: for a very few (for example Families First) the evidence, gathered in a Dutch context, is quite robust; for the big majority of programs the evidence is much less convincing (Jansen et al., 2019). A rather new approach in researching the effectiveness of interventions is to take a closer look at what are the specific elements in intervention programs that make them work for what problems of help-seekers. It is this recognition of the "one size does *not* fit all" rule that can help us to get ahead in our search for approaches and interventions in the child welfare and protection field "that work" (cf. Van Yperen et al., 2019).

References

Alink, L., Prevoo, M., Van Berkel, S., Linting, M., Klein Velderman, M., and Pannebakker, F. (2018). *NPM 2017: Nationale Prevalentiestudie Mishandeling van kinderen en jeugdigen.* Leiden University, Institute of Education and Child Studies/TNO Child Health.

Arbeiter, E. and Toros, K. (2017). Parental engagement in child protection assessment: A qualitative analysis of worker and parent perspectives. *International Social Work*, 60(6), 1469–1481.

Asscher, J. J., Deković, M., Manders, W., Van der Laan, P. H., Prins, P. J. M., Van Arum, S., and Dutch MST Cost-Effectiveness Group [Jansen, D. E. M. C., Vermeulen, K. M., Buskens, E., Knorth, E. J., Reijneveld, S. A.]. (2014). Sustainability of the effects of multisystemic therapy for juvenile delinquents in the Netherlands: Effects on delinquency and recidivism. *Journal of Experimental Criminology*, 10(2), 227–243.

Baartman, H. (2009). *Het begrip kindermishandeling; pleidooi voor een herbezinning en voor bezonnen beleid.* Augeo Foundation.

Baeten, P. (2014). *VNG-model handelingsprotocol voor het Advies- en Meldpunt Huiselijk geweld en Kindermishandeling "Veilig Thuis".* VNG.

Bakker, R. (2018). *Jeugdzorg voor en na de Jeugdwet: Overzicht van het gebruik van jeugdzorg 2011–2016.* CBS.

Bartelink, C., Knorth, E. J., López López, M., Koopmans, C., Ten Berge, I. J., Witteman, C. L. M., and Van Yperen, T. A. (2018). Reasons for placement decisions in a case of suspected child abuse: The role of reasoning, work experience, and attitudes in decision-making. *Child Abuse and Neglect*, 83, 129–141.

Bartelink, C., Van Yperen, T. A., Ten Berge, I. J., and Knorth, E. J. (2021). The use and usability of decision-making theory in child welfare policy and practice. In J. D. Fluke, M. López López, R. Benbenishty, E. J. Knorth, and D. J. Baumann (Eds.), *Decision making and judgement in child welfare and protection: Theory, research, and practice.* Oxford University Press.

Benbenishty, R., Davidson-Arad, B., López, M., Devaney, J., Spratt, T., Koopmans, C., Knorth, E. J., Witteman, C. L. M., Del Valle, J. F., and Hayes, D. (2015). Decision making in child protection: An international comparative study on maltreatment substantiation, risk assessment and interventions recommendations, and the role of professionals' child welfare attitudes. *Child Abuse and Neglect*, 49, 63–75.

Bonnet, R. (2016). *De kleine gids kindermishandeling: Achtergronden, signaleren en de meldcode* (4th ed.). Wolters Kluwer.

Bouma, H., Grietens, H., López López, M., and Knorth, E. J. (2020). Learning from parents: A qualitative interview study on parents' experiences with a trajectory in the Dutch child protection system. *Child and Family Social Work*, 25(S1), 116–125.

Bouma, H., López López, M., Knorth, E., and Grietens, H. (2016). *HESTIA factsheet: Briefing on the Dutch child protection system.* University of Groningen, Department of Special Needs Education and Youth Care.

Bouma, H., López López, M., Knorth, E. J., and Grietens, H. (2018). Meaningful participation for children in the Dutch child protection system: A critical analysis of relevant provisions in policy documents. *Child Abuse and Neglect*, 79, 279–292.

CBS. (2018a). *Veilig Thuis, stand van zaken 2017.* CBS.

CBS. (2018b). *Jeugdbescherming en jeugdreclassering 2017.* CBS.

CBS. (2018c). *Jeugdhulp 1e halfjaar 2018*. CBS.

Cruyff, M. J. L. F., Van Dijk, J., and Van der Heijden, P. G. M. (2017). The challenge of counting victims of human trafficking. Not on the record: A multiple systems estimation of the numbers of human trafficking victims in the Netherlands in 2010–2015 by year, age, gender, and type of exploitation. *Chance*, 30(3), 41–49.

EM Youth Act (2013, July). Available at: https://zoek.officielebekendmakingen.nl/kst-33684-3.html.

Euser, E. M., Van IJzendoorn, M. H., Prinzie, P., and Bakermans-Kranenburg, M. J. (2010). Prevalence of child maltreatment in the Netherlands. *Child Maltreatment*, 15(1), 5–17.

Euser, S., Alink, L. R. A., Pannebakker, F., Vogels, T., Bakermans-Kranenburg, M., and Van IJzendoorn, M. H. (2013). The prevalence of child maltreatment in the Netherlands across a 5-year period. *Child Abuse and Neglect*, 37(10), 841–851.

Fluke, J. D. and Merkel-Holguin, L. (2018). Introduction. In L. Merkel-Holguin, J. D. Fluke, and R. D. Krugman (Eds.), *National systems of child protection: Understanding the international variability and context for developing policy and practice* (pp. 1–5). Springer.

Friele, R. D., Bruning, M. R., Bastiaanssen, I. L. W., De Boer, R., Bucx, A. J. E. H., De Groot, J. F., Pehlivan, T., Rutjes, L., Sondeijker, F., Van Yperen, T. A., and Hageraats, R. (2018). *Eerste evaluatie Jeugdwet: Na de transitie nu de transformatie*. ZonMw.

Friele, R. D., Hageraats, R., Fermin, A., Bouwman, R., and Van der Zwaan, J. (2019). *De jeugd-GGZ na de Jeugdwet: een onderzoek naar knelpunten en kansen*. Nivel.

Healy, K., Darlington, Y., and Feeney, J. A. (2011). Parents' participation in child protection practice: Towards respect and inclusion. *Families in Society*, 92(3), 282–288.

HESTIA (2016). *Overview of the Dutch child protection system*. [Graphic]. Available at: http://www.projecthestia.com/wp-content/uploads/2016/09/Figure-1.-Overview-of-the-Dutch-child-protection-system1.pdf.

Jansen, D. E. M. C., Reijneveld, S. A., and Evenboer, K. E. (2019). Effects of interventions for families with multiple and complex problems: a national research overview. In J. Knot-Dickscheit and E. J. Knorth (Eds.), *Families with multiple and complex problems: Theory and practice* (pp. 296–331). Lemniscaat.

Kinderombudsman. (2015). *De zorg waar ze recht op hebben. Onderzoek naar de toegang tot en kwaliteit van de jeugdhulp na de decentralisatie*. Kinderombudsman.

Knijn, T. and Van Nijnatten, C. (2011). Child welfare in the Netherlands: Between privacy and protection. In N. Gilbert, N. Parton, and M. Skivenes (Eds.), *Child protection systems: International trends and orientations* (pp. 223–240). Oxford University Press.

Knorth, E. J. (2016). *Easing the burden of problematic child rearing and child development. Research on care and treatment of children and youth with emotional, behavioural and family problems*. Garant.

Knorth, E. J. (2017, August 21). *The Dutch decentralisation policy: risks for child protection and child welfare?* Paper presented at Summer School "The Future of Child and Family Welfare Policy: Looking through different Lenses" (pp. 1–8). University of Groningen, The Netherlands.

Knorth, E. J., Evenboer, K. E., and Harder, A. T. (2016). Jeugdhulp, wetenschappelijk verantwoord. In M. H. van IJzendoorn and L. van Rosmalen (Eds.), *Pedagogiek in beeld: Een inleiding in de pedagogische studie van opvoeding, onderwijs en hulpverlening* (3rd ed.) (pp. 193–204). Bohn Stafleu van Loghum.

Leyen, E. A., Stelk, G. C. P., and Isaac, M. (2015). *De effectiviteit van de Meldcode Kindermishandeling in de kinderopvang*. GGD Amsterdam, Department of Hygiene and Inspection.

López López, M., Bouma, H., Knorth, E. J., and Grietens, H. (2019). The Dutch child protection system: Historical overview and recent transformations. In L. Merkel-Holguin, J. D. Fluke, and R. D. Krugman (Eds.), *National systems of child protection: Understanding the international variability and context for developing policy and practice* (pp. 173–192). Springer.

Meima, B. and Van Yperen, T. A. (2013). *Beleidsinformatie stelselherziening jeugd: Meetbare preventie*. Budget Memorandum 2017. Ministry of Finances.

Ministry of Health, Welfare and Sport, Ministry of Security and Justice, and Association of Netherlands Municipalities. (2014). *Factsheet Jeugdwet: Naar goede jeugdhulp die bij ons past*. Ministry of Health, Welfare and Sport, Ministry of Security and Justice, and Association of Netherlands Municipalities.

Nanninga, M., Jansen, D. E. M. C., Knorth, E. J., and Reijneveld, S. A. (2018). Enrolment of children in psychosocial care: Problems upon entry, care received, and outcomes achieved. *European Child and Adolescent Psychiatry*, 27(5), 625–635.

OM. (2016). *Aanwijzing huiselijk geweld en kindermishandeling*. Available at: https://wetten.overheid.nl/BWBR0037818/2016-05-01.

OM. (n.d.). *Kindermishandeling.* Available at: https://www.om.nl/onderwerpen/kindermishandeling.

Paganini, A. (2018, January 8). Child porn investigators help free 130 Dutch kids from abuse last year; 380 arrests. *NlTimes.nl.* Available at: https://nltimes.nl/2018/01/08/child-porn-investigators-help-free-130-dutch-kids-abuse-last-year-380-arrests.

Pattje, W. (2015). *Model voor samenwerkingsafspraken tussen Veilig Thuis, politie en OM.* VNG.

Raad voor Maatschappelijke Ontwikkeling. (2012). *Ontzorgen en normaliseren. Naar een sterke eerstelijns jeugd- en gezinszorg.* Raad voor Maatschappelijke Ontwikkeling.

Rijksoverheid. (2019). *Meldcode Huiselijk Geweld en Kindermishandeling.* Rijksoverheid. Available at: https://www.rijksoverheid.nl/onderwerpen/huiselijk-geweld/meldcode.

Rijskamp, M., Dekker, B., and Roggen, T. (2013). *Geef mij een signaal. Een meldcode voor kindermishandeling en huiselijk geweld.* SWP Publishers.

RvdK. (2014). *Het Adviesteam van de Raad voor de Kinderbescherming: Betrokken en gericht op samenwerking.* RvdK.

RvdK. (2015a). *Het Kwaliteitskader van de Raad voor de Kinderbescherming.* RvdK.

RvdK. (2015b). *Protocol Beschermingszaken.* RvdK.

RvdK. (2016). *Protocol Strafzaken.* RvdK.

RvdK. (n.d.). *De uitkomst van het onderzoek.* Available at: http://www.kinderbescherming.nl/hoe_werkt_de_raad/de_uitkomst_van_het_onderzoek/.

Schellingerhout, R. and Ramakers, C. (2017). *Scholierenonderzoek Kindermishandeling 2016.* Radboud University, ITS.

Schouten, M. (2017). *Systematic screening for child abuse in the out-of-hours primary care* [Unpublished doctoral thesis]. Utrecht University.

Sedlak, A. J., Mettenburg, J., Basena, M., Petta, I., McPherson, K., Greene, A., and Li, S. (2010). *Fourth national incidence study of child abuse and neglect (NIS–4): Report to Congress.* US Department of Health and Human Services, Administration for Children and Families.

Simons, M., Meertens, R., and Tielen, N. (2015). *De kleine gids Jeugdwet.* Wolters Kluwer.

Smit, W., Van den Tillaart, J., and Snijdewint, M. (2015). *Evaluatie van de Methode Voogdij.* Regioplan.

Smithson, R. and Gibson, M. (2017). Less than human: A qualitative study into the experiences of parents involved in the child protection system. *Child and Family Social Work, 22*(2), 565–574.

Slot, N. W., Theunissen, A., Esmeijer, F. J., and Duivenvoorden, Y. (2001). *909 Zorgen. Een onderzoek naar de doelmatigheid van de ondertoezichtstelling.* Vrije Universiteit, Faculty of Psychology and Pedagogy.

Ten Brummelaar, M. D. C., Knorth, E. J., Post, W. J., Harder, A. T., and Kalverboer, M. E. (2018). Space between the borders? Perceptions of professionals on the participation in decision-making of young people in coercive care. *Qualitative Social Work, 17*(5), 692–711.

Thoburn, J. (2010). Achieving safety, stability and belonging for children in out-of-home care: the search for "what works" across national boundaries. *International Journal of Child and Family Welfare, 13*(1/2), 34–49.

Thoburn, J., Cooper, N., Connoly, S., and Brandon, M. (2013). The place of "think family" approaches in child and family social work. *Children and Youth Services Review, 35,* 228–236.

Topberaad Jeugd. (2014). *Procesmodel jeugdbeschermingsketen 2015. Versie 0.8, concept.* Available at: https://vng.nl/onderwerpenindex/jeugd/jeugdhulp/publicaties/procesmodel-jeugdbeschermingsketen-2015.

Van Assen, A. G., Knot-Dickscheit, J., Post, W. J., and Grietens, H. (2019a). The effect of intensive home-based family interventions on child outcomes, child maltreatment, and out-of-home placement: an international study. In J. Knot-Dickscheit and E. J. Knorth (Eds.), *Families with multiple and complex problems: Theory and practice* (pp. 332–356). Lemniscaat.

Van Assen, A. G., Knot-Dickscheit, J., Post, W. J., and Grietens, H. (2019b). Child and Youth Coaching: the importance of child-focused support in families with multiple and complex problems. In J. Knot-Dickscheit and E. J. Knorth (Eds.), *Families with multiple and complex problems: Theory and practice* (pp. 453–467). Lemniscaat.

Van Bijleveld, G. G., Dedding, C. W. M., and Bunders-Aelen, J. F. G. (2014). Seeing eye to eye or not? Young people's and child protection workers' perspectives on children's participation within the Dutch protection and welfare services. *Children and Youth Services Review, 47,* 253–259.

Van der Laan, A. M. and Beerthuizen, M. G. C. J. (Eds.) (2018). *Monitor Jeugdcriminaliteit 2017. Ontwikkelingen in de geregistreerde jeugdcriminaliteit in de jaren 2000–2017.* WODC.

Van Rooijen, K., Berg, T., and Bartelink, C. (2013). *Wat werkt bij de aanpak van kindermishandeling?.* Netherlands Youth Institute.

Van Yperen, T. A., Scholte, R. H. J., and Visscher, L. (2019). Working elements in supporting families with multiple and complex problems. In J. Knot-Dickscheit and E. J. Knorth (Eds.), *Families with multiple and complex problems: Theory and practice* (pp. 402–423). Lemniscaat.

Veerman, J. W. and De Meyer, R. E. (2015). Consistency of outcomes of home-based family treatment in the Netherlands as an indicator of effectiveness. *Children and Youth Services Review*, 59, 113–119.

Vink, R., Van der Pal, S., Eekhout, I., Pannebakker, F., and Mulder, T. (2016). *Ik heb al veel meegemaakt: Ingrijpende jeugdervaringen (ACE's) bij leerlingen in groep 7/8 van het regulier basisonderwijs.* TNO.

Zeijlmans, K., López López, M., Grietens, H., and Knorth, E. J. (2019). Participation of children, birth parents and foster carers in the matching decision: Paternalism or partnership? *Child Abuse Review*, 28, 1–13.

Zijlstra, E., Rip, J. A., Beltman, D., Van Os, C., Knorth, E. J., and Kalverboer, M. (2017). Unaccompanied minors in the Netherlands: Legislation, policy and care. *Social Work and Society*, 15(2), 1–20.

The Development of the Korean Child Protection System: Cultural Influences, Unique Challenges, and Policy Strategies

Yiyoon Chung *and* T. J. Lah

Abstract

This chapter explicates the development, cultural influences, unique challenges, and policy strategies of the child protection system in Korea. The Korean government fronted its critical challenge of enforcing an indigenous Korean child protection philosophy and institutions. Traditionally, child-rearing is a task for individuals instead of government intervention. The chapter expounds on the CPS system of social allocations, social provisions, delivery, and finance dimensions. The delivery and financing of services proved to be a significant policy issue. The chapter also emphasizes how the definition of child-rearing and child maltreatment are heavily influenced by cultural traditions and beliefs. Family preservation has been the ultimate goal of Korean child protection services.

Key Words: Korea, policy strategies, finance, delivery, service, child-rearing, child protection system, tradition, family preservation, maltreatment

Introduction

In the past two decades, Korea has experienced a wide range of changes in the area of child protection services as the government initiated, implemented, and adjusted a public system to address child maltreatment. Establishing an indigenous Korean child protection philosophy and institutions, whether addressed consciously or not, has been one of the most critical challenges faced by the Korean government. Traditional cultural norms in Korea have long considered child-rearing a task to be handled by individual families rather than a matter suited to government intervention. Cultural influences have also affected Korean people's definitions of child maltreatment and their attitudes about the appropriate response when child maltreatment occurs (e.g., there is an emphasis on family preservation).

Before the 1970s, extended families and neighborhood surveillance offered some child protection. In the following decades, the protection provided by extended family and communities largely disappeared as Korea became an industrialized nation. But there was still no public system for child protection. During the 1980s, civil society and scholars in health and social work began raising explicit concerns about the prevalence of child maltreatment. However, neither the public nor the government paid much attention to the issue until the end of the 1990s, when media coverage of tragic incidences of child maltreatment in 1998[1] created opportunities for civil society to push the issue of child maltreatment to the fore of the public agenda.

Over the last 20 years, the Korean government has enacted and revised a series of child protection laws, most prominently the 2000 amendment to the Child Welfare Act and the 2013 Special Act on the Punishment of Child Abuse, thereby shifting child protection from a task left solely to families or private organizations to a matter of public policy. The policy reforms enacted by the Korean government include the establishment of public child protection agencies—currently one National Child Protection Agency (NCPA) and 62 local child protection service (CPS) agencies—providing an official definition of maltreatment, formalizing the process of reporting intake, investigation, documentation, and decision making, and strengthening mandatory reporting systems. Since 2001, the NCPA has published an annual report on CPS policy outcomes, and since 2016 the agency has managed an integrated national electronic system that collects information on reports and substantiation of child maltreatment from child support agencies and the police. Furthermore, the government has expanded (at least moderately) public services for children and families who are contacted by the child protection system.

The consensus among scholars in the field, however, is that the Korean child protection service system remains incomplete, fragmented, and under-resourced (Ahn et al., 2017; Ryu, 2017; Kim, 2018). The fragmentation of the government departments responsible for child protection services in Korea has reduced the efficiency and effectiveness of policy implementation. The Korean government's budget for child protection services is unstable and too small. This funding comes primarily from a special fund (collected from criminal offenders and designated for crime victims) rather than from general tax revenues, which reduces funding stability and creates the potential for zero-sum competition for this funding between child protection services and other beneficiaries of the fund, such as battered women. Scholars and policymakers have also suggested that the budget itself is too small (Ryu, 2016; Ahn et al., 2017).

The goal of this chapter is to describe the child protection system from a comparative perspective; report current realities, including the risk of child maltreatment in Korea; identify policy challenges; and consider potential implications for future policies. Child maltreatment has been an understudied area in Korea, due to both a lack of data and the traditional absence of the perspective of children in policy practice. However, there have been recent advances in the empirical research on the estimation

---

[1] One notable case involved a father and stepmother who starved two young children and beat them until one child died.

of child maltreatment risk (Hahm & Guterman, 2001; Kim et al., 2013; Lee et al., 2016; Ahn et al., 2017) as well as critical reviews of the systems (Lee, 2015; Kim, 2017; Ryu, 2017). In this chapter, we build on the growing body of the literature on Korean child maltreatment and contribute to this literature by reviewing the system using the frameworks of benefit eligibility, benefit allocation, delivery, and finance (Gilbert & Terrell, 2005). These frameworks deepen the scholarly understanding of the structure of the current Korean child welfare system as a welfare policy because they help identify the potentially conflicting values, as well as the advantages and disadvantages, of policy choices associated with each of the (often interdependent) dimensions above. The study also offers a complete review of the history of policy changes in Korea in the field of child protection services—while previous literature has discussed certain parts of the law, no prior work has offered a complete history. Although the primary focus of this chapter is to review the Korean child protection system and draw policy implications for Korea, it also has a broader implication for other countries: the Korean example can illustrate the difficulties involved in establishing culturally sensitive definitions of child maltreatment as well as the need for professionals to be culturally competent when working with families from a different culture.

Background: Economic, Policy, and Cultural Context

The child poverty rate in Korea is low relative to other OECD countries; in 2015, the poverty rate among Korean children was 7.1%, while the OECD average was 13.4% (the poverty threshold is set at 50% of median disposable income) (OECD, 2018a). However, the low rate of overall poverty among children obscures certain negative aspects of the welfare of children in Korea. Children in Korea report the lowest level of happiness among the children surveyed from 22 OECD countries (Ryu, 2017). Korea is a highly competitive society (Yoon, 2018) in which private education often starts early in childhood and increases stress for both parents and children, which in turn increases the risk of child maltreatment.[2]

One alarming issue is that child maltreatment reports are increasing over time. The number of reported child maltreatment incidents in Korea rose from 4,144 in 2001 to 29,674 in 2016.[3] A portion of this increase may be due to heightened awareness, the strengthened system of mandated reporting, and newly systemized child protection services—all of which should improve the welfare of children in Korea. However, there is a fair amount of concern that the true incidence of child maltreatment may

---

[2] Parents' intense identification with their children and very high expectations of success for their children are also factors that leads to highly competitive education in Korea (Hahm & Guterman, 2001). On a related note, Korea is experiencing the lowest fertility rates in the world, in part because of these factors as well as the high and increasing cost of raising children in the nation.

[3] We compare the statistics in 2001 and those in 2016, because the NCPA started counting reports of suspected child maltreatments in 2001 and the most recent year for which data are available is 2016.

be increasing in the highly competitive context of Korean society. Economic crises, increases in family separation, and the increasing social isolation of caregivers may have contributed to the increase in the reports of suspected child maltreatment (Ahn et al., 2017). However, there are no empirical studies of whether actual incidences of child maltreatment have increased. There is some population-based survey research on child maltreatment risk (Hong, 2000; Ahn et al., 2017) (see below for details), but these studies produced cross-sectional data and have not used the same measurement methods with the same target group over time to gain information about trends in child maltreatment risk.

Although Korea is often categorized in the typology of welfare capitalism as a liberal welfare state, like the United States, some scholars categorize the nation as a conservative or hybrid state or a distinct East Asian welfare model (Choi, 2012; Powell & Kim, 2014). Public spending on family benefits is relatively low in Korea compared to other OECD countries. Korea has neither a universal allowance for children nor a guaranteed child support system. In 2013, the proportion of GDP dedicated to public spending on family benefits was about 1.1% in Korea, while the OECD average was 2.1% (United States 0.7%, Japan 1.3%, Norway 3.0%, Finland 3.2%, Sweden 3.6%, United Kingdom 3.8%) (OECD, 2018b).

Family preservation has always been the ultimate goal of child protection services in Korea (NCPA, 2017, p. 129), while the government emphasis in the United States has shifted between family preservation and child protection. The Korean focus on family preservation has resulted in many Korean children remaining with their parents even when the parents were abusive; in 2016, 79% of child maltreatment victims were returned to their homes immediately and 91% were returned home within a year (NCPA, 2017). The high home-return rate of Korean child maltreatment victims may be partially driven by the nation's lack of options for the placement of children who have been separated from their families.

Budgets for welfare in Korea are relatively small compared to those in OECD countries, and the situation is even more pronounced for child protection services. Public expenditures on child protection services and other child welfare services (including in-home care, foster care, group homes, residential child care facilities, adoption, and financial support for children who have aged out of the child welfare system) were about $63 million in 2018, or about 0.057% of the total public expenditure on children and adolescents (Choi, 2018).[4] Within the typology of child welfare arrangements (Gilbert, 2012; Berrick et al., 2015), Korea's system follows a child development model—the state-parent relationship in the child protection system is paternalistic rather than collaborative (unlike the family service model, in which the state-parent partnership is emphasized),

---

[4] Authors' calculation based on Choi (2018). In the calculation, the exchange rate as of June 18, 2018 was applied: 1105.8 won to 1 dollar.

and intervention into family life remains very restricted and justified by children's developmental needs (unlike the child protection model, in which government intervention is investigative, coercive, and punitive toward parents).

The child protection system is an under-developed policy area in Korea due to several aspects of the nation's cultural history and traditions. First, within the Confucian tradition, hierarchical subordination within the family creates a social order that rationalizes gender and age inequality, and thus places special emphasis on the virtues of filial piety and familism (Hahm & Guterman, 2001). Confucian philosophy has also contributed to a predominant cultural belief that children are essentially the property of their parents, often the possessions of male heads of households. This belief has supported punishment-oriented childrearing practices (Xu et al., 2018), and in turn, inhibited the public focus on government intervention in child maltreatment. For example, *sarangeei mae* (whip of love) is the belief that the use of corporal punishment is an expression of concern or caring (Hahm & Guterman, 2001). There is some ambiguity in this matter—a certain amount of limited, planned corporal punishment might be a cultural practice, not to be judged from the perspective of outsiders; however, excessive corporal punishments have also been justified by cultural beliefs. A related consideration involves the Confucian ideal of family harmony (Hahm & Guterman, 2001). Because of the primacy of family harmony as a Korean value, child maltreatment is considered shameful and kept private. This limits the ability of child maltreatment victims to frankly report their situation outside. This also affects neighbors, schoolteachers, and professionals, making them reluctant to report suspected domestic child maltreatment because intervening in other families' "private" matters can cause dramatic shame and anger. All of these have helped delay government intervention into child protection services in Korea.

The second reason the Korean government has played a limited role in securing child welfare is related to the relationship between the family and the state. Traditional cultural norms emphasize a stronger role for the family and a weaker role for the government in matters of the welfare of families and children (Wang, 2012, cited in Xu et al., 2018). The prevailing belief is that children should be protected within the family, including the extended family. There has been a disproportionate emphasis on paternal extended families, rather than maternal extended families, although it has become less pervasive in recent years. This traditional belief is partially responsible for the notably weak system of out-of-home care for children such as foster care in Korea.

Third, the limited child protection policy reflects an overall absence of the perspective of children from Korean policy, partly due to the influence of Confucian culture as discussed above. The government does not have a single department that integrates services for children and their families; instead, welfare programs for children are currently managed by the Ministry of Health and Welfare, the Ministry of Gender Equality and Family, and the Ministry of Education. The child protection system also relies on multiple government and non-government agencies, and there is no single government body independently responsible for the child protection system in Korea.[5] Finally, official statistics in Korea are not often offered from the perspective of children (Chung, 2016a). Since 2001, national statistics on child maltreatment (e.g., reports and substantiation) have been produced annually by NCPA, but national statistics on children living in out-of-home care are unavailable, in part because there is no single government body responsible for the matter.[6]

Legal Changes

The Child Welfare Law, originally enacted in 1962 under the name *Adong-boklee-bup* and then revised and renamed *Adong-bokjee-Bup* in 1981, concerns the welfare of children in general but also includes specific measures to prohibit child maltreatment. For example, in both the 1962 and 1981 versions, the law prohibited child maltreatment. However, it did not specify what constitutes child maltreatment. Further, the law did not designate mandatory reporters (i.e., those required by law to report any time they observe suspected child maltreatment) or provide for either a separately responsible government body, a public system of reporting suspected child maltreatment, or the collection of national statistics about child maltreatment in Korea.

During this time, public efforts to prevent child maltreatment were quite limited and reports of alleged child maltreatment, often serious ones, were not handled in a public system. The received reports of alleged child maltreatment were usually handled by the police, who did not have specialized training in dealing with child maltreatment cases and had little dedicated resources to address these incidents. Thus, the reports, unless they were perceived as urgent and life-threatening, were not really addressed by public agencies. Private agencies played a role in taking reports of suspected child maltreatment and providing services to victims of child maltreatment, and often received public funding. However, these organizations had no legal authority to investigate the cases or intervene beyond providing support services. In part because of the low level of public awareness of child maltreatment in Korea, which was influenced by the culture as described above,

---

[5] As discussed at other points in this chapter, NCPA is under the supervision of the Ministry of Health and Welfare, a department of the central government, but most local CPS agencies are run by non-profit organizations that are contracted by local governments. Korean CPS workers have limited authority to investigate cases of suspected child maltreatment, while the criminal justice system, including police and prosecutors, still takes on much of the work of child protection services. The budgets of NCPA and local CPS agencies are drawn from an unstable special fund, instead of general tax revenues, and these budgets are determined by the Ministry of Justice, not the Ministry of Health and Welfare that is generally responsible for the implementation of the child protection system. In addition, much of the out-of-home care budget is determined by the Ministry of Economy and Finance (except for the budget for foster care, which is covered by the Ministry of Health and Welfare). The lack of the perspective of children in Korean public policy is responsible for the fragmentation of the system, which has then impeded the further development of the system to improve the well-being of children and their families.

[6] National statistics on how many children are newly placed into out-of-home care services each year are reported annually.

these private agencies received an extremely low number of reports of suspected child maltreatment. For example, in 1989, the Korean Child Welfare Prevention Association established 16 child maltreatment reporting centers across the nation, but during the first three years, they received only 239 reported cases (Lee, 1993, cited in Hahm & Guterman, 2001).

In 1991, the Korean government ratified the UN Convention on the Rights of the Child, taking public responsibility for the welfare of children. However, it was not until the 2000s that child maltreatment was perceived as a public issue that the government should address. The Korean Child Welfare Act's most significant amendment in 2000 represented the start of the formal public child protection system in Korea. It defined child maltreatment (Article 2), established public child protection agencies (Article 24), and explicitly laid out a procedure for mandatory reporting and listed those who have mandatory reporting responsibilities (Article 26). Since this amendment, child protection in Korea has become systematized and has been monitored by the NCPA, with an increasing workforce in the area.

The National Child Protection Agency, established in 2001, is a central public agency that manages other local agencies, develops measures to monitor and evaluate the activities of local child protection agencies, collects data from local CPS agencies and the police, publishes annual child maltreatment reports, and makes efforts to increase public awareness to prevent child maltreatment. Local CPS agencies, which were first established in 2001, are public agencies that receive reports of alleged child maltreatment, investigate, and provide services to support victims and prevent child maltreatment in the region.[7] There are currently 62 local CPA agencies (NCPA 2018).

In 2013, an extremely tragic case,[8] along with several following incidences, increased public awareness of the system's limitations and inspired public consensus about the need to make fundamental changes to the child protective system in Korea. In response to the public outcry, the Korean government enacted the 2013 Special Act on the Punishment of Child Abuse (implemented in September 2014), which strengthened the mandatory reporting system. It simplified the system for reporting suspected child maltreatment, which created the current system in which reports are made to either local CPS agencies or the police's crime call center, whose phone number is 112.[9] Notably, the police still receive

---

[7] The NCPA does not directly receive reports. Local CPS agencies receive reports and investigate the cases of alleged child maltreatment, but compared to the police, they still have limited compulsory investigation authority.

[8] A stepmother abused and tortured two daughters that her new husband brought to the family (7 and 11 years old, respectively). After she murdered the 7-year-old daughter, she tried to impute the crime to the 11-year-old daughter. At first, the older daughter said that she committed the crime and was accused of murder. However, three months after she was separated from her parents, she came to tell the truth that she did not commit the murder and it was her stepmother who beat her sister to death.

[9] Previously, besides calling 112, there were other routes to report to the police (e.g., to the Ministry of Health and Human Services, a designated call center for women, etc.), but the 2013 Special Act on the Punishment of Child Abuse simplified these different numbers to create the current arrangement of using only 112.

substantial reports of suspected child maltreatment and make independent investigation and assessment (see below for details). The 2013 Special Act on the Punishment of Child Abuse also increased the number of mandatory reporting categories from 22 to 24 by adding childcare workers and public service workers for low-income families and children. Yet, CPS agency workers and directors are still not included as mandatory reporters of child maltreatment for reasons that are not documented.[10] The 2016 amendment to the Special Act on the Punishment of Child Abuse strengthened the penalty when mandatory reporters fail to report a suspected child maltreatment case and added measures to protect those who make a report.

The CPS System in Four Dimensions: Social Allocations, Social Provisions, Delivery, and Finance

The Bases of Social Allocations
DEFINITIONS AND MEASUREMENTS OF CHILD MALTREATMENT
The current Korean Child Welfare Act (Article 3) defines child maltreatment as the physical, mental, and sexual violence or act of cruelty committed by adults including caregivers that causes damage to the health and welfare of children or hinders their ordinary development, and child neglect and abandonment committed by caregivers.[11] The Child Welfare Act (Article 17) also defines eleven specific prohibited acts. The eleven acts prohibited are: (1) abusive acts that injure a child's body; (2) abusive acts including sexual harassment, sexual assault, and other acts that cause sexual humiliation; (3) emotionally abusive acts that harm a child's mental health or development; (4) abandoning a child under one's protection or neglecting basic protection, care, and medical treatment including clothing, food, and housing; (5) selling or buying a child; (6) asking a child to do sexual acts or any acts related to sex; (7) exhibiting a child with disability in public for the purpose of entertainment; (8) forcing a child to be involved in begging; (9) pushing a child to do acrobatic stunts that are harmful to their health and safety for the purposes of entertainment or commercial success; (10) with the exception of agencies with legal authority, offering child placements and receiving monetary benefits; and (11) spending money or other valuables that are designated to help raise a child for other purposes (National Law Information Center, 2018).

---

[10] In 2016, an amendment to the Child Welfare Law (implemented in September 2016) further extended mandatory reporter categories by adding CPS agency workers and directors as mandatory reporters of child maltreatment, but two months later, an amendment to the Special Act on the Punishment of Child Abuse (implemented in November 2016) excepted these groups from the mandatory reporter category. This amendment added domestic violence center service workers, adoption agency workers, and childcare service center workers as mandatory reporters.

[11] Under the Child Welfare Act, children are defined as those under age 18.

Defining what constitutes child maltreatment is a social process, and Korea is a good example of this. Traditionally, the influence of Confucianism led to the popularity of punishment-oriented childrearing practices among Korean parents. This focus is reflected in the definition of child maltreatment in the current Child Welfare Act: a corporal punishment may not be considered child maltreatment if it does not cause damage to children. However, which acts Koreans consider child maltreatment has changed over time in concert with other changes. Specifically, family structure has changed—for example, the dominant family form has shifted from extended families to nuclear families, and the number of children per family has decreased dramatically, which creates an environment in which child rearing without corporal punishment is more effective and more affordable. Although no official empirical evidence exists, anecdotal evidence suggests that the number of families who exercise corporal punishment has declined, and people's attitudes toward corporal punishments have changed such that people are less accepting of the use of this type of punishment as an appropriate educational tool for children. All corporal punishments are now prohibited in Korean schools. Within the home, however, corporal punishment is still left to the judgement of families, although any corporal punishment on children under age three is prohibited by law. Another characteristic of the definition of child maltreatment in Korea is the lack of a clear definition of child neglect (Ryu, 2017). Neither laws nor conventional regulations suggest a clear minimum standard of care for children's needs, reflecting a relatively high social acceptance of potentially neglectful behaviors such as leaving young children alone at home for hours.

Despite the wide range of acts that constitute child maltreatment, there is no validated measure that reflects the Korean definition of child maltreatment, and most Korean studies have employed measures developed in other countries (Han et al., 2006). Using the self-reports of a nationally representative sample of caregivers and children, Hong and colleagues (2000) estimated that, overall, 43% of Korean children experience child abuse. This was considered too high and critics argued that the definition of child maltreatment did not reflect the cultural context of Korea. Using the Child Physical and Psychological Maltreatment (CPPM) measure,[12] Ahn and colleagues (2017) found a 25.3% rate of physical and psychological maltreatment among Korean children in 2011. Specifically, the risk of physical abuse, emotional abuse, and child neglect was 7.1%, 10.9%, and 15.4%, respectively.

According to NCPA (2017), child maltreatment is grouped into four broad categories: physical, emotional, sexual, and neglect. In 2016, 65.5% of child abuse victims were psychologically or emotionally abused (19% experienced emotional abuse only), 58.2% were physically abused (14.5% experienced physical abuse only), 24.4% were neglected

---

[12] The CPPM measure is based on a common self-report measure for child maltreatment called the CTS-PC, which was developed by Straus and colleagues (1998), and adjusted for the Korean situation (e.g., excluding sexual abuse for cultural reasons).

(15.6% experienced neglect only), and 3.7% were sexually abused (2.6% experienced sexual abuse only). With the exception of sexual abuse cases, over 80% of the acts of child maltreatment were committed by the parents of the focal child (NCPA, 2017).

CORRELATES OF THE RISK OF CHILD MALTREATMENT

Ahn and colleagues (2017) reported that household income is negatively associated with the risk of child maltreatment, and this association is particularly strong for child neglect. Poverty is consistently associated with the heightened risk of child maltreatment, as is living in a large city compared to living in a mid-sized to small city. Boys experience a higher risk of physical abuse than girls, but this gender pattern does not emerge for other types of child maltreatment.

Family structure, along with income, also affects the risk of child maltreatment. As mentioned previously, the child poverty rate in Korea is relatively low among OECD countries. However, an important issue to consider is that relative economic vulnerability among single-parent families, compared to two-parent families, is a more serious problem in Korea than in other OECD countries, including the United States (Chung, 2016b; Chung & Kim, 2018). In previous studies, children living in single-parent families experience a higher risk of child maltreatment, in part because these families tend to experience a lack of time and financial resources, which are important determinants of child maltreatment (Berger, 2004). Indeed, single-parent families are over-represented in child maltreatment reports in Korea; families with single parents constitute 8% of all families with children under age 18, but 29% of families in the Korean CPS system in 2016 (NCPA, 2017).

Other studies conducted in Korea suggest some empirical evidence consistent with the negative consequences of child maltreatment for the varied outcomes of depression, anxiety, low self-esteem, delinquency, and school maladjustment among children (Kwon et al., 2013; Ju & Lee, 2018; Park & Kim, 2018). Kim (2017) also reported correlations between adverse childhood experiences and alcohol abusive behaviors among Korean college students.

PROCEDURES FOR INVESTIGATION AND ASSESSMENT

In Korea, reports of alleged child maltreatment are received via multiple channels. In 2017, Korean CPS agencies received only 34.5% of child maltreatment reports (51.3% if cases that CPS workers additionally reported during field investigations, such as abused siblings, are included); the police received 48.2% of reports; and other public and private organizations received the remaining 0.6% of reports (NCPA, 2018). As explained above, mandatory reporting categories have been expanded, and 32.0% of all reports received in 2016 were made by mandated reporters (NCPA, 2017), compared to 28.4% of reports in 2002 (NCPA, 2003).

After a report is received, an investigation is initiated by protective service workers or police, or the two together. The 2013 Special Act on the Punishment of Child Abuse indicates that an investigation should be conducted "immediately" after a report is received but does not mandate a specific timeline; in practice, the first investigation is usually conducted within a few hours. The need for an "immediate" investigation is especially emphasized if the alleged victim is aged 3 or younger. In 2016, an average of 2.1 field investigations were conducted for each case of suspected child maltreatment (NCPA, 2017).

The current Child Welfare Law grants the police and prosecutors extensive authority to investigate, while granting CPS agency workers a more limited ability to investigate.[13] However, the 2013 Special Act on the Punishment of Child Abuse, CPS workers can ask the police to accompany them on field investigations in order to enhance their investigation ability. In 2016, 56.6% of investigations were conducted by a CPS worker(s) alone; 27.3% were conducted by CPS workers and the police; 10.7% were conducted the police alone; and 3.8% were conducted jointly by CPS workers, the police, and public social workers.[14] Because the majority of investigations involved only CPS workers, the limited authority of these workers to investigate is an important issue to address.

Once an investigation of alleged child maltreatment is completed, the results are classified as 1) substantiated cases (i.e., child maltreatment occurred), 2) unsubstantiated cases, and 3) early support cases (unsubstantiated but support is needed). In 2016, 72.3% of cases were substantiated, 8.6% were unsubstantiated, and 18.6% were early support cases (cases that are not substantiated but are regarded to benefit from support services). Workers file field reports about each case and then a team of CPS workers makes a final decision about substantiation and develops a plan for support and/or legal actions to pursue court orders (for more details, see below).

Social Provisions: Benefits and Services Available for Maltreated Children

CPS agencies provide various programs and services for children at risk of maltreatment and their families. The services that CPS agencies provide tend to be in-kind benefits (e.g., personal services) rather than cash benefits. They include intake counseling, individual counseling (including home visitations that occur once a month or more frequently for a serious case), group counseling, medical and psychological tests, medical services including in-hospital or commuting services, and various therapies including art therapy and play therapy. In addition, CPS agencies offer services for strengthening families (including various educational programs and services connected to local social service agencies and public benefit programs), temporary care services (through connections to temporary

---

[13] For example, CPSA staff are limited to making observations and asking questions specifically related to the protection of the child who is alleged to have been maltreated (Special Act on the Punishment of Child Abuse, Article 11), while the police have the authority to conduct a complete investigation.

[14] Public social workers refer to government employees who work for local governments and specialize in social welfare in the region.

protection facilities and shelters), and urgent care for children. Finally, CPS agencies can pursue a legal procedure for mandated services for perpetrators or for the protection of a child (e.g., court orders for protecting the child, restricting the perpetrators' access to the child, and filing an accusation against the perpetrator).

In practice, the services CPS agencies provide are largely oriented toward counseling services; in 2016, 52.5% of children involved in the CPS system received counseling, 32.5% received temporary care services, and only 3.1% received family-strengthening services (in-home services or being connected to other service agencies or public programs). Few cases result in providing the child an alternative, stable, long-term shelter in the aftermath of serious abuse. According to a 2017 NCPA report, 79% of child maltreatment victims were returned to their homes almost immediately, while 21.9% were separated from caregivers; 12.4% were placed in temporary care, 6.3% were placed with relatives, and 1.7% were placed in long-term care, including foster care, group homes, and residential childcare facilities. Note that only seven children were placed in foster care (constituting 0.0%). Furthermore, 44.3% of the children who were separated from their homes (i.e., the 21.9% above) were returned to their homes within one month, and almost all children, 99.8%, were returned to their homes within one year. Statistics on voluntary and involuntary service use are not available. The options for in-home and out-of-home services for maltreated children and their children tend to be narrow in range and insufficient in number in Korea.

Delivery

The fragmentation of the government departments responsible for child protection services and other child welfare services in Korea has reduced the efficiency and effectiveness of policy implementation (Anh et al., 2017; Ryu, 2017; Kim, 2018). The Korean CPS (NCPA and local CPS agencies) is not responsible for all aspects of child protection services and, indeed, does not have full authority to manage these services. For example, CPS agency workers have only limited authority to investigate suspected child maltreatment cases, while the criminal justice system, including police and prosecutors—who do not specialize in this field and thus may not have the sensitivity, specialized knowledge, and practical skills required—take on much of the work of child protection services.

Further, in Korea, child protection services and other child welfare services are not well connected with each other (Ryu, 2017). Thus, the flow of services from providers to clients is often impeded. Child welfare services such as in-home services, foster care, and group homes are primarily run by non-profit organizations, which are often contracted by local governments (i.e., funding is provided by the government, but the implementation is managed by organizations). The target of local child welfare services includes abandoned children, and children left alone,[15] but many of these children have

---

[15] Children may be left alone due to parents' death, poverty, or unemployment. Or children may be lost or run away.

been sent to the out-of-home care system by the local government official, without any interaction with CPS agencies. These cases tend to be managed separately from the cases initiated by CPS agencies. Under the current system, CPS agencies are involved in child maltreatment cases only when there is an alleged perpetrator. Experts report that the lack of coordination of placement services between local governments and CPS agencies is one of the most critical challenges in the delivery of the child protection system (Ryu, 2017).

Both the absolute number and the diversity of the organizations that provide in-home and out-of-home care services are insufficient, and the organizations are not well connected with local CPS agencies. Further, 60 of 62 local CPS agencies are run by non-profit organizations (contracted by the government), and their workers are often non-standard workers receiving low wages. The other two local CPS agencies are run directly by local governments, while NCPA is a public agency within a department of the central government, the Ministry of Health and Welfare.

In response to the fragmentation of the child protection system, broad support emerged among scholars in the field for the establishment of an independent child welfare department with greater authority to investigate and provide support, as well as specialized training (e.g., enhanced professional knowledge, deliberate caution, sensitivity, and skillful relational practices, and authority to sanction and penalize individuals for noncompliance). Developing a child protection system that is simple, unified, and centralized is a critical issue (Kim, 2018). In addition, as scholars, policymakers, and practitioners continue to develop and implement the child protection system in Korea, it will be also important to actualize democratic values by considering measures to increase the rights of alleged perpetrators to challenge decisions of CPS authorities.

Finance

Major financing for the child protection system comes from a special fund (collected from criminal offenders and designated for crime victims) rather than from general tax revenues, which reduces funding stability and creates the potential for zero-sum competition for this funding between child protection services and other beneficiaries of the fund, such as battered women. Further, NCPA belongs to the Ministry of Health and Welfare, but the budget for NCPA is determined by the Ministry of Justice. Thus, the Ministry of Justice has little incentive to increase the budget, which is a potential reason for the slow growth of the NCPA budget. Scholars in the field agree that financing for the child protection system should be drawn from general revenues, instead of unstable special funds (Ryu, 2017; Kim, 2018).

When also considering other child welfare services including in-home and out-of-home care, the picture becomes even more complicated. The budget for foster care services, as well as some (one-time) financial support for children who have aged out of the child welfare system, comes from general tax revenues and is managed by the Ministry of

Health and Welfare.[16] However, the financing for many in-home services, group homes, residential child care facilities, support for adopted children, and programs for local centers for children comes from another special fund (collected from the public lottery business), which is managed by the Ministry of Economy and Finance. Most of the funds for these services are given to non-profit organizations as a lump-sum contribution for relevant programs. The central government collects no statistics on how the money is spent, how child protection services are coordinated (e.g., the bases on which children who need public care are being assigned into foster care, group homes, or residential childcare facilities), or the extent of regional disparities in these practices and policy outcomes.

Conclusion

This chapter has reviewed the Korean child protection system using the frameworks of social allocations, social provisions, delivery, and finance. In the process of investigation and assessment, effective child protection services require workers to exhibit a high degree of sensitivity and cautiousness and possess highly specialized knowledge and practical skills; thus, a system that sufficiently educates and trains CPS workers is essential. While it is important for CPS workers to have the authority to sanction and penalize individuals for noncompliance, those who are accused must have guaranteed access to channels for disagreeing with the decisions of CPS authorities. Our examination also reveals that within the Korean child protection system, the fragmentation of both the delivery and financing of services is a significant policy challenge. Thus, the first order of business involves developing a coherent and unified child protection system (Kim, 2018). The establishment of an independent child welfare department with greater authority to investigate and provide support may be an option.

Increasing the Korean government's budget for child protection services is important. If the government believes that children are important public goods (Folbre, 1994), it is appropriate for the child protection system to be financed via general tax revenues (rather than special funds) to increase funding stability. Further, increasing preventative child welfare services supportive of families and children, as well as quality in-home and out-of-home care services, is also important.

Although practitioners and policymakers have placed increasing emphasis on evidence-based policymaking, there is limited empirical evidence that can inform policymaking decisions in the field of child protection services in Korea. Because of the nation's unique cultural and policy contexts, applying findings from empirical research conducted in other parts of the world will not guarantee successful results. Thus, gathering appropriate data should be a high priority of the Korean government and scholars in the field in Korea.

---

[16] There are no official data on the kindship care budget.

Developing a clear definition of child maltreatment that reflects the Korean Child Welfare Act and is adjusted to Korean culture remains another significant task in the field of Korean child protection policy. Which types of corporal punishment should be considered an extension of discipline rather than child maltreatment remains an open question for Korean government to address. Researchers should neither adopt today's measures to understand the past nor use an outsider's measure to understand Korean culture, but at the same time, cultural differences, or complexities in understanding the issue, should not mask the importance of children's rights.

Acknowledgments

This work was supported by the Ministry of Education of the Republic of Korea and the National Research Foundation of Korea (NRF-2016S1A3A2923475). An article on the child welfare system in Korea that is an expanded and revised version of the chapter is forthcoming in the *International Journal of Social Welfare*.

References

Ahn, J., Lee, B. J., Kahng, S. K., Hye, L. K., Hwang, O. K., Lee, E. J., and Yoo, J. P. (2017). Estimating the prevalence rate of child physical and psychological maltreatment in South Korea. *Child Indicators Research*, 10(1), 187–203.

Berger, L. M. (2004). Income, family structure, and child maltreatment risk. *Children and Youth Services Review*, 26(8), 725–748.

Berrick, J. D., Peckover, S., Pösö, T., and Skivenes, M. (2015). The formalized framework for decision-making in child protection care orders: A cross-country analysis. *Journal of European Social Policy*, 25(4), 366–378.

Choi, Y. J. (2012). End of the era of productivist welfare capitalism? Diverging welfare regimes in East Asia. *Asian Journal of Social Science*, 40(3), 275–294.

Choi, Y. (2017). *Analysis of the 2018 budget for the Ministry of Health and Welfare-areas of children and adolescents*. People's Solidarity for Participatory Democracy. Available at: http://www.peoplepower21.org/Welfare/1534365.

Choi, Y. (2018). *Analysis of the 2019 budget for the Ministry of Health and Welfare-areas of children and adolescents*. People's Solidarity for Participatory Democracy. Available at: http://www.peoplepower21.org/Welfare/1593001.

Chung, Y. (2016a). Economic vulnerability among single mother families and social inclusiveness: Facts and policy issues. Korean Presidential Committee for National Cohesion. *Policy Issue Report*, 8, 98–143.

Chung, Y. (2016b). Divorced single mothers and their child support receipt in Korea. *Family and Culture*, 28, 271–231.

Chung, Y. and Kim, Y. (2018). How cultural and policy contexts interact with child support policy: A case study of child support receipt in Korea and the United States. *Children and Youth Services Review*. Available at: https://doi.org/10.1016/j.childyouth.2018.11.026.

Folbre, N. (1994). Children as public goods. *The American Economic Review*, 84(2), 86–90.

Gilbert, N. and Terrell, P. (2005). *Dimensions of social welfare policy*. Pearson Allyn and Bacon.

Gilbert, N. (2012). A comparative study of child welfare systems: Abstract orientations and concrete results. *Children and Youth Services Review*, 34(3), 532–536.

Han, I. Y., Yoo, S. K., Park, M. S., Park, H. W., and Lee, Y. W. (2006). Development of a physical abuse assessment scale for children. *Journal of the Korean Society of Child Welfare*, 21, 7–27.

Hahm, H. C. and Guterman, N. B. (2001). The emerging problem of physical child abuse in South Korea. *Child Maltreatment*, 6(2), 169–179.

Hong, K. E., Lee, J. Y., Cho, H. S., Lee, Y. H., Ahn, D. H., Kwak, Y. S., and Han, J. S. (2000). *The national survey of child abuse and outcome of abuse*. Ministry of Health and Welfare.

Ju, S. and Lee, Y. (2018). Developmental trajectories and longitudinal mediation effects of self-esteem, peer attachment, child maltreatment and depression on early adolescents. *Child Abuse & Neglect*, 76, 353–363.

Kim, A. (2018). *Measures to strengthen the public policy to address child maltreatment*. Issue paper no. 2018-08. Korea Institute of Child Care and Education.

Kim, M. (2017). A study on the measures to prevent child abuse-emotional abuse in the home. *Korean Criminal Information Research*, 3(4), 1–22.

Kim, M., Jun, J., Ha, T., Kim, H., Oh, M., Jung, E., Choi, E., Lee, B., and Kim, S. (2013). *Child welfare survey*. Policy report to the Ministry of Health & Welfare.

Kwon, J., Lee, E. and Nho, C. (2013). Mediating effects of teacher and peer relationship on the association between child abuse and neglect and school performance. *Journal of Korean Society of Child Welfare*, 42, 29–54.

Lee, E. (2015). Changes and improvement plans for child abuse protection systems. *Korean Journal of Family Welfare*, 20(1), 69–85.

Lee, I., Jang, M., Whang, J. Lee, M. Joo, J., and Jung, S. (2016). *The domestic violence survey in 2016*. Research report no. 2016-46. Report to the Ministry of Gender Equality and Family.

National Law Information Center. (2018). *Child Welfare Act*. MGL. Available at: http://www.law.go.kr/LSW/eng/engMain.do.

NCPA. (2003). *Report on the incidents of child maltreatment in Korea*. National Child Protection Agency.

NCPA. (2017). *Report on the incidents of child maltreatment in Korea*. National Child Protection Agency.

NCPA. (2018). *Preliminary report on the incidents of child maltreatment in Korea*. National Child Protection Agency.

OECD. (2018a). *Poverty rate* [Graph]. doi: 10.1787/0fe1315d-en.

OECD. (2018b). *Family benefits public spending* [Graph]. doi: 10.1787/8e8b3273-en.

Park, A. and Kim, Y. (2016). Investigating a longitudinal trajectory of child obesity and its association with child maltreatment in south Korea. *Asian Social Work and Policy Review*, 10(2), 237–247.

Park, A. and Kim, Y. (2018). The longitudinal influence of child maltreatment on child obesity in South Korea: The mediating effects of low self-esteem and depressive symptoms. *Children and Youth Services Review*, 87, 34–40.

Powell, M. and Kim, K. (2014). The "chameleon" Korean welfare regime. *Social Policy & Administration*, 48(6), 626–646.

Ryu, J. (2017). Child maltreatment and improvement direction for child protection system. *Health and Social Welfare Review*, (5), 5–23.

Straus, M. A., Hamby, S. L., Finkelhor, D., Moore, D. W., and Runyan, D. (1998). Identification of child maltreatment with the parent–child conflict tactics scales: Development and psychometric data for a national sample of American parents. *Child Abuse & Neglect*, 22(4), 249–270.

Xu, Y., Bright, C. L., and Ahn, H. (2018). Responding to child maltreatment: Comparison between the USA and China. *International Journal of Social Welfare*, 27(2), 107–120.

Yoon, J. (2018). Peer relations and tensions in the school life of Finnish and Korean students: a cross-cultural perspective. *Pedagogy, Culture & Society*, 27(4), 1–18.

Child Protection Systems in Spain

Sagrario Segado

Abstract

This chapter expounds on the child protection systems in Spain. It cites the range of international, national, and regional legislations impacting the Spanish child protection system. The social protection system for minors aims to protect the rights of children and adolescents, guarantee their well-being, families, safe environment, and belonging. Regardless of the parties involved, the measures will be catered to the minor's best interests. The chapter notes how there is still a long way to go in addressing the violence against minors, unaccompanied foreign minors and child poverty, despite Spain being family-oriented. It notes the models of support intervention in child protection such as theories of attachment, child needs, ecological-systematic model, empowerment and protection factors.

Key Words: Spain, legislation, child protection system, well-being, minors, violence, attachment, empowerment, family, belonging

Introduction

Spain is a parliamentary monarchy. The Constitution of 1978 politically and administratively divided the territory into 17 autonomous communities and two autonomous cities (Ceuta and Melilla). This territorial division undoubtedly marked the configuration of the Spanish child protection system. Many intervention structures and protocols, particularly those establishing the foundation and enacted by law, are standardized across the autonomous communities. The promotion and defense of children's rights are organized in two areas throughout the nation: on the one hand, prevention actions, which involve a detailed analysis of the child and their family's situation, and interventions to face situations of risk; on the other hand, actions derived from situations of risk or abandonment, aimed at the protection of children at risk of/or who already suffered abuse or neglect. The 17 communities also share similar organizational hierarchies, such as two levels of the division of social services: basic social services and specific social services. The latter is contained within "childhood, youth and family," where local entities govern the needs of affected minors by creating specific agencies, such as local councils for children and adolescents (where child/youth voice and active participation in matters of policy are promoted) present in most of the Spanish municipalities, or specific bodies in the autonomous communities, such as the childcare center (Centro de Atención a la Infancia; CAI) in Madrid. In general, every social services measure taken by the administration to protect the minor requires notification to the Public Prosecutor for Minors' Office for monitoring and follow-up.

The basic objectives of the social protection system for minors are to: 1) protect the rights of children and adolescents; 2) guarantee their well-being and that of their families; 3) ensure that they have a stable and safe environment in which their basic needs are met; and 4) guarantee the continuity of their environment and persons within it, their attachment references, and their significant relationships, so that the child can develop the feeling of continuity and belonging necessary for healthy growth.

The following is a description of the childhood protection system in Spain.

Legal International, National and Regional Framework

A variety of international, national, and regional laws that affect the Spanish child protection system are detailed below.

International

The first international point of reference for our current child protection system is the United Nation's Convention on the Rights of the Child (CRC) (1989), which was ratified by Spain in 1990. The CRC establishes a broad framework of protection for minors as subjects of rights that must be recognized, practiced, and defended by all, especially by parents and responsible institutions. European legislation contributes to the Spanish child protection system with both the European Charter of the Rights of the Child, adopted by the European Parliament in 1990, and The Hague Convention of 1993 on the protection of children and cooperation on the subject of International Adoption, ratified by Spain in 1995.

National

However, it is Law 21 in 1987, an amendment to the civil code, that profoundly transformed Spain's child protection system. The Spanish Constitution of 1978 states in Article 39 that the public powers will ensure the social, economic and legal protection of the family, as well as the integral protection of the child(ren). Yet with the 1987 reform, the amendment of the civil code included terms of adoption and other forms of child protection. It included decisions on measures to protect minors, including their removal from the home. These decisions became mainly administrative, although judges decide in the case of appeal, or when the child protection measures appear within other cases that are in court (e.g., a divorce). The additional terms generally referred to the adaptation of administrative responsibilities to adhere to childhood and adolescence needs in Spain. In addition, a thorough review of children and adolescent protection institutions was carried out with the reform (Berrocal Lanzarot, 2015). This amendment later became organic Law 1 in 1996, known as Legal Protection of the Minor, and included a partial modification of the Civil Code (LOPJM). Law 1 is the highest level of comprehensive regulation in minors' protection.

These successive laws emphasize, particularly since 1996, the process of adaptation to emerging social changes, of which lawyers, professionals, and non-governmental organizations spanning all areas related to minors have been involved. This allowed educational, psychological, and social aspects to be introduced in legal drafts, thus bringing their understanding and application to these groups. These aspects aimed to achieve the integral development of the child by integrating principles of minors' rights with the cultural, material, and technical resources of the State (Moreno Torres, 2015). As a result of this long legislative process, Laws 8 and 26 were created in 2015 to modify the wording in the 1996 Law 1 specific to the protection system of childhood and adolescence. An organic law, Law 8, for everything affecting fundamental rights and public liberties, and an ordinary law, Law 26, for remaining matters.

The urgency of protection criteria standardization across the different autonomous communities led to organic Law 8/2015. In issuing it, Spain satisfied the CRC's requests, in that it claimed that the rights of the child should be guaranteed throughout the entire country. The law also required reinforcement of the best interests of the child as a guiding principle of actions aimed at the protection of minors. Organic Law 8/2015 regulates issues such as placement in centers in the case of conduct disorder and permits entry into the home to implement protection measures in cases when freedom and fundamental rights of minors and their families are impacted.

However, our system of protection is not only based on laws. Theoretical social frames of reference support intervention in child protection. They have led to the clarification of the different explanatory and intervention models that have empirically proven to be useful and relevant in the evaluation and intervention with families where situations of child vulnerability have occurred. The following are some of these models:

- the theory of attachment;
- the theory of the child needs;
- the ecological-systemic model;
- models of empowerment (promotion of competition); and
- models to strengthen protection factors.

Regional
Each autonomous community has the discretion to create their own laws focused on developing and adapting the abovementioned regulations. In its Article 148.1, the Spanish Constitution empowers the communities to assume full power in matters of

social assistance. Thus, the map of child protection is configured in a series of regional and local competences.

By the statute of autonomy of the Community of Madrid, approved by Organic Law 3 in 1983, Madrid is entitled to a legislative function in social assistance matters, including all child protection matters. Among its competences is that of "the protection and guardianship of minors and the development of policies of integral promotion of youth," as shown in Article 26.1.24.

The community of Madrid also approved Law 6 on March 28, 1995, which guarantees that rights are legally granted to the child and the adolescent. In its Article 50, this law states that protection of minors in a social risk situation corresponds to the public system of social services, and that necessary prevention, care, and reintegration activities will be developed in the respective programs. This law also declares that, in order to reinforce and provide support for general social services, municipal administrations will create specialized social services for childhood care according to the needs detected within their population.

The principles and procedures for the social and legal protection of minors are included in title III, chapter V: *Guarantees of care and protection of children and adolescents, principles and procedures for the social and legal protection of minors*. Law 11, enacted in 2003, complements the legal framework with social services for the protection of minors in the Autonomous Community of Madrid.

To conclude this section, we revisit autonomous Law 6/1995. It is worth reading its general principles since in most of them reference is made to the "state" order from which they emanate, as well as to the international system:

- Prioritize the best interests of minors over any other legitimate concurrent interest, under the terms established in the civil code and the Convention on the Rights of the Child.
- Ensure the full exercise of the minor's subjective rights and, in all cases, the right to be heard in all decisions he might be involved in, under the terms established in the civil code.
- Eliminate any form of discrimination based on birth, sex, color, race, religion, nationality, ethnic or social origin, language, opinion, physical impediments, economic or personal social conditions of minors or their families, or any other discriminatory circumstance.
- Promote the necessary conditions so that the responsibility of the parents or guardians in the effective exercise of the rights of their children or guardians can be fulfilled in an appropriate way.
- The public administrations of the community of Madrid will assume this responsibility when the parents or guardians cannot exercise it or do so in a

way contrary to the best interests of the child, under the terms established in the civil code and the Convention on the Rights of the Child.

- Guarantee the educational nature of all measures adopted so that socialization is sought.
- Promote the values of tolerance, solidarity, respect, equality, and, in general, the democratic principles of coexistence established in the constitution.
- Promote the participation of social initiatives in relation to the care and promotion of childhood and adolescence, seeking their participation into the care plans and programs promoted by the public administrations.
- Encourage intergenerational relations through the volunteering of older and younger people to collaborate in activities with children and adolescents.

Bases of Social Allocation

In order to examine the actions and standards used to identify children at risk, it is convenient at this point to recall that national laws allow for different Autonomous Communities to have their own child protection system, processes and structures. However, differences are not significant from the qualitative point of view. This is mainly because the aforementioned two laws of 2015 to modify the system of protection for childhood and adolescence standardized the protection measures across national autonomies and encouraged communication and coordination between protection systems. In this chapter, we focus on the community of Madrid, as it host the capital city and 6.7 millions of inhabitants, also, it is the reference with which this author currently participates in several international comparative research projects[1] on the protection of minors. The description of this community reflects the functioning of the protection system in Spain.

Eligibility Criteria: Standards Used to Identify Children Who Are Maltreated or at Risk
We begin at the state level. Nationwide, Spanish laws establish that every minor has the right to be raised with their family. The administration acts in accordance with the principle of progressive subsidiarity with respect to the legal obligations of parents or guardians. Therefore, it is important for the courts to clearly delimit situations of risk, neglect, and abandonment and the need to restrictively interpret the legal concept of abandonment. Thus, in situations of child vulnerability, the administration is obliged to adopt protection measures in the child's family environment, including separation when deficiencies in basic needs cannot be covered by any other measures.

---

[1] "The Acceptability of Child Protection Interventions: A Cross-Country Analysis." This project has received funding from the Research Council of Norway under the Independent Projects – Humanities and Social Science program (grant no. 262773). "DISCRETION." This project has received funding from the European Research Council (ERC) under the European Union's Horizon 2020 research and innovation program (grant agreement no. 724460).

On a national scale, Organic Law 1/1996 (LOPJM) made one of the most important innovations in distinguishing between situations of risk and situations of abandonment. While the law kept the concept of abandonment under the terms of the previous legislation, it introduced a new legal institution: that of risk. Two laws reflect this distinction.

Article 17 of the LOPJM states that the local, public child protection entity will intervene 1) in situations of risk of any kind deemed mild, moderate, or serious; 2) where the state does not assume legal guardianship; and 3) where the personal or social development of the child could be harmed. The entity will: 1) implement relevant actions to reduce risk factors and social difficulty that, if ignored, could lead to the separation of the child from its family; and 2) monitor the evolution of the child in the family. Additionally, in Article 172.1, the Civil Code states that parental abandonment is a situation of fact, which occurs because of non-compliance, or the impossible or inadequate exercise of protection duties (i.e., moral or material deprivation) established by the laws for the custody of minors. Abandonment and risk interventions vary, and they are usually detected by the community services, social services, the school, the health system, people from the family environment, or any other social agent. Figure 17.1 details both interventions' trajectories.

A final concept important to the child protection system is that of social conflict (Law 6/1995, Article 67). It is applied when the behavior of minors, who have reached the age of 12, seriously alters the family dynamic and disregards generally accepted social

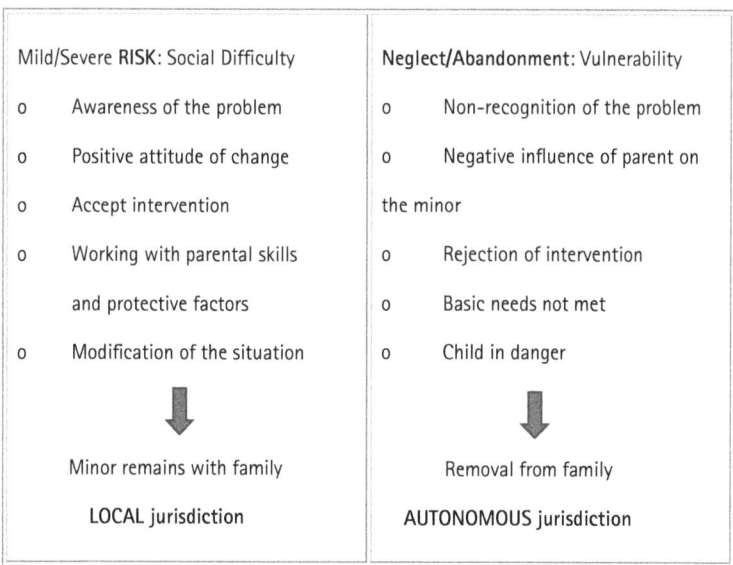

Figure 17.1 Distinction between risk and abandonment trajectories

behavior, with the risk of causing harm to third parties. Social conflict can be deemed so with or without a judicial measure and with or without an allegation of lack of protection.

Given these various concepts and interventions, the administration performance must be *flexible*, adapting to the circumstances of the minor and his family at all times. To proceed accordingly, the protection measures agreed by the social services must be periodically reviewed. Likewise, protection interventions are subject to the principle of family reunification, which requires that in cases of abandonment where the separation of the minor from their family has been determined, the public administration must establish the measures and programs necessary to pursue the return to the family of origin in the shortest possible time. Throughout this process, both principles of the best interests of the minor and the minor's right to be heard in all decisions that affect him, are mandatory, and must be permanently present. Finally, it is worth remembering that all these decisions must be adopted in accordance with the legal principle of objectivity, impartiality, and legal certainty in the protective action, guaranteeing the collegial and interdisciplinary nature of the measures taken.

Very often reports of abandonment result in guardianship "ex lege" of the minor by the administration, which implies suspension of parental custody due to non-compliance or impossible or inappropriate exercise of the duties of protection. Similarly, risk situations are usually protected with a guardian measure which can be voluntary or involuntary, and which does not imply the withdrawal of parental rights. Risk situations may occur at the request of the parent or guardian if they cannot take care of the minor due to serious circumstances. Finally, both tutelage and guardianship can result in an unlikely return to the parents, leading to either adoption (per judicial resolution) or placement in a residential care center. Figure 17.2 details the child protection system's processes determined by the aforementioned laws.

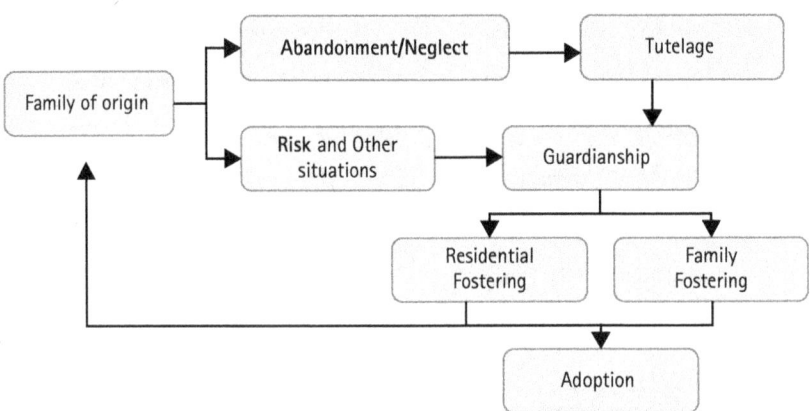

Figure 17.2 A simplified sequence of the most significant processes that have shaped the child protection system according to Law 1/1996, Law 26/2015, and Organic Law 8/2015. *Source: Observatory for childhood.* 2017. Statistical data bulletin of protection measures to childhood, number 18. Data 2015. Ministry of Health, Social Services and Equality, Spain.

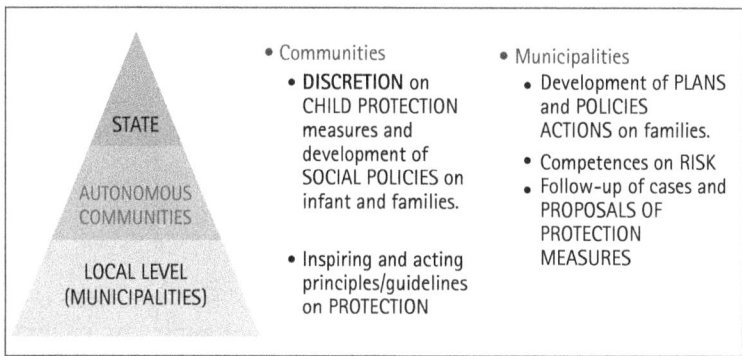

Figure 17.3 Autonomous and governmental competences in the Spanish territory *Source*: Adaptation based on information provided by Esther Abad, head of the Child Protection Area of the Community of Madrid.

Nature of Social Provisions Allocated to Protect Children

As mentioned throughout this chapter, full power in the matter of social assistance is transferred to the Autonomous Communities. Law 6/1995 declares that the General Directorate of the Family and the Minor assumes the role of public entity of protection and the tutelage and guardianship responsibilities within the Community of Madrid. However, its work is dependent on the indispensable and necessary role of the Local Entities: City Council Social Services, CAIs, Family Support Commissions and other social agents, which, together, form the Public System of Protection in the Community of Madrid. The principle of local control is very strong in Spain. Regardless of the jurisdiction (the municipality of Madrid, for example, has approximately 3.5 million residents whereas some other municipalities of the Community of Madrid may have no more than 150 residents), local area have a child protection network, though they range widely in their resources.

Social Provisions at the Local Level

As shown in Figure 17.3, the interaction and distinction between the local and regional level are the backbone of the child protection system in Spain. At the local level (Madrid city or municipality), the social services and resources of the municipality are mainly devoted to the detection of cases (i.e., prevention), through interventions that deal with risk. Similarly, as dictated by social services' decisions at the regional level (Community of Madrid), these services monitor and apply intervention measures with children and families who are within the protection system. Within Madrid's social services, there is a specialized social care area called the Children and Family Area, which provides a total of 11 main resources for families, children, and adolescents. They are primarily the CAIs, Support Center to Families (CAF), and other resources such as: Children's Day Care Center, Big House Project, Leisure Spaces for Adolescents, Centers for Adolescents and Youth ASPA, Social Education Service, Family Support Service with Minors, support and accommodation resources, Family Meeting Point (PEF), and Access to Minor Data and Family. CAIs and CAFs are detailed below.

The Community of Madrid has a population of 6,578,079 inhabitants; 786,164 (~12%) of them are under the age of 18 (Municipal Register of Madrid, 2017). The latest report of the statistical bulletin of the Observatory of Youth (Statistical Bulletin on Child Protection Measures, 2017, p. 59) shows that 5,496 (~1%) children were subject to protection measures, of which 2,768 were "ex lege" guardianships. These minors enter the protection system through the basic social services center (CSS) or the childcare centers (CAIs), which constitute Madrid's organizational infrastructure for the protection of minors. The CAI centers, of which there are 13, receive all cases in which the child is suspected of being at serious risk or presumed to be neglected. Cases of sexual abuse, petitions from the courts and public prosecutor's office, and communications from other services related to minors are directly received in these centers. They are all public institutions dependent on the city council. In the CAIs, psychological, social, and educational interventions are implemented with minors and their families with social or abandonment risk. The following services are offered:

1) *Initial risk evaluation of minors.* Appropriate investigation is initiated in the event of a possible risk situation for a child or adolescent.
2) *Evaluation of the family situation* and, where appropriate, the lack of protection of the minors. Once completed, the results of the evaluation and a family improvement plan will be presented to the family.
3) *Special family treatment.* Develop the family improvement plan with the objective of avoiding the separation of the child from the family or reunifying in the shortest possible time.
4) *Accompaniment and supervision of families that are not in treatment.* Develop the family improvement plan with families that do not accept or do not need treatment.
5) *Solution of conflicts.* Specific attention to minors and families, users of the CAI, who face conflict situations within their family dynamic.
6) *Technical support* to professionals and resources that work with minors. Advice given to professionals in the field of child protection.
7) *Prevention of child maltreatment.* Training for professionals in education and health, and for social entities to promote early detection.
8) *Family follow-up once the care is finished.* Interviews with the family to verify their situation six and 12 months after the intervention.

Another important specialized resource is the Support Center or Families (CAFs)of which there are seven centers in Madrid's municipality. The CAFs are devoted to prevention for slight risks with minors and their families in social difficulty where there is no lack of protection but who need intervention or support. CAF programs include parent training, mediation between parents and child, and attention to violence in the family. CAFs have interdisciplinary teams of family intervention experts formed by professionals from the fields of psychology, law, social work, mediation and administrative staff. Access to the CAF can also be direct, without requiring a referral. CAF services are free of charge to families in the city of Madrid.

The CAFs provide the following services:

- *Information to families and professionals*: face-to-face, telephone or telematics.
- *Social orientation*: social attention to families. Information and referral to programs or resources, if applicable.
- *Legal advice*: information and guidance from the legal point of view in matters related to the family (filiation, dissolution of marital economic regime, divorce, breakup of couple, inheritance, etc.).
- *Psychological care in the event of family difficulty*: orientation and intervention, depending on the family situation.
- *Care and prevention of violent relationships in the family*: intervention aimed at all family members, both those who suffer and those who exercise violence, to reduce it and prevent future situations of violence.
- *Family mediation*: professional support to help cope with and manage conflict situations, promoting consensual agreements (amidst breakup of couple, care of the elderly or dependents, intergenerational discrepancies, etc.).
- *A relationship space for families with children from 0 to 3 years old*: groups of fathers and mothers and children in which, through play and information, they develop affective bonding, exchange experiences and create networks.
- *Family training*: group reflection and training activities, aimed at families and professionals, for the improvement of family coexistence conditions. Monthly training program at https://www.comunidad.madrid/servicios/asuntos-sociales/centros-apoyo-encuentro-familiar.
- *Community participation (collaborate with the social network)*: promotion and coordination of social networking and the participation of families in community activities.
- *Banks of Time*: networks of mutual help among citizens with services exchange where the value unit is time.

Social Provisions by the Autonomous Communities

With the purpose of situating the protection system within the Community of Madrid, a brief (though simplified) explanation of its governance structure follows. The same way there is a president of the state government with his Ministry of the Presidency, the regional level also has a president of the Community with a Counsellor of the

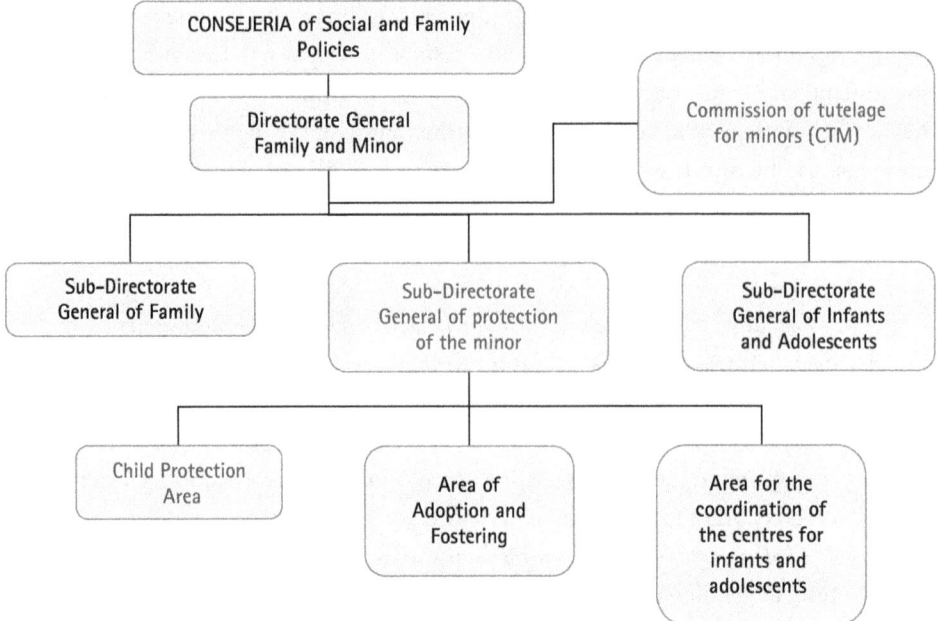

Figure 17.4 The organizational chart of the Social and Family Policy *Consejeria Source*: Adaptation based on information provided by Esther Abad, head of the Child Protection Area of the Community of Madrid.

Presidency. Likewise, just as the state level has several ministries, the regional level (the communities) has several councils (i.e., *Consejeria*). The entire system of protection of minors is allocated to the Community of Madrid under the Ministry of Social Policies and Family. Figure 17.4 displays the complete organization chart of the Social and Family Policy *Consejeria*.

Within this Ministry, the General Directorate of the Family and the Minor, in accordance with Laws 121/1988[2] and 71/92, regulates the guardianship and custody of children procedure. Within this process, the Guardianship Commission of the Minor assumes responsibility for children who are in a situation of abandonment in the Community of Madrid and provides care in residential centers. This is one of the measures to ensure children's subjective needs are met, and full moral and material assistance of the minors are protected (under tutelage) and/or saved (guardianship) by the Community of Madrid.

The Commission for the Guardianship of Minors (CTM) was created in 1988 (Law 49/1988) as a collegial body where tutelary action resides. This occurred as a result of two processes: one is the nationwide legal dismantling of child protection, and the other is decentralization (i.e., creating specific institutions for the protection of minors in each

---

[2] Exercise of Guardianship and Custody for Minors; see http://www.madrid.org/wleg_pub/secure/normativas/contenidoNormativa.jsf?opcion=VerHtml&idnorma=489&word=S&wordperfect=N&pdf=S#no-back-button.

of the different Autonomous Communities). The CTM is a collegiate body of higher decision and execution regarding the protection of minors in the community of Madrid. Some of its functions are as follows:

- Assume and exercise the measures for the protection of minors within the territory of the community of Madrid, while considering the best interests of the minor in accordance with legislation.
- Confirm suitability and acceptance of national and international offers for adoption and foster care applicants.
- Establish guidelines and general criteria for the best exercise of protection actions for minor's residence in the Community of Madrid.

CTM's decisions are supervised by the public prosecutor, and their agreements can be challenged directly by corresponding parties at the family courts of Madrid, with no requirement of claim or prior administrative appeal.

The members of such a commission are:

- President: the Director-Manager of the Madrid Institute for the Family and the Minor (IMFM);
- Vice President: the Assistant Director General of Resources and Programs of the IMFM;
- Secretary: an IMFM official;
- Members: responsible for the different IMFM Areas (i.e., Protection, Adoption and Foster Care, Coordination of Centers, and Children and Adolescents) and Manager of the ARRMI (Madrid Community Agency for the Reeducation and Reinsertion of the Minor Offender);
- A lawyer of the General Law of the Community of Madrid.

A series of guidelines dictates CTM decision-making: 1) act in the best interest of the minor, 2) keep the child in his/her own partner/family environment, 3) utilize preventive interventions, 4) provide resources to children after removal, 5) keep siblings together, 6) limit interventions to a maximum of two years, 7) coordinate between institutions. CTM's ordinary procedure is detailed in Figure 17.5, and for comparison their emergency procedure is detailed in Figure 17.6.

Financing Child Protection Services

Budget allocation for the protection of children is a complex task. It requires reviewing nationwide health, social welfare, and education or benefits then estimating child protection processes within each. To add complexity, many of the competences regarding child protection are transferred to the regional and local level Autonomous Communities

C.T.M. ORDINARY PROCEDURE

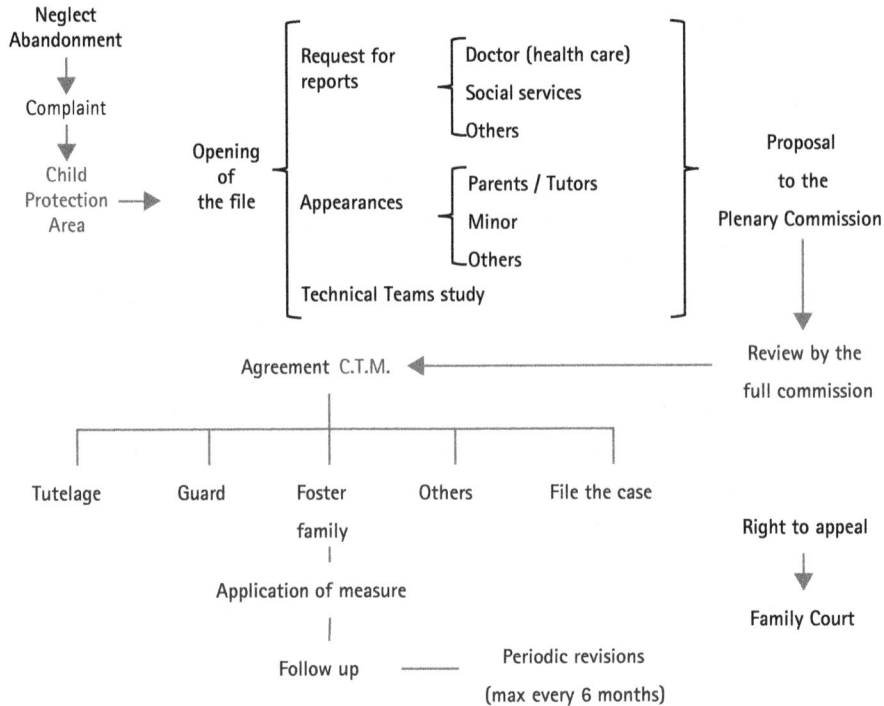

Figure 17.5 CTM ordinary procedure *Source*: Adaptation based on information provided by Esther Abad, head of the Child Protection Area of the Community of Madrid

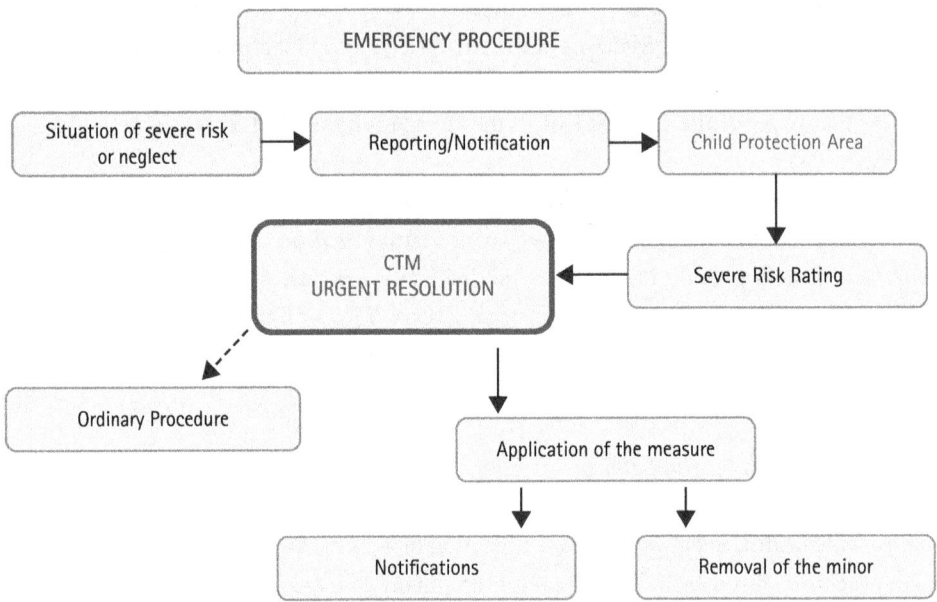

Figure 17.6 CTM emergency procedure *Source*: Adaptation based on information provided by Esther Abad, head of the Child Protection Area of the Community of Madrid.

and municipalities, respectively. Organizations, such as UNICEF or the Platform for Children, have been involved in budget tracking for years, and provide the following information.

According to data from the Observatory of Childhood (2017), social protection expenditure of family and children from all public administrations was reduced from 8,832 million euros in 2009 to 6,431 million euros in 2014 (2,401 million euros (27%) less). A small part was recovered in 2015, yet still remaining 21% less than in 2009. The cumulative reduction in these six years was 11,544 million euros. Spain allocates 1.3% of its GDP to child social protection, far short of the European Union's average of 2.3%.

At present, the community of Madrid does not provide specific statistics on the cost in protection assigned to children and families. According to a UNICEF report (2018), data provided by Madrid's regional ministry of economy and finance are based on a functional classification of expenditure that was established in the 2015 community budget. Thus, in the general budget of the community of Madrid for 2017, there are two programs assigned to the care and protection of children and families. Total investment budgeted in both programs totals 98,045,753 euros, which represents 0.0465% of the GDP of the community of Madrid. A comparison over the last five years reveals that investment in childhood and family in Madrid experienced an increase of more than 5 million euros between 2013 (105,166,375 euros) and 2015 (110,266,978 euros) with a reduction by more than 12 million in 2017 (98,045,753). The evolution of expenditures attributed to family and minors demonstrates a cumulative decrease of 14% over the last five years.

Reports on the Spanish compliance to the Convention on the Rights of the Child (Committee on the Rights of the Child, 2018) expressed great concern about the country's little investment for the protection of children. It also recommended that:

> the State: (a) Adopts a child-rights approach when drawing up public budgets, specifying clear allocations to children, including specific indicators and a tracking system to monitor and assess the adequacy, efficacy, and equitability of the distribution of resources allocated for implementation; define budgetary lines for children in disadvantaged or marginalized situations that may require affirmative social measures and make sure those budgetary lines are protected even in situations of economic crisis, natural disasters or any other emergencies. (Committee on the Rights of the Child, 2018, p. 3)

Additionally, although not easily quantifiable though comparable by the resources offered to children in different communities, an uneven distribution of wealth throughout the Spanish territory creates a difference in budgetary items destined to protect children in the different communities.

Table 17.1 Minors served by the system from 2012 to 2017

		2012	2013	2014	2015	2016	2017
Tutelage "ex lege"	Abs.	29,703	29,291	27,626	25,952	27,160	29,583
	Rate	356.9	350.7	311.5	311.3	325.7	354.7
Total guardianships	Abs.	4,413	5,033	4,177	4,724	4,753	5,161
	Rate	53.0	60.3	52.4	56.7	57.0	61.9
In assessment/measure of previous support, a protective measure	Abs.	SD	7,157	11,064	11,952	11,989	12,749
	Rate	—	85.7	145.4	160.5	143.8	157.1
Rate 1/100,000 people under 18 years old							

Source: *Observatory for childhood*. 2020. Statistical data bulletin of protection measures to childhood, number 18. Data 2017. Ministry of Health, Social Services and Equality, Spain

How Many Children? Reasons and Types of Measures

The Ministry of Health, Consumption and Social Welfare has a Directorate General for Services for the Family and Children, with a dependent Children's Observatory.[3] The latter launched an online application in 2014 called BOLETINF to collect data on child protection throughout the Spanish territory and has managed to quantify the data in detail since 2015. There are no published comparative and detailed data with public access prior to this initiative, so BOLETINF represents a tremendous advancement in terms of information, practices and homogenization of services in the different autonomies. Its annual report allows access to the most updated data.

STATISTICS: NATIONAL LEVEL

To start, in 2015, there were an estimated 8,119,000 children aged 0 to 17 years (INE [Instituto Nacional de Estadísticas], 2017; Ministry of Education, Culture, and Sport, 2016; UNICEF, 2016b). The same year, there was an increase in the number of minors under some form of protection, from 42,628 in 2015 to 43,902 in 2016. This is attributed to the significant rise in "guardianships ex-lege,"[4] from 25,952 in 2015 to 27,160 in 2016. The time series in Table 17.1 reveals a constant fall in the number of "ex lege" guardianships from 2012 to 2015. In 2016, however, the trend is reversed, although it does not reach the height of the 2014 figures. As for custodians, the figures remain very stable, and have even fallen below the maximum reached in 2013. Also stable are the number of minors in assessment or with a measure of support prior to the adoption of a protective measure.

---

[3] http://www.observatoriodelainfancia.mscbs.gob.es/.

[4] In the case of parental rights' abandonment, resolutions are adopted by the corresponding public entity and the child's protection is assumed by law. A different resolution is issued for each affected child. In practice, the exercise of guardianship is implicit.

Data indicate a clear tendency for short stays in centers and a preference, in the medium and long term, for measures representative of family permanence. The total number of children in residential care increased, from 13,596 in 2015 to 14,104 in 2016. As in previous years, the most remarkable differences by sex occur in residential care, with a clear predominance of males in age groups 11–14 and 15–17. Foster care decreased slightly, from 20,172 in 2015 to 19,641 in 2016. Aligned with historical trends, in absolute terms, foster care (70.7% with extended family and 29.3% with non-family) is still the main protection measure adopted by the protection services of autonomous communities and cities. Age groups of 11–14 years are prevalent, without any differences in the number of girls and boys (Statistical Bulletin of Child Protection Measures, 2017, p. 19).

STATISTICS: REGIONAL LEVEL

Turning to the regional level, the number of children in out-of-home care in the community of Madrid are 4,048, as of December 31, 2016, of which 1,586 (39.17%) are in residential care and 2,462 (60.82%) in foster care. In comparison with other autonomies, Madrid ranked second in number of supervised children in 2015, behind Andalusia, with 9,552 (UNICEF, 2018).

CHILD ABUSE

In Article 19 of the United Nations Convention on the Rights of the Child (1989), maltreatment is defined as: "All violence, physical or mental harm or abuse, negligence or negligent treatment, mistreatment or exploitation, while the child is under the custody of their parents, a guardian or any other person who is in charge of them." Article 172 of the Spanish Civil Code defines maltreatment as a "situation that occurs in fact because of non-compliance, or the impossible or inadequate exercise of the protection duties established by the laws for the custody of minors, when they are deprived of the necessary moral or material assistance." To track protection interventions related to maltreatment, cases are registered in our country by an online application of the unified registry of cases of suspected child maltreatment (RUMI). Unlike the data on protection measures (which are downloaded into the BULLETINby a single person in charge of each Community), RUMI collects notifications of both individual cases and those from pre-existing databases by operators throughout different protection services (e.g., police, education), bolstering the reliability of the records. Before 2012, not all operators used the RUMI database. However, since 2014, all the Autonomous Communities upload data to RUMI and in accordance with Law 26/2015, which states the necessity to develop and maintain this statistical operation. Table 17.2 provides statistics about reported cases by severity and Table 17.3 provides reported cases by child's age. Looking at the age group, trends demonstrate significant increases in the age groups 11–14 and 15–17.

However, the Childhood Observatory explains that the real prevalence of child maltreatment is unknown, since most of the cases are not detected. Given that the very nature

Table 17.2 Trend of notifications by severity

		2012	2013	2014	2015	2016	2017
Severe	Abs.	4,469	4,966	6,531	5,730	5,462	5,713
	Rate	54.8	59.5	73.6	68.7	68.7	71.8
Light-moderate	Abs.	4,591	7,406	7,882	8,088	9,107	11,064
	Rate	56.2	88.7	88.9	97.0	114.5	139.1
TOTAL	Abs.	9,060	12,372	14,413	13,818	14,569	16,777
	Rate	111.0	148.1	162.5	165.8	183.2	211.0
Rate 1/100,000 people under 18 years old							

Source: *Observatory for childhood 2020*. Statistical data bulletin of protection measures to childhood, number 18. Data 2017. Ministry of Health, Social Services and Equality, Spain.

Table 17.3 Trend of notifications by age group

		2012	2013	2014	2015	2016	2017
0–3 years old	Abs.	2,088	2,366	2,592	2,324	2,240	2,498
	Rate	25.6	28.3	29.2	27.9	28.2	31,4
4–6	Abs.	1,311	1,718	2,034	1,810	1,751	1,787
	Rate	16.1	20.6	22.9	21.7	22.0	22.5
7–10	Abs.	1,645	2,316	2,676	2,664	2,708	2,928
	Rate	20.2	27.7	30.2	32.0	34.1	36.8
11–14	Abs.	2,116	3,289	3,840	3,760	3,992	4,329
	Rate	25.9	39.4	43.3	45.1	50.2	54.4
15–17	Abs.	1,900	2,683	3,271	3,260	3,878	5,223
	Rate	23.3	32.1	36.9	39.1	48.8	65.7
TOTAL	Abs.	9,060	12,372	14,413	13,818	14,569	16,765
	Rate	111.0	148.1	162.5	165.8	183.2	210.8
Rate 1/100,000 people under 18 years old							

Source: *Observatory for childhood*. 2020. Statistical data bulletin of protection measures to childhood, number 18. Data 2017. Ministry of Health, Social Services and Equality, Spain.

of the problem is often originating within the family itself, barriers to reporting include the fear of reporting by the assaulted child and insufficient training of professionals. It is estimated that the cases detected are only a portion of actual incidence. Regarding the number of cases detected, the most relevant fact is that there is a constant growth in the number of recorded cases of abuse since RUMI's inception.

As for the types of abuse, displayed in Table 17.4, two aspects are noteworthy. First, and standing out above the others, is negligence, which represents almost 50% of the

Table 17.4 Types of maltreatment									
Sexual abuse		Emotional		Physical		Neglect		TOTAL	
Abs.	Rate	Abs.	Rate	Abs.	Rate	Abs.	Rate		
828	10.4	4,752	59.8	3,535	44.5	8,999	113.2	18,114	
Rate 1/100,000 people under 18 years old									

Notes: Sexual abuse: involvement of children in sexual activities to meet the needs of an adult. Forms as per action type: 1) With physical contact: rape, incest, pornography, child prostitution, sodomy, touching, sexual stimulation. 2) No physical contact: indecent solicitation of a child or explicit verbal seduction, sexual act performance or masturbation in the presence of a child, exposure of the sexual organs to a child, promoting child prostitution, pornography. a) Forms by omission: Do not attend to the needs of the child and their protection in the area of sexuality b) Forms: Do not give credibility to the child, neglect demand for help, do not educate in assertiveness, mother who prefers "not seeing"—passive consent in incest, lack of training/ information, lack of protection.

Emotional abuse: Action capable of originating psychological-psychiatric symptoms by affecting child's needs according to the different developmental states and characteristics of the child. Forms: reject, ignore, terrorize, isolate, corrupt or involve a child in antisocial activities. Forms by omission: affective deprivation, not addressing the affective needs of the child (love, stability, security, stimulation, support, protection, role in the family, self-esteem, etc.), pedagogical abuse.

Physical abuse: Any act, not accidental, that causes physical damage or illness in the child or places him in a situation of serious risk of suffering. Forms: skin lesions (ecchymosis, wounds, bruises, abrasions, scalds, burns, bites, traumatic alopecia), fractures, mechanical asphyxiation, stripping, poisoning, Münchausen syndrome by proxy.

Neglect: A form of physical abuse exercised by omission by neglecting the needs of the child and the duties of care and protection or inadequate care of the child. Forms: inattention, abandonment, non-organic growth retardation, "street children" or unaccompanied minors, constantly dirty, physical problems or unsatisfied medical needs or absence of routine medical care (e.g., vaccinations).

total notifications. Second, this data is collected from almost all autonomous communities, with the notable exception of the Balearic Islands (i.e., a Spanish archipelago with a population of over 1 million inhabitants).

Each of the protection measures with minors in our country is exhaustively monitored, involving the coordination of various sectors in child protection, as can be seen in Figure 17.7.

Issues and Trends

In this section, we will briefly describe some of the most urgent challenges facing the protection system in our country, such as the work to determine the best interest of the child, the urgent reality of unaccompanied foreign minors, and the extreme poverty of a large number of minors, including the violence suffered by children.

Best Interest of the Child

Dating back to Organic Law 1/1996, the principle of the "best interests of the minor" is expressly included in Article 2, and we find references to it throughout the legal system, motivated by the special situation of vulnerability of minors and their need for protection.

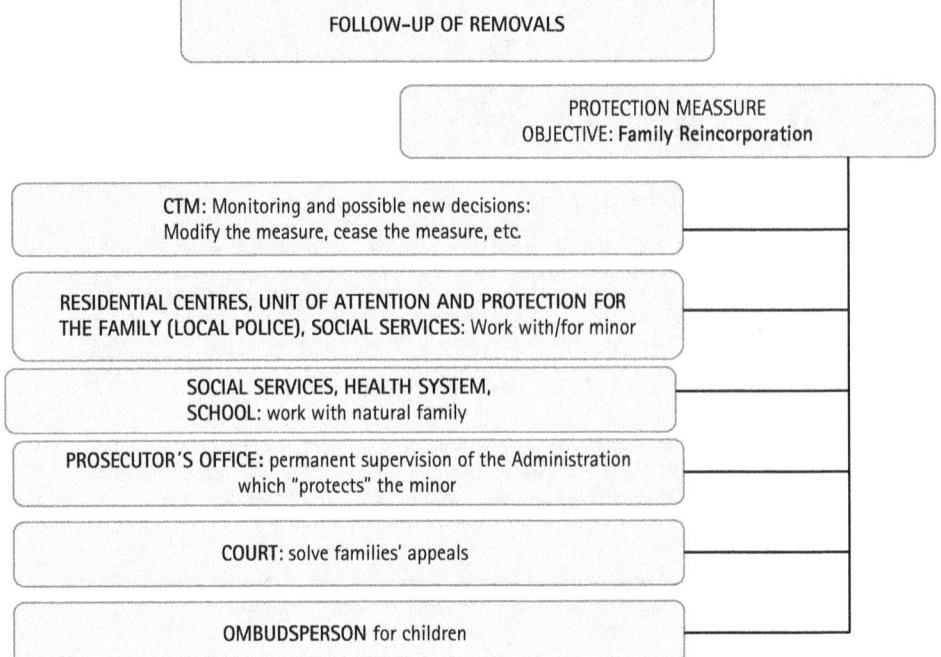

Figure 17.7 Sectors of child protection.

Over the years, this concept has experienced different interpretations since it is an undefined legal concept. Its flexible meaning depends on several social, intellectual, and legal variables among others, which results in a study of each individual case depending on the specific circumstances.

Until the publication of Law 8/2015 and Law 26/2015, state regulation did not include a technique for evaluating the child's best interests. Finding a determination for this concept was one of the most complicated tasks judges faced when making decisions affecting minors. Although this principle is included in legislation, and in fact is considered by the administration and the judiciary in decisions affecting children, a uniform process was missing. With enactment of these laws, the understanding and application of the aforementioned principle was standardized to account for the persistent differences in practice in each Autonomous Community. Therefore, the general principle has been established in law, but it is applied differently, case by case. It also reinforces the right of children to be heard and participate in all matters that concern them (UNICEF, 2018).

The best interests of the child has become a concept in the protection of minors with the following connotations (Moreno Torres Sanz, 2017: 1) a substantive and subjective right of the minor, which requires that when making a decision about a minor, his "best interest" "has been previously evaluated"; 2) as a general principle of information and interpretation, and when arising different interpretations of a rule, the one that reflects the best interests of the child will always be chosen; 3) as a procedural rule. If the procedure stipulated for each case is not followed, the best interest of the child is undoubtedly prejudiced and court appeals will occur.

The measures adopted will be in the minor's best interest, regardless of what is requested by the parties. The new regulation establishes a technique for assessing this condition[5] should other interests concur, as administrative and judicial proceedings include affected third parties, including parents, grandparents, siblings and close friends. In anticipation of this scenario, this regulation prioritizes the best interests of the child while valuing the fundamental rights of these parties (Save the Children, 2017). With the implementation of the new laws, the best interests of the child must always be evaluated by professionals and legal operators, as well as by institutions (whether public or private), courts, and legislative bodies. With the ruling of each decision, resolution or technical report issued, decision makers must specify the criteria and values that have been considered to confirm their accurate application.

However, even today, after the laws of 2015, it is argued that the criteria and elements established for this concept are broad and their formulation still leaves a gap for interpretation. Sometimes, even the scope and meaning of the notion can vary from one Autonomous Community to another. Ultimately, and regardless of the importance and significance of these measures, a more explicit consideration is needed: "that the child's right to have his or her best interests taken as a primary consideration is appropriately integrated and consistently interpreted and applied in all legislative, administrative and judicial proceedings and decisions and in all relevant policies, programs and projects that have an impact on children" (Committee on the Rights of the Child, 2018, p. 4).

Unaccompanied Minors

It is well known that Spain is the natural border of southern Europe and the Mediterranean. Additionally, Ceuta and Melilla, the only "autonomous" cities, are among the four recognized main immigration entry routes into Europe. Moreover, 98% of unaccompanied foreign minors who enter the country do so through these Spanish territories—a relevant fact when considering social and political implications for ervening with unaccompanied foreign minors (UAMs).

The arrival of UAMs in Spain has increased year after year. Some 6,600 minors were placed in residential care in 2017, that is, 60% more than in 2016, when 4,087 minors were under custody (State Attorney General's Office, 2016). Similarly, this is a 42% increase on 2015, when UAMs accounted for 85% more than in 2014. Out of the

---

[5] Evaluating and Determining the Best Interests of the Minor: https://www.savethechildren.es/sites/defa ult/files/imce/docs/ism_pdf_6_octubre_docx_0.pdf.

unaccompanied minors who arrived in 2016, rough estimates indicate that 89% were male compared to 13.6% female.[6] A significant increase in minors of foreign origin in residential care is evident, with 27.02% of the total children received in 2015 compared to 28.9% in 2016 (Observatory of Childhood, 2017).

According to Observatory of Childhood and Youth data (2017), both in 2015 and 2016, Ceuta and Melilla were the regions with the highest rates of assisted children (Tutelages and guardianships). These minors represent 90% of the protective measures carried out in these regions, leading this author to recall the aforementioned 98% who access the country through these cities, which are ports of entry for migrant children. The Committee on the Rights of the Child (2018) warn of the extreme emergency that these children convey: 16% of foreign arrivals to Spain are unaccompanied minors. Debate is intense in Spain about the question of their status as "foreigners" since this condition may prevail over that of minor (UNICEF Madrid, 2018), overriding the application of the best interest of the minor. The Community of Madrid, as well as Ceuta and Melilla (the main recipients of these minors) have attempted a number of strategies and intervention models to respond to the protection needs of these children, in coordination with local entities and social organizations. There is still a long way to go to identify protection measures that respond to the general needs of these children, as well as to their specific needs as unaccompanied foreigners. In any case, it is essential to adopt a human rights approach to fight the stigma that surrounds these children at the community, local, and regional levels (UNICEF, 2018).

Extreme Poverty and Violence

To conclude, there are two urgent child protection issues in Spain.

The first is a problem that would not seem relevant to a country like Spain, given its 14th place in the world economic ranking of the International Monetary Fund (2020)—extreme child poverty. A total of 1,300,000 children in the country are in a situation of severe poverty (ECV, 2016). In most cases, these are children whose parents have a very low educational level; children with parents of foreign origin; or children who come from single-parent families (85% of cases are single mothers, a profile which is becoming an increasingly strong predictor of extreme poverty for the child; UNICEF, 2018).

The second problem, also partially invisible, is that of violence against minors. One in every two crimes of sexual abuse in Spain is committed against a minor, and between 20% and 40% of these abuses are committed by older children, adolescents, and people under

---

[6] Because data are collected at the local level, the aggregated data do not necessarily equal 100%.

21 (UNICEF, 2016a). Half of the sexual abuse cases reported are suffered by children and adolescents (3,725 complaints of violence against children recorded; Fernández-Oruña et al., 2016). This high rate of violence against children is mostly attributed to cultural patterns where children are considered family property, not full citizens and/or adults. Even the Committee on the Rights of the Child (2018) has drawn attention to the lack of laws to protect children from violence and the need for a comprehensive law against violence to children to raise awareness of the problem.

Conclusion

Throughout this summary of the Spanish child protection system, continuous reference has been made to areas of improvement identified by the Committee on the Rights of the Child (2018), but there are strengths as well. The observations of the Committee on the Rights of the Child also include the positive actions that have been carried out in recent years, such as the approval of the *Second Strategic Plan for Children and Adolescents 2013–2016*, the National Action Plan for social inclusion, and the implementation of extraordinary funds for child poverty and the comprehensive plan to support the family.

Progress in child protection has been very considerable in just 21 years, since the 1996 law. In fact, the last two laws of 2015 have put the country on the right direction. However, as shown throughout this chapter, there is still a long way to go, mainly in terms of violence against minors, unaccompanied foreign minors, and child poverty. These are inexplicable paradoxes in a country that shines for being family-oriented, a country that has also internationally led the number of donations and transplants for 26 years. Spain is a generous and intergenerationally committed country, but it is in desperate need of more education and training regarding the child protection issues mentioned. With this improvement, Spain can celebrate her cultural imagery, and flourish, giving way to more awareness and commitment to non-violence against children in this Mediterranean society.

References

Berrocal Lanzarot, A. I. (2015). *Las instituciones de protección a la infancia y adolescencia: atención inmediata, situación de riesgo y desamparo, tutela administrativa, y acogimiento familiar y residencial tras la Ley 26/2015.* La Ley, Derecho de Familia: Revista Jurídica sobre Familia y Menores, Nº3.

Boletín Estadístico de Medidas de protección a la infancia. (2017). *Statistical Bulletin on Child Protection Measures. Bulletin number.* Observatorio de la Infancia. Informes, Estudios e Investigación 2017. Madrid: Ministerio de Sanidad, Servicios Sociales e Igualdad.

Committee on the Rights of the Child. (2018, March 5). *Concluding observations on the combined fifth and sixth periodic reports of Spain: Committee on the Rights of the Child.* Retrieved from: https://digitallibrary. un.org/record/1476613. Available at: http://tbinternet.ohchr.org/_layouts/treatybodyexternal/Download. aspx?symbolno=CRC/C/ESP/CO/5-6&Lang=en.

ECV (2016). Living conditions Survey. Retrieved from www.ine.es/prensa/ecv_2016.pdf.

Fernández-Oruña, J. C, Álvarez, J. L. G., Jiménez, F. S., Sánchez, D. H., Ossorio, J. J. L., Moreno, F. M., García, M. R., Pérez, V. G., Orozco, A. M. S., and Martín, M. A. G. (2017). *Informe sobre delitos contra la libertad e indemnidad sexual en España*. Ministerio del Interior. Available at: http://www.interior.gob. es/documents/10180/0/Informe+delitos+contra+la+libertad+e+indemnidad+sexual+2017.pdf/da546c6c-36c5-4854-864b-a133f31b4dde.

INE. (2017, June 29). *Cifras de Población a 1 de enero de 2017: Estadística de Migraciones 2016*. Available at: http://www.ine.es/prensa/cp_2017_p.pdf.

International Monetary Fund (2020). Spain: Selected Issues; IMF Country Report nº. 20/299.

Mármol, S., Serrano, H., and UNICEF Comité Andalucía. (2014). *Guía Básica para la creación de Consejos de infancia y adolescencia en el ámbito local con enfoque de género*. UNICEF and Ciudades amigas de la infancia. Available at: http://ciudadesamigas.org/wp-content/uploads/2015/09/consejos_enfoque_ genero.pdf.

Ministry of Education, Culture, and Sport. (2016). *Main characteristics of Spanish families according to the level of participation in school education*. Available at: https://sede.educacion.gob.es/publiventa/principales-cara cteristicas-de-las-familias-espanolas-segun-el-nivel-de-participacion-en-la-educacion-escolar/educacion-politica-educativa/20767.

Moreno Torres, J. (2015). *Modificación del Sistema de Protección a la infancia y a la adolescencia. Guia para profesionales y agentes sociales*. Save the Children.

Moreno Torres Sanz, J. (2017). *Cómo aplicar el Interés superior del menor en casos de desamparo: Una Herramienta Para Profesionales*: Save the Children.

Municipal Register of Madrid. (2017). *Statistics*. Available at: http://www.madrid.es/portales/munimadrid/ es/Inicio/El-Ayuntamiento/Estadistica/Areas-de-informacion-estadistica/Demografia-y-poblacion/Cifras-de-poblacion/Padron-Municipal-de-Habitantes-explotacion-estadistica%20/?vgnextfmt=default&vgnext oid=e5613f8b73639210VgnVCM1000000b205a0aRCRD&vgnextchannel=a4eba53620e1a210VgnVC M1000000b205a0aRCRD.

Observatory of Childhood. (2017). *Boletín de datos estadísticos de medidas de protección a la infancia número 18*. Statistical data bulletin on child protection measures number 18. Available at: https://observatoriodelai nfancia.mdsocialesa2030.gob.es/productos/pdf/Boletinproteccionalainfancia18accesible.pdf. Available at: https://observatoriodelainfancia.mdsocialesa2030.gob.es/.

Observatory of childhood. (2020). *Boletín de datos estadísticos de medidas de protección a la infancia número 21*. Statistical data bulletin of protection measures to childhood, number 21. Data 2018. Ministry of Health, Social Services and Equality, Spain. Available at: https://observatoriodelainfancia.mdsocialesa2030.gob.es/ estadisticas/estadisticas/PDF/Boletin_21_proteccion_accesible.pdf.

Platform for Children in Spain. (2017). Diagnosis of the situation for children in Spain before the implementa-tion of the European Child Guarantee. Available at: https://www.unicef.org/eca/sites/unicef.org.eca/files/ 2021-11/Spanish%20Deep%20Dive%20Literature%20review%20EN.pdf.

Save the Children. (2017). *Instrumento para la evaluación y determinación del interés superior del menor en la declaración de la situación de desamparo*. Available at: https://www.savethechildren.es/sites/default/files/ imce/docs/ism_pdf_6_octubre_docx_0.pdf.

State Attorney General's Office. (2016). Conclusions of Immigration Delegate Prosecutors Sessions. Available at: https://www.fiscal.es/documents/20142/160400/CONCLUSIONES+JORNA DAS+EXTRANJER%C3%8DA+2016.pdf/eaed6951-b285-d996-376a-32269b8971df?t=153260 5078839.

UNICEF. (2016a). *Abuso sexual contra niños, niñas y adolescentes: Una guía para tomar acciones y proteger sus derechos*. Fondo de Naciones Unidas para la infancia. Available at: https://www.unicef.org/ecuador/protecc ion-AbusoSexual_contra_NNyA-2016_(1).pdf.

UNICEF. (2016b). *The state of the world's children 2016 statistical tables*. Available at: https://data.unicef.org/ resources/state-worlds-children-2016-statistical-tables.

UNICEF (2018). Children´s participation in the work of NHRIs. National human rights institutions (NHRIs) Series. Available at: www.unicef.org/eca/sites/unicef.org.eca/files/2019-02/NHRI_Participation.pdf.

UNICEF Madrid. (2018). *Los Derechos de la Infancia y la Adolescencia en la Comunidad de Madrid: Agenda 2030*. Available at: https://www.unicef.es/sites/unicef.es/files/comunicacion/derechos_infancia_y_adolescencia_en_comunidad_de_madrid.pdf.

Child Protection and Children's Services in Switzerland

Stefan Schnurr *and* Joel Gautschi

Abstract

This chapter notes Switzerland's child protection and children's services. The core principles of subsidiary and federalism are upheld at all levels of policy-making and policy implementation. Thus, the country's political system and federalism have a significant impact on the institutionalization of child protection and children's services. The distinctiveness of child protection in Switzerland is due to the diversity of its institutional arrangements linked to numerous policies, programs, and cultures of decision making. Decisions on child protection measures are related to the requirement that a child's best interests are threatened and the parents are unwilling or unable to remedy the situation.

Key Words: Switzerland, child protection, children's services, subsidiary, federalism, policy-making, decisions, maltreatment, political system

Switzerland is a multilingual country of 8.6 million inhabitants, including a total of 1.5 million (17.9%) children under the age of 18 years (as of 2019; Swiss Statistics, 2020b) and 1.3 million family households with children under the age of 25 years (as of 2018, Swiss Statistics, 2020a). The four national languages are German (62%), French (23%), Italian (8%) and Romansch (0.5%) (Federal Chancellery, 2021). Switzerland is a federation of 26 cantons divided into 2,172 municipalities (as of 2021; ibid.). With regard to the political system, the core principles of subsidiarity and federalism are upheld at all levels of policymaking and policy implementation. The understanding of subsidiarity is that responsibilities are best located at the lowest possible level. The Federal Constitution grants the cantons far-reaching powers, competences and responsibilities. The cantons' sizes vary from 16,000 to 1.5 million inhabitants. The cantons have their own constitutions, parliaments, governments, and legislation, and are important players in policymaking at the federal level. Among other policy areas, education, health, and social affairs are the responsibility of the cantons. Thus, the policy capacity of the federal state is limited (Mach & Trampusch, 2011). Similarly, the municipalities have considerable autonomy from the cantons. Both cantons and municipalities have fiscal competences and therefore the capacity to gain resources and set priorities with respect to the design and implementation of programs. Switzerland's political system and its small-scale federalism have a significant impact on the institutionalization of child protection and children's services. Instead of a uniform system, there is a patchwork of 26 variations in the cantons. The resulting commonalities and differences in children's services and child protection are assessed in more detail below. Before considering them, an overview of the extent of child maltreatment in Switzerland is provided.

Child Maltreatment in Switzerland

On a national level, there is no statistics on child maltreatment in Switzerland. The Conference of the Cantons on Child and Adult Protection (*Konferenz der Kantone für Kindes- und Erwachsenenschutz*; KOKES) maintains statistics (KOKES-Statistics) on the decisions of Child and Adult Protection Authorities (CAPAs). These statistics provide information on the measures taken on behalf of the child protection authorities in order to respond to a spectrum of children's maltreatment and endangerment. However—according to their function—they do not collect information on the reasons for responding. Therefore, to provide an (admittedly incomplete) picture of the prevalence of child maltreatment, as well as the problems triggering action by the relevant authorities and agencies, it is necessary to bring together data from different sets of statistics and data from (a limited number) of studies.

In Switzerland, the incidence of child maltreatment became a topic of public interest and research in the 1980s (Bundesrat, 1995). Schönbucher and colleagues (2011) conducted the first systematic review of 15 studies on the prevalence of child sexual abuse in Switzerland, covering the years from 1997 to 2007. The heterogeneity of the studies under review allowed only a cautious and limited conclusion. The authors concluded that, compared to international mean prevalence rates of child sexual abuse such as those presented in Pereda and colleagues (2009), which are "around 20% for girls and 8% for boys, the results reported by Swiss studies fit quite well into this picture" (Schönbucher et al., 2011, p. E6).

The first representative and standardized national population survey on the prevalence of sexual victimization among adolescents included answers from 6,749 students (15-year-olds). It revealed that "22% of girls and 8% of boys reported having experienced contact victimization" in their lives, with the most frequent type "being touched and kissed with sexual intention against your will." Furthermore, "2.6% of the girls and 0.5% of the boys reported having been victims of non-consensual (anal, oral or vaginal) penetration" (Averdijk et al., 2012, p. 7). Further findings were that "[m]ost perpetrators reported by the 15-year old respondents were estimated to be between ages 14 and 18" and "42% of victims reported that at least one incident of contact victimization was perpetrated by their partner or date" (Averdijk et al., 2012, p. 8).

The prevalence of parental corporal punishment has been examined in a recent study. Baier and colleagues (2018) conducted online-classroom interviews with 8,317 adolescents (mainly aged 17–18) in 10 cantons. The results demonstrate that 22% respondents had experienced severe violence (5% of them frequently), 54% reported they had been slapped across the face (8% of them frequently), and 36% reported they had been punched. At least one form of corporal punishment was experienced by 62% of all respondents, which amounts to almost two thirds of all young people.

The Swiss Society of Pediatrics collects data on the number of children treated in Swiss pediatric clinics (and pediatric departments) for suspected or substantiated maltreatment (see Table 18.1). In 2018, the participating pediatric units reported a total of 1,502 cases (Wopmann, 2019); in 2019, a total of 1,568 cases (Wopmann, 2020).

Another source of data on agency responses to child maltreatment are the Statistics on Victim Assistance, according to the regulations of the Federal Act on Assistance to Victims of Crime (Victims Assistance Act [VAA], 2007; see below). This law entitles individuals affected by a criminal offence against his or her physical, mental, or sexual integrity to counseling and assistance ("victim assistance"). Swiss Statistics collects data on victim consultations under the VAA, which are provided in mandatory statistics. In 2019, a total of 7,614 victim consultations referred to children (3,359 to children under 10 years; 4,225 to children aged 10–17) (Swiss Statistics, 2020c).

A recent study on the incidence of agency responses to child maltreatment in Switzerland on a national level provides further insights (Jud et al., 2018; Schmid et al., 2018; Jud et al., 2021). In an innovative, collaborative process of data collection, the research team invited organizations of the wider child protection system (social and

Table 18.1 Children treated in pediatric clinics for suspected or substantiated maltreatment in 2018 and 2019

	Cases		Proportion of types of maltreatment		Cases per 10,000 children[a]	
	2018	2019	2018	2019	2018	2019
Neglect	405	470	27.0%	30.0%	2.6	3.0
Psychological maltreatment (including exposure to domestic violence)	354	321	23.6%	20.5%	2.3	2.1
Physical maltreatment	436	486	29.0%	31.0%	2.8	3.2
Sexual abuse	297	279	19.8%	17.8%	1.9	1.8
Munchhausen-by-proxy	10	12	0.7%	0.8%	0.1	0.1
Total	1,502	1,568	100%	100%	9.7	10.2

Notes: [a] Based on the number of children (0–17) in the permanent resident population in Switzerland 2018 (1,530,231) and 2019 (1,542,361). Calculations by Stefan Schnurr using STAT-TAB of Swiss Statistics.

Source: Wopmann (2019, 2020).

health sectors, public child protection, and the penal sector) to make their standardized data available for research (Jud et al., 2018). The stratified sample included 351 agencies (participation rate of 81%), with a total *n* = 7,651 newly reported cases in the three-month period (September–November 2016) (Jud et al., 2021). The study estimated that 2.0–3.3% of all children living in Switzerland came into contact with an organization in the wider child protection system in 2016. Of the recorded cases in the three-month period in which a primary form of child endangerment was recorded (62% of the total number of cases), neglect was most prevalent (22.4%), followed by physical maltreatment (20.2%), psychological maltreatment (19.3%), exposure to intimate partner violence (18.7%), sexual abuse (15.2%), and other forms (4.3%) (Schmid et al., 2018; see Table 18.2). However, due to the large proportion of cases without a documented type of maltreatment, these statistics might be biased. Jud and colleagues (2021) assume that the proportion of neglect might be underestimated.

The average age of children in the respective case records (see Table 18.2) was the lowest for exposure to intimate partner violence (6.8 years) and the highest for physical maltreatment (10.4 years). According to Schmid et al. (2018, p. 28) these results "may be an indication that in Switzerland physical maltreatment is in some areas of care first recognized and recorded as such at a very late stage." There were significant differences for gender (see Table 18.2). This was most pronounced for sexual abuse, where it was estimated that in 73% of cases the gender of the child was female.

In addition, the results showed significant differences in the spatial distribution of agency responses across seven greater regions of Switzerland (Jud et al., 2021). In regions with multifaceted services and organizations related to family support and child

Table 18.2 Estimated frequency of forms of child endangerment, average age, and gender distribution of children

Form	Proportion of recorded cases of the primary forms of child endangerment	Lower and upper limit per 10,000 children in 2016	Average age of children in respective case records	Proportion of females
Neglect	22.4%	28–46	7.8 years	46%
Physical maltreatment	20.2%	25–41	10.4 years	46%
Psychological maltreatment	19.3%	24–39	8.8 years	57%
Exposure to intimate partner violence	18.7%	23–38	6.8 years	49%
Sexual abuse	15.2%	19–31	9.1 years	73%
Other forms	4.3%	5–9	–	42%
No response	–	77–127	–	47%

Source: Schmid et al. (2018); Jud et al. (2021) (supplementary material) for estimates on gender

protection, the number of recorded cases per 10,000 children during the three-month survey period was 107 (canton Zürich), and 76 (predominantly French-speaking Lake Geneva region). By far the lowest number of recorded cases per 10,000 children was 26 in the Italian-speaking canton of Ticino. The other four regions varied between 45 (Eastern Switzerland) and 62 (Northwestern Switzerland) recorded cases per 10,000 children. We agree with Schmid and colleagues (2018) that it is very unlikely that these differences are due to a different distribution of child endangerment in the population. Different levels of trust or skepticism towards professionals in the social and health sector, leading to different number of reported cases, does not seem to be a plausible explanation either, as Swiss statistics on consultation with physicians or treatment for mental health problems do not show a similar pattern (Gautschi, 2021). The same applies for the national distribution of wealth and an association between the regional differences in recorded case numbers and a urban-rural measure (Jud et al., 2021). Jud and colleagues (2021) have raised the assumption that varying concepts of child endangerment might have contributed to the differences between regions. As another hypothesis, we suggest a positive association between the number of reported cases and the extent to which the cantons within in a region have established decentralized services for children and families offering voluntary support (similarly, Schmid et al., 2018, p. 34). In other words, we would weight institutional and organizational factors higher than conceptual factors.

The data and findings collated in the above section to provide a picture of the prevalence of child maltreatment in Switzerland can be summarized as follows. While the incidence rate reported in Schmid and colleagues (2018) and Jud and colleagues (2021) may differ from those in other child protection systems—due to features of the child protection systems under comparison, or due to the agencies included within respective research designs—there is no substantiate reason to claim major differences between the incidence rates for different types of child maltreatment documented by agencies for Switzerland when compared to those reported in international meta-analyses (Stoltenborgh et al., 2011, 2012, 2013), if the reported confidence intervals and estimates of upper and lower limits are taken into account (Gautschi, 2021). Thus, the distinctiveness of the child protection system in Switzerland is not in the prevalence of child maltreatment and endangerment, but in the diversity of its institutional arrangements which—to varying degrees—is associated with a diversity of policies, programs and cultures of decision-making (Schnurr, 2016; Favre et al., 2019).

Owing to the principles of federalism and subsidiarity considered at the outset of this chapter, children's services and child protection are provided by 26 cantonal regimes. The main characteristics of these regimes result from interactions between federal legislation, cantonal legislation (where it exists), and the local/regional pattern of service provision. The following sections give a brief explanation of the legal and institutional framework of child protection in Switzerland.

Child Protection in Switzerland: The Legal Framework

Federal Legislation: Definitions and Forms of State Interventions into Family Autonomy

The federal civil law—the Swiss Civil Code (SCC)[1]—defines the conditions for and forms of compulsory state interventions to protect children, as well as the core organizational and procedural standards of the CAPAs that put the federal legislation on child protection into practice. In principle, decisions on child protection measures[2] are linked to the requirement that "the child's best interests are threatened and the parents are unwilling or unable to remedy the situation" (SCC, Article 307). Furthermore, the SCC sets out a number of child protection measures, which together constitute a graded system of interventions with corresponding limitations on family autonomy. The core child protection measures are:

1) *Appropriate measures (Article 307)*: These include reminding parents, foster parents or the child of their duties; instructions regarding care, upbringing or education; appointing a suitable person or agency with powers to investigate and monitor the situation. These are not exclusive: the law explicitly requires CAPAs to order "all appropriate measures to protect the child." A further measure, which is explicitly mentioned in the SCC, is requesting the parents to participate in mediation (SCC, Article 314).

2) *Deputyship (Article 308)*: The appointment of a child deputy (described in greater detail below) is the most frequent response by far, presumably because the preconditions for such an appointment are vaguely defined ("where circumstances so require") and deputyship can be used in very flexible ways. A child deputy can be appointed in a general sense (to "help the parents look after the child by providing advice and practical support"). Deputyship can also be tailored to specific issues (e.g., the child's medical treatment) and involve corresponding restrictions on parental rights.

3) *Revocation of the right to decide on place of residence (Article 310)*: A decision to remove a child from her/his parents and place him or her in a "suitable location" is linked to the condition that "there is no other way to avert a threat to the child's well-being." A prerequisite for this measure is that less intrusive measures have been tried and proved insufficient.

4) *Withdrawal of parental responsibility (Article 311)*: A withdrawal of parental responsibility is linked to the pre-condition that "other child protection

---

[1] Initially issued in December 1907; important amendments with regards to child protection in 1976, 1998, 2008, 2014, and 2017. Throughout this chapter, the official translation of the most recent version of the SCC (dated January 1, 2019) in English is used, which is available online from the federal administration at www.admin.ch.

[2] Child protection measure is a literal translation of *Kindesschutzmassnahme*; in legal terms, the child protection measures listed in the SCC have the status of orders, that is, limitations to parental autonomy.

measures have failed or offer little prospect of proving adequate" in combination with two other (alternative) conditions: 1) the "parents are unable to exercise parental responsibility as required on account of inexperience, illness, disability, absence, violent behavior or other similar reasons"; or 2) the "parents have not cared for the child to any meaningful degree or have flagrantly violated their duties towards the child." In addition, parental responsibility can be withdrawn, "if the parents request so for good cause" or if they have consented to having the child adopted.

5) *Committal [of a minor] to a secure institution or psychiatric hospital (Article 314b)*: The application of Article 314b is linked to the pre-condition that a severe threat to the well-being of the child in accordance with Article 310 is evident, the need for treatment is necessary, and such treatment cannot be met otherwise.[3]

The SCC also provides the legal basis for emergency placements and for the involvement of the police if this turns out to be necessary in order to enforce a decision of a CAPA (SCC, Article 450g). Mandatory statistics on decisions of the CAPAs are collected through KOKES. As of 2017, statistics on specific measures of the CAPAs are available for all cantons. Table 18.3 shows children with core child protection measures at year-end for 2017–2019 (KOKES, 2018, 2019, 2020). Overall, we see a rather small but steady increase in the absolute and relative number of children with selected child protection measures over these years.

Table 18.3 Number of children with selected child protection measures (SCC), 2017–2019

	Number of children (cases per 10,000 children in the resident population)		
	December 31, 2017	December 31, 2018	December 31, 2019
Appropriate measures (Article 307)	4,874 (32.0)	5,519 (36.1)	6,057 (39.3)
Deputyship (Article 308)	32,376 (212.9)	33,309 (217.7)	34,296 (222.4)
Revocation of the right to decide on place of residence (Article 310)	4,329 (28.5)	4,514 (29.5)	4,535 (29.4)
Withdrawal of parental responsibility (Article 311/312)	286 (1.9)	324 (2.1)	350 (2.3)
Child protection measures in a broader sense (i.e. full spectrum of child protection measures covered by the KOKES-statistics)	41,902 (275.5)	41,993 (274.4)	42,720 (277.0)

Note: Calculations for the relative numbers of the selected measures by Joel Gautschi. More than one measure per child is possible.

Source: Konferenz für Kindes- und Erwachsenenschutz (2018, 2019, 2020).

---

[3] This measure is not covered in the KOKES statistics (KOKES, 2020).

The differences between cantons are significant. For example, the relative number of children with a child protection measures in a broader sense per 10,000 children in the resident population as of December 31, 2019 in the canton of Jura (455.2) is more than three times higher than in the canton of Uri (134.2) (KOKES, 2020). The ratio of cases with child protection measures in general to cases with a measure related to an out-of-home placement (SCC, Articles 310, 311/312) also varies considerably between cantons (Favre et al., 2019). However, Favre and colleagues see no major changes in these cantonal statistics overall between the two time periods of 2009–2011 and 2016–2017, despite a significant institutional reform of the child protection authorities in 2013 (see below). They suggest that the different institutional frameworks and practices in the cantons, which are associated with different cantonal child protection regimes, are a strong influence factor for the inter-cantonal heterogeneity and cantonal persistence in the statistics presented.

Federal Legislation on Mandatory Reporting

Recent amendments to the SCC provide a legal basis for mandatory reporting on a national level. Previously, rights and obligations to report cases of child endangerment had been subject to diverse regulations under the competence of the cantons. As of 2019, all professionals with regular contact with children (in fields like healthcare, childcare, psychology, education, social work, religious/spiritual communities, and sports clubs) as well as "persons who learn of such a case in their official capacity" are "obliged to report if there are clear indications that the physical, psychological or sexual integrity of a child is at risk and that they cannot remedy the threat as part of their professional activities" (SCC, Article 314d). Furthermore, according to the new legislation, doctors, psychologists and lawyers who are subject to confidentiality rules according to the Swiss Criminal Code, have the right to contact a child protection authority if the reporting is in the interest of the child. Before 2019, professionals falling under these confidentiality rules were only entitled to report in cases of criminal acts.

Federal Legislation on Acts Against Sexual Integrity and Corporal Punishment

The Swiss Criminal Code (SCrC) imposes criminal penalties on engaging in sexual acts with a child under 16 years of age as well as inciting a child to commit such an activity or involving a child in a sexual act. The Code further states that no penalty may be imposed if the difference in age between the persons involved is three years or less (SCrC, Article 187). The prostitution of minors is also a punishable offence (Articles 195, 196) as is the production and distribution of child pornography (Article 197). Assault and repeated acts of aggression against a child (Articles 122, 123, 125, 126) are "Offizialdelikte," that is, criminal offences, which a prosecution authority must prosecute if it becomes aware of it. Non-serious injuries to a child or his/her health through negligence (Article 125) as well as acts of aggression that are not committed repeatedly are "Antragsdelikte," that is, criminal offences that cannot be prosecuted without a complaint of the victim. As a result, children are not sufficiently protected from corporal or other degrading forms of punishment insofar as they often lack the knowledge and capabilities required to report what has happened to them, not to mention the inhibitions associated with bringing a lawsuit against one's own parents (Jaffé et al., 2014, p. 28; United Nations Committee on the Rights of the Child, 2015). At present, there is neither legislation containing a right for parents to use corporal punishment towards their children (it was withdrawn from the SCC in 1978), nor is there legislation that explicitly outlaws and penalizes corporal punishment together with other degrading forms of punishment. With respect to the case law of the Federal Supreme Court, it has been argued, that corporal punishment is still tolerated by the judicial system (Luze, 2011; Jaffé et al., 2014, p. 28). As a consequence, there is a cultural and legal indifference towards corporal punishment.

Federal Act on Assistance to Victims of Crime

As noted above, the Victims Assistance Act entitles every person affected by a criminal offence against his or her physical, mental or sexual integrity to counseling and assistance. Age and citizenship of the victim are irrelevant and the entitlement to assistance is irrespective of whether the identity and/or the guilt of the offender(s) has been established. The law obliges the cantons to provide at least one Victim Assistance Agency that responds to a range of experiences of victims and offers short-term and long-term assistance. Victim Assistance Agencies can facilitate assistance and counseling from third parties. Law enforcement authorities are obliged to inform victims about Victim Assistance Agencies. As of 2018, 37 agencies provide counseling and short-term assistance for children and young people. Short-term assistance includes information on rights and entitlements of victims, as well as on therapies, legal procedures, opportunities to involve legal counsel, and so on. Long-term assistance may include therapy and/or legal representation. Depending on the financial situation of the victim, partial costs of long-term assistance are covered. According to the VAA, victims and their relatives are entitled to compensation for damages or death of a victim as a result of the criminal offence and may also be entitled to compensation for personal suffering (VAA, Articles 19, 22). The VAA is the only legal provision in federal legislation that gives children individual legal entitlements to services and benefits.

Cantonal Legislation: Implementation of the CAPAs and Service Provision

The SCC obliges the cantons to establish CAPAs and legislate for their implementation. Furthermore, it remains at the discretion of the cantons to legislate on the provision of services for children and families and the requirements of non-statutory services, that is, the use of services in parental consent, which is often referred to as "voluntary," both in the field and in the literature. The degree to which the cantons have legislated on the provision of services for children and families as well as on features and responsibilities of agencies that may provide or facilitate access to such services in the non-statutory arm of the system varies considerably across the 26 cantons. Legal entitlements to non-statutory services for children and families do not exist, either at the federal or canton level. Moreover, insofar as the cantons have legislation on services for children and families, it is usually restricted to general regulations, such as general statements on the types of services eligible for public funding, on organizations authorized to provide access to services, and on financial responsibilities. Generally, pre-conditions for service provision (who gets what under what circumstances etc.) are not regulated on a legal or formal level. Thus, they are left largely to the discretion of local agencies and individual service workers.

Child Protection in Switzerland: The Institutional Framework

Child and Adult Protection Authorities (CAPAs)

As of 2013, and resulting from a reform of the SCC in 2008, child protection authorities are multi-professional (interdisciplinary) authorities. The CAPAs replaced the former Guardianship Authorities, which (in most German-speaking cantons) had been subdivisions of the elected bodies of municipalities and therefore lay-bodies. Thus, the main results of the 2013 reform were the late professionalization of decision making in the Swiss child protection system and the reduction of the number of authorities from 1,414 to 148 (142 at year-end 2019; KOKES, 2020). The SCC states that the CAPAs must be specialist authorities and make decisions through a quorum of three members. The legislators pursued the idea of a collegial body whose members apply expert knowledge from different fields and disciplines to meet the substantially diverse characteristics and requirements of complex cases. According to recommendations of the inter-canton conference for child and adult protection (Konferenz der kantonalen Vormundschaftsbehörden, 2008), the preferred professions/disciplines to be represented in a CAPA are law, social work, pedagogy/education, and psychology. A recent evaluation survey found that 93% of the CAPAs have multi-professional decision-making bodies, with law and social work being the most frequent combination (Rieder et al., 2016, p. 40). The CAPAs—as their name suggests—hold responsibilities for child *and* adult protection. Up to now, the great majority of CAPAs have refrained from setting up separate sections for child or adult protection. Thus, the same body usually makes decisions on cases of children and (mainly older) adults.

There are one to three CAPAs in the majority of cantons (Rieder et al., 2016, pp. 5–6). The population served by a CAPA varies from 2,700 to 485,000 inhabitants (KOKES, 2017). It is at the discretion of the canton legislatures whether CAPAs are administrative authorities or judicial authorities (courts). In addition, they can be canton, municipality, or intercommunal/regional authorities. Altogether, this has added to the diversity of child protection regimes across the cantons, of which Table 18.4 gives only a superficial impression.

Table 18.4 Basic organizational forms of CAPAs	
Canton administrative authorities	14 cantons
Municipality/municipalities administrative authorities	6 cantons
Canton or regional courts	6 cantons

Source: Rieder et al. (2016, p. 34).

Social Service Agencies and Children's Service Agencies

Decentralized public agencies carrying the responsibilities for 1) facilitating access to non-statutory services for children and families and 2) decision making on non-statutory removals of children to alternative care are widespread in Switzerland, albeit not comprehensive. The responsibilities, target groups, and organizational features of the respective agencies vary across the cantons. In a number of cantons, these tasks and decisions are assigned to social service agencies, which, inter alia, are also responsible for social assistance (i.e., basic social security against poverty) and reintegration into employment. In another group of cantons, they are assigned to specialized children's service agencies. A small number of cantons neither have children's service agencies nor have they assigned these tasks and decisions to social service agencies. Since the implementation of the CAPAs in 2013, it has become quite common for social service agencies and children's service agencies to carry out assessments on behalf of the CAPAs in cases when there appear to be threats to the well-being of a child.

The range and ways in which social service agencies or children's service agencies contribute to child protection and children's services is structured from two directions: first, the canton legislation, especially cantons' legislation on the implementation of the federal provisions on child and adult protection set out in the SCC; second, the regulations of the municipalities where they are located. As mentioned before, the extent to which service provision and access to non-statutory services is institutionalized and organized at a legal or formal level is generally low. This applies equally to cantons where social service agencies or children's service agencies exist, as the thresholds for access to service provision are often opaque. Insofar as agencies are under the supervision of municipalities (or associations of municipalities), access to services is shaped by local policies and cultures. While case-specific decisions are usually made by service workers, they remain in principle under the final discretion of representatives of the municipality, such as an elected body, specialist committee, or the mayor.

Accordingly, social service agencies and children's service agencies usually have their own policies with respect to the question of whether they provide access to services "on their own," or refer a case to the CAPA. From a legal point of view, agencies have to notify a case to a CAPA if they have knowledge about threats to the well-being of a child and assess that their own means are not sufficient to avert the threat and protect the child. However, the extent to which a service agency may be able to improve the situation of a child by providing appropriate services "by its own means" is also dependent on the prevailing understanding of its tasks and competences as well as on organizational and financial rules. The more the legitimacy of non-statutory family support and other services is contested and financial resources are (perceived as) scarce, the more an agency may tend to interpret a case as one that exceeds its capacity and therefore has to be referred to a CAPA.

Deputyships

Among the child protection measures defined in the SCC, deputyship is widely considered as an all-purpose response appropriate to a wide variety of cases and, therefore, it is used very frequently. As a rule, a deputy is appointed when a child is taken into alternative care (both with parental consent or by an order). He or she is supposed to be an intermediary between the child, the parents, the provider of out-of-home care, and the CAPA. Deputyships have also become a standard response when a parent's right to visit a child is controversial or legally restricted. Whereas in legal terms a deputyship is a public office assigned to an individual person in his or her own right, it is much more common to delegate deputyships to service workers located in a social service agency or children's service agency or to individuals who carry out (multiple) deputyships as an occupation (*Berufsbeistände*/Occupational Deputies). In a small number of cantons/authorities, deputyships are regularly located at a CAPA (Rieder et al., 2016). In the majority of cantons, associations of specialist deputies make up a significant part of the child protection infrastructure. According to a survey, the proportion of deputies in 2015 who were private individuals is only 11.5% while 88.5% of deputyships are assigned to service workers and occupational deputies (Rieder et al., 2016, p. 58).

Child Protection Teams

Child Protection Teams, assembling experts from different fields such as pediatrics, psychologists, social workers, and others, have been established in the majority of pediatric clinics. They may carry out assessments, provide treatment, refer cases to the CAPAs, and/or report them to the penal system (Wopmann, 2020). In a number of cantons there are local or canton Child Protection Teams which are located outside the health system. They see their main task as the provision of advice to professionals in schools, social service and children's service agencies, kindergartens, and so on in cases of (alleged) maltreatment of children (Jud & Knüsel, 2019). However, the continuing relevance of these Child Protection Teams has been questioned since the implementation of the CAPAs.

Core Procedures and Standards in the Swiss Child Protection System

In this section an (admittedly simplified) picture of core procedures in the Swiss child protection system is provided, beginning with notification of (alleged) threats to the well-being of a child, then considering assessment and decision-making on needs for care and concluding with appropriate responses including limitations on family autonomy.

Reporting

In general, any person has the right to pass information about a person in need to a CAPA (SCC, Articles 314c, 443). All professionals with regular contact with children are subject to mandatory reporting. A recent study estimated that between September and November 2016, most of the cases were reported to the CAPAs by penal agencies (ca. 30%), followed by the health sector (ca. 26%), social sector (ca. 18%), parents (ca. 13%), schools (ca. 9%), relatives (ca. 3%), and children (less than 1%) (Jud et al., 2021; own estimates by Joel Gautschi based on Figure 3, column 3). The CAPA is responsible for and required to receive notifications and carry out investigations "ex officio." It also holds the responsibility for the entire process from investigation to decision making. However, the option of the CAPA instructing "a suitable person or agency to carry out enquiries" is explicitly provided for in the SCC (Article 446).

Assessment

Assessments of the circumstances when a child's well-being appears to be under threat may be carried out by a member of the decision-making body in a CAPA, an internal specialist unit of a CAPA, an external public agency such as a social service agency or children's service agency, or some other professional or a specialist provider (including for-profit). In practice, the majority of assessments are carried out by external agencies (Rieder, 2016, p. 47) and largely by social service agencies or children's service agencies.

There is a general expectation that a typical child protection assessment stretches over a period of three months. It includes conversations with the parent(s) and the child, home visits, and additional conversations with relevant persons or professionals, such as teachers, medical doctors and so on. In addition, the person in charge of the assessment makes use of available files from earlier encounters with agencies, authorities, and so on. If required and/or requested by the assessing agency, the CAPA may also commission additional expert assessments (e.g., from a child psychiatrist). Finally, the person carrying out the assessment integrates data and knowledge into an assessment report, which is passed to the CAPA. Generally, an assessment report contains:

- A description of the type and severity of the endangerment to the well-being of the child;
- Statements about the need for support, appropriateness of services, and the willingness of the child and the parents to accept and cooperate;
- Recommendations with respect to appropriate types of support;
- Statements about whether there should be limitations on parental autonomy (i.e. child protection measures) and what type of limitations may be necessary to protect the child and safeguard his/her well-being.

Most frequently, CAPAs have developed their own templates for assessment reports (as they have also often done for the reception and appraisal of notifications). Any further obligatory requirements with regard to the process and/or the use of methods and instruments are quite rare. Since the 2013 reform, there has been increasing recognition of the relevance of structured risks and needs assessments in child protection (Lätsch, 2012; Biesel & Schnurr, 2014; Spratt et al., 2014). Meanwhile, an instrument (Hauri et al., 2016) and a "process manual" for the assessment of the well-being of the child (Biesel et al., 2017) has been developed, which are both research-based and designed to meet the requirements of the (diverse) child protection regimes in Switzerland. A small number of CAPAs and agencies have started to adopt these or other standards and frameworks, often taken from Germany. However, the adoption of research-based frameworks for the assessment of the well-being of the child is occurring slowly and the use of such concepts has still not yet become the norm. A recent experimental vignette study found quite large differences between professionals in their assessment of the severity of the endangerment to the well-being of the child and the likelihood of their recommendation for out-of-home placement, at least in certain case constellations (Gautschi, 2021).

Participation and legal representation

As a general rule, the CAPA is obliged to hear a person affected by a decision "in person" (SCC, Article 447). In child protection proceedings the SCC stipulates that "the child is heard in person in an appropriate manner by the child protection authority or by a third party appointed for this purpose, unless this is inadvisable due to the child's age or other good cause" (SCC, Article 314a). It is at the discretion of the CAPA to decide on time, place, and frequency of hearings. Drawing from anecdotal knowledge, hearings with the parents are often conducted in combination with the disclosure of the decision, whereas hearings with the child are more frequently conducted prior to decision making and used as a means to gain information on the case from the child's perspective. Based on survey data, Rieder et al. (2016, p. 59) found that hearings with the child have been conducted in 64% of child protection cases; in 28% of the cases the CAPA did not conduct hearings because of the age or disability of the child; 8% of cases proceeded without a hearing for other reasons.

In addition, independent legal representation of the child has been introduced into the SCC since the 2013 reform. The law gives discretion to the CAPA about whether such representation is provided but stipulates that this should be considered, especially if the proceedings relate to the child's accommodation or "if the parties file differing applications in relation to regulating parental responsibility or important contact issues" (SCC, Article 314a[bis]). In contrast to a deputy, who acts on behalf of a CAPA, an independent representative has the right to file applications and appeals against the CAPA. Statistics on the decisions of the CAPAs reveal that independent representation of the child has been provided in 704 cases at year-end 2018 and in 741 cases at year-end 2019 (KOKES, 2019, 2020). A study on child protection proceedings in three cantons found that the CAPAs are very reluctant to appoint an independent representative for the child (Hitz Quenon & Matthey, 2017). There is reason to believe that the CAPAs make use of their discretion in a way that prevents a great number of children from accessing a legal provision, which grants powers and could be used to strengthen the child's position in the proceedings. What can be said with certainty, however, is that there is considerable inconsistency in the use of the independent representation across the cantons. This is supported by the fact that the ratio of the number of cases with *independent representation of the child* (SCC, Article 314a[bis]) to the number of cases with a *revocation of the right to decide on place of residence* (SCC, Article 310) measure at year-end 2019 (as a very rough indicator) differed by up to 37-fold between cantons.[4]

Decision Making

Decision making takes place in the absence of the parents and the children affected by the decision either in meetings or in a process of consultation between the members of the decision-making body, which relies on written material. Usually, the responsibility for a case is assigned to one member of the collegial body who controls the assessment and later presents the case to the decision-making body together with a recommendation for a particular decision. The material used in decision making generally includes the assessment report and records from hearings involving the parents and the child. If a decision is made, it must be presented to the persons affected by it in a written form that includes information on the right to appeal. The 2013 reform stressed a multi-professional body's potential for decision making. The underlying assumption was that a multi-professional body allows knowledge from different perspectives and disciplines to be used in a deliberative process and therefore contributes to rational and sustainable decisions. However, anecdotal knowledge suggest that the deliberative exchange of views is largely restricted to cases found to be exceptionally challenging. Hence, available knowledge suggests that further developments are needed to maximize the potential for multi-professional decision making in the routine practice of the CAPAs.

Services for Children and Families

The overall spectrum of services for children and families is highly diverse. The types of services that are available and accessible within particular regions vary considerably.

---

[4] Calculations by Joel Gautschi, based on Konferenz für Kindes- und Erwachsenenschutz, 2020. Ratio for the canton of Jura = 0.016 (one case with SCC Article 314a[bis]/64 cases with SCC Article 310). Ratio for the canton of Zug = 0.571 (20 cases with SCC Article 314a[bis]/35 cases with SCC Article 310). Even if we exclude cantons with less than 100 cases of SCC Article 310, the cantons still differ by up to 14-fold: Ratio for the canton of Ticino = 0.027 (6 case with SCC Article 314a[bis]/219 cases with SCC Article 310). Ratio for the canton of Zurich = 0.371 (280 cases with SCC Article 314a[bis]/754 cases with SCC Article 310).

Children and families living in and around cities have fewer difficulties in finding a greater variety of services within reasonable distances. The spectrum of available services is often arbitrary and tends to depend on traditions and supply-side growth, rather than on demand-driven planning. Moreover, it is a feature of the Swiss system of children's services and child protection that there is only very limited knowledge about the distribution of services for children and families at the federal, regional and canton level (Bundesrat, 2012, p. 42), albeit the number of cantons that have started to produce such information has increased over the last few years owing to a federal program that offers financial support for cantons that have decided to do so.[5] Insofar as web-based overviews have been developed, the predominant focus has most often been on residential care.[6]

A report of the federal governmental on "Violence and neglect in families: necessary measures in child welfare and state sanctions" presented a catalogue of basic services for children and families. The term "basic" was used to characterize services that respond to needs that may occur at any place and time and therefore "should be available and accessible to ensure a needs-based provision of services for children, young people and families" (Bundesrat, 2012, p. 23, translation ours). Only these kinds of services for children and families that already existed and were available in the country at the time of the report were listed in the catalog, although their spatial distribution and availability were unknown. Though the catalog only has the status of a recommendation addressed to the cantons (without stipulating any obligations), it marks a tentative step towards service orientation in child protection and children's services in Switzerland, at least at the federal level. The types of services are organized in three groups (Bundesrat 2012, p. 23; Schnurr, 2012; see Figure 18.1): (A) general promotion of children and families (including youth work, childcare, and parental training), (B) counseling and support (including counseling and support for children/for parents and families, and school social work), and (C) aid to upbringing (including in-home services, residential care, and foster care).

The types of service listed are supplemented by two categories that are better understood as functions of institutions and agencies in the field of child protection and children's services: (D) assessment and (E) case responsibility. The services (in categories B and C)

[5] The legal basis is Article 26 of the federal Kinder- und Jugendförderungsgesetz KJFG (Law on the Promotion of Children and Adolescents). The law regulates the provision of federal funds to promote out-of-school education of children and adolescents. Support goes—inter alia—to umbrella organizations and coordination platforms for youth work. In addition, the KJFG provides financial support for projects directed by cantons and municipalities and aimed at developing programs or concepts of national relevance. The program is transitional and limited to eight years (2013–2021).

[6] See casadata.ch, a website produced and maintained by the Federal Office of Justice (FoJ); last accessed May 16, 2019.

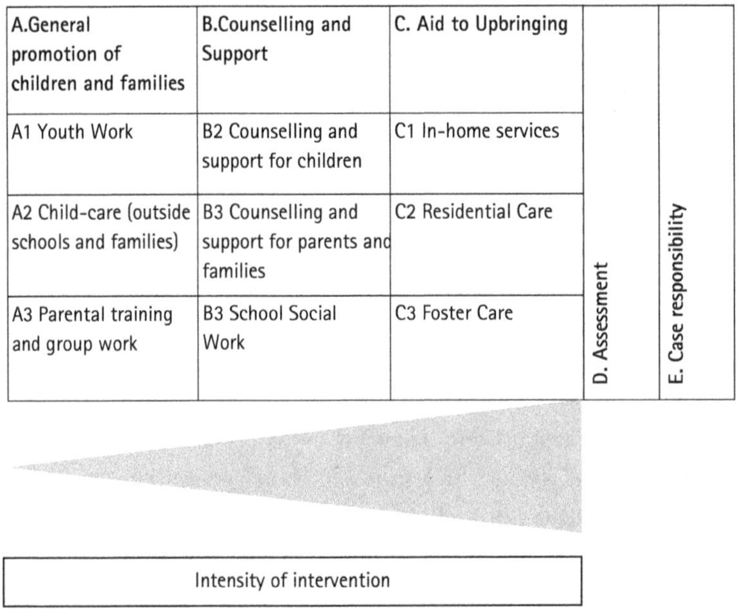

A. General promotion of children and families	B. Counselling and Support	C. Aid to Upbringing	D. Assessment	E. Case responsibility
A1 Youth Work	B2 Counselling and support for children	C1 In-home services		
A2 Child-care (outside schools and families)	B3 Counselling and support for parents and families	C2 Residential Care		
A3 Parental training and group work	B3 School Social Work	C3 Foster Care		

Intensity of intervention

Figure 18.1 Catalogue of basic services for children and families (Schnurr, 2012)

that are both of great relevance in child protection and children's services and widely available throughout the country are as follows:

- *Counseling service for mothers and fathers* (*Mütter- und Väterberatung*): a flexible counseling service for all parents with children aged 0–4, providing knowledge and support around questions of the child's health, care, nutrition, and education, and the multiple challenges of being a mother/father. It is widespread and easily accessible throughout the country.
- *Child and youth counseling*: provided in centers, but increasingly telephone- and web based.
- *Parental counseling/Child guidance*: also provided in centers and via phone and internet. Specialized counseling services for families in crisis, marital counseling, divorce and separation counseling, and so on in different combinations are provided throughout the country, albeit access in terms of available appointments and waiting times varies considerably and is generally much easier in urban areas.
- *School social work*: this has experienced strong growth over the last twenty-five years and has become almost a universal service, albeit concentrated at the secondary level. For children of compulsory school age, a school social worker is probably the simplest entry point to children's services.
- *In-home services*: a rapidly growing type of service in Switzerland. Widespread forms are known as *Social-pedagogical family work* and *Competencies-oriented*

family work (Cassée et al., 2010); the former goes back to developments in Germany in the 1980s (where it is still a pillar of parental support), the latter is a research-based and manualized intervention that has been developed in Switzerland. Other standardized or manualized in-home interventions adopted in Switzerland are "schritt:weise"/"a:primo" and Multi-systemic Therapy (MST-Standard and MST Child Abuse and Neglect) (Henggeler et al., 2009).

- *Residential care* has longstanding traditions in Switzerland. The landscape of residential care units is highly diverse. It ranges from shared apartments to units which are combined with schools (often for disabled children) or vocational training facilities, to institutions with locked units. A (non-complete) survey on behalf of the Federal Department of Finance found a total of 205 residential care units in Switzerland. Eighty-seven percent reported the capacity to facilitate access to internal or external therapeutic resources (Dvorak et al., 2011; Wyl et al., 2017).
- *Foster care*: During the last few years, the relevance of and attention paid to foster care has increased. In Switzerland, similar to Germany, foster care is highly diverse and consists of various forms on a continuum which stretches from short-term foster care to arrangements for long-term continuity (Gassmann, 2013).

In-home Services and Alternative Care

Up until the early 2000s, residential care had been the state's primary response to a child in difficult circumstances (especially between the ages of 7 and 17). It enjoyed the highest reputation, was the most widespread response, and was the easiest for local agencies or authorities to make available. With regard to alternative care, the higher significance of residential care over foster care applies up to the present time. According to a current estimate 67% of children in alternative care in the period 2015–2017 are in residential placements and 33% are in foster care (Seiterle, 2018, p. 9). However, in the last few years, the relevance of foster care and the supply of in-home services has increased.

On the national level, there are no statistics on the use of family and children's services including alternative care. In other words, the Swiss state has no knowledge on the number of children in state care. Only three out of twenty-six cantons collect and publish statistical data on children in alternative care (and other selected services) on a regular basis.[7] The federal state has recently started to collect supply-related data on the field of residential care and information on the organizations and institutions in the cantons involved in child protection and children's services.[8] Hence, an approximation towards a picture

---

[7] Cantons Basel-Landschaft, Basel-Stadt, and Bern; other cantons may also collect but not publish statistical data.

[8] See casadata.ch, last accessed May 16, 2019.

of the proportion of children in care can be gained from the KOKES-statistics (KOKES, 2019, 2020; see above). As decisions on the *Revocation of the right to decide on place of residence* (SCC, Article 310) are linked to care order removals of children in alternative care, the respective data are relevant here. Based on end-of-year data, the number of children in alternative care, based on an order of a CAPA, was 4,514 in 2018 and 4,535 in 2019. This corresponds to 29.5 per 10,000 children in 2018, and 29.4 per 10,000 children in 2019. However, these figures relate to children removed through care orders. There is a common understanding among experts in the field that the proportion of children placed in alternative care through care orders accounts for approximately 40% of all placements, while roughly 60% of children are placed with parental consent. This estimation is supported by statistical data from particular cantons (Schnurr, 2016). With regard to in-home services, on the national level there is hardly any data other than the reports of the Swiss Association of Social-pedagogical Family Work (Fachverband Sozialpädagogische Familienhilfe Schweiz), which produces information from its member-organizations that shows a total of 1,115 families being served in 2016 (Messmer et al., 2019).

Pathways to Services

There are generally three pathways to services in the Swiss system of child protection and children's services:

1) Parents and families themselves decide to request and use a service. This applies mainly to services listed in section A of the above catalog of services.
2) A social service agency or children's service agency or other body (e.g., school authority in some areas) decides on the need and appropriateness of a certain service, drawing from an assessment, and facilitate use of the services by matching users with a service provider.
3) A CAPA decides on the need and appropriateness of a certain service. This may be alternative care, but in principle a CAPA has the competence to decide on any "appropriate measure" (and thus on services a family or child could also have already started to use on their own initiative).

In principle the use of a certain type of service can be facilitated or arranged through each of the above pathways. Therefore, it would be more precise to speak about non-statutory and statutory contexts of service delivery and not about voluntary versus compulsory services. In addition, the term voluntary is to some degree misleading. Parents and children often feel pushed into the use of a certain service, not least because of the capacity of service agencies to involve the child protection authority, such as the CAPA. Threatening parents with making a child the subject of a care order is quite common and creates doubts about the accuracy of the term "voluntary" in a great number of cases. Moreover, the reluctance of the cantons to legislate on non-statutory service provision has led to a situation, where access to services in the statutory arm of the system is often easier than it is in the non-statutory arm.

Financing and Delivery of Services

The delivery of children's services takes place in interactions between 1) the CAPAs, 2) the social service agencies/children's service agencies, and 3) a great variety of public, non-profit, and for-profit service providers. The majority of non-governmental service providers is composed of charitable trusts and non-profit corporations with mixed backgrounds, from faith-based to secular "professional" cultures. For-profit corporations play a minor role, and it is only in the sector of in-home services and the brokerage of foster care placements that they make up a significant proportion of the supply. In highly simplified terms, a social service agency, a children's service agency, or a CAPA makes the decision on what is an appropriate service, guarantees the financing, and matches service users with service providers, with varying degrees of participation of parents and children about the type, place, and provider of the service. However, as has become clear in the above sections, there is no single and uniform organizational regime in the Swiss system of child protection and children's services. There is variation in the ways in which the CAPAs (representing statutory child protection) and service agencies (social services or children's services or other, representing non-statutory child protection) understand and carry out their respective competencies and cooperate with each other. There is also variation in the distribution of financial responsibilities between the cantons and the municipalities, which are often set out in the cantons' legislation on the implementation of the 2013 reform. In a number of cantons, the responsibility for the costs of services linked to a protection order by a CAPA rests with the canton. In other cantons it falls on the municipality where the family is residing. The latter has become a matter of (latent) conflict between the municipalities and the cantons. In the majority of cantons, the financial responsibility for non-statutory services facilitated by social services agencies and/or children's services agencies is located with the municipality where the family resides. A small number of cantons have financial compensation schemes to which the municipalities pay contributions (according to their size or other criteria) into a pool at the canton level, which is then used for the coverage of costs for services regardless of the place of residence of the service users. Whatever regulations on the share of costs between the cantons and municipalities exist, the parents contribute to the costs on a regular basis. The legal basis for this is the definition of the parent's duty of maintenance, set out in the SCC (Article 276). The amount which the parents contribute to the costs is subject to canton legislation and thus varies across the cantons. The same applies to regulations with regard to compensation in cases when the required contributions exceed the financial capacities of parents. In this case, social assistance generally intervenes, which means that municipalities cover the costs.

It has been argued earlier that in the CAPAs, which represent the statutory arm of child protection, decision making and the related procedures are increasingly framed by legislation and formal structures, when compared to the voluntary arm of child protection (service agencies within the competence of the cantons and municipalities). This has consequences for finances. Since funding of services resulting from the decision of a CAPA is more decisive and leaves less room for maneuver, a service worker in an agency is tempted to see the CAPA as a safe harbor to which cost responsibility can be passed. All that is necessary is to interpret a case to make it compatible with the (anticipated) requirements of the CAPA, which can be achieved if the severity of the case is raised and the willingness of the parents to cooperate is called into question. As a result, the parents are forced to accept limitations of autonomy in exchange for services.

The extent to which the cantons put efforts into monitoring, control, and governance of service provision in the field of child protection and children's services is surprisingly low. Even the embedding of responsibility for child and family issues within canton governments and administrations is usually vague, often distributed to various departments (health, education, social affairs, etc.). The less attention canton administrations pay to the field and the less control they exercise, the more issues are at the discretion of the service providers. In the majority of cantons (and more in the German-speaking than in the French-speaking ones) the composition of available services is left to chance rather than a result of policies. The fact that up to now only three out of 26 cantons have collected and published statistics on the supply and use of services illustrates this. A great number of cantons shows similar reluctance with regard to the issues of contracting and quality control. However, during the present decade, some cantons have intensified their efforts to generate knowledge about often inconsistent rules and regulations and set up models for the design of contracts between cantons/municipalities and service providers in combination with models for the development and control of service quality. Against this background, it is an important signal that the inter-cantonal conference of governmental departments for social affairs (a body aiming at coordinating policies between the cantons) agreed on joint recommendations on the continuation and strengthening of these trends (Konferenz der kantonalen Sozialdirektoren, 2016).

Key Challenges and Child Protection Issues Currently under Debate

Public image of the CAPAs: Soon after the 2013 reform, the CAPAs attracted critique and hostility both in the public and in the media. Media coverage of the CAPAs suggested the CAPAs intervene too frequently and too ruthlessly, and take decisions on restricting family autonomy too easily. Criticism was and still is directed to both child and adult protection. As a response, a contact point for child and adult protection (*Anlaufstelle Kindes- und Erwachsenenschutz*; KESCHA) has been established, which is independent and led by a public-private partnership. Citizens who are subject to a CAPA can call the KESCHA and receive information on the procedures, aims, and powers of the CAPA. Nonetheless, the CAPAs face the challenge of building trust both in the public and in direct interactions with the citizens they serve.

Cooperation between CAPAs and agencies: Almost a decade after the implementation of the CAPAs, cooperation between CAPAs (representing the statutory child protection) and service agencies (representing the non-statutory child protection), which had to be established from scratch, has made progress. However, it still needs improvements, namely:

- The development of a common understanding of intervention thresholds;
- Agreements on the division of elements of a shared task (i.e., to protect children in the best way possible) among the four key actors, the family, the service providers, the agencies, and the CAPA;
- Adoption and use of knowledge-based and research-based concepts for the assessment of the well-being of children and families, which link risk and safety assessment with needs assessment and conclusions on necessary interventions and appropriate services (Biesel & Schnurr, 2014; van der Put et al., 2017);
- The hallmark of these processes is respectful interactions with children and parents.

Service provision: Since it seems unrealistic to wait for a successful push towards federal legislation on (entitlements to) services for children and families in the near future, the further development of legislation at the canton level is pressing (Konferenz der Sozialdirektorinnen und Sozialdirektoren, 2016). It should be linked to an expansion of the cantons' policy capacities to shape local and regional patterns of service provision more closely to the needs of children and families, and create effective strategies for quality development and control, which is best done in trustful and cooperative structures with service providers. These efforts should be bound to create a continuum of service alternatives for children and families which can be used in flexible ways according to individual needs and choices. Early help preventive services for young children and their caregivers should become an integral part of these service landscapes. The cantons would then be able to make the best use of the unique potential of small-scale federalism for the benefit of children and families.

References

Averdijk, M., Mueller-Johnson, K., and Eisner, M. (2012). *Sexual victimization of children and adolescents in Switzerland*. Final report for the UBS Optimus Foundation. UBS Optimus Foundation.

Baier, D., Manzoni, P., Haymoz, S., Isenhardt, A., Kamenowski, M., and Jacot, C. (2018). *Elterliche Erziehung unter besonderer Berücksichtigung elterlicher Gewaltanwendung in der Schweiz: Ergebnisse einer Jugendbefragung*. Available at: https://doi.org/10.21256/zhaw-4863.

Biesel, K., Fellmann, L., Müller, B., Schär, C., and Schnurr, S. (2017). *Prozessmanual. Dialogisch-systemische Kindeswohlabklärung*. Haupt.

Biesel, K. and Schnurr, S. (2014). Abklärung im Kindesschutz: Chancen und Risiken in der Anwendung von Verfahren und Instrumenten zur Erfassung von Kindeswohlgefährdung. *Zeitschrift für Kindes- und Erwachsenenschutz*, 69(1), 63–71.

Bundesrat. (1995). *Bericht Kindesmisshandlung Schweiz. Stellungnahme des Bundesrates vom 27. Juni 1995*. Schweizerische Eidgenossenschaft.

Bundesrat. (2012). *Gewalt und Vernachlässigung in der Familie: notwendige Massnahmen im Bereich der Kinder- und Jugendhilfe und der staatlichen Sanktionierung. Bericht des Bundesrates in Erfüllung des Postulats Fehr (07.3725) vom 5. Oktober 2007*. Schweizerische Eidgenossenschaft.

Cassée, K., Los-Schneider, B., Baumeister, B., and Gavez, S. (2010). Kompetenzorientierte Familienarbeit KOFA. Entwicklung, Implementierung und Evaluation eines manualisierten Programms für die Arbeit mit belasteten Familien. Schlussbericht. Available at: https://doi.org/10.21256/zhaw-3339.

Dvorak, A., Schnyder-Walser, K., Ettlin, R., Ruflin, R., and Bütler, C. (2011). *Teilbericht. Eidgenössische Finanzkontrolle (EFK). Befragung von stationären Einrichtungen für Kinder und Jugendliche ohne Subventionen des Bundesamtes für Justiz*. Socialdesign.

Favre, E., Jung, R., and Voll, P. (2019). La protection des enfants en Suisse: variations linguistiques, écologies différentes et pratiques hétérogènes. *Actualité sociale*, (12), 18–20.

Federal Chancellery. (2021). *The Swiss Confederation: A brief guide*. Available at: https://www.bk.admin.ch/dam/bk/en/dokumente/komm-ue/buku2021/buku2021.pdf.download.pdf/EN_BUKU_2021_Einzelseiten.pdf.

Gassmann, Y. (2013). Diversität in der Pflegekinderhilfe. In E. M. Piller and S. Schnurr (Eds.), *Kinder- und Jugendhilfe in der Schweiz* (pp. 129–161). Springer Fachmedien Wiesbaden.

Gautschi, J. (2021). *Urteile und Entscheidungen unter Unsicherheit in Kindeswohlabklärungen: Einflussfaktoren auf Fallbeurteilungen in einer multifaktoriellen, experimentellen Vignettenstudie*. Available at: https://nbn-resolving.org/urn:nbn:de:bsz:frei129-opus4-8835.

Hauri, A., Jud, A., Lätsch, D., and Rosch, D. (2016). Anhang I: Das Berner und Luzerner Abklärungsinstrument zum Kindesschutz. In D. Rosch, C. Fountoulakis, and C. Heck (Eds.), *Handbuch Kindes- und Erwachsenenschutz. Recht und Methodik für Fachleute* (pp. 590–627). Haupt.

Henggeler, S. W., Schoenwald, S. K., Borduin, C. M., Rowland, M. D., and Cunningham, P. B. (2009). *Multisystemic therapy for antisocial behavior in children and adolescents* (2nd ed.). Guilford Press.

Hitz Quenon, N. and Matthey, F. (2017). *Une justice adaptée aux enfants. L'audition de l'enfant lors d'un placement en droit civil et lors du renvoi d'un parent en droit des étrangers*. Available at: https://www.skmr.ch/cms/upload/pdf/170829_etude_audition_enfant.pdf.

Jaffé, P. D., Zermatten, J., Balmer, F., Gaudreau, J., Quenon, N. H., Gapany, P. R., . . . and Zermatten, A. H. (Eds.). (2014). *Umsetzung der Menschenrechte in der Schweiz. Eine Bestandesaufnahme im Bereich der Kinder- und Jugendpolitik*. Editions Weblaw.

Jud, A. and Knüsel, R. (2019). Structure and challenges of child protection in Switzerland. In L. Merkel-Holguin, J. Fluke, and R. Krugman (Eds.), *National Systems of Child Protection* (pp. 207–227). Springer.

Jud, A., Kosirnik, C., Mitrovic, T., Ben Salah, H., Fux, E., Koehler, J., . . . and Knüsel, R. (2018). Mobilizing agencies for incidence surveys on child maltreatment: successful participation in Switzerland and lessons learned. *Child and Adolescent Psychiatry and Mental Health*, 12(1).

Jud, A., Mitrovic, T., Portmann, R., Gonthier, H., Fux, E., Koehler, J., . . . and Knüsel, R. (2021). Multisectoral response to child maltreatment in Switzerland for different age groups: Varying rates of reported incidents and gaps in identification. *Child Abuse & Neglect*, (111).

Konferenz der kantonalen Vormundschaftsbehörden. (2008). Kindes- und Erwachsenenschutzbehörde als Fachbehörde (Analyse und Modellvorschläge). *Zeitschrift für Vormundschaftswesen*, 63(2), 63–128.

Konferenz der Sozialdirektorinnen und Sozialdirektoren. (2016, May 19). *Empfehlungen der Konferenz der kantonalen Sozialdirektorinnen und Sozialdirektoren (SODK) für die Weiterentwicklung der Kinder- und Jugendpolitik in den Kantonen*. Available at: https://ch-sodk.s3.amazonaws.com/media/files/2016.06.21_SODK_Empf_KJP_d_ES_RZ.pdf.

KOKES. (2017). KESB: Organisation in den Kantonen (Stand 1.1.2017): Zusammengestellt durch die KOKES. *Zeitschrift für Kindes- und Erwachsenenschutz*, 72(1), 5.

KOKES. (2018). KOKES-Statistik 2017: Anzahl Personen mit Schutzmassnahmen. *Zeitschrift für Kindes- und Erwachsenenschutz*, 73(5), 394–401.

KOKES. (2019). KOKES-Statistik 2018: Anzahl Personen mit Schutzmassnahmen per 31.12.2018. *Zeitschrift für Kindes- und Erwachsenenschutz*, 74(5), 430–437.

KOKES. (2020). KOKES-Statistik 2019: Anzahl Personen mit Schutzmassnahmen per 31.12.2019. *Zeitschrift für Kindes- und Erwachsenenschutz*, 75(5), 438–447.

Lätsch, D. (2012). Wissenschaftlich fundierte Abklärungen im Kindesschutz: Überblick über den internationalen Entwicklungsstand—und ein Ausblick in die Schweiz. *Zeitschrift für Kindes- und Erwachsenenschutz*, 67(1), 1–20.

Luze, E. D. (2011). *Le droit de correction notamment sous l'angle du bien de l'enfant: Étude de droit Suisse*. Bis et Ter.

Mach, A. and Trampusch, C. (2011). *Switzerland in Europe: Continuity and change in the Swiss political economy*. Routledge.

Messmer, H., Fellmann, L., Wetzel, M., and Käch, O. (2019). Sozialpädagogische Familienhilfe im Spiegel der Forschung. *Neue Praxis*, 49(1), 37–53.

Pereda, N., Guilera, G., Forns, M., and Gómez-Benito, J. (2009). The prevalence of child sexual abuse in community and student samples: A meta-analysis. *Clinical Psychology Review*, 29(4), 328–338.

Rieder, S., Bieri, O., Schwenkel, C., Hertig, V., and Amberg, H. (2016). *Evaluation Kindes- und Erwachsenenschutzrecht. Analyse der organisatorischen Umsetzung und Kennzahlen zu Leistungen und Kosten. Bericht zuhanden des Bundesamts für Justiz (BJ)*. Available at: https://www.bj.admin.ch/dam/bj/de/data/gesellschaft/gesetzgebung/kesr/ber-interface-evaluation-kesr-d.pdf.download.pdf/ber-interface-evaluation-kesr-d.pdf.

Schmid, C., Jud, A., Mitrovic, T., Portmann, R., Knüsel, R., Salah, H. B., and Kosirnik, C. (2018). *Child endangerment in Switzerland: Frequency of incidents, agency responses and political implications*. Available at: https://www.hslu.ch/-/media/campus/common/files/dokumente/sa/forschung/optimus-3-booklet-study-ch-iii-en.pdf.

Schnurr, S. (2012). Grundleistungen der Kinder- und Jugendhilfe. In Bundesrat (Ed.), *Gewalt und Vernachlässigung in der Familie: notwendige Massnahmen im Bereich der Kinder- und Jugendhilfe und der staatlichen Sanktionierung: Bericht des Bundesrates in Erfüllung des Postulats Fehr (07.3725) vom 5. Oktober 2007* (pp. 66–109). Schweizerische Eidgenossenschaft.

Schnurr, S. (2016). Child Removal Poceedings in Switzerland. In K. Burns, T. Pösö, and M. Skivenes (Eds.), *Child welfare removals by the state. A cross-country analysis of decision-making systems* (pp. 117–145). Oxford University Press.

Schönbucher, V., Maier, T., Held, L., Mohler-Kuo, M., Schnyder, U., and Landolt, M. A. (2011). Prevalence of child sexual abuse in Switzerland: A systematic review. *Swiss Medical Weekly*, 140, w13123.

Seiterle, N. (2018). *Schlussbericht Bestandesaufnahme Pflegekinder und Heimkinder Schweiz 2015–2017*. PACH Pflege- und Adoptivkinder Schweiz and Intergras—Fachverband Sozial- und Sonderpädagogik. Available at: https://pa-ch.ch/wp-content/uploads/2018/10/Seiterle-2018_Bestandesaufnahme-2015-2017_d.pdf.

Spratt, T., Nett, J., Bromfield, L., Hietamäki, J., Kindler, H., and Ponnert, L. (2014). Child protection in Europe: Development of an international cross-comparison model to inform national policies and practices. *British Journal of Social Work*, 45(5), 1508–1525.

Stoltenborgh, M., Bakermans-Kranenburg, M. J., Alink, L. R. A., and van Ijzendoorn, M. H. (2012). The universality of childhood emotional abuse: A meta-analysis of worldwide prevalence. *Journal of Aggression, Maltreatment & Trauma*, 21(8), 870–890.

Stoltenborgh, M., Bakermans-Kranenburg, M. J., van Ijzendoorn, M. H., and Alink, L. R. A. (2013). Cultural-geographical differences in the occurrence of child physical abuse? A meta-analysis of global prevalence. *International Journal of Psychology: Journal international de psychologie*, 48(2), 81–94.

Stoltenborgh, M., van Ijzendoorn, M. H., Euser, E. M., and Bakermans-Kranenburg, M. J. (2011). A global perspective on child sexual abuse: meta-analysis of prevalence around the world. *Child Maltreatment*, 16(2), 79–101.

Swiss Statistics. (2020a). *Einfamilienhaushalte mit Kindern in der Schweiz*. Available at: https://www.bfs.admin.ch/bfs/de/home/statistiken/kataloge-datenbanken/tabellen.assetdetail.11947520.html.

Swiss Statistics. (2020b). *Ständige Wohnbevölkerung nach Geschlecht und Alter*. Available at: https://www.bfs.admin.ch/asset/de/px-x-0102030000_101.

Swiss Statistics. (2020c). *Victim consultations by gender, age and nationality*. Available at:https://www.bfs.admin.ch/bfsstatic/dam/assets/12967924/master.

United Nations Committee on the Rights of the Child. (2015, February 26). *Concluding observations on the combined second to fourth periodic reports of Switzerland.* Available at: https://www.eda.admin.ch/dam/eda/en/documents/aussenpolitik/internationale-organisationen/Empfehlungen-Ausschusses-Bericht-Ueberein kommens-Rechte-Kindes-2015_EN.pdf.

van der Put, C. E., Assink, M., and Boekhout van Solinge, N. F. (2017). Predicting child maltreatment: A meta-analysis of the predictive validity of risk assessment instruments. *Child Abuse & Neglect,* 73, 71–88.

Wopmann, M. (2019, May 23). Zehn Jahre Erfassung von Kinderschutzfällen an Schweizerischen Kinderkliniken: Leider keine Erfolgsgeschichte! *Pädiatrie Schweiz.* Available at: https://www.paediatrieschweiz.ch/nationale-kinderschutzstatistik-2018/.

Wopmann, M. (2020, May 8). Kinderschutzfälle an Schweizerischen Kinderkliniken: Unverändert hohe Fallzahlen! *Pädiatrie Schweiz.* Available at: https://www.paediatrieschweiz.ch/kinderschutzstatistik-2019/.

Wyl, A. v., Howard, E. C., Bohleber, L., and Haemmerle, P. (2017). *Psychische Gesundheit und Krankheit von Kindern und Jugendlichen in der Schweiz: Versorgung und Epidemiologie. Eine systematische Zusammenstellung empirischer Berichte von 2006 bis 2016.* Schweizerisches Gesundheitsobservatorium.

Child Protection in the United States

Jennifer Lawson *and* Jill Duerr Berrick

Abstract

This chapter discusses child protection in the United States at the federal level. Federal policies governing the child welfare system need state and local jurisdictions to respond to child maltreatment. Government approaches to child welfare vary from child protection to family service programs. Maltreatment is treated as a product of inadequate parenting that results in substantial harm. Additionally, child welfare system responses range between risk assessment, in-home care, and out-of-home care. Child welfare professionals conduct eligibility determination for child welfare services and make recommendations to the courts about the need and nature of services. The US child welfare system constantly changes through shifts in federal, state, and local policies, as well as ongoing research into effective interventions and approaches.

Key Words: US, federal policies, child welfare system, jurisdictions, child protection, risk assessment, in-home care, out-of-home care, family service

Introduction

The child protection system in the United States is more accurately conceptualized as many state and local systems operating under an umbrella of broad federal mandates. The federal policies governing the child welfare system require state and local jurisdictions to respond to reports of child maltreatment and take steps to ensure the safety of children who are found to have been maltreated or who are at risk of harm due to maltreatment. While these broad guidelines exist to establish reasonably similar systems of protection across all US states and territories, there are substantial variations in policies, practices, and service approaches among state and regional jurisdictions (Berrick, 2012). This chapter provides an overview of the structure and features of the United States child welfare system at the federal level, with some discussion of state and local variations in the execution of child protection functions.

Child Maltreatment

Gilbert (1997) and Gilbert and colleagues (2012) suggest that, broadly, government approaches to child welfare fall on a continuum ranging from child protection to family service orientations. The child protection approach is characterized by a conceptualization that maltreatment is a product of inadequate parenting that results in substantial harm or risk of harm to children, warranting an investigative response by the state to uncover evidence and to respond to that harm. In contrast, the family service orientation conceives of the best interest of the child as responsive to state interventions focused on assessment of need and provision of therapeutic services. In this conceptual framework, the US system is oriented to the child protection paradigm, characterized by investigations of child maltreatment allegations, and a state response that often results in non-voluntary interventions such as court-ordered participation in services or removal of children from homes where they are deemed to be at risk of continuing harm (Gilbert et al., 2012).

Under this child protection approach, eligibility for child welfare services is determined by child welfare professionals who investigate allegations of maltreatment that are reported to abuse and neglect "hotlines" operated by state or county-level child protective services (CPS) agencies. While any person may initiate a child maltreatment investigation by sharing concerns via the reporting hotline (or in some localities, reporting websites), each state has its own laws establishing which individuals are legally mandated to make such reports when there are concerns of possible maltreatment. In all states, professionals who encounter children in the course of their jobs (such as teachers, counselors, medical personnel, and law enforcement officials) are mandated by law to report suspected child maltreatment, and 19 states (including Puerto Rico) require all members of the public to report suspicions of child abuse or neglect (Child Welfare Information Gateway [CWIG], 2019).

When a report is made to a hotline alleging potential abuse or neglect of a child, a CPS professional makes a determination of whether the expressed concerns meet the state-specific statutory guidelines to trigger a child welfare system response. Nationally, close to half (45.8% during the most recent reporting year) of reports are "screened out," or determined not to meet criteria for a child welfare response (USDHHS, 2021a). The reports that are deemed appropriate for a CPS response are "screened-in," and in many states, there are two primary pathways of intervention that a report can take from that point: assessment or investigation. Assessments (also called differential or alternative responses) are reserved for a relatively small proportion of low- to medium-risk circumstances in which families are offered voluntary community-based services to meet identified needs. In these situations, an investigation to produce a legal finding of maltreatment is not required. The philosophy behind the alternative response/assessment approach is to offer non-adversarial assistance to voluntarily engage families who could benefit from community services, but where the families' difficulties do not present immediate threats to child safety (Kaplan & Merkel-Holguin, 2008).

Investigations, by contrast, are utilized to respond to the majority of screened-in reports in which the circumstances and level of concern for a child's safety warrant full evaluation and gathering of evidence to determine whether the child has been maltreated (or is at risk of being maltreated), and whether further intervention or services are needed to ensure child safety (USDHHS, 2021a). Cases that start as assessment-only can move to an investigation track if information arises during the assessment that indicates a higher risk case warranting full investigation. Alternative response is implemented unevenly across states; some states do not utilize alternative response at all and instead investigate all screened-in referrals. In 2020, approximately 3,145,000 children, 13.8% of all 2,120,316 children nationally who were the subject of a screened-in report, received an alternative response rather than an investigative response (USDHHS, 2021a).

Among cases receiving a full investigation, some are "substantiated," where CPS professionals have verified that the circumstances fall within the state's definition of maltreatment, and the children who were the subject of the allegations are considered to be victims of abuse or neglect. A minority of all investigated reports of maltreatment result in a substantiated disposition; in 2020, some 618,000 children (8.4 per 1,000 children in the US population) were found to be victims of maltreatment after substantiated reports (USDHHS, 2021a). These child victims represent about 17% of all children who were subjects of screened-in CPS reports nationally. There are, however, sizable differences across states in the proportion of children who are substantiated as victims of maltreatment; in 2020, the state of Maine had the highest rate of substantiation at 19.0 children per 1,000 in the population, while the state of Pennsylvania had the lowest rate at only 1.7 children per 1,000 (USDHHS, 2021a). While research is scant on the reasons for such dramatic differences in substantiation rates by state, they likely reflect variability in state-specific reporting and screening patterns, as well as differences in local policies and practices related to investigation and substantiation, rather than substantial differences in the underlying incidence of maltreatment.

Definitions for what circumstances are considered maltreatment also vary from state to state, but all fall within the minimum standards established by the federal government in the Child Abuse Prevention and Treatment Act of 1974 (CAPTA). The minimum definition of maltreatment according to CAPTA (1974) is:

> Any recent act or failure to act on the part of a parent or caretaker which results in death, serious physical or emotional harm, sexual abuse, or exploitation; or an act or failure to act which presents an imminent risk of serious harm.

Within these broad parameters, each state has established definitions that formalize the statutory guidelines for what circumstances constitute maltreatment in that state. Testa (2008) has argued that the scope of public interest in the welfare of children ranges between "two opposing conceptions of the proper relationship between the child and the state" (p. 109). The narrow scope of interest reflects the belief that the state should only intervene to protect children when there is threat of immediate bodily harm to a child, while the diffuse scope of interest reflects the belief that public intervention should occur when a child's well-being is seriously compromised, not only when there is an immediate safety threat. Evidence for the diffuse approach is seen in the gradual widening of the criteria for defining maltreatment from physical abuse (the target of early formal CPS intervention) to conditions presenting less immediate safety threats, such as emotional abuse, parental drug use, neglect, and in more recent years, child exposure to domestic violence (Myers, 2006; Casey Family Programs, 2014; Henry, 2017).

Continuing a multi-decade pattern, neglect continues to be the most prevalent maltreatment type in the United States, affecting 76.1% of children determined to be victims of maltreatment in 2020 (USDHHS, 2021a). In the same year, 16.5% of child victims experienced physical abuse, 9.4% experienced sexual abuse, and 14.6% experienced less common types of maltreatment, such as psychological abuse, medical neglect, or sex trafficking (USDHHS, 2021a). Child victims of maltreatment are not evenly distributed across demographic groups. Younger children are substantially overrepresented among victims; in 2020, more than a quarter (28.6%) of child victims were under the age of 3. Consistent with prior years of data, a plurality (43.1%) of child victims in 2020 were White, compared with 23.6% who were Hispanic/Latino, 21.1% who were African American, and 1.5% who were American Indian or Alaskan Native (USDHHS, 2021a). These figures, however, reflect rates of maltreatment that are disproportionately high for African American and Native American children compared to their representation in the US child population (discussed further in a subsequent section). It is also important to note that these statistics only reflect maltreatment that was brought to the attention of CPS and substantiated through an investigation, not all maltreatment that occurred in the population.

Child Welfare System Responses

Risk Assessment

When families become involved with the child protection system, one of the core functions of child welfare professionals is to assess the level of risk to children alleged to have been maltreated. Risk assessment is a difficult but critical task for child welfare workers. If the level of risk is underestimated, children may be seriously or even fatally harmed; if the level of risk is overestimated, families can be subjected to unnecessary government intervention, including loss of custody or even the termination of parental rights. Risk assessment plays a central role across child protection agencies in determining what additional protective interventions may be needed to ensure child safety, but different jurisdictions use different approaches to make the risk determinations that drive case decisions and service responses.

Debate among child welfare stakeholders has been ongoing for many years in relation to appropriate risk assessment strategies to guide CPS decision making. Standardized measurement tools have developed over recent decades to reduce the human error inherent to risk assessment based solely on the clinical judgment of professionals (Carnochan et al., 2013; Gambrill & Shlonsky, 2000; Pecora et al., 2013; Cuccaro-Alamin et al., 2017). Current risk assessment tools used in child welfare practice include consensus-based tools, actuarial tools, and recently in a small number of jurisdictions, the newer strategy of predictive risk modeling. Consensus-based risk assessment tools provide CPS professionals with an organized system for examining maltreatment-related risk factors. Consensus based tools are not statistically validated, but rather they use expert consensus on domains and indicators of risk to help practitioners arrive at a risk determination using a systematized, rather than ad hoc, method (Cuccaro-Alamin et al., 2017). Actuarial tools (such as the widely used Structured Decision-Making system) are also standardized decision aids, yet these are distinguished by the use of empirically-derived risk factors for maltreatment and statistical validation of intrument reliability and validity (Pecora et al., 2013). Research comparing the performance of consensus-based and actuarial risk assessment instruments suggests that actuarial measures assist CPS professionals in more accurately predicting maltreatment risk compared to consensus-based measures (D'Andrade et al., 2005; Cuccaro-Alamin et al., 2017).

A newer risk assessment method that is being utilized in some limited child welfare jurisdictions is predictive risk modeling (PRM), which uses advanced statistical techniques (artificial neural networks) to mine population-level data and produce a unique maltreatment risk score for children reported to CPS. Risk scores generated through PRM can be used to target families for early intervention to prevent child welfare involvement, or to help make determinations of which families reported to CPS should be screened in for investigation. Early research on PRM suggests more accurate maltreatment risk prediction than actuarial and consensus-based methods, though operational, legal, and ethical challenges are still under consideration (for a review of extant research, including benefits, barriers, and ethical considerations, see Cuccaro-Alamin et al., 2017; Drake et al., 2020).

Post-response Services

Risk assessments are used to support decision making for subsequent protective interventions that can be taken at the close of a child welfare investigation or assessment. For cases in which the assessed level of risk is low, CPS professionals may close the case without further action or refer the family to voluntary community-based services. For cases with higher levels of assessed risk, there are two case pathways representing an escalation of CPS involvement with families: in-home services and out-of-home care (also called substitute care or foster care).

IN-HOME SERVICES

In-home services, also referred to as family preservation services, are provided to families based on a multidimensional assessment of their needs and strengths in cases with a level of risk that warrants further protective involvement beyond investigation or assessment. These services (which may include substance abuse treatment, mental health treatment, individual or family counseling, or domestic violence intervention, among many others) are time limited, usually up to a few months, and are meant to reduce or mitigate risks to child safety and strengthen family functioning while the child remains in the custody of the caregivers in his or her home. Typically, in-home services are not directly provided by child welfare professionals in public CPS agencies; rather, child welfare agencies contract with community providers to deliver services to families while CPS professionals continue to monitor the family's services, track progress, link the family to resources, and provide ongoing risk and safety assessments. In 2020, some 1.2 million children (representing 59.7% of children who were substantiated as victims of maltreatment and 27% of children whose cases were assessed or investigated but not substantiated) received in-home services through child welfare agencies (USDHHS, 2021a). In-home services may be provided in conjunction with a court order and judicial oversight, or they may be used in voluntary agreements with families that do not involve the court system (Berrick, 2012; CWIG, 2014).

The effectiveness and quality of in-home services that families receive can vary widely based on the local availability of providers and the service arrays offered by those providers (Berrick, 2012; Institute of Medicine & National Research Council [IOM & NRC], 2014). Recent decades have seen advances in the development of effective child welfare interventions, including therapeutic modalities for treating children who have been exposed to trauma and empirically-supported parent training models (IOM & NRC, 2014). The extent to which families receive effective services, however, depends on many factors that are highly variable across jurisdictions, including the accuracy of the family's assessed needs and strengths, the availability of community providers offering needed services, the use of empirically-supported service arrays among providers, the quality of the child welfare agency's engagement with families and monitoring of progress, and use of culturally responsive practices in both the child welfare agency and the provider community (CWIG, 2015). Determining whether in-home child welfare services as a whole are effective at achieving the aims of reducing risk, strengthening family functioning, and preventing out-of-home placement is difficult because there are so many variations in these dimensions of service delivery, as well as in which families are selected to receive services. Findings from prior research on the effectiveness of family preservation is indeed mixed, probably due to these inconsistencies in targeting and delivery across jurisdictions. A meta-analysis of intensive family preservation programs indicates that families may experience improvements in family functioning, but out-of-home placement prevention is unlikely (Al et al., 2012). A more recent synthesis of studies limited only to child welfare clients suggests that incidents of child maltreatment may not be affected (Schweitzer et al., 2015).

OUT-OF-HOME CARE

The most intensive intervention child welfare authorities can employ to protect children who are at continuing risk of maltreatment is removing them from their families of origin and placing them in out-of-home care. In these instances, the state becomes the legal custodian of the children while the parents receive services to try to remediate the circumstances leading to the out-of-home placement. Recommendations to involuntarily separate children and parents are made by child welfare professionals and must be confirmed by the courts. In court, interested parties' legal interests are represented by counsel. Indigent parents may be provided legal representation, and parents with separate interests in the children may each have their own representation. Federal law requires that courts appoint a guardian ad litem (GAL) to represent the interests of children in child welfare cases that result in legal action. Depending on the state and the local court jurisdiction, the GAL may be an attorney or a trained volunteer from the community (CWIG, 2017; Piraino, 1999).

When children are placed in out-of-home care, parents receive services similar to in-home services, with judicial oversight. This action is typically involuntary and is reserved for cases in which the safety of the children cannot be assured while remaining in the home. Per federal law, parents are given up to 12 months (with a possible extension of up to six more months) to utilize services and address the problems that led to the removal of their children in order to have their children returned to their care.

Younger children are the likeliest to enter out-of-home care; 20% of 2020 foster care entries were children younger than 1, and nearly half (49%) were children under age 6 (USDHHS, 2021b). As with maltreatment victimization, White children represent the largest number of children entering care, although they are underrepresented compared to their proportion of the total child population, while African American and Native American children are overrepresented among foster care entries compared to their representation in the population. Neglect and parental drug abuse are the most common risk factors associated with children's placement into out-of-home care (USDHHS, 2021b).

Nationally, only about one in five children verified as maltreatment victims following a CPS investigation are removed from their homes and placed in out-of-home care (IOM & NRC, 2014; USDHHS, 2021a), amounting to some 216,838 children in the United States entering foster care in 2020 (USDHHS, 2021b). Rates of entry to out-of-home care, however, vary considerably by state; in 2020 rates of entry (among children determined to be maltreatment victims) by states exhibited a staggering range, from a low of 4.4% in Kentucky to a high of 48.1% in South Dakota (USDHHS, 2021a). Research suggests that state-specific cultural orientations and socioeconomic conditions are the primary predictors of state variation in foster care entry rates (Russell & Macgill, 2015).

Nationally and across many states, the number of foster care entries, and relatedly, the total number of children in foster care, has been relatively stable since 2015. Each year the federal government takes a point-in-time measure of all children in foster care nationally, and in each state, on a single day. In 1999, the foster care caseload hit a record with 597,000 children in care at the point-in-time count. This figure decreased every subsequent year through 2012, when the count reached a low of 397,000 children in care and then began an upward trajectory to the current (as of 2020) count of 407,493 children in care (USDHHS, 2021b). Though the precise reasons for the increases in foster care entries are still being determined, some preliminary information from state child welfare agencies suggests that an increase in parental substance abuse, much of which is associated with the opioid epidemic in the United States, may be a primary driver of the increase in out-of-home placements (Administration on Children, Youth, and Families [ACYF], 2016; Sepulveda & Williams, 2019).

Once in out-of-home care, there is also wide variation in how long children remain in care, their living arrangements while placed out-of-home, and the circumstances to which they exit care. Some children placed out-of-home live with extended family members instead of in a foster home with unrelated caregivers. Placements with family members are collectively referred to as kinship placements or relative placements, and these are prioritized in federal law as the preferred placement type when children cannot remain in their own homes. In some states and localities, children may be placed with relatives through voluntary or informal arrangements in order to prevent the state from taking custody of the children. These informal kinship care arrangements are often not supervised by the court system, and they are utilized to divert families away from formal out-of-home placements in which the state assumes custody of the children while services are provided. As such, children in voluntary diversion placements with relatives are not counted in federal statistics as children in out-of-home care. The only estimates currently available suggest that anywhere from 135,000 to 400,000 children live with relatives under kinship diversion (Ehrle et al., 2003; Main et al., 2006; Annie E. Casey Foundation, 2013). Nationally, one-third of all children in formal out-of-home care are placed with relatives (USDHHS, 2021b).

When children cannot remain in their own homes, and there are no relatives able to act as substitute caregivers, child welfare agencies are mandated to place children in the least restrictive setting to meet their needs. For most children, this means placement in a nonrelative foster family home. Some children and youth with higher levels of need, however, are placed in more restrictive group homes or other institutional settings, collectively referred to as congregate care. During the point-in-time measurement in 2020, 10% of all children in out-of-home care were placed in a congregate care setting (USDHHS, 2021b), though recently passed federal policy mandates will limit the use of congregate care placements even further (Family First Prevention Services Act of 2018).

Research is clear that placement stability is associated with more positive emotional and behavioral outcomes for children, even when accounting for any behavioral difficulties upon entering care (Rubin et al., 2007a). Children who are removed to out-of-home care, however, often experience more than one placement during their time in care, especially those placed in nonrelative settings. One study, using a large nationally representative sample of children who entered out-of-home care following a CPS investigation, found that children had an average number of slightly more than three placements while in care (Rubin et al., 2007b). Older youth and children with mental health challenges are more likely to experience placement changes (Rubin et al., 2007b), while children in kinship placements have more stablity (Font, 2015).

Exits from Out-of-home Care

Among children exiting care, almost half (45%) leave within 12 months (CWIG, 2018) and the median length of stay in care is 14.6 months (USDHHS, 2021b). The average duration in care has crept up slightly over the past decade, but the proportion of children in care for extended stays is relatively low and the proportion of children experiencing lengthy stays in care has been steadily declining (Wulczyn, 2020). Children's length of stay in care is strongly associated with the type of permanency they achieve. Children who leave care to reunify with their birth parents typically experience the shortest stays in care. As the probability of reunification falls with time, however, the likelihood of adoption rises.

The majority of children placed in foster care are ultimately reunified with their parent (Wulczyn, 2020; USDHHS, 2021b). Reunification with birth parents, however, is not always durable, as some children who are reunified with their families will later return to foster care. The percentage of children who re-enter care is variable based on the state or local jurisdiction of the case, the age of the child, and the length of time the child initially spent in care. It is estimated that between 15 and 30% of children who have reunified with their birth parent will later re-enter out-of-home care (Lee et al., 2012; Wulczyn et al., 2020). Despite changes in foster care caseloads since 2000, the proportion of all children in foster care who are re-entries to care has remained stable at 20% throughout that time (Roberts et al., 2017). The high re-entry rates speak to the vulnerability of families deeply involved with the child welfare system, the paucity of services available to families following reunification, and the fragility of the changes parents attempt to enact in order to keep their children safe (Font et al., 2018).

When circumstances prevent children from reunifying with their families of origin, child welfare professionals pursue other substitute care arrangements to provide legally binding and emotionally lasting connections with permanent caregivers (Testa, 2005). Federal law privileges adoption as the next best option for children when reunification is deemed impossible. Adoption involves termination of parental rights and the permanent transfer of care, custody, and control of the child to new parents. Children can be legally adopted by relatives or by unrelated caregivers. Adoption from foster care accounts for about 40% of all adoptions in the United States every year; inter-country and private adoptions account for the remainder (Vandiviere et al., 2009). In the most recent year for which data are available, of all children exiting foster care, 25% exited to adoption (USDHHS, 2021b).

In some cases, adoption is not a permanency option for children. Because adoption requires the termination of parents' rights to a child, and is considered an extreme state intervention, it may not suit some children's or caregivers' interests. Older children in kinship foster care, for example, may be reluctant to have their legal ties to their parent severed. Kinship foster parents may also be hesitant to pursue adoption as it may signify a break in the family that is neither necessary nor preferred. In cases such as these, legal guardianship may be an appropriate alternative, offering children and caregivers the legal security afforded by the transfer of custody from the state to the caregiver. Unlike adoption, however, the parents retain their legal parental rights and can petition the court for the return of their child should circumstances change. Federal law allows kinship foster parents who become children's legal guardians the opportunity to receive a subsidy for the continued care of the child up to age 18. Thirty-six states and the District of Columbia have implemented kinship guardianship policies that provide ongoing foster care subsidies to caregivers (Grandfamilies.org, 2018).

Since the early 1980s, multiple child welfare policy and practice reforms have endeavored to support permanency for children; it is widely agreed that long-term foster care, considered a permanency "failure," should be avoided whenever possible. Efforts to promote permanency may be bearing fruit. Children rarely grow up in care. An analysis of infants placed in care during the first year of life and followed for 18 years found that less than 1% spent the duration of childhood in care (Magruder & Berrick, 2022). For older children ages 13 or younger placed in care, the likelihood of remaining in foster care to adulthood is less than 10% (Wulczyn, 2020).

When older youth are placed in care, opportunities for exits to permanency may be limited. As a result, older youth are more likely to exit care via "aging out" (Stott & Gustavsson, 2010). Federal funds are now available for states that elect to extend foster care beyond age 18; 25 states plus the District of Columbia (Washington, DC) currently do so (National Conference of State Legislatures, 2017). In these instances, youth are typically eligible to remain in care if they are in school or working (unless they have a disabling condition that prevents employment or education), and their care arrangement transitions from involuntary to voluntary.

Disproportionality in Child Welfare

The disproportionate representation of African American and Native American children among those reported for maltreatment, designated as victims of maltreatment, and placed in out-of-home care has been well established in recent decades and is the subject of vigorous debate among child welfare researchers, administrators, policymakers, and advocates. The discourse centers on the perceived causes of disproportionalities, and consequently, what actions should be taken to reduce them. Some researchers and advocates view disproportionality as primarily the product of racism at individual-, community-, and institutional-levels, both inside and outside of the child welfare system (e.g., Dettlaff & Boyd, 2020; Roberts, 2002; Roberts, 2022). In recent years, prominent voices with this view have brought public attention to a movement to abolish the child welfare system entirely. Rooted in the view that racism is the main cause of disproportionate maltreatment investigations and involuntary family separations, these perspectives see abolition as the path to eliminate racial inequities in the system and end harm to Black and Indigenous children and families (Dettlaff et al., 2020; Dettlaff & Boyd, 2020; Roberts, 2022). Other perspectives stem from a body of research demonstrating that when individual, family, and/or community poverty is controlled for, group differences by race/ethnicity in child welfare system involvement attenuate, suggesting that differences in macro-level socioeconomic conditions concentrate risk factors for maltreatment in some communities of color and are the primary drivers of disproportionate system involvement (e.g., Barth et al., 2021; Putnam-Hornstein et al., 2013; Kim & Drake, 2018; Drake et al., 2020). For those who view disproportionality as largely stemming from economic disparities, solutions to the problem primarily lie in strategies to reduce poverty and race-based income inequality (Barth et al., 2021). Across perspectives on the causes of and solutions to disproportionality, there is broad agreement that having a robust system of accessible supports for families in need of assistance—such as affordable child care, health care, safe housing, transportation, and disability services—would create a more equitable society with less need for child welfare involvement.

Policy Context

Many dimensions of child welfare system functioning, including important policy mandates such as the degree to which in-home services are prioritized over placement in foster care, have shifted over time as federal policies have redefined US child welfare priorities. The Child Abuse Prevention and Treatment Act of 1974 (CAPTA) was the first major federal law to establish broad national guidelines directing states to put child maltreatment reporting and investigation mechanisms in place, and to support these mandates with federal funding for maltreatment prevention efforts and service provision.

The Adoption Assistance and Child Welfare Act of 1980 (AACWA) was passed several years later to establish a framework of permanency planning for children placed in foster care. With AACWA, permanency became a core concept in child welfare that refers to a child's lifelong connections with stable, secure caregivers. The law set limits on the amount of time children spent in care and prioritized family-based out-of-home care settings (Testa, 2008). These priorities were addressed through the permanency planning provisions of AACWA, which mandated that child welfare agencies make "reasonable efforts" to prevent placement of children into out-of-home care, to reunify children with their caregivers as quickly as possible in cases where out-of-home placement was necessary, and to find adoptive families to serve as permanent caregivers in circumstances when children could not be safely reunified with their families.

In the mid-1990s, new federal legislation responded to ongoing concerns about how long children were staying in foster care. The Adoption and Safe Families Act of 1997 (ASFA) prioritized faster adoptions for children who were not able to be reunified with their families of origin. This legislation narrowed the time frame in which family reunification could occur before other permanency arrangements (such as adoption or permanent placement with extended family) were sought.

In 2008, Congress passed the Fostering Connections to Success and Increasing Adoptions Act, allowing states to extend foster care to age 19, 20, or 21 with federal financial participation. The law was based, in part, on research showing an array of adverse outcomes for transition-age youth following emancipation from foster care at age 18 (Courtney et al., 2007).

Most recently, the Family First Prevention Services Act of 2018 (FFPSA) implemented important changes that will allow federal foster care funds to be used for evidence-based mental health services, substance abuse treatment, and in-home parenting training interventions that are focused on preventing out-of-home placement. The legislation also limits states' use of federal funds to place children in congregate care settings rather than family-based settings. Provisions of the law have generally been heralded as an important opportunity for states to use federal funding more flexibly to support child and family needs (Haskins, 2020). Concerns about the limitation of the law have also been expressed (for a review, see Testa & Kelly, 2020). In particular, FFPSA supports the use of selected evidence-based practices (as determined by a federal government review process) that target specific family concerns (i.e., mental health, substance abuse, and parenting), but ignores one of the primary risk factors for child maltreatment: poverty. In addition, the threshold for determining whether a program or practice is evidence-based is higher than the norms that have traditionally been employed in the field of child welfare, and some of the evidence-based programs are proprietary and therefore expensive for child welfare agencies to initiate. Moreover, funding from the law can only be used for families already involved with the child welfare system, and whose children are defined as "candidates" for foster care placement (those considered at imminent risk of removal). The prevention funding available under FFPSA, therefore, ignores the millions of families who need support to avoid contact with the child welfare system altogether. As FFPSA rollout continues across states, future research will be required to carefully examine whether the law achieves its intended goal of stabilizing vulnerable families and reducing foster care entries.

Service Delivery and Financing

In most states, eligibility determination for child welfare services is conducted by child welfare professionals working within public child welfare agencies. These professionals make recommendations to the courts about the need for and the nature of services that will be provided in the case of involuntary services, and monitor parental progress with case plans in voluntary and involuntary cases.

Child welfare agencies typically contract with community-based organizations (CBOs) for the services that child welfare clients require. These might include parent training, therapy, substance abuse treatment, or domestic violence counseling, for example. In some states, activities associated with case plan compliance may also be conducted by staff in private non-profit agencies under a public contract (Flaherty et al., 2008).

Funding for services includes federal, state, local, and philanthropic resources; child welfare agencies typically blend funding from multiple sources including child welfare, health, and public assistance, to meet child and family needs (Jordan & Connelly, 2016). On average, the federal government pays for the majority of child welfare services, but there are large differences among states regarding the proportion of child welfare funds from federal, state, and local sources (deVooght & Cooper, 2012). The federal government spent about $13 billion on child welfare in the most recent year for which we have data (2012), representing about 0.6% of the total federal budget (Jordan & Connelly, 2016). The largest source of federal funding for child welfare services is provided through a policy mechanism called Title IV-E, which supports foster care, adoption, and guardianship for children placed in out-of-home care. Funding is open-ended, allowing states to claim these funds regardless of the number of children requiring assistance. Federal funding to support families and prevent out-of-home care is more limited; funds are capped and typically do not extend to the number of families requiring preventive services (deVooght et al., 2014).

Efforts in recent years to experiment with Title IV-E dollars (variously called "Title IV-E waivers") have led to a number of child welfare innovations (James Bell Associates, 2015). In most instances, states and jurisdictions engaged in these experiments have used the flexibility of IV-E funding to promote prevention services and reduce reliance on out-of-home care. In fact, the 2018 Family First Prevention Services Act (previously described) was developed in part due to findings from the Title IV-E waivers that suggested investments in evidence-based prevention services might offer benefits to families and give state agencies more autonomy in using federal funds to meet families' individual needs.

Conclusion

The child welfare system in the United States is constantly changing and is characterized by a high degree of experimentation to determine "what works." The evidence base supporting most child welfare interventions is still notably thin, so few child welfare practitioners or policymakers are satisfied with the status quo. The most recent federal law (Family First Prevention Services Act), which requires deployment of evidence-based practices (in circumscribed areas) in exchange for federal funds, is likely to accelerate interest in developing and testing new models of service.

Other trends likely to characterize child welfare in the near term include increasing pressure to reduce utilization of congregate care for children, increasing utilization of kin (either as foster care providers or as informal caregivers outside of the child welfare system), and to reduce entries to care by narrowing eligibility to circumstances only involving considerable danger. Whether these inducements to change are inspired by an interest in children's well-being, fiscal conservativism, decreasing racial disproportionalities, or in reducing the role of the state in the private affairs of families will be revealed in time.

References

ACYF. (2016). Number of children in foster care increases for third consecutive year. *Children's Bureau Express*, 17(8), 1. Available at: https://cbexpress.acf.hhs.gov/index.cfm?event=website.viewArticles&issueid=181&articleid=4855.

Al, C. M., Stams, G. J., Bek, M. S., Damen, E. M., Asscher, J. J., and van der Laan, P. H. (2012). A meta-analysis of intensive family preservation programs: Placement prevention and improvement of family functioning. *Children and Youth Services Review*, 34, 1472–1479.

Annie E. Casey Foundation. (2013). *The kinship diversion debate: Policy and practice implications for children, families, and child welfare agencies*. Annie E. Casey Foundation. Available at: http://www.aecf.org/m/pdf/KinshipDiversionDebate.pdf.

Barth, R. P., Berrick, J. D., Garcia, A., Drake, B., Jonson-Reid, M., Greeson, J., and Gyourko, J. (2021). *Research to consider prior to effectively re-designing child welfare services*. Research on Social Work Practice.

Berrick, J. D. (2012). Trends and issues in the US child welfare system. In N. Gilbert, N. Parton, and M. Skivenes (Eds.), *Child protection systems: International trends and orientations* (pp. 17–36). Oxford University Press.

Carnochan, S., Rizik-Baer, D., and Austin, M. J. (2013). Preventing re-entry to foster care. *Journal of Evidence-Based Social Work*, 10, 196–209.

Casey Family Programs. (2014). *Addressing child sex trafficking from a child welfare perspective*. Casey Family Programs.

Child Abuse Prevention and Treatment Act. (1974). (42 U.S.C.A. 5106g) amended by Keeping Children and Families Safe Act, 2003.

CWIG. (2014). *In-home services in child welfare*. US Department of Health and Human Services, Children's Bureau.

CWIG. (2017). *Representation of children in child abuse and neglect proceedings*. US Department of Health and Human Services, Children's Bureau.

CWIG. (2018). *Foster care statistics, 2016*. US Department of Health and Human Services, Children's Bureau.

CWIG. (2019). *Mandatory reporters of child abuse and neglect*. US Department of Health and Human Services, Children's Bureau.

Courtney, M. E., Dworsky, A., Cusick, G. R., Havlicek, J., and Perez, A. (2007). *Midwest evaluation of the adult functioning of former foster youth: Outcomes at age 21*. Chapin Hall Center for Children.

Cuccaro-Alamin, S., Foust, R., Vaithianathan, R., and Putnam-Hornstein, E. (2017). Risk assessment and decision-making in child protective services: Predictive risk modeling in context. *Children and Youth Services Review*, 79, 291–298.

D'Andrade, A., Benton, A., and Austin, M. J. (2005). *Risk and safety assessment in child welfare: Instrument comparisons*. Bay Area Social Services Consortium.

Dettlaff, A. J. and Boyd, R. (2020). Racial disproportionalities and disparities in the child welfare system: Why do they exist and what can be done to address them? *Annals of the American Academy of Political and Social Sciences*, 692, 253–274.

Dettlaff, A. J., Weber, K., Pendleton, M., Boyd, R., Bettencourt, B., and Burton, L. (2020). It is not a broken system, it is a system that needs to be broken: the upEND movement to abolish the child welfare system. Journal of Public Child Welfare, 14(5), 500–517.

Drake, B., Jonson-Reid, M., Kim, H., Chiang, C.-J., and Davalishvili, D. (2020). Disproportionate need as a factor explaining racial disproportionality in the CW system. In A. J. Dettlaff (Ed.), *Racial disproportionality and disparities in the child welfare system*. Child maltreatment (contemporary issues in research and policy) (vol. 11, pp. 159–176). Springer.

deVooght, K. and Cooper, H. (2012). *Child welfare financing in the United States*. State Policy Advocacy and Reform Center, Annie E. Casey Foundation.

deVooght, K., Fletcher, M., and Cooper, H. (2014). *Federal, state, and local spending to address child abuse and neglect in 2012*. Child Trends.

Ehrle, J., Geen, R., and Main, R. (2003). *Kinship foster care: Custody, hardships, and services.* Urban Institute. Available at: http://webarchive.urban.org/publications/310893.html.

Flaherty, C., Collins-Camargo, C., and Lee, E. (2008). Privatization of child welfare services: Lessons learned from experienced states regarding site readiness assessment and planning. *Children and Youth Services Review*, 30(7), 809–820.

Font, S. A. (2015). Is higher placement stability in kinship foster care by virtue or design? *Child Abuse & Neglect*, 42, 99–111.

Font, S. A., Sattler, K. M., and Gershoff, E. (2018). When home is still unsafe: From family reunification to foster care reentry. *Journal of Marriage and Family*, 80, 1333–1343.

Gambrill, E., and Shlonsky, A. (2000). Risk assessment in context. *Children and Youth Services Review*, 22(11–12), 813–837.

Gilbert, N. (1997). *Combatting child abuse: International perspectives and trends.* Oxford University Press.

Gilbert, N., Parton, N., and Skivenes, M. (2012). *Child protection systems: International trends and orientations.* Oxford University Press.

Grandfamilies.org. (2018). Subsidized guardianship: Summary and analysis. Available at: http://www.grandfamilies.org/Topics/Subsidized-Guardianship/Subsidized-Guardianship-Summary-Analysis.

Haskins, R. (2020). Child welfare financing: What do we fund, how, and what could be improved? *Annals of the American Academy of Political and Social Sciences*, 692, 50–67.

Henry, C. (2017). Expanding the legal framework for child protection: Recognition of and response to child exposure to domestic violence in California law. *Social Service Review*, 91(2), 203–232.

Institute of Medicine and National Research Council. (2014). *New directions in child abuse and neglect research.* The National Academies Press.

James Bell Associates. (2015). *Summary of the title IV-E child welfare waiver demonstrations.* James Bell Associates.

Jordan, E. and Connelly, D. D. (2016). *An introduction to child welfare funding and how states use it.* Child Trends.

Kaplan, C. and Merkel-Holguin, L. (2008). Another look at the national study on differential response in child welfare. *Protecting Children*, 23, 5–21.

Kim, H. and Drake, B. (2018). Child maltreatment risk as a function of poverty and race/ethnicity in the USA. *International Journal of Epidemiology*, 47(3), 780–787.

Lee, S., Jonson-Reid, M., and Drake, B. (2012). Foster care re-entry: Exploring the role of foster care characteristics, in-home child welfare services, and cross-sector services. *Children and Youth Services Review*, 34(9), 1825–1833.

Magruder, J. and Berrick, J. D. (2022). A longitudinal investigation of infants and out-of-home care. *Journal of Public Child Welfare*, 1–18. doi.org/10.1080/15548732.2022.2036294.

Main, R., Macomber, J. E., and Geen, R. (2006). *Trends in service receipt: Children in kinship care gaining ground* (Series B. No. B-68). Urban Institute.

Myers, J. E. B. (2006). *Child protection in America: Past, present, and future.* Oxford University Press.

National Conference of State Legislatures. (2017). *Extending foster care beyond 18.* Available at: http://www.ncsl.org/research/human-services/extending-foster-care-to-18.aspx.

Pecora, P. J., Chahine, Z., and Graham, J. C. (2013). Safety and risk assessment frameworks: Overview and implications for child maltreatment fatalities. *Child Welfare*, 92(2), 143–160.

Putnam-Hornstein, E., Needell, B., King, B., and Johnson-Motoyama, M. (2013). Racial and ethnic disparities: A population-based examination of risk factors for involvement with child protective services. *Child Abuse & Neglect*, 37, 33–46.

Roberts, D. (2002). *Shattered bonds: The color of child welfare.* Basic Civitas Books.

Roberts, Y. H., O'Brien, K., and Pecora, P. J. (2017). *Supporting lifelong families: Ensuring long-lasting permanency and well-being.* Casey Family Programs.

Roberts, D. (2022). *Torn apart: How the child welfare system destroys Black families and how abolition can build a safer world.* Basic Books.

Rubin, D. M., O'Reilly, A. L. R., Hafner, L., Luan, X., and Localio, R. (2007a). Placement stability and early behavioral outcomes among children in out-of-home care. In R. Haskins, F. Wulczyn, and M. Webb (Eds.), *Child protection: Using research to improve policy and practice* (pp. 171–186). Brookings Institution.

Rubin, D. M., O'Reilly, A. L. R., Luan, X., and Localio, A. R. (2007b). The impact of placement stability on behavioral well-being for children. *Pediatrics*, 119(2), 336–344.

Russell, J. R. and Macgill, S. (2015). Demographics, policy, and foster care rates: a predictive analytics approach. *Children and Youth Services Review*, 58, 118–126.

Schweitzer, D. D., Pecora, P. J., Nelson, K., Walters, B., and Blythe, B. J. (2015). Building the evidence base for intensive family preservation services. *Journal of Public Child Welfare*, 9, 423–443.

Sepulveda, K. and Williams, S. C. (2019). *One in three children entered foster care in 2017 because of parental drug abuse.* Child Trends. Available at: https://www.childtrends.org/blog/one-in-three-children-entered-fos ter-care-in-fy-2017-because-of-parental-drug-abuse.

Stott, T. and Gustavsson, N. (2010). Balancing permanency and stability for youth in foster care. *Children and Youth Services Review*, 32(4), 619–625.

Testa, M. (2005). The quality of permanence: lasting or binding? Subsidized guardianship and kinship foster care as alternatives to adoption. *Virginia Journal of Social Policy and Law*, 12(13), 499–534.

Testa, M. (2008). New permanency strategies for children in foster care. In D. Lindsey and A. Shlonsky (Eds.), *Child welfare research* (pp. 108–124). Oxford University Press.

Testa, M. and Kelly, D. (2020). The evolution of federal child welfare policy through the Family First Prevention Services Act of 2018: opportunities, barriers, and unintended consequences. *Annals of the American Academy of Political and Social Sciences*, 692, 68–96.

US Department of Health and Human Services [USDHHS]. (2021a). *Child Maltreatment 2020.* Administration for Children and Families, Administration on Children, Youth, and Families, Children's Bureau. Available at: https://www.acf.hhs.gov/cb/report/child-maltreatment-2020.

US Department of Health and Human Services [USDHHS]. (2021b). *The AFCARS report no. 28.* Administration for Children and Families, Administration on Children, Youth, and Families, Children's Bureau.

Vandiviere, S., Malm, K., and Radel, L. (2009). *Adoption USA: A chartbook based on the 2007 National Survey of Adoptive parents.* US Department of Health and Human Services.

Wulczyn, F. (2020). Foster care in a life course perspective. *Annals of the American Academy of Political and Social Sciences*, 692, 227–252.

Wulczyn, F., Parolini, A., Schmits, F., Magruder, J., and Webster, D. (2020). Returning to foster care: Age and other risk factors. *Children and Youth Services Review*, 116, 105166.

PART II

Emerging

The Chilean Child Protection System

Carolina Muñoz-Guzman, Miguel Cillero Bruñol, *and* Mariana Bernasconi

Abstract

This chapter explores the child protection system in Chile. Social services have been shifting since the return of civilian rule in 1990 and the ratification of the UNCRC. Children are more affected by the geography of poverty than the rest of the Chilean population. Overall, the Chilean population benefited from modernization, but good policy design ideas and successful implementation would improve the living conditions of the population. Additionally, the state defines children as objects of intervention and state responsibility will only be invoked in the presence of social risks. The chapter also highlights the work and models enforced by the National Service for Minors (SENAME).

Key Words: Chile, social services, child protection system, poverty, modernization, population, SENAME, state responsibility, children, UNCRC

Introduction

This chapter describes the Chilean child protection system, which from the 1990s has been challenged to implement a rights-based approach to policy for children, a fundamental shift in the framework for public policy. Transforming social services for children in Chile has taken, until now, 28 years, since the return in 1990 to civilian rule after 17 years of military dictatorship, and the ratification of the United Nations Children's Rights Convention by the Chilean government in the same year. There is no research evaluating the whole process of implementation of the new policy, but a few studies suggest that the goal of installing a rights perspective has been hindered mainly because of lack of appropriate resources: legal, professional, financial, and political will, among others (SENAME, 2005; UNICEF, 2005; Comisión Expertos RPA, 2006; Comisión Expertos RPA, 2007).

The chapter is organized as follows: first, the reader is familiarized with the Chilean context; second, core Chilean child welfare policies and programs exemplifying this system are explored; then recent Chilean child protection policy trends and issues are described; and the chapter finalizes with a review of Chilean child protection results.

Chile, the Context of the Policy for Children

Chile is located in the Southern Cone of South America, bordering the South Pacific Ocean, south of Peru and west of Argentina. It has been commonly considered an archetype of privatization and neoliberal economic and social policies as strategies for economic growth and social equity (Marcus, 2004). However, the neoliberal model of development has increased long-standing forms of social and economic stratification, negatively affecting the perception of economic and social security, equity and trust among Chileans (Marcus, 2004; UNDP, 2009). According to Marcus (2004), Chile's labor market is organized roughly in two segments: permanent, more skilled, and better paid employees; and temporary, less skilled, and poorly paid workers. These differences underlie a persistent inequity in access to social security and health insurance (services privatized in the 1980s) for a group of the population, since access is mediated by permanent and formal employment. The poorest segments in Chilean society, thus, are users of the lower cost and lower quality social services provided by the state (Larragaña & Rodríguez, 2014).

Demographic data and information about governmental social spending is presented below with the aim of helping readers contextualize this research. The last census was carried out in Chile in 2017. Official figures from this census indicate a population of 17,327,192 inhabitants, with a rate of population growth of 1.3 people for each 100 inhabitants. This figure puts Chile as one of the countries with the weakest population growth in Latin America, compared to a regional average for Latin America and the Caribbean of around 8% growth (INE, 2003; PRB, 2011). 4,250,155 are children and adolescents under 18 years old (24.2% of the total population). Most of the population (88%) lives in urban areas; a trend produced by population displacement as well as accelerated urbanization. The population is greatly concentrated in the central region of the country, with 40% inhabiting the Metropolitan Region of the capital city, Santiago.

Turning now to quality of life indices, measures of economic growth show large and sustained progress for the past 30 years, well above the Latin American average. The increase in the size of Chile's economy has helped reduce poverty. The estimation of the magnitude of poverty in Chile, as in most of Latin American countries, is based on identifying poor households whose income is lower than the poverty line. The poverty line is set at the monetary value of the goods and services needed to satisfy essential needs. In Chile, economic growth and social policy in the period from 2006 to 2017 reduced poverty from 29% of the population to 9% (CASEN, 2017). This figure put 1.1 million Chileans in a situation of poverty, and over 400,000 in extreme poverty.

Children and adolescents are more affected by poverty and extreme poverty than the rest of the Chilean population; 23% live in poverty (CASEN, 2017). Poverty and extreme poverty were higher among households headed by women, a fraction of households that has been on the rise in the last decade, reaching now almost one-third of all homes. Children are especially affected by the geography of poverty, based on large economic disparities across the regions of the country (UNICEF, 2005).

In sum, the Chilean population has benefited from modernization, as attested by the country's age structure, improvements of social indices, and several sociodemographic changes produced by increases in schooling, female labor, and changes in family formation, among others. We have also seen that poverty in Chilean families is rooted in structural, unequal social factors, so that even though their quality of life has improved, there remains the challenge of transforming the life conditions of the poorest families. Advances in improving the living conditions of these groups requires not only the design of good policy ideas, but also successful implementation.

Hantrais (2004) distinguishes between four family policy patterns—de-familiarized, partly de-familiarized, familiarized, and re-familiarized—types of welfare states. "These regimes reflect different ways to mix social service providers with family responsibilities, leading to highly variable consequences in terms of the role of the family, but also in terms of resource distribution between richer and poorer, men and women, generations, immigrants and natives, etc." (Nygren, 2013). Chile fits the "familiarized" regime, characterized by a non-interventionist approach by the state and people's well-being is deeply embedded in, and supported by, family relationships.

Related to Hantrais' proposal, Gilbert and colleagues (2011) indicate that even though there are two main orientations in child welfare—a "child protection orientation" and a "family service orientation," child protection-oriented states have moved towards focusing on early intervention and family support. And those states that seemed family service oriented increasingly focus on dysfunctional features affecting children. Chilean child protection and family services have practices that are more family service-orientated and focus on family dysfunction and therapeutic orientations (Ursin et al., 2017).

These features respond to a transition of family policies from a view concerned with "social deviation," towards a rights perspective. The first view presents families facing social problems as in conditions or behaviors labeled as "situations of moral or material risk" or "irregular situations," under the framework of what is called in most of the Latin American countries the "Doctrine of Social Irregularity" (Congreso de Chile, 2005).

Core Child Welfare Policies and Programs that Exemplify the Chilean System

Main Developments in Social Care for Children in Chile: 1970–1990

The development of a framework for social care for childhood has been a long process in Chilean policy. Children have not had a public space as social actors with fundamental rights assured by the state, as free and equal citizens. What happened, instead, is that "throughout the twentieth century children appeared as a specific category of public policy only as part of problems in the private familial space, such as physical or sexual abuse, issues previously invisible to public policy, which later became social problems demanding state intervention" (Pilotti, 2000, p. 15).

Children were defined by the state as *objects of intervention*. State responsibility to children was activated only in the presence of social risk. Since social risk indices have been generally associated with precarious social contexts, the intersection between state and childhood involved children of the lower social classes. This explains why in Chile the social concern for children is focused on children in poverty. Thus, the objective of public action has been not to guarantee their rights, but to improve their social condition.

The system serving children in Chile up to 1990 was a tutelary one, as organized originally by Act 4.447, LM, in 1928, which aimed to deal with infractions of the law, abandonment, need for protection, and, generally, "irregular social situations" affecting children (Tello, 2003). This system was reinforced by Act 16.618 of 1967, which focused on irregular family relationships and children's behavior. During this period, children and families facing social problems were understood in terms of this notion of social irregularity.

The concept of "irregular" families and children, as Donzelot (1979) explains, was convenient because although not strictly medical, it did suggest a deficit of socialization, with moral connotations. Of course, all of this required an idea of the "regular," which coincided with the characteristics of middle-class families. The irregular, then, would be the pattern of behavior of poor families and children. Together with this labeling of some children and their families as deviant, there was a reformulation of the role of the state, which incorporated a protective "*parens patriae*" responsibility to children, in the place of parents, as it were (Pilotti, 2000, p. 18), whereby the state has a duty to supervise the discharge of parental responsibilities and other tasks associated with the satisfaction of basic needs of children.

This vigilant role over children's lives derived from social control practices exerted upon children and their families, justified by the families' alleged failure to properly raise their children. From this followed the policy of separating children from their families, and segregating them for long periods in out-of-home care institutions, which were to act as substitute parents.

The medical model underlying the understanding of these social processes, typical of early 20th-century social intervention, led to a classification of parental roles as dysfunctional when they affected the system, legitimating state intervention and affecting families' self-perception. The previous description constitutes the ideological basis for a state paternalistic perspective in children's services and an institutionalized view of children and families as deviant, a view particularly acute in Chile between 1973 and 1990, a period characterized by an authoritarian government and its systematic violation of human rights.

The National Service for Minors (SENAME) was established early in this period (1979), with the mission of stimulating, guiding, coordinating and technically supervising public and private institutions sharing its objectives (MIDEPLAN, 1997, p. 19). SENAME was to carry on with the work done until then by a National Council of

Minors, and to transfer some of its programs to private organizations. SENAME was created as a public service under the authority of the Ministry of Justice. Both SENAME and its predecessor organization worked under the sway of the Doctrine of Social Irregularity and saw their role as one of providing assistance to children by taking charge of them in substitution of the natural family, when that family was deemed dysfunctional for their developmental process (SENAME, 2005, p. 5).

The model implemented by SENAME had characteristics that, later on, would affect the context for the reforms introduced by future democratic governments (Tello, 2003). Specifically, these features are: 1) the ample powers given to Minors Tutelary Judges; 2) jurisdiction over issues ranging from social protection to juvenile law infractions under the same social service; and 3) outsourcing of some social care programs to the private sector through agencies appointed as collaborative organisms.

These characteristics, reminiscent of the history of childcare services in the industrialized world (Donzelet, 1969, p. 88), form the basic constitutive elements of the Doctrine of Social Irregularity. Under a functionalistic model, with the influence of the paternalistic perspective, state services defined some children's environments as poor and inadequate, and marked some social and familial configurations as risky. One of the main characteristics of this period was the increasing numbers of children living in residential care.

At the end of the 1980s, SENAME had increased its coverage of children in care by 55% compared to 1970. By the end of the 1990s, 45.1% of the children in SENAME's care were in residential care (MIDEPLAN, 1997 p. 19). This large proportion was in part a result of a perverse incentive carried by the funding mechanism for private agencies collaborating with SENAME, which paid four times as much for a child living in residential care than for home-based or agency-based services. Not surprisingly, a 1989 evaluation carried out by SENAME found that 40% of the children living in out-of-home care services did not need such services, that more than 20% had been institutionalized for more than five years, and that close to 40% stayed for more than a year, developing institutional patterns of replacement of the parental role (Contreras, 2003 p. 145).

We can see Chile following in the steps of 20th-century child welfare policy in developed countries: beneficent state action to protect children's welfare; courts and social workers as key decision makers on what would be best for the child; and disregard for any likely negative effects of state surveillance and intervention in child rearing, compared to the benefits of "saving" children in distress by transferring them to what were defined as better homes, which basically meant traditional families[1] (Freeman, 1983, p. 51; Fox, 1997).

Political changes in Chilean society, following the recovery of democracy in 1990, created an opportunity for renovation of this longstanding framework. The new aims of

---

[1] Family structure that consists of a man, woman, and one or more of their biological or adopted child(ren).

social care for children were framed under international agreements and more elaborated technical approaches to social policy.

Child Protection under a Rights Perspective from 1990

In the course of the late 20th century, society underwent a deep process of legalization and recognition of children's rights, whose landmark was the ratification of the United Nations Convention on the Rights of the Child (UNCRC) in 1989. The UNCRC reflects the most progressive and universal approach to the guarantee and protection of human rights, through the adoption of legal instruments that benefit from representative power and universal consensus. With the UNCRC ratification, roles and ideas about social actors were transformed under the principles of citizenship and human rights. This process included an ample debate about the conception Chileans had about children and the services provided for neglected children and young offenders. After Chile subscribed in 1990 to the UNCRC, the reform of national childcare began.[2]

The reform entailed a departure from the prior perspectives framing children's services towards promotional ones, where children's rights as human beings are at the core of child development, and where a rights perspective becomes the framework for social services for children. Children are thus seen today as bearers of multiple needs and potentials, able to participate and contribute to solving their own problems, according to their developmental stage (MIDEPLAN, 2000). The rights perspective underpinning the new paradigm proposes a new conception of childhood, and its relations with family, society and state, leaving behind the predominant idea of a child defined on the basis of his or her needs.

The new policy perspective considers that children require an integral and special protection system, configuring a new kind of social relation and culture that recognizes, values, and promotes children's rights. This requires stronger support of families so that they can fulfill their protective role, and the regulation of the mechanisms used by the state when facing the neglected rights of children. It also defines a role for the community, which should strengthen a culture of rights (MIDEPLAN, 2000). Under this framework, family is seen as the best provider of care for children, even when in need of external support, while the role of the state is defined as *preventing children from entering state care* through monitoring and supportive intervention, rather than coercive, punitive, or intrusive ones (Fox, 1997, p. 71). Explanations about how families come to need external support are not based on cause–effect rationalities, like those prevailing in the former perspective. Poor parenting is seen as a consequence of environmental conditions such as unemployment, single parenthood, social disadvantage, or deprived neighborhoods, for

---

[2] This reform took notice of similar developments elsewhere: the Estatuto del Niño y Adolescente del Brasil (Law No. 8,069, 1990); the Ley Orgánica para la Protección del Niño y del Adolescente de Venezuela (1998), and, at later stages, the Ley Orgánica de Protección Jurídica del Menor from Spain, 1996.

example, all of which influence parenting behavior and child-rearing methods. Ultimately, multi-causal conditions make families unable to meet the essential norms for childcare expected by society (Holman, 1987, p. 86).

In sum, the Chilean reform rests on three core principles enfolding the already discussed conceptualization of childhood: children's centrality, family as mainly responsible in children's care, and a support role for the state and community in ensuring children's (and families') rights. These principles imply a new configuration of the child's world: children themselves go from being seen as "objects" of interventions to rights holders, in a position of centrality, protected by the principles of non-discrimination and the gender perspective (UN, 2009, p. 7). Children's families are defined as the most important and natural group for children's upbringing, so that social services must strive for the child and family to stay together or reunify, or, when appropriate, find support in other close family members.

Regarding the role of state and social services, states should grant support for families, respecting always the child's view, but considering his/her developmental stage and his/her access to information. Interventions should take place only when the family, even with suitable backing, is unable to care for the child by itself. In this case, alternative care ought to be provided by authorities at the local level, or by duly authorized organizations of civil society. Finally, the community also has a role defining and achieving rights-based environments (UN, 2009, p. 6).

Chilean policy has incorporated the orientation of the UN, which constitutes the policy's core values. In the following section we will describe the policy's legal framework and guidelines, and sources of the specific requirements social services for children should meet to favor a rights-based perspective in the delivery of services. Even though Chile signed the UNCRC in 1990, only in 2000 did SENAME redefine its mission to protect and promote children's rights when these are infringed, and to contribute to young offenders' social inclusion. The reform of the Children Justice and Protection System challenged SENAME to specialize its programs in coordination with public and private actors. The proposals and institutional changes contained in this reform aimed at improving public and private support systems for children, in order to make them coherent with the UNCRC (Bulletin No. 3.792-07 2005). The measures adopted sought to modernize the legal system and the social policies available to guarantee and promote the integral development of children.

To set the grounds for this Integral Reform, the main legal changes were the creation of Family Courts, the new Subsidization Act of 2005, and the establishment of a specialized Social Services System for young offenders. Family Courts were created in 2004 through Act No. 19.968, with specialized jurisdiction over family problems and their resolution, complemented with a system of alternative means of conflict resolution (mediation), which was outsourced from the courts. This Act also established legal procedures for the protection of children, where Courts are slated to replace the figure of the Judge of Minors (SENAME, 2004, p. 7). The approval of the Subsidization Law in 2005 established a new welfare system for children, which favors non-institutionalization and family life. The new financial scheme replaced the subsidy paid for each child being served with a system of calls for proposal, where each private agency periodically presents its projects for funding and is evaluated according to the achievement of its goals.

The approval in 2007 of Act No. 20.084, after five years of discussion in Congress, created a specialized judicial system for young offenders, establishing procedures to investigate and assign responsibility for acts committed by adolescents between 14 and 18 years of age who break the law. The system's objectives are, among others, to introduce penal and procedural guarantees, to eliminate the declaration of moral awareness which was required to prosecute an adolescent between the ages of 16 and 18, and to apply less severe sanctions together with socio educative measures. These measures are administered directly by SENAME and by private organizations. This law brought a momentous change in how justice was administered for young offenders, as the figure of the Court of Minors disappeared, and children older than 14 were to be considered accountable for their actions, if found guilty in a trial with all the guarantees of the due process of law.

Chile's progress cannot be overlooked: subscribing to the UNCRC, launching a policy for children based on the UNCRC, and sanctioning specific laws to sustain the policy. But these advances are limited in their impact by the dearth of monitoring mechanisms to ensure the effective guarantee of rights, which, as asserted earlier, is a requirement to ensure the exercise of rights. In this regard, one characteristic defect of the Chilean legislative process is not identifying clear and measurable objectives for new laws that would enable the assessment of their efficacy in terms of outcomes or impacts (Manzi et al., 2011). During these 28 years there has been an important advance favoring program differentiation, at least in the creation of formal units such as Prevention and Participation, Adoption, Protection, and Juvenile Justice. All these units have an expression at the regional level, across the whole country. Currently this organization is under review to be reorganized, but this process is not discussed in this chapter.

Chilean Child Protection Policy Trends

Since the onset of the new policy for children, SENAME has been working to develop programmatic offerings in line with the UNCRC. To fulfill this responsibility SENAME divided its functions into two departments: the Rights Protection Department (RPD) and Department of Juvenile Criminal Responsibility (DJCR). In this chapter we will only focus on RPD services.

RPD produced policy guidelines for programmatic offerings establishing different and specialized systems, including financial channels and support programs, according to the characteristics of each child (SENAME, 2005). SENAME call for bids to non-profit organizations specialized in children's services; 96.2% of SENAME services are implemented by these organizations, the rest of the services are implemented by SENAME, and correspond to part of the alternative care services offered by the system.

RPD pursues children's best interests, protecting and restituting their rights through different services (DIPRESS, 2015–2018). The goals of the RPD are to promote and prevent children's maltreatment (DIPRESS, 2015–2018), as well as supervise service quality and efficient use of resources, and permanently adjust the services to improve quality (DIPRESS, 2015–2018).

SENAME works in coordination with different institutions to carry out the full process of services, from defining the protection measure to implementing and evaluating programs. Courts always will be involved if alternative care is mandated, and in order to grant access to services, courts also must be involved; given the scarcity of services, the judicial order gives priority to get services. Institutions involved with SENAME and their functions are:

1) *Family courts*: In charge of carrying out a judicial process to verify a rights violation that does not qualify as a criminal act, and to guarantee the following actions: ensuring judicial representation for each child asking an audit; ensuring a first assessment to refer children to the most appropriate programs, ordering access to the selected program, and monitoring the advances of children during the process of care, as well as providing support when required.

2) *Prosecutor's offices*: Receive complaints for investigation about children's violations, and when it is required, refer children to family courts.

3) *SENAME network*: Corresponds to the full offer of services; the fundamental role here is played by non-state agencies implementing SENAME programs.

4) *Local inter-sectorial services*: Correspond to the full range of services at the local level that should be available for children, from public schools, health services, justice, police, and so on.

5) *Chilean police*: A point of access for children less than 14 years of age who have committed an illegal act (Chilean children older than 14 are considered legally responsible for their acts so they are referred to juvenile justice) or for children under 18 who were registered as living in risk of vulnerability.

6) *Local rights protection offices*: Services implemented at the local level, with preventive aims, conceived as the entrance to the system of children's services. Rather than treatment, these offices develop community work promoting a children's rights culture, and offer a referral service through which neglected children can be assessed and directed to specialized services.

Basis of Social Allocation and Nature of Social Provisions

According to Law 20.032, SENAME must provide three areas of child protection services: alternative care for children, protection programs, and assessment programs. During 2017, the number of children receiving services from SENAME was equivalent to 4.17% (177,915) of the child population (4,250,155). SENAME's programs are mainly implemented through nonprofit partner organizations (OCAS, for its abbreviation in Spanish) that participate in a bidding process for projects and receive per-child transfers. SENAME supervises and oversees the service provision.

Funding for SENAME was increased 8.2% for 2018, providing SENAME with a budget of more than 300,000,000 Chilean pesos (SENAME, 2017). This works under a subsidized logic whereby the state funds part of the resources needed to implement the programs; OCAS are accredited by SENAME and manage 96.18% of the annual services for children. SENAME provides technical and financial oversight to programs implemented by OCAS. The main programs developed by SENAME are described next.

ALTERNATIVE CARE SERVICES

Alternative care services correspond to foster care and residential care services. SENAME implements some of these programs, but most of them are executed by nonprofit organizations and funded by SENAME. In 2019, 10% of children in child protection (19,642) were under alternative care, either residential or foster care. Children are referred to alternative care when their parents have temporarily lost parental rights. In Chile this occurs only by court order, stemming from a violation of rights suffered by a child and for which the parents are deemed responsible. Subsequently, the child is referred to an alternative care state program. A Family Court magistrate makes the mandate and it is compulsory (Muñoz et al., 2015). It is expected that parents will change the conditions of their parenting so that families can be reunited. Based on these expectations, courts typically do not terminate parental rights permanently.

De Iruarrizaga (2016) in her research to develop a better understanding of the child protection system and to design solutions tailored for each case, described intake causes into the child protection system. The more common intake causes were neglect, inability of the parents, and different types of maltreatment. For all children participating in alternative care, the main cause was maltreatment or abuse, children with a specific diagnosis, or because of their parents' inability to care for them (see Graph 1). Table 20.1 shows the proportion of children in child protection in relation to the national population of children considering data from the National Institute of Statistics (2017) and SENAME (2017).

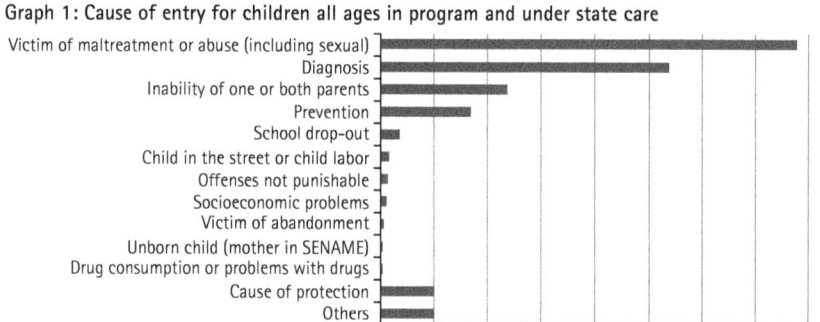

Graph 1: Cause of entry for children all ages in program and under state care

Figure 20.1 Distribution of intake causes

Table 20.1 Children in child protection, 2017

	2017	
	Frequency	Rate per 1,000
Child population 0–17 years measured on January 1, the following year. *n*=children	4,259,155	
Child protection services (total all, types), end of year. Services per 1,000 children 0–17 years	177,915	41,7723703
New children with child protection services	135,073	
In-home measures, total end of year (Se KL)	163,682	38,43
Out of home placements, total end of year	14,233	3,34
Adoptions from care	428	

Source: Own elaboration with data from annual data SENAME (2017) and Instituto Nacional de Estadísticas (2017).

Residential service is provided at institutions for groups of children through a shift system of non-relative caregivers. During January and December of 2019, 4.7% (9,317) of the children in the child protection system were in residential programs; over 80% of them were in programs executed by private agencies, and the rest were in state residential programs.

Table 20.1 shows statistics of children involved in the Chilean child protection system in 2017. Because the Chilean informational system is being revised now with limited access for research matters, it is not possible to present statistics over time.

Within this type of care service, there is a period of transitory residential program while the best care option is assessed; hence, it is a transitory short-term measure, aiming to provide immediate protection and assess best alternatives. There is also a medium to long-term residential service, which seeks to provide shelter while improving a family situation. The number of children in this type of residence is variable. There are facilities for infants (aged 0 to 4) in large numbers, such as *Casa Nacional del Niño* (National Home for the Child), which can host more than 90 children, and smaller residential facilities hosting 20 to 30 children on average. International recommendations indicate residences with a reduced number of children (aged 6 to 8) are preferable. The residences provide for the children's basic needs, ensure they are going to school, and attempt to work with the children's biological family to promote reunification, but some lack the specialized tools and personnel to do this (Muñoz et al., 2015).

Even though in 2004, with the creation of the Family Courts, removing a child from its family was established as the last option and required a judicial order, in practice this is not always the case and not all alternatives are exhausted (De Iruarrizaga, 2016). The current Chilean child protection system negatively affects children's right to live in family. Unlike the world trend, the Chilean system is characterized by a clear state intervention in the family sphere, prioritizing judicial action over administrative ones. In addition, it has a deficient regulatory framework for protecting children's rights, since it lacks a true preventive and integral child protection policy. This system allows wrong procedures such as judges requiring alternative care for children while their cases are investigated, contrary to the norm of ordering the entry of children and adolescents into residence systems only when all other protective measures have been explored. Additionally, children spend excessive periods in care due to lengthy court procedures, complexity of family reintegration processes and the extended periods of time it takes to complete adoption. This situation is being partially addressed by a bill that seeks to establish a regulatory framework for the comprehensive protection of children's rights.

RESIDENTIAL ALTERNATIVE CARE SERVICES FUNDING

Non-state agencies hold service agreements awarded by SENAME to provide residential care. The basic allowance per capita is 153,000 pesos per month (approximately US$230); this amount will vary, depending if the service corresponds to state or non-state agencies implementing the services. State agency residential services receive up to 900,000 pesos monthly per child (1,353 US$). This amount is expected to cover all costs relating to staffing, physical, infrastructure, food, clothing and social activities. Additional allowances are available for complex cases, as for example children who have a drug addiction or require psychological support. There is a general agreement about the fact that the amount they receive from the government is unrealistic and leaves the non-state agencies with the burden of having to find additional funds (Fundación León Bloy para la Promoción Integral de la Familia, 2009). Most of the children in residential services are in non-state agencies. State agencies have the higher funding; however, those programs have been sanctioned by UN observers because children's rights are neglected in state residences.

FOSTER CARE AS ALTERNATIVE CARE SERVICES

A foster family is another program SENAME offers as alternative care. It provides care in a home for one or two children, who may or may not be siblings. This service is implemented mainly through kinship families. It can also be provided by an external family—a family not blood related to the child—which can provide specialized or simple care, depending on the case. Implementation of these alternatives will depend on the existence or not of a kinship family prepared to protect the child while a decision is made regarding whether the birth family can recover their care. It will also depend on the special needs the child might have (Muñoz et al., 2015).

In 2005, Law 20.032 allowed non state agencies to manage foster care programs. The program gives assistance and protection to children deprived of parental care because of an infringement to their rights (Iruarrizaga, 2016). These children, through a judicial order, are incorporated into an alternative family as a temporary placement solution (RELAF et al., 2013). In 2013, Chile had 47 foster care programs in 14 (of 15) regions of the country, with 3,374 children in care. Over three-quarters of children were placed with extended families (RELAF et al., 2013). Therefore, only 5% of the children under alternative care lived with a non-relative foster family; this means only around 700 children nationwide receive this solution. The selection of foster families is made by the judge in conjunction with the non-state agencies, through a "clearance process" of who in the family can receive the child. The screening process, if implemented, is not systematic (Iruarrizaga, 2016). By 2019 the number of children in foster care was 10,325, representing 52% of children in alternative care. For first time in Chile, there were more children in foster care than in residential care.

FOSTER CARE FUNDING

Regarding external or non-relative foster families, there is no formal recruitment process and SENAME is not active in doing recruitment or awareness campaigns. The program managing foster families receives a transfer of 93,527 or 134,164 pesos depending on the type of program (approximate US$150 and US$210 dollars) and at least 50% has to be assigned to the foster family or to the biological family if needed for the reunification process. The rest is used for the non-state agencies, administration and professionals that work with the child and both families. There is considerable debate among experts about how much money foster families should receive, and this is an aspect that should be revised when designing a new program. Foster care programs that have been successful in other countries paid families an average wage to replace the cost of having a family member taking care of the child instead of working.

SENAME found that only 50% of foster parents had been evaluated for their parental abilities. In most of the cases, they only went through a social evaluation (80%) and psychological evaluation through tests that did not distinguish their capacity to take care of a foster child. They recommended that programs need to establish requirements and a screening process for all foster families including the relatives chosen by the Family Courts (SENAME, 2019). Regarding duration, residences and foster care exceed the time stipulated with children staying three years on average. The results for re-entry vary among the different care models; for residences it is 63% and for foster care 75%. The results are more worrisome for residences for infants, with values around 40% (Focus, 2013).

Protection services correspond to protection and rights restitution programs, framed by geography and gender. At the national level, there are 10 types of programs:

1) *Ambulatory assessment*: Programs offering judicial and forensic advice for family court decision making about the protection measures for children whose rights have been seriously damaged and to avoid secondary victimization in the persecution processes carried out by penal courts.

2) *Judicial representation program*: Pursues guaranteeing children's access to justice undertaking their legal representation in front of Family Courts, Penal Courts, and Superior Justice Courts, and giving legal advice to children under alternative care.

3) *Focalized prevention programs*: These programs provide services to children affected by moderate maltreatment related to family contexts where severity does not force the removal of children from their family. The program's objective is to strengthen parental and family skills to care and raise their children.

4) *Maltreatment and sexual abuse protection programs*: This is a socio- and psychotherapeutic program that searches to restore the well-being of children who suffered severe physical and/or psychological maltreatment, constituting criminal and/or sexual aggression. The service provides interventions to interrupt these actions, through the activation of judicial mechanisms required to solve the victims' legal situation and access to justice, and to favor the victims' re-elaboration of these experiences and strengthen family resources to enhance children's psychological well-being.

5) *Integral specialized intervention programs*: These are offered when children suffer severe violations of rights such as serious neglect, abandonment, and exploitation, through stopping these actions, developing competences of responsible adults in charge of the victims to provide protection, and psychosocial and therapeutic interventions.

6) *Ambulatory protection for children with disabilities*: These programs attempt to solve vulnerability of children living with disabilities through strengthening inclusion skills at the personal, familial and social levels. The oldest age of children being served by this program is 24.

7) *Specialized program for street children*: This helps in ending the street situation, ensuring children's protection and well-being, to be provided by their families or responsible adults willing to care for these children. The program develops parental skills and strengthens familial attachment; additionally, local services are activated to protect and reinforce personal resources to achieve children's autonomy and independent living skills for those children who lack networks.

8) *Specialized protection program for commercial and sexual exploitation*: This is a socio- and psychotherapeutic program that searches to restitute the rights of children who are victims of sexual exploitation (commercial-sexual exploitation, sexual tourism, trafficking with sexual ends, child pornography). The service provides interventions to interrupt these actions, heal the psychosocial damage, and guarantee access to pertinent services at the local level. Family and children's protector resources are evaluated to guide the intervention plan.

9) *Specialized intervention programs for adolescents indicating sexual abusive behaviors*: The program pursues the immediate and permanent interruption of the adolescent's sexualized abusive behavior by developing and/or strengthening adolescents' competences to face dynamic factors[3] affecting the recurrence of these behaviors, by strengthening the re-elaboration of experiences of maltreatment or sexual abuse if these occurred in childhood, and by promoting their socio-communitarian integration. Targets of this program are children from 10 to 18 years old who present sexualized abusive behavior, especially those in residential alternative care, and those adolescents between 14 and 18 years who have been formalized by sexual abuse (i.e., adolescents who have been accused of abuse but who have not been assigned to prison) and receive a non- incarceration sanction.

10) *24-hour programs*: These include integral specialized 24-hour intervention programs, integral specialized back to school programs (i.e., a school reinsertion program), and integral specialized intervention programs for children with alcohol and drug abuse issues. These three programs should act in coordination and target children between 10 to 17 years of age. The main features of the services offered by these programs are: rights restitution of children who are victims of abusive situations, by providing interventions to interrupt these actions, healing psychosocial damage, and guaranteeing access to pertinent services at the local level. Additionally, the back-to-school program offers support to children who are drop-outs, as well as those attending school but presenting poor school attendance and/or school delay. Lastly, the program for children abusing alcohol and other drugs offers help to build a life free of abusive consumption of drugs or alcohol, by including children in community activities and improving family patterns of interaction.

Outpatient placements offered by SENAME for these programs are financed through the Budget Law, without contributions from third parties, mainly through the Ministry of Justice and Human Rights. Data suggests that these funds have been rising since 2015,

---

[3] Motivation to commit the sexual aggression, accept responsibility, empathy towards the victim, quality of peer relations, levels of general and sexual autoregulation, consumption of substances, mental health.

however, other data show that expenditures exceed the budget suggesting that funding provided for these programs is not sufficient to cover the needs of these children (CJS, 2018).

Chile has had a national Adoption System since 1999, when Law No. 19.620 was passed. This law mandated powers of oversight of the adoption system to SENAME and legal authority to Family Courts in granting adoption status when in the best interest of the child. Administration of adoption programs is run by SENAME and four accredited non-state agencies. The physical, psychological, moral, and social criteria to be met by prospective adopters are defined by this law. Those eligible to adopt are married heterosexual couples, unmarried females, and female widows, though these criteria are under revision. The law allows for the prenatal consent of mothers who decide to give their child for adoption before birth and establishes safeguards with respect to inter-country adoption. Only if parents have either relinquished parental rights, or have been deprived of them by a court, is a child considered suitable for adoption.

Gale (2016) indicates that in all cases, a Family Court Judge must assess the competency of adoptive parents and any efforts to ensure the safety of children within their own family before a decision about adoption is reached. The author states that in 2015 although there were an estimated of 11,500 children in residential facilities, only 5% have adoption status. Members of one government and one non-state provider of adoption services were interviewed for Gale's study, and both mentioned lack of understanding and/or belief among residential workers regarding adoption and their failure to follow proper case management procedures in these cases. Table 20.2 shows the number of children adopted by agency in Chile from 2010 to 2015. The total number of adoptions has increased modestly from about 500 to 600 children per year.

Table 20.2 Number of children matched to adopters by agency in 2010–2015

Year	Total number of children given adoption status	Total number of children adopted
2006	1,168	433
2007	1,124	442
2008	837	492
2009	787	503
2010	923	660
2011	1,100	605
2012	1,383	605
2013	1,346	596
2014	1,352	590
2015	1,388	510

Source: Gale (2016).

Reviewing Policies and Programs of Chilean Child Protection

The protection system for children whose rights have been neglected has become particularly visible in Chile since 2013 because of the dramatic findings of a study conducted by the United Nations International Children's Emergency Fund (UNICEF) and the Family Courts, which came into public light in July that year (Muñoz et al., 2015). The confirmation of serious violations of rights occurring within the SENAME residential system has made evident the need to review the protection models implemented to date. The report indicates that children currently in state residences suffer sexual abuse, violence, and ill treatment. These violations are present throughout the entire system. The report radically questions the protection provided to these children and places at the heart of the discussion the urgent need for an intervention in these programs (Muñoz et al., 2015).

In 2018, SENAME audited residential services implemented by state agencies and found that among the 758 children being served, 365 dropped out of school, 48% had a school delay, 55% presented mental health problems, 54% suffered a psychological aggression, and 42% had problems with drugs and/or alcohol (SENAME, 2018). The audit raised public concern about the situation of these children and has mobilized diverse state action to improve these critical situations. The most worrying dimensions in urgent need of change, reached by the audit were: the massiveness of some residential settings with 40 to 120 children, the large number of children under 5 years old living in residential settings, and the predominance of residential care over foster care programs. Muñoz and colleagues (2015) showed that:

> in residential services children usually do not have meaningful contact with their families or friends; there have been revelations about physical and sexual abuse in residential care over several decades, and monitoring to ensure that children are safe, healthy and receiving proper services, appears as a permanent weakness of the system; at the same time, residential care for children is perceived as staffed by a largely unqualified workforce. There is a great deal of concern regarding the tendency to continue giving priority to residential care as an alternative, over and above the possibility of strengthening and extending the use of foster families. (p. 220)

There has been a trend to increase the percentage of children in foster care with extended families and reduce the number of children entering residential care. In 2012, from the total number of children in alternative care (7,850), 20% (1,628 children) were in foster care and 80% (6,222) were in residential care. In contrast, in 2019, 45% of children under care were in residences and 52% of them were in foster care.

Still, implementation studies give account of services that are far from reaching the goals established by Chilean child protection policy. In their research on the alternative care system in Chile, Munoz-Guzman and colleagues (2015) noted how "poor outcomes have led to question capacities to successfully achieve family reunification" (p. 49). Gale (2016) found "methodological shortcomings addressing family reunification intervention. In general, professionals see themselves with lack of required specialization in order to work with this population and its complexities" (p. 79). Gales' research raises the concerns of practitioners about the complexity involved in children being able to safely return to many households where serious violations have occurred. This included lack of professional skills to effectively facilitate family reunification and poor access for some families to the range of services they needed, as for example, support for those with drug and alcohol addictions. Other practitioners noted how some residential settings still develop children's care plans without goals for reunification and how "sometimes it isn't even considered, the reunification is not considered as a goal in the intervention plans" (p. 49).

Additional limitations of the system are: weak leadership to conduct technical and administrative management, key positions empty for long periods, a lack of coordination among work teams, large numbers of young people receiving inadequate care, meagre professional services, low accomplishment of daily routines, incomplete records of children, and lack of intervention with families (only 64% of intervention plans include objectives of family unification). Part of the findings of the social audit (SENAME, 2017) revealed that, as a system, SENAME does not have complete information regarding the health status of the child and adolescent service users. This impedes its ability to adequately weigh the damage to which children have been exposed in order to react appropriately to restitute children's rights.

The following brings to discussion the findings of Muñoz and colleagues (2015), which review difficulties in the implementation processes of child protection policies in Chile. Some of these shortcomings are related to the technical guidelines; however, the great majority are based in structural conditions. The result is that in most of the programs, the interventions actually implemented fall within some intermediary point between the model as designed and what the contextual restrictions actually allow.

Below is a summary of the main nodes of conflict, common to SENAME's programs. The overview begins with those embedded in the programs, moving towards those in the institutional and legal framework.

Critical Node 1: Insufficient Technical Guidelines

In all of the programs, what first stands out is the lack of clear protocols for acting in crucial stages of treatment, including recruitment in the case of foster care programs, staff selection, or intervention for family reunification in the case of residential programs. In the case of foster families' recruitment, the lack of interested families threatens the prospect of reducing residential services and extending foster families. In this sense, strategically designed recruitment actions are urgently required. The limited number of foster families ultimately blankets the discussion about caregiver minimum standards or professional intervention with a highly complex population. Furthermore, although official guidelines make appropriate distinctions between children with different needs, and even consider assigning them to different sub-programs, the interventions are actually quite homogeneous. This homogeneity does not come as a consequence of the existence of homogenizing protocols, but rather the absence of any specific procedures. Hence the main part of the intervention relies heavily on the criteria of the professionals involved. Lastly, clinical work with children, biological families, and foster families is left to the discretion of each professional team working with the families. With such a framework, it comes as no surprise that favorable programs are associated with the volunteering spirit of program stakeholders rather than objective characteristics that could be made available to other programs.

Critical Node 2: Low Specialization

Shortcomings are aggravated in light of the low level of specialization present among most professionals in practice. They mostly have limited knowledge about interventions that have proven to be effective with children who have faced trauma, families that have lost custody of their children, and with foster families. Neither have they received specific training in the skills required to work with children whose rights violations can be categorized as highly complex.

In general, programs show difficulty in recruiting and retaining specialized professionals and caregivers, and an overall appropriate level of staffing. Precarious working conditions, low wages, and the difficulty of the task, make this field unattractive to specialized professionals. This leads to a greater proportion of young under-specialized professionals and high turnover. In the case of direct caregivers, the shift system is increasingly unattractive in urban sectors where there is greater availability of jobs, and where wages are too low for the market.

Critical Node 3: Stigmatization of Biological Families

The behaviors of professionals and staff who work directly with children appear suspicious and somewhat stigmatizing of birth families, who tend to be defined as inadequate and not deserving of care over their children. This attitude is rooted in a pro-institutionalizing organizational culture that prevails and has been legitimized for many decades. The recent introduction of children's rights and a pro-family-reunification approach has been unable to substantially modify this attitude.

Critical Node 4: Fragmentation of Services for the Child

In Chile, access to public goods and services operates in a highly compartmentalized manner and by service sector. Thus, child protection programs are challenged to resolve access to basic services that should be safeguarded by right (health, education, justice) but that are scarcely available and, by default, fall under the responsibility of a single service. In addition, within SENAME there is also great disarticulation among the various institutional services. The radical separation between foster care and adoption programs is one of the clearest examples of this. In fact, in many cases the child stays with a foster family for a considerable period (more than one year) and significant attachment is forged, whereby the child, especially infants, see their caregivers as their parents. This can lead to a significant sentiment of loss and mourning, both for the foster family as well as for the child at the time of separation. The question that arises here is why the foster family is not given top priority for adoption of the child, in contrast to adoptive parents who have followed the adoption process for the child in parallel.

Critical Node 5: Discretionary Work of Judges within the Framework of the Minors Act

The Minors Act allows Family Judges almost absolute powers when making decisions about family life, usually with limited information and a lack of standardized criteria to determine the future of the child. Professional teams who implement these decisions see that Family Judges too often end up making inappropriate decisions that go against the best interests of the child. Examples of this situation include the tendency to give priority to a relative to take care of the child, despite the fact that that option may not be ideal (in families entirely linked to drug trafficking, sexual abuse, family violence, or simply the inability to provide care in the long-term).

Critical Node 6: Lack of Resources

Several of the indicated deficits have a common structural background: the state subsidy does not cover the actual cost of the programs required to work with these populations. The shortage of funding is particularly evident with regard to the precarious working conditions of the professionals as well as the technical staff. Low wages, overburdened teams, reduced staffing, high turnover, and under-specialization are all aspects that are having a drastic negative impact on the quality of the interventions, and especially on the coaching received by the biological families and foster families. Furthermore, in the case of residential services, funding is insufficient to provide appropriate infrastructure, which results in homes with a shortage of space and privacy for daily living. Most recent information about the status of residential care suggests that various centers have difficulty satisfying the basic material needs of children.

Many explanations have been given for not having higher funding: the financial contribution being symbolic because all the services required by the child (health, education, social services, and so on) are provided separately; or foster families should not use the subsidy as a business, referring to the risk that families could take financial advantage of the money received. The first explanation does not consider that the quality of services provided is often insufficient, or that waiting lists to access public services are long. The second argument shows prejudice toward foster families that does not suggest collaborative work between staff and families.

The issue of funding for residential and foster care programs is a crucial dimension when explaining the success or failure of the implementation of a program. Nevertheless, this is inexplicably one of the points systematically avoided by policymakers. In this sense, if in Chile it has been proven that budgets for programs are well below the actual cost of the planned interventions, the origin of the failure or insufficient performance should be initially sought in the funding difficulties and not the judges, professionals, families, or institutions. Ultimately, aside from their specific actions or omissions, the structural impact of the underpinning financing system and legal framework is far greater.

Conclusion

To close this chapter, this last section presents the challenges and guidelines Chilean child protection should embrace in order to accomplish its obligations towards children's rights. In 1990, Chile ratified its position as a signatory to the International Convention on the Rights of the Child (CRC), thereby committing to gradually modify its institutional framework regarding policies for the child, in order to adapt them to the rights approach underpinning the CRC (Munoz-Guzman et al., 2015). In this new paradigm, judicial protection of rights should recognize and promote rights, not restrict them; judges should exercise their activity limited by guarantees.

During the 1990s, but with much greater force as of 2011, Chile began a gradual reform of its child welfare institutional framework in order make these rights effective. Despite the important progress made, civil society organizations that work with children (many of these being organizations that collaborate with SENAME) have on innumerable occasions indicated that transition towards a comprehensive protection model is far from finished. This view is shared by the National Institute of Human Rights (INDH—*Instituto Nacional de Derechos Humanos*) and by international organizations such as UNICEF and the Committee on the Rights of the Child that indicate the Chilean state must embark on a series of reforms to have a modern and effective institutional framework respectful of the rights of all children and adolescents. Specifically, the Committee on the Rights of the Child, in its regular examinations in 2002 and 2007, recommended Chile reform the Minors Act since its spirit contradicts the CRC principles in substantive terms, and establish a single regulation for comprehensive protection of children and adolescents, guaranteeing their effective enjoyment of rights.

The authors suggest relevant changes at the structural level, which should be approached promoting social solidarity and the construction of citizenship based on rights. From this frame and a comprehensive protection of children approach, the following recommendations should be considered, which are understood as basic conditions for the improvement of the Chilean child protection system:

- Integrate child protection services with universal social protection to enable the provision of a broad array of care options for covering the individual needs of children and their families.

- Provide mechanisms for children and their families to participate systematically and effectively in decision making about the most appropriate care options and the long-term aims of the placement; these changes may be easier under a decentralized system.

- Establish criteria to guide decisions of the judicial system.

- Regularly review protection measures for their continuous adaptation and justification.

Lastly, the authors call for the same adjustments that they have made elsewhere (Munoz-Guzman et al., 2015): once and for all, give children the place they deserve on the public policy agenda and assign the necessary budgets to guarantee what is owed by right.

References

CASEN. (2017). Encuesta de caracterización socioeconómica nacional Ministerio de Desarrollo Social y familia, Observatorio Social. Santiago Chile. Available at: http://observatorio.ministeriodesarrollosocial. gob.cl/encuesta-casen-2017.

Centro Justicia y Sociedad CJS. (2018). Estudio para el fortalecimiento de los Programas Ambulatorios del Servicio Nacional de Menóres UNICEF Santiago de Chile. Available at: ttps://www.unicef.org/chile/media/2441/file/desinternacion.pdf.

Comisión de Expertos. (Octubre 2006). *Responsabilidad Penal Adolescente.* Santiago de Chile: Primer Informe de la Comisión de Expertos (68 páginas). Available at: https://pazciudadana.cl/biblioteca/documentos/primer-informe-comision-de-expertos-responsabilidad-penal-adolescente/.

Comisión Expertos RPA. (2007). *Segundo Informe Comisión de Expertos: Responsabilidad Penal Adolescente.* Gobierno de Chile.

Congreso de Chile. (2005). Informe de la comisión de Constitución, Legislación, Justicia y Reglamento sobre Boletín 3.792-07 (10).

Consejo Presidencial de la Infancia. (2006). *Propuestas del Consejo Asesor Presidencial para la Reforma de las Políticas de la Infancia.* Available at: unicef.cl/web/informe-consejo-asesor-presidencial-para-la-reforma-de-las-politicas-de-infancia-2/.

Contreras, C. (2003). El Sistema de Protección a los derechos de los Niños, Niñas y Adolescentes. Las Oficinas de Protección de Derechos: Un servicio a Nivel Local. Revista de Derechos del NIño. Programa de derechos del niño Centro de Investigacion Juridicas de la Universidad Diego Portales (2), 140–153. Available at: https://www.unicef.cl/archivos_documento/92/Derechos2.pdf.

De Iruarrizaga, F. (2016). Rediseñando el sistema de protección a la infancia en Chile. *Estudios Públicos*, 141, 7–57.

Departamento Protección de Derechos Servicio Nacional de Menores. (2004). *Orientaciones Técnicas Familias de Acogida.* Available at: http://www.sename.cl/wsename/otros/proteccion/FAMILIAS_DE_ACOGIDA. pdf.2004.

Donzelot, J. (1979). *La policia de las familias.* Pre-textos.

Focus. (2013). *Evolución del gasto institucional del Servicio Nacional de Menores. Resumen Ejecutivo. Evaluation commissioned by the Budget Division (DIPRES).* Available at: http://www.dipres.gob.cl/595/articles-109121_doc_pdf.pdf.

Fox Harding, L. (1997). *Perspectives in child care policy.* Longman Group.

Freeman, M. (1983). *The rights and wrongs of children.* Frances Pinter.

Fundación León Bloy para la Promoción Integral de la Familia. (2009). *Proyecto "EVA-Estudio de Gastos de las Líneas de Acción Centros Residenciales, Programas de Familias de Acogida y Programas de Protección*

Especializada, Específicamente de Explotación Sexual Comercial Infantil. Available at: http://www.sename.cl/wsename/otros/estudios_2012/Infrome_Final_EVA.pdf.

Gale, C. (2016). *Alternative child care and deinstitutionalisation: A case study of Chile CELCIS.* Available at: https://www.oecd.org/eco/surveys/Chile-2018-OECD-economic-sruvey-Spanish.pdf.

Gilbert, N., Parton, N., and Skivenes, M. (2011). *Child protection systems: International trends and orientations.* Oxford Scholarship Online. DOI:10.1093/acprof:oso/9780199793358.001.0001.

Hantrais, L. (2004). *Family policy matters: Responding to family change in Europe.* Policy.

Holman, R. (1987). *Putting families first.* Macmillan.

INE (2003) Síntesis de Resultados Comisión Nacional del VIII censo de población y de vivienda. Santiago de Chile, Marzo de 2003. Available at: https://www.ine.cl/docs/default-source/censo-de-poblacion-y-vivienda/publicaciones-y-anuarios/2002/sintesiscensal-2002.pdf.

Instituto Nacional de Estadísticas. (2017). *CENSO 2017.* Available at: https://resultados.censo2017.cl/.

Larragaña, O., and Rodríguez, M. E. (2014). *Desigualdad de Ingresos y Pobreza en Chile 1990 a 2013 (Programa de las Naciones Unidas para el Desarrollo-Chile. Área de Reducción de la Pobreza y la Desigualdad).* Available at: https://www.undp.org/content/dam/chile/docs/pobreza/undp_cl_pobreza_cap_7_desiguypob.pdf.

MIDEPLAN. (1997). *Diagnóstico sobre el Sistema de Protección Simple del SENAME.* Gobierno de Chile.

MIDEPLAN. (2000). Política nacional a favor de la infancia y la adolescencia 2001–2010. Gobierno de Chile.

Manzi, J., Mardones, R., Riveros, A., Toro, S., and Cortés, F. (2011). Un enfoque de gestión para mejorar la eficacia legislativa en Chile. In I. Irarrazaval (Ed.), *Concurso Políticas Públicas/2011 Propuestas para Chile* (pp. 23–60). Pontificia Universidad Católica de Chile.

Marcus, B. (2004). Growth without equity: Inequality, social citizenship, and the neoliberal model of development in Chile. Dissertation Presented to the Faculty of the Graduate School of the University of Texas at Austin, United States. Available at: https://repositories.lib.utexas.edu/handle/2152/2238.

Muñoz-Guzmán, C., Fischer, C., Chia, E., and LaBrenz, C. (2015). Child welfare in Chile: Learning from International Experiences to Improve Family Interventions. *Social Sciences,* 4(1), 219–238.

Nygren, L. (2013). *Family complexity and social work: A comparative study of family-based welfare work in different welfare regimes.* NORFACE Welfare State Future Application Template Outline Proposal. Published at: https://welfarestatefutures.wordpress.com/research-network/facsk-family-complexity-and-social-work-a-comparative-study-of-family-based-welfare-work-in-different-welfare-regimes/

Pilotti, F. (2000). *Globalización y Convención sobre los Derechos del Niño : el contexto del texto.* Naciones Unidas, CEPAL, Division de Desarrollo Social, marzo 2001 Available at: https://digitallibrary.un.org/record/441693?ln=es.

PRB. (2011). Cuadro de datos de población mundial 2011. Population Reference Bureau, Washington, DC 20009 EE.UU. Available at: https://www.prb.org/wp-content/uploads/2011/07/wpds-2011-population-data-sheet_sp.pdf.

RELAF, UNICEF, SENAME. (2013). Proyecto piloto para la desinstitucionalización y mejoramiento de los cuidados alternativos para niños(as) menores de 3 años en Chile. Santiago de Chile, abril. Available at: https://www.relaf.org/materiales/Informe%20FINAL%20PP%20Chile.pdf.

SENAME. (2005). Orientaciones Técnicas Departamento de Protección de Derechos. Gobierno de Chile.

SENAME. (2017). *Balance de Gestión Integral Año 2017.* Ministerio de Justicia y Derechos Humanos Santiago, Chile: Gobierno de Chile. Available at: http://www.sename.cl/web/wp-content/uploads/2015/10/BGI100700032017_00162.pdf.

SENAME. (2018). *Informe Auditoría Social.* Available at: http://losninosprimero.cumplimiento.gob.cl/documents/InformeAuditoriaSocialCentrosSename.pdf.

Servicio Nacional de Menores, Sename. (2019). Recomendaciones estudios UNICEF. Programa Familias de Acogida y programas ambulatorios UNICEF Chile. Disponible en: http://www.sename.cl/web/wp-content/uploads/2019/06/RESULTADOS-ESTUDIOS-CFS-FINAL.pdf.

Tello, C. (2003). Niños, adolescentes y el Sistema Chile Solidario: ¿una oportunidad para constituir un nuevo actor estratégico de las políticas públicas en Chile? Revista de Derechos del Niño - Año 2003 No. 2, 9-52 Available at: https://app.vlex.com/#vid/651229897.

UNDP. (2009). Informe de Desarrollo Humano 2009. La Manera de Hacer las Cosas. Santiago: UN Available at: https://www.cl.undp.org/content/chile/es/home/library/human_development/publication_1.html DP.

UN General Assembly. (64th sess. : 2009–2010). Guidelines for the Alternative Care of Children: resolution/ adopted by the General Assembly.

UNICEF. (2005, March). *Desinternación en Chile: Algunas lecciones aprendidas*. Serie reflexiones: Infancia y Adolescencia, no. 4. Available at: http://www.unicef.cl/archivos_documento/125/WORKINGPAPE R4a.pdf.

Ursin, M., Oltedal, S., and Munoz, C. (2017). Recognizing the "big things" and the "little things" in child protection cases. *Child & Family Social Work,* 22(2), 932–941.

Czech Child Protection after 1989: Between Socialist Legacy and the European Call for Democratic Legitimacy

Victoria Shmidt

Abstract

This chapter explains the child protection system in Czech Republic after 1989 in relation to the socialist legacy and the European call for democratic legitimacy. It notes the legitimacy crisis of diverse institutions such as child protection in Eastern Europe. The ideal performance of child protection should coincide with the ideals of democratic legitimacy and reduction of democratic deficit. Democratic legitimacy is used as an analytic tool for exploring the transformation of child protection in the Czech Republic. The shift in child protection came in waves of battling residential care, focusing on the empowerment of biological families, and campaigning against domestic violence.

Key Words: Czech Republic, socialist, democratic legitimacy, biological families, residential care, domestic violence, institutions, Eastern Europe, child protection

Czech Child Protection: The Phantoms of the Past Meet the Challenges of the Present

Among the other clichés about late Eastern European socialism, the famous Oscar-winning film *Kolya* (Jan Svěrák, 1996) exemplifies the insensitive cruelty of socialist child protection. Zubatá (literally Toothy), a social worker, arrives late by half a year upon the request of a Czech cellist, Franta Louka (literally Meadow). The latter, a single man and under life's pressure, desperate and unemployed, meets and accepts the offer of mock marriage to a young Russian beauty, who is dreaming about her German fiancé. After acquiring Czechoslovak citizenship, she unites with her actual fiancé. However, she leaves Kolya, her 5-year-old son, in Franta's care. Not speaking Russian and lacking the skills to raise a child, Franta asks social services for help. By the time the social worker finally visits, Franta and Kolya have overcome their cultural gap and developed strong emotional bonds. Unsurprisingly, Zubatá ignores what Franta says, and what Kolya wants. She offers only one possible solution for authoritative child protection: removal of Kolya from Franta's care, and placement in an institution that is akin to a Soviet shelter. Franta and Kolya are left with no other option than to escape and hide. The Velvet Revolution—the transition of power—finally rescues not only Franta and his Czech friends but also Kolya—who reunites with his mother.

The character of Zubatá portrays the legitimacy crisis of diverse institutions including child protection in Eastern Europe, particularly in the Czech Republic during the early 1990s. After the fall of communism, the Czech Republic was besieged with legitimacy challenges pursuant to the loss of geopolitical influence after separation from Slovakia in 1992, an aggravating economic crisis, and "the divisiveness and volatility of the new democratic regime that persisted until the elite and the citizenry became accustomed to the norms of democratic participation" (Frankland & Cox, 1995, p. 146). The demographic crisis, a direct consequence of political turbulence after 1989, led to a dramatic decline in the natural growth of the population: birth rates fell until 1999 and the height of the revival of fertility from 2004 to 2008 was again halted by economic crisis (Němečková et al., 2015). In contrast to the period of late socialism, when children consisted of approximately 22% of the total population, in 2007 this proportion was less than 15%. Comparatively, in 2017, the approximate rate was 16% with 1,671,000 children between the ages of 0 and 14 among a total population of 10,610,000 (Český statistický úřad, 2018). In a country with a strong, long-term tradition of familialization in welfare policy, the decline in the child population negatively impacted the value of social benefits for families with children (Saxonberg & Hašková, 2016). Like other post-socialist countries, mobilizing the negative effect of the socialist past, including child protection, was done in two ways: encouraging the newly formed democratic regime of the independent Czech state and legitimizing its agencies.

In the 1990s, child protection was compared to other institutions of previous political repression, especially residential care because of its massive number of children placed in diverse children's homes, boarding schools, and other residential care centers. *Liga lidských práv* (The League of Human Rights, 2007) directly stressed this in their reports by providing impressive statistical data: according to them, in 2005, 48 children out of 1,000 between the ages of 3 and 18 lived in such institutions. However, other experts expressed uncertainty about such numbers due to unclear approaches in differentiating substitute family care from residential settings, as well as the various lengths of stay of the children under residential care (Carter, 2005).

In the early 2000s, the focus shifted to the inhumanity of socialist residential care with an eye to replacing the socialist legacy of child protection. That legacy was characterized by pervasive forced removal of children due to parents' insufficient housing conditions, lack of control over school attendance, and inability to ensure children's socialization. In the early years of child protection reform, few questioned the process of decision making concerning forced removal or duration in care.

More than two decades after the fall of socialism, the historical trajectories of child protection continue to result in abnormally high numbers of children in large-scale institutions (Shmidt & Bailey, 2014). Obviously, this challenge reverberated throughout western Europe in the early 1990s and was summed up by Christine Hallett (1993, p. 29), who emphasized the necessity to transform the "simply established systems for the identification and referral of child abuse." By accepting the critical lack of "availability and effectiveness of subsequent intervention to help the children and their families," Hallett stressed the inevitable rejection of "over-simplified espousals of either therapy or social control" that would question "the balance between the conflicting principles of paramountcy of the welfare of the individual child, and the interests of the wider community and of justice" (Hallett, 1993, p. 29).

Thus, the ideal performance of child protection should align with the ideals of democratic legitimacy and should aspire to reduce the democratic deficit. This chapter interprets the transformation of Czech child protection after 1989 within the limits of democratic legitimacy—referencing a civil society that reflects sustainable, transparent, and participative models of policymaking (Barker, 2007). Within this approach, child protection, as well as its outcomes and measures, is explored as a structure shaped by the vicissitudes of democratic legitimacy that simultaneously influence the degree of public trust in government authorities. One of the main aims of this text is to indicate the complex obstacles that can thwart achievement of a sustainable strategy against institutional and domestic violence within the larger legitimacy crisis in post-socialist child protection.

The chapter is divided into two parts. The first introduces democratic legitimacy as an analytic tool for exploring the transformation of child protection in the Czech Republic after 1989. The second analyzes three main waves of transforming child protection in the Czech Republic: 1) combatting residential care and attempting to replace it with substitute family care in the 2000s; 2) focusing on the empowerment of biological families after 2008; and 3) providing campaigns against domestic violence, including the maltreatment of children. The annual statistical reports of the Ministry of Education, Youth, and Physical Culture; Ministry of Health; Ministry of Labor and Social Affairs; and the Ministry of Justice provide core information concerning the various realms of child protection measures during the first three post-socialist decades. The reports of the Human Rights Ombudsman regarding complaints of individuals and regular monitoring under residential care institutions were used for the period from 2009 until today.

Czech Child Protection after 1989: Solving the Deficit of Democratic Legitimacy

Child Protection as a Component of Democratic Legitimacy

Understanding child protection systems as clearly political is rooted in historically diverse attitudes about the relationship between the family, the child, and the state in constituting a good society (Gilbert et al., 2011). By establishing, practicing, and substantiating an array of procedures regulating the distribution of power between parents, children, and the state, child protection remains a key agent responsible for the state's legitimacy together with the education system, welfare policy, and healthcare. In democratic states, policies should be designed that gain popular acceptance and to which citizens will typically comply (Frankland & Cox, 1995). The concept of legitimacy covers very different realms of governing from the European Union (EU) level to the level of particular services and their direct communication with citizens.

This multilevel framework of legitimacy reverberates within the multilevel operations of child protection. In developed democracies, "engagement is felt to produce not only better policies but better citizens who believe their government to be more legitimate" (Johnson, 2015, p. 766). Experts stress that when welfare policy agents, including child protection, enact unjust practices, young European citizens lose sight of state legitimacy. Yet initiatives that involve children in policymaking or organize parents to prevent child abuse are two examples of direct European influence on Czech strategies of child protection.

Fair child protection is an important part of the "grand narrative" of the European Union. There is increasing attention on the civil/political participation of children and young people as an indispensable part of "thicker identity" (i.e., historically closed and traditional, incorporating national and local levels of identity) European values (Davidson, 2008, p. 33) that are especially indicative of the newer members of the EU (Forbrig, 2014). Does child protection in the contemporary Czech Republic operate in line with democratic legitimacy? With which authorities—European, national, or local—is the country aligned? Answering these questions requires focus on child protection development as an example of a transnational community (i.e., the EU) changing policymaking patterns at the national level.

Czech Child Protection: Moving through Multiple Legitimacy Crises

The transformation of child protection has become an indispensable part of Europeanization that infiltrates interrelated domains of child and family policymaking, such as communication of governmental bodies with local authorities and inter-country relationships. For example, EU policy asserts that "minority interests can gain a voice even without majority support" (Schmidt, 2012). Relevant to the Czech Republic, the rights of the Roma (i.e., a historically marginalized community) children have received special attention and brought the national standards of child protection in the Czech Republic into multiple contestations regarding EU expectations. Two judgments of the European Court of Human Rights (ECtHR)—*Wallová and Walla v the Czech Republic* (2006) and *D. H. and others v the Czech Republic* (2007)—frame the main priorities of monitoring child protection in the Czech Republic. These judgments respectively limited the forced removal of children due to insufficient social conditions and replaced the practice of special education for Roma children with inclusive education (Peleg, 2018). Also, the Czech Republic was called upon to develop alternatives to residential care for specific groups, in particular children with disabilities and those in conflict with the law. The pressure to introduce integration and replace residential care with various forms of substitute family care produced multiple arguments from practitioners and some institutions (Drahokoupil, 2017). It significantly complicated the formation of a trusting relationship between the national government, EU bureaucracy, and the local authorities culminating in reduced potential for democratic legitimacy of both the national and European governments.

Emergent in the complicated relationship between the national and European levels of child protection is increasing contention between Czech families living in other European countries, mainly Scandinavia, and the local child protection services. Due to different thresholds for a state response to domestic violence Czech parents face increased risk for involvement with child protection in countries like Norway and Finland. Much as in other post-socialist countries, the Czech public views cases of forced removal of children by foreign authorities as "stealing." Moral panic and related campaigns have been the most common response of the Czech public to foreign authorities limiting parental rights because of concerns about physical or sexual abuse.

The case of the Michaláková sons remains the most visible example among more than 20 cases of forced removal of Czech children in Finland and Norway during the last decade (Ferebauer, 2018). The sons of Czech parents, Denis (b. 2005) and David (b. 2008), were removed by Norwegian local child protection authorities in 2011 due to accusations of parental violence, including sexual abuse. The Czech media stressed that despite lack of evidence and a halted criminal investigation both boys have remained in foster families with limited contact with their mother and grandparents. After exhausting all options to solve the case at both Czech and Norwegian national levels, Michaláková appealed to the European Court of Human Rights in September 2017. The legal proceedings of the case were accompanied by several rallies in Prague, always concluding in front of the Embassy of Norway.

The case of the Michaláks disrupted the collective Czech identity of "caring parents" and united different groups within the nation. The public response to the suffering of the children and their mother engaged the Czech public in the emotional politics of child protection that resembled many western countries' public discourse concerning children's rights in the 1980s (Warner, 2015). The question of "how 'they' could be allowed to do such a thing to 'us'" echoed in public debates concerning the comparable patterns of Czech child protection. But the most palpable consequence of this campaign was decreased public trust in national authorities, who remained limited in their ability to protect their citizens living abroad, especially the vulnerable, such as children (Lhoťan, 2014). In order to draw attention to the comparability of arbitrary practices against Roma parents and children typical of Norwegian and Czech child protection services, human rights activists (Albert, 2015) disseminated the Report by the Council of Europe's Commissioner for Human Rights concerning Norway that stressed the necessity of preventing family separation and preserving family unity (Muižnieks, 2015, p. 18). The obvious differences in the states' policies concerning the Roma population should also be taken into account for embedding the desirable changes in child protection strategies along more general pathways of reconciliation already introduced in public policy in Norway (Engebrigtsen, 2016, pp. 87–88) and still missing in the Czech contexts (Shmidt, 2019, p. 203).

Undoubtedly, blaming the Scandinavian model of child protection, viewed as arbitrary, confirmed an overall defensive attitude toward the EU governments' prescriptions and expectations relating to child welfare and the prevention of violence. Comparable to other Central and Eastern European countries, the Czech audience is inclined to liken the shadow sides of Scandinavian child protection with current trends in European policymaking, noted for violating country norms about family autonomy (Mazancová, 2015). Amy McEwan-Strand and Marit Skivenes (2018) explain the paradox of Norway's consistently good reputation of child protection among international organizations with its negative image recently shaped by several campaigns in the media from post-socialist countries. This is indicative that child protection is at a crossroads of values and approaches.

Child protection remains either an issue of democratic legitimacy or one of the vehicles for overcoming the deficit of legitimacy. Multiple debates between different levels of child protection operation aggravate the deficit of democratic legitimacy when it is alleged to actually further democracy in contemporary Europe. The approaches to revise democratic legitimacy towards minimizing the conflicts of interests among European, national and local levels are directly reflected in the fast-paced transformation of ideal models of child protection (Gilbert et al., 2011). Which trajectories of post-socialist transformation have led Czech child protection to these conflicts?

Transformation of Czech Child Protection: Eliminating Residential Care to Preventing Domestic Violence

Residential Care vs Substitute Family Care: The First Wave of Transformation during the 2000s

In the early 1990s, public opposition to residential care divided the experts into two camps: those who likened placement in residential care settings to inhumane treatment calling for total deinstitutionalization, and those who shared a critical view of the state of residential care while indicating the necessity to transform it into better standards. As in other post-socialist countries, the debate between these pro-family and pro-residential care placement camps reflected the competition for resources from the state and district budgets, as well as the support of non-governmental donors. This trend was felt in several former Soviet republics where residential care was perceived as a national scapegoat (Shmidt & Shchurko, 2014). In the Czech Republic the struggle concerning residential care stemmed from the well-known and popular studies of attachment by the Czech psychologists Zdeněk Matějček and Josef Langmeier (1963), who were among the propagandists of SOS-Children's villages in socialist Czechoslovakia, and who conducted several studies aimed at exploring the deprivation of children placed in institutions. The main argument against residential care was extremely utilitarian: being placed in an institution would irreplaceably result in the loss of important developmental potential (Matějček, 1968). Psychologists who advanced this approach augmented the general trend of "social engineering" typical of socialist education and care for children (Henschel, 2016). In addition, the persecution of scholars during the socialist period legitimized the institutional approach and eliminated the opportunity for critical discourse and remediation.

In the early 2000s, the argument was framed as promoting good parenting in lieu of bad institutions. This led to mainstream reforms, namely the replacement of residential care with family placement, predominantly foster care. Factors considered in this reform were the relative economic and social costs, and the future implications for children (Macela, 2014). The main target of the reform was to improve the recruitment and preparation of foster caregivers for a sustainable alternative to residential care, or in terms of democratic legitimacy to improve input legitimacy of family placement and involve as many as possible potential foster caregivers.

One of the first laws reforming child protection, *Zákon o sociálně právní ochraně dětí* (Law on Child Protection, 1999) reflected this stream: the law introduced several forms of substitute family placement that later were amended by supplementary legal regulations focusing on prevention. Tellingly, the law separated child protection from the politics of welfare because the latter recognized the inevitability of residential care. Indeed, the law missed the mark of redefining the eligibility criteria for child protection's core mission: preventing child maltreatment and minimizing youth delinquency. Ignoring the corresponding operationalization of social provisions made it impossible to protect the right of children to their family. Rather, the tokenistic nature of the measures that were introduced by the law led to more than 30 additional acts aimed at specifying the concepts introduced therein and the options of their implementation—for instance, in 2006 concerning foster care and in 2012 introducing case management to child protection practice (Krístek, 2014).

In practice, deinstitutionalization occurred at a modest pace, especially concerning the largest share of institutions that belonged to the Ministry of Education, Youth, and Physical Culture (see Figure 21.1) for children older than three years. Neither the general number of institutions nor the number of children in this group declined significantly. Also, the notable decline in the number of children in assessment centers after 2011 can be explained by changes in the procedures concerning the placement of the child after removal from the family. At that time, the courts became responsible for the removal decision in contrast to administrative decision making in previous years, also the opinion of child protection remains the most decisive for the legal judgment (Shmidt & Bailey, 2014, p. 63).

The success in developing foster care was also modest in contrast to the intractably high rates of children in residential care settings. Between 1985 and 2016, the number of

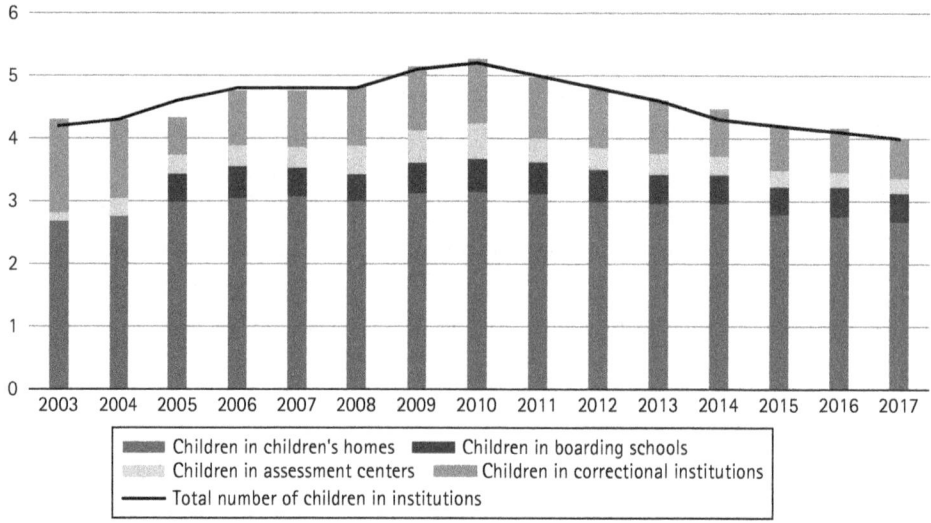

Figure 21.1 The number of children older than three years in an institution under the Ministry of Education, Youth, and Physical Culture per 1,000 children *Source*: Ministerstvo práce a sociální věcí (2017).

children annually placed in foster care increased from 780 or 0.32 per 1,000 children to 1,892 or 1.2 per 1,000 children. Grandparents and other relatives remain the main target group for recruiting foster caregivers; in 2016 they comprised 72% of the total number of foster caregivers. Among foster caregivers, non-relatives are those who work at the SOS children's villages and foster care centers (*Klokanek*). Additionally, substitute family care remains a rare option for children with a disability in contrast to placing them in residential settings. In 2016, only 14.4% of all children with disabilities who lived away from their biological families were placed with substitute families. In comparison, children with disabilities among all children under foster care remained less than 3% (Mikanová, 2017). State experts directly stressed that

> physical or mental disability or difficult behavior can be an inapproachable obstacle for placing the child into a family especially if the deficient state of health coexists with belonging to [an] ethnic minority. (Kuchařová, 2010, p. 171)

Accordingly, these children were not included in the registration system for warranting a substitute family search. Not until 2010 did the Ombudsman declare this practice as anachronistic, representative of the socialist period and ultimately a violation of children's rights.

In summarizing the possibilities and limitations for developing substitute family placement, the Ombudsman stressed that child protection had to guarantee a sufficient level of care in line with general levels of social provision not "the right to family which cannot be understood in terms of equal opportunities" (Ochránce lidských práv, 2010,

p. 1). For example, regarding family placement for children with disabilities, several projects aimed at searching for alternatives expanded the expectations on the welfare system. As a result, a more flexible approach relies on cooperation between residential care settings and child authorities (Kořínková et al., 2013).

Care for children under 3 years of age draws serious public attention and a united desire to replace residential care with substitute family care. For young offenders, a new orientation toward a restorative justice approach is gaining traction. Despite the obvious differences in populations and approach, both realms of child protection face comparable challenges.

CHILD PROTECTION FOR CHILDREN UNDER 3 YEARS OF AGE: RESCUING THE FUTURE OF THE NATION

In contrast to very modest success in transforming substitute care for children older than three, residential care for children under three has significantly changed. Since the end of the socialist period, the number of institutions and the number of children under three years of age significantly declined; from 52 centers in 1980 to 28 in 2016 and from 2,986 children (3.5 per 1000 children) to 1,559 (2.7 children), respectively. The percentage of children reunified with biological families significantly increased after the late socialist period, in excess of 70% in 2016 (see Figure 21.2). The increase in reunifications is related

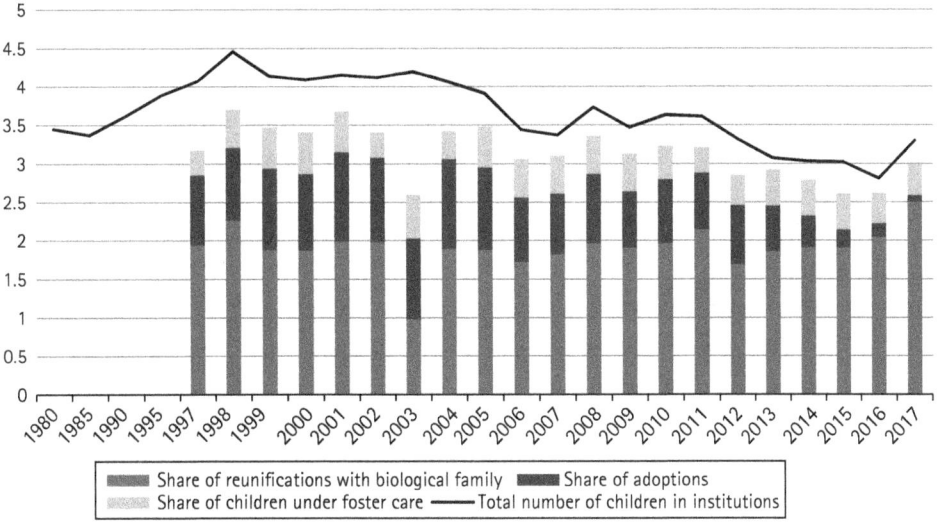

Figure 21.2 The trajectories of aftercare for children under three following placement in residential care units within the Ministry of Health per 1,000 children *Note*: The Ministry of Health has not provided information related to differentiation of baby homes (i.e., children's homes for children under 3 years) because this division is very formal. In the beginning, *kojenický ustav* (institution for infants) was the priority setting for healthcare. A children's home was distinguished by its larger number of pedagogues, and the children's center (there have been only two since 2003) combines various forms of care including services for young mothers who can reside up to four months with the child and learn more about care.

Source: Institute of Health Information and Statistics of the Czech Republic.

to a reduction in long-term placements (more than six months) in residential care, from 22% in 1997 to less than 10% after 2003. While the percentage of children older than 3 placed in mainstream residential care institutions changed significantly from 22.2% in 1997 to 9.3% in 2016, the share of those sent to units for children with disabilities decreased slightly from 4.9% to 1.2%, respectively. In combination with data on the increasing complexity of children's disabilities, this trend can be explained by the current politics of inclusion. Children with disabilities tend to be placed in mainstream institutions especially until commencement of primary school attendance.

The actions of the Ministry of Health suggest that even the priority of family placement would not replace the necessity for residential care for children less than 3 years of age. The Ministry mainly interprets the development away from residential care in extended historical contexts and avoids associations with the political regime (Bruthansová et al., 2005). Rather, it emphasizes societal changes and demographic waves for explaining the transformation in the new service approach. According to the Ministry, among those young children who require residential care are the children of mothers with addiction, those infected by HIV/AIDS or hepatitis, and children with multiple developmental disorders. The motivation for utilizing residential care for younger children is ostensibly based on knowledge from medical science and healthcare. Due to the regulations for processing personal data, the Ministry of Health remains the only one among officials that continues to register the ethnicity of the children placed into settings—specifically the number of Roma children. Compared to child protection statistics in other countries, there are no indications how the Ministry of Health collects the data, who makes decisions about what ethnicity is recorded (i.e., staff or parents), and how those who have "mixed" ethnic identity are registered (Bywaters et al., 2017, p. 1887). Though this practice is contested, the Ministry of Health shows that the share of Roma children in institutions remains significant. In 2016, there were 2.81 per 1,000 children aged 3 or younger in residential care. Among similarly aged Roma children, the rate was 8.9 per 1,000 children. Older Roma children are especially likely to be placed in residential institutions. Although common perceptions might suggest that children placed in residential institutions at an early age are raised there for the duration of childhood, the evidence suggests that that may not be so. Reunification rates for Roma children are higher than rates of reunification for other children; about 85% of Roma children placed in residential institutions reunify with their original family.

The number of adopted children increased from the early 1990s until 2004. Children seen as suitable for adoption in terms of their legal status (either the parents had their parental rights terminated or officially gave up their rights) started to be placed into foster care families since 2004 (instead of placing them in residential care). While 2.8 per 1,000 children under 3 were placed into infant homes (i.e., residential institutions) in 2003, this number declined to 1.1 per 1,000 children in 2016. Most of these children were considered high prospects for adoption and were therefore unlikely to experience long-term foster care.

PROTECTION OF MINORS IN CONFLICT WITH THE LAW: THE FRONTIERS OF RESTORATIVE JUSTICE

From the very beginning of the transformation of child protection in the mid-2000s and due to an enormous number of violations of children's rights, the task to replace residential care for children in conflict with the law with community services was seen as a main priority. Since 2004, the number of correctional institutions (*výchovný ústav*) as well as the number of children there did not decrease significantly. In 2005, 2.1 per 1,000 children between the ages of 10 and 15 years were placed in 34 correctional institutions; comparatively, this number had declined slightly by 2017 to 1.85 per 1,000 children housed in 27 institutions (Ministerstvo školství, 2018).

Similar to the socialist period, *výchovný ústav* aims to provide care for two target groups of children: those of minimum age of criminal responsibility (currently 15 years) who have committed a crime and children with long-term delinquent behavior including absence from school, addiction to drugs, participation in youth gangs, and so on. The correctional institutions accept children between 10 and 15 years of age who are ordered there by the court. The Ministry of Education operates correctional institutions with an approach that limits freedom and autonomy. The settings restrict children by not permitting them to leave without educator accompaniment, and obliging them to attend special trainings, psychological counseling, and other activities.

Undoubtedly, one of the main reasons explaining the slow pace of deinstitutionalization is inadequate alternative strategies to re-socialize children who are in conflict with the law. Probation and mediation programs for children and youth were introduced by *Zákon o odpovědnosti mládeže za protiprávní jednání a o soudnictví ve věcech mládeže* (Law on Responsibility of Youth for Criminal Acts and on Judiciary, 2003). This law aimed to apply restorative justice practices and reinforce community participation to achieve the task of resocialization. The law established a framework of mutually complementary procedures and penal sanctions: diversion of criminal proceedings, educational and protective measures, alternative sanctions to imprisonment, and diverse strategies to constrain the freedom of those who would need a strict educational approach (Válková, 2006). Probation strategies included social learning, psychological assistance, therapeutic intervention, general socially useful activity, education, vocational counseling, and retraining aimed at improving the social competencies of young people. The law also established regulations for licensing regional programs.

In 2009, the Czech Republic introduced restorative justice practices for children, and like other European countries, did so only after introducing similar options for adults. Established in 2008, the Probation and Mediation Service of the Czech Republic, allowed for probation for minors in conflict with the law. The program is considered a success as in 2009, 1,837 young participants were accepted into more than fifty programs

(Ochmanová, 2010). These programs varied in terms of addressing different target groups as well as offering different strategies of resocialization. However, despite a promising start, regions were unable to offer the courts a suitable range of probation services, so further development of mediation and probation for minors lost steam; the number of participants and the variety of programs significantly decreased after 2010.

Probation and mediation programs operate independently of child protection authorities. Rather, the majority of decisions on applying probation rest with the courts under the direct recommendation of police and prosecution offices. Only 5% of decisions at the stage of investigation and less than 1% at the stage of accusation are made under the recommendations of child protection officers (Probační a mediační služba, 2014). The involvement of civil initiatives in transforming residential care to community care remains on the margins of the local authorities' priorities.

When the Ombudsman, Anna Šabatová, offered an alternative to the practices found in institutions, namely integration of children in conflict with the law into community life, she was severely attacked by the public. The main argument against Šabatová's position was the necessity to practice a tough response with those children who "did not experience proper rearing and lost the sensitive moments of accepting the rules" (Lysáková, 2017). Events at one of the correctional institutions, in Chrastava, Liberec Region (detailed below), exemplify attempts by Šabatová to advance deinstitutionalization of correctional institutions while at the same time illustrating the limitations of these efforts.

In May 2016, the Ombudsman published a report on the situation in a correctional institution for boys in Chrastava, a small town situated in the Northern part of Bohemia (Ochránce lidských práv, 2016). The report indicated the wide range of arbitrary practices against boys placed in the institution, such as forced hair cutting, a special system of evaluating behavior leading to limitations on freedom of movement, and the predominance of punishment strategies as educational methods. The report called for urgent action, especially in the context of a School Inspection from six months prior which not only concluded no specific violation of children's rights but was extremely positive and recommended the model for further dissemination. This resulted in immediate mass media debates about the appropriateness of tough measures on children placed in institutions (Lysáková, 2017) and caused conflict between local authorities and human rights activists.

A solution to the conditions at the Chrastava correctional institution culminated in two ministers (one from Education and the other from Labor and Social Affairs) proposing the radical solution of transforming the correctional institution into a mainstream children's home. As a result, the grounds for placing children were revised; more than half of the children were sent back to their families after achieving the options of local monitoring and probation. Some children with behavioral issues were sent to other correctional institutions. The remaining children stayed at the institution, which was transformed into an ordinary children's home with completely different and less restrictive living conditions

(Trachtová, 2016). Although this incident was significant, the number of institutions, as well as the number of children in them, has not changed appreciably since that time.

In terms of democratic legitimacy, the first wave of transforming child protection worked through the experience of illegitimating residential care and revising the approach to its operation as a part of new child protection. This turn reinforced the role of the biological family and started to be seen as a key alternative to the risks of institutional violence against children after 2009.

Residential Care vs Biological Family: The Second Wave of Child Protection Reform (the 2010s)

Shifting the focus to prevention and empowering biological families as a key alternative to residential care was established in the *Národní akční plán k transformaci a sjednocení systému péče o ohrožené děti na období 2009 až 2011* (National Action Plan of Transformation and Uniting the System of Care for Children at Risk). The plan of transformation introduced new strategies for treating families at risk of child removal, including case management, family visits, and training for parents. The strategy was revised in 2013 and included more focus on the standards of care for children placed in crisis centers by reinforcing the options of reunifying the child with the biological family.

The dynamics of decision making concerning the regulation of parental rights reflect the changes in strategies aimed at empowering biological families. Between 2005 and 2011, the number of parental rights' terminations increased and other more flexible approaches to regulating parental rights remained on the margins of the courts' activity. However, since 2012, the number of terminations has decreased and the application of temporal and partial limitations increased (see Figure 21.3). This trend directly correlates with the extension of several practices: prescribing parents to attend special training, monitoring families, and distributing forms of prevention such as voluntary and temporary placement of children with delinquent behavior in newly established crisis centers. At initial service implementation, in 2011, 0.044 per 1,000 children between the ages of 7 and 18 were voluntarily placed for two to four months' duration at the request of parents; in 2016 this number rose to 1.1 per 1,000 children.

The introduction of this new legal order aggravated a pre-existing issue of the Czech justice system—the courts' lack of capacity to process cases in a timely fashion—and resulted in an extension of the pre-trial period. In 2004, more than one-third of all cases concerning termination of parental rights were delayed by more than six months beyond the period mandated by the law. The average period for making decisions about foster care placement took 274 days and adoption 232 days (Kristková, 2005). While there are time limits for making decisions concerning removal (four hours) and placement into care (seven days), there are also no such regulations for revising the decision (e.g., reunifying the child with the family).

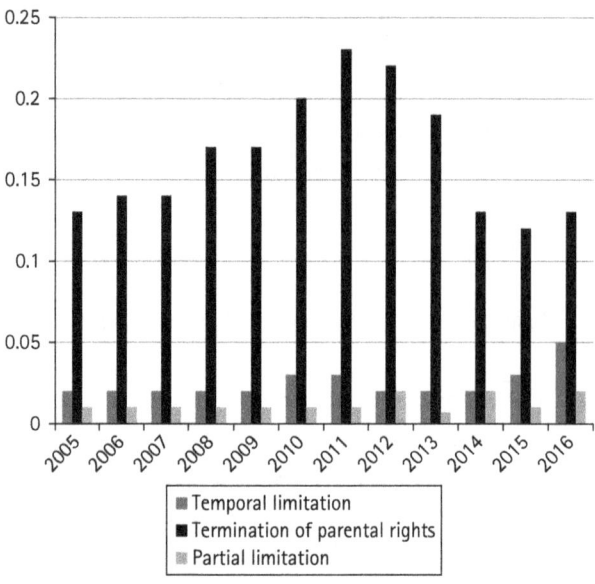

Figure 21.3 The approaches to regulate parental rights in case of risk of abuse and neglect—number of parental limitation per 1,000 children *Source:* Ministry of Labor and Social Affairs

Despite significant moves towards more transparent decision making, parents' access to independent experts is limited. Courts face pressure to make more nuanced decisions aimed at increasing the options for family reunification (see Figure 21.3), but their principal source of information for decision making is solely the child protection worker. These staff are not obliged to ensure the participation of parents or children. Thus, parents and children remain alienated from participation in decision making, thereby reducing the potential for throughput legitimacy in child protection. Among other obstacles for improving coherence between the different stages of intervention with the families, some experts suggest an imbalance in financing prevention and crisis intervention services. The budget for services aimed at preventing crisis situations, mainly community care centers and non-government organizations, is 700 million Czech crowns (approximately 25 million euros); comparatively, the budget of child protection services responsible for implementing crisis intervention and further treatment is 1,200 million Czech crowns (approximately 44 million euros). A major portion of the budget targets the corresponding legal procedures of child protection officers and child placement into institutions.

Both budgets address the same target group, approximately 400,000 families, which is one-third of all households with children. However, child protection services implement prevention only for one tenth of the total number of families that need such services. Such disparities between prevention and crisis intervention are reflected in complaints that were recently analyzed by the office of the Ombudsman (Ochránce lidských práv, 2017).

Transitioning to biological families stemmed from the revision of residential care practices. Two interrelated issues were argued by national and international experts, who advocated the necessity to transform residential care: the inappropriateness of long-term residential care as the main strategy for solving child removal placements and the inhumane treatment of children in institutions. Typical of publications during the first wave of reform, alarmists of residential care were replaced by more thoughtful critiques. Revising transformation approaches of residential care was determined by an overhaul of the deinstitutionalization general strategy. In early 2007, Resolution No. 127 of the Czech Government ratified the *Koncepce podpory transformace pobytových sociálních služeb v jiné typy sociálních služeb, poskytovaných v přirozené komunitě uživatele a podporující sociální začlenění uživatele do společnosti* ("Conception of transforming the residential care settings directly framed the options for embedding residential care settings into the system of community care"). The specifics attached to the transformed residential care approach became clear, including respite care for parents of children with multiple disorders of development, or short-term placement for children whose parents needed some training. In contrast to the negative public attitude toward residential care accompanying the reforms of the 1990s, in the 2010s, short-term residential care started to be seen as part of the strategy targeting improvements to family placement by remedying and redefining communication between residential settings, child protection services, and local community services (Lukášová, 2013). The main institutional outcome of this wave of transforming child protection—the predominance of professionals active in prevention—directly framed more recent attempts to meet the challenge of domestic violence against children.

Domestic Violence against Children: A Not Yet Accepted Challenge?

Czech parents used to be the most violent parents in the European Union. The global study of youth victimization indicates that the Czech Republic has one of the highest rates of parental physical punishment or parental maltreatment among European countries (Marshall et al., 2015). This international measurement of family violence against children reflects similar data gathered at the national level. The recent survey of adverse childhood experiences in the Czech Republic also confirms the large number of cases of parental violence against children, more than a fourfold increase reported within the last decade (Velemínský et al., 2017).

Systematic data concerning the type of domestic violence, as well as the typical trajectory of decision making started to be gathered and published in 2005 (the year when Parliament began debating the draft of the Law on Domestic Violence) and continued to be collected until 2013. Experts stressed particular difficulties in tracing the dynamics of violence and the role of preventive programs due to an unclear definition of family violence in both practice and legal regulations (Podaná, 2016). The indicators against children included: in 2005, only child pornography, child prostituion, sexual maltreatment, physical abuse, and psychological abuse as forms of violence. Neglect was added to this list in 2009. Introducing neglect (i.e., the systematic lack of care and inattention to the child's needs) significantly changed the composition of data; mothers, those typically accused of neglect, assumed the first position among perpetrators. Before 2009, fathers and partners of mothers held the lead position due to the number of cases of physical and psychological violence. Not surprisingly, after 2009, the number of cases increased even though the number of physical and psychological violence incidents remained approximately the same. After 2013, data regarding perpetrators and the trajectory of the cases ceased to be logged in official statistics. However, neglect as a consequence of social issues moved to the forefront.

In 2013, the Ministry of Labor and Social Affairs published an approximately 300-page report titled *Sociodemografická analýza Mapy rozložení ohrožení dětí a rodin v ČR* (Sociodemographic analysis: The maps of distribution of risk factors for children and families; Sociofaktor, 2017) that introduced a new approach to measure violence against children as determined by family living conditions. The report comprised maps and graphs exploring the role of three main groups of risk factors, including social risks (e.g., housing conditions, lack of education), economic risks (unemplyment, number of social benefits recipients), and disfunctional families (number of divorces, number of foreigners under 18 years old, number of Roma). From this perspective, it is easy to recognize the international trend of operating with a mindset of risk in child protection, specifically that "the boundary between families and professionals seems impermeable from both sides" (Haan & Connoly, 2017, p. 31). Under the pressure of professionals' prejudices,

> families see acceptance of services as opening their lives to scrutiny by people who will never understand their circumstances . . . A perception that professional services provision is troublemaking interference, threatening rather than supportive. (ibid.)

Illegitimacy of child protection for those who need it is directly linked to an extremely fragmented and incoherent institutional response to domestic violence.

In 2013, the year when collecting data about family violence was the most rigorous, among 7,408 indicated cases, only 1,278 were passed to either police or child protection services for further investigation. Of these, 1,019 cases were accepted for further investigation, broken down into: 252 cases of family member guilt, 415 cases postponed due to lack of evidence, and 163 cases closed; information concerning the rest of the cases was not provided.

The rupture between the needs of children and the strategic vision against domestic violence could be clearly recognized in the core message of the National Strategy of Preventing Violence Against Children for 2008–2018, ratified in late 2007 (Úřad vlády ČR, 2009). In contrast to the national strategies of other European countries accepted during the same period (e.g., Norway and Poland), the Czech strategy was minimal—not more than 13 pages. The main focus, "zero tolerance to any type of violence including applying physical force," directly addressed problematic parenting behaviors. It also embedded the strategy into a wide range of disputable suggestions concerning the decay of traditional family values as the main source of violence. Last among the priorities of the strategy were 1) promoting a healthy family life, 2) establishing the network of services for children exposed to violence, and 3) collecting data about violence in a systematic way, touching upon children's participation, and rather exceptionally, in terms of "recruiting the children as those who also should improve the environment towards eliminating violence."

The role of healthcare workers remains central to addressing the issue of domestic violence. The Ministry of Health established *Národní koordinační centrum pro prevenci násilí a zranění na dětech* (National Coordinative Centre for Preventing Violence and Injuries to children) and introduced a corresponding online program for preventing violence. The central hospitals within the universities' infrastructure in Prague and Brno situated domestic violence as an issue related to physical injury to children. The Prague project initiated several actions within the network of safe schools and kindergartens; by comparison, in Brno, the second biggest city in the country, a new approach for recording cases of injuries with particular focus on violence was introduced. Together with schools, hospitals report more than half of the cases of domestic violence. Police and the prosecution office inform and initiate the investigation of violence against children in more than 20% of all cases. The child protection authorities rank third in this field, indicating between 15–20% of all cases. Family members, neighbors, and local communities remain significantly behind the professionals in activities recognizing domestic violence against children (Ministerstvo práce, 2017).

Generally, this systematic lack of participation across the aforementioned levels of society can be explained by the fragmented legitimacy of the legal grounds for preventing domestic violence. In 2006, attempts were made to remedy fragmentation with the *Zákon na ochranu před domácím násilím* (Law No. 135 On Protection from Domestic Violence). This introduced a new national practice of separating the victim and the perpetrator by forbidding the perpetrator to gain access to previously held joint housing. The law transformed the police and the trial procedures towards more rapid decision making concerning separation of the perpetrator.

Tellingly, this practice launched one of the first strategies to prevent violence against children. However, experts still stressed that tolerance for physical violence against children is higher than against women. More than one fifth of respondents express their uncertainty regarding the necessity to punish parents for applying physical force for educating their children (i.e., correcting "bad" behavior) (Topinka, 2016). Also, more than half of respondents do not share the opinion that physical force is applied only by those parents who are unable to practice other more suitable forms of educating. Other experts interpret this trend as the Czech public not recognizing corporal punishment as violence, which is the source of debate between the public and professionals blocking campaigns aimed at minimizing violence against children (Vávrová et al., 2016). However, in this resistance of the public to accept the new approach to violence, it is obviously possible to recognize the systematic crisis of legitimacy. Several reasons for this crisis are the ambiguous attitude toward residential care and its opposition to family care in terms of the slogan "Any family is better than the best children's home"; a lack of coherence in empowering parents to advocate for their rights in court to contest child protection services; and the narrow focus of prevention programs.

Conclusion

The development of child protection can be seen as an ongoing process to extend citizen participation into new procedures and practices that target the dissemination of diverse expectations of proper parenting and childhood. These are the key prerequisites for nurturing future citizens. Finding the ways to generate and reinforce democratic legitimacy of child protection relies on particular institutions and procedures. The elaboration of child protection in the Czech Republic can be seen as a process of rebuilding organizational frames and revising discourses concerning childhood, parenthood, and children's rights towards becoming more legitimized. While at the beginning this task was also linked with the necessity to emancipate from the authoritative socialist past, currently its main concern is uniting the expectations of different actors within the child protection transformation.

By making attempts to align with EU expectations, national authorities face conflicts with the local level of child protection, inevitably reducing the potential for legitimizing child protection and cooperating with local authorities by gathering data, making decisions, and preventing intervention with families based on prejudices concerning ethnicity and poverty. The Czech public often blames child protection for late intervention in cases of injury to the child, at the same time that it criticizes arbitrary decision making and undeserved violations of family autonomy. These negative attitudes to child protection are not opposite extremes but complementary beliefs. The willingness of the public to accept such serious interventions against family autonomy, such as forced removal and limitations on parental rights, directly depends on the public image of substitute care, either residential or family, as well as effective participation of the communities in diverse strategies aimed at preventing crisis intervention.

Effective child protection can be developed within the context of democratic legitimacy that includes the interaction between shared values, sustainable participation, and transparency of decision making. Together, these legitimacy mechanisms can affect each stage of child protection: prevention, crisis intervention, and care. The task to transform child protection into a virtuous circle of democratic legitimacy is embedded in the mission to bring together the strategies concerning institutional and domestic violence against children.

Czech child protection remains more focused on institutional violence—noted by the shift from residential care to procedures of decision making in situations of high risk of violence to children and families. The interrelation between measures against institutional and domestic violence remains an unsolved challenge due to systematic alienation of parents and children from decision-making processes and a glaring lack of recognition about the issue of domestic violence by the public. Therefore, it is reasonable to conclude that in the near future a new, positive phase of cooperation between local non-government initiatives and international Human Rights activists should aim for an interdisciplinary approach to violence and improvement in parent and child access to services that advocates for their best interests.

Acknowledgments

The research for this chapter was sponsored by the Grant Agency of the Czech Republic, as part of the project "Child welfare discourses and practices in the Czech lands: The segregation of Roma and disabled children during the nineteenth and twentieth centuries" (15-10625S).

References

Albert, G. (2015). Council of Europe Human Rights Commissioner criticizes Norway for taking Romani children into care. Available at: http://www.romea.cz/en/news/world/council-of-europe-human-rights-commissioner-criticizes-norway-for-taking-romani-children-into-care.

Barker, R. (2007). Democratic legitimation: What is it, who wants it, and why? In A. Hurrelmann, S. Schneider, and J. Steffek (Eds.), *Legitimacy in an age of global politics* (pp. 19–34). Palgrave Macmillan.

Bruthansová, D., Červenková, A., Pechanová, M., Novotný, Z., and Schneiberg F. (2005). *Zdravotně sociální služby v kojeneckých ústavech a dětských domovech pro děti do tří let věku*. Ústav zdravotnických informací a statistiky ČR.

Bywaters, P., Kwhali, J., Brady, J., Sparks, T., and Bos, E. (2017). Out of sight, out of mind: Ethnic inequalities in child protection and out-of-home care intervention rates. *British Journal of Social Work*, 47, 1884–1902.

Carter, R. (2005). *Family matters: A study of institutional childcare in Central and Eastern Europe and the Former Soviet Union*. Every Child.

Český statistický úřad. (2018). Česká republika od roku 1989 v číslech. Available at: https://www.czso.cz/csu/czso/ceska-republika-od-roku-1989-v-cislech-2017-8jcopi31rm.

Davidson, A. C. (2008). Through thick and thin: "European identification" for a justified and legitimate European Union. *Journal of Contemporary European Research*, 4(1), 32–47.

Divoká, L. (2017). Professionalization of child protection in the Czech Republic from the perspective of sociological theories. *Sociální práce*, 4, 30–47.

Drahokoupil, Š. (2017). Discrimination against Roma in education: Waiting for changes on the ground. *European Implementation Network*. Available at: https://www.einnetwork.org/ein-voices-archives/2017/3/22/discrimination-against-roma-in-education-waiting-for-changes-on-the-ground-VkDd8.

Engebrigtsen, A. (2016). Lost between protective regimes: Roma in the Norwegian state. In M. Seeberg and E. Goździak (Eds.), *Contested childhoods: Growing up in migrancy* (pp. 81–98). Springer.

Ferebauer, V. (2018). *Soud ve Štrasburku projedná případ Michaláková: Výsledek bude do půl roku 31.1.2018*. Available at: https://www.idnes.cz/zpravy/domaci/eva-michalakova-peticni-vybor-evropsky-soud-pro-lidska-prava-jitka-chalankova.A180131_163411_zahranicni_fer_.

Forbrig, J. (2014). A school of democracy? Civil society and youth participation in the multicultural Europe. In Y. Ohana and H. Otten (Eds.), *Where do you stand? Intercultural learning and political education in contemporary Europe* (pp. 135–160). Springer.

Frankland, E. G. and Cox R. H. (1995). The legitimation problems of new democracies: postcommunist dilemmas in Czechoslovakia and Hungary. *Environment and Planning C: Government and Policy*, 13, 141–158.

Gilbert, N., Parton, N., and Skivenes, M. (Eds.). (2011). *Child protection systems: International trends and orientations*. Oxford University Press.

Haan, I. and Connoly, M. (2017). Anticipating risk: Predictive risk modelling as a signal of adversity. In M. Connolly (Ed.), *Beyond the risk paradigm in child protection* (pp. 29–45). Palgrave.

Hallett, C. (1993). Child protection in Europe: Convergence or divergence. *Adoption & Fostering*, 17(4), 27–32.

Henschel, F. (2016). A project of social engineering: Childhood experts and "childhood question" in socialist Czechoslovakia. *Acta historica Universitatis Silesiane Opaviensis*, 9, 143–158.

Johnson, C. (2015). Local civic participation and democratic legitimacy: Evidence from England and Wales. *Political Studies*, 63, 765–792.

Kořínková, D., Johnová, M., and Strnad, J. (2013). *Analýza ústavní a ochranné výchovy vykonávané v pobytových sociálních službách z hlediska transformace sociálních služeb*. Národní centrum podpory.

Krístek, A. (2014). Půlkulaté jubileum. K patnácti letům zákona o sociálně- právní ochraně dětí. *Sociální práce*, 4, 23–31.

Kristková, V. (2005). Práva dítěte a procesní praxe českých soudů. *VIA JURIS*, 4, 73–92.

Kuchařová, V. (2010). *Zhodnocení a optimalizace řízení systému sociálně-právní ochrany (ohrožených) dětí a rodin ve vybraných regionech*. VÚPSV.

Langmeir, J. and Matějček, Z. (1963). *Psychická deprivace*. SZN.

Lhoťan, L. (2014, December 10). Proč lže ministryně Marksová o únosu českých dětí v Norsku? *Bez Cenzury*. Available at: http://bez-cenzury.com/clanek/proc-lze-ministryne-marksova-unosu-ceskych-deti-v-norsku-lukas-lhotan.

Liga lidských prav. (2007). Péče o děti odebírané z biologické rodiny Systémové doporučení Ligy lidských práv. No 3. Available at: http://www.knihovnanrp.cz/wp-content/uploads/2017/03/pece-o-deti-odebirane-z-bio logicke-rodiny.pdf.

Lukášová, M. (2013). Speciální potřeby dítěte jako důvod pro život v instituci: poznatky z agendy veřejného ochránce práv. *Sociální práce*, 1, 34–36.

Lysáková, D. (2016, June 8). Delikventní menšina má větší práva? *Parlamentní listy*. Available at: https://www.parlamentnilisty.cz/profily/Mgr-Dana-Lysakova-10767/clanek/Delikventni-mens ina-ma-vetsi-prava-70273.

Macela, M. (2014). *Analýza financování systému ochrany dětí a péče o ohrožené děti*. Ministerstvo práce a sociálních věcí.

Marshall, I., Enzmann D., Hough M., Killias M., Kivivuori, J., and Steketee, M. (2015). *Youth victimization and reporting to police: First results from the third round of the international self-report delinquency study (ISRD3)*. Northeastern University.

Matějček, Z. (1968). Typy deprovované osobnosti dítěte a indikace pro adopci. *Československá pediatrie*, 23(7), 644–646.

Mazancová, H. (2015, June 2). Proč chtějí Michalákové odebrat syny? Případ zveřejnila, na dětech jí nezáleží, tvrdí úřad. *Lidové noviny*.

McEwan-Strand, A. and Skivenes, M. (2018, January 3). A child-centred court of human rights? Strand Lobben v. Norway (30. Nov. 2017). *Strasbourg Observers*. Available at: https://strasbourgobservers.com/2018/01/03/a-child-centred-court-of-human-rights-strand-lobben-v-norway-30-nov-2017/.

Mikanová, M. (2017). *Děti se z ústavů přesouvají do náhradních rodin*. Available at: http://www.statistikaamy.cz/2017/12/deti-se-z-ustavu-presouvaji-do-nahradnich-rodin/.

Ministerstvo práce a sociální věcí. (2017). *Roční výkaz o výkonu sociálně-právní ochrany dětí*. Available at: https://www.mpsv.cz/statistiky-1.

Ministerstvo školství. (2018). *Statistické ročenky školství: Zařízení pro výkon ústavní výchovy a ochranné výchovy*. Available at: www.msmt.cz/file/21328/download/.

Muižnieks, N. (2015). *Report by Commissioner of Human Rights of the Council of Europe following his visit to Norway from 19 to 23 January 2015*. Council of Europe: Commissioner for Human Rights. Available at: https://tandis.odihr.pl/handle/20.500.12389/22067.

Němečková, M., Kurkin, R., and Štyglerová, T. (2015). Family pattern in the Czech Republic: First child later and outside marriage. *Eurostat*. Available at: https://ec.europa.eu/eurostat/statistics-explained/index.php/Marriages_and_births_in_the_Czech_Republic.

Ochmanová, V. (2010). *Zpráva o průběhu a výsledcích výběrového dotačního řízení pro poskytování finančních prostředků ze státního rozpočtu ČR nestátním neziskovým subjektům realizujícím probační programy pro rok 2009*. Ministerstvo vnitra.

Ochránce lidských práv. (2010). *Stanovisko veřejného ochránce práv k rovnému zacházení s dětmi pří zařazování do evidence náhradní rodinné péče V Brně dne 28. dubna 2010.* Available at: https://www.mpsv.cz/docume nts/20142/225508/Stanoviskoochrance.pdf/0f0fdb40-0ce3-c369-c3f1-6d237014f238.

Ochránce lidských práv. (2016). Zařízení v Chrastavě deset let neplnilo své povinnosti. Available at: https:// www.ochrance.cz/aktualne/tiskove-zpravy-2016/zarizeni-v-chrastave-deset-let-neplnilo-sve-povinnosti/.

Ochránce lidských práv. (2017). Stanoviska Rodina a dítě II. Available at: https://www.ochrance.cz/fileadmin/ user_upload/Publikace/sborniky_stanoviska/Sbornik_Rodina_a_dite-2.pdf.

Peleg, N. (2018). Marginalisation by the court: The case of Roma children and the European Court of Human Rights. *Human Rights Law Review*, 18(1), 111–131.

Podaná, Z. (2016). Násilí na dětech současná situace v ČR a vývoj od roku 1999. *Forum sociální práce*, 1, 52–66.

Probační a mediační služba České republiky. (2014). *Zpráva o realizaci probačních programů v roce 2013.* Ministerstvo vnitra.

Saxonberg, S. and Hašková, H. (2016). The revenge of history: The institutional roots of post-Communist family policy in the Czech Republic, Hungary and Poland. *Social Policy and Administration*, 50(5), 559–579.

Schmidt, V. (2012). Democracy and legitimacy in the European Union. In E. Jones, A. Menon, and S. Weatherill (Eds.), *The Oxford handbook of the European Union* (pp. 661–675). Oxford University Press.

Shmidt, V. and Bailey, J. (2014). Institutionalisation of children in the Czech Rep: A case of path dependency. *Journal of Sociology and Social Welfare*, 1, 53–75.

Shmidt, V. and Shchurko, T. (2014). Children's rights in post-Soviet countries: The case of Russia and Belarus. *International Social Work*, 57(5), 447–458.

Shmidt, V (Ed.). (2019). *The politics of disability in interwar and socialist Czechoslovakia segregating in the name of the nation.* Amsterdam University Press.

Topinka, D. (2016). *Domácí násilí z perspektivy aplikovaného výzkumu Základní fakta a výsledky.* SocioFactor s.r.o.

Trachtová, Z. (2016). *Výchovný ústav v Chrastavě bude zrušen, oznámila Valachová.* Available at: https://zpravy. idnes.cz/polepsovna-v-chrastave-bude-zrucena-d7e-/domaci.aspx?c=A160608_154716_domaci_jj.

Úřad vlády, Č. R. (2009). *Národní strategie prevence násilí na dětech v ČR na období 2008–2018.* Úřad vlády ČR. Available at: https://www.vlada.cz/cz/urad-vlady/vydavatelstvi/vydane-publikace/narodni-strategie-prevence-nasili-na-detech-v-cr-na-obdobi-2008-2018-79428/.

Válková, H. (2006). Restorative approaches and alternative methods: Juvenile justice reform in the Czech Republic. In J. Junger-Tas and H. Decker Scott (Eds.), *International handbook of juvenile justice* (pp. 377–395). Springer.

Vávrová, S., Vaculiková, J., and Kalenda, J. (2016). Selected aspects of social and legal protection of children" expert approach versus public opinion. *Sociální pedagogika*, 4 (2), 56–74.

Velemínský, M. st, Velemínský, M., Jr., Rost, M., Samková, J., Samek, J., and Sethi, D. (2017). Studie negativních zážitků z dětství (ACE) v České republice. *Česko-slovenská pediatrie*, 72(7), 409–420.

Warner, J. (2015). *The emotional politics of social work and child protection.* Policy Press.

Child Protection Systems in Estonia and Latvia

Merle Linno *and* Judit Strömpl

Abstract

This chapter focuses on the historical process of transformation from the paternalistic Soviet state system of child protection in Estonia and Latvia. Moreover, it tackles the criticism of the deinstitutionalization of residential care and changes in juvenile justice. The Soviet concept of the child sees parents as dangerous for the kids, while the educational system was empowered to take responsibility for rearing the new generation. Population growth is found to have a significant impact on children's well-being. Both countries acknowledge the child's right to family as a core principle in child protection work. Local governments are required to develop measures based on the needs of children and families.

Key Words: Soviet, Estonia, Latvia, population growth, child protection, local government, families, deinstitutionalization, juvenile justice, residential care

Introduction

Whilst Estonian and Latvian social policy are influenced by a common background in terms of state socialist legacies, transition, and EU accession processes (Javornik, 2014), the development of child protection systems over the previous 20–30 years presents some differences. Therefore, the main focus of this chapter is on the process of transformation from the paternalistic Soviet state system of child protection to a liberal system based on children's rights and well-being. In addition to describing and comparing the Estonian and Latvian child protection systems, deinstitutionalization of residential care and changes in juvenile justice will also be scrutinized.

Both Estonia and Latvia are small countries with few inhabitants. Therefore, the question of population growth and the quality of children's well-being are questions central to the future existence of these countries. The total number of children in Estonia (to age 18) at the beginning of 2020 was 263,867 (20.2% of the population); a rate relatively unchanged from the previous year.[1] The total number of children in Latvia was also

---

[1] Estonian Statistics, https://www.stat.ee/en, retrieved December 19, 2020.

Table 22.1 Fertility rate, pulation growth, birth Rate and youth dependency rate in Estonian and Latvia, 2020

	Fertility rate, 2020 (no. per female) (CIA, 2020)	Population growth, 2020	Birth rate (no. per 1,000)	Youth dependency ratio (CIA, 2020)
Estonia	1.61	–0.65	9.3	26.1
Latvia	1.53	–1.12	9.2	26.1

relatively stable at 376,731 (20% of the population) in 2020.[2] Data showing low fertility rates, low population growth, and the youth dependency rate can be seen in Table 22.1.

Although no full analysis has been conducted of the child protection systems in Estonia and Latvia based on the scheme of Gilbert and colleagues (2011), it is possible to see evidence of a child protection orientation in both countries.

For a better understanding of the processes of change, a brief overview of the historical and socio-legal background of child welfare in both countries is presented. This will be followed by a description of the main characteristics of child protection policies and programs, including recent trends and issues.

Historical and Socio-legal Context of Child Protection in Estonia and Latvia

Estonia and Latvia have a long, common history, dating back to at least the 18th century when both countries were integrated into the Russian Empire after the Russian victory of the Great Northern War in 1710. As a result of events of the Russian Revolution and World War I, both states gained independence in 1918. This was maintained for less than 20 years and ended with an annexation by the Soviet Union in 1940. The Soviet occupation lasted nearly 50 years, ending in 1991 when both Estonia and Latvia restored independence.

During the 50 years that Estonia and Latvia belonged to the Soviet Union, principles of legislation were the same as Article 14 of the Soviet Constitution, which set forth the extensive limits of the Soviet Republic. This granted the highest structures of state authority and structures of government of the Soviet Union jurisdiction in significant areas, including legislation on the judicial system and procedure, and criminal and civil codes (Kerikmäe et al., 2017). Hence, in both Estonia and Latvia the legal framework was similar. Thus, their constitutions stated that all the laws of the Soviet Union were binding on their territory (Kerikmäe et al., 2017).

There was no special child protection or social work legislation in the Soviet Union; the Code on Marriage and the Family was the law stating the mutual rights and obligations on parents and children, together with rules about how authorities must deal with

---

[2] Central Statistical Bureau of Latvia, http://data.csb.gov.lv/pxweb/en/?rxid=147633eb-6654-4065-ab82-b4d2a1368945, retrieved December 19, 2020.

children left without parental care. Technically, according to the federal structure of the Soviet state, the Soviet Republics were granted—at least in theory—the right to their own family law (Khazova, 2010). However, the Republics had no freedom in designing these laws. Instead, according to Khazova (2010), they were obliged to follow the federal law (the Fundamentals of the Legislation of the USSR and Soviet Republics on Marriage and the Family of 1968), which covered the main family law issues. These related to principles about treatment of parents, the basis for the determination of parental rights, further possibilities for children left without parental care, adoption, and custody regulation. All procedures which formed the basis of taking care of families in need were fundamentally the same in both Estonia and Latvia. Khazova (2010), who analyzed family laws in post-Soviet territories, states that differences between the republican family codes were slight. Further, they all had the Russian Soviet Federative Socialist Republic Code on Marriage and the Family of 1969 as a common compulsory model. According to Bernstein (2001), who analyzed Soviet Supreme Court decisions on adoption, the child's best interests were central, and the judicial framework emphasized the need to understand the child's interests beyond just material conditions (at least in adoption cases).

Child Protection System and Policies in Soviet Estonia and Latvia: 1940–1991

Child protection is one of the social spheres that was already in existence in the Soviet Union. However, official Soviet policy did not recognize the existence of social problems, and if difficulties arose, these were to be dealt with by militia, teachers, employers, and other representatives of the Communist Party and trade unions (Aidukaite, 2003; Kiik & Sirotkina, 2005; Iarskaia-Smirnova & Lyon, 2018).

The legal regulation of child protection during the Soviet period was similar in Estonia and Latvia. Overall, social policy in the Soviet Union focused on supporting labor productivity, creating a collectivist consciousness, and ensuring at least a minimal standard of living for the work force (Tobis, 2000). Within this framework, child protection policy was aimed at supporting parents'—especially mothers'—ability to work, liberating them from the responsibility of taking care of their children. Thus, Soviet child protection was a state paternalistic system, meaning the state took total responsibility for every child. For example, in the Estonian Code for Marriage and Family, it is stated that motherhood should be under the protection of the state. Furthermore, the Code states:

> To protect mother's and child's rights the state provides and develops a network of maternity homes, day-care, kindergarten, boarding schools, and other children's institutions, enables paid maternity leave, provides protection for mothers on their working places, pays special finance support to single mothers and extended families, and provides other kinds of state-run and communal help to family. (Estonian SSR Code for Marriage and Family, 1969)

First, this meant that governance of childrearing and education was in state hands, and educational institutions were empowered to work with children and families. For example, in 1956 (to promote industrialization and increase productivity), Khrushchev[3] used boarding schools (*internati*), nurseries, and kindergartens to educate children and free their mothers for employment (Tobis, 2000). Although the aim was that by the 1980s all children would be educated in boarding schools, according to Tobis (2000) they remained for children from underprivileged families.

For children separated from parents due to the parents' lack of capability to take care of their children, institutionalization was the main option, although the law offered the possibility to raise children in non-biological families through adoption and guardianship. Adoption was meant for families with difficulties in having their own children; there was then also a list of children not suitable for adoption, because of either a disability or their parents' mental or social problems (Luhamaa & Strömpl, 2021). The Soviet foster care system favored biological relatives, believing they could provide the most consistent care, having greater responsibility for the care of their progeny (Bernstein, 2001).

According to Tobis (2000), residential institutions in the Soviet Union served the dual roles of social protection and social regulation. Children's residential institutions were used for the socialization of individuals into the collectivist culture, for education and training of children, preparing and channeling them into the work force, for the re-education of juvenile delinquents, and for the protection of orphans and children at risk of abuse or neglect (Tobis, 2000; Bernstein, 2001). There were special boarding schools for children with learning difficulties and for gifted children, as their parents and teachers sought specialized boarding schools as a better option. Additionally, boarding schools were sometimes used when children were living far from a neighborhood school. Special types of institutions were meant for children with disabilities, and parents were forced to place their child into such an institution if they were found to be disabled. Tobis (2000)—citing Madison (1968) and Kadushin (1982)—argues that schoolteachers and nurses in polyclinics also recommended the placement of children in residential institutions, and parents themselves petitioned for permission to place a child in an institution. Thus, child residential care was normalized as an acceptable solution and the only possibility in cases of specific difficulties.

Special educational facilities were provided exclusively for children with behavioral difficulties, built on the principles of Soviet pedagogy developed by Makarenko. These were based on vocational and ideological education, a strong sense of the collective, and pedagogical control. After completing special school, young people were directed to labor where their discipline was provided by the working collective. However, special schools as

---

[3] Khrushchev was the First Secretary of the Communist Party of the Soviet Union from 1953–1964 and Chairman of the Council of Ministers from 1958–1964. The position is comparable to the prime minister; he (and other leaders of the SU) held undivided authority.

total institutions often did not have the desired effect, instead providing the first step in the development of a criminal career (Saar, 2003).

Characteristic of the Soviet residential care system was the separation of children according to age. There were separate orphanages for infants aged 0–3 years, children's homes for pre-schoolers aged 3–6 years, and children's homes for school-age children. This meant that in the case of removal, siblings would also be separated according to their age (Sindi, 2015).

During the 1970s, with the development of child psychology and empirical studies in the Soviet Union, the negative impact of child separation from the mother and the negative outcomes of institutional care became topics of professional discussion. During *perestroika*,[4] information about child abuse in children's institutions were revealed (Tobis, 2000).

In the latter part of the 1970s, moderate familialization replaced the previous monopoly of public care; direct and indirect benefits for families were introduced, and the main intention of the new policy was to shift responsibility for children from state institutions back to parents (Bernstein, 2001; Schmidt & Shchurko, 2014). According to Harwin (1996, cited in Tobis, 2000), although the government encouraged the development of services to assist troubled families, these initiatives remained modest and few. Alongside changes in family policy, new measures were established that were aimed at more consistent monitoring of families, with strict criteria related to child removal and limitation of parental rights being introduced in 1979 (Schmidt & Shchurko, 2014). Since 1987, institutions recruited psychologists and speech therapists, child protection inspectors in local government responsible for cooperation with youth militia, and local child commissions were established (Aus, 1984; Schmidt & Shchurko, 2014). Child protection inspectors were tasked with oversight of the situation for children in need, reacting when a child's safety was in danger. It was their responsibility to make a claim to the courts for determination of parental custody and place the child into either an institution or a substitute family. According to Schmidt and Shchurko (2014), the late Soviet policy opposed the interests of both children and parents—with the latter being viewed as potentially less competent than professionals.

Independence and Times of Transition: Some Background Information

After the collapse of the Soviet Union, "the newly independent Baltic states, virtually overnight, had to abandon the old social security network and healthcare management systems, since these were based on the Soviet currency, all-Union budget, and total state control of all resources, infrastructures and employment" (Lauristin, 2011, p. 10).

---

[4] *Perestroika* (restructuring) was a period of Mikhail Gorbachev's time in power started in 1985 with economic reforms.

Lauristin (2011) divides the transition time into three periods, culminating in the joining of the European Union (EU). During the first period of transition, several western practices were implemented; one such practice from the child protection field is the SOS Children's Village, which is discussed later in this chapter.

The transition started from the creation of a new constitutional and social order, establishing economic reforms that transferred from a central planning economy to a market economy (Simpura, 1995). These transition strategies can be characterized as fast (*big bang*) reform or gradual reform (Svejnar, 2002). The transition in both Estonia and Latvia was characterized as the *big bang* type, which meant a radical and comprehensive economic program in which macroeconomic stabilization, microeconomic liberalization, and fundamental institutional restructuring were launched at about the same time and implemented as quickly as possible (Lenger, 2008). As a result, the Baltic states stand out for their convergence on radical neoliberal macroeconomic, structural, and social policies (Bohle & Greskovits, 2012). Bohle and Greskovits (2012) argue that the Baltic states rapidly instituted market economies, but did little to mitigate business risks and losses, or help them through adequate industrial policies to capture promising market niches.

The reform of the social system began with the establishment of health insurance and pension insurance systems. This was a difficult period, when poverty and the stratification of society developed quickly—particularly in Latvia. Bohle and Greskovits (2012) argue that similarly, with the lack of mitigation of economic risks, the Baltic welfare states fell short in providing sufficient protection against inequality and social anomie.

The authors of the Alternative Report to the UN (Ebela et al., 2015) about protection of children's rights, and the implementation of the United Nations Convention on the Rights of the Child, are critical of accomplishments made in Latvia during the first transition period. According to the report, stability was not achieved, poverty increased, and sufficient attention was not given to making the child's best interests central in decision making. Corruption among the "old" elite leaders of the Latvian Communist Party, who maintained their power, were seen by the authors of the report as the main reason for these outcomes. By comparison, Estonia is described in the report as an example of good practice in managing the transition and the subsequent rapid changes in society.

The second period of transition relates to preparations to join the European Union. Estonia was invited to join the EU in 1997, whilst Latvia and Lithuania were invited in 1999. This period could be called a period of disappointment when public support for government and parliament was at its lowest during the transition. The third period refers to joining the EU in 2004. The period started with GDP growth of 10%, further increasing from spring 2005 to the autumn of 2007. There was an increase in well-being for a while; however, social spending and the level of social protection was the lowest in the EU. In 2008, Estonia spent 15.1% of GDP on social protection; Lithuania spent 16.2%, and Latvia 12.6% (Lauristin, 2011, p. 11).

One characteristic of the Baltic states during this time was the low level of solidarity, which as Lauristin explains was a result of the ethnic split of the population. It might be borne in mind that Soviet Union immigration policy supported the movement of citizens between Soviet Republics (for details, see Misiunas & Taagepera, 1993; Zepa et al., 2015), and as a result, in early 1990 ethnic Latvians formed only 52% of the population in Latvia, whilst there were 61.5% ethnic Estonians in the Estonian population. The development of industry in certain regions of both countries needed working personnel; however, a characteristic of independence was that large numbers of Russian-speaking immigrants were segregated from the main population—mainly because of language and regional location (Linno & Strömpl, 2015). Those people who had previously identified themselves as equal citizens of both Estonia and Latvia became immigrants upon the restoration of independence. The societies were indeed divided ethnically, and both states still struggle today with the integration of their descendants. A rapidly instituted market economy was accompanied by an orientation to material values and a move toward individualism, opposing the previous rigid rules of collectivism (Aidukaite, 2006).

Child Protection System Today

According to OECD[5] data, in 2015 Estonian and Latvian expenditures on family benefits were 2.93% and 2.13% of GDP, respectively. In Estonia, most support is provided by the state as benefits paid in cash; about one-fifth of expenditures go to services and less is provided in the form of tax breaks for families. In Latvia the situation is similar, despite the fact that GDP is lower than in Estonia, and there are no tax breaks for families.

International Law and the Evolution of National Law

During the first period of transition, rapid changes in legislation relating to social work took place. One of the important features of developing a modern child protection system has been the acceptance of the United Nations Convention on the Rights of the Child (CRC). This happened almost at the same time for both countries: it was one of the first international treaties that the Estonian Republic signed in 1991, whilst Latvia accepted the CRC in 1992. The first Estonian Child Protection Act came into force in 1993 and was replaced by the new Act in 2016. In Latvia, the Protection of the Rights of the Child Law was adopted in 1998. The first difference between these acts can be seen in their titles, reflecting essential differences between the concept of the child as the subject of law and the state activity to protect children. Latvia focused on the protection of the *rights* of children, while Estonia focused on the *protection* of children. The difference is substantial, and here it is evident that Estonia continued to pursue a more paternalistic approach to child protection, seeing the child as less competent and in need of adult protection. Meanwhile,

---

[5] Public spending on family benefits: http://www.oecd.org/els/soc/PF1_1_Public_spending_on_family_benefits.pdf.

Latvian legislation placed the child at the center of activity, as the bearer of human rights, and fully participatory.

Although the CRC was accepted, and social welfare law was established in the early and mid-1990s, the everyday practice of child protection in Estonia was performed through family law (entered into force in 1995). It has been suggested that family law was influenced by Soviet rules, but compared to other states in Europe, family law in the Soviet Union was more liberal and therefore in Estonia there was no need for considerable change (Kerikmäe et al., 2017). The new family law was enacted in 2010 and replaced principles of parental rights with a system of the parental right of custody (e.g., custody over the person and custody over property) (see Family Law Act, 2009). Thus, until 2010, relationships between children and parents were addressed through certain principles, which included the abolition of parental rights where parents might be considered a risk to the child. From 2010, in cases where a child's well-being might be endangered, the local government could apply to the courts for a restriction of parental rights of custody, and the courts could then restrict the right of custody over a person or property by prohibiting the performance of certain acts (Family Law Act, 2009).

Latvia (unlike Estonia) re-established its civil law, which had originally come into force in 1938 but was replaced after incorporation into the Soviet Union with the Soviet Civil Code (Bebre & Gjortlere, 2016). Latvian civil law does not differentiate various custodies.

Organization of Child Protection Work

Both Estonia and Latvia recognize the child's right to family as a core principle in child protection work. If the parents and children need help, the main responsibility for providing support rests with local government in both countries (Protection of the Rights of the Child Law, 1998; Child Protection Act, 2016).

Besides local government, child protection workers, and social workers, both countries also have a central institution established for supervising local child protection work and make recommendations at the municipal level. In Estonia, this role has been undertaken since 2016 by the Social Insurance Boards Child Protection Department, which has units in each of the four regions of Estonia (Child Protection Department, n.d.; Nikonov, 2016). According to para. 6, Section 2 of the Child Protection Act, the state and local governments must develop measures to evaluate and prevent children's problems and reduce the number of children who need help or support (Nikonov, 2016). By the end of 2019, there were 269 child protection workers in Estonia, of whom 87% were employed full-time (the remainder being part-time).[6] Of the total number of workers, 78% had a

---

[6] Not every local government has employed child protection workers; sometimes child protection work is performed by a social worker, youth worker, or some other professional.

social work education (although annual statistics do not differentiate between the BA and MA level).

Child protection by local governments should develop measures that are based on the needs of children and their families, and have a long-lasting, positive effect. The state identifies four tasks in developing a better child protection system to work in harmony with the new Child Protection Act. First, child protection workers from the social insurance body assist local governments both in their development programs and in solving concrete difficult cases. Second, with the help of the state, guidance and assessment materials are developed. One of the recent developments is adopting the child and family assessment tool from Sweden (BBIC system), which actually originated from the UK Common Assessment Framework (ibid.). Although recruitment of child protection workers is financed by municipalities, training and supervision is the responsibility of the state, and financed by the state. Third, the state thus offers free training to child protection workers employed by local governments. The training is a two-year program, designed according to the needs of practitioners and organized in a way that is suitable for working specialists.[7] Fourth and finally, the state develops services for particularly troubled target groups, for example services for young offenders.

Until 2009, the Latvian Ministry of Children and Family and Integration Affairs (MCFIA) was the leading state administration institution, with the function to develop national policy in the areas of protection of children's rights and implementation of policy. That same year, the Ministry of Welfare, Ministry of Justice, and Ministry of Education and Science together took over the functions of MCFIA. Since then, the State Inspectorate for the Protection of Children's Rights (Inspectorate) was established (Committee on the Rights of the Child. Latvia, 2013). The Inspectorate—an institution of direct administration under the supervision of the Ministry of Welfare—supervises and controls the observance of the Protection of the Rights of the Child Law (PRCL) and other regulatory enactments that regulate the protection of the rights of the child. The functions of the Inspectorate include analyzing the situation in the field of protection of the rights of the child and providing suggestions to institutions to ensure and improve the protection of the rights of the child. To perform these specified tasks, the Inspectorate has the right to request and receive (free of charge) from private individuals and institutions the necessary information to examine administrative violation matters and impose administrative fines, and to form advisory expert councils (Grävere et al., 2015, p. 20). State protection officers have their visiting hours and places of work in three areas of Latvia (State Inspectorate for the Protection of Children's Rights, n.d.).

Latvia has a special administrative institution named the Orphan's and Custody Court, established in 2007. This is a guardianship and trusteeship institution established

---

[7] The training program consists of four modules: 1) prevention and community work, 2) legal basis for child protection work, 3) child well-being, assessment, and case management, and 4) social work with child and his/her family (Lastekaitsetöötajate koolitused, 2018).

by a municipality (Law on Orphan's and Custody Court, 2006). Although the court system in Latvia is clearly established as a three-level system (as in Estonia), questions about parental responsibility are addressed through two institutions. First, general courts deal with custody, access rights, place of residence, and maintenance, whilst all other issues concerning child protection (including suspension of custody rights, establishment of out-of-family care, and appointment of the guardian) are addressed through the Orphan's and Custody Court (Kucina, 2017; Central Statistical Bureau of Latvia, 2020, p. 75). At the end of 2019, 117 Orphan's and Custody Courts operated in 119 Latvian municipalities. During a personal interview, Dr. Ilona Kronberga, a Latvian expert told us that there is a schedule to reduce the number of these courts according to administrative-territorial reform[8] and rename them Child's Rights Court. This will respond to the efforts of law and harmonize the policy and practice.

Mandatory Reporting about Children in Need of Assistance and in Danger

According to both countries' law everyone has an obligation to notice and report about a child in need of assistance or in danger. In Estonia, the first Child Protection Act (1993) included Article 59, which obligated everyone to report children in need of assistance and/or those in danger. In 2009, a child helpline telephone-service (Lasteabi.ee) was introduced to enable reporting about children in need of assistance and/or in danger, which also enables children to ask for help themselves. Presently, several other services are offered for children, including forums and chat services. Informers are guaranteed anonymity, and all persons (civilians or professionals) who have information either of a child in need of assistance or in danger are required by law to notify (Child Protection Law, 2016, sections 27 and 31; FRA, 2015).

According to the Latvian Protection of the Rights of the Child Law (PRCL), the same notions of the child in danger and the child in need of assistance are used, and the obligation to report rests on all inhabitants (FRA, 2015). Healthcare, pedagogical, social field, or police employees, and elected state and local government officials who have received information regarding violations of rights of the child and who have failed to inform the institutions referred to in regard to such, shall be held liable as laid down in law for such failure to inform (Protection of the Rights of the Child Law, 1998, para. 73). A child hotline has been available in Latvia since 2006 (State Inspectorate for the Protection of Children's Rights, 2020).

The Estonian helpline joined the European system in 2011, while Latvia did so in 2008 (Child Helpline International, 2017). In both countries, the helpline is run by the central institution with responsibility for child protection, is financed by the state, and is free of charge.

---

[8] On Latvian administrative-territorial reform, see https://www.saeima.lv/en/news/saeima-news/29027-saeima-adopts-administrative-territorial-reform.

Helping Families: Supporting Services

Ensuring children's rights in professional child protection work can be divided briefly into open family care (such as helping children and families without separating the child and family), and substitute care, where there are several possibilities: residential care, foster care, guardianship, and adoption.

ESTONIA

In Estonia, helping families in need is the responsibility of local government. Therefore, open family care is provided mainly through institutions in municipal ownership or non-profit organizations (Linno & Strömpl, 2015). These kinds of services are financed by the municipalities, and the quality and range of services vary. As Estonian child protection policy follows the risk-oriented model, the activity of local government child protection workers first focuses on protecting children from abusive parents (see Toros, 2011). In family assessment processes, a deficit-based approach (i.e., parents are viewed as lacking capabilities) dominates (Toros & LaScala, 2018; Toros et al., 2018), regardless of the clear aim stated by law to enhance the capability of parents in their role as carers. In recent years, efforts have been made to introduce programs financed by the state to support parents and to prevent child abuse and removal. The Incredible Years program has been tested and adapted from its 2014 inception, and according to an evaluation, the program has reached its aims, with changes in parent behavior occurring (Kasvandik et al., 2014; Trummal, 2018). Multidimensional family therapy (funded by the state) has been offered since 2015 for children and families with multiple problems, and again, evaluations of implementation have found it to be helpful and useful, with school truancy and delinquency diminishing (Aaben et al., 2017). In local governments, there are other initiatives to educate parents and to avoid the placement of children into substitute care, though these have not been evaluated and services provided in different areas of the country are rather different.

LATVIA

Providing support services for families is also the responsibility of municipalities in Latvia. However, due to disparities in human resources and financial capacity between municipalities, the availability, quality, and diversity of social services and family support measures differ greatly between municipalities (Opening Doors, 2017). Particularly in rural areas, there is a lack of specialized social workers who can respond to the individual needs of children and families at risk. Alternative Report to the UN (Ebela et al., 2015) was critical of the situation in municipalities with regard to support for families, stating that in Latvia, residential care is still the prevailing method of supporting children and families.

Aligned with this method, one of the initiatives introduced in Latvia in 2009 is a system of baby boxes (i.e., a location parents can anonymously bring their baby to leave in the care of others). The project came to fruition after years of careful planning and research to answer the social problems of poverty, child maltreatment, and infanticide. The aim is to avoid infanticide, and to support parents in difficulties at a particular moment, unable to see a way out. There are eight "baby boxes" in different locations in Latvia, and since the scheme's inception, 40 children have been placed in the boxes for safety (Glabejsilites Latvija, n.d.). Parents who place their newborn in the baby box relinquish custody rights, and after monitoring the baby's health and condition, the baby can then be adopted. There is a six-month interim period, during which time parents have the possibility of applying to the orphan's court to regain parental rights and have their child returned. The orphan's court makes the decision based on the child's best interests (Glabejsilites Latvija, n.d.). However, the UN Committee on the Rights of the Child does not approve of the baby boxes because it states that it violates several articles of the UNCRC. Instead, the committee urges the state to increase their efforts to address the root causes that lead to the abandonment of infants, including the provision of family planning, adequate counselling, social support for unplanned pregnancies, and the prevention of high-risk pregnancies. (The rights of vulnerable children under the age of three, n.d.)

Child Removal and Substitute Care

Estonia and Latvia both inherited the Soviet institutional care system of big institutions (Suni, 1995; Paulovica, 1995). In conjunction with independence, deinstitutionalization began and is still in process today (Frindt, 2007a, 2007b; Ismayilova et al., 2014; Rajevska et al., 2016; Kuuse & Toros 2017; Sindi et al., 2018).

In Estonia, the first step in reorganizing of institutional care was ending the system of dividing children by age into different orphanages. New, smaller orphanages were opened in addition to existing ones. For example, in Tartu, Estonia, a home (*Mäe-kodu*) was opened in 1994 for just 24 children. Moreover, siblings previously living in different orphanages were reunited. In the mid-1990s (with international help), other large institutions were reorganized into more family-like substitute homes, where smaller groups of children—mostly siblings—could stay (Sindi, 2015).

In 1995 in Estonia, and in 1997 in Latvia, the first SOS children's villages (SOS CV) were introduced and operated under the auspices of the NGO, SOS (SOS Children's Village in Latvia, n.d.; SOS Children Village in Estonia, n.d.). According to SOS concepts, principal caregiving rests with women, known as SOS-mothers (SOS Children's Village in Latvia, n.d.; SOS Children Village in Estonia, n.d.). This was a new development in residential childcare, differing from the old Soviet model of residential institutions where children were cared for by staff who worked in shifts making any sort of caregiver attachment complicated. In SOS CV, the SOS-mother lives and works in an SOS family house, with a maximum of six children. Today, there are four SOS CVs in different parts of Estonia and two homes in Latvia. The Estonian SOS CVs are in permanent reorganization, with the plan being to move SOS families into ordinary flats where they become integrated members of the neighborhood, more like foster families (Sindi et al., 2018).

ESTONIA

In Estonia, there are 42 residential childcare institutions called substitute homes. By the end of 2018, there were 2,451 children[9] in public care (9.7 per 1,000 children), 801 of them living in institutions (3.2 per 1,000), and only 115 children (0.5 per 1,000 children) in foster families (Jõks, 2020). Additionally, there were 1,284 children (5.1 per 1,000 children) living in guardianship, full data presented in Table 22.2. In 2013, approximately 40% of children living in institutions had some kind of health concern, including mental health issues (EV Sotsiaalministeerium, 2014). Presently, a clear direction to increase family-based care has been adopted and attempts are being made to make children's substitute homes more family-like (ibid.). Initial achievements reported are as follows: many institutions are now situated in smaller buildings; the size of the children's groups has been reduced to a maximum of six children; and family-like care is offered. Furthermore, studies have revealed that many children leaving care will face different problems connected with the quality of the care (Turk, 2011; Osila et al., 2016; Civitta, 2022). In 2018, changes were made to the way substitute residential care is financed, as well as changes to special means for young people leaving care. Simultaneously, attempts were made to raise the number and quality of foster families, however we can see that this number is rather decreasing every year.

LATVIA

In Latvia, residential care is provided in state social care centers, which are subordinated to the Ministry of Welfare to provide long-term social care and rehabilitation services and social care centers of local governments and other organizations. At the end of 2018, there were 207 children in 14 state social care centers and 645 children in 29 social care centers of local governments and other organizations (Central Statistical Bureau of Latvia, 2019, p. 78).

Funded by the state, these centers support orphans and children left without parental care under the age of two, children with mental and physical special needs or disabilities (under 4 years of age), and children with multiple mental special needs or disabilities from 4 to 18 years of age (Grāvere et al., 2015).

Deinstitutionalization is also in process in Latvia. According to Legzdina and Rajevska (2017), although the physical size of institutions is being reduced, the total number of institutionalized children is still high. For example, by the end of 2016, there were 4,548 children (12.3 per 1,000 children) in foster care and under guardianship, and the other 1,257 (3.4 per 1,000 children) lived in residential care. Deinstitutionalization in Latvia began in 2015 when initial documents were approved to start the transition from institutional to community-based care, and in 2016, the implementation of deinstitutionalization reforms commenced (Opening Doors, 2017).

Individual needs assessments and the development of individual support plans for all children in institutional care were undertaken in 2016–2017, to find suitable solutions

---

[9] Children aged 0–17.

Table 22.2 Children (ages 0–17) child protection services in Estonia and Latvia, 2010–2018 (total *n* and per 1,000 child population)

	2010		2016		2018	
	EST[a]	LV[b]	EST[a]	LV[b]	EST[a]	LV[c]
Population on 1 January	1,333,290	2,120,504	1,315,944	1,968,957	1,319,133	1,934,379
Child population measured on 1 January the following year. *n*=children	245,360 (184)	375, 015 (177)	246,991 (187.7)	352,298 (179)	252,117 (191)	358,762 (185.5)
Referrals investigated, *n*= children, end of year (per 1,000 children)	2,852 (11.6)	3,851 (10.3)	2,599 (10.5)	2,887 (8.2)	2,451 (9.7)	2,773 (7.7)
Lost custody rights, *n*= children (per 1,000 children)	172 (0.7)	1,953 (5.2)	353 (1.4)	1,378 (3.9)	287 (1.1)	1,321 (3.7)
Children living in residential care, end of year, *n*=children (per 1,000 children)	1,096 (4.5)	1,870 (5)	862 (3.5)	1,225 (3.5)	801 (3.2)	852 (2.4)
Children living in guardianship, end of year, *n*= children (per 1,000 children)	1,348 (5.5)	5,565 (14.8)	1,395 (5.6)	4,548 (12.9)	1,284 (5.1)	4, 398 (12.3)
Foster families, *n*=children (per 1,000 children)	-	884 (2.4)	174 (0.7)	1,193 (3.4)	115 (0.5)	1,246 (3.5)
Domestic adoptions from care, *n*=children (per 1,000 children)	73 (0.3)	99 (0.3)	38 (0.2)	127 (0.4)	22 (0.1)	102 (0.3)
Intercountry adoption from care, *n*=children (per 1,000 children)	28 (0.1)	136 (0.4)	11 (0.04)	119 (0.3)	00	50 (0.1)

Source: [a] Statistics Estonian and Estonian Ministry of Social Affairs (2010–2018); [b] Children in Latvia 2017; [c] Children in Latvia 2019.

for everyone (Opening Doors, 2017). Since 2017, important steps have been taken to improve alternative care. For example, professional foster care has been introduced in the country, and training and selection processes for foster families will be reviewed (Opening Doors, 2017). Early results are promising; according to the May 2018 data released by the State Inspectorate for the Protection of Children's Rights, for the first time, the number of children without parental care raised in foster families exceeded the number of children living in institutions. The number of social care centers decreased during the last 10 years from 58 institutions (with 1,870 children) in 2010 to 33 (with 801 children) in 2018. Thus, family-based care in 2018 prevailed over institutions for children in Latvia.

Juvenile Justice in Estonia and Latvia

Today in both Baltic States children in conflict with the law are handled as children in need of assistance (in Estonia) or as children whose rights are broken (Latvia) and as such they belong to the child protection system. In this section, we will briefly explain developments during the years of independence when juvenile offenders became subjects of child protection systems.

In the 1990s, juvenile crime increased in both Estonia and Latvia. The percentage of child offenders in Estonia varied between 16% and 20% of all offenders. The rate was at its highest in 1995 at more than 20%, with 5.6 per 1,000 children classified as child offenders, and the lowest in 2000 at less than 14%, with 5.4 per 1,000 children classified as the same. The difference is minimal because of the reduced child population in 2000. Of the total number of homicides, the number committed by children varies between 5% and 9%, whilst the number of convicted minors was highest in 1997 with 1,668 (18% of all convicted persons) being children—meaning 4.4 per 1,000 children (Saar et al., 2002).

Further statistics indicate that in Latvia in 1994, some 5% of all criminal offenses were committed by children, and by the following year this had risen to 7%. In 1996, there were 3,014 children aged 7 to 18 (4.4 per 1,000 child population) who were under police supervision, meaning they were suspected or guilty of an offense (Kinis, 1996, pp. 176–177). In 1998, juvenile crime reached its peak with 4,023 (6.3 per 1,000 child population) offences by juveniles.

In the new century, juvenile crime has continued to decrease in both countries. This is partly attributed to a decreasing child population, and partly related to new legislation and development of the juvenile justice systems in both countries during the 1990s.

Legislation

In the early 1990s, instead of Soviet legislation and institutions, some temporary solutions were adapted for juveniles in the system (see Strömpl, 2002; Saar, 2003). In the Soviet Union, there was no separate criminal system for children and juveniles; all criminal cases were processed by the adult courts. The same was true in both Baltic countries. Despite the wish to protect underage offenders from a criminal career and direct them to the child protection system, there are problems with realization of such a policy. Therefore today, severe criminal cases committed by minors are processed in the general court system and are regulated in Estonia by the Estonian Penal Code, the Code of Criminal Procedure, and the Imprisonment Act. In Latvia, the Criminal Law, the Criminal Procedure Law, the Penalty Enforcement Code of Latvia, and the Law on Detention Procedure all regulate the criminal proceeding and deprivation of liberty of juveniles (Grāvere et al., 2015).

Since the 1960s, cases of juvenile offenses were investigated by juvenile committees—public establishments operated by local Soviets. The aim was to keep minors from criminal proceedings. The ideology behind this move was that using pedagogical methods of control and influence could be effective in fighting youth delinquency. In both Latvia and Estonia, similar systems were developed during the 1990s. In Estonia, the Juvenile Sanctions Act, and in Latvia, the Child's Rights Law both came into force in 1998. In Estonia, the Juvenile Sanction Act regulated among others, the function of juvenile committees—an alternative non-juridical organization dealing with young people (under 18 years) in conflict with the law. Juvenile committees were formed by county governors and worked within the limits of local municipalities. Members of committees were experts in the areas of education, health, social welfare, and youth police (Strömpl & Markina, 2017).

In Latvia, similar to Estonia, the adult court observes cases of severe juvenile offences. According to Article 58 of PRCL, local governments, the state police, and the state probation service (if the child is directed to probation) work with children involved with the law. When a criminal offense is proven, several public organizations and institutions also intervene. In Latvia, the prevention of juvenile delinquency is the focus, which aligns with the ideological concept of the PRCL. Accordingly, when a child commits an antisocial or criminal act, they lose their rights (Kronberga, 2017). Therefore, the law stipulates focusing on prevention to avoid a child's loss of rights (Grāvere et al., 2015).

Article 66 of PRCL defines the competence of local municipalities, who have to analyze the situation and develop programs to protect the rights of children in their administrative territory. It is intended that this work is approached first with regard to assistance and support for families, but also to develop out-of-home services for children whose family is not capable of caring for them. Local municipalities are obligated: 1) to provide primary healthcare for mothers and children; 2) to organize parental education, to provide primary schools and extracurricular child institutions; 3) to ensure the rights of the child in acquiring general secondary education; 4) to provide vocational training; and 5) to provide public libraries and organize child recreation. Thus, in Latvia, most preventive measures focus on all children at risk, not only those who are in conflict with the law (Kronberga & Zermatten, 2012; Kronberga & Sile, 2015). Therefore, all children and families are included in welfare's primary prevention level.

Education for Juvenile Offenders

In the 1990s, both in Estonia and Latvia, most young offenders were placed in closed special educational institutions—special schools. After the emancipation from Soviet ideology, a belief in the power of education still existed. These institutions gave opportunities for many neglected children to have accommodation, daily food, and to fulfil their obligatory basic education. As residential care in response to children's problems was normalized, the scope of special schools' support was broad, and both young offenders and neglected children lived together (Strömpl, 2002).

In Estonia at the beginning of 1990s, there were five correctional educational and special vocational institutions. Children in conflict with the law and at risk of delinquency were separated into different institutions according to age, gender, language of instruction (Estonian and Russian), and the severity of the offense. In addition to special schools, there was an educational labor camp in Viljandi for male minors under the authority of the Ministry of Interior (Home Office). Special vocational schools were closed, then reorganized as special schools for minors. The labor camp was reorganized as the Viljandi Youth Prison. It was closed in 2008. Since 2015, there has been one special school (Estonian: *Maarjamaa Hariduskolleegium*), working in two centers. In one center, there are children who have committed more severe criminal offenses, and in the other, those who have committed less serious offenses.[10]

In Latvia, reorganization began with a law, passed in 1993, applying compulsory measures of educational character to juveniles. This development had a similar beginning to the reorganization in Estonia: the most important expectation of dealing with youth delinquency was the educational correction of children. However, by 1992, some former correctional educational institutions had been closed. Some old institutions are still operating, although they have been rebuilt and reorganized (similar to the Estonian system).

Transitioning Juvenile Justice into Child Protection

Reforms of the juvenile justice system have taken place in Estonia since the beginning of 2018. Significant changes are expected in Latvia.

The principle of both sanctions and juvenile committees were reminiscent of those from the Soviet era, but these committees were not as powerful as their former namesake. The reorganization aimed to avoid the legislative contradiction in the Constitution of Estonia (July 3, 1992, Articles 20 and 21)[11] according to which only the court decision can deprive a person, including a child, of their liberty. Therefore, in the case of applying the most severe solution of the juvenile committee, directing the child into a special school should be provided with permission from the court. This made the job difficult because receiving such an allowance was timely—from one month to as much as one year (Strömpl & Markina, 2014). However, research shows that after 20 years of operation, juvenile committees evidence little capacity to help children stay away from crime (Rannala, 2014; Tamm & Salla, 2016a).

---

[10] See the institution's homepage at https://mhk.edu.ee/en.
[11] https://www.riigiteataja.ee/akt/12846827?leiaKehtiv.

After 2018, the juvenile committee was terminated, and the Juvenile Sanctions Act ceased to function. Since this time, juvenile justice has bene absorbed into the child protection system, and juvenile offenders are defined as children in need of help. Accordingly, measures of help and support are applied instead of blame and punishment. These changes are connected to the new Child Protection Act that was enacted in 2016 (Tamm & Salla, 2016b).

At the end of January 2021, there were only five male minors and one female minor in Estonian prisons.[12] Child offenders are now directed into special institutions called closed children's institutions,[13] where, in addition to compulsory education, they are provided with psychological and medical services if needed.

Both in Latvia and Estonia ideas of restorative justice are replacing the traditional ideology of punishment-centered approaches to working with young offenders. In Latvia probation officers and in Estonia police officers and prosecutors provide restorative justice measures while working with children and young people (Markina et al., 2021). During 3 years of reform in Estonia, improvements in reform are visible first of all in decreasing the number of offences among children (Markina et al., 2021).

Conclusion

The story of child protection in Latvia and Estonia begins with the Soviet concept of the child as a soft material to be molded by the hands of the state into a new type of personality—the Soviet human being. Parents were seen as dangerous for the child, and the educational system was empowered to take responsibility for rearing the new generation.

Although moderate processes of familialization began in the 1970s and family support measures were introduced, the influences of previous times are still visible in child protection work. Estonian and Latvian child protection systems have not been analyzed according to Gilbert and colleagues' (2011) scheme to establish if they are more child-protection-oriented or family-service-oriented. However, it is likely there is more evidence of child protection orientation in both countries. Social policy in post-Soviet Baltic states overall is characterized as neoliberal, with low social spending and a low degree of decommodification. The individual's responsibility is reflected in social work, as both Estonia and Latvia quickly switched from a collectivist to an individualist ideology after the restoration of independence. In both countries, deinstitutionalization processes have achieved some success, and in Latvia data released by the State Inspectorate for the Protection of the

---

[12] https://www.vangla.ee/et/uudised-ja-arvud/vangide-ja-kriminaalhooldusaluste-arv, accessed January 30, 2021.

[13] https://sotsiaalkindlustusamet.ee/et/lapsed-pered/lastekaitse/kinnise-lasteasutuse-teenus-0, accessed January 30, 2021.

Children's Rights (spring 2018) indicates the number of children without parental care growing up in foster families now exceeds the number of children living in institutions.

Both countries have joined the CRC and recognize the child's right to family as a core principle in child protection work. Efforts are made to develop programs supporting parents, and some of the programs implemented in Estonia (e.g., Incredible Years, Multidimensional Family Therapy) have been evaluated as effective.

The intriguing difference lies in the names and contents of children's rights laws at a local level. The Latvian Protection of the Rights of the Child Law (June 19, 1998) focuses on the *rights* of the child and declares the child as a subject of rights, while in the Estonian Child Protection Act the management of child *protection* is key. Additionally, the child appears in a passive role as someone "in need of assistance" or "in danger"; conversely, Latvian law recognizes the child behind the problem, as one whose rights were broken. Responsibility is placed on adults to fulfil the rights of the child. Thus, in Estonian law, the child is seen as a victim of either maltreatment or bad management of child protection work.

Overall, based on the analysis, it can be concluded that even if the basis for building modern child protection systems in both Estonia and Latvia had been the same, choices made by the state in each case has led them in different directions. However, the core concept for working with children and their families is the same: the child's rights.

Acknowledgments

Thanks to Dr Ilona Kronberga for her assistance with this chapter. Chapter was supported by Estonian Research Council, grant PRG700.

References

Aaben, L., Tammik, M., and Kallavus, K. (2017). *Mitmedimensioonilise pereteraapia tõhususe uuring.* Poliitikauuringute keskus Praxis.

Aidukaite, J. (2003). From universal system of social policy to particularistic? The case of the Baltic States. *Communist and Post-Communist Studies*, 36, 405–426.

Aidukaite, J. (2006). Reforming family policy in the Baltic States: The views of the elites. *Communist and Post-Communist Studies*, 39, 1–23.

Aus, H. (1984). *Lastekaitse. Kogumik normatiivmaterjale.* Valgus.

Bebre, B. and Gjortlere, L. (2016). *Guide to Latvian legal system and legal research.* Available at: https://web.archive.org/web/20190326181041/https:/www.nyulawglobal.org/globalex/Latvia1.html. Retrieved June 20, 2022.

Bernstein, L. (2001). Communist custodial contests: Adoption rulings in the USSR after the Second World War. *Journal of Social History*, 34(4), 843–861.

Bohle, D. and Greskovits, B. (2012). *Capitalist diversity in Europe's peripheria.* Cornell University Press.

CIA. *The World Factbook.* https://www.cia.gov/the-world-factbook/. Retrieved January 1, 2021.

Central Statistical Bureau of Latvia. (2020). *Children of Latvia. Collection of Statistics.* Riga.

Central Statistical Bureau of Latvia. (2018). *Children in Latvia: Collection of statistics.* Riga.

Central Statistical Bureau of Latvia. (2019). *Children in Latvia: Collection of statistics.* Riga.

Child Helpline International. (2017). Voices of Children and Young People in Europe. Looking Back: Ten years of 116 111. https://resourcecentre.savethechildren.net/pdf/chi_global_web_final1.pdf/. Retrieved June 20, 2022.

Child Protection Act. (1993). RT 1992, 28, 370.

Child Protection Act. (2016). RT I, 06.11.2014, 1. Available at: https://www.riigiteataja.ee/en/eli/506052015 001/consolide. Retrieved January 30, 2021.

Child Protection Department. (n.d.). Social Insurance Board. Available at: http://www.sotsiaalkindlustusa met.ee/en/family-and-child-protection/child-protection#Child%20Protection%20Department. Retrieved January 30, 2021.

Civitta (2022). *Asendushoolduselt iseseisvasse ellu astuvate noorte uuring. Lõpparuanne.* Tallinn: Civitta Eesti AS.

Committee on the Rights of the Child. (2013). *Consideration of reports submitted by States parties under article 44 of the Convention: Combined third to fifth periodic reports of States parties due in 2009. Latvia.* Available at: https://www.refworld.org/docid/56a1eb154.html.

Ebela, I., Rektiņa, A., Pūķis, M., Leiškalns, P., and Meţs, I. (2015). Alternative Report to the UN on the Situation of the Protection of Children's Rights and the Implementation of the UN CRC Recommendations in Latvia. Latvijas biedrība "Glābiet bērnus". http://www.glabietbernus.lv/projects/. Retrieved June 20, 2022.

Estonian SSR Code for Marriage and Family. (1969). Tallinn.

European Union Agency for Fundamental Rights (FRA). (2015). Mapping Child Protection Systems in Europe. (2015). FRANET. https://fra.europa.eu/en/publication/2016/mapping-child-protection-systems-eu#publication-tab-3 – aga see on 2016 materjal. Retrieved January 30, 2021.

EV Sotsiaalministeerium. (2014). *Vanemliku hoolitsuseta laste asendushoolduse poliitika roheline raamat.* Tallinn, Ministry of Social Affairs of Estonia.

Family Law Act. (2009). RT I 2009, 60, 395. Available at: https://www.riigiteataja.ee/en/eli/ee/Riigikogu/act/507022018005/consolide. Retrieved January 30, 2021.

Frindt, A. (2007a). Country Report: Estonia. In J. Beadle-Brown and A. Kozma (Eds.), *Deinstitutionalisation and community living—outcomes and costs: Report of a European study* (vol. 3, pp. 110–130). Tizard Centre, University of Kent.

Frindt, A. (2007b). Country Report: Latvia. In J. Beadle-Brown and A. Kozma (Eds.), *Deinstitutionalisation and community living—outcomes and costs: Report of a European study* (vol. 3, pp. 312–336). Tizard Centre, University of Kent.

Gilbert, N., Parton, N., and Skivenes, M. (Eds). (2011). *Child protection systems: International trends and orientations.* Oxford University Press.

Glabejsilites Latvija. (n.d.). *Baby Boxes in Latvia.* https://babybox.lv/glabejsilites-latvija/. Retrieved June 20, 2022.

Grāvere, L., Haružika, A., Rūsiņa, Z., Caune, T., and Anskaite, S. (2015, April). *Children's rights behind bars. Human rights of children deprived of liberty: Improving monitoring mechanisms (JUST/2013/JPEN/AG/4581). National report Latvia.* Available at: http://www.childrensrightsbehindbars.eu/images/national-reports-2014/LATVIA-FINAL-REPORT.pdf. Retrieved January 30, 2021.

Iarskaia-Smirnova, E. and Lyons, K. (2018). Social work in FSU countries: Mapping the progress of "the professional project." *European Journal of Social Work*, 21(1), 114–127.

Ismayilova, L., Ssewamala, F., and Huseynli, A. (2014). Reforming child institutional care in the post-Soviet bloc: the potential role of family-based empowerment strategies. *Child and Youth Service Review*, 47, 136–148.

Javornik, J. (2014). Measuring state de-familialism: Contesting post-socialist exceptionalism. *Journal of European Social Policy*, 24(3), 240–257.

Jõks, H. (2020). Kuidas on rakendatud muudatused asendus- ja järelhooldusteenuse valdkonnas? *Sotsiaaltöö [Social Work]*, 2, 25–29. Available at: https://tai.ee/images/ST2_2020_25kuni29.pdf. Retrieved January 30, 2021.

Kasvandik, L., Edovald, T., Treial, K., and Vajakas, K. (2014). *Vanemlusprogrammide Triple P ja Incredible Years süsteemide võrdlev analüüs.* Ministry of Social Affairs.

Khazova, O. A. (2010). Family law on post-Soviet European territory: A comparative overview of some recent trends. *Electronic Journal of Comparative Law*, 14(1). Available at: https://www.ejcl.org/141/art141-3.pdf. Retrieved April 8, 2018.

Kerikmäe, T., Hoffmann, T., and Särav, S. (2017). The historical development. In T. Kerikmäe, K. Joamets, J. Pleps, A. Rodina, T. Berkmanas, and E. Gruodyte (Eds.), *The law of the Baltic states* (pp. 4–11). Springer.

Kiik, R. and Sirotkina, R. (2005). The development of social work as a speciality and the profession in Estonia. *Social Work & Society*, 3, 128–133.

Kinis, U. (1996). Child Criminality in Latvia. In P. Cavadino (Ed.), *Children who kill. An examination of the treatment of juveniles who kill in different European countries* (pp. 176–177). Waterside Press in association with British Juvenile and Family Court Society.

Kronberga, I. (2017). Life without crime as a fundamental right of the child: On the prevention of juvenile delinquency. *Juridica International*, 25, 74–81. Available at: https://doi.org/10.12697/JI.2017.25.08. Retrieved April 8, 2018.

Kronberga, I. and Sile, S. (2015) *Keeping youth away from crime: Searching for best European practices. Summary.* Providus. Available at: http://providus.lv/article_files/2886/original/keeping_eng.pdf?1427889591. Retrieved March 5, 2018.

Kronberga, I. and Zermatten, J. (2012). *Child-friendly justice in Latvia: Focusing on crime prevention.* Providus.

Kucina, I. (2017). Latvia. In P. Beaumont, M. Danov, K. Trimmings, and B. Yürkel (Eds.), *Cross-border Litigation in Europe* (pp. 351–360). Blumsbury Publishing.

Kuuse, R. and Toros K. (2017). Estonian social policy: From Soviet heritage to understanding the principles of deinstitutionalisation. *European Journal of Social Work*, 22(3), 388–399. Available at: doi.org/10.1080/13691457.2017.1357024.

Lastekaitsetöötajate koolitused. (2018). *Tervise Arengu Instituut.* Available at: http://www.tai.ee/et/tegevused/koolituskeskus/koolitused/lastekaitsetootajate-koolitused. Retrieved January 30, 2021.

Lauristin, M. (2011). Introduction. Human development during the transition: the challenges faced by the Baltic States. In M. Lauristin (Ed.), *Estonian Human Development Report 2010/2011* (pp. 10–12). Eesti Koostöö Kogu.

Law on Orphan's and Custody Court. (2006). Legal Acts of Latvian Republic. Riga, Likumi. https://likumi.lv/ta/en/en/id/139369. Retrieved June 20, 2022.

Legzdina, K. and Rajevska, F. (2017, April 27–28). Step towards alternative child care: Analysis of child care deinstitutionalization components (based on the research in Vidzeme region, Latvia). 2017 International Conference "Economic science for rural development." Jelgava, LLU ESAF, pp. 92–100. Available at: http://llufb.llu.lv/conference/economic_science_rural/2017/Latvia_ESRD_46_2017-92-100.pdf. Retrieved July 23, 2018.

Lenger, A. (2008, April 10–11). *Big-bang versus gradualism? Towards a framework for understanding institutional change in central and eastern Europe.* Ökonomik, Politische Ökonomie und Psychologie staatlicher Reformen in Europa Manheim.

Luhamaa, K. and Strömpl, J. (2021). Overcoming the soviet legacy? Adoption from care in Estonia. In T. Pösö, M. Skivenes, and J. Thoburn (Eds.), *Adoption from Care: International Perspectives on Children's Rights, Family Preservation and State Intervention* (pp.33–48). Bristol University Press, Policy Press.

Linno, M. and Strömpl, J. (2015). Immigrant children and families in the Estonian child protection system. In M. Skivenes, R. Barn, K. Križ, and T. Pösö (Eds.), *Child welfare systems and migrant children: A cross country study of policies and practices* (pp. 241–260). Oxford University Press.

Markina, A., Strömpl, J., Tamm, G., Ilves, K., Luhamaa, K., Ginter, J., Tubelt, E., Puur, S. M., Roos, L., and Espenberg, S. (2021). *Noorte õigusrikkujate uuring.* TÜ Sotsiaalteaduslike Rakendusuuringute Keskus ja Justiitsministeerium.

Misiunas, R. J. and Taagepera, R. (1993). *The Baltic states: Years of dependence, 1940–1990.* University of California Press.

Nikonov, E. (2016). Õigusrikkumise toime pannud lapse abistamine. *Sotsiaaltöö*, (4), 71–76.

OECD. (n.d). Social spending. Available at: https://www.oecd.org/els/soc/PF1_1_Public_spending_on_family_benefits.pdf. Retrieved January 4, 2021.

Opening Doors for Europe's Children. (2017). Latvia. Country Fact Sheet. https://www.openingdoors.eu/wp-content/uploads/2018/02/country-fiche-Latvia-2017.pdf. Retrieved June 20, 2022.

Osila, L., Turk, P., Piirits, M., Biin, H., Anniste, K., and Masso, M. (2016). *Asendushooldusel elluastuvate noorte uuring.* Praxis.

Paulovica, I. (1995). The situation of the disabled in Latvia. In J. Simpura (Ed.), *Social policy in transition societies: Experience from the Baltic countries and Russia* (pp. 76–88). Finnish ICSW Committee and Finnish Federation for Social Welfare.

Rajevska. F., Silina, G., and Stavausis, D. (2016, April 21–22). *Deinstitutionalization: Challenges for policymakers in Latvia*. 2016 International Conference, Economic Science for Rural Development. Jelgava, LLU ESAF. Available at: http://llufb.llu.lv/conference/economic_science_rural/2016/Latvia_ESRD_43_2016-99-107.pdf. Retrieved March 25, 2018.

Rannala, I.-E. (2014). *Dialoogi olulisusest töös riskikäitumisega noortega. Alaealiste komisjonide näitel*. Tallinn University.

United Nations Human Rights Office of the High Commisioner. (n.d.). *The rights of vulnerable children under the age of three*. Available at: https://europe.ohchr.org/_layouts/15/WopiFrame.aspx?sourcedoc=/Docume nts/Publications/Children_under_3.pdf&action=default&DefaultItemOpen=1. Retrieved January 30, 2021.

Saar, J. (2003). *Delinquent conduct in the minority age and the subsequent criminal careers (as based on longitudinal research 1985–1999, Estonia*. University of Tartu Press.

Saar, J., Markina, A., Ahven, A., Annist, A., and Ginter, J. (2002). *Crime in Estonia 1991–2001*. Institute of International Social Studies of Tallinn Polytechnic University and ER Ministry of Justice.

Schmidt, V. and Shchurko, T. (2014). Children's rights in post-Soviet countries: The case of Russia and Belarus. *International Social Work*, 57(5), 447–458.

Simpura, J. (Ed.). (1995). *Social policy in transition societies: Experience from the Baltic countries and Russia*. Finnish ICSW Committee and Finnish Federation for Social Welfare.

Sindi, I. (2015). Changing discourse and changing institutional child substitute care: new terms and processes toward family-like and family-based care. *Child Care in Practice*, 22(1), 50–63. Available at: http://dx.doi.org/10.1080/13575279.2015.1054785.

Sindi, I., Strömpl, J., and Toros., K. (2018). The Estonian way of deinstitutionalisation. Staff members' perspective on residential substitute care: Experiences from an ethnography research in an Estonian SOS Children's Village. *Child and Youth Services*, 39(4), 305–332.

SOS Children Village Estonia. (n.d.). Homepage. https://www.sos-lastekyla.ee/en. Retrieved January 30, 2021.

SOS Children's Village Latvia homepage. (n.d.). Homepage. https://www.sosbernuciemati.lv/lv. Available at: January 30, 2021.

State Inspectorate for the Protection of Children's Rights. (2020). Child Hotline. http://www.bti.gov.lv/eng/vbta_inspekcija/uzticibas_talrunis/. Retrieved January 30, 2021.

State Inspectorate for the Protection of Children's Rights. (n.d.). Homepage. https://www.bti.gov.lv/en. Retrieved January 30, 2021.

Statistics Estonia. (n.d.). Homepage. https://www.stat.ee/en. Retrieved January 30, 2021.

Strömpl, J. (2002). *The K. School. Residential Management of Troubled Girls in Transition-time Estonia*. Acta Electronica Universitatis Tamperensis 215. https://dspace.ut.ee/handle/10062/54912. Retrieved June 20, 2022.

Strömpl, J. and Markina A. (2014, August). *Children's rights behind bars. Human rights of children deprived of liberty: improving monitoring mechanisms. Estonian national report*. Available at: www.childrensrightsbeh indbars.eu. Retrieved September 14, 2018.

Strömpl, J. and Markina, A. (2017). Children's rights and the juvenile system in Estonia. *Juridica International*, 25, 66–73.

Suni, M. (1995). Social welfare and law in Estonia. In J. Simpura (Ed.), *Social policy in transition societies: Experience from the Baltic countries and Russia* (pp. 31–43). Finnish ICSW Committee and Finnish Federation for Social Welfare.

Svejnar, J. (2002). Transition economies: Performance and challenges. *Journal of Economic Perspectives*, 16(1), 3–28.

Tamm, K. ja Salla, K. A. (2016a). Laste toime pandud süütegudele reageerimise analüüs. *Kriminaalpoliitika analüüs, 5/2016*. https://www.kriminaalpoliitika.ee/sites/krimipoliitika/files/elfinder/dokumendid/tamm._k_salla_k-a_2016._laste_toime_pandud_suutegudele_reageerimise_analuus.pdf. Retrieved July 23, 2021.

Tamm, K. and Salla, K. A. (2016b). Tulemuslikum ja lapsesõbralikum õigussüsteem: laste mõjutamise põhimõtted ja võimalused. *Sotsiaaltöö* (4), 76–82.

Tobis, D. (2000). *Moving from residential institutions to community-based social services in central and eastern Europe and the former Soviet Union*. World Bank.

Toros, K. (2011). *Assessment of child well-being: Child protection practice in Estonia*. Tallinn University.

Toros, K., DiNitto, D., and Tiko, A. (2018). Family engagement in the child welfare system: A scoping review. *Children and Youth Services Review*, 88, 598–607.

Toros, K. and LaSala, M. (2018). Estonian child protection workers' assessment perspectives: The need for competence and confidence. *International Social Work*, 61(1), 93–105.

Trummal, A. (2018). *Vanemlusprogrammi "Imelised aastad" tulemused 2017. aasta teise poole kokkuvõte*. Tervise Arengu Institut.

Turk, P. (2011). *Asenduskodudes kasvanud noorte valmisolek iseseisvaks eluks*. Praxis.

Zepa, B., Kļave, E., and Šupule, I. (2015). Russian-Latvian language conflict in urban settings in Latvia. *Humanities and Social Scencies Latvia*, 23(1), 42–64.

Child Protection in Lithuania

Ilona Tamutienė *and* Dalija Snieškienė

Abstract

This chapter expounds on the child protection system in Lithuania. The development of a system of child protection coincides with the necessity to create a political and administrative apparatus for state administration. Additionally, large-scale residential childcare is a prominent form of guardianship of children deprived of parental care. Thus, the separation of siblings, isolation of disabled children, and delinquent children are widespread across the country. Changes in the institution of social work and child psychologists were influenced by the desire to create an independent child protection system in Lithuania and Lithuania's ambition to join the EU. Child protection reform was enacted slowly following the ratification of the UNCRC.

Key Words: Lithuania, child protection, state administration, social work, separation, residential childcare, EU, UNCRC, children

Welfare and Child Protection in a Development Context

Lithuania broke away from the Soviet Union in 1990. After the restoration of the country's independence, it was necessary to create a political and administrative apparatus for state administration, with modest resources. This included the development of a system of child protection. It was necessary not only to create a new protection system for children in an independent state, but also to deal with the Soviet legacy, in which human rights and children's rights were not addressed. Large-scale residential childcare was prominent as a form of guardianship of children deprived of parental care in Lithuania. Separation of brothers and sisters and, in particular, the isolation of disabled children and delinquent children in large, rather closed institutional structures was widespread. The country did not have an institution of social work, child psychologists, and so on. Changes in this area were influenced both by the desire to create an independent child protection system in Lithuania and Lithuania's aspiration to join the EU.

The population of contemporary Lithuania consists mainly of Lithuanians, the majority of whom are Roman Catholics (78%) and the national language is Lithuanian (Department of Statistics of Lithuania, 2017). According to data from the Department of Statistics, the population has declined since 1990 (3.587 million) due to emigration, declining indigenous populations, and an aging population. At the end of the year 2017, there were 2.8 million inhabitants in Lithuania, of whom 503,000 were children. The Gross Domestic Product (GDP) in Lithuania was recorded at 13,483 euros per capita in 2016 (Department of Statistics of Lithuania, 2017). Since 1990, Lithuania has faced insufficient financing of social protection, which, despite GDP growth, has gradually declined from 14.2% in 1995, to 13.4% in 2004, to 11.2% of GDP allocated to social protection in 2016 (Eurostat, 2017). Using a western typology, the Lithuanian welfare state can be ascribed to the hybrid "corporatist—Bismarckian—clientelistic" model slowly drifting towards a liberal-marginal one (Aidukaitė et al., 2016). The current extreme market orientation is not modified by social support institutions and is combined with conservative ideologies about women and the family (Kabašinskaitė & Bak, 2006). Therefore, a high percentage of the population lives in poverty: in 2016, 21.9% of the population were at risk of poverty; the rate for children was 25.6%. In 2016, 27.1% of all children were raised with one parent (23% only with the mother), and in these families the poverty level after benefits was 41.7% (Stankūnienė et al., 2016).

Family/child benefits are also very small. Until 2004, Lithuania was spending less than 70 euros per inhabitant on family/children benefits, while the figure for the EU-15 was about 560 euros per inhabitant. Starting with 2004, expenditures on the family/children started increasing and reached its peak in 2009 at 183 euros per inhabitant. The increase in expenditure can be explained by the gradual introduction of universal benefits in Lithuania during the period 2004–2008 and with the introduction of a generous parental leave policy (period 2006–2009) (Aidukaite et al., 2016). According to the latest Eurostat data for 2014, Lithuania spends 135 euros per inhabitant for family/children benefits. On average in the EU, expenditures on family/child benefits in that same year amounted to 651 euros per inhabitant (Eurostat, 2016).

During the period of 2004–2008, universal family benefits were gradually introduced, which in 2008 were payable to every child up to his/her 16th birthday. These benefits were abolished as soon as the financial crisis of 2008 hit the country (Aidukaite et al., 2016). The universal benefit of 30 euros per child (until the child reaches 18 years old) was introduced in January of 2018 (Law of Child Benefits of Lithuania, 2018). At present, children from poor families are eligible to receive family benefits on a means-tested basis. For those who do not qualify for maternity and parental benefits, the state also gives support on a means-tested basis. In Lithuania, means-tested benefits are quite wide-ranging, such as a social benefit, compensation for heating, cold and hot water, free school meals, a lump sum benefit, and a benefit for families with children. To qualify for means-tested benefits the claimant has to pass not only an income test, but also property and assets tests. There are also some categorical benefits in Lithuania, such as special benefits for children of parents who are on military duty, benefits for orphans, and parents on guardian duties (Aidukaite et al., 2016, p. 436).

Child protection reform in Lithuania was launched very slowly after the ratification of the United Nations Convention on the Rights of the Child (CRC, 1995). This process was in line with the emergence of the first social work professionals in 1995 and the creation of new NGOs such as the organization developed by parents of children with mental disabilities.[1] Hope, Save the Children, Lithuania's Caritas, and others developed innovative, better-performing alternative services for the rights of the child and actively initiated new changes to the law and changes in public opinion. The recommendations of the United Nations Committee on the Rights of the Child were also a serious stimulus to start reforms. However, in the field of legal and service development, the changes took place very slowly and did not meet the needs of socially vulnerable families.[2]

According to the State Children's Rights Protection and Adoption Service, in 2016, 0.5% of all children in Lithuania suffered from violence (physical, sexual, and psychological). In 2017, a significant increase of up to 0.98% in such cases was observed. Despite the fact that the rate of "child murders" (which include a combination of deaths resulting from interpersonal violence, i.e., maltreatment, neglect, abuse, and peer-to-peer violence) has decreased from 2.8 per 100,000 in 2004 to 1.7 per 100,000 in 2014, Lithuania remains among the countries where this rate is highest (Lazutka et al., 2017). In 2017, the number of children growing up in socially vulnerable families (identified through the List of Child Protection) made up 3.6% of all Lithuanian children. The number of children in the care system in 2017 comprised 1.74% of all Lithuanian children, an increase since 2014 (State Children's Rights Protection and Adoption Service, 2014, 2017).

In the child protection system, there is still a significant gap between the stated goals and the practical effectiveness of child protection (Muižnieks, 2017). The child protection system is not centered on the child, the difficulties faced by children are not disclosed, children very rarely participate in their protection processes, social support measures for the family prior to the separation of the child from the family are actually focused on adults, and the problems of children are frequently ignored (Tamutienė, 2018; Tamutienė & Jogaitė, 2018). These challenges have signaled the need for reform.

Political processes and child protection practices that took place after the restoration of independence are partially summarized in three stages: 1) state and public initiatives in reforming the system (1990–2004), 2) absorption of Structural Funds to support institutionalization (2005–2014), 3) and the reform of child protection caused by public

---

[1] We use the term "children with mental disabilities" as suggested by many authors and public authorities at both national and European levels despite the pejorative and stigmatizing meaning of it. (See European Union Agency for Fundamental Rights, 2014).

[2] We will use the English term socially vulnerable families instead of the direct translation of "risk families," which is widely used in child policy documents by the legislature. Risk families implies not only the risks for the child but also has a pejorative meaning and stigmatizing effect, whereas vulnerability implies that not the family itself causes risk for the child, but the conditions to which this family (e.g., poverty, single parenthood) is exposed make children vulnerable.

pressure (in 2015–to present). The chapter also describes the effectiveness of child protection and changes in the child protection system which started in July of 2018.

Development in Law and Policy

Period of State and Public Initiatives (1990–2004)

During this period, the foundations of the child protection system were formulated, the goals were set, and the legal and institutional environment for their implementation was created. The modern child protection model of the Soviet system was very different from the one that the UNCRC developed in independent Lithuania, which reflected the model that has been developed in more advanced countries. The Soviet child protection system itself was a source of institutional violence against the child. Given the Soviet legacy of child protection, policymakers had a double challenge to transform the old and harmful system into a modern system, more in line with the interests of the child. In 1992, the Department of Juvenile Rights Protection and Guardianship[3] was established by the Government of Lithuania. The human and financial resources of this institution were quite modest with one Head Office, two referees, and one consultant (0.5-time involvement). In addition, the government required cities and district municipalities to organize local child protection and guardianship services (which later turned into Children's Rights Protection Agencies [CRPA]) and assign them to guarantee child protection, including childcare organizations and the care of children who are prone to delinquency. The functions of these services have been continuously expanded.

After the re-establishment of independence, numerous non-governmental organizations began to change the public sphere. Various civic organizations, whose activities were linked to the protection of children, including the disabled, were particularly active. NGOs representing the interests of the child were the key actors in the development of child protection policies and influenced the policymaking process. With the support of national and international NGOs a number of civic activities took place with representation of children's rights as human rights at the core. In 1992, Lithuania joined the UNCRC and the act was ratified by Parliament in 1995. Such political action laid the foundation for further development of the protection of the rights of the child in the country. Lithuanian nongovernmental organizations working in the field were the initiators of new and effective forms of organization of services and methods, their representatives were invited as consultants to develop standards for social services, and to seek ways to improve the quality and efficiency of services (Žalimienė & Rimšaitė, 2007, p. 92). Social work professionals also

---

[3] We will use English term "guardianship" in this text as it is generally used in current EU policy documents. By this term we mean foster care both in institutions and guardian families. (See European Union Agency for Fundamental Rights, 2018; European Union Agency for Fundamental Rights, 2014.) We will use term "custody" instead of care or guardianship when there is implication of a criminal juvenile justice system.

set up the first postgraduate program in social work at the re-established Vytautas Magnus University in 1995 and later in other institutions (Snieškiene, 2012).

Two important legal acts were adopted in 1996. First, the Concept of Family Policy (1996) and the Law on the Fundamentals of the Protection of the Rights of the Child (1996). The latter act has strengthened the goals of protecting the child, defining the rights, freedoms, and duties of the child, and the responsibilities of the protection institutions. Finally, the Child Guardianship Act (1998) regulated the guardianship of children in families and private residential group homes run by families. These documents incorporated the objectives of child protection into a common family policy. The objectives are complex, but their common denominator is to ensure the rights of the child to grow and develop in a safe family. It was acknowledged that this goal can only be realized in a strong biological family, and in the case of absence of parental care, in the family of guardians or adoptive parents. According to such acts, legal regulations regarding the search for guardianship families was legally established, including training of guardians and the provision of services. Two categories of child guardianship were established: temporary and permanent. These developments were essential in order to move away from Soviet residential care to guardianship in the family. This was the beginning of a change in state policy and the essence of the reform of the child protection system in the country.

Six years after the ratification of the UNCRC, the Office of the Ombudsman for the Protection of the Rights of the Child was established (Law of the Office of the Ombudsman for the Protection of the Rights of the Child, 2000) In order to ensure the functioning of the system of protection of the rights of the child, the development of a network of Children's Rights Protection Services of the municipalities was initiated. In addition, in 2003, documents devoted to work with socially vulnerable families with a high risk of children suffering various forms of violence, abuse and abandonment (Order of the Minister of Social security and Labour Ministry, 2003) were implemented. Since 2006 the state has allocated special centralized funding to municipalities for the training of staff for work with socially vulnerable families.

The Lithuanian Parliament also adopted the Concept of Child Welfare State Policy in 2003 which once again emphasized and strengthened the provisions of the UNCRC, distinguishing between protection, provision, and participation, which meant that it directed the policy towards the child, and entrusted the Government with the establishment of a strategy and action plans for the implementation of state child welfare policy.

Since 1999, juvenile justice reforms were launched in order to improve the legal regulation of juvenile justice. The procedures for the execution of sentences and punishments imposed on juveniles were established with an emphasis on the re-socialization of minors, relegating punishment of juveniles to an extreme measure. One alternative form of punishment other than imprisonment is placement in a special education institution from six months to three years (prior to age 18) (Vitkauskas, 2010, p. 119). It should be noted that four special-detention homes for children's custody and education which were founded in the Soviet era functioned until 2008 and later were reformed into six resocialization centers for children. The Concept of Minor and Medium Custody of Minors was approved by the Government in 2003 and established in law in 2010, thereby establishing guidelines for the development of a system of alternative punishment (Vitkauskas, 2010, p. 120).

The current system of protection of the rights of the child was formed at the state level and was very much influenced by public initiatives and civil society. It was formed in different policy-making stages and integrated the state and the municipal levels as well as case law, which is performed by independent courts.

The state level, at which the Parliament and the Ombudsman for the Protection of the Rights of the Child are based, is directly linked to the formation of a child protection policy. The government manages and creates administrative rules for child protection including its standards, licensing activities, financial allocations, and other activities that directly deal with the practical implications of the legislation. The Ministry of Social Security and Labor and the State Children's Rights Protection and Adoption Service under this Ministry play the main coordinating role in the implementation of child protection policy.

The role of independent courts in the implementation of child protection is also very important because violence against children may entail administrative or criminal liability. The courts make decisions about permanent custody and adoption of a child, and the temporal or permanent limitation of the power of parents. It should be noted that there are no specialized family courts in Lithuania.

The majority of child protection practice takes place at the municipal level, according to the Law on Social Services of the Republic of Lithuania (1996 and 2006). The actions of staff at this level are directed by guidelines, standards and targeted resources set by the higher levels of government. Each municipality has a department for the protection of the rights of the child. Implementation of the protection of the rights of the child at the local level is financed from state and municipal budgets. Municipalities may have their own child protection policies and approaches, including the number of professionals working in the child rights protection unit, how child guardianship is organized, whether to refer children to institutions, the provision of additional incentives to guardians, and how services will be provided to children. The work of municipalities in these areas is very uneven, with a particularly striking gap between the big cities, where the spectrum of services is much higher in comparison to the rest of Lithuania.

During this period (1990–2004), the effectiveness of child protection in cases of child abuse was poor and, in some cases, harmful due to lack of services, neglect of the needs of the child, failure to enter into the protection process, multiple interviews, lack of child lawyers, lack of resources, and lack of expertise of child protection staff (Tamutienė, 2004).

European Structural Funds and Their Impact on Child Policy in 2005–2014

Before Lithuania's accession to the EU, child protection reform was based on resources from the EU PHARE program, individual state and private organizations' funds, and state funds (Snieškienė, 2009). After Lithuania's accession to the EU, financial resources from the EU Structural Funds were opened and many structural changes occurred. The substitute childcare system was underdeveloped, there was a lack of social services to the families with children, and there was an increase in the number of children guarded by institutions. After 2004, the number of children in institutional care began to grow (up to 44.8% of all children in care in 2005). The increase can be directly linked with the focusing of structural supports on the renovation of children's care homes rather than being used for the development of an alternative childcare system (Tamutiene, 2017). In fact, according to the State Audit report, from 2004 to 2012, including EU Structural Funds and other financial mechanisms, 27 projects were financed comprising a total of 51.8 million LTL (approximately 15 million euros). These funds were directed at the renovation of children's care homes and the construction of new homes for care. Clearly, the goals of the reorganization of the childcare system were not achieved. The focus of the child's guardianship in the family was limited only to an increase of the childcare allowance of 7 euros.

In 2008, NGOs started to search, prepare, select, counsel, and assist guardians and adoptive parents (State Audit, 2014), but the development of services for these families was minimal in comparison to investments in care homes. Despite the declared principles, 38.4% of children without parental care are raised in large institutions (2017), where the maintenance of children is almost five times more expensive than childcare (State Audit, 2014). In Lithuania, the number of children in the youngest age group (0–3 years old) living in institutions is relatively stable (56% out of a total 800), despite the fact that long-term negative consequences of this kind of childcare have been proven by research (Delap, 2011). Nevertheless, professional guardianship was not institutionalized in Lithuania until 2016.

Although the de-institutionalization of child guardianship and the provision of services for families and children during the support period of the Structural Funds did not work, significant legislative changes that directly influenced the protection of the child occurred during this period. Social work with vulnerable families was developed, and funding for the training of social workers was provided. The plan also provided for the launch of trained specialists for the search and counseling of guardians and adoptive parents using the US PRIDE program (Government of the Republic of Lithuania 2007–2012 plan). The EC Convention on the Protection of Children against Sexual Exploitation and Sexual Abuse (Law on the ratification of EC Convention on the Protection of Children against Sexual Exploitation and Sexual Abuse, 2012), the Law on Social Services (2006), the Law on the Protection against Violence in the Immediate Environment (2011) and the Law on Minimum Supervision of the Child (2010), were extremely positive and promising breakthroughs in positive child policy. The Law on Social Services regulates the responsibility for the organization of social services to municipal governments, provides for licensing at the national level, defines the guidelines for the need for social services, planning and supervision and control. With regard to family violence, the law is significant particularly with regard to the perpetrator. The police now have an obligation to inform the child rights department in case of family violence in the presence of a minor.

The Law on Minor and Medium Supervision of the Republic of Lithuania (2010) establishes a system of support for the rights of the child, his interests, and the needs of society. It also aims to help the child deal with inappropriate behavior and developing standards for a fair life. In 2012 the Ministry of Social Security and Labor adopted the Children's Welfare Program aimed at the creation of a system of services to ensure the child's well-being and suitable conditions for his or her family growth (Order of the Minister of Social security and Labour Minister, 2012). Under the Program, a lot of attention is paid to the attraction of guardians, and the training, selection, and development of the support system. Also in 2012 The Ministry Order approved strategic guidelines for the deinstitutionalization of social care homes for disabled children (children without parental care) and for adults with disabilities. This became the basis for improvements in children's residential care (Gvaldaitė & Šimkonytė, 2016).

Child Protection Reform (2015—to Present) Caused by Public Pressure

In 2015, the public was outraged following the tragedy of a four-year-old boy, Matukas, who was beaten to death by his mother and her partner. The investigation revealed that the child had been neglected and exposed to harmful behavior by his parents for a long time, and that childcare teachers had informed the formal authorities and reported physical abuse of the child. In the wake of this great outrage and political pressure, the child's rights protection reform was initiated in 2017.

The National Social Security Campaign "For a Safe Lithuania," initiated by the President, initiated a process of de-institutionalization of child guardianship (Presidential Palace of the Republic of Lithuania, 2016). Since 2014, residential care rates have been declining marginally. During this period, an action plan was established to transition from residential care to guardianship in the family and communities for children who are disabled or who are deprived of parental care. The Action plan for the period of 2014–2020 was approved by the Minister of Social Security and Labor. A new provision of the Law on Benefits for Children entered into force in 2017, according to which the child's guardian (caretaker) receives one basic social benefit (38 euros) per child for whom the guardianship (caretaker) is established, and from January 2017 onwards the target supplement of guardianship (care) benefit payments (152 euros) will be available (Lithuania Benefit Law, 2018). It seems that the targeted supplement introduced in 2016 was not sufficient to change the rate of residential care (children guarded by institutions decreased by only 0.7 per cent in 2017 compared to 2015). Children's rights protection specialists are faced with pressure to reduce residential care of children; on the other hand, they are limited by lack of guardians (Snieškienė & Tamutienė, 2014). These indicators may also reflect the inadequacies of social work with socially vulnerable families due to late intervention, the choice of working methods, the lack of inter-institutional cooperation in services, and the lack of services which are directed towards families and children in municipalities.

Child Protection Reform

In Lithuania, after the change of political forces (in 2016 a new Lithuanian political party, Peasants and Greens, was elected to the Seimas, replacing the changing conservatives and social democrats of several decades prior), many social policy areas were reformed. Resonant events such as the Matukas tragedy (Stažytė, 2017) caused public dissatisfaction with the existing policy. It was exacerbated by the inability of those working in this area to identify the problem with vulnerable families in advance, the lack of preventive assistance, the unequal treatment of family support and removing children away from families, and lack of human and material resources. There was an urgent need to focus on support to families where violence against children prevails and also on greater cooperation between the relevant authorities in addressing specific child protection policy issues (Order of the Minister of Social Security and Labour on the case management approval, 2018). The discussions of definitions of violence against children and their prohibition in the Law on the Protection of the Rights of the Child of the Republic of Lithuania took far too long for politicians, who instead debated about children's discipline. Many politicians indicated that they were disciplined using physical punishment in their childhood, which, according to them, led to better adoption of values and good career prospects. Only after the Matukas tragedy were the media and general public affected, and physical punishment and all forms of violence were defined and prohibited in February 2017. The law defines physical punishment as follows: "Any punishment when physical force is used to cause physical pain, even small, to cause or physically torture a child." The same law defined abuse against children in general:

> the act or omission of an act which causes child a direct or indirect deliberate physical, psychological, sexual influence, disregard or neglect of honor and dignity, which causes the child to be harmed or endangers life, health, development

The following forms of violence against children have been identified and defined in Lithuania:

1) *Physical violence*: direct or indirect deliberate physical activity against the child, as well as physical punishment which causes pain to a child, causing harm or endangering his or her life, health, or development, or damage to honor and dignity.

2) *Psychological violence*: permanent violation of the rights of the child to individuality, the humiliation of a child, bullying, intimidation which causes disturbance for the child's development, promotion of antisocial behavior or other behavior of non-physical contact, causing harm or endangering the child's life, health, or development, or damage to honor and dignity.

3) *Sexual violence*: sexual acts with a child, who, according to the provisions of the legal acts of the Republic of Lithuania, has not reached the age from which sexual activity with him or her does not give rise to criminal liability, or sexual acts with the child in cases of coercion, force or threats, or abuse of trust, power or influence on the child, including in the family, or abuse of a particularly vulnerable position of the child, in particular because of his or her mental or physical disability or dependence; as well as exploitation of children for prostitution purposes, child pornography, recruitment, translation, or participation in a pornographic event; pornography or other forms of child sexual abuse; child molestation.

4) *Neglect*: permanent neglect of the physical, emotional, and social needs necessary for the child, causing harm or endangering the child's life, health, or development.

The prohibition against physical punishment and the definition of forms of violence, including the neglect of a child, is indeed a big step forward.

In order to ensure that these guiding principles could be effectively implemented in practice, the reform of the system of protection of the rights of the child has begun. In 2017 the Seimas of the Republic of Lithuania adopted the new edition of the Law on the Fundamentals of the Protection of the Rights of the Child (2017), the purpose of which is to establish a coordinated system of child protection institutions that increases the child's security and ensures the proper representation of his interests and rights. In 2018 the State Child Protection and Adoption Service became the central institution for the protection of children. It is responsible for ensuring a uniform, harmonized, and compatible child protection system, including implementation of uniform practices, standards, rules and principles, and the appointment of specialists working in this field. It is also expected that such safeguarding measures will provide prompt assistance for each child and decision making in a particular situation will not be slowed down, helping to avoid tragedies in the field of child protection policy.

In parallel to the process of centralization of child protection policy, innovations of a system of protection of the rights of the child will be implemented (State, 2018). Some of the essential changes are legal (analysis of reports of violations, representation of a child in court proceedings, coordination of guardianship, support of interinstitutional cooperation) and social (provision of preventive programs, provision of services, implementation of guardianship, including finding of carers, their assignment, placement of guardianship, etc.). Legal and social child protection were separated but based on close inter-institutional cooperation Legal protection of the child is ensured by the State Child Rights Protection Service through the central and territorial offices. Meanwhile, more actors are involved in the social protection of the child, that is, municipality administration with its subordinate structural units, other municipalities and state institutions, and non-governmental organizations.

New childcare policy measures were also implemented in 2018, enabling the child at risk to get help as soon as possible. Children under the age of 6 cannot be left alone in the care of people under the age of 14 years; institutions must respond to reports of violence against children on the same day and at the latest within six hours, and to other non-violent referrals as soon as possible, but not later than three days. The law stipulates what action is to be taken. Upon receipt of a report of allegedly violated rights of the child, the child is first transferred to his or her place of residence, the child and the members of his family are interviewed, the existing environment is assessed, and the appropriate level of threat is determined on the basis of available information. The reform provides for two levels of threat to the child. At Level 1, CRPA specialists identify the child's risk factors; that is, their rights are not guaranteed, but they do not endanger the child's health or life. Level 2 defines a situation where identifiable threats to the child's safety, health, or life relate to the various risk factors on which further specialist actions depend. When specialists estimate that the situation can be assigned to the second level of threat, the territorial unit decides to remove a child from the family, but its reasonableness must be assessed and approved by the court, by accepting or rejecting the execution of the permission (no court authorization has been requested so far). If the court complies with the request of the unit's specialists, the director of the municipality's administration issues temporary custody, mobile teams are set up for help, an aid plan is drawn up, and, depending on the parent's actions, the child is returned to the family, or decisions are taken regarding restrictions of parental authority, permanent guardianship, or adoption organization.

As previously mentioned, the new version of the Law on the Fundamentals of the Protection of the Rights of the Child also introduces the definition of functions of mobile teams and case managers, which are of particular importance for improving the system of child protection policy. The above mobile teams are made up of professionals who respond promptly to the threats posed to the child or family and urgently provide various kinds of collective or individual assistance (legal, psychological, medical, etc.). Within one working day of receiving the notification, the team, in cooperation with the case manager, begins intensive work with the family. The team provides appropriate assistance and conclusions on the current situation of the family within the timeframe. The law also provides for a number of mobile teams: the establishment of 11 teams, which will carry out their functions in 10 Lithuanian counties and Vilnius. The law also regulates a case management process where a designated person, based on the identified threat level, forms and implements an aid plan (service provision) by monitoring the family and each time reviewing the need for services provided to them. NGOs can also engage in its implementation, for example, by providing specific family-related services (Order of the Minister of Social Security and Labour, 2018).

One of the main areas of the reform's change involves distinguishing the functions of child protection institutions and specialists working there, separating social and legal protection of the rights of the child, introducing case management and mobile teams, and determining the levels of threat. These changes will aim to respond promptly to the threats posed to the child or the family, urgently, in accordance with the needs of the clients, to provide various kinds of collective or individual assistance and intensive work with the family. The reform was hastily begun, poorly prepared, and did not have fully trained specialists engaged. Specialists in this area feel great uncertainty, anxiety, and ignorance, saying that the standards of child protection are unrealistic and impossible to implement in practice because of the lack of specialists and services for children and families (Tamutienė & Auglytė, 2018).

Assessment of the Effectiveness of Child Protection

Munro (2011) recommends measuring the effectiveness of the implementation of child protection by measuring the answer to the question of whether the services were effective for children. Tamutienė and Jogaitė (2018) conducted a qualitative study to assess the effectiveness of social assistance for children at risk of alcohol abuse among children at risk. Parents' alcohol abuse and the work of a social worker with the family were the criteria for the selection of children. The results of the study revealed a painful reality: children who were living in the alcohol misusing families had experienced neglect and physical abuse, there was violence in the immediate environment, suicide by parents, witnesses of murder, and some of the children had thoughts of suicide and had tried to kill themselves. In many cases, safeguarding measures were not applied. By providing social services to families, children's individual needs become "invisible." Social workers, school professionals, police officers, or other professionals ignore children's needs. Only children who attend child daycare centers (CDCC) seem to experience limited attempts to help them from the social work specialists.

Many children who attended CDCCs evaluated their experiences quite well (Tamutienė & Jogaitė, 2018). Similar trends in the assessment of CDCCs were obtained in 2015 (Eurointegration, 2015). The current study revealed that access to CDCCs is problematic because only 35% of children in vulnerable families have the opportunity to attend CDCCs. Furthermore, it shows that there is a high customer satisfaction with CDCC services, and the continuous adequacy of financing from the government for several decades. It is obvious that access to CDCC services needs to be expanded, as well as solving the problems of CDCC financing, particularly for CDCCs run by NGOs (Tamutienė & Jogaitė, 2018).

Other research confirms similar facts that children growing up in vulnerable families, when safeguarding measures do not arrive in time, experience long-term harm which destroys their childhood. Gvaldaitė and Šimkonytė (2016) conducted qualitative interviews with the experts of childcare institutions. Their qualitative research suggests that some children experience delays from abusive homes in order to show reductions in the use of residential care.

A management audit was carried out in 2012 aimed at assessing the protection of the rights of the child. The evidence suggested that legal representation of the child is not well organized. Finally, the data indicated that the organization of social work services was not sufficiently effective. The audit report states that:

> threats to the child's life, health and safety were assessed inappropriately, because the criteria for assessing this threat and the procedure for taking the child are not set. As a result, there are cases when the children are left in the families and died or were removed from their families several times for a short period and returned to their abusive homes back again . . . In some municipalities, the plan for individual work with families is inadequate and inaccurate, or tasks of it were not related to the family problem solving. There were cases when social workers do not reconcile their plan with the CRPUs, because of the workload of employees. Some work with families is organized formally. Some of the tasks in the plan are not fulfilled because families lack motivation to change . . . Work with children at social risk families is not sufficiently effective because the legislation does not oblige municipalities to collect data on such children living in their territory, therefore, only half of the municipalities execute this function. (State Audit Report, 2012, pp. 26–34)

In sum, it can be argued that, even with a significant increase in funding, without changing the skills of professionals, the situation for vulnerable children in Lithuania would not improve.

Many children fall into the guardianship system. The State Audit Office conducted an audit "Does the childcare system fit in with the best interests of the child under guardianship?" in 2014 and concluded that the existing childcare system is ineffective and does not ensure the best interests of the child. Due to social work measures that were not appropriate or that were not taken in time, the majority of the results of the reform of the child guardianship system were not achieved by 2013 as planned and the deadline for implementation of the reform has been postponed for almost eighteen years (until 2030). The planned reduction in the proportion of children under guardianship did not decrease by 1% but increased by 2%. The audit report states that the financing of guardianship has not encouraged child's guardianship in families (rather than institutions), and the selection of the child's guardian does not always ensure the best interests of the child. When a child is placed with a new family, the legislation determines the eligibility requirements for only a single guardian (other members of the household are not assessed for their suitability).

Therefore, children who are separated from their parents receive placements which may not be favorable for their safeguarding. As examples, in two of the four municipalities audited, alcohol-dependent persons lived together with the child's guardian. Similarly, it is not assessed whether the guardian family is itself socially or financially vulnerable. In six municipalities, persons appointed to be the child's guardians were having problems with their own children, that is, they were included in the list of vulnerable families. In two of the four municipalities audited, children under guardianship lived with guardian partners or spouses who were suspected, accused or convicted persons and had no permanent income, and were dependent on benefits (State Audit Report, 2014, p. 9).

The Lithuanian Ombudswoman for the Protection of the Rights of the Child conducted a study on the guardianship of children under 3 years of age in residential care homes for children with development issues. (It should be noted that the above-mentioned State Audit Report does not assess residential care homes of children under the age of 3 years.) The study revealed a number of systemic gaps that could theoretically be called systemic violence against children. The investigator's findings were submitted to the Seimas and the Government, the Ministry of Social Security and Labor, and the Ministry of Health. However, no substantial changes were made (the Ombudsman for the Protection of the Rights of the Child, 2015). As is stated elsewhere, residential care for children under the age of 3 remains a violation of the rights of the child (Pūras, 2012). However, one can assume that the situation will improve in the future, as the law prohibits sending healthy infants into residential care for children with disabilities. Since 2017, professional guardians are available for young children and children in need of emergency care.

The fact that the goals of the State Child Welfare Policy were not realized were related to an adult-centered (paternalistic) approach, unprofessional implementation of policy documents that were essential for the absorption of financial EU resources, and the channeling of resources to building renovation and construction rather than to the development of family homes. For example, the declarative and promising Child Welfare Program and its Implementation Plan for 2013–2018 did not include the health, living conditions, education, participation of children, prevention of poverty risk, and other important issues necessary for the welfare of the child (Poviliūnas, 2014, p. 8). The support from the EU funds has not been sufficiently used due to lack of capacity for EU funds administration (Frazer & Marlier, 2014, p. 18). Furthermore, the use of EU finances toward residential care buildings and renovation has slowed the de-institutionalization of children.

It would seem that initiatives of the past years could be a breakthrough approach to child protection and well-being. However, an overview of several policy documents (the 2016–2018 Action Plan on Child Welfare; Complex Family Services, 2016–2020; The Action Plan; Transition from Residential Care to the Family and Community Services for the Disabled and for the Children Without Parental Guidance 2014–2020 Action Plan) clearly shows that there is a risk of familialism as children can "dissolve" in the context of family services. Further, deinstutionalization is confined to a mechanical redistribution of children to smaller residential care institutions which function in apartments, rather than transitioning to families. Moreover, there is still a harmful practice that the performance of the institutions is not measured by the criteria of effectiveness, but by the number of services provided, which is easy to manipulate.

Based on its name, the Action Plan for the Child's Welfare 2016–2018 should focus on child welfare measures. However, the purpose of this plan is to reduce the preconditions that would put children at risk for guardianship. The goal is to provide five objectives focused on adults, that is, parents and specialists. These include prevention services for families, reunification services, higher standards for staff, inter-organizational cooperation, and program monitoring. A great deal of emphasis is placed on training, without which a qualitative breakthrough in the practical work cannot be expected.

As is stated in the report of the Commissioner for Human Rights of the Council of Europe, Lithuania has developed a child protection system which has set goals, but there is a very large gap between the stated goals and the practical protection of the child (Muižnieks, 2017). There is no integral, systematic research in Lithuania which would deal with the reasons for this situation. Moreover, there are no active discussions on the measurement of safeguarding and guardianship of children in the Lithuanian context because of the conflicting views on the different concepts of the interests of the child (Žalimienė, 2007; Kairienė, 2012). There are serious obstacles to the practical organization of assistance in the field of violence against children. Foreign research shows that alcohol abuse is one of the main causes of ill-treatment of children (Velleman & Templeton, 2016), longer duration of guardianship and re-admission to guardianship (Laslett et al., 2012). International studies show that between 13% and 80% of neglected children are associated with problem alcohol use in parents (Laslett et al., 2013). One of the reasons for the ineffectiveness of child protection is the gap between the treatment of addictions and social work with families. But social workers cannot solve this problem. Governmental measures to build bridges between the treatment of addictions, child protection, and social work will still have to wait for years, as this issue does not come into play in either the public discourse or the political agenda. In order to improve the protection of children in Lithuania, both addiction and domestic violence should be addressed in parallel.

A situation in which municipalities are obliged to collect data on vulnerable families, but not necessarily about their children and their well-being, has revealed a clear tendency for familialism. The National Child Rights Protection and Adoption Service issues an annual report that draws a picture of a child growing up in a group of families at risk. It provides data only about children's gender and age, and the territory of a resident's municipality (State Children's Rights, 2016). The neglect of child neglect can be seen as the neglect of the child's well-being, the lack of prevention of violence, and the inability of state institutions to minimize the effects of family dysfunctions that have already occurred. The emphasis on preventing child neglect would help to focus political debate on child well-being and its determinants, such as child poverty reduction, development and empowerment of the child daycare centers, social work with the child, and reconciliation of work and family responsibilities.

Conclusions

Lithuania joined the European Union with few financial resources, but has achieved a great deal in a short period of time: the UN Convention on the Rights of the Child has been ratified; the system of protection of children's rights, including the network of child rights protection services has been established; guardianship of children in families has been legalized and prioritized; alternatives to imprisonment for minors have been created ; the Ombudsman for the Protection of the Rights of the Child has been established; and intensive training of social workers has been developed. A significant contribution to such achievement was done by active non-governmental organizations working in the field of child protection.

The period of financial assistance from the EU Structural Funds is particularly closely linked to the continuation of the Soviet childcare tradition and the failure of the administrative system to direct financial support from the EU towards the development of the child protection system. Support from the EU Structural Funds was harmful, as the highest-ranking officials who were responsible for coordinating the implementation of policy goals turned the funding into an objective toward infrastructure and the major part of the financing went to building childcare institutions. However, common child welfare processes could have been reformed and could have had a more positive impact on the child protection system. It is worth mentioning the Law on Violence in the Immediate Environment, which, as a result of publicity on the prevalence of domestic violence, enacted the viewpoint that violence isn't just a private affair of the family, but also a responsibility of the state. The Law on Social Services was also significant as it provided the basis for the administration of social services: it obligated municipalities to investigate the need for services, to plan, organize, supervise, and control them, and to finance them. During this period, the resources for financing the function of social work, including work with children's rights protection was increased. Since 2012, the State Audit Office and the Office of the Ombudsman for Children have begun to raise the problem of child safeguarding and the ineffectiveness of services for cases of abuse. However, fundamental changes had to wait until 2017.

A new reform of the protection of the child was launched in 2017. It obliges attention from the "top down" to include the child's participation, the child's needs, assessment of the level of threat to the child, and the organization of inter-institutional assistance. The organization and assessment of assistance provides a case management approach, and in the case of extremely complex cases, interdisciplinary mobile assistance, which will operate under the central government.

Although in theory, the reform provides much hope that child protection will improve, there are still many challenges in the practical implementation of child protection. First of all, this relates to the human resources of the child's protection, which have been criticized for lack of professionalism. This reform is really a big step forward, but in order to take effective protection of the child, it will have to overcome the challenges of developing human resources and services without losing the interests of the child.

In the development of the Lithuanian child protection system, child-focused protection should start by improving the ability of professionals to recognize neglect and abuse. One can definitely say that the focus of the future should be on training professionals working with children and the family. The knowledge of working with children should be strengthened to recognize the risks and manifestations of negligence and violence and their effects on the development of the child, emphasizing that work with parents is important, but only one of the child protection measures. Getting good practice, especially by building bridges between addiction treatment, child protection, and social work with the family, is very important.

References

Aidukaite, J., Moskvina, J., and Skuciene, D. (2016). Lithuanian welfare system in times of recent crisis. In K. Schubert, P. De Villota, and J. Kuhlmann (Eds.), *Challenges to European welfare systems* (pp. 419–441). Springer.

Child Guardianship Act of 1998, Pub. L. No. VIII-674, Stat. 35-933 (Lithuan.).

Concept of Family Policy of 1996, Pub. L. No. 362, Stat. 28-684 (Lithuan.).

Delap, E. (2011). *Scaling down. Reducing, reshaping and improving residential care around the world.* Positive care choices: working paper No.1. Every Child.

Department of Statistics of Lithuania. (2017). *Residents of Lithuania.* Available at: https://osp.stat.gov.lt/gyve ntojai1.

Eurointegration projects and Ministry of Social Security and Labour. (2015). *Report on the research of the activities of the children's day care centers, the evaluation and development possibilities of the social services provided in them.* Available at: https://socmin.lrv.lt/uploads/socmin/documents/files/pdf/10601_galutine-tyrimo-atask aita_suderinta_2015-08-19_maketas_galutinis.pdf.

European Union Agency for Fundamental Rights. (2014). *Guardianship for children deprived of parental care. A handbook to reinforce guardianship systems to cater for the specific needs of child victims of trafficking.* Publications Office of the European Union. Available at: http://fra.europa.eu.

European Union Agency for Fundamental Rights. (2018). *Guardianship systems for children deprived of parental care in the European Union. Summary.* Publications Office of the European Union. Available at: https://publications.europa.eu.

Eurostat. (2016). *Family and child benefits in the EU.* Available at: http://ec.europa.eu/eurostat/web/products-eurostat-news/-/EDN-20170512-1?inheritRedirect=true.

Eurostat. (2017). *Total general government expenditure on social protection* [Graphic]. Available at: http://ec.eur opa.eu/eurostat/statistics-explained/images/0/05/Total_general_government_expenditure_on_social_pro tection%2C_2016_%28%25_of_GDP_%25_of_total_expenditure%29.png.

Frazer, H. and Marlier, E. (2014). *Investing in children: Breaking the cycle of disadvantage: A study of national policies. Synthesis Report.* Publications Office of the European Union.

Gvaldaitė, l. and Šimkonytė, S. (2016). De-institutionalisation of child foster care system in Lithuania: Will the "carriage" move forward?. *Social theory, empiricism, politics and practice*, 12, 55–73.

Kabašinskaitė, D. and Bak, M. (2006). Lithuania's children's policy in the period of transition. *International journal of social welfare*, 15(3), 247–256.

Kairienė, B. (2012). Legal status of the child: problems of implementation. *Societal Studies*, 4, 1443–1455.

Laslett, A. M. L., Dietze, P. M., and Room, R. G. (2013). Carer drinking and more serious child protection case outcomes. *British Journal of Social Work*, 43(7), 1384–1402.

Laslett, A. M., Room, R., Dietze, P., and Ferris, J. (2012). Alcohol's involvement in recurrent child abuse and neglect cases. *Addiction*, 107(10), 1786–1793.

Law of Child Benefits of Lithuania of 1994 Pub. L. No. I-621, Stat. 89-1706 (2018). Available at: https://www.e-tar.lt/portal/lt/legalAct/TAR.1DEDD43B92AE/UJcoAfonsR.

Law of the Office of the Ombudsman for the Protection of the Rights of the Child of 2000. (2000). Pub. L. No. VIII-1708, Stat. 50-1432 (Lithuan.).

Law on Minimum Supervision of the Child of 2010, Pub. L. No. XI-1232, Stat. 157–7969…

Law on Social Services of 2006, Pub. L. No. X-493, Stat 17-589 (Lithuan.).

Law on the Fundamentals of the Protection of the Rights of the Child of 1996, Pub. L. No. I-1234., Stat. 33-807 (Lithuan).

Law on the Fundamentals of the Protection of the Rights of the Child of 2017, Pub. L. No. Lietuvos No XIII-643, Stat. 16087 (Lithun.). Internet access: https://e-seimas.lrs.lt/portal/legalAct/lt/TAD/e711b850aa6011e7a65c90dfe4655c64.

Law on the Protection against Violence in the Immediate Environment of 2011, No. Pub. L. No. XI-1425, Stat. 72-3475 (Lithuan).

Law on the Ratification of EC Convention on the Protection of Children against Sexual Exploitation and Sexual Abuse of 2012, Pub. L. No. XI-2368, Stat.. 132-6694 (Lithuan.).

Lazutka, R., Poviliūnas, A., and Žalimienė, L. (2017). *Lithuania to tackle deficiencies in the policy on the protection of children's rights and child welfare*. ESPN Flash Report, (26). Available at: http://www.ec.europa.eu/social/BlobServlet?docId=17807&langId=en.

The Concept of Child Welfare State Policy of 2003, Pub. L. No. IX-1569, Stat. Valstybės žinios, 2003-05-30, Nr. 52–2316. (Lithuan.).

Muižnieks, N. (2017). *Report by commissioner for human rights of the Council of Europe following his visit to Lithuania from 5 to 9 December 2016*. https://www.refworld.org/docid/594908124.html.

Munro, E. (2011). *The Munro review of child protection: Final report, a child-centred system, Vol. 8062*. The Stationery Office.

Ombudsman for the Protection of the Rights of the Child. (2015). *The report about changes in child under 3(4) years old and disabled children care in institutions and A. Bandzos institutional childcare home*. Available at: http://vtaki.lt/lt/teisine-informacija/vaiko-teisiu-padeties-vertinimas/atlikti-tyrimai-ir-apibendrini mai?page=3.

Order of Minister of the Ministry of Social Security and Labor on Methodological recommendation of 2003. No. A1-207. Available at: https://e-seimas.lrs.lt/portal/legalAct/lt/TAD/TAIS.225359.

Order of the Minister of Social Security and Labour on the Case Management Approval of 2018, Pub. L. No. 41—141, Stat. 4881. (Lithuan.).

Poviliūnas, A. (2014). *Investing in children: Breaking the cycle of disadvantage. A study of national policies Lithuania*. EU Network of Independent Experts on Social Inclusion. Available at: http://ec.europa.eu/social/main.jsp?pager.offset=10&catId=89&langId=lt&newsId=2061&tableName=news&moreDocume nts=yes.

Presidential Palace of the Republic of Lithuania. (2016). *Nacionalinė socialinio saugumo kampanija "Už saugią Lietuvą"*. Avaiable at: http://uzsaugialietuva.lt/apie-projekta.

Pūras, D. (2012). *Institucinė globa: Vaikų iki trejų metų amžiaus teisių pažeidimas*. Lietuvos Respublikos Seimas. Available at: http://www3. lrs. lt/docs2/TJSYLCNC.PDF.

Snieškienė, D. (2009). The development of foster family care in post-Communist countries: The experience of Lithuania. *Adoption & Fostering*, 33 34–43.

Snieškienė, D. and Tamutienė, I. (2014). *Comparative analysis of ensuring the human rights of children in institutions and families. Research report*. 1-42. Vytautas Magnus University.

Stankūnienė, V., Baublytė, M., and Maslauskaitė, A. (2016). Single mother families in Lithuania: Demographic and socio-economic characteristics. *Sociology. Thought and Action*, 38, 64–85.

State Audit report. (2012). *Is the protection of the rights of the child effectively organized?* Report No. VA-P-10-3-21. (Lithuan.).

State Audit. report. (2014). *Does the childcare system meet the best interests of the child under care?* Report No. VA-P-10-3-1. (Lithuan.).

State Children's Rights Protection and Adoption Service under the Ministry of Social Security and Labor. (2014). *Report of activities in 2014*. Available at: http://vaikoteises.lt/media/file/SPIS%20ataskaita%20sut varkyta.pdf. https://vaikoteises.lt/media/file/ataskaitos/2014%20m.%20ataskaita.pdf.

State Children's Rights Protection and Adoption Service under the Ministry of Social Security and Labor. (2016). *Report of activities in 2016*. Available at: https://vaikoteises.lt/media/file/ataskaitos/2016_m.%20at askaita.pdf.

State Children's Rights Protection and Adoption Service under the Ministry of Social Security and Labor. (2017). *Report of activities in 2017*. Available at: https://vaikoteises.lt/media/file/2017%20m.%20ataska ita%20GALUTIN%C4%96(1).pdf.

State Children's Rights Protection and Adoption Service under the Ministry of Social Security and Labor. (2018). *Innovations in the system of protection of the rights of the child in the context of the Framework Law on the Protection of the Rights of the Child News About Child Protection System*. Available at: http://www.vaik oteises.lt/media/image/VTA%20sistemos%20pertvarka%20VTAPI%20kontekste%202017-11-16.pptx.

Stažytė, K. (2017, May 7). Keturmečio Matuko nužudymo tyrimas baigtas: pareigūnai baisisi abiejų įtariamųjų emociniu intelektu. *15min.lt*. Available at: https://www.15min.lt/naujiena/aktualu/nusikaltimaiirnelai mes/keturmecio-matuko-nuzudymo-tyrimas-baigtas-pareigunai-baisisi-abieju-itariamuju-emociniu-intele ktu-59-821976.

Tamutienė, I. (2004). *Vaiko teisių apsaugos institutai ir jų sąveika prievartos prieš vaiką atvejais* [Unpublished doctoral dissertation]. Vytauto Didžiojo universitetas.

Tamutienė, I. (2017, January 27). *Vaikų globos reformai ES fondų parama buvo žalinga*. Available at: http://www.vdu.lt/lt/vaiku-globos-reformai-es-fondu-parama-buvo-zalinga/.

Tamutienė, I. (2018). Efficiency problems of child protection in Lithuania. *Public Policy and Administration*, 17(1), 24–37.

Tamutienė, I. and Auglytė, V. (2018). Societal and political pressure on child protection: The perspective of child protection professionals. *Public Policy and Administration*, 17(3), 385–398.

Tamutienė, I. and Jogaitė, B. (2018). Disclosure of alcohol-related harm to children: Children's experiences. *Nordic Studies on Alcohol and Drugs*, 36(3), 209–222.

Velleman, R. and Templeton, L. J. (2016). Impact of parents' substance misuse on children: An update. *BJPsych Advances*, 22(2), 108–117.

Vitkauskas, K. (2010). Resocialization of delinquent children in the system of the average care for the juvenile. *Public Policy and Administration*, 33, 115–127.

Žalimienė, L. (2007). *Vaikų socialinės globos kokybė ir jos vertinimas*. Available at: http://www.sppd.lt/media/ mce_filebrowser/2015/01/09/Vaiku_socialines_globos kokybe_ir_jos_vertinimas.pdf.

Žalimienė, L. and Rimšaitė, E. (2007). The metamorphosis of the role of nongovernmental organizations: From charity in XVIII century to market of social services in modern society. *Social Work*, 6(1), 83–95.

Child Protection in Poland

Violetta Tanaś

Abstract

This chapter discusses the child protection system in Poland. Since children should be protected against maltreatment and exploitation, formal, psychopedagogical and socio-political considerations should be taken into consideration when looking into the consequences of actions to protect children against violence. The Convention on the Rights of the Child (CRC) became the bases of numerous documents defining the responsibilities of the state and local entities in the field of protecting children against abuse since the European Parliament recognized that violence is a violation of human rights to life, personal security, freedom, dignity, and integrity. Moreover, the policy of protection against abuse has been prepared in line with the applicable law.

Key Words: Poland, child protection system, children, applicable law, human rights, violation, CRC, European Parliament, abuse, consequences

Children, just like other citizens, should be protected against improper treatment and exploitation and against the breaking of their rights in everyday life, including the right to protection against violence and cruel treatment in all living environments—family, school, community, and society. The basis of this position and the consequence of actions to protect children against violence, are formal, psycho-pedagogical, and sociopolitical considerations. Among the formal reasons included in various documents and international agreements signed by states are provisions prohibiting the use of violence against children, including the beating of children. The fundamental act in this area is the Convention on the Rights of the Child and related documents such as Comments of the UN Committee on the Protection of Children's Rights, as well as various recommendations of the Council of Europe and the European Union. These documents present the position of the international community regarding violence against children and postulate about specific actions; they also formulate obligations and recommendations for introducing appropriate solutions in countries to protect the youngest from various forms of violence.

The Convention on the Rights of the Child has become the basis for many subsequent documents defining the responsibilities of the state and local entities in the field of protecting children against abuse. The convention has exerted and still exerts influence on undertaking various initiatives aimed at the implementation of children's rights and the protection of life as well as decent conditions for its development in various cultures and societies. The Convention also puts political pressure on those countries that have ratified it, gradually enforcing the introduction of appropriate state solutions and measures. Since the 1970s, the Council of Europe has introduced resolutions and conventions aimed at setting standards in the field of social policy and solving various social problems.

With the creation of the European Union, the process of unifying legal solutions in the field of social policy in the Member States took place. In the 1990s, domestic violence began to be perceived in Europe as a human rights problem. The European Parliament has recognized that violence is a violation of human rights to life, personal security, freedom, dignity, and physical and mental integrity, and thus constitutes an obstacle to the full development of individuals. Many European laws contain recommendations on the treatment of children and references to ill-treatment in families.

The Polish Response

As a country that ratified the Convention on the Rights of the Child and as a member state of the Council of Europe and the European Union—in accordance with international standards—Poland has introduced several important legislative measures for the protection of children against violence. In accordance with international recommendations, in Poland the law has been reformed for better protection of children against violence. In Poland, the problem of child abuse has been recognized by non-governmental organizations since the early 1990s. It should be noted, however, that Polish researchers were already interested in this phenomenon, although this was incidental. In the scientific literature—mainly medical and then psychological—there have been scientific articles about abused children and violence against a child in the family since the late 1960s. The development of democracy in Poland after 1989 and subsequent aspirations for accession to the European Union have positively influenced the implementation of legal reforms in the field of domestic violence and child protection. In 2000, the Act on the Ombudsman for Children was passed in Poland. This Act—after the Constitution of the Republic of Poland and alongside the Convention on the Rights of the Child ratified by Poland—was at the time the most important legal act regarding children and the protection of their rights.

In 2005, the Polish Parliament passed the Act on Counteracting Domestic Violence, which became the basic, official interpretation of the approach to the problem, and which formulated the responsibility of specific state entities for counteracting domestic violence. This act enabled the launch of many measures to prevent and reduce domestic violence. Analysis and verification of the several-year functioning of this act led to its amendment in 2010. The amendments included a total ban on violence in raising and taking care of children. The Family and Guardianship Code, Article 96, prohibits the use of corporal punishment for persons exercising parental authority, protection or care over minors. A number of additional administrative provisions have been introduced, which set out more detailed directions and procedures to address the problems of domestic violence (Jarosz & Nowak, 2012). The amendment of the Act on Counteracting Domestic Violence defined in a more detailed way the actions that should be organized and undertaken against the phenomenon of domestic violence and its cases, and pointed to institutions and persons responsible for it. On the one hand, the act is perceived as a modern legal solution that refers in its content and formulated obligations to world standards in the field of counteracting domestic violence and to solutions applied for years in other countries. On the other hand, the law has raised a lot of controversy and has led to public discussion regarding some of its provisions.

Definitions of Violence against Children

Violence against children is mainly defined as: physical, psychological, sexual, and violence through neglect. The Act on Preventing and Counteracting Domestic Violence also distinguishes less characteristic forms, such as indirect violence, economic violence, overprotection, excessive control, and others (Jarosz, 2008).

Psychological violence includes all behaviors and omissions (lack of behavior) that can cause emotional, cognitive, or behavioral disorders as well as psychological problems and destructive tendencies in the child. In essence, psychological violence means destroying the dignity of a child; it includes all behaviors of neglect and rejection, which is the cause of a disturbing constructive image of the child, causing or threatening the development of a sense of worthlessness, being unloved, unwanted, and so on. Psychological violence can take the form of repeated patterns of behavior of parents (attitudes) and individual acts (Jarosz, 2008).

Researchers have so far isolated a wide range of behaviors treated as psychological violence, such as insults, threats, and other forms of verbal aggression; terrorization; scaring; isolation; blackmail (something that a child is afraid of—including, for example, his own suicide); excessive requirements; negating the child's developmental abilities; excessive control; excessive restriction of freedom; guilt-inducing, blaming, and criticizing; making a scapegoat; opposing demands; emotional rejection and neglecting his or her emotional needs; and corrupting, leading to dissociation (subcultural socialization). Within the main categories of psychological violence there are several main types of psychological violence in the literature: rejecting and degrading, terrorizing and scaring, isolating and exploiting, and corrupting.

Physical abuse includes any non-accidental use of physical force against a child, as a result of which the child suffers physical pain and (possibly) injuries. Physical abuse also includes other behaviors that can cause these consequences. In addition to commonly understood behaviors, such as hitting a child, physical violence is also poisoning, introducing foreign bodies into the child's body or restraining physical freedom (e.g., attachment to various household appliances). Physical punishment is also a form of violence that includes spanking. However, this approach often meets with social protest, expressed by the claim that "spanking is not violence," the scientific stand and political position is quite clear in this matter (Wójcik, 2012).

Physical punishment has been defined by the UN Committee on the Rights of the Child as: "any punishment with the use of physical force, which is intended to cause some pain or discomfort." In a detailed interpretation, a physical punishment includes any hitting a child with a hand or any other object, kicking a child, shaking a child, throwing objects at a child, scratching a child, pinching, biting, pulling hair or ears, ordering to maintain some uncomfortable position (e.g., kneeling, standing with raised hands), scalding or burning, doing painful activities (washing lips with soap, forcing to swallow hot food), and other similar acts.

Neglect and mistreatment of a child means not meeting the necessities for the proper development of the child, his existential needs related to nutrition, clothing, shelter, hygiene, medical care and education. Neglect also means exposing a child to danger by those who are responsible for the well-being of the child. Neglect can refer to different developmental needs of the child. There are several variations of neglect (Jarosz & Nowak, 2012):

- Physical: inadequate nutrition, clothing, hygiene, shelter and lack of supervision and care, as well as jeopardizing the health and life of a child to danger through their behavior or conditions created by a child;
- Medical: not seeking medical help or significant delay in looking for it in the event of serious injuries or diseases or health problems of the child, failure to take the actions recommended in the treatment of the child on the basis of medical knowledge;
- Abandonment: leaving the child unattended or supervised for a long time or with the intention of getting rid of the child, including throwing from home or refusing to accept back after an escape;
- Educational: lack of cognitive stimulation of a small child, failure to fulfill school compulsion, consent to truancy, allowing for unjustified leaving school, lack of care for providing special educational activities for the child who has such indications, lack of interest in the child's school situation and lack of cooperation between parents and school;
- Educational: lack of consent and/or lack of action in the situation of the child's problem behavior, lack of psycho-pedagogical support, refusal to subject the child to corrective and therapeutic procedures in situations when the child has behavioral problems, emotional disorders, etc.;
- Emotional: lack of support for a child in situations difficult for him, lack of interest in a child, lack of attention to a child, lack of behaviors of contact

with a small child, admission to a child in situations that are harmful to him in a psychological sense (acts of violence between parents, violence in the media, etc.).

Sexual abuse includes all types of behaviors that use the child for stimulation and sexual satisfaction by an adult or a much older person. These behaviors may take forms from exhibitionism or drawing into pornography, to full sexual contact. Sexual exploitation means engaging a child in sexual activity, which he or she cannot or does not want to give consent to, which he or she does not understand, but which he or she perceives as harmful at the time of the incident or later. The term "sexual violence" can also be used in a situation where a mature person does something consciously or neglects his social duties or obligations resulting from specific responsibility for a child, and thus allows the child to engage in any activity aimed at sexual satisfaction of an adult (Sajkowska & Włodarczyk, 2010). The way of understanding what is violence against a child is dynamic—it changes with the passage of time and conditions. Taking into account factors influencing what is meant as violence against a child and what behaviors are included in this scope, it can be assumed that if there will be development of knowledge and improvement of living conditions of societies, there will be increased social sensitivity to a child's harm or risk of its occurrence.

Scope of Violence against Children in Poland

At the end of 2016, there were nearly 6.9 million children in Poland aged 0–17 (Central Statistical Office [GUS], 2017). The share of children in the general population of Poland has been decreasing since the 1990s. In 1990, children under 18 years of age accounted for about 30% of the total population (GUS, 2001), while in 2016 they were less than 18% (GUS, 2017). Fifty-one percent of children are boys. In cities, the share of children in the population is smaller than in rural areas and is less than 17%, while in rural areas—nearly 20%. However, the fall in the number of children in the village is faster than in the city. In 1999–2016, the share of children in the rural population dropped by 8.3 percentage points, while in the city the decline was 6.6 points (GUS, 2017).

The scale of the problem of violence against children in Poland can be estimated from two basic sources—official statistics and social research. Various types of statistics on violence against children are collected by the police, courts, but also Interdisciplinary Teams on Domestic Violence, as well as help and crisis intervention centers. It is worth noting that police and judicial statistics only represent a slice of reality—they usually contain information about crimes committed, so they do not take into account some forms of violence that are not penalized. In addition, these are only cases that have been reported to law enforcement authorities. This is a particularly important factor in the case of violence against children on the part of parents or guardians—children have a limited opportunity to report such situations. Official statistics are often a good indicator of trends. Social research shows a much more defined definition of violence, including those behaviors that are not included in the codes. Social research also shows a greater scale of violence—they can include not only experiences not reported to law enforcement agencies, but also those about which the child has not yet told anyone.

The main statistics on violence against children are data collected under the "Blue Cards" procedure introduced in Poland in 1998. This is an integrated system of help and monitoring families in which cases of violence were reported (Wójcik, 2012). The Blue Card can be created by representatives of the police, social welfare, education, health protection and municipal commissions for solving alcohol-related problems. In fact, the vast majority of procedures are initiated by the police—75.68%, 12.78% by social assistance, 6.18% by education representatives, 4.8% by communal commissions solving alcohol problems, and only 0.56% by healthcare workers. It would be particularly important to include analyzes of the Blue Cards established by the representatives of education, because in all these cases the victim was certainly a child. In 2013, 2014, and 2015 the police completed over 70,000 Blue Card forms—in 2016, it was 73,531 forms (Ministerstwo Rodziny, Pracy i Polityki Społecznej [MRPiPS], 2016).

According to the National Police Headquarters (2017), the number of minor victims of domestic violence in Poland is declining—from 56,500 in 2006 to 14,223 in 2016 (7,074 are girls, 7,149 are boys). The proportion of juvenile victims in relation to the total number of victims of domestic violence also changed, from 36% in 2006 to 15% in 2016. In 2016, as part of the Blue Card procedure, 598 children were placed in a non-threatening place (e.g., foster family, extended family, care facility) due to domestic violence. This is more than twice as many as in 2015, when there were 275 children. Reports of police officers who take part in the interventions of the Blue Card procedure show that they most often face psychological and physical violence. The important fact is that there is rarely a family situation that can only be classified as one type of violence.

In Poland, particularly violent cases of violence against children are recorded in police statistics as crimes according to Article 207 of the Penal Code. This article deals with the physical or mental abuse of a close relative or other person who is in a permanent or temporary relationship of dependence to the offender. This article also applies to abuse of a minor or a person who is clumsy due to a mental or physical condition. Annually, between 3,000 to more than 4,000 minors are victims of this crime. The vast majority are cases considered as domestic violence—child abuse by family members. In other cases, the perpetrator of child abuse may be, for example, a teacher, a neighbor or a foreign person. In 2015, victims of crime in accordance with Article 207 of the Penal Code (qualified as domestic violence), there were 3,789 children (49% girls and 51% boys) (Ministerstwo Sprawiedliwości [MS], 2016).

As already mentioned, in the case of children who are victims of physical violence on the part of parents, reporting such a case to law enforcement agencies is difficult—there must be a person who knows about violence and wants to report it—it can be difficult when the parent is a perpetrator of violence.

This is particularly difficult for young children (up to 3 years of age) who are not already in kindergarten or school and therefore do not have regular contact with adults from outside the family who might observe that something bad is happening in the child's home and react to it. Young children are also more vulnerable to violence and neglect, because they need constant care. In such a situation, healthcare workers are important to monitor the child's situation. They should be in regular contact with young children because they have the opportunity to report suspicion of violence against a child. However, healthcare representatives initiate only 1% of cases—627 procedures of the Blue Card (NIK, 2016).

Doctors also have their own case report system for children, whose injuries indicate that they may be victims of a diagnosis coded as the battered child syndrome. It is important that this code covers various forms of violence against children: not only physical violence, but also psychological, sexual and neglect. In Poland, only just over 20 such codes are reported annually. In 2015, there were 23; 17 of them concerned girls and six boys. These data do not indicate the scale of the problem, because the code on the cause—in this case the battered child's code—is an additional and optional addition to the basic code, describing the direct reason for the child to go to the doctor (Włodarczyk, 2017).

A much greater scale of the problem of violence against children in Poland than the scale emerging from official statistics, shows research conducted among both children (studying their own experiences) and adults (retrospective studies on their own experiences of childhood or research related to the use of violence by parents towards their children). In the case of teenagers, every third (32%) knows at least one peer in their environment who experiences some form of domestic violence. Almost every second (46%) young person thinks that almost all or more than half of his peers are victims of at least one examined manifestation of physical violence, and almost every fourth peer (23%) is a victim of psychological violence (Miedzik, 2014).

In the case of own experiences of violence in childhood, available statistics seem to indicate a much smaller scale of the problem. According to data, 13.4% of adults experienced physical violence in childhood; the same percentage (13.4%) of the respondents experienced psychological violence (Miedzik & Godlewska-Szurkowa, 2014). These are much lower interest rates than those obtained in a similar study carried out in 2008—27.5% and 21.6% (Miedzik & Godlewska-Szurkowa, 2014). This difference cannot certainly attest to the fact that the scale of physical violence against children has fallen to such a large extent, because the vast majority of the surveyed population of adult Polish people has not changed, and thus the childhood experience has largely remained unchanged. This difference can therefore be explained primarily by various methodological approaches and a change in public awareness of violence against children. The ban on physical punishment introduced in 2010 and the accompanying public debate on the negative consequences of abuse could have led to a greater reluctance to acknowledge that one was experiencing violence from close relatives.

It is important that research carried out among adults shows the situation from several dozen years ago. More accurate data on the current situation is shown by research conducted among children and adolescents. According to data from the Nationwide Diagnosis of the Problem of Violence Against Children (Wfodarczyk & Makaruk, 2013) conducted by the Empowering Children Foundation (Fundacja Dajemy Dzieciom Siłę), every third (34%) child aged 11–17 has ever experienced violence from an adult friend, and 18% during the year preceding the survey. The study shows that the scale of the two discussed forms of violence—psychological and physical—is similar in the case of questions about experiences from the whole child's life (22% and 21%). In the year preceding the study conducted among children and adolescents, children more often experienced psychological violence (14%) than physical (9%). The form of violence to which the child is more vulnerable depends on his or her sex. Mental abuse is more often experienced by girls, while boys are more exposed to physical violence (Wójcik 2013b; Miedzik & Godlewska-Szurkowa, 2014).

The perpetrators of both physical and mental violence against children are most often parents, more often fathers than mothers. Boys are more often victims of emotional abuse on the part of fathers, and girls on the part of mothers. No such dependencies have been established in the case of physical violence (Wójcik, 2013b; Miedzik & Godlewska-Szurkowa, 2014).

Physical punishment is the most common form of physical violence against children, including in Poland. Apart from raising the voice, the slap is the form of reaction to undesirable behavior most commonly used by Polish parents (Makaruk, 2013; RPD, 2016). Most parents, according to a study by Makaruk (2013) and the Ombudsman for Children (2016), spank at least once in their lives, and every fifth parent (21%) spanked their child many times. A much smaller percentage of parents admitted to being beaten by hand (24%) or by a belt (11%). Polish parents are definitely the least likely to hit children in the face—4% of parents according to Makaruk (2013) and 3% of parents according to the Ombudsman for Children (RPD, 2016). In addition to the above, Polish parents also use other methods of physical disciplining of children. Every seventh Polish parent (14%) happened to jerk or shake a child, while a tenth pinch or squeeze angrily (11%) or spank (10%). Eight percent of parents pulled the child by hair or ears, and 7% hit the child with a belt or other object (RPD, 2016).

An important fact is that all forms of physical punishment are currently used less frequently in Poland than a few years ago (Makaruk, 2013). It is certainly influenced by the penalization of physical punishments and parents' education about the consequences of their application and the promotion of other ways to raise children. A particularly large change in public awareness about physical punishment can be seen in the case of punishment. Over a dozen or so years, the percentage of parents who spanked their child at least once in the month preceding the survey dropped from 10% in 1998 to 2% in 2012. The percentage of parents who never spank a child increased from 43% to 74% (Center for Public Opinion Research [CBOS], 2012).

Sexual abuse of a child is the inclusion of a child in sexual activity, which the child cannot fully understand and give informed consent. Sexual abuse of a child is also the inclusion of a child in sexual activity when the child has not matured and cannot agree in a valid legal way. According to the WHO, sexual exploitation occurs when such an activity occurs between a child and an adult or other child if, due to differences in age or development, the child and adult remain in the relationship of care, dependence, or power. The definition of sexual exploitation of children has not been formulated in Polish law. The concept can consist of many behaviors, separately penalized in the Penal Code. The lack of a legal definition of sexual abuse is not a negligence of the legislator. It results from the diversity of forms and contexts of sexual activities with the participation of the child and enables penalization of newly emerging sexual behaviors, victims of which are minors.

Crimes of child sexual abuse are described in Chapter 25 of the Criminal Code ("Crimes against sexual freedom and decency"). The legislator placed the following crimes there: rape (Article 197 § 1 of the Penal Code), rape of a minor under 15 (qualified type of rape, Article 197 § 3 of the Penal Code), abuse of the dependency ratio (Article 199 of the Penal Code), communion with minors under 15 (Article 200 of the Penal Code); grooming children via the Internet (article 200a of the Penal Code), incest (article 201 of the Penal Code), pornography (Article 202 of the Penal Code), pimping and procuring (Articles 203 and 204 of the Penal Code).

The delicacy of the problem of sexual abuse of children means that many cases of abuse are not reported, and many of the victims do not tell anyone, even when they are already adults. The hidden nature of the phenomenon is the main limitation of the possibility of its measurement and the answer to the question about its scale and character. Researchers constantly improve research methods to obtain the most complete data possible. It must be understood, however, that the scope disclosed will never coincide with the real scope of the phenomenon. The estimation of the scale of the problem of sexual abuse of children can be made on the basis of various data. Generally, two types of such data allow a systematic assessment of the scale and dynamics of the phenomenon. However, the different methodology of obtaining them makes us remember the correct interpretation of the given data category and limitations in the generalization of results.

In Poland, despite the growing number of institutions helping abused children, there is still no system of institutions covering the whole country, offering assistance in all forms of abuse, according to common standards. Therefore, there are no registers to assess the scale of the problem of abuse, including sexual abuse of children. The only data that allow estimating the trend of the phenomenon are data from police and judicial statistics. These data, however, only concern the small percentage of cases in which legal intervention was undertaken. The relation of these data to the real scale of the phenomenon depends on many factors, such as the effectiveness of justice institutions, or social attitudes towards sexual abuse of children.

Number of proceedings reported to the police in cases of sexual contact with minors up to 15 years of age has remained relatively stable over the last decade—nearly 2,000 proceedings instituted annually. The number of proceedings in connection with presenting minors below 15 years of age pornographic content and the dissemination, production, or possession of pornographic content involving minors is growing rapidly in recent years. Police statistics show that crimes related to the sexual abuse of children are committed about 1,500 each year. In the last years, their highest number was recorded in 2004: 1,904; in 2016 there were 1,533 cases.

Social Provisions to Protect Children

At the national level, the Act on Counteracting Violence imposed on the Council of Ministers the obligation to adopt the National Program for Counteracting Domestic Violence in order to create conditions for more effective prevention of domestic violence. The previous Program defined specific actions in the scope of providing protection and assistance to persons affected by domestic violence, programs of corrective and educational actions towards people using violence, and raising social awareness about the causes and effects of domestic violence. The program was adopted by resolution of the Council of Ministers of September 25, 2006 for the years 2006–2016, and then this program was implemented by the government administration and the local government. On August 1, 2010, the Act of June 10, 2010 amending the Act on the Prevention of Domestic Violence and Certain Other Acts (Journal of Laws No. 125, item 842) entered into force, which introduced many new regulations regarding both the improvement of existing as well as new legal institutions. It was necessary to develop a new document—the National Program for Counteracting Domestic Violence for the years 2014–2020.

Statutory provisions require more detailed and regular implementation of the activities carried out. The new document complements the provisions of the Act and systematizes priorities in the area of counteracting domestic violence. In addition, the development of the new Program is conditioned by the need to comply with the legislative technique. The preamble to the amended law emphasizes that domestic violence violates basic human rights, including the right to life and health, and respect for personal dignity. The preamble of the Act also points out that public authorities are obliged to ensure equal treatment and respect for the rights and freedoms for all citizens. The provisions of the Act have expanded the scope of activities within the framework of raising public awareness about the promotion of non-violent educational methods. The regulations also expanded the scope of disseminating information on the possibilities and forms of providing assistance to both those affected by violence and those using domestic violence, in order to create conditions for effective prevention of domestic violence.

The Program contains references to the objectives contained in the EU programming document EUROPA 2020—a strategy for smart, sustainable, and inclusive growth. The methods and tools for achieving the objectives of the Program will apply nationally. The Program is universal and it takes into account the priorities in the field of preventing domestic violence. The Program was created as a result of the work of the Monitoring Team for Counteracting Domestic Violence with the Minister responsible for social security, in cooperation with the Ministry of Interior, Ministry of Justice, Ministry of Health, Ministry of National Education, Ministry of Culture and National Heritage, Government Plenipotentiary for Equal Treatment, The General Prosecutor's Office, and non-governmental organizations. The financial consequences of the implementation of individual tasks were also identified and the sources of financing the activities in subsequent years of implementation and the rules for reporting on the tasks completed were indicated.

The Program has a long-term perspective, as the objectives and areas of action included in it impose an obligation on all levels of public administration to carry out long-term tasks in order to reduce the phenomenon of domestic violence. Reducing the scale of domestic violence in Poland is a process that requires time, effort, financial outlay, the involvement of all services, and a change in public awareness. The implementation of the Program should contribute to limiting the phenomenon of domestic violence.

The Blue Card procedure is an institutional tool for counteracting domestic violence. The amendment to the Act on Counteracting Domestic Violence of 2010 defines this procedure as follows: "Blue Card procedure covers all activities undertaken and implemented by representatives of social assistance organizational units, municipal committees for solving alcohol problems, police, education and health protection, with reasonable suspicion of the existence of domestic violence" (Journal of Laws No. 125, item 842). The provisions of this amendment point to the Council of Ministers as the body that determines the procedure and develops specimens of forms used during its implementation.

The current procedure in the original version was developed by the Police Headquarters and the Warsaw Metropolitan Police Headquarters in cooperation with the State Agency for Solving Alcohol Related Problems and introduced to the practice of police activities in 1998. Conducting the Blue Card Procedure belonged to the tasks of social assistance units since 2004. The idea of the procedure is cooperation between services working to counter domestic violence, actions against people using violence, and for the protection of abused children. The aim was to change the way in which services are handled in a situation of domestic violence—to establish cooperation and interdisciplinary action—assuming that violence in the family is not only a legal and criminal issue, but also a social, psychological and health issue. To help the family, specialists in various fields should cooperate with each other.

In 2011, the Council of Ministers issued an Ordinance on the Blue Card procedure and templates for the Blue Card forms. In the regulation, we can read about the rules regarding participation in the procedure of interdisciplinary teams and working groups (which each municipality was obliged to create under the mentioned amendment) and tasks imposed on police officers, healthcare representatives, education, municipal commissions for solving alcohol problems and social workers (Policja, 2012). The regulation indicates how to start and guide the Blue Card procedure, and when it can be completed.

The initiation of the procedure begins when the Blue Card form part A is completed by a police officer, a social worker, or a representative of the municipal commission for solving alcohol problems, health protection or education. This should happen in the presence of a person suspected of being violent in the family, or in a situation where this contact is impossible without the participation of that person. In a situation where a person who is suspected of experiencing domestic violence, the person is transported to the treatment entity and the form A is filled in by the healthcare representative.

The Blue Card form part B is given to a person affected by domestic violence, or, in the case of violence against a child, a parent, legal guardian, or other person who has reported a suspicion of domestic violence. Form B is a document for victims, which contains a definition of violence, human rights and information about places where you can get help. Form B is not passed on to a person suspected of using domestic violence.

Both the child and the adult have the right to know what actions will be taken in their case and where they can turn to for help, and they have the right to know what the procedure will look like. It is important to provide all the information to victims (children without form B). When a child is harmed, it may mean that both parents are violent towards him or her and that the minor does not have another closest family. It is important to then notify the family court and minors and ask for insight into the child's family situation. Form B remains at the beginning of the procedure until the child's situation is resolved.

The procedure requires that a conversation with a person suspected of being violent in the family is carried out in conditions guaranteeing freedom of expression and respect for the dignity of that person and ensuring their safety. It is necessary to create such conditions that a person affected by violence could safely describe the situation in which they found themselves.

If the person experiencing violence is a child, the activities of the Blue Cards procedure are carried out in the presence of a parent or legal or factual guardian. When a parent, legal guardian, or actual guardian are suspected of using violence against a child, these activities are carried out in the presence of an adult closest to the child (if possible, also in the presence of a psychologist). The presence of a psychologist is not necessary, because it often happens that he is not in the staff resources of a given institution or place.

The Act on Counteracting Domestic Violence indicates that assistance activities are not conditional upon consent and do not require such consent. None of Blue Card forms require the signature of a person suspected of experiencing or using domestic violence. The commencement of the Blue Cards procedure does not require the acceptance of a person suspected of experiencing domestic violence—domestic violence is a crime prosecuted *ex officio.* The form should be submitted immediately, but not later than within seven days from the date of initiation of the procedure to the chairman of the interdisciplinary team. A copy of form A remains at the initiating procedure. Completing form A does not exempt from the obligation to take intervention measures that ensure the safety of the person experiencing violence.

The chairman of the interdisciplinary team submits the Blue Card part A to the other members of the team or working group immediately, no later than three days from the date of receipt. Transferring the form to other members in such a short time can be a challenge, considering that some teams can have up to 20 people. In practice, this may be solved in such a way that the chairman informs members that he has received the form, for example by e-mail or telephone, and each member will have to go to the Social Welfare Center, where the form will be stored in order to familiarize themselves with it before a team meeting is called.

At the meeting of a working group or interdisciplinary team, an invitation is given to a person who is suspected of experiencing domestic violence. At this meeting, the family situation is analyzed and the Blue Card form C is completed. Meeting a team or group with a person who experiences violence is very important for the actions undertaken and their effectiveness. The injured person has the place and time to determine the needs, ideas for the situation and whether the person is ready to take action. In addition, at this meeting, an individual support plan is formulated together with the person experiencing violence. Thus, the person experiencing violence has an impact on what is happening in the case of her family. If the person who suffered violence does not come to the meeting, it does not stop the work of the interdisciplinary team or the working group. Children are not invited to this meeting.

It should be remembered that the entry into force of the regulation does not exempt services from their current duties. In many interpretations of the regulation, there is an opinion that the team's regulations should introduce a record that says a team or group meeting for a given matter is preceded by the actions of services in the environment, and only if these actions do not bring the desired effect should one reach for the tool—the team or group. The point here is to make the best use of resources. The regulation does not specify whether a meeting of a team or a working group should be convened for each case. All activities of the interdisciplinary team or working group are documented. Documentation is forwarded to the police or the public prosecutor's office in case of suspicion of a crime.

The task of a social worker—a representative of the municipal commission for solving alcohol problems, healthcare (whose representative is a doctor, paramedic, nurse, or midwife), and education—is primarily to inform the person experiencing violence about forms and places of assistance to people involved in violence, as well as providing access for medical help if the state of health of a person affected by violence so requires. The healthcare representative should inform the person about the possibility of obtaining a certificate about the types and causes of injury in connection with the use of domestic violence. In addition, the representative of education and social assistance as well as the municipal committee for solving alcohol problems should diagnose the situation and needs of the person experiencing violence, and he or she may conduct conversations with persons using violence. A social worker is to additionally provide shelter to a person experiencing violence if the situation so requires. As part of the procedure, a police officer provides the necessary assistance to a person suffering violence, including access to medical help; undertakes activities protecting life, health, and property; talks to a person using violence with criminal responsibility; protects traces and evidence of crime; and takes measures to prevent further threats that may occur in this family (including visits).

The tasks of members of an interdisciplinary team or working group within the framework of the Blue Card procedure are to provide assistance to a person experiencing violence, to take action against a person using violence, and to develop an individual help plan.

Completion of the procedure takes place when the domestic violence has been eliminated or reasonable assumption of the cessation of further use of domestic violence, and after the implementation of an individual assistance plan. The completion of the procedure must be documented in the form of a protocol signed by the chairman of the interdisciplinary team. The participants participating in the procedure after the end of the procedure shall be notified.

The basic unit of common court in Poland is the district court. In every district court there is a criminal department and a family department as well as teams of probation court services executing criminal decisions and teams of the probation court service that execute judgments in family and juvenile matters.

The fact of revealing domestic violence, especially when minor children are brought up in a family, may become the subject of both criminal and civil proceedings. The purpose of criminal proceedings is to punish the perpetrator of a crime, while the aim of civil-guardian proceedings is to take intervention measures towards the child's family environment, which are supposed to lead to protecting the child from further harm, and then in the long term aim to change the child's caring environment, which will allow the child to function and develop in it in a child-friendly way.

It is obvious that the criminal and family criminal proceedings I have mentioned in the case of violence in a family in which the children are brought up are not mutually exclusive, but they are a complementary action aimed at ensuring full protection for children who are involved in domestic violence, help and support from various services.

The policy of protecting children against abuse is an internal document established by employees of an educational or nursing institution, containing rules for providing children with safety and conduct in case of risk of child abuse. This policy is prepared in accordance with the applicable law. It gathers in one place the principles of creating a child-safe environment, as well as establishes internal and external intervention procedures that are comprehensible and binding for all staff members, enabling a quick response to threats to the safety of children's well-being and helping meet legal requirements to protect children from harm. Establishing a policy to protect children from abuse is the first standard for the protection of children. This policy regulates these areas of the institution's operation, which involve the possibility of violating children's rights: from security and support to intervention in situations that threaten his or her life, health, and well-being. In particular, the provisions of the Child Protection Policy against Injury include (Prusinowska-Marek, 2010):

- procedures for reporting suspicions and interventions that determine what action should be taken in the event of a child being harmed or a security risk posed by strangers, family members, school or facility personnel, and peers;
- principles of personal data protection of a child, which specify the manner of storing and sharing information about a child and the principles of protecting a child's image, which determine the manner of its recording and sharing;
- principles of children's access to the Internet and protection of children against harmful content on the internet;
- principles of safe relations between the school's or institution's staff and the child, specifying which behaviors are not allowed in contact with the child.

These rules should be adapted to the specifics of a given facility in "out-of-home" care (foster care, extended care, other facility).

It should be remembered that in the response procedure, two stages must be considered—internal and external. The internal stage consists of taking steps inside any facility. It always takes place in situations where:

- the employee suspects that the child is hurt;
- the child revealed the experience of abuse;
- suspected child abuse or abuse by someone from the staff;
- suspicion of child abuse was reported by another mentee in a situation of advantage due to age or dependence. In many cases (which do not involve a legal obligation to notify external bodies), intervention can be positively concluded already at this stage.

The external stage consists in taking legal steps—that is, notifying the competent institutions.

Usually, external intervention results from legal provisions that require representatives of educational institutions to notify relevant institutions (e.g., police or prosecutors). External intervention also results from the ineffectiveness of actions taken inside the facility. The policy of protecting children against abuse should also include provisions that are clear guidelines on how to help a child victim of abuse. Examples of activities in such cases may be contact with a parent or other person who looks after a child (in the case of child abuse in a family—with a parent or guardian) or a child's conversation with a psychologist or pedagogue.

Tasks implemented in the local system of protection of children against violence in the family are mentioned in standards and recommendations. Some are more general, others more specific in character, others are set depending on the level of activity. Tasks at the individual level are based on early identification of the problem in the family, in-depth, interdisciplinary diagnosis of the child and family situation, prevention of the risk of child abuse or restraining, minimization of the consequences of harm suffered, psychosocial rehabilitation of victims, rehabilitation and reintegration of parents who are hurting, prevention of recurrence of the problem, and transgenerational transmission of abuse (Jarosz & Nowak, 2012).

The system's tasks at the social and environmental level are a gradual allocation of activities to general prevention and risk prevention, change of social attitudes and cultural behavior patterns that are harmful to children, raising public awareness of the phenomenon, gaining animators to protect children from harm, and developing positive parenting.

There are also programs supporting parenthood. These include educational programs raising parental competences for families at risk and families with the problem of child abuse already identified.

Delivery through Interdisciplinary Teams and Special Support Centers

The standard of activities in local systems for the protection of children against harm is the interaction of institutions and services in interdisciplinary teams. The phenomenon of child abuse is complex and multidimensional, and its reduction and counteraction requires the involvement of many disciplines and many different professionals.

Cooperation and integration of sector activities is carried out at the level of individual activities, but also at the level of local activities. The implementation of a multi-sectoral approach requires certain conditions. In Poland, the tradition of interdisciplinary teams is not very long and Poland does not have much experience in this area. In the beginning, these were bottom-up and unregulated activities. The Act on Counteracting Domestic Violence of 2005 did not recommend the creation of teams, but only recommended creating communal systems to counteract the phenomenon (Dz.U. z 2005 r. Nr 180, poz. 1493). Teams were also not mentioned in the National Program of Counteracting Domestic Violence adopted in 2006. The Act of June 10, 2010 contains in particular the creation of a communal system for counteracting domestic violence, including the creation of interdisciplinary teams.

The purpose of the new institutions introduced by the Act on Counteracting Domestic Violence is to effectively influence the perpetrator of violence by isolating him or her and responding appropriately to further violent crimes. The Ministry of Justice has no data on the number of judgments about taking the child away from the family, including the number of children who were taken away by the family in connection with family violence and the number of complaints that the parties filed with the courts regarding the collection of children in relation to domestic violence, or about the number of cases of unreasonable withdrawal of a child from a family in connection with domestic violence. It should be emphasized that analysis of the functionality of the measures introduced by the amending Act of 2010 in the area of improving children's safety and protection against violence must be based on properly collected data, which may be the basic parameters of the measurement monitoring the functioning of the Act. The most desirable solution would be to establish standard indicators to monitor the size of the phenomenon and the measures applied. It is worth considering inserting in the statistical forms of judicial decisions data that would distinguish the number of penal and probation measures imposed for violent crimes against children, data on the number of children taken away from the family in connection with domestic violence, data on various forms of assistance provided to children—victims of violence in the family—and data on parents' participation in corrective and educational programs for perpetrators of domestic violence.

Summarizing the analysis of executive acts issued from the perspective of a child victim of domestic violence, it should be recognized that such acts have expanded the services related to counteracting violence, which may significantly improve the protection of the child against abuse. It seems that Poland is currently unable to provide comprehensive information about the circumstances of protective actions for children as victims of domestic violence. This indicates the need for a separate legal act in the future, which would include a more detailed approach to protect children from abuse, and a model from other countries that recognizes the complexity of violence against children and its specificity against the background of the general problem of domestic violence. It is also necessary to disseminate knowledge about child abuse and modern solutions in the area of its reduction among relevant services and decision makers.

Specialized support centers for victims of domestic violence are units whose purpose is to provide adequate assistance to persons harmed by domestic violence, including providing them with a safe haven. These centers provide comprehensive assistance, among others legal, psychological, medical, social, as well as counseling in the above field. There are 35 specialized support centers for victims of domestic violence in Poland (MRPiPS, 2018). Running centers is a task assigned to regional governments, and the financial resources for their maintenance are provided by the state budget.

The centers provide: 1) children shelter, without referral and irrespective of income, for a period of up to three months with the possibility of extending it in cases justified by the situation of that person; 2) protection against a person using domestic violence; 3) immediate psychological and legal assistance and access to medical assistance in the event that the state of health of a person affected by domestic violence requires it; and 4) assessment of the situation and of the risk in terms of the threat to safety. In terms of therapy and support the centers can: 1) diagnose the problem of domestic violence; 2) develop an individual plan to help the victim of domestic violence, including: needs, goals, methods, and time of assistance; 3) provide counseling including medical, psychological, legal, and social; 4) run support groups or therapeutic groups for victims of domestic violence; 5) conduct individual therapy aimed at supporting a victim of domestic violence and acquiring protection skills against a person using domestic violence; 6) provide access to medical help; 7) assess the situation of children on the basis of family-based family intelligence and providing them with support or psychological support as well as specialist sociotherapeutic and therapeutic help; and 8) provide educational consultations. And in terms of assistance with basic living needs, the centers can provide: 1) a 24-hour period of stay for no more than 30 people, with the reservation that this number may be increased depending on the accommodation capacity of the specialist support center for victims of domestic violence and after obtaining the consent of the leading authority; 2) sleeping rooms intended for a maximum of five persons, taking into account the family situation of the victim of domestic violence; 3) a common day-stay room with a children's play area and a place to learn; 4) generally accessible bathrooms, equipped in a way that allows both adults and children to use, respectively, one bathroom for five persons; 5) places for washing and drying; 6) a communal kitchen; and 7) food, clothing, and footwear for personal hygiene and cleaning products (MS, 2011).

The Minister of Justice, after conducting the competition procedure, decides on the award of a subsidy to entrust the implementation of tasks from the Assistance Fund to the Victims and Post-penitentiary Assistance—the Justice Fund in the field of providing assistance to victims of crime and their immediate relatives and providing assistance to witnesses and their loved ones, for entities not included in the public and non-profit sector in order to achieve profit, including associations, foundations, organizations, and institutions.

Victims of crime, including crimes of domestic violence, can receive: 1) legal assistance, including access to alternative methods of conflict resolution; 2) an interpreter's help in order to provide legal aid to an entitled person, if he or she does not speak Polish sufficiently, until the preparatory proceedings are initiated; 3) help of a sign language interpreter or guide translator for legal assistance; 4) access to psychotherapy or psychological help, including assistance by a first contact person; 5) funding to support the costs of health services, medicines to the extent that the drug is not refundable or in the part in which it is not refunded, medical devices, including dressing materials, orthopedic items, and auxiliaries, to the extent necessary in the treatment process to suffer damage to health resulting from the crime or its consequences; 6) funding to support costs related to education in public schools, including individual tuition, as well as in the case of compulsory schooling or the obligation to learn outside of school according to the age and educational needs of the entitled persons; 7) access to training and courses improving professional qualifications and covering the costs of exams confirming professional qualifications; 8) funding for the costs of temporary accommodation or providing shelter; 9) financing periodic subsidies to current rent commitments and payments for heating energy, electricity, gas, water, fuel, collection of solid and liquid waste for a dwelling or a single-family house, to which the right holder holds a legal title, in proportion to the number of permanent residents in this place or house; 10) the service of adaptation of a flat or a single-family home to the needs of a crime victim in the event that the loss of physical fitness occurred as a result of a crime; 11) financing travel by means of public transport or covering transport costs related to obtaining benefits and regulating matters; 12) covering costs of food or food stamps; 13) covering the purchase of clothes, underwear, footwear, cleaning products, and personal hygiene; 14) financing the costs of organized departure of an eligible minor; 15) financing of some travel expenses (MS, 2011).

In Poland, after the period of systemic transformation, various non-governmental organizations have been established and are helping people who are involved in violence. Associations and foundations use various sources of financing for their activities. Although there appear to be a lot of these sources, financial problems are the most serious obstacle to their development or the reason for termination of activities.

Most of the associations and foundations operate in a project. The project is submitted to the financing institution in the form of a grant application (co-financing of the project). In addition to substantive activities, organizations must also finance administrative costs. Unfortunately, these costs are usually very reluctantly funded, especially by public administration, which makes project implementation very difficult. Not all sources are available for all types of organizations, for example, the implementation of projects financed from EU funds requires a lot of knowledge, professional technical background (e.g., good accounting), or own monetary contribution.

References

CBOS. (2012). *O dopuszczalności stosowania kar cielesnych i prawie chroniącym dzieci przed przemocą. Komunikat z badań nr BS/74*. CBOS.

Jarosz, E. (2008). *Ochrona dzieci przed krzywdzeniem. Perspektywa globalna i lokalna*. Wydawnictwo Uniwersytetu Śląskiego.

Jarosz, E. and Nowak, A. (2012). *Dzieci ofiary przemocy w rodzinie*. Biuro Rzecznika Praw Dziecka.

Makaruk, K. (2013). Postawy Polaków wobec kar fizycznych a ich stosowanie w praktyce rodzicielskiej. *Dziecko krzywdzone. Teoria, badania, praktyka*, 12(4), 40–53.

Miedzik, M. (2014). *Diagnoza zjawiska przemocy i możliwości uzyskania pomocy w sytuacji doświadczania przemocy w percepcji dzieci i młodzieży*. Ministerstwo Pracy i Polityki Społecznej.

Miedzik, M. and Godlewska-Szurkowa, J. (2014). *Badania porównawcze oraz diagnoza skali występowania przemocy w rodzinie wśród osób dorosłych i dzieci, z podziałem na poszczególne formy przemocy wraz z opisem charakterystyki ofiar przemocy i sprawców. Raport cząstkowy. Wyniki badań PSDB dla Ministerstwa Pracy i Polityki Społecznej*. Ministerstwo Pracy i Polityki Społecznej.

MRPiPS. (2016). *Polityka rodzinna. Raport*. Ministerstwo Rodziny, Pracy i Polityki Społecznej.

MRPiPS. (2018). *Wykaz Specjalistycznych Ośrodków Wsparcia dla Ofiar Przemocy w Rodzinie*. Ministerstwo Rodziny, Pracy i Polityki Społecznej.

MS. (2011). *Zasady postępowania interwencyjnego w sytuacji występowania przemocy w rodzinie*. Ministerstwo Sprawiedliwości.

MS. (2016). *Przeciwdziałanie przemocy w rodzinie w Polsce. Raport.* Ministerstwo Sprawiedliwości.

Policja. (2012). *Informacja dotycząca realizacji przez jednostki organizacyjne Policji w 2011 roku procedury „Niebieskie Karty" oraz inicjatyw podejmowanych w obszarze przeciwdziałania przemocy w rodzinie.* Biuro Prewencji i Ruchu Drogowego KGP.

Prusinowska-Marek, A. (2010). *Sady i kuratorska służba sadowa. Niebieska linia 4/2010.* Available at: http://www.niebieskalinia.pl. 12.04.2018.

Sajkowska, M. and Włodarczyk, J. (2010). *Wykorzystywanie seksualne wychowanków domów dziecka. Raport z badań.* Fundacja Dzieci Niczyje.

Wfodarczyk, J. and Makaruk, K. (2013). *National survey of child and youth victimization in Poland.* Nobody's Children Foundation. Retrieved June 28, 2022: chrome-extension://efaidnbmnnnibpcajpcglclefindmkaj/http://www.canee.net/files/National_Survey_of_Child_and_Youth_Victimization_in_Poland_2013.pdf.

Włodarczyk, J. (2017). Przemoc wobec dzieci. Raport o zagrożeniach bezpieczeństwa i rozwoju dzieci w Polsce. *Dziecko krzywdzone. Teoria, badania, praktyka*, 16(1), 197–203.

Wójcik, S. (2012). Przemoc fizyczna wobec dzieci. *Dziecko krzywdzone. Teoria, badania, praktyka*, 2(39), 7–27.

Child Protection in Portugal

Jorge Ferreira

Abstract

This chapter looks into child protection in Portugal. The state has been called upon to address the field of childhood through policies and education guided by the principles of equality, opportunity, citizenship, responsibility, participation, multicultural and local intervention. The Portuguese child protection and welfare system fits the Southern European model, which is characterized by mixed social protection, cash transfers, and universal health services, and is based on the role of the social partners in income guarantee policies. The Children and Youth Protection Commission applies measures of keeping the kids in their natural living environment or enforcing placement measures if their conditions are not met.

Key Words: Portugal, child protection, intervention, equality, opportunity, social protection, placements, CPCJ, policies, education

Introduction

Portugal is a small country in the context of the European Union, with a population of 10.5 million residents, of which about 1.5 million are children aged 15 and under, representing 14% of the total population; about 7 million (65%) are in the active population group (15–64 years); and foreign residents in the country represent 4%. Most of the families are Catholic (66%), on average they have 2.6 members and 22% are single-parent families, with a 64% divorce rate associated with this indicator. The birth rate is low at 1.38 per woman of childbearing age, the first child is born at 30 years of age and about 55% of children are born out of wedlock. Life expectancy is 77.8 for men and 83.4 for women and the child mortality rate is 2.7% (https:www.pordata.pt; https://www.dgs.pt).

The state has been increasingly called upon to intervene in the field of childhood through policies for social protection, preventing risks and dangers, and through education and policies for strengthening family life through measures such as support for maternity and reconciling work and family life. These policies are guided by principles of equality of opportunity, citizenship, responsibility, participation, multicultural and local intervention (Portuguese Institute of Social Security, 2007). The state recognizes children and young persons as social actors and develops protective measures designed to foster their individual economic, social, and cultural rights.

The child protection and welfare system in Portugal fits the so-called Southern European model (Esping-Andersen, 1990; Ferreira, 2011), characterized by mixed social protection, that is, the existence of cash transfers although fragmented and the existence of universal health services. It is a model based on the role of the social partners in income guarantee policies and in which taxes mainly support Social and Health Services. About children we have identified examples of applying an intervention model centered on a systemic approach where the principle of collaborative intervention and inter-institutional partnership is privileged, and a model of network intervention, whose guiding principles of intervention are articulation, cooperation, and partnership.

There are currently two intervention models underlying the social protection of children/young people: a social intervention model directly related to the Child and Youth Protection Commissions and local social action services; and a judicial intervention model related to the public ministry, the courts, and the Education Centers of the Directorate General of Social Reinsertion.

Since 1999, the Portuguese state has intervened in the welfare system to protect and educate children in a relationship involving the interaction and cooperation between the social security system and the legal system. The consolidation of norms, "on the one hand, expanding the process of equal opportunities, . . . and, furthermore, reducing social inequalities . . . form the constitutional matrix and the principles for action by the Welfare State" (Mozzicafreddo, 2001, p. 15).

In 2018, according to data provided by the child protection system (Children and Youth Protection Commission [CPCJ] 2018 annual activity assessment report; www.cnp dcj.gov.pt/cpcj), the main situations of child protection are: 1) negligence, at 31.2% (the data also show that negligence (the main situation of diagnosed danger), shows a slight increase between 2017 and 2018); 2) domestic violence, at 22.7%; 3) hazardous behaviors in childhood and youth at 17.5%; and 4) situations that call into question the right to education at 16.1%.

Regarding the situation of domestic violence, in the case of children, we speak essentially of vicarious violence involving 3,789 diagnoses, with a higher incidence in males of 52.7%. Almost all diagnoses of domestic violence (99%) refer to situations of exposure to violent behaviors. However, in 1% of situations children are also victims of physical offense. Diagnoses of physical abuse total 997 situations, including two cases of female genital mutilation and 120 cases of corporal punishment (0.0008 per 1,000) (12% of the total), with a higher incidence in boys (52%). A total of 333 sexual abuse situations were diagnosed, mainly related to females, 81%.

Domestic violence and dangerous behaviors of children or young people increased by 0.5 and 0.7% respectively from 2017–2018, and situations related to education stabilized at 16%. It should be noted that reports of physical abuse represent 5% of the total and those of sexual abuse 2%, representing an increase of 86 and 73 cases, respectively, compared to 2017 (CPCJ 2018 annual activity assessment report (https://www.cnpdpcj. gov.pt).

Social Welfare and Assistance

In the system of child promotion and protection in Portugal we find two types of measure that have as a principle to protect the best interests of the child and constitute as an alternative to the biological family.

The CPCJ, in accordance with the principle of the best interests of the child and the prevalence of the family (Article 4 of the LPCJP), applies measures keeping the child in his or her natural environment, whenever certain conditions are met. Only when this is not possible are placement measures resorted to.

The measures in the natural environment of life include support of parents, support of another family member or trusted person, and support for the autonomy of life. The placement measures are host family and residential placement.

Natural living environment measures have a typical maximum duration of 12 months, although this can be extended up to 18 months. The duration of family and residential placement measures will be set in the promotion and protection agreement or in the court ruling.

The total number of promotion and protection measures implemented and monitored by CPCJ for children aged 0–17 in 2018 was 41,498. Of these, 79.1% (32,825) of children remained at their parents' home and 20.9% (8,673) were away from their parents.

The largest number of measures implemented with children and young, as 56%. This incidence increases in proportion to age, namely the 15–21 age group accounts for 42% of the measures implemented and the 11–14 age group for 23% of the total, that is, 3/4 of the measures are implemented on children over 10 years old. An analysis of the data shows that 9.7% of measures are implemented in the natural environment in which children live, in particular support for parents.

A more detailed analysis shows that:

- Support of parents is consistently the measure most applied by the CPCJ. For the 15–17 age group, there is a greater tendency to apply it;
- The second most widely applied measure is residential placement care and focuses mainly on young people in the 15–17 age group;
- The support measure for other family members is more focused on male youths and the value tends to increase when the age group is higher.

The distribution of child/youth protection measures is as follows:

- support of parents (biological family)—79.1% (32 825);
- residential placement—9.4% (3 901);
- support measure from another family member (extended family)—9.3% (3 859);
- trusted person (possible adoption family)—1.1% (456);
- support for life autonomy—0.8% (332);[1]
- host family (foster families)—0.3% (125).

The support measure with parents is the most applied measure; the second most applied measure is residential care and focuses mainly on young people aged 15–17 years. The support measure with another family member has a higher incidence in males and the value tends to increase when the age group is higher.

The social worker's function under the law of child protection is highly specific: "the external Social Work is due to investigate the antecedents of each minor, study the conditions of their family, professional and social surroundings and stimulate the independent factors that these environments may have to provide for the social reintegration of minors" (Article 120, no. 1). Regarding social intervention in the family, "the families are visited regularly by Social Assistants that shall seek to conserve and strengthen the family bonds, feelings and responsibilities and cooperate in the resolution of their difficulties" (Article 143, no. 2).

Amendments made in 1978 (D.L.314, 27/10) to the Organization of the Guardianship of Minors (OTM) of 1962 established a new formality for determining the means of juridical intervention. The minor's courts were endowed with the purpose of "the judicial protection of minors and the defence of their rights and interests about the application of guardianship measures for protection, assistance and education" (OTM 1978, Article 2). Amendments to the prevailing legislation, the OTM 1978, limited the judicial protection of minors to the field of criminal law.

Where there is a present or imminent danger to the life or serious impairment of the physical or mental integrity of the child or young person, and in the absence of consent of the holders of parental responsibility or de facto custodian, the CPCJ shall take appropriate measures to immediate protection and request the intervention of the court or law enforcement authorities (LPCJP, Article 91).

Juridical Framework for the Child Protection System in Portugal

Portugal was one of the first countries to enact protective measures for children. Three significant landmarks in the Portuguese legal system include: the 1911 "Law of Infant Protection," the 1962 OTM, and the 1978 amendments to the OTM. The social and

---

[1] Support for life autonomy is a measure applied to children aged 12–21.

judicial intervention in the field of minors (civil and educational guardianship) then fell within the political-ideological context characterized by the dictatorship.

The Infant Protection Law of 1911 (coinciding with the setting up of the first court for minors in Portugal) conveys a political context centralized in the Republican Government that held maximum authority for determining the core social policies for the country. The government proceeded according to an ideology based on the good, the moral, and a well-structured society in which there was only space for unanimity (Ferreira, 2011). The second Organization of Guardianship for Minors in 1978 emerged out of a decentralized political context in which there were both legislative and consultative powers (for example: the Government, the Assembly of the Republic, and active social movements implemented at the community level), with the political parties taking on an equally active role in political life as a guarantee of the heterogeneity of ideologies, specifically as regards the well-being of the population. Over the period from 1911 to 1978, other legislation was enacted for the protection of minors, in particular the following.

In 1926, legislators attributed to "the guardians of infants the competences to declare minors in moral danger through to twenty-one years of age . . . the protection measures established by the law, including the restoration of paternal powers or the guardianship functions and the provision of foodstuffs" (D.L.12:74,26/11, Article 30, 1926).

In the 1960s, there appeared a new definition as regards the purposes and goals of courts for minors following the publication of the law of the Organization of Guardianship for Minors (D.L.44 288, 20/4, 1962). According to this law, guardians of minors are responsible for "the judicial protection of minors, within the domain of criminal prevention, through the application of measures for protection, assistance, education and in the field of defense of their rights and interests" (Article 2).

Child protection intervention agents have specific responsibilities. In particular:

- The judge is responsible for preparing and deciding on all cases involving minors (OTM 1962, Article 12);
- Under the current protection law in Portugal, any child 12 years of age and older may be represented in a social service or protection committee or in court by a lawyer;
- "The persons attributed to the Social Assistance service only perform those functions that are expressly charged to them by the judge, in their exercise, they hold the same attributions, rights and duties as Social Assistants or Auxiliaries" (OTM 1986, Article 17).

The professional (social worker) makes an intervention with the child and family, which can be developed either in the institutional context or at the person's home and assuming some characteristics appropriate to the type of "intervention populations," based on a theoretical-methodological framework of knowledge. This includes:

- Screening the situation: this is the first step to providing help/protection to the subject and family;
- Identifying the social and risk indicators: the professional uses a set of indicators that facilitate the reading of the problem and analysis of the needs of the child and/or family, namely: the state of the subject, needs of the subject, behavioral problems of the subject, specific family characteristics and social context, housing, territorial space of residence, and so on;
- Investigation or in-depth study: this has as its principle proving the validity of the problem situation, through fundamental evidence and analysis of the subject's needs;
- Case evaluation: this consists in identifying the possibilities and potentialities that motivated the problem, determining the aspects/factors that represent the weak points of the family, and seeking to identify obstacles to intervention.

In executing their work, social workers resort to the technical-methodological procedures, using a diverse set of instruments/technical tools that support their intervention as scientific and technical practice:

- social information Criminal Procedure Code (Article 1 al.) H);
- social report Criminal Procedure Code, (Article 1 al.) H);
- psychosocial assessment report;
- social expertise.

In the performance of professional activity their work might include:

- Providing social assistance to children, young people, and families in urgent situations (e.g., emergency financing, repatriation, situations of violence and or mistreatment);
- Drawing up a social contract as a means of explanation, clarification, accountability, and reciprocal cooperation, in the construction of social responses to the subject's problem assuming a technical dimension and an administrative dimension, in the negotiation process;
- Providing fundamental social support in promoting the relationship of closeness, inclusion, and social integration, and in promoting the active social citizenship of the person in distress.

Child and Youth Protection: The Reform of the System

The Portuguese legislation on "Mistreatment of Minors" covers all the behaviors or attitudes that inflict:

> Physical mistreatment, treating cruelly, or not providing them with the care or assistance to their health that the duties stemming from their functions require of them, or employing them in dangerous, forbidden or inhuman activities, or overloading them physically or intellectually, with excessive or inappropriate work in a way that offends their health or their intellectual development or exposes them to serious danger (Penal Code, 1984, Article 153.a) and b)).

In 1998, the designated "Reform of the system for implementing penalties and measures" led to the separation of Children and Youths at risk from Children and Youths in breach of the law, integrating the former under the auspices of Social Intervention[2] (the Ministry of Employment and Social Security) and the latter within the scope of Judicial Intervention[3] (by the Ministry of Justice).

The law for the Protection of Children and Youths in Danger (Law 147/99, of September 1, 1999), revoked by Law 142/2015, had the objective of fostering the rights and the protection of children and young persons at risk to guarantee their well-being and integral development. This understands children or young persons as under the age of 18 or a person aged under 21 who requested the continuation of an intervention that began before they turned 18 years of age. According to Law 142/2015, children and youth are in danger whenever: 1) they are abandoned or live under their own supervision; 2) suffer from physical or psychological mistreatment or are victims of sexual abuse; 3) they do not receive the care or attention appropriate to their age and personal situation; 4) are obliged to undertake excessive amounts of labor or inappropriate to their age, dignity, and personal situation, or otherwise prejudicial to their training and development; 5) are subject, whether directly or indirectly, to behaviors that seriously affect their security or their emotional balance; or 6) display behaviors or give themselves over to activities or consumption that seriously affect their health, security, formation, education, or development without their parents, legal representatives, or whoever is their de facto guardian opposing this in a means able to resolve the situation.

Within this legal framework, a governmental administrative structure was founded with the title of the CNPCJR—the National Commission for the Promotion of the Rights and Protection of Children and Youth, established by Decree-Law no. 98/

---

[2] Law 147/99, of September 1, 1999 Law of Protection for Children and Youths, revoked by law 142/2015, of September 8, 2015.

[3] Law 166/99, Education Guardians Law, revoked by the Education Guardianship law no. 4/2015, of January 15.

98—with functions for state planning and intervention and the coordination of the child protection system (CNPCJR, 2013). According to Article 31 of Law no. 142/2015, the National Commission provides for 1) specialist and informed training on promoting the rights and the protection of children and youths at risk; 2) setting out recommendations for the commission's regular functioning and composition; 3) intervening in situations where a child or young person is in danger (LPCJP, Article 21, no. 1); 4) implementing programs, as well as promoting and actively implementing cooperation protocols; and 5) fostering mechanisms for the supervision of local commissions.

Each protection committee is empowered to apply measures in the natural environment of life (parents, extended family, or third persons) and institutional care measures according to the diagnosis of the situation of the child or youth. Within this framework, they intervene through multidisciplinary teams, nurturing interdisciplinary interventions to ensure wide-reaching protection of children/youths.

Measures for the promotion of rights and the protection of children and the young are the exclusive jurisdiction of the Protection Commissions and the courts. Their work takes place within children's natural living environment and includes (Law no. 142/2015, of September 8, Articles 34, 35, and 56): 1) support for parents; 2) support for other family members; 3) welcoming the children in reputable families; 4) support for autonomy in life; 5) analyis and facilitation of the process of child adoption through families already selected by the social security system; 6) civil sponsorship (a family that supports a child in solidarity); 7) family accommodation; and 8) institutional care (shelters and homes). The Protection Committees function in two formats: plenary (extended) mode and restricted mode.

- The plenary/extended format serves as a forum for discussion and reflection on child/youth problematic issues and developing an appropriate response.
- The restricted format operates constantly and serves as the technical staff of the Protection Commission, providing services in the local community whenever children or youth are at risk or in danger. The Commission may review cases and refer to the judicial system, if necessary; it will ensure collaboration with other public and/or private entities; and will decide on the application, supervision and/or revision of Protective Measures.

The Law of Educational Guardianship applies to youth aged 12 to 16, with circumstances that qualify as a crime under the law, and who are susceptible to restraining measures. These include: 1) warnings and cautions; 2) removing the right to drive motorbikes; 3) compensation to the injured party; 4) community service duties; 5) behavioral restrictions and other obligations; 6) attending training programs; 7) educational supervision; and 8) internment in an education center. Interventions are based on the public policies enacted by the General Directorate of Social Reinsertion and Prisoner Services (https://dgrsp.just ica.gov.pt). Interventions target the prevention of criminality and social reinsertion as well as guardianship measures (as above) in addition to the implementation of community sentence penalties (alternatives to prison custody) and preventive imprisonment denominated as "electronic surveillance."

Education centers are used with some frequency in Portugal. In an open regime, the child/youth lives and is educated in the establishment but may be authorized to leave the grounds and spend holidays or weekends with parents or others. In a semi-open regime the child/youth lives and is educated at the center. He or she may be authorized to leave the grounds, but these excursions are normally accompanied by staff. In a closed regime, the child/young person resides in and is educated at the center. Should the court provide authorization, following a proposal from the social reinsertion services, unaccompanied excursions may take place for limited periods.

We may thus conclude that the response to child related problems has evolved with greater autonomy from political or government powers. While in the legal dispositions of 1911 interventions were almost exclusively through state courts and institutions focusing on issues around protection and prevention, the current legal framework maintains the diversification and strengthening of the role of partners in the application of justice to minors. From the 1980s onwards, non-state interventions have expanded with the emergence of a highly diverse range of institutions under the auspices of Private Social Solidarity Institutions.

Focusing on the problems of fostering social well-being among the children and youth of Portugal, we would highlight the role of the Center for Judicial Studies (http:// www.cej.mj.pt/cej/home/home.php) as the institution responsible for training judicial magistrates and the Public Ministry. The center is also involved in child/youth promotion under the "Jurisdictions of Minors and Families," when necessary, regularly promoting multidisciplinary interventions.

Another important facet of this law that directly interrelates with the promotion of the greater interests of children is establishing agreement over the exercising of parental responsibilities (Article 1776-A) and over the amounts of maintenance (Article 2016-A). Within this scope there is intervention by the ECJ—Children and Youth Teams, integrated into the social security social development unit (http://www.seg-social.pt/ iss-ip-instituto-da-seguranca-social-ip), which undertake a process of mediation between spouses in conflict, seeking to establish agreements between the parties. In conclusion, we may affirm that fostering the rights and protection of children and young persons at risk/ in danger is the responsibility of the entities with skills in the field of children and youth, the Commissions of Children and Youths at Risk, and ultimately the minors and family courts.

In summary, we may depict the child protection system in Portugal as in Figure 25.1.

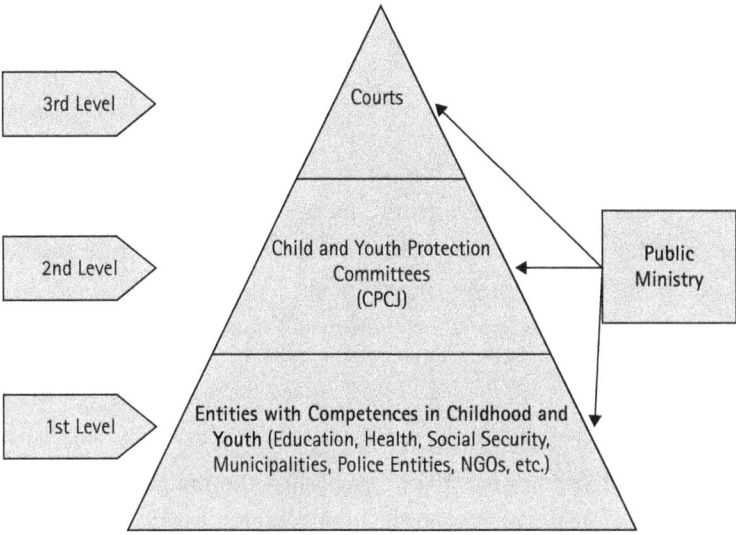

Figure 25.1 Pyramid of the child protection system in Portugal *Source*: Ferreira (2011).

Differentiation criteria between the three levels of intervention

3rd Level (Public Ministry, Family & Minors Courts)	- Intervention in specific situations; - Application of Guardianship measures and Protection measures; - Validation or not of the 2nd line intervention.
2nd Level (CPCYP)	- Collaborative approach with first line services; - Diagnostic deepening; - Integrated intervention plan; - Application of protective measures - Integrated social prevention plan
1st level (Services with competence in the field of childhood)	- Identification of cases; - Diagnosis - Integrated primary intervention plan (child, family, community)

In this pyramidal system we identified some communication and articulation difficulties:

- understanding of literacy in the protection system;
- communication flows (+ top-down/- bottom-up);
- ethical dilemmas in the intervention of the first and second lines.

Evolution of the System of Child Protection in Portugal

In the system for the protection of children, defending their rights and applying measures for their protection, assistance, and education, different systems interact across Portugal including health, social security, employment, income, education, and community services.

1911 to 1919

In 1911, courts for minors were established in Lisbon, Oporto, and Coimbra, with the supreme function as the guardian organs in the application of measures for the protection, defense, and promotion of the rights of children (Infancy Protection Law, 1911, Article 1). This also involved the setting up of child support institutions, in particular Infancy Guardianship, the National Federation of Friends, and Defenders of Children (Article 2).

1919 to 1962

In 1919, Decree-Law 5611 (10/5/1919) established the first central service, founded under the Ministry of Justice as the coordination organism for the activities of guardianship of minors and then entitled—the General Inspectorate of Child Protection. This service was subsequently converted into an Administration and the General Inspectorate of Jurisdictional Services and Guardianship of Minors (D.L. 10767 1923). Through Decree-Law 15:162 5/3: 1928, the Directorate of Jurisdictional Services and Guardianship of Minors expressed the need to stimulate and promote collaboration among the private entities and institutions with the courts. This raised interest in social action on behalf of youth and children, although the state was yet to organize and deploy the necessary means of action.

1980 to 1998

The Judiciary statute of 1944 (D.L. 33547, 24/2) altered the designation of guardianship to the court of minors. Law 82 of 1977 specified the separation between courts for minors and courts for families. The family courts took on actions relating to the separation of persons, assets, divorce, and allocating guardianship (Law 38, 1978, Article 60–61).

The Ministry of Solidarity and Social Security targets the less advantaged including the homeless, the poor, and children. This required setting up support structures such as homes for children and youth at risk or deprived of their normal family environment, creche and infant facilities (schools for different social strata and age groups of children), and local social action services with the objective of providing social and economic support to members of the population with the greatest difficulties. The Ministry studied the situations of minors at risk and defined prevention strategies. It also developed alternative responses such as infant nurses, host families, and temporary accommodation centers to host children, orphans, and those abandoned, maltreated, neglected, or in moral danger, in conjunction with the jurisdiction of the Courts of Minors and Families. Other important organizations and actors include:

- health centers, which, through family doctors, have taken on a fundamental function in identifying and preventing situations of risk/maltreatment;
- child psychiatric centers, which deal with and accompany children with disabilities or with irregular patterns of development.

Another structure that constituted a fundamental pillar of local social action in the city of Lisbon is the Santa Casa de Misericórdia de Lisboa. This institution runs teams of Social Assistants with the objective of providing support and assistance to groups most in need.

The Particular Institutions of Social Solidarity set up by the Ministry of Social Affairs (State Secretary for Social Security) are institutions that propose the resolution of social problems for which state interventions are insufficient (D. L. 119 1983, 25/2). These institutions have become a major partner of the state in its response to social problems. Within this institutional framework there are creches; pre-schools; homes under interned and semi-interned regimes; free time activity centers; host centers for children abandoned or removed from parents due to serious illness (AIDS) or abnormal behaviors (e.g. drug addiction, prisoners, etc.); centers of early intervention; homes for single mothers, prostitutes, or children abandoned or maltreated by the parents or by the husband; centers for children deprived of normal family environments; and the Casa Pia home and training centers of Lisbon providing multiple services for protection, welcoming, and education.

In 1992, the Council of Ministers resolution no. 30/92 created the inter-ministerial PAFAC—the Project for Support to the Family and to Children—with representatives from the ministries of justice, health, employment, and social security, and Santa Casa da Misericórdia de Lisboa, with the purpose of providing services targeting maltreated children through psycho-social family intervention teams, which function in conjunction with the hospital network.

- Child abuse emergency line and the mobile crisis intervention team, which act in situations of child emergency in response to urgent appeals received via the telephone hotline from children, parents, teachers, neighbors, friends, and the community in general.

In 1986, the Portuguese Association for the Rights of Minors and the Family was founded with a national scope and objectives of undertaking interdisciplinary studies on issues regarding the judicial and administrative protection of minors and the family as well as fostering, organizing, and dynamically running community support services for children, youth, and the family.

In 1995, new alterations were introduced into the Portuguese juridical system within the scope of the organic law structuring the Institute of Social Reinsertion D.L.58: 1995. Under the auspices of the Social Interventions of Justice, the Social Institute of Reinsertion integrated all the activities carried out by the General Directorate of Guardian Services to Minors. The Institute set up CAEF—the Colleges of Accommodation, Education and Training—with skills for ensuring the accommodation, education, and training framework for minors who are completing judicial measures in institutions.

1999 to 2015

This period is marked by both reform of the Law for Minors in Portugal, and the enactment of the Law of Protection for Children and Youths (Law no. 147/99, of September 1) and the Guardianship Education Law (Law no. 166/99, of September 14), bringing about certain reforms to the response structures for children and youth and handing down new and more appropriate ethical-political orientations for the social protection system.

Law no. 147/99 implements the Protection Commissions for Children and Youths in a renewed fashion and configured into a model of participation and social responsibility, in both a wide-reaching approach (with the greater involvement of civil society) and with a restricted (more technical) focus with the objectives of deepening the participative and interdisciplinary diagnosis of the problems facing children and youth. This new legal framework also acknowledged parents as a factor in the effectiveness of any intervention with children, recognizing their obligations and social responsibilities (Article 9) and the consent of the child/youth aged 12 or over (Article 10), apart from situations deemed urgent (Article 91). The law of protection also provides a legal government representative for children and young persons aged 12 or over. This new legislative landmark reflects a philosophy centered on the family, lower levels of child institutionalization, and greater responsibility of the family in the promotion of the well-being of children/youths. This philosophy was further deepened by the legislative framework currently in effect for the child protection system (Law of protection no. 142/2015, and the Guardian Education Law no. 4/2015) with the alignment of the means of an institutional response.[4]

Partnerships were also designed and launched with universities and centers of study of preventive based programs, highlighting the Safe School Program (Dispatch no. 25 650/2006) and the Choices Program (Resolution of the Council of Ministers no. 80/2006).

Social Policies for the Protection of Children and Families in Portugal

Social policies fall within the scope of the public policy context, understood as "a set of mutually interrelated actions, taken by an actor or a set of political actors as regards the choice of objectives and the means to achieve them within the context of a specific situation, due to these decisions, in principle, located within the range of the powers these actors have to achieve them" (Jenkins, 1978, quoted in Pereirinha, 2008, p. 17). The public policies are defined in legal norms that express their goals in accordance with their

---

[4] These include: center of family support and parental counseling, street team for child and youth support, host families for children and young persons, temporary accommodation centers, apartment of autonomy, early intervention units, social sponsorship, and care homes.

area of action (Ferreira, 2017). Social policy distinguishes itself from other areas of public policy intervention by the fact that the former targets goals around the fostering of well-being in society, meaning that this is about meeting social needs that seek to improve social justice in society. "This means understanding the concept of need as a social construction, relative to society" (Pereirinha, 2008, p. 20).

In the social protection system for children and the family, we encounter direct responses and indirect responses that, as Pereirinha (2008) defines, are "actions targeted directly at a social problem, whether a general situation of society (unemployment, financial sustainability of social security, the existence of regions in economic depression, and poverty), or that characterize a social group (problems of persons caring for the elderly, problems of failure and school dropout in youths attending secondary schooling)" (p. 94). The indirect responses, thus, are those that are not directly targeted at the problem in itself but that are to indirectly impact on it. These include how "economic growth acts favorably on employment and the earnings of households and family and so fostering growth may resolve problems with unemployment and poverty, without having the need to target actions on the unemployed or the poor population" (Ferreira, 2016).

Within the scope of child protection, the social security sub-system acts in conjunction with the citizen in promoting well-being through family-based payments, with the objective of compensating for the costs incurred with the family. These payments may be made to national and international citizens, refugees, and stateless persons, resident in the national territory in accordance with the requirements defined by law. The type of family payments made by the state include family subsidy for children and young persons,[5] a monthly payment made to the parents or guardians of children with the objective of offsetting some of the costs of maintaining and educating children and young persons. Family subsidies are paid through to the age of 16 and continue until 18 whenever the child/youth is attending secondary school or equivalent and 24 years of age when attending higher education. These subsidies are part of the social action policy known as Family Allowances for families with social needs or in situations of poverty, and the child is more an indicator of formal requirement in the granting of support than is often the direct beneficiary.

For the purposes of awarding this payment, Portuguese legislation considers the concepts of Aggregate Family and Family Economy. The Aggregate Family includes, in addition to the child or youth, all members who live in the household to include parents and similar, directly and collaterally through to the second level; adopters and adopted; guardians and their charges; children and youth entrusted into care by a judicial or administrative decision; and spouse of the youth or person in de facto unions for longer than two years.

---

[5] Law no. 53-B/2006 and Decree no. 106/2007; D-L. No. 176/2003, of August 2; D-L. No. 41/2006, of February 21; Decree no. 458/2006, of May 18.

For the purposes of awarding this subsidy payment, children and youths are considered eligible in isolation when in situations of internment in public or private non-profit establishments, as well as residents in care homes, guardian education, or detention centers.

We now have some child protection measures that form part of the formal and public child protection system in Portugal:

- The protection regime[6] of benefits for disability consists of an additional payment to the family subsidy in the case of children and youth aged under 24 and registered as disabled (currently, as special needs), and who are attending or are interned at a specialist rehabilitation establishment or are in conditions to attend or require residential care and that need specialist individual support either of a pedagogical or therapeutic nature.

- Subsidy to attend a special education establishment, attributed to children and youth, registered as disabled, aged under 24 and in attendance at a specialist teaching establishment, receiving individual educational support by this specialized entity, needing to attend a private establishment for regular education following attendance in specialist teaching, or attending creche or pre-school, as a specific means of social integration.

- Third person[7] career subsidy, attributed to children and young persons in receipt of the Family Subsidy, with additional payments due to disability, depending on and effectively receiving assistance from a third person to ensure their basic needs.

- Lifetime monthly subsidy,[8] given to descendants of beneficiaries aged over 24, registered as disabled on physical, organic, sensorial, motor, or mental grounds, which renders impossible their ensuring their own subsistence through exercising a professional activity.

- Additional extraordinary solidarity payments[9] are a pecuniary amount paid monthly in addition to the amount of the lifetime monthly subsidy.

- Orphan's pension,[10] attributed to children and youths through to attaining adulthood or independence, who are orphans of persons not covered by any social protection regime and that meet the requirements set down in the law.

---

[6] D-L. No. 133-C/97, of May 30.
[7] Law no. 4/2007, of 16 January (base social security law).
[8] Law no. 2/2008, of 7 January.
[9] D-L. no. 208/2001 of 27 July.
[10] Regulatory Decree no. 71/80, of November 12.

Indirect Child Protection Measures

In Portugal, the RSI measure (Income support) is part of a social protection policy called Public and Social Policy for the family and the child, against poverty and social exclusion. In terms of child protection, it is of relevance because it aims to prevent social deprivation within the family and promote the integration of children into school, access to the National Health Service and the overcoming of balanced dietary needs.

The Income Support social policy[11] is important, given its scope covering families with children and the role it plays in the improvement of their well-being. The RSI consists of a payment integrated into the solidarity subsystem under the auspices of the public social security system and in an insertion program that provides support adapted to individual and family situations, contributing to meeting their essential needs and their social and community integration. These insertion programs consist of a set of actions of social integration for direct beneficiaries and members of their household (Law no. 13/2003, Article 3). These actions might include employment, professional training, attending education, participation in occupation programs or others of a temporary character that favor the subsequent integration into the employment market, actions of a vocational type, professional rehabilitation initiatives, prevention action, drug treatment and rehabilitation programs, the development of activities ongoing under the auspices of the particular social solidarity institutions, utilization of social support equipment, and domestic support and incentives for the launching of activities whether as self-employed or through the creation of employment (Law no. 13/2003, Article 18).

In Portugal, the child protection system, is part of a large group of public policies that directly and indirectly promote the protection and well-being of the child/youth. They are part of a transversal model of public policies, of which we highlight:

- Support measures for reconciling family life and working life, especially domestic support services;
- Strengthening RSI insertion payments considered as the minimum income guaranteed by the state to each person;
- Facilitating the access of families to new technologies as a means of educating the family for a knowledge-based society and also as a form of child internet protection and prevention;
- Developing family mediation services[12] and parental training programs as a means of supporting households facing situations of crisis;

---

[11] Law no. 13/2003 of May 21.
[12] Dispatch no. 5524/2005, of the Ministry of Justice.

- Support for families experiencing domestic violence as well as vulnerable families at risk of social exclusion, especially single parent families;
- Promoting the social participation of families in NGOs and social solidarity institutions to build on household access to the social support rendered by the state;
- Social support and fiscal benefits to large families.

In the field of health, Portugal provides some benefits that are indirectly supportive of children. For example, the sickness subsidy consists of a pecuniary payment awarded to compensate for the loss of earnings resulting from a temporary incapacity to work due to illness.

Compensation subsidy payments for holidays[13] and Christmas are made when the beneficiaries, due to disease (and receiving subsidies), do not have the right and have not been paid the holiday and Christmas subsidies by their respective employer in accordance with that established in the collective working regulations based upon the right to work.

Social Responses

What other countries might describe as "foster care," Portugal describes as family hosting, defined as "attributing the trust of a child or youth to a single person or a family, qualified for such purpose, seeking their integration into the household environment and the provision of the care appropriate to their needs and well-being and the education necessary to their integral development" (Law no. 142/15). Family hosting is a temporary measure of protection for the child, which is achieved through the placement of the child or young person with a family, with a view to integrating into the family environment, as well as the provision of personal and educational care appropriate to the child's needs. The purpose of the host families is to provide the child or young person with a socio-family environment suitable for the development of his or her personality in place of the natural family (https://www.seg-social.pt/familia).

Services put into practice through the support and social assistance programs/projects essentially consist of undertaking activities targeting groups or communities with the objective of preventing and/or responding to specific problems, as well as research-action initiatives. These programs/projects may take on a local, regional, or national scope and are designed to respond to and improve the quality of life of children and families. In other words, they are programs that articulate a professional intervention profile based on the action research method. In some cases these programs become social policy initiatives at the central government level.

---

[13] Decree-Law no. 28/2004 of February 4, rewritten by Decree-Law no. 146/2005, of August 26.

In the Portuguese protection system, we may identify prevention programs especially in terms of behaviors incurring risk and the transmission of contagious diseases, programs of personal, social, and parenting skills, and research-action programs with the objectives of studying, analyzing, and reviewing intervention methodologies.

One of the measures that best portrays this social policy approach at the local level, and with clear reflections on the social intervention models and methodologies, is that called the Social Network. This initiative strives to bring together efforts at the local level to provide a diagnosis and a solution to social problems, with an emphasis on poverty and social exclusion. The approaches use a logic of proximity and hence "at the level of congregating efforts" should take place at "a level as proximate as is feasible to the location registering the social problems, beginning with the parish, and whenever there exists the means for possible solutions" (Introductory Preamble to the Resolution of the Council of Ministers no. 197/97).

In 2018, the XXII Constitutional Government of Portugal (council of ministers of March 8, 2018) implemented a new social protection program called 3 Online, a program for the reconciliation of professional, personal, and family life. This program proposes a cultural change in thinking about public policies in an integrated and cross-sectoral rather than sectoral way, in line with the EU's open coordination model strategy, which calls on society to make a collective commitment to impact measures in the short, medium and long term. There are 33 measures aimed at promoting a better balance between work, personal, and family life (exclusive of initial parental leave of the father from 15 to 20 days, the exemption of three hours for civil servants to accompany their children (up to 12 years) in the first school hours or the exemption of annual hours so that workers can deal with personal and/or family matters), recognized as essential tools to promote the reduction of absenteeism and also contributing to demographic sustainability.

The program aims to promote a better balance between professional, personal, and family life, as a condition for effective equality between men and women and for full citizenship and free choice. The importance of this balance is recognized in the European Pillar of Social Rights as one of the just conditions of work, referred to as Program 3.

Program 3 Online is structured along four axes:

- Axis 1: (Im)Pact for Conciliation—adds measures that mobilize different types of employers for the development of practices promoting proactive family policies and their embodiment;
- Axis 2: Harmonization in Public Administration—adds measures that represent the commitment of the central and Local Public Administration with the promotion of proactive family policies;

- Axis 3: Equipment and services sector—should encourage to promote pro-active family policies, in particular in the fields of care, education, transport and health;
- Axis 4; Knowing to Reconcile—adds measures that lead to the production of knowledge and its dissemination, which can support the development of new actions.

The program promotes cross-sectoral and sectoral measures, pilot projects, and public and social policy measures targeting diverse target groups, including public, social, and private organizations; women and men at different stages of their life cycle (children, young people, adults/older people); and families in their diversity of models.

Conclusion

Today, social problems are not isolated, but they assume a systemic and multidimensional configuration. In this context, we must consider the constructivist paradigm (Parton, 2009), centered on the skills and capacities of the citizen, guided by a logic of action in partnership, and using network interventions. Social citizenship (recognition of all citizens as subjects of rights and essentially of their Human Dignity) and human rights should be central to a policy and program approach (Ferreira et al., 2016).

Child protection should integrate the legal model with the community model. Therefore, child protection should include the development of a community intervention focused on the development of skills in the family; promotion of specific local proximity networks; prevention; evaluation; training and intervention; and the application of the cartographic method in the definition of specific territories of high, medium, and low priority. Other challenges include the professional service and the related organizational culture and politics, namely the ecological sustainability frameworks of protection and well-being for children and family, for example, the eco-social model in vulnerable communities (Ferreira & Rocha, 2016).

The professional must know how to respect and use in its intervention the principles of individuality, freedom, and self-determination of each citizen, the respect for privacy (confidentiality) and private life of the subject and its autonomy, recognizing their skills and capacities, and its interdependence facing rights and duties that are recognized for every citizen in the society.

The conception of the family in an integral bio-psycho-social dimension requires an approach that takes into account the family's social relations, and its belonging to the community. Interventions should be centered on the relationship between personality, means, resources, social relations, and groups (Ferreira, 2011, 2016a).

We conclude that the Portuguese model of child and youth protection is:

- a well-established system with an evolutionary history in terms of the transverse welfare policies and the diversity of the target group;
- a system that, while still very child-centered, is beginning to integrate other important actors as a focus of its own resources (host families, support families, etc.);
- a system that is well structured and defined, with several legally implicated actors (education, police, social security, environment, security, justice, etc.).

While on the one hand it can be seen as synonymous with a hierarchical and rigid system, it can also be seen as ripe for a reconfiguration of the protection system, renewal of professional practices with the interaction of collaborative working methodologies, networking, integration of community resources, inter-professionality, and ready to embrace professional literacy in the area of child protection as a true expression of recognition of their citizenship.

References

CNPDPCJ. (2018). Relatório Anual de Avaliação da Atividade das CPCJ 2018. ISSN: 2184-559X. Comissão Nacional de Promoção dos Direitos e Proteção das Crianças e Jovens (CNPDPCJ). Lisboa/Portugal.

Convenção dos Direitos da Criança. ed. Instituto de Apoio à Criança. Lisboa. 1990.

Convenção sobre os Direitos da Criança. Organização das Nações Unidas. (1989). Aprovação para ratificação da alteração do nº 2 do artigo 43º da Convenção sobre os Direitos da Criança. Resolução da Assembleia da República nº 12/98, de 22/1/1998, in DR nº 66, de 19/03/1998.

Convenção Relativa à Proteção das Crianças e à Cooperação em Matéria de Adoção Internacional (Decreto do Presidente, nº 6/2003. Resolução da Assembleia da República nº 8/2003, de 25/2.

Decreto-Lei nº 164/99, de 13 de Maio. 1999.

Despacho n.º 12 388197—2ª Série. D.R. de 9/12/1997.

Esping-Andersen, G. (1990). *The three worlds of welfare capitalism*. Polity Press.

Ferreira, J. M. L. (2011). *Serviço Social e Modelos de Bem-Estar para a Infância: Modus Operandi do Assistente Social na Promoção da Protecção à Criança e à Família*. Quid Juris.

Ferreira, J. M. L. (2016). Un análise crítico de la investigación cuantitativa y cualitativa en el trabajo social en la promoción del conocimiento de la ciudadania de la infancia. In A. Picornielli-Lucas and E. Pastor Soller (Eds.), *Politicas de inclusión social de la infancia y la adolescencia: Una perspetiva internacional* (pp. 259–270). Grupo 5.

Ferreira, J. M. L. (2017). As políticas de família na contemporaneidade: a dimensão eco-social na intervenção territorializada. In M. Conserva (Ed.), *Multiterritorialidades e os desafios da proteção social no Brasil e na Europa* (pp. 228–255). Editora do CCTA. Universidade Federal de Paraíba.

Ferreira, J. M. L. and Pérez, P. A. (2017). Pobreza y exclusión: reinterpretación desde el trabajo social para un sistema de bienestar sostenible. In E. P. Seller (Ed.), *Sistemas y políticos de bienestar: Una perspectiva internacional* (pp. 197–211). Editora Dykinson.

Ferreira, J. M. L. and Rocha, H. B. (2016). Social policies and social work: A commitment for social welfare. In A. L. Peláez and S. S. Sánchez-Cabezudo (Eds.), *Politicas Sociales*. Thomson Reuters Aranzadi.

Ferreira, J. M. L., Rocha, H. B., Ferreira, P., and Perez, P. A. (2016). Derechos Humanos y Justicia Social en la formacion en trabajo social. In E. P. Seller and E. R. Diez (Eds.), *Trabajo social, derechos humanos e innovación social* (pp. 287–300). Thomas Reuters Aranzadi.

Friedmann, M. (1984). *Capitalismo e Liberdade*. Abril Cultural.

Law no. 61/2008, Altera o regime jurídico do divórcio de 31 de Outubro. 2008.

Law no. 75/98. D.R. nº 268/98 Série I-A, de 19 de Novembro de 1998.

Law no. 142/2015, de 8 de Setembro.

Law no. 147/99 (1 de Setembro). *Lei de proteção de Crianças e Jovens em Perigo*. 1999.

Law no. 166/99 (14 de Setembro). *Lei Tutelar Educativa*. 1999.

Lei Tutelar Educativa n.º4/2015, de 15 de Janeiro.

Martins, I. C. (2018). *Modelos de proteção social em sociedades com programas de austeridade* [Unpublished doctoral dissertation]. Instituto Universitário de Lisboa.

Mendes, H. (2015). A condução da política orçamental durante o programa de ajustamento. In M. L. Rodrigues and P. A. e Silva (Eds.), *Governar com a Troika: Políticas Públicas em Tempo de Austeridade* (pp. 57–118). Almedina.

Menezes, M. (2017). *Práticas do serviço social com crianças num contexto de políticas neoliberais* [Unpublished doctoral dissertation]. Instituto Universitário de Lisboa.

Moreira, C. (2007). *Teorias e Praticas de investigação*. Instituto Superior Ciências Sociais e Políticas.

Mozzicaffredo, J. (2001). *Estado Providência e Cidadania em Portugal*. Celta.

Offe, C. (1984). *Problemas estruturais do Estado capitalista*. Tempo Brasileiro.

Parton, N. (2009). Challenges to practice and knowledge in child welfare social work: From the "social" to the "I, formational"? *Children and Youth Services Review*, 31(7), 715–721.

Pereirinha, J. A. (2008). *Política social: Fundamentos da actuação das políticas públicas*. Universidade Aberta.

Programa 3 em linha: Programa de conciliação da vida profissional, pessoal e familiar, (conselho de ministros de 8 de Março de 2018). (https://www.portugal.gov.pt/pt/gc21/comunicacao/documento?i=3-em-linha-programa-para-a-conciliacao-da-vida-profissional-pessoal-e-familiar-2018-2019-).

Regime Jurídico da Adopção. Alteração do Código Civil e Organização Tutelar de Menores em 1998— Decreto-lei 120/98, de 8/5.

Regime Jurídico do acolhimento familiar. Decreto-lei nº 190/92, de 3/9.

Resolução 451113 da Assembleia Geral das Nações Unidas. Directriz das Nações Unidas para a Prevenção da delinquência Juvenil (Diretrizes de Riade). 1990.

Resolução da Assembleia da República n.º 21/91 Aprova, para ratificação, a Carta Social Europeia. 1991.

Rodrigues, F. (1999). *Assistência social e políticas sociais em Portugal*. Instituto Superior de Serviço Social.

Torres, A. et al. (2008). *Estudo de diagnóstico e avaliação das comissões de protecção de crianças e jovens*. ISCTE-IUL.

UNICEF. (2014). *As Crianças e a Crise em Portugal: Vozes de Crianças*. Comité Português UNICEF. http://www.unicef.pt.

The Child Protection System in the Slovak Republic

Lenka Kvašňáková *and* Beáta Balogová

Abstract

This chapter explores the child protection system in the Slovak Republic. Following the split with Czech, Slovakia's documents on the protection of children's rights are based on the EU's European Charter of Fundamental Rights and the UNCRC's optional protocols. Additionally, Slovak children are a target of socio-legal protection which protects the rights and legitimate interests of minors. Intervention is required in line with the failure of the natural family environment to preserve the children's rights and needs. The chapter expounds on the legislative changes that sparked the process of transformation and deinstitutionalization of substitute care. The legislation is based on the principles or preferences like a natural family environment or substitute care.

Key Words: Slovakia, EU, UNCRC, substitute care, legislation, deinstitutionalization, child protection system

Introduction

An independent Slovak Republic was established on January 1, 1993 by splitting the Czech and Slovak Federal Republic. Many changes were made in Slovakia during the 1990s, which were subsequently gradually reflected in new legislative arrangements.

Slovakia, as one of the member states of the European Union (since May 2004), respects the legislative standards adopted on its soil. The EU explicitly recognized children's rights in the European Charter of Fundamental Rights (2000). The United Nations Convention on the Rights of the Child (1989) and the respective optional protocols became binding for the Slovak Republic in 1993. As a basic reference for international documents aimed at protecting children, it also serves as the basis for all incoming documents related to the protection of children's rights in Slovakia.

Fundamental legislation relating to children's protection in the Slovak Republic includes, among others:

- The Constitution of the Slovak Republic warrants children and the juvenile with exclusive protection;

- The principle of the child's best possible interest (similar to other European countries), or taking into consideration the interest of a child is reflected in the Family Act No. 36/2005 Coll.;
- The Social-legal Protection of Children and Social Guardianship Act No. 305/2005 Coll. (Zákon č. 305/2005 Z. z. o sociálnoprávnej ochrane detí a sociálnej kuratele a o zmene a doplnení niektorých zákonov, 2005; SLPC&SG Act) regulates the social protection of children and social care to prevent the emergence of crisis situations in the family, the protection of children rights, prevention of the deepening and recurrence of mental development disorders, physical development and social development of children and adults, and the prevention of sociopathological phenomena;
- Social Work Act No. 219/2014 Coll. (Zákon č. 219/2014 Z. z. o sociálne práci a o podmienkach na výkon niektorých odborných činností v oblasti sociálnych vecí a rodiny a o zmene a doplnení niektorých zákonov, 2014), which regulates social work, the conditions for the performance of social work and the establishment, the status and scope of the Slovak Chamber of Social Workers and Assistants of Social Work, and the conditions for carrying out some professional activities in the field of social affairs and family;
- Foster Care and Foster Benefits Act No. 265/1998 Coll., which regulates conditions for the provision of foster care;
- Act No. 176/2015 Coll. On the Commissioner for Children and the Commissioner for Persons with Disabilities, the Commissioner for Persons with Disabilities;
- the Code of Civil Court Procedures and the Civil Code and criminal orders.•

Children are a target of sociolegal protection in the Slovak Republic. The system aims to protect the rights and legitimate interests of minors who, due to the failure of the natural family environment, require intervention in order to preserve their rights and needs. Through children's sociolegal protection, the state provides the prevention of crisis situations in the family, protection of rights and legitimate interests of children, and the prevention and recurrence of disorders of the mental, physical, and social development of children to prevent the rise of sociopathological phenomena.

Sociolegal protection of children, according to the SLPC&SG Act, is a set of measures to ensure protection of the child, which is necessary for his or her well-being and respecting his or her best interests under the International Convention on the Rights of the Child, together with the education and universal development of the child in his or her natural and family environment; and also providing a substitute environment for a child that cannot be raised in his or her own family. These are fundamental principles in child protection in Slovakia.

Legal and Policy Changes: Process of Transformation and Deinstitutionalization of Substitute Care

Significant legislative change in 2005 allowed the improvement of social work in the field of child protection mainly through new legislative measures such as SLPC&SG Act and the Family Act. Based on the SLPC&SG Act, the prevention of family crises is achieved by organizing or mediating participation in programs, trainings, and activities to promote the fulfillment of parental rights and duties; fulfillment of family functions; the formation and consolidation of relations between spouses and between parents and children; and development of the capacity to solve problematic situations and adapt to new situations. The Act also supports programs and activities aimed at the prevention of sociopathological phenomena and the procurement of cultural, leisure, and other activities to promote the appropriate use of children's free time.

The basic legal status of the child is derived from constitutional law—the right conferred by the protection of the marriage, parenthood, and family, as well as the specific protection of children and adolescents. The National Action Plan for Children for 2013–2017 is the basic instrument for a targeted and coordinated approach to fulfill the obligations arising from the Convention on the national level. The coordinator of the tasks contained in the Action Plan is the Secretariat of the Committee for Children and Youth (part of the Government Council for Human Rights, National Minorities, and Gender Equality).

The strategic aim of the action plan is to contribute to building a coherent and effective system for the protection of the rights and interests of children and to ensure progress in the implementation and protection of the rights and interests of children. In line with this objective, the partial strategic objectives in the area of support and protection of children's rights focus on strengthening and consolidating the status of the child as a bearer of rights and of a human being with his or her own dignity and evolving capacities and opinions. They also focus on supporting and developing family competencies as a natural environment for the growth and well-being of the child and promoting positive parenthood. On the third side is the important coordination of policies related to children at all levels—in horizontal and vertical planes (promoting interdisciplinary collaboration and increasing the professional training and professionalism of specialists working with children), accordingly raising the level of awareness and information about all areas of the Convention between children and the public.

In the European regional context, the Council of Europe fulfills the role as a catalyst for the implementation of the Convention on the Rights of the Child, primarily through the Building a Europe for and with Children program. The program was launched in Monaco in 2006. The latest strategy document related to the protection of children against violence is the National Strategy for the Protection of Children against Violence (adopted in 2014), which is based on the identification of weaknesses and risks in child protection policy against violence. In the Slovak Republic, several organizations and individuals are involved in the protection of children's rights, including the Slovak National Center for Human Rights, The National Coordination Center for Resolving the Issues of Violence against Children, Ombudsman for children, and the Commissioner for Children. Various governmental and non-governmental organizations are involved as well. After long persuasion by interested parties, the Government of the Slovak Republic realized that visible results can only be achieved with prepared individuals and institutions and a well-constructed system. In 2015, the national strategy for the protection and promotion of human rights in the Slovak Republic was approved. One outcome of the proposal was the *Coordination of Child Protection against Violence* guidebook, which briefly introduces the model of coordination across sectors to protect children against violence.

The ongoing processes of transformation and deinstitutionalization of care also resulted in the development and implementation of important documents such as: *Planning of social work in the implementation of measures for the sociolegal protection of children and social guardianship* ((Central Office of Labor, Social Affairs and Family, 2012) and the *Innovative model of family preservation management* (Litavská et al., 2013). Previous legislation did not follow a best interest standard or focus on the protection and promotion of children's well-being (Brenner, 2004, in Bernhauserová, 2007). At the same time, however, the implementation document was limited in scope and was re-drafted in 2015. The current approach corresponds to the family services model described by Gilbert and colleagues (2011).

Application of SLPC&SG measures in Slovakia is financed from the state budget and from national projects funded by the EU. These include the national project called Development Support of Social Work in the Client's Family Environment in Social Work and Family Area (2015–2020). The national project's aim is to provide for the Social Affairs and Family Department, specifically the Department of Material Need, State Social Support Benefits departments, and Severe Disabilities departments. The national project Support of Deinstitualization of Substitute Family Care (2007–2013) is focused on the deinstitutionalization process primarily through workforce development. Monitored indicators are the number of new SLPC&SG cases during the year, the overall number of cases during the year, and the number of cases at the end of a monitored year.

Child Maltreatment: Current Situation

Slovak social policy has elements of the welfare state reflected in current and past legislative standards. The latest success is the adoption of the Social Work Act no. 219/2014 Coll., which may have contributed to a modest decline in the number of new families and children in need of social protection or social guardianship in 2016. Data come from a national database that tracks children and the services they receive say that there was a modest decline in the incidence of maltreatment cases, but more recent years have shown an increase. This is related to the ability to detect and help these children. More detailed data are shown in Figure 26.1 and Table 26.1.

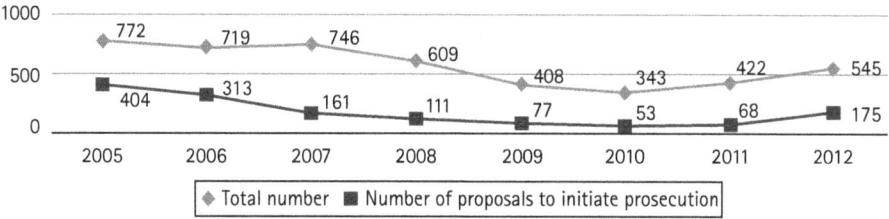

Figure 26.1 Year-on-year development of the number of cases of reasonable suspicion of children abused, sexually abused, and bullied, and the number of proposals to initiate prosecution *Source*: Fico (2013); Ministry of Labor, Social Affairs, and Family (2017)

The data say there are about 0.008 per 1,000 children registered for child protection services. As reported by Fico (2013), one third of children who have experienced some form of violence have never trusted anyone. Also, up to 90% of cases of violence against children aged between 1 and 3 years remain undetected.

Substitute Care in Slovakia

Discussions about the potential risks that emerged from collective, institutional types of children's homes started around 1997. Children's houses and nursery institutions under the common heading "orphanages" were transferred into the scope of the Ministry of Labor, Social Affairs and Family (MLSAF), which created the framework for change. These changes have resulted in current legislation that is based on six principles. The first, the principle of the preference of a natural family environment says that children remain in the natural family environment and the return of children to the natural family environment in the case of their exclusion is an absolute priority. The second principle is about preferability of placing children who cannot grow up in their natural family environment into substitute care (with a primary focus on a child's relatives), if that is not possible, so they are placed in foster care before residential care. The third principle prefers the placement of children stationed in facilities for the sociolegal protection of children and social guardianship by decision of a court in professional families before other organizational units of these facilities. The next principle is based on the implementation of a court decision in independently organized groups established in separate houses or apartments, if it is not possible to place a child in a professional family or facility. The principle of preservation of sibling relationships and the avoidance of separation is based on placing children as close as possible to their natural family environment in case their parents cannot take care of them. And the last principle is focused on the integration of children requiring special, respectively increased care.

The substitute care of children and young people is governed mainly by Family Act no. 36/2005 Coll. (Zákon č. 36/2005 Z. z. o rodine a o zmene a doplnení niektorých zákonov, 2005). The forms of substitute care in Slovakia correspond with the above principles and are as follows:

Table 26.1 Assistance provided to maltreated, sexually abused, and bullied children in 2016

			Physical abuse	Psychological abuse	Sexual abuse	Bullying	Exploitation for commercial purposes (pornography, prostitution)	Child abuse and neglect (CAN syndrome)	Total
Number of registered children	Total		88	41	60	2	4	519	714
	Of which	Up to 6 years	17	7	5	0	0	201	230
		Up to 15 years	50	20	31	2	3	252	358
		Up to 18 years	21	14	24	0	1	66	126
Number of proposals to initiate criminal proceedings	Total		9	7	2	0	0	9	27
Total number of children in Slovakia in 2016 (0–14)		840,228							

1) *Substitute personal care*: this is equivalent to foster care by relatives or non-relatives, though relatives are preferred. There is no need to complete the preparation training for providing this kind of substitute care by Offices for Labor, Social Affairs, and Family (OLSAF) or accredited subject of sociolegal child protection measures.

2) *Foster care*: this form of care is preferred to institutional care. OLSAF, in accordance with the SLPC&SG Act, decides on the educational measures in accordance with *Articles 12 to 15*, on temporary custody of a child in care of a natural person who is interested in becoming a foster parent and a cash contribution for resocialization;

3) *Institutional care (residential)*:
   a) *institutional care facilities*: until 2018, there was more variability in offering institutional care facilities: for example, children's homes, re-educational children's homes and re-educational youth centers, crisis facilities, diagnostic centers, resocialization centers, therapeutic and educational sanatoriums, social services at children's home (providing care for a child with physical disabilities, mental and behavioral disorders, or sensory disabilty as part of the child's home). (More information about recent efforts to de-institutionalize children's care is provided below.)

   b) *special institute professional parenthood*: this constitutes a separate body of residential care and has been legally stipulated in the Slovak legal system since 1993. The aim is to provide temporary or long-term care for a child from a substitute upbringing facility. It is not a family in a legal sense, but an industrial/labor law relation. A professional parent signs an employment contract with a facility and becomes its employee. They have to pass through the process of evaluation and preparation with specialized in-service training. Usually, a professional parent has between 1 and 6 children in care. They provide the care in their households, not in a facility. Research on young people leaving children's homes (Lukšík, 2017) reveals that the "quality of life of young residential care leavers is typically lower than the quality of life of their peers in regular population" (p. 133).

   c) *adoption*: the law provides for adoption if it is in the child's best interest. Adoption by married couples is privileged and both biological parents have to agree to the adoption.

The data in Tables 26.2 and 26.3 show the downward trend of overall placement of children and young adults in children's homes in the reporting period from 2015 to 2017 as a result of child protection measures to work with the family in its natural environment in order to optimize its functioning.

Table 26.2 Number of children entrusted to substitute family care in 2015, 2016, and 2017

	Substitute personal care	Foster care	Tutor care (guardianship)	Total
2015	6,484	1,847	571	8,902
2016	6,518	1,719	562	8,799
2017	6,634	1,548	557	8,739

Source: Ministry of Labor, Social Affairs, and Family (2017b).

Care for children and young adults in Slovak residential facilities is terminated for various reasons. The care ends most commonly upon reaching the age of majority while an increasing number of children return to their biological family.

In 2006, 2007, and 2010 a nationwide study was conducted to analyze the reasons children are removed from their families, the families they are being removed from, and the conditions for their return to their biological families.[1] The authors divided the reasons for removing into two basic groups: reasons relating to the child and reasons relating to the parent. Reasons for removing on the part of children prevail in older age groups, while parental reasons are present in all age groups.

As the results of the research show, the most important reason for removing children from the family on the parents' side was neglectful childcare, loss of housing, parental alcoholism, mismanagement of the child's health, and loss of employment. The background for the removal of children shows parents' inability to manage their life and parental roles. The most important finding of the research is that up to 56% of children removed from their homes have a chance to return to their original family following family support and rehabilitation of the family environment. More than half of the mothers cooperated with the authorities before the child was removed. On the other hand, there was low interest among fathers in cooperating with the authorities both before and after the removal. However, only 5.5% of children return to their families.

The law stipulates that substitute care should be avoided and children should be maintained in their family home whenever possible. In order to determine the nature of services needed, a social worker (a representative of OLSAF) conducts a social assessment to examine the family circumstances, housing, and social circumstances of the child for the purposes of a court decision. A proposal may be submitted to the court as an interim measure under a special regulation for determining or denying paternity under a special regulation to initiate proceedings on the fulfillment of the conditions of adoptability, on

---

[1] The authors of the study are Mikloško et al. (2008, 2010) in collaboration with the NGO Society of Friends of Children from Orphanages Smile as a Gift, the Centre for LSAF, and the Faculty of Health and Social Work, Trnava University. Reasons for the exclusion of the family are assessed in the monograph *Vulnerable families in Slovakia in the context of the causes of exclusion of children from biological families* (staff of the OLSAF). Data for 2006 were obtained from 482 questionnaires for 2007 of 493 questionnaires, and in 2010 a lot of data from 553 questionnaires. Total evaluated questionnaires: 851.

Table 26.3 Termination of care for children and young adults in children's homes

Number of children / % of total		2010		2011		2012		2013	
		Number	%	Number	%	Number	%	Number	%
Total number of children in children's home (residential care)		4,423		4,622		4,701		4,798	
Care termination in children's homes		1,577	100	1,347	100	1,372	100	1,147	100
From this	By reason of return to biological family	236	14,97	262	19,45	261	1,902	278	2,424
	By reason of placement to substitute family care	443	2,809	365	271	387	2,821	308	2,685
	By reason of reaching the age of majority or independence	482	3,056	456	3,385	441	3,214	448	3,906
	By other reasons	416	2,638	264	196	282	2,063	113	985

Source: based on the reports on Slovak republic population's social situation in 2010 – 2013.

the institution or abolition of institutional care, or on the institution or abolition of an educational measure imposed by the court, to perform a parental intervention.

The Center for the International Protection of Children and Youth (hereinafter referred to as the Center) is a body of state administration which implements measures for the social protection of children and social carers. The Center carries out child protection tasks at the international level against the harmful effects of unauthorized relocation (so-called parental abduction), and fulfills the role of ensuring children's rights to contact with both parents, the rights of children to grow up in the family environment, and child support payments. Under the SLPC&SG Act, counseling services are also available to children and families, specifically in cases of divorce or when children may need assistance with problematic behaviors (e.g., truancy, crime, bullying, drug addiction).

How Is a Child's Maltreatment Assessed?

The Internal Standard no. IN—067/2012 Planning Social Work to Implement Measures for The Social Legal Protection of Children and Social Guardianship was adopted in 2012 and describes and characterizes the process of child and family assessment. Many actors and institutions have a right to notify authorities about children's needs or circumstances, including the child's parent or person taking care of the child, or another institution (such as a school, medical facility, or court). Areas of assessment of the life situation of the child and his or her family include assessing the physical, psychological, and social condition of the child (taking into account individual aspects such as specific needs and health problems); evaluating the functioning of the family, parental competencies, and family relationships; and determining the degree of danger to the child.

Social workers provide continuous protection for the life, health, and well-being of children, which is done in practice through the 24-hour standby service of one of the SLPC&SG department's staff. The social worker is required to assess the child and his or her family, and create, execute, and evaluate a social work plan that addresses the unique needs of the child. The social worker offers specialized programs aimed at preventing the child from being removed from the natural family environment and supporting the preservation of the family environment from which the child was removed.

Based on many years of family preservation practice, the Innovative Model of Family Preservation Management[2] (hereinafter referred to as the Model; Litavská et al., 2013) was created within the national project Support for Deinstitutionalization of Substitute Care. The Model places emphasis on multidisciplinarity, cooperation (parents as partners), coordination, and support for active family participation. There is the multidisciplinary team

---

[2] The model was created under the operational program Employment and Social Inclusion and the national project Supporting the Deinstitutionalization of Substitution Care; the professional guarantor was the Department for the SLPC&SG of the Center for Labor, Social Affairs, and Family. It is available at the OLSAF website.

coordinator as the optimally responsible employee of the department of SLPC&SG. He or she is responsible for a comprehensive assessment of the situation of the child and his or her family, and this process is ongoing. The other prerequisites for successful family preservation are the implementation of regular case conferences as a tool to support the child and his or her family, and naming the family preservation goal and the time period in which it is necessary to work on qualitative changes, according to the intended goal: a plan for social work with the child, his or her parents or a person who personally takes care of the child, are signs of effective work with a family in crisis. Family preservation is based on intensive, acute field social work in the natural environment of the family, limited by time, need, and agreement. It can be provided as a preliminary measure, as a measure to prevent institutional placement, and as a service following other placements (Bechyňová & Konvičková, 2008). Field experience confirms the family's dependence on the system (help and support); often many generations of families remain in care (most often Roma families).

Evidence: Examples of Good Practice

Since the Slovak Republic committed, during its 25 years of existence, to adhere to a set of important human-legal international documents, it could not always ratify them compared to the 28 countries of the EU. Therefore, certain corrective actions and measures had to be taken. Optimal conditions were not always being created.

Joining the EU intensified efforts to respect the rights and fulfill the individual needs of all citizens. Historical relations from the beginning of the last century led to the creation of an institutional system of providing social benefits, a dominant strategy in several former communist countries. Similarly, the field of childcare was dominated by an institutional approach to collective education (Central Office of Labor, Social Affairs and Family, 2011). Despite efforts to deinstitutionalize social services, this did not produce the desired effects. It was therefore necessary to adopt several corrective measures including professional training and "mandatory supervision" of workers, which began in 2013 with regular group supervision.

Another example of good practice is the implementation of case conferences. In Slovakia, these started after 2010. Currently, the major aspect of these is that they are used today by the departments of the SLPC&SG as an effective method of social work. At the same time, the employees of the departments of the SLPC&SG and employees of the counseling-psychological services participate on case conferences in children's homes. The Centre for Labor, Social Affairs, and Family (CLSAF) created conditions to train the employees of the departments of the SLPC&SG, employees of counseling-psychological services, and professional teams in children's homes responsible for organizing and implementing case conferences. Currently, we are encountering the opinion the case conferences in particular are applied in cases which are difficult to solve, or they represent some dilemma for the social worker. To avoid demotivation and burnout, often this method is chosen using "collective decision making," divergent forms of solving the situation, and the participation of all stakeholders (the client, wider family, school representative, town mayor, social worker, psychologist, doctor, neighbors, or friends). Since this is the most relevant circle of people, those who know the client's situation, it is likely that the healing of this family will be successful.

Key Issues in Current Child Protection

In fulfilling its obligations for its participation in the EU, Slovakia is required to annually evaluate the implementation of the social-legal protection of children and social guardianship. In recent years Slovakia has been reproached for its shortcomings in these areas. A report (UN Committee on the Rights of the Child, 2016) summarized a variety of challenges relating to child welfare in Slovakia that must be addressed by 2020. These challenges include some of the following components.

Improvements in the data collection system are urged in order to provide an analysis of the situation of all children, especially those in a vulnerable situation, and to share data across relevant ministries to formulate, monitor, and evaluate policies, programs, and projects designed to effectively implement the UN Convention. The Committee further recommends that Slovakia: 1) ensures adequate and long-term funding for the Children's Commissioner's Institute (Children's Ombudsman) and sets up an appropriate monitoring system; 2) ensures that all past, current, and future reports of the Ombudsman as well as the Commissioner for Children on Children's Rights, including those dealing with sensitive issues, are adequately assessed and conducted on the basis of these; 3) request technical cooperation, inter alia, from the Office of the United Nations High Commissioner for Human Rights and the United Nations Development Program.

The report charges Slovakia with cooperating more closely with civil society, including funding for NGOs for innovative practices, and engagement with NGOs in planning and implementation of programs.

Other requirements include full implementation of the Anti-Discrimination Act as well as other laws prohibiting discrimination. Despite the recent legislative amendments to the Family Act of 2005, the Committee is concerned about the interpretation of Article 3 of the Convention and its implementation in the Agreement State, relating to the best interests of the child. It reports that the concept of best interests of the child is becoming increasingly abused in the activities and campaigns of certain groups and is misinterpreted by the media (for example, the integration of Roma children). Children's rights are sometimes compromised, in particular with regard to the child's right to consider his or her own best interests. The Committee recommends that the Agreement State: 1) increases its efforts to ensure that this right is consistently interpreted and applied in all legislative, administrative, and judicial proceedings and decisions, as well as in all policies, programs, and projects that are relevant to children and have an impact on them; 2) develops procedures and criteria for providing guidance to all relevant persons with the competence to assess the best interest of the child in each area; 3) performs public awareness activities as a counterbalance to all malicious interpretations of the principle of best interest.

The report also urges Slovakia to do more to respect the views of the child including developing tools to consult children on issues that have an impact on them; to implement awareness-raising programs and activities to promote meaningful and empowered participation of all children in the family, community, and schools, including student counselors, with special attention to girls, Roma children, and disabled children; and to institutionalize permanent participatory structures to ensure that a meaningful mandate and adequate human, technical, and financial resources are provided to ensure the effective involvement of children in the issues that have an impact on them.

Other recommendations include provisions to reduce acts of police brutality and unlawful conduct of the police, particularly relating to Roma children. The report also encourages Slovakia to prohibit physical punishment in the family. Other concerns are raised about minimal reporting of suspected physical or sexual abuse by public or other competent institutions, and sanctions for not reporting that are either not imposed or are too lenient. In some cases, the child victim is exposed to various detention/corrective measures/arrangements and placed in a detention center instead of being helped. Therefore, the Committee urges improved cooperation and coordination among all actors involved in child protection, including crisis centers, and standard procedures and operating methodologies. Furthermore, Slovakia is encouraged to protect all types of families without discrimination. Family law in Slovakia (Article 3 of the Family Law, 2015) identifies a stable family as consisting of a father of the child and the mother of the child and indicates that this family type is the most suitable environment for the complex and harmonious development of the child. The UN Convention, however, focuses on the well-being of the child more than family composition.

While Slovakia's national legislation provides support for community services to help identify and provide assistance to children and parents exposed to social risk, it is clear that these services are not available throughout the country. A series of other related shortcomings include: 1) a lack of services to prevent removing children from the family and the lack of programs to prevent the abandonment of children after childbirth; 2) uniform standards of quality work for professionals in nursing and foster care systems; 3) limited monitoring of children in alternative care; 4) few services to families at the community level; 5) insufficient support for biological parents to maintain contact with their children who are located in foster care, and for youth who are leaving institutional and foster care; and 6) insufficient information for children placed in institutional care to learn about their new placement: their location often ignores the geographical location of their biological family, culture, or language.

Finally, in the report, Slovakia is urged to adopt strategies to support positive parenting to prevent family crises that lead to the exclusion of children from their families, provide access to professional help for families in crisis, and ensure that children can stay in contact with their parents if their separation becomes necessary.

There is also an urgent need to re-establish specialized judicial proceedings for juveniles with adequate human, technical, and financial resources, including specialized, fully trained judges. In addition, children who have broken the law should be provided qualified, independent legal services. Childcare procedures (in the cases of child protection) for all children under the age of 18 should be provided with an emphasis on protecting and preventing secondary victimization. Protocols should be developed to ensure that children are only interviewed in the presence of their lawyers, parents or other people they trust. And, of course, Slovakia is encouraged to ratify all outstanding international human rights documents.

Conclusion, or What Is the Future of Child Protection in Slovakia?

A 2018 amendment to the SLPC&SG Act indicates a shift from a child protection model to a family service model. The family, as a system, is becoming a focus of interest, and the task of the government is to support and empower parents in their role, mainly through family needs assessment and subsequent therapeutic help in their natural environment. The activities of the national projects mentioned above correspond to these principles.

In 2018, particular types of SLPC&SG facilities (children's homes and crisis and resocialization centers) will be transformed into "multifunctional facilities." The new amendment of the SLPC&SG Act allows the development of outpatient help, care, and support for families in need in this new kind of facility to include specialized diagnostic, intervention, and resocialization programs. According to the *Reasoning Report—General Part* (2017) the change in application of measures in facilities will be built on the principle of the preservation of the distinction between government control and help. The new approach is state-run, though non-governmental agencies will also provide services with accreditation standards set by the state. Families served by the centers include those from marginalized Roma communities, incomplete families, families with one or more addicted members, low-income families, and families with one or more long-term unemployed members, and families at social exclusion risk. Substitute families, including Romani children in non-Roma families, face a number of difficulties, including feelings of disappointment among foster parents and feelings of failure where the goal might be to become accepting of the child, and to empower the parental skills of the foster parents. The reasons that interventions are typically required include school neglect, complex childcare neglect by parents, and neglect of a child's health care (not in compliance with a pediatrician's recommendation, neglecting personal hygiene of minors), educational problems, committing of antisocial activities by minors, and problems in substitute families.

Resulting from the complexity of social protection of children, the most common dilemma which social workers should encounter is focused on situations when we have to decide between: help a family with the child/children in its natural environment or temporarily to take the child from its family environment, which is currently harmful (Balogová & Kvašňáková, 2017; Fabian, 2018; Kvašňáková, 2011, 2016). The other questions are aimed at "identification of the best interest of the child," for example, who is the best parent for a child—biological parent, foster parent, carers in a post-divorce situation. Or questions connected to decisions about a child's home; issues about keeping false hope of "going home." Other question is about the hope in the ability of parents to change their behavior quickly enough. Or question how to support contacts between child and parent, despite evident child abuse.

One of most common problems is related to children from marginalized groups—mostly Romani children. The Romas comprise 6–8% of the Slovak population, yet Romani children make up a significant proportion of the children placed in residential care. It is not possible to register children by ethnicity, so it is difficult to provide specific numbers. Most Romani children are living in segregated Roma communities, which include geographic isolation, insufficient infrastructure, bad hygienic and living conditions, poor nutrition, and very low education level (Šramatá & Kállay, 2012). Those conditions have a great impact on the quality of life among Roma people in Slovakia. As it appears from the criticism of a report entitled *A lesson in discrimination: Segregation of Romani children in primary education in Slovakia* (Amnesty International & European Roma Rights Centre, 2017) it is necessary to eliminate the incorrect assignment of Romani children to special schools and classes for children with a "mild degree of mental retardation." Those practices create a space in which human rights are violated and the government has not yet solved that problem. Low quality of education in segregated environments restricts access of Romani children to secondary education.

In conclusion, we can state that the conditions for children and youth are comparable with other European countries. The priority interest is to keep a child in his or her natural environment—in a family, but we must not forget the child's best interest.

Acknowledgments

This chapter was written under VEGA research project No. 1/0134/17, "The importance of value orientation—expectations and perspectives of the young generation in the context of its application on the labor market."

References

Amnesty International and European Roma Rights Centre. (2017). *A lesson in discrimination: Segregation of Romani children in primary education in Slovakia.* Available at: http://www.errc.org/uploads/upload_en/file/report-lesson-in-discrimination-english.pdf.

Balogová, B. and Kvašňáková, L. (2017). Residential child and youth care in the Slovak republic. In I. Tuhinul and L. Fulcher L. (Eds.), *Residential child and youth care in a developing world: European perspectives* (pp. 187–204). The CYC-Net Press.

Bechyňová, V. and Konvičková, M. (2008). *Sanace rodiny. Sociální práce s dysfunkčními rodinami.* Portál.

Bernhauserová, E. (2007, December). *Efektivita zabezpečovania náhradného rodinného prostredia pre deti.* Available at: http://www.ceit.sk/IVPR/images/IVPR/vyskum/2007/Bernhauserova/Bernhauserova.pdf.

Central Office of Labor, Social Affairs and Family. (2011). *Koncepcia zabezpečovania výkonu súdnych rozhodnutí v detských domovoch na roky 2012–2015 s výhľadom do roku 2020: Plán transformácie a deinštitucionalizácie náhradnej starostlivosti.* MPSVR. Available at: https://adoc.pub/ustredie-prace-socialnych-veci-a-rodiny. html

Central Office of Labor, Social Affairs and Family. (2012). Interná norma č. IN—067/2012 *Plánovanie sociálnej práce pri vykonávaní opatrení sociálnoprávnej ochrany detí a sociálnej kurately.* Ústredie práce, sociálnych vecí a rodiny. Available at: http://www.otcovia.sk/docs/IN_067_planovanie_socialnej_prace.pdf.

Fabián, P. (2018). Práce sociálního pracovníka v systému sociálně-právní ochrany dětí v současnosti nejen ČR. *Logos Polytechnikos*, 2, 35–48.

Fico, M. (2013). *Prevalencia násilia páchaného na deťoch v Slovenskej republike.* Inštitút pre výskum práce a rodiny.

Gilbert, N., Parton, N., and Skivenes, M. (Eds.). (2011). *Child protection systems: International trends and orientations.* Oxford University Press.

Kvašňáková, L. and Balogová, B. (2014). Significant factors for the process of assessment of vulnerable families with children: A qualitative study. *SGEM2014 Conference on Psychology and Psychiatry, Sociology and Healthcare, Education*, 2, 765–772.

Kvašňáková, L. (2011). Ethical problems and dilemmas in child protection. In I. Kovalčíková and T. Matulayová (Eds.), *Professional ethics as a part of professional competence of supporting professions* (pp. 118–122). University of Prešov in Prešov.

Kvašňáková, L. (2016). *Vybrané otázky posúdenia životnej situácie ohrozenej rodiny s deťmi v kontexte sociálnoprávnej ochrany.* Prešovská univerzita v Prešove. Available at: http://www.pulib.sk/web/kniznica/elpub/dokument/Kvasnakova2.

Litavská, E. et al. (2013). *Inovatívny model manažmentu sanácie rodiny.* Ústredie práce, sociálnych vecí a rodiny. Available at: http://www.upsvar.sk/buxus/docs/SSVaR/SPODaSK/Inovativny_model_manazmentu_sanacie_rodiny.pdf.

Lukšík, I. (Ed.). (2017). *Kvalita života detí a mladých ľudí v ústavnej starostlivosti.* Typi Universitatis Tyrnaviensis.

Mikloško, J. (Ed.). (2011). *Ohrozená rodina na Slovensku v kontexte príčin vyňatia detí z biologických rodín.* SPDD.

Ministry of Labor, Social Affairs, and Family. (2010–2013). *Reports on the social situation of the Slovak Republic.* MLSAF. Available at: https://www.employment.gov.sk/sk/ministerstvo/vyskum-oblasti-prace-socialnych-veci-institut-socialnej-politiky/spravy-soc-situacii.html

Ministry of Labor, Social Affairs, and Family. (2014). National strategy for the protection of children against violence. MLSAF. Available at: http://detstvobeznasilia.gov.sk/en/wp-content/uploads/2015/09/Národná-stratégia-na-ochranu-detí-pred-násilím.pdf.

Ministry of Labor, Social Affairs, and Family. (2015). *Coordination of child protection against violence guidebook.* MLSAF. Available at: http://detstvobeznasilia.gov.sk/en/wp-content/uploads/2015/09/Koordinácia-ochrany-detí-pred-násilím.pdf.

Ministry of Labor, Social Affairs, and Family. (2017a). Dôvodová správa—všeobecná časť k vládnemu návrhu zákona, ktorým sa mení a dopĺňa zákon č. 305/2005 Z. z. o sociálnoprávnej ochrane detí a o sociálnej kuratele a o zmene a doplnení niektorých zákonov v znení neskorších predpisov a ktorým sa menia a dopĺňajú niektoré zákony. Available at: https://www.nrsr.sk/web/Dynamic/DocumentPreview.aspx?DocID=445276.

Ministry of Labor, Social Affairs, and Family. (2017b). *Report on the social situation of the Slovak Republic for 2016.* MLSAF. Available at: https://www.employment.gov.sk/files/slovensky/ministerstvo/analyticke-centrum/report-on-social-situation-2016.pdf.

Šramatá, M. and Kállay, A. (2012). Evolution of child protection in Slovakia. In J. Hämäläinen, B. Littlechild, O. Chytil, M. Sramata, and E. Jovelin (Eds.), *Evolution of child protection and child welfare policies in selected European countries* (pp. 257–276). University of Ostrava, ERIS.

UN Committee on the Rights of the Child. (2016). *Concluding observations on the combined third to fifth periodic reports of Slovakia.* Available at: http://tbinternet.ohchr.org/_layouts/treatybodyexternal/Download.aspx?symbolno=CRC%2fC%2fSVK%2fCO%2f3-5&Lang=en.

Zákon č. 36/2005 Z. z. o rodine a o zmene a doplnení niektorých zákonov. (2005). Available at: http://www.zakonypreludi.sk/zz/2005-36.

Zákon č. 305/2005 Z. z. o sociálnoprávnej ochrane detí a sociálnej kuratele a o zmene a doplnení niektorých zákonov. (2005). Available at: https://www.slov-lex.sk/pravne-predpisy/SK/ZZ/2005/305/.

Zákon č. 219/2014 Z. z. o sociálne práci a o podmienkach na výkon niektorých odborných činností v oblasti sociálnych vecí a rodiny a o zmene a doplnení niektorých zákonov. (2014). Available at: https://www.slov-lex.sk/pravne-predpisy/SK/ZZ/2014/219/20160101.

Child Protection in South Africa

Julia Sloth-Nielsen

Abstract

This chapter discusses South African child protection in line with the transition from an apartheid regime to a democratic multi-party democracy. The child protection system remains shaped by the apartheid history, thus it recently underwent an overhaul with the Children's Act 38 of 2005. The legislation, additionally, became fully operational by 2010. Child protection in South Africa also covers the parent-child relationship, domestication of Hague Abduction and Intercountry Adoption Conventions, and contractual surrogacy. Moreover, non-governmental organizations and church groups mostly delivered child protection services despite its result of racially skewed, patchy, and unequal network of services at the conclusion of the apartheid.

Key Words: South Africa, child protection, apartheid, regime, legislation, NGOs, Hague Abduction, Children's Act 38

Introduction and Context

South Africa is renowned for its peaceful transition from a repressive apartheid regime to a democratic multi-party democracy in 1994. The child protection system inherited from the apartheid era, and indeed the system in practice today, remains deeply shaped by this history and by the place of welfare services in the national and provincial governmental hierarchy, as well as by shifting policy in the post-apartheid era. In 1996, the country established a legal basis for the protection of children against all forms of abuse, neglect, maltreatment, and degradation, enshrined in the constitution's Bill of Rights (section 28(1)(d)). Law reform notwithstanding, the situation of children exposed to abuse, neglect, maltreatment, and degradation, and the responses to violence against children, including sexual violence, remain deeply concerning. In fact, in its response to the report of South Africa, the UN Committee on the Rights of the Child said in 2016 that:

> 33. The Committee is concerned at the very high prevalence of violence against children, which includes corporal punishment, gender-based violence and harmful practices.

34. With reference to its general comment No. 13 (2011) on the right of the child to freedom from all forms of violence and taking note of target 16.2 of the Sustainable Development Goals on ending abuse, exploitation, trafficking and all forms of violence against and torture of children, the Committee urges the State party to develop, adopt and implement effectively a comprehensive national strategy to prevent and address all forms of violence against children and to protect and support child victims of violence.

Similar concerns were expressed by the regional monitoring body, the African Committee of Experts on the Rights and Welfare of the Child (ACERWC) in 2019. The ACERWC noted with concern the prevalence of violence, corruption, poverty and inequality, as well as the lack of training for persons who work for and with children (ACERWC, 2019, par 18).

The true extent of child abuse in the country is only now beginning to emerge with greater clarity. The 2016 Optimus National Prevalence Study (the first ever national evidence-based study on the incidence of violence upon children in South Africa, for which 10,000 participants aged 15–17 were polled) found that one in three children experience sexual violence or physical abuse before the age of 18. Twelve percent of children report neglect, and 16% emotional abuse. The 2013–2014 police crime statistics indicate that 29% of cases of sexual abuse (18,524 cases) concerned victims who were under 18. This equates to 51 cases per day. It has also been estimated that 35–45% of children witness violence against a mother by an intimate partner (Seedat et al., 2009). It is suggested that the problem of sexual violence originates in a deeply patriarchal and child rights-negating society, exacerbated by policies and apathetic responses to violations which do not, in practice, place children first.

In addition, there is an extremely wide gap between the "haves" and the "have nots," South Africa being one of the most unequal societies in the world (World Bank, 2015). This huge disparity fuels violence in many forms. Violence against individuals with fewer resources means they have little recourse for justice. The population of South Africa is now estimated at around 60 million (Statistics South Africa, 2021), with 17.8 million below age 18. Of these children, 65% lived below the Statistics South Africa upper bound poverty line of R1138 per capita, per month in 2017 (Alternative Rights Coalition, 2018), and 22% of children were living below the international poverty line ($1.90/day or R351/month).

In one respect, South Africa has made huge advances which are characterized as world-leading, including the establishment and roll out of a dedicated social security net targeting children, the Child Support Grant (CSG), which was introduced in 1999. Providing a basic safety net against extreme poverty, thereby reducing the potential for non-deliberate neglect due to parental poverty, the CSG initially targeted children ages 0–7. This age threshold was eventually raised, gradually, and now the CSG is available (on a means-tested basis) to all children under the age of 18. Although not a large or even significant sum of money—now ZAR460 or 29 USD per month—it does provide a social safety net for the country's many poor children. In 2020, the grant reached nearly 13 million children (Children's Institute, 2021). The universal old age pension policy also plays a role in supporting children financially. The elderly are frequently the primary caregivers for children, especially in the context of HIV/Aids, and in a society in which kinship care networks are customary. It has been estimated that each old age pension can extend support to as many as eight household members and hence serves an important role as a social safety net.

Having described the most pressing risks to child health and safety, including their historic and cultural underpinnings, this chapter continues with a discussion of the child protection system, recently strengthened by the promulgation of the Children's Act 38 of 2005. Its various constituent components are described as detailed in the Act. This is followed by a review of social provisions relating to the child protection system (notably foster and kinship care, and residential care), and a discussion of the methods by which child protection services are delivered and financed. A brief comment on informal child protection systems is ventured, along with concluding remarks and recommendations.

The Bases of Social Allocations

Introduction

The child protection system in South Africa recently underwent an overhaul. The Children's Act 38 of 2005 came into operation partially in 2007 and became fully operational in 2010. It replaced the Child Care Act 74 of 1983, which was not compliant with the UN Convention on the Rights of the Child (CRC) and was regarded as being an apartheid era relic. Efforts to review the child protection system (and child law more broadly) commenced in the 1990s, shortly after the new constitution took effect in 1996. These efforts were marked by the appointment of an inter-ministerial task team to investigate the child protection system for young people at risk (Sloth-Nielsen, 2007). The appointment followed efforts to reduce the detention of young people in conflict with the law in prisons, which at the same time brought attention to the crisis in the alternative care system more generally. At the same time that the inter-ministerial committee on young people at risk was investigating policy options for child protection and alternative care, the need for legislative revision became patent. The omnibus Children's Act was thus developed after an extensive and highly consultative process by a project committee of the South African Law Reform Commission (SALRC). Prior to its adoption by Parliament, in an innovative and important move, the draft bill (as it then was) was costed to determine the financial implications of implementation (Cornerstone Economic Research, 2006). The findings of the costing analysis will be alluded to later.

The principal Act is accompanied by detailed regulations (and forms), altogether comprising a lengthy statute of nearly 500 pages. Child protection, broadly speaking, is not the only terrain covered by the Act, which also deals with the parent–child relationship (acquisition and loss of parental responsibility, exercise of parental responsibility, etc.), domesticates the Hague Abduction and Intercountry Adoption Conventions, and deals with contractual surrogacy, amongst a raft of topics. However, child protection occupies a central place in the statute.

Child protection services have historically been provided by non-governmental organizations and church groups, under a racially motivated policy developed in the 1930s that was premised on families and communities looking after their own needy members (on a segregated basis), rather than the state funding such endeavors (SALRC Report on the Child Care Act, 2000). Although this resulted in a racially skewed, patchy, and deeply unequal network of services, it was this system that prevailed at the end of apartheid. The splitting of the service delivery functions between private sector actors and faith-based organizations, and state employees, continues to characterize the welfare sector today.

Welfare—renamed social development around the turn of the millennium—is a concurrent national and provincial function according to the Constitution; this means that national government is responsible for legal and policy formation and certain assigned national functions (such as maintaining the national child protection register, discussed briefly below), whilst the bulk of services are located at the provincial level, where most staff are employed. Provincial budgets are funded through a system of allocations to provinces by a national fiscal commission (health and education are similarly concurrent national and provincial responsibilities). South Africa is currently divided into nine provinces. Whilst provincial departments employ social workers to render statutory services, such as those involved in child protection, a large (but unknown) percentage of cases entering the child protection system continue to be dealt with by external agencies. In November of 2017, there were nearly 30,000 registered social workers in South Africa (they must register with the South Africa Council for Social Services Professions annually in order to practice). However, it cannot be determined how many are employed by the state (i.e., the national department and the provincial departments which carry out its mandates), the private sector (such as companies), non-governmental organizations, or other employers (such as schools, hospitals, and those in private practice). Other complications hinder an accurate assessment of the work force. Some social workers may be registered but not currently employed. The array of workers enabled to register (separately) include social auxiliary workers (just over 10,000 were registered in November 2017), learner student auxiliary workers (nearly 10,000), and social work students (17,700) (South African Council for Social Service Professions, 2017).

The Children's Act considered child protection services to be a specialized social work role, and therefore for the first time called for the accreditation of what are termed "designated child protection services." Only such accredited bodies and their employees may perform child protection work, and then only in accordance with the norms and standards contemplated in section 106 of the Children's Act and fleshed out in the Regulations to the Act. Designated child protection services may, however, also be provided by the national or provincial departments of Social Development, who do not need to register an accreditation, but are *ex lege* permitted to perform child protection functions.

The costing report referred to above identified a serious shortage of social workers in the country as a primary impediment to implementation of the Children's Act. The government responded by declaring social work a "scarce skill" (enabling the payment of more attractive salaries in the public sector), and for the last decade has funded social work studies. This has borne fruit, with numbers of graduates increasing measurably.

Reporting of Child Abuse and Neglect

The Children's Act establishes a system for the reporting of child abuse and neglect (not for the first time in South African law, but now in a much more elaborate and deliberate fashion). The Act mandates reporting for designated professionals (e.g., doctors, nurses, dentists, and teachers, among others), while allowing for voluntary reporting among community members. This distinction was based on research that claimed mandatory community reporting led to a large number of unsubstantiated reports that overwhelmed the system (SALRC Discussion Paper 2000: 338).

The requirements for each form of reporting differ. First, professionals are required to report "a conclusion on reasonable grounds" that a child has been abused in a manner causing physical injury or has been sexually abused or deliberately neglected. This must be reported to a designated child protection organization, a provincial department of social development, or a police official (section 110(1) Children's Act). Details of the report must be recorded in prescribed forms (specifically, Form 22) that were developed to enable accurate recording of information for the National Child Protection Register (see below).

Voluntary reporting, by contrast, is provided for when a member of the community believes on reasonable grounds that a child is in need of care and protection (section 110(2) Children's Act). No civil claim for damages can be instituted if a report made in good faith turns out to be unfounded (section 110(3)(b) Children's Act), and the identity of the community reporter does not have to be disclosed. It has been pointed out that the standard of proof for the two different forms of reporting differs, insofar as for mandated reporters a mere suspicion would not suffice; rather, a conclusion on reasonable grounds must be substantiated on Form 22 (which stretches to five pages in length). The provision concerning community reporting relates not to a particular form of child abuse or neglect, but to the question as to whether a child is potentially in need of care and protection. That is something of a "term of art," which is explained further in the Act at section 150. This section provides a comprehensive list of which children are to be regarded as being "in need of care and protection," including orphaned or abandoned children, children living or begging on the street, children whose behavior cannot be controlled by their caregivers, children who have been abused or neglected, children who have been exploited or are living in circumstances that may expose the child to exploitation, and children who live in, or are exposed to, circumstances that may seriously harm their physical, mental, or social well-being. Child victims of child labor (an estimated 577,000 children were working in 2015; Alternative Rights Coalition, 2018), and children living in child-headed households *may* be designated children in need of care and protection, after an investigation into their individual circumstances. Section 150 lies at the heart of children's entry into the child protection and alternative care system (e.g., foster care, temporary safe care, and placement in a child and youth care center) once a children's court determines that a child is in need of care and protection.

Children's courts have been in existence since the 1930s, and are quasi-civil courts established specifically to deal with child protection matters. Their jurisdiction is founded solely in the provisions of the Children's Act (Chapter 4), and the orders that they can make are regulated by section 46 of the Act, and include alternative care orders, adoption orders, orders placing a child, or parent (or both) under the supervision of a social worker, a child protection order and so forth: section 46 lists more than 20 possible orders. Their criminal jurisdiction is restricted to offences prescribed in the Children's Act, and they are intended to function in tandem. Their proceedings are supposed to be as informal and conducive to the participation of all parties as possible, including children (Rohrs, 2017). Children's courts have otherwise limited functions. They do not deal with divorce, for instance, or recovery of child support, or juvenile justice matters. They function at the lowest level of the judiciary, at the local or district magistrates' court level, and although more specialized staff are available in large urban courts, in smaller towns and districts the children's court is staffed by a generalist judicial officer who also performs many other judicial tasks including presiding over both civil and criminal trials. There are currently 700 children's courts located in various magistrate's courts around the country, including periodical and branch courts, which do not function full-time (Rohrs, 2017).

The powers of the children's court were considerably augmented in the Children's Act, which now provides for a wider variety of orders that a children's court can make, and for the court to review its own interim decisions. One reason for this was the need to provide for family reunification and reconstruction services. Previously, a court order confirming a removal of the child from the family was in place for a two-year period, after which it could be extended or altered; now authorities consider court orders of shorter duration. Moreover, the Children's Act authorizes a vastly expanded range of potential orders that enable children's courts to operate with more creativity. Examples of these creative solutions include designating adults to supervise child-headed households or ordering parents or caregivers to arrange for a facility to care for the child during specific hours of the day or night, or for a specific period (Children's Act, section 46). Some further possible orders are discussed below.

The Children's Act provides instructions for responding to reports of child abuse or neglect. In the case of the police, after securing the immediate safety and well-being of the reported child at risk, the police official must notify the provincial department of social development within 24 hours.

In the case of a report made to a social worker at the provincial department of social development, the social worker must ensure the immediate safety and well-being of the child, and if there is risk, make an initial assessment of the report. Unless the report is obviously frivolous, the social worker must investigate it or cause it to be investigated, and if the report is substantiated, the worker must institute further proceedings specified in the Children's Act without delay, as specified below. If the report was received by a designated child protection agency, this must be reported to the provincial department of social development, which must monitor the progress of all matters related to the report. The designated child protection agency carries out the case work and investigation, however.

The Act calls for one of three intervention responses after the social worker (whether employed by the state or by a designated child protection agency) completes the investigation. The first assists the child while the child remains in the care of his or her current caregivers (including mediation, counselling, early intervention or prevention services, family reconstruction and rehabilitation, behavior modification, problem-solving, and referral to another suitably qualified person or organization). This is deliberately listed as the first option, indicating preference for service to the child within the family environment. Second, new provisions in the Act (section 110 (7)(b)) allow for removal of the offender from the child's home, if this would serve the best interests of the child. Despite the addition of this removal mechanism, years of personal communication with social service professionals suggest that this option is rarely, if ever, implemented.

Third, the matter can be referred to the children's court for an inquiry, in accordance with the provisions of Chapter 9 of the Children's Act. This chapter provides for two types of removals: removals of children into temporary safe care with an order of court (section 151), or emergency removals without such an order, but where it is reasonable to believe that the child is in need of immediate emergency care and protection, and that the delay caused by obtaining a court order would jeopardize the child's safety and well-being (section 152). In the Constitutional Court case of *C v Minister of Health and Welfare Gauteng* (2012), the Court found that an emergency removal must be brought to the children's court for a judicial review of the measure to take place within 48 hours of that removal. The basis for the finding was, in essence, the drastic interference with family life caused by such an emergency removal, necessitating judicial oversight. Before this decision, the Act permitted a 90-day period to elapse before the social worker's investigative report needed to be presented at a children's court inquiry. In 2012, this provision was struck down as unconstitutional, and the Act has since been amended to mandate judicial confirmation of a removal within 48 hours (Children's Act Amendment Act 7 of 2016, inserting a new section 152A in the principal Act to this effect). Once an inquiry has been opened, the children's court must consider the background investigative report of a social worker within 90 days. The social worker's input is central to the children's court processes; social workers complete a social inquiry report (Form 38) that informs the court as to whether the child is in need of care and protection, and which measures should be taken to secure the child's needs.

As noted, the Act provides the children's court with a commendably wide range of orders, illustrating the range of therapeutic interventions that the court can employ. Among others, the court can: 1) order that a child remain in, be released from, or return to the care of a specific individual, subject to conditions; 2) give consent to medical treatment for a child, including surgery; 3) instruct a parent or caregiver to undergo professional counselling, or to participate in mediation, a family group conference, or other problem-solving forum; 4) instruct the child and other involved parties to participate in a professional assessment; 5) instruct a person to undergo a specified skills development training, treatment, or rehabilitation program where this is necessary for the protection or well-being of the child; 6) place the child in alternative care (which includes foster care or placement in a child or youth care center), an adoption order, and so forth. Section 46 of the Act is expansive in the variety of options it provides, to spur creativity amongst presiding officers.

The National Child Protection Register, and the Reporting of Sexual Offences

The Children's Act recently established the National Child Protection Register (NCPR), consisting of two parts. Part A (section 114 of the Act) establishes the child register, which provides the details of all children reported to have been abused or neglected. It is intended to facilitate monitoring and surveillance of cases and their follow up, to assist in planning so that policymakers can target resources to where they are most needed, and to prevent to the extent possible the re-victimization of already victimized children (since it is considered that children who have been victims once are more likely to be victims again). The social inquiry report (Form 23) is a standardized tool that captures information required to be loaded onto Part A of the Register, which is then transmitted to the Director General of the (national) Department of Social Development (hereafter DSD).

Whilst NCPR Part A has several important goals, among them the collection of national data on the prevalence of child abuse and neglect, indications are that the Register is not functioning optimally. This is at least partly due to inadequate information on reports of child abuse and neglect being captured at the district and provincial level, so that data is incomplete and not fit for purpose. Inadequacy of information on reports may be the result of human resources deficits, particularly the lack of social workers, which were identified in the costing report. The need for careful deployment of existing resources is patent, and the NCPR child register is one tool that helps achieve this objective. It is therefore of some concern that the register is apparently not serving its goals.

Part B (section 118 of the Act) establishes the offender register, which records the details of persons found (by a court) unsuitable to work with children. Unsuitability may be the consequence of a criminal conviction, or a determination that the person was the cause of a child being found in need of care and protection. It could also be a finding of a tribunal (e.g., dismissal). The offender register is supposed to be a screening tool: to prevent persons who have committed abuse against children from working in environments where they have access to children. Employers are required to check the names of applicants against those in the offender register.

Indications are that the data on the national offender register is woefully inadequate. Employers cannot rely on the efficacy of any vetting process, due to its gaps. One reason for this is the fact that some reports filed with the offender register may also be filed with the Department of Justice and Correctional Services's sex offender registry (NRSO), which was established under the Criminal Law (Sexual Offences and Related Matters) Amendment Act of 2007. The NRSO contains the names of persons convicted of a sexual offence against a child or a person with a mental disability. As with the offender register, the aim of the NRSO is to prevent registered sex offenders from working or operating in environments that will expose them to children, and from becoming foster parents, kinship caregivers, temporary safe caregivers, adoptive parents, or curators, unless they receive a clearance certificate from the NRSO. It has been anecdotally suggested that confusion exists about whether to document sex offender convictions in the NRSO, the NCPR, or both. The civil society group which prepared the civil society input to the CRC Committee reporting process has argued that the two registers should be merged to improve data integrity, and to save scarce resources (Alternative Coalition Report, 2017, para. 250). Another reason for the inadequacy of the offender register is social workers' poor compliance completing applicable forms (Alternative Coalition Report 2017 par 249, citing the Child Abuse Tracking study discussed below).

What Social Provisions Are Allocated to Protect Children?

Foster Care and Kinship Care

In South Africa, a large proportion of children (22% or just over 4 million children) do not live with their biological parents. The majority of these children are cared for by extended family members (Hall & Sambu, 2016), though the prevalence of such informal kinship care is unknown.

Foster care results from an order of the children's court that formally places a child in the care of a foster parent, who may be (and most often is) a relative. It is regulated by the Children's Act in a dedicated chapter titled "Foster Care," which prescribes the responsibilities of the foster parent, the duration of orders, and the renewal process for orders that have expired, including the documentation social workers must submit to the children's court. A foster care grant (FGC) is payable to the foster parent in whose care the child has been placed. At the time of writing, the amount for this grant is ZAR1040 or roughly 67USD, which is 2.5 times the amount of the CSG payable to a primary caregiver caring for his or her own child. Whereas the CSG is means tested and payable only until the age of 18, the FGC is not means tested and is payable until the child reaches 21 years of age, provided the child is still legally in foster care and pursuing education.

Understanding the foster care system requires an explanation of the sociopolitical context. From 2002 to 2012, the number of children in foster care increased dramatically (from 30,000 to 500,000 children), with the number of children receiving FGC peaking at 550,000 (approximately 30 per 1,000 children) in 2012. (Information about the racial characteristics of children in care is not available.) These increases were the results of government policies that proactively addressed the impending orphan crisis at the height of the HIV/Aids pandemic by promoting FGC as the preferred grant for orphans living with relatives (Alternative Coalition Report, 2017, para. 226). The number of children on FGC has decreased since then, however; as of March 2017, only 420,000 children (21.4 per 1,000 children) were receiving FGC (Alternative Report Coalition, 2017, para. 226). Information on the number of children admitted to foster care in each year (as opposed to the cumulative number of FGCs being paid) is not available (Alternative Coalition Report, 2017, para. 208). According to the Alternative Coalition Report, the decline is attributable to the "inability of the child protection system to place South Africa's uniquely high numbers of orphans into foster care" (as above).

This is borne out by the litigation around the renewal of children's court orders that commenced in 2012. The Children's Act (fully operational from April 1, 2010) had introduced (newly) the requirement of a court-ordered renewal, which previously had been effected administratively (i.e., without requiring court approval). This was motivated by the need to comply with CRC Article 25, which required periodic review of placements in alternative care. Absent a court ordered placement or renewal, the electronic systems driving grants payments cannot initiate any further cash transfers, as there is no case number to enter on the system.

By 2011, 120,000 FGCs ceased to be paid because social workers had not extended the court orders in time. The department cited capacity constraints; social worker shortages were such that the lapsed orders could not be reinstated. In a court settlement agreement, temporary authority was granted to the department until 2014 to extend foster care orders without a court order—by that time a comprehensive legal solution had to be devised. By December 2014, a further 300,000 foster care orders had lapsed, necessitating an extension of the timeframe within which the department would need to devise a solution. An extension until December 2017, and then thereafter until 2022 was granted, but the department now needed to report progress every six months back to the court.

At the time of writing (July 2022), amendments to the Children's Act to address the need for a systemic are almost finalized in Parliament. An updated version of the envisaged provisions is not yet available, but according to what was envisaged in the Bill tabled in 2020, the intention is to permit to order an extended period for foster care orders to subsist, where the child has been placed in foster care with a family member. They will then endure until the child turns 18. (Bill 28 of 2020). Also the Social Assistance Act has been amended; this is the comprehensive law dealing with all forms of social security and the eligibility requirements for each grant. In reporting to the UN Committee on Economic Social and Cultural Rights in October 2018, government referred to the implementation of a "top-up grant" to the CSG, specifically for orphans placed in kinship care, to obviate the need for foster care in what is actually a family-based solution, and to minimize labour-intensive social work and court interventions that have torpedoed the foster care system and led to the cessation of FGC payments to vulnerable care-givers (frequently grandmothers). This amendment has now been effected (in 2022), although it seems that, as yet, no funding has been made available for implementation by Treasury. If the CSG Top-Up is implemented effectively, it will provide orphans with a CSG of higher value than non-orphans, although the amount that might be payable is presently unknown. Civil society has been calling for this reform for over 10 years because the current use of the Foster Child Grant is ineffective in reaching the majority of orphans in need, and is reducing the capacity of social workers and court to respond to serious cases of child abuse.

A recent report of the DSD found that "[t]he strain on the foster care system results in children who are abandoned, abused or neglected not receiving the level of service they require, as a great deal of social workers' time is spent on dealing with the administrative and court processes relating to foster care" (DSD, 2016, p. 364). The reality is that children in the day-to-day care of relatives are not in need of elaborate social work services, as they are not children in need of care and protection, as defined in section 150 of the Children's Act.

A comprehensive solution to the woes befalling the foster care system will undoubtedly yield benefits for the child protection system more broadly, in that scarce social work skills can be devoted to specialized child protection work instead of "paper pushing" FGC applications through the children's court system.

Residential Care in Facilities

The Children's Act has renamed all residential facilities "child and youth care centers" (CYCCs), rather than the polyglot of former labels applied to orphanages, homes for adolescent delinquents, and so forth. Residential facilities are extensively regulated by in Chapter 15 of the Act, accompanied by detailed regulations. These regulations have their origin in the work of the Inter-ministerial Committee on Young People at Risk in the 1990s, which documented extensive abuses and malpractices in existing children's welfare institutions at the time. Now, institutions must be registered according to the program they present (secure care, substance addiction treatment, care for abandoned children aged below 2 years, and so forth).

The main tool for the regulation of children's residential care institutions is the process of registration, which in turn is accompanied by the requirement of adherence to the provisions of the Act (e.g., in relation to their governance, behavior management practices, and management systems) and compliance with minimum norms and standards (such as those related to programs and individual development plans for each child in a

CYCC). The monitoring requirement that the Act prescribes is a developmental quality assurance (DQA) process that must take place every three years (Children's Act, section 211, read with Regulation 89), to be conducted first by a team connected to the CYCC, followed by a review by an independent team. The intended result is an organizational development plan for addressing any improvements required, which is submitted to the provincial department of social development.

At the practical level, three main issues present themselves. First, the Government of South Africa's (GOSA) report to the African Committee of Experts on the Rights and Welfare of the Child in 2016, at par 251, is vague about registration of facilities, beyond the development of guidelines. In 2019 the Committee responded to the first periodic report submitted by the GOSA that:

The Committee takes this opportunity to recommend that the Government direct efforts towards determining the number of such facilities that exist, their registration status, as well as do a quality audit to ensure that they comply with minimum standards to ensure the rights of children living there are protected. Furthermore, the Committee recommends to the Government to make available effective reunification services to ensure that children having biological parents reunify with their parents instead of staying in CYCCs (par 23).

It is still not known how many children are admitted to CYCCs each year, and how many are reunified with their families. One estimate, which could not be verified, is that there are about 21 000 children residing in approximately 360 registered CYCCs (this includes children in conflict with the law awaiting trial or sentenced to a CYCC).

Shelters for street children are also classified as CYCCs. A 2013 study found that there were 60 such registered institutions, accommodating 4,662 resident children (Review of the Welfare White Paper, 2016, p. 167). The same source indicates that there are no reliable figures on the total numbers of street children, but that they are likely to far exceed the guesstimate of 10,000 provided in the 1994 Welfare White Paper.

Second, due to a lack of reunification services or monitoring system, children are essentially "forgotten" in CYCCs even though they have biological families they could return to (Alternative Report, 2017, para. 238). A 2016 study of foreign children in CYCCs in one province in South African found that insurmountable difficulties presented themselves when foreign children were caught up in residential care, including lack of documentation and the inability of social workers to arrange for any identification documentation, lack of contact with birth families in the country of origin, and social workers' inability to navigate the immigration and asylum-seeker system (Sloth-Nielsen & Ackerman, 2016). Although this study found the numbers of foreign children in the formal care system to be low (approximately 4% of the total number of children in that province recorded as being resident on a CYCC for that month), the lack of durable solutions meant that these children will, to all practical extent, remain in care until they reach adulthood.

Third, the problem of unregistered facilities continues to bedevil effective implementation of child welfare interventions such as reunification services. Children in unregistered facilities often lack social work services, and thus miss out on opportunities to be reunified with their families, or to be fostered or adopted. Such children are in many cases not known to the care and protection system, and this could make them vulnerable to unlawful adoption or trafficking. At the same time, it is also important to highlight the positive role that these facilities play, in view of the fact that social workers have in the past utilized them for the placement of children, and the support that most of them enjoy from the communities.

Facilities may be unregistered for a number of reasons, including that they cannot comply with physical requirements (space, sanitation, equipment, etc.) due to their location in poor township areas; that they are taking in children in order to collect FGCs (CYCCs are defined in the Children's Act as facilities that accommodate more than six children); or that owners or managers or those running unregistered facilities are unaware of or ill-equipped to engage with registration processes due to low literacy levels; amongst others. A 2013 study found that the most common registration challenges experienced by unregistered facilities were a lack of knowledge and understanding of the registration procedures and requirements, and a lack of clear information and guidance from the DSD on registration procedures (Centre for Child Law, 2013). The Children's Act does not provide for financial assistance from the department for complying with the registration requirements, and absent state funding, for centers with limited means, it is at times "a choice between feeding the children in our care or paying for another basin or toilet" (IOL, 2014). And although section 192 of the Children's Act requires the Minister of Social Development to include "a comprehensive national strategy aimed at ensuring an appropriate spread of child and youth care centres throughout the Republic providing the required range of residential care programs in the various regions," this has to date not been done (Alternative Coalition Report, 2017, para. 234).

What Are the Methods for the Delivery of These Provisions?

The model envisaged in the Children's Act is based on a cooperative implementation model and the Act specifically requires government to adopt a "comprehensive, intersectoral strategy aimed at securing a properly resourced and coordinated child protection system" (Children's Act, sections 104 and 105).

Yet a recent pilot study has revealed the extent of the gap between the law as crafted, and its practical implementation (Children's Institute, 2017). The first of its kind, the study sought to establish the extent to which the role players tasked with child protection services were in fact following protocol. The study was conducted in two provinces, Kwa Zulu Natal and the Eastern Cape Province, deliberately selected due to their urban/rural mix, large child populations, and high rates of child abuse. The study used data from police files, departmental social work records, and records from accredited child protection agencies. Based on a pilot study, about 200 closed case files from 2012 were reviewed and data were extracted and analyzed. Qualitative semi-structured interviews were conducted with key informants: staff attached to the specialized Family Violence, Child Protection, and Sexual Offences Police units (FCS) and social workers from DSD and the child protection agencies. This allowed investigators to track how cases are managed within an agency, whether cases are completed (court outcomes), how cases are documented, and the extent of inter-agency collaboration. Overall, 23 agencies were involved in the study: 20 police stations falling under five FCS units; 10 social development service offices in five districts; and three designated child protection organizations in three districts. Despite its small sample size, the study's findings are nonetheless instructive. In some sites, there were no designated child protection organizations functioning at all. The police unit responsible for following up on reported instances of child abuse and neglect is the FCS (except in the case of death, which is dealt with by the homicide division). The study revealed a distinction between cases reported to the FCS units and to social services (e.g., neglect by a parent or caregiver was usually reported to social services authorities). Most cases of sexual abuse were reported to the police, who were also the report recipients in 62% of the cases of abuse. Sixteen percent of the cases in the sample were reported by mandated reporters, and 84% were reported voluntarily, usually by close family members. The study reports that when physical abuse was reported to the police, they did not take it seriously and rarely referred it to social workers (Children's Institute, 2017, p. 23). Physical abuse was often put down as justifiable punishment. South Africa has, until a very recent Constitutional Court decision, allowed the defense of reasonable chastisement to be raised in connection with parental corporal punishment. It has now been ruled unconstitutional (FORSA v Minister of Justice and Constitutional Development, 2019).

Despite the clear and unambiguous forms provided by the Children's Act to capture reports of child abuse and neglect, the study found that only 5% of reports were recorded on the prescribed forms, with police and social workers using a variety of "informal" ways of recording information, such as making a note in their investigation diary or keeping process notes. This in turn meant that vital information was likely omitted or not captured.

Only 8% of cases that reported physical abuse were cross-referred to the other agency (e.g., police to social services and vice versa), and none were jointly managed, in stark contrast to the intended model of cooperative implementation (Children's Institute, 2017, p. 55). No cases were forwarded to the Director General of Social Development for entry in the NCPR child register.

The results of the study are even more concerning with regard to sexual offences against children. South Africa has some of the highest incidences of child and infant rape in the world. The 2015/2016 crime statistics report 15,790 child victims of rape (about 8 children per 10,000 children), representing 37% out of a total of 42,596 all rape cases in that period (Alternative Coalition Report, 2017, para. 266). In a third of cases, the perpetrator is a family member or close relative. Child sexual abuse is primarily reported to the South African Police Services and fewer than one in three cases are referred by police to social services for therapeutic services. According to the report:

> Inter-sectoral collaboration in the management of child abuse cases is absent with limited evidence that children are accessing temporary safe care. Inter-sector protocols on the coordinated management of child abuse are outdated and unused. In addition, research suggests that social service professionals lack the capacity to adequately manage cases of sexual abuse and most children remain at continued risk with perpetrators still around.[1] (Alternative Coalition Report, 2017, para. 265)

The attitude of government to addressing violence against children (and women) and sexual offences in particular has flip-flopped in recent times: specialized Family Violence, Child Protection, and Sexual Offences police units were disbanded in 2005, with a loss of specialized skills—though they were re-established in 2010. The same happened with regards to specialized sexual offences courts, which were decommissioned in around 2010 despite their proven ability to secure a higher conviction rate. Happily, these too were re-established in 2017, though progress on implementing the courts is evidently slow. Lack of political will to hold duty bearers accountable is at least one factor contributing to the failure of the Children's Act to ensure the necessary protective services to children in practice.

Perhaps in recognition of the difficulties in ensuring the requisite coordination and inter-sectoral service delivery, the recently tabled Children's Act Amendment Bill (2018) includes a new proposed section 5D which will establish a National Inter-sectoral Committee for the Management of Child Care and Protection Matters, comprised of a large number of stakeholder Departments. The functions are proposed to be as follows: monitoring and evaluating the implementation of the priorities and strategies contained in the national child care and protection policy and the Act; measuring progress on the achievement of the goals and objectives; ensuring that the different organs of state comply with the primary and supporting roles and responsibilities allocated to them in terms of the national child care and protection policy and this Act; and monitoring the implementation of the national child care and protection policy and of this Act. For now, however, recent reports show that Parliament is only considering finalizing the aspects of the Bill related to foster care, leaving all the other omnibus amendments aside for the time being (Parliamentary Monitoring Group May 2022).

---

[1] Because there is not an intervention from the police or the child protection service.

How Are Child Protection Services Financed?

As noted, the funding of welfare services is both a national and provincial issue. The provincial allocations are determined annually by a central commission, the Fiscal and Finance Commission, out of monies appropriated from the central revenue fund collected through taxation. Private expenditure on child protection is unknown but likely to be extremely limited and concentrated around services such as domestic adoptions. In these scenarios, well-off families may pay for social workers and psychologists to write reports that support their adoption applications. In fact, domestic adoption is declining, with only 1034 domestic adoptions were registered during the period April 2018–March 2019, half of the figure of a decade earlier (Sloth-Nielsen, 2022, p. 77). 150 Intercountry adoptions were approved, a number which is also dropping steadily.

Registered non-profit organizations, such as children's homes and accredited child protection organizations, are allowed to receive donations and to raise funds. The issue of government subsidies to such organizations came under the spotlight in the court cases of *NAWONGO and others v Member for the Executive Social Development, Free State Province* in the High Court between 2010 and 2014. The National Association of Welfare Organisations and Non-Governmental Organisations (NAWONGO) argued that the provincial government had chronically underfunded them, even though they were fulfilling their governmental obligations by providing residential care services to the elderly, to children with disabilities, and to children in the care and protection system. Nonetheless, their government subsidies—one third the amount of what the government was spending per capita on children in its own, state run, facilities—were woefully inadequate to meet the care needs of the children or the elderly.

The Department of Social Development in turn recognized that approximately 2,000 beds in child and youth care centers are needed in the Free State Province. Presently, approximately 1,085 such beds are available. Only approximately 320 beds in CYCCs are provided by the department itself in two children's homes. In line with the department's policies, one NGO moved away from large children's homes or orphanages to a decentralized care model based on an emulation of a normal family home and incurred considerable costs in implementing this model.

The applicable national and provincial financing policy that outlined the respective role of state and non-profit organizations (NPOs) was premised on the recognition that, in addition to funding from state sources, NPOs were in the position to raise some funds themselves, through other state departments, donor organizations, corporate social responsibility programs from the private business sector, trusts and foundations, and the proceeds from lotteries. The funding payable to NPOs would be based on set formulae, related to the costs of the program, the NPO's ability to leverage other funds, the purpose for which the funds were requested, and the NPO's ability to deliver the program or service, amongst other factors. The provincial financing policy also set out the department's strategic priorities (which included vulnerable children). However, a disclaimer was in place to the effect that the distribution of funds would be dependent on the availability of provincial revenue. There was also a clause to the effect that due to limited funds, the department could not support the full cost of services it supported, and that the determination of the final award was the prerogative of the department. If the NPO objected, no agreement with the department would be signed—a "take it or leave it approach," as the court noted. With allocated funding from the province being wholly inadequate to meet the care needs of the respective vulnerable groups, NAWONGO argued that the financing policy was insufficient to guarantee children's rights "to family care or parental care, or to appropriate alternative care when removed from the family environment . . . to basic nutrition, shelter, basic health care services and social services; and . . . to be protected from maltreatment, neglect, abuse or degradation" (Constitution, section 28).

Was the department reasonable in its disclaimer that it could unilaterally reduce required subsidies to NPOs performing statutory functions on behalf of the state? The court's answer, at first, was no; the court ruled that a reasonable policy must contain a fair, equitable, and transparent method of determination of what these NPOs are able and should contribute to the provision of care for children, older children, and vulnerable persons in need. The financing policy lacked any method of such determination, because its premise was that it did not require one. The department was ordered to return to court within four months with a revised policy which met constitutional imperatives.

The department returned to court on three subsequent occasions. The financing policy was founding wanting each time, save the last, on the basis that although the services to children and the elderly around which this case revolved had been prioritized by the department, the department continued to hold on to the limitation of budgetary control by adjusting downward any award if available funds were insufficient to fund the service required.

Finally, four years after its first judgment, the court was satisfied that the funding policy met constitutional specifications, in that it ranked programs according to their core costs. Programs qualifying according to the ranking would be fully funded, less any contribution the NPO could make. Funding would be applied down the ranking until available funds were exhausted. The court ultimately agreed that the revised model would withstand constitutional muster, as it was reasonable, whilst at the same time being geared towards progressive realization of social welfare rights. The court was careful to note that due to the doctrine of separation of powers, the court could not determine any monetary award itself, but was restricted to deciding whether the policy adopted met with constitutional standards.

The issue of funding remains unresolved, however, evident in the fact that the share of provincial children and families' budgets allocated to NPO subsidies dropped from 64% in 2012/2013 to 55% in 2016/2017 (Alternative Report Coalition, 2017, para. 30). This decline is in part due to increased expenditure on state funded posts and state services, a response to a burgeoning public sector wage bill driven by a unionized public sector that demanded higher than cost of living wage increases). In the context of a faltering economy, this has led to the closure of some NPOs and threats to the continued existence of others.

Informal Justice Systems

In the African context (and indeed in other development world contexts), child protection responses are frequently effected through informal and traditional justice systems within the extended family and community, with outcomes being determined according to customary law and practice. While researchers are starting to explore the operation of community-based child protection responses (African Child Policy Forum, 2018), little to nothing has been done in South Africa and information about informal justice systems and child protection is scant and anecdotal.

The African Child Policy Study found that the perseverance of community, traditional, and informal justice systems is fostered by the inaccessibility of formal justice systems, especially in rural and remote areas. But because these systems are invariably oral, and no written records of dispute resolution processes are kept, it is difficult for researchers to ascertain with any authority the extent to which child protection interests (and other justice matters involving children, such as juvenile justice and custody disputes) are furthered. Suffice it to say that informal justice mechanisms typically involve mediation and restorative justice modes of dispute resolution. They typically operate according to the notion of collective rather than individual responsibility, in which parties are perceived as part of the wider social and kinship network, and senior family members are most often the main interlocutors (speakers) during processes. Much more field work at the grassroots level is needed to understand fully the role of informal justice systems in child protection, both in South Africa as elsewhere.

Conclusions

The legal framework for responding to reports of child abuse and neglect is arguably sufficient in most respects and provides the necessary tools and guidance to stakeholders involved in the child protection system as to the actions and steps at their disposal. However, as the Alternative Report Coalition notes,

[v]iolence against children is also pervasive, with 824 cases of child murder reported in 2016, and a child homicide rate of 5.5/100 000, more than double the global rate of 2.4/100 000 with child homicides peaking amongst adolescent boys, yet nearly half of child homicides occur in the context of child abuse and neglect; with these cases concentrated in young children aged 0-4. An estimated one in three children are victims of sexual violence and physical abuse, 12% of children report neglect and 16% report emotional abuse. In other words, many children experience and/or witness multiple forms of violence in the home,

family, community and school, often at the hands of a trusted adult, which is likely to lead to complex and continuous trauma. (Alternative Report Coalition, 2017, para. 80)

Much more training is needed to ensure health and other professionals uphold their reporting obligations under the Children's Act and Sexual Offences Amendment Act to ensure children's safety and access to therapeutic and mental health services. Moreover, Police responses to reports of child abuse and neglect need to be sharpened, and intersectoral cooperation between all agencies involved in child protection prioritized if the constitutional injunction to protect all children from abuse, neglect, maltreatment, and degradation is to hold meaning.

References

African Child Policy Forum. (2018). *Spotlighting the invisible: Justice for children in Africa*. The Africa Child Policy Forum.

African Committee of Experts on the Rights and Welfare of the Child. (2019). *Concluding Observations South Africa*. Available at: www.acerwc.org.

Alternative Report Coalition. (2017). *Complimentary report to the African Committee of Experts on the Rights and Welfare of the Child: A response to South Africa's second report to the African Committee of Experts on the Rights and Welfare of the Child on the African Charter on the Rights and Welfare of the Child*.

Alternative Report Coalition. (2018, October 9–13). *List of issues submitted to working group on South Africa: Committee on economic, social and cultural rights*. Available at: https://tbinternet.ohchr.org/_layouts/treatyb odyexternal/Download.aspx?symbolno=INT%2fCESCR%2fCSS%2fZAF%2f28794&Lang=en.

Barberton, C. (2006). *Costing the tmplementation of the children's bill*. Cornerstone Economic Research.

Burton, P., Ward, C. L., Artz, L., and Leoschut, L. (2015). *The Optimus study on child abuse, violence and neglect in South Africa*. Centre for Justice and Crime Prevention.

Centre for Child Law. (2013). *Addressing the registration issues experienced by unregistered child care facilities*. Available at: https://dgmt.co.za/tackling-the-registration-issues-experienced-by-unregistered-child-care-fac ilities/.

Children's Institute. (2021). Children's Institute: Children Count. Available at: http://childrencount.uct.ac.za/ indicator.php?domain=2&indicator=10.

Department of Social Development. (2016). *Comprehensive report on the review of the white paper for social welfare, 1997 Government of the Republic of South Africa*.

Government of the Republic of South Africa. (2016). *South Africa's second country report to the African committee of experts on the rights and welfare of the child on the African Charter on the Rights and Welfare of the Child*. Independent Online.

Hall, K. and Sambu, W. (2016). Demography of South Africa's children. In S. Delany, S. Jehoma, and L. Lake (Eds.), *South African child gauge 2016* (pp. 1–66). Children's Institute.

IOL. (2014). *SA's childcare system in crisis*. Available at: https://www.iol.co.za/pretoria-news/opinion/sas-childc are-system-in-crisis-1697472. Children's Institute at the University of Cape Town.

Jamieson, L., Sambu, W., and Mathews, S. (2017). *Out of harm's way? Tracking child abuse cases through the child protection system in five selected sites in South Africa*. Children's Institute.

Meintjes, H., Moses, S., Berry, L., and Mampane, R. (2007). *Home truths: The phenomenon of children's residential care for children in a time of AIDS*. Children's Institute.

Parliamentary Monitoring Group: minutes of meeting of the Social Development Parliamentary Committee on 18 May 2022. Available at: https://pmg.org.za/committee-meeting/34960/?utm_source=transactio nal&utm_medium=email&utm_campaign=minute-alert (accessed June 16, 2022).

Rohr, S. (2017). The child in need of care and protection. In T. Boezaart (Ed.), *Child law in South Africa* (2nd ed.) (pp. 280–305). Juta and Co.

Seedat, M. I., Van Niekerk, A., Jewkes, R., Suffla, S., and Ratele, K. (2009). Violence and injuries in South Africa: Prioritising an agenda for prevention. *Lancet*, 374(9694), 978, 1011–1022.

Sloth-Nielsen, J. (2007). Child protection. In T. Davel and A. M. Skelton (Eds.), *Commentary on the Children's Act* (pp. 1–21). Juta and Co.

Sloth-Nielsen, J. and Ackerman, M. (2016). Unaccompanied and separated children in child and youth care facilities in the Western Cape: A socio-legal study. *Potchefstroom Electronic Law Journal*, 19, 121, 1–27.

Sloth-Nielsen, J (2022). Lessons from the South African Experience of Intercountry Adoption FJR 77-84.

SALRC. (2001). *Discussion Paper 103 on the Review of the Child Care Act*. Government of the Republic of South Africa.

SALRC. (2002). *Project 110: Report on the Review of the Child Care Act*. Government of thte Republic of South Africa.

South African Council for Social Service Professions. (2018). *Bi-annual Newsletter 2017*. Available at: https://www.sacssp.co.za/2021/SACSSP%20Newsletter%201%20of%202018.pdf. https://www.sacssp.co.za/2021/SACSSP%20Newsletter%201%20of%202018.pdf

Statistics South Africa. (2018). *Mid-Year Population Estimates 2017*. Available at: https://www.statssa.gov.za/publications/P0302/P03022017.pdf.

UN Committee on the Rights of the Child. (2016). *Concluding observations on the second periodic report of South Africa*. Available at: http://www.refworld.org/publisher,CRC,CONCOBSERVATIONS,ZAF,587ce86b4,0.html.

World Bank. (2015). *South Africa Economic Update*. UN Committee on the Rights of the Child.

Legislation

Children's Act 38 of 2005, published in Government Gazette of the Republic of South Africa Vol. 492, No. 28944 dated June 19, 2006. Commencement date April 1, 2010.

Social Assistance Act 13 of 2004, published in Government Gazette Vol. 468, No. 26446 dated June 10, 2004, commencement date April 1, 2006.

Children's Act Amendment Bill. (20 of 2018).

Cases

C v Minister of Health and Welfare Gauteng. (2012). (2) SA 208 (CC).

FORSA v Minister of Justice and Constitutional Development 2019 ZACC 34.

NAWONGO and others v Minister of the Executive Social Development, Free State Province. (2010). ZAFSHC 73; (2011) ZAFSHC 84; (2013) ZAFSHC 49; (2014) ZAFSHC 127.

The Child Protection System in Uruguay

María del Luján González Tornaría *and* Delfina Miller

Abstract

This chapter notes the child protection system in Uruguay. The social allocations are presented with social, political, and legal landscapes while specifying the conception of violence and maltreatment of minors. The Comprehensive System for the Protection of Children and Adolescents against Violence aims to deal with the problem of violence against boys, girls and adolescents. Additionally, SIPIAV is regulated by the Uruguayan Institute for Children and Adolescents of Uruguay. The definitions of maltreatment and violence in Uruguay are adopted from the World Health Organization. SIPIAV's principles range from the prevention of revictimization to the acknowledgement of the BGA who are witnesses of gender violence.

Key Words: Uruguay, violence, maltreatment, revictimization, gender violence, WHO, INAU, SIPIAV, social allocations, child protection system

What Are the Bases of Social Allocations?

To provide an overview of the social allocations in Uruguay we will present the social, political, and legal landscape, illustrated by specific data about our population and our conception of violence and maltreatment, and we will offer data collected by different institutions that take care of children and adolescents.

Presentation of the Child Protection System in Uruguay

In Uruguay, since 2007, there is an institution called Comprehensive System for the Protection of Children and Adolescents against Violence (SIPIAV.)[1] This institution, whose main goal is to deal with the problem of violence against boys, girls, and adolescents (henceforth BGA), in a joint and integral manner, is regulated by the Uruguayan Institute for Children and Adolescents of Uruguay (INAU). The SIPIAV includes members of the Ministry of Social Development (MIDES), the Ministry of Public Health (MSP), the State Health Services Administration (ASSE), the Ministry

---

[1] Translator's note: all Uruguayan acronyms for institutions are transcribed in the Spanish original.

of the Interior (MI), and the National Public Education Administration (ANEP), and it receives the support of the United Nations Children's Fund (UNICEF). Its Administrative Committee is integrated by the Judiciary Branch, the Public Prosecutor's Office, and civil society organizations (CSOs) that have an agreement with INAU to address this issue. INAU is the state agency whose mission is to guarantee the effective exercise of the citizenship of all BGAs in Uruguay, according to their status of full subjects of law.

According to SIPIAV (2016c), it is possible to envisage two large collective agents acting to promote the recognition of children's rights and the need to provide them with protection: children's/adolescents' defense movements, and women's rights and feminist movements. These groups work together in the National Advisory Council against Domestic Violence (CNCLVD) and, specifically, since 2012, they have developed a conjoint strategy to address gender-based and generational violence.

Definition of Violence and Maltreatment
SIPIAV (2016c, p. 9) adopted the definition of violence from the World Health Organization (WHO, 2002):

> The intentional use of physical force or power, threatened or actual, against oneself, another person, or against a group or community, that either results in or has a high likelihood of resulting in injury, death, psychological harm, maldevelopment, or deprivation.

SIPIAV (2016a) identifies the most widely accepted typologies, both internationally and also enshrined in the National Law on Domestic Violence (Law 17.514, from 2002). The classification of violence that is recognized is: physical, psychological/emotional, sexual, patrimonial, and neglect. This same document warns that these classifications are not rigid, insofar as the types of violence can coexist or even vary according to, for example, the age of the victims, their reactions, or the environmental conditions.

The ANEP (2013) defines child maltreatment as any intentional act or omission that causes physical or psychological harm to BGA which is practiced by the adults who are responsible for their care and development. The following types of maltreatment are recognized: emotional or psychological, sexual (commercial and non-commercial), physical or chemical, abandonment or neglect. There is also a description of the kind of violence that results from witnessing violent acts, and a description of institutional violence. SIPIAV (2016a) also distinguishes social violence, which is described as the result of interconnected forms of harm production: differential access to social recognition, and differential access to socially produced wealth, participation, and decision making. It should be pointed out that this classification has increased in complexity in successive documents produced by SIPIAV and by its participant institutions.

Basic Principles of the Operation of SIPIAV

The basic principles mentioned in SIPIAV (2016c) are: the need to deal with each case in its entirety and uniqueness, the prevention of revictimization, the need to consider the words of the BGA, and the acknowledgment of BGAs who are witnesses of gender violence. Likewise, there is mention of the need to include the siblings as victims of violence, even when the violence was not inflicted directly on them.

From an ecological perspective of the phenomenon, the SIPIAV recognizes four levels: the responses must take into account first the BGA, then their families, those groups or institutions involved, and, lastly, the community to which they belong. These levels refer to the conception of violence against BGA as a collective responsibility.

The system of responses encompasses five steps, which are not necessarily sequential, and can overlap in time and may not always occur. These steps include: promotion and prevention, care and protection, access to justice, the reparation of harm, and follow-up. These levels will be described in turn in the present chapter.

Registry of Violence against BGA

UNICEF (2017) gathers data from the Multiple Indicator Cluster Survey (MICS, 2013), which is part of the fourth round of surveys conducted by UNICEF (MIDES & UNICEF, 2015), and which constitutes the last record which is available in Uruguay. MICS surveys apply the Parent-Child Conflict Tactics Scale (CTSPC) method, which allows measurement of the use of violent disciplinary methods at home.

According to this study, a total of 3,568 households participated, which ensures national representation, since the last census counted 1,166,292 households. About 55% (54.6%) of the BGAs from age 2 to 14 years have been subjected to some form of violent disciplinary practices within the last month. This includes psychological aggression and any form of physical aggression. Fifty percent of boys and girls suffered psychological aggression and 25.8% physical punishment. The survey showed that only 34.4% experienced non-violent discipline exclusively. About 11% of the households surveyed did not offer data.

Three hundred and fifty thousand BGAs from ages 2 to 14 years had been exposed to some form of violent disciplinary method within the previous month. According to the last national census, carried out in 2011, the figures regarding BGAs are: 21.8% children and adolescents ages 0–14 years (Calvo, 2014). According to a report of UNICEF, there were 714,965 children up to 14 years, almost half of whom (48.9%) were subject to some kind of violence. The MICS survey (2013), which was published conjointly by UNICEF and MIDES, reports that 54.6% of children between 2 and 14 years of age have been subjected to some violent disciplinary method by their father, mother, or an adult member of the household.

Boys are exposed to violent disciplinary methods to a greater extent than girls (58.4% versus 51.2%). The tendency towards a more violent disciplinary pattern for boys is quite evident regarding physical punishment: overall, males are physically punished twice as much as females (34% versus 18.3%).

In Uruguay, 2.8% of BGAs received a severe corporal punishment from their caregivers in the month previous to the survey. (This means approximately 11,000 boys and approximately 7,000 girls.)

Among the types of psychological violence, yelling is predominant (48.1%) and among physical punishment practices, the two most significant methods are shaking and spanking (17. 4% and 18.7%, respectively).

The use of some kind of violent disciplinary method is most frequently found among younger boys and girls: 60.6% of children aged 2 to 4 years have experienced violent disciplinary methods, while the percentage is less for boys and girls aged 5 to 9 years (52%) and for boys aged 10 to 14 years (53.6%). Violent disciplinary methods permeate all sectors and do not depend on socioeconomic variables. While in the poorest 40% of households 57.5% of children experience some kind of violent disciplinary method, in the richest 60% of households, violent disciplinary methods are applied in 52% of cases. The most significant difference is observed in the case of physical punishment: in the poorest 40% of households, one in every three children receives this kind of punishment and in the richest 60%, one in every five (UNICEF, 2017).

If we take into consideration the educational level of the head of the household, the use of physical punishment represents 28.4% when he or she has primary education and 19.1% when he or she has tertiary education. Rural areas and areas with fewer than 5,000 inhabitants stand out for reporting the lowest rates of application of some violent method (42%). The distributions by race or ethnic group show no significant differences.

The MICS survey reports that 26.8% of women aged 15 years or older have suffered physical violence during childhood, and that 18.3% of the present-day population of girls are victims of physical violence according to well-informed sources. According to the First National Survey on the Prevalence of Gender-based and Generational Violence (EVBGG) (MIDES & National Statistics Institute, 2013), aggression towards these women when they were girls was committed initially by their mothers (45.1%), followed by their fathers (26%). The younger generations report having been exposed to less violent experiences than previous generations.

It is estimated that one in every five girls live in a household in which women suffer violence exerted by a cohabiting intimate partner. The EVBGG 2013 survey enables us to inquire about the circumstances of children to these situations. According to this scale, 20.3% of boys/girls live in a household in which women over 15 years old have suffered gender-based violence exerted by the cohabiting partner during the previous year. This amounts to around 150,000 BGAs in urban areas. The figures are slightly higher in childhood than in adolescents (22.3% and 18.1%, respectively). Since the approval of the law 19.580 (2018) Gender Violence against Women, the child witness is also considered a victim.

A higher prevalence of reports of violence has been observed involving adolescents compared with children. Among adolescents of both sexes, a rate of 9.1 for every 100,000 has been registered, while between 5 and 14 years of age the rate is 6, and between 0 and 4 years, 4.7. Each year, approximately 1,000 cases of domestic violence against boys and girls between 0 and 4 years of age are reported to the police, and around 1,500 cases in other age groups.

Up to 13 years of age, victims of domestic violence are distributed in similar proportions among male and female groups. From 13 years of age onwards, the majority of victims are women. Among women, figures increase with age.

while among male victims, figures oscillate among the different age groups.

According to the report of the Ministry of the Interior, between 1996 and 2016, 264 women lost their lives in the hands of their domestic partner or former domestic partner; 42.3% of whom had dependent minor children. The loss of the primary caregiver exposes children and adolescents to suffer other situations which involve the violation of rights, such as placement in foster-care homes. Insofar as BGA victims of homicide are concerned, in the last five years there were 108 cases, of which 30.6% involved children 0–5 years of age, 7.4% children 6–12 years of age and 62% children 13–17 years of age. Intra-family violence is the motive that is identified in the first place in 27.8% of cases.

This information is provided to SIPIAV by the operators who work at the official institutions as well as those who work in institutions that operate in agreement with INAU. This constitutes the First Information System (SIPI), which is the best available source of data on childhood and adolescence in situations of violence.

It is important to highlight that the information is limited to those situations registered in the SIPI, not the total of maltreatment and abuse situations experienced by BGA in the country, or the total of those that were addressed by the response system. The data refers to situations that have been detected, addressed, and registered in the SIPI by operators who work with childhood and adolescence within the sphere of INAU and SIPIAV (SIPIAV, 2016b).

Some prevention services are offered to children and families by CSOs and by local reception committees (CRLs).

Specific services include facilities with a specific profile for the response to violence towards BGA; they are managed by CSOs in a partnership agreement with INAU. The Blue Line is INAU's telephone service to report situations of rights violations related to BGAs (SIPIAV, 2016b).

During the last 10 years, SIPIAV has made a great effort from the point of view of inter-institutional coordination between public and private sectors, to generate and promote conjoint actions oriented to take preventive measures and give better responses to situations of violence against BGAs (SIPIAV, 2016b).

The Perception of Maltreatment

UNICEF (2017) reports a recent study carried out by the consulting firm Cifra about the attitudes of the population in relation to the issue of violence towards boys and girls. This study shows Uruguayan explicit parental standards regarding what "ought to be done" excludes physical punishment. Paradoxically, at the same time, the use of verbal or physical violence is still perceived by most parents as an effective way of solving conflicts or problems. The participants in the study took part in 10 focus groups. They remembered having received a "smack on the bottom" at least once during their childhood, and some of them much more than once. Besides, they argued: "I wasn't traumatized at all and I learned." That is why parents use smacks or ear pulling as "a last resort," being convinced that it is something good for their children.

Both fathers and mothers spank their children, and they do not feel they are being violent; according to them, they do it occasionally and for "a good cause." Some parents even questioned those who did not apply this method. Furthermore, it was observed that slapping, shaking, or yelling are considered adequate forms of putting a child on the right track and setting clear limits. What seems harder to observe is psychological maltreatment at home. When this issue was explored some examples of verbal violence emerged, but participants were not aware of them.

Poverty and Deprivation in Childhood in Uruguay

If we take into account the concern for the rights of BGAs and the definition of social violence, as evidence of the differential access to socially produced wealth, it is necessary to report that Uruguay is among the countries in the region with the lowest incidence of multiple deprivation for which we have available data. In 2000, it was the country with the lowest incidence (26.1%), and in the next two measurements (2007, 2011) it occupied the second position, behind Costa Rica in 2007, and behind Chile in 2011. A strong decrease is noticeable during that period, even considering that the point of departure was from low values of the indicator. Between 2000 and 2011, a decline of almost 9 percentage points can be observed, reaching just 17.4% of children and adolescents in 2011.

In all dimensions a decrease was observed during the period that was analyzed. Housing is the dimension with the highest levels of deficiencies (7.7% in 2014), followed by education (4.5%). The latter is the dimension for which the lowest decrease can be observed during the period that was analyzed (Colacce & Tanembaum, 2016, p. 49).

Adolescents between 15 and 17 years of age have the highest rates of multiple deprivation, and they are those for whom the reduction was more moderate. These facts do not coincide with monetary poverty, since in this case the rate decreases systematically with age, in such a way that the highest rates are observed among the youngest children. The differences among the groups are mainly due to the educational dimension. The rates of non-attendance and educational lag are high among adolescents between 15 and 17 years of age: in 2014, 20% of adolescents in this age group did not attend any educational institution, and 14% of those who did attend were lagging behind. For school-aged children, non-attendance, as well as educational lag, was below 1%.

Legal Framework

The regulatory antecedents of the struggle for the rights of BGAs evince two well-differentiated stages. On the one hand, the international regulations for which Uruguay has accepted responsibility, and on the other, national initiatives.

Among the former, we find two laws that relate to national jurisprudence with international treaties: Law 15.737 from 1985 (at the end of the dictatorial regime) acknowledges, in its Articles 15 and 16, the competence of the American Convention on Human Rights for an undetermined period, and accepts the so called Pact of San José, Costa Rica, "signed in the city of San José, on November 22, 1969" (p. 3). In turn, Law 16.137 from 1990 ratifies and consecrates the UN Convention on the Rights of the Child, and sets down in its Article 1 the need to establish legislative, administrative, social, and educational measures which are appropriate to protect the child against all forms of physical or mental injury or abuse, neglect or negligent treatment, maltreatment, or exploitation, including sexual abuse. Furthermore, in Part 3, Article 50, it ratifies the obligation of the State parties to accept "the provisions of the present Convention" (p. 16). Complementary to the former provisions, an Inter-American Convention was summoned for the prevention, punishment, and eradication of violence against women, whereby the "Convention of Belem do Para" was created, which was adopted in 1994, in Brazil. This requires state parties to adjust the entire normative system (administrative, civil, penal, procedural) for the prevention of gender-based violence, the protection of women facing this type of violence, the prosecution of the perpetrator, penalties for violent behavior, and reparation and restitution for the victims (Article 7).

Law 17.823 published in 2004 represents the link between both stages; it takes the first step, at a national level, towards the creation of a Code of Childhood and Adolescence, and it also takes into account the international treaties. In its first article, it establishes its mandatory application to all living beings, and determines that "a child is defined as every human being under the age of thirteen years and an adolescent as those over thirteen and under eighteen years" (p. 1). Article 15 establishes "the obligation to grant special protection to children and adolescents against all forms of neglect, sexual abuse or exploitation, discriminatory treatment, harassment; economic exploitation or any other kind of work that is harmful to their health; cruel, inhuman or degrading treatment; life endangering situations or those that incite violence; situations that endanger a child's safety and identity" (p. 3). Furthermore, Chapter 4, Articles 18 to 22 underlines the obligatory nature of promoting and protecting childhood and adolescence through social policies, and establishes the guiding criteria for ensuring the harmonious development of children and adolescents, while the state's responsibility for the creation of integral care programs is set down.

As part of the second stage, and in order to reinforce the above-mentioned law, in 2007, Law 18.214 was approved, which includes and modifies provisions of the Code of Childhood and Adolescence and the Civil Code. In particular, Article 12 emphasizes the prohibition "for parents or legal tutors, as well as any person in charge of the care, treatment, education or supervision of children and adolescents" to "use physical punishment or any type of humiliating treatment as a way of correcting or disciplining boys, girls or adolescents" (p. 2). At the same time, it is necessary to review some subsequent rules that introduce changes to the code, such as Law 18.590 (2009) and Law 19.092 (2013) that modify provisions related to adoption, and Laws 18.777 (2011), 18.778 (2011), and 19.055 (2013) that introduce modifications regarding adolescents in conflict with the law.

Lastly, it is necessary to mention Law 18.651 from 2010, which enshrines the integral protection of persons with disabilities. Article 2 defines as disabled "any person who suffers from or has a functional disorder, be it permanent or prolonged, physical (motor, sensory, organic, visceral) or mental (intellectual and/or psychological) that, in relation to his/her age and social environment involves considerable disadvantages for her/his family, social, educational or occupational integration" (p. 1), and Articles 3 and 4 promote prevention and integral rehabilitation.

Adjoining and complementary to the above-mentioned provisions, in 2002, Law 17.514 on domestic violence was promulgated, whose Article 21 establishes the responsibility of the State to adopt the measures required to prevent, punish and eradicate domestic violence. It was supplemented by Law 18.850 from 2011, which establishes the reparation to daughters and sons of persons who died as a result of domestic violence. As mentioned before, Law 19.580 of 2018 introduces important changes in the consideration of violence against children: in case of domestic violence the child is always a victim, even though the violence is not directly perpetrated against him.

Law 19.747, enacted in 2019, strengthens access to justice for NNA through all the process. Changes refer to the International Convention on the Rights of the Child and the Committee on the Elimination of Discrimination against Women. The law offers orientation to professionals with respect to the interview with children, the information that can be offered to them, their rights, and the importance of actively listening to their needs. The professional must avoid child revictimization, mediation, confrontation, or reconciliation in cases of violence between the victim and the aggressor. The consent of the child should not be considered to decrease adult responsibility.

In case of violence, the professional cannot re-link with the offender unless the victim requests it and the professional team gives approval. Children must remain always with protective family members. The precautionary measures are to stop mistreatment and prevent repetition and retaliation. The child must receive immediate attention from SIPIAV, and he/she has the right to receive medical treatment, psychosocial intervention, and therapeutic monitoring, which must be reported every six months.

What Is the Nature of Social Provisions Allocated to Protect Children?

Based on the information just provided about what we consider the bases of social allocation in Uruguay, we now describe the child protection system. Although we have no official documentation, we can offer approximate numbers. In the publication INAU Memoria Anual 2019 (latest available data) there are 4517 children from 0 to 18 years cared for in full-time centers. These centres offer full attention for children when their rights are violated and their families cannot serve them (the cause is not only violence, it can be too, for example, abandonment).

Different Levels of Protection

The levels of care planned by the SIPIAV (2016c) are: prevention and promotion, care and protection, access to justice, damage reparation, and follow-up.

LEVEL OF PREVENTION AND PROMOTION

This level implies anticipating the occurrence of acts of violence, promoting bonds based on respect, rights and responsibilities, and the consideration of the BGA as subjects of law. These measures are addressed to BGA as well as to adults and they involve the strengthening of community participation. Some measures specific to this level are detailed as follows. The SIPIAV (2016b) has implemented a series of specific actions for the eradication of violence by organizing campaigns to fulfill this primary level of prevention.

The measures are, for example, the use of SMS text messages, in cooperation with Uruguay Crece Contigo (Uruguay Grows with You, UCC), which is a public policy program of national coverage that aims to consolidate a system of integral protection for early childhood with the National Administration of Telecommunications (ANTEL), which broadcasts a spot on television networks and social media (SIPIAV 2016b, p. 13).

Likewise, work has been developed jointly with the Plan Ceibal (a state program whose goal is to promote the integration of technology in the service of education) through the creation of short films that address issues such as bullying, maltreatment, and sexual abuse. These audiovisual materials are available to teachers for their work with children in the manner they find most convenient.

The measures for primary prevention also include brochures addressed to the general population, which furnish information about the rights of BGA, and which define violence as an act or behavior that jeopardizes their integral health. The different types of violence are identified and information on how to detect signs of violence is provided. Lastly, orientation is provided about where to turn in case of suspicion that a child is experiencing violent situations.

LEVEL OF CARE/PROTECTION

In case of suspicion or actual existence of situations of violence, immediate and integral responses must be implemented. The adults responsible for the BGA must be prepared to detect signs related to situations of violence. The SIPIAV (2016c) describes non-specific indicators of violence such as physical, behavioral, or emotional signs that should be analyzed contextually, in an integral manner and through teamwork. The signs considered include distress, irritability, inhibition, overt behavioral disorders, domestic accidents, difficulties or poor school achievement, and so on.

Detection results from the evaluation of certain non-specific indicators or from specific indicators of violence. The latter refers to narratives of BGA, verified domestic violence, sexually transmitted infections, pregnancy of girls under 15 years of age or of adolescents under circumstances of abuse. Many complaints of maltreatment and intrafamily abuse arrive through the Educational Centers, Afterschool Children Clubs,[2] NGOs, INAU, and the Ministry of Public Health. This fact shows the degree to which Uruguayan society shows its concern for the protection of childhood and adolescence.

The next step is the report to the competent authority, according to whether the case has been detected within the healthcare, educational, or police environment, the corresponding Road Map documents are to be taken into consideration according to the institution in question. To date, there are judiciary proceedings that are described by the Ministry of the Interior available, and Road Maps at the educational level (National Public Education Administration, ANEP, 2013), and at the level of the healthcare system (Ministry of Public Health, MSP) (SIPIAV & UNICEF, 2009).

Regarding the Road Map in the context of education (ANEP, 2013), it contains conceptual definitions of different types of maltreatment and it describes the stages that should be taken into account: detection and initial assessment, risk assessment and diagnosis of the situation, intervention, and follow-up. Emphasis is placed on networking and on the identification, from the very start, of an adult who can fulfill the role of child protector and who is willing to get involved in the search for solutions in cases of maltreatment. Those who report the situation of violence can be educators, social workers, or members of teams working in the field, and they can do the initial assessment and the risk assessment. The diagnosis in general is entrusted to teams of psychologists, and the intervention and follow up involves all the team.

It is the policy of the Ministry of the Interior to emphasize the child as a subject of law, and to highlight the harms produced by violence (Ministerio del Interior et al., 2015). Among the main damages the document mentions: low self-esteem, poor academic performance, learning disabilities and social interaction difficulties, and physical and emotional consequences. The text focuses particularly on cases of children who have witnessed domestic violence, intrafamily sexual abuse, sexual exploitation, and adolescents in conflict with the law. Its aim is to differentiate myths from actual facts in relation to these issues. The document provides criteria to ensure the respectful communication of

---

[2] Translator's note: in Spanish: *Club de Niños*. They are centers that operate in agreement with INAU to offer to part-time care low-income families for school-aged children for their caregivers to be able to work.

facts that involve BGAs, which take into account the ways to refer to them, and the image that is conveyed so as to avoid lapsing into revictimization.

The response system also involves listening and supporting the BGA, and risk assessment, which determines whether the response must be urgent (in cases of life-threatening risk or evident maltreatment). Risk assessment implies taking into account aspects related to the child (age, presence of disabilities, emotional or behavioral problems, available resources, present crisis situation), the situation (type of maltreatment, the significance of the signs observed, the chronicity of the situation, the naturalization of violence, previous interventions, intensity and frequency of violent acts), the adult (failure to comply with measures taken previously, threats, access to or possession of guns, alcohol or drug abuse, mental disorders, history of maltreatment in childhood, violent behaviors in settings other than those related to the BGA), and the context (responses given by adults in the immediate environment, unavailability of adults to play the role of protector for BGA, history of domestic violence incidents, siblings in institutional confinement due to violence, previous reports of violence).

Risk assessment serves to guide the teams that are operating and does not entail an evaluation of the specific case. From the assessment, urgent responses can result and the beginning of the articulation of the services that are appropriate for the case, the design or strategies for violence interruption and the registry of the case, as forms of safeguarding the BGA and all those operating in the situation. The institutions that have competence are in general terms all the institutions that are part of the SIPIAV. Therefore, the professional profiles are diverse: physicians, psychologists, social workers, lawyers, judges, and prosecutors. In urgent cases, judicial actors may be involved to protect and exercise the rights of the child or youth and to punish the responsible party, if necessary. The state must guarantee the speed and quality of the proceedings so that the child and the adult referent can obtain prompt and effective responses, and access to free legal assistance and representation. The sanction of the individual responsible is considered part of the repair of damage and the judge can also manage assistance for the aggressor in rehabilitation programs. This assistance is compulsory.

Generally, a team is responsible for this risk assessment. In these teams there are social workers, teachers, doctors, and a psychologist, according to the place where the case is identified. Then, a report is produced and the child is oriented to the corresponding center for a more thorough assessment.

DAMAGE REPARATION

In some cases, when it is considered necessary, children and youth can get therapeutic services that have been proven effective, educational actions, measures for social inclusion, and pain and damage reduction. Specifically, educational and social inclusion strategies are oriented to develop individual, family, and community protective factors. Measures taken at this level can be combined.

This level includes a multi-disciplinary, team-based evaluation of the strategies applied, monitoring of the agreements reached through the intervention strategies, watching for the emergence of indicators that may suggest the need for a new intervention, and providing input for the revision of the functioning of the system and for its improvement. Of course, if the case comes to justice, its monitoring and constant evaluation will depend especially on this system.

ASSISTANCE IN OVERT CASES OF VIOLENCE

When there are clear and visible signs, the teams operating in healthcare centers request an expert evaluation to the MSP or to the services of INAU. Once the evaluation is carried out, the judicial system should be informed. It is noted that it is important that the team follows the entire process.

In the case of the Children and Family Care Centers (CAIF), which offer daycare services for children up to 3 years of age, the process starts with the evaluation of the child before establishing contact with the family and following the requirements of keeping strict confidentiality.

Based on consultation with field operators, it should be pointed out that there may be a lack of articulation between the different agents involved in cases of violence. For instance, the Forensic Investigation Office (ITF), which depends on the Judiciary Branch, has a Multidisciplinary Expert Team that is integrated by experts from the fields of Psychology, Social Work and Psychiatry. Their immediate supervisors are the judges from each court who are the professionals requesting the evaluations and the addressees of the special reports.

Concerning contact among the different organisms, communication of the ITF with the Institutions of Education and Health is unusual, except for the Ministry of the Interior when an urgent evaluation is requested. Instead, the SIPIAV, CAIF and Non-Governmental Organizations maintain contact with the different systems: health, education, and international organizations such as UNICEF.

Thus, it is possible to point out that Uruguay has the statutes and norms that define diagnostic criteria and the age limits required to determine the need for protection. Even though, as a unified regulatory framework for action, route maps by sectors are the principal unifying mechanism, once a BGA enters the evaluation process there are no consensual protocols for the evaluation available. Some inconsistencies are found in the classification of sexual abuse when the signs are not entirely visible; there is also a gap between the guidelines of the SIPIAV and the legal statutes. Not all organizations have access to SIPIAV but only those that have an agreement with INAU, which are only three or four (those operating in Montevideo and the metropolitan area).

Regarding the therapeutic measures and the models of care for the children and their families, a diagnosis is made and only on some occasions is the assistance of a multidisciplinary team required.

Beyond this, in healthcare centers, psychologically focused diagnoses are carried out, the possibility of brief therapeutic interventions is evaluated, child patients are followed periodically, and, on some occasions, hospitalization is required.

In cases of psychological assessment, a diagnostic evaluation of the specific situation of abuse or violence is made. Since there is no specific approach that psychological experts must follow, the guidelines depend on the field of specialization of the professional in charge. Nevertheless, the most commonly used strategies are based on the psychodynamic approach to personality and on the systemic perspective that is applied to approach family situations. In a document that deals specifically with situations of sexual violence against children and adolescents (MSP et al., 2018), cognitive behavioral therapy is recommended for the consideration of these cases that are suffering symptoms of post-traumatic stress.

The most frequently used evaluation techniques are semi-structured interviews (carried out with the individual and/or close relatives, according to what the judge determines), graphic projective tests, and intelligence tests, either to complement or to contrast with the information elicited in the interview.[3]

The interventions for the most part are non-compulsory. Compulsory treatments are ordered, for instance, when violence persists. In such cases, judicialization of the situation is required to establish the obligatory nature of the intervention for the persons involved. The persons who seek the services of a non-profit organization (NPO) are then referred by the Judiciary Branch, INAU or other public or private entity. Care is provided at the center corresponding to each institution.

The goal of the therapeutic intervention is reparation of the damage caused to the BGA individually and in groups. On the other hand, psychoeducational interventions are carried out with adults in charge of these BGAs. It is recommended to begin the intervention at a place of easy access for those involved, so as to ensure its continuity.

Progress has been made over the years in search of a model of integral care by working with the family and the community, trying to identify a significant protective family member capable of taking charge of the BGA's well-being and of generating changes in relationship patterns. The work is centered on the BGA and on their protective caregivers to develop their awareness of the harm produced and the violation of rights. If there is no available adult with the appropriate characteristics, the INAU team in charge must inform the competent court so as to give the child the necessary protection.

---

[3] The information about diagnoses, assessment techniques, and therapeutic measures provided in these paragraphs was elicited by means of interviews with authorities and professionals involved in the system of care.

Regarding the intervention process and its stages, a maximum of 18 months is stipulated by INAU. The follow-up may be carried out by INAU itself.

In case of institutionalization, the intervention is integrated to the daily routine of the center through coordinated work between the team in charge of the treatment (NGO, or the Family Therapy Unit of INAU) and the team of the center, to design the intervention strategies. The aim is to articulate networking with public and private organizations and persons who are significant to the family, according to the requirements of each situation.

Services Offered by INAU

The Division for the Integral Care of the Family provides care through the Department of Family Therapy. In 2014, this department carried out interventions with 180 families per year (400 girls and boys) who were referred and registered by INAU. Services include evaluation, mediation, and family therapy. Cases are referred by the entire INAU system and other judicial or educational institutions at a national level, mostly from Montevideo and the metropolitan area. The issues that are addressed include: Domestic Violence, school performance problems, developmental stage crises, sexual abuse, parental conflicts with repercussions for their children such as custody problems, visitation schedules, and agreement violations.

Highlights of the Protection Systems for BGA

The total number of BGAs who go through the services of INAU are 131,551 (Annual Report, 2019). This figure covers several services: community care (includes diagnosis and referral services, family referral centers), part-time comprehensive care modality (such as childhood and family centers), full-time comprehensive care modality (in this case children and adolescents live in centers because their rights have been violated, this attention may be temporary or permanent and its cause may be abandonment, violence situation). Finally, there is the alternative modality of foster care.

Child protection programs in Uruguay are centralized within the INAU. There are also quota agreements with NGOs through which the state pays the NGO for children's care and treatment.

In case of violence, in the service community care, individual, or group therapeutic treatments are offered for BGAs, as well as treatments with their caregivers. The approaches range from voluntary to compulsory in relation to the persistence of violence and its possible judicialization. It must be pointed out that even if treatments are prescribed, there are delays at the treatment centers and sometimes treatments are not carried out or, if they are initiated, they cannot be sustained over time.

According to the professionals who work in the field, assistance organizations receive an overwhelming number of care requests related to these issues, as well as INAU, and psychological care is unaffordable by the majority of the population.

There is a persistent concern related to the need to provide whole family services, including services to the offender. Funding limitations and too few qualified professionals are available to provide these treatments.

There is no specific policy for hiring staff beyond the customary requirement of having knowledge and experience related to that field of work. Although maltreatment and abuse are relevant issues in our present-day society, on many occasions it is difficult to find professionals interested in working in this area, such is the case, for instance, for pediatric psychiatrists. In the 2016 annual report of INAU (2017), it is accepted that in cases of violence the manifestation of the problem exceeds the capacity of the professional teams suitable for its response. In this sense, INAU accepts in this document the need to insist on training and to make calls according to the needs of each region. Some of the primary challenges to child protection in Uruguay include the lack of uniform criteria across sectors regarding definitions of harm and thresholds of response. The lack of financial resources across the system also hinders response time for prevention and intervention. Higher efficiency within the judicial system and greater guarantees from the police for effective protection are also needed. Children and youth also require more supports. And professionals working in these sectors need additional specialized and postgraduate training.

What Are the Methods for the Delivery of These Provisions?

When the cases are serious, and pass to the justice system, the situation of the child can vary depending on the type of violence that the child has suffered and who is the offender (father or mother, or both). The situation as a whole is assessed in all cases. There are some extremes that merit the loss of parental authority (*patria potestad*). Article 285 of the Civil Code establishes that parental authority is lost in the case of common crimes. Extreme physical aggression against their own child is a crime.

Once parental authority is lost, the adoption process can begin according to Article 249 of the Civil Code, provided that the requirements are met according to the regulations. In Uruguay, there are no child residency services with specialized personnel for addressing this type of situation. When there is a loss of parental authority in case of violence against minors the Specialized Family Judge deals with the subject according to Article 117 of the Childhood and Adolescence Code. Close relatives such as older siblings, uncles, or grandparents are sought as adoptive caregivers.

If relatives are not considered capable, children are referred to the INAU for a period of time and then they are assigned to what is called "surrogate mothers" who take care of them under the supervision of INAU until alternative adoptive parents can be identified.

On the other hand, the Foster Care Program is a temporary support resource, which has a national scope. When coexistence with the family of origin of the child or adolescent is no longer possible, assistance can be requested to INAU.

The INAU will seek a solution to ensure the child's development in a new family environment, trying to stimulate respect for their identity and their emotional ties. Each case will be evaluated and programs aimed at family strengthening can be implemented, or protective measures based on different types of family arrangements can be carried out.

It is important to remember that children can always choose to maintain the link with their family of origin. The intervention of INAU will end once the competent authority (s) deems it pertinent. There is, for example, the "Amiga Family" (Friend Family) program, which is an initiative of the INAU, which seeks that every child and adolescent can exercise their right to live within a family even if there are obstacles to do so with the family of origin. The idea is to convene solidarity families that temporarily receive the child or adolescent until they can return to their family of origin, or until a definitive family solution is found, through a family registered in the Sole Registry of Applicants to Adoption (Registro Unico de Adopción). The number of evaluations of applications for Adoption in 2017 was 110 (Memoria Annual INAU, 2019).

In 2020, new authorities presented for "urgent consideration" Law 19.889, which takes into account different subjects: economy, education, housing, penal right. In this law there is a new consideration for child adoption. The judge who studies the case can decide the child's adjudication for a new family without the INAU's report in those situations in which a boy, a girl, or an adolescent is fully integrated into a family, provided that this tenure started in a lawful way. Beyond the fact that the intention of this law is to expedite the adoption process favoring family integration as soon as possible, and although it is early to know the consequences of this change, a concern is present in reference to the families who are not selected or evaluated by the INAU and because work with the family of origin can be reduced. In several cases, the latter families, with support, could take care of the child again.

INAU also has support for families so that they can exercise their functions, for example, part-time programs, such as CAIF, Afterschool Children Clubs, and Youth Centers.

The CAIF provide maternal and child health services from pregnancy through early childhood. These services include nutrition, health, and parenting.

There are also Youth Centers that offer different educational and recreational activities for adolescents, with the aim of promoting socialization, pedagogical support, training, and/or job placement. They are open throughout the year and have multidisciplinary technical teams. The lines of work include educational activities, citizen participation activities, sports, health, and nutrition training.

How Are the Child Protection Services Financed?

Social public spending (henceforth SPP) refers to the state fiscal effort on activities that are oriented toward poverty reduction and the redistribution of income; the training, expansion, or renewal of human capabilities; and the observance, respect, protection, and promotion of citizens' rights. Since the beginning of the 20th century, Uruguay has been outstanding for having a high SPP within the regional context, resulting from the construction of an early social protection matrix. During the last 10 years, the country has registered an increase in cumulative SPP and there was also a reorientation addressed to a policy on early childhood, childhood, and adolescence. The implementation of reforms in the healthcare system, the tax reform, the new system of family allowances, and the increase in public policies directed towards persons from 0 to 18 years of age had an effect on the reduction of poverty and inequality: from 32.5% in 2006 to 9.7% in 2014. According to the United Nations, the Economic Commission for Latin America and the Caribbean, and UNICEF (2013), during the period 2005–2013, the average growth of SPP was 8.1% per year, due to the increase in healthcare and education; in the case of healthcare 200%, and in education 122.4% (National Office for Monitoring and Evaluation& MIDES 2015).[4]

The highest cumulative increase between 2006 and 2013 occurred in the 0–17 age group, with a relative weight increase of 5 percentage points, reaching at present almost 25% of the SPP. In turn, the remaining age groups decreased their relative weight, especially the older groups.

Starting with the creation of the National Plan for Early Childhood, Childhood and Adolescence 2016–2020 (Uruguay Social, 2016), a goal was set to prepare a road map to guide actions at a national level and by the institutions that compose the social protection fabric. Concerning early childhood, a five-year plan of investment has been devised to respond to the challenges that are constantly emerging, both at an inter-institutional level as well as within each organization. As one of the priorities concerning early childhood, there is a plan to implement and operationalize the Integrated National System of Care (SNIC). The SNIC acknowledges the right to receive care, reinforcing and amplifying the fabric of social protection of Uruguay. The SNIC has as its principal goal to generate a model of co-responsible care between the families, the state, the community and the market. The priorities outlined by the government related to early childhood include: to continue reduction of childhood mortality, prematurity, and low birth weight, to stimulate natural childbirth and reduce Caesarean section occurrences, to support food safety and the provision of childrearing guidelines, to improve parenting and family skills and child development, and reduce violent practices within the family. Other goals that are highlighted are the progressive universalization of access to education of 3-year-old children and to expand and diversify educational opportunities for children 0–2 years of age with the aim of improving the availability of care services and education in early childhood. The goals also include advancing the implementation of a common curriculum framework for the 0–6 age group, reducing the prevalence of developmental disorders in

---

[4] Dirección Nacional de Evaluación y Monitoreo.

children between 0 and 5 years of age, and attenuating the severity of the disorders already diagnosed in this age group.

Regarding childhood, the plan envisages implementation of the Protection System of Educational Trajectories, which implies the achievement of educational inclusion, the monitoring of educational trajectories and the completion of educational cycles.

The relation between the educational system and the healthcare system for the integral approach to learning difficulties and the psychosocial support for boys, girls, and their families is of great importance. Among the problems prioritized in childhood is to prevent nutritional disorders, such as overweight and obesity, as well as the need for providing integral healthcare with special attention to eye and dental checkups. Special attention is paid to the need to improve the quality of the detection systems and of timely and effective administrative and technical procedures to respond to situations of maltreatment in all its forms.

With regard to adolescence, in the same document (Uruguay Social, 2016), the priorities identified refer to educational inclusion, the opening up of spaces for participation, and the approach to pregnancy and sports. All of these priorities have a bearing on the integral development and the empowerment of adolescents, who are going through a crucial stage in the construction of their identity and citizenship.

In 2016, the National Agency of Investigation and Innovation (ANII) approved projects in the area of Education and Social Development that aim to foster, among other subjects, research that focuses on these age groups. This year, 28% of the projects approved focused on this area, and they ranked in the second place below projects on Human and Animal Health. Education and Social Development were ranked higher than other projects that are also considered priorities, such as energy, environment, and environmental services; agricultural, livestock, and agro-industrial production; and software for data-processing and logistic services and transport (ANII, 2018).

Finally, the document Uruguay Social (2016) cautions that an increase in the SPP is a necessary but insufficient condition for the improvement of the quality of the services that produce well-being, and points out that it is necessary to keep up the political commitment to improve the quality of public services.

Pending Challenges

The challenges identified in the document elaborated by Uruguay Social (2016) refer to the relation between the civil society and the state, which requires constant analysis and rethinking. Some specific challenges include a need to strengthen community agencies so that they are able to go beyond the mere execution of public policies and promote their long-term sustainability. A further challenge concerns the relation between universal and targeted public policies. Universal systems can adopt rigid formats that do not correspond to the different life situations of people. Additionally, there is insufficient funding to support some universal programs. On the other hand, targeted programs need to extend their scope. Regarding intervention practices, child protection in Uruguay needs to respond to different family configurations as family types take on greater diversity. Further coordination between the central government and the territories is necessary, with sensitivity to the needs of local actors and communities. Coordination between departments within metropolitan and rural areas is also needed. And efforts to conduct follow-up and continuous evaluation of policies is also needed.

In the same document, as far as the weaknesses are concerned, it was pointed out that there was a gap between the design of actions, programs and policies and their implementation in the territories. In this sense, two aspects must be mentioned: first, differences between the actions planned and the potential execution, and second, the heterogeneity observed in the actual implementation of the plan in different territories. On the other hand, in relation to the deployment of the policies, it was observed that there is a bias towards early childhood stages of development to the detriment of the other stages: childhood and adolescence. The recommendation includes the need to reflect on the institutionality of early childhood, childhood, and adolescence policies based on current reality. The planning, actions, and the present responses still reflect the current sectorialization, in spite of the efforts to attain integration (Uruguay Social, 2016).

In summary, we can say that child protection policies and their implementation in Uruguay as systems are relatively recent. Although in legal material we have provisions since many decades, only about 10 years ago, with the creation of SIPIAV, the institutions that are in charge of ensuring the development of BGAs began to work as a system. There are few evaluations of these efforts, and there is room for improvement in relation to detection and the care provided to victims and their families. Moreover, little data is collected to document processes and outcomes for children and families. In some passages of this chapter, this lack of concrete data is noted. Efforts to prepare and train personnel who are capable of implementing child protection collectively through their coordinated performance is also a new important challenge.

References

Agencia Nacional de Investigación e Innovación. (2018). *Informe de seguimiento de actividades 2016.* Available at: www.anii.org.uy.

ANEP. (2013). *Mapa de ruta para las situaciones de maltrato y abuso sexual en niños, niñas y adolescentes detectadas en el ámbito escolar.* ANEP, SIPIAV, UNICEF.

Calvo, J. J. (2014). *Atlas sociodemográfico y de la desigualdad en el Uruguay. Jóvenes en el Uruguay: demografía, educación, mercado laboral y emancipación.* Instituto Nacional de Estadística.

CNCLVD. (2015). *Plan de acción 2016–2019: por una vida libre de violencia de género, con una mirada generacional.* CNCLVD.

Colacce, M. and Tenenbaum, V. (2016). *Pobreza y privaciones múltiples en la infancia en Uruguay.* UNICEF.

Convención de Belén do Para. (1994). *Convención interamericana para prevenir, sancionar y erradicar la violencia contra la mujer.* Available at: https://www.oas.org/dil/esp/convencion_belem_do_para.pdf.

Dirección Nacional de Evaluación y Monitoreo and MIDES. (2015). *Monitoreo de la Situación de la Infancia en Uruguay.* MIDES.

INAU. (2017). *Memoria anual 2016*. INAU. Available at: www.inau.gub.uy.

INAU. (2018). *División de Atención Integral para la Familia*. INAU. Available at: http://www.inau.gub.uy/institucional/oficinas-de-inau/division-atencion-integral-a-la-familia-daif.

INAU. (2018). *Memoria Anual 2017*. INAU. Available at: www.inau.gub.uy.

INAU. 2020. *Memoria Anual 2019*. INAU. Available at: www.inau.gub.uy.

Instituto Nacional de Estadística. *Anuario 2017*. INE. Available at: www.ine.gub.uy.

Instituto Nacional de Estadística. *Anuario 2020*. INE. Available at: www.ine.gub.uy.

MIDES and INE. (2013). *Primera Encuesta basada en Género y Generaciones*. Ministerio de Desarrollo Social.

MIDES and UNICEF. (2015). *Encuesta nacional de indicadores múltiples*. MIDES-UNICEF.

Ministerio del Interior, Voz y Vos, and UNICEF. (2015). *Protocolo de comunicación para la policía frente a situaciones de violencia que involucren a niños, niñas y/o adolescentes*. Ministerio del Interior-UNICEF.

MSP, SIPIAV, and UNICEF. (2009). *Mapa de ruta para la prevención y la atención de situaciones de maltrato y abuso sexual infantil en el sector salud*. MSP, SIPIAV, and UNICEF.

MSP, SIPIAV, and UNICEF. (2018). *Protocolo para el abordaje de situaciones de violencia sexual hacia niños, niñas y adolescentes en el marco del Sistema Nacional Integrado de Salud*. Ministerio de Salud-SIPIAV-UNICEF.

OMS. (2002). *Informe mundial sobre la violencia y la salud. sinopsis*. OMS.

SIPIAV. (2016a). *Hoja de ruta 2016–2019*. SIPIAV.

SIPIAV. (2016b). *Informe de Gestión*. SIPIAV.

SIPIAV. (2016c). *Sistema de protección contra la violencia hacia NNA*. SIPIAV.

UNICEF. (1989). Convention on the Rights of the Child. Available at: https://www.unicef.org/panama/spanish/convencion(3).pdf.

UNICEF. (2017). *Panorama de la violencia hacia la infancia en Uruguay 2017*. UNICEF.

Uruguay Social. (2016). *Plan Nacional de Primera Infancia, infancia y adolescencia 2016–2020*. MIDES, INAU.

WHO. (2002). *Guidelines for medico-legal care in cases of sexual violence*. Available at: http://apps.who.int/iris/bitstream/10665/42788/1/924154628X.pdf.

Legislation

Law No. 15.737. Amnistía. (1985).

Law No. 16.137. Convención sobre los Derechos del Niño. (1990).

Law No. 17.514. Violencia doméstica. (2002).

Law No. 17.823. Código de la niñez y la adolescencia. (2004).

Law No. 18.211. Sistema Nacional Integrado de Salud. (2007).

Law No. 18.214. Integridad personal de niños, niños y adolescentes. (2007).

Law No. 18.590. Código de la niñez y la adolescencia. Se modifican disposiciones relativas a adopción. (2009).

Law No. 18.651. Protección integral de personas con discapacidad. (2010).

Law No. 18.778. Adolescente en conflicto con la ley. (2011).

Law No. 18.777. Adolescente infractores de la ley penal. (2011).

Law No. 18.850. Hijos de personas fallecidas como consecuencia de hechos de violencia doméstica. (2011).

Law Nº 19.055. Código de la niñez y la adolescencia. Modificación artículos 72 y 76. (2013).

Law Nº 19.092. Código de la niñez y la adolescencia. Modificación de varias disposiciones. (2013).

Law No. 19.580. Violencia hacia las mujeres basada en género. (2018).

Law 19. 747 Código de la Niñez y la Adolescencia. Modificación del Capítulo XI Ley 17.823. (2019).

Law 19.889 Ley de Urgente Consideración. (2020).

PART III

Nascent

Building the Child Protection System in Argentina

Carla Villalta *and* Valeria Llobet

Abstract

This chapter explores the construction of the Argentinian child protection system. Whilst Argentina was one of the first countries to develop a strong Welfare State in Latin America, the nation's child protection matters did not perform nearly as well. The expansion of children's rights occurred parallel to the retraction of citizenship and welfare protection and the rise of poverty. Thus, transformation in education, social protection, and family laws was framed by rights focused on children's interests and needs. The chapter expounds on the process of local reception and institutionalization of children's rights discourse, the local debates, and disputes over the definition of the aforementioned rights and their actors.

Key Words: Argentina, child protection system, Latin America, Welfare State, education, family laws, institutionalization, children's rights, poverty, citizenship

Introduction

Argentina was one of the first Latin American countries to develop a strong welfare state; however, the nation did not perform nearly as well in the area of child protection issues. While the United Nations Convention on the Rights of the Child (CRC) was included in the Constitution during the 1994 reform, the principles of children's rights did not inform federal laws until 2005, when an extensive body of laws on children's rights, comprised of education, health, and special protection were introduced. During the 1990s, the institutionalization of children's rights and the CRC, in the context of a neoliberal state and the dominance of the Washington Consensus, marked the conjunction of children's rights and the transformation of the welfare state. Deemed a paradoxical process, the expansion of rights occurred parallel to the retraction of citizenship and welfare protection and the rise of poverty (Llobet, 2009a; Villalta, 2010a). In the 2000s, the financial crisis of 1999–2002 marked the end of the neoliberal wave and the beginning of a left-wing era—the so called Pink Wave—due to the government's support for human rights and emphasis on inequality. A change in the role of state institutions and the development of policies and laws in favor of human rights strongly marked the decade. Children were at the center of political discourse as the legitimate subject of rights and protection policies. Changes in education, social protection, and family laws were framed by rights focused on children's interests and needs.

In 2015, the rise of an openly right-wing government marked the end of the consensus of children's rights, and new voices took control of the stage. The new government shifted the main focus of the debate to the age of full penal prosecution. This coincided with a criminal characterization of political engagement by children and youth, while implementing budget cuts that put pressure on the provision of social rights. The social protection system, previously based on ideas of social and economic rights, has slowly moved into a more defined model of individual activation. Moreover, the new political actors in power are contesting human rights discourses as part of a past from which the new policy focus needs to move away. Children's and human rights activists strategically use discourses and meanings to delegitimize these changes, but the very meanings and scope of rights seem to be currently under siege; the institutions and policies that support these ideas are being eliminated and transformed.

In this chapter, we will focus on the process of local reception and institutionalization of children's rights discourse, the local debates and disputes over the meaning and extension of those rights, and the local actors that have been active in these disputes. The struggles over the meaning of childhood and rights have not only contributed to the vernacularization of human rights (Merry, 2006), but have also taken part in the re-drawing of the social place and meaning of childhood, parenthood and parental responsibilities and entitlements, as well as the State's obligations and responsibilities. Therefore, the chapter will also discuss the architecture of rights (Haney, 2002), which are comprised of the institutions and policies of child protection and acknowledge the challenges of realizing children's rights in a socio-political context of budget constraints and a "minimal-state."

Several key points frame this chapter. Institutionalization of rights is a contested process that involves struggles over redistribution and interpretation of needs (Fraser, 1989; Fonseca, 2004; Haney, 2006), and the community, market, and private realms interact in complex ways to produce both the ideological and the material forms of state regimes (Haney, 2002; Milanich, 2002). Therefore, the social and material conditions for the institutionalization of rights are not merely contextual, but the main components of institutionalization. Public authority and the private sphere draw on a common well of cultural beliefs and practices and, therefore, they are not dichotomous. The rights of children are at the center of debates with respect to the institutionalization of the state, to the relationships and exercising of family authority, and to the extension of social protection (Schuch, 2009). This is reminiscent of the beginning of the 20th century when debates about the protection of childhood constituted an important stage for a broader pan-American debate about family, maternity, and social protection (Guy, 2009; Rojas Novoa, 2017).

The Local Reception of the CRC

The national debates on child protection arose in Latin American countries mainly at two historical moments. The first period was during the late 19th century and early 20th century, when these countries were building the core institutions of nation states, and at the pan-American level; the governability of the Americas was a fertile terrain for debates. Following a clear regional pattern, while also responding to local debates, Argentina condensed 30 years of debates on child education and child protection into a national law in 1919—the National Law of "Patronato de Menores" number 10.903. It established new regulations on parenting and parental responsibility and rights, including the possibility of losing parental rights if the children were considered "at risk" by educational, police, or philanthropic authorities (Villalta, 2010a). The "tutelary complex" (i.e., a system of institutions imposing child-rearing norms and regulations; Donzelot, 1990) put in place by that law included not only state regulations on poor families and their children, but implied the re-drawing of state agencies' functions and power as well as the creation of a new actor, a judge, the *Juez de Menores* ("Judge of Minors"), who became the authority in issues of reform and protection of minors. The *Juez* developed progressively greater centrality and power, as well as a range of interventions that covered: crimes committed by underage children, children who were victims of crime and abuse, and children deemed to be "abandoned." The *Juez* acted in an institutional context of massive institutions, labeled as "total" (Goffman, 2001) by the critical scholarship after the dictatorship. Despite the centrality of those institutions throughout the Americas—starting in the 1950s and 60s and lasting through the 1990s—attempts at reform were made, including the creation of foster care programs in family settings.

The law—and that complex collection of institutions, practices, meanings, and regulations that it reorganized—was widely criticized through the 1980s and 90s. The core criticisms were, first and foremost, that the focus on poverty as a moral deficit deemed parenting strategies and practices of poor families wrong and harmful. Second, critics claimed that the treatment framed children as mere objects justifying intervention and control, as opposed to conceptualizing children as rights bearers—an argument that arose from the debates over the formulation of the CRC during the 1980s. Third, critics condemned the size and types of institutions in which children under state custody were placed.

This criticism arose in Argentina during the post-dictatorship democratization. Evidence emerged of child abduction performed by the military dictatorship with the assistance of those involved with the minors tutelary complex contributing to mistrust and moral rejection. Kidnapped "nietos" were under the custody of institutions of foster care and in placements selected by the judiciary because they were labeled as orphans. In effect, this evidence linking foster care practices and institutions for minors with the illegally missing children of the "Desaparecidos" (i.e., people who disappeared during 1974–1983 dictatorship known in anglophone countries as the Dirty War), was a main reason that the *Abuelas de Plaza de Mayo*, a key player in the inclusion of the right to an identity in the CRC, was able to find some of the children (Villalta, 2012).

Despite the consensus of the critics, it took 11 years from the incorporation of the CRC into the Argentine Constitution to become a federal law, in 2005, which repealed the 1919 law. One of the main reasons for the lengthy transition is analyzed in the literature on the resistance of the judiciary. The *Jueces de Menores*, if not a powerful body among the judiciary in itself (Lugones, 2012), was a dominant actor capable of restraining the ability of other state agencies to maneuver (Haney, 2006; Villalta, 2010b). The 1919 Law, known as the "Agote" Law or "10.903," established an ample set of functions and an uncontestable power in the figure of the judge. His own criteria (most of the *Jueces de Menores* were male for most of the 20th century) was enough to decide the fate of a child, and the other state agencies (e.g., school, health agencies, orphanages) were designed as auxiliary— dependent on the judge's authority if a child was under his tutelar control. In this context, the transformation of the law under the influence of the CRC was seen, first and foremost, as the restriction of the discretionary power of the *Juez de Menores*. More recent research has shown that this picture was correct but incomplete; it did not analyze child protection as a complex field in which many actors confront and dispute meanings, resources, and power (Villalta & Llobet, 2015).

In a transitional lapse during the 1990s, several federal and local entities passed laws that enforced the CRC perspective in local governments, restricted the authority of the *Juez de Menores*, and created new administrative authorities for child protection. Those new agencies, called *Defensorías* ("defense offices"), were devoted to the protection of vulnerable children from abusive and arbitrary state interventions. They were a paradoxical place for more than one reason, since first, the welfare state was being dismantled and poverty was on the rise, and second, the *Defensorías* were named as a judicial office but were a branch of executive power and therefore, lacking very relevant power. The decade was analyzed as showing three interrelated processes that impacted the situation of children: the democratization after the most recent dictatorship, the increased impoverishment of the population, and the crisis of the education system (Carli, 2006).

In effect, during the 1990s, there was a first cycle of reforms that included a CRC perspective narrowly focused on the judiciary. In 1995, the province of Mendoza, in the center-west of the country, passed the first local law that was inspired by the CRC and created a local authority, namely the Provincial Child Council, that aimed to replace the judiciary in all social matters, and created Family Courts to replace the former *Juez de Menores*, now confined to juvenile justice. That reform is emblematic of the 1990s. Whereas the "discretionary power" of the judiciary was deconstructed by replacing the penal system for civil courts, administrative agents were still treated as mere auxiliary agents. Also, with the creation of Family Courts, nearly every case was still managed through judicial power. The same type of reform was in place in the eight provinces that engaged in changes during the

1990s (Ciudad Autónoma de Buenos Aires (CABA), Chubut, Mendoza, Neuquén, San Juan, Tierra del Fuego, San Luis, and Jujuy).

If the institutional changes of the 1990s were limited in scope and confined to a minority of provinces—although some of those provinces were among the most populated and affluent—they were widely debated by civil society, and the local governments that championed the changes were deemed progressive and applauded. Nevertheless, the changes were developed in the midst of devolution as the core paradigm for the necessary reform of the state: decentralization, municipality level services, and deconcentration of funds were seen as key features in bureaucratic administration in order to achieve a human rights-based approach (UNPD, 2005). This context of ideas was paramount to understand the limitations and the imprint that marked the nascent Child Protection Services. Within a short period of time, hundreds of NGOs were funded nationwide, developing services previously provided by the State, and becoming prominent and vocal actors in the debate on the needed reforms. The CRC promoted the inclusion of NGOs as relevant actors in the institutionalization of rights, considering them capable of improving democracy and holding the public administration accountable. Since the inception of the modern state, child protection issues were taken into the hands of Catholic philanthropic associations, usually run by prominent ladies. The novelty that the nineties brought to the field was the emergence of professionalized NGOs, with newer practices of funding and newer social groups organized in grassroots organizations that were considered in the children's rights agenda.

However, since the financial sources for the NGOs mostly came from the state, the devolution process took the form of a semi-privatization that contributed to the nationwide neoliberal reform and the expansion of the "market of childhood" (Donzelot, 1990). Furthermore, the fact that the criticism and questioning of child protection services provided by the state was coming from "outside" (i.e., voiced by NGOs, social movements, and activists) emerged consequentially as a corporative defense of the old ways, in a boomerang effect that complicated the dialogue (Beloff, 2005). The new children's rights discourse was formulaic and tokenistic. Specifically, it was useful for giving a new look to old practices (Fonseca & Schuch, 2009) and for galvanizing the dominant perception of a field divided into two coexisting sub-systems: the old ways of tutelary power concentrated in the *Juez de Menores*, and the children's rights approach developed by the new but weak programs.

The limited achievements of the 1990s were widely debated in light of the negative social outcomes that followed the privatization and shrinkage of the welfare state: high rates of unemployment and child poverty, an unprecedented rise in hunger and the growth of urban slums, and an increase in crime. Informal labor reached 40% in 2002, and under-employment rose to 19% that same year. In terms of poverty, 42% of households in 2002 had income under the poverty line, which represented three out of four children under 18 in poverty (CEPAL, 2004). Furthermore, Argentina was condemned several times for not presenting the periodic state report to the CRC committee and for their poor results when doing so. Additionally, social movements were vocal in criticizing the violations of children's rights. *Los Chicos del Pueblo* (Children of the People), a nationwide grassroots and union organization, and other social movements claimed that child poverty was a matter of human rights and an outrageous source of injustice. Demands to tackle child poverty and child protection services became intertwined; changes in child protection services were deemed necessary in order to tackle child poverty under the auspices of children's rights. As the country moved closer to the socioeconomic and political crash of 2001, those demands became more and more urgent and dramatic.

The rise in 2003 of a new political cycle, after the political and economic turmoil of 2001–2002, resulted in the launch of child protection services reform under a new light. As a consequence, the 2005 Law, welcomed by the many actors promoting children's rights, involved a major change in the institutions and the case management in child protection as well as the re-drafting of the borders between the judiciary and the executive branches of government. It also implied the development of a body of rights that were at the heart of a redefinition of the relationship between state, families, and children in order to fulfill the expectation of a citizen-childhood. The law also renewed the interactions between NGOs, the subsectors of the welfare state (education and health primarily), and Child Protection Services. But, after at least ten years of debates, the ground in which to build the new institutions was not a virgin one (Beloff, 2004). The consequences of the layers of partial reforms and disputes shifted solutions to the microlevel of institutional practices and interactions.

The Normative Reform: Law 26.061 and the Emergence of a New Child Protection Institutionality

During the 1990s, only eight provinces launched child protection laws to incorporate the CRC. However, after 2005, every Argentinian province adapted new laws following the federal Integral Protection Law (26061/2005). This law was part of a set of interrelated laws that configured a new definition of state protection: Law 26206 for National Education, Law 25763 for Sexual Health and Family Planning, Law 26233 for Children's Early Development Centers, Law 26150 for Sexual Education, Law 26390 for Child Labor, and, in 2009, Law 26579 reforming the age of civil rights. These legislative innovations were included in the new Civil Code (effective August 2015), and together represent revolutionary transformations in family law in areas including filiation, parent-child responsibilities and obligations, and divorce.

The Child Protection Law:

- mandated the jurisdiction of the CRC in each juridical act and administrative decision for children under the age of 18 (Article 2);

- defined the Best Interest Principle [of children] as "the maximum, integral and simultaneous satisfaction of rights and guarantees" (Article 3);
- stipulated the state undertake public policies (Article 4);
- defined the approach of state responsibilities as well as those of family and community in the provision of protection and rights (Articles 5 to 7).

The federal law also advanced the ongoing debate of tutelary power exercised by the judiciary by restricting prerogatives and strengthening administrative agencies. In doing so, the law dismantled the former national agency—the National Council for Childhood, Adolescence and Family—that was the executive branch of the *Patronato* established in 1919 and replaced it with the National Secretariat for Children's Rights (SENAF).

After approval of the law, it became imperative to redesign the institutional architecture in order to comply with the nascent "Integral Protection System." Although many actors agreed with the need for redesign and compliance, the implementation was much debated. The government opened a cycle of consultation and political negotiation with different sectors, actors, and institutions, including provinces, national ministries, international institutions, unions, civil society movements, and scholars, among others (Burgues & Lerner, 2006) that both shaped the institutionality as well as gave it legitimacy and political purchase. Law 26061 included in its provisions that the implementation of child protection was to be articulated by the national, provincial, and municipal governments. Also, it explicitly defined the Integral Protection System as comprising the following: policy, plans, and programs; administrative and judicial rights protection agencies; financial resources; procedures; rights protection measures; and exceptional rights protection measures (Article 32).

That process led to the creation, in December 2006, of the Federal Council for Childhood, Adolescence, and Family, constituted by representatives of each province, with the mission of leading the planning process for children's public policy nationwide. The peculiarity of the Council was that, for the first time, it was provided with a budget and the power to establish the approach that should be adopted by each province's child protection policies. The Federal Fund for Children, in place since 2008 and active until 2015, provided the resources for the creation of child protection agencies in each province and many municipalities. The Fund was, therefore, correcting the errors and problems that followed the state reforms during the 1990s, especially those related to administrative capabilities and the labor conditions in the sector. The Council encountered a variety of situations in each province, such as reforming the previous institutionality (e.g., the city of Buenos Aires) or having to start from scratch. The former faced the challenge of reforming organizations that acted as an auxiliary of the judiciary and as administration of orphanages and foster placement institutions. That reform redefined case management, intensified old disputes with the judiciary, and introduced a new area of conflict with other executive agencies, especially those in education and health. The second cases—those that needed to build agencies anew—usually built the Child Protection system at a provincial level, which saved resources and allowed the administration to operate though implied that the system would be concentrated in the main city/cities, typically the provincial capital. Therefore, the initial agenda of the Council was dominated by the development and placement of an effective child protection agency in every province. In 2009, the National Plan of Action for Children's Rights was enacted as a national strategy for the implementation of the CRC, focusing on human resources training. The reform of juvenile justice, the second core goal of the National Plan, was deemed politically too risky, and only was developed at the level of debating institutional practices, putting the law reform aside.

The process of rebuilding the child protection system with better articulation of social protection reached its apex in October 2009 when the *Asignación Universal por Hijo* (AUH—Children's Universal Monetary Transfer; i.e., a conditional cash transfer program that was much more generous and less punitive than the other programs in the Latin American region) was put in place. The AUH extended the system of family pension from the formal workers to those families with both unemployed parents and those working in informal sectors. Most importantly, the AUH framed the cash transfers as citizen's rights and as a means for redistributive justice, extending the violation of children's rights to poverty and pushing the idea of child protection to explicitly include socioeconomic rights.

By 2010, the process of reforms was considered to have reached acceptable stability, and therefore, the national focus shifted to developing agents' capabilities, to professionalizing them, and to creating tools for intervention. Several changes occurred: many postgraduate programs were developed that focused on the workers, institutional practices, and procedures; nationwide workshops and conferences were held; and the debate finally focused on the improvement of everyday needs. But, what needed to be improved? In what follows, we focus on the methods for delivering child protection services.

Child Protection Services: The Design of Rights Interventions and the Focus on De-institutionalization

Given that Argentina is a federal nation, the implementation of Child Protection Services varies from province to province, though most provinces signed rights protection laws or subscribed to the national law in the last decade (see Table 29.1). Along with these federal and provincial laws, there were national and provincial laws on family and gender violence and child maltreatment called *Violencia Doméstica*. The emergence of these laws was a result of the demands of the women's movement, together with the institutionalization of the Convention of the Elimination of All Forms of Discrimination Against Women (CEDAW) and other women's rights treaties. The laws were enforced by programs that promoted changes in social practices and behavior regarding gender violence; established new procedures to receive complaints and allegations; and registered, systematized, and researched the problem.

Table 29.1 Laws relating to child protection by province

Province	Child protection laws	Domestic/family violence laws
Buenos Aires	Law 13298	Law 12569
CABA	Law 114/Law 26061	Law 1688/Law 26485
Chaco	Law 7162 Law 26061	Law 4175 Law 26485
Chubut	Law III 21/Law 26061	Law XV 12
Cordoba	Law 9944	Law 9283
Corrientes	Law 5773 (Adhere to Law 26061)	Law 5903 Adhere to Law 26485. Law 5019 Law 5663
Entre Rios	Law 9861 (Adhere to Law 26061).	Law 9198 (Adhere to Law 26485)
Formosa	Law 26061	Law 1160 and modified 1191/96
Jujuy	Law 5288	Law 510
La Pampa	Law 2703	Law 1918
La Rioja	Law 8848/Law 26061	Law 6580
Mendoza	Law 6.354 Law 26.061	Law 6672/ Law 6551 Law 8226 Adhere to Law 26485
Misiones	Law II 16 (Ex 3820) Regulation Decree 1.852/10, Resolution 471/10	Law 3325 (Modified by Law 4405), Regulation Decree 2668/08
Neuquén	Law 2302	Law 2212/Law 2786
Rio Negro	Law 4109 (Adhere to Law 26061)	Law 4241
Salta	Law 7039. (Adhere to Law 26061)	Law 7403
San Juan	Law 7338 (Modified by Law 7511) Law 7889. Adhere to Law 26061	Law 6542
San Luis	Law 5430/2004 Adhere to CRC/Law I-0808-2012 Strategic Plan for Childhood and Adolescence/Law IV 0871-2013 Foster Care System	Law I—0009
Santa Cruz	Law 3.062	Law 24417
Santa Fe	Law 12967 (Modified by Law 13237)	Law 11529
Santiago del Estero	Law 6915	Law 6970/Adhere to Law 24417. Law 7032
Tierra del Fuego	Law 521/Law 26061	Law 39/Law 26485
Tucuman	Law 8293/Law 26061	Law 7264/Law 24417

Starting in 2005, each province established specific areas of government to implement these laws, called "Application Organism," with territorial agencies named "decentralized services" (see Table 29.2). These agencies receive allegations and cases from other institutions (hospitals, schools, police, judiciary) of children

Table 29.2 A description and organization of services by province

Province	Application organism	Decentralized services
Buenos Aires	Child and Adolescence Secretariat	23 Zone Services for the Promotion and Protection of Children's Rights
CABA	Children's Rights Council	17 Zone "*Defensorías*"
Catamarca	Family Under Secretariat	No services
Chaco	Childhood, Adolescence and Family Under Secretariat	5 Integral Protection Units—UPI
Chubut	Ministry of Family and Social Promotion, Under Secretariat for Human Development and Family	8 decentralized services
Cordoba	Ministry of Social Development, Secretary of Childhood, Adolescence and Family	16 Regional Development Unit (UDER)
Corrientes	Childhood, Adolescence and Family Council	6 Territorial Technical Teams
Entre Rios	Provincial Council of Child, Adolescent and Family COPNAF	1 Central Department, 13 Department coordination, and 71 Childhood Areas
Formosa	Childhood, Adolescence and Family Under Secretariat	7 decentralized services
Jujuy	Childhood, Adolescence and Family Secretariat and Direction of Childhood and Adolescence	2 offices
La Pampa	General Direction for Childhood and Adolescence	4 decentralized services
La Rioja	General Direction for Childhood and Adolescence	No services
Mendoza	Ministry of Social Development and Human Rights Direction of Childhood, Adolescence and Family DINAF	16 decentralized services
Misiones	Ministry of Social Development Direction of Minor and Family	3 Agencies of Integral Rights Protection
Neuquén	Childhood, Adolescence and Family Under Secretariat	9 Community Units
Rio Negro	Under Secretariat for Integral Protection of children and adolescents	9 decentralized services
Salta	Ministry of Human Rights Secretariat for Equality of Opportunities.	59 decentralized services
San Juan	Direction of Childhood, Adolescence and Family	19 decentralized services
San Luis	Ministry of Social Inclusion, Program of Promotion and Protection of the Family	3 regional areas

Table 29.2 *Continued*

Province	Application organism	Decentralized services
Santa Cruz	Ministry of Social Development Childhood, Adolescence and Family Under Secretariat	14 Local Protection Offices
Santa Fe	Childhood, Adolescence and Family Secretariat	5 nodes
Santiago del Estero	Childhood, Adolescence and Family Under Secretariat	6 Rights Protection Centers
Tierra del Fuego	Direction of Integral Protection Direction of Institutional Protection	2 decentralized services
Tucuman	Childhood, Adolescence and Family State Secretariat SENAYF	13 decentralized services

Source: SENAF & UNICEF (2014).

whose rights were vulnerable, *niños con derechos vulnerados*. These rights deprivations may include lack of housing, school absences, or difficulties in healthcare. Child neglect cases are also included, which could entail child maltreatment, witnessing gender violence, or being the victim of sexual abuse or any other crime. The agencies must also intervene in cases of teenagers under 16 who are suspected of committing a felony or a crime, in order to include these children in special programs and to restitute any rights unmet.

Also, each provincial state differs in its relational and administrative capabilities (Rodríguez Gustá, 2004), including the agents' professional training and skills, and the ideas and values about gender, class, and family that infuse the institutional culture. In shifting from provinces to a local context, each local context consists of a different kind of civil society, from more traditional ones with Catholic charity organizations to more "modern" ones, comprised of NGOs and social movements.

Despite the variability in governance, and after 13 years of legal implementation, a common understanding of the meanings and practices of "integral protection" intervention was found. That understanding impacted, in particular, the definition of clients, targets, and general goals. However, it did not prevail in the interactions and interrelations between programs and agencies, in which the more therapeutic and individualized logistics permeated everyday practices and interventions.

In effect, the 26.061 law defined two types of interventions aimed at the "restitution of children's rights". The first type of measure (see Table 29.3), defined in Article 33, is for *integral protection of rights* as all actions restoring the rights that are not provided for (i.e., healthcare, education, home). Examples of measures are housing subsidies, fellowships for elementary or middle schooling, or cash transfers or special provisions for specific medication. The goal of the intervention is to strengthen family and community ties. Furthermore, the article tackles the criticism elaborated during the 1980s and 90s

Table 29.3 A description of child protection services

	Integral protection measures	Exceptional protection	Foster care (Acogimiento)
Types of measures	Financial aid, assistance with attendance compliance, healthcare, family-support programs.	Placement in childcare services in residential programs, in other family members' homes or in foster care families	Small institutions (state run and NGOs contracted by the state) organized by age and sex. Foster care programs (state run and NGOs contracted by the state). Other family members or community members.
Targets	Children with rights unmet, families unable to safeguard those rights.	Children that, following the Best Interest principle, needed to be removed from their homes and to be severed from their families. Main issues include: child abuse and neglect, maltreatment and violence, street-children, children with parents abusing drugs, and newborns left in hospitals.	Children under exceptional protection measure
Resources (e.g., social policies, funding)	Healthcare provisions, medicine and drugs, educational special programs, housing programs and subsidies, financial aid, day centers, food supplies, etc.	Per capita funding, financial aid depending upon the number of children under residential care. Healthcare provisions, medicine and drugs, special education programs, housing programs and subsidies, financial aid, daycare centers, food supplies, etc.	Per capita funding directed to NGOs; special aid for families, upon discretionary decision; and risk evaluation.

Table 29.3 *Continued*

	Integral protection measures	Exceptional protection	Foster care (*Acogimiento*)
Involvement of family members	Working with families is a priority. Some provinces include parents in child-care programs, family-support programs or psychological treatment. The caseworkers sign agreements and rules of conduct with parents that imply changes in their care arrangements and proof of compliance with treatments, if needed.	The aim of the measure is "family re-vinculation" (i.e., reorganization of family ties). But the work with families varies by province though typically there are only a few programs to support families while the child protection measure is underway.	Usually, families—or parents specifically—are no longer involved in the intervention when the children are placed in foster care, since the child is eligible for adoption.
Organizational arrangements (who delivers services)	Territorial services and offices that implement the Child Protection Laws. Child Directions, usually in the Ministry of Social Development. Educational System and Healthcare.	Special programs that supervise the residential service. Judiciary—usually Family Courts— that supervise administrative decisions.	Family Courts and Programs for Child Placement. 10% of children under exceptional protection are in family foster care programs. 60% of the interventions are exceptional protection measures.
Decision maker	Agents in territorial services	Agents and child protection authorities with Family Courts Supervision. Different degree of involvement of NGOs.	Family Court and Child Protection Authorities.
Centralization/ decentralization	Maximum decentralization	Involves a degree of centralization in the decision making process	Mixture of centralization and decentralization
Funding	There is a combination of funds: national, provincial and eventually, local.	Sources of funds may include private donors and NGOs, and the judicial budget.	Sources of funds may include private donors and NGOs, and the judicial budget. Some programs may include international agencies' support.

by clearly stating that parental or family poverty must not be the reason for removing the child from her or his home (Article 33).

The second type of measure, *exceptional protection* (Article 39), is put into place after the integral protection has been declared depleted by the agencies implementing it. It comprises the removal of the child from their home for a maximum of six months due to a finding of high risk and imminent danger. State agencies have to follow specific requirements: an administrative protocol conformed by the judiciary, in which all the previous measures must be detailed; and the out-of-home placement must be in an institution, organization, or family evaluated by state officials. After the lapse of six months, the exceptional measure expires. According to the new Civil and Commercial Code,[1] the child is either declared for adoption, or sent back to his or her family, including an opportunity for formal guardianship through extended family.

The concrete implementation of these provisions varies by multiple factors, including jurisdiction, situation, and corresponding case worker procedures, length, and outcomes. However, this variability may be clarified if analyzed within three main heuristic dimensions: interpretive, institutional, and regional.

INTERPRETIVE

The meanings and values of rights protection and children's needs constructed and disputed by actors in the field are central to understanding the institutionalization of rights process and the building of welfare regimes (Fraser, 1989; Bourdieu, 1999; Haney & Pollard, 2003). The interpretation and administration of children's needs and rights through welfare, specific protection institutions, and policies relies on the gendered and class underpinnings of the welfare state. Therefore, the child protection system as a whole is prone to punitive practices, or the culpability of parents (typically mothers) as principal perpetrators of rights violations, similar to other familial discourses (Haney, 2002; Nari, 2005). When understanding rights protection and welfare regimes with a focus on highly gendered family capabilities, the consequences are practices of moral regulation, psychologization, and familiarization of needs (Llobet, 2009; Schuch, 2009).

INSTITUTIONAL

Nevertheless, the familial and psychological principles, patterns, and norms underlying children's rights do not go uncontested. As Fraser (1989) states, there is an ongoing dispute on the extension and entitlements of welfare provision and rights, as well as who is

---

[1] In 2015, the new Civil Code was enacted. It included the change of many family relations and the juridical status of children and adolescents: replaced the *patria potestas* for "parental responsibility," included the "will of procreation" as a new type of filiation, and changed stigma-charged categories of "minors and disabled" for children (0–12) and adolescents (13–18). It modified the principle of capability, including the principle of progressive autonomy, by including the child's lawyer and taking into account the child's opinion and their right to be heard.

going to be held accountable, for what, and to whom. Contesting the familial ideologies, there are discourses on community and "territorialization" (Magistris, 2016; Medan et al., 2019) of state intervention that focus on inequality. These discussions shift individual and motherhood regulation to a more comprehensive understanding of vulnerability. It is usually in school and the healthcare system where the moral discourse on motherhood and the individualization and psychologization of social problems are more successful. Therefore, both areas tend to be more problematic from the point of view of case workers and children's rights agencies. For the former (health and educational institutions), the rights protection agencies do not intervene promptly, and therefore teachers and health workers tend to portray the rights protection agencies as inactive, indifferent, and inefficient. From the point of view of caseworkers and agencies, schools and healthcare institutions do not fulfill the requirements of co-responsibility established by the law. On the contrary, they consider schools and healthcare systems as moving far too quickly to dispose of the "problem."

Especially difficult are the cases in which the distinction between poverty and child abuse is debatable. Cases in which schools "diagnose" the situation are seen by Child Protection agents as highly selective and morally biased. For instance, schools called attention to cases of child maltreatment when children came poorly dressed or dirty, with no other signs of real violence, relying on old protocols and customary practices that permit or enforce expulsive practices contradictory to current Child Protection Law. In the healthcare systems, on the other hand, the agents held expectations of a fast resolution, as provided by the old *Juez de Menores*, which were a fruitful source of conflict between healthcare professionals and the new Child Protection agencies. Therefore, many cases were still managed through the judiciary, in open contradiction of the new law and executive agencies guidance.

These bureaucratic resistances—especially those in health and education—expose the disagreement and dispute over the meaning of "child protection," and what kind of practices it comprises and enables. Further, it shows us how debates are influenced by prestige and professional pride wherein "specialists" defend types of practices as their own expertise and competence. Change is then perceived as a threat to their power, social place, and recognition, which is evident in the Bourdieusian-like field of child protection. Consequently, Child Protection System implementation is heavily dependent on the characteristics of the inter-institutional and interpersonal relations, alliances, and disputes; the contingent intensity of the conflicts around specific cases; their correct interpretation and course of action; and the moral values underpinning the agencies and agents' actions.

One solution for the varied implementation dependencies was the development and implementation of case management protocols, rules, definition of practices, and timeframes for case management. The joint work of the National Secretariat (SENNAF) and the provincial governments resulted in the elaboration and implementation of such protocols in at least 15 provinces (UNICEF, 2016). In order to achieve coherence and consistent criteria, the SENNAF developed procedures for rights protection measures and for standards in institutional quality. Both were approved by the Federal Council and acted as guides for action, although there has been little evidence of effective implementation (UNICEF, 2016).

One of the most relevant problems faced by the Child Protection System is the lack of systematic information and periodic statistical reports. Therefore, information must be gathered by research usually developed in partnership with national universities and/or UNICEF. One of these research projects showed that the most common child protection measure implemented by Child Services in 15 provinces was the creation of specific programs that "supervise parental care of the child in their own home, aiming to support the parents or adult family members in complying with their responsibilities." In another five provinces, the measure implemented is the inclusion of the child and her family in family-support programs; two other provinces indicated that the first measure was economic assistance for the family; one more showed that the most implemented measure was medical or psychological treatment for the child and/or the parents; and the last one stated that the most implemented measure was integral assistance for at-risk pregnant women.

Despite the statistical limitations, the census and national surveys conducted in the last decade show the following data: the number of children and adolescents from 0 to 15 years of age in 2010 was 10,222,317. In 2011, according to a survey carried out by SENAF and UNICEF, there were 14,675 children and adolescents in Argentina "without parental care," that is, children who had been separated from their families by various reasons and were under some form of institutional care (both residential and family). In March 2014, 9,219 girls and boys were identified in that situation (roughly 0.9 per 1,000 children). The interprovincial distribution of girls and boys without parental care is not exactly congruent with the distribution of the population. According to the most recent survey, more children were without parental care in three jurisdictions: Neuquén (0.21%), La Pampa (0.17%) and Santa Cruz (0.16%). The incidence of girls and boys in this condition changes in very short periods, which suggests that the situation is sensitive both to the evolution of socioeconomic conditions and to those of public policies (UNICEF, 2016).

REGIONAL

Another dimension of the variable implementation of Child Protection Services is the cultural, political, and economic diversity between provincial states. The following differences between provinces emphasize the complexity in variability: the strength and variability of civil society and non-governmental organizations, the rates of professionalization of the population, the strength or weakness of state institutions, and other types of differences such as geography. From the geographical equity in the localization of child protection agencies to the ability to fill all positions with qualified professionals, regional variability is a critical consideration for implementation.

Sociopolitical factors within the provinces impact the implementation of Child Protection Services. Rich provinces with enough professionals, and lively and strong social organizations and political actors, tend to present a more democratic and much more debated institutionalization of child protection agencies. The poorest provinces, however, or those that lack strong civil movements and instead have Catholic charities in a prominent place, have had more limitations in the development of new agencies, relying more on judiciary power and practices.

Also, each province had a different way of depending on national funds to operate. Between 2007 and 2010, the Federal Council funded the new agencies, including salaries, but required an agreement from the province. Usually, the agreements detailed the allocation of national funds to cover salaries from March to December while provincial funds completed year-round employee contracts. The poorest states were unable to meet the agreements, and as a consequence, offered fewer positions that attracted the best qualified professionals, who preferred private practice or the judiciary as employment. The values-fueled feud between the executive and the judiciary was complemented, in many provinces, by a professional expertise and competence rift explained by the administration's lack of resources.

Another noticeable characteristic of the Integral Protection System is its geographical concentration. In other words, child protection services are primarily confined to territories, namely the capitals or the most populated cities, leaving the smaller cities or rural areas with no specific governance for rights protection, nor the possibility for the inter-relation with other cities. This causes regional complexities to intertwine with the aforementioned institutional dimension. Furthermore, the development of protocols for case management, the institutionalization of Local Councils with a variety of local actors, and the establishment of thematic round tables, are relevant dimensions of variability.

The New Sociopolitical Scenario

The end of 2015 marked the change of the political scenario with a new administration taking office. The impact of the new government's first measures increased poverty sharply. According to the *Observatorio de la Deuda Social* (UCA), by the first semester of newly elected President Mauricio Macri's right-wing government in mid-2016, more than one million children had fallen into poverty, and in the two first years of the government, the child poverty rates increased by 2.1%, reaching 62.5% of the child population.[2] By October 2018, almost one and a half million children had lost AUH because of failure to meet new requirements, which represented a harsh change in tightening of controls.

The political shift had negative implications for the budget of Child Protection Services. The National Secretariat for Children failed to use their entire, allocated budget.

---

[2] https://www.infobae.com/politica/2018/04/29/segun-la-uca-la-pobreza-infantil-aumento-al-625-y-hay-8-millones-de-ninos-privados-de-algun-derecho/.

In 2016, only 41% of the annual budget was spent, and in the first half of 2017, the level of budget implementation was as low as about 17% of the allocation. Furthermore, since 2017, the Secretary position has been vacant, meaning that the national child protection system lacks political direction (Coalision *Infancia en Deuda*, 2017). To add complexity, the demise of the former authority took place amidst a juvenile justice debate; the existing law is a decree signed during the last dictatorship and the age of penal prosecution is still debated (Kessler, 2004). The Juvenile Justice Law 22278 (1982) does not comply with international human rights recommendations and it was sanctioned under the previous dictatorship. One of the main reasons why it was not reformed, despite the many voices favoring a reform, was the fear of the lowering of the age of penal prosecution, now established as 16 years. The reform of the penal prosecution at 14 is promoted by those who seek the protection of a regular penal procedure, who claim that the high age does not protect the youngest and leaves them at the mercy of discretionary judges who seek to punish feeble crimes. Emerging from this is the organization of social movements, activists, and scholars that are against the lowering of the age of penal prosecution. Two examples in particular are: Network Against the Lowering of Age (*No a la Baja en Argentina*), and Argentine not Descent (*Argentina No Baja*).

Both the national government and the province of Buenos Aires declare that developing early childhood policies is a main goal, yet policies do not reflect this. A new policy on Child Development Centers—drawn from the United Kingdom's Sure Start model— was presented in early 2016. But the 2017 budget showed an implementation of only 4.34%, reaching 536 children in Child Development Centers throughout the country (Coalición Infancia en Deuda, 2017). The child protection offices in both the national administration and the Buenos Aires province were moved down within the hierarchy of their organization, with a considerable loss in budget and autonomy. State agencies' budgets were partially transferred to NGOs, especially in foster care, drug abuse, and child development. In several provinces, contracts were signed with extremely conservative NGOs, such as CONIN Foundation in child development and nutrition programs, and Catholic organizations in foster family programs, as *Movimiento Familiar Cristiano* and *Hogares de Belén*.

Paradoxically, the government promoted the fulfillment of the Child Ombudsman position, established in Law 26061 yet unfilled since 2005. After a democratic and careful selection process coordinated by a Special Commission formed by representatives of the lower house and the senate, the Defensor will be appointed by the end of November 2018. Their responsibilities will include the supervision and monitoring of public policy, design of special programs, and the management of judicial and administrative claims.

In summary, the change of government shows a striking demise in the relevance of child protection programs and the empowerment of a rights discourse on juvenile justice, emphasizing lowering the age of penal punishment and the moral punitive discourse

(Levitas, 2005). The current context, therefore, permits us to identify trends of increasing privatization and the marked restraint of state-based services.

Conclusion

The legal and institutional reforms after the 1990s have been remarkable. Most of the provinces developed laws that reflected a rights paradigm, and have either reformed their institutions or created institutions in order to provide for child protection. In fact, since 2005 onward, there were advances in decentralization processes and legal and administrative changes that promoted the principles of co-responsibility, integrality, and mainstream children's rights. Even in a context of institutional frailty, and the persistence of weakness in treating structural poverty and its consequences, gradually all jurisdictions built child protection areas and services. Furthermore, the right to be heard, to have their opinion taken into account, and the right to have a lawyer of their own, signals a significant change in institutional practices with children, even if more progress is needed.

The reform in education and health policies extended children's rights protections. With the National Education Law 26206 (2006), programs were implemented to facilitate access and stability to school and to facilitate the return of those who had previously failed school. It extended opportunities for attendance in the initial level (children from 3 to 5 years) and in high school (children from 13 to 17 years). High school coverage reached 93% of the population, among the highest in the region (although with great differences among provinces). Within health, improvements were made. The obligatory immunization as well as the implementation of primary care and special programs in mobile units throughout the country (e.g., dental care, newborns' special assistance) helped to improve several indicators. In 2010–2014, child mortality decreased from 12/1,000 to 9.7/1,000. Nevertheless, the striking inequalities between provinces and regions in the country still persist.

As we have pointed out, the new administration took a different path in their definition of the function of the state, canceling many programs or lowering their budgets to levels that made them, in effect, not operative. The most affected programs were the provision and distribution of drugs and medicines and the program targeting digital inequalities reduction among elementary and high-school students through the distribution of computers (*Conectar Igualdad*).

The 2019 budget shows a marked reduction in both health and education funding, as well as the Child Protection areas, and was criticized by many agencies and organizations, including UNICEF. The obstacles that persist include: 1) the institutional dimension of Child Protection Systems (e.g., "demoting" a former national secretariat to a department in a ministry); precariousness of labor conditions; high rates of case worker turnover; lack of adequate infrastructure; and lack of an adequate budget; and 2) inter-institutional relations (e.g., little articulation between child protection, the educational system and healthcare agencies; insufficient variety of resources and programs to work with families with specific problems (e.g. drug abuse); and persistence of conflicts with the judiciary.

The current context of budget constraint and austerity conspire against the development of strategies to overcome these obstacles and endangers some of the gains achieved during this laborious process. Moreover, the unresolved problem of an inadequate juvenile law haunts the system with a less democratic approach and a backlash that furthers right-wing movements with an anti-rights discourse.

References

Beloff, M. (2004). *Los derechos del niño en el sistema interamericano.* Editores del Puerto.

Bourdieu, P. (1999). *Razones prácticas.* Anagrama.

Burgués, M. and Lerner, G. (2006). Alcances, límites y delimitaciones de la reglamentación de la ley 26.061: Desafíos pendientes. *Revista Jurisprudencia Argentina, tomo II.*

Carli, S (comp). (2006). *La cuestión de la infancia: entre la escuela, la calle y el shopping.* Paidós.

CEPAL. (2004). *Pobreza y políticas sociales en Argentina de los años noventa.* Pablo Vinocur Leopoldo Halperin Serie Políticas Sociales Nro. 85.

Colectivo de Derechos de la Infancia. (2017). Alternative Monitoring Report of Argentine's fulfillment of Children's Rights to the Children's Rights Commission. https://www.colectivoinfancia.org.ar/wp/wp-content/uploads/2020/07/Informe-Sombra-FINAL-PDF.pdf.

Donzelot, J. (1990). *La policía de las familias.* Pretextos.

Fonseca, C. (2004). Os direitos da criança. Dialogando com o ECA. In C. Fonseca, V. Terto, and A. Caleb Farias (Eds.), *Antropologia, diversidade e direitos humanos. Diálogos interdisciplinares* (pp. 103–115). Universidade Federal de Rio Grande do Sul Editora.

Fonseca, C. and Schuch, P. (Eds.). (2009). *Políticas de proteção à infância. Um olhar antropológico.* Editora UFRGS.

Fraser, N. (1991). La lucha por las necesidades: esbozo de una teoría crítica socialista-feminista de la cultura política del capitalismo tardío. *Debate Feminista,* 3(1), 3–40.

Fraser, N. and Gordon, L. (1997). Decoding "dependency": Inscriptions of power in a keyword of the US welfare state. In M. Shanley and U. Narayan (Eds.), *Reconstructing political theory: Feminist perspectives.* (pp. 25–47) Pennsylvania State University Press.

Goffman, I. (2001). *Internados: Ensayo sobre la situación social de los enfermos mentales.* Amorrortu.

Guy, D. (2009). *Women build the welfare state: Performing charity and creating rights in Argentina, 1880–1955.* Duke University Press.

Haney, L. (1996). Homeboys, babies, men in suits: The state and the reproduction of male dominance. *American Sociological Review,* 61, 759–778.

Haney, L. (2002). *Inventing the needy: Gender and the politics of welfare in Hungary.* University of California Press.

Haney, L. and Pollard, L. (Eds.). (2003). *Families of a new world: Gender, politics, and state development in a global context.* Routledege.

Kay, E. M., Tisdall, M., and Hill, M. (2010). Policy change under devolution: The prism of children's policy. *Social Policy & Society,* 10(1), 29–40.

Kessler, G. (2004). *Sociología del delito amateur.* Paidós.

Levitas, R. (2005). *The inclusive society? Social exclusion and new labour.* Palgrave.

Llobet, V. (2009a). *¿Fábricas de niños? Las instituciones en la era de los derechos.* Editorial Novedades Educativas.

Llobet, V. (2009b). *Las políticas sociales para la infancia, la psicología y el problema del reconocimiento. Revista Investigaciones en Psicología,* 14(2), 1–20.

Lugones, M. G. (2012). Obrando en autos, obrando en vidas: Formas y fórmulas de Protección Judicial en los tribunales Prevencionales de Menores de Córdoba, Argentina, a comienzos del siglo XXI. LACED, UFRJ.

Medan, M., Llobet, V., and Gaitán, A. C. (2019). El Estado local y el territorio. Aspiraciones de cercanía y transformaciones en la institucionalidad de los sistemas de protección y promoción de niños y jóvenes. In V. Llobet and C. Villalta (Eds.), *De la desjudicialización a la refundación de los derechos. Transformaciones en las disputas por los derechos de los niños y las niñas (2005-2015)* (pp. 315–352) Ed. TeseoPress, Buenos Aires.

Merry, S. E. (2006). Transnational human rights and local activism: Mapping the middle. *American Anthropologist*, 108(1), 38–51.

Milanich, N. (2002). Illegitimacy and illegitimates. In T. Hecht (Ed.), *Minor omissions: Children in Latin American history and society* (pp. 72–101). University of Wisconsin Press.

Ministerio de Salud, Presidencia de la Nación. Indicadores básicos, Argentina. (2017). Organización Panamericana de la Salud, *Organización Mundial de la Salud*. Available at: http://www.deis.msal.gov.ar/wp-content/uploads/2018/04/IndicadoresBasicos2017.pdf.

Nari, M. (2005). *Políticas de maternidad y maternalismo político: Buenos Aires, 1890–1940*. Biblos.

Rodríguez Gustá, A. L. (2004). *Capacidades estatales: Reflexiones en torno a un programa de investigación* [Conference presentation]. IX Congreso del CLAD sobre Reforma del Estado y de la Administración Pública, Madrid.

Rojas Novoa, S. (2017). *La protección de la infancia en América: una problematización histórica del presente. El caso del Instituto Interamericano del Niño, la Niña, y los Adolescentes (1927–1989)* [Unpublished doctoral dissertation]. University of Buenos Aires.

Schuch, P. (2009). *Práticas de justiça. Antropologia dos modos de governo da infância e juventude no contexto pós-ECA*. Universidade Federal de Rio Grande do Sul Editora.

SENAF-UNICEF. (2014). *Relevamiento de niños, niñas y adolescentes sin cuidados parentales en la República Argentina*. UNICEF.

UNICEF. (2016). *Estado de situación de la niñez y la adolescencia en la Argentina*. Buenos Aires.

Villalta, C. (2012). *Entregas y secuestros. El rol del Estado en la apropiación de niños*. Ed. Del Puerto.

Villalta, C. (2010a). La *administración* de la infancia en debate. Entre tensiones y reconfiguraciones institucionales. *Estudios en Antropología Social*, 1(2), 81–99.

Villalta, C. (2010b). Introducción. In C. Villalta (Ed.), *Infancia, justicia y derechos humanos*. Editorial de la Universidad Nacional de Quilmes.

Villalta, C. and Llobet, V. (2015). Resignificando la protección. Nuevas normativas y circuitos en el campo de las políticas y dispositivos jurídico-burocráticos destinados a la infancia en la Argentina. *Revista Latinoamericana de Ciencias Sociales, Niñez y Juventud*, 13(1), 167–180.

Child Protection Systems in Brazil

Diene Monique Carlos, Ailton de Souza Aragão, Eliana Mendes de Souza Teixeira Roque, *and* Lygia Maria Pereira da Silva

Abstract

This chapter explicates the child protection systems in Brazil. Brazilian children and adolescents living in extreme poverty have the highest percentage among all age groups. Important advances have been made in Brazilian legislation regarding the social protection of children and adolescents. The organizational structure of services in this area is also coherent and thoughtfully designed. How these policies and structures are conducted in practice, however, still presents challenges. A care network between child protection services and other sectors may be an appropriate mechanism to face these challenges, with intersectoral and interprofessional articulation to protect children, adolescents, and their families.

Key Words: Brazil, child, adolescent, family, inequality, Brazilian law, social support network, interprofesional care

Introduction

There are approximately 190 million people in Brazil; of these, 59.7 million are children and adolescents (0–18 years of age) and, following the current aging trend, the proportion of Brazilians up to 19 years of age fell from 45% to 33% between 1991 and 2010 (Instituto Brasileiro de Geografia e Estatística [IBGE], 2010; UNICEF, 2015). This demographic transition is due to two main factors—the reduction of fertility and mortality rates. However, since it is a continental country, this change is not uniform. The Northern and Northeastern regions, respectively, are the youngest in Brazil, with this aspect being related, in part, to the high fertility rates that were still present in these regions up to 1980.

The number of people who self-identified themselves as black and brown grew in the young population. Currently, more than half the population aged up to 18 years is Afro-Brazilian. In 1991, 70% of Brazilian children and adolescents lived in poor households, declining to 52% by 2010 (IBGE, 2010; UNICEF, 2015). The population of children and adolescents living in urban areas increased from 72% to 82% between 1991 and 2010 (IBGE, 2010).

The percentage of Brazilian children and adolescents living in extreme poverty—in families with a monthly income of less than R$70.00 per person (equivalent to U$18.03)—is highest among all groups. A total of 13.3% of children aged between 0 and 6 years are considered extremely poor; 12.4% of those aged between 7 and 15 years; 7.9% of people between aged 16 and 24 years; 6.8% between 25 and 39 years; 5.9% between 40 and 59 years; and 3% of those aged over 60 years (IBGE, 2010). This situation is more serious considering the ethnic profile—while 37% of white children and adolescents live in poverty (families with a monthly income of less than R$140.00 per person, equivalent to US$35.35), this percentage increases to 61% when black and brown children are considered. This aspect denotes the fact that Brazil is considered one of the most unequal countries in the world (World Bank Group, 2015).

In the last two decades, Brazil has made considerable educational advancements. More children have access to school, and more children are persisting with it; educational outcomes are improving as well. In addition, the mandatory school age has been increased. The percentage of children and adolescents of compulsory school age that were not in school fell by 64% between 1990 and 2013. The mean illiteracy rate fell among those aged 10 to 18 years, dropping from 12.5% to 1.4% in this period. However, more than 3 million children and adolescents are not in school (IBGE, 2010). This exclusion affects mainly poor, black, indigenous, and quilombola people (descendants of escaped slaves). The aspects related to expulsion and/or dropping out of school are varied—some children work and contribute to the family income; others have some kind of disability; while others reside in regions such as the peripheries of large urban centers, the semi-arid region, the Amazon region, and the rural area where access to school is limited (UNICEF, 2015).

This dynamic of advances and setbacks coupled with demographic transitions, among other issues such as the implementation of public policies for children and adolescents, has had a considerable impact on health indicators, such as the reduction of child mortality. Between 1990 and 2012, the infant mortality rate fell 68.4%, reaching 14.9 deaths per 1,000 live births, according to the Ministry of Health (Ministério da Saúde, 2012). This rate is quite close to the level considered acceptable by the World Health Organization (WHO), which is 10 deaths per 1,000 live births. Thus, Brazil achieved the goal of reducing child mortality present in the Millennium Development Goals (MDG), prior to the agreed deadline. The Northeastern Region of the country, which had a critical situation of infant mortality, presented the sharpest decline (UNICEF, 2015). Changes in the organization of the health system and public policies directed toward children, adolescents, and their families (covered in more detail later); the increase in education levels of mothers; increased vaccination coverage; improved access to basic sanitation; and social stimulation for breastfeeding are other contributing factors (UNICEF, 2015).

However, inequalities also exist—indigenous children are twice as likely to die during the first year as other Brazilian children. This mortality is mainly related to malnutrition: approximately 40% of the indigenous children living in the Northern Region have chronic malnutrition, with a mean of 7% in the country (UNICEF, 2015). Furthermore, the reduction of maternal mortality presents another challenge, as, despite the reduction of this rate, it has not yet reached the rates established in the MDGs. The quality of prenatal services also needs to be improved—there was a significant increase in cases of congenital syphilis and low coverage of the tetanus vaccine in the last 10 years (UNICEF, 2015).

In this scenario, accidents and violence are important causes of morbidity and mortality among children over the age of one and adolescents (Ministério da Saúde, 2013). In 1980, they accounted for 6.7% of all deaths in this age group; while by 2010, the mortality rate had risen, reaching the level of 26.5%. In children older than one year and adolescents, accidents and violence accounted for 53.2% of all deaths (Waiselfisz, 2012). Homicides of adolescents have become the most worrying face of this violation of rights. In 2014, it appeared as the highest cause of mortality among adolescent males. In 2013 alone, more than 10,000 adolescents were murdered. Furthermore, in most cases, the perpetrators of these crimes were not brought to justice, generating a cycle of impunity that fuels a growing wave of violence. In Brazil, between 92% and 95% of homicide cases remain unsolved (UNICEF, 2015).

These statistics represent only the apex of the pyramid, which is the best configuration to comprehend the magnitude of the problem. Thousands of people in Brazil are victims of non-fatal violence every day. Among these, some people are assisted by health services and receive urgent medical-legal care or other types of assistance. In 2006, the Ministry of Health of Brazil instituted the Violence and Accident Surveillance System (*Sistema de Vigilância de Violências e Acidentes* [VIVA]), in order to identify the magnitude of accidents and violence that do not lead to death or hospitalization. The VIVA system was structured in two components, Continuous VIVA and Sentinel VIVA. The Continuous VIVA, incorporated into the National System of Notifiable Diseases, allows the continuous surveillance of domestic, sexual, and/or other interpersonal violence and self-harm, while the Sentinel VIVA permits the surveillance of violence and accidents in hospital emergency wards (Ministério da Saúde, 2013). Access to these data makes it possible to plan preventive actions and interventions considering these injuries, avoiding fatal consequences.

According to a report of this system containing data collected between 2009 and 2010, children and adolescents are the main victims of domestic violence, sexual violence, or other types of interpersonal violence, accounting for 44.7% of total reported cases (Ministério da Saúde, 2013). Boys ages 0 to 9 years are the most affected by violence (26.5% of cases), followed by 10 to 19 years (24.1% of cases). For females, violent incidents are most likely between 10 to 19 years (25.7% of cases), followed by 0 to 9 year-olds (15.9% of cases). Violent acts are predominantly carried out in the home (61.9% for children and 42.6% for adolescents), with approximately 26% of subjects reporting being victims of repetitive violence, due to having previously been subjected to these injuries (Ministério da Saúde, 2013).

According to the nomenclature proposed by the World Health Organization (WHO), the predominant violence was neglect (35.6%), sexual violence (35.6%) and physical violence (32.8%). For males, neglect (42.8%) and physical violence (37.2%) were highlighted. For females, sexual violence (45.5%) and neglect (30.1%) were more frequent. The most likely perpetrator of violence was the mother (31.8%) and the father (20.9%) (Ministério da Saúde, 2013).

Physical violence (76.1%) and psychological/moral violence (14.3%) were highlighted in male adolescents. Among female adolescents, physical violence (53.2%), sexual violence (41.9%), and psychological/moral violence (29.4%) predominated. The probable perpetrator of the violence maintained a relation of proximity with the victim; being a friend (18%), an unknown person (16.8%), or the mother (10.6%) in the case of violence against males. Among females, it was a friend (18.8%), an unknown person (16.1%), or the father (8.5%) (Ministério da Saúde, 2013). Despite these statistics, a large proportion of the population, representing the base of the pyramid, suffer violence daily; however, they never report it to protective services. Research indicates that the main populations suffering from violence in silence are children, adolescents, women, and older adults (WHO, 2010; WHO, 2014).

Considering the scenario presented, it can be noticed that, despite important advances, there are still challenges and inequalities that generate barriers for integral protection and the guarantee of the rights of children and adolescents. According to the latest UNICEF report, "in order to overcome these, it is necessary, above all, to adopt public policies capable of combating the geographical, social and ethnic inequalities of the country and to celebrate the richness of its diversity" (UNICEF, 2015).

Thus, in this chapter we will discuss the historical course of public policies directed toward children and adolescents, the current scenario of these policies and programs, and the main scientific evidence related to the integral protection of children, adolescents, and their families. This evidence will be essentially based on the current literature and our experience in the Study, Teaching and Research Center of the School Primary Health Care Program (PROASE), which has been operating since 1986.

From Irregular Situation to Integral Protection: Conceptual Aspects and Tendencies in the Brazilian Context

Child Protection Processes

The perspective of children and adolescents as subjects of rights and the focus of integral protection (as opposed to the view of these subjects as "miniature adults"), appears in legal terms in Article 227 of the Brazilian Federal Constitution of 1988 and its subsequent regulation through the Statute of the Child and Adolescent (ECA), Law No. 8069/90. Integral protection designates a system in which children and adolescents, up to the age of 18, are considered to be holders of subordinate interests, in relation to the family, society, and the state.

However, it should be emphasized that the primary movement for guaranteeing the non-violation and exercise, by all citizens, of a list of basic rights to a dignified life, called human rights, began with the adoption of the Universal Declaration of Human Rights in 1948, through the United Nations. The contents of this declaration have changed and expanded due to the new social conditions that have arisen, with international pacts being established.

Aiming for the solidification of these universal rights, the need was recognized to create specific measures for some segments more vulnerable to violations of their rights. Thus, a special system of protection was created for some subjects, such as black people, women, children, adolescents, older adults, and the disabled, materializing in the various conventions signed by the United Nations.

At the national level, Brazil grants through the Federal Constitution, the democratic institutionalization of human rights in the country, especially for children and adolescents.

> Article 227: It is the duty of the family, society and the State to ensure the right to life, health, food, education, leisure, professionalization, culture, dignity, respect, freedom and family and community coexistence, and to protect them from all forms of neglect, discrimination, exploitation, violence, cruelty and oppression. (Ministério da Justiça, 1988)

Regulating the aforementioned article, the Child and Adolescent Statute (*Estatuto da Criança e do Adolescente* [ECA]) was enacted in 1990, positively affecting the citizenship of children and adolescents in Brazil. It is considered one of the most advanced pieces of legislation in the world in this area. To place the ECA in context, it is necessary to draw a parallel to what previously existed as a protection policy for children and adolescents.

The abandonment of children in Brazil has historical roots to Colonial Brazil. In this period, abandoned children were entrusted to the care of the Catholic Church, with the support of the state. The system of the Foundling Wheel and House (*Roda e Casa dos Expostos*) was structured in the Empire of Brazil, with religious institutions responsible for the education of abandoned children. Poor and abandoned children and adolescents were understood as deprived of rights (Belluzzo & Victorino, 2004).

At the end of the 19th century, the state began to worry about the increase in the number of children on the streets, arousing pity for the situation of abandonment and fear of potential danger. In order to more directly manage this social issue, in 1927 the state created the first Minors Code, also known as the Melo Mattos Code, revised and replaced in 1932. This dealt with the care, protection, and supervision of those who had not yet reached the age of 18 years. It therefore applied exclusively to "minors" who were in an irregular situation, considered thus when they were abandoned by their parents or guardians, even partially, from a poor family, a victim of crime, badly behaved, or the author of a criminal offense.

If the child was found in any of these conditions, the juvenile court could apply one of the so-called "assistance or protection measures" (from admonition to incarceration) that would be appropriate to the case, without due process of law, since these sought, "fundamentally, their social and family integration." During this time, the principle of social control and criminalization of poverty was strongly associated with the policies of cleansing of the public space (Bertolli Filho, 2008).

This legislation shows that children and adolescents were seen as "objects of intervention of the adult world," not as subjects that had family, society, and state rights. Public and private initiatives emerged from the 1930s to the 1970s, with the creation of the Children's Assistance Service (*Serviço de Assistência ao Menor* [SAM]) in 1940 and its closure in 1964, and the creation of the National Foundation for the Well-Being of Minors (*Fundação Nacional do Bem-Estar do Menor* [FUNABEM]). In 1979, the new Minors' Code was designed to reinforce the "irregular situation," categorizing children and adolescents as marginal, marginalized, or integrated (Silva & Motti, 2001; Santos, 2004; Aragão, 2011).

The literature shows that from the 1970s, new studies were carried out focused on the "abandoned child." Researchers sought to understand the circumstances of children and adolescents of the lower classes, especially those institutionalized and living on the streets, as well as questioning the term "minor" (related to this people exclusion) and examined whether welfare policies contributed to the detriment of the wills and desires of these adolescents (Souza Neto, 2002; Aragão, 2011). Parallel to these questions in the academic world, in the 1970s and 1980s Brazilian society experienced a period of intense change, marked by the process of democratization and widespread mobilization of society (direct elections, freedom of the press, amnesty), initiating claims for better conditions for children (Silva & Motti, 2001).

In the 1970s, the deaths of children and adolescents that lived on the streets of big cities were motivated by businessmen who saw sales plummet in the presence of these "minors." In defense of the lives of these subjects, the National Movement of Street Boys and Girls (*Movimento Nacional de Meninos e Meninas de Rua* [MNMMR]) was organized. The Movement began in 1985 and signaled a shift toward the defense of childhood and adolescence; children and youth became protagonists of their own history (Silva & Motti, 2001). These movements sparked a sensitization and mobilization of civil society, resulting in policies for the protection of childhood and adolescence, such as the Amendment of the Federal Constitution and later in the ECA.

In this way, this "ill-fated principle of the irregular situation" was replaced, at least on paper, by the doctrine of integral protection, through which the ECA indistinctly supports the fundamental rights of children and adolescents for the full exercise of citizenship. As quoted by Minayo (2006, p. 15), the "theory of integral protection starts from the comprehension that the rules of care for children and adolescents should conceive them as full citizens, however, subject to priority protection, since they are people in [the special condition of] physical, psychological and moral development." Thus, with the enactment of these laws, children and adolescents were no longer considered "latent and potential citizens," but rather full citizens, with all their rights guaranteed. In addition, these laws emphasize the priority in meeting the needs of this age group, organizing them in a system in which the laws recognize guarantees for these groups, protect their private interests, and create instruments for the realization of their rights.

An important aspect of the ECA is the change in concepts regarding public intervention for children and adolescents: prior to its implementation, the institutionalization of children and adolescents that were abandoned, victims of violence, or offenders was one of the main pillars of the policies directed toward this population. The ECA advocates deinstitutionalization, favoring family orientation, school insertion and family/community articulation, with placement into a surrogate family or an orphanage being used in exceptional circumstances (Silva & Motti, 2001). In this way, it is important to highlight several components of the law:

Article 98: The measures for the protection of children and adolescents are applicable whenever the rights recognized in this Law are threatened or violated:

1) due to action or omission by society or the state;
2) due to lack, omission or abuse by parents or guardians;
3) due to their conduct.

Article 101: Having verified any of the hypotheses provided for in Art. 98, the competent authority may determine, among others, the following measures:

1) referral to the parents or guardian, by means of a term of responsibility;
2) temporary guidance, support and monitoring;
3) compulsory enrollment and attendance at an official elementary education establishment;
4) inclusion in a community or official services and programs to protect, support, and promote the family, children, and adolescents;
5) request for medical, psychological, or psychiatric treatment, in a hospital or outpatient regimen;
6) inclusion in official or community care programs, guidance, and treatment for alcoholics and drug addicts;
7) shelter welcoming;
8) inclusion in family welcoming;
9) placement with a surrogate family.

The children and adolescents who reach this level of care are evaluated through the Childhood and Youth Courts, distributed among the states and municipalities. These courts are able to provide support so that rights are guaranteed, such as the implementation of socio-educational measures, adoption and situations of institutional reception. The courts have services, comprised of Social Workers and Psychologists, with interprofessional teams able to provide contributions through written reports or verbally at the hearing, as well as develop counseling, guidance, and prevention work.

Criticism of individuals and entities involved in the protection of children and youth led to changes in the law, which in turn favored the adoption of less punitive practices with children and adolescents facing legal proceedings. The interest in improving the quality of the approach to victims has been discussed across several institutions responsible for children, including the Judiciary.

Care actions aimed at preventing children from being revictimized in the judicial process have been modeled in other countries since the 1980s. In Brazil, the main documents used to substantiate demands for such measures are the Declaration of the Rights of the Child and the Statute of the Child and Adolescent, following the principles of integral protection. The discussion about taking the child's testimony has been a frequent theme within the Judiciary, based on the Testimony Without Harm (*Depoimento Sem Dano* [DSD]) methodology.

In 2007, the Chamber of Deputies approved the Project of Law No. 4126/04, which "allows a special procedure for expert examination of children and adolescents in case of sexual abuse, as well as the preparation of a psychosocial report to establish elements indicative of abuse." It should be noted that the Project changed the ECA and not the Criminal Procedure Code (*Código de Processo Penal* [CPP]), which is the instrument most used by legal professionals.

The methodology of the special hearing has been used by several Brazilian states and is currently a recommendation issued by the National Council of Justice. As legal grounds, it is supported by the Statute of the Child and Adolescent, in particular Article 98, and the Federal Constitution, Articles 5, 226, and 227. The early production of proof was now allowed under Article 156 i of the Criminal Procedure Code, through Law No. 11.690 of 2008.

In the state of Pernambuco, in 2010, the Center for the Special Testimony of Victims and Witnesses of Violence of the Court of Justice of Pernambuco was established. The special inquiry department was made up of professionals from the staff of the court, with the job of taking the testimonies of child and adolescent victims or witnesses of the legal processes of the Courts of Crimes against Children and Adolescents, Family Courts, and Children and Youth Courts. The sector began its work following a rigorous and detailed protocol that determines that the interviews are recorded and filed so that the records can be consulted by the legal professionals that work on the process.

In 2017, Law No. 13.431/17 was published nationally, with a one-year *vacatio legis* (Article 29), which establishes the system for guaranteeing the rights of child and adolescent victims or witnesses of violence, providing important innovations. This law established the specialized hearing as "an interview procedure about the situation of violence with children or adolescents in a service of the protection network, limiting the report strictly to what is necessary for the fulfillment of its purpose" (Article 7). Thus, the special testimony is the "procedure of hearing the child or adolescent victims or witnesses of violence by a police or judicial authority" (Article 8). This is done in a multidisciplinary way, with the participation of a social worker or psychologist, favoring a less upsetting environment that is more conducive to seeking the truth.

The above document is designed to prevent revictimization by determining that all the services that the victim experiences to stop the violence and repair the harm suffered, must have professionals trained for qualified listening. However, the discussion regarding the specialized hearing or special testimony of children and adolescents will not end with the appearance of new laws as, in some cases, the child or adolescent can only make the revelation when undergoing psychotherapy and after some time, which may be months or years. Therefore, even considering the importance of the revelation for the legal process the tempo of the victim must be respected. Accordingly, the Judiciary needs to go further, rethinking the procedures to replace the investigation of the child victim of sexual violence with a more complete evaluation of the family system. It is understood that such a modification will require deeper changes in the Judiciary, specifically in the law. In order for the changes to be effective, there must be a change in the CPP, as this is the law that provides the basis for the legal professionals to judge the crimes.

Policies and Programs for the Protection of Children and Adolescents in the Brazilian Context

Bases of Social Allocations

In order to comprehend the types of violence against children and adolescents, the concepts presented in the most recent legislation of the System of Guarantee of Rights of the Child and the Adolescent Victim or Witness of Violence (Brazil, 2017) will be described: physical violence, psychological violence, sexual violence, and negligence.

Physical violence is recognized as any action inflicted on children and adolescents that affects their integrity or physical health. Psychological violence presents itself as a conduct of "discrimination, depreciation or disrespect towards the child or adolescent through threat, embarrassment, humiliation, manipulation, isolation, verbal aggression and cursing, ridicule, indifference, exploitation or bullying that can compromise their psychic or emotional development." In addition to these acts, parental alienation and other actions of direct or indirect exposure of the child or adolescent to violent crime against family members or people of the support network, regardless of the environment were included as violence. This covers situations in which the child or adolescent witnesses violence.

Sexual violence is "conduct that obligates the child or adolescent to practice or witness sexual intercourse or any other libidinous act, including exposure of the body in photo or video by electronic means or not." This classification includes sexual abuse, commercial sexual exploitation, and people trafficking. The legislation also considers institutional violence, which can be practiced by a public or contracted institution, including the generation of situations of revictimization.

Negligence is mentioned in this legislation, as in other official documents; however, it is not typified. It is included in psychological violence. This legislation also reinforces the importance of articulating the child protection sectors in coordinated and effective actions, as well as establishing a requirement for specialized hearing and special testimony aimed at receiving and providing comprehensive care to victims of violence (Brazil, 2017).

The organization of the actions aimed at the social protection of children, adolescents and their families is performed by the Social Welfare sector. This is a public non-contributory social security policy, structured in the Unified Social Welfare System (*Sistema Único de Assistência Social* [SUAS]), which provides services, programs, projects, and socio-assistance benefits for the population in situations of social vulnerability. The SUAS was created by the National Social Welfare Policy (Ministério do Desenvolvimento Social e Combate à Fome & Secretaria Nacional de Assistência Social, 2004), resulting from the Organic Social Welfare Law No. 8.742/1993, which was updated in 2011 by Law No. 12.435. Social welfare actions are organized under Basic Social Protection (BSP) and Special Social Protection (SSP) of Medium and High Complexity.

Nature of Social Provisions Allocated to Protect Children

Family Support Services

Basic Social Protection is configured as a set of social welfare services, programs, projects, and benefits aimed at preventing situations of vulnerability through the development of potential and capacity, as well as the strengthening of family and community bonds. The BSP seeks to organize its work in order to respond to this demand, developing actions offered by the Reference Centers of Social Assistance (*Centros de Referência de Assistência Social* [CRAS]). These, which are the first steps to the public policies, are structural axes of the SUAS, acting in the area together with the families and communities.

The CRAS performs the following actions: Service of Protection and Integral Care to the Family (*Serviço de Proteção e Atendimento Integral à Família* [PAIF]); Service of Coexistence and Strengthening of Bonds (*Serviço de Convivência e Fortalecimento de Vínculos* [SCFV]); and Income Transfer Programs, which are the Family Grant (*Bolsa Família*), Youth Action, Citizen Income, and Continuous Provision Benefit (*Benefício de Prestação Continuada* [BPC]). Due to the importance of actions directed toward children and adolescents, we will deepen the explanation of the PAIF and SCFV services.

In accordance with the prerogatives established by the Ministry of Social Development (*Ministério do Desenvolvimento Social* [MDS]) and the National Social Welfare Council

(*Conselho Nacional de Assistência Social* [CNAS]), the PAIF, through Decree No. 5.085/ 2004 and Resolution No. 109, of November 11, 2009,

> consists of social work with families, of a continuous nature, with the purpose of strengthening the protective function of families, preventing the breaking of their bonds, promoting their access and enjoyment of rights and contributing to the improvement of their quality of life. It aims to develop potentialities and acquisitions of the families and strengthen family and community bonds, through preventive, protective and proactive actions. The social work of the PAIF should also use actions in the cultural areas to fulfill its objectives, in order to expand the information universe and provide new experiences for the families that use the service. The actions of the PAIF should not have a therapeutic nature. (Ministério do Desenvolvimento Social e Combate à Fome, 2014, p. 12)

These theoretical prerogatives indicate the recognition that welfare, as a charitable and historical practice of helping the poor, had failed to promote family groups in terms of access to constitutional rights, according to the 1988 Federal Constitution of Brazil.

The SCFVs are organized into groups based on pathways, according to the specificities of the life cycle and the requirements of the area and community. This service acknowledges the importance of human relationships. Thus, the bonds extend to different areas of life, such as the family sphere, public services, and other places in which social relationships are strengthened or weakened. The SSP provides specialized services, programs and projects for individuals and families who are vulnerable due to the violation of rights, for example: 1) violence (physical, psychological, neglect, sexual) against children, adolescents, women and older adults; 2) psychoactive substance abuse; 3) compliance with socio-educational measures; 4) situation of homelessness; 5) child labor; and 6) need for specialized care due to disability or aging.

The Medium Complexity SSP serves families and individuals who have had their rights violated, however, have not yet broken the family and community bonds. The Specialized Reference Center for Social Welfare (*Centro de Referência Especializado de Assistência Social* [CREAS]) is the center for the reference, articulation, and coordination of this modality, with its aim being to provide continuous and specialized support and guidance to families and individuals whose rights have been violated. The Protection and Specialized Care Service for Families and Individuals (*Serviço de Proteção e Atendimento Especializado a Famílias e Indivíduos* [PAEFI]) is the main service provided by the SSP of Medium Complexity.

The PAEFI's consultations and guidelines have sought 1) the promotion of rights; 2) the preservation and strengthening of family, community, and social bonds; and 3) the strengthening of the protective function of families faced with a set of conditions that make them vulnerable. In addition to the PAEFI, the Medium Complexity SSP performs its actions through the:

- Specialized Social Approach Service;
- Service of Social Protection to Adolescents fulfilling the socio-educational measure of Assisted Freedom and of Provision of Community Services;
- Specialized Care Service for People with Disabilities, Older Adults, and their Families;
- Program for the Eradication of Child Labor.

Out-of-home Care

The High Complexity SSP is directed towards the integral protection of families and individuals whose rights have been violated, and whose community and family bonds have been broken. High complexity services are provided through the reception in care institutions—such as institutional orphanages, nursing homes, boarding houses and inclusive residences, in shared housing and in foster families—as well as through protection services in situations of public disasters and emergencies.

As already indicated, an important aspect present in the ECA is the change of concept regarding public intervention with children and adolescents. Also in article 101, in its sole paragraph, it is emphasized that "the shelter is a provisional and exceptional measure, usable as a form of transition for placement in a foster family, not implying deprivation of liberty" (Ministério do Desenvolvimento Social e Combate à Fome & Secretaria Nacional de Assistência Social, 2004, p. 42). The shelter is characterized, according to the ECA, by personalized attention, physical conditions of health, safety and appropriate education, where respect and care necessary for children and adolescents are guaranteed. It is understood as a space of reception, not of segregation (Souza Neto, 2002).

The ECA establishes that, from the placement of the child or adolescent in the institution until their departure at the age of 18, preparation for their withdrawal must be considered, including working with the promotion of guarantees of rights such as schooling, employment, and the maintenance of some type of bond outside of the institution, whether parental or not.

Institutional reordering is a new paradigm in social policy that must be incorporated throughout the entire care network of the country. Reordering care means reorienting the public and private networks that historically practiced under the orphanage regime, for them to align with the proposed paradigm shift. This new paradigm selects the family as the basic unit of social action and no longer conceives the child and adolescent isolated and/or excluded from their social and family context. According to the National Plan for the Promotion, Protection, and Defense of the Right of Children and Adolescents to Family and Community Life (Presidência da República et al., 2006), and the National Typification of Social Welfare Services (Ministério do Desenvolvimento Social e Combate à Fome, 2014), the organization service should guarantee privacy and respect for the clients, ethnic traditions and diversities, family members, and gender. The units should not geographically or socioeconomically distant from the community of origin of the children and adolescents served. Groups of children and adolescents with kinship links must be cared for in the same unit. They will be cared for until it is possible to return them to the family of origin (nuclear or extended) or be placed in a surrogate family.

According to the National Typification of Social Welfare Services, this care should be carried out in the following modalities:

1) Care in a residential unit where a person or couple works as resident educators/caregivers, providing care to a group of up to 10 children and/or adolescents;

2) Care in an institutional unit similar to a residence, intended for the care of groups of up to 20 children and/or adolescents. In this unit it is proposed that the educators/caregivers work in fixed daily shifts, in order to guarantee stability of the routine daily tasks, reference and predictability in the contact with the children and adolescents. There will be a specific space for immediate and emergency reception, with professionals prepared to receive the child/adolescent, at any time of day or night, while conducting a detailed diagnostic study of each situation for the necessary referrals. (Ministério do Desenvolvimento Social e Combate à Fome, 2014, p. 44)

In addition to the institutional care service, the legislation provides for the "Foster Family Shelter Service," which receives children and adolescents, separated from the family due to protection measures, in the residence of registered families. The service is particularly appropriate and a priority for the care of children and adolescents whose evaluation indicates the possibility of returning to the family of origin (nuclear or extended). This service is responsible for selecting, qualifying, registering, and monitoring the foster families, as well as monitoring the child and/or adolescent and his/her family of origin. It is essentially directed toward promoting the deinstitutionalization of children and adolescents. Data are not currently available to indicate the percentage of children in institutional care versus foster care.

Methods for the Delivery of These Provisions

The social protection services are financed by the three federative entities from the Social Security Budget, which is remitted to the National Social Welfare Fund (FNAS) and then passed on to state and municipal social welfare funds. State and municipal entities also contribute financially and use the combined resources for the operation, provision, and improvement of the services, programs, projects, and benefits of this policy. The estimated budget for 2019 is R$62.17 billion, corresponding to 2.03% of public expenditures. Due to recent changes in the delivery and specificities of the social protection services, we do not have valid evaluations of the effectiveness of these services.

Final Considerations: The Perspective of the Care Network

Important advances have been made in Brazilian legislation regarding the social protection of children and adolescents. The organizational structure of services in this area is also coherent and thoughtfully designed. How these policies and structures are conducted in practice, however, still presents challenges.

Scientific evidence suggests that a care network between child protection services and other sectors may be an appropriate mechanism to face these challenges. A study by Carlos, Padua, Silva, and colleagues (2017) showed that for primary health care professionals, the care networks for violence were small, homogeneous, with large gaps and a lack of density. These networks were characterized by relationships that were not institutionalized, with people-centered bonds, difficult dialogues during ordinary practices in professional life, and directed by fragmented and reactive social policies. These findings corroborate a study by Ferriani and colleagues (2017), who found weaknesses in the institutional network of services responding to school violence.

Some characteristics of the traditional paradigm were present in these relationships: the logic of referral, the lack of cooperation, the lack of knowledge of partners, the lack of responsibility for care, and the power relations of "dominant" institutions over "dominated" ones. This last aspect is well evidenced in the Judiciary System, with studies by Roque and colleagues (2014) and Silva and colleagues (2013) explaining these issues and problematizing the secondary victimization of child and adolescent victims of sexual violence during their hearings. It is suggested that this aspect can be overcome through the Testimony Without Harm, highlighted in this chapter.

The consequences of this traditional model were institutional isolation and fragmented care for families, with intervention still directed only toward the child and adolescent victims of domestic violence (Carlos et al., 2016; Carlos, Padua, and Ferriani, 2017). The families themselves showed that they remained "in transit" and "detached" in this service network (Carlos et al., 2016). In two studies carried out in two large Brazilian cities, deficits in social support were evidenced—this was configured by informal, affectionless, and reactive relationships (Carlos et al., 2014; Rodarte et al., 2015). Human interpersonal relationships, which allow attachment and co-responsibility for the protection of children and adolescents, can change cycles of vulnerability.

It is important to emphasize the academic training of professionals, which is still based on biomedical models and focused on curativism. Interdisciplinary teamwork and the comprehension of the dialogic "autonomy-dependence" as inherent to the practice of teams has been put forward as a strategy to overcome this logic (Carlos et al., 2016). The studies of Aragão and colleagues (2013) and Leite and colleagues (2016) demonstrate that nurses still have difficulties in understanding violence as an object for their care, not being part of their professional *habitus*, which remains strongly anchored in the biomedical model. As well as the articulation to the protection network, it is important to emphasize the vicarious trauma to which these professionals are exposed, with it being necessary to include this still incipient issue in the Brazilian research agenda.

In addition to the issues cited and the existence of general public policies, it is necessary to return to the specific: the life contexts of these families. Within this ambit, the context is referenced by Edgar Morin (REF), who considers spaces where the ties are woven together and there is an interdependent fabric that unites them. This aspect is essential for the discussion of child protection in low- and middle-income countries, where diverse powers act in various areas, among them drug trafficking and organized crime (Leite et al., 2016; Carlos, Padua, Silva et al., 2017). The very space where violence against children and adolescents generally emerges—the intrafamily space—is a "sacred" place, where it is difficult to intervene (Carlos et al., 2016).

It should be emphasized that in Brazil, social control is the right and duty of the population, legitimized and guaranteed by the Federal Constitution of 1988. Social control guarantees citizen participation in the formulation and implementation of public policies. In particular, Articles 198, 204, and 206 of the Constitution gave rise to the creation of public policy councils in health, social welfare and education at all three levels of government. Emancipatory and empowering strategies for these families and communities are recommended.

Finally, we end the chapter with some recommendations for action: 1) intersectoral and interprofessional articulation to face the challenges in the protection of children, adolescents, and their families; 2) professional training that goes beyond the biomedical model of practice, with actions aimed at health promotion; 3) support for families, considering the construction and promotion of affective bonds; and 4) community and family empowerment.

References

Aragão, A. S. (2011). "Lapidando pedras brutas": formação disciplinar de adolescentes *uma instituição assistencial para o (incerto) mundo do trabalho*. Revista Jurídica Direito & Realidade. 1(1):1–16.

Aragão, A. S., Ferriani, M. G. C., Vendruscollo, T. S., Souza, S. L., and Gomes, R. (2013). Primary care nurses' approach to cases of violence against children. *Revista Latino-Americana de Enfermagem*, 21(spe), 172–179.

Belluzzo, L. and Victorino, R. C. (2004). A juventude nos caminhos da ação pública. *São Paulo em perspectiva*, 18(4), 8–19.

Bertolli Filho, C. (2008). *História da saúde pública no Brasil* (11th ed.). Ática.

Brasil. *Lei nº 13.431, de 4 de abril de 2017*. Estabelece o sistema de garantia de direitos da criança e do adolescente vítima ou testemunha de violência e altera a Lei nº 8.069, de 13 de julho de 1990 (Estatuto da Criança e do Adolescente). Brasília, DF: Presidência da República, 2017.Brasil. Conselho Nacional de Justiça. *Recomendação nº 33, de 23 de novembro de 2010*. Recomenda aos tribunais a criação de serviços especializados para escuta de crianças e adolescentes vítimas ou testemunhas de violência nos processos judiciais. Depoimento Especial. (Publicada no DJ-e nº 215/2010, em 25/11/2010, pág. 33-34).

Carlos, D. M., Padua, E. M. M., and Ferriani, M. G. C. (2017). Violence against children and adolescents: The perspective of Primary Health Care. *Revista Brasileira de Enfermagem*, 70(3), 511–518.

Carlos, D. M., Pádua, E. M. M., Fernandes, M. I. D., Leitão, M. N. C., and Ferriani, M. G. C. (2016). Domestic violence against children and adolescents: social support network perspectives. *Revista Gaúcha de Enfermagem*, 37, e72859.

Carlos, D. M., Pádua, E. M. M., Silva, L. M. P., Silva, M. A. I., Marques, W. E. U., Leitão, M. N. C., and Ferriani, M. G. C. (2017). The care network of the families involved in family violence against children and adolescents: The Primary Health Care perspective. *Journal of Clinical Nursing*, 27, 2452–2467.

Carlos, D. M., Ferriani, M. G. C., Esteves, M. R., Silva, L. M. P., and Scatena, L. (2014). Social support from the perspective of adolescent victims of domestic violence. *Revista da Escola de Enfermagem da USP*, 48(4), 571–763.

Cezar, J. A. (2010). A escuta das crianças e adolescentes em juízo. Uma questão legal ou um exercício de direitos? In L. Potter (Ed.), *Depoimento sem dano: uma política criminal de redução de danos* (pp. 71–86). Lumen Juris.

Dayrell, J. (2003). O jovem como sujeito social. *Revista Brasileira de Educação*, 24, 40–52.

Ferriani, M. G. C., Carlos, D. M., Oliveira, A. J., Esteves, M. R., and Martins, J. E. (2017). Institutional links to cope with school violence: an exploratory study. *Revista de Enfermagem Escola Anna Nery*, 21(4), e20160347.

IBGE. (2010). Estudo e Pesquisas: Informação demográfica Socioeconômica. Síntese de Indicadores Sociais: uma analise das condições de vida da população brasileira. no. 27. Gráfica Digital, IBGE.

Law no. 11.690 (2008, June 9). Altera dispositivos do Decreto-Lei no 3.689, de 3 de outubro de 1941— Código de Processo Penal, relativos à prova, e dá outras providências. Brasília, 2008. Available at: www.planalto.gov.br/ccivil_03/_ato2007-2010/2008/lei/l11690.htm. Retrieved March 12, 2018.

Law no. 13.431 (2017, April 4). *Estabelece o sistema de garantia de direitos da criança e do adolescente vítima ou testemunha de violência e altera a Lei no 8.069, de 13 de julho de 1990 (Estatuto da Criança e do Adolescente).* Casa Civil, Subchefia para assuntos jurídicos.

Law no. 8.069 (1990, July 13). *Dispõe o Estatuto da Criança e do Adolescente e dá outras providências.* Casa Civil, Subchefia para assuntos jurídicos.

Leite, J. T., Beserra, M. A., Scatena, L., Silva, L. M. P., and Ferriani, M. G. C. (2016). Coping with domestic violence against children and adolescents from the perspective of primary care nurses. *Revista Gaúcha de Enfermagem*, 37(2), e55796.

Minayo, M. C. S. (2006). Violência e saúde. Rio de Janeiro: Editora Fiocruz.

Ministério da Justiça. (1988). *Constituição da República Federativa do Brasil*. Atlas.

Ministério da Saúde, Secretaria de Atenção à Saúde, and Departamento de Atenção Básica. (2012). *Saúde da criança: crescimento e desenvolvimento*. Ministério da Saúde.

Ministério da Saúde, Secretaria de Vigilância em Saúde, Departamento de Vigilância de Doenças e Agravos não Transmissíveis e Promoção da Saúde. (2013). *Sistema de Vigilância de Violências e Acidentes (VIVA): 2009, 2010 e 2011*. Ministério da Saúde.

Ministério do Desenvolvimento Social e Combate à Fome and Secretaria Nacional de Assistência Social. (2004). *Política Nacional de Assistência Social*. CNAS.

Ministério do Desenvolvimento Social e Combate à Fome. (2014). Tipificação Nacional de Serviços Socioassistenciais. CNAS.

Presidência da República, Secretaria Especial dos Direitos Humanos, and Conselho Nacional dos Direitos da Criança e do Adolescente. (2006). *Plano Nacional de Promoção, Proteção e Defesa do Direito de Crianças e Adolescentes à Convivência Familiar e Comunitária*. Conanda.

Rodarte, B. C., Carlos, D. M., Totti Leite, J., Beserra, M. A., Garcia Oliveira, V., and Ferriani, M. G. C. (2015). Protective factors from the perspective of victimised and institutionalised adolescents. *Referência— Revista de Enfermagem*, 4(7), 73–80.

Roque, E. M. S. T., Ferriani, M. G. C., Gomes, R., Silva, L. M. P., and Carlos, D. M. (2014). Justice system and secondary victimization of children and or adolescents victims of sexual violence in the family. *Saúde e Sociedade*, 23(3), 801–813.

Santos, B. R. (2004). Cronologia histórica das intervenções na vida de crianças e adolescentes pobres no Brasil. *Estudos*, 31(December), 11–44.

Silva, E. and Motti, A. (2001). *Estatuto da criança e do adolescente, uma década de direitos: avaliando resultados e projetando o futuro*. Ed. UFMS.

Silva, L. M. P., Ferriani, M. G. C., Beserra, M. A., Roque, E. M. S. T., and Carlos, D. M.. (2013). *A escuta de crianças e adolescentes nos processos de crimes sexuais*. Ciência & Saúde Coletiva, 18(8), 2285–2294.

Souza Neto, J. C. S. (2002). *Crianças e adolescentes abandonados: estratégias de sobrevivência* (2nd ed.). Arte Impressa.

UNICEF. (2015). *Estatuto da Criança e do Adolescente 25 anos: Avanços e desafios para a infância e a adolescência no Brasil*. UNICEF.

Waiselfisz, J. J. (2012). *Mapa da violência 2012: A cor dos homicídios no Brasil Rio de Janeiro: CEBELA, FLACSO*. SEPPIR/PR.

WHO. (2010). *Violence prevention: The evidence*. World Health Organization.

WHO. (2014). *Global status report on violence prevention 2014*. World Health Organization.

World Bank Group. (2015). World Open Data. Available at: http://data.worldbank.org.

Child Protection Policy and Service in China

Fang Zhao *and* Yanfeng Xu

Abstract

This chapter discusses China's child protection policies and services. Children are considered as a family's private property in China following its Confucianism influence. Since the establishment of the People's Republic of China, the child protection policy has been influenced by its sociopolitical system and transitioned from a residual welfare system to a modest institutional system. While the country witnessed the rapid development of its policies and practices, China is still fronting issues such as insufficient supportive measures to implement child protection legislation, and lack of clarification on the concept of child abuse and neglect. Building a family-centred child welfare policy and comprehensive welfare services are vital in improving the Chinese child protection system.

Key Words: China, child protection, family, Confucianism, sociopolitcal system, welfare system, child abuse, development, policies, legislation

Introduction

The deep influence of Confucianism means that children are considered a family's private property in China, and it is a family's responsibility to protect children. Since the establishment of the People's Republic of China in 1949, China's child protection policy has been deeply influenced by its sociopolitical system, which brought forth a residual child welfare system for the most vulnerable children. After the reforms of 1978, child welfare policy has been gradually transitioning from a residual welfare system to a modest institutional one. In recent years, China has seen a rapid development of child protection policy and practice, including the establishment of a mandatory reporting system, legislation for surrogate care for vulnerable children, legal practice of custody transfer of parental custody, comprehensive promotion of a grassroots child welfare director's policy, and active involvement of nonprofit organizations in child protection. However, China is still confronted with a series of child protection challenges: lack of supportive measures to implement child protection legislation; lack of an effective government authority involved in protecting children; lack of clarification of concepts of child abuse and neglect, cultural barriers to the enforcement of the mandatory reporting system, lack of clear and specific procedures for interventions, lack of a system design for surrogate care for maltreated children, lack of satisfactory temporary settlement services, lack of interventions from professionals and professional service organizations, and lack of sufficient family support services. Although China faces multiple challenges, constructing a family-centered child welfare policy and fostering comprehensive child welfare services are pivotal pathways to further develop a family-centered child protection system in China.

Background

China, the most populous countries in the world, has about 295 million children, which comprises 12% of children in the world (UNICEF, 2016). Child maltreatment is a serious social and public health problem, and child protection is a sensitive but widely discussed issue around the world. Although there is no national prevalence of child maltreatment in China, an estimated 26.6% of children had experienced physical abuse, 19.6% emotional abuse, 8.7% sexual abuse, and 26.0% neglect, according to a meta-analysis of 68 empirical studies conducted in China (Fang et al., 2015).

The response to child maltreatment is closely related to a country's level of socioeconomic development and civilization. With a rapid social transformation in China, social problems have emerged abruptly in the past few years, among which are frequent cases of child abuse and neglect. The current child protection policy and services do not effectively respond to child maltreatment cases and meet the needs of these children and families. Although China currently has implemented the revised Minor Protection Law since June 2021, how to establish a specific and effective system to protect children's rights and interests is still unclear. Topics hotly debated have emerged: how this child protection act can respond to the needs of maltreated children and their families, and how to balance the ideology between traditional Chinese culture and a modern child protection system in intervening in child maltreatment.

Evolution of Child Protection Policy in China

China's child protection policy has been evolving alongside social development, constantly adapting itself in response to the practical needs of social development.

Child Protection Policy Under the Deep Influence of Confucianism

The establishment of the traditional social order in China is greatly influenced by Confucianism. The Confucian traditions permeate every aspect of the social structure, which has influenced China's child protection policy in return (Zhao et al., 2017). Under the impact of Confucianism, a family is a major, even an exclusive bearer of child welfare. As long as individuals have a family, their basic needs can be met within families. Only those who are from poverty-stricken families and are homeless are eligible to be recipients of social relief benefits. "Family" and "child protection" have traditionally been separated from the range of social relief benefits.

In such a cultural context, the responsibility of child protection falls naturally on the family. The government only plays the residual function and is the last resort for child protection; other organizations and neighbors are neither allowed nor able to be involved in family affairs. Similarly, family members are not encouraged to seek external assistance or support so as to avoid being deemed incapable of taking care of their family, for which they may be discriminated against.

In addition, in the Confucian patriarchal culture that focuses on filial piety, children are deemed no more than an instrument for family reproduction and prosperity and are disciplined and educated by adults based on the family tradition. Not considered to be independent individuals, children inherit the prospects of the family rather than their own development. Children are asked to sacrifice part of their interests for the family's benefit and are also partially deprived of freedom and the right to make any decisions or choices of their own. Today's China is still considerably influenced by Confucianism, as Yang (2002) stated that most of the values and beliefs pursed in traditional Chinese culture last long into modern times. Despite repeated clashes with exoteric cultural values and the dramatic transformation in the social and economic structure, the distinctive "China-ness" remains largely intact (Yang, 2002).

China's Child Protection Policy in the Context of the Sociopolitical Structure

From the establishment of the People's Republic of China in 1949 to 1966, the nation's political and economic power increased. With this and the start of the women's liberation movement, some progress was made in child development and welfare. Child welfare policy, during this period, was aimed at guaranteeing children's right to survival, and child welfare services were only provided to orphans, children with disabilities, and abandoned children under extremely difficult circumstances. Child welfare agencies provided family-like or parent-substitute services at child welfare homes, adoption centers, and residential care, as well as children's education organizations to these children.

During the 10-year Cultural Revolution from 1966 to 1976, child protection grounded to a halt. With economic reform in 1978 and the furtherance of industrialization and urbanization, China entered a period of massive transformation. Child protection policy in this period saw a big developmental leap. China signed the Convention on the Rights of the Child in 1990 (UN, 1994), and the World Declaration on the Survival, Protection, and Development of Children in 1991 (UNICEF, n.d.), which connected China's child welfare affairs to those of the international community and substantially raised public awareness of children's rights in society. This progress was marked by two significant pieces of legislation.

First, the Law on the Protection of Minors was enacted in 1991[1] (Standing Committee of the National People's Congress, 1991), followed by the Law on the Prevention of

---

[1] The terms "minors" and "children" are used interchangeably in Chinese, and both refer to children between ages 0 and 18.

Juvenile Delinquency (Standing Committee of the National People's Congress, 1999, 2012). The Law on the Protection of Minors (1991) Article 5 states:

> Any organization or individual shall have the right to dissuade or stop any act encroaching upon the lawful rights and interests of minors, or report to or complain before a department concerned there against.

The Law on the Prevention of Juvenile Delinquency (1999), Article 41 further states:

> Minors who are abandoned by their parents or other guardians, or are subject to maltreatment, shall have the right to seek protection from local police stations, civil affairs departments, the Communist Youth League, the Women's Federation, or protection organizations for minors. These departments and organizations shall respond to the appeal and take necessary and effective measures to provide proper aid and assistance.

The enactment of the two laws ensures basic legal protection for children. However, due to the lack of regulations on child abuse and neglect reporting, initial protection against child abuse and neglect is restricted to conciliation and dissuasion. In addition, a case can go through proper legal procedures only when the victimized child appeals for protection. However, children with limited autonomy and independence can hardly appeal for aid. Even in rare cases where such an appeal is made, only offenders who have caused severe harm to the child get punished. As a consequence, the initially developed child protection policy had little practical application.

The Development of a New Child Protection System in the Past 15 Years

In the past 15 years, from 2005 to 2020, with the furtherance of social transformation, China's child protection policy has entered a phase of rapid development.

Transitioning from a Residual Welfare System to a Modest Welfare System

The recently issued National Program for Child Development in China (2011–2020) (State Council, 2011) mentions that child welfare should gradually transform from a residual system to a modestly inclusive one, stressing the need to increase foster and adoption rates for orphaned children. It also discusses issues regarding the protection of AIDS affected children and children of incarcerated parents, which further expands the scope of child welfare service populations.

According to the Pilot Work to Establish a Modestly Inclusive Child Welfare System for All Children issued by the Ministry of Civil Affairs (Ministry of Civil Affairs, 2013a), children are subdivided into orphans, children living under deprived circumstances, children from vulnerable families, and children under ordinary circumstances. Some of these subdivisions are further elaborated. Children living under deprived circumstances are further divided into three categories: the disabled, the severely ill, and the homeless. Children from vulnerable families are subdivided as: 1) children in the custody of parents who are profoundly disabled or are suffering from severe diseases; 2) children whose parents are serving prison sentences or are forced into rehabilitation programs; 3) children with a deceased parent and the other parent incapable of providing custody or acting as a guardian; and 4) children from poverty-stricken families. This policy first defines vulnerable children in China. Despite the limit to basic life protection, these policies brought forth a socialized child welfare service system, which to some extent meets the needs of children living in deprived circumstances, as well as abused and neglected children.

In recent years, protecting left-behind children, who are at a high risk of experiencing child maltreatment, has been a priority of child protection work in China. Left-behind children are those who are left in rural homes under the care of relatives or without any adult supervision while their parents or one of their parents migrate to urban regions to look for jobs (Wen & Lin, 2012). To protect left-behind children, the State Council on Further Strengthening the Protection of Left-behind Children in Rural China has been enacted since 2016 (State Council of China, 2016a). This administrative measure requires to establish a well-developed social services system to protect left-behind children (State Council of China, 2016a). Following this administrative measure, the State Council further enacted the State Council on Strengthening the Protection of Vulnerable Children, which guided the specific child protection mechanisms to protect different types of vulnerable children as we elaborated earlier in accordance with the nation's socioeconomic status (State Council of China, 2016b).

These policies expanded the scope of child welfare services beyond orphans, children with disabilities, and abandoned children, and included more vulnerable children in the country's child welfare services coverage. It serves a vital turning point in the development of China's child protection system from a residual model to a modestly inclusive one.

The Establishment of a Mandatory Reporting System and Surrogate Care System for Child Abuse

A mandatory reporting system was established in the Law of the People's Republic of China against Domestic Violence 2016 (Standing Committee of the National People's Congress, 2015). This is to date the most pertinent law related to child abuse, as child abuse is a common form of domestic violence. According to the Law against Domestic Violence, those who work in kindergartens, elementary, middle and high schools, medical institutions, and other related units shall report suspected domestic violence cases to police officers if they suspect that a person with limited or no civil conduct capacity experiences domestic violence; otherwise, these mandated reporters shall bear legal responsibility. The Supreme People's Procuratorate (2020), along with other government agencies, issued the Opinions on Establishing a Compulsory Reporting System for Cases Against Minors, which offered specific measures to establish a mandatory reporting system and further refined the system. In October 2020, China's Law on the Protection of Minors (Standing Committee of the National People's Congress, 2020) was amended. The mandatory reporting system in child protection has been further defined and emphasized by the law.

With regard to surrogate care, the Measures for the Administration of Family Foster Care (Ministry of Civil Affairs, 2014a) expanded family foster care from orphans, children with disabilities, and abandoned children to street children for the first time in history. Followed by this, the amendment to the Law on the Protection of Minors (Standing Committee of the National People's Congress, 2020) stated that "the People's Governments at or above the county level and Departments of Civil Affairs shall, in light of need, establish institutions for the relief and protection of minors and institutions for the welfare of children to take in minors under the guardianship of Departments of Civil Affairs." This is the very first step to set surrogate care for maltreated children, and this is no small progress.

THE LEGISLATIVE PRACTICE OF CUSTODY TRANSFER AND THE ESTABLISHMENT OF ITS LEGISLATION

In addition to the establishment of a mandatory reporting system and surrogate care, the legislative practice of custody transfer has made progress. The Beijing Municipal Bureau of Civil Affairs proposed in 2013, to launch a pilot program to improve public child protection in three districts: Chao Yang, Feng Tai, and Mi Yun. According to this proposal, guardians' custody could be revoked if they fail to perform their duties (China News, 2014). Early in 2014, the Supreme People's Court, the Ministry of Public Security, and the Ministry of Civil Affairs jointly drafted the Opinions on Guidelines for Custody Transfer of a Minor in Improper Family Custody (Consultation Paper) (Ministry of Civil Affairs, 2014d). The document stipulates seven categories in which the guardianship of the offender shall be abrogated, children's new guardianship upon guardianship abrogation, guardianship restoration, and a series of essential issues concerning mandatory termination of guardianship and state guardianship.

Later that year, the definition of and principle in handling a guardian's infringement were detailed. In December 2014, these four departments, the Supreme People's Court, the Supreme People's Procuratorate, the Ministry of Public Security, and the Ministry of Civil Affairs, jointly promulgated the Opinions on Legally Handling Several Issues on Guardian's Infringement upon the Rights and Interests of Minors (hereafter: the Opinions) (Four Departments, 2014). It also specifies major duties of four departments with regard to report and disposal, temporary shelter and personal safety protection, applying for revocation of a guardian's qualification, case hearing, procedures after the hearing, and the major responsibilities of these four departments. Additionally, even possible situations are detailed concerning departments' requirement to take immediate measures to deter and investigate harmful behaviors and to take the minor away from the custodian under particularly serious circumstances. The Opinions officially took effect on January 1, 2015. Though custodianship abrogation was first introduced in 1987 with the General Principles of the Civil Law (National People's Congress, 1986) and later the Law on the Protection of Minors in 2006 (Standing Committee of the National People's Congress, 2006), it was not effectively implemented.

Furthermore, at the national level, the Civil Code of the People's Republic of China in 2020, and the Law on the Protection of Minors (newly amended in 2020) stated that the Civil Affairs authority, the residents' committee, or the villagers' committee shall act as the state guardian of children if parents and relatives are not capable (National People's Congress, 2020). Hailed as a giant step forward in China's child protection policy, for the first time in history, custody transfer was specified in the Law, which demonstrates China's commitment to and substantive progress in child protection.

In practice, the first case of custody deprivation due to child abuse in China occurred in July 2014: a mother lost custody of her biological son by a county court in Fujian Province (Ifeng News, 2014). On February 4, 2015, Tongshan District People's Court of Xuzhou Municipality in Jiangsu Province heard a case where a female child was sexually abused by her biological father. The father was charged with rape and child molestation and sentenced to 11 years; the mother, due to child abandonment, had her custody revoked along with the father (China Court, 2015). Since the implementation of the Opinions by the four departments, this was the first lawsuit where custody of both parents was revoked. Moreover, Shanghai Child Temporary Care Center, as an administrative department of the government, pursued a lawsuit against a single mother who abandoned her nonmarital child in a hospital for three years in 2017. The court not only revoked the mother's custody but also sentenced her for a year (Sohu News, 2015). These were the very first cases of the deprivation of parental custody with a governmental entity as a prosecutor of child maltreatment lawsuits, which was a significant milestone of custody transfer practice in China. By August 2017, 69 cases of guardianship revocation, which included: 28 cases (41%) of abandonment or refusing to fulfill guardian duties; 18 cases (26%) of rape, sexual abuse or sexual assault; and 11 cases (16%) of abuse or violence were documented (Zhang, 2017). This marks the beginning of custody deprivation judicial practices.

PILOT PROGRAMS TO IMPLEMENT CHILD PROTECTION POLICY AND ITS GRADUAL PROMOTION

Some pilot programs have been implemented in the past few years. On May 6, 2013 and July 31, 2014, the Ministry of Civil Affairs launched the Notice on Implementing a Pilot Program for Minor Protection by the Society (Ministry of Civil Affairs, 2013b) and Notice of the Ministry of Civil Affairs on Launching the Second Batch of National Social Protection Pilot Projects for Minors (Ministry of Civil Affairs, 2014c), respectively. The Ministry of Civil Affairs endeavored to accomplish the pilot project for the social protection of minors by the year 2016 and to promote the program nationally. Pilot programs for minor protection have since been launched by two groups in 98 locations (Ministry of Civil Affairs, 2013b; Ministry of Civil Affairs, 2014c). Holding the principle of "maximizing the rights of the minors," these programs have extended protection to children, reinforced foundational work on screening and prevention, established a reporting system for minors in difficult circumstances, improved intervention measures to assist minors in difficult circumstances and their families, and built a social service network for child protection. Based on the pilot work of the 98 national-level locations, another 105 pilot locations were founded at the province level. Through the pilot project, a guardianship system centering on the family, with social supervision as the guarantee and state guardianship as the supplement, was established, and a trinity of social protection for minors was formed: family, society, and government.

To solve the last mile issue of child welfare services in rural regions, the Ministry of Civil Affairs with other nine departments further passed Opinions on Further Strengthening the Caring Services System for Left-behind Children in Rural China and Vulnerable Children in 2019 (Ministry of Civil Affairs, 2019). This administrative measure further emphasized the establishment of children's homes and having child welfare directors at the village level and child supervisors at the township levels nationally (Ministry of Civil Affairs, 2019). Moreover, the Ministry of Civil Affairs aimed to have 620,000 registered child directors and 45,000 child supervisors nationally (People Society, 2019). In Guangdong Province, there were 25,000 registered child welfare directors as of April 2019 (People's Government of Guangzhou Province, 2019). This policy strengthened child welfare workforce development and clarified the role of child welfare directors and supervisors in promoting the well-being of left-behind children and vulnerable children.

From 2010 to 2015, a pilot child welfare director model was implemented in five western/central provinces (i.e., Shanxi, Henan, Sichuan, Yunnan, and Xinjiang) where there was a high proportion of left-behind children (Child Welfare Demonstration Project Office & China Philanthropy Research Institute Child Welfare Research Center, 2013). The evaluation research of this pilot project demonstrated that having child welfare directors at the village level expanded child welfare services to the last mile, which improved the service accessibility and promoted child well-being (Child Welfare Demonstration Project Office & China Philanthropy Research Institute Child Welfare Research Center, 2013). By June 2020, China had set up 663,000 child welfare directors in rural villages and urban communities, which indicated a nationwide coverage of child welfare directors (Ministry of Civil Affairs, 2020). It has been a giant leap forward for China's child protection from policymaking to policy implementation.

CIVIL NON-PROFIT ORGANIZATIONS BECOMING AN IMPORTANT FORCE IN CHILD PROTECTION

Recently, the emergence of social governance in China has promoted a mixed public/private welfare service model, involving more and more civil non-profit organizations in child protection. Among these are: "Home of Little Hope" in Shanghai; Beijing Juvenile

Legal Aid Research Center; Nanjing Tongxin Juvenile Protection and Service Center; and "Girls' Protecting," started by the Beijing Times and People.cn (Zhao et al., 2018).

As an example, X institution is a civil organization founded in 2013 for the protection of abused children. Their vision is "protecting the children, safeguarding the future". X institution is devoted to propagating legislation on child protection, providing legal aid for victims of child abuse and violence against women, and providing assistance at individual and family levels. The founders of X institution have a strong ideology of child protection, emphasizing that children shall not be separated from their parents. Additional values include:

- in case of conflicts of interest between guardians and children, the interest of children is the priority;
- there shall be clear legislation safeguarding the interests of children;
- in case of families' inability to safeguard the interest of children, the state shall intervene in a timely manner;
- civil organizations shall exercise their compensatory functions in case of state safeguard deficiency.

Between 2013 and 2015, X institution established five group homes for children in difficult circumstances, registered 1,500 volunteers, and aided 136 victims of child abuse and neglect in difficult circumstances. In addition to aiding children under difficult circumstances, X institution has also been actively engaged with policy advocacy, striving to promote the advancement of policy and regulations in child protection. For example, in September 2014, a homeless woman was found begging with her daughter. This woman suffered from mental illness, and the girl was in bad condition. X institution followed up through visits and reporting, yet no real progress was made. Not until the implementation of the Opinions by the Four Departments on January 1, 2015, did local volunteers report for a second time to the police, in accordance with the Opinions. After reporting, local police and staff from the Bureau of Civil Affairs intervened, sending the child for a physical exam and the mother for medical treatment. The child was brought to a temporary shelter for minors operated by the Department of Civil Affairs. A thorough investigation of this case was conducted by the Bureau of Civil Affairs to decide a long-term placement plan for the child (State Council, 2016a, 2016b).

After its first two years of operation, X institution gradually became familiar with the most current policies and created a set of practical workflow procedures and methods of intervention. The approach to intervention has shifted from an assertive involuntary intervention to a positive and modest serving one. This is demonstrated in X institution's fostering collaborative relationships with local police and the Women's Federation, exploring local charity organizations that can provide direct services, and allocating local resources. After the Opinions, X institution further made an initial summary of past cases, had discussions with legal experts in seminars, and propagated some cases to improve public awareness of child protection and facilitate implementations of relevant policies. In recent cases, staff and volunteers from X institution actively advocated the police, the Women's Federation and the Department of Civil Affairs to intervene in child protection collaboratively and achieved satisfactory intervention outcomes.

PROFESSIONAL SOCIAL WORKERS ENTERING CHILD PROTECTION

Guidelines have emerged in the past few years for the social work profession. The Ministry of Civil Affairs (2014b) passed the Service Guideline for Social Work with Children, which stipulates in detail the principles, subjects, categories, procedures, skills, supervision, administration, and staff qualifications of child social work services. This is evident in both domestic violence and child protection. The Law against Domestic Violence (2016) legally confirmed for the first time the role of social workers in intervening in domestic violence. The Law on the Protection of Minors amended in 2020 further defined the important role and status of social workers in child protection in legal provisions. The State Council and Ministry of Civil Affairs both stated the role of social work professionals in care and protection of left-behind children and vulnerable children (State Council of China, 2016a, 2016b; Ministry of Civil Affairs, 2019). Since then, child protection social work has obtained both assurances from legislation and policy and support from professional guidelines; thus, social work services in child protection are provided gradually. In Guangzhou by August 2020, for example, the government purchased professional services provided by 54 social organizations, including 42 social service agencies (e.g., Guangzhou Caring Center for Children in Difficulty), nine social groups, and nine foundations. Furthermore, the government offered 22 training courses and trained 1,763 child welfare social workers. Since the COVID-19 pandemic, the Civil Affairs Bureau of Shanghai has raised RMB 5.9 million and purchased services from 16 professional social services organizations to serve vulnerable children. In this service model, a professional child welfare social worker was matched to serve a child in difficulty during the pandemic. In this way, a long-term mechanism for "one-on-one" interactive feedback between social workers and children in difficulty was established (Zhao et al., 2021).

Creation of and collaboration with social work research institutions with the participation of universities have also emerged. In March 2014, seeking to involve social work intervention in child protection, joint efforts were made to start the building of a child protection system and initiate family group conference interventions in Guangzhou. The coalition behind these efforts included the Sun Yat-sen University Center for Education and Research of Social Work, the Social Work Department at the University of Bath in the UK, the Qi Chuang Social Work Service Center, and the Bai Yun District Social Work Association. In 2016, the Sino-Finnish Center for Child Protection Research was founded at Fudan University's Department of Social Work. The center conducts research on legislation and interventions in child protection and directly participates in the assessment and intervention of vulnerable children through the purchase of services from the government. In 2017, the Resource Center for Child Protection and Development in collaboration with Yunnan University was founded in Kunming (Zhao et al., 2018).

In sum, through an interactive platform that involves government departments, universities, social organizations, and communities, the construction of a child protection system and the development of child social work have thus been implemented.

Challenges in Child Protection System

Although China has made significant progress, it is undeniable that much remains to be done. The current child protection practice faces multiple challenges at the policy, administrative, professional, and cultural levels. These challenges include lack of supporting measures to implement child protection legislation, lack of an effective government authority involved in protecting children, lack of clarification with concepts of child abuse and neglect, cultural barriers to the enforcement of the mandatory reporting system, lack of clear and specific procedures for intervention, lack of a system design for surrogate care for maltreated children, lack of satisfactory temporary settlement services, lack of interventions from professionals and professional service organizations, and lack of sufficient family supportive services (Zhao et al., 2018). A description of each is detailed below.

Lack of Supporting Measures to Implement Child Protection Legislation

The Law on the Protection of Minors was revised in 2020. The newly amended law, which has 132 articles, is based on children's rights of survival, protection, participation, and development, and covers six major areas of child protection: family protection, social protection, school protection, judicial protection, government protection, and internet protection. It is a big step forward to have very detailed child protection measures. However, although the law has been in effect since June 1, 2021, there is still a need for a series of supporting mechanisms to implement the law. Many institutional barriers also hinder the practice. For example, although the law clearly states that governmental authorities can be children's state guardians when caregivers are incompetent, it does not have practical guidelines, particularly lacking instructions to guide practice when child custody is transferred to the state, and the child is in need of alternative care (Yao, 2019). Taken together, China still has not successfully built an effective and comprehensive child protection system (Man et al., 2017), and there is still a long way to go.

Lack of an Effective Government Authority Responding to Child Protection

In the child protection system of other countries, a government agency or a government-designated organization usually takes major responsibilities in child protection. In the newly revised Law on the Protection of Minors, the People's Governments at or above the county level shall establish a coordination mechanism for the protection of minors. The specific work of the coordination mechanism shall be undertaken by Departments of Civil Affairs in the People's Governments above the county level. Therefore, the law establishes the leading role of Civil Affairs Departments in child protection. In practice, however, child welfare services are provided by numerous administrative departments, including the Department of Medical Relief in the Ministry of Labor and Social Security, the Department of Social Assistance and Social Affairs in the Ministry of Civil Affairs, the Department of Women and Children's Care and Community Health in the Ministry of Health, and the Department of Basic Education in the Ministry of Education. The major civil organizations involved in child protection are the Department of Women's Development, the Department of Rights and Benefits, the China's Disabled Persons' Federation, the Department of Children's Work in All-China Women's Federation, the Department of Youth Work, the Department of Rural Youth, the Department of Schools, the Department of Adolescence, and the Department of Community and Protecting Youth and Children's Rights and Benefits in the Central Committee of the Communist Youth League (Shang & Zhang, 2011). In addition to this multitude of departments, child protection needs multisectoral collaboration from public security, court, procuratorate, and other representatives of state authorities. Although Departments of Civil Affairs take the lead, it has been difficult to coordinate resources and share information among all these departments.

To resolve this challenge, the Child Welfare Department under the Ministry of Civil Affairs was newly established in January 2019, which aimed to coordinate resources among multiple state agencies. However, it has not been that effective because the Child Welfare Department has no authority as a parallel, even subordinate agency among these governmental entities. In addition, this new setting has only been implemented at the central governmental level but has not been extended to local governments. As a result, limited collaboration among multiple state agencies is still a significant challenge in the implementation process of child protection services due to a lack of an effective government authority responding to child maltreatment.

Lack of Clarification with Concepts of Abuse and Neglect

The concepts of abuse and neglect are not well defined. Although the current policy recognizes child abuse as a social problem, it does not provide a practical definition of it. In terms of child neglect, there are no direct responses to or definitions of neglect. Specifically, domestic violence, including child abuse, is defined in the Law against Domestic Violence; however, guidelines to identify domestic violence and determine levels of injuries are missing. Also, provisions for child neglect are not mentioned. Without a clear and working definition of child maltreatment in the context of Chinese culture, it is challenging to diagnose child maltreatment and assess children's risky and vulnerable situations (Xu et al., 2018). As such, child protection programs have faced significant barriers to intervene in child abuse and neglect but end up with providing general child services to improve child well-being (Man et al., 2017).

Cultural Barriers to the Enforcement of the Mandatory Reporting System

In terms of the reporting system, the newly released Law against Domestic Violence marks significant progress in the prevention of child maltreatment. It has expanded the reporting from the victim's self-reporting to mandated reporting of certain organizations and voluntary reporting of all other individuals. However, only limited mandated reporting is stipulated because of the deep belief in traditional Chinese culture. Some proverbs, such as "each one sweeps the snow from his own doorstep and doesn't heed the frost on his neighbor's roof," and "family discipline privilege," and a deep-rooted parenting theory of "spare the rod and spoil the child" reflect Chinese culture in family affairs and child education. The strong concept of family privacy and high tolerance of corporal punishment make it challenging for the public to accept child maltreatment as a public health and social problem and participate in disclosing child abuse and neglect. In more conservative rural areas, in particular, more efforts are needed to increase the public's awareness through education, public campaigns, and extra support.

Lack of Clear and Specific Procedures for Interventions

With respect to the procedures to implement child protection policy, the first challenge is no clear standard to distinguish between low degrees of maltreatment and more severe maltreatment cases. Traditionally, in cases with a comparatively low degree of maltreatment, an educative mediation between parents and the child is employed by community authorities. The judicial department and public security only get involved in cases when children have severe injuries. Of note, the involvement of public security agencies and the judicial department as public authorities have not been widely recognized. Furthermore, the procedures from investigations, in-home services, or out-of-home practices to reunification or adoption are not detailed. Moreover, family and children's participation have been overlooked, which gets away from a family-centered approach.

Lack of a System Design for Surrogate Care

Currently, surrogate care has been used in China, particularly for orphans (Xu et al., 2018). For children living under difficult circumstances where their guardians are incompetent to provide adequate care, a systemic and well-developed surrogate care plan is still lacking. Before the introduction of the Opinions, guardianship revocation was never truly implemented, putting children's long-term safety at risk when parents abused or neglected their children. When placing children back to their family of origin without any family support services, children may still have a high risk of being maltreated by their guardians and suffer more severe harm. Substantial efforts have been made to bolster surrogate care in recent years, such as a series of regulations concerning guardianship revocation and settlement and the establishment of children's homes and shelters and foster care homes for vulnerable children. Yet these efforts still do not adequately serve maltreated children.

Lack of Satisfactory Temporary Settlement Services

The current placements for children's alternative care often include welfare centers, senior living centers, and relief centers, which are not originally designed to provide a temporary settlement for children. Additionally, staff members in these facilities are not professionally trained to provide services to protect children's safety and improve children's well-being. Other civil organizations, however, are neither qualified nor equipped with adequate resources to provide temporary care for children. Although current policies stipulate that it is the state's responsibility to provide temporary placements for children under difficult circumstances, it is unclear that the extent to these placements have been established and whether they are able to take care of children in an effective way. Temporary settlement is an area of child protection services that requires more in-depth analysis.

Lack of Interventions from Professionals and Professional Service Organizations

Professional service organizations and professionals should actively participate in child welfare services, including preventing child maltreatment, intervening in child maltreatment, preserving families, and promoting permanency. Due to a very short history of social work education, China still has not trained a substantial number of professionals involved in child protection services. Although social workers are expected to serve as child welfare directors and supervisors, unprofessional trained community workers also function in these roles (Child Welfare Demonstration Project Office & China Philanthropy Research Institute Child Welfare Research Center, 2013). Additionally, many unprofessional behaviors have been observed during the service process, leading to unnecessary harm to children and their families from time to time.

Lack of Sufficient Family Supportive Services

A healthy biological family is the best place to promote child well-being. It is also the case that when delivering child protection services, the first choice is to restore the biological family's healthy functioning. The ultimate goal of child protection policy is to promote children's healthy development in a healthy family rather than taking children away from their family. The current Chinese policies somehow follow this philosophy. For instance, the Opinions stipulate that in efforts to maintain the guardian's custodianship, multiple departments shall engage in follow-up to enhance protection for the minors and supervision of the guardians within the family. Except for a few serious cases described in the stipulation, guardians may apply for guardianship restoration between three months and one year from the time when their guardianship was revoked (Four Departments, 2014). Whether it be guidance to either families with intact guardianship or children returning to their biological family, building and strengthening the healthy functions of a family and creating a healthy familial environment are the first steps. This calls for more effective family-support services that are provided to parents and other caregivers, but these services in China remain limited.

Table 31.1 Characteristics of child-focused and family-focused child protection policy

	Child protection-oriented	Family service-oriented
Problem framework	Individualism/morality	Society/psychology (family system, poverty, inequality)
Initial intervention	Legal regulation/investigation	Treatment/needs assessment
Motivation for intervention	Parents taking care of children inappropriately	Family needing assistance
Goal of intervention	Protection/harm reduction	Prevention/social connection
Government-parents relationship	Suggestive: government functioning as "night watchman" to ensure child safety	Partnership: government ameliorating relationship with family
Out-of-home placement	Involuntary	Voluntary
Balance between rights	Children's/parents' rights enforced by law	Parents' rights adjusted by social workers

Source: Gilbert (1997, p. 223).

The Construction of China's Child Protection System

Child protection is an issue involving policy as well as implementation; policymaking without implementation is like building castles in the air. Although China does not currently enjoy a national policy in the area of child protection, what follows is a review of the context that would likely shape such a policy in the future.

Comparing Child-focused and Family-focused Child Protection Approaches

Child protection policy can be divided into two classifications: one is child-focused, the other is family-focused. Table 31.1 (Gilbert, 1997, p. 223) displays a comparison between these two policy orientations. The former tends to be identified with the Anglo-American system, including England, the United States, and Canada, while the latter is represented by the Nordic system, including Denmark, Finland, and Norway. These two orientations can also be distinguished along four dimensions (Gilbert et al., 2011):

1) Perspectives on child abuse and neglect: in a child-focused orientation, child abuse is regarded as harm from parents. Thus, the children themselves need protection. In a family-focused orientation, however, child abuse is viewed as an issue stemming from the psychosocial conflicts and dysfunctions within a family. Thus, the family as a unit needs more assistance and support.

2) Interventions for child abuse and neglect: a child-focused orientation depends highly on legal interventions investigating children's family, while a family-focused orientation focuses on providing treatments and services based on the needs of the family.

3) Relationship between staff member and family: in a child-focused orientation, staff often have a difficult relationship with children's family, while in a family-focused orientation, staff build a collaborative relationship with the family.

4) Decisions for out-of-home placement: in the child-focused orientation, settlement decisions are made mandatorily by the government and the court, while in the family-focused orientation, parents are invited to participate in decision making.

An assessment on several countries' child risk coefficient conducted by the Organization for Economic Cooperation and Development (OECD) in 2009 reveals that the risk coefficient is highest in child-focused England and the United States and lowest among family-focused countries (Gilbert et al., 2011). Therefore, a family-oriented approach protects the best interest of the child. Some countries, such as the United States, are shifting to family-centered practice in child welfare (Pecora et al., 2009). A family-focused model is a process in which parents are encouraged to express their thoughts in decision-making concerning child and family service needs. Sample components in a family-centered approach include: parents as peer mentors could provide mentorship to other newly child welfare involved parents; extended family members may also be encouraged to participate in supporting children and parents (Gilbert et al., 2011).

Constructing a Family-Focused Child Protection System

A family-focused child protection policy is more aligned with Chinese culture than the child-focused approach for several reasons. Chinese people view family affairs as an issue that stems from an interaction of multiple factors inside and outside a family. Poverty, inadequate social welfare resources, illness, disability, social discrimination, and inequality are factors associated with family difficulties as well as consequences of weakened family functioning. Simply taking the child away from the family would undoubtedly reduce the immediate potential for harm to the child. But in the long run, it does not solve the problematic functioning within families and is far from being the best choice for children's growth and social development. Furthermore, mutual trust and support between family members, including extended family members, is highly emphasized in Chinese culture. Parents' and relatives' responsibilities to take care of children are well-esteemed. Thus, family support services are very likely to be highly valued and accepted by family members.

Additionally, Chinese culture is a family-focused culture in which parents are granted the rights to discipline children mentally and physically, as is expressed in sayings like "an untaught child is a father's fault" and "spare the rod and spoil the child." Child protection, however, aims to bring the public authority to private areas—a process indicative of public authority challenging patriarchy and paternity. Even though this action aims to protect children's safety, it is likely to be resisted by families due to the influences of traditional Chinese cultures. The authority of family or parents are being constantly challenged by child protection social workers during the processes of investigation, needs assessment, family interventions, and determination of surrogate care. In the meantime, the involvement of a public authority challenges traditions with thousands of years' history, like "do not air your dirty laundry in public," or "even the most upright judge cannot settle a family quarrel." Such involvement is likely to encounter several difficulties, including a power imbalance between public authority and private authority, and potential conflicts between affections, relationships, and mandated child protection. Therefore, in Chinese culture where affection, relationship, and the family as a unit are heavily stressed, the "intrusion" of social workers and other professionals into family affairs (such as child abuse and neglect) can ignite anger and resistance from parents, who would fight back in every possible way. Thus, respecting each family's culture and engaging family members in the decision-making process should be widely employed across child welfare services.

Considering the above, more effective protection could be achieved through a family-focused child protection policy and services in collaboration with the family. Family engagement and participation is a key principle in the process of strengthening family functioning.

Establishing a Child Protection System with Cross-Departmental Collaboration

If a well-functioning family-focused child protection policy were to be established in China, a number of elements would be essential to its. These elements include: a government department that oversees child protection issues and coordinates multiple departments; professional interventions by social organizations with public credibility; a formal and working definition of abuse and neglect; well-developed procedures of reporting and intervention; and intensive family support services, surrogate care (e.g., kinship care, non-kin foster care), and reunification and adoption services. The establishment of this system includes structural elements and technical elements. Figure 31.1 displays a child protection system with cross-departmental collaboration.

Establishing the Structural Elements

Structural elements include three aspects. First, valuation underlines an in-depth understanding of child protection, which includes giving priority to children's rights, maximizing the rights of children, and balancing the relationship between children, family, state, and society. This is a process where the society gradually comes to a universal understanding and reaches consensus concerning child protection. Second, relevant child protection systems and mechanisms should be formulated so that the Law on the Protection of Minors can be truly and effectively implemented a national and authoritative law on child welfare or child protection needs to be enacted. Additionally, corresponding

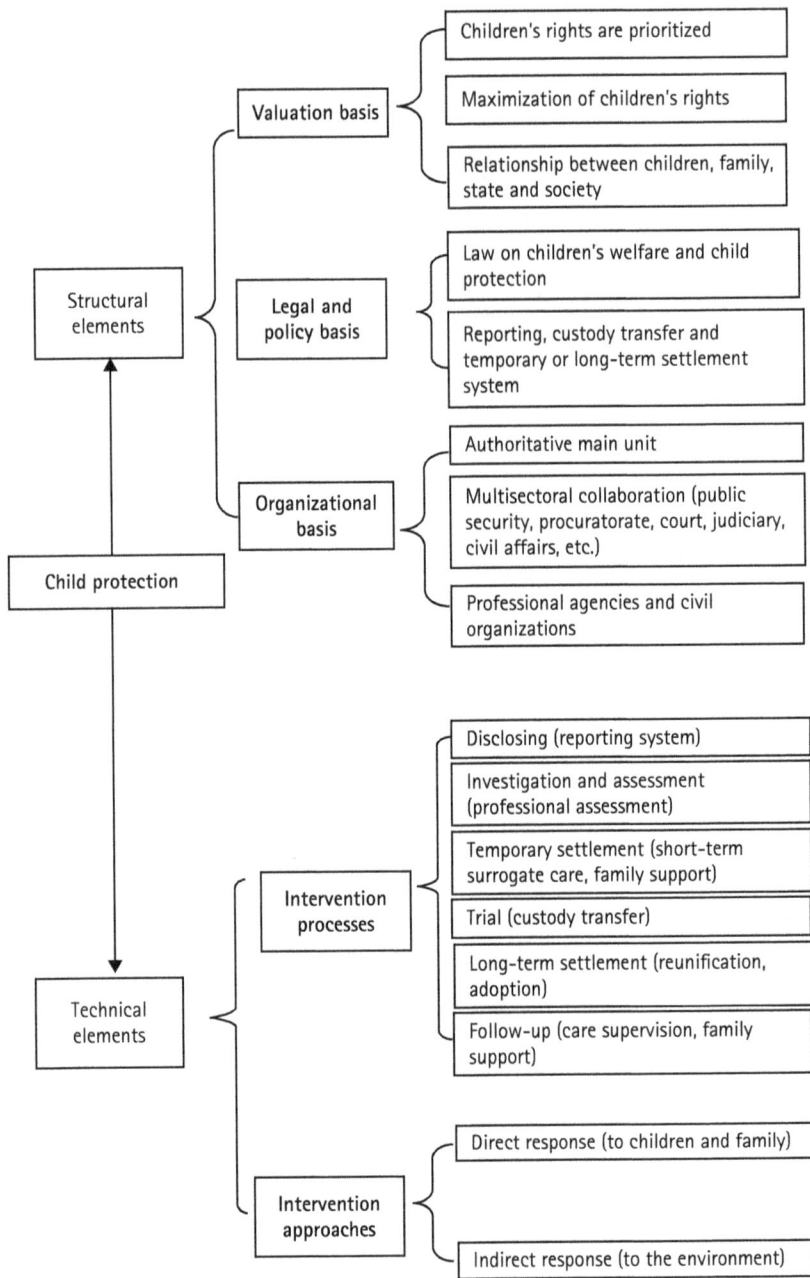

Figure 31.1 Construction of a cross-departmental collaborative child protection system (Zhao et al., 2018)

top-down regulations from central to local governments, including a reporting system, a custody transfer system, a temporary and long-term settlement system, and pathways to achieve permanency, are required. Whether it be general guidance or specific instructions, a series of professional processes need to be developed, from assessment and investigation, custody transfer, temporary settlement, long-term placement, and reunification, to adoption. Third, an authoritative main unit of child protection at the national and local levels needs to take the lead in child protection affairs and coordinate and integrate different departments. A number of departments, including public security, procuratorate, court, judiciary, hospital, school, and community, need to collaborate with each other to foster a smooth relationship and integrate essential resources to implement the policy in a rational and legitimate way. In the meanwhile, special emphasis should be given to the functions of civil organizations and professional non-profit organizations to integrate their resources and make full use of their timely, individualized, and professional services during child protection interventions.

Establishing the Technical Elements

The technical elements required to ensure the process of child protection service delivery, including the professional intervention process and specific services, are elaborated below. A national reporting hotline should be set up for mandated reporting and voluntary reporting. Mandated reporting is designed for staff who work closely with children while voluntary reporting is for civilians' use. Confidentiality is of great importance in the reporting system with some exceptions when the reporters are required to testify in court. During the investigation phase, social workers conduct investigation and assessment in collaboration with other professionals. If the investigation team identifies unsubstantiated child maltreatment, cases are closed but preventive services are provided if needed. If cases are substantiated, follow-up intervention services are provided by a multidisciplinary team. Additionally, intensive family support services are needed across the child protection services continuum. Preventive services should be provided to prevent occurrence and reoccurrence of abuse and neglect. Families, especially those at high risk, are the target for preventive services. These services aim to enhance caregivers' parenting skills and build healthy home environments for children. Holistic services in the community, such as mental health services, housing support services, financial assistance, are needed to provide to caregivers and their children. For children who stay in surrogate care, educational, mental health, and physical health services are needed to promote child well-being. To protect child safety, a monitoring and supervision mechanism that includes regular home visits, regular check-ins with children, and continuous foster family evaluation is needed to prevent any further abuse and neglect occurrence in surrogate care.

Specific intervention components include: building a professional team, establishing a standardized system for professional services, and providing indirect and direct services. Professional child protection social workers, along with other professionals, are needed to effectively work together and support children and families. Intensive training is needed to ensure these professionals have clear understandings of their roles and responsibilities, uphold professional ethics, and have the professional knowledge and skills to effectively serve maltreated children and their families. The establishment of comprehensive child protection services involves conducting investigations, making assessments, placing children in appropriate settings, and conducting follow-up services. Other countries' established standards and successful practical experiences can be good references to develop China's child protection services standards. However, a culturally sensitive definition of child abuse and neglect and socioeconomically appropriate child welfare services are needed. Furthermore, to monitor the quality of services, establishing a national child protection case monitoring system and database is needed. With regard to assessment, in addition to assessing abuse and neglect, social workers also need to engage family members to assess the family's capacity during the process of investigation and out-of-home placement. The provision of direct and indirect services is needed. Direct services involve providing services directly to families and children, like clinical therapies (e.g., trauma-informed therapy, family therapy), financial aid, crisis interventions, short-term and long-term settlements, reunification, and adoption. During the service delivery process, professionals shall follow professional standards to assure the quality of child welfare services. Indirect services aim to improve family functioning through the alteration of the environment and through making structural changes, such as policy advocacy, public campaign, community development, and community education.

Conclusion

China is in the early stages of developing a national child protection system. Child protection policy has been promoted in China, but looking ahead, more efforts are needed to establish a family-centered child protection system. Looking at other countries' experiences, no matter if it is a child-oriented or a family-oriented child protection country, building an effective child protection system is a long process. The history of child protection policy in the United States started with setting the standard of child abuse and neglect over a period of 87 years (1875–1962), underwent policymaking regarding child abuse and neglect prevention in a period of 12 years (1962–1974), and has continued to refine how the system of child protection functions under the Child Abuse Prevention and Treatment Act of 2003 (Myers, 2004, 2008). It took the United States a total of 128 years to develop legislation and services for child protection. Take a family-oriented country, Finland as an example. From the first Finnish Child Welfare Act in 1936 to the Child Welfare Act of 1983 until the most recent Child Welfare Act (Revised) in 2008 (Hearn et al., 2004; Satka & Harrikari, 2008), 72 years have been spent in formulating and refining child protection legislation and services. Developing a child protection system is a complex ongoing process rather than a once and for all matter; it is the same in China.

Note

Portions of this chapter were originally published in the *International Journal of Social Welfare.* Copyright (2017) Wiley, as F. Zhao, J. E. A. Hämäläinen, and H. L. Chen, Child protection in China: Changing policies and reactions from the field of social work.

Used with permission. Portions of this chapter were also originally published in China in the journal *Social Work and Management*, as Child protection policy analysis and family-centered child protection system construction" (儿童保护政策分析及以家庭为中心的儿童保护体系建构) (2018). Translated text has been reprinted with permission from *Social Work and Management*.

To provide a more comprehensive and updated picture of child protection in China, this chapter further integrates recent child welfare policies and services.

References

Child Welfare Demonstration Project Office and China Philanthropy Research Institute Child Welfare Research Center. (2013). 中国儿童福利示范项目中期评估报告 [Chinese child welfare demonstration program midterm evaluation report 2010–2012]. Available at: http://www.bnu1.org/show_962.html.

China Court. (2015). 全国首例父母双双被撤销女儿监护权案件判决：民政局担任监护人 [The first custody revocation case in the nation: The Civil Affairs authority becomes the child's guardian]. Available at: https://www.chinacourt.org/article/detail/2015/02/id/1546258.shtml.

China News. (2014). 未成年人监护权转移将实践 失责父母将失监护权 [*The opinions on guidelines for custody transfer of a minor in improper family custody (consultation paper)*]. Available at: http://www.chinan ews.com/sh/2014/06-21/6305331.shtml.

Fang, X., Fry, D. A., Ji, K., Finkelhor, D., Chen, J., Lannen, P., and Dunne, M. P. (2015). The burden of child maltreatment in China: A systematic review. *Bulletin of the World Health Organization*, 93(3), 176–185C.

Four Departments. (2014). 最高人民法院、最高人民检察院、公安部、民政部关于依法处理监护人侵害未成年人权益行为若干问题的意见 [Opinions of the Supreme People's Court, the Supreme People's Procuratorate, the Ministry of Public Security, and the Ministry of Civil Affairs on legally handling several issues on guardian's infringement upon the rights and interests of minors.] Available at: http://pku law.cn/%28S%28pvgj1x45wuwnwm5555df4e55%29%29/fulltext_form.aspx?Gid=240239.

Gilbert, N. (Ed.). (1997). *Combatting child abuse: International perspectives and trends*. Oxford University Press.

Gilbert, N., Parton, N., and Skivenes, M. (Eds.). (2011). *Child protection systems: International trends and orientations*. Oxford University Press.

Hearn, J., Pösö, T., Smith, C., White, S., and Korpinen, J. (2004). What is child protection? Historical and methodological issues in comparative research on lastensuojelu/child protection. *International Journal of Social Welfare*, 13(1), 28–41.

Ifeng News. (2014). 父母失当，撤销监护权. [Incompetent parents: Custody revoked]. Avaiable at: http://news.ifeng.com/a/20140905/41884156_0.shtml.

Man, X., Barth, R. P., Li, Y. E., and Wang, Z. (2017). Exploring the new child protection system in Mainland China: How does it work?. *Children and Youth Services Review*, 76, 196–202.

Ministry of Civil Affairs of the People's Republic of China. (2013a). 民政部关于开展适度普惠型儿童福利制度建设试点工作的通知 [*Pilot work to establish a modestly inclusive child welfare system for all children*]. Available at: http://fgcx.bjcourt.gov.cn:4601/law?fn=chl393s652.txt.

Ministry of Civil Affairs of the People's Republic of China. (2013b). 民政部关于开展未成年人社会保护试点工作的通知 [The notice on implementing a pilot program for minor protection by the society]. Available at: http://www. gov.cn/zwgk/2013-05/14/content_2401998.htm.

Ministry of Civil Affairs of the People's Republic of China. (2014a). 家庭寄养管理办法 [The measures for the administration of family foster care]. Available at: http://www.lawinfochina.com/display.aspx?id=685e6 7f6378e620dbdfb&lib=law.

Ministry of Civil Affairs of the People's Republic of China. (2014b). 儿童社会工作服务指南[Service guide-line for social work with children]. Available at: http://files2.mca.gov.cn/sw/201412/20141230133842 478.pdf.

Ministry of Civil Affairs of the People's Republic of China. (2014c). 全国未成年人社会保护第二批试点工作确定78个地区 [Notice of the Ministry of Civil Affairs on launching the second batch of national social protection pilot projects for minors in 78 regions]. Available at: http://www.gov.cn/xinwen/2014-08/19/content_2736857.htm.

Ministry of Civil Affairs of the People's Republic of China. (2014d). 关于开展家庭监护失当未成年人监护权转移工作的指导意见（征求意见稿）[The Opinions on Guidelines for Custody Transfer of a Minor in Improper Family Custody (Consultation Paper)]. Unpublished internal document.

Ministry of Civil Affairs of the People's Republic of China. (2019). 关于关于进一步健全农村留守儿童和困境儿童关爱服务体系的意见 [Opinions on further improving the caring service system for left-behind children in rural regions and vulnerable children]. Available at: http://www.mca.gov.cn/article/gk/wj/201905/20190500017508.shtml.

Ministry of Civil Affairs of the People's Republic of China. (2020). 民政部关于充分利用村级文化活动中心全面提升留守儿童综合素质答复的函 [The Ministry of Civil Affairs' letter of reply on making full use of village-level cultural activity center to improve the comprehensive quality of left-behind children]. Available at: http://xxgk.mca.gov.cn:8011/gdnps/pc/content.jsp?id=14781&mtype=4.

Myers, J. E. (2004). *A history of child protection in America*. Xlibris.

Myers, J. E. (2008). A short history of child protection in America. *Family Law Quarterly*, 42(3), 449–463.

National People's Congress of People's Republic of China. (1986). 中华人民共和国民法通则 [General principles of the civil law of the People's Republic of China]. Available at: http://www.lawinfochina.com/display.aspx?id=5b0d6fe8c67e52c4bdfb&lib=law.

National People's Congress of People's Republic of China. (2020). 中华人民共和国民法典 [Civil Code of the People's Republic of China]. Available at: http://www.lawinfochina.com/display.aspx?id=32806&lib=law.

Pecora, P. J., Whittaker, J. K., Maluccio, A. N., Barth, R. P., DePanfilis, D., and Plotnick, R. D. (2009). *The child welfare challenge: Policy, practice, and research (modern applications of social work)* (3rd ed.). Aldine Transaction.

People Society. (2019). 民政部：已实名配备66.5万名服务儿童工作者. [Ministry of Civil Affairs: 665,000 registered child welfare workers]. Available at:http://society.people.com.cn/n1/2019/0527/c1008-31105286.html.

People's Government of Guangdong Province. (2019). 让困难儿童得到及时救助 2.5万名基层儿童主任实现全省覆盖 [To help vulnerable children: 25,000 child welfare directors are in place in this province]. Available at: http://www.gd.gov.cn/zwgk/zcjd/snzcsd/content/post_2283496.html.

Satka, M. and Harrikari, T. (2008). The present Finnish formation of child welfare and history. *British Journal of Social Work*, 38(4), 645–661.

Shang, X. and Zhang, Y. (2011). *Establishing an effective system of child protection in China*. Social Sciences Academic Press.

Sohu News. (2015). 上海首例行政部门起诉父母剥夺监护权案宣判 [Shanghai's first administrative department sued parents for deprivation of custody]. Available at: http://www.sohu.com/a/157715924_162758.

Standing Committee of the National People's Congress of People's Republic of China. (1991). 中华人民共和国未成年人保护法 [Law of the People's Republic of China on the protection of minors]. Available at: http://www.lawinfochina.com/display.aspx?id=36cc820787004e95bdfb&lib=law.

Standing Committee of the National People's Congress of People's Republic of China. (1999). 中华人民共和国预防未成年人犯罪法 [Law of the People's Republic of China on prevention of juvenile delinquency]. Available at: http://www.lawinfochina.com/display.aspx?id=4a1ebc24d1141674bdfb&lib=law.

Standing Committee of the National People's Congress of People's Republic of China. (2006). 中华人民共和国未成年人保护法(2006修订)中华人民共和国未成年人保护法(2006修订) [Law of the People's Republic of China on the protection of minors (2006 revision)]. Available at: http://www.lawinfochina.com/display.aspx?id=6b73590a1c01ca78bdfb&lib=law.

Standing Committee of the National People's Congress of People's Republic of China. (2012). 中华人民共和国预防未成年人犯罪法(2012 修订案) [Law of the People's Republic of China on prevention of juvenile delinquency (2012 amendment)]. Available at: http://en.pkulaw.cn/display.aspx?id=12577&lib=law&SearchKeyword=juvenile%20delinquency&SearchCKeyword=.

Standing Committee of the National People's Congress of People's Republic of China. (2015). 中华人民共和国反家庭暴力法 [Anti-domestic violence law of the People's Republic of China]. Available at: http://en.pkulaw.cn/display.aspx?id=20841&lib=law&SearchKeyword=Anti-domestic%20Violence%20Law&SearchCKeyword=.

State Council of People's Republic of China. (2011). 中国儿童发展纲要（2011-2020年) [*China national program for child development (2011–2020)*]. Available at: http://www.gov.cn/gongbao/content/2011/content_1927200.htm.

State Council of People's Republic of China. (2016a). 国务院关于加强农村留守儿童关爱保护工作的意见 [The State Council on further strengthening the protection of left-behind children in rural China]. Available at: http://www.gov.cn/zhengce/content/2016-02/14/content_5041066.htm.

State Council of People's Republic of China. (2016b). 国务院印发《关于加强困境儿童保障工作的意见》 [The State Council on strengthening the protection of vulnerable children]. Available at: http://www.gov.cn/xinwen/2016-06/16/content_5082862.htm.

Supreme People's Procuratorate. (2020). 关于建立侵害未成年人案件强制报告制度的意见（试行）[Suggestions on establishing compulsory reporting system of cases against minors (Trial)]. Avaiable at: https://www.spp.gov.cn/xwfbh/wsfbt/202005/t20200529_463482.shtml#1.

Standing Committee of the National People's Congress. (2020). 中华人民共和国未成年人保护法 [Law of the People's Republic of China on the protection of minors]. Available at: http://lawdb.cncourt.org/show.php?fid=152560.

UNICEF. (2016). *The state of the world's children 2016* [Statistical tables]. Available at: https://data.unicef.org/resources/state-worlds-children-2016-statistical-tables/.

UNICEF. (n.d.). *World declaration on the survival, protection and development of children.* Available at: https://www.unicef.org/wsc/declare.htm.

UN. (1994). *Convention on the rights of the child.* Available at: https://www.refworld.org/pdfid/3ae6aeda4.pdf.

Wen, M. and Lin, D. (2012). Child development in rural China: Children left behind by their migrant parents and children of nonmigrant families. *Child Development*, 83(1), 120–136.

Xu, Y., Bright, C. L., and Ahn, H. (2018). Responding to child maltreatment: Comparison between the USA and China. *International Journal of Social Welfare*, 27(2), 107–120.

Yang, X. H. (2002). 危机与转折:心理学的中国化问题研究 [Crisis and transition: The Chineseization of psychology]. Heilongjiang People's Publishing House.

Yao, J. L. (2019). 未成年人法的困境和出路—论《未成年人保护法》和《预防未成年人犯罪法的修改》 [The dilemma and outlet of the juvenile law: Discussion on the Law on the Protection of Minors and the Amendment of the Law on the Prevention of Juvenile Delinquency]. *Youth Research*, 424(1), 5–19, 98.

Zhang, W. (2017). 全国至少69例撤销监护权案件 遗弃强奸虐待三类最为高发. [At least 69 cases of guardianship termination nationwide, and abandonment, rape and abuse are among the highest]. Available at: http://www.legaldaily.com.cn/index/content/2017-08/18/content_7286382.htm?node=20908.

Zhao, F., Hämäläinen, J. E. A., and Chen, H. L. (2017). Child protection in China: Changing policies and reactions from the field of social work. *International Journal of Social Welfare*, 26(4), 329–339.

Zhao, F., Xu, Y., and Chen, H. L. (2018). 儿童保护政策分析及以家庭为中心的儿童保护体系建构 [An analysis of child protection policy and a construction of a family-centered child protection system in China]. *Social Work and Management*, 18(5), 67–77.

Zhao, F., Zhu, N., and Hämäläinen, J. (2021). Protection of children in difficulty in China during the COVID-19 Pandemic. *Sustainability*, 13(1), 279.

The Colombian Child Protection System

María Cristina Torrado P. *and* Ernesto Duran Strauch

Abstract

This chapter looks into the child protection system in Colombia. The protection of childhood is divided among the purposes of philanthropy, morality, social control devices, and equitable societies. Additionally, child protection systems justify their existence in an alleged inability of poor families to care for their children. Cases of abuse and violence against children are understood as situations of threat or violation of their rights due to omissions or non-compliance with the obligations of the state and society. Significant improvements have been recorded in the last few years concerning the quality of life of the child population. However, ethnicity, area of residence, and home characteristics remain as factors of the social service's accessibility.

Key Words: Colombia, child protection system, philanthropy, morality, social service, accessibility, ethnicity, abuse, rights, quality of life

Introduction

As the literature on the subject indicates, the term child protection system does not have a single meaning and also acquires multiple meanings in "the real practices that give body to what has been called 'protection of childhood'" (Villalta & Llobet, 2015, p. 168). From the beginning, the protection of childhood is divided among philanthropic purposes, moralistic judgments, social control devices, and the search for equitable societies. Even so, and faithful to their origin, child protection systems justify their existence in an alleged inability of poor families to care for their children.

Today we speak of the systems of integral protection of childhood—or protection of the rights of children in the sense proposed by the Comisión Interamericana de Derechos Humanos (2017), which includes both legislative and public policy measures as the institutional organization adopted by states, to make effective the recognized rights of children and adolescents. Comprehensive protection refers to the obligation to "respect, promote, protect, and restore the rights of children and repair the damage in the face of their violation" (Morlachetti, 2013, p. 12). The perspective introduced by the International Convention on the Rights of the Child, the CRC, proposes a new way of understanding child protection and requires states to develop appropriate legal frameworks, reorient policies and programs aimed at children, and, in particular, transform practices and knowledge of those who work directly with them.

Which perspective does this chapter in order assume to talk about the Colombian system of child protection? As in other countries and in spite of continued efforts in the last 20 years, in Colombia the integral protection of the rights of children continues to be a goal that is yet to be achieved. It is not only necessary to overcome the conditions of inequality in which part of the country's children and adolescents grow, derived from poverty and exclusion, but also to make effective the guidelines of Law 1098: Código de infancia y adolescencia, based on the principles of the CRC and approved in 2006.

Nowadays, all the actions of the Colombian state as well as the set of policies and programs aimed at the welfare of children are oriented from the perspective of integral protection of the rights of children. For this reason, cases of abuse and violence against them are understood as situations of threat or violation of their rights due to omissions or non-compliance with the obligations of society and the state as guarantors of them. Consequently, in the following pages dedicated to characterizing the Colombian model of child protection, the reader will perceive the efforts of the authors to overcome the restricted sense understood by such protection as state intervention when there is a risk for the child to settle in a broader perspective of comprehensive guarantee of rights for this group of the population. The text is organized in three sections: the first one provides some necessary data to contextualize the protection model, described in the second section; and at the end, a critical analysis is proposed.

Some Elements of Context

Colombia is one of the largest countries in Latin America, both due to the extension of its territory and the size of its population. Today, with 45 million inhabitants, it is the third most populous country in the region, after Brazil and Mexico, and its economy ranks fourth. It is a country characterized by its ethnic and cultural diversity and recognized for its enormous biodiversity, formed of varied regions that extend from the Caribbean Sea to the Amazon, passing through large mountain ranges and fertile valleys where one of the best coffees in the world is grown.

It is also known for illicit crops (marijuana, coca, and opium poppy), the presence of organized crime dedicated to the processing and trafficking of narcotics, and for having lived through one of the lengthiest and bloodiest armed conflicts of the 20th century. The confrontation between various illegal armed groups and the dispute for territorial control over several decades turned important rural areas of the national territory into a scene of atrocious events and serious crimes against the civilian population, including children and adolescents. In fact, according to the unique registry of victims of the internal armed conflict, during the last 33 years more than eight million Colombians (18% of the population) were victims of forced displacement, sexual crimes, kidnapping, forced disappearance, and anti-personnel mines. According to Save the Children (2017), Colombia ranks fifth among the top 10 countries that experienced internal armed conflicts because of the number of children and adolescent victims of forced displacement (more than two million), and the fourth among 172 countries in 2015 in the rate of child homicides (22 per 100,000 inhabitants).

In the last years, the dynamics of the Colombian armed conflict have undergone a major change, following the agreement signed in November 2016 between the national government and the Revolutionary Armed Forces of Colombia-FARC, the oldest and largest Marxist-oriented guerrilla group in Colombia. With the agreed ceasefire, the disarmament and subsequent demobilization of more than 10,000 combatants, armed confrontations and violent actions against the civilian population have decreased significantly. However, the active presence of other actors and the complex dynamics of the conflict do not allow us to speak of true peace in Colombia.

As established in the first article of the Political Constitution of 1991, "Colombia is a social State governed by law, organized as a unitary republic." This means that the country is committed to social justice and the protection of the rights of the citizens; organizationally, there is a President of the Republic as Head of State, Head of Government, and supreme administrative authority of the country (Political Constitution of Colombia, Article 115). Although some autonomy is granted to municipalities and departments, local authorities cannot depart from the national normative, political, and administrative framework. Consequently, the national ministries and institutes are responsible for the design of public policies in each of the sectors in which the Colombian State is organized (health, education, work, finance, security, etc.). As the integral protection of the rights of children requires the participation of several of these sectors, the Colombian Family Welfare Institute (ICBF) is in charge of:

> the articulation of the entities responsible for the guarantee of rights, the prevention of their violation, the protection and the reestablishment of the same, in the national, departmental, district, municipal and indigenous territories. (Law 1098, 2006, Article 205)

As will be seen below, the ICBF has a fundamental role in the process of restoring the rights of children when they have been threatened or violated and especially when it comes to the right to personal integrity that is to be protected against all kinds of abuse. (Law 1098, 2006, Article 18). The same article establishes:

> For the purposes of this Code, child abuse is understood as any form of harm, punishment, humiliation or physical or psychological abuse, neglect, omission or negligent treatment, mistreatment or sexual exploitation, including abusive sexual acts and the violation and in

general any form of violence or aggression on the child, the girl or the adolescent on the part of their parents, legal representatives or any other person.

Although the ICBF is responsible for defining the policies and technical guidelines for the entire country, the attention of children and adolescents with violated rights is provided by the local offices of the ICBF or those created for this purpose by the municipal authorities: Family Defenders Offices and Family Commissaries.

Colombian Children and Adolescents

Like other countries in Latin America, Colombia has experienced a process of demographic transition in the last 20 years as a result of the decrease in both birth rates and mortality rates. As a consequence, there is lower population growth and there has been a significant change in the distribution by age groups which is summarized in a decrease among people under 15 years and an increase in adults over 65 years. According to population estimates in Colombia there were 14,144,000 people under 18 years of age in 2015 (about 29% of the total population; UNICEF, 2016), distributed relatively evenly by sex and age groups. Children and adolescents are overrepresented in rural areas and especially in indigenous communities where birth rates exceed the national average. According to data from the 2005 census, while the national fertility rate (number of live births per thousand women of fertile age) was 75, for indigenous women it was 124 and 89 for Afro-Colombian women. According to data from CEPAL and UNICEF (2012), the number of indigenous Colombian children and adolescents is estimated at 639,000, representing 46% of the population recognized as such.

Regarding the quality of life of the child population, many indicators show significant improvements in last years. For example, the infant mortality rate declined from 18 to 14 per 1,000 live births in the past five years (Colombia: Encuesta Nacional de Demografía y Salud—ENDS, 2015). But these gains are not evenly distributed among the population or throughout the country. Indeed, ethnicity, the area or region of residence, and some characteristics of the home are determining factors in the access of Colombian children and adolescents to essential social services and to the necessary conditions for their well-being, which generates considerable equity gaps (Vélez & Torres, 2014).

A few data allow us to appreciate the magnitude of the welfare gaps between groups of the country's children and adolescents. According to a study conducted by García and colleagues (2014), in 2011 more than a third of Colombian children and adolescents (34%) lived in multidimensional poverty and only 11.9% were free from deprivation. Eight out of ten children and adolescents suffered at least one deprivation in one of the dimensions that make up the Infantile Multidimensional Poverty Index.

The study identified large inter-regional differences: for example, in the department of Chocó, whose population is mostly Afro-descendant, the percentage of multidimensional child poverty was more than twice the national average and four times than in

Bogotá. It was also established that the lack of drinking water, typical of some regions of the rural area, is one of the variables with the highest incidence in multidimensional child poverty in all age groups (between 15% and 19%) (García et al., 2014).

As is well known, poverty during childhood has a greater impact on the life trajectory of people due to its cumulative nature and the risk of generating irreversible effects on the development of their individual potential and capacity:

> Among children living in poverty, the lack of adequate nutrition, lack of health care or education, experiences of violence and abandonment, among other deprivations, add up and result in limited access to endless numbers of opportunities, which facilitates poverty to extend throughout life, and reproduce through generations. (CEPAL & UNICEF, 2017, p. 11)

One more proof of the profound inequality characteristic of Colombian society is the situation of poverty and exclusion for children and families living in the rural areas; especially those who are far from the urban centers or in regions of the country historically lagging behind. The rural area concentrates the poorest households in the country, both for the level of income and for deprivation in basic indicators of quality of life. In the year 2017, 26.9% of the Colombian population was considered poor by income (measured as the value of a basket of goods in a geographic area); in rural areas, poor people represent 36% (Departamento Administrativo Nacional de Estadistica [DANE], 2018).

According to the Multidimensional Poverty Index (IPM), in 2017, 77% of rural households have low educational achievement compared to 34.6% in urban areas. As expected, in the other dimensions included in this index related to access to drinking water and housing quality, the same gap is observed (DANE, 2018). As reported by numerous studies, the sociodemographic conditions of the households, such as the number of children or the educational level of the parents, increase the vulnerability of children, putting their rights at risk. Analyses carried out for all of Latin America show that children "are overrepresented in the lowest income quintiles and that from the outset, households with children are more vulnerable" (Acosta et al., 2016, p. 33).

In the Colombian case, all these conditions worsen in the rural areas where indigenous peoples and some Afro-descendant communities live, who have also suffered more intensely the impact of the armed conflict and the violence generated by the illegal economies. For this reason, it is the indigenous children and peasants of some regions of the country who are at greater risk of dying from hunger during the first years of life or leaving school to work, among many other consequences of poverty and inequality (Therborn, 2013). This reality highlights the enormous gap between the legal equality of Colombian children and adolescents recognized by national and international standards—especially the Law 1098 (2016)—and the existing inequality in living conditions and the opportunities between groups of the child and adolescent population in the country.

Situations of Non-observance and Violation of the Rights of Children and Adolescents

The continued effort of the Colombian state through various public policies has reduced the poverty rates of the population in the last 10 years and has improved access and coverage of health, education, and culture services for children and adolescents in the country. It is still yet to ensure equity and non-discrimination generated by precarious social policy models, access barriers, and the low quality of services in some regions of the country and for certain groups of the population. Although the great majority of Colombian children and adolescents are enrolled in the health system, many of them do not access timely and quality medical services for different reasons, among which the economic interests of those who operate many of these services stand out. This explains why while the probability of a child dying in the country before reaching their first year is 14 per 1,000 children; in rural areas it is 22 and can reach 51% in the case of mothers without education (Encuesta Nacional de Demografía y Salud [ENDS], 2015).

In the same sense, according to the National Consultation to Children and Adolescents, (UNICEF Colombia, 2018), children living in remote rural areas lack health services near their homes, so their families must travel long distances at very high costs and without guarantees of being adequately cared for at the next destination. This situation increases the risk of dying or becoming more ill for the child.

As a result of public policies related to the importation, production, and commercialization of food, more than half of Colombian households have difficulties in accessing sufficient and adequate food, a situation that is even more serious for some sectors of the population such as the indigenous towns. Consequently, the chronic malnutrition rate, defined as the delay in height for children less than 5 years of age, in indigenous children (29.6%) is three times the national average (10.8%) (Encuesta Nacional de Situación Nutricional [ENSIN], 2015). According to official data, by 2016 the country reached 100% coverage in primary education and 80% in secondary education; however, on average, the education of the Colombian population does not exceed 8 years. As expected, indicators related to quality and school retention favor children and adolescents in large cities.

Girls and adolescent women are another of the subgroups that require special attention from public policies and the protection system of their rights. "Among the injustices and inequalities suffered by girls, and that contribute to the generation of conditions of poverty, is teenage pregnancy, gender violence, domestic work and child marriage" (CEPAL & UNICEF, 2017, p. 7). In relation to gender-based violence, it should be noted that sexual abuse against girls and adolescents is a particularly serious situation in Colombia. During the year 2017, 23,798 examinations were carried out in the country for alleged sexual offenses, of which 86.83% were among children and adolescents, with females being the main victims (Forensis, 2017). Since there are so many cases of sexual abuse reported to the authorities, it is not surprising that this is the main reason for

Colombian children and adolescents to enter the protection system, followed by physical, psychological or negligent mistreatment (ICBF, 2018). Between 2014 and 2015, cases of negligence and child abandonment doubled, from 7,719 cases to 15,454 (Forensis, 2017). These two situations constitute the main risks in the immediate family and social environment, to which the Colombian state has responded with prevention policies and an institutional offer for the denunciation and protection available to children and their families.

In the broader social contexts, both urban and rural, there are other risks, especially the recruitment of children and adolescents for criminal activities by armed groups linked to illegal economies (trafficking in persons, drug trafficking, mining, etc.) or by insurgent groups that maintain confrontations with the state. The confrontations between different actors in conflict in some areas of the country make the youngest people victims of forced displacement, death or mutilation due to anti-personnel mines, or orphanage, among other situations that generate risks to their lives and their physical and emotional integrity. Since 2011, the country has provided specialized assistance and reparation programs for over 2,300,000 children and adolescent victims of the armed conflict.

Protection of Children and Restoration of Violated Rights

In the history of child protection policies in Colombia, an important milestone is the creation in 1968 of the Instituto colombiano de bienestar familiar ICBF, an entity charged with "providing protection to minors and, in general, improving stability and of the welfare of Colombian families" (Law 75 (1968), Article 3). Within this institution, the "Family Defenders" emerged as specialized units to intervene in the different situations of child protection. The Family Defender Office consists of an interdisciplinary team including a lawyer (the defender), a social worker, a psychologist, and a nutritionist. As the responsible authority, Colombian law assigns the Family Defender various competences that allow him to act in civil and criminal jurisdictions (Jiménez-Barros, 2012).

In 1979, the National System of Family Welfare was created with the following functions: "a) To promote the integration and harmonious realization of the family; b) protect the child and guarantee the rights of the child; and c) link the largest number of people and coordinate the competent state entities in the handling of the problems of the family and the minor, in order to raise the standard of living of our society" (Law 7, 1979, Article 2). In this system, public and private institutions responsible for the protection of children collaborate, both at the national level and at the different territorial levels, coordinated by the ICBF. It was the first attempt to articulate services and social actors around the protection of childhood and system has been maintained ever since.

In 1989, days after the signing of the CRC, and as a product of a national discussion that came from previous years, Colombia issued the Code of the Minor, which organizes legislation on the protection of children and incorporates some of the rights, as well as the principle of the best interests of the child. This law defined when the child must receive protection from the State from the perspective of irregular situations, defining as such:

1) Is in a situation of abandonment or danger; 2) lacks sufficient attention for the satisfaction of their basic needs; 3) the estate is threatened by those who administer it; 4) has been the author or participant of a criminal offense; 5) lacks legal representation; 6) has a present physical, sensory or mental deficiency; 7) is addicted to substances that cause dependence or are exposed to addiction; 8) is a worker under conditions not authorized by law; or 9) is in a special situation that violates rights or integrity. (Decree 2737, 1989, Article 30)

The same law established precisely the functions of the Family Defender as the authority responsible for acting "ex officio or request" in any situation of abandonment or danger to a child or adolescent and the ICBF as the institution responsible for the protection actions (Decree 2737, 1989, Article 277). Likewise, it created the "Family Commissaries," institutions with municipal police functions, dependent on the mayors' offices, whose objective is "to collaborate with the Colombian Family Welfare Institute and with the other competent authorities in the function of protecting minors who are found in an irregular situation and in cases of family conflicts" (Article 296). Family Commissaries have a lawyer (the commissioner) supported by a team consisting preferably of a doctor, a psychologist, and a social worker (Decree 2737, 1989, Article 297). In both cases, the professional teams perform the assessment of the situation of the children and their families and advise the family advocates in the decision making before, during, and after the process of restoration of rights.

Both the Family Defenders Offices and the Family Commissaries were extended throughout the country, to the capitals and some intermediate cities, leaving an important part of the rural area without coverage. For several decades these institutions applied the doctrine of irregular situation and officials' decisions were mediated by the preconceptions they had of the children and their protection based on social or ethnic prejudices. According to Carreño (2017), even today, many of the actions related to the protection of children are based on social imaginaries according to which

> the families and mothers of the highest seats and those who are presumed to have the greatest purchasing power are more responsible with childhood. On the other hand, the rights of girls and boys from families with the lowest social seats and those with the lowest purchasing power would be at risk. (Carreño, 2017, p. 190)

In this context, poor or indigenous families are considered incompetent to care for their children and as a result, they are often institutionalized. In Carreño's words, "state institutions ignore structural inequalities and, at the same time, have transferred the demand for children's rights to mothers and families, blaming them for their non-compliance." (2017, p. 191). This position is heir to the so-called tutelary system that prevailed during the last century, which Cussianovich (2004) has characterized by the three P's: property (of the adult world), dangerous for society (Spanish: *peligroso*), and dispensable (Spanish:

prescindible). Within this system, the risk category was widely used, which at the same time makes the structural character of social and economic problems invisible, and contributes to what has been called the "criminalization of poverty" (García-Méndez, 1993).

Progressively, the Catholic Church continued to lose the central role it played for several centuries in the protection of childhood and a sector of lay philanthropy was strengthened; NGOs gained strength, evolving towards what has been called the third sector, which henceforth will play an important role in dealing with situations of violation of rights. Institutions increasingly specialize in addressing certain problems such as homeless children, abandoned children, sexually exploited children, and working children.

Seventeen years after the Code of the Minor, the Code of Children and Adolescents was issued, which has as its objective the comprehensive protection of children and adolescents, the guarantee of their rights and freedoms, and the restoration of violated rights (Law 1098, 2006, Article 2). This law establishes a process of re-establishing the rights of children for cases in which there is an identified threat situation (imminent danger to the exercise of rights), non-compliance (omission or denial of access to a service or the obligation of protection), or a violation of the rights of children and adolescents. It should be noted that Law 1878 of 2018 establishes that in cases of non-observance of rights it is not always necessary to open the administrative process of restoration of rights, but rather that institutions may be ordered to guarantee the rights of children.

Although the Code of Children and Adolescents defines new rules for the process of protection, which from this point on will be referred to as the process of re-establishing rights, it does not substantially reform the institutional structure. Its application remains in the hands of the same institutions and officials that are heirs of the tutelary system which has generated in its application frequent conflicts between paternalistic perspectives, heirs of the previous legislation, and the perspective of rights that the Code incorporates. Indeed, the Administrative Procedure of Restoration of Rights (PARD) is still the responsibility of the aforementioned institutions: Family Defenders and Family Commissaries.

In the reestablishment of rights, in addition to the aforementioned institutions that have a role in the administrative procedure, the "family courts" also intervene. The courts respond to conflicts of competence of the administrative authorities, the reinstatement appeal of the decisions of the administrative authorities, the rectification of errors in the administrative process, and the homologation of protection measures, such as adoptability, when this is required (Law 1098, 2006; Law 1878, 2018).

The Code of Children and Adolescents of Colombia also regulates everything related to the Criminal Responsibility System for Adolescents, with the intention that this is understood as a process of restoration of rights, which is considered an important advance, although so far it has not been fully achieved. In the development of the Code, Family Welfare was redefined as a public service made up of the actions developed to guarantee the recognition, protection, and restoration of the rights of children and adolescents, as well as those aimed at the prevention of their threat or violation and family strengthening

(Decree 1084, 2015, Article 2.4). This broad definition of the National Family Welfare System, in addition to the restoration, also includes the actions of promotion, prevention, and guarantee of rights, expanding what in other countries is called a child protection system. In this part of the chapter, we will not refer to the system in a broad sense, but we will limit ourselves to actions aimed at the restoration of violated rights.

Administrative Process of Restoration of Rights

The process of restoration of rights is regulated by the Code of Childhood and Adolescence, by Decrees that regulate specific aspects, and some documents called technical guidelines, issued by the ICBF as rectors of the system. These guidelines regulate the competences and functions that correspond to the different actors in the restoration of rights and specify the conditions that must be fulfilled by the institutions that provide services oriented to the restoration of rights. Often these guidelines contradict the protective spirit of the rights that the Code has, which establishes that the process has the purpose of restoring "the dignity and integrity as subjects and the capacity to exercise the rights that have been violated" (Law 1098, Article 50).

The competences of the entities in charge of the process at the level of the territories are given in the order of prevalence: Family Defender–Family Commissary–Police Inspector. If, in a certain territory, there is only a Family Defender, it assumes all cases. The same happens if there is only one Family Commissary in a territory; if in a territory the Family Defender and the Family Commissary are present, the last one will only know the cases of intra-familial violence and the Family Defender all the others. This distribution often generates conflicts of competence. If neither of the two institutions is present, the functions are performed by the Police Inspector (Durán et al., 2009).

According to information from the Mission Information System of the ICBF, between 2011 and 2017 a total of 260,000 Colombian children and adolescents entered the administrative process of restoration of rights (PARD), with an average of 37,143 cases per year (2.4 per 1,000). It is important to clarify that these are not all cases known by the protection system because they do not include those in which, in the opinion of the Defender or Family Commissioner, there was no justification to start such a process. When analyzing the variations in the number of cases per year, a significant increase is observed, going from 32,536 in 2011 to 46,339 in 2017 (3 per 1,000). This can be explained by a lower tolerance for violence against children in Colombian society as well as a greater presence and capacity of action of the competent authorities in all the municipalities of the country, as a result of the implementation of what is established in the Code of Childhood and Adolescence of 2006.

PARD takes place in four phases: 1) receipt of the case and verification of compliance with rights; 2) conciliation or opening and development of an investigation; 3) resolution and provisions for the re-establishment of rights; 4) closure of the process and follow-up. In the first phase, the actions are aimed at identification, initial diagnosis and reception and assessing the situation of the child's and adolescent's rights. In the second phase, it is decided whether to close the process with a conciliation or to open and develop the evidentiary phase. In the third phase, actions aimed at the re-establishment of rights are decided and implemented, and the last phase is oriented to the preparation of the child or adolescent and his family for the process of reintegration or of his entrance to adoptability.

Identification, Diagnosis, and Reception Phase

The relevant authority may be made aware of a possible situation of threat or violation, either by a complaint or report: because it acts ex officio in a situation of violation of rights; because an activity threatens or violates their rights; or at the request of children, adolescents, parents, caregivers or legal representatives. The first action is the verification of the guarantee of all rights, which includes in all cases the verification of at least the following aspects: 1) psychological and emotional situation; 2) nutrition and review of the vaccination scheme; 3) initial assessment of the family environment, linking networks and identification of protective and risk elements for the guarantee of rights; 4) registration in the civil registry of birth; 5) linkage to the health and social security system; and 6) linkage to the education system (Law 1878, 2018, Article 1). The verification is intended to solve the problem that gave rise to the state intervention, and to identify all the gaps of guarantee of rights in order to plan concrete actions to solve them. However, with some frequency, the verification becomes a routine process that does not lead to specific actions, or the families are given the responsibility of processing the corresponding documents, generating an obstacle to access to the system (Durán et al., 2009).

In cases of non-compliance, when the child has been denied access to a service essential to the enjoyment of his or her rights, the administrative authority must order the respective entities of the National Family Welfare System to carry out the necessary actions to guarantee the rights in a term not greater than 10 days, after which, if the situation is maintained, the administrative procedure will begin.

Second and Third Phases

Once the verification of rights and the initial investigation have been carried out, it must be decided whether the case is reconcilable, if it is conciliated, if the conciliation is not achieved, or if the case was considered as not reconcilable. Then, the administrative process of restoration of rights begins. If a process is opened, it must be carried out taking into account the particular situation of each child or adolescent and respond to the specific needs evidenced in the first phase. The actions that follow depend on the determination of the existence of a threat or violation of rights and the specific needs of the child or adolescent and the family.

Both the Code and the norms that develop or regulate it establish that priority should be given to staying in the family environment, either in one's own family or in the extended family network, expressly stating that the lack of economic resources cannot be a reason for the child's withdrawal from the family environment and that it is the responsibility of the entities of the National Family Welfare System "to provide families with adequate resources while they can guarantee them" (Law 1878, 2018, Article 2).

Similarly, if the decision is to separate the child or adolescent from the family, the preference is their location in a family environment. The Constitutional Court has ratified this principle in several of its judgments, which have occurred because in practice this is not what happens: "As a general rule, the child must always remain in his family nucleus, unless there are compelling reasons and determinants, depending on the best interests of the former, to choose to separate him from his family. In any case, the separation must be exceptional and, preferably, temporary" (Corte Constitucional, Sentencia T-572, 2009).

Once the process is opened, the official in charge must take a provisional measure, which can be modified as many times as deemed necessary, always in the perspective of the best interests of the child. The measures include: admonition to the family with the obligation to take a course on children's rights, administrative, or judicial actions when necessary. If the situation justifies it, a relevant authority can place the child or adolescent in one of the modalities of care defined by the ICBF: 1) initial location, 2) support and strengthening of the family, and 3) support and strengthening in a different environment from the family of origin or the linking network (ICBF, 2017). These measures are summarized in Table 32.1.

The initial and temporary placement of the child outside the family can be done for a period no longer than eight days in a Home of Passage (a family that has met certain requirements and is approved as a protective environment for up to four children or teenagers at a time), or an emergency center (an institution when it is not possible to go to a Home of Passage). Once the time corresponding to the transitory measure of initial placement has elapsed, the child or adolescent can be sent with his family to a support and strengthening program or separated from it and placed in the care of another family or institution.

The support and strengthening of the family are aimed at strengthening the protective capacities of the family of origin of the child or of the link network. It includes: 1) psychosocial support intervention actions; 2) assistance to a protection institution on a day contrary to school, or full-time; 3) home manager, which consists of psychosocial support and financial support, aimed at the family of origin or the family network of children and adolescents with disabilities or separated from armed groups.

When the child or adolescent is separated from the family, he or she can go to a substitute home that is committed to giving attention and care to the child or adolescent during the development of the entire process of restoration of rights. These are families that have gone through a selection and training process and receive a sum of money from ICBF for each child or adolescent in their care. The House Home is an institution accompanied by a team of professionals in an environment similar to the family, with a capacity of up to 12 children or adolescents. Finally, there would be the internship, the shelter and

Table 32.1 Modalities of care

Phases		Modality	For whom
Initial location	Family mode	Home of passage	Preferably children under 6 years old
	Institutional modality	Emergency center	Children and adolescents from 6 to 18 years old
Support and strengthening the family		Psychosocial	Permanence of the child or adolescent in their family environment or with their link network
		Extended half a day	
		Extended full day	
		Home manager	
Support and strengthening in a different environment than the family of origin or the link network	Modality of foster family	Substitute home	Children and adolescents of all ages and all violations
	Modality of institutional care	House home	Institution with a maximum of 12 places with a family atmosphere
		Internship	Two kinds of institution: Specialize or for different rights violations
		Shelter	Adolescents separated from armed groups
		Protection house	Adolescents that have come out of illegal groups

Source: ICBF (2017).

the protection house, institutions that have a permanent team of professionals, defined in the guidelines that accompany children and adolescents throughout the process of re-establishment of rights.

For various reasons, Colombia does not have enough information to analyze the evolution of protection measures and, therefore, the location of children and adolescents. Although Family Advocates and Commissioners must report the information to a single information system, only some of them do so and not all of them completely; technological difficulties or the high number of cases explain this situation. It should not be forgotten that there are more than 2,000 professionals located in 1,100 municipalities throughout the country.

Despite this limitation, analysis of the data available in the Mission Information System of the ICBF allows us to establish a certain tendency: the majority of children and adolescents with a measure of protection (76.6%) remain under the care of their own family network with follow-up by the authorities. About one-quarter (23.4%) are separated from their family and placed in similar proportions in residential units or in foster homes until the situation is overcome or an adoption process begins. This means that by decision of the competent authorities, only one of every four children who enter PARD temporarily or permanently lose the care of their biological family.

This distribution shows a clear orientation of the Colombian policy that on the one hand privileges the strengthening of the family network as the main strategy for protecting the rights of children and adolescents and, on the other hand, works on the implementation of alternatives to institutionalization following the United Nations guidelines.

Closure of the Process and Follow-up

The administrative processes of the re-establishment of rights must be closed within a maximum period of six months, extendable in special situations justified by the authority in charge. After completing all phases of the process, the decision can be oriented in one of two ways: the child or adolescent returns to his family environment (family of origin or his network link), or he or she is declared adoptable and remains in the charge of the state until adoption or the child reaches the age of majority. In the last months of the administrative process, each child or adolescent must be prepared for what goes on in the process, as well as their families, in case they are going to return with them.

The children and adolescents declared adoptable go to institutions, and if they are very small they can remain with substitute families. A new process is then initiated for them that is also regulated by the Childhood and Adolescence Code. According to the ICBF, in the last 20 years, 45,658 Colombian children and adolescents were given up for adoption, showing a significant decrease in the number of cases from 2012 moving to an annual average of 1,200 cases per year.

Follow-up depends on the institution in charge. The follow-up after the final decision of the case is under the responsibility of the coordinator of the Zonal Center (territorial reference) of the ICBF as established by the regulations (ICBF, 2016b). Some Zonal Centers do not have enough staff to provide follow-up and there are few in the country (they are located in less than 200 municipalities of the 1,100 in the country). In a study carried out in 2010, it was found that only 28.6% of the definitive protection measures ordered by the family commissioners were followed up (Procuraduría General de la Nación, 2012). This weak follow-up of the child, as well as the lack of accompaniment to the families, can help explain the recidivism of cases that occur in the process of re-establishment of rights.

A special situation exists in the protection of children and adolescents belonging to indigenous communities, as the Constitutional Court has expressed in several of its judgments and which is summarized in the following sentence:

> In the case of jurisdictional or administrative proceedings in which an indigenous child is involved, their individual rights must be jointly protected with the collective rights to cultural identity and their ethnic identity. In principle, the competence to resolve conflicts

related to indigenous children are within the community to which they belong and must be resolved by their authorities according to their habits and customs. (Corte Constitucional, 2012)

Analysis of the Protection Model and Issues under Discussion

Colombia never developed a welfare state model capable of guaranteeing a basic quality of life to the entire population. Throughout the 20th century the State concentrated its efforts on the provision of some goods and services focused on the population with fewer economic resources through social assistance programs and the allocation of insufficient subsidies. The rest of the population was expected to acquire these goods in a segmented market. Thus, the welfare of children and adolescents depends to a large extent on the resources of the family, which would bring the country closer to the so-called liberal welfare systems.

Only in 1991, when a new constitution was issued, was Colombia defined as a Social State of Law, paradoxically at a moment of full boom in the country of the neoliberal model that restricts the size and responsibilities of the state while also decreasing public investment in social benefits directed to welfare. For this reason, in the last 25 years, social policies, including policies for children, have been debated between a guarantee discourse on rights and assistance practices. Consequently, the country has not had a social policy model that assures families their basic well-being so that they can guarantee dignified living conditions for their children. The most recent policies transfer financial resources to families with children from the poorest sectors of the population with the requirement that their children receive education and attend health checks. These are referred to as conditioned subsidies.

The focus of social policy, coupled with the suspicion of low-income families that predominates in those responsible for services, has contributed to Colombia's failure to consolidate a child and adolescent protection model oriented towards the well-being of children and families. On the contrary, even when family-society-state co-responsibility is recognized in the protection of the rights of children and adolescents as a concurrent action, in practice the State acts to replace the family when it considers that it has failed and society is relatively indolent in situations of violation of rights.

Thus, the country has developed a protection model focused on intrusive intervention on children and adolescents with violated rights, without taking care to accompany and improve the conditions of families. This is a model of protection of children at risk, not necessarily of protection of their rights; a model that is not of early intervention or prevention, but of intervention before flagrant violations of rights. It is a model that for this reason has been ineffective in the results it achieves.

A strength of the country for the protection of children whose rights have been violated is the existence of specialized institutions with presence throughout the territory, as well as defined processes, routes and modes of care that create a regulatory framework for decision making by the responsible professionals. However, there are limitations of economic and human resources; in 2010, the ICBF had just over 1,000 Family Defenders, a number insufficient to cover all the violations of children's rights that occur in the country. Although the law was created more than 35 years ago, the National System of Family Welfare, with the participation of different institutions of the public and private sector, does not work in an articulated way. The ICBF, an institution that attends to multiple issues related to childhood and adolescence and other population groups, leaves the protection system relegated to the background.

The functioning of the country's comprehensive protection system requires a high degree of inter-sectoral and inter-institutional coordination; however, a recent study found that at both the national and subnational level, "there are pathways for coordination within each agency and among agencies and sectors, however, many public officials are unaware of them or are unclear about how they work, or they do not understand the purpose behind these mechanisms, which creates friction in interpersonal and inter-institutional relations" (UNICEF & Global Affairs Canada, 2015, p. 32).

The coverage of the institutions responsible for the restoration of rights has been extended throughout the national territory in recent years, thanks to an expansion of the Family Commissary that today has a presence in 99.4% of the municipalities. However, the coverage does not guarantee an adequate fulfilment of its functions given that the vast majority (78.1%) of the Family Commissaries do not have a full professional team (Procuraduría General de la Nación, 2011). There are also significant shortcomings in the provision of necessary elements to fulfil its mission, such as vehicles, furniture and adequate spaces. Despite these limitations, the officials in charge make an effort to adequately fulfill their function. Another characteristic of the Colombian model is the delegation of protection to private actors who contract with the state for the provision of services. This results in diverse quality conditions that do not always guarantee children's rights. In all cases, the economic resources come from a high percentage of the national state budget that monitors the performance of the institutions that care for children.

Conclusion

Colombia is living the contrast between a legal framework that protects the rights of children and adolescents, with a reality of great economic and social inequities, and a context of social and political violence that seriously affects children and adolescents from the poorest and most excluded sectors. The country is far from policies for children that, from a rights perspective, guarantee the same benefits with homogeneous quality for all in the sense proposed by Filgueiras (2014) as a strategy to strengthen citizenship from the first years of life. Likewise, the country is torn between a model based on a discourse of comprehensive protection of children's rights and an institutional structure and culture of bureaucracy responsible for services anchored in a tutelary model of social control.

A retrospective look at Colombian child protection policies in the last 25 years allows us to identify three important trends. First, despite the challenges it poses, the country has adopted the rights perspective as the guiding framework of all state actions aimed at ensuring the well-being of children and adolescents. The Code of Childhood and Adolescence of 2006, which adopts this perspective, has been one of the main tools to promote changes in the way of thinking and relating to children in all social life scenarios. It is still necessary to overcome numerous institutional obstacles and contradictions in the implementation of policies. Second, institutions specializing in the care of children with rights that have been violated—Family Defenders Offices and Family Commissaries—have been extended to all municipalities in the country and have defined guidelines for their actions. This has strengthened the reporting of cases and the collective rejection of violence against children and adolescents. Even so, there are still great technical and resource deficiencies in the processes that hinder a true restoration of rights for these children. Finally, in line with the guidelines on alternative care of the United Nations of 2009, incorporated into the model of care for children with violated rights, in Colombia the family's own network is privileged as the main protective environment. Likewise, in case of loss of parental care the location of the child in a substitute home is preferred, seeking to minimize its institutionalization.

Acknowledgments

The authors appreciate the contributions to the preparation of this chapter by Astrid Torres Quintero and Margarita Chaustre, professionals linked to our academic group.

References

Acosta, O., Botiva M., Ramírez, J., and Uribe, L. (2016). *La protección social de la población rural en Colombia.* Serie estudios y perspectivas, 32. CEPAL.

Carreño, C. (2017). *Las madres, las familias y los hijos del sur: Miradas etnográficas a la protección infantil contemporánea en la ciudad de Bogotá.* [Unpublished doctoral thesis]. Universidad Nacional de Colombia.

CEPAL and UNICEF. (2012). *Pobreza infantil en pueblos indígenas y afrodescendientes de América Latina.* CEPAL/UNICEF.

CEPAL and UNICEF. (2017). *Medición multidimensional de la pobreza infantil.* CEPAL/UNICEF.

ENDS. (2015). Encuesta Nacional de Demografía y Salud. ENDS 2015. Profamilia-Ministerio Protección Social.

ENSIN. (2015). Encuesta Nacional de Situación Nutricional. ENSIN 2015. -Ministerio Protección Social.

Comisión Interamericana de Derechos Humanos (2017). *Hacia la garantía efectiva de los derechos de niñas, niños y adolescentes: Sistemas Nacionales de Protección.* Available at: http://www.oas.org/es/cidh/informes/pdfs/NNA-GarantiaDerechos.pdf.

Corte Constitucional. (2009). Sentencia T-572 M.P. Humberto Antonio Sierra Porto.

Corte Constitucional. (2012). Sentencia T-001 M.P. Juan Carlos Henao Mejía.

Cussiánovich, A. (2004). *Historia del pensamiento social sobre la infancia.* Fondo Editorial de la Facultad de Ciencias Sociales, Universidad de San Marcos.

DANE. (2018). *Pobreza Monetaria y Multidimensional en Colombia—Año 2017.* DANE.

Durán, E., Guáqueta, C., and Torres, A. (2009). *Proceso de restablecimiento de derechos de niños y adolescentes en el marco del SNBF: Estudio de caso en la localidad de Engativá-Bogotá.* Unpublished report.

Filgueiras, F. (2014). *Hacia un modelo de protección social universal en América Latina.* Serie Políticas Sociales, 188. CEPAL.

García, S., Ritterbusch, A., Bautista, E., Mosquera, J., and Martín, T. (2014). *Análisis de la pobreza multidimensional en niños, niñas y adolescentes en Colombia: metodología y principales resultados.* Serie Documentos de Trabajo EGOB. Universidad de los Andes.

García-Méndez, E. (1993). Legislaciones infanto-juveniles en América Latina: modelos y tendencias. UNICEF (Ed.), *Derecho a tener derecho. Infancia, Derecho y Políticas Sociales en América Latina*. UNICEF. Vol. 1, pp. 31–42.

Gilbert, N., Parton N., and Skivenes, M. (2011). *Child protection systems: International trends and orientations*. Oxford University Press.

Forensis (2017). Instituto Nacional de Medicina Legal y Ciencias Forenl.gov.co/documents/20143/262076/Forensis+2017+Interactivo.pdf/0a09fedb-f5e8-11f8-71ed-2d3b475e9b82.

Instituto Nacional de Salud. (2016). *Informe sobre violencia de género en Colombia*. Available at: https://www.ins.gov.co/buscador-eventos/Informesdeevento/Violencia%20de%20g%C3%A9nero%202016.pdf.

ICBF. (2016a). *Lineamiento técnico administrativo de la ruta de actuaciones para el restablecimiento de derechos de niños, niñas y adolescentes con derechos inobservados, amenazados o vulnerados*. ICBF.

ICBF. (2016b). *Lineamiento técnico para el proceso administrativo de restablecimiento de derechos*. ICBF.

ICBF. (2017). *Lineamiento técnico del modelo para la atención de los niños, niñas y adolescentes con derechos amenazados o vulnerados*. ICBF.

ICBF. (2018). *Infografía Ingreso de Niños y Adolescentes al Proceso Administrativo de Restablecimiento de Derechos (PARD) por Motivo de Maltrato*. ICBF. Available at: https://www.icbf.gov.co/bienestar/observatorio-bienestar-ninez/infografias.

Jiménez-Barros, R. (2012). Naturaleza del defensor de familia como institución garante de la eficacia de los derechos de la niñez y la adolescencia. ¿Conciliador o juez? *Universitas*, 124, 169–199.

Morlachetti, A. (2013). *Sistemas nacionales de protección integral de la infancia: Fundamentos jurídicos y estado de aplicación en América Latina y el Caribe*. CEPAL/UNICEF.

Procuraduría General de la Nación. (2011). Procurando la Equidad No. 6.

Procuraduría General de la Nación. (2012). Procurando la Equidad No. 7.

Save the Children. (2017). *En deuda con la niñez: Informe sobre la niñez en el mundo 2017*. Save the Children.

Therborn, G. (2013). *La desigualdad mata*. Alianza editorial. g/resources/state-worlds-children-2016-statistical-tables/.

UNICEF and Global Affairs Canada. (2015). *Building a comprehensive child protection system in Colombia: The architecture, cost and gaps*. Available at: https://www.unicef.org/protection/files/Colombia_CP_system_case_study.pdf.

UNICEF Colombia. (2018). *Consulta nacional a niños, niñas y adolescentes ¿Y La Niñez Qué?* Available at: https://www.unicef.org.co/sites/default/files/informes/Consulta_nacional_a_ninos_ninas_y_adolecentes.pdf.

Vélez, C. and Torres, M. (2014). *La desigualdad de oportunidades entre los niños colombianos: avances y retos del desarrollo humano en la última década*. Serie Documentos de Trabajo EGOB. Universidad de los Andes.

Villalta, C. and Llobet, V. (2015). Resignificando la protección: los sistemas de protección de derechos de niños y niñas en Argentina. *Revista Latinoamericana de Ciencias Sociales, Niñez y Juventud*, 13(1), 167–180.

Legislation

ICBF. (2015). Decree 1084.

Law 75. (1968).

Law 7. (1979).

Law 1098. (2006). Código de la Infancia y la Adolescencia.

Law 1878. (2018).

Political Constitution of Colombia (1991).

President of Colombia. (1989). Decree 2737. (1989).

Child and Adolescent Protection Systems in Ecuador

Verónica Jiménez Borja, Micaela Jiménez-Borja, *and* Teresita Borja-Álvarez

Abstract

This chapter outlines Ecuador's child protection systems. Ecuador's signing of the Convention of the Rights of the Child in 1989 was the result of a long struggle to institutionalize and legislate children's rights in the country. There have been important improvements in terms of the availability of a comprehensive public child protection system. However, ongoing political, economic, institutional, and legislative upheaval in the country poses difficulties to the implementation of the rights of children. As such, this chapter explores difficulties in the implementation of the National Decentralized Comprehensive Child Protection System. In particular, it highlights how Ecuador is suffering from deep structural socio-economic, regional, ethnic, and gender inequality.

Key Words: Ecuador, child protection, CRC, children's rights, upheaval, inequality

Ecuador was the first country in Latin America to sign the UN Convention of the Rights of the Child (CRC) in 1989 (UN, 1989). This was the product of a long struggle by local activists who, in line with nascent global trends, sought to institutionalize and legislate the rights of children. Since then, the country has made considerable strides in its quest to ensure the availability of a public comprehensive child protection system and in its efforts to improve the lives of children and their families. However, these achievements, and the considerable challenges the country still faces in order to guarantee the full exercise of the rights of children, can only be understood in the context of the significant political, economic, institutional, and legislative upheaval the country underwent over the past three decades. This chapter begins by charting the country's shift from the neoliberal policies of the 1990s towards the welfare policies of the 21st century that fundamentally changed the normative, political, and institutional structure of the country's child protection system. The chapter then outlines the National Decentralized Comprehensive Child and Adolescent Protection System currently in place. Finally, it explores the challenges of providing child protection services in a country that is currently in the midst of an uncertain political and institutional transition.

Like most Latin America countries, Ecuador suffers from deep structural socioeconomic, regional, ethnic, and gender inequality. As such, one of its greatest challenges has been providing marginalized communities and territories equal access to protection services. Poverty affects about 35% of the population (Observatorio Social del Ecuador [OSE], 2018) and is especially prevalent amongst indigenous communities (59%) and in rural areas (45%). The country is ethnically diverse (9% indigenous, 8% Afro-Ecuadorian, 7% montubio, and 76% mestizo) (INEC, 2010). In 2015, the child population (0–17 years) was estimated at 5,588,000, constituting about 35% of the country's 16 million people (UNICEF, 2016). This age range is unevenly distributed amongst ethnic and territorial lines. Forty percent of minors (under the age of 18) live in two provinces: Pichincha and Guayas. In coastal regions, in the Amazon province of Morona Santiago, and amongst indigenous people and Afro-Ecuadorians half of the population is under 18 years of age. Universal access to social services has been enshrined in the country's Constitution since 2008. As such, the state offers free education and healthcare to all the country's inhabitants (this includes the migrant population). The country has high levels of infant and child mortality (up to 5 years of age) (1.14%), and a high rate of teenage pregnancies (5.1%)—especially in the Amazonian and coastal regions. It also has high suicide rates amongst adolescents (10 in every 100,000 persons between the age of 12 and 18), particularly amongst indigenous communities (25% of all adolescent deaths).

Historical Overview

The 1990s: A Decade of Political and Economic Upheaval

During the last two decades of the 20th century Ecuador tended towards the implementation of neoliberal policies including limited state intervention in economic and social affairs and reduced social expenditure. Social services were privatized, and the few existing rural development programs were dismantled. Throughout the last decade of the 20th century, Ecuador suffered from slow economic growth, increasing inflation, fiscal instability, political upheaval, and the general degradation of the rule of law and of the democratic regime, along with a sharp increase in inequality and poverty rates throughout the decade. The percentage of people living in situations of poverty grew from 39% to 50% between 1995 and 1999 (OSE, 2012). Between 1996 and 2006, three democratically elected governments where deposed (Bustamante et al., 2006; Camacho & Hernández, 2009). The state struggled to attain economic stability by cutting social investment, thus putting economic and social policies at odds with each other (Ortiz, 2017). The decade was marked by civil unrest as a powerful wave of social movements called for the inclusion of marginalized actors, and the general consolidation of social rights (OSE, 2012). These movements paved the way for burgeoning forms of activism; amongst these were various organizations calling for the institutionalization and legislation of the rights of children. Still, what few social services were developed in the country at the time tended to be dispersed and disarticulated. This posed a significant limitation to the development of a comprehensive child protection system. Not only was there no clear overarching institutional or planification framework underlying these projects, but they had limited territorial range and were thus unable to reach the most vulnerable populations. What few social policies were developed during the decade tended to be subsidiary in nature—a limited sector of the population considered to be living under the poverty line would receive benefit or assistance packages, with little focus on the economic and socially excluding structural problems and distribution mechanisms that perpetuated poverty and inequality (OSE, 2012).

On the other hand, by the beginning of the 1990s, along with regional trends, Ecuador developed policies for the decentralization of public functions (Ortiz, 2017). While decentralization efforts were hard to apply in practice, due to a lack of political will and the absence of a coherent national project able to coordinate political, social, and corporate interests, these structural changes offered social actors the possibility of expanding their territorial presence and of pressuring municipalities into assuming responsibility for promoting and guaranteeing protection systems and rights. In general, movements advocating for children's rights were successful in inserting initiatives into the public agenda; particularly those relating to priority attention for children between the ages of 0 and 6, access to health and education services for children, and policies related to child maltreatment (Ortiz, 2017). Forums, summits, and consultations brought indigenous-rights groups, political leaders, cooperation agencies, non-governmental organizations, and activists into dialogue. While these movements did not extend to the entire nation, they did have significant presence and would become the basis for advances in the legislation of children's rights.

As a signatory of the CRC, the Ecuadorian state committed to making the institutional and legislative changes necessary in order to guarantee the full exercise of the rights of children. The Code for Minors, developed in 1992, officially recognized children as legal subjects (OSE, 2012). The 1998 Constitution explicitly recognized the specific rights and citizenship of vulnerable or marginalized groups including children and adolescents, women, and indigenous people. This normative framework legitimized and ensured the presence of the rights of children in public policy agendas and set an important foundation for the Ecuadorian protection system during the decade that followed.

By the mid-to-late 1990s Ecuador entered an unprecedented economic and political crisis which deeply affected Ecuadorian families. During the crisis, approximately 6% of households migrated out of the country (Bertoli et al., 2011). Between 1998 and 1999, the country's economy shrunk by over 7%, urban unemployment almost doubled, and inflation went over 60% (OSE, 2012). The lack of general protections for the population had a particularly negative impact on children and adolescents. By 2001, the number of children who worked had increased by 20%. The deterioration in quality of life affected the coastal and urban areas more drastically. Along the coast, three in every four children lived in conditions of poverty. The situation was even more dire amongst the most marginalized populations: 43% of indigenous children and 31%

of Afro-Ecuadorian children worked, and 56% of indigenous children did not attend school (OSE, 2012).

The 21st Century: The 2008 Constitution and the Construction of the Welfare State

Ecuador began the 21st century with a slow but constant economic recovery process due in great part to an increase in the price of petroleum upon which the country is greatly dependent. In 2003 the efforts of children's rights movements in the country came to fruition with the approval of the Childhood and Adolescence Code (Código de la Niñez y Adolescencia, CAC, 2003). The development of the CAC was the result of growing consensus that a normative framework for the rights of children and adolescence was necessary. The CAC is a legal instrument built according to the superior interest of children and adolescents and founded on a comprehensive protection doctrine which establishes the co-responsibility of the state, society, and the family in guaranteeing the full exercise of the rights of minors (Article 1). The Code offers a normative framework for regulating the exercise and protection of the rights of children—all those under the age of 12; and adolescents—all those between the ages of 12 and 18 (Article 4). As such, the CAC required that legal reforms be made in order to specify, expand, organize, and guarantee the rights of minors. It also calls for the creation of the National Decentralized System of Comprehensive Protection for Children and Adolescence in order to guarantee the rights enshrined in the Code. CAC Book III (Articles 193–254) outlines the organizational framework for the country's comprehensive child protection system, along with the objectives, policies, and protocols through which the system should operate. The decentralized system is made up of various state institutions at the local, provincial, and national levels, which work in coordination amongst each other in order to optimize, restructure, and strengthen public and private institutions.

The Code also lays out five fundamental priorities which must intersect with and pervade all judicial, health, education, and social services, and must be articulated in the country's legal system, as well as in all institutions that monitor and protect the rights of children and adolescents. These include 1) basic social policies such as the protection of the family unit, and access to education, health, nutrition, housing, and social security; 2) policies prioritizing programs and services for children and adolescents living in extreme poverty, natural disasters, or armed conflict; 3) special protection policies focusing on protecting children whose rights are under threat; 4) defense and protection policies aiming to ensure the full exercise and protection of the rights of children and adolescents; and, finally, 5) policies oriented towards ensuring the full exercise of the right to participative citizenship of minors. The CAC also requires that all institutions providing services for children should be integrated into the public protection system. Affiliated institutions are responsible for enforcing all public policies related to the rights of children. While the CAC offered an important normative platform for the elaboration of a fully comprehensive child protection system, the process was hindered by a general failure to create public policies with common parameters and weak institutions. Indeed, while the Code set the foundation for the current comprehensive child protection system, it was not until 2008 that an institutional framework capable of executing these policies was laid out.

By the beginning of the 20th century, Latin America had undergone a fundamental paradigm shift towards universal social welfare systems which entailed a tendency towards the deprivatization of social services along with increased investment in social security systems. This set the stage for the entrance of Rafael Correa and his party Alianza Pais in the political life of the country. Correa ran on a platform of radical socioeconomic change founded on the "Good Living" principles—the integral and comprehensive well-being of citizens (Secretaría Nacional de Planificación y Desarrollo, 2009). He was elected president of Ecuador in 2007 and Alianza Pais gained control of congress. Soon after the elections, Correa called for the formation of a new Constituent Assembly with the purpose of renovating and transforming the state's social model. The new Constitution was enacted in September 2008. The processes of deep constitutional, legal, and institutional transformation that followed meant a profound change to the scene in which the children's rights movement had worked thus far.

The Constitutional Framework of the Ecuadorian Child and Adolescent Protection System

The 2008 Constitution (Asamblea Constituyente, 2008) was founded on a multidimensional concept of social welfare based on the premise that socioeconomic inequality is intersectional—the result of overlapping and interdependent social, historical, racial, and gender contexts which create systems of discrimination or disadvantage. For this reason, the Constitution puts forth a comprehensive intergenerational protection paradigm that takes into account three intersectional dimensions: the vertical dimension (differences in access to means and resources), the horizontal dimension (gender and ethnic differences), and the intergenerational dimension (differences throughout the lifecycle).

The state took on the key role of redistributor of social wealth (Article 261). It is the obligation of the state to generate the necessary conditions for the comprehensive protection of its citizens throughout their lives (Article 341). The state must also ensure the availability and effective allocation of resources for the permanent function and management of its institutional framework (Article 342).

For the first time in the country's history social protection systems were the constitutionally mandated responsibility of the state. As the head steward of the country's child protection system, the state is in charge of generating laws, guidelines, and protocols, and regulating all of the country's diverse protection services (both public and private). It must also ensure that all social programs are in compliance with the Constitution and with all international conventions to which the country subscribes. In order to enact this responsibility, the Constitution calls for the creation of National Councils for Equality (Article 156). The 2003 CAC required the creation of The National Council for Children and Adolescents NCCA (Consejo Nacional De La Niñez Y Adolescencia; CNNA, 2004) as the chief managing body of the country's child protection system. The sixth transitional provision of the 2008 Constitution, stipulated that the NCCA must transition into the National Council for Intergenerational Equality (NCIE) as the chief overseer of the nation's child protection system. This provision was included in order to ensure that the guiding concept of intergenerational protection enshrined in the Constitution be translated into the country's normative framework and operationalized through its institutional framework. As such, the NCIE expanded its mandate to the protection of the rights of children, adolescents, young people, and senior citizens.

The intergenerational comprehensive protection doctrine places children and adolescents as the utmost priority group when allocating resources (i.e., free access to all public services and preferential treatment to those under the age of 6) and when formulating and executing public policies (Article 44, 12). Additionally, the Constitution provides a framework for social participation (Articles 95–97) that favored the rights of children by broadening opportunities for direct democracy and participation in the development of the public agenda. Together these diverse actors produced analysis, studies, assessments, and proposals which resulted in the country's Ten-Year National Plan for the Comprehensive Protection of Children and Adolescents (CNNA, 2004).

The state's National Plan for Good Living sets the guidelines for the development and implementation of all public policy and for all allocation of resources. Its objectives are mandatory for all state functions and levels of government (Article 340). Since 2009, the National Plan explicitly outlines public policies aiming to protect the rights of children with a focus on intergenerational equality, and prioritizes special protection services for children and adolescents, particularly those in vulnerable situations (Article 35, 40–42). This has resulted in policies extending education coverage, expanding health services for children, and programs combating gender violence and child labor. These public policies have been ratified in the current National Plan "Toda una Vida" (2017–2021), which has added to its stated objectives free access to childcare centers for preschool-aged children (Secretaría Nacional de Planificación y Desarrollo, 2017).

The Organizational Framework of the Ecuadorian Child and Adolescent Protection System

Following the organizational framework of the CAC, the National Decentralized Comprehensive Protection System is divided into three institutional levels (Article 192). The first level is made up of all institutions that define, plan, and evaluate policies related to childhood and adolescence with NCIE at its head.

The NCIE is chaired by the minister of the Ministry of Economic and Social Inclusion (MIES) and is made-up of four state delegates and four civil society delegates (including national and international NGO representatives). It is responsible for formulating, mainstreaming, evaluating, and monitoring all public policies related to intergenerational rights. Its activities are guided by three leading principles: 1) the need for parity amongst public policies; 2) the need for comprehensive protection measures; and 3) the need to develop services to execute these protection measures. The NCIE's National Agenda for Intergenerational Equality 2019–2021 serves as the guiding instrument for policymaking at all institutional and government levels.

The NCIE is also in charge of coordinating amongst the different sectoral agencies providing rights protection services. As such, it works with the executive branch for the articulation and execution of intergenerational policies, with the legislative branch in order to define a normative framework that may guarantee the exercise of intergenerational rights, and with judicial branches in order to strengthen the application of intergenerational justice for priority groups.

Additionally, it works with the Electoral College in order to ensure that adolescents and seniors may effectively exercise their right to a participative citizenship. Finally, the NCIE works with the Cantonal Councils for the Protection of Rights (CCCA) in order to coordinate the implementation of all policies (Articles 201–204).

As stipulated in the Childhood and Adolescence Code, the CCCA are collegial bodies working on a cantonal level that must be put together by their corresponding municipal government. These councils have administrative and functional autonomy and are responsible for the protection of all children and adolescents living in their respective Canton. The CCCA are presided over by their corresponding mayor and are made up of equal parts of state and civil society delegates. The councils have organic, functional, and budget autonomy, and are in charge of developing and proposing local policies for the consideration of the Municipal Council.

The Ministry of Economic and Social Inclusion (Ministerio de Inclusión Económica y Social; MIES) is the state body whose primary role is to guarantee, execute, and design policies oriented towards guaranteeing access to special protection systems for vulnerable people (MIES, 2018a). MIES serves as the government entity in charge of the approval, coordination, supervision, and evaluation of all protection services for priority groups. It must also ensure these services respect all constitutionally guaranteed rights and that they follow the official guidelines, methodologies, standards, and models stipulated in the National Plan.

The second organizational level of the National Decentralized Comprehensive Child Protection System is made up of all institutions responsible for the protection and enforceability of rights at the local level. This level includes the Cantonal Boards for the Protection of Rights (CBPR), the specialized judicial system, and the Ombudsperson.

The CBPR are administrative institutions rooted in local governments which, according to the CAC, have functional autonomy and are organized and financed by each municipality (Articles 205–207). Their members are democratically elected professionals trained to deal with situations in which the rights of children may have been violated. These professionals are also charged with ensuring that all judicial or administrative protection measures ordered by a judge be followed appropriately.

As stipulated in the CAC, a specialized judiciary system for children and adolescents working at the second organizational level must be in place. This judiciary system is in charge of administrating and resolving all legal issues regarding the protection of minors and is made up of judges trained in all matters pertaining to the rights of children and adolescents (Article 225). The qualified personnel that make up the judicial system for minors include: the Childhood and Adolescence Judges, the special prosecutor for juvenile offenders, and the Child Welfare Police (DINAPEN) (Article 208). The judiciary system has its own special chambers with a team of doctors, psychologists, social workers, and other relevant professionals at its disposal in each province (Article 260). All judge-mandated evaluations are conducted within these chambers. During the entire administrative and judiciary process the child's best interests must be prioritized. A minor's testimony must be conducted behind closed chambers or employing Gessel chambers (a separate, safe space for children's testimony) in order to avoid re-victimization; and the system must always protect the physical and emotional integrity of the child. People under the age of 18 are not sworn in when they give testimony (Article 258).

In recognition of the collective nature of the country's rural communities, the child protection system has an office of the Ombudsperson as well as Communal Ombudspeople. These are forms of communal organizations in parishes, neighborhoods, and rural areas that seek to promote, defend, and monitor the rights of children and adolescents. They may intervene in cases where rights have been violated and exercise administrative and judicial actions at their disposal. When necessary, they coordinate their efforts with the office of the Ombudsperson (Article 208).

The third institutional level of the country's child protection system is made up of all institutions tasked with executing policies, plans, and programs (Article 209). These include all government bodies and NGOs that provide protection services to families, children, and adolescents.

Protocols for the National Decentralized Child and Adolescent Protection System

Protection services can be provided by either government bodies or approved NGOs. However, all child protection centers are regulated by the MIES. In order to operate, these entities must be approved by and registered in the MIES (Article 212). All protection services must follow the guidelines established by the appropriate government institution (i.e., MIES; Ministry of Justice, Human Rights and Worship; Ministry of Public Health). These organizations are subject to control, auditing, and annual evaluations.

The MIES's general operational rules are founded on three guiding principles. All protection service centers must respect the principle of universal access, they must be exceptionally sensitive to the particular vulnerability to which women and girls are exposed (including sexual abuse and violence), and they must cater to the cultural realities and contexts of the territories in which they work.

Protection Measures for Children and Adolescents

Protection measures for vulnerable children and adolescents can be either judicial or administrative. According to the CAC, judicial measures can only be ordered by a Childhood and Adolescence Judge (Article 217). The aim of these measures must always be to protect, care, and restore the child's rights and safety as soon as possible (Article 79). These measures may include foster family placement, residential care placement, police raids, and protection, restraining, or eviction orders, amongst others.

Administrative Measures (Article 218) can either be ordered by a Childhood and Adolescence Judge or by the Cantonal Rights Protection Boards. These measures may be educational, therapeutic, psychological, or can provide family support (i.e., family re-insertion, temporal housing, emergency guardianship for minors, order to care for children in the home). These measures must be monitored and evaluated and can only be modified or revoked by the authority that so ordered them (Article 219).

Custody Laws and Protocols

According to the CAC, both parents are equally responsible for the fulfillment of all parental duties to the child (Article 100). Custody of a child is only lost in cases when there has been unjustified parental absence, physical, psychological, economic or sexual abuse, a mental or physical condition which impedes the parents' ability to care for the minor, or addiction to narcotic or psychotropic substances. Importantly, neither an absence of economic resources nor forced migration due to a lack of resources can be considered reason enough to remove custody of a child (Article 114). When only one parent loses custody of the child, custody immediately goes to the other parent. In cases where both parents are unable to care for the child, custody may be granted to a legal guardian (Article 112). All custody and adoption decisions prioritize the biological family (Article 153). A child's biological family extends up to the fourth-degree of consanguinity (Article 98). National adoptions are given priority over international adoptions (Article 153) which may only occur in exceptional circumstances. Adoptive parents must be over 25 years old. Priority is given to heterosexual couples over single parents, and to members of the minor's cultural background (Article 159). The law requires that siblings only be separated in exceptional circumstances (Article 156). In cases when siblings must be separated, custodians must ensure that their relationship and communication channels be maintained. Differently than with children, judges may not order an adoption against the will of an adolescent (Article 156). Minors who have been or are in the process of being adopted have the right to know their history and the origin of their biological family (Article 153).

Special Protection for Children and Adolescents

As the chief guardian of the rights of vulnerable citizens, the MIES offers various special protection services. Those which cater specifically to children and adolescents include foster family placement, adoption centers, and residential care facilities. Additionally, the Family Support Units work to maintain the family unit and avoid family breakdown, disenfranchisement, conflict, or social exclusion through preventative, educational, or rehabilitation measures. The Eradication of Child Labor Project oversees a net of public-private alliances to combat child labor. In 2008, the MIES's Family Protection Secretariat developed Comprehensive Attention Centers and Shelter Homes with the aim of safe-guarding and ensuring the restitution of the rights of children, adolescents, and women victims of intrafamily sexual violence and/or exploitation (Ministerio de Justicia, Derechos Humanos y Cultos, 2015). Both the attention centers and the homes provide counseling services for families. When necessary, they also provide custody and care services for minors. Since 2014, the Ministry of Justice, Human Rights, and Worship has provided support to these centers through civil society alliances. These centers can be operated by the public sector, the private sector, or public/private partnerships. Many of these centers are managed by religious orders or national and international non-profits. However, all centers are monitored and regulated by the MIES.

Special Protection Centers for Children and Adolescents

The fundamental purpose of special protection centers is to care for at risk children and adolescents. The fundamental objective of the centers is that the child may be able to return, whenever possible and without risk, to the care of their direct or extended family (Ministerio de Justicia, Derechos Humanos y Cultos, 2015). Centers must coordinate with local organizations. As such, local community leaders must be included in the center's team. Additionally, they must have a team of cultural mediators and translators available, and all informational material must be offered in the local language. Also, centers must respect and incorporate the attention protocols and norms developed by the culture in which they are working (i.e., ancestral healing methods). Child protection services may be accessed through referrals by informed acquaintances (teachers, family members, or other people who have become aware of the need to protect the rights of the minor), or through institutional referral.

All protection centers must offer at least three levels of professional attention (MIES, 2018a): social workers, psychologists, and lawyers. These experts must hold professional degrees certified by the National Secretariat for Higher Education, Science, Technology and Innovation. Social workers constitute the primary contact for people requiring protection services. Minors who arrive at protection centers are given an interview or crisis attention as necessary by a social worker. All interviews to minors must be conducted with an adult family member present. During this initial evaluation a social worker applies a standardized risk assessment measure in order to ascertain the level of risk there is that the minor has been or will be exposed to physical, sexual, or emotional violence. This instrument also helps the social worker recommend the kinds of social, psychological, and legal services that will be required. Any intervention by social workers must follow an "ecological" model (MIES, 2018a). This consists of gathering information through home visits and interviews with the victim's family and people from their social environment. The social worker must identify the minor's family support network, as well as social and public institutions that may provide the minor with the necessary support for the restoration of their rights.

The fundamental role of psychologists is that of evaluating the mental state of victims and mitigating the psychological damage to which victims are exposed. The government has established a humanistic attention model whose protocols must be followed independently from each therapist's personal therapeutic approach.

Lawyers provide legal counseling and information to victims. They also serve as legal representatives helping victims through all required legal processes. According to protocol, it is the responsibility of lawyers to prevent the victimization or re-victimization of the minor. As such, they may request emergency hearings or the use of Gessell chambers when interviewing minors—especially in cases of sexual violence. They must also ensure that minors are always accompanied by an adult.

The CAC requires the availability of institutional care centers (Articles 232–244). These are transitory units which serve as last resorts used only when foster care is not possible (Article 232). The centers care for minors on a transitory basis. Their primary objective is family reunification or, in cases when that is not possible, foster care placement or adoption (Article 232). In order to access foster care services, a Childhood and Adolescence Judge must first order that temporary protection measures be taken to ensure the safety and well-being of the child. These measures may only be ordered when the Judge considers that both the child's parents and their extended family are not able to care for the child. Once such a protection measure is ordered, the judge establishes a fixed monthly fee which, when possible, must be paid by the child's family. If the family is unable to pay the monthly fee, the state will do so (Article 223). Foster care may only be provided by families or institutions which have been authorized by the government agency in charge of managing these services (Article 225). In order to be considered as foster care providers (Articles 220–231), families must be able to offer a single-family home in which a maximum of eight children may be housed. Foster care providers may not profit from the services provided (Article 230). When possible, children must be placed in houses as close to their family and community context as possible. Preference is always given to groups of siblings. In fact, siblings must not be separated unless justified (i.e., sexual violence or abuse). Foster care services may be terminated when the child is reunited with their biological family; or when the child becomes eligible for adoption or emancipation (Article 229). Minors who are being cared for in these centers must be enrolled in and attend school. Children between the ages of 1 and 3 must attend public child development centers. The attention model for residential care must follow all of the MIES's standards and protocols. These may be managed by authorized public or private organizations. The centers must be staffed with a multidisciplinary team of qualified professionals (psychologists, lawyers, and social workers). There must be a minimum of one psychologist and social worker available for every 30 children. Additionally, there are specialized centers for children under the age of 3 who are not in the care of a responsible adult or who are in situations of extreme vulnerability.

According to the MIES, there were 2,462 (F = 58%, M = 42%) children in foster care in 2018. Most of these children were between 7 and 17 years old (71%) and were mestizo (85%) (MIES, 2018b). The main reason children enter foster care is either mistreatment (26%) or negligence (30%). Up to 51% of children who enter foster care stay in the system for up to 2 years, and 25% stay in the system for between 2 and 4 years. Sixty-one percent of these children do not have family available for future reunification. In 2018, there were 82 national adoptions, two international adoptions, and 72 families were in the process of adopting a child. These adoptions showed no gender preference, but there was a thirty percent ethnic preference for mestizos. There were 224 minors who could be adopted, most of these were mestizo (78%) and did not have a disability (65%).

In order to fulfill its commitment to create programs and services that ensure the full exercise of rights for vulnerable groups the MIES has also developed "Growing with Our Children" centers, which offer early stimulation and care to children between 0 and 3 years of age, and "Youth Spaces", which provide attention to marginalized adolescents (12 to 17). The MIES also offers various Non-contributive Social Schemes related to monetary transfers, discount schemes, credits, pension plans, and special assistance for mothers, seniors, and people with disabilities. These schemes are particularly geared towards families.

Protection System for Juvenile Offenders

The Ecuadorian Constitution (Articles 46–51) states that special protection services for juvenile offenders must be available to ensure their health and development. The public body in charge of overseeing and executing all public policy related to juvenile offenders is the Ministry of Justice, Human Rights, and Worship. According to protocol, custodial sanctions can only be applied as a last resort. Additionally, when custodial sanctions are applied, these must have a socioeducational goal and must be proportional to the infraction. Juvenile offenders can only be held in specialized centers administered by the state. These must always be separate from retention centers for adults.

An undersecretary of the Ministry of Justice, Human Rights, and Worship has been appointed to administer and oversee these detention facilities. Protocol also specifies that these centers must provide comprehensive psycho-pedagogical care that encourages the maintenance or restitution of family and affective bonds. The centers must guarantee full enrollment in the education system and aim towards school retention. All detention facilities must guarantee the comprehensive physical, emotional and social health of juvenile offenders. Juvenile offenders over the age of 15 should be offered occupational skill training in order to ensure future insertion in the work force. All forms of intervention must embrace activities that include the juvenile's family.

Protection for Migrants in Vulnerable Situations

The Constitution considers migrants to be a priority group (Article 35 and 40), in recognition of the complex and particularly vulnerable situations of migrants. As such, since 2008, the Ecuadorian state has officially maintained a migration policy that seeks to ensure the fulfillment of the rights of migrants, to guarantee free and universal access to public services, and to offer migrant families in vulnerable situations special protection services (Secretaria Nacional del Migrante, n.d.). According to the CAC, legally, all minors in Ecuadorian territory are under Ecuadorian jurisdiction and enjoy the same constitutional rights and guarantees as nationals, regardless of their migratory status (Article 15). As such, these children have the right to receive an education, to have their birth certificate issued by the state, and to access all services provided by the Ecuadorian Social Security Institute.

The two public entities in charge of designing and executing policies regarding migrants are the Ministry of Foreign Affairs, which designs all migratory policies, and the National Secretariat of Migrants. The Secretariat manages, regulates, coordinates, monitors, and authorizes all centers offering special protection services to migrants in situations of vulnerability. There is particular emphasis on providing refuge for families who are escaping social and political violence. Most protection centers for migrants are managed by national and international NGOs or by the church (Camacho & Hernández, 2008).

Funding Schemes for the Child Protection System

According to the Constitution, the state is responsible for the allocation of resources in such a way as to ensure the effective functioning and management of the National Decentralized Comprehensive Child and Adolescent Protection System. The CAC (Articles 298–304) stipulates that all financial resources available to the child protection system must serve to finance all three levels of the system.

The NCIE is in charge of making budgetary recommendations and of managing and allocating funds to all public and private institutions within the National Decentralized Comprehensive Child Protection System. It also monitors these funds and serves to guarantee the implementation of the policies and guidelines outlined in the National Agenda (2018–2021) (Secretaria Nacional del Migrante, n.d.). International funding is monitored by the Ministry of Foreign Affairs (MIES, 2018a). Child protection programs managed by NGOs are co-financed. These programs receive state funds proportional to their financial contribution (MIES, 2018a).

State funds are divided into the current expenditure budget, which is mostly fixed and goes to support the state's administrative apparatus, and the investment expenditure budget which is greatly dependent on the country's economic situation (Ministerio de Economia y Finanzas, 2018). Most of the budget necessary to sustain the country's protection systems are considered to be investment expenditures. Since the country is strongly dependent on the price of oil, it suffers from constant economic instability. As such, funding for child protection services has fluctuated greatly along with the country's economic situation.

The current state budget (2019) is US$34,818 million. This is 5.34% less than its 2018 budget. The state's total social investment is divided amongst education (50%), health (20%), and social welfare (15%). The budget for the child protection system is allocated to the different state sectors whose functions are directly related to or have specialized programs working within said system (Ministerio de Economia y Finanzas, 2018).

The shift from monetary transfer programs, which had been the foundation of social policy since the 1980s, towards the establishment of an integrated social service model required a reorientation in terms of the allocation of fiscal resources. While between 1990 and 2007 the state's social investment remained relatively constant, since 2007 the state has exponentially increased social investment (Ruiz, 2018). Investment in education remained at about 2.6% from the 1990s to 2006 and is currently at 5.2%. Likewise, state investment in health remained at about 1.4% until 2008. It is currently at 4%.

Achievements 1990–2019

The most important achievement of the past three decades in terms of the provision of child protection services is undoubtedly the creation of a normative and organizational framework for a public comprehensive protection system. Legal reforms and extended coverage of child protection services have resulted in an important decrease in child-labor rates from 18% in 2006 to 5% in 2016. Data collected by the Ministry of Justice shows an exponential increase in the number of child maltreatment and sexual abuse cases reported. While the District Attorney's office only had 897 reported complaints on file between 2003 and 2016, there were 919 complaints filed between 2014 and 2017 (OSE, 2018).

Moreover, exponentially larger state social investment has provided an important foundation for tackling historical inequalities in the country. Indeed, while the 1990s were starkly deficient in terms of socioeconomic development (UNICEF, 2003), during the first few decades of the current century the country has experienced improved social and economic mobility that have positively impacted the lives of the country's children. These changes include increased access and more extensive coverage of education, health, and social protection services (OSE, 2012, 2016, 2018). Indeed, poverty rates have decreased from 39% in 1995 to 30% in 2016. Education attendance rates up to 9th grade are at 96% regardless of gender, ethnic, or territorial differences. Between 2006 and 2016 high school enrollment rates increased from 42% to 71%, and pre-school attendance increased from 18% to 23%. Additionally, between 2006 and 2016 infant mortality rates decreased from 43 deaths for every 1,000 births, to 11.46 for every 1,000 births.

Challenges and Recommendations

During the past decade, Ecuador has experienced undeniable achievements in its efforts to ensure the full enforceability of the rights of children. The construction of a normative and organizational framework founded on the provision of a comprehensive social protection doctrine is promising. However, old challenges such as social inequality and the exclusion of marginalized groups prevent access to equal opportunities amongst the children and adolescents of the country. In practice these persistent territorial, ethnic, and gender inequalities continue to pose one the greatest difficulties to the construction of a comprehensive child protection system able to coordinate services across territorial divides. As long as the social protection system in Ecuador is unable to provide service to all its citizens, a truly comprehensive child protection system remains out of grasp. Particularly vulnerable are marginalized children from rural areas, indigenous and Afro-Ecuadorian children, migrant children, and girls (OSE, 2018).

These problems are compounded by the rapid institutional changes the country has undergone in the past decade. In practice these transitions have created confusion and rifts in terms of the territorial coordination of protection services. The result has been a persistently disarticulated system, which has made the task of operationalizing the system at a local level tremendously difficult. Indeed, given the limited institutional development of the majority of the more than 1,000 autonomous local governments, only a few municipalities have effectively adopted and operationalized specific child protection policies (OSE, 2016). For this reason, the Committee for the Rights of the Child (2017) has recommended the development of a high-level inter-ministerial coordination body, endowed with a clear mandate and sufficient authority to coordinate all policies, activities, and programs. It is also necessary to ensure sufficient human, technical, and financial resources to comply with the functioning of the National Decentralized Comprehensive Child Protection System.

The Committee for the Rights of the Child also recommends developing indexes in order to produce more data regarding progress made in terms of access and coverage. Additionally, the country has yet to develop indicators specifically developed for observing and analyzing the situation of children's rights in the country. Without this, the country lacks the necessary information for the future planning and development of policies. For this reason, the Committee goes on to recommend the creation of a national data collection system (OSE, 2018).

In order to improve the quality of healthcare, the country must encourage training and specialization opportunities for its health professionals. Specialized professionals are particularly lacking in rural and marginalized areas. The development of mental health services for marginalized communities is particularly urgent in order to tackle the high rates of suicide amongst indigenous adolescents. On the other hand, while there have been considerable achievements in terms of access to education, in order to improve the quality of the education system the state must provide adequate educational resources and foster the professionalization of teachers. Also, there is an urgent need to institutionalize gender-specific policies aiming to reduce the high rate of teenage pregnancies, sexual abuse, and gender-specific violence. Indeed, policies directed at the specific vulnerabilities that girls are exposed to have not been sufficiently developed. However, while the Law for the Prevention and Eradication of Violence Against Women only came into force in 2018 (Asamblea Nacional, 2018), it sets a promising precedent for future intervention.

Additionally, Ecuador must respond to the increasingly complex migration processes in which it has become inserted in recent decades. Indeed, the overflow of the Colombian conflict to neighboring countries and the more recent Venezuelan migrant crisis has meant that Ecuador has become the country with the largest number of refugees in Latin America and the Caribbean region. Moreover, the insertion of Ecuador in global migrant circuits has meant that Ecuador is not only a country of emigrants and a destiny country for immigrants, but also a country of transit for those seeking to go to the United States. Children who arrive as refugees or through clandestine channels and who must be inserted in the country's health, education, and legal system pose a strain to the child protection system that must be tackled. These are children exposed to particular risk of sexual and physical violence and abuse, as they often end up in the hands of coyotes or in human trafficking rings. Constructing a protection system able to confront these situations of extreme vulnerability is one of the greatest challenges the state faces. As such, the legal code must integrate concrete measures that meet the particular protection needs of migrant families and children.

References

Asamblea Constituyente. (2008). *Constitución de la República del Ecuador*. Government Printing Office. Available at: https://www.asambleanacional.gob.ec/sites/default/files/documents/old/constitucion_de_b olsillo.pdf.

Asamblea Nacional. (2018). *Ley para prevenir y erradicar la violencia contra las mujeres*. Government Printing Office. Available at: https://www.igualdad.gob.ec/wp-content/uploads/downloads/2018/05/ley_prevenir_ y_erradicar_violencia_mujeres.pdf.

Bertoli S., Fernández-Huertas Moraga J., and Ortega, F. (2011). Immigration policies and the Ecuadorian exodus. *World Bank Economic Review*, 25(1), 57–76.

Bustamante, F., Durán, L., and Andretti, A. C. (2006). *Una sociedad civil eficaz mas allá de sus debilidades, Informe Final del Índice de la Sociedad Civil en el Ecuador*. Civicus Esquel.

Camacho, G. and Hernández, K. (2008). *Niñez y migración en el Ecuador: Diagnóstico de la situación*. CEPLAES, INNFA, UNICEF.

Childhood and Adolescence Code. (2003). Available at: https://www.igualdad.gob.ec/wp-content/uploads/ downloads/2017/11/codigo_ninezyadolescencia.pdf.

CNNA. (2004). *Plan Nacional Decenal De Protección Integral A La Niñez Y Adolescencia*. Government Printing Office. Available at: http://www.oei.es/historico/quipu/ecuador/plan_decenal_ninez.pdf.

Committee for the Rights of the Child. (2017). *Observaciones finales sobre los informes periódicos quinto y sexto combinados del Ecuador*. Available at: http://acnudh.org/comite-sobre-los-derechos-del-nino-crc-ecua dor-2017.

INEC. (2010). *Censo de la poblacion y vivienda 2010*. Government Printing Office. Available at: http://www.ecuadorencifras.gob.ec/base-de-datos-censo-de-poblacion-y-vivienda/.

MIES. (2018a). *Acuerdo Ministerial #14*. Government Printing Office. Available at: https://www.inclusion.gob.ec/wp-content/uploads/downloads/2018/03/ACUERDO-014-y-PROTOCOLO-COMPLETO.pdf.

MIES. (2018b). *Informe Acogimiento Familiar*. Internal document.

Ministerio de Economía y Finanzas. (2018). *Rendición de cuentas*. Available at: https://www.finanzas.gob.ec/rendicion-de-cuentas/.

Ministerio de Justicia, Derechos Humanos y Cultos. (2015). *Modelo de atención integral y protocolos para los centros de atención a niñas, niños, adolescentes y mujeres víctimas de violencia intrafamiliar y/o sexual*. Government Printing Office. Avaiable at: https://www.justicia.gob.ec/wp-content/uploads/2014/08/plan_erradicacionviolencia_ecuador.pdf.

Ortiz, S. (2017). *Balance de la descentralización en el Ecuador: 1998–2016*. Cooperación Alemana, GIZ. Available at: http://www.amevirtual.gob.ec/wp-content/uploads/2018/01/Balance-de-la-Descentralizacion-en-Ecuador-2017.pdf.

OSE. (2012). *Estado de los derechos de la niñez y la adolescencia en Ecuador 1990–2011*. Government Printing Office. Available at: https://www.unicef.org/ecuador/Edna2011_web_Parte1.pdf.

OSE. (2016). *Niñez y adolescencia desde la intergeneracionalidad*. Government Printing Office. Available at: https://www.worldvision.org.ec/wp-content/uploads/2016/04/ninez.pdf.

OSE. (2018). *Situación de la niñez y adolescencia en Ecuador, una mirada a través de los ODS*. Government Printing Office. Available at: https://www.unicef.org/ecuador/SITAN_2019_Web.pdf.

Ruiz, M. E. (2018). La inversión social y el índice de Sen en Ecuador. *Revista Científica Hermes—FIPEN*, 20, 87–109.

Secretaria Nacional del Migrante. (n.d.). *Manual de procedimientos de protección a niños, niñas y adolescentes en situación de movilidad humana*. Government Printing Office. Available at: https://www.unicef.org/ecuador/Sustento_teorico_Migracion.pdf.

Secretaría Nacional de Planificación y Desarrollo. (n.d.). *Plan nacional para el buen vivir. 2013–2017*. Government Printing Office. Available at: http://www.buenvivir.gob.ec/versiones-plan-nacional.

Secretaría Nacional de Planificación y Desarrollo. (2009). *Plan nacional para el buen vivir. 2009–2013*. Government Printing Office. Available at: http://www.planificacion.gob.ec/wp-content/uploads/downloads/2012/07/Plan_Nacional_para_el_Buen_Vivir.pdf.

UNICEF. (2003). *Estado mundial de la infancia: Fondo de las Naciones Unidas para la infancia*. Available at: https://www.unicef.org/spanish/sowc/archive/SPANISH/Estado%20Mundial%20de%20la%20Infancia%202004.pdf.

UNICEF. (2016). *The state of the world's children 2016* [Statistical tables]. Available at: https://data.unicef.org/resources/state-worlds-children-2016-statistical-tables/.

UN. (1989). *Convention on the rights of the child*. Available at: https://treaties.un.org/pages/ViewDetails.aspx?src=IND&mtdsg_no=IV-11&chapter=4&lang=en.

Child Protection in Egypt

Hmoud S. Olimat *and* Amal A. ElGamal

Abstract

This chapter notes child protection in Egypt. The population in urban areas continued to grow steadily over the years. Egypt also recorded a spike in inflation due to domestic inflation, fuel subsidy cuts, and value-added tax. The legal framework of Egypt's child protection system sparked policy and institutional changes which included policies, strategies, and programs focused on child protection. The government has committed great efforts in battling child labor by adopting relevant UN conventions and international instruments. Moreover, the National Council for Childhood and Motherhood has the highest authority to implement children's and mothers' rights whilst being simultaneously being responsible for the formulation, implementation, and monitoring of social protection policies. This chapter notes child protection in Egypt. The population in urban areas continued to grow steadily over the years. Egypt also recorded a spike in inflation due to domestic inflation, fuel subsidy cuts, and value-added tax. The legal framework of Egypt's child protection system sparked policy and institutional changes which included policies, strategies, and programs focused on child protection. The government has committed great efforts in battling child labor by adopting relevant UN conventions and international instruments. Moreover, the National Council for Childhood and Motherhood has the highest authority to implement children's and mothers' rights whilst being simultaneously being responsible for the formulation, implementation, and monitoring of social protection policies.

Key Words: Egypt, child protection, inflation, child labor, NCCM, social protection, population, UN, rights

Background Information

Egypt is one of the most populous nations in the Middle East and Africa. The total population grew at a rate of roughly 2% annually between 2000 and 2015. The proportion of people living in urban areas has remained steady over the past 10 years, with almost 43% of the population located in urban areas. Children aged 0–17 years constitute 33.4 million, representing (37.1%) of the total population (Central Agency for Public Mobilization and Statistics [CAPMAS and UNICEF, 2017). The current population of Egypt is estimated to reach approximately 103.5 million in 2022 (CAPMAS, 2022).

The Egyptian population is exceptionally young with about 60% under the age of 30 and 40% of the population between the ages of 10 and 29, being equally distributed among males and females. This population could be perceived as a challenge for the Egyptian government in providing education and health services, suitable housing, and employment opportunities to accommodate the needs of this massive generation of young people. It could also be seen as a demographic opportunity of huge potential for achieving progress and prosperity for the country if those human resources are properly utilized and directed toward work, production, and active participation in building the nation (Roushdy & Sieverding, 2015).

Egypt experienced a spike in inflation, increasing from 14% to nearly 30% over 2016–2017. This strong inflationary pressure on Egypt reflects the effects of a pass-through exchange rate on import prices due to domestic inflation, coupled with price increases caused by fuel subsidy cuts and a value added tax (United Nations Economic and Social Commission for Western Asia [ESCWA], 2018).

In Egypt, where unemployment had been on an upward trend since 2010, there was a small but positive improvement in 2017 in the labor participation rate, which increased to 73% for men and to 22% for women. Employment that lacks affordable childcare facilities, flexible working arrangements, and supportive labor market policies presents a high opportunity cost for active married women with children (Nazier & Ramadan, 2016 in ESCWA, 2018, p. 75; CAPMAS, 2017).

Chapter Organization and Content

This chapter is organized into three sections. The first section describes international instruments and the national legal framework for child protection. The legal framework triggered a wide range of policy and institutional changes. The second section explains policies, strategies, and programs tailored to child protection in Egypt. The third section looks into the real situation of Egypt's children. It explains the wide range of challenges and problems faced by Egypt's children followed by descriptions of the various services provided to them. The fourth section presents a brief evaluation of the child social protection system in Egypt, offering some recommendations for improvement. Figure 34.1 explains the logical flow of the chapter content that hopefully reflects the logical development of child protection in Egypt.

The Legal Framework for Social Protection for Children

According to Bonilla Garcia and Gruat (2003, p. 54):

> Social Protection in order to be effective, requires a comprehensive legal and policy framework, which . . . gives a legal basis to entitlement and makes a commitment to putting in place the appropriate mechanisms. The greater the precision, the better the framing of obligations, rights and entitlements.

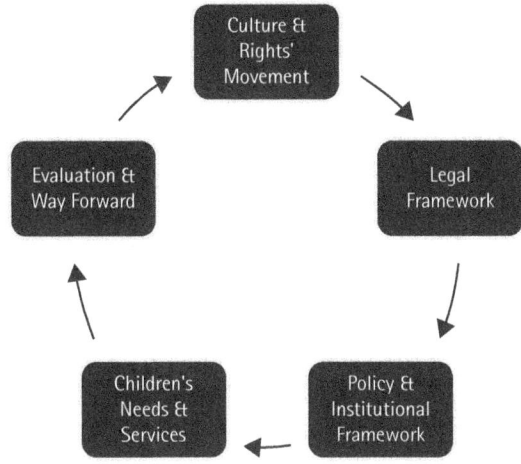

Figure 34.1 The child social protection framework in Egypt

In its report for the implementation of the Convention of the Rights of the Child (CRC; UN, 1989) and its optional Protocol, the Government of Egypt asserted that its legislation has treated issues of children with great importance for a long time. Since the 1930s, Egypt's laws contained articles pertaining to combating child endangerment (e.g., kidnapping, rape, prostitution, pimping, sexual exploitation, inducing children into prostitution) with relevant penalties. (A list of most relevant laws is mentioned below.) Efforts on child welfare were accelerated. Since the 1980s, Egypt's government expressed its concern for children in accordance with global efforts. This commitment to the welfare of children has resulted in the signing and ratification of the CRC. Egypt was one of the six initiator countries to call for convening the World Summit for Children in 1990 and was also among the first 20 countries to ratify the CRC, showing its firm commitment to this issue. Egypt then established the National Council for Motherhood and Childhood (NCCM; http://www.nccm-egypt.org/e7/e2392/e2391/index_eng.html) in 1991.

Building on the achievements of the first decade and responding to the new challenges, another presidential announcement was made declaring the period from 2000–2010 as the second decade for children. The goals of the second decade encompassed education, health, social solidarity, culture, and legislation. As evident, all of these areas of concerns are crucial for children's development and prosperity. However, for the current chapter, only the section on social solidarity is considered. The social solidarity section (State Information Service [SIS] 2009: Fact 3, Third section) has the following goals:

> The Second Declaration for the Protection and Welfare of the Egyptian Child is launched at a time when Egypt is set to explore the horizons of a comprehensive social development, in the qualitative and quantitative sense of progress for all segments of society. However, children and women, in their capacity as mothers, should be given special attention as follows:

1) Children at risk, especially school dropouts, working and street children, and those incarcerated and placed in social institutions should be protected and a program should be devised to address their problems and provide them with a proper psychological, social and occupational upbringing.
2) Problems of single mothers and of mothers facing difficult conditions should be addressed; training should be provided so that they would acquire new skills and new occupations. This should be linked to illiteracy projects and to the funding of small enterprises.
3) All problems of the female child should be addressed.
4) It is essential that every child should join a sporting, social or cultural club and/or be part of an extra-curriculum activity as a means of refining their character and providing them with new social skills.

International and Regional Instruments

Based on various efforts of the Government of Egypt and its agencies, and with the spirit of the rights movement especially for children and women, a cluster of international and national legal instruments were issued as the base for children's social protection. The following is a brief list of major international and regional instruments to which Egypt is a signatory and active party; the next section considers relevant national legislation.

- International Labour Organization [ILO] Convention No. 129 for the year 1969 on Labor Inspection in Agriculture.
- ILO Convention No. 138 for the year 1973 on the Minimum Age for Employment.
- UN Convention on the Rights of the Child, 1989.
- Convention concerning the prohibition and immediate action for the elimination of worst forms of child labor, 1999, No. 182.
- A world fit for children: resolution/adopted by the General Assembly, 2002.
- Cairo Declaration on CRC and Islamic Jurisprudence, Cairo, November 23–24, 2009.
- CRC optional protocols on combating human trafficking, No. 64 for the year 2010.

National Instruments

Child protection is included in Egyptian Child Law No. 126 (2008), and in Labor Law No. 12 (2003). The child law stresses child protection in several of its articles, in particular, protecting children from any type of discrimination based on origin, gender, religion, race, or disability, and any other means of discrimination. This stated that children should enjoy real equality in assuming their various rights. For example, child age was extended to 18 years, aiming to protect children from practices that may hinder the normal development and quality of life (e.g., early marriage and child labor). According to the Government of Egypt (SIS, 2010), the single most important legal instrument for child rights is Child Law No. 12 (1996), amended by Law No. 126 (2008). This law resembles exemplary law for children and came as Egypt's response to all the rights contained in the CRC and its optional protocols. The law is a comprehensive instrument that implied all the content of the optional protocol, indicating that Egypt has accepted all the crimes included in the optional protocol. Most important is what the law asserts are the assurance of child rights for protection from violence in its broader meaning. In that spirit, the law dictated the need for a special judicial system for children, establishing a decentralized protection system with community involvement and participation.

Care for child protection in Egypt is not a recent development. Rather, it has a long history going back almost a century. As noted above, Egypt's government asserted that its legislation has long treated issues of children with great importance. Examples of these legal instruments are:

- Law No. 49, 1933, on Beggary;
- Penal Law No. 58, 1937;
- Law No. 128, 1960, on Combating Drugs, amended with Law No. 122, 1989 (on combating drugs and regulating its use and trading);
- Law for Combating Prostitution No. 10, 1961;
- Arab Republic of Egypt's Constitution, 1971;
- Child Law No. 12, 1996, (Amended by Law No. 126, 2008);
- Law for Combating Money Laundering No. 80, 2002;
- Unified Labor Law No. 12, 2003.

The Government of Egypt has committed to exerting utmost efforts in combating child labor, principally by adopting relevant UN conventions and international instruments pertinent to combating child labor. The previous section mentioned the international conventions, protocols, and covenants that the government had signed and ratified. The following are national legal frameworks adopted for the elimination of child labor in its various forms and shapes that confirm this commitment (Egypt Ministry of Manpower & ILO, 2018):[1]

- Child Law No. 12 of 1996, amended by Law No. 126 of 2008 and its executive regulation issued by decree No. 2075 of 2010;
- Labor Law No. 12 of 2003;

---

[1] Ministry of Manpower and ILO (2018, p. 13) cites several sources for the availability of these conventions and laws.

- Ministry of Manpower's Decree No. 118 of 2003 prohibiting employment of children in hazardous work.

The national commitment was reiterated by the 2014 Constitution:

- Prohibiting child employment before the age of compulsory education (Article 80);
- Ensuring the right to compulsory and free education (Article 19);
- Ensuring vocational and technical training (Article 20);
- Providing social security (Article 17).

Institutions, Policies, and Strategies

According to Pereznieto and colleagues (2011), well-designed, evidence-based, child-sensitive social protection can be instrumental in improving the equitable development of children in the region. Egypt's legal and political commitment to child rights and protection were translated into policies, strategies, and national frames of action. In response to the movement of child rights and in accordance with Egypt's commitments, several public and semipublic institutions were established to implement the state's obligations. However, as previously mentioned and as an outcome of the child rights movement, one important institution—the NCCM—was established to deal directly with children and mothers' issues and concerns.

The National Council for Childhood and Motherhood

The NCCM was established by presidential (executive order) decree no. 54 for the year 1988, modified by decree no. 273 in 1989. The NCCM is the highest authority in Egypt for the implementation of children's and mothers' rights. Article 214 of the constitution grants NCCM its legal status as an independent national entity. Consequently, the NCCM is responsible for the formulation, implementation, and monitoring of social protection polices for children and mothers in accordance with other government and relevant institutions. NCCM's (n.d.) main duties include:

- Propose public policy in the field of childhood and motherhood;
- Formulate the project for a national plan for children and motherhood within the framework of the general plan for the government;
- Monitor and evaluate the implementation of the public policy and national plan for childhood and motherhood in light of the assessment report provided by various ministries, commissions, and concerned parties;
- Data collection and statistics, and possible studies in areas relevant to childhood and motherhood, and to evaluate its indicators;

- Propose training programs that assist in enhancing the level of performance in implementing childhood and motherhood activities;
- Cooperate with government and non-government organizations at the local, national, and international levels.

Strategies Relevant to Child Protection

Strategies relevant to child protection came as an outcome of the movement of rights and due to the establishment of several government and semi-government institutions. The list of major strategies below is followed by a brief discussion of the major and relevant ones.

- National strategy for childhood and motherhood, 2017–2022;
- National action plan for combating the worst forms of child labor in Egypt and supporting family, 2018–2025;
- National strategy to combat female circumcision;
- Early child development strategy, 2005–2010;
- National plan for combatting child trafficking, 2009;
- National strategy of addiction treatment and rehabilitation in Egypt, 2008;
- National plan to combat violence against children, 2006;
- National strategy and the work plan to eliminate child labor, 2006;
- National strategy to protect young children from drugs, 2005;
- National strategy to protect and rehabilitate street children, 2003;
- National plan for girls' education, 2002.

THE NATIONAL STRATEGY FOR CHILDHOOD AND MOTHERHOOD, 2017–2022

This is the umbrella national strategy that organizes government and non-government efforts for the improvement of the situation of children and their mothers. The strategy includes a national vision and unified framework of action for government and non-government organizations concerned with childhood and motherhood affairs. The complicated situation of the country and the wide variation among various governorates (i.e., geographic regions) in Egypt necessitates the existence of a strategy. Therefore, the strategy is an attempt to translate into programs and services what the Constitution stipulates as rights for citizens in general and children in particular. It is of utmost importance to have such strategies with real work plans and implementation efforts. The strategy covers the following six major rights: children's right to protection, children's right to health (development, life, and survival), rights to education, rights of poor children, rights to participation, and motherhood rights and welfare.

The strategy suggests providing support for poor families to ensure that their children enroll in schools and ensuring programs provide small grants and microfinances to start their own income-generating projects. The strategy also suggests providing training programs for women head of households and that businessmen adopt development programs to improve the conditions of poor families. One suggestion was to establish a hybrid school that, in addition to traditional education, offers training on trades and skills for hand and semi-skilled work, which would give students some financial return at the same time. These measures are meant to give some meaning to education for poor children and other children who see no hope in education. Poor children's rights include free participation in all matters about them. However, the general conditions of the country make it difficult to achieve this right, even for other children and adults. Particular to children, their participation is not valued, and it has no space in the public sphere. It is understandable that poor children are not well trained for participation, with a lack of awareness on the part of their parents. Poor children do not have time for leisure and community participation; schooling and work takes their time. In addition, poor areas lack clubs and cultural centers to facilitate children's participation.

EARLY CHILD DEVELOPMENT STRATEGY, 2005–2010

The Early Child Development Strategy calls for enlisting the support of all political, social, psychological, and economic actors and powers in Egypt to promote and support policies and programs that could enable children in their critical developmental stage, specifically in providing children with services and high-level education that foster the optimal development of children, psychologically, socially, intellectually, spiritually, and mentally. The proper development and nurturing of children will eventually contribute to the progress and development of society.

Situation Analysis of Egypt's Children

Political changes from 2011 to the present have immensely affected the situation of Egypt's population. Indicators from various sources show considerable deterioration in all aspects of population and development. Official government sources show that the number of individuals living below the poverty line has risen from 22% in 2009 to 28% in 2015. This percentage ranges from 25% to 40% in six governorates and exceeds 40% in five governorates, which is commensurate with deteriorated services (National Population Council et al., 2016; Osman, 2016).

As evident from various sources and from observing current conditions in Egypt, the situation in Egypt is very problematic and somewhat conflictual, with deteriorated socioeconomic conditions. The overall troubled and destabilized political condition has a negative impact on various socioeconomic conditions and the delivery of health services, economic development, and employment, accompanied with increased poverty rates. Socioeconomic indicators from various sources show that the impact of the political disturbances on the demographic situation is immense. Amongst these adverse and turbulent conditions, vulnerable and marginalized people are suffering the most. In such adverse conditions, children suffer the most. The consequences of such troubled conditions are reflected in children facing excessive use of violence as a way of discipline, child labor, early marriages, child trafficking and illegal migration (without their families), homeless and street children, imprisonment, and disability, to name but a few (Osman, 2016, p. 50).

A statistical analysis based on five Demographic Health Survey (DHS) rounds showed that 29% of the children-under-5-years were stunted, 7% were wasted, and 6% were underweight in 2008. Also found was a robust statistically significant negative association between economic growth, at the governorate level, and four indicators of child malnutrition, namely, underweight, wasting, extreme wasting, and extreme stunting (Rashad & Sharaf, 2018). The plight of Egypt's children is put succinctly by Ragab (2010, p. 135):

> Under the fierce rays of the desert sun, in the heat of the summer, young children are forced to remove pests from cotton crops for eleven hours per day, search for recyclable goods among animals and the pungent stench of city dumps, and are sold to elderly male tourists through temporary marriages by their parents.

Violence against Children

Many children in Egypt face various forms of violence, exploitation, trafficking, and inadequate family care. There is a widespread use of violence as a socially acceptable disciplinary practice. The 2014 DHS showed that 93% of children aged 1–14 years have been exposed to violent disciplinary practices, including psychological aggression and/or physical punishment. Furthermore, 43 percent were exposed to extreme physical punishment, including being hit or slapped on the face, head, or ears; repeated beating; and being hit with a hard object, such as a belt (Ministry of Health and Population et al., 2015). Moreover, according to the National Centre for Social and Criminological Research and the Special Rapporteur on trafficking in persons in 2011, child trafficking in Egypt includes seasonal or temporary marriages, slavery or forced labor, and trafficking for removal of organs and sexual exploitation. The exact number of children who are trafficked is unknown and no reliable surveys or data collection systems on child trafficking exist (Home Office, 2017).

One of the major facts about violence against children in Egypt is that it is a widespread problem, with thousands of cases annually, some of them leading to death. A high percentage of children in Egypt were (are) subject to violence (NCCM and UNICEF, 2015; Ministry of Health and Population & NCCM, 2018). A study conducted by UNICEF and NCCM (2015) shows that children are often exposed to violence in their own homes by their parents or other caregivers, followed by violence in school by other students, and finally, by teachers. Thus, the sources of love, care, and education may turn out to be harmful places for children.

Violence is an acceptable means of discipline in Egypt. Not only does society, including parents, approve of such behavior, children do too. This means that violence is socially and culturally acceptable. The implied acceptable of violence is detrimental to the efforts of combating violence against children. The NCCM finds it difficult in the case of family violence because no legal measures can be enforced for the protection of the child without an official complaint. The complaint should be submitted by a parent or relative of the child that has been abused. In various cases neighbors and people who may witness or hear children screaming do not typically call to inform the concerned agencies or call the hotline.

The NCCM is the starting point for all kinds of responses to violence against children. With concerned government agencies and organizations, it established the committee for child protection. Members of this committee offer various kinds of services necessary for abused and homeless children. Even before the newly established committee, the council established the help line (hotline) in 2005. The council receives calls and acts upon them based on the severity of cases. The council has working relationships with concerned government and non-government institutions. A major and important partner to the council is the office of the Attorney General (AG). The AG reviews violence cases and decides upon them. This may entail sending abusers to court, taking children out of their families, and other legal and protection consequences. Children may be sent to hospital in case of injury or illness, sent to residential institutions, or in some cases, children may be sent to some of their relatives. Referring a child to a relative is a somewhat socially and culturally acceptable alternative to institutionalization.

The NCCM is the focal point for all issues concerning the welfare and protection of children. The NCCM coordinates the responses and services provided to children and families in need. In the case of child victims of violence, the NCCM with the office of the Attorney General decides on the cases, and children may be placed in residential houses, NGOs' houses, or with their relatives. Children who are deprived of families who are found astray in the streets, or children with unknown parents, may be picked up by the police from streets or from their hiding. The police, in consultation with NCCM, refer children to Ministry of Health centers for motherhood and childhood for medical checks and treatment. Then children are sent to residential care centers. Young children aged 0–6 years are sent to residential kindergartens. After the age of 6 children are sent to residential institutions. Residential institutions are either governmental or non-governmental. The main government institution that offers placement services is the Ministry of Social Solidarity (MoSS). The MoSS either refers children to its institutions or sends them to NGOs, of which 21 are available.

Child Poverty

Poverty is one of the major challenges to Egypt's children's welfare and well-being. Based on government statistics (CAPMAS, 2015), in 2014, three in 10 children in Egypt lived in multidimensional poverty; this represents 10 million children. Poverty disproportionally affects children with long-term consequences, reducing their chances of living and development. In 2012–2013, 9.2 million Egyptian children (0–17 years) lived in extreme poverty. An additional 7.5 million children were vulnerable to extreme poverty, with meager consumption rate above the poverty line. The percentage head count of children living in extreme poverty is increasing during the last 15 years, from 21% in 1999–2000 to 29% in 2012–2013 (CAPMAS and UNICEF, 2015).

Child poverty is multidimensional in its nature; it manifests in deprivation from health, nutrition, weak education outcomes, lack of decent housing, difficulty in having clean water, lack of sanitation, inadequate socialization and development, and lack of mobility chances. In order to combat poverty in an effective way and to support human and economic development at the national level, there needs to be a reform of the social protection system—from a system directed to subsidize consumption of which the main beneficiaries are the rich people to a system of cash transfer that targets the poor people, specifically families with children, accompanied with an increase in investment in quality social services (Cockburn et al., 2014).

Social safety nets, adequately designed and delivered, are an essential component of a poverty reduction strategy. Until these long-term development goals are achieved, there must be policies to ensure that the poor survive. The focus on economic growth is not sufficient to address the immediate needs of the large, and probably increasing, number of poor people in Egypt (Sabry, 2005).

Child Labor

A major issue of concern to various countries in the world, including Egypt, is the problem and challenge of child labor. Child labor, according to Egypt's Ministry of Manpower and the ILO (2018), is one of the obstacles facing children. Child labor drastically reduces the quality of the state's human capital through its detriment to education as well as damaging the physical and mental health of children. Moreover, an impaired work force produces sluggish economic development. Child labor also plays a significant role in the underestimation of the GDP of developing economies through increased activity in the informal economy. Poverty is one of the main factors associated with child labor (Olimat, 2018). Child labor is a manifestation of the pains of extreme poverty on the world's most vulnerable population (Ragab, 2010, p. 135).

Child labor has damaging effects on children's present life and future prospects. There is a reverse relationship between child labor and school attendance. Compared to their counterpart children, working children (6–17 years) have lower levels of school attendance. In addition, child labor consequences include health problems, more vulnerability, deviance, and susceptibility to physical and sexual exploitation (Al-Esawi, 2017; Saleh, 2013).

Children's Health Problems

Inequality in health is a major challenge to Egypt's people in general and to children in particular. The lack of adequate nutrition to mothers and their children usually is reflected in their health and development. According to the World Health Organization (WHO, 2018, para. 1), "Malnutrition, in all its forms, includes undernutrition (wasting, stunting, underweight), inadequate vitamins or minerals, overweight, obesity, and resulting diet-related noncommunicable diseases." According to UNICEF (2018), in Egypt, despite the investment in the health sector, and a notable decline in child mortality, malnutrition rates remain high for young children under five years of age.

Egypt's Ministry of Health and Population (2014) showed that there is considerable chronic malnutrition among Egyptian children. Based on comparisons with the WHO Child Growth Standards population, around one in five children under age 5 are stunted and one in 10 children are severely stunted. Considering age patterns, stunting peaks among children aged 1–23 months (25%). Urban children are only slightly more likely to be stunted than rural children (23% and 21%, respectively). Considering place of residence, the percentage who are stunted is higher in urban Upper Egypt (30%) than in other areas. Children whose mothers never attended school or who attended but did not complete primary school are somewhat more likely to be stunted than children whose mothers have completed the primary level or higher (Ministry of Health and Population, 2014, p. 40). These finding are also supported by Rashad and Sharaf (2018), who reported that statistics show that 29% of the children under 5 years were stunted, 7.2% were wasted, and 6% were underweight in 2008 (pp. 769–795). They found a robust statistically significant negative association between economic growth, at the governorate level, and four indicators of child malnutrition, namely: underweight, wasting, extreme wasting, and extreme stunting. Anemia is widespread among Egypt's children. In general, more than one in four children in Egypt suffers from some degree of anemia. Rural children are more likely to be anemic than urban children (29% and 23%, respectively). The anemic situation is variable according to the geographic locations. Children in the three Frontier Governorates and in rural Upper Egypt were more likely than children in other areas to be anemic (45% and 30%, respectively) (Ministry of Health and Population, 2014).

Reproductive Health

Adolescents and youth are a group at risk of HIV/AIDS and other sexually transmitted diseases. Adolescents and youth are deprived of health and preventive services in general and of sexual and reproductive health in particular. This is accompanied by a lack of proper life skills and health education. Early health and behavioral health are crucial to the development of youth and their smooth transfer to adult life. With this problematic situation and the lack of proper health services, adolescents and youth are vulnerable to all kind of diseases, illnesses, and poor health, which will be reflected in their education and work life. Pregnancy among adolescents not only affects the health, education, and employment of the young women but also affects their children. The newborns of mothers in the 15–19-year age range suffer higher rates of morbidity and mortality (Ministry of Health and Population, 2014; Osman, 2016). The fertility rate in the adolescents' group was 72 per 1,000 in 1988, declined to 48 in 2005, then rose to 50 in 2008 and to 56 in 2014 (Ministry of Health and Population, 2014).

Street Children

The street children problem is a manifestation of the effect of various interrelated factors in Egypt. Poverty, family breakdown, and child abuse and neglect seem to be the leading causes. Many Egyptian families who are economically marginalized have become seriously dysfunctional and have placed their children in circumstances that have resulted in such youth leaving home and trying to survive in the often unprotected and hazardous street environment (Ray et al., 2011). Factors associated with the problem of street children in Egypt are multidimensional in which a combination of factors often leads to a single child ending up being on the street. Most research seems to agree that the leading causes of the problem are poverty, unemployment, family breakdown, child abuse and neglect, dropping out of school, child labor, the effect of peers, and other social and psychological reasons related to the social environment or to the personality of the child such as behavioral disorders or sensation seeking (Ray et al., 2011).

Some researchers and practitioners (e.g., Ray et al., 2011) have presented a wide range of microstructural factors. These include poverty and social exclusion, conflict, disasters and climate change, migration and urbanization, cultural attitudes and behaviors, violence against children, lack of access to quality education, the HIV pandemic, exploitative and hazardous child work, and what the future holds (expecting a bleaker future for children due to expected socioeconomic disturbances globally).

Street children lead unhealthy, dangerous, and hazardous lives. They are deprived of their basic needs for protection and supervision, while exposed to various types of exploitation and maltreatment. Consequently, living in the street means beggary, sexual exploitation by adults, violence, community disapproval, police arrest, theft of savings, inability to cope, and lack of attachment, to name but a few problems (Osman, 2016; Ray et al., 2011). The hazardous lifestyle of the streets creates various health problems for children, ranging from headaches to cancer, with a high prevalence of mental illness; dental problems are considered an epidemic among street children, followed by scabies (mange) and skin diseases, with other incidents of cold weather diseases and burns from fire used for heating in winter (Osman, 2016).

Interventions to address the issue of street involvement by children are generally categorized according to the following program's phases (Ray et al., 2011):

- Prevention (work to stem the flow of children onto the streets);
- Protection and support (interventions to address the rights of children on the streets);
- Rehabilitation (activities aimed at supporting children to stabilize their lives);

- Reintegration (returning them to their families or placement in an alternative setting).

Substance Abuse

Elkoussi and Bakheet (2011) conducted a study to assess the extent, patterns, attitudes, motivations, and impacts of volatile substance misuse (VSM) among street children in Upper Egypt in 2009. The study consisted of a 36-item questionnaire that was administered to a randomly selected sample of 120 street children aged 10–18 years. Nearly 91% of street children were misusing products containing VS because they are inexpensive, legal, and easy to acquire. About one-third reported inhaling "Kolla," a commercial glue that contains a mixture of 15 toxic solvents. Children reported both benefits and hazards in regard to VSM and that VSM was prevalent among the subjects' peers and family members. As indicated by Elkoussi and Bakheet (2011), single and repeated Kolla inhalation in rats dose-dependently increased locomotor activity, decreased motor coordination, induced both a depressant and excitatory response in the central nervous system, and led to pathological changes in the liver. It is expected that these effects would be much more hazardous in underprivileged, neglected, and malnourished street children, who indicated that familial neglect and lack of supervision were the main social motivations reported by street youth for misusing volatile substances.

In their study, Ray and colleagues (2011), reported that substance abuse is rampant among street children. Almost 66% of the selected sample of street children consumed various substances or drugs on a habitual basis, whereas 34% did not refer to use at the time when interviews were conducted. Drugs consumed included cigarettes, sniffing glue, Bango, tablets, and combinations of substances. Unfortunately, street children have access to these illicit drugs through many people or dealers who exchange drugs with them in return for various forms of exploitation. The tragedy of street children's substance abuse is that the purpose of their use is to relieve them from the hardship of street life, relief from the pressures of the street (70%), peer pressure (60%), to sleep easily (50%), and to be able to endure pain, violence, and hunger (30%).

Female Circumcision (Female Genital Mutilation)

On November 14, 2015, and in concomitance with the National Day to Combat Female Circumcision, Egypt's State Ministry of Population and the United Nations (2015) announced the National Strategy to combat Female Circumcision. The date was not chosen arbitrarily but denotes the date when a child—Bdor Shaker—died from a circumcision operation in 2007. Girls are particularly vulnerable to various forms of abuse such as female genital mutilation and child marriage.

The prevalence of female genital mutilation/cutting (FGM/C) in girls aged 15–17 has steadily decreased in the past decade from 77% in 2005 to 61% in 2014, according to the

2014 DHS. However, regional disparities exist. For example, the percentage of girls aged 0–17 who are expected to undergo FGM/C reaches 90% in some Upper Egypt governorates. The general prevalence rate of female circumcision in the reproductive age (15–49 years) is 92%, while the prevalence rate has declined among the younger age group (15–17 years) to 61% (Ministry of Health and Population, 2014).

The World Convention on Population and Development in 1994 was a turning point for non-governmental efforts to combat female circumcision. Several coalitions from government and non-government organizations were formed throughout the country. The purpose was to support the effort to eradicate this harmful practice. In 1996, the Minister of Health and Population issued a ministerial decree prohibiting the practice. More government ministries and agencies (e.g., Ministry of Health & Population, Ministry of Social Affairs, Ministry of Education) adopted programs to eradicate female circumcision in Egypt. Despite the governmental efforts, non-governmental efforts have a longer history. However, there is no convincing evidence for their success and effectiveness (Abdel-Tawwab & Hijazi, 2000). Although in general, medical authorities are key players in indicating the risks and dangers females face due to circumcision and genital mutilations, surprisingly most of those who conduct the practice are physicians. This shows the power of customs and traditions to override medical knowledge and convictions.

THE NATIONAL PROGRAM TO COMBAT FEMALE CIRCUMCISION

The National Program to Combat Female Circumcision was enacted by the Egyptian Government since 2003 that was adopted by the NCCM. Later, the goals of the program were expanded to cover family empowerment and combating female circumcision. The goals of the National Plan are to combat FGM/c and to reduce its prevalence and incidence rates. The plan is designed to:

- Enact and enforce laws and ministerial decrees to prevent FGM/c and to punish those who practice it;
- Support the general polices of the government and NGOs that aim to disseminate (scientific, religious, legal) authentic information and facts that can counteract the mythical culture of female circumcision;
- Establish a system for monitoring the practice of FGM at the national level;
- Support and promote a cultural and social environment that encourages the Egyptian family to resist the practice of female circumcision (State Ministry of Population & UN, 2015).

Early Marriage

Early marriage is a common practice in several societies; Egypt is not an exception. Thus, a critical issue facing females in Egypt, specifically poor girls, is early marriage. Early marriage deprives a girl of education and employment opportunities and places her at risk of early and repeat pregnancy, gender-based violence, and sexually transmitted infections (Abdel-Tawwab, 2018). Although the median age of marriage has increased to 21 years for women and 23 years for men, and despite the presence of a law that sets the minimum age for marriage at 18 years, child marriage continues to exist. According to the 2014 Survey of Young People in Egypt (Roushdy & Sieverding, 2015), 21% of married female youth aged 25–29 were married before 18 while 33% of young women residing in rural Upper Egypt were reported to be married before age 18. According to Egypt's Demographic and Health Survey 2014 (Ministry of Health et al., 2015), Marriages among girls aged 15–17 was 6% (See also Abdel-Tawwab, 2018).

Although the prevalence of early marriage appears to be declining among younger cohorts of women, substantial percentages still marry before the legal age of 18. In addition, over a third of married young women report that they had no say in their decision to marry. There is, therefore, a need for continued programs to prevent early marriage and to ensure the protection of young women's right to decide when they marry and to whom (Roushdy & Sieverding, 2015, p. 93).

Young women remain at risk of early marriage, particularly in rural areas and in Upper Egypt. "Female youth in rural areas continue to face the greatest risk of early marriage. Among married female youth aged 30–34 in 2014, 23.0% of those in rural Upper Egypt had been married by age 16 and 11.2% of those in rural Lower Egypt" (Roushdy & Sieverding, 2015, p. 17).

As noted above, the Child Law of 2008 sets the minimum age of marriage in Egypt at 18 years for females and males. Despite this legislation, many girls are still married before the age of 18. In fact, data from Egypt's DHS (2014) reveals that though the percentage of women aged 20–24 years who were married before the age of 18 had declined from 20% in 2000 to 17% in 2005; it remained steady at 17% from 2005 to 2008 and increased slightly to 17% in 2014. In contrast, the percentage of women aged 20–24 years who married before the age of 15 years has remained low and declined steadily during the same time frame, going from 4% in 2000 to 2% in 2014 (UNICEF MENA Regional Office and International Center for Research on Women [ICRW], 2017). The government has shown interest in curbing early marriages with a five-year national strategy to prevent child marriage that was launched in 2014. However, the implementation and momentum for such developments have abated due to the politically restrictive environment (UNICEF MENA Regional Office and IRCW, 2017).

Services to Children

The main service provider for vulnerable children and their families is the Ministry of Social Solidarity (http://www.moss.gov.eg/ar-eg/Pages/default.aspx).[2] Ministry work is

---

[2] Main sources for information on services to children are found on the Ministry of Social Solidarity website: http://www.moss.gov.eg/ar-eg/Pages/default.aspx.

divided into three categories: protection, welfare, and development. The Ministry's services are divided into two major categories: programs and initiatives. Programs are longer in term, while initiatives are occasional and may be dependent on funding.

ElGamal (2014) asserted that there is a positive correlation between the availability of human services and the feeling of social safety for children. The order of importance of the MoSS services is social, health, education, economic, and protection. Direct services are an important sign of the truthfulness and commitment of the state and society toward the welfare of children. A brief description of the main social protection services and programs for children follow.

Cash Assistance Schemas

There are several cash schemas available for children and their families.

CASH ASSISTANCE TO CHILDREN

The Ministry of Social Solidarity offers financial assistance and monthly stipends for children in extraordinary circumstances, including:

1) Orphaned children and children born out-of-wedlock (unknown parents);
2) Children of divorced women in case of their mothers' remarriage or mothers' imprisonment or death;
3) Children of fathers imprisoned for at least three years.

CHILD CONDITIONAL CASH TRANSFER

Children under 18 years of age are granted a scholastic stipend provided that they enroll in basic education until the middle school level. The maximum amount given is 200 Egyptian pounds for eight months from October until May. Eligible children are the same as for the Cash Assistance to Children program (above).

MONTHLY INSURANCE (SOLIDARITY) ASSISTANCE

This subsidy is allocated to poor individuals and families. The amount is based on the family's size. Additional assistance is given to families with children enrolled in basic education or intermediate education. This allowance is given for 8 months from October to May in each academic (school) year. The assistance is offered if the family has no income. If the family has some income, then a supplement is given with (50%) deduction for seasonable employment.

EXCEPTIONAL (EXTRAORDINARY) INSURANCE ASSISTANCE

This is a one-time payment to individuals and families who receive monthly assistance from the insurance fund. This assistance is given in extraordinary circumstances (e.g., education costs, funerals, delivery of children (maximum of two), income supplement projects, etc.). The exceptional assistance requires that beneficiary individuals and families commit to education and visiting health and reproductive health centers as well as striving to improve family resources.

Homeless Children Program

This program is operated by the Ministry of Social Solidarity. The program aims at protecting street and homeless children (http://www.moss.gov.eg//ar-eg/Pages/program-details.aspx?pid=6). It offers protection and rehabilitation and inclusion into society services. The program seeks to prevent new cases and direct intervention. The program covers 10 of the most populated governorates in Egypt based on the 2014 census. According to the ministry, the program will extend its coverage to the remaining four governorates. The target beneficiaries of the program are homeless children. A comprehensive survey of homeless children at the national level is among the main goals of the program. Taking into consideration that NGOs are active contributors in extending help to disadvantaged people in general and to homeless children in particular, the ministry seeks active partnership with civil society organizations and the business world as well as to support non-governmental societies and organizations. As part of government efforts to upgrade services to children in need of protection, the ministry is planning to stipulate standards and quality checks for NGOs.

Our Country Players

This initiative works with homeless and children deprived from family care (http://www.moss.gov.eg//ar-eg/Pages/initiative-details.aspx?pid=10). It is a sport program aimed at preparing children psychologically, socially, and behaviorally to be immersed in society and family. The program is designed after similar experiences by other countries, based on the belief that sports and arts contribute to the development of positive thinking and creativity. Also, the program will help in developing children positively, thus contributing to their character and creativity development. The program has organized several activities that included hundreds of eligible children in various activities and places. It is expected that this program will use sports to attract children to participate in meaningful activities and create an enabling community environment for homeless and street children.

Evaluation of Social Protection for Children

Egypt is one of the developing countries that has a long history of using different social protection tools to maintain social cohesion and promote equitable development, yet the programs offered are highly fragmented, poorly targeted, and suffer from leakages. The system also suffers from misallocation of resources given that large amounts are spent on untargeted subsidies while few resources are allocated for a number of fragmented programs.

Social protection policies, legislation, institutions, programs, and services have been the subject of investigation and scrutiny (Saleh, 2013; ElGamal, 2014; Hosni, 2014; Izzedine, 2016; Rashad & Sharaf, 2018). Despite good intentions and good laws, however, laws do not specify standards of quality for services and care provided for children (Zahran, 2015)—laws on paper are not a reality of life.

Inadequacy of the Child Protection System

The Government of Egypt in its child rights report (SIS, 2010) mentioned several shortcomings and deficiencies in various government and non-government institutions and services provided to children. For example, NGOs' regulations limit their services to homeless and street children up to 14 years of age, thus, children older than 14 have no place to go. Another consideration is that most of these places are for daytime only. The cases of children with disabilities or who need health care are more difficult. This is true for residence houses of NGOs as well as the government ones.

One major cross-cutting deficiency that is noted in the government report (SIS, 2010) is that both government and non-government institutions, including police and the judicial system, is the lack of qualified, trained staff and social workers who are able to deal with children with various problems, especially those children with disabilities and health problems, victims of violence and abuse, and addicts. Therefore, the need is dire for capacity building and training programs for workers with children in various settings, including but not limited to residence houses, care institutions, health services, NGOs, government agencies, and schools.

Egypt's Constitution includes several articles on social protection, and the national budget has allocations for social protection, including child protection. These efforts resulted in laws, regulations, policies, institutions, and programs for the implementation of social protection in general and for child protection in particular (see Tanash, 2011). However, while some successes were achieved, more is needed to be done, taking into consideration the dramatic political and violent changes in Egypt since 2011 that resulted in complicated, pressing socioeconomic conditions.

On the other hand, Sieverding and Selwaness (2012) echoed the need for reformulating the social protection system in Egypt. As noticed in other countries in the region, social protection systems are fragmented and lack efficient coordination. The lack of coordination is a noticeable obstacle for effective social policies and social protection. There are various players in the arena of social welfare in general (e.g., government, private sector, NGOs, civil society organization, the general public). Consequently, the lack of coordination among these players result in wasting resources, weak targeting, inadequate services, and lack of necessary monitoring and evaluation (Olimat, 2005; Tanash, 2011; ElGamal, 2014).

Lack of Coordination and Inefficiency in Using Resources

Several sources (Tanash, 2011; ElGamal, 2014; Al-Hadidy, 2015) noticed the major issue of the lack of coordination among various government and non-government players in the field of child protection. Lack of coordination resulted in misuse of resources, duplication, conflict, and interference, which leads to depriving children of their rights and needed services. Tanash (2011) noticed the lack of proper communication among those players. The problems of lack of coordination and weakness of integrated roles of various organizations and institutions involved in social protection have led to the mismanagement of scarce resources and even in wasting them. The lack of coordination is a lingering hindrance, not only among government and non-government and international organizations but also with each sector. More government institutions lack coordination, and more of the civil society lacks coordination among themselves.

The absence of a holistic and comprehensive strategic vision that can mainstream social protection programs within the general policy of the state is critical. One major cross-cutting issue that is lacking is data (SIS, 2010); there is a need for authentic and reliable data on poverty, unemployment, poor families, disadvantaged populations, homeless and street children, and so on. Most of the pressing issues and concerns of child protection lack proper data, which hinders the effectiveness of policy making and program development and implementation.

Most of the programs on social protection in general, and on child protection in particular, focus on symptoms of the problem and offer direct assistance, while not focusing on developmental and empowerment strategies. Keeping the vulnerable segment of society under the mercy of other people and organizations contributes to their vicious circle of poverty and vulnerability. Therefore, special attention should be given to vulnerable people's empowerment, education, improvement of resilience, and strength in their communities. Sadly, with the deteriorated and complicated socioeconomic changes in Egypt—especially with cuts in subsidies that increase taxes and devaluation of the Egyptian Pounds—the prospects for improvement are grim at least for the foreseeable future.

Recommendations

More attention is needed in the form of adequate policies and programs as well as improving the service delivery mechanisms of the government bodies that deliver them. The Government of Egypt must also review where its actions actually contribute to the vulnerability of the poor. Moreover, *poor* and *vulnerable* are terms that conceal a lot of diversity; the unexamined use of these terms can result in broad generic policies that do not address the real needs of the poor (Sabry, 2005). For a better and an effective social protection system, Bonilla Garcia and Guart (2003) suggested the following measures:

- There should be adequate monitoring, inspection, and enforcement of schemes.
- Adequate resources need to be made available on a sustained basis.
- Integration of social protection schemes should be actively promoted. Responsibilities and resources among the different sectors and levels of government should be clearly established to avoid fragmentation, duplication, or even multiplication of schemes.
- Dissemination and exchange of information should be encouraged. This is essential for the proper monitoring and implementation of social protection objectives. In particular, specific campaigns should be designed for vulnerable and marginalized groups.
- The psychological and sociocultural obstacles that prevent some men and women from realizing their social protection rights should be recognized and addressed in the delivery of benefits and services.
- Vulnerable groups and regions need to be targeted for specific attention.

Specifically, to combat child multidimensional poverty there is a dire need for comprehensive development accompanied with an integrated and effective child-rights-based social protection system (Ministry of Social Solidarity et al., 2017).

References

Abdel-Tawwab, N. (2018). *Married adolescent girls in rural Assiut and Souhag: Limited choices and unfulfilled reproductive health needs* (GIRL Center Dataverse; Version , V2) [Data set], https://doi.org/10.7910/DVN/21IXV4 (Harvard Dataverse).

Abdel-Tawwab, N. and Hijazi, S. (2000). *An analysis to the programs for eradicating female circumcision: The summative report for the project New Horizons in reproductive health.* International Population Council.

Al-Esawi, H. R. (2017). Child labor phenomenon in Egypt: Indicators and implications. *Social Work Journal,* 10(58), 104–123.

Al-Hadidy, M. (2015, February 16–18). *Social protection policies for the welfare and empowerment of the family in Egypt* [Conference presentation]. 17th Annual Conference of the National Center for Social and Criminal Research, Cairo.

Bonilla García, A. and Gruat, J. V. (2003). "Social Protection: A Life Cycle Continuum Investment for Social Justice, Poverty Reduction and Sustainable Development," Version 1.0, ILO, Geneva.

The Central Agency for Public Mobilization and Statistics (CMAS), Egypt and United Nations Children's Fund (UNICEF), Egypt. (2015). Child Poverty in Egypt. (Statistics in Focus: 01). CAPMAS and UNICEF.

The Central Agency for Public Mobilization and Statistics (CAPMAS), Egypt and United Nations Children's Fund (UNICEF), Egypt. (January 2017). *Children in Egypt 2016 Statistical Digest.* CAPMAS and UNICEF.

The Central Agency for Public Mobilization and Statistics (CAPMAS). (2017). *Quarterly bulletin labour force survey.* Available at: http://www.capmas.gov.eg/Pages/Publications.aspx?page_ id=5106.

The Central Agency for Public Mobilization and Statistics (CAPMAS). (2019). *Egypt in numbers.* CAPMAS.

The Central Agency for Public Mobilization and Statistics (CAPMAS). (2022). Current Population. Retrieved on June 24, 2022, https://www.capmas.gov.eg/HomePage.aspx.

Cockburn, J., El Lahga A.-R., Robichaud, V., Tiberti, L., and Zaki, C. (2014). *Enhancing equity for children in the context of the reform of energy subsidies in Egypt.* A.R.E. Ministry of Finance, and UNICEF.

ElGamal, A. A. (2014). Human service as an approach to fulfil social safety for homeless children: A study on Risalah Society for Charity and its branches. *Journal of Studies in Social Work and Human Sciences, Faculty of Social Work, Helwan University -Egypt.* Volume 36, Part 15, 3907-3975-3907.

Elkoussi, A. and Bakheet, S. (2011). Volatile substance misuse among street children in Upper Egypt. *Substance use and misuse*, 46, 35–39.

ESCWA. (2018). *Survey of economic and social developments in the Arab region 2017–2018*. ESCWA.

Home Office. (2017). *Country policy and information note Egypt: Background information, including actors of protection, and internal relocation*. Home Office.

Hosni, H. M. (2014). Homeless children welfare organizations current status and prospects. *Social Work Journal*, July, (52), 469–492.

Izzedine, I. (2016). Evaluating the effectiveness of the role of the social work organizer in implementing child social policies: Non-governmental social care organization for homeless children. *Social Work Journal (the Egyptian Social Workers Society-Egypt)*, 55, 57.

Ministry of Health and Population. (2014). *Egypt's demographic and health survey 2014: Main findings*. Ministry of Health and Population.

Ministry of Health and Population, El-Zanaty and Associates, and ICF International. (2015). *Egypt demographic and health survey 2014*. Ministry of Health and Population and ICF International.

Ministry of Health and Population and NCCM. (2018). *Ending violence against children in Egypt national strategic framework*. The National Strategy.

Ministry of Manpower and ILO. (2018). *National action plan for combating the worst forms of child labour in Egypt and supporting family (2018–2025)*. International Labour Organization.

Ministry of Social Solidarity, CAPMAS, and UNICEF. (2017). *Understanding child multidimensional poverty in Egypt*. Ministry of Social Solidarity, CAPMAS, and UNICEF.

National Council for Childhood and Motherhood (NCCM) and UNICEF. (2015). Violence against Children in Egypt. A Quantitative Survey and Qualitative Study in Cairo, Alexandria and Assiut, NCCM and UNICEF Egypt, Cairo.

National Population Council, UNFPA, and Baseera. (2016). *Analysis of the demographic situation—Egypt 2016*, the Egyptian Center for Public Opinion Research.

Nazier, H. and Ramadan, R. (2016). *Women's participation in labor market in Egypt: Constraints and opportunities*. ERF Working Paper, No. 999. Economic Research Forum.

NCCM. (n.d.). *NCCM mandate and functions*. Available at: http://www.nccm-egypt.org/e3/e1101/index_eng.html.

Olimat, H. S. (2005, June 29–30). *The successive changes to social safety net in Jordan, yet leaky?* [Presentation]. World Bank and Lebanese Council of Ministers workshop "Poverty alleviation," Beirut.

Olimat, H. S. (2018). Child poverty and youth unemployment in Jordan. *Poverty and Public Policy*, 10(3), 317–337.

Osman, M. (2016). *Analyzing population situation in Egypt—2016*. The National Population Council, UNFPA and Baseera.

Pereznieto, P., Marcus, R., and Cullen, E. (2011). *Children and social protection in the Middle East and North Africa* (Project Briefing No 64). Overseas Development Institute.

Rashad, A. S. and Sharaf, M. F. (2018). Economic growth and child malnutrition in Egypt: New Evidence from National Demographic and Health Survey. *Social Indicators Research*, 135(2), 769–795.

Ray, P., Davey, C., and Nolan, P. (2011). *Still on the street–still short of rights: Analysis of Policy and Programmes Related to Street-involved Children*. Consortium for Street Children and Plan Geneva.

Roushdy, R. and Sieverding, M. (2015). *Panel survey of young people in Egypt 2014: Generating evidence for policy, programs, and research*. Population Council.

Sabry, S. (2005). The social aid and assistance programme of the Government of Egypt: A critical review. *Environment & Urbanization*, 17(2), 27–41.

Saleh, E. M. (2008). *The extent of implementing labor laws on child labor in firms in urban governorates in Arab Republic of Egypt: Population research and studies*, 76, 1–20.

Saleh, E. M. (2013). Child labor legislation between legal texts and actual reality in Arab Republic of Egypt—2010. *Population Research and Studies*, 86, 195–233.

Sieverding, M. and Selwaness, I. (2012) "Social protection in Egypt: A policy overview." Gender and Work in the MENA Region Working Paper no. 23. Population Council.

SIS. (2009). *Declaration of the second decade for the protection and welfare of the Egyptian child, 2000–2010*. Available at: http://www.sis.gov.eg/Story/1690/Declaration-of-the-Second-Decade-for-the-Protection-and-Welfare-of-the-Egyptian-Child%2c2000-2010?lang=en-us.

SIS. (2010). *Report submitted by Arab Republic of Egypt on the measures taken to implement the optional protocol of CRC on child trafficking and Exploiting children in prostitution and pornography.* United Nations, Convention on the Rights of the Child.

State Ministry of Population and UN. (2015). *The national strategy to combat female circumcision.* State Ministry of Population.

Tanash, Osama Ali El-Sayed Ahmed. (2011). Social protection in Egypt towards an integrated social policy. *The Scientific Journal of Economics and Trade*, 4, 744–776. Retrieved from http://search.mandumah.com/Record/113530.

UN. (1989). *Convention on the rights of the child.* Available at: https://www.unicef.org/child-rights-convention/convention-text.

United Nations Children's Fund (UNICEF). (2018, October). *Child malnutrition: Unfolding the situation in Egypt. Data Snapshot*, (1). UNICEF.

United Nations Children's Fund (UNICEF) Middle East and North Africa Regional Office in collaboration with the International Center for Research on Women (IRCW). (2017). 'Child Marriage in the Middle East and North Africa – Egypt Country Brief', 2017. UNICEF & IRCW.

WHO. (2018). *Malnutrition: Key facts.* Available at: https://www.who.int/news-room/fact-sheets/detail/malnutrition. Geneva: WHO.

Zahran, S. A. (2015). Formulating social care policies for homeless children. *Journal of Social Work*, 54, 307–334. 699706/Record/com.mandumah.search://hN.

Child Protection Systems in Ghana

Mavis Dako-Gyeke, Abigail Adubea Mills, *and* Doris Akyere Boateng

Abstract

This chapter discusses the child protection systems in Ghana. Extended family still participates in the protection and support activities for children in the possibility of stretching the care environment of children beyond their nuclear family. Building a protective environment for children is indispensable for their optimal growth and development since it ensures that suffering children are easier to identify and protect. Additionally, child protection encompasses prevention and response to violence, neglect, abuse, and exploitation against children. However, the implementation of laws for the protection of children remained weak. Some of the provisions of the Children's Act based on the UNCRC were considered socio-culturally unsuitable for Ghana.

Key Words: Ghana, extended family, child protection, violence, exploitation, laws, Children's Act, UNCRC

Introduction

Many countries around the world, including Ghana, have designed and implemented measures and structures or systems that aim to protect children from experiencing violence, neglect, abuse, and exploitation, and to provide a response to child maltreatment. Although formal child protection systems exist in Ghana, the extended family still participates in the protection and support activities for children in view of the fact that the care environment of children goes beyond the nuclear family. Building a protective environment for children is indispensable for their optimal growth and development because it ensures that children exposed to suffering are easily identified and protected.

History of Child Protection Policy Enactment in Ghana

Child protection encompasses prevention and response to violence, neglect, abuse, and exploitation against children, including commercial sexual exploitation, trafficking, child labor, and injurious traditional practices, like female genital mutilation/cutting and child marriage (UNICEF, 2006). Given that a strengthened child protection system is likely to guarantee justice for all children, international, regional, and national conventions and agreements have been enacted to protect children. The Convention on the Rights of the Child (CRC, 1989) emphasizes the fundamental rights of children, which include the right to be protected from economic exploitation and harmful work, from all forms of sexual exploitation and abuse, and from physical or mental violence (UN, 2013). Illustrating Ghana's commitment and responsibilities towards ensuring the rights of children, the country was the first to ratify the CRC in 1990. Subsequent to the ratification of the CRC, governments were required to put measures in place to ensure that children in their respective countries were able to enjoy the rights stipulated in the CRC.

Key among the requirements of the CRC was the harmonization of all national laws with the Convention's standards. The process was facilitated by the return to democracy in Ghana in 1992 and the passage of the 1992 Constitution by Parliament. The Ghanaian Constitution thus included specific provisions on the rights of children (Articles 25, 26, and 28). In 1995, the government initiated a comprehensive law reform process to guarantee compatibility between national laws and the CRC. The exercise resulted in the establishment of the Law Reform Advisory Committee by the Ghana National Commission on Children, to review the status of, and laws regarding, children (Agbényiga, 2012). The committee recommended the enactment of a comprehensive law that would ensure prompt and effective administration of justice for children. The passage of the Children's Act (Act 560) in 1998 was the result of the recommendation by the committee.

The Children's Act, 1998 (Act 560) merged all laws relating to children into a single, child-focused legislation and at the same time integrated the CRC into the country's national laws. The Act was enforced in 1999 and has since been the major point of reference for all child-related actions. After the Children's Act, other policies were designed and implemented to serve numerous purposes that aim at enhancing children's rights and protection. Table 35.1 shows some of the major international and national child protection laws that have been ratified or introduced in Ghana since 1990.

Despite Ghana's comprehensive child welfare policies, many children continue to experience various forms of abuse, violence, neglect, maltreatment, and exploitation, which could have adverse effects on their growth, development, and well-being. Many children are subjected to various forms of abuse and exploitation due to the limited child protection system (Dako-Gyeke, 2018; Twum-Danso, 2012). In addition, many challenges associated with the implementation of child protection policies have contributed to their poor performance, including institutional constraints (particularly lack of or limited resources), absence of inter-agency coordination, and inadequate awareness of the Children's Act on the part of many parents/guardians, professionals, policymakers, and the general public (Twum-Danso, 2012).

Children in Vulnerable Circumstances

Although Ghana has enacted laws for the protection of children, implementation remains weak (UNICEF, 2013). Thus, child protection policies seem to be more relevant on paper than in practice, and as a result, many children are left inadequately protected. For

Table 35.1 International and national child protection laws ratified or introduced in Ghana since 1990

Law	Year of enactment	A key improvement or issue addressed by the Act
Criminal Code (Amendment) Act (Act 484)	1994	Recognizes and includes female genital mutilation as an offence punishable by law and abolishes the practice.
Criminal Code (Amendment) Act (Act 554)	1998	Increases age of criminal and sexual responsibility; includes specific offence of indecent assault and revised provisions regarding sexual offences. Also abolishes customary or ritual servitude, e.g., *trokosi*
Children's Act (Act 560)	1998	Harmonized child care legislation in Ghana to conform to the United Nations Convention on the Rights of the Child
UN/ILO Convention on the Worst Forms of Child Labor	1999	Provides guidance for governments on hazardous child labor activities which should be prohibited in their countries
The Child Rights Regulations (Legislative Instrument, LI 1705)	2003	Provides the necessary measures for the establishment and maintenance of residential homes and regulates the activities of these residential homes for the best interest of children in Ghana.
Labor Act (Act 651)	2003	Amends and consolidates the laws relating to labor, employers, trade unions, and industrial relations, and establishes a National Labor Commission to provide for matters related to these.
Juvenile Justice Act (Act 653)	2003	Provides a juvenile justice system to protect the rights of juveniles, ensures an appropriate response to juvenile offenders, and makes legal provisions for young offenders.
National Gender and Children's Policy	2004	Sets out a wide range of strategies for the improvement of living standards of women and children. Seeks the elimination of child labor, protection of children and young persons; and ensure quality of opportunity and treatment
Early Childhood Care and Development Policy	2004	Promotes holistic early childhood development and program packages that address the physical, mental, social, moral, and spiritual needs of the child.

Table 35.1 *Continued*

Law	Year of enactment	A key improvement or issue addressed by the Act
Human Trafficking Act (Act 694)	2005	Prevents and combats human trafficking, protects and assists victims of trafficking, investigates and prosecutes offenders of human trafficking, and collaborates with and promotes cooperation among stakeholders and civil society groups.
National Disability Act (Act 715)	2006	Makes provisions for persons with disability, promotes and protectes the rights of persons with disabilities (PWDs), and ensures their equitable and effective participation and inclusion in Ghanaian society at all levels.
Domestic Violence Act (Act 732)	2007	Defines domestic violence to include various forms of economic abuse, in addition to more conventional definitions of sexual and physical violence. Provides a working definition of domestic violence and outlines a comprehensive legal framework for the prevention of and protection against domestic violence.
National Plan of Action for the Elimination of the Worst Forms of Child Labor	2008–2015	Addresses the high number of children involved in child labor and seeks to eliminate the worst forms of child labor in Ghana
National Plan of Action for Orphans and Vulnerable Children	2010–2012	Promotes the welfare, care, and protection of children as provided in the Constitution and the provisions of the Children's Act through social measures such as cash transfers, improves access to education and health.
Child and Family Welfare Policy	2015	The policy has the objective to design child and family welfare programs and activities to more effectively protect children from all forms of violence, abuse, neglect, and exploitation, and to ensure an effective coordination of the child and family welfare service at all levels.

instance, the Children's Act is based on the CRC with some provisions that are considered socio-culturally unsuitable for Ghana. The CRC and Children's Act stipulate that:

> No person shall deprive a child capable of forming views the right to express an opinion, to be listened to and to participate in decisions which affect his wellbeing, the opinion of the child being given due weight in accordance with the age and maturity of the child.

While this is an important clause in dealing with matters concerning children, many children in Ghana are socialized to defer to adults and would hardly voice an opinion even in matters concerning their own well-being. Besides, many families and children do not generally understand abusive situations and are therefore unable to make choices that would prevent and respond to situations that expose children to risk. In consequence, levels of violence, exploitation, maltreatment, and abuse of children, including sexual abuse, continue to be high, with over 90% of children reported to have experienced physical violence, both at home and school settings (UNICEF, 2013). The Ghana 2011 Multiple Indicator Cluster Survey (MICS) findings revealed that 94% of children aged 2–14 years were subjected to some form of violent (physical and/or psychological) disciplinary method. Also, 14% of children aged 2–14 years were subjected to severe physical punishment and 73% to minor punishment (Ghana Statistical Service, 2012).

It is important to emphasize that, compared to those on boys, abuses inflicted on girls are likely to have more far-reaching consequences because girls seem to be more vulnerable than boys in comparable situations. Findings from a nationwide child protection baseline study conducted by UNICEF in 2012 indicated that prevailing socio-cultural attitudes attributed higher social status and more power to males than females. Sexual abuse and exploitation of girls were reported in every region. Even though traditional cultural practices echo the values and beliefs held by members of ethnic groups in Ghana, some of these are harmful and could negatively affect the physical, mental and socioemotional health of girls. These harmful cultural practices are more predominant in rural areas where they are deeply rooted. Many girls suffered from abusive and exploitative conditions, some of which were rooted in harmful cultural values and practices, such as female genital mutilation, child marriage, and *trokosi* (MoGCSP, 2014).

Trokosi is a traditional custom that involves the ritual servitude of girls. *Trokosi* (meaning slaves of the gods), is practiced in some southeastern communities of the Volta Region (Ame, 2012). In this practice, girls sometimes as young as 3 years old are abandoned at a shrine to atone for a crime committed by other family members, most often males (Ame, 2012). The practice is part of the traditional, religious, and crime-control system of the Ewes, the main ethnic group that occupies southeastern Ghana and the southern parts of neighboring Togo and Benin. It takes the form of girls having to spend a few years at the shrine. Unfortunately, a few years typically turns into a lifetime of servitude (Ame, 2012).

In 2013, there were about 4,000 to 6,000 (0.02%–0.03%) women and children under bondage as *trokosi* slaves in Ghana (Mistiaen, 2013).

Notwithstanding Ghana's efforts aimed at eliminating FGM/C among girls by 2030 (UNICEF, 2012), there are regional differences with high prevalence rates in the Upper West (41%) and Upper East (28%) regions as indicated by the 2011 MICS (Ghana Statistical Service, 2012). In addition, a study conducted in 2012 revealed that 50% of girls under age 15 had been subjected to FGM/C in the Bawku municipality in the Upper East region of Ghana (UNICEF, 2012).

Child marriage is another dangerous traditional practice that is common among girls and could have dire consequences for their health, as well as their physical, emotional, and cognitive development. Child marriage denies girls of their childhood, interrupts their education, and restricts their ability to participate in economic and social activities (UNICEF, 2014). It is an issue of public concern because both the 1992 Constitution and the 1998 Children's Act of Ghana set the legal age for marriage at 18 years for girls and boys, which makes the practice illegal. Nonetheless, the 2010 Population and Housing Census report revealed that over 5% of children aged 12–17 were married while 0.8% were in informal or consensual unions (Ghana Statistical Service, 2012). Additionally, the MICS data indicated that among women aged 15–49 years who were married, 6% were married before the age of 15, and 27% were married before age 18; marriages before age 15 in rural areas were 8% and 4% in urban areas (Ghana Statistical Service, 2012). The statistics suggest that the phenomenon is prevalent in many regions of the country and therefore needs urgent attention.

Child labor is prevalent in Ghana even though the government and civil society organizations have made efforts to address these problems. Most often, children engaged in economic activities and other forms of hazardous work in the areas of agriculture, stone-quarrying, hawking, and artisanal activities are exposed to various forms of abuse in the workplace. The sixth round of the Ghana Living Standards Survey (GLSS 6) Child Labor Report indicated that in 2013, 21.8% of children aged 5–17 years were engaged in child labor, and this was higher in rural areas as compared to urban areas with 30.2% and 12.4%, respectively (Ghana Statistical Service, 2014). The report further revealed that of the children aged 5–17 years who participated in economic activities, 76.4% were involved in child labor, out of which 49.7% participated in hazardous work. In addition, about 9 in 10 (91%) children who suffered abuses were engaged in child labor while 87.4% of them worked under hazardous conditions.

Another issue of concern is child trafficking, which affects a startling proportion of children (49,000/10,467,808, aged 0–17 years) in Ghana (Adepoju, 2005). Many trafficked children engage in agriculture (farming and fishing), gold mining, stone quarrying, manufacturing, hospitality, commercial sex industries, and domestic labor. Ironically, affected children are generally treated as commodities due to the exchange of money.

Buyers of the children are likely to exploit them to the fullest by engaging them in many hours of daily work and this could lead to physical and emotional abuses, among others.

A child protection baseline study conducted in 2012 found that children are mainly trafficked for child labor in five regions: Eastern, Greater Accra, Upper East, Volta, and Western (UNICEF, 2012). Further, anecdotal data gathered during the study indicated that money earned by trafficked children was often taken by adults, including trafficking agents and their parents. The children received nothing more than their food and board, which tended to be of poor quality (UNICEF, 2012). Besides, the Anti-Human Trafficking Unit of the Ghana Police Service reported 238 child-trafficking-related investigations and referred 21 individuals for prosecution for trafficking-related crimes in 2015 (US Department of State, 2016).

In Ghana, street living is another menace with adverse effects on children's development and well-being. Many children live and work on the streets, especially in urban areas of the country. Not all of these children are orphans though, as most of them have either migrated or were brought into the cities by other adults for work. This notwithstanding, these children remain invisible as they are among the most difficult to protect, as well as the hardest to reach in terms of service provision, such as education and healthcare (UNICEF, 2006). While it is difficult to estimate the number of street children in Ghana due to their itinerant lifestyles, a study conducted by Boakye-Boaten (2008) estimated that there were about 20,000 street children (out of an estimated 1.4 million children) in Accra, the capital city of Ghana (Ghana Statistical Service, 2012). The number of street children is likely to be higher since the phenomenon is prevalent in other parts of the country, particularly regional capitals. Many street children are vulnerable to different forms of violence, exploitation, maltreatment, and abuse, and are exposed to the vagaries of the weather. They experience abuses ranging from physical to sexual as they are often raped, coerced into prostitution, exploited by strangers, and their savings are usually stolen as they are not safely kept (Boakye-Boaten, 2011).

Moreover, more than 4,000 children in Ghana live in residential facilities, generally referred to as orphanages (UNICEF, 2013). Although the statistics on the total number of children in care in Ghana are not readily available, orphanages constitute the primary care facilities for children who require care outside the extended family, with a few being in foster care. Generally, many children are placed in orphanages due to poverty, and in these settings they may encounter challenges like depersonalization (through lack of personal belongings, care relationships, or symbols of individuality), rigorous routines, group treatment, and seclusion from wider society (UNICEF, 2016). Moreover, Ghana has a high rate of adoption of children, including inter-country adoptions that are often shrouded in secrecy due to lack of transparency and control in the processes and procedures (UNICEF, 2013).

Children in correctional facilities are vulnerable to many of the same abuses as children in residential facilities, as well as the criminal guilt that is associated with them;

they suffer triple vulnerability—as children, criminals, and detainees (Ayete-Nyampong, 2012). Given the challenges that many juvenile offenders encounter in correctional facilities, some scholars (e.g., Ayete-Nyampong, 2012) have questioned whether human rights promotion in the country apply to juvenile offenders too. The few correctional facilities in the country are not well-resourced, suffering from inadequate funding and professional staff, poor quality food and accommodations, and lack of access to education by the children. Of major concern is the fact that child offenders are usually stigmatized and discriminated against by society as they are often perceived as criminals. Also, generally, the criminal justice system and other policing agencies view juvenile offenders as uncontrollable, defiant, and stubborn, and therefore excessively target and monitor them (Trulson, 2007). These opinions could result in unjust treatment, which may expose the juveniles to maltreatment, abuse, and neglect with adverse consequences for their development and well-being.

Bases of Social Allocations

Generally, a person under 18 years of age is considered a child in Ghana (Children's Act, 1998, Act 560) and thus all policies and legal instruments pertaining to children in the country apply as such. In other words, being below the age of 18 years could be considered the primary eligibility criterion for the application of child-related laws and policies. Beyond the age factor, however, there are other parameters that add to a child's eligibility to access certain services. The first key instrument to be examined is the Children's Act, 1998 (Act 560), which resulted from one of the earliest efforts to protect children's rights in Ghana.

Legal Protections for Children's Rights

The Children's Act, 1998 (Act 560) mandates that district social welfare officers[1] remove children in need of protection from their homes, conduct investigations, and prepare reports for the Family Tribunal, as well as make decisions and arrangements for foster care and institutional placements (Child Frontiers, 2011). Section 16 of the Act 560 (sub-section 1) states that "the District Assembly shall protect the welfare and promote the rights of children within its area of authority and shall ensure that within the district, governmental agencies liaise with each other in matters concerning children." The Department of Social Welfare (DSW), under the Ministry of Children, Gender and Social Protection (MoGCSP), is responsible for investigating cases of children's rights violations. Any person with information on child abuse or a child in need of care and protection can report to the Department (Children's Act of Ghana, Act 560, section 17).

---

[1] In Ghana, not all social welfare officers are necessarily social workers. There are some people who may be working in the provision of social welfare services but do not have the academic qualification to be called social workers.

The Children's Act (1998, Act 560) defines a child in need of care and protection to cover a wide range of descriptions, such as a child who: is an orphan or has been deserted by his or her relatives; has been neglected or ill-treated by the person under whose care and custody the child is; has a parent or guardian who does not exercise proper guardianship; is destitute; or is under the care of a parent or guardian who, by reason of criminal or drunken habits, is unfit to have the care of the child. Additional descriptions include: a child who is wandering and has no home or settled place of abode or visible means of subsistence, is begging or receiving alms, accompanies any person when that person is begging or receiving alms, or frequents the company of a person noted to have an immoral lifestyle (such as a reputed thief or commercial sex worker).

Furthermore, in section 13 (1) of the Children's Act (Act 560, 1998), it is stated that:

> No person shall subject a child to torture or other cruel, inhuman or degrading treatment or punishment including any cultural practice which dehumanises or is injurious to the physical and mental well-being of a child.

The afore-mentioned legal provision sums up the need for all Ghanaian children to be protected from harmful customary practices such as forced marriage, *trokosi*, FGM/C, and child slavery, among others. Other laws in Ghana which protect children in this regard are the Criminal Code (Amendment) Act 1994 (Act 484) and the Criminal Code (Amendment) Act 1998 (Act 554), which abolish FGM/C and *trokosi*, respectively. These amendments to the Criminal Code of Ghana are applied when a child's rights are violated through these cultural practices. While FGM/C is a phenomenon applying to females, it is noteworthy that victims of *trokosi* are mostly girls as well. This makes girls more vulnerable, and, as such, a lot of focus is placed on protecting them through these legal provisions.

The Domestic Violence Act, 2007

Another major legislation enacted in Ghana which clearly identifies children as one of the main groups that require protection is the Domestic Violence Act (Act 732, 2007). This law outlines some of the actions that constitute abuse or violence in domestic relationships and provides directives on how matters pertaining to domestic violence, including those involving children, should be addressed. Reports about domestic violence may be filed with the police by various categories of people, including the victims themselves (in the case of a child, with assistance from a next friend), a social worker, probation officer or healthcare provider, the victim's family member, or any other person mandated to represent the victim in case the victim is deceased. Upon filing the complaint, the victim is entitled to services, such as free medical treatment where necessary and provision of a safe place (if required by the victim), among others. Article 18 of the Domestic Violence Act states that "where there is a need for special protection for a child, the Court may refer matters concerned with the temporary custody of a child in a situation of domestic violence, to a Family Tribunal." Family Tribunals are established under the Courts Act, 1993 (Act 459) and "have jurisdiction in matters concerning parentage, custody, access and maintenance of children" (Children's Act, 1998, Act 560, section 35).

Child Labor

The UN/ILO Convention on the Worst Forms of Child Labor (Convention 182, 1999) and the Labor Act 2003 (Act 651) are among other legal instruments that directly address child labor issues in Ghana. The worst forms of child labor include but are not limited to all forms of slavery, child trafficking, sexual abuse and commercial sex work, children used in armed conflict, children used to traffic drugs, and "work which, by its nature or the circumstances in which it is carried out, is likely to harm the health, safety or morals of children" (ILO Convention 182, 1999, Article 3). Ghana, like other countries that have signed the ILO Convention on the elimination of worst forms of child labor, is enjoined to identify and reach out to children at special risk, and also to take account of the special situation of girls. Whereas both boys and girls experience trafficking and labor exploitation, girls in particular tend to be sexually exploited more than boys.

The Human Trafficking Act, 2005

The Department of Social Welfare, along with several NGOs, work at the community, district, and national levels to identify and rescue children who have been exploited or who are at special risk. Unfortunately, some of these children are never reached. A related legislation, the Human Trafficking Act, 2005 (Act 694), section 4, highlights the fact that in the case of child trafficking, consent cannot be used as defense during prosecution, whether given by the child, parent(s) or guardian(s). This is key in dealing with child trafficking matters because in many instances, the traffickers may not use force at the point of taking the child, but may have received consent from either the child, the parent, or guardian.

The Juvenile Justice Act, 2003

When dealing with children who come into conflict with the law, Ghana has the Juvenile Justice Act of 2003 (Act 653), which was passed to provide a child-friendly justice system to protect the rights of children and to ensure an appropriate response to juvenile offenders. Section 1, sub-section (2) of the Juvenile Justice Act states that "a juvenile shall be dealt with in a manner which is different from an adult, except under exceptional circumstances under section 17." The exceptions in Section 17 are provided in sub-sections 2, 3, and 4, and cover situations where a juvenile court is unavailable to process bail, where a charge has been made jointly against a juvenile and a person who has attained the age of 18 years, and where the charged offence would be punishable by death if it had been committed by an adult. Apart from these instances, juvenile offenders are to be tried in juvenile courts.

Children with Disabilities

Children with disabilities, orphans, and other vulnerable children constitute additional special categories of children who are protected by various legal instruments and policies. Key among these are the National Disability Act of 2006 (Act 715), the Children's Act, the National Plan of Action for Orphans and Vulnerable Children (2010–2012), as well as the Child and Family Welfare Policy (2015). Specific provisions relating to children in the Disability Act focus on education. Sections 16 and 17 provide that children with disabilities shall be enrolled in school, and that failure of a guardian to do so will attract punishment. Educational institutions are also enjoined to provide the necessary facilities and equipment that will enable children with disabilities to fully benefit from the school or institution. The National Plan of Action for Orphans and Vulnerable Children (2010–2012) and the Child and Family Welfare Policy (2015) address various susceptibilities that orphans and other vulnerable children, like children living on the streets or those encountering various forms of abuse, may encounter. The next section throws more light on the nature of social provisions allocated to protect children in Ghana.

Nature of Social Provisions Allocated to Protect Children

The Child and Family Welfare System in Ghana is comprised of "laws and policies, programs, services, practices and structures designed to promote the well-being of children by ensuring safety and protection from harm; achieving permanency and strengthening families to care for their children successfully" (MoGCSP, 2015, p. vii). There are many formal and informal actors involved in child protection in Ghana, and these include families, communities, government, traditional authorities, civil society, private organizations, and religious bodies, as well as children themselves.

Since the year 2000, a range of social protection programs have been rolled out in Ghana, many with a specific focus on children. These include social assistance programs, notably the School Feeding Programme, the Education Capitation Grant (ECG) and the Livelihood Empowerment Against Poverty (LEAP) cash transfer program, which was launched in March 2008. There have also been social insurance schemes, in particular the National Health Insurance Scheme (NHIS), which is substantially supported by the government, along with a range of payment exemptions for groups considered to be vulnerable in the society, such as pregnant and postpartum women and children under 18 years of age. In addition to these programs, several social welfare services, including programs to prevent and respond to child protection problems, such as child labor, trafficking, and sexual exploitation have also been put in place (UNICEF, 2009, pp. 11–12).

In 2015, MoGCSP launched the Child and Family Welfare policy, whose main objectives were to:

> design child and family welfare programmes and activities to more effectively prevent and protect children from all forms of violence, abuse, neglect and exploitation; ensure effective

coordination of the child and family welfare system at all levels; empower children and families to better understand abusive situations and make choices to prevent and respond to situations of risk; build capacity of institutions and service providers to ensure quality of services for children and families in urban and rural areas; reform existing laws and policies to conform to the Child and Family Welfare system; and ensure provision of adequate human, technical and financial resources required for the functioning of the Child and Family Welfare system at all levels. (MoGCSP, 2015, p. x)

The numerous legislations that have been previously discussed in this chapter, as well as programs like the LEAP, NHIS, School Feeding Programme, among others, have resulted in the provision of various services for children, and by extension, their families. Extant research studies have reported some of the benefits of the School Feeding Programme—improvement in school attendance, learning, and children's physical and psycho-social health (Alderman & Bundy, 2011; Gelli et al., 2016). Pertaining to the NHIS, however, Williams and colleagues (2017) noted that within the scheme, socially excluded children did not have equal access due to a range of challenges. Key among these challenges are the linkage of children's enrolment to parental membership, as well as additional registration fees, which very poor families are unable to pay. Thus, de-linking of premium waiver entitlements from parental membership and the removal of additional registration fees will go a long way to help children who are from very poor families (Williams et al., 2017).

In connection with LEAP cash transfer, the selection of qualified recipients is based on three sets of criteria: 1) single parents with orphaned or vulnerable children, particularly children affected by AIDS; 2) persons with extreme disability who are not in any productive capacity; and 3) the extremely poor aged 65 years and above (Debrah, 2013, p. 50). The cash transfers help caregivers to provide food, clothing, and other basic needs for children in their care, while part of the money is used in some cases to offset educational expenses, such as school fees, uniforms, and books (Roelen et al., 2015). The LEAP has been found to play a crucial role in keeping children with their parents by ensuring that parents could provide adequate shelter for their children, and not give them away as a result of accommodation challenges (Roelen et al., 2015, p. 80).

Social protection for children in Ghana merges formal and informal structures to provide for the needs of children. While programs such as LEAP, NHIS, and the School Feeding Programme are ongoing, they are limited in terms of coverage and, as a result, may not be reaching all socially excluded children. In spite of the challenges associated with the administration of these interventions, some children in need of protection have been provided with the needed services. The bigger challenge relates to how many or all children, especially those in difficult situations, may be contacted and served.

Methods for the Delivery of Child Protection Services

The government of Ghana has consistently shown commitment to the protection of children in the ratification and passage of several instruments since the 1990s. In addition to these, there has been some monitoring and evaluation of programs and policies in order to identify loopholes, strengthen existing systems, and make suggestions for the improvement of service provision. Delivery of child protection services in Ghana has often been vested in government ministries, departments, and agencies, as well as non-state actors, such as NGOs and international development partners that promote the protection of children's rights (UNDP, 2010). Typically, the main entry points into the formal child protection system are the police and social welfare agencies, although informal structures exist as well, such as community volunteers, community-based organizations, and traditional leaders (MoGCSP, 2015). Nonetheless, these institutions are hampered by lack of financial and human resources to effectively deliver services. Community structures—mostly led by family heads, religious leaders, chiefs, queen mothers,[2] and assembly members—often emphasize compensation, reconciliation, and restoration of harmony in the family and community over the needs of the child who has been harmed (MoGCSP, 2015, p. x).

While both formal and informal institutions provide invaluable services to protect and secure the rights of children, their activities are largely uncoordinated, and this often results in replication of projects and programs (UNICEF, 2015). The Children's Act mandates District Assemblies with the overall responsibility to protect the welfare and promote the rights of children in their areas, but does little to spell out terms that should govern the delivery of child welfare services, or the types of prevention and family support services that should be made available. Consequently, many of the child protection interventions tend to be reactive in nature, with limited focus on protection and prevention (Child Frontiers, 2011). At the national level, the Department of Children, under MoGCSP, has been given the responsibility of implementing programs and activities affecting children in Ghana. Its mandate is to improve the welfare of children and promote their full integration into the development process through advocacy, research, policy formulation, networking and collaborating with stakeholders in a well-resourced environment (MoGCSP, 2015).

In addition to the Department of Children, the DSW is mainly responsible for the delivery of child and family welfare services. The DSW is staffed by social workers, welfare and probation officers, and community development officers who provide child protection services at the district and community levels. With over 170 offices across the country, the DSW is better positioned to provide decentralized services in the areas of child justice, family welfare, and general welfare issues in the local communities (Child Frontiers, 2011). At the district level, delivery of child protection services is undertaken by a number

---

[2] Queen mothers are female traditional leaders.

of private organizations in addition to the Ministries, Municipal, and District Assemblies (MMDAs). The MMDAs are mandated by government to spearhead the implementation of the Child and Family Welfare Policy and to facilitate the mainstreaming of child protection issues into the country's Medium-Term Development Plans (MoGSCP, 2014). Although there is no clear structure for delivery of social welfare and child justice services, many of these organizations focus on specific child protection issues only and do not have clear linkages to district-level social welfare authorities (UNICEF, 2015).

The activities of formal child protection agencies and institutions are complemented by community-based structures, such as traditional authorities, comprising chiefs, queen mothers, family elders, teachers, community health workers, and women's groups, who could be co-opted as part of the child protection service delivery system in communities. Traditional rulers, especially queen mothers, play important roles in their local communities, particularly in matters relating to the general welfare of community members (Mensah et al., 2014). With respect to child protection, queen mothers investigate and address child abuse and related cases, and conduct informal, community-based mediation. They also have the mandate to issue punishment and prevention orders. However, the authority of the queen mother is vested in tradition and geographically bound and can therefore be limited in scope and effectiveness.

The invaluable contribution of civil society and international development organizations cannot be overlooked in the delivery of child protection services in Ghana. These organizations work both at the national and community levels to prevent and protect children from abuse, exploitation, violence and other harmful practices, as well as general vulnerabilities. They commission research into social and traditional practices that are considered harmful to children and make recommendations to government on how to address such issues. Some of the key civil society and international development organizations that operate in the country are UNICEF, PLAN Ghana, Action Aid, World Vision, and numerous local NGOs that together form the Ghana NGOs Coalition on the Rights of the Child (GNCRC). The GNCRC is a network of over 60 NGOs that work with or for children, and their activities impact on the rights of children (GNCRC, 2014).

The Child and Family Welfare Policy (2015) was formulated to address the lack of a clear national policy framework for child and family welfare services in the country. The child protection system used to be guided largely by a series of issue-specific national plans of actions, which were overlapping and duplicative both in terms of the target group covered and the types of activities that are carried out. While a significant amount of training has been undertaken across the country on specific child protection issues, there is still the need for standardized, certificate-based training for all stakeholders in child protection, especially the police, social workers, probation officers, teachers, and health workers. With the passage of the Child and Family Welfare Policy (2014), the provision of adequate resources for the effective protection of the child is expected to be assured at the national, district and community levels. Nevertheless, there is an urgent need for the creation of clear coordination pathways in the delivery of child protection services to prevent duplication and overlap of projects and programs, as well as reduce the waste of resources that result from such overlaps.

Financing Child Protection Services

Generally, social protection in Ghana is funded by various sources, including the Government's consolidated budget, direct inflows from international donors, allocations from statutory funds, and social security contributions (ILO, 2014). Child protection services, therefore, have been and continue to be financed by a combination of internal budgetary allocations and external donor support. Donor funding and support have been very crucial during the inception, delivery, monitoring, and evaluation of many child protection services and programs. Since then, the government of Ghana, as well as civil society organizations that provide child protection services have relied heavily on funding from international development partners and organizations in the implementation of child protection policies.

Before the introduction of the Child and Family Welfare Policy, generally there were no clear and consolidated national policies and programs for child protection. As a result, many NGOs and civil society groups mushroomed across the country to provide different kinds of services that are geared towards the protection of children. These NGOs were largely partnered and financed by international organizations, such as UNICEF, ILO, Plan Ghana, and others. While external donor support has been invaluable in the delivery of child protection services in Ghana, it has over the years resulted in the cessation of important services when funds run out. Although there are yearly budgetary allocations by the government of Ghana for the delivery of social protection programs in the country, there is a general lack of disaggregated data on specific allocations for child protection.

There are also major inconsistencies in budgetary allocations to child protection from different sources, which make it difficult to map out government spending with accuracy. Irrespective of this, over the years, the government's social budget has been small and spread across various programs with very little coordination among the various sectors that provide child protection services (Adu-Gyamfi, 2014; DFID, 2006). Ghana's national budget derives from a combination of taxes, internally generated funds from the MMDAs, and support from international development partners. The MMDAs are the government's decentralization machinery vested with the responsibility for the provision of services, advancing the cause of equal opportunity, redistribution of wealth and poverty reduction (Adu-Gyamfi, 2014).

Although the MMDAs rely on the District Assemblies' Common Fund (government's budgetary allocations), they are also required to generate funds internally to support programs and policies at the local level. In recent times, however, government has urged the MMDAs to explore other innovative means of generating funds, as there appears to be over-reliance on donor funding to support programs, like the provision of child protection services in the country. The problem with dependence on donor funding to support programs is that when such funds cease, the programs are likely to be discontinued. In 2010, the World Bank reclassified Ghana as a lower middle income country, and this resulted in a drastic reduction in development assistance to the country. Since many social programs, of which child protection is one, are mainly funded by international donors, such reductions in funding tend to adversely affect the successful implementation and sustainability of these programs.

Conclusion

Child protection systems in Ghana manifest in both formal and informal structures. Due to the various levels at which children may experience abuse, violence, or other vulnerabilities, it is imperative that formal and informal institutions work together to protect children in the country. As the first signatory to the CRC, Ghana demonstrated political and moral commitment to ensuring that children within her jurisdiction are duly protected. A notable outcome of this commitment was the enactment of the Children's Act of Ghana (Act 560 1998), which is a localized version of the numerous provisions spelt out in the CRC.

As discussed in this chapter, several past and ongoing efforts have culminated in the formulation of a Child and Family Welfare Policy (2015), which seeks to synchronize the many different formal child protection interventions in Ghana. With support from the government and development partners, as well as funds generated within districts through innovative measures that will sustainably protect children, the country's child protection systems could be strengthened. The time has come, now more than ever, for Ghana to explore bold and new approaches of raising funds internally for its child protection programs. Creating incentives and mechanisms for innovation, experimentation, and replication of best practices in child protection, and taking steps to increase the life chances of children, would go a long way to secure and safeguard the future of Ghana's children.

References

Adepoju, A. (2005). Review of research and data on human trafficking in sub-Saharan Africa. In F. Laczko and E. Gozdziak (Eds.), *Data and research on human trafficking: A global survey* (pp. 75–98). International Organization for Migration.

Adu-Gyamfi, E. (2014). Effective revenue mobilisation by Districts Assemblies: A case study of Upper Denkyira East Municipal Assembly of Ghana. *Public Policy and Administration Review*, 2(1), 97–122.

Agbényiga, D. L. (2012). Defining childhood: A historical developmental perspective. In R. K. Ame, D. L. Agbényiga, and N. A. Apt (Eds.), *Children's rights in Ghana: Reality or rhetoric?* (pp. 15–36). Mot Juste Limited.

Alderman, H. and Bundy, D. A. P. (2011). School feeding programs and development: Are we framing the question correctly? *World Bank Research Observer*, 27(2), 204–221.

Ame, R. (2012). Children's rights, controversial traditional practices and the Trokosi system: A critical sociolegal perspective. In R. K. Ame, D. L. Agbényiga, and N. A. Apt (Eds.), *Children's rights in Ghana: Reality or rhetoric?* (pp. 107–123). Mot Juste Limited.

Ayete-Nyampong, L. (2012). Situating CRC implementation processes in the local contexts of correctional institutions for children in conflict with the law in Ghana. In R. K. Ame, D. L. Agbényiga, and N. A. Apt (Eds.), *Children's rights in Ghana: Reality or rhetoric?* (pp. 139-158). Mot Juste Limited.

Boakye-Boaten, A. (2008). Street children: Experiences from the streets of Accra. *Research Journal of International Studies*, 8, 76–84.

Boakye-Boaten, A. (2011). Surviving in the streets: The story of a street girl from Ghana. *International Journal of Humanities and Social Science*, 1(18), 244–250.

Child Frontiers. (2011). *Report of the mapping and analysis of Ghana's child protection system*. UNICEF.

Dako-Gyeke, M. (2018). Perspectives of key informants on child abuse: Qualitative evidence from Northern Ghana. *Child and Adolescent Social Work Journal*, 36(2), 155–169.

Debrah, E. (2013). Alleviating poverty in Ghana: The case of livelihood empowerment against poverty (LEAP). *Africa Today*, 59(4), 40–67.

DFID (2006). Eliminating world poverty – making governance work for the poor. A White Paper on International Development. DFID.

Gelli, A., Masset, E., Folson, G., Kusi, A., Arhinful, D. K., Asante, F., Ayi, I., Bosompem, K. M., Watkins, K., Abdul-Rahman, L., and Agble, R. (2016). Evaluation of alternative school feeding models on nutrition, education, agriculture and other social outcomes in Ghana: Rationale, randomised design and baseline data. *Trials*, 17(37), 1–19.

GNCRC. (2014). Convention on the rights of children (CRC) report to UN Committee on the Rights of the Child. GNCRC.

Ghana Statistical Service. (2012). *2010 population and housing census, summary report of final results*. Ghana Statistical Service.

Ghana Statistical Service. (2014). *Ghana living standards survey (GLSS 6): Child labour report*. Available at: http://www.statsghana.gov.gh/docfiles/glss6/GLSS6_Child%20Labour%20Report.pdf.

ILO. (2014). *Rationalizing social protection expenditure in Ghana*. ILO.

Mensah, C. A., Antwi, K. B., and Dauda, S. (2014). Female traditional leaders (Queen Mothers) and community planning and development in Ghana. *Environmental Management and Sustainable Development*, 3(1), 205–220.

Mistiaen, V. (2013, October 4). Virgin wives of the fetish Gods: Ghana's trokosi tradition. *Thomson Reuters Foundation News*. Available at: http://news.trust.org//item/20131003122159-3cmei/.

MoGCSP. (2015). *Child and family welfare policy*. Government of Ghana.

MoGCSP. (2014). *Child Protection Baseline Research Report*. Government of Ghana.

Roelen, K., Chettri, H. K., and Delap, E. (2015). Little cash to large households: Cash transfers and children's care in disadvantaged families in Ghana. *International Social Security Review*, 68(2), 63–83.

Trulson, C. R. (2007). Determinants of disruption: Institutional misconduct among state committed delinquents. *Youth Violence and Juvenile Justice*, 5(1), 7–34.

Twum-Danso, A. (2012). Assessing the progress of the 1998 Children's Act of Ghana: Achievements, opportunities, and challenges in its first ten years. In R. Ame, D. L. Agbényiga, and N. A. Apt (Eds.), *Children's rights in Ghana: Reality or rhetoric?* (pp. 151–168). Mot Juste Limited.

UN. (1989). *Convention on the rights of the child 1989*. Available at: http://www.ohchr.org/en/professionalinterest/pages/crc.aspx.

UN. (2013). *Convention on the rights of the child*. General comment No. 14 (2013) on the right of the child to have his or her best interests taken as a primary consideration (art. 3, para. 1). Available at: http://www2.ohchr.org/English/bodies/crc/docs/GC/CRC_C_GC_14_ENG.pdf.

UN and ILO. (1999). Convention on the Worst Forms of Child Labour Convention, C182. Available at: http://www.refworld.org/docid/3ddb6e0c4.html.

UNDP. (2010). *Ghana country analysis*. United Nations.

UNICEF. (2006). *What is child protection?* Available at: https://www.unicef.org/protection/files/What_is_Child_Protection.pdf.

UNICEF. (2009). *Social protection and children: Opportunities and challenges in Ghana*. UNICEF (Ghana) and Ministry of Employment and Social Welfare.

UNICEF and UIS. (2012). *Global initiative on out-of-school children: Ghana country study*. UNICEF.

UNICEF. (2013). *Ghana: Advocating for development that leaves no child behind*. Available at: 2017 from https://www.unicef.org/ghana/Ghana_Booklet_Final.pdf.

UNICEF. (2014). *Ending child marriage: Progress and prospects.* Available at: https://data.unicef.org/wp-cont ent/uploads/2015/12/Child-Marriage-Brochure-HR_164.pdf.

UNICEF. (2015). *Building a national child protection system in Ghana: From evidence to policy and practice.* United Nations.

UNICEF. (2016). *Institutionalization of needy children not the best way: It must be a last resort.* Available at: https://www.unicef.org/ghana/media_10500.html.

US Department of State. (2016). *Trafficking in persons' report: Ghana.* Available at: http://www.refworld.org/ docid/577f960215.html.

Williams, G. A., Parmar, D., Dkhimi, F., Asante, F., Arhinful, D., and Mladovsky P. (2017). Equitable access to health insurance for socially excluded children? The case of the National Health Insurance Scheme (NHIS) in Ghana. *Social Science & Medicine,* 186, 10–19.

Legislation

Children's Act (Act 560). (1998).

Labour Act (Act 651). (2003).

Juvenile Justice Act (Act 653). (2003).

Human Trafficking Act (Act 694). (2005).

Disability Act, Act 715. (2006).

Domestic Violence Act (Act 732). (2007).

The Child Protection System in India: An Overview

Sanjai Bhatt *and* Subhashree Sanyal

Abstract

This chapter provides an overview of the Indian child protection system. As most of India's development initiatives considers the best interests of children, the country has adopted numerous laws and formulated policies to ensure the protection and improvement of children's situation. The Juvenile Justice Act is comprehensive legislation focusing on children in need of care and protection, and children in conflict with the law. The chapter also notes how the definition of a child is mostly based on age, which is all people below eighteen years old. Thus, the definition does not refer to the context and experiences associated with childhood, which could be treated as a social construction.

Key Words: child protection system, India, age, best interests, laws, Juvenile Justice Act, initiatives, childhood

Background

India is a country with the largest child population in the world. As children are at the center of most of the development programs, every initiative takes into consideration the best interest of the child. India has adopted a number of laws and formulated a range of policies to ensure the protection and improvement of children's situations. Amongst all these laws, the Juvenile Justice (Care and Protection of Children) Act, 2015 is comprehensive legislation that deals with two major aspects: children in need of care and protection, and children in conflict with the law. The Act was introduced to enable the processes and systems to become more child friendly and sensitive to the needs and rights of children. The term "child friendly" implies physical space provided, language used, accessibility of child welfare policies and programs, quality of intervention, procedures followed, access to legal aid and respecting the wishes of the child, and so on. Children are the most important asset of any nation and need to be nurtured in a dignified manner where they are protected and have access to all their entitlements for their overall development. It is because of this fact that they are also more vulnerable to abuse, exploitation, and violence. The Juvenile Justice Act was initially passed in 1986 (herein after referred to as the JJ Act) as a progressive piece of legislation that provides for proper care, treatment, development, and rehabilitation of the most vulnerable children of our society, including children in conflict with the law and children in need of care and protection.

The term "child protection" refers to preventing and responding to violence, exploitation, and abuse against children—including commercial sexual exploitation, trafficking, child labor, and harmful traditional practices, such as child marriage (UNICEF, 2018). Child protection programs also target children who are uniquely vulnerable to these abuses such as when living without parental care, in conflict with the law, and in armed conflict. Violations of the child's right to protection take place in every country and are massive, under-recognized, and under-reported barriers to child survival and development, in addition to being human rights violationsChild protection is a tool that protects both children and staff by clearly defining what action is required to keep children safe and ensuring a consistency of behavior so that all staff follows the same process. Millions of children are not fully protected. Many of them deal with violence, abuse, neglect, exploitation, exclusion, and/or discrimination every day. Such violations limit their chances of surviving, growing, developing, and pursuing their dreams.

"Child" in the Indian Context: The Dilemma of "Age"

Starting from the Indian Majority Act, 1875 which laid down the age of majority as 18 years and meant by implications that a person below 18 years is a child, a majority of laws have attempted to define the term "child" in terms of an age limit. The Child Marriage Restraint Act, 1929 puts this limit at 21 years for males and 18 years for females. The Children (Pledging of Labour) Act, 1933, fixed the age limit to 15 years for the purposes of the Act. The Factories Act, 1948, brought down the age to 14 years and the Apprentices Act, 1961, and the Child Labour (Prohibition and Regulation) Act, 1986, followed suit. However, the Immora Traffic (Prevention) Act, 1986, passed in the same year as the Child Labour (Prohibition and Regulation) Act, lifted the age bar to 16 years. Under pressure from the United Nations Convention on the Rights of the Child, the JJ Act 2001 defined a child as a person younger than 18 years (Bhatt & Jha, 2006, p. 114).

It has to be highlighted that age-based definitions for "child" do not take into account the "context and experiences" associated with childhood (Norozi & Moen, 2016). Several scholars have opined that childhood can be treated as a social construction that is open to cultural and historical change and interpretation (Qvortrup, 1984; James & Prout, 1997). In India, while chronological age is used to define a "child" for all legal purposes, census enumeration, and implementation of government programs, the notion of a "child" varies across different communities in the country and is shaped by local customs and beliefs. In most rural and urban communities, the onset of menarche marks the end of "childhood" for girls. In the case of boys, it is the appearance of visible secondary sexual characteristics. It has also been observed that in most Indian patriarchal societies a male child is treated by his parents, specifically by his mother, as a "child" even after the appearance of secondary sexual characteristics.

The population of children in India (0–17 years) is estimated at 452 million (UNICEF, 2016). This constitutes 35% of the country's total population. Out of this population, about 52.4% are male and 47.6% are female. Further, with 19% of the world's children living in India, the country is also home to the largest number of children in the world (NIUA, 2016). The Working Group on Development of Children for the Eleventh Five Year Plan (2007–2012) has reported that "nineteen per cent of world children live in India. India is home to more than one billion people, of which 42 per cent are children, defined as persons under 18 years of age. In international comparisons of the status and condition of children, India continues to rank poorly on several key counts. The world tenth largest economy unfortunately ranks 127 on the Human Development Index (HDI). If all child rights indicators were to become a critical measure for HDI, India would fare even worse, because of its low levels of achievement on accepted national goals for the survival, development and protection of its children" (Government of India, 2010).

Children in India: Issues and Challenges

In the present context in India, children are in several difficult circumstances and are vulnerable to the situations in their environment which include female feticide, crimes against children, juvenile delinquency, abandoned children, and disaster affected children. The relevant causes of these vulnerable situations include poor households without family income; children denied educational opportunities and forced into labor, abused/trafficked children, children on the streets, children affected by substance abuse, by armed conflict/civil unrest/natural calamity, and so on. Hence, protection of these children is one of the main concerns (UNICEF, 2011). While protection is a right of every child, some children are more vulnerable than others and need special attention. The government recognizes these children as "children in difficult circumstances," characterized by their specific social, economic, and geopolitical situations. There are various categories and subcategories of children who are in need of care and protection as well as children in conflict with the law, only children belonging to some extreme forms are explained in detail. However, it does not mean that children in other categories are not important.

Juvenile delinquency: Juvenile crimes (under the Indian Penal Code (IPC) have shown rising trends in India as the number of cases registered against juveniles has gone up from 18,939 in 2005 to 31,396 in 2015 (NCRB, 2016). Children are found involved in petty as well as heinous crimes. Their involvement in crimes of a non-serious nature such as theft, burglary, and snatching, to serious crimes such as robbery, dacoity (gang robbery), murder, and even rape is on the rise across the country. All these types of crimes are also being committed by children below the age of 18 years. The major crimes committed by juveniles in 2014 were theft (20%), rape (5.9%), grievous hurt (4.7%), and assault on a woman with intent to outrage her modesty (4.7%). Following a shameful case of gang rape in 2012, the JJ Act was amended for juveniles 16 years or older to be tried as adults for heinous offenses. Heinous offenses are those which are punishable with imprisonment of seven years or more. From 2003–2013 there was a substantial increase in other crimes by children. The increase has been in the age group of 16–18 years, with a substantial decrease among younger children. The major causes of such an increase may be due to lack of employment, leading to frustrations gradually increasing in India (Wani, 2014). According to Times of India- a National daily, Cases against 3.1 percent of juveniles apprehended and produced before various juvenile boards in 2014 were disposed of with fine, while 5.8 percent were acquitted. No more than 14.4 percent were sent to special homes last year. Interestingly, the low figure is despite the fact that 73.7 percent of the juvenile offenders arrested under IPC last year were aged between 16 and 18 years (TOI, 2015).

Child marriage: Child marriage is one of the major issues of child protection along with teenage pregnancy. Both deprive children of all their rights, denying them the opportunity to develop into fully empowered individuals. These harmful social practices are very often cited as a prime cause for high maternal and infant mortality and inter-generational cycles of malnutrition. In India, about 43% of women are married before attaining the age of 18 years. The rural–urban difference is very significant; 48% of women in rural areas are married before attaining the legal age of 18 (UNICEF, 2011). However, it is a matter of great satisfaction that the incidence of child marriage has declined barring two states (Himachal Pradesh and Manipur), which means that efforts of better education, awareness, and empowerment are ensuring results. Most child marriages result in teenage pregnancy due to societal pressure and a lack of knowledge of family planning. Almost one in three girls who get married between 15 and 19 years have babies while they are still teenagers themselves. Almost a quarter of them had a child by age 17, and 31% by age 18. More than a quarter (27.3%) of married teenage girls have given birth to one child while 4.2% of married girls have two or more children (NCPCR, 2018).

Child labor: There are 33 million child laborers between the ages of 5 and 18 years in India and 10.13 million between the ages of 5 and 14 years, as per the 2011 census. Figures from different stakeholders vary. Non-government organizations working in this field give an estimate of 60 million child laborers. As per the Census of India, the marginal workers (who had worked for less than six months during the major part of the reference period) contribute 63% of the total child labor while the rest (37%) is being contributed by main workers (who had worked for six months or more during the reference period) (Prognosys, 2012). UNICEF states that 12.66 million children are engaged as child laborers in different activities such as domestic workers, pan (a dessert sweet), bidi (cigarette making and selling), spinning, and weaving (UNICEF, 2011). The recent round of the National Sample Survey (NSSO) suggests that child labor in the country is around 8.9 million in 2004/2005 with a workforce participation rate of 3.4% (Progynosys, 2012, p. 10). The world's largest democracy is yet to ratify the Minimum Age Convention, 1973 (No. 138) of the International Labour Organisation (ILO), which lays down ground rules for employment of minors across the globe. Another NGO, Action Aid India, has claimed that one in every 11 children in India works to earn a living.

Child sexual abuse: Child sexual abuse is another major modern-day crime against children. Cases registered for child sexual abuse rose from 8904 to 14,913 from 2014 to 2015. A total of 33,098 cases of sexual abuse of children were reported in the nation during the year 2011 when compared to 26,694 reported in 2010, an increase of 24%. A total of 7,112 cases of child rape were reported during 2011, a 30% increase from the previous year (Government of India, 2007). The researchers from the University of Barcelona have analyzed 65 research studies across 22 countries to estimate an "overall international figure" for such abuse. The study found that an estimated 7.9 per cent of men and 19.7 per cent of women globally experienced sexual abuse prior to the age of 18's authors note that "the studies all agree that child sexual abuse is a much more widespread problem than previously estimated . . . and even the lowest prevalence rates include a large number of victims who need to be taken into account. . . . Indeed, research confirms the importance of the problem among both men and women in all the countries studied" (Whibey, 2011).

Child Trafficking: Information from the National Crime Data Bureau (NCRB) shows 5,466 incidents of crime relating to human trafficking in 2014 compared to 3,940 during the year 2013. The country has made effective laws and efforts to check trafficking of children.

Missing children: The definition of a missing child as mentioned in the Standard Operating Procedure for handling cases of missing children issued by the Ministry of Women and Child Development and the CHILDLINE foundation, says that "a child whose whereabouts are not known to the parents, legal guardian or any other person or institution legally entrusted with the custody of the child, whatever may be the circumstances or causes of disappearance, and shall be considered missing and in need of care and protection until located or his safety and wellbeing established." According to figures from India's National Crime Records Bureau (NCRB), one child goes missing in the country every eight minutes and 40% of these children are never found. In reply to a question, India's Minister of State for Home Affairs said in the parliament's upper house that 60,000 children had been reported missing in the country in 2011, an increase from 44,000 in 2004. A good number of the lost children end up as prostitutes and bonded laborers or join the homeless population in big cities. They are prone to high chances of being trafficked or kidnapped for various purposes like prostitution, organ trade, slavery, beggary, or labor, and thus are at very high risk of being subjected to exploitation and being forced to be part of chains of organized and unorganized crimes. Since most of these children belong to families with a very weak socioeconomic background, their parents lack the resources to help them trace their children on their own and hence seek help from governmental or non-governmental organizations to trace them. The National Human Rights Commission (NHRC) has constituted a committee on Missing Children, after the infamous Nithari incident of missing children, under the Chairmanship of its member P C Sharma on 12th February 2007, to examine the issue of missing children in depth and to evolve simple, practical guidelines so that appropriate recommendations. The Committee has made several observations. One of the observations worth mentioning is a veritable black hole in law enforcement. The Committee reported that "not much has been achieved to protect the rights of children in the last 60 years. The world of missing children is unknown and there is no proper study or research on this issue. Even today the exact figures of missing or traced children are not available. The existing legislation requires the State and district authorities to periodically carry out inspections/surveys of places where children are employed to identify missing children and those engaged in bonded labor/child labor. This task has remained a low priority area" (NHRC, n.d., pp. 37–38).

Considering the enormity of the problem, especially in an under-developed country like India, where more than half the population belongs to socioeconomically weaker sections and numerous other challenges, the care and protection of missing children is a serious challenge. Finding a suitable solution is a distant dream in the absence of strong legal backup, swift police action, proper networking between responsible institutions, and inadequate data.

Legal Environment for Protecting Children in India

The Constitution of India, which came into force in 1950, is the supreme law of the country. It has several provisions which address the special needs of children. Part III of the Constitution contains the "Fundamental Rights" (Articles 12–35), which are the legally enforceable rights guaranteed to all citizens. Article 15(3) of the Constitution of India indicates that states must make special provisions for children. In addition to the fundamental rights guaranteed to the children as citizens of the country, Article 21A was inserted by the Constitution's 86th Amendment Act, 2002, to provide free and compulsory education to all children in the age group of 6 to 14 years as a Fundamental Right in such a manner as Statetate may, by law, determine. Article 24 of the Constitution states that "No child below the age of 14 years shall be employed to work in any factory or mine or engaged in hazardous employment." Part IV of the Constitution contains the "Directive Principles of State Policy (DPSP)" (Articles 36–51). While these guidelines are legally not enforceable, they are referred to for promulgating legislation and formulating policies for the country. Article 39 asks the state to direct its policy towards securing (among other things), that children are not abused; not forced by economic necessity to enter avocations unsuited to their age or strength; and that they are given opportunities to develop in a healthy manner and conditions of freedom and dignity, protected against moral and material abandonment. Article 39(e) and (f) of the DPSP states that the state "shall, in particular, direct its policy to ensure that towards securing that the health and strength of workers, men and women, and the tender age of children are not abused." In the Indian constitution, "to provide opportunities for education by the parent or guardian, to his child, or a ward between the age of 6–14 years as the case may be" has been accepted as a fundamental duty of a citizen (Article 51A (k)).

Efforts at the international level have reinforced and re-strengthened our commitment. The United Nations Convention on the Rights of the Child (CRC) is one of the major conventions which is universally accepted by the nations of the world, and the CRC covers the whole range of human rights. It also sets standards for three other international instruments for dealing with juvenile justice: the Beijing Rules (1985), the Riyadh Guidelines (1990), and the Havana Rules (1990). Thus, by becoming a part of the treaty, the state is bound to fulfill all the duties and provisions set out in the conventions (Plan International, 2003). Fortunately, the CRC provided a system for Juvenile Justice which India ratified in 1992 and consequently amended three times (in 2000, 2006, and 2015). The JJ Act hence focuses on protecting the rights of children in conflict with the law and in need of care and protection and ensuring the best interests of children (UNICEF, 2011).

The JJ Act, 2000, amendment stated that individuals below the age of 18 years who commit heinous crimes (rape, murder, assault) are to be tried as juveniles and sent to a Juvenile Justice Board. If they are found guilty, they will be placed in a place of safety and sent for rehabilitation for three years. As stated previously, the JJ Act was amended in 2015 to indicate that individuals between 16 and 18 years committing serious or heinous crimes will be tried as adults. Heinous offences include a minimum punishment of imprisonment for seven years or more; serious offences call for three to seven years of imprisonment. Juveniles cannot be inflicted with life imprisonment or the death penalty. The board, aided by a team of experts, determines on a case-by-case basis whether youth will be tried as an adult or child based on an assessment of the mental state of the accused. Delinquent juveniles may be sent to a children's home or tried as an adult (Goel, 2015). Most often, the police are the first point of contact for children in difficult circumstances. Keeping in view the significant role of the police, the Act mandates that the state governments have to create a Special Juvenile Police Unit in every district of the state. The Act further requires that such police officers who frequently or exclusively engage with children or are primarily engaged in the prevention of offences committed by children go through special training, instruction and orientation on how to deal with such children in a child-friendly manner. The Act also proposes that at every police station, at least one police officer shall be designated as the "Juvenile or Child Welfare Officer" to deal with children and coordinate with others.

In the past 15 years, India has added a few other important pieces of legislation to protect children. The Child Labour (Prohibition and Regulation) Act, 1986, prohibits the employment of children below the age of 14 years in 13 occupations and 57 processes that are hazardous to the lives and health of the children. Under the new Section 370, trafficking of persons for physical exploitation or any form of sexual exploitation, slavery or practices similar to slavery, servitude, and the forced removal of organs is prohibited (Vidushy, 2016). New legislation, the Prohibition of Child Marriage Act (2006), declares that child marriage is voidable and the law gives power to the child to nullify the marriage within two years after attaining majority. In such cases, the husband has to pay the maintenance for the girl/woman until her remarriage from the male contracting party or his parents. To stop child sexual abuse, the country has promulgated new legislation—the Protection of Children from Sexual Offences (POCSO) Act (2012)—which provides protection for children from the offences of sexual assault, sexual harassment, and pornography, while safeguarding the interests of the child at every stage of the judicial process by incorporating child-friendly mechanisms for reporting, recording of evidence, investigation, and speedy trial of offences through designated Special Courts. Above all, India has accepted education as a fundamental right and brought the Right to Education Act (2009), which provides compulsory and free education for all children aged 6–14 years. This act is being implemented across India except in Jammu and Kashmir. This act includes free education, and all basic amenities in school along with the mid-day meal in schools (Government of India, 2009). The act ensures that no child shall be held back, expelled, or required to pass a board examination until the completion of elementary education. The act also ensures the child will be admitted in the class appropriate to his or her age. A requirement of the birth registration certificate is required for the proof of age for admission, and the child is awarded a certificate at the completion of elementary education. Another important feature of this act is also improving the quality of education and the infrastructure of schools.

Policy Framework on Child Protection in India

Since independence, the government has focused on children and their welfare. From child welfare to child rights, children in India have received adequate attention in the constitution and remained part of planned program development. We can see a gradual transgression from corrective to more right-based approach of child protection in India.

Children in Five-Year Plans

The government of India has, every five years, developed a new plan to address the needs of children. These five-year plans were initiated in 1952 and continued until 2015, when their main body was revamped as the National Institution for Transforming India in place of the Planning Commission. From the first five-year plan (1951–1956), which identified health, nutrition, and education as major areas of concern with regard to children, it has met several milestones in the last seven decades, such as:

1) strengthening the child welfare system (1956–1961);
2) coordinated welfare extension projects (1958);
3) the Children's Act in 1960;
4) nutrition programs (1959);
5) the national education policy in 1968;
6) the National Policy for Children in 1974;
7) the Special Nutrition Programme;
8) the Balwadi Nutrition Programme;
9) the prophylaxis scheme against blindness due to vitamin A deficiency among children of 1969–1974;
10) the shift from child welfare to child development in 1974–1979;
11) the Integrated Child Development Scheme (ICDS) in 1975;
12) the scheme of Crèches/Daycare Centers for Children of Working and Ailing Mothers;
13) the setting up of the National Children's Fund in 1979;
14) emphasis on the needs of working children in 1980–1985;
15) the formulation of the Indian National Code for Protection and Promotion of Breast Feeding in 1980–1985;
16) the establishment of the Department of Women and Child Development in the Ministry of Human Resource Development in 1985;
17) the Juvenile Justice Act in 1986;
18) the National Child Labour Project in 1987;
19) setting up of the Central Adoption Resource Agency in 1990;
20) ratification of the first comprehensive convention for child rights (UN Convention on the Rights of the Child);
21) the National Plan of Action for the Girl Child in 1992, and to address the plight of the girl child, the declining sex-ratio as well as female feticide and infanticide.

In the field of health, the government introduced the Reproductive and Child Health Program (RCH). The JJ Act was significantly amended to welcome the new century. In the field of education, the government launched Sarva Shiksha Abhiyan (SSA) in 2001–2002. In the 10th five-year plan (2002–2007), the approach shifted to a right-based one ensuring the survival, development, and protection of children. During this period, the Pre-natal Diagnostic Techniques (Regulation and Prevention of Misuse) Act was amended in 2003 to further address the problems of female feticide and infanticide. The scope of existing schemes such as ICDS, universal immunization, Sarva Shiksha Abhiyan, and a few others was expanded. Major accomplishments have been a constitutional amendment making the right to education a fundamental right, the revision of the National Health Policy to take into consideration more recent health concerns like HIV/AIDS and the amendment of the JJ act, and the adoption of the Goa Children's Act of 2003. The 11th five-year plan (2007–2012) clearly stated that "Development of the child is at the centre of this Plan."

There were four key areas in the National Plan of Action for Children: ICDS, Early Childhood Education, Girl Child, and Child Protection. The 11th plan recognizes the need for child protection programs and initiatives. According to the MWCD report the eleventh plan's idea of child protection is very limited and does not cover all commitments of NPAC. The Ministry is committed to strengthening the justice delivery mechanism to comprehensively address child sexual abuse, trafficking, and violence against women and children (Ministry of Women and Child Development, 2012). The Integrated Child Protection Scheme (ICPS)—with the aim to provide care, protection, and a safe and secure environment for children in conflict with the law as well as children in need of care and protection—was launched in last plan period. It focuses on the effective implementation and consolidation of the scheme and worksto promote quality non-institutional care, professionalized institutional support, the expansion of Child Line, and the development of a credible database on missing children and those in difficult circumstances. With the inception of NITI Ayog in 2015, to achieve Sustainable Development Goals and cooperative federalism, the government has developed 15-year road maps of forward development.

National Policy for Children, 2013

On April 18, 2013, the Union Cabinet approved the National Policy for Children to help in the implementation of programs and schemes for children all over the country. The policy gives utmost priority to the right to life, health, and nutrition, and also gives importance to development, education, protection, and participation. Through this policy the state is committed to take affirmative measures—legislative, policy, or otherwise— to promote and safeguard the right of all children to live and grow with equity, dignity, security, and freedom, to ensure that all children have equal opportunities; and that no custom, tradition, cultural, or religious practice is allowed to violate or restrict or prevent children from enjoying their rights.

The National Policy for Children, 2013, recognizes that a child is any person below the age of 18 years, childhood is an integral part of life with a value of its own, and children are not a homogenous group and their different needs require different responses, especially the multi-dimensional vulnerabilities experienced by children in different circumstances. A long-term, sustainable, multi-sectoral, integrated, and inclusive approach is necessary for the overall and harmonious development and protection of children. The policy reaffirms that every child is unique and a supremely important national asset; as such, special measures and affirmative action are required to diminish or eliminate conditions that cause discrimination. All children have the right to grow in a family environment, in an atmosphere of happiness, love, and understanding, and families are to be supported by a strong social safety net in caring for and nurturing their children. The key priorities of the policy are survival, health and nutrition, education and development, protection, advocacy and partnerships, coordination, action and monitoring, research, documentation and capacity building, and resource allocation.

National Plan of Action for Children, 2005

The National Plan of Action for Children (NPAC), 2005 is by far the most comprehensive planning document concerning children. It clearly outlines goals, objectives, and strategies to achieve the objectives outlined and recognizes the needs of all children up to the age of 18. It is divided into four basic child right categories as per the United Nations Convention on the Rights of the Child: child survival, child development, child protection, and child participation.

Child survival first refers to child health. The plan outlines goals to reduce children's risk of contracting malaria, tuberculosis, and cholera, and exposure to HIV/AIDS, and to provide them with full immunization, access to quality health care, water, food, and sanitation. The goal is also to reduce the poor health indicators in the infant mortality rate, child mortality rate, and neonatal mortality rate. In order to do this, services need to provide mothers with adequate pre-natal medical attention and nutrition, encourage safe birth practises, encourage breast feeding as essential to having healthy babies, cover all children and women within the reproductive age with necessary immunizations, ensure proper coverage of all families under the Integrated Child Development Services (ICDS) scheme, educate communities about proper infant care, universalize use of oral rehydration to prevent dehydration in children, make efforts to detect and treat all diseases such as malaria and Dengue, take steps to prevent mother–child transmission of HIV/AIDS, and provide children with the necessary care and medication to fight infections and disease.

The second aspect of child survival is maternal health which is to be achieved by improving anaemia in mothers and girls, generating awareness about maternal health practices and child spacing, preventing and treating sexually transmitted diseases and infections, and ensuring that health centers are fully equipped to handle the needs of mothers and offer appropriate referrals. The third aspect of child survival is nutrition to be achieved by promoting breast feeding and prohibiting milk substitutes for infants, conducting constant screening of children to ensure they are not underweight; and by empowering families with information about child nutrition and making low cost complementary food products. It is also important to address anaemia and vitamin A deficiency, and address macro and micro malnutrition via midday meal and public distribution food systems. In order to provide enough water for all, there is a need to begin water conservation practices such as rain water harvesting, and recycling and reusing water.

The National Plan of Action for Children also focuses on child development, with an emphasis on the development of pre-school centers and crèches, promoting community-based initiatives, and creating awareness regarding birth registration and good parenting skills. The Plan also aims to promote equality and special opportunities for the girl child, including survival, development and protection, elimination of sex selection and child marriage, protection against sexual and non-sexual abuse, protection from neglect, the breaking down of gender stereotypes, and increasing access to education facilities. Some of the strategies outlined in the plan for the girl child are advocacy through social, political, and religious leaders and well as the government, proper enforcement of laws, support of non-government organizations and initiatives, and monitoring clinics to ensure that diagnostic tests are not being run illegally. The primary concerns with adolescents are child marriage, STDs, higher education curriculum, protection from exploitation, and providing rehabilitation and support programs so that they grow into responsible and aware citizens. This age group especially requires support and counseling services.

The Plan for Child Development also relates to children with disabilities. The aim is to reduce the risk of living with a disability by taking preventive measures during pregnancy and right after birth, providing disabled children with facilities that will ensure their mental and physical development, and providing help for children with disabilities to participate fully in society. Children, like all other human beings, are connected to the environment. In order to safeguard natural resources for our children the plan outlines the need to create recreational spaces for children, prevent toxic and harmful effects on the natural environment, use sustainable forms of production and energy, encourage children's understanding of their own surroundings, and ensure better sanitation and hygiene in communities. Finally, one of the most important aspects of child development is education. The plan discusses the importance of increasing access to public education for children with disabilities, girls, and children living in remote areas, improving infrastructure of schools, improving the quality of education, providing teachers with the correct training, reducing school drop-outs, supporting marginalized groups of society, establishing counseling services in school, and providing children with healthy midday meals.

The National Plan for Child Protection covers six main areas: children in difficult circumstances, children in conflict with the law, sexual exploitation and child pornography, child trafficking, combating child labor, and children affected by HIV/AIDS. Children in difficult circumstances require protection from exploitation, abuse, and neglect. The aim is to protect vulnerable groups by providing them with the proper facilities and services according to their needs. While keeping the best interest of the child in mind, the services should reunite families, rehabilitate and reintegrate children into society, and then provide for special needs of children with disabilities, homeless children, street children, destitute and orphan children, and so on.

Integrated Child Protection Services (ICPS) in India

Child protection is an integral part of programs, strategies and plans for achieving the millennium development goals as well as sustainable development goals. The issue of child protection is a complex subject and needs a comprehensive and multi-pronged approach. Children have manifold needs starting from health, nutrition, care, protection, development, education, love, affection, and recreation. Some children, like those affected by HIV/AIDS or disabilities, have special needs that should be taken care of. Apart from these, children either in conflict or contact with the law have additional needs that require interventions from the police, judiciary, and local level institutions like Panchayati raj institutions, urban local bodies, and local administration. ICPS is a centrally sponsored program and is implemented through the State Governments or Union Territories (UT) Administrations with the bulk of financial assistance from the central government.

The scheme primarily aims to institutionalize essential services and strengthen structures for emergency outreach, institutional care, family and community-based care, counseling, and support services at the national, regional, state, and district levels. The scheme aims to create a database and knowledge base for child protection services, including a MIS and child tracking system in the country for effective implementation and monitoring of child protection services, undertake research and documentation, strengthen child protection at the family and community level, create and promote preventive measures to protect children from situations of vulnerability, risk and abuse, raise public awareness, educate the public on children's rights and protection, on situations and vulnerabilities of children and families, on available child protection services, and on schemes and structures at all levels.

The ICPS is based on 10 guiding principles, which include: the components of child protection; a primary responsibility of the family; the support of community, government, and civil society; loving and caring family, the best place for the child; privacy and confidentiality; non-stigmatization and non-discrimination; child-centered planning and implementation; good governance; accountability; and responsibility. Various approaches are used like prevention through outreach programs to identify and support vulnerable families and to promote family-based care, including sponsorship, kinship care, foster care, and adoption. Partnerships, information sharing, and strategy building between government structures and civil society are encouraged through regular training and capacity building. Monitoring and evaluation also occur through a child protection data management system and other strategies to monitor outcomes.

The ICPS scheme targets children in need of care and protection and children in conflict with the law either as victims or as a witness or due to any other circumstance. It intends to provide preventive, statutory care and rehabilitation services to any other vulnerable child including, but not limited to: children of potentially vulnerable families and families at risk, children of socially excluded groups like migrant families, families living in extreme poverty, scheduled castes, scheduled tribes and other backward classes, families subjected to or affected by discrimination, minorities, children infected and/or affected by HIV/AIDS, orphans, child drug abusers, children of substance abusers, child beggars, trafficked or sexually exploited children, children of prisoners, and street and working children. The Government of India has shouldered the primary responsibility for the development and funding of the scheme as well as ensuring flexibility by cutting down rigid structures and norms. The IPCS scheme is depicted in Table 36.1.

ICPS is implemented by the State Child Protection Society (SCPS) and District Child Protection Units (DCPUs). A State Adoption Resource Agency (SARA) functions as a unit under the SCPS. The Structure of the District Child Protection Unit is as shown in Figure 36.1.

The SCPS follows national and state priorities, rules, and guidelines. The Central Adoption Resource Agency (CARA) was set up to function as the Central Authority in all matters concerning adoption and to implement various provisions of the Hague Convention on Inter-country Adoption 1993 regarding rights, safeguards, and procedures involving children who are orphaned, abandoned, or surrendered. CARA functions as an advisory body and think-tank for the Ministry of Women and Child Development (MWCD).

The MWCD implements the ICPS at its Child Welfare Bureau, whose responsibilities include: formulation of policies and legislation for children; advocacy for effective implementation of policies, programs, and services for children; ensuring implementation of various international norms and standards related to children; and representing the Government of India at various national and international child related forums. The implementation of a scheme as large and comprehensive as ICPS requires a fully-fledged, dedicated, and professionally equipped team working closely with state governments and other stakeholders to ensure the successful and speedy implementation of this massive task. The scheme is implemented on a cost sharing basis between centers and states/NGOs.

The ICPS has significantly contributed to the realization of government/state responsibility for creating a system that will efficiently and effectively protect children. It has strengthened prevention of children's rights violations, enhanced infrastructure for protection services, provided financial support for implementation of the JJ Act 2000, increased access to a wider range and better quality of protection services, and increased investment in child protection, and is continuously drawing focus to the rights of all children to be safe. Based on the cardinal principles of "protection of child rights" and "best interest of the child," ICPS is achieving its objectives to contribute to improvements in the well-being of children in difficult circumstances, as well as to the reduction of vulnerabilities to situations and actions that lead to abuse, neglect, exploitation, abandonment, and separation of children from their families.

Table 36.1 ICPS in India at a glance

Aspects	Description		
Service delivery structures	At central level: Central Project Support Unit (CPSU), Central Adoption Resource Authority (CARA), and National Institute for Public Cooperation and Child Development (NIPCCD)		
	At state level: State Child Protection Society (SCPS), State Adoption Resource Agency (SARA), and State Project Support Unit (SPSU)		
	At district level: District Child Protection Unit (DCPU)		
Implementation plan	Implementation plan to be developed in advance of convergence of services		
Funding pattern	Defined funding pattern and fund flow between center and states There is 100% support from center for many activities and for other activities, funds will be shared between center and states in ratios of 90:10 and 75:25.		
Services and other activities	Program and activities		
	Care, support, and rehabilitation services	a)	Emergency outreach services
		b)	Open shelters
		c)	Family-based non-institutional care through sponsorship, foster care, adoption, and aftercare
		d)	Institutional services
		e)	Institutional care through various kinds of homes
		e)	General grant in aid
	Statutory support services	a)	Child welfare committee
		b)	Juvenile justice board
		c)	Special juvenile police units
	Other activities	a)	Human resource development
		b)	Training and capacity building
		c)	Strengthening knowledge base
		d)	Child tracking system
		e)	Advocacy, public education and communication
		f)	Monitoring
		g)	Audit
		h)	Evaluation

Table 36.1 Continued	
Aspects	Description
Output indicators	a) State child protection structures in place and functioning including SCPS, SCPC, and SARA b) District child protection structures in place and functioning, including DCPU, DCPC, CWC, JJB, SJPU, and SAA c) Needs assessment and resource mapping of each district carried out d) State and district child protection plans developed and under implementation e) Open shelters for children in need, cradle baby reception centers, shelter homes, children's homes, observation homes, special homes, and place of safety established in a district or group of districts f) Child line services established in all districts g) Minimum standards of care for all childcare institutions and service providers developed and implemented h) Protocol of care for all service providers developed and implemented i) Individual care plans for all children prepared within the prescribed time limit, followed, and regularly updated j) Capacity-building plan formulated and implemented for ICPS functionaries and service providers k) All childcare institutions registered under the Juvenile Justice (Care andProtection of Children) Act, 2000 and its Amendment Act, 2006 l) Family-based, non-institutional care services mainstreamed m) Sponsorship and foster care program available within the DCPU n) After-care program available within the DCPU for children exiting care and in need of such services o) Child tracking system developed and functional p) Website for missing children and MIS on child protection set up and functioning q) Monitoring system for the ICPS in place and implemented r) Timely allocation, disbursement, and utilization of funds at all levels and services
Outcome indicators	a) Information/knowledge base of children and families at risk b) Reduced vulnerabilities of children c) Better child protection services d) Fewer children in need of care and protection e) Increase in the proportion of children in family-based non-institutional care services f) Increase in the proportion of children placed in in-country adoption g) Better quality care for children in institutional care h) Increased availability and accessibility of a variety of child protection services i) Increase in the proportion of children/young people leaving institutional care who are self-sufficient and gainfully engaged in productive activity

Source: Compiled from The Integrated Child Protection Scheme (ICPS): A Centrally Sponsored Scheme of Government—Civil Society Partnership, Ministry of Women & Child Development Government of India, 2016.

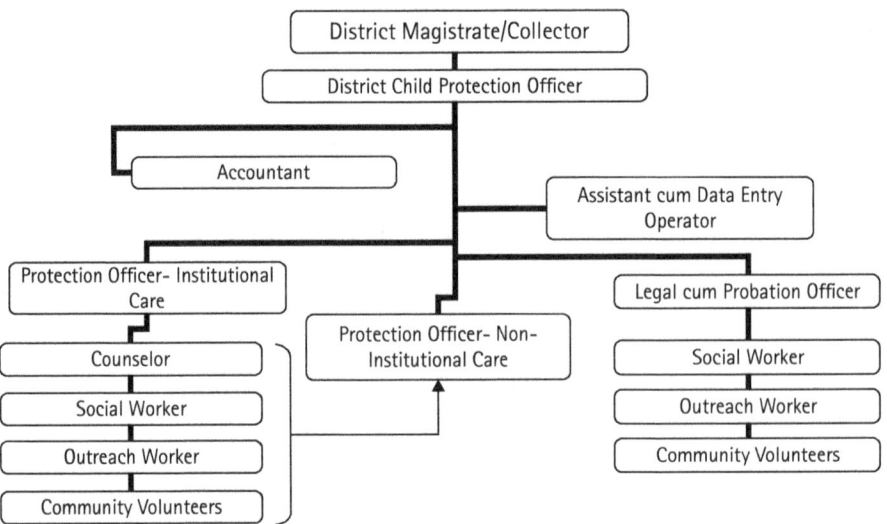

Figure 36.1 Structure of child protection unit at district level

Role of Non-Government Sector in Child Protection

NGOs are working in the field of child development and are providing direct services in health, hygiene, education, care, protection, awareness, research, and advocacy. While some NGOs work in close collaboration with government, international agencies, international NGOs, or donor supports, there are many working without any support. The government has promoted the voluntary sector through its national policy, which is a commitment to encourage, enable, and empower an independent, creative and effective voluntary sector, with diversity in form and function, so that it can contribute to the social, cultural and economic advancement of the people of India (Government of India, 2007 a). It intends to create an enabling environment for voluntary organizations that stimulates their enterprise and effectiveness and safeguards their autonomy. The emphasis is on partnership between the government and the voluntary sector.

ICPS is an ambitious scheme which seeks coordination of all departments and ministries and NGOs involved. Despite insistent attempts to implement a pro-child rights policy environment, India still needs the support of civil society, and concerned citizens to help children. At every stage, India's children face difficult challenges. The voluntary sector has made a robust contribution in implementing schemes/programs for children, improving the working environment, pointing out deficiencies and bottlenecks, and advocating for rights and values for children's well-being. The voluntary sector has tirelessly provided on-ground support and activism while working with officials in realizing goals—be it ICDS, midday meals, immunization, polio drive, education, or protection against exploitation, vulnerabilities, and child abuse. The NGO-DARPAN started out as an initiative of the Prime Minister's Office, to create and promote a healthy partnership between VOs/NGOs and the Government of India. The portal is managed at present by NITI Aayog. On this portal, there are 69,795 registered NGOs and 25,071 NGOs are solely dedicated for children. (NITI Ayog, 2019). These NGOs work hand in hand with the government in pursuit of a better world for the society. Some notable NGOs working for the welfare, development, and protection of children are Child-Line India—a 24-hour helpline—SOS Villages of India, Save the Children, Child Rights and You (CRY), Pratham, Plan India, Bachpan Bachao Andolan, the Kailash Satyarthi Foundation, the Akshay Patra Foundation, and Smile Foundations Teach for India, among many more.

Under the ICPS scheme, the role of civil society as stakeholders has been highlighted. They are to provide vibrant, responsive, and child-friendly services for detection, counseling, care, and rehabilitation for all children in need, and to raise awareness, capacity development, innovations, and monitoring. The media and advocacy groups are to promote rights of the child and child protection issues with sensitivity and sustain a media discourse on protection issues. The corporate sector should partner with government and civil society initiatives under the scheme, financially support child protection initiatives, and contribute to government efforts to improve the situation of children of India by adhering to the laws pertaining to child protection. Community groups and local leaders, volunteers, youth groups, families, and children should provide protective and conducive environments for children, to act as a watchdog and monitor child protection services by participating inter alia in the village and block level child protection committees.

The ministry is implementing the ICPS under which financial assistance is provided to State Governments/UT Administrations for setting up and managing childcare institutions (CCIs) by themselves or in association with voluntary organizations/NGOs. There are 1,626 institutional homes, 306 open centers, and 351 specialized adoption agencies supported under ICPS for care and protection of children. The primary responsibility of maintaining the CCIs rests with the states/UT Administration. From time to time, the ministry has requested the state Governments/UT Administrations to identify and register all CCIs under the provisions of the JJ Act, 2015 so as to ensure that minimum standards of care can be maintained. Under Section 41 of the Act, registration of CCIs has been made mandatory with penalties in case of non-compliance. Under Section 54 of the Act, state governments are required to appoint inspection committees for the state and district for mandatory inspection of all facilities housing children, at least once every three months (Ministry of Women and Child Development, 2017).

HAQ – Centre for Child Rights, a leading NGO, made an analysis of the Union Budget 2018–2019 for children. It presented an interesting analysis that "India is one of the world's youngest countries with the largest young population with significant 37% belong to the age group of 0–18 years. Children, in the Union Budget 2018–2019, received only 3.24% of the total financial resources, a decline of 0.08 percentage points from the 2017–2018 budget, despite the government adopting the National Plan of Action for Children in the year 2016 with specific goals and strategies to meet its commitment to

India's children." Child Protection Services has received Rs 108.333 billion in this budget. Mentioning the Economic Survey 2018, HAQ's report on its budget analysis has pointed out that "the rationalization, restructuring and continuation of four child centric schemes such as: Anganwadi Services (in place of ICDS); Scheme for Adolescent Girls (SAG) (in place of SABLA); Child Protection Services (in place of ICPS); and National Crèche Scheme (in place of Rajiv Gandhi National Crèche Scheme) of the Ministry under the "Umbrella Integrated Child Development Services" Scheme has been approved by the Government. These four schemes combined together have sought Rs 413.537 billion. As per the government's own projection, more than 110 million children, pregnant women and lactating mothers, and adolescent girls will benefit through this scheme ' (HAQ, 2018).

Under corporate social responsibility program, which had funds for Rs 240 billion, there are a good number of projects for children's well-being. NGOs are therefore trying to take the initiative by emphasizing the importance of education to children and communities; working to establish "safe schools" that do not discriminate on gender, caste, or socioeconomic background; creating inclusive Learner Friendly Environments (children aged 3–18 years); pushing for a financial framework supporting the Right to Free and Compulsory Education Act, 2009; creating fun school environments, using child-friendly and interactive methods; driving funding for libraries, computers, sports equipment, and mobile learning centers; bringing out-of-school children back to the classroom; and bringing street children and child laborers back to school.

Through awareness campaigns on nutrition and essential healthcare, NGOs like Save the Children have reduced newborn and child deaths (Save the Children, 2016). The NGO programs are closely linked with the ICDS Scheme, the Department of Health and Family Welfare, and Panchayat raj institutions, through whom it pushes for better policies and their implementation. Additionally, it provides on-the-ground assistance to community healthcare workers so they can help mothers, newborns, and pregnant women. Communities are educated about the importance of natal checkups, hospital deliveries, breastfeeding, and access to nutrition. Malnourished mothers and children are provided cooking demonstrations as well as health camps. In disaster situations, the NGO generates massive fundraising to provide non-stop aid to communities. It does so by reaching out to millions who support NGO rescue operations at such adverse times.

Dealing with Child Abuse

India has two strong legislations—the JJ and POCSO Acts—to deal with child abuse and child sexual abuse along with the Indian Penal Code. In 2012, the POCSO Act was established to protect children against offences like sexual abuse, sexual harassment, and pornography. It was formed to provide a child-friendly system for trial under which perpetrators could be punished. India has laws pertaining to child physical abuse, including parents physically hurting children. The JJ Act, 2016, is the comprehensive legislation that also deals with child physical abuse by parents. Though the primary responsibility for safety, security, and providing a conducive environment to children for their development lies with the parents, the law does not spare even parents who cause hurt to and abuse their own children. Such children, who have been physically abused by parents, come in the category of children in need of care and protection. The incidents of child physical abuse by parents are dealt by the Child Welfare Committees (CWCs) established under the JJ Act. Chapter V of the legislation contains the detailed procedure about the formation of CWCs, and their procedures, powers, functions, and responsibilities. The specific sections of the Act pertaining to CWCs are sections 27–30.

The child may be produced in front of CWC by any police officer or special juvenile police unit or a designated Child Welfare Police Officer or any officer of a District Child Protection Unit or inspector appointed under any labor law for the time being in force; any public servant; Childline Services or any voluntary or non-governmental organization or any agency as may be recognized by the State Government; a Child Welfare Officer or probation officer, any social worker or a public spirited citizen; by the child himself; or any nurse, doctor, or management of a nursing home, hospital, or maternity home. Also, CWC can take *suo motu* notice of a child in need of care and protection. Generally, CWCs are involved with cases of a child in need of care and protection, and can take decisions in the best interest of the child who has been physically abused by the parents. CWC actions can include: admonition; conduct inquiry; direct the Child Welfare Officers or probation officers or District Child Protection Unit or non-governmental organizations to conduct social investigation and submit a report before the Committee; ensure care, protection, appropriate rehabilitation, or restoration of a child in need of care and protection, based on the child's individual care plan and passing necessary directions to parents or guardians or fit persons or children's homes or fit facility in this regard; select a registered institution for placement of each child requiring institutional support, based on the child's age, gender, disability, and needs, and keeping in mind the available capacity of the institution; or access appropriate legal services for the child. The CWC makes decisions in the best interest of the child and it may or may not place the child in institutional care arrangements, kinship, or foster care. The CWC is empowered to pass the appropriate orders in respect of the child and can provide custody of the child to any person or agency which ensures the best interest of the child.

The different forms of sexual abuse, like penetrative and non-penetrative assault, sexual harassment, pornography, and so on, are included under the POCSO Act. Under certain specific circumstances POCSO states a sexual assault is to be considered "aggravated when the abuse is committed by a person in a position of trust or authority of the child, like a family member." It describes strict action against the offender according to the gravity of the offence and it prescribes rigorous imprisonment for a term which shall not be less than ten years but which may extend to imprisonment for life. There are circumstances when children and families are given support and services to change their behaviors or situation. If there is a severe situation the CWC can take children away from parents involuntarily. The Indian Law, while keeping in mind the parents' right to the custody of a child, holds the welfare of the child as the most important factor of consideration when deciding upon who gets the custody of a minor child. Broadly, the welfare of the child includes safekeeping of the child, an ethical upbringing, conditions for imparting a good education, and the guardian's economic well-being. However, no legal right, preferential right, or any other right holds more importance than the well-being of the child. Any court of law grants custody to that party who can assure the court that the welfare of the child best lies with them.[1] India is not averse to institutional care arrangements and there are thousands of children living in foster care. The promotion of adoption in view of institutional care is also encouraged as CARA is functioning across the country under government directives.

Case Studies from India

Two case studies are provided as representative of the situation of vulnerability and exploitation of children.

Child marriage: Cases of child marriage are still prevalent in India and have been one of the major concerns with respect to health, social, and physiological issues. Thus is one of the case studies of child marriage from the district of Warangal, Telengana state. Mrs. Manga is a resident of village Dammannapet, belonging to the Backward Class—low in the social hierarchy. She was only 10 years old and was studying in primary section along with her two elder sisters who were also victims of child marriage at an early age due to the pressure of their grandparents. At present, she is only 21 years old and a mother of three girls; the family is pressuring her for a male child. She had little knowledge about family life when she got married and always wanted to pursue education but the culture in their community enforced their family members to get their children married off at a very early age. Along with this, she also added that she was a victim of physical and mental harassment both by her husband and in-laws. Thus this picture shows that this is one of the cultures which are still prevalent in India, even in this modern era of the 21st century (Lal, 2016).

Child labor: This is a case study of an adolescent girl named Nisha Khora aged about 12 years and coming from a scheduled caste background that is an officially designated group of historically disadvantaged people in India, the lowest in the social hierarchy and untouchable. The family of this girl includes three brothers and she is the eldest among her siblings. Both the parents are working, her father works as a coolie, meaning a laborer, sometimes regarded as offensive or a pejorative, depending upon the historical and geographical context, and her mother works in a factory. Nisha was a student

---

[1] http://www.fortunelegal.in/child-custody-laws-in-india.html.

at a special school for child labor at Umuri three years back. She left education when the school was physically shifted to a new place named Jayanagar. She was very happy in attending the NCLP School as the school uniform, reading-writing materials, and textbooks were provided free of charge. Though she is still interested in attending the school, her parents are not interested in educating her because of losing her as an earning member of the family as well as providing for safety and security of their child. As Nisha's mother works in a cashew nut processing factory, Nisha has no option except to stay at home to take care of her younger siblings, or to do other household chores during the absence of her mother at home. Later on, Nisha joined in cashew nut-related employment with her mother and earns about Rs 150/(US$2.2) per week. She often prepares garlands and sells them. It has also been reported that the child's name is enrolled in Government Upper Primary School, but she does not attend since her parents view her as an economic asset to the family (Pradhan et al., 2006)

To conclude, the child protection system in India has evolved and is receiving increasing and adequate attention from its stakeholders. It has evolved from child welfare to child development to child protection and aspires to empower children in the truest sense of the term.

References

Bhatt, S. and Jha, A. K. (2006). Social care of children in India. In N. T. Tan and S. Vasoo (Eds.), *Challenge of Social Care in Asia* (pp.113–140). Marshall Cavendish Academic.

Goel, S. (2015). Children in Conflict with Law: Indian and International Perspective (June 18, 2015). Available at SSRN: https://ssrn.com/abstract=2620325 or http://dx.doi.org/10.2139/ssrn.2620325

Government of India. (2007a). *National policy on the voluntary sector, voluntary action cell planning commission.* Available at: http://planningcommission.nic.in/data/ngo/npvol07.pdf.

Government of India. (2007b). *Study on child abuse in India, Ministry of Women and Child Development.* Available at: wcd.nic.in/childabuse.pdf.

Government of India. (2009). The Right of Children to Free and Compulsory Education Act, 2009. Available at: https://legislative.gov.in/sites/default/files/The%20Right%20of%20Children%20to%20Free%20and%20Compulsory%20Education%20Act,%202009.pdf.

Government of India Ministry of Women and Child Development (2010). "Working Group on Development of Children for the Eleventh Five Year Plan (2007-2012): (Volume One)," Working Papers id:2873, eSocial Sciences. Available at: https://ideas.repec.org/p/ess/wpaper/id2873.html.

Government of India, Ministry of Women & Child Development. (2016). The Integrated Child Protection Scheme (ICPS): A Centrally Sponsored Scheme of Government—Civil Society Partnership. Available at: http://cara.nic.in/pdf/revised%20icps%20scheme.pdf.

HAQ. (2018). *Union budget 2018–19: Budget for children in #NewIndia.* Available at: http://haqcrc.org/wp-content/uploads/2018/02/haq-budget-for-children-2018-19.pdf.

Hindustan Times. (2017, February 21). *Children go missing every hour.* Available at: https://www.hindustantimes.com/delhi/7-children-go-missing-every-hour/story-oVkhqnOEQJUPsFIfmE6UjN.html.

James, A. and Prout, A. (Eds.). (1997). *Constructing and reconstructing childhood: Contemporary issues in the sociological study of childhood.* Falmer Press.

James, A. and Prout, A. (Eds.). (1997b). Re-presenting childhood: Time and transition in the study of childhood. In *Constructing and reconstructing childhood: Contemporary issues in the sociological study of childhood* (pp. 230–250). Falmer Press.

Juvenile Justice Care and Protection of Children Act. (2015). Available at: www.trackthemissingchild.gov.in>jjact.

The Plantations Labour Act (1952). https://labour.gov.in/sites/default/files/The-Plantation-Labour-Act-1951.pdf.

Lal, B. (2015). Child marriage in India: Factors and problems. *International Journal of Science and Research*, 4(4), 2993–2998.

Lal, S. (2016). Child marriage in India: Case studies in Warangal District of Telangana state. *International Journal of Current Research*, 8(10), 40268–40272.

Ministry of Women and Child Development. (2012). *Model guidelines under section 39 of the Protection of Children from Sexual Offenses Act, 2012*. https://wcd.nic.in/sites/default/files/POCSO-ModelGuidelines.pdf.

Ministry of Women and Child Development. (2017, April 6). *There are 1626 Institutional Homes supported under ICPS for care and protection of children*. http://pib.nic.in/newsite/PrintRelease.aspx?relid=160622.

NCPCR. (2018). *India child marriage and teenage pregnancy based on NFHS-4 (2015–16)*. Young Lives and NCPCR.

National Human Rights Commission. (n.d). Report of the NHRC Committee on Missing Children. https://nhrc.nic.in/sites/default/files/misc_MCRReport.PDF.

NITI Ayog. (2019). *NGO-DARPAN*. https://ngodarpan.gov.in/index.php/home/sectorwise.

NIUA. (2016). *Status of children in urban India: Baseline study*, 2016. National Institute of Urban Affairs, Delhi, India. http://cfsc.niua.org/sites/default/files/Status_of_children_in_urban_India-Baseline_study_2016.pdf.

Norozi, T. and Moen S. A. (2016). Childhood as a social construction. *Journal of Educational and Social Research*, 6(2), 75–80.

Plan International. (2003). *Kids behind bars: An international study*. Stenco.

Pradhan N., Mishra, R N., and Anuradha, K. (2006). *Perspectives of child labour in Koraput District and related issues in education at primary stage: A case study*. Society for Promoting Rural Education and Development. https://spread.org.in/document/childLabour.pdf.

Prognosys. (2012). Child Labour Always right in front of you But why constantly hidden from your view, Progynosys e services Pvt Ltd. Available at: chrome-extension://efaidnbmnnnibpcajpcglclefindmkaj/ https://niti.gov.in/planningcommission.gov.in/docs/reports/sereport/ser/ser_nclp1709.pdf.

Qvortrup, J. (1989). *On change of children and childhood*. In S. Doxiadis and S. Stewart (Eds.), *Early influences shaping the individual*. NATO ASI Series (Series A: Life Sciences), 161 (pp. 85–92). Springer.

Save the Children. (2016). *Recent statistics of child abuse*. Available at: www.savethechildren.in/resource-centre/articles/recent-statistics-of-child-abuse.

The Plantations Labour Act (1952). Available at: https://labour.gov.in/sites/default/files/The-Plantation-Labour-Act-1951.pdf.

Times of India. (2015, December 19). *85% delinquents are let off lightly*, New Delhi. Available at: http://timesofindia.indiatimes.com/articleshow/50239425.cms?utm_source=contentofinterest&utm_medium=text&utm_campaign=cppst.

UN. (1989). *Convention on the rights of the child*. New Delhi. Available at: https://www.childlineindia.org/pdf/Convention-on-the-Rights-of-the-Child-1989.pdf.

UNICEF. (2011). *The situation of children in India: A profile*. UNICEF.

UNICEF. (2016). *The state of the world's children 2016* [Statistical tables]. Available at: https://data.unicef.org/resources/state-worlds-children-2016-statistical-tables/.

UNICEF. (2018). Child Protection. Available at: https://www.unicef.org/protection.

Vidushy, V. (2016). Human trafficking in India: An analysis. *International Journal of Applied Research*, 2(6), 168–171.

Wani, S. (2014, December 3–4). *Child rights and the law: An emperical study of deprivation of rights and humane treatment of juveniles in conflict with law in India* [Conference presentation]. 6th International Conference of the International Justice Observatory, Brussels, Belgium.

Wihbey, J. (2011). Global prevalence of child sexual abuse. *Journalist Resource*. Available at: Journalistsresource.org/studies/./global-prevalence-child-sexual-abuse.

The Social Construction and Development of an Integrated Child Protection System: In Search of Core Templates in a Diversified and Decentralized Indonesia

Erna Dinata

Abstract

This chapter expounds on the social construction and development of an integrated child protection system in Indonesia as the country continues to reconstruct its identity as a nation and renegotiate its structural and institutional boundaries through social-cultural, political, and economic changes. While progress has been made in realizing the critical role of intermediary structures and intersectoral coordination in the decentralized governance of social service provisions, Indonesia continues to front the challenges of having millions of children living in poverty and the risk of child labor, trafficking, and early marriage. Despite the decline in the national poverty rate, levels of income and gender inequality are soaring, and the poverty rate reduction is slowing. The chapter identifies key challenges in building critical public discourse about child abuse and neglect, translating, and implementing the laws, policies, and strategies in protecting children and their families.

Key Words: Indonesia, social construction, child protection, identity, poverty, child marriages, child labor, trafficking

Introduction

An archipelago of approximately 17,000 islands, stretching about 5,236 kilometers between the West and the East, Indonesia is one of the world's most ethnically diverse nations with more than 1,200 self-identified ethnic groups living on roughly 6,000 islands (Ananta et al., 2015). The world's fourth largest child population, about 80 million from the total population of 270.2 million are under 18 years of age (UNICEF, 2020; BPS, 2018; BPS, 2020) and are, according to Law No. 35/2014, the amendment of the Law on Child Protection No. 23/2002, categorized as children. However, Indonesia still faces challenges ahead: more than half of the child population, an estimated 45 million, live in poverty and at risk of child labor, trafficking, and early marriage (SMERU Research Institute & UNICEF, 2013). Over half of Indonesia's children live in 5 provinces out of a total of 34 provinces, and the country experiences rapid urbanization in which two third of total population will reside in cities by 2030, which will impact the quality of children's life (UNICEF, 2020). Historically, child protection in Indonesia included programs targeted to address specific problems, based largely on the involvement of international non-governmental agencies in Indonesia, such as street-children, child labor, trafficked children, child domestic workers, children in contact with the law, or children affected by HIV or AIDS (Needham, 2007; UNICEF, 2008). Today, these international agencies continue to engage in stimulating, initiating, and guiding the development of a more comprehensive child protection system than merely addressing those fragmented areas. Under these physical boundaries and characteristics, Indonesia continues to reconstruct its identity as a nation, and renegotiate its structural and institutional boundaries through social-cultural, political, and economic transformations (Aspinall & Berger, 2001; Aspinall, 2004; Carnegie, 2008; Bräuchler, 2015; Bazzi et al., 2017). The shift from a highly centralized state to a decentralized governance system in post-reformation Indonesia in 1999 marked an important transformation in which the political economy of local contexts and diversity grew increasingly relevant (Fitrani et al., 2005; Smith, 2008; Bräuchler, 2015). In addition, the shifting of reform dynamics to local contexts under a great deal of variation of resources and child protection elements among regions in Indonesia could challenge equitable public services, including services for children and families (UNICEF, 2020; Eaton, 2010; Kaybryn, 2015; Cummings et al., 2014). Could the decentralized governance structure be seen as a source for bottom-up reconciliation and empowerment, bridging local initiatives to a national child protection agenda? Indonesia has been among countries that use the language of rights in its public discourse on child protection and continues to face challenges in translating and implementing a rights-based system, closing the gaps between the legal framework, policy formulation, and practice implementation.

Complex Set of Interrelated Issues in Protecting Children

In Law No. 35 of 2014 amending the Law on Child Protection (No. 23 of 2002) the term child protection is defined broadly as "all activities to guarantee and protect children and their rights so that they can live, grow, develop optimally in accordance with inherent human dignity and worth, and get protection from violence and discrimination." In their Baseline Report on Children in Indonesia, BAPPENAS and UNICEF (2017) address the 2030 Sustainable Development Goals Agenda that links the social, economic, and environmental aspects of development. Those interrelated circumstances are fundamentally complex in understanding the interconnectedness between the social protection and child protection system in Indonesia. Poverty, a risk factor for child development, is linked to worse-than-average outcomes in other dimensions of sustainable development goals like nutrition, health, education, child marriage, water and sanitation, and birth registration. Monetary poverty lines are complex phenomena as households experience dynamics over time such as illness, unemployment, drought, disability, death, and birth. Even though the national poverty rate fell from 24% in 1990 to 11% in 2015, levels of income inequality are rising, and the rate of poverty reduction is slowing. In addition, the notion of a national child poverty rate is intricate for several reasons: the continuous cycle of poverty, large family size of the poor, lack of social protection coverage for children under the age of 6, and the fact that poverty rates vary across provinces. Children in the three provinces of West, Central, and East Java make up 42% of all children living below the national poverty line. The Indonesian Central Bureau of Statistics (BPS) and UNICEF recently applied the Multiple Overlap Deprivation Analysis (MODA) to investigate children's experience of deprivation in six domains of well-being (food and nutrition, health, education, housing, water and sanitation, and protection) and found that 65% of children were deprived in at least two non-income dimensions of poverty in 2016; rural children experienced substantially higher rates.

Nationwide, over 37% of children under 5 years of age were stunted in 2013—roughly 8.4 million children (Bappenas & UNICEF, 2017; Rokx et.al, 2018; Save the Children, 2018). National data also shows that 37% of pregnant women were anemic, thus the mother's nutrition and her children's nutrition are compromised. Early childbearing has been a concern: about 10% of adolescent girls aged 15–19 years were mothers or pregnant with their first child, about 13% for rural compared to 6% for urban teenagers. Child marriage rates vary by region (higher in rural areas), by education (child marriage rates are lower for women living in a household where the household head has completed senior secondary and university education), and by income. Some studies show that even though poor households consider child marriage benefits economically in the short term, it does not provide financial security for the long term, and likely maintains and exacerbates poverty, rather than alleviates it (Kalamar et al., 2016; Marinescu & Triyana, 2016; Rumble et al., 2018). Therefore, gender inequality and gender-based violence has been a critical context for understanding the complexity of child protection in this country. The Women's Health and Life Experiences Survey (SPHPN), conducted by the Indonesian Central Bureau of Statistics (BPS) in 2016 found that about 28% of women and girls aged 15–64 years who have ever been married or in union had experienced physical, sexual, and/or psychological intimate-partner violence. Living in urban areas, school, and work environments increases the likelihood of women and girls experiencing physical and/or sexual violence. The National Commission of Violence Against Women (Komnas Perempuan, 2018) documented a 74% increase in the number of cases reported. Most of domestic violence data comes from District and Religious Courts and the Commission's partner service institutions, which reported an increase from 259,150 cases in 2016 to 348,446 cases in 2017. Violence against girls in the context of domestic violence is quite high (23%), including some sexual abuse cases perpetrated by the biological father. Courage to report these cases to service institutions showed progress as women and girls previously tended to foster impunity for perpetrators. Sixteen percent of reported trafficking victims in Indonesia are children, mostly girls, traded internally and abroad for commercial sexual exploitation, including tourism, domestic work, and mining.

The mid-term evaluation of the National Medium Term Development Plan 2015–2019 (RPJMN, 2015–2019) documented the baseline prevalence rate of violence against children (including other types of violence and not limited to intrafamilial violence) in 2014 as 21% and 39% for girls and boys, respectively. Unlike in many western industrialized countries, child maltreatment in Indonesia does not serve as the focal point for defining the child protection system. It is an aspect of the development of child protection: to improve the quality of life and growth of children optimally; increase the protection of children from acts of violence, exploitation, neglect, and other mistreatment; and increase the effectiveness of child protection institutions. Nevertheless, child maltreatment becomes relevant as severe cases of intrafamilial family violence are increasingly discovered and reported. In addition, the low percentage of birth registration continues to be a problem in Indonesia overall, though it is getting better in some regions and worse in others. More than 24 million Indonesian children are undocumented (Summer & Kusumaningrum, 2014), which is linked to problems such as increased school dropout, child trafficking and labor, and reduced access to health services, social services, and education. Without effective civil registration and vital statistics (CRVS), the government cannot inform and monitor various social policies and programs. Contributing factors to the invisibility of some children include unaffordable costs and hidden fees, incomplete prerequisite documents, complex navigation of the CRVS system, and long distances and remote locations for registration.

The Institutional Environment of Child Protection System

The many forms of adversity experienced by children do not occur in a vacuum. In fact, the definition of neglected children in Law No. 35/2014 on Child Protection reflects those critical contexts, that is, neglected children are those whose needs—including their physical, mental, spiritual, and social needs—are not naturally fulfilled. Interestingly, the term abuse is not explicitly used in the law; instead, the closest term to abuse that is included in the law is violence, which is defined as any act against a child which results in physical, psychological, sexual, and/or neglectful misery or suffering, including unlawful threats to commit certain acts, coercion, or deprivation of liberty. While complex interconnectedness between the physical and mental aspects of children's needs and problems are evidenced, the intricacy of spiritual and social contexts is pivotal. These larger institutional contexts have been significantly influential in contributing to and shaping the public discourse on conceptions of abuse, neglect, and protection. Hasenfeld (2010) insightfully underlines the primacy of the institutional environment and the nature of human services as *institutionalized organizations*[1] in which any efforts to alleviate pain and

---

[1] Meyer and Rowan (1977) noted that the growth and survival of 'insitutionalized organizations' rely less on the technical proficiency of their work and more on their conformity with institutional rules—dominant cultural symbols and belief systems (Hasenfeld, 2010, pp. 14–15).

suffering through human services would involve moral work and must constantly seek and maintain legitimacy and support by making reference to institutionalized moral systems and elaborating rules and requirements from various elements in the environment. Scott (2008) specifically noted critical elements in the institutional environments:

> they adopt and uphold moral systems and cultural frames that resonate well with their significant audiences, such as legislative bodies, government bureaucracies, regulatory agencies, professional associations, other human service organizations, various civic and political associations, and clients. (Hasenfeld, 2010, p. 14)

The institutional environment in a multicultural pluralistic society like Indonesia, in which child protection systems are embedded, is diverse and tumultuous, adopting conflicting values, norms, and institutional logics that affect the development as well as the implementation of child protection efforts. The gravity of child marriage, which is a common phenomenon throughout Indonesia, shows that poverty is not the only contributing factor. Its occurrence has been supported by intricate interactions of local demographic and geographic contexts, religious and traditional values, and legal frameworks (Grijn & Horii, 2018; Prameswari & Agustin, 2018; Rumble et al., 2018; Sumanti et al., 2018; PUSKAPA UI et al., 2020a). When questions of child marriage come before the courts, judges must practice discretion as they attempt to reconcile state laws with local norms and religious preferences. At the national level, the Indonesian government may attempt to comply with international goals and policies to reduce child marriage, yet the national public discourse on this issue is heavily influenced by a conservative Islamic perspective. Other moderate perspectives including from female clerics and women and children's rights practitioners, are not sufficient to counter the dominant discourse.

The issue of translation and implementation of law and regulations also continues to be open to discretion and various conflicting interests. In their analysis of the nationally representative Indonesian Demographic and Health Survey and the Adolescent Reproductive Health Survey, Rumble and colleagues (2018) also found that unmarried females (aged 15–24) reject child marriage and prefer partnerships as adults. This growing norm to support broader child marriage prevention in Indonesia faces challenges and dilemmas as rising religious conservatism reflects the continuous struggles and compromises on the diversity of values related to gender equality. Providentially, the Indonesian Constitutional Court finally reversed its controversial 2015 decision in regard to a provision in the 1974 Marriage Law. The court agreed that defining the marriageable age as 16 for girls and 19 for boys was a form of discrimination against women and that the current marriageable age of 16 for girls was unconstitutional (Sapiie, 2018; Afrianty, 2019). The court also determined that child marriage violates children's rights to education and to live a healthy life, and gave the legislature three years to revise the provisions.

Recent agreement between the Indonesia House of Representatives together with various Ministries (i.e., Ministry of Women's Empowerment and Child Protection, the Ministry of Religion, the Ministry of Health, and the Ministry of Law and Human Rights) to raise a minimum age for marriage to 19 both for women and men, during the house's working committee meeting, is a hopeful sign, considering eight of the 10 factions present support the decision.

Nevertheless, the rise of social conservatism that emphasizes traditional gender roles and identities might impede efforts to support legislative bills and challenge its implementation. The recent debate on a legislative bill related to sexual violence was politicized and linked to religious and morality issues, especially during the election, and stalled due to strong opposition from the religious conservative political party within the House of Representatives, which argued that the bill has a "liberal perspective," inconsistent with religious values, and promotes other sexual relations like free sex and lesbian, gay, bisexual, and transgender relations (Farisa, 2019; Suryakusuma, 2019). The tensions between various institutionalized elements in relation to the moral system, cultural framework, legislative and court processes, state law, and government bureaucracy have been intricate both in the law making and implementation process under a decentralized governance system.

> At the local level, village bureaucrats create their semi-autonomous social field, which sustains customs, rules, and symbols internally but is also vulnerable to rules and decisions from outside the field. They use their unofficial support system to solve legal issues in accordance with local cultural and religious norms and values. Such a system is created to meet the needs of their local community. Villagers almost always resort to this unofficial system without any involvement of state institutions. (Grijn & Horii, 2018, p. 464)

The implementation of current and future child protection policies might continue to face challenges. Political turmoil and polarization has been linked, within the context of the increased political influence of Indonesian Islamists' in late 2016 and early 2017, with the successful mobilization of hundreds of thousands of people (known as the 212 movement) to remove the then governor of Jakarta, a Chinese-Christian, who was accused of blasphemy (IPAC, 2019). This mass mobilization contributed to the continuing significant rise of political identity and the role of religion in politics and public life as the party system has been fragmented along the Islamist–pluralist spectrum rather than polarized by policy issues, in which politicians frame inequality in ethno-religious terms and invoke a sectarian reading of socio-economic disparity that deepen social divisions and distrust (Aspinall et al., 2018; Aspinall, 2019; Tapsell, 2019; Warburton, 2019, Warburton & Muhtadi, 2019). In line with this tension, the rise of the conservative women's movement has challenged the progress of gender equality in Indonesia (Kartika, 2019b; Mazrieva, 2019). While the participation of women's partisan groups from the full spectrum has been advocating issues within a patriarchal state-propagated gender ideology, the rise of the conservative women's movement, through social media and an organized Islamic study circle, has larger consequences (Kartika, 2019a, 2019b; Fachriansyah, 2019; Mazrieva, 2019). This movement fears that the "pluralist" agenda might mean the inclusion of communism and other moral threats associated with parenting, family life, and morality issues, such as abortion, extra-marital sex, bodily autonomy, homosexuality, and women working overseas unaccompanied by their families. Social media has become their campaign tool by using slogans like *Indonesia Without Feminism*, *Uninstall Feminism*, *Indonesia Without Dating*, *Let's have Polygamy*. The implementation of a gender quota in parliament in 2004 may provide opportunities for both the pluralist and Islamist women representatives, feminist and anti-feminists, to pursue their agendas, shape gender-related public discourse, and initiate policy that effects issues and resources related to women, family, and child protection (Kartika 2019b; Prihartini, 2018a; Prihartini, 2018b).

Indonesia has adopted progressive legal instruments and policies, and participated in ratifying various international treaties in relation to child rights. Table 37.1 lists some of those significant instruments, policies, and treaties.

In spite of these legal instruments, there is currently little effort to translate these instruments into regulations, instructions, or resources to develop national policies and programs. Some of them have been translated into presidential and ministerial instructions and decrees, especially developed by the Ministry of Social Affairs (Kemensos) and

Table 37.1 List of instruments, policies, and treaties relating to children's rights and welfare

- Ratification the UN Convention on Child Rights of 1990
- Act No. 39 of 1999 on Human Rights
- Act No. 23 of 2002 on Child Protection
- Act No. 20 of 2003 on National Education System
- Act No. 23 of 2004 on Elimination of Domestic Violence
- Act No. 12 of 2006 on Indonesian Nationality
- Act No. 17 of 2007 on National Long-Term Development Plan 2005–2025
- Act No. 21 of 2007 on Eradication of Human Trafficking Crimes
- Act No. 40 of 2008 on Elimination of Racial and Ethnic Discrimination
- Government Regulation No. 47 of 2008 on Compulsory Education
- Act No.44 of 2008 on Pornography
- Act No. 24 of 2011 on Social Security Management Body
- Ratification of the Convention on Rights of the Disabled of 2011
- Act No. 11 of 2012 on Child Justice System
- Act No. 7 of 2012 on Management of Social Conflict
- Act No. 24 of 2013 on Population Administration
- Ratification of Optional Protocol of Convention on the Rights of the Child and Child Involvement in Armed Conflict of 2012
- Ratification of International Convention on Protection for the Rights of Migrant Workers and their families of 2012
- Act No. 35 of 2014 on Child Protection (Revision of the Child Protection Act No. 23 of 2002)

Source: Ministry for Women's Empowerment and Child Rights Republic of Indonesia (2016).

the Ministry for Women's Empowerment and Child Protection (KPPPA), which are the two key stakeholders with critical roles in the provision of social services, and policy advocacy, strategy, and coordination.

Some instruments reflect the broad issues and challenges children face (i.e., education, birth status, human trafficking), such as the National Strategy for Elimination of Violence Against Children 2016–2020 (STRANAS PKTA,[2] 2016–2020) and the National Medium Term Development Plan (RPJMN). The National Strategy for Elimination of Violence Against Children was mutually formulated by various key stakeholders, consisted of 75 participants from 17 ministries/institutions, seven NGOs, four religious organizations, and six youth organizations. They developed the strategy with a clear timeframe, emphasizing prevention and coordination at all levels of government (i.e., provincial, district/city, sub-district, and villages). The main objective of STRANAS PKTA was for "All children in Indonesia to be able to grow and develop optimally based on their respective potentials and are free from all forms of violence, including neglect and exploitation." The six strategies include:

1) *Legislation and application of policies protecting children from all forms of violence.* By 2020, legal instruments and policies would be available to eliminate all forms of violence against children from all backgrounds, and align these with government commitments to international conventions and protocols. A study at the ASEAN (Association of Southeast Asian Nations) level noted that of all Indonesia's legal instruments and policies, only 42% were in compliance with the International Human Rights standards (UNICEF, 2015). Challenges include the rules and regulations in regard to prohibiting physical punishment toward children; the scope of official or legal definitions of "emotional violence," "neglect," and "rape"; discriminatory treatment toward the minimum age of marriage for girls; and minimal legal instruments to identify children as victims of sexual exploitation. The socialization of these policies, together with law enforcement, are critical for the implementation process.

2) *Change in social norms and cultural practices that accept, justify or disregard violence.* This strategy is targeted at children, caretakers, and community figures for them to be aware of the rights of children to have protection from all forms of violence and methods of preventing violence. Community empowerment and mobilization for capacity building and social-behavioral change would be achieved through advocacy, training, counseling, and

---

[2] STRANAS PKTA stands for Strategi National Penghapusan Kekerasan Terhadap Anak.

campaigns through the existing structures in cross sectoral government agencies under decentralized structural arrangements.

3) *Childcare that supports safe and loving relations between care giver and child to prevent violence.* This strategy encompasses programs related to positive parenting to help parents develop communication and interaction, including methods for identifying abuses that can significantly reduce the risk and exposure to any forms of violence.

4) *Improving life skills and survival skills of the child in preventing violence and supporting child compulsory education programs.* A variety of programs are anticipated to provide children with knowledge and skills in controlling emotions, appreciating cooperation, mutual support and diversity, and understanding sexual and reproductive health.

5) *Providing accessible and quality supportive services for victims, perpetrators, and children at risk.* This strategy focuses on connecting children to various service systems across sectors and agencies, and requires the interaction and coordination of various policies and programs from social protection, social assistance, and child protection. Child welfare assistance funds, low-income family assistance, and a variety of case screening and management, educational, advocacy, and counseling services would be included in this strategy.

6) *Improved quality of supporting data and evidence on violence against children.* Establishing an integrated child protection database that includes epidemiology data, case management, and supervision from data collection, analysis, and evaluation. This strategy would utilize data across agencies in various ministries, especially the Coordinating Ministry for Human Development and Cultural Affairs (Kemenko PMK), Ministry for Women's Empowerment and Child Protection (KPPPA), Ministry for National Development Planning (PPN/Bappenas), Ministry of Social Affairs, and Central Bureau of Statistics. The development and coordination across ministries is at a very preliminary stage to establish its own data structures and communicate what they collect.

In the process of planning, implementation, monitoring, and evaluation of STRANAS PKTA, some basic principles, rooted in the International Standards of Human Rights and Child Rights, as stipulated in the Convention on the Rights of the Child, guide the process. These principles include: a) the best interest of the child; b) child participation; c) the child's right to live, survive, and develop; and d) non-discrimination. Other national policies that have critical importance in relation to child protection are: the National Medium Term Development Plan/RPJMN; the National Action Plan for Child Protection/RAN PA; the National Action Plan for Health of School Age Children and Adolescents/RANKES AUSREM; the National Action Plan on Human Rights/

RAN HAM; the National Action Plan on Protection and Empowerment of Women and Children in Social Conflict/RAN P3AKS; and the National Action Plan for Acceleration of Implementation of Gender Mainstreaming and Child Rights through the Forum of Religious Organizations. It is within this interweaving of various institutional contexts, contradictory institutional norms, and logics (i.e., legal frameworks, cultural, and religious norms and values) and decentralized governance that the child protection system in Indonesia is embedded. The translation and implementation of these principles and strategies depend on mutual understanding and ongoing dialog within and between key stakeholders and intermediary structures on the contexts, policy issues, and strategies in child protection.

Negotiating Spaces of Child Protection: Decentralization Context

The transformation from a centralized to a decentralized governance structure after the 1998 reformation reflected more of the political uncertainty during that period than merely a change of structural arrangement (Rabasa & Chalk, 2001; Bjork, 2003; Hosen, 2003; Fitrani et al., 2005; Guess, 2005; Aspinall & Fealy, 2010; Mietzner, 2010; Unicef, 2011; Hamid, 2014; Malesky & Hutchinson, 2016; Prasetyawan, 2018). Precipitated by the Asian financial crisis, political discontent, the fragmentation of the political party system, and power concentration in Java, decentralization seemed unavoidable. Allocating power to the provinces was highly precarious as the most affluent provinces might separate and seek independence, thus, the option to diminish that risk was to transfer power to lower administrative units, to the districts. The central government is responsible for defense, fiscal policy, foreign relations, religious affairs, justice, and economic planning; the provinces are expected to assume a coordinating and supervisory role, and the districts are in charge of delivering most government services, that is, healthcare, education, and social and civil services (Brodjonegoro, 2009; Pepinski & Wihardja, 2011; Pisani, 2014). Thus, the delivery of services for children and families is provided at the district level of government. Changes in the decentralized structural arrangement are reflected in the growing number of divisions, in which the number of districts and cities increased the most, 80% and 70%, respectively, since the decentralization decision was in effect at the early Indonesian reformation period.

Bureaucratization continues with the expansion in the number of civil servants, although is not necessarily followed by higher performance and quality of human resources; this challenges the efficiency and effectiveness of various local service provisions. While decentralization might be associated with developing good local governance based on local context and needs, some studies indicate that a few successful reform efforts at the local level have been driven by a handful of exceptionally well-performing administrators, not a reflection of broader trends (Aspinall & Mietzner, 2010; Buehler, 2010). It also changes the power dynamic between the central and local governments, which results in wide variation of fiscal effects and experiences across regions, lobbying relationships and coalitions between central and local governments:

> This devolution has created a new class of regional political elites and has shifted significant power back to sub-national levels in Indonesia's centuries' long history of centre-local tensions. While the political motivations of mitigating centrifugal pressures appear to be vindicated, the anticipated gains in service provision and downstream economic impacts have not uniformly materialized: efficiency gains in some regions have been offset by the widespread emergence of clientalistic practices and fiscal inefficiencies. Recent efforts towards limited administrative and political recentralization underscore the tension that remains between the centre and local governments. (Ostwald et al., 2016, p. 139)

Pepinsky and Wiharja (2011) note that high levels of heterogeneity across districts challenge the competition over productive resources and, unfortunately, socioeconomically disadvantaged districts, for which the benefits of decentralization are crucial, are left behind. Geographic and demographic variations across regions affect the implementation and funding for the child protection system as well as the complex coordination of various elements of stakeholders cross-sectorally. This complicates the various levels of decision making in negotiating resource allocation, operating procedures, service domain and coverages.

Under decentralized governance, about 40% of a government budgeted income of IDR 2,142 trillion was transferred to the regions, 90% of which was allocated to all districts/cities (total of 514) and 10% went to 34 provinces as block grants. Regions have discretion to spend according to regional needs and priorities, to accelerate development, expand regional access, and improve the quality of public services, including for child protection. However, 70% of the local budget at the district level (APBD) is spent on overhead costs, leaving 30% for public services such as education and health, and almost none for social services. A very small proportion of child protection funds is allocated to two ministries, the Ministry of Women Empowerment and Child Protection, and the Ministry of Social Affairs. The actual allocations might be different from the proposed ones considering political and economic uncertainties, which might create policy windows that affect decisions on resource allocations. The Ministry of Social Affairs, one of the 10 ministries and institutions with the highest budget allocation, allocated most of its funds, IDR 41 trillion in fiscal year 2018 and IDR 59 trillion in 2019, to social assistance. This decision underlines the crucial interconnectedness and interdependence between the social protection and child protection system in Indonesia. Lacking access to resources and various services might increase children's risks in experiencing violence, neglect, and abuse. Indonesia's social protection system, which accounts for about 0.73% of GDP, consists of contributory schemes (social insurance) and non-contributory schemes (social assistance) is seen as a crucial part of child protection policy. Indonesia's national health insurance (Jaminan Kesehatan Nasional) is funded primarily by members' contributions while the poorest 40% of the population are supported through the health insurance subsidy system. Social assistance, which includes food assistance programs, conditional cash transfers, and a cash transfer for students from poor and vulnerable families, provides emergency assistance as children and families navigate life trajectories, develop capacities, and build their support systems. A significantly smaller budget for the Ministry of Women Empowerment and Child Protection, compared to the Ministry of Social Affairs, around IDR1 trillion, is allocated for child development and child protection.

From Fragmentation to Integration: In Search of Core Templates and Locus of Discretion

The political-economic, social, and cultural contexts of child related issues in Indonesia have inevitably shaped the policy directions of child protection in this country. Most policies have aimed to increase access of quality services in order to support growth and development of all children, to strengthen the child protection system, which includes prevention, case management, and rehabilitation of children as victims of violence, exploitation, neglect, and other mistreatments, and to increase the effectiveness of child protection institutions. Indonesia does not have a single registry (i.e., child maltreatment referral and removal); multiple stakeholders engage in various levels of policy and practice that might overlap between the national, provincial, and district/city levels. Two main institutions, KPPPA (Ministry of Women Empowerment and Child Protection) and Kemsos (Ministry of Social Affairs) are two ministries which directly focus on the development and implementation of child and family policies, advocacy, and service provision. The National Planning Agency (BAPPENAS)[3] forsees an increased cross sectoral synergy between various ministries to support and improve the national child protection system along with KPPPA and Kemsos to work cross-sectorally with other ministries such as the Ministry of Education and Culture (Kemendikbud), Ministry of Health (Kemkes), Ministry of Manpower (Kemnaker), Ministry of Communication and Information Technology (Kemkominfo), Ministry of Law and Human Rights (Kemkumham), National Anti-Narcotics Agency of the Republic of Indonesia (BNN), Indonesian National Police (POLRI), and Indonesian Child Protection Commission (KPAI). Generally, the Ministry of Law and Human Rights oversees and participates in the implementation of restorative justice to protect the rights of children in violation of the law, the Ministry of Manpower handles aspects of child labor issues, and the Anti-Narcotics Agency works to prevent and manage cases related to substance abuse. The National Police Agency and the Ministry of

---

[3] Discussion with Ir. Yosi Diani Tresna, MPM at her office, Sub-Directorate of Child Protection, Directorate of Population, Women Empowerment and Child Protection National Planning Agency (BAPPENAS), and materials provided in regard to Coordination and Challenges for developing an integrated model of child protection (Jakarta, February 7, 2018).

Health play critical roles as few possible entry gates of receiving reports of child and family abuse, neglect, or violence, as well as coordinating their services network to provide necessary services. The Ministry of Education and Ministry of Communication's roles are to provide resources for educational services and socialization/advocacy on various child protection topics including the various trainings and seminars for building capacities.

The Indonesian Child Protection Commission (KPAI, 2016, 2018) is responsible for supervising the implementation of the fulfillment of the Rights of the Child. If needed, the Regional Government (Pemda) could form a Regional Child Protection Commission or other similar institution to support the supervision of the implementation of Child Protection in the regions. The commission's membership consists of elements from the government, religious leaders, community leaders, professional organizations, non-governmental organizations, corporations, and other elements of civil society who care about child protection. The commission collects data and information, receives and reviews community complaints, mediates disputes, reports to authorities about violations of the Right of the Child Act, and provides input for policy formulation on child protection. The KPAI documented 4885 cases of violence against children in 2018, showing an increased trend of reported cases since 2011. The highest proportion, 29.3%, are categories of children in conflict with the law, including children as victims of physical, psychological and sexual abuse, victims of murder, abortion, accident, robbery, suicide, gun violence, and kidnapping. The second most reported cases, about 17.5%, are related to family disputes and care problems, including child custody battles, lack of access for child visitation, child neglect, missing, and abduction. Next, about 14%, are children as victims of pornography and cyber-criminal activities. Cases from schools, about 9%, include children as victims and perpetrators of bullying, children as victims and perpetrators of customary mass street fighting between gangs of particular schools (*tawuran*), and other cases related to problems with violation of school policy. Health and substance abuse problems, 7.45%, are related to medical malpractice, poison, and children as substance abusers and distributors. Children as victims of human trafficking and exploitation has a similar proportion, about 7%, to children as victim of social and emergency circumstances (i.e, social conflict, war, and natural disasters). Five percent of the reported cases are children situated in complex circumstances related to conflict with religious norms and cultural values such as having sex outside marriage, child marriage, and as victims of conflict between religions. The rest of the cases, about 3%, are problems linked to civil rights and participation such as children without a birth certificate, and children from mixed parental marriages and citizenship. While these numbers provide rough estimates and a depiction of complex children and family issues, the many categories reflect the challenges in classifying, addressing the overlapping, and understanding the root causes of those categories, contexts, and contingencies.

Law No. 35 of 2014 on Child Protection describes the circumstances when children are eligible to receive services such as: 1) children in emergency situations; 2) children who are in contact with the law; 3) children from minority and isolated groups; 4) children who are exploited economically and/or sexually; 5) children who are victims of narcotics, alcohol, psychotropic, and other addictive substances; 6) children who are victims of pornography; 7) children with HIV/AIDS; 8) child victims of abduction, sales, and/or trade; 9) child victims of physical and/or psychological violence; 10) child victims of sexual crimes; 11) child victims of terrorism networks; 12) children with disabilities; 13) child victims of mistreatment and neglect; 14) children with deviant social behavior; and 15) children who are victims of stigmatization because of the labels attached to the condition of their parents. The performance report from the Directorate of Social Rehabilitation under the Ministry of Social Affairs documented that 130,000 children from various groups received services in 2018, including neglected and street children, children in conflict with the law, children with disabilities, and children and families in need for protection and capacity building. Under the decentralized governance structure, the provision and coordination of services across sectors requires coordination of social service provision from the central to district level. Currently, most policies, programs, and services for children and families at the district level are coordinated and implemented through a Technical Implementation Unit (UPT) from the Ministry of Social Affairs (Kemsos) and the Ministry of Women Empowerment and Child Protection (KPPPA).

In 2015, Kemsos released an Indonesia Child Help Line (TePSA), which is a hotline that operates 24/7 to provide referral and counseling services. However, the capacities of the hotline staff to grasp the complexity of the children's problems and available resources through social protection, social assistance and service programs needs to be improved with ongoing training (Rusmana, 2017). The training for hotline services also includes UPT local staff from other ministries other than Kemsos. From 2015 to 2018, the number of cases reported from regions across Indonesia and handled through TePSA were 88 (0.001), 1,387 (0.017), 1,626 (0.020), and 1,096 (0.014),[4] respectively. The increased number of reported cases from 2015 to the following years, with a slight decrease in 2018, might be attributed to the increased capacity of the system to receive and handle reports. Cases reported most frequently are for child abuse and neglect, especially cases of sexual violence, and children in contact with the law. The call center staff will then connect with the social workers at the respective regions where the cases are located.

To receive services, children should be younger than age 18, bring the recommendation from UPT at the district level, and receive guidance from a social worker. Social workers, hired by the Ministry of Social Affairs, provide assessment and referral, on a voluntary basis, for children/families in the form of case management and needed services such as school, health services, civil registry, child protection and rehabilitation institutions, court, and other types of socioeconomic-related needs. In fact, at the district level,

---

[4] Rates per 1,000 are provided in the parentheses derived from total case reported divided by 80 million (total children population in Indonesia).

social workers at the Center of Social Welfare for Children (PKSA), under the Ministry of Social Affairs, collaborates closely with other UPT workers under various ministries and elements of civil society to identify high risk and vulnerable families to access various types of resources from public and private entities and communities, especially in further development of an Integrated Child Welfare Service Model PKSAI.[5] This model, which aims to strengthen PKSA, combines cash assistance with complementary social welfare interventions supported by a social worker. The Directorate of Social Rehabilitation for Children in collaboration with two other directorates under the Ministry of Social Affairs (i.e., the Directorate of Individual, Family, and Community Institutional Empowerment, and the Directorate of Social Protection and Insurance) utilize a database from the Data and Information Center to identify high risk groups eligible for social assistance and discuss cases and contexts to provide case management and intervention plans, including preventive efforts to access birth certificates, improve nutrition, and develop capacities for social and economic empowerment programs. The capacities and level of coordination among these institutional and government level structures vary greatly across regions, provinces, and districts in Indonesia, only a few of which have developed these capacities.[6] Children and families might also report and seek help from the Center of Integrated Services for Empowering Women and Children (P2TP2A), under KPPPA at the province and district level. The center will provide assessment and case management through case conference and can access various short-term services, such as medical referrals to inpatient or outpatient facilities, legal aid, psychological services, temporary safe house, and home visit. The center also engages in preventive programs to educate various stakeholders and community members through seminars, training, and capacity building especially for police officers, doctors, nurses, and teachers.

Adoption. The Directorate of Social Rehabilitation for Children (under Sub-Directorate for Children under age 5) has a unit that is in charge of providing adoption[7] because of various circumstances, including out of wedlock children, parents' physical

---

[5] Since 2015, the Ministry of Social Affairs of the Republic of Indonesia and UNICEF have been developing an Integrated Child Welfare Service Model (PKSAI), piloted in five regions, three districts (Tulungagung in East Java, Klaten in Central Java, and Gowa in South Sulawesi), and two cities (Surakarta in Central Java and Makassar in South Sulawesi), to protect vulnerable children and families, particularly child victims of violence, abuse, exploitation, and neglect. This service model strives to address complex challenges related to policy implementation, service delivery and decentralization. The total number of cases reported to the PKSAI in those piloted regions increased from 957 in 2017 to 1,960 in 2018. The most common reasons for cases reported or referred to PKSAI in those regions are problems in acquiring birth certificates, needs for service provision of family support and social/psychosocial rehabilitation, parenting issues, and education access (Child Frontiers, 2019).

[6] Among the piloted regions for PKSAI, the front-runner district is Tulung Agung in East Java.

[7] Law No. 35/2014, the amendment of the Law on Child Protection No. 23/2002, Articles 39–41; Government Regulation on the Implementation of Adoption for Children No. 54/2007; Ministry of Social Affairs Regulations No. 110/HUK/2009 on the Procedure of Adoption for Children; Directorate Regulations No. 02/2012 on Technical Guidance of Adoption for Children; Circulation Letters of the Supreme Court No. 6, 1983.

and/or mental illness, children abandoned in a public space or hospital, children taken care of by relatives, and economic difficulties. Three categories of adopted children are as follows: 1) children under age 6 are the main priority, namely children who experience neglect, children who are in emergency situations, and children who need special protection; 2) children aged 6 to 12 years as long as there are urgent reasons based on social reports, such as abandoned children in an emergency situation; 3) children aged 12 years old up to age 18, such as neglected children who need special protection. The adoption should be conducted for the best interests of the child and carried out based on local customs and statutory provisions. However, the adoption does not terminate the parental rights, it must be recorded in the birth certificate without removing the child's initial identity. Prospective adoptive parents must meet a number of requirements, such as having the same religion as the adopted child; if the child's origin is unknown, the child's religion will be adapted to the religion of the majority of the local population. While intercountry adoption is allowed, the adoption of children by foreign nationals should be taken as a last resort. Adopted parents would have to receive consultation, a permit document, home visits, social reports, a progress development report of the child, a court team report from the Center for Child Adoption Licensing, and a permission letter for adoption. It takes about nine months to one year to complete the adoption process.

Foster care and guardianship. Other placement possibilities in the case that children cannot stay with biological parents are foster care and guardianship. Foster homes provide the last resort options for relatives and non-relatives to be foster parents. There would be no court involvement in this process, however, relative foster parents must obtain at the district/city government social service a recommendation from a professional or trained social worker's assessment. Non-relative foster parents still have to obtain the same permission, and a recommendation from an accredited foster care agency. Foster parents would take care of the child for a maximum of one year with an extension if family reunification is not a possible outcome after that period. Foster parents are required to pass the selection and verification process and write a signed agreement that they will not commit violence, exploitation, neglect, or mistreatment of the child. Guardianship proceeds in similar ways with foster parents in terms of children's circumstances, that is, the parents are not present, their information is unavailable, or they are not able to carry out their responsibilities. The main difference is that court decisions are required for a relative, a non-relative, or legal entity to be declared a guardian. Guardianship ends when children reach age 18, they are deceased, or if the legal entity is dissolved or bankrupt. The guardian's power can also be revoked and terminated pursuant to a court's order if the guardian commits neglect or abuse against children, abuse their guardian power, mishandle legal matters, or neglect their obligations, or if the biological parents are considered ready for reunification. Both central and regional governments, and elements of the community provide guidance for foster care and guardianship through various programs such as counseling, consultation, training, technical guidance, and supervision.

Children in contact with the law. One manifestation of the state's obligation and consequences of ratification of the international law in the context of child protection, in addition to Law No. 35 of 2014 on child protection, is the implementation of Law Number 11 of 2012 concerning the Child Criminal Justice System (SPPA). This law focuses on regulations for children in conflict with the law: children as perpetrators compared to children as victims or witnesses and their social rehabilitation process. Served under the Social Rehabilitation for Children Directorate, the protection of Children in Conflict with Law (ABH) is carried out to ensure the well-being of children under investigation, to avoid violence, discrimination, neglect, and negative effects of the justice system, and to make child punishment as a last resort. Since the enactment of the SPPA Law in 2014, the implementation of the law has not been fully achieved and faces challenges in translating the restorative and diversionary justice, which is intended to avoid children going through the judicial process, thus avoiding stigmatization, and to support smooth reintegration into the community. Restorative Justice is the principle of settlement process in criminal cases by involving the perpetrators, victims, families of the perpetrators/victims, and other related parties to jointly seek a just solution by emphasizing recovery and integration to society. The possibility of diversion is taken into consideration during the investigation and examination of cases. Children in the district court must seek diversion especially for cases threatened for imprisonment under 7 years of age, and not a repetition of a crime. The agreement to go for diversion typically includes the consent of the victim and/or family and their willingness to go through the process. In 2019, the data that were collected and reported from 29 correctional centers, under the direction of the Indonesian Ministry of Law and Human Rights, showed that 6,704 children with delinquency filed in court, and 4,748 of them (70.82%) were sentenced to criminal cases, which was a similar trend with the proportion of cases in 2018 (Ministry of Social Affairs, 2018). In fact, the figures are likely to be higher since the data reported come only from 29 out of a total of 62 correctional centers. Generally, the children are involved in crimes of theft, narcotics, and beatings or violence with potential sanction of over seven years in prison. Children who undergo the judicial process can be placed in the Special Guidance Institution for Children (LPKA), and an assessment will be conducted by social workers as a guide to follow up on needed services and actions.

Under the complex context of the institutional environment and the political economy of child protection, the translation and implementation of restorative justice into diversion decisions or other types of intervention plans in decentralized Indonesia provide locus for discretion. The emphasis on children in conflict with the law framework might underestimate and reduce the problems to criminal and other legal violations, instead of investigating the root of the conflicts, which could be abuse or neglect. In fiscal year 2018, the Sub-Directorate of Social Rehabilitation attempted to translate the restorative justice framework by developing regulations, conducting socialization on those regulations, providing guidance and consolidation, and other various social assistance programs to address children's basic needs. The outcome and performance of those programs and systems require further empirical investigation, especially to identify variation across regions under a decentralized structure of governance. The studies from the Institute for Criminal Justice Reform (ICJR) and PUSKAPA UI (Anggara et.al, 2016; PUSKAPA UI et al., 2020b) underlined some important overlapping findings such as lack of legal and non-legal assistance (social workers, community advocates/counselors) and access to effective legal assistance, including lack of good research on this issue that could be utilized by the judges in deliberating court decisions in various types of placements. Furthermore, while cases with diversion increase, its impact and accountability have not been carried out transparently, and mechanisms for monitoring and evaluation are almost non-existent. The decision to place children in detention is still very likely; thus children who enter the trial process are generally detained, even if there are possibilities to suspend them from detention. Lack of resources lead to lack of appropriate institutions, infrastructure of detention, rehabilitation, and reintegration programs, which also lead to the utilization of some unregistered places. Imprisonment continues to dominate the demand from the prosecutor, while the use of alternative paths outside the prison has not been sufficiently included in the deliberation process. For children who are narcotics users, the police, prosecutors, and judges have usually considered them as criminal users who require imprisonment instead of rehabilitation and treatment. Lastly, a limited service for translators and assistance for foreign children has been challenging. This matter might also be relevant considering the complex diversity of the Indonesian cultural context in which the child protection system operates, including the increasing number of children in the refugee community.

Intermediary Structures as Spaces for Negotiation and Public Discourse

Indonesia's child protection system has moved away from its reliance on institutional care and various programs targeted on specific children's problems to community-based care. This shift seems logical considering the intricate and interrelated set of issues of child protection and social protection—poverty, inequality, and gender-based violence, to name a few—that require an integrated and comprehensive approach on policy, service provision, and practice levels. The move to a decentralized governance structure in post reformation Indonesia might also need a community-based care approach since resource allocation, social construction, and validation of the meanings of protection, abuse, and neglect are often negotiated and decided at lower government levels. Furthermore, the enactment of Law No. 40/2004 on the National Social Security System (Sistem Jaminan Sosial Nasional; SJSN) that implements universal and compulsory social security for all citizens and residents of Indonesia would benefit children and families, which could reduce various risk factors that might lead to abuse and neglect. The SJSN transforms the traditional features of the Indonesian welfare system, which relies on informal and family-based welfare (Dostal & Naskoshi, 2017) and provides a framework for social security in Indonesia—social insurance, social assistance programs, and voluntary private social insurance (Joedadibrata, 2012).

Nevertheless, policy decisions at the local level are affected by public discourse on child protection and the intersection of various legal frameworks and social and cultural contexts. That is, while 40% of the national budget is transferred to the regional governments, the amount to be allocated for child protection would still continue under the discretion of local government officials. Therefore, it is critical to have an international legal framework such as the United Nations Convention on the Rights of the Child (CRC) to set the standards and priorities, and encourage the public discourse to address issues related to child protection. Yet applying the rights-based approach can be in conflict with or undermine the local context of child protection and community practices (Forrester & Harwin, 2000; Rosen, 2007; O'Leary et al., 2018). The history of child protection under Muslim-majority nations like Indonesia may not align with western understandings of childhood (Mohan & Holland, 2001; James, 2007; Rajabi-Ardeshiri, 2009; Hutchinson et al., 2014; O'Leary et al., 2018). At the same time, the rise of the conservative women's movement and religious fundamentalism might compromise progress in addressing the root causes and underlying factors of gender inequality, socioeconomic deprivation, and exclusion that can result in various forms of abuse and neglect. Thus it makes sense to have an ongoing dialogue among these frameworks to balance the views from various stakeholders that would translate into policies and practices for the best interest and well-being of the children, families, and communities. "It emphasizes the need for partnership within the global child protection movement and social work profession, as well as the need for ongoing development of an Indonesian approach to child protection and social work" (O'Leary et al., 2018, p. 2).

Shifting paradigms in child protection in Indonesia from a fragmented view of child protection issues and reliance on institutional care arrangements to a decentralized integrative structure of delivery will continue to require a shift in various stakeholders' perceptions, interactions, and functions in the system. The development of an Integrated Child Welfare Service Model (PKSAI) at the district level and its replication to over 100 districts is underway. It comprises early detection and identification, referral, and follow-up for child-centered case management, and has shown some positive results in serving children's needs, with a primary strength in improving the access of children and families to health services, law enforcement, education, and birth registration (PUSKAPA UI et al., 2017; Child Frontiers, 2019). The model has a case management focus, and includes four critical dimensions of child and family welfare services: 1) working horizontally from early detection and identification to referral and follow-up; 2) coordinating and integrating a range of sectors including social protection, child protection, and family support; 3) addressing poverty, risks. and vulnerabilities across the life- cycle; and 4) developing vertical coordination from the district to the national level to ensure that management of the pilots is effective, sufficiently resourced and staffed, regularly monitored and evaluated, and well-positioned for eventual dissemination. Nevertheless, the evaluation of PKSAI indicated that social workers appear to be less well-equipped and lack skills in responding to high-risk child protection cases involving violence, abuse and other sensitive issues, despite provision of training on different topics related to child protection. In addition, the presence of PKSAI appears to have had less impact on community awareness or knowledge about available services (Child Frontiers, 2019). Strengthening social work, engagement of national and provincial level government agencies and academic institutions, data collection and management, the inclusion of children in institutional care as beneficiaries, and empowerment of the role of various child protection agency and local organizations were crucial in taking the lead and facilitating the establishment and functioning of child welfare systems in a decentralized governance. Social workers play various roles including, but not limited to, brokers and advocates in facilitating community-based responses, and facilitating birth registration services and education scholarships for the children in institutions, health care needs, regional court, and police. Nevertheless, reunifying children from nearby institutional care with their families/communities has been challenging since children usually come from various regions.

It is critical to note that in addition to the technical implementation units of regional governments, there have been working groups that work collaboratively with various elements of community and regional government to increase access to quality services, and allow the voices of children to be heard and included in the policy making process. "Child Friendly Districts/Cities" (KLA) are initiated in approximately 307 districts/cities using 24 indicators to develop a child rights-based sustainable system and ensure the fulfillment of children's rights and protection by integrating commitments and resources from the government, community, and private sectors. The establishment of KLA in districts/cities varies and further efforts are required to evaluate its conception, implementation, and progress. Children's Forum, which was formed in 34 provinces, 377 districts/cities, and 508 sub-districts, allows children's participation to accommodate their voices and aspirations to be taken into consideration in the planning, monitoring, and evaluation of regional policies and program development. The Women's and Children's Protection Task Force (Satgas PPA), with 68 members in 34 provinces in 2016, carries out outreach and assistance for victims of violence against women and children. Community Based Integrated Child Protection (PATBM) programs in 136 villages aim to increase the ability of the community to prevent violence and provide early response. In addition, the Task Force for the Prevention and Handling of Crimes of Human Trafficking (Gugus Tugas TPPPO) engages various ministries to coordinate efforts for managing human trafficking cases, including children. Through various mechanisms and structures initiated at the province, district/city, and lower levels of government, it is expected that an ongoing public discourse will be strengthened, the voices of children, families, and communities will be encouraged, and the creation of civic spaces for dialog and negotiations will bring empowerment and innovative solutions. The critical ongoing task is to stimulate and develop intermediary structures that arise from the bottom-up and facilitate the link between policy and practice.

References

Afrianty, D. (2019, January 31). Reversing Indonesia's child marriage laws. *Legal Affairs* [University of Melbourne]. Available at: https://pursuit.unimelb.edu.au/articles/reversing-indonesia-s-child-marriage-laws.

Ananta, A., Arifin, E., Hasbullah, M., Handayani, N., and Pramono, A. (2015). *Demography of Indonesia's ethnicity*. Institute of Southeast Asian Studies ISEAS–Yusof Ishak Institute.

Anggara, N., Erasmus, A., and Hernowo, A. (2016). Study on the implementation of children's care in courts based on the Juvenile Criminal Justice System Law. Institute for Criminal Justice Reform, 1–54.

Aspinall, E. (2004). Indonesia: Transformation of civil Society and democratic breakthrough. In M. Alagappa (Ed.), *Civil society and political change in Asia: Expanding and contracting democratic space* (pp. 25–60). Stanford University Press.

Aspinall, E. and Berger, M. T. (2001). The break-up of Indonesia? Nationalisms after Decolonisation and the limits of the nation-state in post-Cold War Southeast Asia. *Third World Quarterly*, 22(6), 1003–1024.

Aspinall, E. and Fealy, G. (2010). *Soeharto's new order and its legacy: Essays in honour of Harold Crouch*. Asian Studies Series Monograph 2. The Australian National University E Press.

Aspinall, E., Fossati, D., Muhtadi, B., and Warburton, E. (2018, April 24). Mapping the Indonesian political spectrum. *New Mandala, New Perspectives on Southeast Asia*. Available at: https://www.newmandala.org/mapping-indonesian-political-spectrum/.

Aspinall, E. and Mietzner, M. (2010). *Problems of democratisation in Indonesia: Elections, instituand society*. Institute of Southeast Asian Studies ISEAS Publishing.

Aspinall, E. (2019). Indonesia's election and the return of ideological competition. New Mandala, New Perspective on Southeast Asia. Available at: https://www.newmandala.org/indonesias-election-and-the-return-of-ideological-competition/.

BAPPENAS (Indonesia Ministry of National Development Planning) and UNICEF. (2017). *Sustainable development goals (SDG) baseline report on children in Indonesia*. Jakarta: BAPPENAS and UNICEF, 1–120.

BPS-Badan Pusat Statistik. (2018). Statistik Indonesia: Statistical yearbook of Indonesia 2018. BPS-Statistics Indonesia, 1–719.

BPS-Badan Pusat Statistik. (2020). Berita Resmi Statistik, Hasil Data Sensus 2020. BPS-Statistics Indonesia, 1–12.

Bazzi, S., Gaduh, A., Rothenberg, A., and Wong, M. (2017). Unity in diversity? Ethnicity, migration, and nation building in Indonesia. *CEPR Discussion Papers* 12377, C.E.P.R. Discussion Papers, 1–62.

Bjork, C. (2003). Local responses to decentralization policy in Indonesia. *Comparative Education Review*, 47(2), 184–216.

Bräuchler, B. (2015). *The cultural dimension of peace: Decentralization and reconciliation in Indonesia*. Palgrave Macmillan.

Brodjonegoro, B. (2009). Fiscal decentralization and its impact on regional economic development and fiscal sustainability. In C. Holtzappel and M. Ramstedt (Eds.), *Decentralization and regional autonomy in Indonesia: Implementation and challenges* (pp. 196–221). Institute for Southeast Asian Studies.

Buehler, M. (2010). Decentralisation and local democracy in Indonesia: The marginalisation of the public sphere. In E. Aspinall and M. Mietzner (Eds.), *Problems of democratisation in Indonesia: Elections, institutions and society.* (pp. 267–285) Institute of Southeast Asian Studies ISEAS–Yusof Ishak Institute.

Carnegie, P. (2008). Political Islam and democratic change in Indonesia. *Asian Social Science*, 4(11), 1–7.

Child Frontiers. (2019). *Formative evaluation of the Integrated Child Welfare Program (PKSAI), the collaboration of Ministry of Social Affairs and UNICEF Indonesia*. Child Frontiers.

Cummings, H., Ferrazzi, G., and Kaur, I. (2014). *Equity-focused formative evaluation of UNICEF's engagement in the decentralization process in Indonesia*. Harry Cummings and Associates Inc. and UNICEF Indonesia, 1–133.

Dostal, J. M. and Naskoshi, G. E. (2017). The Indonesian welfare state system with special reference to social security extension in the development context. In C. Aspalter (Ed.), *The Routledge international handbook of welfare state systems* (pp. 366–382). Routledge.

Eaton, K., Kaiser, K., and Smoke, P. (2010). *The political economy of decentralization reforms: Implications for aid effectiveness.* The World Bank, 1–92.

Fachriansyah, R. (2019, April 1). "My body is not Mine": Indonesia without feminists group starts online campaign. *The Jakarta Post.* Available at: https://www.thejakartapost.com/news/2019/04/01/my-body-is-not-mine-indonesia-without-feminists-group-starts-online-campaign.html.

Farisa, F. C. (2019, August 30). Komnas Perempuan: RUU PKS Sudah Banyak Dipolitisasi, Saatnya DPR Serius Bekerja. *Kompas.*

Fitrani, F., Kaiser, K., and Hofman, B. (2005). Unity in diversity? The creation of new local governments in a decentralizing Indonesia. *Bulletin of Indonesian Economic Studies,* 41(1), 57–79.

Forrester, D. and Harwin, J. (2000). Monitoring children's rights globally: can child abuse be measured internationally? *Child Abuse Review* 9(6), 427–38.

Grijns, M. and Horii, H. (2018). Child marriage in a village in West Java (Indonesia): Compromises between legal obligations and religious concerns. *Asian Journal of Law and Society,* (5), 453–466.

Guess, G. (2005). Comparative decentralization lessons from Pakistan, Indonesia, and the Philippines. *Public Administration Review,* 65(2), 217–230.

Hamid, S. (2014, October 1). In Indonesia, decentralization and direct elections two sides of the same coin. *Asia Weekly Insights and Analysis.* Available at: https://asiafoundation.org/2014/10/01/in-indonesia-decentralization-and-direct-elections-two-sides-of-the-same-coin/.

Hasenfeld, Y. (Ed.). (2010). *Human services as complex organizations.* Sage Publications.

Hosen, N. (2003). Indonesian political laws in Habibie era: Between political struggle and law reform. *Nordic Journal of International Law,* 72, 483–518.

Hutchinson, A., O'Leary, P., Squire, J. and Hope, K. (2014). Child protection in islamic contexts: identifying cultural and religious appropriate mechanisms and processes using a roundtable methodology., *Child Abuse Review,* 24, 395–408.

IPAC. (2019, March 15). *Anti-Ahok to Anti-Jokowi: Islamist influence on Indonesia's 2019 election campaign.* Report No. 55.

James, A. (2007). Giving voice to children's voices: Practices and problems, pitfalls and potentials. *American Anthropologist,* 109(2), 261–72.

Joedadibrata, D. (2012), A Study of the Shift Towards Universal Social Policy in Indonesia, International Institute of Social Studies, A Research Paper, Erasmus University, The Hague, December, 1–34.

Kalamar, A., Lee-Rife, S., and Hindin, M. (2016). Interventions to prevent child marriage among young people in low- and middle-income countries: A systematic review. *Journal of Adolescent Health,* 59(3), 16–21.

Kartika, D. (2019a, May 2). Talking Indonesia: Anti-feminism. *Talking Indonesia* [Podcast]. https://indonesiaatmelbourne.unimelb.edu.au/talking-indonesia-anti-feminism/.

Kartika, D. (2019b, April 14). An anti-feminist wave in Indonesia's election? *New Mandala, New Perspectives on Southeast Asia.* Available at: https://www.newmandala.org/an-anti-feminist-wave-in-indonesias-election/.

Kaybryn, Jo. (2015). Formative Evaluation of UNICEF's Systems Building Approach to Child Protection in Indonesia. UNICEF, 1–148.

KPAI. (2016). *End of year report.* Office of Secretary of Indonesian Child Protection Commission.

KPAI. (2018). *Performance report.* Office of Secretary of Indonesian Child Protection Commission.

Malesky, E. and Hutchinson, F. (2016). Varieties of disappointment: Why has decentralization not delivered on its promises in Southeast Asia? *Journal of Southeast Asian Economies,* 33(2), 125–138.

Marinescu, I. and Triyana, M. (2016). The sources of wage growth in a developing country. *IZA Journal of Labor & Development* N d, 5(2), 1–43.

Mazrieva, E. (2019, February 4). "Indonesia tanpa feminis," Kritik atau Bunga Tidur? *Voice of America Indonesia.* Available at: https://www.voaindonesia.com/a/indonesia-tanpa-feminis-kritik-atau-bunga-tidur-/4858116.html.

Meyer, J. and Rowan, B. (1977). Institutional organizations: Formal structure as myth and ceremony. *American Journal of Sociology,* 83, 340–363.

Mietzner, M. (2010). Political conflict resolution and democratic consolidation in Indonesia: The role of the constitutional court. *Journal of East Asian Studies,* 10, 397–424.

Ministry of Social Affairs. (2018). *Performance report on social rehabilitation program for children, government agency performance accountability system report on annual performance plan, indicators, work program of Children's Social Rehabilitation Program (PKSA), Directorate Social Rehabilitation for Children, Directorate General for Social Rehabilitation. Office of Ministry of Social Affairs.*

Ministry for Women's Empowerment and Child Rights Republic of Indonesia. (2016). *National Strategy: Elimination of Violence Against Children 2016–2020.*

Mohan, G. and Holland, J. (2001). Human Rights and Development in Africa: Moral Intrusion or Empowering Opportunity? *Review of African Political Economy*, 28(8), 177–196.

Komnas Perempuan. (2018, March 7). *The elimination of women's safe space in the politics of populism movement: Note on violence against women in 2017.* National Commission of Anti Violence Against Women (Komnas Perempuan) Report, 1–100.

Needham, E. (2007). *A mapping of national child protections systems: Summary report.* Save the Children, 1–47.

O'Leary, P. J., Young, A., McAuliffe, D., and Wismayanti, Y. (2018). Developing the social work role in the Indonesian child protection system. *International Social Work*, 62(2), 814–828.

Ostwald, K., Tajima Y., and Samphanth, K. (2016). Indonesia's decentralization experiment: Motivations, successes, and unintended consequences. *Journal of Southeast Asian Economies*, 33(2), 139–156.

Pepinsky, T. B. and Wihardja M. M. (2011). Decentralization and economic performance in Indonesia. *Journal of East Asian Studies*, 11(3), 337–371.

Pisani, E. (2014). Indonesia in pieces: The downside of decentralization. *Council of Foreign Affairs*, 93(4), 142–152.

Prameswari, Z. W. and Agustin, E. (2018). Indonesian marriage law reform: The way to strengthen the protection of children's rights against child marriage. *Journal of Southeast Asian Human Rights*, 2(1), 286–301.

Prasetyawan, W. (2018). Networked: Business and Politics in Decentralizing Indonesia, 1998–2004. Kyoto CSEAS Series on Asian Studies. Kyoto University Press and NUS Press.

Prihartini, E. (2018a). On the same page? Support for gender quotas among Indonesian lawmakers. *Asian Social Science*, 14(5), 48–59.

Prihartini, E. (2018b, June 21). On the same page? In Indonesia, some male lawmakers are sceptical of quotas for women in politics. *The Conversation (Indonesia)*. Available at: http://theconversation.com/on-the-same-page-in-indonesia-some-male-lawmakers-are-sceptical-of-quotas-for-women-in-politics-90824.

PUSKAPA UI, Maestral, and UNICEF. (2017, April 2017). *Development of a pilot model of child and family welfare in Indonesia.* Final report. PUSKAPA - Mestral, 1–12.

PUSKAPA UI, UNICEF, BPS, Kementrian PPN/BAPPENAS (2020a). *Preventing child marriage.* PUSKAPA, UNICEF, BPS, Kementrian PPN/BAPPENAS, 1–71.

PUSKAPA UI, UNICEF, BAPPENAS (2020b). *Restoring Opportunities for children in Indonesia's Juvenile Criminal Justice System: Study on the implementation of the Juvenile Criminal Justice System in the Tangerang, Surabaya, Palembang, and Kendari Regions.* PUSKAPA, UNICEF, BAPPENAS, 1–115.

Rabasa, A. and Chalk, P. (2001). Reinventing Indonesia: The challenge of decentralization. In A. Rabasa and P. Chalk, *Indonesia's transformation and the stability of Southeast Asia.* Rand Corporation Publication, 47–51.

Rajabi-Ardeshiri, M. (2009). The rights of the child in the Islamic context: The challenges of the local and the global. *The International Journal of Children's Rights*, 17, 475–489.

Rokx, C., Subandoro, A., and Gallagher, P. (2018). *Aiming high: Indonesia's ambition to reduce stunting.* World Bank Publications.

Rosen, D. (2007). Child soldiers, international humanitarian law, and the globalization of childhood. *American Anthropologist*, 109(2), 296–306.

Rumble, L., Peterman, A., Irdiana, N., Triyana, M., and Minnick, E. (2018). An empirical exploration of female child marriage determinants in Indonesia. *BMC Public Health*, 18(407), 1–13.

Rusmana, M. (2017, July 22). Directorate of Child Social Rehabilitation improves the competence of TEPSA officers. Directorate of Child Social Rehabilitation, Ministry of Social Affairs. Available at: http://anak.kemsos.go.id/2017/07/22/direktorat-rehabilitasi-sosial-anak-tingkatkan-kompetensi-petugas-tepsa/.

Sapiie, M. (2018, December 13). Court orders revision of minimum age for women to marry. *The Jakarta Post.* Available at: https://www.thejakartapost.com/news/2018/12/13/breaking-court-orders-revision-of-minimum-age-for-women-to-marry.html.

Save the Children. (2018). *The many faces of exclusion: End of childhood report.* Save the Children.

Scott, W. R. (2008). *Institutions and organizations: Ideas and interests.* Sage.

SMERU Research Institute and UNICEF. (2013). *Policy brief: The urgency of addressing multi-dimensional child poverty in Indonesia, No. 2/13*. Available at: http://www.smeru.or.id/sites/default/files/publication/child poverty_eng.pdf.

Smith, B. (2008). The origins of regional autonomy in Indonesia: Experts and the marketing of political interests. *Journal of East Asian Studies*, 8, 211–234.

Sumanti, R., Handayani, S., and Astuti, D. (2018). The correlation between knowledge of marriageable age, education, matchmaking and child marriage in females in Banjarnegara Indonesia. *Belitung Nursing Journal*, 4(5), 502–509.

Summer, C. and Kusumaningrum, S. (2014). *The Australia Indonesia partnership for justice (AIPJ) legal identity baseline study: Indonesia's missing millions*. AIPJ, PUSKAPA UI, PEKKA, SMERU Research and Analytical Teams.

Suryakusuma, J. (2019, March 6). "When the PKS party collides with the PKS bill." *The Jakarta Post*. Available at: https://www.thejakartapost.com/academia/2019/03/06/when-the-pks-party-collides-with-the-pks-bill.html.

Tapsell, R. (2019, March 22). The polarisation paradox in Indonesia's 2019 elections. *New Mandala, New Perspectives on Southeast Asia*. Available at: https://www.newmandala.org/the-polarisation-paradox-in-indonesias-2019-elections/.

UNICEF. (2008). *The significance of child protection systems: Key findings from a systems mapping exercise in six provinces of Indonesia*. Unicef Global Child Protection Strategy, Issues Briefs. UNICEF Indonesia, 1–6.

UNICEF. (2011). *The situation of women and children in Indonesia 2000–2010: Working towards progress with equity under decentralization*. Available at: https://www.unicef.org/sitan/files/Indonesia_SitAn_2010.pdf.

UNICEF. (2015). Legal Protection from Violence: Analysis of domestic laws related to violence against children in ASEAN member States. Evidence: Strengthening Child Protection Systems. UNICEF EAPRO, 1–276.

UNICEF. (2020). The State of children in Indonesia - Trends, opportunities and challenges for realizing children's Rights. UNICEF Indonesia.

Warburton, E. and Muhtadi, B. (2019, April 8). *Politicizing inequality in Indonesian elections*. The Brookings Institution. Available at: https://www.brookings.edu/blog/order-from-chaos/2019/04/08/politicizing-inequality-in-indonesian-elections/.

Warburton, E. (2019, April 16). Polarisation in Indonesia: what if perception is reality? New Mandala, New Perspective on Southeast Asia. Available at: https://www.newmandala.org/how-polarised-is-indonesia/.

Child Protection in Iran

Marzieh Takaffoli, Meroe Vameghi, Maliheh Arshi, *and* Leila Ostadhashemi

Abstract

This chapter explores child protection in Iran. The Child Development Index, based on the indicators of health, education, and nutrition, shows growth and development. Additionally, the definition of a child is based on the age of maturity in Islam: nine years old for girls and fifteen years old for boys. The physical health and moral nurture of children are vital factors that would lead to an intervention and court decisions to child custody. However, the criteria for mistreatment are not comprehensive enough to only have a single interpretation in courts. On other hand, the Orphaned and with Inappropriate Care Givers Children and Youth Protection Act facilitates the adoption process, especially for kids with inappropriate caregivers.

Key Words: Iran, child protection, CDI, maturity, Islam, OICGCYP, adoption, caregivers, intervention

Introduction

The Islamic Republic of Iran is an upper-middle-income country (WHO, 2016) located in western Asia, with a population of more than 80 million, of which 22,149,000 are children (28%) (UNICEF, 2017). The government of Iran has been in power since the 1979 Islamic revolution and the Constitution, adopted by a referendum, uses a separation of powers model with Executive, Legislative, and Judicial Bodies. The President of Iran is the executive body's leader, appointed by direct election. The Islamic Consultative Assembly (ICA) is the national legislative body of Iran. The parliament (ICA) representatives are elected by direct vote. The Guardian Council of the Constitution (GCC) approves all laws passed by the ICA before they come into law to ensure they do not violate Islam and the Constitution. Finally, the chief of the Judicial Body is appointed by the Supreme Leader.[1]

In recent years, Iran has been making significant efforts to improve the status of children. The 2012 Child Development Index (CDI) also shows growth and development.

---

[1] In Iran, the Supreme Leader is selected and monitored by the Assembly of Experts of the Leadership. The members of the assembly are elected by direct vote. The Supreme Leader has the authority to appoint the chief of the Judicial Body.

The CDI is based on an aggregate of three indicators of health, education, and nutrition. Countries are ranked according to their scores regarding a child's chances of dying before their fifth birthday, not enrolling in school, and being underweight. The lower the score, the better. According to these indicators, Iran is succeeding and is among the countries with the most progress in the area of child well-being. During 1995–2010, Iran moved 15 steps up the ranking to reach 60 of 141 countries worldwide (score = 7.93) (Save the Children, 2012).

This chapter begins with a brief review of social welfare in Iran to make familiar with the context in which child protection policies and practices are being developed and implemented. The following sections provide general information on the definition of at-risk children, trends and highlights of child regulations and policies, and the roles and responsibilities of different authorities. Next, the process of intervention, from assessing eligibility to evaluating services, is described. Finally, some key challenges for fulfilling children's rights and developing a child protection system are briefly discussed.

Social Welfare System in Iran

Articles 3, 29, 30, 31, and 43 of the Constitution of Iran address concepts such as eliminating poverty, developing welfare, and fundamental rights for everyone. Regarding welfare models, social policy studies classify Iran as a developing country with an informal social security regime (Mardoukh Rouhani, 2012; Vesali & Basatian, 2012). Concerning the socioeconomic status of Iran, national and international statistics indicate the growth rate in Iran, especially in the fields of health and education. Iran's Human Development Index (HDI) value for 2017 was 0.798, ranking 60 out of 189 countries. This is above the average of 0.638 for countries in South Asia. Between 1990 and 2017, Iran's HDI value increased from 0.577 to 0.798, an increase of 38.3% (United Nations Development Programme [UNDP], 2018). In 2014,[2] the Transformation Plan (HTP) was launched as a health reform program to ensure complete coverage of essential health needs. According to a WHO assessment in late 2016 and national reports, insurance coverage for over 10 million low-income and disadvantaged people and a reduction in out-of-pocket payments from 30% to 10% have been some of the most significant achievements of this plan (Ministry of Cooperatives, Labor and Social Welfare [MCLSW], 2015). Almost universal coverage of immunizations and reduction in maternal and neonatal mortality rates are some of the other health achievements in Iran (WHO, 2016). In terms of education indicators, in 2016, the literacy rate (over 6 years old) was 87.6% overall (84.2% and 91% among women and men, respectively, and 90.79% in urban areas and 78.50%

---

[2] Reviewing different HDI dimensions, between 1990 and 2017, life expectancy at birth increased by 12.4 years (76.2 years in 2017), mean number of years of schooling increased by 5.6 years (9.8 years in 2017), expected years of schooling increased by 5.7 years (14.9 years in 2017), and gross national income per capita increased by about 67.5% (19,130 in 2017) (UNDP, 2018).

in rural areas) (Statistical Center of Iran, 2018b). On the other hand, according to the International Monetary Fund (IMF), Iran, with an unemployment rate of 12.8% in 2018, ranked 13th in the world according to its high unemployment rate (IMF, 2018). This rate was reported to be 13.4% in urban areas and 2.8% in rural areas (Statistical Center of Iran, 2018a) and 10.2% and 19.8% among men and women, respectively (MCLSW, 2017). The high unemployment rate in Iran is one of the country's main economic problems and seriously affects disadvantaged people. Also, the existence of inequalities and disparities in some spheres is still evident; the provinces of Iran have unbalanced growth and development according to the various indicators (Mowlaei, 2007; Sheykh Beygloo et al., 2012; Mohaqeqi Kamal et al., 2015, Shahiki Tash et al., 2015; Karimi Moughari & Barati, 2017). Concerning children, in 2007, there were significant differences among the provinces of Iran for indicators such as mortality rates among children under 5 years, child labor among those aged 5–15 years, and teen fertility among those aged 10–18 years (UNICEF, 2012).

Child Protection System in Iran

In recent years, the significance of children's rights and protecting them against harm has been considered by civil society, legislators, government officials, and the general public. On September 5, 1990, Iran signed the UN Convention on the Rights of the Child (CRC) (1989), which was conditionally ratified in August 1994.[3] Based on existing laws and policies, different organizations and institutions in Iran provide services to children in general, and the State Welfare Organization (SWO) is primarily responsible for protecting and supporting maltreated and at-risk children. Before reviewing and discussing child protection in the context of existing programs, laws, and the entities responsible, it is necessary to address the meaning of childhood in Iran.

Childhood age has undergone considerable developments in Iranian law in the areas of delinquency, victimization, and rights (civil, political, and social). According to Iran's penal laws, Iranian legislators have three approaches to the age range of victimized children. There are laws on the different types of crimes against children in which they are mentioned with titles such as minor, immature, child, and so on, and not defined as a specific age. In these cases, according to the definition of "child" in some other laws and according to the age of maturity in Islam, girls under the age of 9 (lunar years) and boys under the age of 15 (lunar years) are considered children.[4] Thus, the legislation supports this age group in some contexts, such as the punishment of a sexual offender of an immature girl even if she gives consent (Articles 658 and 224 of the Islamic Penal Law, 2013).

---

[3] "In each case and each time do not violate domestic laws and Islamic rules."

[4] The age of religious maturity is calculated by lunar year, that is, boys who are about 14 years and 7 months, and girls who are about 8 years and 9 months, have reached puberty or have become mature. At such age, he or she is obliged to obey religious laws and follow some acts of worship such as praying and fasting.

The second category includes laws in which those under 15 years of age are defined as children; for example, employing children under the age of 15 is prohibited (Articles 79 to 84 of the Labor Law of Iran 1990). The third category includes laws in which the legislator, without defining a "child" explicitly, considers those under 18 years old subject to special protection; for example, the Children and Adolescents Protection Act (2002, 2020).

Concerning the age of criminal responsibility, in the Islamic Penal Law of 2013, the same as in the previous law of 1996, the age of criminal responsibility is defined according to the age of physical and sexual maturation (9 lunar years for girls and 15 lunar years for boys). In the Islamic Penal Law of 2013, although the age of criminal responsibility was not increased, legislators defined a system of gradual responsibility for different age groups: up to 9 years old (exemption from criminal responsibility), 9–12 years (correctional educational reactions), 12–15 years (educational and less punitive reactions in comparison to previous law of 1996), and 15–18 (less punitive reactions in comparison to last law of 1996). The most important innovation of this law (Article 91) concerns *Qiṣāṣ* and *Hudud* offenses and punishments in children between the ages of 15 and 18. If they do not realize they have committed a crime or there is a doubt about their developmental wisdom, they are sentenced to a Youth Detention Center and pay Diya and a fine.[5] Although this change is a considerable improvement (especially the inclusion of gradual criminal responsibility), children are still held to be criminally responsible, and the judge is required to assess their competency and maturity. So, according to these multiple and diverse age limits, legislation concerning children needs to be revised and integrated in terms of childhood and age as a proxy for competency and maturity (Fehresti & Nazari Khakshour, 2008; Saboori Pour & Alavi Sadr, 2015; Zeinali & Karimi Tachara, 2017; Kahzadi Baseri, 2018).

Defining At-risk Children

In 1997, Iran's laws addressed the conditions under which children are exposed to risks (the amendment of Article 1173 of the Civil Code) for the first time. According to this law, instances of "inappropriate care" or "moral corruption" of parents that lead to risks to the "physical health" or "moral nurture" of the child give the court the right to terminate parental custody of the child. Such instances include: 1) harmful addiction to alcohol, drugs, and gambling; 2) moral corruption and prostitution; 3) mental disorder; 4) exploiting a child or forcing them to be involved in immoral and illegal jobs such as prostitution, trafficking, and begging; and 5) repeated beating over the normal limits (unusual corporal punishment). According to this law, the "physical health" and "moral nurture" of children are the two important factors that lead to intervention and a court

---

[5] *Qiṣāṣ* is an Islamic term meaning retaliation in kind. In Islamic law, *Hudud* refers to punishments that under Islamic law are mandated and fixed by God, and *Diya* is the financial compensation paid to the victim or the heirs/heiresses of a victim.

decision to take custody of a child. However, it seems that these criteria and examples of mistreatment are not sufficiently comprehensive and can lead to different interpretations by the courts (Akbarineh, 2013; Pur Abdollah & Sharifi, 2014; Zeinali, 2015).

The Children and Adolescents Protection Act (2002), the first significant law on child protection, gave more precise definitions of child abuse. The law defined child abuse as 1) maltreating a child in such a way as to cause physical, psychological, or moral harm or to endanger their physical, psychological, or moral health; 2) physical and psychological torture of a child; 3) deliberate neglect of a child's physical and psychological health; 4) prohibiting a child from education;[6] 5) buying and selling of a child;[7] 6) exploiting a child, and 7) using a child to commit offenses such as drug trafficking.[8] These criteria mainly address the situation after the occurrence of harm, but conditions that can lead to harm and their prevention were not considered. Finally, given the lack of precise definitions of at-risk children in the laws, in the Children and Adolescents Protection Act (2020), related concepts and 14 risky situations are precisely defined:

(a) Being orphaned or neglecting a child by failing to carry out legal caring duties by any person who is responsible for doing so;
(b) When any of the parents or caretakers has behavioral, psychological, or personality disorders or severe contagious diseases;
(c) Imprisonment of any of the parents or caretakers;
(d) Addiction of any of the parents or caretakers to drugs or gambling;
(e) Setting up, running, or committing prostitution by any of the parents or caretakers;
(f) Continuous violence of the parents, caretakers, or other family members towards each other;
(g) Failure to register the birth of a child or to take the identity documents for a child without any valid justification;
(h) Keeping a child out of school;
(i) Exclusion and rejection of a child by the family;
(j) Physical and mental disabilities of the child, or having certain diseases or sexual dysfunction;

---

[6] Prior to this law, in the Law on Providing Educational Facilities for Iranian Children and Youth (1974), prohibiting children from education by parents or caregivers was criminalized and was punished by a financial penalty and imprisonment; but this law was old and, with a lack of executive guarantee, it was not considered or used by the courts (Zeinali, 2003a).

[7] Prior to this law, the Penal Law for Passing Unauthorized Persons from the Borders of the Country (1988) referred to intensification of the punishment for trading children, and Article 631 of the previous 1996 Islamic Penal Law also addressed the punishment for kidnapping a child.

[8] Prior to this law, only the previous 1996 Islamic Penal Law addressed the punishment of child beggary, and there was a gap on using children in criminal activities.

(k) Child and youth delinquency, exploiting or involving them in illegal and criminal activities, as well as child addiction to drugs or alcohol;

(l) Any damage caused by extreme poverty, asylum, refugee, immigration, or being without nationality (statelessness);

(m) Frequent running away from home or school and dropping out of school;

(n) Child and youth maltreatment or exploitation. (Authors' translation)

With this law, this widespread definition of at-risk children will positively affect identifying them and timely interventions. In the previous laws, the situations were primarily defined individually (e.g., features and conditions of abuse) based on the relationship between caretaker and child. In the new law, risky situations have become slightly broader and more diverse. These 14 conditions are either caused by the status of the parents (such as (b) and (c)) or their interaction with the child (such as (n) and (i)), or the child has circumstances that may cause maltreatment (such as (j) and (k)); or family interactions create the situation (f) or, most importantly, the social and economic structure underlying the child's risky situation (l). This diversity in how to view the problem can improve the macro and systemic approach. As a result, the interventions go beyond legal and judicial interventions that focus solely on caretakers and their punishment. The development of general comprehensive services and primary prevention could be positive consequences of this law.

Responsible Bodies and Agencies

In Iran, different government institutions have responsibilities for the welfare and protection of children, and no specific institution is responsible for managing and coordinating all their affairs. Thus, according to the Social Problem Database of MCLSW (2018) and the guidelines of the State Welfare Organization, the duties of the most important institutions related to child abuse and neglect (child protection) are explained in the following.

The MCLSW is an organ of the Executive Body, established in 2004 and responsible for the welfare of general and disadvantaged groups of people in Iran. The ministry has responsibilities for reforming and enforcing child-related laws; developing, strengthening, and organizing social insurance and supportive services for children; improving methods and mechanisms for identifying and protecting at-risk children; and so on.

The SWO is one of the most important institutions associated with children. It is a subsidiary of MCLSW, and its overall mission is to control the risks facing vulnerable groups in society, including children, women, low-income groups, and the disabled. This organization is mainly responsible for the care and support of orphan children and children with inappropriate caregivers. In particular, it is responsible for protecting maltreated and at-risk children by preventing child abuse; identifying and supporting abused and at-risk children directly and in collaboration with the Iran Police Force; providing permanent support for abused children, and improving the possibility of reuniting the child with the family. Following The SWO offers its services directly to the child and the family or by outsourcing services to non-governmental organizations, which they monitor directly. The organizational plans and child protection services are elaborated on in the following sections. The SWO has paid considerable attention to a child protection system in recent years and has expanded its services, but its policies and services are more based on the individual; they do not pay much attention to prevention, and the organization's activities are means-tested. Therefore, children come under the organization's care when they have already faced severe harm (Ghafari & Hosseini, 2016).

The Judicial Body is another governmental institution with a vital decision-making role in programming, implementing, and monitoring policies and programs about children, especially child protection. Regarding child abuse, the main tasks of the institution include identifying and protecting at-risk or abused children; judicial intervention and referral to relevant institutions; indictment against child-related offenses; providing counseling and legal assistance; terminating or addressing various types of custody orders for these children; decision making about the competency of applicants for child adoption; and drafting related bills for child protection.

MCLSW and SWO guidelines have attempted inter-sectoral and inter-organizational collaboration among all related governmental and non-governmental organizations in the child protection system. However, still there is growing criticism of the numerous duties and responsibilities shared by various organizations. Most of these duties are defined according to the instructions and guidelines of the Executive Body, not the laws. Therefore, they do not have a high priority, and enforcement is weak. Also, the monitoring process and accountability of these organizations are not defined; these tasks are mainly focused on the situation after the incidence of harm, mostly severe, and have not addressed primary prevention; and finally, a sufficient budget required for all authorities has not been allocated.

Policies and Legislation

In recent decades, there has been considerable development in legislation enacted for children in Iran. In addition to the international approach to the human rights of children, Iran also considered child protection in welfare, civil and criminal rights through laws associated with issues including compulsory family responsibilities, differential criminalization, and punishment for behaviors that violate children's rights (Zeinali & Jomepour, 2012). Along with the ratification of the CRC in 1994, the amendment to the CRC (1995) and the Convention Concerning the Prohibition and Immediate Action for the Elimination of the Worst Forms of Child Labor (1999) were accepted by Iran in 2001. Accession to the CRC and other international commitments to children's rights led to increased attempts by child rights activists to develop laws in line with the fulfillment of the CRC. The Children and Adolescents Protection Act (2002) was one such achievement. This was the first specific law on the protection of children and was considered a milestone in child rights in Iran. This law included a number of innovations: the age of a child has been increased to 18 years in terms of protection;[9] the term "child abuse" appears for the first time in Iran's legal literature; and particular behaviors that endanger children have been criminalized.

The brief trend of child legislation on related topics, addressed in the following section, indicates the increased conformity of domestic laws with international documents on children's rights. Iran's laws address different groups of children, including maltreated children, undocumented children, orphaned children, children from deprived areas, disabled children, delinquent children, children of divorced parents, children with the mother as head of the family, and children in labor.

FUNDAMENTAL LAWS OF IRAN

There are two fundamental laws in Iran: the Constitution of the Islamic Republic of Iran (1979) and the Civil Code of the Islamic Republic of Iran (1928), which address and highlight the status of the family and children and support them.

According to the third Article of the Constitution of Iran (1979), the government is responsible for providing facilities for free education for all, creating justice, welfare, elimination of poverty, and removing any kind of deprivation in the context of nutrition, housing, job, health, and insurance. In addition, Article 30 obliges the government to provide free education for everyone up to the end of high school and expand free academic education within the country's self-sufficiency. The Constitution of Iran considers the family as a fundamental unit of society. It asserts that all the laws and regulations have to facilitate the formation and consolidation of the family (Article 10). Article 21 clearly obliges the government to support mothers, particularly during their pregnancy and for custody of their child and protection of orphaned children.

The Civil Code of the Islamic Republic of Iran (1928) addresses child protection issues in different Articles, including citizenship and identity of the child, custody, guardianship, child maintenance, child adoption, and children of divorce, and, in case of any disagreement, allows the court to intervene and make decisions on children's issues. Based on Article 1178, rearing children is a parental duty, and parents should not neglect it. Further, Article 1199 addresses that the father, paternal grandfather, and mother must pay child maintenance. Some criticisms of this Article are that child maintenance is limited to basic needs such as housing, clothing, and so on, and also the weakness of its enforcement.

---

[9] Until this law was passed, the victimization age of the child in various crimes was not mentioned. But according to previous Islamic Penal Law (1996) and the Civil Code, this age could be adopted implicitly as 9 (lunar years) for girls and 15 (lunar years) for boys (Zeinali, 2003a). Passing of this law in 2002 led to an increase in the age of childhood supported by government.

CUSTODY AND GUARDIANSHIP OF CHILDREN

In accordance with the law, "custody" means keeping and taking care of the child, and regulating their relationships with others, which is primarily a parent's right and duty. With the death of a parent, the other parent takes custody, and in the event of the death of both parents, custody is given to the child's paternal grandfather; after that, the custody of the child will be determined by the priority to the closest relatives. Regarding the custody situation after divorce, the mother can have custody of a child up to 7 years of age whether boy or girl, and after the age of 7 years, custody is given to the father; in the case of disagreement, the court will decide according to their competency (Katouzian, quoted in Saei & Kamyab Mansouri, 2016; Hedayat & Hashemi, 2017; Nourzad Laleh & Ghayoum Zadeh, 2017).

Article 1173 was passed in 1986, according to which, whenever the child's physical or moral health is at risk due to lack of care or moral corruption of the father or mother of the child, the court may, upon the request of the child's relatives or the request of the child's guardian or the request of the head of the judicial district, make any decision in the best interest of the child. In 1997, an amendment to Article 1173 defined instances when a child is at risk, and conditions for termination of custody by parents were added to the previous law in five cases (which are addressed in the section "Defining at-risk children" above). This Article is limited to parents (other caregivers are not mentioned), the lack of supportive and protective measures for children after substantiation, and the fact that the process of judicial and supportive proceedings is undefined are some of its criticisms (Akbarineh, 2013; Pur Abdollah & Sharifi, 2014; Zeinali, 2015).

There are differences in the law of Iran between custody and guardianship. First, custody relates to the physical, mental, and psychological care of the child, while guardianship is associated with monitoring property, financial rights, and the marriage of children. Second, custody is something that is essentially entrusted to both parents, while "inherent guardianship" is left to the father and paternal grandfather (or the successor appointed by them as "special guardian") (Najafi, quoted in Saei & Kamyab Mansouri, 2016). According to these definitions, although the mother of a child can take custody of the child, she is not the "natural guardian." However, she may be determined as a successor by the father or paternal grandfather of the child; in this case, she becomes the "special guardian" of the child (Saei & Kamyab Mansouri, 2016). Whenever the child does not have a natural or special guardian, the court gives the guardianship to another person, and the priority is with the mother (Orphaned and with Inappropriate Care Givers Children and Youth Protection [OICGCYP] Act, 2013).

Articles 1184 and 1187 of the Civil Code state that if the natural guardian (father or paternal grandfather) is alive but unable to deal with issues related to a child for some reason, such as sickness, old age, or imprisonment, and has not appointed a person himself, the court can determine a person as the "temporary trustee." The mother has the first priority, and then the child's relatives have the priority to become the temporary trustee of the child. The temporary trustee has the same responsibilities as the natural guardian, so childcare, administration of property, and the child's financial rights are delegated to the temporary trustee (Civil Code and the OICGCYP Act, 2013). This type of custody can be considered to be equivalent to fostering or kinship care in other countries.

By passing the Family Protection Law (2012), the child's interests are considered before the custody rights of parents. This law addresses issues related to decision-making by the court about the custody of the child; facilitating and expediting the process in favor of the child; the possibility of re-deciding a court judgment according to the best interests of the child or when the custodian does not correctly carry out their duties and responsibilities; and punishment of crimes committed against children. According to the law, any person who does not comply with the court's order, prohibits its enforcement, or neglects it will be punished (Articles 40, 41, and 54). In addition, the law also considers imprisonment for any person who is responsible for child maintenance but does not carry out his/her duties (Article 53).

SUPPORTING ORPHANED CHILDREN AND YOUTH AND THOSE WITH INAPPROPRIATE CAREGIVERS

Adoption has been accepted in Iran since ratification of the Supporting Orphaned Children Act in 1974, the first law in Iran on this issue. The Protection of Headless Women and Orphaned Children Act (1992)[10] was one of the first special laws for children after the revolution. This law specifically and explicitly addressed institutional placement of orphaned children in formal care centers of the SWO or adoption for the first time. In this law, an orphaned child refers to a child who has lost his/her caretaker for any reason, permanently or temporarily (Article 2). But this law did not specifically define the factors that cause the child to lose his/her caretaker temporarily, and it did not address the circumstances and criteria in which the parent or caretaker is incapable of caring for the child. Thus, decision-making about the custody of the child in these situations was open to interpretation by the court, and a considerable number of these children were living in formal care centers (institutions).

To overcome this problem, the Orphaned and with Inappropriate Care Givers Children and Youth Protection Act (OICGCYP) (2013) was passed to facilitate the adoption process, especially for children with inappropriate caregivers (Article 1). It explicitly defines a child with inappropriate caregivers, and the responsibility to support these children was entrusted to the SWO (Article 2). According to this law, children with inappropriate caregivers are those under the legal guardianship of the SWO whose father or paternal grandfather or the mother have not taken custody within two years from the date of their legal guardianship, or none of them are competent to have custody (even with the appointment of a supervisor) (Article 8).[11] The law also highlights the consultative role of

---

[10] "Headless Women" in Persian can be roughly translated to "women who are head of the family."

[11] The supervisor is a person who supervises a child's care based on a court order to ensure that the child's needs are met by the caretaker but does not necessarily live with the child.

social workers and experts from the SWO at all stages of decision-making for children. However, there are still some other concerns that this law does not account for, including the possibility of termination of an adoption order to unify the child with his/her biological family; the need to insert the real name of the child's family in his/her birth certificate; and lack of declaration of an illegal marriage of the adopted child and caretaker (which is discussed later) (Akbarineh, 2013; Shariati Nasab, 2017).

EXPLOITATION AND MALTREATMENT OF CHILDREN

The Labor Law of Iran (1990), Articles 79 to 84, provided a section on "working conditions for youth." According to this law, the employment of people under the age of 15 years is prohibited; a physician must approve the proportion and type of work according to the ability of the young worker (15 to 18 years); daily working hours of a young worker are half an hour less than the regular hours of workers, and punishment is considered in terms of any deviation from these rules. On the other hand, this law does not include family workplaces and workplaces with less than ten workers; this is a serious criticism of this law (Fehresti & Nazari Khakshour, 2008).

As mentioned, the Children and Adolescents Protection Act (2002) had notable points, such as defining child abuse and neglect as "any physical, psychological and moral harm to children and the deliberate neglect of mental and physical health and education"; criminalization of particular behaviors that endanger children; determining criminal enforcement for criminal offenses toward children; and providing the possibility of reporting child abuse without the need for a private complainant. In regulating this law, the legislature specifically sought to protect children when abused by their parents and caretakers, because children cannot sue, and relatives may not wish to file a complaint. Thus, child abuse reports provided by authorities and institutes associated with caring and supporting children become obligatory, and punishment is considered in terms of any delinquency (Zeinali, 2003a; Mehra, 2010; Zeinali, 2010; Vameghi, 2011; Ghafari & Hosseini, 2016; Raghfar & Yousefvand, 2017; Nobahar & Saffari, 2018).

The Law on Combating Human Trafficking (2004) also protects at-risk children, and when a trafficked person is less than 18 years old, the offense is subject to a higher sentence (Article 3). In 2007, Iran ratified the Optional Protocol to the Convention on the Rights of the Child on the Sale of Children, Child Prostitution, and Child Pornography (2000).

The Islamic Penal Law (2013) also refers to the punishment of sexual abuse and explicitly states that if a person has sexual intercourse with an immature girl (under the age of 9 years) by deceiving her or without her consent, the sentence is the death penalty (Articles 658 and 224). However, it does not refer to other forms of child sexual abuse, sexual abuse of girls aged 9 to 18 years, and sexual abuse of boys. The law also includes significant innovations in the context of penalties and punitive measures for children and youth and determining the ages of criminal responsibility compared with previous laws.

The Criminal Procedure Law (2015) addresses crimes against children and deals with child crimes. With regard to crimes against children, Article 237 addresses the temporary arrest of offenders in cases of child abuse and child harassment. Article 31 stipulates that the Police Force of Iran should include special police for children and youth, which has been drafted into a bill in the Judicial Body. According to the draft of the bill, the children's police will address both delinquent and maltreated children. One of the other strengths of this law is Article 66, which makes it possible for NGOs supporting children to report child maltreatment and participate in all stages of the proceedings. This can have a considerable impact on fulfilling the best interests of the child during the proceedings process. In this law, in addition to imposing financial compensation, a court may impose compensation for spiritual damage to restore the comfort of the abused child by obliging the offender to make an apology to the child, publishing this in newspapers (taking into account the best interests of the child) or other methods ordered by judges.

Following the efforts made by civil society and the Judicial Body of Iran, the Children and Adolescents Protection Act was passed by the Iranian parliament in May 2020 to overcome the shortcomings of the old laws and coincide with the international developments regarding the protection of children. This law is applicable to all children under the age of 18 years. It explicitly provides definitions of concepts related to child maltreatment, such as neglect, abuse, economic exploitation, and imminent and immediate danger, to resolve previous ambiguities. It also defines 14 risky situations that may expose the child to physical, psychological, educational, social, or moral harm or risk for which intervention is necessary and provides legal protection for children in these circumstances (Article 3) (these 14 situations are listed in the section on "Defining at-risk children," above). This law classifies offenses against children and specifically different types of child sexual abuse. Articles 7 to 27 elaborate on the types of crimes committed by parents, legal caretakers of a child, and whoever is responsible for caring for the child and specifies the punishments. In this law, the penalty is intensified for certain crimes such as child sexual abuse if the offender is a parent or a person responsible for caring for and protecting the child. Contrary to previous laws, the duties of other institutions, including the SWO, the Police Force, the Ministry of the Interior, MCLSW, the Ministry of Health and Medical Education, the Ministry of Education, and the Islamic Republic of Iran Broadcasting, are explained in detail at various stages from prevention to providing specialized services for abused children. One of the remarkable points of this law is the detailed description of the duties and role of social workers of the SWO and courts in the proceedings process. In this law, mandatory reporting of child abuse is increasingly highlighted and includes all citizens, and more severe punishment is imposed on responsible individuals (such as doctors and care providers) in comparison with the 2002 act.

Notable points of this law are that there is no need for harm to occur before intervention can take place; a particular procedure has been defined for child maltreatment; the child's opinion is valid in this law; the rights of the child are considered in the process;

non-Iranian children are considered; the SWO is allowed to intervene directly and is supported by police; and the priority of keeping the at-risk child with his/her family has been emphasized. Of course, there are some critiques of this law: for instance, the definition of at-risk children is still limited, it does not include all groups of at-risk children, and it does not include the general population of children. The preventive approach, the enforcement of laws, and the supporting aspects are still unclear, and in some cases, there is no proportionality between the crime and the punishment (Hedayat & Hashemi, 2017; Raghfar & Yousefvand, 2017; Marzban, 2018).

Given the review of laws in Iran, it can be said that, in recent years, significant efforts have been made to regulate the laws to promote child protection. These efforts follow the approach of addressing situations after the occurrence of harm, and as in many countries, this risk management approach is a priority; a preventive and systemic approach to support the child and family is not considered (Schmid, 2010; Akbarineh, 2013; Hayes & Spratt, 2014; Ghafari & Hosseini, 2016; Marzban, 2018).

Child Protection Process of Providing Services

The admission process until discharging children from the SWO care process is described below, according to the Protection of Headless Women and Orphaned Children Act (1992), the *Guideline for Caring for Children under Protection of a Legal Guardian* (SWO, 2009), the OICGCYP Act (2013), and the *Guidelines for Caring for Orphans and with Inappropriate Care Givers Children and Youth in Family* (SWO, 2018a). The prevailing approach of these guidelines is to preserve the family and deinstitutionalization.

Assessing Eligibility and Decision Making

The SWO carries out primary admission at the local level (cities) by various procedures, such as the Social Emergency Plan (SEP), which is discussed later, the SWO Admissions Committee, various organizations such as schools, NGOs, police, and the State Prisons and Security and Corrective Measure Organization (referring children with parents who have been sentenced to life imprisonment or the death penalty). After initial investigations and legal proceedings, they are directed through judicial authorities to the Children and Youth Office of the SWO to assess and monitor child custody, his or her eligibility, and then planning for interventions. According to the laws, children are referred to and accepted by the Children and Youth Office for the following reasons: 1) the death of caretakers or a single caretaker; 2) imprisonment of caretakers or a single caretaker; 3) disappearance of caretakers or a single caretaker; 4) an unidentified child; 5) disqualification of caretakers according to a judicial order (under the defined criteria of exiting laws); 6) having severe contagious diseases or psychologic disorders in the family that put the child's health and development at risk; and 7) addiction of the caretakers or a single caretaker that puts the child's health and development at risk. According to the 2016 report of the SWO (2017), of 6,733 newly referred children in 2016, 26.96% were accepted due to addiction, 26.37% due to disqualification, 10.76% due to imprisonment, 9.01% due to death, 6.77% due to disappearance of caretakers or a single caretaker, and 4.45% due to caretakers or a single caretaker having severe contagious diseases or psychological disorders. In addition, 15.65% were accepted because the child was unidentified.

After the child's admission, the first step is to try to empower the family with financial and non-financial support in caring for the child under the supervision of the SWO to prevent the child from entering the organization's formal care process. However, suppose it is necessary to put the child under the protection of legal guardianship. In that case, the SWO offers the judicial authorities the type of child care with the priority on family care (versus institutional care).

TYPES OF CARE IN CHILD PROTECTION

The SWO offers care services in two models: family care and institutional care. Family care involves care of the child under the supervision of the SWO through the biological family (father, mother, or paternal grandfather) or a foster family and adoption (with a temporary custody or adoption order with relatives or non-relatives). The final aim of institutional care is the successful reunification of the child into the family or community. Currently, there are six types of residential care centers according to the age and status of the children. These centers are called homes in Iran, as ultimately, 20 children are living together in a place designed like a home.

The first priority in the care of children is to provide them with safe and stable living conditions with their parents or paternal grandfather. Based on the opinion of the SWO's social workers, if these caregivers are not fully qualified to have custody, the court will grant them custody but will also appoint a supervisor for the child. If neither of the parents nor the paternal grandfather is qualified enough to take custody, even with a supervisor, the court may, based on the opinion of the SWO's social workers, determine a temporary trustee for the child and grant temporary custody of the child to another person who is usually a relative of the child. To ensure the best interests of the child and according to the conditions described in the law of 2013 for the adoption of a child, the court can grant permanent custody and guardianship of the child to applicants for adoption.[12] Ultimately, if the family cannot provide care, institutional care is considered a temporary solution for the child, and necessary follow-up is considered to provide care to the family in the future. The SWO is responsible for supporting these children until the age of 18 years. Still, some young adults (more than 18 years old) live in specific institutions to prepare for independent living in society (SWO, 2018b, reported that 372 young adults

---

[12] Article 8 of OICGCYP Act (2013): a) There is no possibility of recognition by any father, mother, or paternal grandfather; b) father, mother, paternal grandfather are not alive; c) children who are under the protection of a legal guardian and until two years from the date of their legal guardian transfer to the SWO, the parent or paternal grandfather have not applied for custody of the child; d) none of father, mother or paternal grandfather are qualified for custody.

were under institutional care in 2017). Also, after moving into society, the SWO supports them with housing, insurance, university allowance, and so on as aftercare support (SWO, 2018b, reported that 607 young adults were supported in 2017). The court orders all care orders (family and institutional) in Iran except voluntary biological family care, for which the SWO supports the family to prevent other types of care.

In 2017, 26,285 orphans and children with inappropriate caregivers were supported by the SWO, of which 15,821 were in family care. Also, in 2017, 1,594 new adoption orders and 391 new temporary trustee orders were registered (SWO, 2018b). As shown in Table 38.1, the percentage of the total number of children in care who are under family care has been about 60% since 2011. Table 38.1 provides information on different types of care in Iran in recent years.

After the child comes under one of the types of care, the SWO, directly or through charities or private organizations, provides various types of social, psychological, and financial support and monitors the best interests of the child in every kind of care; adherence of caretakers to their financial and nonfinancial obligations is also monitored through periodic house visits. The SWO is required to carry out particular interventions and review the child custody arrangements in cooperation with the judicial authorities in several situations: awareness of the child's inappropriate situation in the family; the marriage, death, or divorce of the caretaker; the biological family apply to take back the child.[13]

MONITORING AND EVALUATING SERVICES

The monitoring and evaluation strategies of related programs include continuous visits to service providers or residential care centers by the local (cities), province, and state levels of the SWO; accurate recording and documentation of data; and continuous reporting. However, it is significant that the performance evaluating indicators of MCLSW in 2018 do not define any accurate quantitative and qualitative indicators and outcome-related factors for the child protection system; only the final measure, that is, the number of in-care children, is counted.

Reviewing the Related National Programs

Nowadays, in Iran, various programs and plans are implemented for different groups of children by various institutions. The main program of governmental organizations to protect children is the Social Emergency Plan (SEP), implemented by the SWO to identify and provide services to all types of vulnerable groups, including children. This plan can be considered one of the most important national child protection initiatives in Iran. SEP's

---

[13] In Article 25 of OICGCYP Act (2013): After consultation with the SWO, the custody order shall be terminated in the following cases: a) the initial conditions and entitlement of the caregivers are eliminated; b) the request of caregivers if the child's misbehavior is intolerable; c) mature child's agreements with caregivers; e) recognizing the father or mother or paternal grandfather of the child if they are qualified to have custody, even with a supervisor decided by the court.

Table 38.1 Overview of basic child protection statistics

	2011	2012	2013	2014	2015	2016
Child population 0–17 years measured	20,819,000[a]	21,774,000	21,920,000	–	21,747,000	22,149,000
Total no. of children in care at the end of the year per 1,000 children aged 0–17 years	1.05	1.00	1.03	–	1.13	1.14
Children in institutional care at the end of the year per 1,000 children aged 0–17 years	0.45	0.42	0.43	–	0.45	0.45
Children in family care at the end of the year per 1,000 children aged 0–17 years	0.61	0.58	0.59	–	0.68	0.69
No. of new adoption orders	–	–	–	–	1257[g]	1408[h]
Young adults >18 years in aftercare support	–	–	–	–	743	652
Young adults > 18 years in institutional care	–	–	–	–	–	403

Sources: Data for 2011–2012 adopted from SWO (2016b). Data for 2013–2017 adopted from SWO (2016b, 2017, 2018b); UNICEF (2013, 2014a, 2014b, 2016, 2017).

Notes: Total number of children in care includes both orphaned and children with inappropriate caregivers.

Institutional care refers to a kind of out-of-home placement but includes both orphaned and children with inappropriate caregivers.

Family care consists of supporting biological family (in-home measures) or foster family and adoption (out-of-home placements). There is no available data reporting these separately. There is also no data that distinguishes between voluntary or coercive out-of-home placements.

services are provided free within 24 hours through 1) a social emergency center, 2) a social emergency hotline (or 123 hotline), 3) social emergency mobile services (in disadvantaged urban and rural areas), and 4) social community service centers (in informal settlements). The SWO has developed a *Guideline for Child Abuse Interventions* for the SEP at all stages of service provision that provides operational information and categorization for decision-making and delivering interventions. In 2017, 232 social emergency centers, 223 social community service centers, 255 mobile services, and 211 hotline services were active throughout the country (SWO, 2018b).

The activities of the social emergency centers began in 1999 and are currently active in all 31 provinces. In each center, various professionals provide outpatient and residential services 24 hours per day, seven days per week. The head of the center is responsible for coordinating the activities of the social emergency mobile service, the 123 hotline, and the center. As the official body is responsible for dealing with child abuse, the centers have the tasks of admission and initial assessment, providing outpatient and specialized services for the child and family, and protecting children reported to have experienced abuse or neglect. Discharge from these centers occurs either by returning the child to the family or referring the child to other departments of the SWO (such as the Children and Youth Office to monitor the child's custody) or other organizations, and necessary follow-ups are conducted.

The social emergency hotline (123) was launched in 2004 for child abuse cases, and currently, services are provided 24 hours per day, seven days per week, in all provinces of Iran. The admission process is by self-reports by children or reports of child maltreatment by any citizen or organization. Telephone counseling is provided as much as possible, and then internal or external referrals occur. The official statistics for the 123 hotline are not publicly available. Still, according to the Social Department of the SWO, in 2016, about 700,000 telephone calls were made to the 123 hotline, with about 160,000 (8.5%) related to child abuse (Masufi Farid, 2017).

The services of the SEP, in particular the 123 hotline, have played a significant role in public awareness of child abuse in recent years. However, these services are still unavailable in all cities and regions of Iran. The lack of publicity about the SEP, problems with financial and human resources, and lack of inter-organizational cooperation are some of the current challenges of the SEP.

In addition to these state programs, public and non-governmental organizations implement various local and national programs to develop the welfare and protection of children. Still , there is no national and accepted indicator or measure for evaluating and comparing these various plans and programs in Iran. There is no national research or evidence that has evaluated them. Therefore, there is no possibility of introducing best practices at the local or national levels.

In terms of the professionals working in the child protection system, given that in the existing reports and statistics, the status of professionals working in different offices of the SWO is not reported separately, accurate statistics about child protection professionals' field of study and academic degree cannot be provided. But according to the rules and guidelines, in the early stages of decision-making and formulating a care plan, social workers of the SEP and the Department of Children and Youth have responsibility for the main tasks. Accurate data are not available, but the fact that professionals are working as social workers without a related academic degree is one of the challenges of SWO; one of the reasons for this is the lack of graduates in social work in the past decades. Currently, there has been an increase in all levels of graduates in social work, and they have priority for these organizational posts. In the next stage, services and interventions within the family care model are provided by social workers of the Department of Children and Youth as well as the private and non-government sectors, primarily within social work clinics. In 2017, 483 social work clinics cooperated with the SWO (SWO, 2018b); a bachelor's degree in social work is the minimum requirement to establish these clinics. Children under the institutional model of care also live in state or non-governmental centers. These centers must employ social workers and psychologists with at least a BA in their academic field. In 2017, 546 psychologists were employed in the state (10.80%) and non-governmental (89.19%) centers, of which 57.32% had a BA, 39.55% had an MA, and the remainder had a Ph.D. or higher degree. Also, 585 social workers were employed in the state (9.4%) and non-governmental (90.6%) centers, of which 7.35% did not have a BA, 82.6% had a BA, and 10.09% had an MA (SWO, 2018b).

Regarding the financial resources of the child protection system, SWO services and programs are funded by state and provincial budgets, as well as contributions from charities and NGOs, but the details are not available to report.

Current Challenges

Despite all the positive developments in legislation, policymaking, and planning about child protection, Iran still faces many challenges in the field of children and child protection, such as the lack of public awareness about current effective laws and programs; the challenges of existing laws, limitations of financial and human resources for law enforcement, the lack of a monitoring mechanism and accountability of organizations; and the lack of integration on documenting and reporting data. These factors cause some issues in child protection, including ambiguity about the age of childhood and criminal responsibility (as discussed earlier), the conflict between the rights of the child and the family, corporal punishment by parents, domination of a patriarchy culture, and ambiguities and conflicts in child adoption. These are addressed in the following section.

Corporal Punishment of Children: The Balance between the Child's Rights and the Parent's Rights

The family in Iran is of great significance and with reference to the laws, caring and nurturing the child is the parents' duty. But to what extent parents have this right is a challenge. Article 9 of the Children and Adolescents Protection Act (2020) excludes parents and caregivers from child abuse definitions according to Article 1179 of the Civil Code and Article 158 of the Islamic Penal Law. Article 1179 of the Civil Code (1928) gives the right of corporal punishment of the child to parents but states that they should not be punished beyond the usual and accepted punishment. Article 158 of the Islamic Penal Law (2013) also indicates that the activities of parents and caregivers in order to care for and nurture a child are not punishable if such actions are compatible with social norms and religion. However, the extent of these norms is not defined in either of these laws. Therefore, this can lead to personal interpretation of child abuse within the family by families and the judge and limits the child protection services to acute and severe maltreatment (Zeinali, 2003b; Akbarineh, 2013). This right of corporal punishment is considered inappropriate and offensive to Islamic values by many researchers of Islamic jurisprudence. They believe that, according to Islamic rules, if parents are to punish the child in a way that even the face of the child gets red, it is forbidden, and they should pay the *Diya* (Fehresti & Nazari Khakshour, 2008; Mehra, 2010; Borhani, 2012; Basiri & Besharati, 2015).

Family Care of Children with Inappropriate Caregivers

As already mentioned, if it is in the best interests of the child, the court can temporarily and permanently grant custody of a child with inappropriate caregivers to another person or family. In practice, however, these laws have not yet been widely enforced, and currently, a significant proportion of children living in residential care are children with inappropriate caregivers. The following are some of the most critical challenges to achieving the goals of family care measures.

Nowadays, temporary trustee orders have been limited to the child's relatives, and few non-relative families volunteer as temporary trustees because of problems such as the emotional insecurity that is caused by a temporary and unstable relationship between the child and family members as well as the religious argument that the child is not *mahram* to the temporary trustee and their family members. Most of the applicants prefer to adopt an orphaned child.[14]

In Iran, adoption builds a legal relationship between the adopted child and the caregiver. After the adoption, most of the rights and duties of the biological child are built into the relationship between the adopted child and the caregiver, such as the care, maintenance, and custody of the child. The birth certificate of the adopted child is also issued based on the new parents' identification. But there are two differences from a biological child: first, being deprived of inheritance; second, marriage between the child and the caregiver (new parent) is not declared illegal by law. The first issue has been solved concerning adoption obligations, such as the possession of the property in the name of the

---

[14] In Islam, a *mahram* is an unmarriageable kin with whom marriage or sexual intercourse would be considered *haram*, illegal in Islam.

child, the life insurance of the child, and the child's entitlement to retirement and death pensions (Akbarineh, 2013; Hedayat & Hashemi, 2017). The permissibility of marriage between caregiver and adopted child is one of the challenging issues in this area. There are no national reports about its prevalence, but some informal reports estimate 2 or 3 cases since the establishment of the SWO (1980) (Talani, 2014; Salamat News, 2018). Such marriages are rare and therefore contrary to the norms and culture of Iran, so the law should be reviewed and revised to prevent such marriages and eliminate child and family concerns. In particular, it is believed that there are numerous jurisprudential justifications for this marriage to be forbidden and declared illegal (Shariati Nasab, 2017).

The conditions described in the OICGCYP Act (2013) for adopting a child are very limited, and a significant proportion of children with inappropriate caregivers cannot be considered for adoption by a family. Of course, the goal of the legislation is to support the child's biological family and to consider the best interests of the child in his/her biological family, but it is necessary to make exceptions in this respect. The next point is the conditions for the abolition of the court's permanent custody (adoption) order and the possibility of returning the child to his/her biological family. If the child's biological family has the right and opportunity to take back the child at any time after he or she has been given to another family, the applicants will be reluctant to adopt a child with an inappropriate caregiver because of this emotional insecurity. Therefore, the criteria beyond the "necessary eligibility of custody" for the biological family to claim back an adopted child should be considered; for example, the return of the child to the parents and not the paternal grandfather of the child; the legitimacy of the reason for leaving the child; reasonable demands and motivations; child participation in decision making; and the best interests of the child (Akbarineh, 2013; Hedayat & Hashemi, 2017; Shariati Nasab, 2017).

Conclusions

Nowadays, in Iran, various laws, policies, and programs for child welfare and the efforts made by children's rights activists to promote them indicate the significance of protecting children against risks. However, there is a dispersed approach and lack of integration in the child protection system, and it has not yet been taken seriously as an independent concept with an integrated executive mechanism to support different groups of at-risk children. This dispersion exists both in the theoretical approach to child protection and in its executive structure, so this lack of concentration is an obstacle to creating a single and holistic approach to the various aspects of children's needs and rights; it also makes it challenging to coordinate the policies, programs, and resources of the multiple organizations responsible for children.

In addition, there is a significant lack of accurate information about children's problems and risks that are impeding a comprehensive understanding and assessment of the current situation, which is thus hampering the design of urgent and timely interventions.

Although important and precise data are available in areas such as child health and education, and efforts have been made to document more data on children's social problems, these activities are primarily cross-sectional studies, and data are not collected regularly and systematically for different groups of children. As mentioned, the Children and Adolescents Protection Act (2020) is an essential step in defining various groups of at-risk children and accepting legal intervention for these children. This law not only helps with the inter-sectoral and inter-organizational planning for these children as the initial steps but also helps policymakers develop policies to improve integrated data collection and provision of services for these groups of children.

References

Akbarineh, P. (2013). Examining legal solutions to protect a child in an inappropriate family. *Woman and Family Study*, 19, 37–54. (In Persian).

Basiri, H. R. and Besharati, Z. (2015). Analysis of corporal punishment of children in the family based on the semantic reading of traditional Islamic narratives including the word "dharb" [hitting]. *Family Research*, 12(45), 93–113. (In Persian).

Borhani, M. (2012). Fiqh and law on the parental child treatment. *Law Quarterly*, 42(3), 73–85. (In Persian).

Fehresti, Z. and Nazari Khakshour, G. (2008). Investigating child abuse on legal dimensions and the need for review. *Islamic Jurisprudence and History of Islamic Civilization*, 4(15), 113–140. (In Persian).

Ghafari, G. and Hosseini, M. (2016). The readout of social policies regarding child risks in contemporary Iran. *Sociological Review*, 22(2), 177–209. (In Persian).

Hayes, D. and Spratt, T. (2014). Child welfare as child protection then and now: What social workers did and continue to do. *The British Journal of Social Work*, 44(3), 615–635. (In Persian).

Hedayat, H. and Hashemi, S. H. (2017). The necessity of family-centered cares for child victim and its exceptions (with emphasis on the Iranian legal system). *Criminal Law Research*, 5(19), 127–163. (In Persian).

IMF. (2018). *World economic outlook: Challenges to steady growth.* (In Persian).

Kahzadi Baseri, M. (2018). Studying and reviewing the criminal and civil responsibility of children and adolescents. *Ghanoon Yar*, 2(6), 121–147. (In Persian).

Karimi Moughari, Z., and Barati, J. (2017). Determining the level of regional inequality in provinces of Iran: Analysis of multidimensional composite index. *Economic Growth and Development Research*, 7(26), 49–70. (In Persian).

Mardoukh Rouhani, E. (2012). Reviewing welfare regimes in Iran and other countries. *Social Development and Welfare Planning.* Special Issue of the First Iranian Social Welfare Conference, 4, 249–285. (In Persian).

Marzban, S. (2018, September 2). Reviewing Children and Youth Act. *Ghanoon Daily News.* (In Persian). Available at: http://www.ghanoondaily.ir/fa/print/main/109007.

Masufi Farid, H. (2017, August 5). 8.5% of 123 calls have been related to child abuse. *Tasnim News.* (In Persian). Available at: http://tn.ai/1483858.

MCLSW. (2015). *The most important achievement of MCLSW.* Public Relation and Information Office. (In Persian).

MCLSW. (2017). *Statistics of Ministry of Cooperatives, Labor and Social Welfare in 2017.* Strategic Data and Information Center. Available at: http://amarkar.ir/Main/time. (In Persian).

MCLSW. (2018). *Social problem database.* (In Persian). Available at: https://asibha.mcls.gov.ir/fa/ghorop/sti eetchildren/intro. Retrieved 13 September 2019.

Mehra, N. (2010). Socio-legal approach towards child abuse. *Social Welfare*, 9 (35), 251–270. (In Persian).

Mohaqeqi Kamal, S. H. et al. 2015. *Territorial analysis of social welfare in Iran.* International and Comparative Social Policy, 31(3), 271–282. doi:10.1080/21699763.2015.1095580.

Mowlaei, M. (2007). The study and comparison of social welfare and services development degree among Iran's provinces in 1994 and 2004. *Social Welfare*, 6(24), 241–258. (In Persian).

Nobahar, R. and Saffari, F. (2018). The requirements of a protective criminalization for street children. *Criminal Law Research*, 8(2), 211–231. (In Persian).

Nourzad Laleh, M. and Ghayoum Zadeh, M. (2017). Legal review of custody in Iranian and British law. *Law Studies*, 9, 127–144. (In Persian).

Pur Abdollah, K. and Sharifi, F. (2014). The loan condition of child's guardianship in the legal system of Iran. *Policing and Social Studies of women and Family*, 2(2), 204–222. (In Persian).

Raghfar, H. and Yousefvand, F. (2017). Shelter and nutrition poverty of children in Tehran in 2011. *The Economic Research*, 17(3), 159–191. (In Persian).

Saboori Pour, M. and Alavi Sadr, F. (2015). Juveniles' age of criminal responsibility in Islamic Penal Code of 2013. *Criminal Law Research*, 6(1), 171–194. (In Persian).

Saei, S. M. H. and Kamyab Mansouri, N. (2016). Remarriage of the mother, custody and the best interest of the child. *Public Law Studies Quarterly*, 46(4), 771–801. (In Persian).

Salamat News. (2018, August 11). Only two marriage between adoptive parent and child have occurred since 40 years ago. *Salamat News*. (In Persian). Available at: http://www.salamatnews.com/news/250806.

Save the Children. (2012). *The child development index 2012: Progress, challenges and inequality*. Save the Children.

Schmid, J. (2010). A history of the Present: Uncovering discourses in (South African) child welfare. *The British Journal of Social Work*, 40(7), 2102–2118. (In Persian).

Shahiki Tash, M. N., Yaghfoori, H., and Darvishi, B. (2015). Review of the intensity of spatial and regional imbalance of welfare (Comparative study of welfare in Iran provinces based on Harvey and Smith approaches). *Scientific Journal Management System*, 5(17), 15–30.

Shariati Nasab, S. (2017). Iranian legislative politics about orphan children. *Iranian Association for Cultural Studies and Communication*, 13(46), 91–112. (In Persian).

Sheykh Beygloo, R., Taghvaeei, M. and Varesi, H. (2012). The spatial analysis of deprivation and inequalities of development in sub-provinces of Iran. *Social Welfare*, 12(46), 215–245. (In Persian).

Statistical Center of Iran. (2018a). *A selection of labor force survey results: The year 1396 (March 21, 2017– March 20, 2018)*. Presidency of Iran: Plan and Budget Organization, Statistical Center of Iran. Available at: https://www.amar.org.ir/english/Latest-Releases-Page/ArticleType/ArchiveView/year/2018.

Statistical Center of Iran. (2018b). *Selected findings of the 2016 national population and housing census*. Presidency of Iran: Plan and Budget Organization. Available at: https://www.amar.org.ir/english/Latest-ReleasesPage/ArticleType/ArchiveView/year/2018.

SWO. (2009). *Guideline for caring for children under protection of a legal guardian*. State Welfare Organization of Iran, Children and Youth Office. (In Persian).

SWO. (2016a). *Guideline for child abuse interventions (For social emergency experts)*. State Welfare Organization of Iran, Social Disadvantages Office. (In Persian).

SWO. (2016b). *Statistical Yearbook of 2015*. State Welfare Organization of Iran, Public Relations and International Affairs Office. (In Persian).

SWO. (2017). *Statistical yearbook of 2016*. State Welfare Organization of Iran, Public Relations and International Affairs Office. (In Persian).

SWO. (2018a). *Guidelines for caring orphan and with inappropriate care givers children and youth in family*. State Welfare Organization of Iran, Children and Youth Office. (In Persian).

SWO. (2018b). *Statistical yearbook of 2017*. State Welfare Organization of Iran, Public Relations and International Affairs Office. (In Persian).

Talani, Z. (2014, March 25). The marriage of adoptive parent and child is not accepted by Iranian convention. *Khabaronline News*. (In Persian). Available at: khabaronline.ir/news/346206.

UNDP. (2018). *Human development indices and indicators: 2018 statistical update. Briefing note for countries on the 2018 Statistical Update: Iran (the Islamic Republic of)*. Available at: http://hdr.undp.org/sites/all/themes/hdr_theme/country-notes/IRN.pdf.

UNICEF. (2012). *The country program action plan between the government of the Islamic Republic of Iran and UNICEF (2012–2016)*. Available at: https://www.unicef.org/iran/children.html.

UNICEF. (2013, May). *The state of the world's children 2013: Children with disabilities*. United Nations Children's Fund.

UNICEF. (2014a, January). *The state of the world's children 2014 in numbers: Every child counts, revealing disparities, advancing children's rights*. United Nations Children's Fund.

UNICEF. (2014b, November). *The state of the world's children 2015: Executive summary, reimagine the future, innovation for every child*. United Nations Children's Fund.

UNICEF. (2016, June). *The State of the World's children 2016: A fair chance for every child*. United Nations Children's Fund.

UNICEF. (2017). *The state of the world's children 2017: Children in a digital world*. United Nations Children's Fund.

Vameghi, M. (2011). *Report of the social status of Iran 2001–2009: Domestic violence*. Aghah Publication. (In Persian).

Vesali, S. S. and Basatian, S. M. (2012). The status of active state in Iran: A study concerning adaptation of state welfare function with social welfare function. *Social Development and Welfare Planning*, 3(11), 69–92. (In Persian).

WHO. (2016). *Country cooperation strategy at glance: Iran (the Islamic Republic of)*. Available at: https://www.who.int/countries/irn/en/.

Zeinali, A. H. (2003a). The legal innovation on Children Protection Act and the fore coming obstacles. *Social Welfare*, 2(7), 59–92. (In Persian).

Zeinali, A. H. (2003b). Children support law. *Social Welfare*, 3(9), 109–132. (In Persian).

Zeinali, A. H. (2010). The globalization of special protection of children. *Social Welfare*, 9(35), 51–87. (In Persian).

Zeinali, A. H. (2015, September). *Protecting at-risk children: Basis and needs*. National Conference of Childhood in Iran, Newsletters (2). Rahman Institute. (In Persian).

Zeinali, A. H. and Jomepour, H. (2012). Corporal Punishment of Children: An Instance of the Challenge of Cultural Relativism and the Universality of Human Rights of Children. *Human Rights*, 7(1), 49–68. (In Persian).

Zeinali, A. H. and Karimi Tachara, R. (2017). Iranian legislative politics about orphan children. *Iranian Association for Cultural Studies and Communication*, 13(46), 71–90. (In Persian).

Child Protection in Lebanon

Hoda Rizk

Abstract

This chapter looks into Lebanon's child protection system. It highlights the significance of the National Social Development Strategy which includes measures for improved protection of children. Higher Council for Childhood is the principal body established for the coordination of children's issues with the governmental, non-governmental and international parties concerned with children's rights. Additionally, the HCC pursued the implementation of the Committee on the Rights of the Child and its respective recommendation. The legal system gives religious communities judicial autonomy on issues of custody and maintenance. All religions, moreover, agree on the responsibility of the parents to provide for their children.

Key Words: Lebanon, child protection, NSDS, HCC, children's rights, CRC, judicial autonomy, religions, parents

The population of Lebanon is estimated at approximately 6 million, though a formal census has not been taken since 1932. Estimates of the proportion of children in the country are difficult to discern, but some estimates indicate that approximately 23% of the population includes children aged 0–14, while the child population aged 0–17 years is estimated to be 1,733,000 (approximately 28%) (UNICEF, 2016).

Approach to Social Welfare in Lebanon

In 2011, Lebanon's Ministry of Social Affairs led the preparation and publication of a National Social Development Strategy (2011–2015). This strategy is the result of a process that began in early 2007.

This strategy represents an important milestone for Lebanon because it constitutes the first consultative, inter-sector strategic commitment by the government to map where priority action is needed for the development of inclusive and equitable social security system and access to services. The National Social Development Strategy (NSDS) is significant because it states a number of important principles:

a) The strategy states that the government will "intervene to regulate and monitor but not to implement (social services)," creating a subsidiary relationship whereby civil society, the family, and the individual become the actors of social change.

b) The strategy recognizes the importance of both universal social services (broad, inclusive initiatives for the whole society) and targeted social services (tailored, inclusive interventions that address inequity of access for the most disadvantaged).

c) The strategy recognizes the marked disparities of income and development across different geographical regions of the country and commits the government to undertake practical efforts to address inequity in some regards.

The strategy reiterates a focus on key areas of social protection, including measures for improved protection of children, who are identified as one priority vulnerable group. The Higher Council for Childhood (HCC) is an inter-ministerial coordinating planning body, designated to ensure that these principles are incorporated into policy across all sectors (education, health, justice, and welfare). The factors above demonstrate a positive commitment that, if applied rigorously, could shape the ability of services at the local level to better protection outcomes for children. The five priority objectives of the NSDS are identified in Table 39.1.

National Coordination of Children's Issues

The principal body established for the coordination of children's issues is the Higher Council for Childhood (HCC). This council was formed in 1994 under Decree No 29/

Table 39.1 National social development strategy	
General objectives	Priority interventions
Achieve better health	Work toward ensuring coverage to all Strengthen the regulatory role of Ministry of Public Health
Strengthen social protection	Develop a pension scheme Address issues related to institutionalized children Strengthen the governance and the institutional capacity of NSSF (National social security food)
Provide quality education	Work towards achieving free compulsory basic education for ages 6–15 years Institutionalize coordination between the Lebanese University and the labor market
Improve opportunities for equitable and safe employment	Encourage and enforce formalization of enterprises and workers Strengthen labor market institutions
Revitalize communities and encourage development of social capital	Reinforce Lebanese identity shared by all citizens Promote home ownership by middle- and lower- income households

94 issued by the Council of Ministers after the ratification by Lebanon of the Convention on the Rights of the Child. The Minister of Social Affairs acts as chairperson of HCC. The mandate of this inter-ministerial council is to coordinate between the governmental, non-governmental, and international parties concerned with children's rights. This council has significantly pursued the implementation of the UN Convention on the Rights of the Child, and the recommendations made by the Committee on the Rights of the Child. In addition, the HCC is mandated to initiate and oversee policy relating to children's issues and build the capacity and skills of persons working on children's issues (Save the Children, 2008). Lebanon created a Parliamentary Committee on Women and Children in 1991 to amend national legislation in line with the CRC. This body can potentially still act as a conduit for wider national dialogue on children's matters, but its current focus and priorities are not set out in any specific document.

Since its inception, the HCC has been pivotal to the advancement of the child welfare agenda. The HCC coordinates a series of sub-committees on children's issues and prepares the sector plans of these respective sub-committees, bringing them into one comprehensive plan for childhood. Unfortunately, it has been very difficult to assure funding and to promote solid, integrated sector plans through these sub-committees.

The HCC has assumed a wider role than coordination between ministries. As demonstrated by its action plan in 2011, the HCC has developed a significant role in the development of the national child welfare sector, including: the review and development of legislation, research on issues of violence in schools and trafficking, developing children's services, and reporting on international commitments. The action plan of 2011 was highly ambitious, but due to funding and human resource constraints some of the activities are on hold.

One of the challenges that HCC faces in the inter-ministerial coordinator role concerns the lack of robust information and statistics about the situation of children. Although Lebanon has a special Central Administration of Statistics under the Prime Minister's Office, there are few published statistics upon which to advocate for policy reform, new initiatives or a revised budget for children's issues. UNICEF supported the development of the Multiple Indicator Cluster Survey in 2000 and in 2009, although the latter remains in draft form. Since 2006, the DevInfo knowledge management system has proved a useful source of information for the development of the report for the Committee on the Rights of the Child, although it has not been systematically updated or maintained. The remit for managing information on DevInfo is located with the Central Administration of Statistics and it appears that HCC and MOSA (Ministry of Social Affairs) are not able to access or publish helpful information. The lack of a reliable evidence base is a challenge for coordinated planning and programming on child welfare issues across ministries.

At the present time, the HCC is represented at the central level only. There is a longer-term vision, however, to replicate the coordination mechanism in each of the regions, if not in all districts eventually. One of the aspirations of this potential structure would bring together senior officials from education, health, law enforcement, and social affairs, as well as civil society organizations to design and implement tailored services and initiatives at the local level.

The Legal Framework for Child Protection

Lebanon has its own Code of Obligations and Contracts promulgated in 1932 during the French Mandate, though personal status matters such as marriage, divorce and child custody are governed by different laws within each religious community, as discussed in detail below.

The Constitution of Lebanon adopted in 1926 (amended in 1990) states principles such as respect for public liberties, respect for social justice, and equality of rights and duties among all citizens, without discrimination (Preamble (c). Article 7). However, in many issues of family and child welfare law, religious communities are given significant autonomy in matters such as child custody and adoption to make decisions based on local cultural norms and practices. Within the legal framework, there are therefore a number of different approaches and procedures that affect children, according to their community affiliation.

Lebanon has ratified the Convention on the Rights of the Child as well as the vast majority of other international and regional instruments concerning child protection. However, the country has neither signed nor ratified the Hague Convention on Protection of Children and Cooperation in Respect of Inter-country Adoption, nor the 1951 Convention Relating to the Status of Refugees.

Childhood is defined based on context and—in some cases—religion. Table 39.2 identifies the legal frame for defining childhood in Lebanon.

What follows is an overview of several child-related laws that shape the context for child protection.

Child Custody and Maintenance

The legal system gives religious communities judicial autonomy on custody and maintenance issues. All religions agree on the responsibility of parents to provide for their children. Maintenance provisions for children are not restricted to food, clothing and housing expenses, but also cover medical expenses, education, and recreation. The Laws of the Personal Status of each community give the religious courts the right to put into practice these obligations. The Civil Court has the jurisdiction to look at these matters in the case of non-religious marriages made abroad. Civil marriage is not a possibility in Lebanon, despite an attempt to make it optional in 1998. Many couples go to foreign—often European—countries to make a civil marriage.

Child custody laws, under the Family Status Laws, largely determine custody on fixed age and gender criteria rather than through a "best interest" assessment. In cases of civil marriages made abroad, the foreign law is applied by the Lebanese civil judge on custody

Table 39.2 Legal definitions of the child

Legal definition of the child	
Definition of the child according to child protection laws (Law 422, Article 1, 2002)	Ages 0–18
Minimum age for marriage	Determined by law of religious community. Family status laws allow for early marriage (as young as 9 for certain groups) and, in some cases, allow parents to arrange marriage without the consent of the child
Minimum age for completion of compulsory education (Law of 2011, but still lacking implementation decree)	15
Minimum age for employment (Law of 1946 Labor Code Modified 1993 & 1996, Article 22), though Lebanon is signatory to ILO Convention No. 138, which sets the minimum age for employment at 15 years. The Labor Law of Lebanon, Article 7, explicitly includes domestic workers.	13
Minimum age for engaging in hazardous work (Law of 1946 Labor Code Article 23, also Labor Ministry Decree No. 700 of 1999 lists specific industries prohibited for children younger than 16 and a different list for those younger than 17.)	16/17
Minimum age for consenting to sexual activities (Penal Code Article 505).	18
Age of criminal responsibility (Law 422/2002, Articles 3 & 6).	7
Maximum age for juvenile justice protections	18
Age for voluntary recruitment to the armed forces www.lebarmy.gov.lb/arabic/ConditionSoldier.asp (2002)	17

issues. However, if two Muslim Lebanese make a civil marriage abroad, the competent court in Lebanon will always be the religious court applying religious legal norms.

Domestic Violence

A draft law proposal (293) protecting women from domestic violence has been prepared and debated by civil society organizations since 2010. However only sections of the proposal were approved in Parliament in 2014.

Inheritance

In terms of inheritance, Lebanese Muslims are subject to the religious laws of their community, while a 1959 secular law applies to "non-Muslims," mainly Christians.

Adoption

There is no national law on the adoption of children as the practice is managed independently by each of the religious communities. Formal adoption is not recognized in Islam, although informal processes exist for the placement of children with extended family and beyond. Some Christian communities have their own personal status legislation concerning adoption recognized by the state. The implementation of these practices is not monitored by the state. However, the penal code prohibits in its Article 500(4) any adoption involving money transactions.

Child Labor

The Labor Law of 1946 (which excludes domestic servants and agricultural workers from most provisions) specifies a minimum age of 14 for employment, and a minimum age for hazardous work of age 18.

Physical Abuse and Corporal Punishment

The Penal Code (Article 186) permits discipline inflicted on children by their parents and teachers as sanctioned by general custom. This provision is currently under review in preparation for a new penal code.

Sexual Abuse

Penalties for sexual abuse are increased when committed on a child (Penal Code, Articles 505–520). Law 422 of 2002 is the principal law that provides for a statutory child protection response and for judicial decisions about a child's welfare to be made.

Child Prostitution

The Penal Code (Article 523) criminalizes prostitution, including where a child is involved, while Law 422 of 2002, Article 25, considers a child engaged in prostitution as a child at risk and in need of protection. Law 164 of 2011 on human trafficking increases the penalty for trafficking and exploitation leading to the prostitution of a minor.

Child Pornography

The Penal Code (Article 533) criminalizes commercial pornography in general, but Law 164 of 2011 on human trafficking can be applied as a penalty for trafficking and exploitation leading to child pornography (Article 586 (1)).

Child Trafficking and Slavery

Law 164 of 2011 on human trafficking introduces for the first time the notion of exploitation. The law provides more severe penalties for trafficking and exploitation offences which force children to participate in the following acts: breaking the law, prostitution, sexual exploitation, begging, slavery or similar practices, forced labor, implication in armed conflicts, terrorist acts, or organ removal (Article 586(5)). It also widens the category of "trafficking" when a minor is involved, by making unnecessary any proof of force, violence, deception, abduction, or material favors (Article 586(1)).

Children in Armed Conflict

Law 164 of 2011 on human trafficking criminalizes exploitation/trafficking leading to the participation of minors in armed conflicts.

Children Living and Working on the Streets

Law 422 of 2002, Article 25, includes street children within the definition of children at risk. However, current legal debate has a tendency to consider these children as young offenders. Article 610 onwards of the Penal Code also criminalizes many actions associated with begging, living and working in the streets. It also has special provisions for the punishment of adults/parents that permit or force a child to beg/work in the street (Articles 617 and 618). Law 164, Article 586(5), on human trafficking increases penalties for trafficking and exploitation offences that result in a child begging.

Early Childhood Education

Elementary education up to the age of 12 is free and compulsory under Act No. 686 of 1998. An amendment to the Law in 2011 increased the age at which compulsory schooling ends to 15 years. However, the implementing decrees and protocols for the Act of 1998 have still to be developed, rendering the latest changes somewhat artificial.

Ministerial Decision 47 of 2003 exempts all public education students, including non-Lebanese, in pre-school, first, and second grade levels from registration fees, although foreign students cannot register in public schools if they do not have relevant identification papers (Save the Children, 2011). A fee of LBP 50,000 is still charged for the Parent Council which may prove an obstacle to enrolment for some families.

Children with Disabilities

Law 220 of 2000 on the rights of persons with disabilities mentions the right of the disabled child to have a proper education (Article 59) and the right to join all educational institutions (Article 60). It forbids any discriminatory practices against disabled children in this respect. However, this law still lacks the implementation decrees necessary to ensure its full implementation in the future.

Policies and Strategies for Child Protection

There are a number of national policies and strategies across a range of different social and justice sectors enacted to protect children. Several are presented but this description is not exhaustive.

Ministry of Social Affairs

The Ministry of Social Affairs does not have a unified child welfare policy or strategy. However, as the leading welfare agency, it has been intrinsically involved in the development of a number of strategies that affect the welfare and protection of children.

The National Social Development Strategy (NSDS, 2011–2015) is the most recent broad inter-sector plan for the welfare of the Lebanese population. Among several other recommended actions for improved social protection for livelihood assistance and support to vulnerable groups such as the elderly, disabled and extremely poor households, the National Social Development Strategy has the following specific recommendations for action for the better protection of children.

- *Address issues related to the institutionalization of children*: Provide assistance to allow families to support their children within their homes and establish measures that leave institutionalization as the absolute last resort to be decided upon with a legal and procedural framework.
- *Eradicate the worst forms of child labor and keep children off the streets*: Establish a comprehensive social, health, and educational program to protect working children and enforce the Higher Council for Childhood's strategy to address the problem of street children.
- *Protect and guide children at risk or in conflict with the law*: Enforce the differential treatment of children in the penal system and institute school support programs and community activities that protect minors against risky social behaviors, including drugs and violence.
- *Protect women and children from violence*: Establish legal and institutional mechanisms to protect women from abuse in home and work settings, beginning with a civil personal status law, and institute and enforce harsh penalties to protect children from violence and abuse within their families and in schools.

A National Action Plan for the Prevention and Protection of Children from all Forms of Violence and Neglect was drafted by the HCC (on behalf of MOSA) and approved by the Ministry in 2012. The plan recognizes certain core child rights principles within its approach to protection including non-discrimination, the indivisibility of rights, best interest of the child, child participation, gender sensitivity, and inclusive programming.

The action plan outlines a series of important principles for protecting children from violence and neglect, underpinned by the findings of the UN Secretary-General's Report on Violence Against Children (2005). For example, the action plan commits to:

1) Protection for all categories of children and in whatever circumstances they find themselves.

2) Ownership and responsibility of a range of different sectors (a multi-sector approach) through partnership and collaboration with Government agencies, civil society, media, academia, and international organizations.

3) Extension of cooperation to international and regional actors to ensure cohesion and funding of projects.

4) Development of prevention strategies as well as multi-disciplinary rehabilitation services.

The action plan has five components, each with several subsections outlining broad strategic objectives:

1) Legislative and legal framework for child protection from all forms of violence and neglect;

2) Develop and build human and institutional capacity for child protection;

3) Raise awareness and educate on child protection issues;

4) Monitoring, warning, and complaints mechanisms;

5) Ensure children's participation in fighting violence against them.

These actions are subsequently broken down into subsequent duties such as:

1) Develop quality standards for social care institutions, including licensing and accreditation;

2) Special code of conduct for employers who receive working children;

3) Modify school curricula to ensure they are free from violence.

Separately, in 2011, the HCC and MOSA developed an annual Plan of Action. Within this plan there are a number of priority projects. These include:

- The potential development of a Child Helpline;
- The legal and social protection of street children, for which a draft "Strategy for Protection, Rehabilitation and Integration of Street Children" has been developed;
- A friendly cities initiative in urban areas;
- The establishment of a Children's Parliament;
- Development of standards and protocols to protect children online;
- The development of ethical standards for journalists.

Ministry of Justice

Although the Ministry of Justice has a number of policies and strategies that underpin its work, a specific policy for the promotion of child justice has yet to be developed.

However, the Department of Juveniles works closely with the HCC to develop n strategic priorities and an action plan for each year.

Ministry of Education and Higher Education

The Education Sector Development Plan (2010–2015), guided by the National Education Strategy of 2007, includes the following objectives:

- Guide the reform of public education, including the development and strengthening of vocational and technical education to meet a growing demand in Lebanon's development and construction sectors;
- Reach the goal to have compulsory education until age 15 instead of 12 (which corresponds with the new age set out in a recent ministerial decree);
- Develop and implement academic, psychological, and social support programs for children at risk.

Corporal punishment is prohibited in public schools under Ministerial Directive, Article 41 of the Decision No. 1130/m/2001, which stipulates that: "Employees in the education sector are prohibited to inflict any physical punishment on pupils, nor to address verbal retribution that is humiliating and is against the principle of education and personal dignity." In 2018, the Ministry of Education adopted a global policy to protect children at schools from physical violence and train more school counselors in a joint strategy between the MOE and UNICEF. The role of these counselors is: to look after the general well-being of students; to raise awareness on child welfare issues with parents and teachers; and to provide social and educational assistance. The strategy was welcomed but has suffered from under-investment and lack of specialized training for counselors. Because the position was never truly formalized or institutionalized, it has not been subject to regulations, standardization, or evaluation.

Ministry of Public Health

Under the Ministry of Health Strategic Plan, 2007, priorities relating to the promotion of child welfare include:

- The development of a basic care service package for children;
- The promotion of the primary healthcare system, including targeted programs to reduce maternal and child mortality (significant progress 1990–2009);
- An enhanced emphasis on the promotion of children's health through the school system.

The MOPH has yet to develop a special child protection policy, or standard or national protocol for handling cases of abuse.

Ministry of Labor

The National Policy and Program Framework for Child Labor, 2002 (adopted 2005), was the first official policy paper focusing on child labor. The issue was highlighted again in the agenda of the National Social Action Plan, a pillar of the Economic Reform Plan submitted to the international Lebanon Donor Conference (Paris III 2007) and incorporated in a Ministerial Declaration in 2009.

The Child Labor Unit has developed a series of priorities to address child labor in Lebanon and has formed a national committee comprised of both government and civil society agencies (e.g., International Labour Organization). The stated focus areas include: 1) harmonizing and disseminating international and national laws, including creation of common definitions; 2) raising awareness and education about the child labor problem with communities and employers; 3) promoting children's rights, access to free education, and basic services to prevent child labor; 4) maintaining a database of child labor statistics and cases, as well as a specialized library and website for resources; 5) responding to individual cases and complaints about child labor; and 6) developing vocational training programs for working children.

Government Welfare Services for Families and Children

A number of government social welfare initiatives and services have been designed to provide general support and help for families and children in Lebanon. While the majority of services in the country have been established by civil society organizations (NGOs, CBOs), the government provides some direct social assistance to families and children, even if these have not been conceived primarily as protection services.

Social Development Centers (SDCs) have been a universal feature of local level service delivery in Lebanon since the late 1960s. At that time, international agencies and the United Nations supported the previous Office for Social Development in the Ministry of Labor and Social Affairs to establish a mechanism for comprehensive social service delivery at the community level. After a period of piloting centers in the 1970s, the SDCs have been become ubiquitous across Lebanon.

Today, there are approximately 260 SDCs in the country, including both primary centers (89) and secondary centers (171). The secondary centers tend to be located in more rural areas and may be satellites of the primary centers. These centers constitute the most important local-level executive arm of MOSA. As part of the ministry's policy of decentralization, each SDC is supposed to target a specific locale and reach between 30,000 and 40,000 inhabitants. The SDC mandate includes the development of local action plans and resource allocation, field assessments, oversight of projects taking place in their geographical area, as well as coordination with public and private bodies. While the central office overseas the major programs, the SDCs have relative autonomy to decide their own activities. MOSA reported that in 2009, SDCs delivered social services to 61,619 adult and child beneficiaries, health services to 309,164 beneficiaries, training to 6,894 beneficiaries, and education services (including nursing, volunteer work, foreign language and literacy classes, and courses for children who do not attend school) to 16,486 beneficiaries all across the country (Ministry of Social Affairs, 2011).

In 2010, MOSA prioritized reform and strengthening of the SDCs, given their importance as a provider of basic social services at the local level. For example, MOPH pays the salaries of mobile doctors, dentists, and other medical staff. Together with the Ministry of Public Health and the Ministry of Interior and Municipalities, MOSA signed a joint Memorandum of Understanding in 2010 to improve coordination in the delivery of healthcare services at the local level. Four pilot SDCs were selected in two regions for which the local administration provides the premises, the MOPH provides the medical services and the MOSA provides the social services. This pilot is aimed at addressing overlap in the provision of health services at the local level. If successful, the pilot will be replicated at the national level. In the future, MOSA envisions that SDCs will have a stronger role in identifying, selecting, and monitoring community social development projects.

Under Law 422, SDC staff have not been legally mandated to participate in the protection of children. Although social workers may report a case to the Union for the Protection of Children in Lebanon (UPEL), they are under no legal obligation or duty to do so and have no other powers of intervention (such as to remove a child in emergency situations). Rather, SDC staff may simply act as a conduit to the police and UPEL by encouraging parents and families to seek judicial assistance and statutory child protection services. In some cases, however, judges may order a child in conflict with the law to be supervised by SDC staff or to join one of the educational centers or vocational programs.

Government Contracted Children's Services

As the government does not provide many direct services itself, it contracts out a number of child welfare and protection services to civil society organizations. The Social Welfare Department of MOSA is responsible for the development of partnership and contracting arrangements with civil society organizations, although the provision of services by these organizations is not specifically mandated under Law 422. Traditionally, these contracts were arranged with organizations that provide residential care and educational support for vulnerable children, although more specialized protection facilities were also contracted for those with particular needs. These services are described in more detail in the later section on non-statutory child protection services.

Special Protection Facilities

The Department for Juvenile Protection is responsible for ensuring that a range of services are available for children who are deemed to be at high risk (such as street children and victims of sexual exploitation). Since 2003, the Department has contracted with a number of agencies (currently 11 NGOs) to provide protective and rehabilitative services:

- Seven day centers in Beirut, Mount Lebanon, and Tripoli. Children attending these centers tend to live with their families and participate in activities voluntarily. They are offered basic services such as food and clothing, psychological counseling, skills development classes, information, and advice. Two agencies focus exclusively on social reinsertion.
- Four residential centers, mostly for children at high levels of risk (such as street children and child beggars). Many of these children are placed on the order of a judge.

It is important to note here that the goal of contracting with these day centers is to maintain children within their families rather than being sent to residential facilities. This is a positive shift in approach.

Residential Institutions

One of the most important challenges to child welfare in Lebanon is the widespread practice of institutionalizing children. There is a long history of enrolling children of destitute families into residential institutions for purposes of maintenance and education in Lebanon. Social and economic factors led to a continuation of these institutions under the auspices of different religious groups, even during the Shehabi administration (post-1958 war) when the newly created Social Welfare Department took up a financially supportive (rather than a strong monitoring and regulatory) role (Consultation and Research Institute, 2007). However, it should be noted that the majority of children in these institutions are not orphans or abandoned children, nor are they generally children in need of special temporary protection.

The Social Welfare Department has 183 contracts with civil society organizations to provide institutional care for children, mostly in residential schools or homes in which children continue to access the public education system. Approximately 35,000 children under the age of 18 are in such care, the majority of them from poor or broken families. Families may present to social workers at the SDC or may be referred by teachers and community leaders.

Although the government acknowledges the need to promote family-based care arrangements, it invests considerable social welfare resources in the maintenance of institutions for children. The Social Welfare Department spends an estimated 60% of its annual budget on the provision of care to children in welfare institutions. Although these figures over-simplify the situation, it is possible that as many as half of the nearly 35,000 children receiving free education or vocational training at the residential schools actually go home at night to their families even though they are formally registered as "residential."

The Legal Framework for the Delivery of Child Protection Services

Legal Mandate and Authority for Child Protection Services

Law 422, Article 52, calls for the Department of Juveniles of the Ministry of Justice (MOJ) to organize and coordinate all matters related to children under the Law. However, the law states that, until this department is fully organized, the Union for the Protection of Juveniles in Lebanon is to continue to practice the tasks within its charge according to "previous laws and the provisions of this law" (Article 53). The Ministry of Justice may contract with specialized agencies to support the implementation of the provisions of the law. Although the basis for contracting these agencies and the scope of potential collaboration remains undefined in the law, the MOJ has already begun this process.

The Ministry of Social Affairs has the broader mandate of attending to welfare services for children in need of assistance, ensuring their rights to live in a stable family environment (Law 212, 1993). The Higher Council for Childhood has a mandate to coordinate between the government, non-government and international parties concerned with children's rights. The council was established in 1994 by virtue of Decision No. 2994, issued by the Council of Ministers (see www.atfalouna.gov.lb/en for more details).

Child Protection Measures and Services

Under Law 422, a child is entitled to legal protection if threatened or at risk (see Figure 39.1).[1] The category of a "threatened" child includes: 1) a child in a situation that exposes him or her to exploitation, or threatens his or her health, safety, morals, or upbringing; 2) a child exposed to sexual abuse or physical violence that exceeds non-harmful, culturally acceptable disciplinary beating, or 3) a child found begging or vagabonding (Law 422, Article 25). The law establishes a competent authority (the judge), for hearing child protection cases. In practice, this authority is a special judge assigned to deal with children's cases (Law 422, Article 26). If a child is found to be threatened, a complaint or report can be submitted to the court by the child, a parent, guardian, social worker, or the prosecutor's office. In general, before making a decision on how or whether to intervene, the judge (or public prosecutor) must either ask for a "social inquiry" or hear testimony from the child and their parents or legal guardian (Law 422, Article 26). The judge is required to act quickly to intervene in cases that require immediate action and, if the judge deems the case to be a matter of great urgency, has the authority to take protective measures before the social inquiry is made (Law 422, Article 26).

The judge has three primary options upon assessing a child to be at risk. A judge can order: 1) protection, 2) supervised freedom, or 3) rehabilitation (Law 422, Article 26).

---

[1] It is worth noting that some of the original terms used, such as "at risk" have not been adequately defined or translated in the English version of the law. Beyond the fact that no definitions have been provided for these terms the translated terms are not commonly used in relation to child protection. It is suggested that the term "at risk" (rather than "in danger") be used in the context of these protection articles.

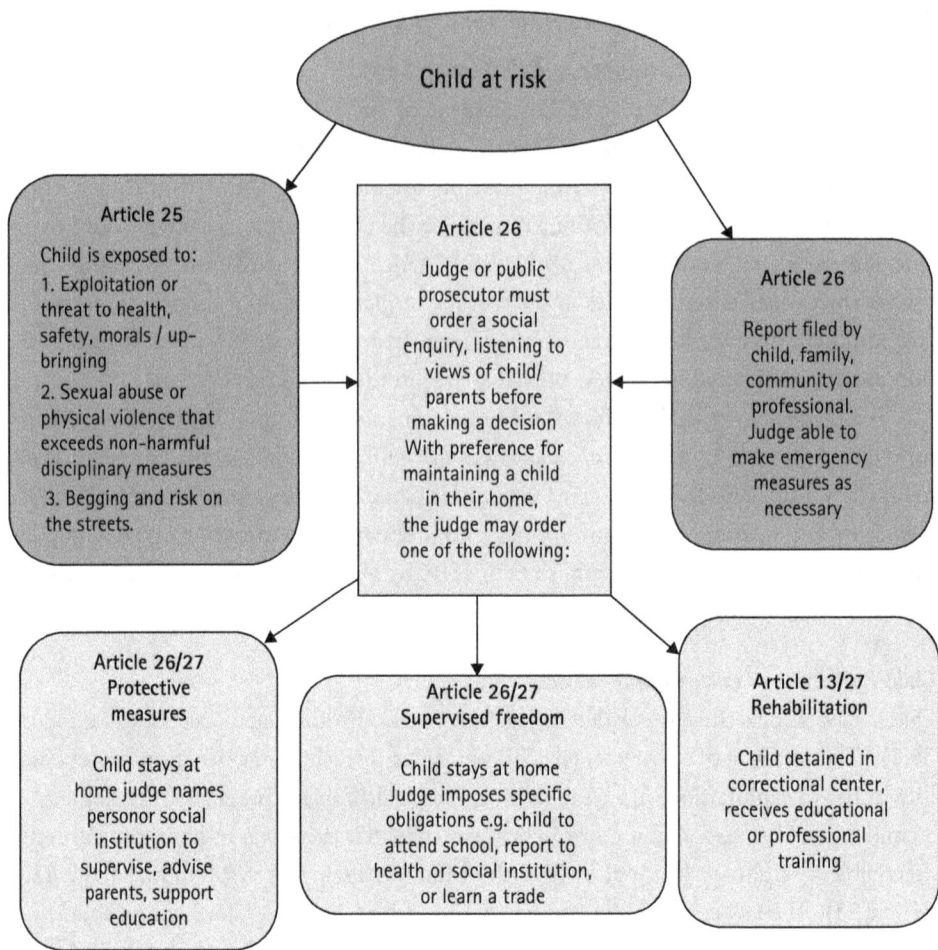

Figure 39.1 Flow chart of protective measures under Law 422

These options are defined in Law 422 in the context of judicial responses to children in conflict with the law and the terms are not tailored to the context of children at risk (Law 422, Articles 9, 10, and 13). Protection and supervised freedom are home-based measures that do not deprive the child of liberty, while rehabilitation is an out-of-home measure that is more corrective in nature. Protection is defined as returning the juvenile to one or both parents, to a legal guardian or to an extended family member as long as the adult has "good morals," under the supervision of a social representative (Law 422, Article 9). In the absence of a person with "good morals," the child can be placed with a trustworthy family or in a social or health institution. Supervised freedom is defined as placing the child under the surveillance of a social representative who observes the behavior, conduct, work, and cultural background of the child for a period of one to five years. Rehabilitation means the detention of a child in a correctional institution for a minimum of six months, with education and professional training provided along with supervision of the child's physical and mental health and morality (Law 422, Article 13).

In terms of legal principles, Law 422 has undefined provisions for guiding judges on how to respond to children at risk. On one hand, judges are to make their order "in the child's interest" (Law 422, Article 26),[2] and there is a specific instruction for keeping juveniles in "their natural environment" to the extent possible (Law 422, Article 27). On the other hand, Law 422 allows judges to use rehabilitation, which is primarily a response to criminal means, in cases of child protection. Further, the law instructs judges to provide the "appropriate measures" when a threatened child's risk of delinquency constitutes a penal issue, "such as in homelessness or vagabondage" (Law 422, Article 28). This provision suggests both that homelessness and begging are criminal acts and that the appropriate response is criminal rather than protective. This conflation of protective and delinquency responses is inconsistent with international standards and with the protective approach to children in difficult situations.

Lebanese legislation lacks details concerning out of home care for children, as expected under the UN Guidelines for the Alternative Care of Children. While Law 422 allows for children to be placed with a trustworthy family, a social or health institution, or a correctional institution, the law does not detail how placements are assessed, determined, or managed.

Social Service Response

Under Law 422, the UPEL is the main mandated agency to provide protective services to children who are referred to the statutory system, whether as victims of abuse or children in conflict with the law. After the promulgation of Law 422, UPEL became the only named and contracted agency with a statutory mandate to manage the follow up of individual child protection and family cases, as well as for compiling the necessary forensic, psychological, and social reports for court.

Since 2005 other agencies, notably the Association pour la Protection de l'Enfant de la Guerre and Mouvement Sociale, have been contracted by the MOJ to implement the provisions under Law 422.

Police Investigations

In some regional headquarters there is a unit for dealing with all children's cases; in others, juvenile cases—both child victims and children in conflict with the law—are dealt with under the regular criminal investigation department. The police tend to receive far more cases of children in conflict with the law than child victims of abuse and exploitation.

---

[2] This is in contrast to the section on children in conflict with the law where judges are to consider both the child's interest, the circumstances of the crime committed and the need to protect society. See Law 422, Article 6.

However, this statement needs to be qualified: many of these children are picked up by urban police patrols for status offences under the Penal Code (begging, street vending, or selling sexual services). They are of course considered under Law 422 as children at risk.

In all cases of sexual abuse, a child-friendly investigative interview is supposed to be conducted in the presence of an UPEL social worker. The MOJ has established a small room in the Palace of Justice in Beirut and contracts the NGO Association pour la Protection de l'Enfant de la Guerre to undertake interviews with victims of sexual abuse. Through the practice of play therapy, the interview aims to gather evidence using specialized audio-visual recordings. This process enables the judge to decide whether to pursue the case through the judicial process and means that children do not have to provide testimonies multiple times.

The community level police are usually the first point of contact for children, often through a home visit. In all situations involving children (whether in conflict with the law or victims of abuse and exploitation), the police will first assess the seriousness of the situation through dialogue with the parents.

Medical Services

Children suspected of being abused may be sent to a hospital for treatment and, if appropriate, for examination by a forensic doctor. According to respondents, the physical and mental symptoms of abuse are rarely identified by pediatricians and nurses. Of particular concern is that those medical officers working in the emergency ward often do not identify the abuse in the first instance. When they do recognize abuse, the majority are said to be unaware of their legal duties to report under Law 422 (Article 151). Indeed, some medical staff may prefer not to take matters further due to fear of becoming embroiled in a legal case.

Within Lebanon, there is one official hospital-based child protection unit (CPU), which is the Hotel de Dieu (University Hospital of USJ) in Beirut, launched in 2011 (though the operational status of the CPU was not clear at the time of writing). While a standard operating procedure has been established for the CPU, other hospitals have not developed a specialized protocol for responding to suspected cases of abuse.

There is no institute of forensics in Lebanon. Forensic doctors are not appointed by the MOPH, but rather by the MOJ in collaboration with the Ministry of Interior. A minority of the doctors conducting forensic examinations of abused children have received specialized training for this purpose.

Forensic doctors are usually requested by the General Prosecutor or the Brigade des Moeurs to examine a child and make a report for the purposes of a criminal investigation. There is an increasing trend of parents to privately request examinations of children by forensic doctors (at a fee of approximately US$40). This usually comes about as a result of a custody dispute when one party claims the other has abused the child in order to avoid the question of custody being decided in the religious courts. While an allegation of abuse may be absolutely legitimate, it is also indicated that the claims may be fictitious, but nonetheless subject the child to an intimate physical examination. All cases of sexual abuse are supposed to be reported to a forensic doctor, although cases of neglect and physical violence are also reported.

Children's Judges

There are six children's judges across Lebanon, one in each region. These judges maintain multiple other functions but are appointed by the Higher Institute of Magistrates. These children's judges (except the judge for Beirut) have a part-time portfolio. They have a case load of approximately 50 children's cases every month in each region. The vast majority of cases are related to children in conflict with the law and it is estimated that less than 10% are children at risk. The meaning of at risk may be interpreted loosely here: it seems that many such cases are not children at immediate risk of abuse but rather children who have missed or truanted from school.

According to the judges, they rely heavily upon the report and recommendations of the UPEL social worker, especially if there are outstanding questions about whether to return the child to the family home or not. They may act unilaterally when an emergency order needs to be made to protect the child. Due to cultural norms and limitations in the law, judges are unable to order suspected perpetrators to be removed from the family home except when the wife owns the family property herself. Therefore, they are often forced to find shelter for the entire family, usually the mother and all the children of the household. Unfortunately, many of the Palestinian and non-Lebanese children that appear before them do not have extended families with whom they can be placed and are therefore more likely to be ordered to an institution.

The power of the judges is somewhat restricted as many private service providers, even residential institutions contracted by the government, refuse to accept children placed by the judge. This creates a severe lack of service options for ensuring the care and protection of children and, it is suggested, many placements are made by default or through personal connections, rather than tailored to the individual needs of the child. Hence, some girls accused of "crimes against morality" have been sent to Roumieh Prison rather than protective shelters.

Application of Law 422 within the Legal Traditions of Religious Communities

Lebanese religious communities have a relatively high degree of legal and jurisdictional autonomy from the State in all matters of "personal status" or family law. There is no common state law covering personal or family matters. Rather, through a state recognition mechanism, each of the 18 communities has its own legal system, producing and applying independent legal standards through their own courts for matters such as marriage, custody, and inheritance (though inheritance issues for Christians are not relevant to the religious courts).

This multiplicity of family laws results in a diverse range of possible legal situations for the child with the Lebanese family. The handling of custody (approximate translation of the notion of *hadana*) varies considerably from one community to another, for example. In the case of a separation of the parents, most communities systematically grant custody to the father once the child has reached an age that is often very young but which varies depending on the religious community.

It is important to understand the commonalities between the various legal situations because they have important consequences for establishing a general child protection system across the communities. Today, judges and legal professionals working in religious courts have increasing access to the terminology of "child rights" within the context of Islam and the Church. In this interpretation children tend to be perceived as belonging to the family, and the family belong to the religious community. This is a significant variation from the notion of child rights envisaged within the broader global discourse on rights that recognizes a child's status as an autonomous subject of law.

The benign nature of Law 422 is reflected in the remarkably vague powers and autonomy of judges to make decisions. This law was voted in following a campaign by local NGOs and IOs and aims, in particular, to make Lebanese law more compliant with the Convention on the Rights of the Child (1989). Because Law 422 leaves room for interpretation, some children's judges have taken certain articles (especially Article 25 onward) in a way that gives them the possibility to intervene in family arrangements, particularly during proceedings for parental separation. A problematic example is where the religious judge grants custody of the child to the father—based on the age of the child—only for the children's judge to decide that this measure would put the child at risk and make a protection order for the child to stay with the mother.

By interpreting the vague notions within Law 422 of a "child at risk" and "the child's interest," children's judges can in practice intervene and indirectly suspend a ruling of the religious court. This extrajudicial and controversial discussion has had a lasting effect on civil judges: they have been accused of harming religion and have seen their attempts to install new protection standards as severely curbed.

Only a relatively small number of child protection files have been opened for children at risk since 2002. Despite the legal process becoming more well-known, the number of protection files seems to have stagnated between 2006 and 2010. Magistrates explicitly mention the controversy around the area of jurisdiction of the religious courts as a reason for their cautious approach, admitting that they now think twice about the consequences of their decisions. The vague notions contained within Law 422 that previously enabled judges to make bold and sometimes controversial decisions, have come to represent a double-edged sword. In their efforts to avoid confrontation, judges now tend to make diluted and restricted decisions on protection cases.

In the functioning of the statutory mechanism under Law 422, it is important to understand the different rationales that are at play. Judges do not consider the social inquiries or psychological assessment as simple technical processes. Rather, in their eyes, these processes—aimed at enhancing justice—hold great symbolic meaning and are qualified as "scientific." In the designation of roles between the social worker and the judge, the former will often put forward arguments in the interests of the child while the judge presents himself as the protector of social values, such as the family or the law, that transcend the individual. The involvement of the courts and judges in assessing psychological or emotional danger has brought the civil courts and the religious courts into conflict.

The politicization of the issue of childhood continues to be felt through extrajudicial interventions and influence from senior figures within communities who have no connection to the case, such as ministers, deputies, high ranked judges, and religious leaders. While the principle of protecting the child at risk now seems to have been taken on board, at least nominally, by most judicial and legislative actors in Lebanon, the definition of risk as well as the protection procedures are still not really debated today. This leaves room for significant differences in actions and interpretations which constantly affect the work of legal professionals and thereby the effectiveness of the child protection system.

References

Consultation and Research Institute. (2007). *Children deprived of family care in Lebanon: Present situation and available alternatives*. Consultation and Research Institute.

Osseiran, H. (2012). *Action against child labour in Lebanon: A mapping of policy*. International Labour Office.

Ministry of Social Affairs. (2011). *National social development strategy*. Ministry of Social Affairs. Retrieved June 28, 2022. Available at: chrome-extension://efaidnbmnnnibpcajpcglclefindmkaj/http://extwprlegs1.fao.org/docs/pdf/leb181091E.pdf.

Pinheiro, P. S. (2005). *World report on violence against children*. United Nations.

Save the Children. (2008). *Child rights situation analysis in Lebanon*. Save the Children.

Save the Children. (2011). *Regional Middle East and North Africa Situation Report*. Save the Children.

UNICEF. (2009). Lebanon: Statistics. UNICEF. Retrieved June 28, 2022: https://data.unicef.org/country/lbn/; www.unicef.org/infobycountry/lebanon_statistics.html. Retrieved June 28, 2022

UNICEF. (2012). *Strengthening the child protection system in Lebanon*. University Saint Joseph, Faculty des Lettres, Ecole Libanaise de Formation Sociale, Government of Lebanon, Ministry of Social Affairs.

UNICEF. (2016). *The state of the world's children 2016* [Statistical tables]. Available at: https://data.unicef.org/resources/state-worlds-children-2016-statistical-tables/.

Children at Risk in Mexico: Issues, Policies, and Interventions

Martha Frías-Armenta

Abstract

Children represent approximately one-third of the population of Mexico, home to around 39.2 million individuals under the age of 18 (Instituto Nacional Estadística Geografía e Informática [INEGI], 2015a). One of the main problems children in Mexico face is poverty, which increases the risk of malnourishment and the likelihood of suboptimal social, cognitive, physical, and emotional development. Poverty is also a potent predictor of antisocial behaviors and violence. This chapter will review key issues faced by children in Mexico, highlight core policies and laws that protect children's rights and criminalize maltreatment, and explore current policies and interventions aimed at addressing maltreatment.

Key Words: Mexico, child violence, children at risk, poverty, malnourishment, antisocial behaviors, early childhood

Issues Faced by Children in Mexico

Poverty is the most important issue facing many children in Mexico. Currently, more than half of Mexicans under the age of 18 lack the economic ability to meet their basic needs. Moreover, data demonstrate that children currently lack the security, educational, and health conditions required for their optimal development.

Poverty

Poverty and malnutrition disproportionately affect children and single parent homes in Mexico. In 2010, 53.8% of children were classified as "poor" and approximately one in five children in single family homes lived in poverty (Fuentes et al., 2016). Similarly, 61% of children have unmet basic needs when compared to 52% of the adult population (Consejo Nacional de Evaluación [CONEVAL], 2010). Additionally, around 12% of children ages 5 to 17 work to contribute to household income (UNICEF/Instituto Nacional de Salud Pública (INSP), 2015). A Save the Children survey estimated that 36% of Mexican children face food insecurity and 12.5% struggle with chronic malnutrition (Save the Children, 2014). Furthermore, a national survey of Mexico estimated that low birthweight (less than 2.5 kilograms) in 2013 and 2015 was as high as 15% and 10.5% respectively (UNICEF/Instituto Nacional de Salud Pública (INSP), 2015).

Early childhood is a crucial period of social, cognitive, physical, and emotional development. Lack of positive environmental, educational, and nutritional conditions can endanger the healthy development of a child. Brain development requires a stimulating environment as well as adequate care and nutrition (Uauy & Dangour, 2006; Georgieff, 2007; Rosales et al., 2009). Despite what is known about promoting healthy child development, the National Poll of Children and Women estimated that whereas around 91% of Mexican children ages five to 16 attended school, only around 63% of children ages 3 to 5 did (UNICEF/Instituto Nacional de Salud Pública (INSP), 2015).

Poverty can affect a child's academic success. While numerous factors influence the decision to drop out of school, around 41.4% of children reported that they stopped studying for economic reasons (INEGI, 2014). Many children who attend school demonstrate low aacademic performance. A little less than half (41% and 47%) demonstrate low academic performance in reading and sciences respectively, and more than half (54%) have poor performance in mathematics (CONEVAL, 2014).

Violence

Violence is another central problem for children and adolescents in Mexico who are vulnerable to both internal and external factors. Violence occurs within the family, school, hospitals, work, community, and institutional environments, as well as in the justice system. The rate of child injury due to violence rose 56% from 3.6 children per 1,000 in 2010 to 5.6 children per 1,000 in 2014 (Programa Nacional de Protección de Niñas, Niños y Adolescentes [PRONAPINNA], 2016–2018).

Corporal punishment is prevalent throughout the country, with 40% of children indicating that they have been hit by their parents or caregivers within the past year (Consejo Nacional para Prevenir la Discriminación, 2010). Around 20% of the population in Mexico believes corporal punishment is justifiable (Consejo Nacional para Prevenir la Discriminación, 2010), and a recent survey indicates that 26% of people believe children should be granted only the rights deemed appropriate by parents and not those guaranteed by the law (Fuentes et al., 2016). Perhaps most concerning, around 5.3% of parents believe children do not have any rights at all (Fuentes et al., 2016).

A national service survey indicated that 40% of Mexican children had been victims of violence inside their homes at some point in their childhood (INEGI, 2014). Another national survey indicated that 63% of children had been physically or psychologically mistreated during their childhood. However, in Mexico only a fraction of maltreatment cases is reported. In 2002, 24,563 (65/100,000) cases were reported nationwide (Secretaría de Salud, 2006). The Mexican Office for the Defense of Minors and The Family indicates that 48,591 (130/100,000) cases of child maltreatment were reported in 2009 and 49,805 (132/100,000) in 2014 (National System for Integral Family Development [DIF], 2014) (see Table 40.1). The minutes of the first session of the Commission to Stop Any Form of

Violence Against Children (Acta de la Primera sesión de la Comisión para poner fin toda forma de violencia contra niñas, niños y adolescentes, 2017) indicate that approximately 30% of the people that were treated for injuries in the country in 2017 were under 18 years old.

The Program for International Student Assessment (PISA) reports that, in Mexico, 20% of 15-year-old students have suffered some type of abuse in school, which is similar to the international average of 18.7% (OECD, 2017). The International Survey on Teaching and Learning ranks Mexico as the nation with the highest level of bullying or school harassment (Backhoff & Perez-Morán, 2015). According to data from the National Survey of Intolerance and Violence in Public Middle Schools (Encuesta Nacional de Exclusión, Intolerancia y Violencia en Escuelas Públicas de Educación Media Superior, ENEIVEEMS, 2009), 18.4% of students reported assaults from peers within the past year. However, some surveys indicate that these rates may be underreported. The Survey for Social Cohesion and Prevention of Delinquency estimates 32.2% have been victims of bullying within the past year (INEGI, 2014).

The advent of new information technologies has opened the door to new forms of child violence. One of these new manifestations is known as cyberbullying. Twenty-four percent of the children in 2015 (INEGI, 2020) in Mexico are victims of cyberbullying. The National Survey of Availability and Use of New Information Technologies in Homes

Table 40.1 Reports of maltreatment received and verified by the Procurator for the Defense of Minors and the Family

Year	Reports Verified	Rate (per 100,000)
1995	15,391	43
1996	19,995	54
1997	25,378	71
1998	23,109	63
1999	25,046	71
2000	27,735	73
2001	30,540	86
2002	24,563	65
2003	32,218	88
2004	38,554	102
2009	48,591	130
2010	33,082*	90
2014	49,805	132

Source: Maltreatment of Children and Adolescents in Family (2007) and data from INEGI.

Notes: No data are available for 2005–2008, 2011, 2012, and 2013. Data in 2010 were missing from many states.

(Encuesta Nacional sobre Disponibilidad y Uso de las TIC en Hogares; INEGI, 2015b) reported that 26.7% of children from 12 to 19 years of age have been victims of cyberbullying within the past year.

According to the 2005 Mexican National Report on Violence and Health, over the last 25 years, two children under the age of 14 are murdered each day in Mexico. The leading causes of death due to homicide for children under the age of one were hanging, constriction, and suffocation; for children aged 1–4, the leading causes were hanging and submersion; and for children aged 5–14, the leading cause was gunshot wounds (Secretaría de Salud, 2006). The annual average of adolescent victims of homicide was 871 (70/100,000) (2001–2006), 1,743 (120/100,000) (2007–2012), and 1,407 (95/100,000) (2013–2015) (Comisión Nacional de Derechos Humanos, I2016).

Institutionalization

Children and adolescents are often both the victims and perpetrators of violence and may be involved in, or party to, criminal acts. Rates of juvenile incarceration had been consistent over the past few decades with some fluctuation; however, those rates have risen sharply in the past couple of years. In 1990, around 4,000 juvenile delinquents were incarcerated; between 1995 and 2000 that number decreased to around 3,000 (Vázquez, 2012). However, the number of juvenile offenders committed to a secure facility rose from 4,959 in 2013 (Azaola, 2015) to 7,785 in 2016 (INEGI, 2016). These rates may be even higher depending on the source and/or definition of commitment and incarceration. INEGI estimated that 8,843 adolescents were incarcerated in 2015 (INEGI, 2018) (see Table 40.2).

The Mexican Minor Council indicates that 34,682 minors (11 to 19 years old) were in treatment for antisocial behavior in 2002. While in treatment, they also received educational, psychological, and work training as well as access to social assistance programs (INEGI, 2004). The Political Constitution of the United States of Mexico was reformed in 2005, which established that incarceration should be applied as the last recourse for adolescents older than 14 years old. As a result, recent institutional juvenile incarceration rates have decreased dramatically (see Table 40.2).

Table 40.2 Adolescents institutionalized per year

Year	Institutionalized	Rate (per 100,000)
2011	11,239	31
2012	11,684	31
2013	10,583	30
2014	10,963	30
2015	8,843	24
2016	7,785	21

Source: Based on data from INEGI.

Teen Pregnancy

Pregnancy under the age of 18 endangers the health and the development of the mother as well as the child. However, 17.2% of adolescents between 15 and 19 years old have had a baby in recent years (UNICEF/Instituto Nacional de Salud Pública (INSP), 2015). The security of the children is likewise jeopardized when they lack adult childcare. In Mexico, 5% of children are left under the care of another child (less than 10 years old) or alone more than one hour at least once a week (UNICEF/Instituto Nacional de Salud Pública (INSP), 2015).

Policies and Laws Aimed at Protecting Children's Rights

Mexico is a Federal Republic consisting of a tiered system of federal and local laws. The Political Constitution of the United States of Mexico is the apex of this hierarchy, with federal laws representing the second tier and local laws the third. As a result, there are sometimes varying legal definitions for criminal acts committed against children (including child abuse) in federal and local codes. The following section outlines a brief chronology of the legal development of children's rights in Mexico.

Until the end of the 20th century, Mexican law allowed parents and guardians "correctional rights" that permitted caregivers to physically punish or use moderate corrective measures such as hitting and spanking to discipline their children (Código Civil del Estado de Sonora, Article 590). Furthermore, authorities could assist in the implementation of these corrective measures. The Criminal Code (Código Penal del Estado de Sonora, Article 244) established that injuries would not be punishable if they healed in fewer than 15 days. During this period, maltreatment or abuse was not mentioned in Mexican codes. Consequently, parents or guardians could cause injuries to their children when they believed correction or discipline was required.

UN Convention on the Rights of the Child (1990)

The Convention on the Rights of the Child was signed in 1990 by Mexico, representing the first legislative protections aimed at promoting the rights of children. Since this legislative ratification, multiple laws have been modified. The Mexican Political Constitution was firstly revised to include principles and child protections provisions aimed at promoting the best interest of the child, such as integral protection, non-discrimination and due process rights.

Political Constitution of the United Mexican States (Modifications from 2000 to 2011)

Article 4 was then transformed in 2000 to include health, educational, nutritional, and recreational requirements for integral development and protection of minors. The underlying concept of integral protection is that children are the *subjects* of rights (rather than objects of protection) with autonomy and a guarantee of those rights. The state must provide the necessary means to promote respect and dignity for children and allow the full exercise of these rights (Congreso de la Unión de los Estados Unidos Mexicanos, 2000). In 2005, a modification of the 18th Article was published (Congreso de la Unión de los Estados Unidos Mexicanos, 2005) establishing an Integral System for the Attention to Adolescents (Sistema Integral de Justicia para Adolescentes). The revised Article stated that the best interest of the child should be of utmost importance in the decision-making process and must drive policy design, execution, follow-up, and evaluation. Caregivers are obliged to preserve and demand the fulfillment of these rights (Congreso de la Unión de los Estados Unidos Mexicanos, 2011).

Law for the Protection for Children and Adolescents (2000)

In 2000, the Law for the Protection for Children and Adolescents was created (Ley para la Protección de los Derechos de los niñas, niños y Adolescentes, 2000) which regulates the 4th Constitutional Article. Its main objective is to secure the optimal development of children and provide an equitable opportunity for physical, mental, social, emotional, and moral growth. Like previous iterations, the principles that underlie this Article are focused on promoting the best interest of the child, non-discrimination and equal rights. The Law expands upon these protections by including language on the right to live with a family; to live free of violence; of the joint responsibility of family, state, and society; and respect for human rights and constitutional guarantees.

The best interest of the child is understood as the care and assistance required for optimal family development and a guarantee of social welfare. It establishes that parents must protect children from maltreatment, prejudice, danger, aggression, abuse, trade, exploitation, drug abuse, kidnapping, armed conflict, natural disaster, recruitment for armed conflict, refuge, and displacement (Article 21). This law also institutes due process rights for adolescents who break the law (Article 44). Moreover, it protects children and adolescents from torture, cruel, inhumane, or humiliating punishment. Deprivation of liberty for juvenile offenders should be a last resort and should respect laws and guarantees for audience, defense, and due process (Article 45).

Human rights and dignity are to be respected in adolescents deprived of their freedom. According to the law, treatment for juvenile offenders should be different from that applied to adults. It should have specialized institutions and authorities whose primary objective should be the reintegration or social adaptation of the child. Adolescents should also receive legal assistance or any other support to safeguard their rights. In addition, they have the right of the presence of any descendent, parent, or guardian during legal proceedings.

General Law of the Rights of Children and Adolescents (2014)

Recently, the National Development Plan 2013–2018 (2013) established five national goals and three transversal strategies. The goals are peace, inclusion, quality education, prosperity, and global responsibility, and the three transversal strategies are democratization, gender perspective, and close and modern government (Poder ejecutivo, 2013). The development plan was followed, in 2014, by the General Law of the Rights of Children and Adolescents (Ley General de los Derechos de Niñas, Niños y Adolescentes [LGDNNA], 2014) which itself replaced the 2000 Law for the Protection for Children and Adolescents. The first part of the law guarantees substantive equality; all children must have the same treatment, rights, and opportunities. Furthermore, it establishes that each child has the right to quality healthcare, protection, education, and access to new technologies and forms of communication. The LGDNNA thus establishes that minors have the right to have their opinions heard and taken into consideration as it relates to decisions that affect their welfare (dependent upon to their age and developmental phase).

With respect to adolescents' judicial procedures, Article 82 establishes that children and adolescents enjoy the rights and guaranties of legal security and due process outlined in the Political Constitution of the United States of Mexico (Constitución Política de los Estados Unidos Mexicanos, 2018). All judicial or administrative proceedings or authoritative acts at federal, state, or municipal levels that involve children should be drafted according to the age, development, and maturity level of the child and must consider their best interest. According to the Constitutional Rights of Children, children should be provided clear and intelligible information about the administrative and judicial proceedings that influence their welfare. The authorities should provide mechanisms for a myriad of services from the ability to lodge formal complaints to receiving assistance from legal professionals or translators. Authorities should weigh the need to call a child or an adolescent to an audience and guarantee the right to parental or guardian accompaniment in all judicial proceedings. However, the LGDNNA also states that children should be kept apart from adults that may have a negative or detrimental influence on their behavior or emotional stability. This law also provides measures of protection from suffering any danger during the process and guarantees the security of personal data (Article 83). Should any state authority become aware of a criminal charge, they must notify the procurator (administrative officer). If there is a possibility of an arrest of a child or if they may be deprived of their personal liberty, the procurator must request the necessary measures for their integral protection and proper social assistance.

The second part of the LGDNNA establishes procedures to fortify Mexican institutions and to improve the state's ability to protect the rights of children and adolescents. It features the creation of the office of the Protection Procurator (Procuradurías de Protección) at both the federal and state levels. The main objective of these offices is to coordinate joint efforts between various authorities. The LGDNNA also regulates Social Assistance Centers whose primary aim is to secure the best conditions for children, and further establishes rules for collaboration and coordination among government and private institutions.

Protection System for the Rights of Children and Adolescents

The LGDNNA also proposed the creation of a national child protection program and was the impetus for the formation in 2015 of the National System of Integral Protection for Children (Sistema Nacional de Protección Integral de Niñas, Niños y Adolescentes [SPINNA]). SPINNA focused on coordinating rights protection programs at the various governmental tiers. The LGDNNA also mandates that each state and municipality must explicitly protect the rights of children through the establishment of a Protection System for the Rights of Children and Adolescents (Sistema de Protección de los Derechos de Niñas, Niños y Adolescentes) and a Department of Protection Procuracy.

The Protection System for the Rights of Children (PRONAPINNA) was created in 2016 to further promote rights outlined in the LGDNNA. The law established that the program must be created with the participation of public, private and social sectors and should encompass policies, purposes, strategies, lines of action, and indicators related to the promotion, respect, and integral protection of children and adolescents.

Civil Federal Code (2018)

Civil laws also establish guidelines for the protection of children. The Civil Federal Code (Código Civil Federal, 2018) establishes that parents have the obligation to provide alimony to their children. If it is impossible for the parents to provide financial support, then any member of the direct family must carry out the obligation. In the cases where no party can provide such support, the state will afford required resources (Article 303). Alimony should be used to provide food, clothing, household necessities, and assistance in case of illness (Article 308). Similarly, the Code specifies that all the members of the family should respect the physical and psychological integrity of the children and are obligated to avoid any behavior that may promote family violence.

Family violence is defined as the use of physical or psychological force, as well as serious omissions, that are repeatedly executed by one member of the family against another in an attempt to physically or psychologically harm an individuals' integrity. This definition is not dependent upon physical injury and refers to situations where the aggressor and the victim live in the same household and represent a relationship of kinship, marriage or concubinage (Article, 323ter).

Mexican Federal Criminal Code (2018)

The Mexican Federal Criminal Code (Código Penal Federal, 2018, Article, 260) establishes that sexual abuse is the performance, or pressure to perform, sexual acts without the purpose of copulation and without consent. Sexual acts are defined as touching, molesting or acts that are explicitly of a sexual nature or any activity that may represent them. It is also considered sexual abuse when the victim is forced to observe a sexual act or expose their body without consent (Article 261). The punishment increases when the victim is a minor younger than 15 years old. Legally, a sexual act is considered statutory rape if copulation without violence is performed, or if any object is introduced into the vagina or anus of a minor younger than 15 years old (Article 266). Injuries inflicted upon children, including rape, by their parents or guardians will result in punishment and it could lead to loss of custody (Código Penal Federal, 2018, Article, 295).

The Article 335 of Federal Criminal Code (2018) stipulates any person who abandons a child who is incapable of caring for his or herself will be punished and may lose custody of that child. The crime of *minor trafficking* is defined as the mobilization of a minor less than 16 years of age out of the country, with the purpose of obtaining an economic profit (Mexican Federal Criminal Code, 2018, Article, 343).

The Mexican Federal Criminal Code (Article, 201[bis]) also establishes crimes against development and dignity of people. One of them is corruption of minors younger than 18 years old. It established that the promotion, coercion, or facilitation of a child or adolescent to commit an action or omission related to sexual acts or perverted behaviors will be punished. Similarly, adults that contribute to minor consumption of alcohol or any other drug or minor participation in organized crime will be prosecuted. Importantly, it stipulates that the minor victim of the crime is entitled to treatment. Parents and owners of a tavern or bar that serves a person under 18 years old will also be penalized. Similarly, the law establishes a system of penalties for people that allow minors younger than 18 years old access to pornographic spectacles or sexual exhibitions, or for those who sell pornographic material to minors. Moreover, the law penalizes any individual that forces or promotes the performance of erotic or sexual acts in public or private with minors. It also makes explicit that the utilization, support, direction, production, reproduction of voices, videos or pictures of children for pornographic purposes is punishable by law (Article 202).

The issue of family violence is also addressed in the Federal Criminal Code. Family violence is any act of power or intentional omission that aims to dominate, control, submit, attack, or harm physically, verbally, psycho-emotionally, sexually, or financially any member of the family (Federal Criminal Code, Article 343[bis]A). This definition is extended to children subject to custody and clarifies that parents can lose custody in cases of child abuse. Further, it proposes that offenders should participate in psychological treatment.

Policies, Laws, and Interventions Aimed at Addressing Child Abuse

General Law for Children and Adolescents

The General Law for Children and Adolescents (LGDNNA, 2014) does not indicate a specific definition for child abuse; instead it establishes that every child and adolescent has the right to live free of violence (Article 46). Federal, state, and municipal authorities are obligated to prevent, assist with, and punish cases involving children suffering from negligence, corruption or trafficking of minors, child sexual abuse, sexual exploitation of children, child labor (under 15 years old), and adolescent labor (older than 15 years old) in manners that may affect their health, education, and mental or physical development (Article 47). Likewise, authorities are obligated to adopt appropriate measures that promote physical and psychological recovery as well as restitution of their rights (Article 48).

The National Survey for Women and Children in Mexico (UNICEF/Instituto Nacional de Salud Pública (INSP), 2015) defines psychological abuse as yelling at or otherwise deriding a child (such as calling a child stupid, lazy, etc.). Physical abuse occurs when a minor is struck, shaken, or beaten (such as spanked or smacked on the buttocks with a hand, a belt, a hairbrush, a shoe, a stick, or any other hard object or hit on the face, head, ears, hand, arm, or leg).

GENERAL LAW OF CHILDREN'S AND ADOLESCENTS' RIGHTS

The LGDNNA establishes that authorities must provide medical and psychological assistance when any child is a victim of acts or omissions that put their physical or mental health at risk and that they should seek to protect children from all forms of abuse. When abuse occurs within the family, the child has the right to receive protection from the state, and if that is not possible, they have a right—at minimum—to receive assistance from public or private institutions.

COMMISSION TO STOP ALL TYPES OF VIOLENCE AGAINST CHILDREN

The minutes of the first session for the Commission to Stop All Types of Violence Against Children (Comisión para poner fin toda forma de violencia contra niñas, niños y adolescentes, 2017) proposed an action plan for federal agencies that consists of 31 activities divided into seven strategies: implementation and vigilance of law compliance, norms and values, security in the environment, support for caregivers, economic strengthening, response to attention services, and education and aptitudes for life (UNICEF, 2017). This action plan aims to integrate all children's rights efforts from the various federal, state, and local institutions. The goal is to improve infrastructure and provide necessary resources to agencies or procurator's offices and to improve the identification, assistance, and transfer of health services for child victims of violence.

GENERAL HEALTH LAW

The General Health Law situates social assistance within the General Health Law (Ley General de Salud, 2018) and the National System of Health (Sistema Nacional de Salud). Their primary objective is to promote the well-being and optimal development of families, as well as social integration and child development (Article 6). The same law indicates social assistance programs are responsible for child guardianship, placement of abandoned children in specialized institutions, legal assistance, and social orientation efforts (Article

168). Minors in social deprivation have the right to receive necessary services provided by any public institution (Article 170). The National System of Health must give preference to the assistance of abused children (Article 171).

LAW OF SOCIAL ASSISTANCE
According to the Law of Social Assistance (Ley de Asistencia Social, 2018), all children and adolescents have the right to receive social assistance. The law is particularly focused on ensuring equal access for all minors, including immigrants, those accused of violating the law, and those at risk of malnutrition, abuse, developmental deficiencies, negligence, abandonment, exploitation, homelessness, exposure to dangerous working conditions, and victimization (Article 4). The Secretary of Health and the National System of Integral Protection of the Family is responsible for supervising strict legal compliance for all governmental institutions when drafting norms, certifying services, promoting research, personnel training, supervision of the adoption process, as well as other related activities (Article 9).

National System of Integral Protection of the Family
The National System of Integral Protection of the Family (Secretaría de Salud, 2018) was developed in 1977 to create and put into action social assistance public policies that promote family integration. Consequently, the institution develops policies, operates programs of intervention, and coordinates federal, state, and municipal institutions. It also promotes actions that improve the living conditions of vulnerable children, adolescents, older adults, and people with disabilities (LGDNNA, 2014). The law establishes that each state will create a local System of Protection for Children and Adolescents and its function and organization should resemble the National System. Furthermore, a Municipal Protection System should be created that will represent the first source of contact for any child in need (Article 138).

Procedures for Reporting, Investigating, and Intervening on Child Abuse
The system established the Procurator of Protection (Procuradurías de Protección) for the protection and restitution of the rights of children and adolescents. The local procurator is the institution that provides attention to maltreated children. A case is initially identified from a report filed by neighbors, relatives, or any other person that has contact with the child. In this sense, all authorities (education, health, cultural, or recreational) should report any children's rights violation. Specifically, educational and public security authorities are obliged to report incidents to the corresponding legal authority (LGDNNA, 2014, Article 168).

The law outlines the procedures for reporting violation(s) of children's rights. Reports can take place face to face, be provided in written form, or relayed by phone (LGDNNA, 2014). There are cases in which the police may take the child directly to the Procurator of Protection (such as children living alone on the streets). Once the institution receives the report, a social worker within the institution verifies the existence of abuse. He or she then contacts and questions the family, neighbors, and school about the suspected abuse. After this first official visit, social workers follow up on the case to verify if the report constitutes abuse. A psychologist and lawyer may also intervene during this portion of the process. Lawyers evaluate the necessity to take other protective measures, and a psychologist assesses whether the case merits additional health treatment.

The next phase of the administrative process involves the National Child Protection System at the local level. The first step is a visit from a social worker to report on the child's living conditions and advise interested parties on their related roles, rights, and responsibilities. The social worker's evaluation constitutes the initial stage of the investigation and determines whether there is a potential case for child abuse. If imminent risk of abuse is determined and the child must be removed from the family, the procurator is required to notify the prosecutor and judge. The procurator should present evidence of the abuse to facilitate the judge's decision. Lawyers from the family institution system are the primary contact with the judge and should present all the evidence to the justice system.

After the initial social worker visit, local agencies create a case file for each report received. The child and his/her family or guardian must then be given an appointment to visit the responsible agency. The main objective of this process is to provide specialized and individualized psychotherapy to victims and aggressors without charge. A lawyer should notify the family judge to intervene in cases that involve family issues (threats of violence, coercion, etc). The prosecutor should be notified to begin criminal proceedings in a potential child abuse case and to dictate the corresponding precautionary measures (Ley de Asistencia y Prevención de la Violencia Familiar, 1996).

The responsible institution is tasked with locating an extended family member who can care for a child in the case of removal. If no member of the family can take responsibility, a foster family is sought. Placement in a group shelter should be considered solely as a last resort and only for a short time (LGDNNA, 2014). Even in the event of familial maltreatment, home removal may be traumatic for children and their families. For this reason, only 1% of children reported for maltreatment are removed from their homes. The responsible institution should provide in-home or familial services to best facilitate an open and productive dialogue (Procurator of state of Sonora, personal communication). The System of Children Protection always encourages family participation throughout the process. However, if the family is unable or unwilling to involve themselves, the relevant government entity will provide necessary assistance.

Governmental institutions, enabled by the National System of Integral Protection of the Family, are tasked with aiding and services; however, the LGDNNA encourages the participation of private organizations in the implementation of governmental programs (Article 117). In some states, personnel from private institutions work within the government protection system. Ultimately, the procurator is responsible for the restitution of children's rights and, as such, attends to all abuse cases. Attention should be directed to the protection of victims and the re-education of the abuser(s) (Ley de Asistencia y Prevención de la Violencia Familiar, 1996). Treatment for the abuser should be based on psychotherapeutic models directed to decrease or eliminate violence (Article 10).

The government provides most services and funding aimed at protecting and promoting children's rights; however, there are private partners contributing to the network of support. Recently, the Mexican government has invested considerably in child protection programs. The 2016 budget for the "Protection and Restitution of the Rights of Children and Adolescents" program was 120 million Mexican pesos (CONEVAL, 2016). In 2017, the Mexican government spent 760 billion pesos on the protection of rights, education, health, social development, and culture of children (Poder Ejecutivo, 2016, 2017). The budget for 2018 further increased to over 797 billion pesos, representing 15.09% of the total budget (Poder Ejecutivo, 2017, 2018).

A Life Free of Violence is a policy initiative developed by the National Center of Gender Equity and Reproductive Health that has become a human right for children and women. It guarantees access to legal or assistance services, protection, and medical and psychological attention. To avoid revictimization, the policy's action program states that its focus should be integral, respectful, solidary, multidisciplinary, and interinstitutional (Secretaría de Salud, 2018).

The *Manual of Organization and Operation for the National System of Integral Protection for Children and Adolescents* (Manual de Organización y Operación del Sistema Nacional de Protección Integral de Niños, Niñas y Adolescentes, 2018) requires the establishment of local family systems for program evaluation, identification of potential resources, and new operating procedures that inform future policy or guideline adjustment. These local family program evaluation committees must conduct an evaluation that measures the degree to which the fulfillment of children's rights has been successful. The evaluation should be based on the principles of law and the mechanisms established for participation of children and adolescents. This information should be used to inform future policy decisions. The National Council of Evaluation (CONEVAL) is ultimately responsible for program evaluation at the national level.

Conclusion

The signing of the UN Convention of the Rights of Children in Mexico has prompted a legislative shift away from a focus on parental correctional rights toward the protection and promotion of children's human rights. The Convention promoted amendments to the law and the development of public policies aimed at protecting and ensuring the human rights of children. However, there still exists a disconnect between the planning and implementation of these laws and policies as more than half of the population under 18 lives in poverty.

The Mexican Constitution states, in Article 4, that the government must promote children's health, education, nutrition, and recreation needs. Despite substantial budget spending on the protection and care of children, most children are currently unable to meet their basic needs. Several studies have analyzed the child human rights problem as it relates to families. However, understanding the role of government is required for successful implementation of policies aimed at promoting children's rights. Indicators suggest that despite significant improvements in financial support, the optimal conditions for development have not resulted in corresponding improvements in the lives of minors. The situation is worse for children living in public or private shelters, living on the streets, or in conflict with the law (juvenile delinquents) as public policies tend to neglect their protection (Comisión Nacional de Derechos Humanos. Ortega Velázquez, E. (Coordinadora), 2018).

Violence has become generalized in Mexico and children are its principal victims. As such, violence occurs not only within families, but also in schools, hospitals, streets, and governmental institutions. Moreover, children are vulnerable to natural disasters, street and neighborhood violence, work and sexual exploitation, neglect in social assistance systems, and harassment. Although current governmental actions are insufficient for the prevention of everyday violations some advances have been made, such as the promotion of a new law for protection of their rights and a National System for the Protection of the Rights of Children.

The Convention on the Rights of Children paved the way in Mexico for modification of the Mexican Constitution and related laws. A fundamental principle of the 4th Article of the constitution establishes integral protection and emphasizes consideration of the best interests of the child, progressive autonomy, and substantive equity. Two main federal laws for protection of children's rights were enacted in the Law for the Protection for Children and Adolescents (2000) and the General Law of the Rights of Children and Adolescents (2014). The former reflected guidelines established in the Convention of the Rights of Children and the latter expanded to include language on substantive equality, the right to quality health protection and education, access to new information and communication technologies, and the right of children to have their opinions heard and taken into consideration as it relates to decisions that affect their welfare. The General Law of the Rights of Children and Adolescents also established important procedures to support the efforts of Mexican institutions in protecting and promoting children's rights. Regulations in the civil and criminal code further protect children from maltreatment, abandonment, negligence, and the corruption of minors.

Despite the ratification of most international treaties and the development of new laws related to the protection of children's human rights by Mexican authorities the mechanism of implementation appears to be insufficient. Quality education, family support, and efficient protection are required for every child and adolescent. The main paradigm shift brought about in Mexico by the ratification of the Convention on the Rights of Children is to break down the vision of children as objects of protection and consider them beholders of their own rights and obligations (Senado de la Republica, 2014). However, the perception that children are the property of adults persists, which can hamper child protection efforts. Thus, it should be a priority to invest and support the protection of children's rights as well as outreach initiatives aimed at public perceptions of child agency.

The National System for the Protection of Children was established in 1977 with the primary objective of protecting children and families. This system promotes the creation of state and municipal agencies to establish direct contact with children and their families and the establishment of a procurator whose sole responsibility is to protect or restitute children's rights. The LGDNNA (2014) further requires the state to assist child victims of acts or omissions that put their physical or mental health at risk. Similarly, all children have the right to social assistance, the main objective of which is to promote well-being and optimal family development.

The LGDNNA (2014) also provides a framework for reporting children's rights violations. The flexible reporting mechanism can be performed by mail, phone, personal communications, or can sometimes originate directly between the procurator and law enforcement. The latter is an administrative process that begins after the procurator receives a report and investigates its veracity. Afterwards a psychologist and lawyer intervene to make necessary revisions and offer psychological treatment or further legal assistance. A social worker can also verify whether probable cause exists to require the procurator to notify the judge and prosecutor to initiate legal proceedings. The judge should decide protective measures based on evidence presented by the public prosecutor. Removing a child from his or her family should be the last recourse as treatment should be directed towards the protection of victims and treatment of their abusers.

In summary, the last few years have witnessed critical changes in policies and laws related to the protection of children's rights. However, it is necessary for those efforts to be well-implemented for governmental actions to have a measurable impact on people's lives. The high rate of children 18 years and younger living in poverty reflects a disconnect between the goals outlined in the various legislative initiatives discussed here and the infrastructure and support networks required to affect real change. The efficient implementation of policies and laws could improve the health, safety, and quality of life of every Mexican child and represent one of the most tangible contributions to protecting and promoting their human rights.

References

Azaola, E. (2015). *Diagnóstico de las y los adolescentes que cometen delitos graves en México*. UNICEF.

Backhoff, E. and Perez- Morán, J. C. (2015). *Segundo estudio internacional sobre la enseñanza y el aprendizaje (TALIS, 2013)*. Instituto Nacional Para la Evaluación de la Educación. Available at: http://www.oecd.org/edu/school/Mexico-TALIS-2013_es.pdf.

Comisión Nacional de Derechos Humanos. Informe Especial de Adolescentes Vulnerabilidad y Violencia (Special Report of Adolescents Vulnerability and Violence). (2016). Informe Especial de Adolescentes Vulnerabilidad y Violencia. Available at: Retrieved from http://www.cndh.org.mx/sites/all/doc/Informes/Especiales/Informe_adolescentes_20170118.pdf.

Comisión para poner fin toda forma de violencia contra niños, niñas y adolescentes. (2017). *Acta de la primera sesión de la comisión para poner fin toda forma de violencia contra niñas, niños y adolescentes.* Available at: https://www.gob.mx/cms/uploads/attachment/file/325000/Acta_de_la_Primera_Sesi__n_ Ordinaria.PDF.

CONEVAL. Evaluación de Diseño Protección y restitución de los derechos de las niñas, niños y adolescents (Evaluation of the Design of Protection and Restitution of Children and Adolescents rights). 2016). Evaluación de Diseño Protección y restitución de los derechos de las niñas, niños y adolescentes. Available at: file:///C:/Users/52662/AppData/Local/Temp/Temp1_SALUD_2016_Diseno_E041_ Proteccion_y_Restitucion_Derechos_de_ni%C3%B1as_ni%C3%B1os_adolescentes.zip/SALUD_ 2016_Diseno_E041_Proteccion_y_Restitucion_Derechos_de_ni%C3%B1as_ni%C3%B1os_adoles- centes/InformeFinal_E041.pdffile:///C:/Users/MARTHA~1/AppData/Loca.

CONEVAL. (2014). *Anexo estadístico de pobreza en México.* Available at: https://www.coneval.org.mx/Medic ion/MP/Paginas/AE_pobreza_2014.aspx.

Congreso de la Unión de los Estados Unidos Mexicanos. (2000). *Diario oficial de la Federación.* Available at: http://www.diputados.gob.mx/LeyesBiblio/ref/dof/CPEUM_ref_148_07abr00_ima.pdf.

Congreso de la Unión de los Estados Unidos Mexicanos. (2005). *Diario oficial de la Federación.* Available at:http://www.diputados.gob.mx/LeyesBiblio/ref/dof/CPEUM_ref_165_12dic05_ima.pdf.

Congreso de la Unión de los Estados Unidos Mexicanos. (2011). *Diario oficial de la Federación.* Available at: http://www.diputados.gob.mx/LeyesBiblio/ref/dof/CPEUM_ref_198_12oct11.pdf.

Comisión Nacional de Derechos Humanos. Ortega Velázquez, E. (Coordinadora). (2018). *Estudios sobre el cumplimiento e impacto de las recomendaciones generales, informes especiales y pronunciamientos de la Comisión Nacional de Derechos Humanos 2001–2017.* Available at: https://www.gob.mx/cms/uploads/attachment/ file/334849/NNA-PUDH-CNDH-RESUMEN-EJE.pdf.

CONEVAL. (2016). *Evaluación de Diseño Protección y restitución de los derechos de las niñas, niños y adoles- centes.* Available at: file:///C:/Users/52662/AppData/Local/Temp/Temp1_SALUD_2016_Diseno_E041_ Proteccion_y_Restitucion_Derechos_de_ni%C3%B1as_ni%C3%B1os_adolescentes.zip/SALUD_2016_ Diseno_E041_Proteccion_y_Restitucion_Derechos_de_ni%C3%B1as_ni%C3%B1os_adolescentes/ InformeFinal_E041.pdf.

Consejo Nacional para Prevenir la Discriminación. (2010). *Encuesta Nacional sobre la Discriminación en México.* Available at: http://www.conapred.org.mx/documentos_cedoc/Enadis-2010-RG-Accss-002.pdf.

ENEIVEEMS. (2009). *Encuesta Nacional de Exclusión, Intolerancia y Violencia en Escuelas Públicas de Educación Media Superior.* Available at: http://bdsocial.inmujeres.gob.mx/index.php/enece/17-acervo/acervo/265- encuesta-nacional-de-exclusion-intolerancia-y-violencia-en-escuelas-publicas-de-educacion-media-super ior-eneivems-2009.http://educacionmediasuperior.sep.gob.mx/work/models/sems/Resource/6711/2/ima ges/4_reporte_del_trabajo_campo.pdf.

Fuentes-Alcalá, M. L., González Contró, M. Padrón Innamorato, M., and Tapia Nava, E. (2016). *Conocimientos, ideas y representaciones acerca de niños, adolescentes y Jóvenes. ¿Cambio o continuidad? Encuesta Nacional de Niños, Adolescentes y Jóvenes.* UNAM. Available at: http://www.losmexicanos.unam.mx/ninosadolescentesy jovenes/libro/html5forpc.html?page=0.

Georgieff, M. K. (2007). Nutrition and the developing brain: Nutrient priorities and measurement. *The American Journal of Clinical Nutrition*, 85(2), 614–620.

Comisión Nacional de Derechos Humanos. (2016). *Informe Especial de Adolescentes Vulnerabilidad y Violencia.* Available at: http://www.cndh.org.mx/sites/all/doc/Informes/Especiales/Informe_adolescentes_20170 118.pdf.

INEGI. (2004). *Mujeres y hombres en México.* Available at: http://cedoc.inmujeres.gob.mx/documentos_downl oad/100490.pdf.

INEGI. (2014). *Encuesta de Cohesión Social Para la Prevención de la Violencia y la Delincuencia.* Available at: http://internet.contenidos.inegi.org.mx/contenidos/productos/prod_serv/contenidos/espanol/bvinegi/ productos/nueva_estruc/promo/ecopred14_presentacion_ejecutiva.pdf.

INEGI. (2015a). *Encuesta intersensal.* Available at: http://internet.contenidos.inegi.org.mx/contenidos/produc tos/prod_serv/contenidos/espanol/bvinegi/productos/nueva_estruc/promo/eic_2015_presentacion.pdf.

INEGI. (2015b). *Encuesta Nacional sobre Disponibilidad y Uso de las TIC en Hogares* Retrieved from http:// internet.contenidos.inegi.org.mx/contenidos/productos/prod_serv/contenidos/espanol/bvinegi/produc tos/nueva_estruc/promo/mociba2015_principales_resultados.pdf.

INEGI. (2016). *Censo Nacional de Gobierno, Seguridad Pública y Sistema Penitenciario Estatales 2016.* Available at: http://www.beta.inegi.org.mx/temas/poblacion/.

INEGI. (2018). *Censo Nacional de Gobierno, Seguridad Pública y Sistema Penitenciario Estatales 2015.* Available at: http://www.inegi.org.mx/lib/olap/consulta/general_ver4/MDXQueryDatos.asp?proy=cngspspe2015_a doltrat;p=cngspspe2015.

INEGI. (2015). *Módulo sobre Ciberacoso, MOCIBA.* Available at: http://www.beta.inegi.org.mx/contenidos/proyectos/investigacion/ciberacoso/2015/doc/mociba2015_principales_resultados.pdf.

INEGI. (2020). *Módulo sobre Ciberacoso, MOCIBA.* Available at: https://www.inegi.org.mx/contenidos/progra mas/mociba/2020/doc/mociba2020_resultados.pdf.

Maltreatment of Children and Adolescents in Family. (2007). *Maltrato de niños, niñas y adolescentes en el seno familiar.* Available at: http://cedoc.inmujeres.gob.mx/documentos_download/100892.pdf.

Sistema Nacional de Protección Integral de Niñas, Niños y Adolescentes. (2018). *Manual de organización y operación del sistema nacional de protección integral de niños, niñas y adolescentes.* Available at: http://dof.gob. mx/nota_detalle.php?codigo=5428443&fecha=03/03/2016.

OECD. (2017). *PISA 2015 results* (Vol. 3). OECD Publishing. Available at: http://www.oecd-ilibrary.org/education/pisa-2015-results-volume-iii_9789264273856-en.

Poder Ejecutivo. (2013). *Plan Nacional de Desarrollo 2013–2018.* Diario Oficial de la Federación 20/05/2013. Available at: http://dof.gob.mx/nota_detalle.php?codigo=5299465&fecha=20/05/2013.

Poder Ejecutivo. (2017). *Presupuesto de Egresos de la Federación para el Ejercicio Fiscal.* Nuevo Presupuesto publicado en el Diario Oficial de la Federación el 30 de noviembre de 2016. Available at: https://www.diputa dos.gob.mx/LeyesBiblio/abro/pef_2017/PEF_2017_orig_30nov16.pdf.

Poder Ejecutivo. (2018). *Presupuesto de Egresos de la Federación para el Ejercicio Fiscal.* Nuevo Presupuesto publicado en el Diario Oficial de la Federación el 29 de noviembre de 2017. Available at: http://www.diputa dos.gob.mx/LeyesBiblio/pdf/PEF_2018_291117.pdf.

Programa Nacional De Protección De Niñas, Niños Y Adolescentes 2016-2018. PRONAPINNA. (2016–2018). Available at: https://www.gob.mx/cms/uploads/attachment/file/331413/PRONAPINNA_-.pdf.

Rosales, F. J., Reznick, J. S., and Zeisel, S. H. (2009). Understanding the role of nutrition in the brain and behavioral development of toddlers and preschool children: Identifying and addressing methodological barriers. *Nutritional Neuroscience*, 12(5), 190–202.

Save the Children. (2014). *Los peligros para la niñez indicadores para México.* Available at: https://www.savethec hildren.mx/sci-mx/media/documentos/310517-Los-peligros-para-la-Ninez-en-Mexico-Save-the-Child ren.pdf.

Secretaría de Salud. (2018). Prevención y atención a la violencia. Available at: https://www.gob.mx/salud/accio nes-y-programas/prevencion-y-atencion-a-la-violencia.

Secretaría de Salud. (2006). Informe Nacional Sobre Violencia y Salud. Available at: http://www.salud.gob.mx/unidades/cdi/documentos/InformeNalsobreViolenciaySalud.p

Secretaría de Salud. (2018). *Sistema Nacional para la Protección Integral de la Familia.* Available at: https://www.gob.mx/inea/documentos/sistema-nacional-para-el-desarrollo-integral-de-la-familia-dif.

Senado de la Republica. (2014, September 10). Análisis de la Ley General para la Protección de Niñas, Niños y Adolescentes. Available at: http://comunicacion.senado.gob.mx/index.php/informacion/versiones/15159-analisis-de-la-ley-general-para-la-proteccion-de-ninas-ninos-y-adolescentes.html.

Sistema Nacional de Protección Integral de Niñas, Niños y Adolescentes. Manual de Organización y Operación del Sistema Nacional de Protección Integral de Niños, Niñas y Adolescentes (Manual of Organization and Operation for the National System of Integral Protection for Children and Adolescents). (2018). Manual de organización y operación del sistema nacional de protección integral de niños, niñas y adolescentes. Available at: http://dof.gob.mx/nota_detalle.php?codigo=5428443&fecha=03/03/2016.

Uauy, R. and Dangour, A. D. (2006). Nutrition in brain development and aging: Role of essential fatty acids. *Nutrition Reviews*, 64, 24–33.

UN. (1989). *Convention on the Rights of the Child.* Available at: http://www.ohchr.org/EN/ProfessionalInter est/Pages/CRC.aspx.

UNICEF/Instituto Nacional de Salud Pública (INSP), UNICEF/Instituto Nacional de Salud Pública (INSP). (2015). Encuesta de Indicadores Múltiples por Conglomerados. Final report. Instituto Nacional de Salud Pública and UNICEF.

UNICEF. (2017). *INSPIRE: Siete estrategias para poner fin a la violencia contra los niños y las niñas.* OPS. https://www.gob.mx/sipinna/articulos/inspire-estrategia-internacional-que-mexico-asume-para-prote ger-de-la-violencia-a-sus-ninas-ninos-y-adolescentes; https://www.unodc.org/documents/justice-and-pri son-reform/Child-Victims/Report_in_Spanish.pdf.

Vázquez, L. D. (2012). Acercamiento estadístico a la realidad de los menores infractores en México: legislación y crimen organizado, nuevos desafíos. *Universitas Psychológica*, 11(4), 1105–1114.

Legislation

Código civil para el estado libre y soberano de Sonora. (1983). Editorial Cajiga.

Código penal del estado de Sonora y de procedimientos penales para el estado libre y soberano de Sonora. (1985). Editorial Cajiga.

Código Penal del Estado de Sonora. (2018). Available at: http://www.congresoson.gob.mx:81/content/doc_le yes/doc_443.pdf.

Código Penal Federal. (2018). Available at: http://www.diputados.gob.mx/LeyesBiblio/pdf/9_090318.pdf.

Código Penal Federal. Nuevo Código Publicado en el Diario Oficial de la Federación el 14 de agosto de 1931. TEXTO VIGENTE. Última reforma publicada DOF 09-03-2018 .2018. Available at: https://www.diputa dos.gob.mx/LeyesBiblio/pdf/CPF.pdf.

Código Civil Federal. (2018). Available at: http://www.diputados.gob.mx/LeyesBiblio/pdf/2_090318.pdf.

Constitución Política de los Estados Unidos Mexicanos. (2018). Available at: http://www.diputados.gob.mx/ LeyesBiblio/ref/dof/CPEUM_ref_165_12dic05_ima.pdf.

Ley de Asistencia Social. (2018). Available at: http://www.diputados.gob.mx/LeyesBiblio/pdf/270_240 418.pdf.

Ley de Asistencia y Prevención de la Violencia Familiar. (1996). Available at: https://docs.mexico.justia.com/ estatales/distrito-federal/ley-de-asistencia-y-prevencion-de-la-violencia-familiar.pdf.

Ley General de Salud. (2018). Available at: http://www.diputados.gob.mx/LeyesBiblio/pdf/142_110518.pdf.

Ley para la Protección de los Derechos de los niñas, niños y Adolescentes. (2000). Available at: https://www. unicef.org/mexico/spanish/mx_resources_ley_nacional.pdf.

LGDNNA. (2014). Available at: http://www.dof.gob.mx/nota_detalle.php?codigo=5374143&fecha=04/ 12/2014.

UNICEF/Instituto Nacional de Salud Pública (INSP) (2015). Encuesta Nacional de Niños, Niñas y Mujeres. Available at: https://www.unicef.org/mexico/informes/encuesta-nacional-de-ni%C3%B1os-ni%C3%B1as-y-mujeres-2015.

The Child Protection System in Nigeria

Chimezie L. Elekwachi *and* Peter O. Ebigbo

Abstract

This chapter discusses the Nigerian child protection system. Child maltreatment in Nigeria is a significant issue, while HIV/AIDS remains to be a major issue currently influencing child protection. As inequality grows rapidly, the unstable economic growth of Nigeria continued to impose substantial welfare costs on Nigerian households. The lack of job opportunities is the core of high poverty levels, regional inequality, and social and political unrest across Nigeria. Moreover, the majority of children never tell anyone about the physical violence or sexual violence they experienced, while only less than 5% of them receive the support they need to recover. Child labor becomes the focus of the child protection programming in Nigeria and the rest of Africa.

Key Words: Nigeria, child maltreatment, child protection, job opportunities, physical violence, sexual violence, support, child labor, economic growth, HIV/AIDS

Introduction

Nigeria is the most populous nation in Africa with about 182 million people; about 50% (91,855,000) are estimated to be children under 18 years (UNICEF, 2016). Nigeria is a major player in West Africa considering its political, economic, and population input in the sub-region. Nigeria constitutes about 47% of West Africa's population (World Bank, 2019) with one of the largest youth populations in the world. The United Nations estimates that in 2015, one-fifth of children under 18 years in Africa were born in Nigeria, and by 2050 Nigeria will acquire the status of 10th of all global births; a majority of Nigeria's population, including youth, will live in cities (UNICEF, 2014).

Child maltreatment in Nigeria is a significant problem. It is estimated that six in 10 children have experienced physical, psychological, or sexual abuse before their 18th birthday (National Population Commission of Nigeria et al., 2015). To respond to this the government and non-governmental organizations (NGOs) are the key players. The government has largely used legislation and policymaking to address child maltreatment, whereas the NGOs are more focused on developing and implementing child protection programs based on children's needs. The NGOs also complement the government in implementing the laws and also holding government accountable in terms of ensuring that the children are well protected. HIV/AIDS is a major issue currently influencing child protection in Nigeria. The UNAIDS 2010 report indicates that 2.5 million children in Nigeria are orphaned by the AIDS epidemic. Other factors affecting orphaning and vulnerability include food insecurity, poverty, conflict, natural disasters, malaria, and other infectious diseases. Children who lack parental care and support are classified as vulnerable, and some of them consequently migrate alone to urban areas due to parental loss, family breakdown, or escaping early marriage unaccompanied by an adult (National Population Commission, 2008). Poverty, gender inequality, sectarian violence, maternal mortality, and conflict are also responsible for orphaning in Nigeria (Federal Ministry of Women Affairs and Social Development, 2007).

This chapter reviews the current child maltreatment landscape in Nigeria. It takes on a historical review of literature on efforts at child protection, the evolving forms of child maltreatment, and the programs and the system of response to various forms of abuse as they occur in Nigeria.

Background

Nigeria practices a federal system of government. Nigeria's federation consists of 36 autonomous states within a multi-ethnic and culturally diverse society. Nigeria has an abundance of resources, it is one of Africa's biggest crude oil exporters, and also has one of the largest natural gas reserves on the continent (OPEC, 2019). However, the unstable economic growth of Nigeria continues to impose substantial welfare costs on Nigerian households. Inequality in terms of income and opportunities has been growing rapidly and has adversely affected poverty reduction. Historically, Nigeria is an amalgamation of Northern and Southern Protectorates of the British colonial empire since 1914. The North and South are culturally and socioeconomically different. The North–South divide has widened in recent years due to the Boko Haram (a terrorist organization affiliated to ISIS) insurgency. The abduction of over 200 Chibok girls in the northern Borno state of Nigeria by Boko Haram on April 14, 2014 came to global knowledge and outrage through the popular social media twitter protest #bringbackourgirls. The slow-paced economic development in the northern part of the country is attributed to part of the rise of Boko Haram (a name which translates to "No to Western Education"). These cultural and economic differences have implications for the manifestation of child maltreatment in the north and south. UNICEF indicates that about 10.5 million children (though recent reports show that this has risen to 13.2 million children) do not attend school in Nigeria. Sixty-nine percent of this population is in Northern Nigeria while the rest is in the south. This makes Nigeria the country with the largest number of out-of-school children globally. Large pockets of Nigeria's population still live in poverty estimated at 87 million people. This also makes Nigeria the capital of poverty on the globe (Brookings Institute, 2019). The lack of job opportunities is at the core of the high poverty levels, of regional inequality, and of social and political unrest in the country (World Bank, 2019).

Child Maltreatment

One in two children experience physical violence, one in four girls and one in ten boys experience sexual violence, and one in six girls and one in five boys experience emotional violence. The majority of children never tell anyone about their experience and less than 5% of children who experience violence receive the support they need to recover (National Population Commission of Nigeria et al., 2014).

Child Protection Policy Trends and Issues

Historically, programming for child protection in Nigeria and indeed Africa officially took a new tone in 1986 during a conference held in Nigeria (April 27–May 2, 1986) titled "Child Labour in Africa." It is important to note that the focus of that conference was child labor. This was because prior to 1986 child abuse was massively denied in Nigeria (Ebigbo, 2010). Although the theme was centered on child labor, this was a strategy to ensure wide acceptance to be able to gain the buy-in of government and the general public. However, the papers presented during that conference covered various forms of child abuse such as sexual abuse, physical abuse, and emotional abuse among other forms of abuse of children.

A Review of the Pre-1986 conference and Post-1986 Conference

Pre-1986

Nigeria was described as undergoing rapid political and socioeconomic changes without adequate infrastructure or facilities to cope with them. Rural migration of many unskilled and unemployed young persons moved to populate the urban slums. The urban accommodation system lacked recreational facilities and regular water and electricity supplies, thereby creating psychosocial problems which eroded marital harmony for the new urban migrants. The resultant effect on the one hand was incidence of births to single mothers which resulted in child abandonment, especially babies, in such places as public toilets, dustbins, and street corners (Animashaun, 1977; Ikediashi, 1988). On the other hand, some children from large families lived in overcrowded one room accommodations in urban slums and were exposed to abuse by an irritable and stressed parent (Garbarino & Sherman, 1980). Such parents were described to be young, physically ill, alcoholic, unemployed, and suffering from financial and social stresses (Okeahialam, 1984).

The children from large, overcrowded families provided the child labor force for parents from higher socioeconomic status who dwell in urban areas. Such children from rural poor overcrowded families were sent to live in the urban areas as childminders, or house helps in the Nigerian parlance. The new family was typically a nuclear family where both parents/guardians lived in a flat and went to work. In the absence of a grandmother or a senior relative, the young childminder, aged 7–12 years and inexperienced in childcare, took charge of the children of the household. The childminder was integrated into the new home and sometimes benefitted from education— mostly informal—as part of the contractual agreement. In most cases, these children were exploited and worked long hours. Under this circumstance the quality of attention a childminder received from her employers was described as proportional to the attention and care the child(ren) being cared for received. This precipitated physical abuse on the children being cared for in the absence of their parents. The childminder was also vulnerable to various forms of abuse like child labor or deprivation of education (Okeahialam, 1984). To support this, a study by Izuora and Ebigbo (1985) found that the childminders were of below average intelligence and of lower intelligence than the children they looked after.

Female suppression, especially financial suppression, was described as common. Financial suppression occurs when husbands prevent their wives from spending money they earn and Nwamuo (1988) found that this action was associated with child abuse. Low reports of child abuse cases in the media—mostly newspapers—was noted by Obinegbo and Ebigbo (1988).

In northern Nigeria it was reported that many parents believed their children should be brought up strictly with religious training. As such, they sent mostly male, but also some female children to the so-called Koranic Mallams, who are versed in teaching the Koran. Many of their Mallams are not educated in the western sense. These children were sometimes not visited by their parents. The Mallams live off the children by sending them to the streets to beg or forage for food on refuse dumps. The Mallams often move from city to city and when they die these children may become delinquent as street dwellers if male, and prostitutes if female (Kisekka, 1981).

Post-1986

The stories of mismanagement of resources and poverty have not significantly changed in Nigeria. For example, Ebigbo (2003) noted that although Nigeria is endowed with multiple natural and human resources she has been unable to develop the needed technological, industrial, managerial, and political know-how to pull its resources to take care of the basic needs of its citizens. Consequently, poverty and harsh living conditions are prevalent, affecting children in particular. The traditional culture has been greatly affected by this upheaval occasioned by cultural conflict, gradual industrialization, and imperfect attempts at westernization. This has affected the maintenance of the extended family culture and breakdown of such philosophies like "I am my brother's keeper." This has fueled consumerism, get rich quick syndrome, and rural–urban migration with the emergence of the urban poor.

Nigerian women and children have suffered profoundly from lack of sufficient investment in addressing their needs and rights. This has been strongly associated with mismanagement during decades of protracted military rule since independence October 1, 1960. Alongside this has been the decay of public institutions and loss of development opportunities, resulting in widening and deepening poverty, both in terms of household income and access to basic social services (Federal Government of Nigeria & UNICEF, 2001–).

Contemporaneously, the role of women has changed from docile housewives to working women who also work to help sustain the family economically. The new role of working outside the home has made women not only keepers of the home and rearers of children but have in many ways, like their male counterparts, become working-class women in the formal sector. However, they have kept their traditional roles as well as playing their new roles. Managing these two roles often leads to domestic violence such as wife battering, maltreatment, and divorce. Imprisonment of women, divorce, widowhood, separation, and so on are described as factors that lead to child abandonment and consequent abuse and neglect. In the case of single mothers who experience extreme situations of isolation and anguish, some may abandon their babies (Ebigbo, 2003).

The condition of infrequent media reports of cases of child abuse has largely changed, as most cases of child abuse and neglect, especially cases of violence, are well covered in the Nigerian dailies and social media.

There has been an increased social media outcry for justice for children such as #justice4ochanya, a young girl who was raped for several years by a brother in-law and her male cousin son until she had vesico-virginal fistula and other complications which finally led to her death.

The prevailing law for children has changed from the Children and Young Person's Law (Constitution of Federal Republic of Nigeria, 1979) to the current Child Rights Act (Federal Republic of Nigeria, 2003), which is a domestication of the UN Convention on the Rights of the Child, the African Union Charter on the Rights and Welfare of the Child, other international instruments such as the ILO convention 138 (Minimum Age and Convention 182, 138), and the United Nations Standard Minimum Rules for the Administration of Juvenile Justice ("The Beijing Rules"). These were domesticated in Nigeria in the Child Rights Act (CRA) of 2003. Because Nigeria is a federal state, all the federating individual states must adopt the law to make it suit their peculiarities while not negating the fundamental principles of child rights. Currently in Nigeria there are 24 states out of 36 that have passed the CRA into state laws.

Summary of Common Forms of Child Abuse and Neglect in Nigeria

What follows is a summary of the major types of child maltreatment documented in Nigeria, although we do not have data to describe the scope of the problem.

Child Labor/Street Children

This refers to activities whereby children engage in activities for economic gain which prevents their full development. Dyorough (1988) described child labor as occurring in two contexts: the familial and outside familial contexts. The outside familial context includes street hawking/trading, kiosk operating, newspaper vending, bus conducting, public entertainment, and formal employment, that is, in the wage sector such as in the textile industry, mechanic villages, timber market, petrol filling stations, and hotels and restaurants (Ekwurigwe, 1988; Obikeze, 1988; Oloko, 1988; Onwuzurike, 1988). The presence of children in labor seems to have focused attention on a social pathology known as street children.

Street children are young boys and girls often seen roaming in towns, streets, car parks, and gambling places, and by cinemas, and so on (Ngboawaji et al., 2009). The phenomenon of street children has become a prominent issue in child protection in Nigeria (Oloko, 1993; Ebigbo, 1999, 2003; Olley, 2006).

The number of working children in Nigeria is estimated to be 15 million; about 6 million of them can be classified as children in labor. About 2 million of them are classified to be in the worst form of labor and the rest are in various forms of labor (Nigeria Office of Statistics, 2000/2001).

Child Abandonment/Baby Farming

Child abandonment is when a child is totally rejected by his or her biological or adopted parents (Ikeadiashi, 1988). Baby farming refers to the criminal activities in Nigeria which entail the restriction of a person's willful movement for purposes of forced impregnation, sale of babies, and illegal adoptions (Huntley, 2013). This is a relatively new form of child trafficking. The common occurrence of child abandonment seems to have reduced or metamorphosed into a new form of child trafficking in Nigeria known as baby farming or harvesting.

Child Trafficking

This is a sub-form of the broadly known human trafficking. Child trafficking involves the unlawful movement of children for clandestine activities. According to the Palemo protocol (UN, 2000) human trafficking has three main components which involve the act, the means, and the purpose. The act includes recruitment, transportation, transfer, harboring, or receipt of persons through the means of force or other forms of coercion, abduction, fraud, deception, the abuse of power or of a position of vulnerability, or the giving or receiving of payments or benefits to achieve the consent of a person having control over the other person.

Human trafficking in Nigeria is very common although it is a criminal offence. However, according to the Global Slavery Index (2018), Nigeria ranks 32nd out of 167 of the countries with the highest number of slaves (1,386,000). The number of people trafficked for the years 2006, 2007, and 2008 are estimated to be 493, 789, and 1269 people, respectively. Victims aged 0–17 years accounted for 49% of total identified persons.

Emotional Abuse

Emotional abuse is defined as the absence of required quality time that is necessary for the emotional development of children (Kalu, 1988). This may come in the form of scolding, ridicule, and verbal abuse. Kalu (1988) reported that these forms of emotional aggression were often used as complementary measures of traditional child discipline in Nigeria

Physical Abuse

This is a kind of physical aggression that involves putting children in a way that injures or puts him or her at risk of being injured. This includes beating, kicking, knocking, punching, choking, confinement, and killing. The National Population Commission of Nigeria, UNICEF Nigeria, and the US Centers for Disease Control and Prevention reported in the Violence Against Children Survey (2015) that one in two children experience physical abuse.

Tympanic perforation is a unique form of physical abuse that has been described by Obiako (1988) in Nigeria. This is reported to occur in an attempt to discipline. The tympanic membrane injury/perforation that he reported was due to compression and this was indicative of abuse (Obiako, 1988). He described this perforation to occur as a result of a force striking and occluding the external ear canal. This often occurs as a result of a slap on the ear by the open hand.

Infanticide

Infanticide is the intentional killing of babies. This occurs in the Federal Capital Territory, mainly among the Basso Komo ethnic group of Nigeria. These children are killed mainly for the following reasons: 1) twins, Albinos, and children who grow upper teeth first are perceived as bad luck; 2) if a breastfeeding mother dies, her child is buried with her because the child is perceived as bad luck; 3) if a woman dies during child birth, it is also perceived as bad luck and the child should die too.

These killings are based on cultural beliefs that perceive any abnormality such as disability or tragic circumstance during birth as ill luck brought by the child. These children are often killed through poisoning or suffocation; in some instances they are buried alive.

Sexual Abuse

Izuora (1988) reported several cases of children who presented to the hospital with various symptoms such as acute abdominal pain. These was later discovered to be incomplete abortion, septic criminal abortion, and teen pregnancy. The root causes of sexual abuse identified from the cases were emotional neglect, poverty, and ignorance of the father and mother.

Female genital mutilation involves the removal of the clitoral hood or labia minora, the excision of the clitoris and the damaging act of infibulation. This is considered as a form of sexual abuse. The age at which female genital mutilation is performed varies from the first week after a female baby's birth to after a woman delivers her first baby.

Child marriage is also considered a subtype of sexual abuse. It involves giving away a young child for the purposes of marriage. A child here refers to a person who is below the age of 18 years.

Therapeutic/Drug Abuse

Therapeutic abuse is defined as the practice whereby parents or guardians force their children to undertake a number of medications or undergo procedures which may be detrimental to their well-being. Some of these drugs are usually inappropriate, often unnecessary, and sometimes harmful. Examples of such drugs are antimicrobial agents, anti-diarrheal medicines, cough expectorants, steroid creams, and a host of others (Ukabam & Ibe, 1988).

Abuse of Children with Disabilities

Izuorah (1988) appraised the abuse of children with disabilities in Nigeria and identified a three-dimensional phenomenon involving families, society, and the government. In families (father, mother, and extended family), common problems include:

1) Refusal to seek proper medical advice early.
2) Denial of special investigation, mainly due to religious reasons. Many parents or guardians rejected investigation and treatment on religious grounds.
3) Refusal to buy drugs.
4) Failure to take children with epilepsy to the hospital for doctor's appointment. Izuorah (1988) reported about 18% of cases of neglect and apathy of children with disability on the part of the parents and guardians.
5) Inadequate stimulation and care by parents and guardians due to inexperienced and unstable mothers who fail to understand the importance of rehabilitative services for children with a disability.
6) Self-medication.
7) Total absence of care.
8) Starvation by mothers or substitute parent.
9) Abandonment of malformed babies.
10) Fatal poisoning or mutilation of children with a disability.

In society, abuse and neglect occur due to:

1) Abuse by orthodox doctors: this includes observed over dosage or under dosage for children with epilepsy or mental retardation.

2) Abuse by quacks or traditional healers, including such practices as splints for paralytic polio, extensive therapeutic scalp and body scarification in epilepsy, induced burns on the limbs of epileptics, incision of the frequelum linguae in dumb children, or mutilation of limbs or the body.

3) Abuse by drug makers, including the sale of some orthodox drugs that have been proven dangerous, teratogenic, or worthless. Also, the sale of untested drugs and concoctions made locally were also reported.

4) Abuse by religious sects including some prayer houses, spiritualists, and religious sects. These groups were reported to claim possession of a cure to all handicapping diseases like epilepsy, cerebral palsy, and so on. Some religious sects refuse blood transfusion, some believe that healing will be achieved only through prayer and fasting.

5) Lack of informed knowledge leading to ignorance in the general public towards the plight and the need to protect children with disabilities.

Finally, the government is complicit in disabled children's abuse. The following forms of abuse were observed by Izuorah (1988):

1) Failure to ensure preventive measures or adequate primary healthcare.
2) Failure to set up adequate rehabilitation centers or institutions for the disabled.
3) Inadequate funding for the care of the handicapped.
4) Absence and failure to implement already set down laws and regulations for protection of handicapped children.
5) Failure to create adequate awareness in the society about the problems of the handicapped.
6) Failure to adequately check quackery.

Child Witchcraft Branding

In Nigeria, child witchcraft branding has become a serious challenge for child protection professionals. This is a post-1986 development, not listed among the various forms of child abuse and neglect listed in Nigeria during the first conference on child abuse and neglect. The term child witchcraft branding refers to accusing children of witchcraft. The term witchcraft here refers to the use of negative manipulation to bring about bad luck or misfortune (Charles, 2012).

Child Protection System

Section 207 of the Child Rights Act provides for a specialized unit of the Nigerian Police Force known as the Specialized Children Police Unit, for anyone who engages in the various forms of child abuse described previously.

The police officers in this unit should consist of officers who frequently or exclusively deal with children, or are primarily engaged in the prevention of child offences. This unit is also charged with the prevention and control of offences, the apprehension of child offenders, the investigation of child offences, and other functions as may be referred to the unit by this Act or by regulations made under the Act or by other enactments.

Family Court

Family courts are courts of law but they are planned and designed to suit children and their families. The family court constitutes two levels including the High Court (higher court) and Magistrate Court (lower court). They manage civil and criminal proceedings as they relate to children and their families. Civil proceedings such as liability, privilege, interest, obligation, or claim in respect of a child are handled by the court. Criminal proceedings involving or relating to any penalty, forfeiture, liability in respect to an offence committed by a child, against a child, or against the interest of a child are handled by the family court. The personnel of the family court includes the judges, court assessors, and child development officers who work at the ministry of women affairs and social development. This is the ministry that handles affairs of children through the child development department. The court is run in collaboration with the ministry of Justice and the Ministry of Women Affairs.

The Family Courts are structured based on the political arrangement of each state. For example, in Enugu State, the Family Courts are found in the three legislative constituencies. This is with a view to make the courts closer to the people.

Forms of Child Protection Programs and Policies: A Historical Overview

From 1981 onwards, the federal, state, and local governments collaborated to address health issues which relate to rural water and sanitation projects. In the 1983–1985 program, a local government area-based project in health education, and water and sanitation was introduced in addition to programs on nutrition, curriculum development, the training of traditional birth attendants and extension workers, and assistance to daycare centers. In general, the program covered communication, support, social, and community development. By the end of that program four main elements depicted its focus: EPI (Expanded Program on Immunization), ORT (Oral Rehydration and Therapy), WATSAN (water and sanitation), and social mobilization. Social mobilization is the process of carrying along society members to address programs in the community. During this period maternal and infant mortality were very high and the concentration was mainly on health, immunization, control of diarrhea, and supply of clean water. By then the social mobilization and rights-based programming had not been introduced (FGN & UNICEF, 1997, pp. 15–17).

More recently, the HIV/AIDS epidemic has largely influenced child protection policies and programs in Nigeria. This is because the HIV epidemic affects child survival at a direct and indirect level. For example, the sick family member requires resources and attention which diverts family resources away from the children. As such, the children of HIV positive parents experience trauma during the sickness and the death that may follow. This drop in family resources may lead to dropping out of school or diminished household resources due to job loss, healthcare, and nutritional status (Federal Ministry of Women Affairs and Social Development, 2007). This puts a lot of burden on the families and the communities to care for these children (Nigeria Demographic and Health Survey [NDHS], 2008).

National Guidelines to and Practice on Orphans and Vulnerable Children (2014)

In response to the HIV epidemic in Nigeria and its concomitant impact on the lives of orphans and vulnerable children (OVC), Nigeria developed the National Guidelines to and Practice on Orphans and Vulnerable Children (Federal Ministry of Women Affairs and Social Development, 2007). The guidelines have the following objectives:

1) Provide guidance for the development and implementation of interventions for the care, support and protection of orphans and vulnerable children in Nigeria.
2) Provide minimum standards in quality of services and activities related to all areas of care, support, and protection of orphans and vulnerable children that are socially and culturally acceptable, in accordance with the Federal Government of Nigeria policies, international instruments, and internationally accepted best practices.
3) Provide a clear understanding of the guiding principles, and define roles and responsibilities for all stakeholders.
4) Enhance collaboration and strategic partnership among stakeholders through effective referral and coordination.

The latest version of the guideline is the National Standard for Improving the Quality of Life of Vulnerable Children in Nigeria. The main contribution of the new service standard is the introduction of the "improvement science methodology." This is the application of science-based systems oriented toward inputs, processes, outcomes, and evidence-based approaches to reach desired results (Ogazi & Stover, 2014). Another important aspect is the involvement of community members in the process of caring for OVC. This service standard also lists the basic services that should be provided for OVC including protection, education and training, nutrition, shelter and care, household economic strengthening, health, and psychosocial support. The approach is to provide for the needs of children through mobilizing community resources.

The process of enrolling children and communities with these OVC programs is usually based on individuals infected or affected by HIV and AIDS or communities affected by HIV and AIDS. This invariably applies to communities with a high prevalence of HIV/AIDS. The process of enrolment of each child in the program is household focused. A household vulnerability assessment is made. This questionnaire assesses the needs of the child within a household context. Furthermore, for each child a care plan is made to care for the needs of the specific child in the household. Subsequent assessment is made to compare the impact of the program on the child and the entire household.

Alternative Care for Children in Nigeria

The report by UNICEF (2005) indicates that the adoption process in Nigeria is not uniform. A child usually comes into institutional care if they are abandoned at street corners, hospitals or maternity homes. Some of them are brought to the social welfare unit by non-governmental organizations (NGOs); these children are taken to orphanages run by government, NGOs, or faith-based organizations. The UNICEF 2005 report showed that poor equipment and staffing prevent adequate rehabilitation of children with disabilities who are in some of the centers. Poor funding, inadequate facilities, lack of specialized staff, inadequate number of germane objectives for establishment of the centers are reasons why the institutional childcare centers are functioning poorly.

The institutional childcare centers also do not have clear and standard procedures of operation. The core things missing include minimum facilities, adequately qualified caregivers (staff), adequate nutrition (feeding), and education such as a personalized development plan for each child. The institutional childcare centers are supposed to be transitory half-way homes for the children, but the reality is that they are home for many of the children who are there.

Sustainability of the private run centers is a major issue because they lack a strong internal governance structure to keep the center running in the absence of the original founder. For the government funded institutions the problem of adequate funding is the concern. Both the government run and private institutions also lack the ability to manage critically the database of the children they handle. This is characterized by poor information flow and information management.

National Policy on Education

Nigeria's education policy is focused on improving access to education and ensuring that education is a vehicle for a free and democratic society, a just and egalitarian society, a united strong and self-reliant nation, and a great and dynamic economy. The policy addresses issues that impede educational development of children and adults from primary to secondary schools. However, lack of political will, poor leadership, poor planning, and corruption are some of the major impediments towards full realization of the policy's expected results (Okoroma, 2006).

National Policy on Child Labor (2013)

The national policy on child labor was based on the wide prevalence of child labor in Nigeria. The policy is designed to 1) work for the establishment of a national program on child labor; 2) harmonize child labor projects and interventions in the country; 3) provide evidence-based and sustained implementation of programs and projects for the prevention and elimination of child labor; 4) advocate for government commitment and stakeholders' active involvement in initiatives to eliminate child labor; and 5) coordinate and manage information on child labor.

National Policy on Protection and Assistance to Trafficked Persons in Nigeria (2011)

This policy takes into consideration the issue of trafficking in persons in Nigeria. It was designed to provide protection for mainly domestic servitude and commercial sexual exploitation. It also takes on the gender lens of understanding that each gender is vulnerable to specific kinds of trafficking. For example, boys are trafficked primarily for forced labor in street vending, agriculture, mining stone, quarries, and as domestic servants. Young girls are induced to get pregnant in order to produce babies that can be sold. They are also involved in sexual related exploitation such as prostitution or domestic labor. The policy also puts into consideration that people in general are trafficked for other things such as organ harvesting.

The policy also focuses on protection and support for trafficked victims including children. It provides a guide for using a mix of intervention for responding to the challenge of trafficking in persons, and other components including prevention, prosecution, and partnership. These interventions are embedded in the principles of redress, recovery, and reintegration. An important aspect of the policy is the social planning model hinged on empowerment of the victims of human trafficking and meeting their needs. The policy was based on the Nigerian Constitution and Millennium Development Goals, especially the areas of child health and gender inequality.

Child Protection Program for Children in Emergency

In Nigeria, children have been affected by the Boko Haram terrorist attacks. It is estimated that in the last six years 20,000 people have died and over 2.2 million have been internally displaced; this consists mainly of children and women (Plan International, 2018). The terrorist attacks have been centralized in the northeast geopolitical zone of Nigeria. The northeast consists of six states (Adamawa, Bauchi, Borno, Gombe, Taraba, and Yobe).

These terrorist attacks have affected the education of children, nutritional status of children, psychosocial well-being, and the socioeconomic well-being of families, among others. Multiple organizations are providing support to victims, families, and communities affected by the attacks. These programs focus on preventing exploitation, preventing violent conflict, avoiding separation of children from their families, recognizing diversity, responding to emergencies, coordination and community mobilization, child participation and communication, and contingency planning (Save the Children, 2005).

Evaluation of Existing Child Protection Policies in Nigeria

These policies are very important because they address critical child protection needs in various settings such as child labor, trafficking, education, violence, HIV/AIDS, emergency relief, and others. However, they have faced two major problems, including poor implementation primarily because of poor funding and poor coordination of programs, policies, and institutions (government and non-governmental resources). Most of these programs and policies are implemented independently of each other. Efforts to provide a coordinated response system to build cohesion among stakeholders are weak and have lacked strategic focus over the years. This makes it difficult to know where the resources to protect children are and who is doing what, where, when, and how. There are national organizations set up to provide this necessary coordination, but they are institutionally weak and have been unable to provide it. However, such programs as the National Joint Taskforce for the Prevention of Child Sexual Abuse, Violence and Neglect is an effort in this direction. From 2015 to 2018 the African Network for the Prevention and Protection against Child Abuse and Neglect (ANPPCAN) Nigeria chapter implemented a pilot program in the southeast geopolitical zone of Nigeria with a view to provide a draft child abuse response system for Nigeria. ANPPCAN facilitated the formation of a joint task force (JTF). Its members are made up of critical stakeholders with responsibility for preventing child sexual abuse, violence, and neglect of children in Nigeria. The JTF is chaired by the Federal Ministry of Women Affairs and Social Development (FMWASD). Its members include government agencies such as the National Agency for the Prohibition of Trafficking in Persons (NAPTIP), FMWASD, National Human Rights Commission, Legal Aid Council, Federal Ministry of Education, Federal Ministry of Health, National Emergency Management Agency, National News Agency of Nigeria, National Orientation Agency, National Agency for the Control of AIDS, Nigerian Immigration Service, Nigerian Police Force, Nigerian Civil Defense, Federal Ministry of Information, Federal Ministry of Justice, Nigerian Law Reform Commission, Public Complaint Commission, African Network for the Prevention and Protection against Child Abuse & Neglect (ANPPCAN) Nigeria chapter, Christian Association of Nigeria (CAN), Muslim Sisters Association, Child Protection Network (CPN), Widows and Orphans Empowerment Organization (WEWE), and National Council of Child Rights Advocates of Nigeria (NACCRAN). So far, the ANPPCAN Nigeria chapter has co-facilitated three planning meetings for the JTF. The outcomes of the meetings include terms of reference for the taskforce, inauguration of the taskforce in 2014, and an implementation plan.

In 2015, ANPPCAN Nigeria started the pilot southeast child sexual abuse monitoring and response center with the following specific objectives: 1) to mobilize a joint response to child sexual abuse, violence and neglect by strengthening this newly formed JTF to set up a pilot monitoring center in southeast Nigeria; 2) to set up an information sharing mechanism within the JTF to support joint activities between civil society organization networks and public institutions to coordinate responses, incident reports, and enforcement of punitive action against offenders; and 3) to increase awareness and knowledge of the JTF in other geopolitical zones on how to replicate monitoring centers to jointly respond to child sexual abuse, violence and neglect in their zones to achieve a multiplier effect across Nigeria.

The center used a proactive and reactive approach to responding to cases of violence against children. Using the proactive approach, field officers in the monitoring center developed a surveillance system in which they visit hospitals (maternal and child health, paediatric, and accident and emergency clinics), markets, and schools where child abuse or violence against children can be reported or observed, to collect data on the nature and form of abuse reported and what action was taken by the authorities. The reactive method used by the monitoring center involved the centre responding to cases of child sexual abuse, violence, and neglect that were directly reported at the center.

The rationale of the center was that child sexual abuse usually occurs in hiding and many children—especially females—who face abuse may be scared to report because of stigmatization. Also, ignorance about what to do after child sexual abuse, violence, or neglect of a child is common.

Using the proactive method the center deployed field officers who visited various schools, hospitals, and religious institutions like churches to know how they report various forms of violence against children that are reported to their institutions.

Table 41.1 describes the forms of child abuse recorded and the kinds of interventions that the various institutions provide.

Table 41.2 indicates the number of cases reported in the pilot states within Nigeria. Given the large number of children in Nigeria, and the widespread phenomenon of child abuse, these numbers suggest that child maltreatment was only infrequently reported to public authorities.

The child protection system in Nigeria has improved from what it used to be in the 1980s. However, there is still need for a lot of improvement, especially in the area of coordinating institutions and resources available in the sector to ensure that information is shared and resources are properly managed to improve child protection.

Table 41.1 The type of actions various institutions use to respond to child maltreatment that are reported to them

Institutions/ Types of Abuse	Type of Abuse	Symptoms	Action Taken	Who Perpetrates the Abuse
Schools	Physical abuse	Belt/beating marks	Guardian invited to discuss the abuse.	Guardian
		Absence from school	Guardian invited to discuss the absence of the child from school.	Guardian
		Lateness to school	Guardian invited to discuss the child's lateness	Guardian
		Student came to report to the guardian counsellor	Guardian invited to discuss the issue the child reported.	Guardian
	Sexual abuse	Students elope with boy friends	Suspension from school	Boyfriend
		Students caught in the act of sex after school hours within school premises	Counseling by guardian counsellor	Boyfriend
General hospital	Physical abuse	Victim brought to the hospital	Reported to police Provision of medical report.	Neighbor
	Sexual abuse	Counseling and medical treatment	Medical treatment and medical report	Teenage boys known to the victim
	Gang rape	Victim brought to the hospital	Medical treatment and medical report	Neighbors and a group of boys
	Fingering	Medical examination	Medical report for police investigation	Neighbor
Religious institution	Physical abuse	Counseling	Counseling	Guardian

Table 41.2 Number of reported cases in selected states

State	Period	Number of cases
Enugu	February 2015–January 2016	238
	February 2016–January 2017	248
	February 2017–January 2018	113
Imo	February 2015–January 2016	7
	February 2016–January 2017	62
	February 2017–January 2018	29
Ebonyi	February 2015–January 2016	12
	February 2016–January 2017	40
	February 2017–January 2018	45
Anambra	February 2015–January 2016	1
Rivers	February 2015–January 2016	1
Abia	February 2016–January 2018	15
Grand total: 811		

References

Animashun, A. (1977). Abandoned children in Lagos. *Nigeria Medical Journal*, 7, 408–411.

Brookings Institute. (2019, June 19). *The start of a new poverty narrative*. Available at: https://www.brookings.edu/blog/future-development/2018/06/19/the-start-of-a-new-poverty-narrative/.

Charles, J. O. (2012). Witchcraft beliefs and practices: A socio-anthropological discourse on man, religion, church and society. In Ebelebe C.A *Spirits Occultism Principalities & Powers: Acts of the 14th SIST International Missiological Synposui* (pp. 27–60). Spiritan International School of Theology.

Dyorough, A. (1988). The problems of child labour and exploitation in Nigeria. In P. O. Ebigbo, G. I. Izuora, M. E. Obiekezie, E. Okpara, and U. Ekwegbalu (Eds.), *Child labour in Africa* (pp. 46–51). ANPPCAN.

Ebigbo, P. O. (1999). Street children: The core of child abuse and neglect in Nigeria. *ANPPCAN Child Rights Monitor*, 1, 10–21.

Ebigbo, P. O. (2000). Situation analysis of child trafficking in Nigeria: Policy implications. National workshop on trafficking in Nigeria. Enugu.

Ebigbo, P. O. (2003). Child Abuse in Africa: Nigeria as focus. *International Journal of Early Childhood*, 95–113.

Ebigbo, P. O. (2010). *The state of Nigerian children in the last 50 years*. ANPPCAN.

Ewurigwe, F. A. (1988). Exploitation of child labour in Choba, Port Harcourt: A political economy approach. In *Child labour in Africa* (pp. 26–38). ANPPCAN.

Federal Government of Nigeria and UNICEF. (1997). *Masterplan of operations country programme of cooperation for Nigerian children and women*. UNICEF.

Federal Government of Nigeria and UNICEF. (2001). *Situation analysis of women and children*. UNICEF.

Federal Ministry of Women Affairs and Social Development. (2014). *National guidelines and standards of practice*. Federal Ministry of Women Affairs and Social Development.

Federal Republic of Nigeria. (1999). *The constitution of the Federal Republic of Nigeria*.

Federal Republic of Nigeria. (2003). *Child rights act*. Federal Government Press.

Garbarino, J. and Sherman, D. (1980). High risk neighbourhood and high risk families the human ecology of child maltreatment. *Child Development*, 5, 188–198.

Global Slavery Index. (2018). *Country data: Nigeria*. Available at: https://www.globalslaveryindex.org/2018/data/country-data/nigeria/.

Huntley, S. (2013). October. The Phenomenon of "Baby factories" in Nigeria as a new trend in human Trafficking. Available at: https://www.internationalcrimesdatabase.org/upload/documents/20140916T170728-ICD%20Brief%203%20-%20Huntley.pdf.

Ikediashi, A. E. (1988). A study of the epidemiology of child abandonment and deprivation in Imo State Nigeria. In P. O. Ebigbo, G. I. Izuora, M. E. Obiekezie, E. Okpara, and U. Ekwegbalu (Eds.), *Child labour in Africa* (pp. 114–119). ANPPCAN.

Izuora, G. I. and Ebigbo, P. O. (1985). Assessment of house-helps in Enugu using the draw–a–person test. *The Nigerian Medical Practitioner*, 9, 21–23.

Izuora, N. (1988). Sexual abuse and recurrent criminal abortions in Nigeria children: A report of three cases. In P. O. Ebigbo, G. I. Izuora, M. E. Obiekezie, E. Okpara, and U. Ekwegbalu (Eds.), *Child labour in Africa* (pp. 81–82). ANPPCAN.

Kalu, W. J. (1988). Emotional abuse and neglect in contemporary Nigerian family: A reassessment of parenthood skills. In P. O. Ebigbo, G. I. Izuora, M. E. Obiekezie, E. Okpara, and U. Ekwegbalu (Eds.), *Child labour in Africa* (pp. 96–104). ANPPCAN.

Kisekka, M. N. (1981). *Children in Kaduna State, Nigeria: Problems and needs.* Department of Sociology and Kaduna Child Welfare Committee.

National Population Commission and ICF Macro. (2008). *Demographic and health survey.* National Population Commission and ICF Macro.

National Population Commission of Nigeria, UNICEF Nigeria, and the US Centers for Disease Control and Prevention. (2014). *Violence against children in Nigeria: Findings from a national survey, 2014.* UNICEF.

Ngbowaji, D. N., Paul, E., and Igbanibo, S. T. (2009). Street children and the challenges of national security evidence from Nigeria. *Bangladesh e-Journal of Sociology*, 6(2), 3–84.

Nwamuo, P. A. (1988). A survey of the suppression of women and its effect on child care. *Child Labour in Africa* (pp. 131–140). Enugu: ANPPCAN.

Nigeria Office of Statistics. (2000/2001). FOS/ILO/SIMPOC Report on National Child Labour Survey Nigeria. Nigeria Office of Statistics.

Obiako, M. N. (1988). Eardrum perforation as evidence of child abuse. In P. O. Ebigbo, G. I. Izuora, M. E. Obiekezie, E. Okpara, and U. Ekwegbalu (Eds.), *Child labour in Africa* (pp. 252–251). ANPPCAN.

Obiekezie, D. S. (1988). Agricultural child labour in Nigeria: A case study of Anambra State. In P. O. Ebigbo, G. I. Izuora, M. E. Obiekezie, E. Okpara, and U. Ekwegbalu (Eds.), *Child labour in Africa* (pp. 39–45). ANPPCAN.

Obinegbo, J. N. and Ebigbo, P. O. (1988). The print media and child abuse and neglect: The Nigerian situation. In P. O. Ebigbo, G. I. Izuora, M. E. Obiekezie, E. Okpara, and U. Ekwegbalu (Eds.), *Child labour in Africa* (pp. 212–219). ANPPCAN.

Ogazi, J. and Stover, K. E. (2014). *Guide for applying improvement methods to improvement methods to implement the national standards for improving the quality of life of vulnerable children in Nigeria.* USAID ASSIST Project and University Research Co LLC.

Okeahialam, T. C. (1984). Child abuse in Nigeria. *Child Abuse and Neglect*, 8, 69–73.

Okoroma, N. (2006). Educational policies and problems of implementation in Nigeria. *Australian Journal of Adult Learning*, 46(2), 245–263.

Olley, B. (2006). Social and health behaviours in youths of the streets in Ibadan, Nigeria. *Child Abuse and Neglect*, 30, 271–282.

Oloko, B. A. (1988). Children's domestic versus economic work and school achievement. In P. O. Ebigbo, G. I. Izuora, M. E. Obiekezie, E. Okpara, and U. Ekwegbalu (Eds.), *Child labour in Africa* (pp. 1–9). ANPPCAN.

Oloko, B. (1993). Children's street work in urban Nigeria as adaptation and maladaptation to changing socioeconomic circumstances. *International Journal of Behavioural Development*, 16(3), 465–482.

Onwuzurike, C. A. (1988). Child abuse: A cultural norm or misapplied term? In P. O. Ebigbo, G. I. Izuora, M. E. Obiekezie, E. Okpara, and U. Ekwegbalu (Eds.), *Child labour in Africa* (pp. 232–238). ANPPCAN.

OPEC. (2019). *Nigeria profile.* Available at: https://www.opec.org/opec_web/en/about_us/167.htm.

Plan International. (2018). Adolescent girls in crisis: Voice from the Lake Chad basin. Available at: http://plan-international.org/publications/adolescent-girls-crisis-lake-chad-basin.

Plan international Save the children. (2005). *Child Protection in Emergencies.* Save the Children Sweden.

Ukabam, S. O. and Ibe, B. C. (1988). Child abuse therapeutic abuse. In P. O. Ebigbo, G. I. Izuora, M. E. Obiekezie, E. Okpara, and U. Ekwegbalu (Eds.), *Child labour in Africa* (pp. 163–166). ANPPCAN.

UN. (2000, November 15). *Protocol to prevent, suppress and punish trafficking in persons especially woman and children, supplementing the United Nations Convention against Transnational Organized Crime.* Available at: https://www.ohchr.org/Documents/ProfessionalInterest/ProtocolonTrafficking.pdf.

UNAIDS. (2000). *UNAIDS Nigeria page*. Available at: http://www.unaids.org/en/regionscountries/countries/ Nigeria.

UNAIDS. (2010). *UNAIDS Report on Global AIDS Epidemic*. WHO.

UNICEF. (2005). *Report on assessment of institutional child care centers in Nigeria*. United Nations Children's Funds.

UNICEF. (2014). *Generation 30 Africa*. UNICEF.

UNICEF. (2015). Report on assessment of institutional child care centres in Nigeria. United Nations Children Fund.

UNICEF. (2016). *The state of the world's children 2016* [Statistical tables]. Available at: https://data.unicef.org/ resources/state-worlds-children-2016-statistical-tables/

World Bank. (2019, April 9). *The World Bank in Nigeria*. Available at: https://www.worldbank.org/en/coun try/nigeria/overview.

Protecting Children in the Philippines: A System-focused Overview of Policy and Practice

Steven Roche *and* Florence Flores-Pasos

Abstract

This chapter explains the policies and practices of child protection in the Philippines. While the country is experiencing rapid economic, social, and political transformations, there is increasing international awareness of the need for children to be protected from neglect and abuse, particularly in circumstances of significant poverty, inequality, and deprivation. Filipino children experience a strong sense of familial belonging and community connectedness, with a high degree of social and cultural significance placed on the family. However, maltreatment and exploitation are the core risks to the Filipino youth, which are followed by other risks such as child labour, child trafficking, extra-judicial killings, and natural disasters.

Key Words: Philippines, child protection, child labour, child trafficking, extra-judicial killings, maltreatment, exploitation, international awareness, poverty, inequality

Introduction

The Philippines is experiencing rapid economic, social, and political change and the challenges that come with such transformation are confounded by relatively low levels of social assistance and the weakening of traditional social support structures (Asia Development Bank, 2013; Chan et al., 2014; Curato, 2015, 2017). At the same time, there is increasing international awareness of the need for children to be protected from neglect and abuse, and to grow up in safe and stable environments (Price-Robertson et al., 2014), particularly in circumstances of significant poverty and deprivation such as in the Philippines (Philippines Statistics Authority [PSA] & UNICEF, 2015).

Child protection "systems" are receiving increasing international attention in preventing and responding to child maltreatment, yet few studies have explored the Philippines' approaches to child protection, nor related these to system frameworks. In response, this chapter presents current policy settings and approaches to child protection in the Philippines. First, it provides an overview of the Philippines and the context of the lives of children and their families. This is followed by insights into the core risks to child maltreatment in the Philippines, including an analysis of national social policy and governance arrangements. Then, utilizing Wessells' (2015) "top-down," "bottom-up," and "middle-out" framework for child protection systems in developing contexts, we provide an overview of child protection approaches in the Philippines, and in doing so, identify its flaws and areas for policy development. This chapter assists researchers, policymakers, and welfare sectors to gain a more comprehensive overview of child protection practices in the Philippines.

The Context of Child Maltreatment in the Philippines

The Philippines is a nation state in southeast Asia, made up of an archipelago of more than 7,000 islands and geographically divided into three main island groupings of Luzon, the Visayas, and Mindanao. The country has a population of over 100 million people (United Nations Development Programme [UNDP], 2016), with around 36.6 million (36.6% of the total population) children under the age of 18 (PSA & UNICEF, 2015, p. 7). The population is growing with a fertility rate (births per woman) of 2.96, one of the highest of countries in southeast Asia (World Bank, 2017b), and is split evenly between regional and urban areas (Asian Development Bank, 2013).

The Philippines' long colonial history strongly impacts its make-up today. Spanish colonization brought disparate islands with varied languages, histories, and cultures together into a nation presided over by a semi-feudal society dominated by landowners, the Catholic Church, and the upper class (Yu, 2006). Later, the United States of America's control between 1898 and 1946 left behind a collection of political and cultural institutions that continue today (Francia, 2010). Now a democratic presidential republic, the Philippines exhibits the formal features of electoral democracy; however, it is argued that this fails to translate into meaningful democratic functioning and sustained democratic reforms (Curato, 2015), and is hampered by intractable oligarchic structures and dysfunctional political institutions (Curato, 2017). Emerging from these governance conditions is a vibrant civil society with the third largest number of non-governmental organizations in the global south, and the densest network of civil society groups in the world (Curato, 2015), as well as a neoliberal economic orientation that pursues foreign investment and public-private partnerships (Curato, 2017).

The Lives of Children in the Philippines

Children in the Philippines experience a strong sense of familial belonging and community connectedness, with a high degree of social and cultural importance placed on the family (Bessell, 2009). The institution of the family is highly important in the lives of Filipino people, defined by loyalty, sacrifice, and affection, and providing economic, social, and emotional support (Asis et al., 2004). Family membership is expansive, involving extended relatives and strong kinship ties, and is characterized by reciprocal exchange and mutual assistance (Asis et al., 2004; Madianou, 2012). This is reflected in the Philippines' comparatively high scores in measures of subjective well-being, based on strong family and peer relationships (Lau & Bradshaw, 2010).

Families are typically large in the Philippines due to a range of factors. Teen birth rates have increased in the last five years (UNICEF, 2016) while 54% of all pregnancies in the Philippines are unintended (Chiu, 2013), which has much to do with limited access to contraception and the illegality of abortion. To combat this, reproductive health legislation was implemented in 2014 that provides free contraception to poor communities, and provides sex education to children and young people (Gulland, 2014), reducing barriers to access to sexual and reproductive health care and services (Chiu, 2013). The impact of these programs on birth rates is yet to be determined.

Contemporary family dynamics are continually being reshaped by 2.2 million overseas Filipino workers, who are the parents of between 4 and 6 million children, and frequently leave their children in various forms of alternate parental or extra-familial care (Department of Justice [DOJ], 2012). Children growing up apart from their mother or father are changing care environments, family relationships, and functioning, as well as parental roles and capacities (Asis et al., 2004; Parrenas, 2005), and can be viewed as a product of the structural contexts of families' lives in the Philippines.

THE STRUCTURAL CONTEXT OF CHILDREN'S LIVES

The lives and experiences of children and their families vary significantly across the Philippines due to significant levels of inequality and poverty, generated by the interaction of social, political, economic, and historical forces (Yu, 2013). Substantive improvements to poverty and inequality have not been achieved by recent governments (Curato, 2017), despite consistently high economic growth in the last decade, including gross domestic product annual growth at 6.9% in 2016 (World Bank, 2017a). Inequality has increased since 1994 (World Bank, 2015), and the number of people living below the poverty line expanded by approximately 2 million people since 1991 (PSA & UNICEF, 2015), detailing entrenched levels for the last 25 years.

A more in-depth measure, the 2016 United Nations Human Development Index (HDI), which incorporates indicators of Gross National Income (GNI) per capita, as well as measures of life expectancy and education, ranks the Philippines 116th out of 188 countries (UNDP, 2017). In addition, a comparative study investigating child well-being in a range of countries in the Pacific Rim found that the Philippines ranked lowest overall, and last on multidimensional measures across domains of well-being, including material well-being, health, education, risk, and safety (Lau & Bradshaw, 2010). Data from 2009 identified that 6.5 million children live in homes without electricity, and 4.1 million children obtain water from an unsafe source (PSA & UNICEF, 2015). Further, 1.4 million children live in informal settlements and 250,000 experience deprivation of shelter, both strong indicators of insecure tenancy, lack of infrastructure and basic services, and an environment conducive to social problems (PSA & UNICEF, 2015). This has direct ramifications for children's education with 1.46 million primary school aged children not attending school, among the highest number of any country in the world (PSA & UNICEF, 2015).

IMPACT OF STRUCTURAL CONDITIONS ON CHILDREN

There is clear evidence that a vast number of children in the Philippines face a multitude of difficulties relating to poverty and inequality, which can impact their safety and well-being. In these circumstances, children and families have fewer resources and capacities to cope with risks and fewer social protections (Gabel, 2012; Myers & Bourdillon, 2012a; Pells, 2012). Childhood poverty and long-term stressful experiences can have a lifelong impact on children's social, emotional, physical, and neurological development, also leaving children vulnerable to exploitation and maltreatment (Gabel, 2012). Lachman and colleagues (2002) describe the impact of inequality on families as "extra-familial structural abuse," a pervasive threat for children in the global south that is a result of international structures such as poverty, inequality, and global debt, the outcomes of which negate many efforts to reduce child maltreatment.

Family life is characterized by insecurity and poverty for many. Indicators of severe disadvantage beyond income and inequality provide details of child deprivation and the lived experience of children living in poverty in the Philippines, with many deprivations overlapping. A comprehensive report jointly authored by the Philippine Statistics Authority (PSA) and the United Nations Children's Emergency Fund (UNICEF) details multiple indicators of child poverty in the Philippines (PSA & UNICEF, 2015). Using 2009 data, the PSA and UNICEF (2015) detail that approximately 13.4 million (36%) children below the age of 18 were determined "income poor," with these families unable to meet the basic needs of children and had an income less than the predetermined poverty threshold of US$355 per person. The incidence of poverty among children is higher in rural areas, with three in four children "income poor," and 5.9 million children living below the "food poverty line," while one in five children between the age of zero and five is underweight for their age (PSA & UNICEF, 2015). These are clear threats to children's well-being that can impact children's development, and leave them vulnerable to maltreatment, exploitation, and other dangers.

Core Risks to Children and Young People in the Philippines: Maltreatment and Exploitation

The Nature and Incidence of Child Maltreatment in the Philippines

While the Philippine Department of Justice states that increasing numbers of Filipino children are victims of various forms of abuse, exploitation and violence (DOJ, 2012), there is an absence of reliable data on child maltreatment in the Philippines (Madrid et al., 2013), particularly recent official data (DOJ, 2012). The Department of Social

Welfare and Development (DSWD) managed a total of 7,182 child abuse cases in 2007, the most recent officially published figure (DOJ, 2012), a figure likely to reflect just a fraction of cases that meet the Philippines' legislative definition of child maltreatment. The Department of Justice estimates four to six million children are without parental care or at risk of losing parental care, between 60,000 and 100,000 children are prostituted, and a quarter of a million are either living or working on the streets (DOJ, 2012). However, a systematic review of peer-reviewed research on child maltreatment and policy responses in the Philippines indicates varying levels of robust evidence of child maltreatment (Roche, 2017).

Emotional and psychological abuse is the most common form of maltreatment in the Philippines (Ramiro et al., 2010). This is most related to children's exposure to family violence which can impact on the psychosocial well-being of children. In the Philippines, domestic and family violence is widespread (Jeyaseelan et al., 2004) and a major concern (Sarmiento et al., 2017). For example, Mandal and Hindin (2013) found that as children, 44% of females and 47% of males in the Philippines had witnessed physical violence between their parents. Hassan and colleagues (2004) identified that intimate partner violence was experienced by 21.2% of participants in a Filipino community (Hassan et al., 2004). Having an impact on children in the home, Ansara and Hindin (2009) found that nearly 26% of women in their study had either perpetrated or experienced a physically aggressive act with their partner in the last year, while more generally, Ramiro and colleagues (2010) found that psychological and emotional abuse is high in the Philippines, experienced by 22.8% of children. Mandal and Hindin (2015) also identify the intergenerational transmission of family violence in the Philippines, suggesting the culturally entrenched nature of these practices.

Research on the physical abuse of children in the Philippines varies in its findings. While Ramiro and colleagues (2010) found physical abuse in only 1.3% of their sample, as noted above, research has identified higher rates of family violence. Children's exposure to family violence is now accepted as a form of emotional and psychological abuse in research and policy (Australian Institute of Family Studies, 2015). Fehringer and Hindin (2009) found prevalence of partner violence perpetration was 55.8% for female and 25.1% for male participants, and that approximately half of participants witnessed their parents or caretakers physically hurt one another in their childhood. In their study, "pushing, grabbing or shoving," "throwing objects," and "hitting" were the most common forms of physical violence (Fehringer & Hindin, 2009). In a sample of Filipino mothers, 21.2% had experienced physical intimate partner violence across their lifetime, most commonly "slapping" and "hitting" (Hassan et al., 2004).

Studies identify high rates of physical abuse relating to punishment and discipline. Sanapo and Nakamura (2011) found physical punishment among 49.7% of their sample of sixth-grade participants, and Runyan and colleagues (2010) discovered that 83% of their sample experienced high levels of "moderate" physical discipline, and 9.9% high levels of "harsh" discipline. Sarmiento and colleagues (2017) reveal that four out of five young Filipino adults experienced minor physical violence during childhood, and one in four severe physical violence. In a large survey of children and young people, the Council for the Welfare of Children (CWC) and UNICEF (2016) identified 66.3% had experienced physical violence during childhood, most commonly relating to corporal punishment in the home. Corporal punishment remains highly tolerated and an accepted cultural practice in the Philippines (DOJ, 2012; Save the Children, 2008), and current law allows parents to discipline children for character formation and obedience (Daly et al., 2015; Sarmiento et al., 2017).

The neglect of children is widespread in the Philippines (Ramiro et al., 2010; Lansford et al., 2015). Ramiro and colleagues (2010) reveal that 22.5% of a general population sample in the Philippines had experiences of physical neglect as children. However, this has much to do with high levels of material deprivation, such as limited access to food, clean water, and medical care, as well as experiences of child labor and a lack of education, which are all typical measures of neglect.

There is limited research that has examined the extent and characteristics of sexual abuse in the Philippines. However, Ramiro and colleagues' (2010) study found that 6% of girls and 4.5% of boys under the age of 18 had experienced sexual abuse. Using broader definitions, the CWC and UNICEF (2016) found in their sample that 17.1% of children aged between 13 and 18 had experienced sexual violence. This is an area that requires significantly more research.

Other Risks to Children in the Philippines

Children in the Philippines also face serious risks to their safety resulting from wide-ranging concerns, including child labor, commercial sexual exploitation, and extra-judicial killings, as well as natural disasters and armed conflict (Daly et al., 2015; Mapp & Gabel, 2017). A 2011 survey found that 3.2 million children aged 5 to 17 were engaged in child labor, half of whom work in "hazardous" work environments (PSA & UNICEF, 2015, p. 72). In total, 7.5% of 5–14-year-olds work in the Philippines (US Department of Labor, 2016). Poverty is a crucial element of child labor in the Philippines, with families more likely to turn to child labor earnings when in financial crisis (UNICEF, 2016). Poverty and family breakdown also force children into living on the street, a group estimated to number approximately 1.5 million (Njord et al., 2010).

Children in the Philippines are exposed to high levels of conflict and natural disasters. A recent example includes Typhoon Haiyan, which hit the Visayan Islands in 2013 and killed or left missing more than 7,000 people (UNICEF, 2016). Threats to children in disaster and conflict contexts often involve separation from family and parents, displacement, exposure to violence and abuse, and lack of basic services and supports (UNICEF, 2016). Additionally, conflict in the Mindanao region between the government and Islamic separatists, claimed over 120,000 lives up until 2012 (UNICEF, 2016), and continues to have a significant impact on civilians including children (Economist, 2017). The CWC and UNICEF (2016) found that 2.6% of their research participants had been displaced by war, ethnic conflict, or crime.

Child trafficking, and the commercial sexual exploitation of children via prostitution or child pornography is a growing phenomenon in the Philippines (DOJ, 2012). The Department of Justice (2012) estimates that there are between 60,000 and 100,000 children involved in prostitution; most are girls aged between 13 and 18 years old. Online child sexual exploitation has increased significantly in scale, relying on ongoing poverty and the advancements in, and increased access to, information and communications technology (Terre Des Hommes, 2016). A report by international non-government organization Terre Des Hommes (2016) estimates that tens of thousands of children are victims of online child sexual exploitation, often in the form of webcam child sex tourism, and that these numbers are increasing rapidly, despite updated legislation such as the anti-trafficking in Persons Act, Cybercrime Prevention Act, and the Anti-Child Pornography Law (Terre Des Hommes, 2016). This phenomenon is yet is be investigated in-depth, although recent ethnographic work provides important insights into victim and community perceptions and the social circumstances in which online sexual exploitation and abuse occur in Manila, noting high levels of victimization among teenage girls, strong financial motivations, and various social and psychological harms (Ramiro et al., 2019).

The Duterte government's (2016–2022) violent campaign to reduce illicit drug use has posed significant threats to children and their well-being, and provides important insights into the rule of law and capacities of the criminal justice system (Cousins, 2016). President Duterte's administration endorsed members of the public, vigilantes as well as police to murder drug users and dealers, outside of the criminal justice system (Teehankee, 2016; Thompson, 2016), even providing financial rewards to police for every person killed (Coronel, 2017). This has resulted in over 12,000 deaths so far (Human Rights Watch, 2018) and left many children orphaned or killed, including the high profile case of a 17-year-old school boy who was murdered in cold blood by police (De Castro & Mogato, 2017).

Clearly children in the Philippines navigate numerous threats to their safety and well-being in a complex setting involving a unique combination of structural, social, and environmental factors. Poverty and inequality leave children and families vulnerable to abuse and neglect within cultural and social settings in which abuse and neglect, in their multiple forms, occur, requiring a range of government and social policy responses.

Governance and Social Policy in the Philippines

The Social Policy Context of the Philippines

The family unit takes primary responsibility for its own welfare, with the state playing a secondary role in providing social assistance in relation to education, healthcare, housing, and social assistance (Yu, 2013). Numerous national and international non-government organizations also provide welfare programs, in part a legacy of the international goodwill and aid following the fall of the Marcos dictatorship (Yu, 2013). Since the 1980s, NGOs have worked to privilege the role of civil society, and in effect, minimize the role of the state in providing social welfare (Yu, 2013). International NGOs provide much support for the health care, education, and basic needs of children and families, and financial agencies such as the World Bank and the Asian Development Bank provide programs to address poverty (Yu, 2013).

Characteristics of welfare provision are evolving since the national government's introduction of a near universal conditional cash transfer program called *Pantawid Pamilyang Pilipino Program* (Building Bridges for the Filipino Family Program) (Kim & Yoo, 2015). Progressively introduced from 2007, it acts as a financial safety net for poor families and was estimated to cover 21% of the poor population in 2016 (Asian Development Bank, 2015). The program was designed with technical and financial support from the World Bank, the Asian Development Bank, and the Australian Agency for International Development (Kim & Yoo, 2015). It distributes money to poor families (Rawlings & Rubio, 2005), and has conditional behavioral requirements built into it that develop human capital, health, and education outcomes through a "social contract" in which participants must have their children attend school, get immunized and receive health checks in exchange for financial assistance (Kim & Yoo, 2015). In 2017, nearly 4.4 million households participated in Pantawid (Department of Social Welfare and Development, 2015; House of Representatives, 2017), taking up approximately 90% of the social welfare budget of the DSWD (Kim & Yoo, 2015). However, there is growing uncertainty as to how the program will continue to be financed after the World Bank and the Asian Development Bank cease funding loans to support the program after 2019 and 2022 respectively (Pasion, 2017).

Decentralized Governance

Government social policy initiatives and programs, including those relating to child protection, are strongly impacted by the decentralization of government structures and policies in the Philippines. Decentralization has seen the national government to devolve spending, taxation and borrowing powers to various levels of local government (Daly et al., 2015), brought about by the enactment of the Local Government Code in 1991, which articulates areas of responsibility for local governments, including health and social services, and education (UNICEF, 2016).

Seventeen regions make up the decentralized governance of the Philippines, and receive 17% of total government expenditure playing a central role in delivering basic services such as health, education and housing (UNICEF, 2016). Primary national administrative divisions are divided into 79 provinces, 115 cities, 1499 municipalities, and more than 42,000 *barangays* (Daly et al., 2015; UNICEF, 2016). *Barangays* are the smallest administrative division of government in the Philippines. Akin to villages, each *barangay* is led by an elected council and receives direct funding from local government units (a widely used term in the Philippines that denotes the various levels of non-national government) but retains a significant amount of their own autonomy (UNICEF, 2016). *Barangays* are an important mechanism of governance, having a major impact on people's lives, and are guided in part by the national government who provide technical assistance and set standards (Daly et al., 2015), while local government delivers all health and social welfare programs, including funding at a *barangay* level (Daly et al., 2015). The capacities and resources of regions, provinces, municipalities, and *barangays* vary significantly due to high levels of resource and governance disparity between local government units (Daly et al., 2015).

Dominant Ideologies in Philippine Social Policy

A significant welfare policy orientation of the Philippines relates to the "productivist" nature of the Philippine welfare state. Consecutive governments have prioritized accelerating the productive elements of society and promoting economic goals, and left social policy underdeveloped and subordinate to economic growth (Holliday, 2000; Choi, 2012). The Asian Development Bank's "social protection index," a measure of social protection policies that reduce poverty, finds the Philippines comparatively low on social assistance (Asian Development Bank, 2013), indicating low de-commodification, the standard of living that is achieved by citizens outside of market-based activity (Esping-Andersen, 1990). At the same time, high economic growth objectives are supported by government, exemplified by labor exportation and the centrality of remittances from migrant workers to the Filipino economy (Asis, 2015). Within this system, welfare provision relies on social rights flowing from high economic growth (Choi, 2012).

Understandings of welfare in the Philippines tacitly accept that inequality and disadvantage are a fixture of Philippine society, while social policy places large amounts of responsibility on individuals for their own welfare, a result of four centuries of colonial influence, and the view that hierarchical social order and inequality is inevitable, with welfare conceptualized as minimalist and functionalist (Yu, 2006, 2013). Understandings of welfare throughout Spanish colonial intervention centered on Catholic views of fatalism, the virtues of suffering, and poverty as a punishment for sin, while American colonial involvement propagated the view that social problems originated in individuals' lack of education, regressive values, and a lack of modern thinking and practices (Yu, 2006). These colonial interventions frequently saw welfare provided under the auspices of religious orders, rather than government, in the form of institutions such as hospitals, orphanages, and asylums (Yu, 2006).

These orientations to welfare and social policy influence child protection policy and are compounded by the low social protection conditions across the Philippines in which the state takes limited responsibility for providing social services, or protecting children from unequal life outcomes that are a result of their social position. The Philippines mainly relies on the free market, and views employment rather than assistance from government as the desired assistance, with families or NGOs providing crisis assistance. This has implications for the official responses to child maltreatment, the state's relationship and role with children and their families, and the child protection system that it engenders.

Conceptualizing Child Protection Systems in the Global South

System understandings of child protection have emerged as the most accepted conceptual approach to improving child protection in the global south (Connolly et al., 2014). They focus on combining policy, programs, and activities that aim to prevent, respond, and resolve the abuse, neglect, exploitation, and violence experienced by children into a coherent structure (Pells, 2012; Wessells et al., 2012). Child protection systems in the global south need to be conceptualized as distinct to those in high-income contexts, as they typically take a different form, rely on different actors, and need to be responsive to a greater diversity of risks to children and more diverse population groups (Connolly et al., 2014). Low-income countries frequently have limited structures to implement strategies and approaches to protect children (Connolly et al., 2014), and often political and economic circumstances negate attempts to alleviate the difficult situations of children through policy intervention, in circumstances where poverty significantly impacts on the likelihood of child maltreatment (Myers & Bourdillon, 2012a). These efforts are frequently beset by a disconnect between formal child protection systems and local child protection practices, relating to problems of access, as well as social and cultural norms, and general perceptions of formal systems (Wessells et al., 2012). For these reasons, the structure of child protection systems in the global south vary, and often focus on integrating the protective potential of community groups and families, and deploy a system that is more balanced between actors than typically "top-down" approaches in the global north.

It is generally considered that the key components of a child protection "system" include a statutory child protection agency, a process to report suspected cases of child abuse and neglect, and a system that provides alternate care for children at high risk (Bromfield & Higgins, 2005). To achieve these functions, a system can incorporate informal actors such as children, families, communities, and leaders, as well as formal actors such as state and multinational actors, government social welfare workers, police, and magistrates (Wulcyn et al., 2009; Wessells, 2015). These actors are supported by laws, policies, and regulations that traverse welfare, education, health, and justice sectors, and combine into a larger structure (UNICEF, 2016; Jenkins et al., 2017).

Focusing on developing contexts, Wessells (2015) highlights the importance of strengthening and balancing child protection systems across three conceptual domains; "top-down," "middle-out" and "bottom-up." "Top-down" approaches include the national government providing laws, policies, and capacities relating to child protection, while "middle-out" approaches comprise local government working to embed child protection agendas in regional functions of government and power (Wessells, 2015). "Bottom-up" approaches involve community actions at the community level, involving identifying and building on community strengths and actors, as well as community–government collaboration (Wessels, 2015). Community-based child protection mechanisms appear in contexts of limited capacity for formal protection, and are commonly comprised of local level groups or processes that respond to or prevent child maltreatment (Wessells et al., 2012; Wessells, 2015). Their strength within child protection systems is that they are located where children and families live, and in the contexts in which children are exposed to risks. This chapter now describes and evaluates the Philippines' child protection system against these three areas of child protection activity. Across each domain we describe the major actors and functions of the child protection system, as well as provide critique, highlighting key questions over the coverage and funding of child protection programs and activities, as well as the systems' coherence and effectiveness.

Approaches to Child Protection in the Philippines: Top-down, Middle-out and Bottom-up

Top-down Approaches to Child Protection: Definitions, Legislation, and Government Agencies

A systemic "top-down" approach to child protection incorporates national legislation, policies, and capacities relating to preventing child maltreatment (Wessells, 2015). The Philippines exhibits a range of "top-down" approaches to protecting children. A clear focus relates to the recognition of children's rights. The Philippines ratified the UN Convention on the Rights of the Child in 1990, and later ratified two optional protocols pertaining to the involvement of children in armed conflict, and the sale of children (DOJ, 2012). Domestically, the basic premise of the rights of children was first established in the "Child and Youth Welfare Code" (Presidential Decree 603) of 1974, which codifies laws on the rights of children and articulates a number of rights of the child, as well as promoting their well-being and development (The LawPhil Project, 2018b).

Legislation and policy relies on the Philippines' definition of child maltreatment. The definition largely mirrors the World Health Organization's (WHO) understanding of child maltreatment. The WHO articulates four distinct classifications of child maltreatment: physical abuse, sexual abuse, emotional and psychological abuse and neglect (WHO, 2006, p. 10). The Republic Act (No 7610), titled the "Special protection of children against abuse, exploitation and discrimination act", understands child abuse as "the infliction of physical or psychological injury, cruelty to, or neglect, sexual abuse or exploitation of a child" (Saplala, 2007, p. 88). The same legislation defines children as "persons below 18 years old or those over but are unable to take care of themselves from abuse, neglect, cruelty, exploitation or discrimination because of physical or mental disability or condition" (CWC, 2000, p. 11). This suggests that children are viewed as vulnerable, and childhood a period of incompetence in which special protection and adult intervention is required (Bessell, 2009).

To operationalize this definition, the Philippines has a strong legal basis for the protection of children. The 1992 "Special Protection of Children Against Abuse, Exploitation and Discrimination Act" (RA 7610) articulates the Philippines' legislative response to child abuse and neglect. It declares that it is the:

> policy of the State to provide special protection to children from all forms of abuse, neglect, cruelty, exploitation and discrimination and other conditions, prejudicial to their development; provide sanctions for their commission and carry out a program for prevention and deterrence of and crisis intervention in situations of child abuse, exploitation and discrimination. (LawPhil Project, 2018a, Article 1, section 2)

This legislation clearly identifies the state's central role in child protection activities and interventions, based on criteria relating to children's development as well as child maltreatment. Further, article one of this act articulates the state's responsibility to protect and rehabilitate children in response to child maltreatment.

> The State shall intervene on behalf of the child when the parent, guardian, teacher or person having care or custody of the child fails or is unable to protect the child against abuse, exploitation and discrimination. (LawPhil Project, 2018a, Article 1, section 2)

Article 2 of the same legislation commits to responding to child maltreatment through providing prevention, deterrence and crisis intervention (LawPhil Project, 2018a, Article 2, section 4). Other legislation relating to child protection, passed between 2003 and 2009 pertain to people-trafficking, child labor, violence against women and children, and anti-pornography acts (CWC, 2011; DOJ, 2012), amounting to a range of robust and well-defined legislation seeking to protect children from a range of potential maltreatment. In 2022, the Philippines raised the age of sexual consent from 12 to 16 years of age. Previously, the Philippines had one of the lowest ages of sexual consent internationally (Child Wise, 2009), which impacted on the protection of children from abuse, and had major social and health consequences (Philippine Commission on Women, 2019).

National Government Agencies Involved in the Protection of Children

A cluster of national government agencies provide oversight for a range of child protection related functions that cascade into regional and provincial contexts. The Council for the Welfare of Children (CWC) operates as the principal agency for children's issues and policy in the Philippines, observing children's rights and coordinating policy for children in the Philippines (CWC, 2016). Its role is to coordinate, implement, and enforce all laws relating to the promotion of child and youth welfare, develop policies and guidelines, and oversee the monitoring of formal child protection mechanisms (UNICEF, 2016). Despite this role, its capacity to achieve these goals is heavily questioned, with limited funding, few policy and research publications, and a low national profile (Yangco, 2010; UNICEF, 2016). In 2018, the CWC is expected to receive an annual budget of 39.9 million Philippine pesos (approximately US$800,000) (House of Representatives, 2017).

The Department of Social Welfare and Development is the primary welfare agency of the national government. It sets standards and regulations, accredits and guides organizations and institutions involved in social welfare activities, and monitors the performance of organizations (Save the Children, 2011; Department of Social Welfare and Development, 2015). Both government and non-government agencies provide child protection responses in the Philippines. The DSWD also both provides and regulates residential care, as well as domestic and international adoption (PSA & UNICEF, 2015).

A host of committees and governance groups provide direction and support to child protection efforts, although their level of influence is unclear. The Committee for the Special Protection of Children is responsible for investigating and prosecuting child maltreatment related cases, as well as receiving reports from its member agencies relating to child protection issues, and promoting the legal protection of children more broadly (Save the Children, 2011; DOJ, 2012, 2017). The Committee also recently designed a protocol for the case management of victims of child maltreatment for use across multiple welfare contexts, advising on reporting and case management procedures (DOJ, 2013). The committee is co-chaired by representatives from DSWD and has multiple members across various government departments (DOJ, 2017).

Other inter-agency councils aim to respond to various child maltreatment related issues in the country that concern children and attempt to connect government with non-government actors. The National Child Labor Committee advocates for reductions in child labor. There is also an Inter-Agency Council on Violence Against Women and Children (Philippine Commission on Women, 2017), while others relate to juvenile justice, child pornography, and human trafficking. These committees reflect the governance mechanisms of child protection policy and programs in the Philippines and its top-down mechanisms for protecting children.

National Policy Documents Relating to Child Protection
Government agencies have produced policy documents that describe policy approaches and ambitions relating to children's welfare, development and protection. The most central child protection document is produced by the Committee for the Special Protection of Children, titled "The Comprehensive Programme on Child Protection 2012-2016" (CPCP) (DOJ, 2012). It identifies key goals to improve child protection nationally, including establishing a comprehensive data base of child protection data, ensuring all child protection related laws are enforced, and making sure child protection systems are functioning (DOJ, 2012). Other policy ambitions include improving services and creating cultures of child protection through major institutions such as families, schools, and government (DOJ, 2012).

Additional policy documents authored by the Council for the Welfare of Children provide insights into national government policy agendas relating to child protection, although they provide limited detail or analysis of current or previous policy programs, and the ways in which these policy objectives might be achieved (CWC, 2000, 2005, 2010, 2011). They detail explicit rights-based strategies to child welfare and child protection policy, which are closely aligned to international rights and development agendas (Roche, 2019). For example, the "Second National Plan of Action for Children 2011-2016" expresses the commitment of the Philippines to the UNCRC and "progressive realization of the rights of Filipino children" as an objective (CWC, 2011, p. 3). Similarly, "Child 21," a frequently cited policy document authored by the CWC to assist with implementation of the UNCRC, aims to "synchronize family, community, and national efforts towards the full realization of the rights of children by year 2025" (CWC, 2000, p. 4).

The CPCP articulates the need for system strengthening via national responses and engagement by government and non-government organizations, communities, and faith-based organizations (DOJ, 2012). It also highlights the role of national government actors in enforcing child protection related laws, ensuring child protection structures and services are functioning, and child protection cultures are improved (DOJ, 2012). Despite articulating these policy objectives, these national policy documents lack information relating to the implementation and direct funding of child protection programs and measures, and their monitoring and evaluation, and as a government body lack the capacity to promote and enforce the policies they suggest in a meaningful way (Roche, 2019).

"Middle-out" Approaches: Localized Governance and Child Protection Mechanisms

Situated between national and community level approaches to child protection, "middle-out" methods and structures in a child protection system comprise actors such as local government and non-government organizations who work to embed child protection agendas in regional functions of government and power (Wessells, 2015). These approaches to child protection are widespread in the Philippines, largely due to the high levels of local government power and a range of non-governmental efforts to protect children.

Decentralization of Government Responsibility of Child Protection

Local governments have major regulatory powers and the responsibility for the welfare of their citizens, putting an onus on regions, provinces, municipalities, and *barangays* to develop their own primary programs and processes to meet child protection goals (UNICEF, 2016). Recent national policy documents continue to make strong recommendations to utilize local government as the central point for all interventions for children, while guided by higher levels of government (CWC, 2010, p. 35). This has merit due to the numerous social issues experienced in communities, the limited reach of the national government into communities, and the difficult geographical nature of the Philippines, which makes service delivery difficult—all problems requiring local and contextualized responses (UNICEF, 2016). This means that all levels of government and civil society are requested to assist in resolving social issues and addressing child protection issues, and designing children's programs and projects, and child-friendly policies.

Government Child Protection Bodies and Functions

There are a range of localized committees and councils charged with the protection of children which represent the major responsible governing bodies for child protection. The CWC coordinates Regional Sub-Committees for the Welfare of Children, whose role is to translate the CWC's policy directives in regions and assist Local Councils for the Protection of Children (LCPC) in their efforts on child protection (DOJ, 2012; UNICEF, 2016). Legislation (Article 87 of PD 603) mandates that all local councils have an operating LCPC (CWC, 2010). The role of LCPCs is to support the implementation of national policies intended to protect children, as well as develop and integrate policies, programs, and projects for children and make their jurisdictions "child-friendly" (CWC, 2010). While these councils are a crucial component of government efforts in the implementation of these national policy directions, Madrid and colleagues (2013) found that in 2013 there was no official data on how many of these LCPCs were functional, while UNICEF (2016) identified that LCPCs are functional in 36% of provinces, 56% of cities, 44% of municipalities, and 34% of *barangays*. This is due to under-resourcing, unclear or overlapping responsibilities, and the limited capacity and expertise of staff (UNICEF, 2016). LCPCs also support and fund Barangay Councils for the Protection of Children (BCPC), which act as community-level responders to child protection issues and are provided with funding and technical assistance (DOJ, 2012; UNICEF, 2016).

Nationally, the Department of Social Welfare and Development delivers programs and services for children (Sarmiento et al., 2017). Although the coverage of these programs is not published, DSWD offices can be found in communities across the country. Some of the DSWD programs relating to child abuse cases include case management, family violence prevention, child and family counseling services, and child protective behavior programs (Yangco, 2010). Child protection actors based at the DSWD and in other health and local government roles are undergoing training in a "protocol for case management of child victims of abuse, neglect and exploitation" (UNICEF, 2016). This protocol instructs child protection actors to report incidents and disclosures to the relevant authority, and support subsequent processes involving social workers and police (UNICEF, 2016). The DSWD also has a 24-hour crisis intervention program called "Assistance to Individuals and Families in Crisis Situations (AICS)" in which social workers can assess and recommend cash assistance to families in response to a crisis up to 25,000 pesos (US$500) (DSWD, 2018). Filling the gaps of the work of the DSWD are numerous non-government organizations.

Non-government Organizations and Child Protection

The involvement of civil society and non-government actors in child protection activities is encouraged by all levels of government (DOJ, 2012). Hundreds of NGOs are accredited by the DSWD and provide a range of welfare programs relating to children's welfare and their families. Organizations are operated by both domestic and international non-government organizations, and are often faith-based representing a variety of Christian denominations. The most recent information provided by the DSWD (2016) reveals 915 private social welfare agencies licensed by the DSWD. Many of the programs offered by NGOs focus on child and family welfare, as well as more specific services relating to mental health, drug rehabilitation, youth offending, disability, and out-of-home care for children. Services include the provision of basic needs like shelter, food, clothes, education programs, referrals, and case management services, as well as counseling (Madrid et al., 2013).

Organizations also offer preventative programs that assist in reducing the likelihood of child maltreatment or preventing it entirely. Examples of these include programs on responsible parenting, maternal and neonatal health, women's health, breastfeeding and immunization programs, and feeding programs (Madrid et al., 2013). Madrid and colleagues (2013) identified child protection related activities across three *barangays*, finding 20 different programs across early childhood education, parent effectiveness, and child development seminars.

The most active provider of child protection services and interventions is the Child Protection Network, a non-government organization that has established 113 Women and Children Protection Units (WCPUs) across 57 provinces of the Philippines, many of which are based in Department of Health-run hospitals (Child Protection Network, 2021). Funded by government, donors, and trustees, these units provide a raft of multidisciplinary services including medical, forensic, social, and legal, as well as specific violence against women services (Child Protection Network, 2018). The social services include case management and risk and safety assessments, as well as therapeutic interventions and classes for children and their families (Child Protection Network, 2018). In 2016, WCPUs handled nearly 8,000 cases (Child Protection Network, 2016). The organization also provides professional development for workers exposed to child protection issues, such as trained medical specialists on child protection, the National Bureau of Investigation and the Philippine National Police (Child Protection Network, 2018). Most referrals to WCPUs come from law enforcement, followed by walk-ins, then hospitals and social workers, while there are low referrals from schools and teachers (Child Protection Network, 2016).

While WCPUs are the pre-eminent service for children who have experienced maltreatment, and provide important services and child protection infrastructure, they are not able to cover the vast number of children who experience abuse and neglect, with 24 of 81 provinces in the Philippines having no WCPU (Child Protection Network, 2021;

End Violence Against Children, 2021). Researchers have also identified that WCPUs often operate in isolation in addressing cases of abuse, provide a disjointed service, and their programs can be poorly implemented at local levels (Terol, 2009; Ramiro et al., 2010). Recent research on child protection in a regional area of the Philippines found WCPUs with limited staffing capacity, inadequate resources, and poor community reach and uptake which hamper their capacity to provide adequate child protection interventions (Roche, 2020b).

Out-of-home Care

A primary government and non-government programmatic response for victims of child abandonment, neglect, and abuse is through out-of-home care, organized by both government and non-government welfare organizations (Save the Children, 2011). While up-to-date statistics are not provided, in 2010, DSWD placed a total of 1,339 children in alternative forms of care including adoption, foster care and legal guardianship (DOJ, 2012), while the use of residential care (institutional care provided in a non-family group setting) is widespread (Save the Children, 2011; DSWD, 2015, 2016). In 2016 there were 177 NGOs accredited by the DSWD operating a total of 197 residential care facilities for children and young people (DSWD, 2016). The DSWD directly operates 46 residential care facilities for children who are victims of maltreatment, or are experiencing homelessness or mental illness (DSWD, 2016). These residential care facilities vary in capacity, from four to 490 children (DSWD, 2016). A recent DSWD annual report details 5,819 children in the residential care facilities run directly by DSWD; however, it provides limited detail of the numbers nor arrangements of children in the 197 DSWD-licensed residential care facilities (DSWD, 2015). This indicates a high, but unknown number of children in residential care settings operated by non-government organizations.

The reason for young people to be placed in residential care is not necessarily related to abuse and neglect, but also for reasons relating to economic circumstances, and the opportunity that residential care can provide children and families in the form of economic support or secure schooling (Roche, 2020a). There is a distinct lack of research into the experiences of children living in out-of-home care in the Philippines, the conditions and practices of these settings, the extent of children's safety, and children's transition into independent adulthood (Roche, 2017).

Bottom-up Approaches: Community-based Child Protection

"Bottom-up" approaches involve community actions at the grass roots level that utilize community actors and their strengths, and can also employ community-government collaboration (Wessels, 2015). In contexts such as the Philippines, community-based child protection mechanisms also play an important role in responding to and preventing child maltreatment (Wessells, 2015). A significant, yet under-utilized, "bottom-up" approach to child protection in the Philippines involves Barangay Council's for the Protection of

Children (BCPC). The role of BCPCs is to address issues of child maltreatment at a grass-roots level, and where functioning, offer initial responses to issues of child protection (End Child Prostitution, Child Pornography and Trafficking of Children for Sexual Purposes International [ECPAT], 2006; Save the Children, 2011; Madrid et al., 2013).

BCPCs offer an initial response to issues of child protection in local communities, assisting abandoned, maltreated, and abused children, and organizing their safety (ECPAT, 2006; Save the Children, 2011). To achieve this, *barangays* attempt to resolve child protection concerns, particularly through utilizing their strong and direct relationships with their communities (UNICEF, 2016). The assistance of BCPCs is sometimes preferred by families over DSWD workers or NGOs due to limited trust in official responses to child maltreatment, and concern about sensitivity, timeliness, and the judicial process, and the capacity to resolve child abuse and neglect within *barangays* (UNICEF, 2016). In some circumstances, children sit on BCPCs, and provide support and advice in cases of maltreated children (Bessell, 2009).

However, BCPCs remain largely unfunded, informal, and untrained initiatives, and can often be ineffective in preventing or responding to child maltreatment. This is due to poor training and organization, limited funding, and inadequate technical support and monitoring (DOJ, 2012). There are poor practices in *barangays* as well. UNICEF (2016) provides the example of a girl who was raped, and then required to marry the offender, for the family to save face, demonstrating the need for monitoring, training, clear guidelines, and reporting mechanisms for BCPCs.

Family as the Primary Protector of Children

Family is positioned as the primary protector of children, holding significant responsibilities and duties for children's welfare both in Filipino sociocultural relations, as well as in national policy documents relating to children's welfare. The Special Committee for the Protection of Children (SCPC) highlights the importance of family ties and strong family relationships in the prevention of children's abuse and neglect, and emphasizes the responsibility families have in ensuring children's welfare (DOJ, 2006). Further, the SCPC (DOJ, 2006, p. 49) identifies that the challenge for child protection approaches is "to build and strengthen family stability, particularly among the poor and disadvantaged families." These documents draw attention to overarching views of the responsibility and centrality of families to protect children from maltreatment, which equates with the view of the family unit bearing responsibility for its own welfare (Yu, 2013).

National government policy documents describe an "ecological" view of children, situating children at the center of a society of multiple actors and systems that influence their well-being, rights, and protection (CWC, 2000, p. 43, 2010, p. 33). This view holds family as the most central actor relevant to children's welfare, followed by the *barangay*, and then the institutional and programmatic influences on a child's life, such as social services, schools, or religious communities (CWC, 2010).

Community-level Reporting Processes

The reporting of child abuse and neglect, as defined in legislation, is mandatory for the head of a hospital or medical clinic, or a doctor or nurse, and they can break the law if they do not do so (DOJ, 2013). Others, such as government workers, such as teachers, government lawyers, police, or *barangay* officials, have a "duty" to report abuse and neglect (DOJ, 2013). Reports of child abuse, neglect, or exploitation are typically received by a DSWD official or the Philippine National Police, but can also be received by a range of agencies including the National Bureau of Investigation, or a member of a Barangay Council for the Protection of Children (Madrid, 2009; DOJ, 2013). A telephone hotline to report child maltreatment, titled "Bantay Bata 163," is available in many places across the country, and is operated by the charity arm of a major media company in the Philippines (ABS-CBN, 2018). After the receipt of a report, investigations are conducted by the DWSD, who also have protective custody authority if deemed necessary (Madrid, 2009; DOJ, 2013).

Challenges for Child Protection in the Philippines

Coverage and Funding of Programs

Despite the range of child protection-related activities across the three levels, research has identified major failings in their coverage. Madrid and colleagues (2013) reveal that government provided child protection services, interventions and laws are barely funded or provided, identifying 31 laws and 17 pending bills in Congress relating to child protection that have not received funding (Madrid et al., 2013). In a survey of community stakeholders relating to children's welfare, the CWC and UNICEF (2016) found that many local government units have either no Barangay Council for the Protection of Children, or if present, are non-functional. The operation of LCPCs is impacted on by local government unit executives and the availability of funds (CWC & UNICEF, 2016). Other analysis of the child protection activities of three local government units found that coverage of social and health services was low and that there were limited responses to child maltreatment, and minimal child protection programs or activities, particularly in regional areas (Madrid et al., 2013; CWC & UNICEF, 2016). In one study, of those who were aware of available services, only 37% of males, and 25% of females utilized a child protection unit or woman and child protection unit in their province or region (CWC & UNICEF, 2016).

Levels of national government funding to child protection efforts are unclear. There is no specific budget allocated to child protection or the prevention of child maltreatment in the health, education, and social welfare areas of government, leaving the financing of distinct programs relating to children's well-being and protection unidentifiable (Madrid et al., 2013). In addition, lower levels of government do not differentiate child protection funding and programs from broader health and welfare budgets (Madrid et al., 2013). The resourcing of local government units varies significantly, and those in poorer areas typically have less resources (UNICEF, 2016). The Asian Development Bank highlights the weak taxing arrangements and low budget transparency as hindering development and government funding in the Philippines (Asian Development Bank, 2014).

As noted previously, BCPCs differ in resources and capabilities across the country, despite mandated to receive funding from local government (Department of the Interior and Local Government, 2012; UNICEF, 2016). They are reliant on local government unit funding and most BCPC workers are volunteers, despite BCPCs being a LGU requirement (UNICEF, 2016). In one of the *barangays* investigated by Madrid and colleagues (2013), it was found that only 1% of the entire *barangay* budget was allocated to a local BCPC, amounting to approximately US$250 per annum. Acknowledging budgetary constraints and inadequate resources for child protection, particularly at the local government level (DOJ, 2012), the Special Committee for the Protection of Children (DOJ, 2006) has suggested financing child protection programs through the private sector, foreign governments, international NGOs, the World Council of Churches, and international philanthropists, among others (DOJ, 2006), and has encouraged the national government to increase funding to child protection and child rights programs (DOJ, 2006).

SYSTEM INCOHERENCE AND BREAKDOWN

Given the low level of funding and limited coverage of child protection efforts, it is unsurprising that the child protection system, as it currently stands, lacks coherence and frequently breaks down. Sarmiento and colleagues (2017) argue that the Philippines lacks the social welfare infrastructure, budgets, expertise, and capacity to provide the required interventions to prevent and respond to child abuse and neglect the way it intends. UNICEF (2016) relates this to a lack of collaboration between and within welfare sectors and a strong disjuncture between national positions on child protection, and the reality of child protection activities and programs at regional, local, and *barangay* levels. Other research finds that child protection programs are not holistic and comprehensive when applied at local levels (Yangco, 2010).

The Committee for the Special Protection of Children identifies an array of failures across the child protection system relating to weak and inconsistent enforcement of laws relating to child protection, non-functional child protection mechanisms at multiple levels, a lack of technical competency, and an unresponsive judicial system (DOJ, 2012). These issues are compounded by a limited capacity to encourage and enforce national policy programs at local government levels (UNICEF, 2016).

At the community level, there are concerns that Barangay Councils for the Protection of Children work outside of the formal child protection system. BCPC councilors have expressed reservations about reporting child maltreatment issues to DSWD, as they determine that it is not always in the best interest of children and their families (UNICEF, 2016). There are also poor understandings of preventing child maltreatment (Madrid et al., 2013), and community misconceptions around the functions and purpose of BCPCs (UNICEF, 2016). The CWC and UNICEF (2016) have also found that children who are victims of various forms of violence rarely disclose, and that families have a low awareness and utilization of child protection services.

Moving Forward: Child Protection System Strengthening

While top-down child protection approaches, including legislation, discourse on children's rights, and national policy are well developed, there remains a significant gap between these visions and the reality of the Philippine child protection system. Despite institutional frameworks, the system struggles to address and respond to the needs of children and families, mostly due to a disconnect between the optimistic intentions of top-down approaches, and the under-resourced and poorly administered reality of both government and non-government supported child protection policy and programs. In addition, community-based child protection mechanisms are ad hoc, and lack the resources and technical skills required. The child protection system highlights the administrative constraints and institutional challenges in implementing welfare policies in the Philippines (Kim & Yoo, 2015).

The systemic characteristics of child protection in the Philippines can be questioned. While understandings of child protection systems are broad, incorporating both formal and informal actors, the extent to which each works with the other is uncertain, as is the level of resources and coverage of the system as a whole. An extensive national child protection system is incongruent with traditions of social policy and welfare in the Philippines that typically resists intervening in the welfare of families in any significant way.

For this reason, bottom-up child protection responses that are enmeshed in community, and fit the physical, social, and economic contexts in which children live, are an important policy consideration (Myers & Bourdillon, 2012b). While basic legal foundations and rights for children's protection are highly important, they are not necessarily the primary structure through which children are protected in developing contexts. Myers and Bourdillon (2012b) argue strongly for a shift from legal and normative standards to community and social relationships to be at the core of approaches to child protection. Through engaging families and communities—the main protectors of children in the Philippines—to build the protective capacity and strengths of the community, child protection responses can be improved (Lachman et al., 2002; Myers & Bourdillon, 2012b).

The challenge is also to connect national policy agendas on child protection and broader social protection to the activities of local governments and community level actors, while at the same time improve accountability and alignment across child protection programs and activities. Setting minimum standards of practice, collecting data, and raising the profile of child protection issues have been identified as ways to improve the system (UNICEF, 2016). In developing contexts such as the Philippines, reducing child maltreatment relies on more than a child protection system, involving significant reductions to the contexts and environments that foster maltreatment. Social services, such as those related to child protection, are frequently only a small element in determining social outcomes (Piachaud, 2015). Child protection approaches need to acknowledge and incorporate understandings of the influence of broader socioeconomic and political structures that influence life chances and outcomes (Pells, 2012). Reducing multidimensional poverty and vulnerability is a crucial part of reducing incidence of child maltreatment (Gabel, 2012). For the Philippines, views and values relating to acceptable social disadvantage must evolve, and the level of state intervention into the welfare of families lives be reassessed, to better protect children.

References

ABS-CBN. (2018). *Bantay bata 163*. Available at: https://corporate.abs-cbn.com/lingkodkapamilya/bantay-bata/about.

Ansara, D. L. and Hindin, M. J. (2009). Perpetration of intimate partner aggression by men and women in the Philippines. *Journal of Interpersonal Violence*, 24(9), 1579–1590.

Asian Development Bank. (2013). *The social protection index: Assessing results for Asia and the Pacific*. Asian Development Bank.

Asian Development Bank. (2014). *ADB to assist review of Philippines' local government code*. Available at: https://www.adb.org/news/adb-assist-review-philippines-local-government-code.

Asian Development Bank. (2015, July). Social protection brief: The social protection support project in the Philippines. *Asian Development Bank Briefs*, no. 38.

Asis, M. M. (2015). "All in the Family": Remittances, gender and public policies in the Philippines. In T. van Naerssen., L. Smith., T. Davids, and M. H. Marchand (Eds.), *Women, gender, remittances and development in the global south* (pp. 1–14). Ashgate.

Asis, M. M. B., Huang, S., and Yeoh, B. S. A. (2004). When the light of the home is abroad: Unskilled female migration and the Filipino family. *Singapore Journal of Tropical Geography*, 25, 198–215.

Australian Institute of Family Studies. (2015). *What is child abuse and neglect?* Available at: https://aifs.gov.au/cfca/publications/what-child-abuse-and-neglect.

Bessell, S. (2009). Children's participation in decision-making in the Philippines: Understanding the attitudes of policy-makers and service providers. *Childhood*, 16(3), 299–316.

Bromfield, L. and Higgins, D. (2005). National comparison of child protection systems. *Child Abuse Prevention Issues*, 22, 1–31.

Chan, R. K. H., Wang, L., and Zinn, J. O. (2014). Social issues and policies in Asia: An overview. In R. K. H, Chan., L. Wang., and J. O. Zinn (Eds.), *Social issues and policies in Asia: Family, ageing and society* (pp. 1–24). Cambridge Scholars Publishing.

Child Protection Network. (2016). Annual report 2016: Protecting the child from many faces of abuse. Available at: http://childprotectionnetwork.org/wp-content/uploads/2013/06/CPN-Annual-Report-2016.pdf.

Child Protection Network. (2018). *Protecting the child from the many faces of abuse: Annual Report 2018*. Available at: https://www.childprotectionnetwork.org/wp-content/uploads/2020/03/Annual_Report_2018_FINAL.pdf.

Child Protection Network. (2021). *Data visualization of 113 women and children protection units and VAWC desk across the Philippines*. Available at: https://www.childprotectionnetwork.org/wcpu-directory/.

Child Wise. (2009). *Mind the gaps: A comparative analysis of ASEAN legal responses to child-sex tourism*. Available at: https://www.ecoi.net/en/file/local/1054488/1002_1248205476_crin.pdf.

Chiu, T. (2013). Reproductive health on hold in the Philippines. *The Lancet*, 381 (9879), 1707.

Choi, Y. J. (2012). End of the era of productivist welfare capitalism? Diverging welfare regimes in East Asia. *Asian Journal of Social Science*, 40, 275–294.

Connolly, M., Katz, I., Shlonsky, A., and Bromfield, L. (2014). Towards a typology for child protection systems. Save the Children and UNICEF.

Coronel, S. S. (2017). Murder as enterprise: Police profiteering in Duterte's war on drugs. In N. Curato (Eds.), *A Duterte reader: Critical essays on Rodrigo Duterte's early presidency* (pp. 167–198). Bughaw.

Cousins, S. (2016). Five thousand dead and counting: the Philippines' bloody war on drugs. *British Medical Journal*, 355, 1–2.

Curato, N. (2015). Deliberative capacity as an indicator of democratic quality: The case of the Philippines. *International Political Science Review*, 36(1), 99–116.

Curato, N. (2017). Flirting with authoritarian fantasies? Rodrigo Duterte and the new terms of Philippine populism. *Journal of Contemporary Asia*, 47(1), 142–153.

CWC. (2000). *Child 21: The Philippine national strategic framework for plan development for children 2000–2025*. Available at: http://www.cwc.gov.ph/index.php/dls/category/19-misc.

CWC. (2005). *The Philippines national framework for children's participation: A guide for upholding children's participation in the Philippines*. Council for the Welfare of Children.

CWC. (2010). *State of the Filipino children report 2010*. Available at: http://www.cwc.gov.ph/index.php?option=com_phocadownload&view=category&id=19:misc&Itemid=73.

CWC. (2011). *The second national plan of action for children 2011–2016 (2nd NPAC)*. Available at: http://www.cwc.gov.ph/index.php/dls/category/19-misc.

CWC. (2016). *Vision, mission, mandate and legal bases*. Available at: http://www.cwc.gov.ph/index.php/cwc-content-links/50-vision-content.

CWC and UNICEF. (2016). *National baseline study on violence against children: Philippines*. Available at: https://resourcecentre.savethechildren.net/node/10264/pdf/philippine_nbs_vac_results_discussion.pdf.

Daly, M., Bray, R., Bruckauf, Z., Byrne, J., Margaria, A., Pecnik, N., and Samms-Vaughan, M. (2015). *Family and parenting support: Policy and provision in a global context*. Innocenti Insight and UNICEF Office of Research.

De Castro, E. and Mogato, M. (2017, August 18). Furore erupts over killing of teenager as Philippines drugs war escalates. *Reuters*. Available at: https://www.reuters.com/article/us-philippines-drugs/furor-erupts-over-killing-of-teenager-as-philippines-drugs-war-escalates-idUSKCN1AY0BT.

Department of the Interior and Local Government. (2012). *Allocation of one percent (1%) internal revenue allotment (IRA) for the strengthening and implementation of the programs, projects and activities of the local councils for the protection of children*. Available at: http://www.dilg.gov.ph/issuances/mc/Allocation-of-One-Percent-1-Internal-Revenue-Allotment-IRA-for-the-strengthening-and-implementation-of-the-Programs-Projects-and-Activities-of-the-Local-Councils-for-the-Protection-of-Children-LCPC-per-Section-15-of-RA-9344/1669.

DOJ. (2006). *Protecting Filipino children from abuse, exploitation and violence: A comprehensive programme on child protection, 2006–2010*. Special Committee for the Protection of Children, Department of Justice.

DOJ. (2012). *Protecting Filipino children from abuse, exploitation and violence*. Committee for the Special Protection of Children. Available at: https://www.doj.gov.ph/files/2016/CPCP%202012-2016.pdf.

DOJ. (2017). *Committee for the special protection of children*. Available at: https://www.doj.gov.ph/child-protection-program.html.

DOJ. (2013). *Protocol for case management of child victims of abuse, neglect and exploitation*. Available at: https://www.doj.gov.ph/files/transparency_seal/2016-Jan/CPN-CSPC%20Protocol%2026Nov2014.pdf.

DSWD. (2016). *Residential and non-residential facilities*. Available at: http://www.dswd.gov.ph/programs/residential-and-non-residential-facilities/.

DSWD. (2015). *Voices from the islands: Annual report 2015*. Available at: http://www.dswd.gov.ph/download/publications/annual_report/DSWD-AR-2015-PDF-File-Spread.pdf.

DSWD. (2018). *DSWD assistance to individuals and families in crisis situations*. Available at: https://www.fo4b.dswd.gov.ph/2017/08/dswd-assistance-to-individuals-and-families-in-crisis-situation-aics/.

The Economist. (2017, July 22). Winning the war with IS in the Philippines, but losing the peace. *The Economist*. Available at: https://www.economist.com/news/asia/21725287-army-close-recapturing-militant-infested-provincial-capital-winning-war.

ECPAT. (2006). *Report on the status of action against commercial sexual exploitation of children: Philippines*. Available at: http://www.ecpat.org/wp-content/uploads/legacy/global_monitoring_report-philippines.pdf.

End Violence Against Children. (2021). *What's happening to the child protection system in the Philippines? With Bernadette Madrid* [Podcast]. https://www.end-violence.org/knowledge/whats-happening-child-protection-system-philippines-bernadette-madrid.

Esping-Andersen, G. (1990). *The three worlds of welfare capitalism*. Princeton University Press.

Fehringer, J. A. and Hindin, M. J. (2009). Like parent, like child: Intergenerational transmission of partner violence in Cebu, the Philippines. *Journal of Adolescent Health*, 44(4), 363–371.

Francia, L. (2010). *A history of the Philippines: From Indios Bravos to Filipinos*. Overlook Press.

Gabel, S. G. (2012). Social protection and children in developing countries. *Children and Youth Services Review*, 34, 537–545.

Gulland, A. (2014). Law to broaden access to contraception gets green light in Philippines. *BMJ*, 348, 2725.

Hassan, F., Sadowski L. S., Bangdiwala, S. I., Vizcarra, B., Ramiro, L., De Paula, C. S., Bordin, I. A. S., and Mitra, M. D. (2004). Physical intimate partner violence in Chile, Egypt, India and the Philippines. *Injury Control and Safety Prevention*, 11(2), 111–116.

Holliday, I. (2000). Productivist welfare capitalism: Social policy in East Asia. *Political Studies*, 48, 706–723.

House of Representatives. (2017). *Agency budget notes: Department of Social Welfare and Development (for FY 2018)*. Congressional Policy and Budget Research Department, House of Representatives.

Human Rights Watch. (2018). *Philippines: Duterte's "drug war" claims 12,000+ lives*. Available at: https://www.hrw.org/news/2018/01/18/philippines-dutertes-drug-war-claims-12000-lives.

Jenkins, B. Q., Tilbury, C., Mazerolle, P., and Hayes, H. (2017). The complexity of child protection recurrence: The case for a systems approach. *Child Abuse and Neglect*, 63, 162–171.

Jeyaseelan, L., Sadowski, L.S., Kumar, S., Hassan, F., Ramiro, L., and Vizcarra, B. (2004). World studies of abuse in the family environment: Risk factors for physical intimate partner violence. *Injury Control and Safety Promotion*, 11(2), 117–24.

Kim, E. and Yoo, J. (2015). Conditional cash transfer in the Philippines: How to overcome institutional constraints for implementing social protection. *Asia and the Pacific Policy Studies*, 2, 75–89.

Lachman, P., Poblete, X., Ebigbo, P. O., Nyandiya-Bundy, S., Bundy, R. P., Killian, B., and Doek, J. (2002). Challenges facing child protection. *Child Abuse and Neglect*, 26, 587–617.

Lansford, J. E., Godwin, J., Tirado, L. M. U., et al. (2015). Individual, family, and culture level contributions to child physical abuse and neglect: A longitudinal study in nine countries. *Development and Psychopathology*, 27(4), 1417–1428.

Lau, M. and Bradshaw, J. (2010). Child well-being in the Pacific Rim. *Child Indicators Research*, 3(3), 367–383.

LawPhil Project. (2018a). *Republic act 7610: An act providing for stronger deterrence and special protection against child abuse, exploitation and discrimination, and for other purposes*. Available at: http://www.lawphil.net/statutes/repacts/ra1992/ra_7610_1992.html.

LawPhil Project. (2018b). *Title 1, General principles, Presidential Decree 603, 1974*. Available at: http://www.lawphil.net/statutes/presdecs/pd1974/pd_603_1974.html.

Madianou, M. (2012). Migration and the accentuated ambivalence of motherhood: The role of ICTs in Filipino transnational families. *Global Networks*, 12, 277–295.

Madrid, B. J. (2009). Child protection in the Philippines. *International Journal of Child Health and Human Development*, 2(3), 271–276.

Madrid, B. J., Ramiro, L. S., Hernandez, S. S., Go, J. J., and Badilio, J. A. (2013). Child maltreatment prevention in the Philippines: A situationer. *Acta Medica Philippina*, 47(1), 1–11.

Mandal, M. and Hindin, M. J. (2013). From family to friends: Does witnessing interparental violence affect young adults' relationships with friends? *Journal of Adolescent Health*, 53(2), 187–193.

Mandal, M. and Hindin, M. J. (2015). Keeping it in the family: Intergenerational transmission of violence in Cebu, Philippines. *Maternal and Child Health Journal*, 19(3), 598–605.

Mapp, S. and Gabel, S. G. (2017). Government abuses of human rights. *Journal of Human Rights and Social Work*, 2(1), 1–2.

Myers, W. and Bourdillon, M. (2012a). Introduction: Development, children and protection. *Development in Practice*, 22(4), 437–447.

Myers, W. and Bourdillon, M. (2012b). Concluding reflections: How might we really protect children? *Development in practice*, 22(4), 613–620.

Njord, L., Merrill, R. M., Njord, R., Lindsay, R., and Pachano, J. D. (2010). Drug use among street children and non-street children in the Philippines. *Asia Pacific Journal of Public Health*, 22(2), 203–211.

Parrenas, R. (2005). Long distance intimacy: Class, gender and intergenerational relations between mothers and children in Filipino transnational families. *Global Networks*, 5, 317–336.

Pasion, P. (2017, July 17). World Bank loan used for 4Ps ending in 2019. *Rappler*. Available at: https://www.rappler.com/nation/175862-world-bank-loan-4ps-ending-2019-dswd.

Pells, K. (2012). "Risky lives": Risk and protection for children growing-up in poverty. *Development in Practice*, 22(4), 562–573.

Piachaud, D. (2015). The future of social policy: Changing the paradigm. *Asia and the Pacific Policy Studies*, 2(1), 1–7.

Philippine Commission on Women. (2017). *Inter-agency council on violence against women and their children (IACVAWC)*. Available at: http://www.pcw.gov.ph/focus-areas/violence-against-women/initiatives/iacvawc.

Philippine Commission on Women. (2019). *Strengthening the provisions of R.A. 8353: Amending the anti-rape law.* Policy Brief No. 1. Available at: https://www.pcw.gov.ph/wpla/amending-anti-rape-law.

Price-Robertson, R., Bromfield, L., and Lamont A. (2014). *International approaches to child protection: What can Australia learn?* Child Family Community Australia paper no. 23. Australian Institute of Family Studies.

PSA and UNICEF. (2015). *Child poverty in the Philippines*. United Nations Children's Fund.

Ramiro, L. S., Martinez, A. B., Tan, J. R. D., Mariano, K., Miranda, G. M. J., and Bautista, G. (2019). Online child sexual exploitation and abuse: A community diagnosis using the social norms theory. *Child Abuse & Neglect*, 96, 1–13, 104080.

Ramiro, L. S., Madrid, B. J., and Brown, D. W. (2010). Adverse childhood experiences (ACE) and health-risk behaviours among adults in a developing country setting. *Child Abuse and Neglect*, 34(11), 842–855.

Rawlings, L. B. and Rubio, G. M. (2005). Evaluating the impact of conditional cash transfer programs. *The World Bank Research Observer*, 20(1), 29–55.

Roche, S. (2017). Child protection and maltreatment in the Philippines: A systematic review of the literature. *Asia & the Pacific Policy Studies*, 4, 104–128.

Roche, S. (2019). Childhoods in policy: A critical analysis of national child protection policy in the Philippines. *Children & Society*, 33(2), 95–110.

Roche, S. (2020a). Conceptualising children's life histories and reasons for entry into residential care in the Philippines: Social contexts, instabilities and safeguarding. *Children and Youth Services Review*, 110, 1–10, 104820.

Roche, S. (2020b). *Residential care as a child protection mechanism in the Philippines: An analysis of children's life histories and their community-based protection*. [Unpublished doctoral dissertation]. Monash University. Available at: https://bridges.monash.edu/articles/thesis/Residential_care_as_a_child_protection_mechanism_in_the_Philippines_An_analysis_of_children_s_life_histories_and_their_community-based_protection/12838022.

Runyan D. K., Shankar, V., Hassan, F., Hunter, W. M., Jain, D., Paula, C. S., Bangdiwala, S. I., Ramiro, L. S., Munoz, S. R., Vizcarra, B., and Bordin, I. A. (2010). International variations in harsh child discipline. *Pediatrics*, 126(3), 701–711.

Sanapo, M. S. and Nakamura, Y. (2011). Gender and physical punishment: The Filipino children's experience. *Child Abuse Review*, 20(1), 39–56.

Saplala, J. E. G. (2007). Understanding abusive relationships in childhood and violent behaviour among convicted felons. *Philippine Journal of Psychology*, 40(2), 88–110.

Sarmiento, B., Denice, C. R., and Rudolf, R. (2017). The impact of childhood maltreatment on young adults' mental health: Evidence from the Philippines. *Asian Social Work and Policy Review*, 11(1), 76–89.

Save the Children. (2008). *A time for change: Ending all forms of corporal punishment of children. Corporal punishment in the Philippines*. Save the Children.

Save the Children. (2011). *Child protection in the Philippines: A situational analysis*. Save the Children.

Teehankee, J. C. (2016). Duterte's resurgent nationalism in the Philippines: A discursive institutionalist analysis. *Journal of Current Southeast Asian Affairs*, 35(3), 69–89.

Terol, E. H. (2009). Cases of sexually abused adolescent girls with mental retardation in the Philippines. *Journal of Child and Adolescent Trauma*, 2(3), 209–227.

Terre Des Hommes. (2016). *Children of the webcam: Updated report on webcam child sex tourism*. Available at: https://www.terredeshommes.nl/sites/tdh/files/uploads/hr_17021_tdh_report_webcam_manilla.pdf.

Thompson, M. R. (2016). The spector of neo-authoritarianism in the Philippines. *Current History*, 115(782), 220–225.

US Department of Labor. (2016). *Child labor and forced labor reports: Philippines*. Available at: https://www.dol.gov/sites/default/files/images/ilab/child-labor/2016Philippines.pdf.

UNDP. (2016). *Human development report: Philippines*. Available at: http://hdr.undp.org/en/countries/profiles/PHL.

UNDP. (2017). *Human development index (HDI)*. Available at: http://hdr.undp.org/en/content/human-development-index-hdi.

UNICEF. (2016). *Strengthening child protection systems in the Philippines: Child protection in emergencies.* UNICEF.

Wessells, M. G. (2015). Bottom-up approaches to strengthening child protection systems: Placing children, families, and communities at the center. *Child Abuse and Neglect, 43,* 8–21.

Wessells, M. G., Lamin, D. F. M., King, D., Kostelny, K., Stark, L., and Lilley, S. (2012). The disconnect between community-based child protection mechanisms and the formal child protection system in rural Sierra Leone: Challenging to building an effective national child protection system. *Vulnerable Children and Youth Studies, 7*(3), 211–227.

WHO. (2006). *Preventing child maltreatment: A guide to taking action and generating evidence.* Available at: http://apps.who.int/iris/bitstream/10665/43499/1/9241594365_eng.pdf.

World Bank. (2015). *World Bank open data.* Available at: http://data.worldbank.org/indicator/SI.POV. GINI?page=1.

World Bank. (2017a). *GDP annual growth: The Philippines.* Available at: https://data.worldbank.org/indicator/ NY.GDP.MKTP.KD.ZG?locations=PH&year_high_desc=true.

World Bank. (2017b). *Fertility rate, total.* Available at: https://data.worldbank.org/indicator/SP.DYN.TFRT. IN?end=2015&locations=PH&start=2005.

Wulcyn, F., Daro, D., Fluke, J. Feldman, S., Glodek, C., and Lifanda, K. (2009). *Adapting a systems approach to child protection: Key concepts and considerations.* Chapin Hall, University of Chicago.

Yangco, C.C. (2010). *A comprehensive approach to prevention of child maltreatment in the Philippines: Building partnerships among agencies, organizations and the community.* United Nations Asia and Far East Institute. Available at: http://www.unafei.or.jp/english/pdf/PDF_rms/no69/07_P97-111.pdf.

Yu, N. G. (2006). Ideological roots of Philippine social welfare. *International Social Work, 49*(5), 559–570.

Yu, N. G. (2013). The role of social work in Philippine poverty-reduction programs: Ideology, policy and the profession. *Asia Pacific Journal of Social Work and Development, 23*(1), 24–34.

Reforming Russia's Child Protection System: From Residential to Family Care

Meri Kulmala, Maija Jäppinen, *and* Zhanna Chernova

Abstract

This chapter explicates the reformation of Russia's child protection system to family care from residential care. The Russian child protection system had been criticized for its inability to support families at risk. The rise of poverty, alcohol, drug abuse, and unemployment were the dramatic indicators of the fall of the socialist regime, which sparked a wide liberalization of the welfare state. Moreover, the Russian support system is regulated by federal and regional legislation. Thus, the current reform is based on the idea of every kid's right to grow up in a family, even if it is a family-based form of alternative care. Russia's child protection paradigm is shifting towards a combination of child-focused and family supports, at least on a policy level.

Key Words: Russia, child protection, family care, support system, liberalization, poverty, socialist regime, welfare state

Introduction

Russia remains a country with one of the highest proportions of children deprived of parental care and a still relatively high level of residential care among such children (Biryukova & Makarentseva 2021). About 80% of these children have the status that in Russian is called "social orphan": they are children whose parents are alive, but for some reason are not part of their lives (Biryukova & Sinyavskaya, 2017); approximately 20% are "true" orphans whose parents were lost to death. The Russian child protection system has been criticized for its inability to support families at risk and consequently its orientation toward alternative care—in large residential institutions. Since the 2010s, Russia has been fundamentally reforming its alternative care system by dismantling the old system of children's homes and developing foster care and preventive support for families.

The collapse of the socialist regime started a wide liberalization of the Russian welfare state, including the decentralization, privatization, and marketization of many welfare services (Cook, 2011). As Kulmala and colleagues (2014) state, one cannot overestimate the social crisis in the 1990s that emerged as a result of this transition into a market economy. Increases in poverty, alcohol and drug abuse, and unemployment were dramatic indicators. They all contributed to the growing number of children deprived of parental care for socioeconomic reasons. A common risk factor for a child entering the out-of-home care system is their parents living under the minimum income level and/or lacking proper housing (Rykun & Iuzhaninoy, 2009).

The Russian support system for families and children, including those in alternative care, is regulated by federal and regional legislation. Russia is a federal state with 85 regional governments. The federal government sets the general principles of family policy and child protection, but their implementation mostly falls to the regional governments. Most subsidies in the sphere of alternative care, introduced later in this chapter, are stipulated by federal laws but their financing relies on regional budgets according to existing resources. This principle has resulted in remarkable regional variation and inequality among Russian children and families. As Kainu and colleagues (2017, pp. 296–297) show, regional disparities in several social development indicators might range between equivalence to Sudan in the bottom of the indexes and equivalence to Norway in the top.

Starting from 2006, the Russian government began to prioritize social and family policy due to the severe decline in the population. At its worst, the population was shrinking by 700,000 per year during the 1990s (Cook, 2011, p. 21). Among numerous earlier measures to stimulate the birth rate (Kulmala et al., 2014), the increasing attention paid to Russian children and families also encompassed children in alternative care in the 2010s. Although some experiments to promote family-like alternatives were carried out local-regionally (see, e.g., Holm-Hansen et al., 2005; Stryker, 2012), no systemic reform had taken place previously.

The current reform is based on the idea of every child's right to grow up in a family. This does not necessarily refer to the child's birth family, but to the development of family-based forms of alternative care. The government has set a goal that nine of ten children now in alternative care will live in families. This is to be achieved by promoting domestic adoptions, increasing fostering, and creating family support services to prevent children from entering the alternative care system. The remaining institutions are to be restructured into home-like environments. These moves will bring Russia into line with the global deinstitutionalization trend (An & Kulmala, 2020; Kulmala et al., 2021a).

The reorganization of the alternative care system has been implemented throughout the country at a considerable scale and speed. In comparison to the Soviet-rooted, residential care dominated system, the reform represents a fundamental change in the underpinning ideals of care and institutional design, a paradigm shift as Kulmala and colleagues (2017) conceptualize it. The prevailing ideologies of child welfare systems are traditionally characterized by being oriented either to family support or child protection (Gilbert et al., 2011). As Verhallen and colleagues (2019, p. 287) briefly summarize, the family support model can be characterized as services and interventions with poor or struggling families to strengthen the care and capacities of parents, whereas the child protection model directs interventions at identifying and protecting children at risk of abuse or neglect. In other words, one of the models aims to protect children, the other to preserve families. Gilbert and colleagues (2011) note that since the 1990s, a third orientation, a child-focused model, has emerged. This model contains aspects of both child protection and family support and is characterized by early intervention with parents' responsibilities as caregivers both examined and supported to ensure that they provide a good childhood.

In reality, though, no country presents a pure type of any model but combines their elements. Russia is no exception. In this chapter, we argue that at the level of ideals and policy, the Russian paradigm shift is from child protection to a mixture of child-focused and family support. Yet, at the level of practices, many aspects of child protection remain. The Soviet legacy still affects the current institutional arrangements and practices and many serious pitfalls persist, as Jäppinen and Kulmala (2021) have shown in their analysis. Much has happened, yet partly on paper and with unintended, even paradoxical results. As Kulmala (2017) argues, the major risk is to focus on decorative renovation without an awareness of the underlying ideas.

In this chapter, we first provide some statistics concerning the children in alternative care and then review the development of the relevant legislation in Russia. Next, we turn to the practical implementation of the new policy by discussing how children enter alternative care, the related decision making, different forms of preventive support and alternative care as well as the division of labor between the different societal sectors. In the end, we discuss our findings in light of the above-mentioned three orientations.

Children in Russian Alternative Care in Numbers

As Khlinovskaya Rockhill (2010, p. 1) notes, there is no single reliable source for the official statistics on children in alternative care (also Birykova & Makarentseva, 2021; Biryukova & Sinyavskaya, 2017), but the numbers that appear in different sources are usually similar. After World War II, there was a peak in the number of orphans, as many children lost their parents in the war and later in Stalin's terror (Cherniak, 2000). Again, since the 1990s, the trend has been growing, peaking in the mid-2000s with 800,000 children in alternative care. This time, the growth was connected to the turbulent transition from socialism to a market economy and characterized by the increase in so-called social orphans. As Biryukova and Makarentseva (2021) showed, according to the *Rosstat* data, the total number of children deprived of parental care, which includes children in residential care, as well as children in family-type placements, has been shrinking since 2005 (see Figure 43.1).

Over the last decade, the number of children in alternative care has decreased by 15.6%. The number of children entering the care system per year was at the highest in 2005, when 133,000 children entered the system. Within ten years (by 2015), their number had decreased by 56%. As Biryukova and Sinyavskaya (2017, pp. 370–371) analyze,

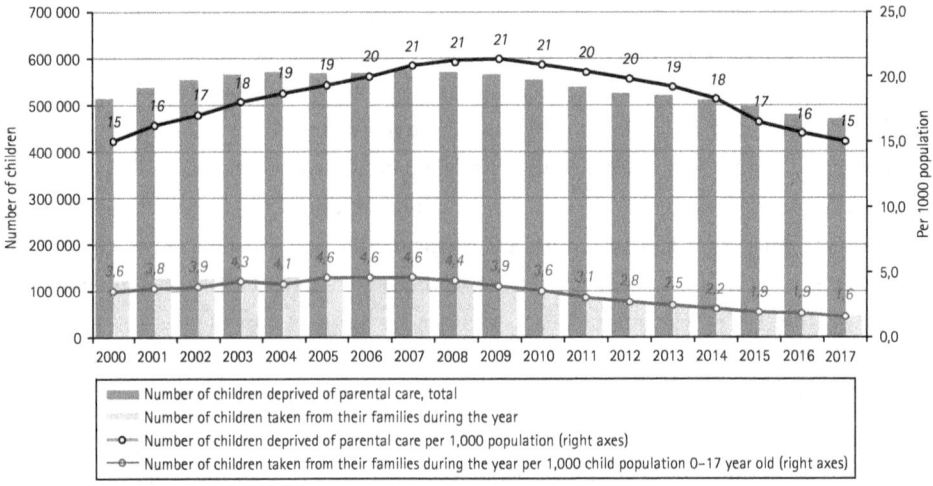

Figure 43.1 Number of children in out-of-home care, 2000–2015 *Source*: Biryukova & Sinyavskaya (2017, p. 371).

the relative indicators show a somewhat different trend. The decline in the number of children without parental care in 2005–2009 was related to the general decline of Russia's child population, while the number of children without parental care among all children in Russia continued to grow, climbing as high as 2.8% in 2009, from where it began to slowly decline. According to the authors, starting from 2009, the share of children entering the care system yearly, in turn, shows a decreasing.

Development of Russian Child Welfare Policy

During the latest years, new ideas and organizational principles shape the lives of those thousands of children in alternative care. Russia has no integral law on child protection, but there are sections related to child welfare in several legislative acts. Next, we review the key changes in Russian child welfare policy and laws, which led to a fundamental reform in Russian child welfare.

Soviet Model of Collective and Residential Care

The dominance of institutional care of the Russian system dates back to the Soviet-era ideal of collective care and upbringing. The Soviet model of child protection was based on the paternalist idea of the state as the primary caregiver and prioritized residential care by state professionals, almost exclusively in large residential institutions with hundreds of children.

Care for orphans appeared for the first time as an actual topic in 1918, when the Soviet state declared all orphaned children to be "children of the state" (*gosudarstvennye deti*) and abolished existing family-based forms of alternative care. By the 1930s, residential institutions had become practically the only form of alternative care. As a result of the peak caused by the war, in 1945, hundreds of new residential institutions were opened

(Nechaeva, 2000, p. 143). Soviet child psychology focused on physical and cognitive functioning in contrast to the theories of attachment and socialization that led to interest in family(-like) care in the west (Disney, 2015, p. 19).

The institutional setting was regarded as a favorable environment for children to grow to be good Soviet citizens (Stryker, 2012, pp. 86–88). It should be noted that the ideal of collective upbringing and education did not concern only alternative care; many other collective forms, which included living in an institutional setting, such as work colonies and pioneer houses, were also established. Institutions were frequently separated from the wider community in terms of location and interaction. They provided services on their own and there was little engagement with local schools, medical or leisure facilities. Life was regimented, with little organized stimulation or play, simply meeting basic needs. All this has led to very poor outcomes in the social adaptation of the "graduates" of these institutions (in education, work, and family life) and accompanying societal stigma (Khlinovskaya Rockhill, 2010; Stryker, 2012). Perhaps somewhat simplifying the picture, one can summarize that the Soviet-type system made children fit into the system, instead of making the system comfortable for children.

Postsocialist-era Conventions, Laws, and Policies

To minimize the negative effects of the post-socialist socioeconomic change in 1992, the Russian government launched the "Children of Russia" program. In 1993, the new Constitution brought the national legislation in line with the international child's rights commitments. Russia ratified the UN Convention on the Rights of the Child as early as 1990. In 1996, Russia joined the Council of Europe, an active advocate for children's rights and deinstitutionalization. In 1998, Russia also ratified the European Convention of Human Rights and thereby became part of the European Court of Human Rights.

The Constitution was followed by the new Family Code (in 1995), which already in principle prioritized family forms of alternative care over institutional ones. It is important to note that instead of the concept of the "child's best interest," the key concepts in the Family Code are the "rights and responsibilities of parents and children." The Family Code stipulates the limitation and termination of parental rights, available forms of alternative care, and social benefits for children deprived of parental care, all discussed later in this chapter.

In the late 1990s, several new laws concerning specific questions of child protection came into force. For instance, Law No 124-FZ 1998 on the Main Guarantees of the Rights of the Child in the Russian Federation defined children deprived of parental care as a category of children in difficult life situations, which gave them the right to particular protection by the state. Law No 159-FZ 1996 on Special Guarantees on Social Protection of Orphans and Children Deprived of Parental Care in the Russian Federation set out to regulate services and provisions to children of this category, as well as the structures of the institutional care system. It also extended the state policy to concern those leaving care up to 23 years old. Law No 48-FZ on Guardianship was set up in 2008 to regulate kinship care and the functioning of guardianship departments. In the same year, the president established the National Foundation for Support of Children in Difficult Life Situations to develop effective preventive mechanisms and forms of support and foster care.

Deinstitutionalization Reform in the 2010s

Russia has been exposed to global ideas of children's rights and the international push towards deinstitutionalization since the early 1990s (An & Kulmala, 2020). By the 2010s, however, Russia was being repeatedly reminded by the UN's Child's Rights Committee about the large number of children in institutions and insufficient efforts to change the situation. Although deinstitutionalization had been somewhat on the policy agenda, systematic reform took place only recently. As often with paradigm changes (Khmelnitskaya, 2015, pp. 16–17), the Russian policy shift was triggered by an exogenous crisis. In 2008, a Russian child adopted from a Russian orphanage to the United States died as a result of negligence by his American adoptive parents (for more information, see High, 2014). This case led to increased attention—also domestically—on children living in state-run institutions in Russia (Bindman et al., 2018). From then, the reorganization of the child welfare system has been a top governmental priority. The issue was emphasized by President Medvedev in his annual address in 2010,[1] which was followed by several policy programs. One of the key documents, "National Strategy to Promote the Interests of Children in 2012–2017"[2] (hereafter: Strategy) was established by presidential decree in June 2012, with the aim of dismantling the system of institutional care. The Strategy recommended children's homes to be reorganized into "family support centers" whose primary task was to return a child to their birth family or place them in a foster family. The document contained frequent references to international treaties and was important in setting out key ideas about alternatives to residential care.

The implementation of the Strategy's proposals started with Presidential Decree #1688 on measures to protect children living without parental care,[3] issued on December 28, 2012, the same day that the ban on adoptions of children by US citizens was signed into law. It was wide-ranging, directing officials to work on improving fostering and adoption processes. It added a specific criterion of the "effectiveness" of regional governors by measuring the proportion of children placed in family care in their region, thus setting a strong top-down incentive to implement the reform in the current non-democratic political environment.

---

[1] http://en.kremlin.ru/events/president/news/9637, retrieved April 23, 2019.

[2] Available at http://static.kremlin.ru/media/acts/files/0001201206040004.pdf, retrieved January 19, 2018.

[3] Available at http://www.kremlin.ru/events/president/news/17234, retrieved January 12, 2018.

Several further policy documents gave impetus to the development of fostering and early support services for birth families under pressure. For instance, in 2013, the presidential party, United Russia, established a nationwide program "Russia Needs All Its Children," which tasked regional branches of the party with developing "road maps" for preventing children from entering care and promoting family placements.[4] Alternative care is also one of the main issues in the current "State Concept for Family Policy in the Russian Federation until 2025," adopted in 2014.[5] Both mentioned programs clearly point to the central priority of the issue for the government.

A key document of the reform, Government Decree RF #481 on the Activities of Organizations for Orphaned Children and Children without Parental Care and on the Placement of Children Without Parental Care in Them (hereafter: Decree 481) came into force in 2015.[6] It fundamentally altered the goals of the child welfare system and the nature of care in institutions, transferring them into temporary family-style units. One of the most prominent NGO campaigners for the reform in September 2015 characterized Decree 481 as revolutionary because "children's life in the orphanages is starting to look like ordinary children's life instead of prison life."[7]

In 2012, Russia also ratified the UN Convention on the Rights of Persons with Disabilities, which is explicit on the right of disabled children to a family life and the need for states to provide services to "prevent concealment, abandonment, neglect and segregation of children with disabilities." Yet the implementation of the Convention is incomplete, and disability certainly poses a major risk for a child to end up in residential care, as shown later.

In sum, the new emphasis on family(-style) care manifests itself in many ways. First, the focus on work with the birth parents is novel as in Russia alternative care has been traditionally long-term with little return to birth families (Khlinovskaya Rockhill, 2010). Second, when the birth family is not an option, a child should be placed into an adoptive or foster family instead of residential care. Third, residential care remains an option but in small, family-like units, which is very different to the previous typically large segregated institutions.

As Kulmala and colleagues (2017) suggest, the shift was driven by a range of factors. Domestic and international scandals and criticism turned attention to the serious shortcomings of Russian alternative care. The prioritization of family-style over institutional care fit well into the increasing level of "family talk" on the government's agenda. As Bindman and colleagues (2018) document, although the final decision-making process

---

[4] See http://council.gov.ru/media/files/41d49b8a57474a8ca104.pdf, retreieved January 19, 2018.

[5] Available at: http://government.ru/media/files/41d4ffd61a02c7a4b206.pdf, retrieved January 19, 2018.

[6] Available at: https://rg.ru/2014/05/27/detdom-site-dok.html, retrieved January 19, 2018.

[7] See https://daily.afisha.ru/archive/gorod/people/eti-deti-stanut-polnocennymi-chlenami-obshestva-kak-izmenitsya-zhizn-sirot/, retrieved April 13, 2018.

clearly depended on governmental actors, NGOs played a crucial role in providing ideas on reform. (Also An & Kulmala, 2020.)

How Do Children Enter the Child Protection System?

In the Russian system, two key concepts organizing the state's concern for children in need of protection are a child/family in a socially unsafe situation and in a difficult life situation. Federal Law FZ-120 on the Prevention of Child Negligence and Youth Offenses (1999) considers the socially unsafe situation of a child/family as parents who neglect their parental responsibilities in raising their child and who abuse or negatively impact on their child, or as children with deviant, criminal or otherwise asocial behavior. The legislation underlines parents' responsibility in raising and socializing a child; a child's deviant behavior in turn is framed as a consequence of negligence rooted in insufficient parental care (Prisiazhniuk et al., 2015, p. 24).

The Authority on Alternative Care Placements

The key state authority responsible for alternative care is the guardianship department, nicknamed *opeka* (shortened from the official name in Russian: *organ opeki i popechitel'stvo*), which is an executive body at the regional level of government. *Opeka* receives information about families in socially unsafe situations from social and health services, police, schools, and individuals (e.g., relatives or neighbors). It then assesses the situation, possibly prepares the case for the court, and implements the alternative care placement.

The "Russia without Orphans" program set a goal to reform the *opeka* departments. They are to become federal-level organs with local branches but uniform working standards and methods. It also seeks a uniform system of monitoring, assessment, and control over these departments. These changes are still underway. Furthermore, with the policy reform the *opeka* no longer functions only as a controlling organ, but it should also support both birth and foster parents. Traditionally the *opeka* has not provided support for families and its former functions of control and assessing the performance of parents (as parents) is still considered the primary one.

Trust will be crucial in the new system. In 2015–2018, we conducted interviews with over 100 regional officials, directors of residential institutions for children, NGOs, and foster parents in several regions of Russia as part of a larger project, "A child's right to a family: Deinstitutionalization of child welfare in Putin's Russia." Our interviews with child welfare professionals suggest that the new double function seems to be one of the greatest challenges, which would require a fundamental change in people's mind-sets. Generally, people do not trust the *opeka*, and do not wish to get in touch with it. This has to do both with the concrete work practices at the *opeka* but also generalized mistrust in state institutions in post-communist Russia (e.g., Offe, 1999, p. 27). As Kulmala and colleagues (2021b) argue, distrust remains one of the most significant dilemmas of the

Russian child welfare. To improve trust in the child welfare system, legal means to appeal court decisions must be made available, if for example a parent finds a decision to be unjustified.

Furthermore, the Russian legislation does not set any requirements on the professional qualifications of the staff of the *opeka*, except having a higher education as state officials generally. Often these people are lawyers and pedagogues; importantly, professional qualification of social worker or any training regarding child's rights or communication with children and their parents is not required. As the competence of the *opeka* officials varies, much of the treatment of the cases depends on the perceptions of individual officials and the local organizational culture. Often, there are real causes for mistrust: *opeka* officials are not free from corruption, a widespread problem in Russian society, and this is actively discussed in the Russian media. Following Marshall's (1993) argument concerning the key factors in the decline of American orphanages, we argue that development of professional social work in the child protection services—in the assessment and decision making and in creating ethical standards—is a necessary condition for real change.

Limitation or Termination of Parental Rights as a Common Practice

After a child has entered the alternative care system, the decision on returning a child to their birth family or on limiting or terminating the parental rights is to be taken within six months. Changes to parental rights always require a decision by a judge of a district court. According to the Family Code, reasons for the termination of parental rights can include negligence of parental responsibilities, child abuse, or a parent's alcohol or drug misuse. Limitation of parental rights is issued if the need for alternative care is caused due to a parent's health problems or "difficult life situation." In Russia, parental rights are more often terminated than limited (Biryukova & Sinyavskaya, 2017). It is possible for birth parents to apply for the restoration of terminated rights, if their situation has changed significantly—if the child has not been adopted. Yet restoration happens quite rarely: in 2015, only 5.8% of children were returned to their birth parents (Biryukova & Sinyavskaya, 2017, p. 378).

With the termination of parental rights, the juridical kinship tie between the child and their birth parent breaks. A parent's liability to maintain their child yet remains. According to the legislation, the child has the right to keep contact with their parents and other relatives, if it is not against the child's best interests. In practice, however, professionals often do not value the role of birth parents in the life of these children; they might even see it as a threat to a child's adaptation to alternative care, and thus do not support keeping the contact (Jäppinen, 2018, 2021). Importantly, with the termination of parental rights, a child can be adopted without permission from their birth parent(s).

As in the UN Convention of the Rights of the Child, placing a child in alternative care and/or termination of parental rights is also in Russian legislation considered as the last resort if all attempts to help the child in the family have failed. Yet so far the accent of the Russian system has been on alternative care. The ongoing reform should mark a major change in the nature of the interventions by setting a clear goal of prioritizing support to birth families to avoid placements, and limitation of parental rights instead of terminating them. In principle, alternative care is now primarily seen as temporary family reunification being the ultimate goal. The State Concept for Family Policy seeks the development of support programs to parents whose parental rights have been limited or terminated in order to make it possible for their child to return. Yet, according to our research, so far the system seems to lack the ability to support families at risk due to professionals' lack of skills and motivation.

New Emphasis on Community-based Early Support

The novel focus of the reform is on early detection and prevention. The municipal child protection authorities are responsible for holding registers, monitoring and providing services for the children and families "in a socially unsafe situation" (Prisiazhniuk et al., 2015, p. 24). There are no uniform federal or regional criteria for either defining this category of families or holding the registers, which complicates preventive work and early intervention (Iarskaia-Smirnova & Sadykov, 2015, p. 7).

Primary versus Secondary Prevention

The Russian system makes a distinction between primary prevention of 'social orphanhood', meaning support for birth families, and secondary prevention, which is about seeking new families for children in institutions. The latter seems to be more dominant in practice. Although the importance of developing social services to assist families to provide care for their children was recognized already in the early 2000s (Klinovskaya Rochill, 2010, p. 322), the system has remained as a combination of punishment and support (Biryukova et al., 2013, p. 61). On the one hand, old punitive methods such as threatening the termination of parental rights, reporting to parents' workplaces and administrative fines still exist, but families are now also provided with different social services.

Primary prevention, that is, providing early support for families in order to prevent the need for out-of-home placements, is one of the new policy ambitions at least on an ideological level. The reform recognizes an effectively functioning system to solve the problems of families and children at an early stage as a primary method to avoid terminations of parental rights and placements of children in alternative care. Recognizing, registering, and helping children in "socially unsafe situations" shall be done through more effective social policies providing socioeconomic, psychological, and pedagogical support to families in difficult life situations. The role of cross-sectoral collaboration, including healthcare and education, is emphasized for effective early prevention.

Already before the reform, the Russian state provided several forms of early support for families in socially unsafe situations. These included, for example, specific social service centers for families and children with psychological, social, juridical and pedagogical counseling, hotlines, and sometimes shelters. Many kinds of (pedagogical) activities designated for children in socially unsafe situations, such as after-school clubs, summer camps and daytime care for children with disabilities are also a common practice. Schools have traditionally played a central role in early intervention and support, and there is much professional literature on how teachers can support children in difficult life situations (Prisiazhniuk et al., 2015, p. 19).

The Strategy and finally Decree 481 reorganized the previous children's homes into family support centers that are now obliged to support and serve both birth and foster parents and care leavers. Referring again to our study, "A child's right to a family," our interviews showed that in different parts of Russia, the centers are better prepared to work with foster and adoptive families and lack skills and motivation to work with birth parents (Jäppinen, 2021). A central challenge is the lack of methods to support families to overcome their "difficult life situations." As Khlinovskaya Rockhill (2010, p. 100) puts it, "working with the family" is still deeply rooted in the old Soviet practice of admonishing the parents expecting them to correct themselves; and if that does not happen, the state agents will use sanctions and place the child into alternative care.

Institutional Placements as Prevention

Offering parents temporary institutional placements for their children as a means of support in difficult life situations is a common practice in Russia. Khlinovskaya Rockhill (2010, pp. 80–88, 103–134), for instance, shows how in the Russian Far East, parents were advised to place their child temporarily into a residential institution because of their unemployment, poverty, or other difficulties in providing care. According to our data, it also still happens that parents are given time and space to solve their problems, while the state takes care of their children, which can be considered as an extreme measure. Often these situations could be solved, for instance, by offering financial aid to a family, improving their housing conditions, and/or empowering parents through psychological support.

Such a measure is considered merely as a preventive service and thus always voluntary. Importantly, these children are not officially in alternative care and thus not seen in the official statistics. Yet, the institutions receive financing for those children. In the current environment this seems to be beneficial for the residential institutions: they can justify their existence without showing growing numbers in alternative care and residential placements (Jäppinen & Kulmala, 2021; Kulmala et al., 2021c). The Child's Rights Ombudsman of St. Petersburg, for example, estimates that 60–70% of the children in residential institutions in her region are such "temporarily" placed and thus without official status, in other words not seen in the statistics.[8]

In sum, the Russian child protection system continues to be oriented rather to alternative care than community-based services for families. Ideologically the reform brings

---

[8] See http://www.spbdeti.org/id6445, retrieved November 7, 2018.

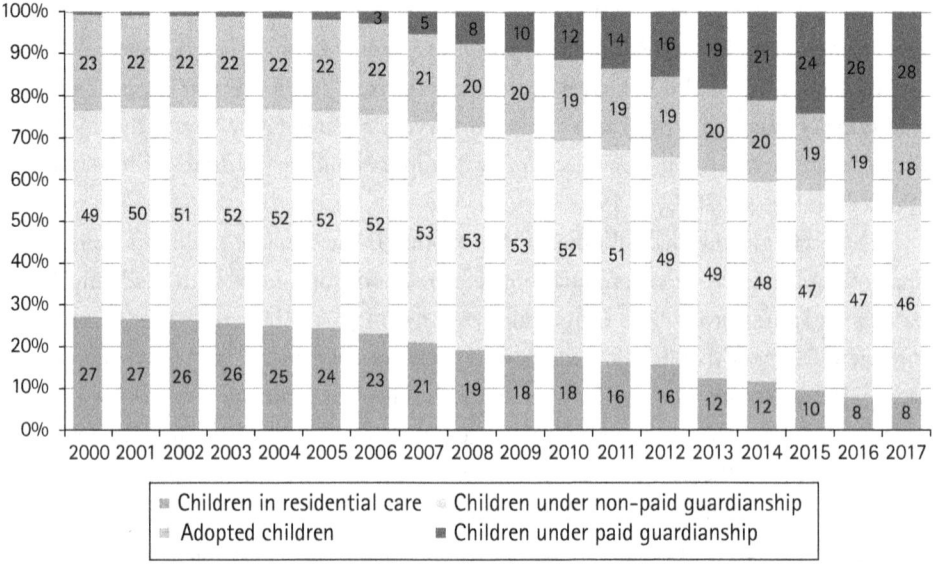

Figure 43.2 Share of children in different forms of alternative care *Source:* Biryukova & Sinyavskaya (2017, p. 374).

a clear shift in the orientation, which is not always realized in the practical implementation. The state seems to be eager to outsource preventive work to NGOs, which indeed are active not only in raising the issues of work with birth parents but also in developing and experimenting with new working methods (Kulmala et al., 2021c; Kulmala & Fomina, 2021).

Changing Forms of Out-of-home Care

According to the Family Code, children in alternative care can be placed either in guardianship care (usually kinship care), in foster families (and in some regions in "patronage families" described below) or given up for adoption. When none of these family forms are possible, a child can be placed in institutional care. Figure 43.2 shows that there is a clear transition from institutional care to care in families, with 27% of the children in institutions in 2000 and 8% in 2017. With regard to adoptions and guardianship care, the trend is quite stable, as the figure shows. Importantly, the above-discussed temporary placements to institutions are not included in the statistics (see also Jäppinen & Kulmala, 2021).

Care in Foster Families

The number of children in foster families has increased more than tenfold in comparison to the early 2000s: while still in 2000 27% of all children in alternative care lived in institutions and basically none in foster families, in 2017 28% of children in alternative care lived in foster families, whereas the share of replacements in institutions had decreased to 8%.

"Foster family" refers to a placement of a child in a family based on a contract between a foster parent (or two parents) and the *opeka*. According to the new legislation, all potential foster parents go through certified training. Training standards are set at the national level, but the *opeka* is responsible for providing the training, typically delegated to a local NGO. There are strict criteria concerning the housing conditions and income level of foster parent(s).

The term of the placement is defined in the contract. In Russia, fostering has often been regarded as a permanent solution, almost equivalent to adoption—except that unlike in adoption, foster parent(s) receive a monthly-based subsidy for providing custody according to regional standards. They are also eligible for many other in-kind benefits, such as housing costs and purchasing certain items such as furniture. In the Russian public imagination, foster parents are often pictured as being motivated because of the monetary and other material support from the Russian state (Iarskaia-Smirnova et al., 2021; also Chernova & Shpakovskaya, 2021). As in any other form of out-home care, a child is eligible for one-time and monthly allowances from the state.

The Russian state recommends a maximum of eight children in one foster family. This is a rather high number, comparable to a unit in an institution, and sets high demands on the foster parents' capacity to address each child's individual needs. In our fieldwork, we met many foster families with more children, even 12. This is especially the case with families who live in so-called "foster villages," typically consisting of 10 families with fostered children, provided with housing and other material and psychological support (Chernova & Kulmala, 2018).

In approximately half of the regions, legislation enables another form, the so-called patronage family, which comes close to professional fostering. Patronage is based on a three-party contract between a foster parent, the *opeka* and a care institution. In such a contract, the foster parent is an employee of that institution and thus has, in addition to a salary, a state employee benefit package. Many experts and foster parents that we interviewed would prefer such official status and being an employee but from the viewpoint of the state it is obviously the most expensive option and thus not typically used.

Kinship Care and Adoption

As seen in Figure 43.2, the most common form of care is guardianship care, in which a child is usually assigned to a relative as their guardian. Thus, in Russia kinship care is the most common alternative care placement. This is worth noting, as the possibilities of kinship care remain underused in many countries even if it is strategically seen as one of the preferred forms of care. The share of children in this form in Russia has stayed stable: around 46–49% for 2000–2017. The regional government pays a small monthly subsidy to a guardian with custody of a child. Criteria for becoming a guardian are less strict than for contracted foster families.

In the Russian context, adoption is regarded as part of the alternative care system. In fact, it is widely considered an ideal solution, as it is permanent. Adoption is also economically the most favorable option for the state, since responsibility for the child passes from the state to the adoptive parents. In adoption, the child receives the same juridical status as with their birth parents. The state provides a one-time allowance for adoptive parent(s) at the moment of signing the adoption but thereafter there are no further benefits as with foster and guardianship parents or for the children themselves. In our interviews with child protection officials, adoption was with almost no hesitation seen as the best possible option. This may be due to the above-discussed negative image of birth parents as lost causes and the underdeveloped competences of social services to work with birth parents (Jäppinen & Kulmala, 2021; Kulmala et al., 2021c). Yet, since the current reform explicitly seeks to see alternative care as a temporary solution, one could expect some changes in people's mindsets and consequently in practices as well. Perhaps public campaigns and increased financial support for fostering have contributed to the slowly decreasing numbers of adopted children seen in Figure 43.2 (also Biryukova & Makarentseva, 2021), and the fact that foreign adoptions are highly restricted. Whereas 47% of adoptions were international in 2006, only 11% were in 2015.[9]

New Family-like Residential Care

Although the number is decreasing, many children still live in residential institutions, nearly all of which are governmental. According to Tarasenko (2021), there 1,302 public institutions of different types in 2019 (in comparison to 4,168 in 2005). Four types of institutions still exist. First, former children homes (*detskii dom*), which are now transformed into family support centers that can accommodate children temporarily. Most of these work under the Ministry of Social Protection and Labor. Second, there are baby homes for children under the age of three (*dom rebenka*) under the healthcare system. Third, there are correctional children's homes for children with special needs due to severe physical and mental disorders (*korrektsionnyi detskii dom*), which, depending on the region, work either under social protection or healthcare. And fourth, there are boarding schools (*shkola-internat*) under the Ministry of Education and Science (Kulmala et al., 2021a). According to Tarasenko (2018b), around 39% of these institutions still offer residential care, while the rest are various types of family support centers (see also Tarasenko, 2021).

As stated earlier, reform brings radical changes to the lives of children living in these institutions. In addition to the new principle of temporality, in the newly arranged institutions the life of children should now resemble family-style living. Children live in small groups with permanent caregivers and siblings together. Instead of previous "corridor-style" living, children live in an apartment-style space with a shared kitchen and living

---

[9] See, e.g., www.usynovite.ru/statistics, retrieved November 7, 2018.

room and a bedroom for each child. Ideally, children go to ordinary schools and have contact with relatives and friends. They have their own hobbies and belongings.

As elsewhere, small and healthy children find their way to family placements (Kulmala et al., 2021c). According to Biryukova and Sinyavskaya (2017, p. 374), children older than 6 years represent the majority who stay in long-term residential care. In 2015, their share was over 90%. Irrespective of age, disability poses a major risk for a child entering and remaining in residential care. Generally, of all children in alternative care, the share of those with some kind of disability is rather high: in the age group under 5 years 33% are disabled, while among those from 5 to 10 years, the share is 45% and among 10 years and older 25% (Semia et al., 2016, pp. 74, 79–80). The share of children under 7 years is high in so-called correctional children's homes, which means that small children not placed in family care are those with problems with health or vital functions (Birykova & Sinyavskaya, 2017, p. 379). For these groups of children (teenagers, those with health problems, and many siblings together), who face difficulties in being placed in families, supported forms of family care (e.g., patronage families and foster villages) are argued to be necessary by many experts. As discussed earlier, in the new situation those children who are placed in residential institutions temporarily (as a preventive measure) are many (also Jäppinen & Kulmala, 2021; Kulmala et al., 2021c).

Division of Labor: State Dominance with Help from NGOs

The Russian child welfare system is predominantly state led, meaning the setting of priorities, organization and funding. As elsewhere, state agencies have the main authority over preparing the decisions for courts about termination and/or limitation of parental rights and further placement of a child in alternative care.

Russian State as the Main Provider

The state is also responsible for funding the system through the regional governments according to their existing resources, which results in the aforementioned wide differences within the country. The earlier discussed laws on the rights and social protection of a child deprived of parental care guarantee these children many kinds of financial and material support. Alongside monthly subsidies for clothing and school supplies, for instance, most notably the state provides an apartment when a child turns 18—if they do not already have one—and free vocational and subsidized higher education. The state also provides a special unemployment benefit. If the parents are not alive, a child receives a pension from the state (Kulmala & Fomina, 2021; Kulmala et al., 2021d).

The providers of out-of-home care can be many. The state, either federal or regional, is responsible for funding the care services in most cases, however. As noted, foster and guardianship parents are eligible for certain subsidies and in-kind benefits. These payments vary largely among the Russian regions. In the Moscow region, the payments are much higher in comparison to other regions, which is why many foster families wish to move there. Yet living in the metropolitan region is of course more expensive. As Granberg and Sätre (2017, pp. 111–117) show, in the Russian countryside, fostering might serve as a means to a substantial improvement of living standards, which obviously contributes to the above-discussed exploitative image of Russian foster parents.

Residential care is basically state-run. Apart from a very few examples (Tarasenko 2021), residential care institutions are governmental. Paradoxically, as in the old system, these institutions still receive funding according to the number of children living in them, even though the new guiding principle is temporality of institutional care. Such path dependency in funding obviously does not encourage returning or placing children in families. These institutions usually no longer provide education, healthcare and other services of their own, but the children go to neighborhood schools and use municipal social and healthcare services, which is seen to better promote their adaptation to society. This has obviously cut the maintenance costs remarkably, but on the other hand, it has been a major reason to resist reform locally because of lost workplaces.

Active Involvement of NGOs

There are only rare non-state alternative care units, run by child welfare NGOs, foundations, and religious organizations (for more information, see Chernova & Kulmala, 2018; Tarasenko, 2018b). Yet NGOs and foundations play a remarkable role in adding—and filling the gaps—to state provision and support (Kulmala et al., 2021c). NGOs run activities to support children living in residential care units throughout the country. Their volunteers take children to events and hobbies, run hobby clubs, and serve as support persons for individual children. NGOs are also often responsible for social adaptation and after-care programs. These are services often outsourced to NGOs through governmental funding (e.g., Tarasenko, 2018a). There are also several child welfare foundations financed by businesses, which provide grants to NGOs to operate in the field. It seems that governmental institutions have become very open to the helping hands of the non-governmental actors, which indeed contribute remarkably to the well-being of institutionalized children by providing a variety of extra support and humanity in their lives (Bindman et al., 2018; also Disney, 2015). In addition, companies are (expected to be) involved in charities ranging from small donations to corporate social programs. Children are perhaps one of the most popular fields for companies and citizens to engage with in charity or voluntarism—perhaps because it is high on the governmental agenda and thus less controversial than many other issues in Russian society.

Outside institutions, many services for foster parents are provided by NGOs. There seems to be both a supplementary and complementary role for NGOs. In the supplementary form, many of the obligatory "schools for foster parents," for instance, are outsourced to NGO providers, with state funding. As to the complementary role, many new associations for foster parents and other NGOs provide a variety of (peer) support services for both fostered children and fostering parents (Kulmala et al., 2021c).

Where the role of non-state actors seems to be major is in preventive work. The public centers so far lack preventive skills, but this new direction is now rapidly developing in the work of NGOs—as is work with those birth parents whose children have already been taken into state care. Religious communities are also engaged in prevention: for instance, the Russian Orthodox Church has parish-level social workers responsible among other things for "prevention of social orphanhood."

Overall, as documented by Bindman and colleagues (2018), Russian child welfare NGOs played a considerable role in shaping the ideas and designing Russia's significant reform. They provided new ideas on care and had a formative role in writing key documents of the reform, thanks to their expertise developed due to their connections to the international child welfare community and street-level realities in their own country.

In sum, the Russian child welfare system remains state-dominated, although with help from other sectors. The conflicts between national policy goals and local circumstances (e.g., inadequate resources, infrastructures) enhance collaboration between the public sector, NGOs and businesses, which produce hybrid service modes. The remaining institutions, though, remain state-dominated, while the main role of the NGOs appears to lie in filling the gaps within the state institutions and providing support for birth and foster families and children leaving the system (after-care). Yet NGOs are clearly in a position to provide much-needed expertise and thus have the ability to change the system.

Conclusions: Will the New Ideas Change the Institutions and Practices?

Undoubtedly, there is a fundamental shift underway in Russia's child welfare policy. Reflecting the Russian system with the conceptualization by Gilbert and colleagues (2011) on the three orientations of child protection systems, the old child protection oriented system is now being reformed toward an interesting combination of child-focused and family support models, at least on a policy level.

One can see several drivers for this change. Russian child welfare experts have been criticizing the predominance of residential care and advocating for change since the 1980s. The ongoing reform is not solely a national project but driven by wider global trends. After the collapse of the Soviet Union, Russia became more closely integrated with global human and child rights norms, which pushed the system toward deinstitutionalization (An & Kulmala, 2020; Kulmala et al., 2021a). Russian child welfare NGOs, linked to the international norms and best domestic practices, contributed significantly to the content of the reform. The reform is, however, also driven by domestic policy. Safeguarding every child's right to grow up in a family-like setting is a beautiful fit with the conservative turn in Russian family policy, which took place due to the severe decline in population and caused moral panics around childhood and family values. Russia needs all its children, as indicated by the program of the presidential party. This need grew from concern around the low birth rate (combined with high mortality) and intertwines with President Putin's wider project to revitalize the nation. Family stands as the core unit of the Russian society in this ideological project.

New Ideals of Children in Focus and Supported Families

At the level of ideas, one can indeed see the shifting orientation toward child-focused and family support. The novel focus on helping birth parents in taking care of their children and this way strengthening Russian families can be interpreted as being driven by the idea of a family unit that needs assistance, which is, according to Gilbert and colleagues (2011, p. 255), characteristic of family service-oriented systems. The programs underline the importance of primary prevention (providing early support for families) in order to prevent children entering alternative care.

The increasing emphasis on the better adaptation of children deprived of parental care into Russian society (through family-based care and social adaptation programs), in turn, speaks to the idea of Russian society's need for healthy and contributory citizens, which is characteristic of child-focused systems. In the end, in Russia, it is the state's obligation to guarantee a good childhood to each child: if this is not possible in the birth family then in a fostering or adoptive one. Such a paternalistic position in which the state assumes a parental role but refamiliarizes a child by foster home, kinship care or adoption is in line with a child-focused orientation. In addition, putting children's rights in the foreground and emphasizing parents' duty as caregivers can be seen in the light of a child-focused model. Ideally, the state-parent relationship (either birth or foster parents) is supposed to be a partnership, as in child-focused and family service-oriented systems (cf. Gilbert et al., 2011, Table 12.2).

Persistent Focus on Alternative Care

Many path dependences and clashes between goals, existing legislation, and daily practices hinder the fulfillment of the goals (Jäppinen & Kulmala, 2021). At the level of many practices, the Russian system is still highly child protection-oriented. Interventions are late and rough, with the aim of protecting children from their maltreating parents. In child protection-oriented systems, parents' neglectful and abusive behavior toward children is typically the key driver of intervention (Gilbert et al., 2011, p. 255). Instead of partnership, the state–parent relationship is adversarial or even punitive in practice. The guardianship department, *opeka*, does not support parents but punishes them for not fulfilling their parental obligations, even if the reform policies assume a new supportive function. Means to support families are still underdeveloped and the accent of interventions is on placing children in alternative care.

Instead of community-based services, an applied form of "preventive" support is often to temporarily place a child in an institution in order to give the parents time and space to solve their problems. The duration of these "temporary" placements, though, might often become years. Further, the termination of parental rights usually breaks the tie between the child and their birth parent(s) permanently, especially if the child is adopted. So far, the system lacks skills in early intervention and prevention, and thus in practice cannot be considered as family service oriented—especially when it comes to birth parents (Jäppinen, 2021). Supportive services for foster families are better developed.

Despite the official goal of prevention, implementation has so far focused on the development of alternative care, namely, increasing foster care and domestic adoptions and renovating the existing institutions to a family-like design. This is seen in the results of the reform. The number of children in alternative care has not decreased substantially, but inside the care system there has been a remarkable change from institutional to family-based care. Notably, though, traditionally common kinship care has stayed as such, comprising almost half of all children in alternative care. In Russia, as in many other countries, adoption is regarded as the part of the alternative care system sometimes serving the best interest of a child—in fact, in the eyes of government officials the ideal solution, being cheapest and permanent; at least for now, when early intervention as a preventive mechanism is still dysfunctional.

Severe path dependencies and institutional traps slow down the development of preventive services. For example, the legislation on the termination of parental rights still directs interventions toward legalistic and investigative means and consequently the system to a child protection orientation (cf. Gilbert et al., 2011, p. 255), in fact by producing "social orphanhood" instead of preventing it. As long as getting in touch with the *opeka* means a major risk of a parent losing their child, there will be no trust in this child protection authority. This poses a serious obstacle for creating low threshold services that families would be willing to use. Moreover, the evaluation of the reform by the number of children placed in foster families as such promotes placements in alternative care instead of support for birth parents and a quantitative measurement of the change that should be qualitative in its essence Furthermore, the old funding scheme of the (temporary) care institutions does not encourage financially returning children to their birth families or placing them in foster families. In addition, the new principle of family-like living in institutions has often meant superficial renovation instead of a real change in staff's mind-sets about the new ideas of care. (Jäppinen & Kulmala, 2021).

Step-by-step Progress and New Openings

So far, we know little what policies and practices are the most effective, but more information should appear as the reform proceeds. Its implementation is regularly monitored. This monitoring is conducted through the regional public chambers, that is, consultative bodies consisting of civil society organizations and other experts at the regional levels of the Russian government. Many visible child rights advocates participate in this work. According to our interviews, at least some of the observed flaws and best practices at the grassroots travel back to decision making. Laws and policies are being amended through this feedback mechanism.

As to the development of evidence-based practice approaches, it is again Russian NGOs who are forerunners: for instance, there is a Moscow-based NGO "Culture of Childhood," financially supported by the Russian Ministry of Economic Development, which coordinates a program "Evaluation of Projects in the Sphere of Childhood." The program brings together scholars, NGO representatives, and other experts on the well-being of children and declares as its major mission that "evidence-based practices would become as the leading principle in the development and realization of any program in the sphere of childhood."[10] So far, we do not see any overarching and systematic application of the evidence-based paradigm in Russian child welfare policymaking, but these baby steps taken by the non-state experts are important in moving into this direction.

As shown, support and practices for foster families have been developing rapidly. According to our observations in the all-Russian meeting of residential care institutions in 2018,[11] now social adaptation programs and after care services are being developed throughout the country. In the resource rich regions (cf. Kainu et al., 2017) the old corridor-type institutions have been transferred into family-like units, but most of the regions still struggle with renovations due to insufficient resources, and sometimes will. For the very first time, there was lots of talk about working with birth parents. Thus, it seems that the changes in ideas push the practices forward step by step.

What is our prognosis for the further direction of the Russian child protection system? We suggest that the child-focused orientation might grow even stronger due to the still existing flaws in work with birth parents. A kind of child-focused discourse has traditionally been strong in Russia, although not focusing on a child's agency but rather on children as the future of the nation. We believe that the paradigm change is likely to proceed, but it still requires time. Many contradictions between the new goals and existing structures remain to be solved. One major issue to overcome is citizens' (fully understandable) distrust of the child protection authorities. How does one deal with the classical tension between support and control? How does one create a system of trustworthy services that do not stigmatize either children or families? How does one empower children and families in vulnerable situations and encourage their participation in the development of the system? The professional standards and ethical guidelines of the *opeka* and remedy mechanisms must develop before the services will be able to gain citizens' trust. What seems promising is the significant role of NGOs, first in designing the ongoing changes, and second in filling the gaps left by the state. These NGOs are forerunners in their efforts to destigmatize the birth parents of children in alternative care and to develop working mechanisms with them. In the long run, this might lead to substantial changes in this still underdeveloped sphere.

---

[10] See, http://ozenka.info/about/dokazatelniy_podhod/ [accessed 7 June, 2018].
[11] See: https://www.profipro.ru/events/detail.php?ELEMENT_ID=936 [accessed 5 December 2018].

Postscript: At the moment of writing this, Russia's invasion of Ukraine in February 2022 with the ever tightening control of domestic sphere sheds a dark shadow over the future development of human rights and social justice in Russia. The NGO sector, which particularly in the field of child welfare has relied on the global discussions over child rights, is under a constantly increasing pressure. Russia is taking distance to the international human rights standards and was excluded from the Council of Europe in March 2022. Most sadly, as always during the crises, it is the most vulnerable groups, including children, who pay the highest price. We will most likely see an increase in numbers of children deprived of parental care. There is already evidence about instrumental use of child's rights in the war. In addition, the economic sanctions most likely shrink down the possibilities to implement the still on-going reforms and in particular the restructuring of the public institutions will be delayed.

References

An, S. and Kulmala, M. (2020). Global deinstitutionalization policy in the post-Soviet space: A comparison of child-welfare reforms in Russia and Kazakhstan. *Global social policy*, 21(1), 51–74.

Bindman, E., Kulmala, M., and Bogdanova, E. (2018). NGOs and the policymaking process in Russia: The case of child welfare reform. *Journal of Public Administration and Governance*, 32(2), 1–16.

Biryukova, S., Varlamova, M., and Sinyavskaya, O. (2013). Sirotstvo v Rossii: Osnovnye tendentsii i prioritety gosudarstvennoy politiki. *SPERO: Sotsial'naya politika: ekspertiza, rekomendatsii, obzory*, 18, 57–80.

Biryukova, S. and Sinyavskaya, O. (2017). Children out of parental care in Russia: What we can learn from the statistics. *Journal for Social Policy Studies*, 15(3), 367–382.

Biryukova, S. and Makarentseva, A. (2021). Statistics on the deinstitutionalization of child welfare in Russia'. In M. Kulmala, M. Jäppinen, A. Tarasenko, and A. Pivovarova (Eds.), *Reforming child welfare in the post-Soviet space: Institutional change in Russia*. (pp. 23–46). Routledge.

Cherniak, M. (2000). Humuroe utro: problemy detei-sirot v Rossii. *Rossiiskaia Federatsiia*, 7, 41–43.

Chernova, Z. and Kulmala, M. (2018). "Po slozhnosti—eto rabota, po sostaianiu dushi—semia": Professionalizatsiia premenogo roditel'stva v sovremennoi Rossii. *Zhurnal sotsiologii i sotsialnoi antropologii*, 21(3), 46–70.

Chernova, Z. and Shpakovskaya, L. (2021). 'Making' a Family: Motives and Practices of Foster Parenting. In M. Kulmala, M. Jäppinen, A. Tarasenko, and A. Pivovarova (Eds.), *Reforming child welfare in the post-soviet space: Institutional change in Russia* (pp. 143–160). Routledge.

Cook, L. (2011). Russia's welfare regime: The shift toward statism. In M. Jäppinen, M. Kulmala and A. Saarinen (Eds.), *Gazing at welfare, gender and agency in post-socialist countries*, (pp, 14–37). Cambridge Scholars.

Disney, T. (2015). The role of emotion in institutional spaces of Russian orphan care: Policy and practical matters. In M. Blazek and P. Kraftl (Eds.), *Children's emotions in policy and practice: Mapping and making spaces of childhood*, (pp. 17–33). Palgrave Macmillan (pp. xx–xx).

Gilbert, N., Parton, N., and Skivenes, M. (2011). Introduction. In N. Gilbert, N. Parton, and M. Skivenes (Eds.), *Child protection systems: International trends and orientations*. Oxford University Press, 3–13.

Granberg, L. and Sätre, A. (2017). *The other Russia: Local experience and societal change*. Routledge.

High, A. (2014). Pondering the politicization of intercountry adoption: Russia's ban on American "forever families." *Cardozo Journal of International and Comparative Law*, 22(3), 497–560.

Holm-Hansen, J., Firsov, M., Kristofersen, L., Malik, L., Mardakhaev, L., and Myrvold, T. (2005). Alternatives to orphanages in northwest Russia: Preconditions and obstacles in policy development. In J. Holm-Hansen (Ed.), *Placement of orphans: Russian and Nordic experiences*. NIBR Working Paper 137.

Iarskaia-Smirnova, E. and Sadykov, R. (2015). Problema opredeleiia sotsial'no opasnogo polozhenii semei i detei v sovremennoi Rossii. In E. Iarskaia-Smirnova and V. Markina (Eds.), *Sotsial'no opasnoe polozhenie sem'i i detei. Analiz poniatiia i metodologiia otsenki* (pp. 7–22). OOO Variant.

Iarskaia-Smirnova, E., Kosova, O., and Kononenko, R. (2021). The 'last-minute children': Where did they come from, where will they go? Media portrayals of children deprived of parental care, 2006–2018'.

In M. Kulmala, M. Jäppinen, A. Tarasenko, and A. Pivovarova (Eds.), *Reforming child welfare in the post-Soviet space: Institutional change in Russia*. Routledge, 47–67.

Jäppinen, M. (2018). Krovnye roditeli detei, iziayh iz sem'i, v diskurse sotrudnikov organov zastcshiti detei. *Zhurnal sotsiologii i sotsialnoi antropologii*, 21(3), 93–114.

Jäppinen, M. (2021) 'No longer parents or parents in need of support? Views of child welfare experts on birth parents', in M. Kulmala, M. Jäppinen, A. Tarasenko, and A. Pivovarova (Eds.), *Reforming child welfare in the post-Soviet space: Institutional change in Russia*, Routledge, pp. (xx–xx).

Jäppinen, M. and Kulmala, M. (2021). One has to stop chasing numbers!' The unintended consequences of Russian child welfare reforms'. In M. Kulmala, M. Jäppinen, A. Tarasenko, and A. Pivovarova (Eds.), *Reforming child welfare in the post-Soviet space: Institutional change in Russia*, Routledge, (pp. xx-xx).

Kainu, M., Kulmala, M., Nikula, J., and Kivinen, M. (2017). The Russian welfare state system: With special reference to regional inequality. In C. Aspalter (Ed.), *The Routledge International Handbook to Welfare State Systems*, Routledge, (pp. xx-xx).

Khmelnitskaya, M. (2015). *The policy-making process and social learning in Russia: The case of housing policy*. Palgrave Macmillan.

Khlinovskaya Rockhill, E. (2010). *Lost to the state: Family discontinuity, social orphanhood and residential care in the Russian Far East*. Berghahn Books.

Kulmala, M. (2017, March 28). Paradigm shift in Russian child welfare policy. *Russian Analytical Digest*, 200, 5–10.

Kulmala, M., Kainu, M., Nikula, J., and Kivinen, M. (2014). Paradoxes of agency: Democracy and welfare in Russia. *Demokratizatsiya: The Journal of Post-Soviet Democratization*, 23(4), 523–552.

Kulmala, M., Rasell, M., and Chernova, Z. (2017). Overhauling Russia's child welfare system: Institutional and ideational factors behind the paradigm shift. *The Journal of Social Policy Studies*, 15(3), 353–366.

Kulmala, M. and Fomina, A. (2021). Planning for the Future: Future Orientation, Agency and Self-Efficacy of Young Adults Leaving Care in the Russian Arctic'. In F. Stammler and R. Toivanen (Eds.), *Young people, wellbeing and placemaking in the Arctic*. Routledge Research in Polar Regions Series, (pp. xx-xx).

Kulmala, M., Jäppinen, M., Tarasenko, A. & Pivovarova, A. (2021a). Introduction: Russian Child Welfare Reform and Institutional Change. M. Kulmala, M. Jäppinen, A. Tarasenko, and A. Pivovarova (Eds.), *Reforming child welfare in the post-Soviet space: Institutional change in Russia*. Routledge, (pp. xx-xx).

Kulmala, M., Jäppinen, M., Tarasenko, A., and Pivovarova, A. (2021b). In Conclusion: The Fragmented Implementation of the New Child Welfare Policy'. In M. Kulmala, M. Jäppinen, A. Tarasenko, and A. Pivovarova (Eds.), *Reforming child welfare in the post-Soviet space: Institutional change in Russia*, Routledge, (pp. xx-xx).

Kulmala, M. Shpakovskaya, L., & Chernova, Z. (2021c) 'The Ideal (Re)organization of Care: Child Welfare Reform as a Battlefield over Resources and Recognition', in M. Kulmala, M. Jäppinen, A. Tarasenko, and A. Pivovarova (Eds.), *Reforming child welfare in the post-Soviet space: Institutional change in Russia*, Routledge, (pp. xx-xx).

Kulmala, M., Chernova, Z., and Fomina, A. (2021d). Young Adults Leaving Care: Agency and Educational Choice'. In M. Kulmala, M. Jäppinen, A. Tarasenko, and A. Pivovarova (Eds.), *Reforming child welfare in the post-Soviet space: Institutional change in Russia*, Routledge, (pp. xx-xx).

Marshall, B. J. (1993). Decline of the American orphanage, 1941–1980. *Social Service Review*, 67(3), 459–480.

Nechaeva A. (2000). *Rossiia i ee deti (rebenok, zakon, gosudarstvo)*. IGT RAN.

Offe, C. (1999). How can we trust our fellow citizens? In M. Warren (Ed.), *Democracy and trust* (pp. 42–87). Cambridge University Press.

Prisiazhniuk, D., Markina, V., and Rozhkova. O. (2015). Analiz sistemy okazaniia pomostcshi sem'iam i det'iam v sotsial'no opasnom polozhenii v RF. In E. Iarskaia-Smirnova, E. and V. Markina (Eds.), *Sotsial'no opasnoe polozhenie sem'i i detei. Analiz poniatiia i metodologiia otsenki* (pp. 23–51). OOO Variant.

Rykun, A. and Iuzaninov, K. (2009). Profilaktika sotsial'nogo sirotsva: Institutsional'nye i diskursivnye aspekty. *Zhurnal issledovanii sotsial'noi politiki*, 7(2), 241–260.

Semia, G., Zaitsev, G., and Zaitseva, N. (2016). Formirovanie rossiiskoi modeli predoleniia sotsial'nogo sirotstva. Psykhologicheskie nauki i obrazovanie, 21(1), 67–82.

Stryker, R. (2012). Emotion socialization and attachment in Russian children's homes. *Global Studies of Childhood*, 2(2), 85–96.

Tarasenko, A. (2018a). Russian non-profit organisations in service delivery: Neoliberal and statist social policy principles intertwined. *Europe-Asia Studies*, 70(4), 514–530.

Tarasenko, A. (2018b). Regional'nye osobennosti reformy sirotkih uchrezhdenii v Rossii. *Zhurnal sotsiologii i sotsial'noi antropologii*, 21(3), 115–139.

Tarasenko, A. (2021). Institutional variety rather than the end of residential care: Regional responses to deinstitutionalisation reform in Russia. In M. Kulmala, M. Jäppinen, A. Tarasenko, and A. Pivovarova (Eds.), *Reforming child welfare in the post-Soviet space: Institutional change in Russia*, Routledge, (pp. xx-xx).

Verhallen, T., Hall, C., and Slembrouck, S. (2019). Family support and child protection approaches: Historicising perspectives on contemporary discourses of social work. *Qualitative Social Work*, 18(2), 286–301.

Child Protection Systems in Uganda

Deogratias Yiga

Abstract

This chapter spotlights the child protection systems in Uganda. Almost three decades have passed since Uganda ratified the UNCRC and African Charter on the Rights and Welfare of the Child . Efforts are underway to ratify the Hague Convention on the Protection of Children and Inter country Adoption to ensure that children grow up in a safe environment free from all forms of maltreatment, violence, and exploitation. Notwithstanding, a strong legal and policy framework children in Uganda continue to experience physical, sexual, and emotional violence and are exposed to varied risk contexts such as child labor, child trafficking, child marriage, and teenage pregnancies. Efforts to translate legal and policy commitments into protection outcomes for children continue to be constrained by limited adherence to established standards, programming pitfalls, limited data, and inadequate investment in child protection systems development and functionality.

Key Words: Uganda, UNCRC, Hague Convention, child labour, child trafficking, child marriage, violence, maltreatment, exploitation, data

Introduction

Uganda is located in the center of the East African region with a population of 40 million people and a population growth rate of 3% per annum. Females are the majority, constituting 51% of the total population. Uganda has one of the youngest populations in the world, with children constituting 53% of the total population (Uganda Bureau of Statistics [UBOS], 2019). Uganda's post-independence history has been characterized by periods of political instability and outright violent conflict. Notwithstanding the relative stability over the last decade, coupled with steady economic growth rates, the country is still ranked among the poorest in the world.

It is almost three decades since Uganda ratified the UN Convention on the Rights of the Child (CRC) in 1990 and subsequently the African Charter on the Rights and Welfare of the Child in 1994. In addition to these key global and regional child rights commitments, Uganda has also ratified several child rights instruments with explicit provisions on the protection rights of children. Notably, the only relevant child protection international instrument that Uganda has not committed to (through signature, accession or ratification) is the Hague Convention on the Protection of Children and Intercountry Adoption. Efforts are underway to have this ratified too. In an effort to domesticate and give effect to its international commitments, the government of Uganda has, over the years, enacted a robust national child protection legal and policy framework that is currently ranked among the best in the region. The overriding aspiration of this framework is to ensure that all children in Uganda grow up in a safe environment free from all forms of maltreatment, violence, and exploitation. Underpinning these commitments is a recognition of the significant and widespread child protection risks to which almost all children in the country are vulnerable.

There is a general appreciation and acceptance among policymakers and practitioners that notwithstanding the substantial legal, policy, and program interventions directed at preventing and mitigating child protection risks over the last three decades, sustainable child protection outcomes remain elusive across the country. This is to a large measure attributed to the disjointed, ad hoc, and project driven nature of social interventions that seek to address these risks. Consequently, there is now a growing momentum to redirect child protection programming in Uganda towards strengthening the child protection system across all delivery levels.

This chapter explores in greater detail and in the context of Uganda, the nature and magnitude of the key child protection risks, the eligibility criteria for accessing services, the nature of child protection provisions, and the delivery methods as well as the child protection financing modalities.

An Overview of the Child Protection Context in Uganda

Throughout the 1990s until recently (2018) the child protection discourse in Uganda has been characterized by an ominous absence of reliable and nationally representative data on the prevalence of various forms of child protection violations and risks. Both policy and program interventions have been largely informed by thematic, geographically limited, and sometimes methodologically questionable studies and surveys conducted largely by NGOs. This reality significantly limits the extent to which prevalence patterns over time can be articulated.

In the early 1990s, an estimated 4 million children, almost half of the total child population then, was categorized as vulnerable and living in difficult circumstances (Barton & Wamai, 1994). These included orphans estimated at between 1.2–1.5 million children, children with disabilities, child laborers, children displaced by armed conflict, children conscripted in the army, and street children. In the 1990s and early 2000s a growing number of girls between 8 and 15 years experienced sexual violence because older men thought they were more likely to be free from HIV/AIDS, unlike their older counterparts. The 1990s also carried a myth that having sexual relations with a virgin would result in a cure for the disease. The age and sex differentials in HIV/AIDs prevalence were most significant in the 15–19 year age group, when girls were three to six times more likely to be infected than boys (Basaza & Kaija, 2002).

To date, the National Violence against Children Survey (Ministry of Gender, Labour, and Social Development [MGLSD], 2018) provides the most reliable and nationally representative overview of the state of evidence on the major forms of violence against children in Uganda. The survey focused on three major forms of violence: sexual, physical, and emotional.

According to the survey, one in three girls (35%) and one in six boys (17%) aged 18–24 years reported experiencing sexual violence during their childhoods. Over 80% of these youths reported experiencing more than one incident of sexual violence. One in four girls (25%) and one in ten boys (11%) aged 13–17 years reported sexual violence in the year preceding the study (MGLSD, 2018). Neighbors, strangers, relatives, intimate friends, boyfriends, and classmates were reported as the common perpetrators of sexual violence. Girls are typically abused in homes of a trusted person, while boys are mostly abused at school (MGLSD, 2018). Six in ten females (59%) and seven in ten males (68%) of Ugandans aged 18–24 years reported experiencing physical violence during their childhoods. On the other hand, four in ten girls (44%) and six in ten boys (59%) ages 13–17 experienced physical violence in the year preceding the study (MGLSD, 2018). With regard to emotional violence, one in three 18–24-year-old Ugandans reported suffering emotional violence during their childhood, with boys in the central region experiencing significantly higher prevalence of emotional violence than their counterparts in the northern and western regions. For children aged 13–17 years, more than one in five reported experiencing emotional abuse in the year preceding the study (MGLSD, 2018). The reported perpetrators of physical and emotional violence include teachers, parents, other adults in the community, and fellow children.

Significant numbers of children in Uganda experience physical, sexual, and emotional violence due to exposure to varied risk contexts which in their own right constitute child protection violations. In this section we explore some of the issues and contexts that constitute or promote child protection violations.

Child labor is on the rise in Uganda due to high levels of household poverty and urbanization. Statistics from the labor force survey (2010) indicated that working children in the age group 5–14 yrs constituted 30.9 % (3,034,126) of the country's population (US Department of Labor, 2015). Majority of the working children (95%) were employed in the agricultural sector with the major activities being crop cultivation, herding and fishing (US Department of Labor, 2015). A total of 2.4 million children are engaged in exploitative child labor (UNICEF, 2015). Girls are at a higher risk of entering child labor to supplement the family income.

Child trafficking is recognized as a hidden but growing problem in Uganda. The country is a source, transit and destination of victims of trafficking with the majority being children and women, although men are also trafficked, albeit on a small scale. Child trafficking has recently mostly involved children from the Karamoja region who are trafficked to Kampala and other urban centres along the way from karamoja. The majority end up emgaged in begging, street vending, domestic work, and commercial sexual exploitation (US Department of Labor, 2018).

Child marriage and teenage pregnancies predominantly impact girls, especially those that are least educated, poorest, and living in rural areas. According to the Uganda Demographic and Health Survey (UBOS and ICF International, 2016), the percentage of children aged 12–17 who had ever been or were currently married was 1.2% for males and 5.7% for females. Teen pregnancies in Uganda which stood at 25% in 2016 (UBOS and ICF International, 2016)), are associated with high maternal mortality, abortions, and cases of obstetric fistula, among other consequences.

The phenomenon of street children has been an intriguing feature of Uganda's child protection landscape for decades. Since the late 1970s, 80s and early 90s, the phenomenon of street children was predominantly attributed to the adverse impact of HIV/AIDS (Barton & Wamai, 1994), abusive parents, broken homes, domestic violence, delinquency, death of parents, and homelessness. In 2006, the face of street children in Uganda changed, with the coming of Karamojong street families (an ethnic group from the North Eastern region of Uganda) on the major streets of various towns of the country who continuously flee insecurity, cattle rustling, harsh climatic conditions, and acute poverty. All in all, there continues to be a close association between violence against children and the street children phenomenon. Children in street situations face overlapping experiences of physical, sexual and psychological violence perpetrated by fellow children, strangers, police and other law enforcement agencies (Walakira and Nyanzi, 2012) . Data relating to the number of street children is scarce and to some extent unreliable (USAID, 2015). Estimates made over 10 years ago suggested that there could be over 10,000 'street children' in Uganda's towns between the ages of 0 and 17 years (USAID, 2015).

Children with disabilities are among the highest at risk category among all vulnerable groups of children. There is a paucity of reliable data on children with disabilities due to a number of reasons, including varied definitions of disability, differing individual and cultural perceptions of impairment, and un-harmonized approaches to data collection (Riche & Anyimuzala, 2014). Regardless, children with disabilities face multiple forms of discrimination that are often rooted in misconceptions and superstitious beliefs about disability. Children with disabilities are often excluded, restricted, and overlooked because of their impairments. They often have the least access to basic social services and are far more vulnerable to multiple forms of abuse and maltreatment.

A substantial number of children, especially adolescents, are infected with HIV/AIDS and growing numbers continue to face considerable risks and vulnerabilities to HIV/AIDS. Whereas significant gains have been registered in the Prevention of Mother to Child Transmission of HIV/AIDS (PMTCT), the pandemic is the second leading cause of death among adolescents in Uganda (UNAIDS, 2014). Most-at-risk adolescents for HIV acquisition or transmission include adolescents vertically infected and living with HIV for many years, those with an early sexual debut, teenage adolescent mothers, and adolescents who are sexually abused or exploited. Adolescent girls often have fewer social assets than their male peers such as reliable peer networks, safe spaces in the community to gather and meet friends, and access to media and public messaging. Many lack the knowledge, skills, and confidence needed to take appropriate preventive or remedial measures.

The ongoing efforts to strengthen the child protection system in Uganda and the institutional arrangements underpinning the system are all geared at preventing, mitigating, and redressing the vulnerabilities and violations associated with the above risks.

In exploring the nature and scope of child protection services, it is important to acknowledge a conceptual blurredness around the definition of what constitutes a child protection system among child welfare professionals. One school of thought looks at the child protection system as a broad framework of preventive and responsive interventions that address the vulnerability of children to denial of all their rights. This broader perspective embraces the rights of children along all the four broad domains namely survival, development, protection, and participation. On the other hand, a more narrow and bounded view posits the child protection system framework along the classical definition of child protection as foreseen in Article 19 of the CRC, focusing on the "protection of children from all forms of physical or mental violence, injury or abuse, neglect or negligent treatment, maltreatment or exploitation, including sexual abuse" (CRC, Article 19). In the subsequent sections of this chapter, child protection services are conceptualized from a broader perspective that includes all services necessary to ensure that children's rights and well-being are respected in all contexts.

Bases for Social Allocation

Within the broad framework of social service provisioning there are normally established criteria for inclusion and exclusion. The overriding child rights legal framework, namely the CRC and its associated optional protocols and complementary instruments, provides an overarching guide for child protection entitlements. By defining "the child" as a person below 18 years, the international legal regime provides an implicit age–based criteria for determining entitlement to child protection services. However, as is clearly known, these instruments leave room for state parties to modify the definition of the child in respect of specific issues through domestic legislation and policy and thus to redefine the applicable child protection entitlements. The wide-ranging child protection laws of Uganda constitute the overriding basis for claiming and delivering child protection services. In Uganda, the legally binding criteria for accessing child protection services is the legal definition of the child. The Constitution of Uganda (1995) and most child related laws in Uganda recognize a child as a person below 18 years. However, there are two exceptions in relation to the minimum age of criminal liability (12 years) and minimum age of employment (16 years). On all other issues, all children below 18 years are entitled to the same legal protection and access to services.

The specific child protection legal entitlements of children are outlined in the Constitution and a wide range of laws and legal instruments focusing on either the broad childcare and protection ambit or on specific child protection issues and risks.

Chapter 4 of the Constitution of Uganda constitutes a bill of rights for all Ugandans including children. It is recognized that the basic rights and freedoms of the individual are inherent (natural) and not given by the state. All rights and freedoms must be respected, and promoted by all organs of Government and by all persons. Some of the rights recognized include: right to life, right to personal liberty, protection from inhuman treatment, and special provisions for disadvantaged groups. Article 34 of the Constitution explicitly recognizes the rights of children. It provides for the right of children to know and be cared for by their parents or those entitled by law to bring them up; a right to basic education and medical treatment; and protection from social or economic exploitation (for children up to 16 years). The Constitution further provides for separation of children in custody from adult offenders and generally for special protection for orphans and other vulnerable children.

One of the key child protection services that also constitutes the foundation for claiming all other services is embedded in the right to birth registration. The Constitution of Uganda; the Births and Deaths Registration Act, Cap 309 of the Laws of Uganda; the Uganda Registration Services Bureau Act; the Local Government Act, Cap 243; and the Children Act, Cap 59 all have provisions relating to birth registration. The provisions in these legislations are in harmony with Article 7 of the CRC, which stipulates that a child shall be registered immediately after birth and shall have the right from birth to a name, nationality, and care by his or her parents.

Article 34 of the 1995 constitution; the Children Act, Cap 59; the Local Government Act 2007 (as amended); the Penal Code Act, Cap 160 (as amended); the Employment Act 2006; the Occupational Safety and Health Act 2006; the Labour Dispute and Settlement Act 2006; the Trafficking in Persons Act 2009; the Occupational Safety and Health Act 2006; and the Education Act 2008 all have provisions that prohibit/regulate involvement of children in hazardous and exploitative work.

Article 32 of the Constitution prohibits laws, cultures, customs and traditions which are against the dignity or interests of women or other disadvantaged groups including children. The specific practices that are prohibited by the law include child marriage and female genital mutilation. The Constitution and the Marriage Act both provide that marriages should be consensual and can only be registered if the parties involved are 18 and over. The ICC Act 2010 also prohibits forced marriage of women and girls especially in conflict situations. The Prohibition of Female Genital Mutilation Act 2010 is the comprehensive law on the subject. The Children's Act Cap 59 in S.7 implicitly prohibits FGM. It provides that "it shall be unlawful to subject a Child to social or customary practices that are harmful to a child's health.

Uganda's legal framework recognizes the role of the family as the fulcrum of the childcare and protection system. The Children's Act provides for the right for children to be cared for by their parents and only to be removed subject to judicial review and determination that it is not in the best interest of the child (section 4(1&2)) and after other alternatives have been sought and exhausted and the risk presenting to the child is severe (section 28).

The Trafficking in Persons Act 2009 consolidates most of the provisions related to child trafficking. Other pieces of legislation are applicable including Article 34 of the 1995 constitution; the Penal Code Act, Cap 160 (as amended); and the Employment Act 2006. Section 12 of the TIPs Act 2009 protects the rights of victims by providing that a victim of trafficking shall not be penalized for any crime committed as a direct result of his or her trafficking. The Act also provides for repatriation, restitution, and compensation of victims of trafficking, and the extradition of offenders. In terms of services, Section 12 of the TIPs Act provides that victims of trafficking in persons shall be accorded available health and social services, medical care, counseling, and psychological assistance. Section 21 provides for establishment of a specific office with a mandate to develop a comprehensive and integrated program to prevent and suppress trafficking in persons.

The protection of children from commercial sexual abuse is encompassed in Article 34 of the 1995 constitution; the Children Act, Cap 59; the Local Government Act 2007 (as amended); the Penal Code Act, Cap 160 (as amended); and the Trafficking in Persons Act 2009.

Access to justice is a critical dimension of child protection. Part 10 of the Children's Act comprehensively outlines the procedures for children in conflict with the law in respect to age of criminal responsibility, arrest, bail, trial, sentencing, detention, and rehabilitation. The Act provides for the right to privacy (section 102) and prohibits detention of children with adults (section 94(6), section 89(8), which is also mirrored by Article 34(6) of the Constitution). The Act prohibits the use of corporal punishment (section 94(9)), provides for detention as a matter of last resort (section 94(4)), and provides for cases involving children to be expedited (section 99(1)). The Article 28 of the Constitution provides for the right to a fair trial and according to the Penal Code Act everyone is innocent until proven guilty. Protection of child witnesses and victims of crime is implicitly provided for in the Magistrates Act (albeit discretionary), the Prevention of Trafficking in Persons Act 2009, the Evidence Act, Domestic Violence Act and the Prohibition of FGM Act.

Matters regarding child protection in emergencies and armed conflicts are provided for under the Refugee Act 2006, which provides for the protection of rights of refugee children. The Amnesty Act 2000 provides for the return and reintegration of ex-child combatants (children are exempted from the rigorous Amnesty processes). The UPDF Act 2005 prohibits the recruitment of children into armed forces.

It is important to note that within the broader legal framework of entitlement to child protection services, various policies, strategies, and programs both public and private have evolved and applied varied targeting criteria which, though not statutorily entrenched, provide insight into alternative bases of social allocation. The overriding consideration across most programs is the level of vulnerability of the child. The concept of child vulnerability, though widely applied, is not clearly and explicitly defined by either law or policy. The national OVC policy outlines different categories of vulnerable children but does not offer an explicit definition. Consequently, there have been, over time, varying estimates of the number of vulnerable children in Uganda depending on the definition of vulnerability applied. It is important to note that whereas orphan hood is generally regarded as the most significant indicator of vulnerability, there are other important individual and household circumstances that expose children to economic, social and health risks (Nkhata et al., 2000). It is indeed important to note that whereas using strict eligibility criteria for selecting children to access social protection programmes may engender efficiency in resource use, it could also exclude many children in need of support and may also introduce "perverse incentives" into the community (Nkhata et al., 2000).

In 2009, the Ministry of Gender, Labour, and Social Development commissioned a national situation analysis of vulnerable children as a precursor to the subsequent development of a National Orphans Vulnerable Children Policy, aimed at improving the quality of life of poor and vulnerable children. This process constituted the first serious effort to conceptualize a usable and Uganda specific criteria for determining "child vulnerability." Through a consultative process with Ugandan experts a criterion that combines multiple factors of children's vulnerability into a single "vulnerability score" was agreed in consultation with national experts. The score has a total of eight vulnerability categories and 50 vulnerability indicators, as shown in Table 44.1.

Based on application of the vulnerability score to household survey data, the situation analysis yielded estimates of vulnerable children under four categories, namely: critically vulnerable (8%), moderately vulnerable (43%), generally vulnerable (45%), and not vulnerable (4%). Overall, more than 96% of children in Uganda were at the time considered to be vulnerable (Kalibala & Elson, 2010).

The other significant effort to systematically define a prospective allocative criteria for social provisioning was the "Situation Analysis of Child Poverty and Deprivation in Uganda (2014)." This analysis developed a methodology for measuring child poverty in Uganda based on an internationally agreed upon framework, stemming from the CRC. The framework used seven criteria, namely: nutrition (stunted, wasted, or underweight); health (immunization, whether their birth was attended by skilled personnel); access to water (use of unimproved water source such as surface water, and distance to clean water sources); sanitation (no access to improved sanitation facilities or having no toilet at all); shelter (overcrowding); education (attendance and completion of primary school); and access to information (household access to radio, television, or mobile phone).

Child poverty was then defined as a situation where a child was deprived in two or more of these seven dimensions. The criteria were applied to household data from the

Table 44.1 Categories and indicators of children's vulnerability

Category	Indicator	Score
1. Household relationships and situation	• Child head of house	2
	• Elderly head of household	1
	• Child <17yrs married	2
	• Child 17 to 18yrs but married	1
	• Illness of at least 3 months in last 1 year of anyone aged 15 to 59yrs in the household	1
	• Number of people in the household >6	1
	• Child rarely or never saw guardian before	1
	• Negative changes in child's life since joining HH (e.g., food, school grades, etc.)	1
	• Not living with siblings	1
	• Does not visit with absent siblings	1
	• Child has no one to talk to in case of problems	1
2. Parental status	• Death of mother	3
	• Death of father	2
	• Serious "impairment" of mother	1
	• Serious "impairment" of father	1
	• Mother illness of at least 3 months in last 1 year	1
	• Father illness in at least 3 months in last 1 year	1
	• Child never visits mother	2
	• Child never visits father	2
3. Household characteristics	• Main source of drinking water (surface water)	1
	• No sustainable source of food	2
	• Household's total current monthly income (<US$30)	1
	• If one in HH aged 18yrs or more reported main activity in last 7 days as paid work	2
4. Child's school attendance	• If child aged 12 to 17yrs and has never attended school	2
	• If child aged <12yrs and has never attended school	1
	• If child aged 12 to 17yrs and did not attend school during 2009	1
	• If child aged <12yrs and did not attend school during 2009	2
	• If reason for absence from school is paid work	3
	• If reason for absence from school is unpaid work for family or any other work	2
	• If reason for absence from school is: not want to go, periods, ceremonies, illness, lack of uniform or stationery, mistreated at school	1
5. Child's health and nutrition	• If when sick place of medical consultation is not health facility	1
	• If unusual number of meals per day	1
	• If child did not eat anything yesterday	3
	• If family had more meals than child yesterday	1
6. Child's disabilities	• If child has complete difficulty in seeing	3
	• If child has complete difficulty in hearing	3
	• If child has complete difficulty in walking or climbing steps	3
	• If child has complete difficulty in communicating	3

Table 44.1 *Continued*

Category	Indicator	Score
7. Child's basic material needs	• If child does not possess blanket	1
	• If child does not possess pair of shoes	1
	• If child does not possess 2 sets of clothes	1
8. Child's risk taking	• If child aged <17yrs is sexually active	2
	• If child aged 17 to 18yrs is sexually active	1
	• If child aged <17yrs and has ever been pregnant	2
	• If child is 17 to 18yrs and has ever been pregnant	1
	• If child has own child and there is someone else >18yrs in HH	1
	• If child has own child and there is no one else >18yrs in HH	2
	• If child often takes alcohol every day or every week	2
	• If child uses drugs (marijuana, petrol, etc.)	3

Source: Kalibala and Elson (2010)

Uganda Demographic and Health Survey 2011 to yield national estimates of the magnitude of child poverty and deprivation. As a result, 55% of children aged 0–4 in Uganda were categorized as living in poverty and 24% in *extreme* poverty. Up to 38% of children aged 6–17 were categorized as living in poverty with 18% in *extreme* poverty (Batana et al. (2014).

Whereas the two foregoing frameworks provide indicative propositions for developing alternative bases for social allocation, over the years there has been very limited progress in exploring the prospects for practical and holistic application of these criteria in social protection programming. It would appear that practitioners selectively pick and use specific elements of the vulnerability categories and indicators that most suit their programming priorities. Consequently, the bases for social allocation of child protection services remain diverse and vary across projects and programs.

The Nature and Scope of Social Provisions Allocated to Protect Children

Child protection services can be framed under two broad but interlinked categories, namely the statutory services and the programmatic services. The statutory services refer to those services which are foreseen and provided for within the legal framework. Normally these services ought to be universally available and accessible to all children in need. In the case of Uganda the major forms of statutory services include child care services and justice services. Programmatic services, on the other hand, include a wide range of prevention and response interventions that seek to mitigate child protection risks or respond to child rights violations and engender a safe environment for children. Most of these services are provided through time bound projects and programs delivered mostly by NGOs with limited government oversight and financial and technical support from external development agencies.

Statutory Child Protection Provisions

As outlined in the preceding section, Uganda's robust child protection legal framework envisions a range of child protection services. Within the broad prism of child protection laws in Uganda, children can be delineated as either being in need of care and protection or in contact or conflict with the law. This categorization, though not mutually exclusive, provides a useful framework for conceptualizing the statutory child protection services.

THE CONTINUUM OF CHILDCARE AND WELFARE SERVICES

The Children's Act 2004 and the Children (Amendment) Act 2016 constitute the overarching legal framework for the provision of services for children in need of care and protection. In Uganda, just like in any other part of the world, the majority of children live with and are cared for within their biological families. However, owing to the wide-ranging vulnerabilities described in the preceding sections of this chapter, primarily associated with orphanhood, poverty, abuse, and neglect, a significant number of children cannot always live and thrive within their biological families. In such circumstances the Children's Act outlines a continuum of care for children including family preservation, kinship care, foster care, adoption, and institutional care. The Act places an obligation on the minister responsible for Gender, Labor, and Social Development to develop a "national strategy" for the provision of prevention and early intervention programmes to families, parents, caregivers, and children across the country.

The most dominant form of alternative care in Uganda is informal foster care/kinship care arrangements. This is a private arrangement provided in a family environment, through which the child is looked after on an ongoing or indefinite basis by relatives of his or her biological parents. For a long time, this kind of arrangement, though widespread, was entirely private without any legal reference. The Children's Amendment Act 2016 accorded legal recognition to this alternative care system. Section 43C of the Act recognizes customary guardianship and provides that under specific circumstances, family members may appoint a guardian of a child in accordance with their customs, culture, or tradition. Kinship care blends well with most local cultures in Uganda, which place a responsibility on the extended family to take care of children in the absence of biological parents. Though now legally recognized and widely used, this care arrangement is not regulated or financially supported by the state. There is neither a national registration system for kinship placements nor a specific mechanism to regulate and monitor such care placements.

Formal Foster Care as provided for under the Children's Act refers to the legal placement of a child under the care of a competent adult(s) through a court of law. In Uganda's context this would be applicable to situations where there is no traceable biological relationship between the child and the foster parents. Two forms of foster care can be delineated: foster care with intention to adopt which is the legally recognized step to adoption and in the case of Uganda lasts for one year (previously three years); and foster care with no intention to adopt, which is very infrequently used.

The lack of government support and effective supervision for foster care arrangements poses a major challenge in guaranteeing the quality of care services provided. The Government of Uganda does not run any foster care program and makes no financial or logistical provision to foster families. Although there are a few NGOs that provide some short-term support to foster families, for the most part these families have to depend on their own resources to look after the children that they take in. Although Probation and Social Welfare Officers have a legal responsibility to supervise foster care placements, they are unable to effectively discharge this responsibility because of human resource and logistical constraints. Consequently, it is not possible to assess the effectiveness and quality of care provided and the outcomes for children in foster care vary widely depending on the capacities of the foster families.

After kinship care, residential/institutional care is the most used formal alternative care option despite policy aspirations that it should be used as a measure of last resort. There is no reliable information on the number of childcare institutions nor on the exact number of children in these institutions. By 2012 there were 420 "known" childcare institutions across the country and an estimated over 100 "hidden or unknown" ones. Only a very small proportion of these were registered and certified to operate. Conservative estimates project a total of 45,000 children to be in institutional care in Uganda (MGLSD, 2012).

There are a number of challenges associated with residential care that adversely impact the quality of care in these institutions. Most of these institutions are run by NGOs and churches and many of the proprietors of such institutions are either unaware of the minimum standards and regulations governing these institutions or are incapable of fulfilling them. One of the key requirements of the law is that children should only be placed in a registered home through a "care order" issued by a court of law. This requirement has been widely ignored and most of the children in residential care do not have placement care orders. As a result, a disproportionately high number of children with surviving biological parents and or extended families have been unnecessarily institutionalized. Residential institutions for children have, over the years, thrived as a point of confluence between two mutually reinforcing "perverse" interests. On one hand there are a growing number of individuals who view the establishment of such institutions as a "business opportunity" to attract funding from gullible foreign donors. These proprietors even go out of their way to entice parents and guardians to send their children into institutions so as to attract the necessary numbers to justify continued funding. On the other hand, in the context of poverty and deprivation as well as sheer parental irresponsibility, there are a number of parents or care givers who conveniently offload the burden of childcare to these institutions and benefit from free feeding, education, and healthcare. Unfortunately for many children in residential institutions, the quality of care and access to basic services is poor, manifested through overcrowding, poor quality feeding, and dependency on inadequate and unqualified caregivers. Many of these institutions are bastions of grave child rights violations.

Bearing in mind the vital role of the family in the proper nurturing of the child, the government policy on institutional care is that it should be temporary and transitory. Until recently, most institutions tended to keep children indefinitely up to 18 years and beyond only to release them into a society for which they are generally unprepared. Very few institutions have a commitment and capacity to reintegrate children into family care. As a result, children aging out of institutional care are often unprepared for the life outside institutions and may end up in situations of being in conflict with the law.

The foregoing gaps in institutional care are underpinned by a dysfunctional monitoring and supervision system for childcare institutions. The MGLSD, through the District Probation and Social Welfare officers, is mandated to monitor the compliance of children's homes with the established regulations through regular inspections. This function is not effectively discharged due to financial and logistical constraints. Most inspections are driven by reports of grave violations and sometimes public outcry.

Adoption is another important alternative care option for children in need. The Children Act (Cap 59, sections 45 and 46) provides for two forms of adoption, namely domestic and inter-country adoption, with specific standards and requirements for each. Courts are required to ensure that adoptions are granted only when they are in the best interest of the child following the guidelines prescribed in the Children Act. Generally, the legal requirements for inter-country adoption were deliberately designed to be more stringent. The concept of legal adoption is not very congruent with most Ugandan cultures. Across most communities "blood lineage" is a major consideration for a child to be co-opted into a family. Thus the dominant practice is to take on "biologically related" children through informal fostering as already described. There have been some initiatives to encourage Ugandans to adopt Ugandan children, but the scope and outcomes of these initiatives have been limited.

The period preceding the amendment of the Children Act (2016) was marked by an exponential growth in the number of foreign applications to adopt Ugandan children. The number of international adoptions grew steadily from 12 adoptions in 2007 to 207 in 2011. In the first half of 2012 alone, more than 600 families had filed applications to adopt from Uganda. Most international adoptions were to the USA, with a few going to UK, Sweden, and other European countries (MGLSD, 2013). Given the legal stringency around inter-country adoption, especially the requirement for prospective adoptive parents to first foster a child for three years, potential adopters were exploiting a loophole in the adoption law, by securing "legal guardianship" and taking children outside the country for subsequent adoption in their respective countries. As a result, an increasing number of children were being taken out of the country without completing the legal adoption process and therefore without the necessary safeguards. The adoption system was gradually becoming a "big business" for lawyers and a potential route for "trafficking" children out of the country.

Following sustained advocacy by child focused organizations and a general public outcry, the 2016 Children Act Amendment closed the legal loophole by providing that "a person who is not a citizen of Uganda shall not be eligible to apply for legal guardianship" (Section 43a). In the absence of up-to-date adoption data, it is not possible to fully assess the exact impact of this legal intervention, but it is bound to have significantly reduced the number of applications for intercountry adoption.

In an effort to streamline the overall continuum of care, the MGLSD, in conjunction with partners, developed an "alternative care framework." The framework is a policy instrument that seeks to guide and regulate the provision of alternative care services for children in need. Among other things, the framework prioritizes family-based care options and institutes mechanisms to ensure that children are only referred for institutional care as a last resort and following due process. However, just like all well intentioned government policies the effective roll out of the alternative care framework requires human and financial resources that are not yet readily available on a sustainable basis. In recent years, significant investment in improving standards and quality of alternative childcare services has been supported through the Displaced Children and Orphans Fund of the United States Agency for International Development (USAID). It is not yet clear if significant and sustainable shifts in the functionality and effectiveness of the alternative care system have been realized.

CHILDREN IN CONTACT WITH THE LAW AND ACCESS TO JUSTICE SERVICES

Within the justice system there are two important categorizations of children namely: children in contact with the law and children in conflict with the law. The term "children in contact with the law" refers to child victims of various forms of abuse, neglect, violence and exploitation, including children forced into crime. It also covers those who are likely to be abused, neglected or exploited as a result of their vulnerability (Government of Uganda & UNICEF, 2016). In most cases this category of children presents as survivors or witnesses. Children in conflict with the law refers to children that are exposed to the criminal justice system owing to their actions that are contrary to the law. It is important to note that much as "children in conflict with the law" are generally viewed as perpetrators of crime, they may simultaneously be outright victims of abuse, neglect, and exploitation. This poses a serious challenge to the justice system to apportion an appropriate category to the complex situations in which vulnerable children find themselves. It is therefore imperative that regardless of the specific category all children interfacing with the justice system should experience a "child friendly" experience that serves the best interests of all children.

Section 89 of the Children Act provides a fairly robust legal framework for delivery of justice to children in conflict with the law. The major characteristics of this framework include minimization of incarceration through diversion, expeditious disposal of children's cases, use of child-friendly procedures and proceedings during arrest and trial, and rehabilitative rather than punitive sentencing options. With respect to children in contact with the law the overarching objective of the justice system is to ensure that child survivors of abuse, violence, and exploitation are able to access justice expeditiously, in a safe environment, without undermining their dignity, and without experiencing further harm or abuse within the justice system.

The justice services for children are delivered through a range of actors and institutions including local council courts, the Uganda police force (through the Child and Family Protection Unit (CFPU), public prosecutors, Courts of Judicature (especially the Family and Children Court), Probation and Social Welfare Officers, and NGOs and legal aid agencies. In Uganda the overall coordination mechanism for children and justice issues is under the Justice Law and Order Sector (JLOS), which is resident within the Ministry of Justice and Constitutional Affairs. JLOS is a sector wide approach adopted by Government bringing together 17 institutions with closely linked mandates of administering justice and maintaining law and order and human rights. Within the JLOS framework are four working groups including one on family justice that supervises the work of the Justice for Children Taskforce. The Steering Committee/Task Force has the mandate to craft a unified strategy to improve services for children within JLOS. Through this framework notable efforts have been made to ensure improved access to child justice services at all levels, challenges notwithstanding.

Currently the major challenges hindering children's access to justice through the formal justice institutions include poor compliance with protective and child friendly standards for children in conflict with the law; inaccessible reporting mechanisms, especially for child survivors of abuse; delays in the investigation and prosecution of child rights violations; inadequate victim support services; lack of legal representation for children in conflict with the law; poor support services (health, psychosocial support, remand facilities); and mis-application of the law by the Local Council Courts.

It is also important to note that beyond the formal institutions, community-based and informal justice systems also play a major role in handling issues of justice for children. These include community/village elders, community/tribal councils, religious leaders and organizations, and extended kinship/clan networks. The work of these institutions as justice mechanisms is yet to be fully documented. However, based on anecdotal evidence, it is clear that informal justice institutions play a significant role in dispensing justice to children. From a community perspective, informal justice systems are sometimes more attractive than formal structures for a variety of reasons. These structures are based on strong and culturally recognized family, clan, and community structures that are more accessible to both children and caregivers. They have greater capacity to respond to the immediate existential needs of children. Considering that these structures are served by community actors working on a voluntary basis, they offer a much-needed low-cost option for accessing justice. It is, however, important to note that these informal structures do not make reference to any established formal guidelines and standards for dispensing justice for children. They operate in a manner that privileges community harmony and reconciliation over justice for the children affected. By and large they are not child rights based and may in some instances condone and perpetuate abusive practices.

PROGRAMMATIC CHILD PROTECTION SERVICES

This category of services combines a range of interventions that are geared at mitigating or redressing child protection risks and vulnerabilities. They include both preventive and responsive interventions. Over the years, child protection programs have been delivered largely through NGOs and development agencies in the form of geographically specific and thematically focused projects. With the enactment of the OVC policy, the government, with support from development partners, rolled out a national multiyear program code-named the "National Strategic Programme Plan of Interventions for orphans and other vulnerable children (NSPPI)." The overall thrust of the program was to respond to and mitigate the child related vulnerabilities that were identified as part of the OVC situation analysis.

The framing of the NSSPI provides a useful conceptual framework for articulating programmatic interventions that target vulnerable children. Though the NSPPI programmatic elements were developed in the context of a specific government program that ended in 2016, they broadly embrace the essential nature and character of programmatic interventions that continue to be delivered by various agencies targeting vulnerable children. The key service provision-related core program areas (CPAs) under the framework include economic strengthening; food and nutrition security; health, water, sanitation, and shelter; education; psychosocial support and basic care; and child protection and legal support (MGLSD, 2011).

There are several concerns about the efficacy and sustainability of the past and current child protection programs. Key among them is the short-term nature of programmatic interventions. The time frames of most intervention projects including those delivered by government is not sufficiently cognizant of the deep-rooted nature of social and economic vulnerabilities and deprivation of children and their households. Many projects come to an end without verifiable and sustainable impacts in terms of redressing the root causes of children's vulnerability. Related to this is the overdependence on external financial support even when such support is channeled through government ministries. As a consequence, even with promising results, there is often no room for replication and scale up.

Methods for the Delivery of Child Protection Services

Key Institutions and Structures

Uganda has made some progress in establishing institutions and structures for responding to child violence, abuse, neglect, and exploitation. At the national level, the Ministry of

Gender, Labour, and Social Development is the lead agency for child protection in the country. The primary responsibility for child protection rests with the Department of Youth Children Affairs. Beyond the Ministry, the mandate for child protection is shared with the Ministry of Internal Affairs, Ministry of Justice and Constitutional Affairs, Ministry of Education and Sports, and Ministry of Health. The MGLSD is responsible for the development and dissemination of policies and guidelines, coordination, provision of technical backstopping, monitoring, and supervision but is not directly responsible for service delivery at the local government level. At the local government level, the mandate for child protection lies with the Community-Based Services Department.

As specific protection issues fall under the purview of different ministries, administrative responsibility for child welfare and protection services is shared across many departments and ministries. The array of structures and coordination mechanisms involved in child protection makes it challenging to ensure that policy development and service delivery are managed in a cohesive and coordinated way. A related challenge is the lack of a clear hierarchy between the structures and coordination mechanisms. The same pattern is evident at the district level.

Child Protection Services in the Context of Decentralization
The Community-Based Services Department, which has the primary mandate for child protection at the sub-national level, is one of the decentralized departments under the current local government structure.

> The Ministry is as such dependent on the local governments to enforce guidelines and directives. Since there is no obligation on the part of the DCDO and PSWO to report back to the Ministry on the progress of implementation of set service standards a lot of policies and practice standards for the delivery of child protection services remain on paper. (MGLSD, 2013)

Consistent with the national level context, even at the district level the responsibility for child protection service delivery is spread across several statutory actors. These include actors in welfare offices and community development, local council authorities, law enforcement actors such as the police and prison authorities, actors in the justice system including prosecutors, and magistrates as well as actors in other social service systems such as teachers and health workers. Civil society groups and community networks and informal community-based structures play a significant role in the delivery of child protection services but often with limited guidance or quality of care oversight.

The staffing structure at the local governments does not fully support the effective delivery of child protection services owing to a significant disconnect between the established staff compliment and the actual staffing levels in almost all districts. This is particularly evident in the department that has the primary responsibility for child protection services.

The Local Government Restructuring Report of 2005 recommends that every district have a Senior Probation and Social Welfare Officer and every sub-county/town council a Community Development Officer and Assistant Community Development Officers to provide childcare and protection services, among other things. Even in the best-resourced districts, the number of child protection staff as a ratio to the population is deficient. As of June 2017, out of the approved establishment of 623 positions, only 277 positions were filled, resulting in a staffing gap of 346 posts (56%).

Overall, it is challenging to accurately determine the human resources available to the child protection system because a variety of actors, both formal and informal, interact with children in need of assistance and have a child protection role. However, almost all child protection structures suffer from severe budgetary and human resource constraints. The severe lack of trained and qualified staff across all child protection service institutions including those that have primary responsibility for child protection continues to undermine the functionality and impair the ability of the system to function as designed.

Community-Based Child Protection Mechanisms

In most cases across the country, direct interface with children is not led by trained or government staff but rather by community-based volunteers who are given child protection roles. There is currently a wide range of community-based structures involved in childcare and protection, including Child Protection Committees, which support delivery of child protection services to children at risk or those abused. Others include family/kinship structures, religious/faith-based groups, and other voluntary groups such as women groups, youth groups, and in some communities, children's clubs.

Strategies implemented by community-based child protection structures are varied and include community mobilization initiatives, monitoring the situation of children in their communities, disseminating information on children's rights and protection, and referring cases of abuse to district authorities. Some have been empowered to respond to incidences of child maltreatment and to handle dispute resolution through mediation.

Community-based child protection mechanisms have regained popularity more recently. As the closest link to families and children, community-based child protection structures often support the work of multiple ministries, NGOs, and international agencies, and are thus often stretched too thin, resource constrained, and unable to provide quality and sustained assistance. Concerns also persist regarding their knowledge and capacity to deal with complex legal cases, as well as the scalability and sustainability of community-based initiatives when initiated and funded externally.

Additionally, a critical gap exists in linking informal child protection systems, such as family referral networks, traditional leaders, and community groups, with formal systems—such as child and family protection units and juvenile justice systems. A mapping of the connections between the formal and informal systems revealed that while child protection cases are referred across these systems, the referrals are made on an ad hoc basis with limited information management system support (MGLSD, 2013).

COOPERATION AND COORDINATION IN THE JUVENILE JUSTICE SYSTEM

The juvenile justice system offers a promising approach where government agencies have been able to streamline their activities under a more unified Justice Law and Order Sector (JLOS) framework. The sector has instituted an overall coordination and monitoring mechanism for children's justice issues through the Justice for Children Steering Committee. As a result of a more harmonized approach JLOS reduced the time spent in detention for juveniles before sentencing from an average of five months to three months through the Justice for Children (J4C) program, which ensures juveniles are fast-tracked in the system. The JLOS Annual Report (2017–2018) indicates that the proportion of juveniles that received non-custodial sentences in 2017/2018 increased to 67.8% while 76.3% of juvenile cases were diverted from the justice system altogether. This notwithstanding, there are still delays in settlement of cases of children in conflict with the law by the High Courts, making them overstay in remand homes and in so doing violating children's constitutional rights. (Ministry of Justice and Constitutional Affairs, 2017).

STANDARDIZATION AND HARMONIZATION OF DATA AND DATA COLLECTION INITIATIVES WITHIN THE CHILD PROTECTION SYSTEM

Implementing child protection strategies outlined in the National Child Policy (MGLSD, 2017b) will require holistic and integrated approaches to coordination that recognize the interconnections between sectors, and that harness potential synergies. One such area is ensuring that reliable, up-to-date, nationally representative, and well-disaggregated data on key child protection indicators are available to inform decision making, and that checks and balances are in place for quality and consistency. Presently, the mechanisms and know-how that are needed to collect the necessary data for child protection already exist. There are several government agencies and civil society agencies collecting data on child protection issues. The problem is that they operate independently of each other. To respond to this challenge, there is need to commit resources and technical capacity to establish a comprehensive and integrated data management system that enables measurement of progress across sectors and thematic issues. Improving the availability and accessibility of child protection data is imperative to bolster resource mobilization and fiscal accountability, trust, and partnership.

THE ROLE OF CIVIL SOCIETY ORGANIZATIONS

Civil society organizations (CSOs) play a very significant role in the delivery of child protection services across the country. Yet it is difficult to properly quantify and account for their contribution. This is because there has been no comprehensive assessment of the quality of performance of CSOs in child protection (MGLSD, 2013). The existing mechanisms for coordination and oversight over the work of CSOs are weak and ineffective. There is a general absence of mechanisms for coordinating and measuring performance and assessing the quality of services delivered through the widespread and diverse CSO interventions. The self-coordination mechanisms of CSOs have not been effective and, as a result, there are significant disparities and overlaps in the provision of services and widespread fragmentation of services due to lack of programmatic convergence within the CSO sector. It is often difficult for children to access a comprehensive package of child protection services in any one center or point (MGLSD, 2013).

SUSTAINING COMMUNITY-BASED CHILD PROTECTION STRUCTURES

Until recently training programs for community-based volunteers focused primarily on raising awareness of children's rights and the national laws related to children, monitoring incidents of violence and exploitation of children at the community level as well as coordination with relevant government agencies to facilitate referrals. More recently, the need for specialized training for volunteers to enable them to offer actual services and assistance to families and children has been recognized and is targeted by the National Child Policy (2017) as an area of priority and a critical step towards strengthening the family and community-based care for all children.

While the involvement of community-based volunteers is necessary and is proven to be effective, the central question remains whether community-based solutions can realistically be based on volunteerism and whether the momentum of community-based volunteers can be sustained when those being called to volunteer their time and energy are often impoverished themselves. Community-based volunteers not only need training, but also need to be empowered to provide actual services and be recognized and rewarded for their work. Local governments should understand that the community-based structures are essential service providers (just as Village Health Teams are widely accepted and utilized in health programs) to implement government and other development partner programs (Muhangi & Begumisa, 2012).

Strengthening the Social Service Workforce

The capacity of the child and family welfare system to prevent, mitigate, and respond to risks of child maltreatment is highly contingent upon the skills and time availability of social workers to work effectively with families and children. A severe shortage of social workers in the formal system impacts on access to services and coordination among service providers for referrals. Social work is viewed predominantly as a voluntary or community endeavor and social work has traditionally been relegated to NGOs or emergency and temporary needs to be addressed as specific projects. In order to mitigate human resource constraints the MGLSD is promoting development and use of para-social workers to augment the delivery of services to children and families. The ministry is developing guidelines for the selection, training, and supervision of para-social workers, developing specific job-descriptions and ongoing training using an approved curriculum (MGLSD, 2017a).

Financing for Child Protection Services

The Budget of the Ministry of Gender, Labor, and Social Development

It is very difficult to determine the total financial resource envelope for strengthening of families and the protection of children in Uganda because there are no resources that are specifically earmarked for this purpose. In most sectors and programs child protection is embedded within broader budget categories.

What is clear, however, is that there is an overwhelming demand for support amidst budgetary constraints. An assessment of the 2014/15 national budget revealed that the inadequate public resourcing of child protection structures, institutions, and programs is a significant impediment to building a comprehensive and functional child protection system in Uganda (Uganda Debt Network, 2014). The MGLSD, which is responsible for child protection, is among the least resourced ministries and receives a minimal percentage of the national budget in comparison with other government sectors (0.5% in fiscal year 2014/2015). The share of the national budget allocated to children services across the various ministries has declined in recent years, from 29% on average in 2008/09 to 25.4% in 2013/14. This reflects a decision to prioritize sectors considered to be direct drivers of economic growth—roads and energy—which have seen an increase from 26.4% to 32% during the same period.

The MGLSD's budget is primarily spent on salaries, with only a small percentage of the annual budgets earmarked for providing direct welfare and protection services to children. Funding for child protection policies and programs is almost exclusively funded by external development partners.

External funding is channeled through various granting mechanisms. The bulk of this support is channeled directly through international and local non-government agencies. Only a very limited proportion is directly channeled through the government ministries.

In conclusion, it is important to note that Uganda demonstrates a commendably high level of commitment to improve the overall environment for the realization of the rights of children through building a strong and vibrant child protection system. If this commitment is to translate into sustainable outcomes for vulnerable children significant public investment in terms of human and financial resources is required. Without this, the glaring disconnect between promising policy commitments and the adverse realities of vulnerable children will persist.

References

Batana, Y. et al. (2014). *Situation analysis of child poverty and deprivation in Uganda.* Partnership for Economic Policy (PEP), Ministry of Gender, Labour and Social Development, Uganda; UNICEF, Uganda, Economic Policy Research Centre, Uganda.

Barton and Wamai. (1994). *Equity and vulnerability: A situation analysis of women, adolescents, and children in Uganda.* Uganda National Council for Children.

Basaza, R. and Kaija, D. (2002). *The impact of HIV/AIDS on children: Lights and shadows in the "Successful Case" of Uganda.* UNICEF.

Government of Uganda and UNICEF. (2016). *Prosecuting child-related cases in Uganda: A handbook for Directorate of Public Prosecutions.*

Greco, G., Knight, L., Ssekadde, W., Namy, S., Naker, D., and Devries, K. (2018). Economic evaluation of the Good School Toolkit: An intervention for reducing violence in primary schools in Uganda. *BMJ Global Health*, 3, e000526.

Kalibala, S. and Elson, L. (2010). *Situation analysis of vulnerable children in Uganda.* Final report. Population Council.

MGLSD. (2012). *National alternative care framework.* Ministry of Gender, Labour, and Social Development.

MGLSD. (2013). *Status of child protection system mapping report.* Ministry of Gender, Labour, and Social Development.

Ministry of Gender Labour and Social Development (MGLSD). (2011). *National Strategic Programme Plan of interventions for orphans and other vulnerable children 2011/12—2015/16.*

MGLSD. (2017a). *Evaluation report of the national strategic programme plan of intervention for orphans and other vulnerable children 2010/11–2015/16.* Ministry of Gender, Labour, and Social Development.

MGLSD. (2017b). *National child policy.* Ministry of Gender, Labour, and Social Development.

MGLSD. (2018). *Uganda violence against children survey: Findings from a national survey.* Ministry of Gender, Labour, and Social Development.

Ministry of Justice and Constitutional Affairs. (2017). *The justice law and order sector annual report 2017/18.* The Justice Law and Order Sector.

Muhangi, D. and Begumisa, A. (2012). *Assessing the effectiveness of approaches, models of care and interventions for orphans and other vulnerable children and their households in Uganda.* UNICEF..

Nkhata, C. (2000) *Who are the vulnerable children? Exploring the implications of different criteria for determining eligibility for program assistance.*

Office of The Auditor General Uganda. (2017). *Report of the Auditor General on the financial statements of the Ministry of Gender, Labour and Social Development for the year ended 30th June 2017.* Government of Uganda.

Owori, M. (2018). *Pro-poor analysis of the 2018/19 Uganda budget: How are government's spending decisions likely to impact poor people?* Development Initiatives.

Riche, N. and Anyimuzala, J. (2014). *Research study on children with disabilities living in Uganda: Situational analysis on the rights of children with disabilities in Uganda.* UNICEF.

Uganda AIDS Commission. (2015a). *An AIDS-free Uganda, my responsibility: Documents for the National HIV and AIDS response, 2015/2016–2019/2020.* Uganda AIDS Commission.

Uganda AIDS Commission. (2015b). *The HIV and AIDS Uganda country progress report 2014.* Uganda AIDS Commission.

Uganda AIDS Commission. (2015c). *National HIV and AIDS strategic plan 2015/2016–2019/2020.* Government of Uganda.

Uganda Bureau of Statistics. (2019). *Statistical Abstract 2019*

US Department of Labour AID. (2015). *Findings on Worst Forms of Child labour; Uganda Child Labor Report.* Available at: file:///C:/My%20Documents%202020/Child%20Protection%20Handbook/Other%20References/Uganda-2015-Child-Labor-Report.pdf.

US Department of Labor. (2018). *Findings on the Worst Forms of Child Labor—Uganda.* Available at: https://www.dol.gov/sites/dolgov/files/ILAB/child_labor_reports/tda2018/Uganda.pdf.

Walakira. E. and Nyanzi, D. (2012) *Violence Against Children in Uganda, A decade of Research and Practice.* Ministry of Gender, Labour and Social Development.

Legislation

Education (Pre-Primary, Primary and Post-Primary) Act. (2008).

The Employment Act. (2008). Available at: http://www.ilo.org/dyn/natlex/docs/SERIAL/74416/76582/F1768664138/UGA74416.pdf.

Employment (Employment of Children) Regulations. (2012). National Development Plan (NDPII) 2015/16–2019/20.

Government of Uganda, GoU. 2015, June. Second.

Making Child Protection Systems Work for Children: Lessons from Zimbabwe

Mildred T. Mushunje

Abstract

This chapter notes the lessons from Zimbabwe on making child protection systems work for children. Poverty reduction and increased social expenditure had been emphasized in the government's plans to address inequalities and shift towards an egalitarian society. Additionally, poverty is a factor in the transformation of the child protection support systems. The Children's Act, which is the key to child protection, underwent several amendments in response to the shifting needs of children. Children who need care can go through a court process to be fostered, adopted, or placed in an institution or under the supervision of a probation officer. However, the institutionalization of children in need of care remained to be the last resort.

Key Words: Zimbabwe, child protection, poverty, social expenditure, egalitarian, institutionalisation, Children's Act, support systems

Introduction

Zimbabwe, which gained independence in 1980, has had a fluctuating population of 10.4 million people in 1992, 11.8 million in 1997, and 11.6 million in 2002. The latest census undertaken in 2022 showing the population is now 15,178,979, 16% higher than in 2012, when the last census was held (Census report, 2022). UNICEF estimates the total child population (0–17 years) at 7,504,000 (UNICEF, 2016). In 1980, Zimbabwe inherited a dual economy characterized by a relatively well-developed modern sector and a largely poor rural sector, the majority of whose population were subsistence farmers. Soon after independence, Zimbabwe sought to provide an egalitarian society through the provision of subsidized education, health and other social amenities (Kaseke, 1998). Government's commitment to addressing some of the inequalities within the economy and country in general was evidenced by a number of key development strategies. In these plans, emphasis was placed on poverty reduction and increased social expenditure.

Social expenditure was evident in the manner in which government introduced child sensitive social protection programs such as immunization programs under the Primary Health care banner and free universal primary education (Government of Zimbabwe, 1995). By 1995, the nation registered a net enrolment rate of 86%, close to universal primary education and one of the highest literacy rates in Sub-Saharan Africa. Social indicators for Zimbabwe during this period were very positive and Zimbabwe was the envy of other African nations (Mupedziswa, 2009).

The 1990s brought a different scenario. The decade from 1990 to 2000 saw a deterioration of services and general quality of life for a large percentage of the population. The economy registered stagnation. Depending on one's persuasion, this was attributed to several factors including recurrent droughts; non-realization of the objectives of the Economic Structural Adjustment Programme, popularly known as ESAP; the impacts of HIV and AIDS; and the infamous fast track land reform program. Without a doubt, ESAP, imposed by the International Monetary Fund as a condition for borrowing money, was one of the key culprits. The advent of ESAPs in the early 1980s in Africa, which were presented as the panacea for all economic ills, contributed to a marked increase in rural poverty and an increased vulnerability to external shocks. Key social indicators such as food security, health, and education began deteriorating. As elsewhere where SAPs have been implemented, the program was characterized by liberating the market, cutting public expenditures for social services like education and healthcare, reducing social safety nets for the poor, deregulation and reduction of government regulation of everything that could diminish profits, privatization of state-owned enterprises, and elimination of the concept of concern for the general public good or the typical community approach to addressing situations of vulnerability to a more inward and individual way of addressing the same.

Compounding ESAP was the impact of HIV and AIDS. For example, life expectancy was estimated at 43 years for the period 2000–2005 (26 years lower than it would have been without AIDS), as compared to 61 years in 1990. In 1992 about 34% of the adult population was HIV infected and because of the ESAP induced removal of social safety nets, many could not access health services. Life-saving anti-retroviral therapy was also not readily available, and when it was, the costs were beyond the reach of the ordinary person. In 2000, HIV prevalence rates were 25% and this rose to 34% in 2003 (UNAIDS, 2005). HIV prevalence has since fallen to 13% (NAC, 2015) owing to consistent efforts underpinned by a social protection linked tax-financed AIDS levy.

Furthermore, in 1999, 13% of under 5s were undernourished, rising to 20% in 2002 (Ministry of Health, 2005). Real GDP in 1990 was 7.0%, declining to 0.2% in 1995, rebounding to 8.2% in 2000, and expanding to 13.9% in 2003. These fluctuations also indicate an instability and inconsistency in the economic system. As with many other countries where neoliberal policies were imposed, the expectation was the benefits would "trickle down" (Sewpaul, 2015, p. 461) but this never was with "inequality being recast as virtuous: a reward for utility and a generator of wealth, which trickles down to enrich everyone."

Between 1996 and 2000, there was a marked acceleration of the deteriorating socio-economic environment in Zimbabwe. ESAP was replaced by a home-grown reform package, "Zimbabwe Programme for Economic and Social Transformation" (ZIMPREST). The reform program was unfortunately undermined by lack of funds for effective implementation. ZIMPREST was then superseded by the Millennium Economic Recovery Programme (MERP), launched in August 2001. This was to be a short-term recovery program spanning a period of 18 months. Its main objective was to restore economic vibrancy and address underlying macro-economic fundamentals. The program faced challenges and became almost impossible to implement as the international donor community withdrew support from the country. In February 2003 another attempt was made towards economic recovery in the form of a 12-month program called the "National Economic Revival Programme" (NERP). This also flopped because there was lack of commitment, inconsistent policy implementation, and a failure to address economic fundamentals (Chronicle commentary, April 22, 2006, cited in Mupedziswa & Mushunje, 2012).

Hyperinflation, which was pegged at over 1,200% in December 2006, was also another enemy of the state. As a result of hyperinflation and before the dollarization of the economy in 2008, economic meltdown, cultural and social changes, low foreign exchange reserves, and a decline in investment became the orders of the day. The 2000s was also unique and the human cost of the economic, political, and fiscal crisis has been catastrophic. Life expectancy at birth dramatically declined in the 2000s, while infant, child, and maternal mortality rose in the same period. Nearly a quarter of children were orphaned, most of them cared for by the elderly, many of whom do not have access to pension payments or other forms of public social transfer payments. While school enrollment rates were still high by African standards, many children dropped out of school since their families could not afford the required user fees. Retention of professional staff in various disciplines was very difficult. For instance, doctors and teachers' retention, in particular in rural areas, has been difficult due to low salaries and brain drain to neighboring countries. The case is the same for social workers, who since the 1990s have been leaving the country for greener pastures with the flight accelerating in the period 2000–2008 (Mupedziswa & Ushamba, 2008).

In another effort to resuscitate the economy, in 2006 the government unveiled yet another recovery plan, dubbed National Economic Development Priority Programme (NEDPP), which aimed to put Zimbabwe on a sound economic footing within nine months. The cornerstone of the program was to harness US$2.5 billion in cash and investments within a three-month period from April 2006. This was a major challenge given that in the previous years, the nation had not been able to achieve similar set targets. One of the main thrusts of NEDPP was agriculture coordination, inputs supply, and food security (Government of Zimbabwe, 2006). As the country continued to experience a decline in basic living standards, especially for already marginalized groups, and a much-contested election outcome, failed governance, deteriorating relations with the east, unprecedented hyperinflation, and a reduced market confidence, a government of national unity was constituted on the September 15, 2008, comprising the political parties represented in the Zimbabwean Parliament.

Under the Government of National Unity (GNU), the government introduced the multi-currency system in which the Zimbabwe dollar was taken out of circulation to be replaced by a basket of currencies—the US dollar, South African Rand, Euro, and British pound, among others. Pursuant to this, the new Inclusive Government took office in the context of an economy that had many challenges (i.e., a failing macro-economic environment, a very poor population, and unequal distribution of economic and social resources). To show its commitment to economic and social recovery the GNU instituted the Short-Term Economic Recovery Programme (STERP). STERP was an emergency short-term stabilization program, whose key goals were to stabilize the macro and micro-economies, recover the levels of savings, investment and growth, and lay the basis of a more transformative midterm to long-term economic program that would turn Zimbabwe into a progressive developmental state (Government of Zimbabwe, 2008). The dollarization period brought in some stability and a sense of order to the economy which by this time was on "life support" (Mupedziswa, 2009). Conditions seemed to improve and there was a sense of hope amongst the majority of Zimbabweans. Prior to the dollarization, the country had been plagued with food shortages, money shortages, drug shortages, and a booming illegal foreign currency exchange system. The economy registered growth again in 2009, and consequently tax collections also rebounded. But the public sector still faced hard choices to meet competing demands within a severely constrained budget. Social sectors received more public resources than before. In 2010, budgeted resources to social sectors reached 11.6% of GDP, almost twice as much as in 2009.

The key priority areas of STERP focused on political and governance issues, social protection, and stabilization. The food security situation improved slightly in 2011. The population of food insecure households in urban areas decreased from 26% in 2009/2010 to 10% in 2011. In rural areas, the proportion of the food insecure population declined from 18% in 2009/2010 to 12% in 2011. In 2012, the food insecure population was 1.4 million people, with approximately 30% living in urban areas (FEWSNET, 2012). In 2013, the GNU was disbanded. Elections, which were highly contested by the Movement for Democratic Change (MDC) opposition party were held, reinstating the current ZANU PF-led government. The new government launched yet another innovative program which was set to place Zimbabwe on a recovery course. In pursuit of a new trajectory of accelerated economic growth and wealth creation, rebuilding and maintaining macroeconomic stability, and restoring the economy's productive capacity, the Government of Zimbabwe crafted a new macro-economic blueprint, the Zimbabwe

Agenda for Sustainable Socio-Economic Transformation (Zim-Asset) (Government of Zimbabwe, 2013).

The Zim-Asset iwasset to run for the period October 2013–December 2018. It was results-based agenda that was built around four strategic clusters that would enable Zimbabwe to achieve economic growth and reposition the country as one of the strongest economies in the region and Africa. The four strategic clusters identified were: Food Security and Nutrition; Social Services and Poverty Eradication; Infrastructure and Utilities; and Value Addition and Beneficiation. Zim-Asset was crafted to achieve sustainable development and social equity anchored on indigenization, empowerment, and employment creation, which was largely propelled by the judicious exploitation of the country's abundant human and natural resources.

Despite all of these seemingly progressive actions on the part of government, economic growth has remained elusive for Zimbabwe. Real GDP growth for 2016 initially forecasted at 2.7% was revised to 1.4% due to the impacts of the El Niño-induced drought of 2016, low international commodity prices, and appreciation of the US dollar (which is one of the currencies used under the multi-currency regime) (Government of Zimbabwe, 2015). These factors combined to trigger further risks to the economy, and this particularly affected vulnerable groups, most of whom are women, the elderly, children, and persons with disabilities. In the midst of all these hardships, the government's commitment towards the protection of the vulnerable has been minimal. For instance, government expenditure on the social sectors which impact highly on child protection has remained very low, as depicted in Figure 45.1.

Prior to the hyperinflationary period of 2008, in 2005, the Government of Zimbabwe used to spend more than 15% of GDP on social expenditures. The economic collapse and hyperinflation left social sectors with limited funding from public sources, and by 2009 social public expenditures accounted for only 6% of GDP, with budgets for education and health cut by more than half, compared to 2005. With funding at minimum levels, by the end of 2008 most schools and many hospitals had closed, and transport and electricity networks were severely compromised. Government-financed social protection programs are currently underfunded, and the amount of money allocated to the social sectors is inadequate to cushion the increasing numbers of poor and vulnerable groups such as orphans, people living with disabilities, and the elderly.

Child Protection Systems in Zimbabwe

Zimbabwe has a strong commitment to and takes seriously child protection, as shown by the number of progressive national laws, regional and international conventions to which it is party. Key to child protection is the Children's Act, which was originally passed in 1971 and has since undergone several amendments in response to the emerging and changing needs of children. Under this Act, children who are identified as being in need of care and/or vulnerable include: orphaned children, those with disabilities, abused children

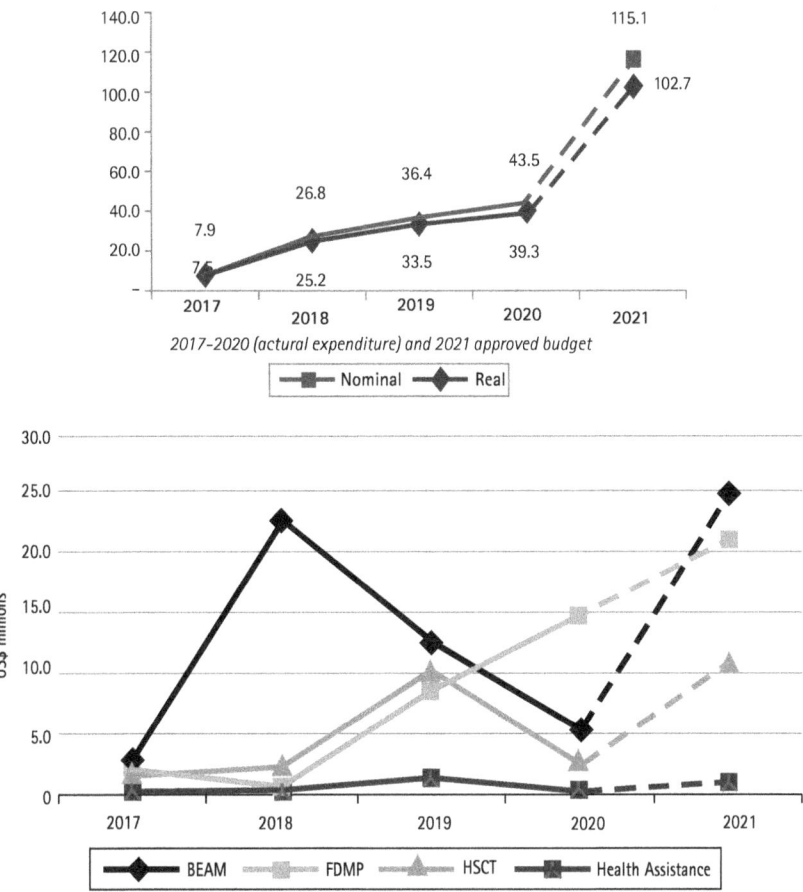

Figure 45.1 Social public expenditure by sector, Ministry of Finance (2011)

(sexually, emotionally, and physically), destitute children, abandoned children, children on the streets, and child parents. The Children's Act is administered by the Department of Social Development (DSs) in the Ministry of Public Service, Labour, and Social Welfare (MPSLSW), and in this context, probation officers (who are qualified social workers), are engaged to enforce the provisions of the Act. Until recently, only social workers from this department[1] had the mandate for statutory child protection work. The recent enactment of the Guardianship of Minors Act is also considered a progressive milestone in the recognition of both parents as having equal rights to the custody of children in cases where custody is contested. Children deemed in need of care can, through a court process

---

[1] In the past, the probation officer had to be an employee of the government under the Department of Social Services. However, with the enactment of the Social Workers Act and statutory instrument on non-public service probation workers of 2013, there is provision for the appointment of a qualified social worker from outside government to carry out statutory work under supervision of the department.

be fostered, adopted, placed in an institution or placed under supervision of the state through the probation officer (Mushunje, 2014). With the increase in orphaned children, foster care has been a major challenge. The National Orphan Care Policy (1999) defines an orphan as those children aged 0–18 whose parents have died. Institutionalization, or residential care of children in need of care is yet another option that is available, although it is considered an option of last resort.

In addition to these national provisions, the government has also ratified a number of international and regional instruments. The UN Convention on the Rights of the Child (CRC) is the first international instrument that is committed to protecting the rights of a child and Zimbabwe is party to this. The government is also a party to the African Charter on the Rights and Welfare of the Child. The African Charter deals with the civil, political, social, economic, and cultural rights of children just like the CRC. It focuses on the plight of children in Africa. Some of the child rights principles that are set out in the African Charter are the best interests of the child, the principle of non-discrimination, survival and development, and child participation (Mushunje, 2006).

A number of factors both endogenous and exogenous have contributed to the increased vulnerability of children, with the worst being HIV and AIDS, which has left an unprecedented number of children orphaned and vulnerable. The debilitating nature of the disease has contributed to families being very poor. Before the roll out of anti-retroviral drugs, families were robbed of breadwinners, leaving children orphaned (Mushunje, 2014). According to the first National Plan for Action, Zimbabwe's orphaned population was 1.8 million in 2005 and estimated at 1.2 million orphans in 2012, of which 890,000 are a result of AIDS, constituting one-quarter of the total child population in Zimbabwe (NAC, 2013).

Poverty is also a factor that has caused a change in the landscape of child protection support systems. There is increased individualism as households strive to cater for their basic needs whereas in the past, households cared for each other during times of hardships. The same cannot be said of today. HIV and economic hardships have weakened and undermined traditional coping systems such as the extended family (Mushunje, 2014). One in four children aged 0–17 live in households considered to be in extreme consumption poverty, living below the food poverty line (Zimstats PICES, 2011/2012). A further one in two children live above the food poverty line but under the total consumption poverty line. HIV/AIDS remains a key driver of poverty in Zimbabwe and has led to high numbers of orphans and "generation gap" households. Over 25% of children are orphaned (living with neither biological parent), often under the care of the elderly (Zimstats & UNICEF, 2011), which increases their exposure to violence and neglect. Children cared for by extended family members are statistically more at risk of neglect, abuse, or exploitation (Mushunje, 2014). Individuals with a disability are more likely to be exposed to physical and sexual violence than others (Government of Zimbabwe, 2013a). About 600,000 children (11% of the child population) live with a disability.

Overall, child protection is the responsibility of the Ministry of Public Service, Labour, and Social Welfare. Within the Ministry, there is a Department of Social Development which administers, coordinates, and monitors the effective and efficient delivery of social protection including child protection (Government of Zimbabwe, 2018). The department has three main functions: family and social protection services, child protection services, and disability and rehabilitation services. The family and social protection services role within the department includes but is not limited to investigating and assessing cases of public assistance, paying fees and grants to institutions, rehabilitating delinquents, and paying school fees through the Basic Education Assistance Module (BEAM). Over the years, Zimbabwe has implemented fairly successful public assistance programs. These include free food to cushion the vulnerable groups (the old, the chronically ill, and the disabled). Introduced in 1982 was a day supplementary feeding/meal for under 5 and early primary school age children. Running currently and since 2001, BEAM was designed to provide educational access and social protection to orphans and vulnerable children. The program utilizes community-based targeting where school selection committees use pre-defined criteria to identify and enroll children meeting eligibility criteria into the program with schools forwarding lists of approved children to the MPSLSW for processing of payments directly to school bank accounts. BEAM is a social protection mechanism which seeks to provide respite for financially hard hit parents and guardians by payment of levies and tuition fees for primary and secondary schools, payment of exam fees, payment of boarding fees, and payment of grants for children with disabilities in specialized institutions. Children have also been assisted to get birth certificates, medical care, and rehabilitative training.

Related to these functions, the department is responsible for the coordination of a National Case Management System for the care and protection of children, assessing suitability of foster and adoptive parents and subsequently processing these for court through a probation officer's report. The national case management system is an effective mechanism for building capacity at the community level to identify and refer child protection cases to district-level social workers and specialist NGOs. However, the current approach as a response (i.e., crisis intervention) mechanism has limited scope for early detection and prevention (DfID, Business Plan, 2013).

The child protection section has the responsibility for assessing foster and adoptive parents through compilation of guardian ad litem reports; identification, documentation, tracing, and reintegration of children living outside the family environment; investigations of cases of children at risk such as neglected and abused children; rehabilitation and protection of children in conflict and contact with the law; presenting cases to court within a prescribed legal period through compilation of probation officers' reports; coordination of the national case management system; coordination of the provision of specialist child protection services for vulnerable children; family casework (support, guidance, and counseling to children in need); advocacy related to justice and human rights with a particular focus on children and families; and use of community approaches through Child Protection Committees and extension cadres (community childcare workers) who are recruited from this structure.

Other key social protection programs run by the ministry include the Harmonized Social Cash Transfers (HSCT) that provide income support to labor-constrained and food-poor households, the Food Deficit Mitigation Program, Public Assistance (PA), and Health Assistance (Assisted Medical Treatment Orders). The department also offers disability and rehabilitation services for children. It is also responsible for statutory support for children outside family environments through setting and reviewing residential care standards at registered children's institutions; paying school fees for committed children in private and government institutions; identification, documentation, tracing, reunification, and re-integration of children living outside the family environment; paying per capita and administrative grants for children in institutions; registration of crèches, pre-schools, and children's homes; and rehabilitation of delinquent children.

Guided by the UN General Assembly Special Session (UNGASS) declaration, Zimbabwe developed a National Action Plan for Children (NAP1), which was adopted by the Cabinet in 2004 and launched in 2005 (Mushunje & Mafico, 2007).[2] Recognizing that children orphaned and affected by HIV and AIDS need special assistance, UNGASS obliged member states to develop and implement national policies and strategies to build and strengthen governmental, family, and community capacities to provide a supportive environment for orphans and children infected and affected by HIV and AIDS. These include providing appropriate counseling and psychosocial support; ensuring their enrolment in school and access to shelter, good nutrition, health, and social services on an equal basis with other children; and protection for orphans and vulnerable children from all forms of abuse, violence, exploitation, discrimination, trafficking, and loss of inheritance. Apart from family, community, and government efforts, there has also been a proliferation of NGOs providing support to underprivileged children including orphans in various forms. With the many challenges that have plagued the country, ranging from the social to the economic and political, several NGOs have come onto the scene to provide childcare and welfare programs. In order to regulate the functioning of these agencies and to come up with a coordinated approach in the provision of care to children, the government in 2001, in conjunction with some donor agencies and NGOs, created the Programme of Support (PoS) initiative, in which funds mobilized for child welfare and protection interventions were pooled and used to promote NAP I (Mushunje & Mafico, 2007). The PoS, which turned out to be an extremely well-coordinated strategy for supporting especially disadvantaged children in Zimbabwe, had two main objectives, namely to strengthen community level organizations providing care and protection for vulnerable

---

[2] UN General Assembly Special Session (UNGASS) Declaration of Commitment on HIV/AIDS set specific targets for all signatory nations to which Zimbabwe is one.

children; and to put in place a mechanism to ensure increased and more predictable funding to organizations assisting these children. These initiatives have largely been driven by resources made available by funding agencies in the NGO sector and their donor governments (Mupedziswa & Mushunje, 2012).

The vision of NAP I was "to reach out to all orphans and vulnerable children in Zimbabwe with basic services that would positively impact on their lives" from 2007 to 2010 (Ministry of Labour and Social Services, 2011). NAP I comprised seven areas of activity: coordination, child participation, birth registration, formal education, social services, extra-curricular education, livelihoods support, and child protection. Resources for NAP I were mobilized under the Programme of Support (PoS I), which was a predictable funding mechanism through which interested donors could pool their resources. NAP I was considered to have achieved positive results as it extended services to 410,000 orphaned and vulnerable children (OVCs), at a time when the capacity for service delivery was declining in government and outside, exceeding the target of reaching at least 25% of OVC (Ministry of Labour and Social Services, 2011). A second phase of the NAP was then introduced.

NAP II was launched and implemented from 2011 to 2015. It integrated actions to help families cope with risks and shocks through three main interventions: 1) cash transfers to the poorest families, 2) education assistance through BEAM, and 3) child protection service delivery for child survivors of abuse, violence, and exploitation (National AIDS Council, 2011). NAP II sought to target vulnerable children and their households to provide a comprehensive package to address the wide range of deprivations experienced by vulnerable children and their families, rebuild capacity of government to deliver the social services needed by children, and strategically position NAP II to become a national child sensitive social protection program for the most vulnerable children (Ministry of Labour and Social Services, 2011). NAP II was set to succeed in providing social protection to OVC as long as it was not affected by a volatile political and economic environment which had affected the nation and impacted negatively on social protection programs (Masuka et al., 2012). The program mobilized US$45 million of the needed US$75 million for the Child Protection Fund (CPF) (NAC, 2011). An evaluation of the program by Coffey International (2015) concluded that CPF was successful in that it was predictable, consistent, transparent, sustainable, and provided for a better quality of life.

NAP II, with CPF funds, adopted a multidimensional approach to child vulnerability and protecting children's rights, which addressed household poverty, access to education, gender disparities, disability, HIV, and risk of violence, exploitation and abuse. In particular, the approach focused on strengthening child protection systems that can deliver coordinated quality services that prevent and respond to violence against children. The HSCT, established within the NAP II in 2012, proved an effective social protection program. It has been the largest and only social protection instrument managed by the government that transparently targets those most in need, and is the kernel upon which a future social protection system can be built. It has reached more than 55,000 food poor and labor-constrained households, the majority caring for orphaned children (82%), 60% elderly or chronically ill, and 19% disabled. The program achieved good results and was able to develop an affordable system for protecting vulnerable children which, with further technical support and strengthening, can continue to achieve good outcomes for the many at risk; and it established the HSCT as a transparently managed, very effective cash transfer that has strengthened household economic resilience and broadened the choices of children and their carers (DfID NAP III business case, 2013). The HSCT program is a "cash plus" social protection program that currently provides cash transfers to approximately 43,000 labor-constrained, food-poor households in 12 districts. Until June 2016, the program was providing payments to over 50,000 households in 19 districts, when 11 districts were subtracted and four new districts were added. The 13,694 households in the four new districts were enrolled with an additional criterion of having at least one adolescent girl and or young woman aged between 10 and 24 years old (Muwoni et al., 2013).

Through NAP II, the National Case Management System (NCMS) was adopted as an approach in child welfare, protection, and child safeguarding by the Ministry of Public Service, Labour and Social Welfare. This is a harmonized and standardized systematic framework for the care and protection of children that provides access to social welfare, social protection, justice, and health services. The system is a community-based approach to prevent and respond to child protection concerns in Zimbabwe. The model was adapted from the South African "isibindi model" to suit the Zimbabwean context. World Education, an NGO operating in Zimbabwe, working with USAID, UNICEF, government, and other partners, was responsible for the development of the NCMS. The pilot program took place in three wards in the Umzingwane district. In less than three years, the NCMS was operating in 47 districts. In total, the program supported a workforce expansion to include 9,365 community childcare workers (CCWs), a front-line, community-level paraprofessional group trained to identify and refer children with child protection issues for assessment and services (Kang, K.T & UNICEF Zimbabwe, 2017).

The objectives of the system NCMS are:

- To establish a standardized response service system that protects children from abuse, violence, exploitation and neglect within a coordinated continuum of care;
- To strengthen child protection systems through linkages of community child protection and the formal system;
- To reduce children's exposure to harm through actions that strengthen the protective environment for children in all settings;
- To establish a system for knowledge management, monitoring, and promotion of quality child protection services informed by ethics and standards of practice.

To date, the Department of Social Welfare has managed to roll out the system to national coverage and trained 9,000 community cadres.

NAP II achieved the following:

- Designed and rolled out the NCMS. The NCMS enhanced reach to almost 50,000 children while minimizing cost: an effective response in a resource-constrained environment.
- Service capacity has been rebuilt and strengthened, creating and training a cadre of volunteer community case workers supervised by government social workers. Case workers provide initial counselling and documentation and facilitate referrals to specialist services. In the case of rape, these include access to legal advice and post-exposure prophylaxis against HIV.
- Regular social transfers under the HSCT have reached 250,000 people in over 52,000 households. Comparing treatment and control groups after just 12 months, early marriage was lower by 6%, school dropouts reduced by 7%, and under-age sex was down by 11%. Recipient households were 9% more likely (than non-recipient but eligible households) to own productive assets and run micro-enterprises, and had increased their consumption by US$2.74 per person per month. The HSCT has effectively targeted the food-poor and labor-constrained, reaching elderly-headed and child-headed households, and including many affected by disability (AIR, 2014).

From 2016 to 2020 Zimbabwe implemented the third National Action Plan for OVC which runs from. The vision was that "by 2020, children live in a safer and more conducive environment that ensures their care and protection and supports their sound growth and development." NAP III set out the broad government approach through the implementation of activities in three strategic pillars:

1) Household economic security, in which adolescents are prepared and ready to join the labor market and families' income is secured and protected;
2) Children are protected from the most severe deprivations that affect their sound growth and development;
3) Access to quality social services: children's developmental needs are fulfilled (health, nutrition, education). Families are strengthened to fulfill children's developmental needs. Child protection and safeguarding: children have the knowledge and skills to recognize situations of risk and to seek help, children are actors of their change, and children live in safe families and communities.

As with previous NAPs, the current NAP III also had its pillars, which were the NCMS and the HSCT. The main activities of the program are:

1) <u>Further strengthening the NCMS:</u> increasing availability, accessibility, and uptake of age/gender-appropriate, affordable, and well-coordinated child protection services.
2) <u>Family and community prevention of violence against children:</u> providing information, knowledge, and skills on detecting, reporting, and preventing violence against children to families and communities.
3) <u>Policy reform to strengthen the enabling environment for child protection</u>: improving and implementing evidence-based policies and legislative instruments to address violence against children, reinforced by institutional capacity.
4) <u>The harmonized social cash transfer (HSCT):</u> improving capacity among households benefitting from social cash transfers to protect children from practices that expose them to violence, abuse, and exploitation.

As part of a comprehensive care for children, the Victim Friendly System (VFS) was also set up. It is designed to improve access to justice and health services for child survivors of sexual violence. The system comprises Victim Friendly Courts (VFCs) and Victim Friendly Units (VFUs) within the police force and comprehensive legal, health, and psychosocial services through a coordinated mechanism that involves different service providers. Regional VFCs allow child survivors of sexual violence to provide evidence in court without fear or intimidation through the use of closed-circuit television or two-way mirrors by which the children can testify without directly facing the offenders. Survivor Friendly Clinics (SFC)—though limited in number—have been established and medical staff have been trained to perform forensic examinations. According to the Multi-Sectoral Protocol, the first port of call for a sexual abuse case is the nearest health care facility. Although nurses are now legally eligible to provide evidence in court, many are reluctant to do so because they fear repercussions and feel insecure in terms of capacity to testify before the court.

Child Protection Committees (CPCs) are in place at national and sub-national levels to coordinate implementation of child protection and safeguarding interventions by various players at each level, including village, ward, district, and provincial and national levels. CCWs, who are selected from members of the CPCs, are the frontline community workers (para-professionals) within the new National Case Management Framework. The framework recognizes the essential role played by CPCs and CCWs as "eyes and ears on the ground" and the importance of a "triggering" role for case detection. They are backstopped by the District Social Workers and Case Management Officers.

Table 45.1 Government contribution to the HSCT, 2013–2017

	Allocated	Released	Used for HSCT	Total HSCT Budget Incl. Donors	Share of Govt Allocation to HSCT Budget (%)
2013 (US$)	3,000,000	300,000	NIL	11,000,000	27.27
2014 (US$)	2,000,000	1,187,000	209,000	15,000,000	20.00
2015 (US$)	1,700,000	1,650,000	300,000	14,000,000	12.14
2016 (US$)	1,800,000	19,000	17,000	11,000,000	0.14
2017 (US$)	7,000,000	4,400,000	1,400,000	15,000,000	47

Source: Davis et al. (2016).

Note: 3,000,000 has been indicated to be under release although the funds had not yet been received in the Ministry as of October 27, 2017.

Funding Child Protection in Zimbabwe

The government's commitment to child protection is not matched by financial resources. Social service provision, of which the bulk impact on child protection are clearly underfunded with the bulk of resources going towards recurrent costs such as salaries. Out of the 2016 health sector budget of US$330.8 million, overall disbursements of US$271 million and 93% was allocated to salaries.

Other funding partners have also come on board to support the child protection system in Zimbabwe. The DfID business case for realization of the National Action Plan for Orphans and Vulnerable Children III (2016 to 2021) commits a total of £20.9 million (initially over three years), for review in 2018/19. The business case reports that the UK will contribute £20.9 million to the multi-donor Child Protection Fund (CPF) II, the principal external financing mechanism for Zimbabwe's NAP III for OVCs. The UK is the lead donor in the child protection sector, complemented by smaller contributions to the fund from the Swedish and Swiss Governments. USAID funds some elements outside of the Fund.

Emerging Child Protection Issues

The question of child protection continues to be key for Zimbabwe's progress towards achieving its child protection national, regional, and international commitments. These efforts are also geared towards responding to emerging child protection issues. One current issue of import is that of child marriages. Whilst probably in existence previously but unreported, child marriages have become more visible and of concern to child protection actors. These are an institutionalized form of child abuse and child sexual abuse. As in many other developing countries, child marriage in Zimbabwe is high. Approximately 21% of children (mostly girls) are married before the age of 18 (Sibanda, 2011). The Zimbabwe Demographic Health Survey (ZDHS, 2015) showed that 17% of girls aged

1–19 were married, a decline from the ZDHS of 2010–11, which estimated that 31% of girls in Zimbabwe marry before they reach the age of 18 years. About 15% of all child-marriages occur before age 15 (Zimbabwe National Statistical Agency (ZIMSTATS, 2010). It is also worth-while to point out that child marriage in Zimbabwe often occurs in the obscurities of poverty, harmful religious and cultural practices, and gender inequality (Sibanda, 2011). Child marriage has been legitimized through institutions such as religion and culture. Following much lobbying by women's rights and child protection activists, a marriage Bill was enacted in 2022 which expressly outlaws child marriages. Marriage to a child below the age of 18 is now a criminal offence The protection of children primarily lies with the custodians of the child, usually the parents, but some of these child marriages are perpetrated with the consent of the parents, thus leaving the child bride vulnerable. Child marriage is a significant problem and both a cause and consequence of teenage pregnancies. Damaging social and gender norms, food and income poverty, and generalized poverty of opportunity for young people are contributing factors. As a way of addressing child marriages, the government has held sector-wide and community dialogues in order to develop sustainable measures for addressing child marriage.

Challenges in the Provision of Child Protection Services

Limited Financing

The most chronic challenge facing Zimbabwe with regards to child protection services is the chronic underfunding of related services and programs. The implementation of all the NAPs have been largely funded by development partners who have borne the huge financial burden on behalf of the government. The implications are that should these actors pull out, children will be even more vulnerable. Financial sustainability is not possible under these circumstances. An MDTF report (2013) showed that over 300,000 pupils under the BEAM may drop out of school if the government does not respond to noted funding needs. One example of the mismatch between funding needs and allocations, the ministry allocated $10M in 2017 in response to a funding request of $105M.

Flight of Social Workers and Other Professionals

At the beginning of 2009, there was an approximate 68% vacancy rate for medical doctors in the sector. The remaining health workers are thinly spread out and therefore overworked. This has implications on the delivery of the VFCs even though there continues to be training for a cadre of nurses. Transport costs as well as unaffordable day to day basic necessities have compounded this crisis. As a result, staff presence at most health institutions average between 15 and 50%. In 2010 there were only 121 documented social workers left in the country, representing a ratio of 1 social worker to 49,587 children. The government, through the Ministry of Public Service, Labour, and Social Welfare, shows considerable commitment to child protection, having increased the number of social workers in the Child Welfare Department by 68% between 2010 and 2014. In

2013 the Department of Child Welfare and Protection Services was created and some 92 new social workers were recruited. This brought the ratio down to a healthier but still insufficient 1:28,152. The current ratio is now at 1:30,000 as attrition and brain drain has started again on the back of worsening socioeconomic indicators.

Absence of a Single Registry System

Information and knowledge management of child protection is weak due to 1) lack of an effective management information system; 2) limited coordination for data collection and collation amongst partners across relevant sectors; 3) limited data to demonstrate impact; and 4) lack of agreement on measurement of system strengthening efforts. The Government of Zimbabwe through the MPSLSW is leading the development of a social protection single registry system in line with the National Social Protection Policy Framework (NSPPF). The Ministry agreed with key UN agencies supporting the single registry process (UNICEF and WFP) as well as the World Bank to consider existing beneficiary and transfer management systems with potential for scalability to be tested as platforms for building on the single registry. Other UN agencies that have supported the idea of a social protection single registry are FAO and UNDP. This would also assist to trace and to target children who periodically move.

Operational Environment

The economic context of Zimbabwe is very complex with unstable exchange rates. Zimbabwe had varying inflation rates with an unstable exchange rate to the US dollar for about six consecutive years since 2001. Such uncertainty and the economic meltdown has had the net effect of creating a speculative environment where goods and services are overpriced and the inflation rate continuously soars. In the financial and banking sector, it has proved to be difficult to withdraw money from the bank and local currency has been known to be in short supply, especially affecting households receiving cash transfers and making children more vulnerable rather than better protected.

Over-reliance on Donor Support

The MPSLSW has a poor record of budget releases to the HSCT due to a combination of fiscal constraints and a lack of harmonization of social protection instruments. It is unlikely the government can achieve sustainability of these programs without significant donor support.

Recommendations

In order to deal with the various challenges brought on by the deterioration of the economy, droughts, HIV and other difficulties, households have been forced to look beyond the state for support and engage in other forms of coping. According to Patel and colleagues (2012), such coping mechanisms have also evolved and changed into new systems of mutual aid and they now play a greater role in the community welfare system. In line with this, these recommendations take into consideration the changing nature of family life and government's seeming shift in priorities.

Community Systems and Strengthening of Informal Systems

Child protection is a multi-faceted function which cannot be successful without the participation of key players (nuclear family, extended family, community, government, and development partners). Strengthening these systems to collaborate should be a key priority for government. Given the waning resources available, the participation of all players could leverage the limited available resources. This is closely linked to a multi-sectorial approach to child protection.

Coordination of Services; Participation of All Stakeholders

Whilst the government, through the social welfare department, already leads in the coordination of child protection services, this function could be strengthened through increased allocation of resources ideally, more resources should be allocated towards social protection services especially those impacting on child protection. Budget should be linked to actual disbursements otherwise the welfare of children will continue to be prejudiced.

References

American Institute for Research. (2014). Process Evaluation of Zimbabwe's Harmonised Social Cash Transfer Programmeme, December 2014, Washington D.C. Handa,S and Seideinfeld.

Davis, B., Handa, S., Hypher, N., Rossi, N., Winters, P., and Yablonkis, J. (2016). *Evidence to action: The story of cash transfers and impact evaluation in Sub-Saharan Africa*. Oxford University Press.

Demographic and Health Survey. (2015). Zimbabwe National Statistics Agency Harare, Zimbabwe.

Department for International development Summary of DFID's work in Zimbabwe 2011–2015, June 2013. Famine Early Warning Systems Network (FEWSNET, April 2012 to September 2012, Zimbabwe, published by USAID.

Government of Zimbabwe. (1999). *Orphan care policy*. Haare, Government Printers.

Government of Zimbabwe. (2005). *National action plan for orphans and vulnerable children*. Government of Zimbabwe.

Government of Zimbabwe. (2006). National Economic Development Priority Programme (NEDPP) strategy document.

Government of Zimbabwe. (2008). *A partnership making a difference, Zimbabwe's programme of support to the national action plan for orphans and vulnerable children*. Ministry of Labour and Social Services, UNICEF, and NAC.

Government of Zimbabwe. (2013), Zimbabwe Agenda for Sustainable Socio-Economic Transformation (Zim-Asset).

Government of Zimbabwe. (2009). *Short term emergency recovery programme (STERP) Getting Zimbabwe Moving Again*. Government Printers.

Government of Zimbabwe. (2016). National Action Plan for Orphans and Vulnerable Children in Zimbabwe Phase III – 2016-2020. Ministry of Public Service Labour and Social Welfare January 2016.

Zimbabwe National Statistics Agency (ZIMSTAT), United Nations Children's Fund (UNICEF) and Collaborating Centre for Operational Research and Evaluation (CCORE). (2013). National Baseline Survey on Life Experiences of Adolescents, 2011.

Government of Zimbabwe, 2022 Census report, Zimbabwe National Statistics office.

Government of Zimbabwe. (2013a). *National survey on living conditions amongst persons with disability.* Ministry of Health and Child Care & UNICEF, Harare, Zimbabwe.

Government of Zimbabwe. (2013b). National budget statement. Available at: https://www.cabri-sbo.org/en/documents/the-2013-national-budget-statement.

Government of Zimbabwe, ZIMBABWE THE 2016 NATIONAL BUDGET STATEMENT "Building a Conducive Environment that attracts Foreign Direct Investment" Presented to the Parliament of Zimbabwe on 26 November, 2015 by Hon. P. A. Chinamasa, MP Minister of Finance and Economic Development.

Kaseke, E. (1998). Structural Adjustment Programmes and problems of urban poverty: An African perspective (pp. 311–320). International Socia Work, Sage, London, Vol. 41.

Government of Zimbabwe with support from UNICEF (2010) Ministry of Labor and Social Welfare. (2010). *Basic Education Assistance Module: Operational Manua.*

Kang, K. T. (2016). *Implementing and Improving: A national case management system for child protection in Zimbabwe.* UNICEF.

Masuka, T., Banda, G. R. Mabvurira, V., and Frank, R. (2012). Preserving the future: Social protection programmes for Orphans and Vulnerable Children (OVC) in Zimbabwe. *International Journal of Humanities and Social Sciences,* 2(12), 59–66.

Mupedziswa, R. and Ushamba, A. (2008). A generation at the edge of a precipice: AIDS and child headed households in Zimbabwe. In T. Maundeni, L. Levers, and G. Jacques (Eds.), *Changing family systems: A global perspective* (pp. 312–327). Bay Publishing.

Mupedziswa, R. (2009). Modelling political leadership responses to the fight against HIV & AIDS in the SADC region. In C. Fombad, R. Mupedziswa, T. Maundeni, and G. Mookodi (Eds.), *HIV/AIDS, vulnerable groups, human rights and development in Botswana* (pp. 104–132). Made Plain Comm.

Mupedziswa, R. and Mushunje, M. (2012). "Between a rock and a hard place": Care of orphaned children in Zimbabwe and social work roles. In J. D. Bailey (Ed.), *Orphan care: The social work role* (pp. 123–154). Kumarian Press.

Mushunje, M. (2006). Child protection in Zimbabwe: Past, present and future. *Journal of Social Development in Africa,* 21(1), 12–34.

Mushunje, M. and Mafico, M. (2007). Walking the talk: Zimbabwe's experience in implementing the national action plan for orphans and vulnerable children. *Journal of Social Development in Africa,* 22(2), 35–62.

Mushunje, M. T. 2014. Interrogating the relevance of the extended family as a social safety net for vulnerable children in Zimbabwe. *African Journal of Social Work,* 4(2), 78–110.

Muwoni, L., Sammon, E., Rumble, L., Mhishi, S., and Schubert, B. (2013). Building resilience to environmental shocks and hazards: Zimbabwe's harmonized social cash transfer (HSCT). In B. Davis, S. Handa, N. Hypher, N. W. Rossi, P. Winters, and J. Yablonski (Eds.), *From Evidence to Action The Story of Cash Transfers and Impact Evaluation in Sub-Saharan Africa.* The Food and Agriculture Organization of the United Nations and The United Nations Children's Fund and Oxford University Press.

National Aids Council, Global Aids Response Progress Report 2015.

Patel, L., Kaseke, E., and Midgley, J. (2012). Indigenous welfare and community-based social development: Lessons from African innovations. *Journal of Community Practice,* 20(1): 12–31.

Sewpaul, V. (2015). Politics with soul: Social work and the legacy of Nelson Mandela. *International Social Work* 59 (6), 1–12.

Sibanda, M. (2011). Married too soon: Child marriage in Zimbabwe. The Research and Advocacy Unit. Available at: http://www.kubatana.net/docs/chiyou/rau_child_marriage_111030.pdf.

UNICEF. (2016). *The state of the world's children 2016* [Statistical tables]. Available at: https://data.unicef.org/resources/state-worlds-children-2016-statistical-tables/.

UNAIDS. (* 2005). Global Report 2005: UNAIDS report on the global AIDS epidemic. UNAIDS.

Zimbabwe Country Report, Reporting Period: January 2014–December 2014.

Zimbabwe National Statistics Agency, Poverty Income Consumption and Expenditure Survey 2011/12 Report.

Conclusion

Child Protection Systems: A Global Typology

Jill Duerr Berrick, Neil Gilbert, *and* Marit Skivenes

Abstract

This chapter discusses the global typology of child protection systems. It also highlights how child protection continues to evolve within and across countries. In line with the UNCRC, countries are mandated to protect children's civil, political, economic, social and cultural rights equal to those of adults. The UNCRC's Article 19 is primarily focused on protecting children from abuse, neglect, and maltreatment when parents or families are incapable of caring for them. Additionally, the legal authority and responsibility of states are the essential features of child protection systems. Research sparked insights into how societal and cultural differences affect protective services and preliminary typologies of child protection systems. Interventions were driven by high-risk situations for the child in the child protection system and their needs in the family service system.

Key Words: child protection, countries, UNCRC, maltreatment, legal authority, states, rights, families, research, interventions

Introduction

As signatories to the UN Convention on the Rights of the Child (CRC), countries are obliged to protect children's rights. The Convention covers all aspects of a child's life, confirming that children have civil, political, economic, social, and cultural rights equal to those of adults. All children, everywhere on the globe, are entitled to these rights. In this volume we examine the systems designed to protect the rights of children under Article 19 of the CRC, which focuses on protection from abuse, neglect, and maltreatment when parents or family are not able to care for their children or they are a direct or indirect threat to their children's well-being. We have termed these *child protection systems*. An essential feature of child protection systems is the legal authority and responsibility of states that prevails when parents do not, or cannot, exercise their parental responsibilities.

As studies of 50 countries in this book show, children everywhere may experience life threatening violence, abuse and deprivation. There is, however, considerable variation among countries in the magnitude of problems and the number of children affected by them. This variation reflects, in part, differences in the living standards and the social, cultural, and religious contexts of family life. We first classified the 50 countries represented in this volume according to three broadly defined living standards roughly corresponding to their wealth reflected in the countries' per capita GDP, an empirical estimate of a government's financial capacity to provide for families and children in a society. Other indicators, such as the KidsRights Index and the Child Flourishing Index, were also used to offer a rough estimate of a state's orientation to children's rights. In this concluding chapter, we seek to refine these broad classifications by proposing a more detailed conceptualization of child protection systems based on the case studies of the 50 countries included in this volume. This detailed classification of countries across the developmental spectrum represents a global typology of child protection systems. The typology consists of five ideal types that have as their emphasis protection against an array of risks to childhood and that represent the focal point for government intervention in the lives of families; these systems are listed below according to the scale of risks covered from a narrow focus limited to child exploitation to the inclusive focus on children's rights.. The five types in the global typology are:

- child exploitation protective systems;
- child deprivation protective systems;
- child maltreatment protective systems;
- child well-being protective systems; and
- child rights protective systems.

In this chapter we offer greater detail about the scope and context of this typology.

Comparative Analyses of Child Protection Systems

Several previous studies have generated insights into how societal and cultural differences impact protective services and formulated preliminary typologies of child protection systems (Gilbert, 1997; Hetherington et al., 1997; Merkel-Holguin et al., 2019). According to Connolly and colleagues (2014, p. 45), "[t]he most well-known typology is based on the fundamental '*orientation*' or approach of the State towards the child and the family on child protection matters." This orientation consisted of a binary formulation, presented in the mid-1990s as a rudimentary typology organized around "child protection" and "family-service" orientations, which was derived from case studies of nine western industrialized countries (Gilbert, 1997). As illustrated in Table 46.1, the child protection approach involved legalistic public investigation to control harmful family behavior, which engendered an adversarial relationship between parents and the state. In contrast, the family service orientation identified the problem as involving psychological difficulties, family troubles, and socioeconomic stress amenable to therapeutic interventions, which sought to advance more of a partnership with parents.

Out-of-home placements were much more likely to be voluntary in family service-oriented systems than in child protective systems, where the majority of child placements usually required court orders. Interventions were driven by high-risk situations for the

Table 46.1 Characteristics of child protection and family service orientations

	Child protection	Family service
Problem frame	Individual/moralistic	Social/psychological
Preliminary intervention	Legalistic/	Therapeutic/needs investigatory assessment
State-parent relationship	Adversarial	Partnership
Out-of-home placement	Involuntary	Voluntary

Source: Gilbert (1997).

child in the child protection system and by children's needs in the family service system. This early comparative analysis was followed by other studies that examined how different countries defined child abuse and the ways in which their child welfare systems operated (Pringle, 1998; Khoo et al., 2002; May-Chahal & Herezog, 2003; Freymond & Cameron, 2006; Cameron et al., 2007).

Building on the child protection/family service typology of the mid-1990s, 15 years later Gilbert, Parton, and Skivenes (2011) organized a follow-up study of the original nine countries plus Norway. This period was characterized by the growing influence of neoliberal policy reforms and the increasing privatization of social services among the modern welfare states, not to mention the great recession of 2008. Assessing the utility of the earlier typology in light of changes that had taken place in child protection policies and the socio-economic context since the mid-1990s, the 2011 follow-up study produced a broader and deeper typology, which included a third orientation and additional descriptive dimensions. As shown in Table 46.2, the "child focused" orientation formed a third pattern of intervention, which combined several features of the two other orientations.

The typologies illustrated above are based on a small number of wealthy countries, which have the economic surplus necessary to support well developed welfare states. Up until recent years there have been limited efforts to broaden the scope of comparative child protection system analysis to include the developing low-to-moderate income countries, which encompass more diverse social, political and cultural communities. Although most countries have signed on to the CRC and all have legislation aspiring to realize the Convention's principles, in practice many of them lack the resources and public structures to provide a substantial systematic program for protecting children. The dearth of comparative research on low-income countries reflects, in part, the difficulty of obtaining data on countries which have limited and often fragmented services. In response to this looming gap in the comparative analysis of child protection systems, UNICEF and Save the Children commissioned a team led by Marie Connolly of the University of Melbourne to develop a more inclusive typology of child protection systems, which would apply to low- and moderate-income countries as well as to the high-income advanced industrialized welfare states. The 2014 report prepared by Connolly's team proposed a theoretical typology that drew upon a set of universal values and beliefs that they deemed as representing essential features of child protection systems:

Table 46.2 Role of the state vis-à-vis child and family in orientations to child maltreatment: Child focus, family service, and child protection

	Child focus	Family service	Child protection
Driver for intervention	The individual child's needs in a present and future perspective/societies need for healthy and contribution citizens.	The family unit needs assistance	Parents being neglectful and abusive towards children (maltreatment)
Role of the state	Paternalistic/defamilialization—state assumes parent role but seeks to refamilialize child by foster home/kinship/ adoption	Parental support—state seeks to strengthen family relations	Sanctioning—state functions as «watchdog» to ensure child's safety
Problem frame	Child's development and unequal outcomes for children	Social/psychological (system, poverty, racism, etc.)	Individual/moralistic
Mode of intervention	Early intervention and regulatory/needs assessment	Therapeutic/needs assessment	Legalistic/investigative
Aim of intervention	Promote well-being via social investment and/or equal opportunity	Prevention/social bonding	Protection/harm reduction
State–parent relationship	Substitutive/partnership	Partnership	Adversarial
Balance of rights	Children's rights/parents' responsibility	Parents' rights to family life mediated by professional social workers	Children's/parents' rights enforced with legal means

Source: Gilbert et al. (2011).

Our read of the academic literature and the span of current child protection systems yields two dimensions that can be used to theoretically inform a typology: *Individualism and Collectivism*; and *Authoritarianism and Permissiveness*. Child protection systems of different sorts can be located along the continua in a way that can capture the essence of a system in two respects: whether it has an individual or collective focus, and whether the system is more or less regulated by authorities, both formal and informal (Connolly et al., 2014, p. 7).

This theoretical framework informed Connolly and colleagues' typology based upon four prototypical dimensions—Authoritarian Individualism, Permissive Individualism, Authoritarian Collectivism, and Permissive Collectivism—with the descriptive characteristics illustrated in Table 46.3. The typology is developed through deductive reasoning, which starts with a theoretical conceptualization of the essential properties of child protection systems.

The report analyzes various concepts drawn from the literature and related to values and beliefs about child protection arrangements. While this approach offers clarity using

Table 46.3 Dimensions and description of the provisional typology

| Description | Dimensions | | | |
	Authoritarian individualism	Permissive individualism	Authoritarian collectivism	Permissive collectivism
"Ideal" type (balance between dimensions)	Regulated independence	Supportive independence	Regulated cooperation	Supportive cooperation
Primary focus	Protecting individual children at risk	Supporting vulnerable children and families	Protecting and regulating communities or populations at risk	Supporting vulnerable communities and populations
Dominant intervention modes	Investigation, assessment, removal	Support, restorative justice, dialogue	Regulation/ inspection, law enforcement	Community development, public health approaches (primary and secondary prevention at the population level)
Main focus of prevention	Targeting high risk children	Targeting vulnerable families	Legal and institutional reform	Media campaigns/ culture change
View of children	Victims	Vulnerable	Community members	Participants
Role of the state	State or state sanctioned organizations act to protect children	State acts to mediate or support change	State regulates communities and organizations	Role of the state downplayed— communities are the major protective bodies.
Balance of rights	Children's right to protection prioritized	Balance of child and parental rights	Communal rights prioritized over individual rights	Communal rights prioritized over individual rights

Source: Connolly et al. (2014).

an abstract conceptual framework, the report provides very few empirical details regarding the actual characteristics of child protection arrangements in specific countries.[1] Their approach is based on the authors' premise "that it is critically important to first understand the underlying values of the system as a means of grouping countries before looking at the

---

[1] The report indicates that four countries/states were examined: Indonesia, Kenya, Malawi, and Balochistan, using information from the UNICEF *Child Protection Systems: Mapping and Assessment Toolkit. Users' Guide*. These countries have the following ranks on the KidsRights Index 2019: Indonesia 106; Kenya

particular attributes of the system" (Connolly et al., 2014, p. 1). The typology, formulated from a theoretical perspective, can be seen as an evolving project that offers a contribution to the ongoing analyses of child protection systems (see also Connolly & Katz, 2019).

An Inductive Approach to Developing a Global Typology

The 2014 report sponsored by UNICEF and Save the Children was a benchmark study, which emphasized the importance of broadening the analytic lens used in the conceptual classification of child protection systems to include low-to-moderate-income countries. In contrast to the theoretical framework and deductive reasoning that informed the inclusive typology developed in the UNICEF report, the global typology presented here (detailed in Table 46.4) is based on inductive reasoning that draws upon specific observations and empirical data on 50 countries to formulate generalizations about the essential characteristics of child protection systems and arrangements.

As outlined above, we see some of the differences across countries shaped, in part, by the resources available to host an extensive web of state protection when parents are unable or unwilling to provide adequate care. At least a decade ago, UNICEF launched a campaign to consider child protection broadly and to encourage new efforts that could be sustainable and systemic, rather than improvised and issue-focused (UNICEF, 2008). The campaign aimed to develop systems of support, urging "laws, policies, regulations and services, capacities, monitoring, and oversight needed across all social sectors—especially social welfare, education, health, security, and justice—to prevent and respond to protection related risks" (as cited in Wulczyn et al., 2010).

Despite these efforts, the establishment of formal and informal systems in support of children and families remains at notably different stages across the globe. We note that these differences roughly parallel the development and institutionalization of a modern welfare state, designed to protect individuals against the unpredictability of the market. Using conceptual labels to characterize these differences, distinguishing between nascent, emerging and institutionalized stages, we recognize that the boundaries between these public administrative structures are porous, and individual countries may have characteristics that straddle at least two types of structural stages.

We describe the structure of many low-to-moderate income countries' public institutions as in a *nascent* stage of development. In these cases, legislation designed to protect children's rights is in place, and some administrative systems have been devised to respond to children's circumstances, but barriers relating to resources, geography, history, and cultural heterogeneity, for example, limit uniform, universal access to protection. The majority of funding in low-income countries is provided by the donor community including UNICEF, Save the Children, and various religious entities, and the delivery of

---

125, Malawi 132, and Balochistan (a region in south Asia; most Balochils live in Pakistan, which is ranked 151 on the KidsRight Index).

Table 46.4 Characteristics of the global child protection typology

Child protection systems	Child exploitation protective system	Child deprivation protective system	Child maltreatment protective system	Child well-being protective system	Child rights protective system
Social, political, and cultural contexts of states					
Rights orientation	Tribal/community rights	Family rights or ambivalent rights	Parental rights	Mixed rights	Child rights
Familialization	Familialized	Familialized and refamilialized	Partly de-familialized	Partly de-familialized	De-familialized
Context of child violence	High	Mixed	Mixed	Low	Low
Definition of childhood	0–15	0–16 or up to 18	0–16 or up to 18	0–18 or up to 23	0–18 or up to 25
State response to cultural and religious diversity	Stark contrasts in practice within cultural/religious enclaves	Recognition of ethnic/racial disproportionalities	Cultural accommodations in law	Universal principles	Universal principles
Protective system characteristics					
Parent/child as active agents	No	No	Parental participation growing. Child participation atypical.	Service-user participation, including parent & child typical.	Service user participation, including parent & child typical. Child participation required
Intervention threshold	High	High	High	Low	Low
Early intervention and family support	No	No	Mixed	Yes	Yes
Array of care settings	Strong reliance on informal kin	Reliance on informal kin and institutional care	Non-kin, formal kin, and institutional care	Non-kin, formal kin, and institutional care	Non-kin, formal kin, and institutional care
Adoption	Little accountability; high intercountry rates	Necessary to solve societal problems	Ease government responsibility and secure permanency for child	Permanency and child's best interest	Child's best interest and child's family life

services is largely conducted by NGOs and private agencies. Social workers are sometimes involved, but voluntary community case workers (supervised by social workers) play a dominant role, as in countries such as Zimbabwe (Mushunje, this volume). Given the resource constraints that many of these countries face, the capacity for data collection and reporting is limited. UNICEF and other international organizations are helpful in collecting periodic information about child and family needs and concerns, but there is little state infrastructure available to assess the scope of service provision or the outcomes for children and families.

In moderate-income countries, historical legacies relating to military and political turmoil, or religious orientations have impacted progress in constructing comprehensive organizational state institutions. These we term *emerging* structures, as the ideal of children's rights is well established in law but the architecture for practice is still developing. The state plays a more substantial role (along with donors) in funding the child protection infrastructure, but reliance on outside assistance is also vital in strengthening bureaucratic capacity. In Lithuania, for example, EU funding was instrumental in efforts to professionalize the workforce and to improve training and support for foster caregivers (Tamutienė & Snieškienė, this volume). NGOs play a large role, though some aspects of the system are shared with state actors. For example, in the Philippines, both state agencies and NGOs provide direct services to children and families, depending on the jurisdiction. That state also aspires to offer services from professionally trained social workers, though resource shortages have limited the capacity to grow the social work workforce quickly (Roche & Flores-Pasos, this volume). In other countries such as Egypt and China, child protection assumes a professional social work workforce, but staff shortages are endemic (Olimat & ElGamal, this volume; Zhao & Xu, this volume).

In many high-income countries a combination of public policy, national (and sometimes state or local) resources, administrative and judicial systems, and professional staff, give rise to a state apparatus that is *institutionalized* in form and function, specifically designed to safeguard children against the vagaries, inadequacies, and inabilities of parents or other caregivers to enact their duties toward children. Particularly in Western Europe, the state plays an especially prominent role and social workers, pedagogues, and other trained professionals provide services to families. Data collection efforts in these nations are growing rapidly and many aspire to employ evidence-based practices.

But within these societal arrangements, what are child protection systems designed to protect? In the Introduction to this volume, we noted that the CRC stipulates that it is the state's responsibility to provide children and young people protection from various forms of maltreatment and abuse when parents or other caregivers are unable or unwilling to enact their responsibilities. The 50 case studies in this Handbook reveal that there are children in all countries who are in dire need of protection, but there is considerable variation among countries in the magnitude of the severity and risks of physical, psychological, and social harms experienced. Depending on the country and community context, parents have greater and lesser capacities to protect their children against harm. Child protection systems also reflect political, economic, social, and cultural contexts that find expression in a focal orientation to children's protection. The *Global Child Protection Typology* therefore focuses on the target of protection and the state's response to children's protection needs. Figure 46.1 illustrates these orientations, suggesting the layered risks that befall children to which the state may respond. At the most basic level, all 50 countries attempt to protect children against the risk of *child exploitation*; going beyond this risk, at the next level some countries are also oriented to protect against *child deprivation*; some are further focused on protecting narrowly against *child maltreatment*; widening the scope of this coverage others also seek to protect *child well-being*; and finally, covering all the levels of risk, a few countries further aspire to protect *child rights*.

We see these levels as both cumulative and fluid. They are cumulative in that all countries attempt to protect children against extreme forms of exploitation, but some countries are resourced and structured such that these issues serve as their focal orientation. By focusing on these different levels of protection, the typology provides an inclusive classification that not only incorporates low- and middle-income countries but also articulates distinctions among the characteristics of child protection schemes in high-income countries. They are also fluid in the sense that there are no stark boundaries between these levels, and some aspects of a country context may emphasize one type of risk but incorporate others as well. The prevalence of risks for children is correlated with the degree to which countries possess sufficient resources and are able to provide adequate living standards for

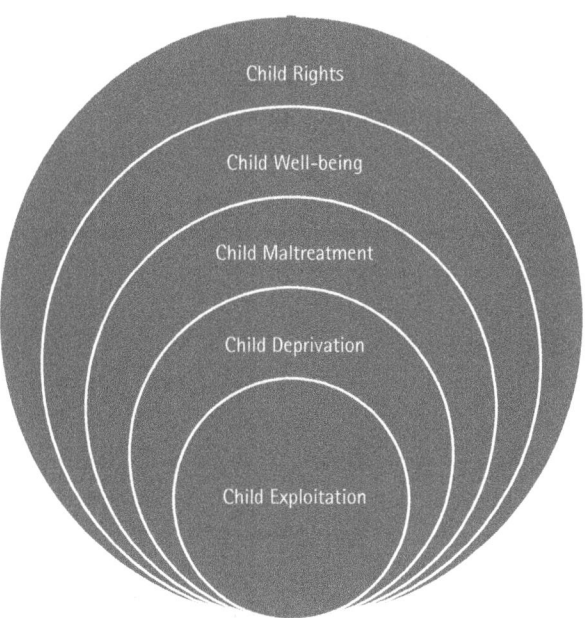

Figure 46.1 Global child protection typology: Protective orientations

families. The prevalence of risk is also correlated with the political resolve to implement programs designed to mitigate child rights violations, to address cultural and religious practices compromising children's rights, and to manage the fundamental tensions that result from protecting children and simultaneously honoring family privacy.

Child Exploitation Protective Systems

Children who lack access to food, clothing, and shelter, and children who risk survival face extreme circumstances. According to UNICEF (2019), approximately 385 million children under 18 years of age live on less than $1.90/day (controlling for purchasing power parity). The large majority of these children live in countries in Sub-Saharan Africa. In South Africa, for example, 65% of children live below the South Africa poverty line, and 22% of children live below the international poverty line ($1.90/day) (Sloth-Nielsen, this volume).

In low- and middle-income countries where vulnerable populations can be more easily targeted for exploitation, protection of children and children's rights tend to focus on child labor, child trafficking, slavery, street children, children engaged in armed conflict, and child marriage. The Philippines and Egypt, for example, both show how children are exploited in child labor and child trafficking, and there are many children living and/or working on the streets (i.e., street children) (Roche & Flores-Pasos, this volume; Olimat & ElGamal, this volume). Uganda has especially high rates of child marriage and early childbearing. Child labor is also endemic; some estimates indicate that approximately half of children work to support family incomes, half of these in hazardous conditions (Yiga, this volume). India has large numbers of "missing" children, many of whom are believed to be homeless, trafficked, kidnapped, or sold (Bhatt & Sanyal, this volume). Low- and middle-income countries are in the initial stages of developing institutionalized welfare states and their focus is broadly oriented to protect children's right to survival and to be free from exploitation and abuse. Lacking a broad welfare system and offering only a minimal safety net, the child protection systems in these countries are just in the early stages of development, and in practice reach a proportionately small number of children in need of protection as the CRC article 19 prescribes.

Child Deprivation Protective Systems

In addition to the risk of extreme poverty, children's survival may be put at risk if they lose a parent to death or abandonment. In this regard, the world AIDS crisis has left millions of children orphaned. At the height of the crisis, over 14 million children were estimated to have been orphaned in Africa alone (UNICEF, 2003). In Zimbabwe, for example, over 1.2 million children have been orphaned by the HIV/AIDS epidemic (Mushunje, this volume), and South Africa experienced a HIV/AIDS pandemic from the beginning of 2000 until 2012, with the number of orphaned children increasing from 30,000 in 2002, to 550,000 in 2012 (Sloth-Nielsen, this volume). In Russia, 2.3% of the child population is left without parental care, either due to substance abuse, poverty, or parental death (Kulmala et al., this volume).

Deprivation of parental care offers one dimension for considering children's risk, but children's survival is also related to their access to health care services to protect against illness and disability, nutrition to protect against stunted growth and disease, and housing to protect against the elements. Low-to-moderate income countries with *emerging* institutional structures tend to focus on the vulnerabilities children may face relating to a lack of basic services. Several of the countries in Latin America and some in Eastern Europe, for example, describe governmental efforts focused on addressing children's basic needs. Countries such as Argentina consider lack of housing, school absences, or healthcare as suggestive of a child rights deprivation (Villalta & Llobet, this volume). In Ecuador, education, health, nutrition, housing, and social security are a focus of concern particularly for refugee and so-called clandestine children (Borja et al., this volume). High levels of poverty in Mexico have dire consequences for children, where more than half of the child population lacks "the economic ability to meet their basic needs. Moreover, data demonstrate that children currently lack the security, educational, and health conditions required for their optimal development" (Armenta, in this volume). Roma children are living in segregated communities in the Slovak Republic, where there is insufficient infrastructure, poor hygienic and living conditions, inadequate nutrition, and little access to education (Lenka & Beáta, in this volume). And in Lithuania, resources are lacking to provide for children's "health, living conditions, education, participation of children, prevention of poverty risk, and other important issues necessary for the welfare of the child" (Tamutienė & Snieškienė, this volume). In these and other countries (China, for example, see Man et al., 2017), child maltreatment is one concern, but overall disadvantage, vulnerability, and deprivation are at the forefront of child protection efforts.

Child Maltreatment Protective Systems

In this group of mostly wealthy countries with *institutionalized* governmental structures, country case studies describe risk-oriented child protection systems that focus narrowly on protection from harm by family members. Child maltreatment includes injuries from physical abuse, sexual abuse, and emotional abuse, including exposure to family violence and long-term chronic neglect. Depending on the context, some countries may show more concern for, or focus greater resources on certain types of maltreatment. In Ireland, for example, the large majority of maltreatment referrals to the child protection system concern child emotional abuse (Burns et al., this volume), whereas in the United States and Canada, the majority of children are identified as suffering from child neglect. These systems are similar to those that would be classified under the "child protection orientation" in Table 46.2 and under "authoritarian individualism" in Table 46.3. The approach is fairly narrow in scope, concerning the state's response to serious harm and risk of harm for children, and reflects a strong family ideology and high threshold for restricting parental freedom. The United States may be considered an exemplar in this area as eligibility for services largely hinges on a substantiated (i.e., verified) assessment of maltreatment (Lawson & Berrick, this volume). Other countries that primarily focus on safety for children, with strong protections for family privacy, in combination with relatively few services to children and families, include Canada, Australia, New Zealand, Japan, South Korea, and some Eastern European countries such as Estonia, Latvia, and Poland. The English child protection system can be categorized as a child maltreatment-focused system, with aspirations to be viewed as a child well-being-oriented system. Due to a systematic lack of resources for child welfare services to realize the ambitions goals set in legislation and policy, it is fairly focused in its orientation to protect against maltreatment (Thoburn, this volume).

Child Well-being Protective Systems

In several high-income countries where a strong and universal safety net provides for health, education, nutrition, and a range of other services, the state's obligation to children extends well beyond securing protection from harm or risk of harm. These states are oriented more broadly to incorporate children's needs and to securing their well-being within a developmental frame. They largely fit within the original Gilbert and colleagues typology of a "family service" system (see Table 46.2), offering a wide range of services to support family life and child wellness. All have highly *institutionalized* structures with laws, protocols, organizational networks, and professional staff providing universal supports. In Belgium, for example, the problem of child abuse or neglect is framed as a health, welfare, or familial problem that is best addressed through a supportive response. The focal point of concern is the child (as opposed to a focal concern on the caregiver and his or her behaviors or intentions) and the need for intervention is, in part, determined by assessing the effects of maltreatment or other concerns on the child's developmental need. Similarly, in the Netherlands, children can be identified as needing services to avoid developmental harm. In these situations, an approach that values parental partnership and voluntary engagement is preferred. Similarly, in countries such as France, Germany, or Switzerland, a range of services are available to support family life that go beyond a narrow response to child maltreatment.

Child Rights Protective Systems

Incorporating an approach that guards against exploitation, deprivation, maltreatment, and developmental harm, the *institutionalized* countries with a child rights orientation are additionally concerned with addressing the child as a person with individual rights. These countries have incorporated the CRC into national legislation, aiming to fulfill the Convention's obligations by also treating the child as a moral subject with individual interests and a right to an open future. Child participation in all administrative and judicial proceedings is valued, together with a recognition of children as equal to adults in society. The Nordic systems of child protection, previously referred to as having a child focus (Table 46.2), have thus developed affirmative approaches for protecting children against rights violations, conceiving of child protection as a broad and comprehensive package of supports and services that respond to children as rights-bearing individuals. As an example of such an approach, Denmark's legislation privileges the child's best interest over the least intrusive principle. Services and interventions, therefore, are adjusted to the child's needs over the family's right to privacy (Hestbæk et al., this volume).

There are challenges, of course, to enacting some of these goals as states make the transition to a child rights framework. In Norway, for example, attention has been focused on finding a balance between children's participation and autonomy on the one hand, and professionals' necessary paternalism on the other hand (Hestbæk et al., this volume). The fundamental challenge for children is to experience the state's recognition of their interests as separate from the family. A study of children's perceptions and experiences by Kosher & Ben-Arieh (2017) suggests that the goals of a child rights orientation can have important effects. They found a correlation between children's right to "participation and, to some degree, their knowledge and thinking about their rights" as an indicator of their well-being (p. 263).

Characteristics of a Global Typology

As noted, all countries have committed to the principles of the CRC, and many have instantiated their ideals in legislation. The global typology aims to capture the evident differences in the degree to which countries have an institutional and ideological frame to carry out their legislative aspirations. Based on the evidence provided across the 50 countries included in this volume, we find ten characteristics relevant to our understanding of the differences among the five types of systems. Table 46.4 offers a schematic of the system differences that are evident across countries. These characteristics are not fixed, nor are they universal for all countries within a single type. They provide, however, a provisional structure upon which to hang a more articulated understanding of countries with different types of child protection systems. Five of these characteristics refer to the *social, political, and cultural context of states*; another five refer to specific *protective system characteristics*.

The protective orientation of a state is shaped, as above, by the history, geography, demography, and resources available. In addition, certain social, and cultural contexts play an especially powerful role in molding a state's orientation to child protection, which we describe briefly below.

Social, Political, and Cultural Contexts of States
RIGHTS ORIENTATION

Although all countries support the CRC, not all countries embrace a strong child rights orientation in the design or execution of their child protection system. Instead, in the global typology, the rights orientation of various countries appears to fall along a continuum from *group rights* (i.e., tribal or community), to *family rights*, to *parents' rights*, to *mixed rights* (parents' and children's rights), to *children's rights*. This is not to suggest that states are exclusive about privileging some rights over others; the differences in emphases are largely a matter of degree.

In Ghana, for example, policies that are responsive to the CRC have been enacted, but implementation at the local level—particularly in more remote villages—is not feasible given resource and infrastructure constraints. Even if resources were ample, there are questions as to whether some local communities would accept formal state involvement (see Wessells et al., 2012). There, *group rights* (tribal or community) typically prevail; the resolution of children's concerns devolve to informal structures such as the tribe or community enclave. Leaders such as chiefs, queen mothers, family elders, or other religious leaders assess and respond, but the resolution does not necessarily tilt toward a child rights orientation. Instead, out of deference to community harmony, the response might include compensation to the victim or supported reconciliation (Dako-Gyeke et al., this volume).

A similar approach is found in Uganda, where an informal system of response serves as an ancillary to the formal system. As in Ghana, there are notable benefits of the informal, community system. The response is essentially cost-free, and it is embedded in the cultural context of the community. Like Ghana, however, and in line with the tribal rights orientation, the goal of preserving community harmony may outweigh the goal of attending to children's rights (Yiga, this volume).

Other countries' child protection systems are oriented toward a *family rights* perspective wherein children and parents are not viewed as separate individuals, but as a single unit with shared interests. Countries that follow the precepts of Confucianism typically align with a family rights orientation. Confucian values suggest that the family is centrally responsible for the welfare and protection of its children. As such, others—including neighbors, community members, or government officials—do not have a natural role in monitoring or responding to children's needs. In China, a family rights orientation appears to dominate, shaping the gradual evolution of its child protection system. Recent legislative activity suggests that the country is developing an infrastructure for child protection, but progress is slow in part due to cultural understandings about family, the role of the family in child protection, and longstanding Confucian values. Family harmony is prized in Confucian teachings, as is the privacy of the family (Zhao & Xu, this volume). Unlike China, South Korea is rapidly developing a system of response to problems of child maltreatment and has established a wide set of child well-being policies (Clarke et al., 2020). The response is nevertheless rooted in a strong family preservation frame, meaning that children are maintained with their parents, even under precarious circumstances (Chung & Lah, this volume).

In contrast to a relatively strict family rights orientation, several countries in Latin America adhere to an ambivalent rights orientation. Many Latin American countries strongly endorse the CRC. In Chile, Muñoz-Guzman and colleagues (this volume) claim that children's rights and interests have been elevated significantly since the UNCRC was ratified. They indicate that "children are thus seen today as bearers of multiple needs and potentials, able to participate and contribute to solving their own problems, according to their developmental stage." And in Mexico, the constitution was amended in 2000 to account for the "integral development and protection of minors" highlighting the role of children as the "subjects of rights," rather than the "objects of protection" (Armenta, this volume). It is equally clear, however, that in many of these nations, children are not considered fully rights-bearing individuals. Brazilian legislation is designed to protect children when their rights are threatened or violated, but also in Brazil, children are considered "holders of subordinate interests, in relation to the family, society, and the state" (Diene et al., this volume).

Further along the continuum, some child protection systems privilege *parents' rights* to an important degree. The United States stands out as an exemplar. Unlike many other countries that include children's rights in the constitutional frame, children are not mentioned in the US constitution. Further, in contrast to many country constitutions that grant positive rights (i.e., the right to benefits from services or supports from the government), the US constitution is based on the notion of negative rights (i.e., the right to be free from government intrusion). As such, in cases where the interests of parents, children, and the state conflict, the US Supreme Court typically privileges the interests of parents' privacy over the interests of the child or the state (see Bartholet, 2020).

Many countries aim to *balance* the rights of children with the rights of their parents simultaneously, providing a mixed rights orientation. Using a "best interest" principle, most Western European countries consider the child's rights and needs in the context of the family, but increasingly recognize that children's rights are parallel to parental rights.

Finally, some countries are recognized for their commitment to a *child rights* orientation, instantiating children's rights in law and in practice. The Nordic countries are illustrative of this (Gilbert et al., 2011; Pösö et al., 2014). Amendments to the Norwegian constitution in 2014 (Section 104) specifically provides children's rights equivalent to those of adults (Hestbæk et al., this volume). Further, because the Danish, Finnish, Norwegian, and Swedish child protection systems emphasize voluntary participation in services, children (of a certain age and maturity) must be consulted regarding their views about the receipt of services.

Some authors have tested these rights orientations empirically and find support for the differences described herein. Ellingsen and colleagues (2019) compared social workers in Chile and Norway to determine their views about children, parents, and families when examining a complex child protection case. Chilean social workers offered responses that were family and adult-oriented, whereas social workers in Norway were more child-oriented, showing concern for the child's individual rights and needs. Furthermore, a study of 54,000 children (ages 8–12 years) across 16 countries examined their subjective perceptions of children's rights (Kosher & Ben-Arieh, 2017), indicating significant country differences. When asked: "I think in my country adults in general respect children's rights," 83% of Norwegian children agreed; in contrast, only 35% of children from South Korea said the same.[2] Denmark has shifted its traditional principles relating to interaction between the state and the family, setting aside the least intrusive principle to instead prioritize children's rights. The least intrusive principle indicates that the state should not intervene in the family more than absolutely necessary. The revised Danish approach suggests that services must be adapted to the child's needs and if the child needs comprehensive assistance measures to be able to continue living at home, the parents must accept this. The implication is also that the child can be moved out of the home without trying in-home services if the child's needs so requires it (Hæstbek et al, this volume).

FAMILIALIZATION

The line between public and private responsibility—between the government and the family's responsibility for children—is a matter of degree. In general, the balance is based on normative and ideological values that are rooted in the cultural, religious, and historical context of a given country and society. Countries where the family is seen as responsible for assuming risks and for protecting its members from the uncertainties of the market are typically referred to as familialized in their approach to public policy, placing responsibility for the care and protection of children on the nuclear or extended family. The reasons for adopting a familialized approach may be related to notions of freedom (i.e., freedom from government interference), trust (i.e., lack of trust in government institutions), or other community values.

Hantrais (2004) has expanded our understanding of the concept of familialization, suggesting that distinctions between familialized and defamilialized (countries where citizens may place greater reliance on the state for supporting individual and family concerns), are too restrictive. Instead, she has expanded the traditional family policy typologies to also include partly defamilialized nations—states with an ideological orientation toward familialization, but with some state supports. She also describes refamilialized nations—those countries that were defamilialized under Soviet rule, but transitioned responsibilities back to the family following the break-up of the Soviet Union.

Some Asian or African countries included in this volume are largely familialized, placing significant emphasis on the family for children's care and support, whereas others—those in Eastern Europe, for example—are refamilialized as family members adjust to the new expectations and obligations for children's care. Among institutionalized structures, some are partly defamilialized and others are strongly defamilialized. Italy and Greece, for example, stand out among Western European nations in the degree to which they are familialized in the European context. That ideological orientation may be expressed more

---

[2] The country rankings (high to low) were: Norway, Turkey, Malta, Nepal, England, Estonia, Germany, Romania, Spain, Israel, Colombia, Algeria, Poland, Ethiopia, South Africa, and South Korea.

or less profoundly depending on the state resources available to enact a more defamilialized system. As Bertotti and colleagues (this volume) suggest, the financial crisis of 2010 saw the retraction of the state from child protection, requiring more of extended families to attend to children's care.

Child protection staff working within these systems are cognizant of the family typology that frames their work, even if they are unaccustomed to the language of familialism. An illustrative study by Oltedal and Nygren (2019) presented child protection staff with a complex child protection vignette. Norwegian child welfare staff were more likely to describe the value of the state in serving the family; in Chile, staff were more inclined to emphasize the family as a source of support.

CONTEXT OF CHILD VIOLENCE

How citizens view family violence powerfully shapes the orientation of their country's child protection system. Evidence from the Multiple Indicator Cluster Survey suggests an important association between a country's level of economic security and inequality, and parents' beliefs in and use of physical discipline and violent physical discipline with their children (Beatriz & Salhi, 2019). Not surprisingly, many of the countries with nascent and emerging public administrative structures also cluster among the societies that are more likely to use physical discipline and violent physical discipline with their children.

In countries such as Uganda and Nigeria, where studies suggest that upwards of 60–70% (Elekwachi, this volume; Yiga, this volume) of children experience serious physical discipline,[3] concepts such as physical child abuse take on a different meaning than in a country where corporal punishment is outlawed or where violence against children is shunned (cf. Chapter 1, this volume). In Egypt, widespread use of corporal punishment is socially acceptable as a disciplinary practice, and 93% of children aged 1–14 years have been exposed to violent disciplinary practices (Olimat & ElGamal, this volume).

In several Eastern European and Latin American countries, family violence and violence towards children are recognized as serious social issues. For example, Tanaś (this volume) indicates that family violence in Poland is a major concern. Lithuania, too, sees high rates of intrafamilial violence (Tamutienė & Snieškienė, this volume). In Brazil, children and adolescents are the main victims of domestic violence, sexual violence, and other types of interpersonal violence (Carlos et al., this volume); in both Brazil and Mexico the annual number of children killed is alarmingly high (Carlos et al., this volume; Armenta, this volume).

In contrast, Sweden and Finland were some of the first countries in the world to outlaw physical discipline (Höjer & Pösö, this volume) and, as mentioned in Chapter 1,

---

[3] Other estimates suggest that these rates are under-estimates. One study of a representative sample of secondary school students indicated that 95% had experienced family violence in the previous month (Ssenyonga et al., 2019).

63 countries have banned corporal punishment. In some countries (e.g., Austria), children's entitlement to a violence-free childhood is included in the federal constitution. Whether national laws follow changes in family parenting practices or vice versa is not clear. Even in countries with a ban on corporal punishment, the general public's acceptance of corporal punishment as an appropriate form of discipline may vary: in Norway, corporal punishment is accepted among about 13% of the population compared to Spain at 39% (Helland et al., 2018).

DEFINITION OF CHILDHOOD

In relatively close alignment with the continuum of types of child protection systems we see patterns associated with how states define childhood itself—with exceptions, of course. In some regards, it appears as though the resource capacity of a state may limit the degree to which it can view the concept of childhood expansively (i.e., up through age 23 or older in some high-income countries), or in a restricted fashion (i.e., childhood defined by the age of menarche for girls, or age nine in some low-income countries). Determining whether childhood ends at age 9, 15, 18, or 2 has implications for who is protected, for how long, and from what.

In Iran, the upper age boundary of childhood has undergone a number of legislative changes in recent years, and the boundary varies depending on the risk being protected. Islam defines the age of maturity for girls and boys as ages 9 and 15 respectively (counted as lunar years). As such, some child legislation, especially relating to sexual abuse, targets these age categories (Takaffoli et al., this volume). Similarly, in Lebanon, the legal definition of childhood is set at age 18, though there are a number of exceptions. For example, the minimum age for marriage is determined by each religious group, with some groups allowing marriage as young as age 9 (Rizk, this volume). Philippine law sets the minimum age for sexual consent at age 12 (Roche & Flores-Pasos, this volume), and in India, particularly in rural villages—childhood ends at puberty (Bhatt & Sanyal, this volume).

The upper boundaries of childhood appear to be most flexible on issues pertaining to sex, labor and criminal responsibility. Child labor is restricted in Lebanon to age 13 (Rizk, this volume). Mexico (Armenta, this volume) and Iran (Takaffoli et al., this volume) set an age limit of 15; India (Bhatt & Sanyal, this volume) and Uganda (Yiga, this volume) limit employment for children under age 16. The age of criminal responsibility is set at age 7 in Lebanon (Rizk, this volume); age 9 (girls) and 15 (boys) in Iran (Takaffoli et al., this volume), age 12 in Uganda (Yiga, this volume), 14 in Chile (Muñoz-Guzman et al., this volume), and 16 in Argentina (Villalta & Llobet, this volume).

In some high-income countries, allowances are made to extend childhood beyond age 18. In Japan, for example, children who have been placed in out-of-home care may remain to age 20, if they choose to do so (Tokunaga et al., this volume). The same is true in many of the US states (Lawson & Berrick, this volume), where children can remain in care until age 21. In Finland and Norway, after-care services can be provided up until age

25; in Sweden mandatory child protection services can be offered up until age 21 (Höjer & Pösö, this volume; Hestbæk et al, this volume). And almost 10% of all children receiving child protection services in France are ages 18–21 (Bolter, this volume).

STATE RESPONSE TO CULTURAL AND RELIGIOUS DIVERSITY

Globalization and many other forces have made national boundaries more permeable and the communities within countries more diverse. None of the countries in this volume include only one ethnic or racial group, and in most, if not all of the countries, child protection disproportionately serves children from ethnic or racial backgrounds that are in the country's minority. These disproportionalities, so common across very different countries, stand out as a disturbing, unifying feature, regardless of nation or continent. Some states *respond to cultural or religious diversity* by tacit acceptance; other states make active accommodations in law or practice, and some uphold universal rights and obligations regardless of cultural or religious difference. But cultural and religious heterogeneity within countries are the norm. Political scientist Parekh (2000) identifies 12 cultural or religious practices that frequently lead to intercultural clashes: female circumcision; polygamy; Muslim and Jewish methods of animal slaughter; arranged marriages; marriages between relatives; scarring children's cheeks and/or body; Muslim exclusion of girls from coeducation; Muslim children's; Sikh turbans; gypsy and Amish not allowing children to attend public schools; Hindu cremation; subordinate status of women. Of these, a majority concern children. How states negotiate protection for children in a context of diversity is, therefore, another distinguishing characteristic of the global typology.

In several of the low- and middle-income countries, the state wittingly or unwittingly allows for stark contrasts in practice within cultural enclaves. In Ghana, for example, although the national laws governing child protection are uniform, their reach into more remote regions or villages is not. The contrasts between secular and customary laws have pronounced effects for children where some cultural enclaves allow practices such as female genital mutilation, child marriage, and girl slaves, but the state does not have the infrastructure to respond effectively (Dako-Gyeke et al., this volume). In other country contexts, active accommodations are made for differences in family practices, typically based on different religious orientations. In Nigeria, crimes against children may not be investigated and treated on religious grounds (Elekwachi, this volume). And in Lebanon, issues relating to marriage, divorce, child custody, and adoption are governed by local, religious communities (Rizk, this volume). Dinata (this volume) shows the difficulties of crafting uniform, national policy relating to child protection in multicultural, pluralistic societies such as Indonesia that are undergoing significant cultural and religious transformations.

Further along the continuum, there is a growing recognition of the disproportionate effects of child protection involvement on ethno-racial minority communities but efforts to address these inequalities are in the early stages of development. As examples, in the Czech Republic (Shmidt, this volume) and Slovak Republic (Kvašňáková & Balogová, this volume), Roma children and families are disproportionately involved in child protection. In Brazil (Carlos et al., this volume), indigenous children face disproportionate risks and are engaged in the child protection system to a greater degree than non-indigenous children.

In contrast to the cultural accommodations made informally in practice in some of the nascent administrative structures, or the acknowledgement that there are disparate effects of child protection on some cultural or ethno-racial groups, some nations have developed separate laws or formal structures to accommodate different communities. In Ecuador, all child protection centers must include community leaders on their interdisciplinary teams to serve as cultural mediators; services offered to families must incorporate practices that are culturally responsive (Borja et al., this volume). In Colombia, both judicial and administrative actions relating to indigenous children must attend to children's individual rights at the same time that their collective rights must be protected (Torrado & Strauch, this volume). In New Zealand and Australia, Family Conference and Care Circles reflect a culturally responsive approach to indigenous families and serve as an alternative to the traditional decision-making system. Policies also specify placement preferences for Aboriginal and Torres Strait children (Cashmore & Taylor, this volume). In the United States, a separate federal law serves all children belonging to any of the over 500 federally recognized Native American or Alaska Native tribes. These legal accommodations are not based on ethno-racial identity but reflect the unique tribal sovereignty of tribal nations within US national boundaries (Lawson & Berrick, this volume). Similarly, in Canada, many of the First Nations have negotiated separate funding and jurisdiction arrangements for their children and families (Trocmé et al., this volume).

Other high-income countries have a universal rights approach, having similar legislation and policy for all children, adhering to the CRC non-discrimination principle set out in Article 2. For example, in France, the nationality of a child is irrelevant, and unaccompanied children do not need residence permits in order to be recognized as children in need of care (Bolter, this volume). In these systems, children's rights to respect for their ethnic, religious, cultural, and linguistic backgrounds are established in legislation, though there are violations in practice, as case law from the European Court of Human rights has shown (see, for example, ECtHR, 2019).

Protective System Characteristics
PARENT/CHILD AS ACTIVE AGENTS

Across child protection systems there are gradations in the degree to which parents and/or children are involved in decisions regarding the receipt of services. Child and parent participation in nascent governmental structures is limited. According to Dako-Gyeke and colleagues (this volume), in Ghana, children are "socialized to defer to adults and would hardly voice out an opinion even in matters concerning their own well-being." In China, children are not viewed as independent individuals and they are not typically free to make independent decisions (Zhao & Xu, this volume); as such, their perspectives are not usually taken into account in the Chinese child protection system.

Although Eastern European countries aspire to include children in decision making in accord with the CRC, many struggle to do so. A recent report by the United Nations urged the Slovak Republic, for example, to develop institutional structures that might facilitate children's involvement in administrative and judicial decisions of import (Kvašňáková & Balogová, this volume). Elsewhere, in Poland, parents are typically invited to participate in interdisciplinary team meetings to develop a plan for services and to resolve family issues, but children are excluded (Tanaś, this volume).

Many of the Western European and North American countries include parents as decision makers and informants in the process, as do both Australia and New Zealand. Family group conferences are used increasingly across countries to engage parents (and children, depending on age and maturity) and to develop plans for safety and support. Children's views, in Australia, are also represented in court by means of a legal representative (Cashmore & Taylor, this volume). In England, the children's guardian is in place and family group conferences are also utilized, though not necessarily in all jurisdictions. Older children may participate in conferences, but all children typically communicate their needs and wishes to intermediary social workers (employed by CAFCASS—Child and Family Court Advisory and Support Service) who then communicate children's expressed concerns to social workers and the courts (Thoburn, this volume). Israeli law stipulates that children can share their views on issues relevant to their well-being; though the weight of their views is considered in light of age and maturity (Gross-Manos et al., this volume).

Along the continuum, the Nordic countries, where a child-rights orientation prevails, are required to consult with children regarding their views about service receipt. Parents, too, must be consulted. A tradition of strong service user involvement is established in the Nordic countries, and this now also includes children. Legislation is focused on children's participation as Article 12 in the UNCRC prescribes, although in practice it has been difficult to fully implement (Hetsbæk et al., this volume; Höjer & Pösö, this volume).

INTERVENTION THRESHOLD

The vast majority of nations place some limitations on parental rights in childrearing, particularly when their actions are injurious to children. But where nations set their threshold to intervene in these rights regarding child rearing vary greatly. In most child protection systems, individual (adults) freedom rights and the principle of "least intrusion" seems to prevail, suggesting that the state will grant the family privacy to the greatest extent possible, assuming the child's safety is protected, setting the threshold for state intrusion in family life high. In part, these thresholds are set in response to a country's capacity for intervention. In Ghana, for example, some cultural practices such as female genital muti-lation, or *trokoski* (i.e., slave of the gods), practiced in more remote regions, are widely viewed in the dominant society as harmful to children, but the state's capacity to intervene even in these high threshold events is limited (Yiga, this volume). In other countries such as the United States, some states set their threshold for public intervention high, only intervening in cases of serious maltreatment. Although state capacity is strong, societal views about government involvement in family life constrain state action. In contrast, and as described previously, recent legislation in Denmark privileges the child's "best interests" over the least intrusive principle when the two ideas are in conflict. That orientation sug-gests much greater tolerance for state intrusion in family life at a relatively low threshold standard of concern rather than harm.

FAMILY AND CHILD SUPPORT ORIENTATION

Whether a nation provides primary prevention services to thwart negative events from occurring to children, secondary prevention to interrupt early signs of risk or harm, or ter-tiary prevention after harmful incidents have occurred, is a matter—at least—of resources, ideology, political will, and cultural context. The degree to which a state orients its child protection system to *early intervention and family support* also falls along a continuum that corresponds to the protective orientations within the global typology. Along the contin-uum of our systems, we find that tertiary or secondary prevention approaches dominate in the nascent and emerging governmental structures. In Zimbabwe or India, for example, the state's resources are constrained so that the delivery of widespread primary prevention services is not currently feasible.

Some countries are developing large-scale campaigns to prevent maltreatment and improve parenting. In Uruguay, a media campaign was launched including television ads, text messaging, and brochures focused on positive parenting, and schools have been offered short videos on maltreatment, sexual abuse, and bullying (Tornaría & Miller, this volume). Other countries have recently introduced a preventive focus to their child protection system. In New Zealand, for example, a national shift in policy and prac-tice was introduced in 2016, oriented toward primary and secondary prevention efforts (Cashmore & Taylor, this volume). And some states might be characterized as aspirational in their orientation to prevention—such as Slovakia, Poland, and Russia—but have not yet garnered the resources or the bureaucratic structure to fully enact their goals.

At the other end of the continuum, some Western European and the Nordic coun-tries provide a range of universal services designed to support parents, strengthen families, and secure children's safety. In these systems, services are provided so that the child can continue living within the family and enable parents' capacities to care for the child. Although services typically are provided on a voluntary basis, the child protection system can require that services are used and control and supervision may follow, as recently enacted in the Norwegian system (Hestbæk et al., this volume).

For children whose safety requires separation from their parents, all states provide mechanisms for identifying alternative care. The *array of care settings* available to children who require substitute care is, in part, a reflection of a state's infrastructure capacity, but the heterogeneity of options is also an indicator of customization designed to meet the unique needs of individual children. These differences across states are notable within the typology. In some societies, children's relatives are often engaged to provide children's care, though these arrangements are typically informal. Caregivers receive neither funding, training, nor support for children's care. From a global perspective, informal kin care is more common than any other type of care: some estimates indicate that well over 160 million children worldwide are cared for by informal kin (Leinaweaver, 2014). Where formal substitute care is required, many countries rely heavily on congregate care, typically funded by donors and unregulated or semi-regulated by the state.

Many countries are undergoing a significant shift in the caregiving arrangements available to children. Most of the Eastern European countries are experiencing a profound transformation from large residential centers to smaller orphanages such as in Estonia and Latvia (Linno & Strömpl, this volume), professional foster care in Latvia (Linno & Strömpl, this volume), and foster care for infants and toddlers in the Czech Republic (Shmidt, this volume). Some of the Latin American countries such as Chile are also transforming their systems from reliance largely on informal kin to the utilization of paid relatives and foster parents (Muñoz-Guzman, this volume).

In institutionalized structures, a wide range of care arrangements are available for children's care. These include paid (and unpaid) kinship care, voluntary foster care, and professional foster care for children who have been separated from their parents. Residential care is used in all systems but efforts to reduce the number of children served in residential centers is a trend seen across all child protection systems, especially in high-income countries (Courtney & Iwaniec, 2009). In Northern Ireland, for example, efforts to reduce reliance on residential care were concerted throughout the 1980s and 90s (Burns et al., this volume). There, and in many other institutionalized countries, the care continuum is wide, including the option of serving children in their birth home, but under court ordered supervision and support. Although the aspiration to shift from residential to family-based care is strong in all countries, some are more successful than others in realizing these aims. In Portugal, for example, the vast majority of children continue to be served in congregate care, in spite of international pressure to do otherwise (Ferreira, this volume). Change seems hard to make, and even child rights-oriented systems vary greatly. About 90% of Norway's children in public care reside in foster homes, whereas in Denmark the corresponding figure is 65% (Hestbæk et al., this volume). There is a strong international push towards family-based care arrangements. In December 2019, all 193 states of the UN General Assembly adopted the Resolution on the Rights of the

Child,[4] committing governments to secure family and community-based alternative care for children. The Resolution includes recognition that many children living in institutionalized care actually have a family that they do not live with due to poverty, a situation that is evidenced by case studies in this Handbook.

ADOPTION

Adoption represents a final response to child exploitation, maltreatment, abandonment, and neglect, permanently transferring the legal care and custody of a child to a new parent. Adoption includes legal permanence—a lifetime, legal relationship between an adult and child—residential permanence, and relational permanence in which an adult and child see each other as family (see Palacios et al., 2019). Article 21 of the CRC states that the best interests of the child are the paramount considerations in adoption and these considerations prevail over the interests of birth parents and prospective adoptive parents. Although informal adoption between parents and extended relatives happens across countries, formal adoption reliant on state sanction falls along a continuum roughly parallel to the five child protective orientations characterized in the global typology.

At one end of the continuum are states that allow a relatively large number of adoptions, many of which involve the transfer of children to homes outside the original country and with relatively weak accountability structures in place to ensure children's ongoing care and protection, or to allow for ongoing contact or connection with birth families (when that might be possible). In Ghana, for example, inter-country adoption happens with some frequency, but the process is often opaque to international monitors (Dako-Gyeke et al., this volume). Further along the child protection orientation continuum, rates of adoption are high, but the large majority occur in-country. Children are adopted from care to secure permanency for the child, but simultaneously reducing state responsibility (and expenses) for a group of children. In some of these countries, such as the United States, efforts to encourage open adoption—where children are allowed ongoing contact with members of the birth family—are growing. In England, case law suggests that adoption is only justified if motivated by the child's best interests principle (Thoburn, this volume). In child well-being and child rights-oriented systems, adoption may be strictly limited. In Sweden, for example, adoption is not considered as a permanency option (Höjer & Pösö, this volume); it is also only considered as a measure for a small group of children in Spain (Segado, this volume) and Germany (Biesel & Kindler, this volume).

Increasingly, adoption is justified using the child's best interest principle turning on children's right to family. In Japan, for example, the government has implemented a New Foster Child Care Vision and the Ministry of Health, Labor, and Welfare has set a goal that the number of Japanese adoptions should be doubled within five years (from 2017 to

---

[4] https://undocs.org/A/74/395

2022) (see Helland & Skivenes, 2019).[5] In Denmark, the government has made clear that adoption should be used if parents permanently lack parental capacities and if adoption is in the best interest of the child otherwise in long-term care (Hestbæk et al., this volume).

The renewed focus on permanency and adoption, based on the child's interests and need for the security of a family, has been supported by the European Court of Human Rights as well. In an analysis of all judgements on adoption from care, Breen and colleagues (2020, p. 741) conclude that "the status and respect of the child's *de facto* family life is changing. This resonates with a view that children do not only have formal rights but that they are recognized as individuals within the family unit that states and courts must address directly." This analysis shows that the ECtHR recognizes the family as including biological parents and children, and—increasingly—foster parents and siblings.

Adoption from care, often portrayed as the ultimate draconian intervention when described from the natural parent's perspective, is from the child's perspective an opportunity to belong in a family for life, recreating the bonds of belonging so vital for an individual's self-esteem. Recently, a multidisciplinary and international team of 11 researchers made a clear conclusion about adoption in child protection systems: "The focus of the argument is that adoption provides a legitimate model for the alternative care of children if undertaken within a rights and ethics framework that emphasizes children's best interests, as set out in international conventions and national laws" (Palacios et al., 2019, p. 57).

Conclusion

Although social and familial circumstances are very different across the globe, and government responses to child and family concerns vary significantly, there are also unifying features. The response to the CRC is evident in all of the countries in this Handbook, and attention to Article 19, specifying governments' responsibilities to protect children from violence, injury, exploitation, and neglect is apparent. Differences in historical, cultural, political, and resource contexts strongly influence states' interpretations of the CRC, both in how problems are defined, and in how formal responses are expressed. There are patterns to these differences that we suggest form an overall global typology. Our global typology of child protection systems, based on evidence from 50 country case studies, indicates that the frame for a public response to children's concerns falls along a continuum of institutional capacity that we characterize as *nascent*, *emerging*, and *institutionalized*. The frame itself is fluid, and various states may possess characteristics that fall within or across structures. With continued globalization and as countries accumulate greater resources, we anticipate that countries may shift their institutional capacity.

Within these broad groups, the case studies reveal five types of child protection systems identified principally by their risk orientation, including protection against *child*

---

[5] The Civil Code of Japan allows for a typical adoption system and special adoption system; for details of special adoption, see: https://www.nippon-foundation.or.jp/en/news/articles/2018/11.html.

exploitation, protection against *child deprivation*, protection against *child maltreatment*, protection of *child well-being*, and protection of *child rights*. The five child protection systems are identified in further detail by 10 characteristics that provide a conceptual tool to identify and categorize existing systems across the world. These five child protection systems respond to a wider scope of risks and are therefore more fully responsive to the letter and intent of Article 19 of the CRC and the concurring Articles in the Convention. According to this typology, classifying a country's system depends on where it falls along the continuum on each of the 10 characteristics.

Child protection is evolving within and across countries. The typology offered herein provides a broad assessment of patterns across country systems, but stark dividing lines between states may be a relic of the past. As knowledge spreads across states, and diversity grows within states, the differences across the global typology will continue to blur. As a unifying statement of values and approach, the CRC will continue to serve as an important guide to the aspirations and functional developments of child protection.

References

Bartholet, E. (2020). Homeschooling: Parent rights absolutism vs child rights to education and protection. *Arizona Law Review*, 62(1), 1–80.

Beatriz, E. and Salhi, C. (2019). Child discipline in low- and middle-income countries: Socioeconomic disparities at the household- and country-level. *Child Abuse and Neglect*, 94(*104023*), 1–11.

Breen, C., Krutzinna, J., Luhamaa, K., and Skivenes, M. (2020). Family life for children in state care. An analysis of the European Court of Human Rights' reasoning on adoption without consent. *International Journal of Children's Rights, 28*, 715–747.

Cameron, G., Coady, N., and Adams, G. R. (Eds.). (2007). *Moving towards positive systems of child and family welfare: Current issues and future direction*. Wilfrid Laurier University Press.

Clark, H., Coll-Seck, A. M., Banerjee, A., Peterson, S., Dalglish, S. L., Ameratunga, S., ... and Claeson, M. (2020). A future for the world's children? A WHO-UNICEF-Lancet Commission. *The Lancet*, 395(10224), 605–658.

Connolly, M., Katz, I., Shlonsky, A., and Bromfield, L. (2014). *Towards a typology for child protection systems: Final report to UNICEF and Save the Children UK*. University of Melbourne Commercial Ltd.

Connolly, M. and Katz, I. (2019). Typologies of child protection systems: An international approach. *Child Abuse Review*, 28, 381–394.

Courtney, M. E. and Iwaniec, D. (Eds.). (2009). *Residential care of children: Comparative perspectives*. Oxford University Press.

ECtHR. (2019, December 17). *Ibrahim v Norway* (Application no. 15379/16). Available at: http://hudoc.echr.coe.int/eng?i=001-199382.

Ellingsen, I., Studsrød, I., and Muñoz-Guzmán, C. (2019). The child, the parents, the family and the state: Chile and Norway compared. *Journal of Comparative Social Work*, 14(1), 1–22.

Freymond, N., and Cameron, G. (Eds.). (2006). *Towards positive systems of child and family welfare: International comparisons of child protection, family service, and community caring systems*. University of Toronto Press.

Gilbert, N. (Ed.). (1997). *Combatting child abuse: International perspectives and trends*. Oxford University Press.

Gilbert, N., Parton, N., and Skivenes, M. (Eds.). (2011). *Child protection systems*. Oxford University Press.

Hantrais, L. (2004). *Family policy matters: Responding to family change in Europe*. Policy Press.

Helland, H. S. and Skivenes, M. (2019). Adoption from care as a child protection measure. *Adopsjon som barneverntiltak*. Universitetet i Bergen, Rapport. [In Norwegian].

Helland, H. S., Kriź, K., Sánchez-Cabezudo, S. S., and Skivenes, M. (2018). Are there population biases against migrant children? An experimental analysis towards corporal punishment in Austria, Norway and Spain. *Children & Youth Services Review*, 85, 151–157.

Hetherington, R., Cooper, A., Smith, P., and Wilford, G. (1997) *Protecting children: Messages from Europe*. Russell House Publishing.

Khoo, E. G., Hyvönen, U., and Nygren, L. (2002). Child welfare protection: Uncovering Swedish and Canadian orientations to social intervention in child maltreatment. *Qualitative Social Work*, 1(4), 451–471

Kosher, H. and Ben-Arieh, A. (2017). What children think about their rights and their well-being: A cross-national comparison. *American Journal of Orthopsychiatry*, 87(3), 256–273.

Leinaweaver, J. (2014). Informal kinship-based fostering around the world: Anthropological findings. *Child Development Perspectives*, 8(3), 131–136.

Man, X., Barth, R.P., Li, Y.-e., and Wang, Z. (2017). Exploring the new child protection system in Mainland China: How does it work? *Children and Youth Services Review, 76*, 196–202.

May-Chahal, C., and Herezog, M. (Eds.). (2003). *Child sexual abuse in Europe*. Council of Europe Publishing.

Merkel-Holguin, L., Fluke, J. D., and Krugman, R. D. (Eds.) (2019). *National systems of child protection: Understanding the international variability and context for developing policy and practice*. Springer.

Oltedal, S. and Nygren, L. (2019). Private and public families: Social workers' views on children's and parents position in Chile, England, Lithuania, and Norway. *Journal of Comparative Social Work*, 14(1), 115–140.

Palacios, J., Adroher, S., Brodzinsky, D. M., Grotevant, H. D., Johnson, D. E., Juffer, F., Martínez-Mora, L., Muhamedrahimov, R. J., Selwyn, J., Simmonds, J., and Tarren-Sweeney, M. (2019) Adoption in the service of child protection: An international interdisciplinary perspective. *Psychology, Public Policy, and Law*, 25(2), 57–72.

Parekh, B. (2000). *Rethinking muliticulturalism: Cultural diversity and political theory*. Harvard University Press.

Pösö, T., Skivenes, M., and Hestbæk, A. (2014). Child protection systems within the Danish, Finnish, and Norwegian welfare states: Time for a child centric approach? *European Journal of Social Work*, 17(4), 475–490.

Pringle, K. (1998). *Children and social welfare in Europe*. Open University Press.

Ssenyonga, J., Muwonga, C. M., and Hecker, T. (2019). Prevalence of family violence and mental health and their relation to peer victimization: A representative study of adolescent students in Southwestern Uganda. *International Journal of Child Abuse and Neglect*, 98(104194), 1–12.

UNICEF. (2003). *Orphans and other children affected by AIDS/HIV*. UNICEF.

UNICEF. (2008). *Child protection systems: Mapping and assessment toolkit*. UNICEF.

UNICEF. (2019). *Poverty eradication begins with children*. UNICEF. Available at: https://www.unicefusa.org/stories/poverty-eradication-begins-children/36503.

Wessells, M., Lamin, D., King, D., Kostelny, K., Stark, L., and Lilley, S. (2012). The disconnect between community-based child protection mechanisms and the formal child protection system in rural Sierra Leone: Challenges to building an effective national child protection system. *Vulnerable Children and Youth Studies*, 7, 211–227.

Wulczyn, F., Daro, D., Fluke, J., Feldman, S., Glodek, C., and Lifanda, K. (2010). *Adapting a systems approach to child protection: Key concepts and considerations*. Chapin Hall Center for Children.

INDEX

For the benefit of digital users, indexed terms that span two pages (e.g., 52–53) may, on occasion, appear on only one of those pages.

Tables and figures are indicated by *t* and *f* following the page number

A

AACWA (Adoption Assistance and Child Welfare Act), United States, 391
abandonment. *See* child abandonment
Aboriginal and Torres Strait Islander (ATSI) children, 25–26, 29, 30, 31–32
Aboriginal and Torres Strait Islander Child Placement Principle (ATSICPP), 31–32
abuse. *See* child abuse
ACERWC (African Committee of Experts on the Rights and Welfare of the Child), 545, 555
Act for the Prevention of Cruelty to and Better Protection of Children (Canada), 96
Act on Cooperation and Information in Child Protection (KKG), Germany, 198, 203, 205–7
Act on Counteracting Domestic Violence (Poland), 487–88, 496, 501–2
Act on Parental Responsibility (Denmark), 114–15
Act Respecting First Nations, Inuit and Métis Children, Youth and Families (Canada), 103
actuarial risk assessment tools, 384–85
Administrative Procedure of Restoration of Rights (PARD), Colombia, 656, 657–62
administrative structure of child welfare services in Canada, 99–102
Adoption and Safe Families Act (ASFA), United States, 15, 391–92

Adoption Assistance and Child Welfare Act (AACWA), United States, 391
adoption of children, 11, 12*t*
in Australia, 32
in Austria, 56–58
in Canada, 98–99
changing rates in, 15
in Chile, 410*t*, 414, 415*t*
in Colombia, 661
in Czech Republic, 431*f*, 432–33
in Denmark, 119*t*, 123–24
in Ecuador, 674, 675, 677
in England, 149–51, 150*t*
in Estonia and Latvia, 457*t*
in global typology, 949*t*, 966–67
in Indonesia, 761–62
in Iran, 780–81, 784, 786*t*, 789–90
in Israel, 249
in Italy, 268*t*
in Japan, 291
in Lebanon, 799
in Norway, 119*t*, 123–24
in Philippines, 867
in Russia, 882, 888*f*, 889–90
in Slovak Republic, 533
in South Africa, 559
in Soviet Union, 447
in Uganda, 912–13
in United States, 389–90, 391–92
in Uruguay, 578–79
adulthood, transition to, 102
Advice and Reporting Centers on Domestic Violence and Child Maltreatment (AMHK), Netherlands, 295*t*, 298–99, 300*f*, 305
Advice Teams (Netherlands), 307
African American children, overrepresentation in United States, 390–91

African Charter on the Rights and Welfare of the Child, 900–1, 928
African Child Policy Study, 561
African Committee of Experts on the Rights and Welfare of the Child (ACERWC), 545, 555
African Network for the Prevention and Protection against Child Abuse and Neglect (ANPPCAN), Nigeria, 845–46
aftercare services (Finland and Sweden), 164
ageing out of care
in Canada, 105–6
in United States, 390
agency social workers, 145–46
age of maturity
in global typology, 960–61
in India, 725–26
in Iran, 773–74
in Lebanon, 798*t*
in Uganda, 904
Agreements with Youth Adults (AYA) program, Canada, 106
aide sociale à l'enfance (ASE), France, 176–78, 180–81, 182–85
Alberta Response Model, 100
Alföldi assessment method, 185
ALI (Organization for Child Protection), 252
allowance policy (Greece), 273
alternative care. *See also* out-of-home care
care settings, in global typology, 949*t*, 965–66
in Chile, 408–11
in Nigeria, 843
in Philippines, 867
in Russia, 878–80, 880*f*, 884–85, 887–92, 888*f*
in Soviet Union, 880–81

alternative care (*cont.*)
  in Switzerland, 373–74
  in Uganda, 913
alternative dispute resolution
    process (Australia), 29
Alternative Report Coalition,
    561–62
ambulatory services
  in Chile, 412
  in Netherlands, 305–6, 306t,
    309–10
AMHK (Advice and Reporting
    Centers on Domestic
    Violence and Child
    Maltreatment), Netherlands,
    295t, 298–99, 300f, 305
anemia, in Egypt, 694
ANEP (National Public Education
    Administration), Uruguay, 565
ANII (National Agency
    of Investigation and
    Innovation), Uruguay, 581
ANPPCAN (African Network
    for the Prevention and
    Protection against Child
    Abuse and Neglect), Nigeria,
    845–46
Anti-Discrimination Act (Slovak
    Republic), 538–39
appeals on interventions, in
    Norway and Denmark,
    121–22
Argentina
  child protection legislation in,
    592–94, 595t
  methods for delivery of
    provisions, 594–603, 596t,
    598t
  out-of-home care in, 12t, 598t,
    602
  overview, 587–88
  sociopolitical scenario in, 603–5
  UNCRC compliance in, 589–92
armed conflict
  in Colombia, 649–50, 654
  in Lebanon, 800
  in Philippines, 856–57
  in Uganda, 906
array of care settings, in global
    typology, 949t, 965–66
ASE (*aide sociale à l'enfance*),
    France, 176–78, 180–81,
    182–85
ASFA (Adoption and Safe Families
    Act), United States, 15,
    391–92
assessments of child welfare
  in Austria, 50

in Chile, 412–14
in Ecuador, 675–76
in Finland and Sweden, 159–60,
    161–62
in France, 185–86
in Germany, 199f, 199–201,
    203–8, 206t
in Netherlands, 298
in Slovak Republic, 536–37
in Switzerland, 368–69
in United States, 382
in Uruguay, 574
asylum, in France, 187–90
at-risk children
  defined, 249
  in Iran, 774–76, 782
  in Lebanon, 807–9, 808f
ATSI (Aboriginal and Torres Strait
    Islander) children, 25–26, 29,
    30, 31–32
ATSICPP (Aboriginal and
    Torres Strait Islander Child
    Placement Principle), 31–32
AUH (Children's Universal
    Monetary Transfer),
    Argentina, 594
Australia
  bases of social allocations in,
    27–28
  child/parent participation in,
    963
  child protection processes in,
    28–29
  evidence-based practice in, 33–34
  family support services in, 30
  methods for delivery of
    provisions in, 32–33
  nature of social provisions in,
    29–30
  out-of-home care in, 12t, 31–32
  overview, 25–27
Austria
  adoption in, 12t, 56–58
  child endangerment
    investigation, 53–54
  child welfare laws and policies,
    48–52
  financing of child protection
    services in, 60–61
  legal system in, 48
  local and regional variation in
    care support, 58–59
  mandatory reporting, 52–53
  methods for delivery of
    provisions in, 59–60
  out-of-home care in, 12t, 14t, 56,
    57t, 63–64
  overview, 47–48

reforms and criticism of child
    welfare system, 61–64
risks to children in, 52
state response to cultural and
    religious diversity in, 961–62
statistics on child protection in,
    55–59, 55t, 57t
support measures, 54–55
UNCRC compliance, 48–49
Austrian Civil Code, 48–50
Austrian Institute for Family
    Research of the University of
    Vienna, 62–63
Authoritarian Collectivism, 946–
    48, 947t
Authoritarian Individualism, 946–
    48, 947t
autonomous communities, in
    Spain
  legislation in, 334–36
  overview, 332–33
  role of, 339f, 339
  social provisions provided by,
    341–43
Averdijk, M., 357
AYA (Agreements with Youth
    Adults) program, Canada,
    106

B

baby boxes (Latvia), 454–55
baby farming (Nigeria), 837
back-to-school program (Chile),
    413
Baier, D., 358
Barangay Councils for the Protection
    of Children (BCPC),
    Philippines, 867–68, 870–71
barangays (Philippines), 858–59,
    867–68, 870
bases of social allocations
  in Australia, 27–28
  in Brazil, 616–17
  in Chile, 408
  in Ghana, 713–16
  in Israel, 242–44
  in Italy, 264–66
  in New Zealand, 34–37
  in South Africa, 546–52
  in South Korea, 323–26
  in Spain, 336–38
  in Uganda, 904–9
  in Uruguay, 564–71
Basic Education Assistance
    Module (BEAM),
    Zimbabwe, 929, 936
Basic Social Protection (BSP),
    Brazil, 617–18

Basso Komo ethnic group
(Nigeria), 838
BCPC (Barangay Councils for
the Protection of Children),
Philippines, 867–68, 870–71
BEAM (Basic Education
Assistance Module),
Zimbabwe, 929, 936
Belgium
child maltreatment definition
in, 68–71
collaboration between judicial
authorities and care
providers, 77–79
extent of child maltreatment in,
72–74, 85–86
federal authorities, judicial
treatment of abuse and
neglect by, 74–77
local child welfare services in,
79–83, 86
out-of-home care in, 12t, 14t,
84–85, 84t, 86–87
overview, 67–68
reporting child maltreatment
in, 71–72
best interest of the child principle
in India, 737
in Slovak Republic, 528
in Spain, 349–51
best practices
in France, 186–87
in Greece, 278
in Italy, 269–71
big bang economic reform, in
Estonia and Latvia, 449
big data (island of Ireland),
230–32
biology principle, 115
birth registration
in Indonesia, 750
in Uganda, 905
Blue Cards procedure (Poland),
491, 496–99
boarding schools
in Canada, 97–98
in Czech Republic, 424, 430f
in Soviet Union, 447
Boko Haram, 833, 844–45
BOLETINF application, 346
bottom-up approach to child
protection (Philippines),
860–61, 867–69, 870–71
Bouckaert, G., 218–19
Brazil
bases of social allocation in,
616–17
care network in, 621–22

child protection legislation in,
611–16
family support services in,
617–19
methods for delivery of
provisions in, 620
nature of social provisions in,
617–20
out-of-home care in, 12t,
619–20
overview, 608–11
rights orientation in, 956–57
Breen, C., 967
Brexit, impact on child safety on
island of Ireland, 228–30
BSP (Basic Social Protection),
Brazil, 617–18
budget allocation. See financing of
child protection services
Building a Europe for and with
Children program, 529–30
Building Bridges for the Filipino
Family Program, 858
bullying
in Greece, 278
in Mexico, 816–17
in Slovak Republic, 532t
in Uruguay, 572, 964
Bywaters, P., 6

C
CAC (Childhood and Adolescence
Code), Ecuador, 669–70
CAF (Support Center to Families),
Spain, 339–41
Cafcass (Children and Family
Court Advisory and Support
Service), England, 144
CAI (Centro de Atención a la
Infancia), Spain, 339–40
CAIF (Children and Family Care
Centers), Uruguay, 575, 579
CAN. See child abuse and neglect
Canada
child maltreatment
investigations in, 91f, 91–93,
92f
emerging practices in, 106–7
First Nations child welfare in,
102–4
historical context in, 95–97
Indigenous communities,
development of services for,
97–99
legislative and administrative
structure in, 99–102
outcomes of child welfare
services in, 104–6

out-of-home care in, 12t, 14t,
93–95, 97, 105–6
overrepresentation of
Indigenous children in,
94–95, 95f
overview, 90–91
state response to cultural
and religious diversity in,
961–62
Canadian Human Rights Tribunal
(CHRT), 102, 104
Canadian Incidence Study of
Reported Child Abuse and
Neglect (CIS), 91–93
Cantonal Boards for the
Protection of Rights (CBPR),
Ecuador, 672–73, 674
Cantonal Councils for the
Protection of Rights
(CCCA), Ecuador, 672
cantons, in Switzerland, 356–57,
364–65, 375–76, 377
CAPA 2000 (Child Abuse
Prevention Act), Japan, 288
CAPAs (Switzerland). See Child
and Adult Protection
Authorities, Switzerland
capitalism, 95–96
CAPTA (Child Abuse Prevention
and Treatment Act), United
States, 383–84, 391
Care and Supervision (Juvenile)
Law, Israel, 240, 242, 245
Care Circles (Australia), 29
care leavers
in France, 184
in Japan, 293
in United States, 386–90
care network (Brazil), 621–22
Care of Young People Act (CYPA),
Sweden, 157–58, 160, 165
care orders
in Australia, 30
in Finland and Sweden, 159–60,
163–64, 165–66
in Switzerland, 373–74
care settings, in global typology,
949t, 965–66
care support measures (Austria),
55–56, 55t, 58–59
Carreño, C., 655–56
CAs (certified agencies),
Netherlands, 302
CAS (Children's Aid Society),
Canada, 96, 99–100
case conferences (Slovak
Republic), 537–38
case coordination (Belgium), 79

case management
  in Argentina, 601–2
  in Lithuania, 477–78
  in Zimbabwe, 929, 932–33
cash transfer programs
  in Argentina, 594
  in Egypt, 699–700
  in Ghana, 716, 717
  in Philippines, 858
  in Zimbabwe, 930, 931–32, 933,
    934, 935*t*
CASS (Consolidation Act on
  Social Services), Denmark,
  114–15, 117, 124–25
CBOs (community-based
  organizations), United States,
  392–93
CBPR (Cantonal Boards for
  the Protection of Rights),
  Ecuador, 672–73, 674
CCCA (Cantonal Councils for
  the Protection of Rights),
  Ecuador, 672
CCCAN (Confidential Centers of
  Child Abuse and Neglect),
  Belgium, 70, 72–73, 73*t*, 80–
  82, 85–86
CCPB (Child Care and Protection
  Board), Netherlands, 296,
  298, 299–302, 307
CDCC (child daycare centers),
  Lithuania, 478
CDI (Child Development Index),
  771–72
Cellule de recueil des informations
  préoccupantes (CRIP), France,
  178–77
Center for Judicial Studies
  (Portugal), 514
Center for the International
  Protection of Children and
  Youth (Slovak Republic), 536
Center of Integrated Services
  for Empowering Women
  and Children (P2TP2A),
  Indonesia, 760–61
Centro de Atención a la Infancia
  (CAI), Spain, 339–40
certified agencies (CAs),
  Netherlands, 302
Ceuta, Spain, 351, 352
CFS (Child and Family Services),
  Belgium, 83
Change Factory, 126
child abandonment
  in Nigeria, 834, 836, 837
  in Spain, 337*f*, 337–38, 338*f*

child abuse
  in Australia, 28
  in Austria, 48–49, 52
  in Belgium, 68–71, 72–77
  in Brazil, 610–11, 616–17
  in China, 626, 636
  in Colombia, 650–51, 653–54
  in Czech Republic, 437–40
  in Egypt, 691–92
  in England, 143*t*, 149
  in France, 180–82
  in Germany, 195–96
  in Ghana, 710–11
  in Greece, 277–78
  in India, 728–29, 742–44
  in Indonesia, 749–51, 759
  in Iran, 774–76, 781–83
  in Israel, 241–42, 241*t*
  in Italy, 267, 268*t*
  in Japan, 288
  in Lebanon, 799–800, 809–11
  in Lithuania, 469, 475–76
  in Mexico, 823–26
  in Netherlands, 294–95, 295*t*
  in New Zealand, 37–39, 42
  in Nigeria, 834, 836–40, 847*t*
  in Poland, 488–95
  in Portugal, 507–8
  poverty and, 6
  right to protection from, 2–4
  in Slovak Republic, 530–31,
    531*f*, 532*t*
  in South Africa, 545, 551–52,
    556–58
  in South Korea, 318–19, 320,
    323, 324–25
  in Spain, 347–49, 348*t*, 349*t*,
    352–53
  in Switzerland, 357–60, 358*t*, 359*t*
  in United States, 381–84
  in Uruguay, 566–69
child abuse and neglect (CAN)
  in Belgium, 68–71, 72–77
  poverty and, 6
  in Slovak Republic, 532*t*
Child Abuse Prevention Act
  (CAPA 2000), Japan, 288
Child Abuse Prevention and
  Treatment Act (CAPTA),
  United States, 383–84, 391
Child Adoption Law (Israel), 249
Child and Adolescent Statute
  (ECA), Brazil, 611, 612, 613–14
Child and Adult Protection
  Authorities (CAPAs),
  Switzerland, 362
  assessment reports, 368–69

cooperation between agencies
  and, 377
financing and delivery of
  services in, 375–76
legal representation of children,
  369–70
legislation, 364–65
organizational forms of, 366*t*
pathways to services, 374
procedures and standards,
  367–70
public image of, 376
Child and Family Services (CFS),
  Belgium, 83
Child and Family Services Act
  (Canada), 96
Child and Family Welfare Policy
  (Ghana), 708*t*, 716–17,
  719–20
child and youth care
  (Netherlands), 297, 305–7,
  306*t*, 309
child and youth care centers
  (CYCCs), South Africa,
  554–56, 559
Child and Youth Committee
  (CY-Committee), Denmark,
  121–22
child and youth welfare offices
  (Germany), 198–201, 203–5,
  207–8
Child and Youth Wellbeing
  Strategy (New Zealand), 43
Child Care and Protection Board
  (CCPB), Netherlands, 296,
  298, 299–302, 307
childcare institutions
  in India, 741
  in Japan, 290
child-centric approach, 17, 18, 114
Child Criminal Justice System
  (SPPA), Indonesia, 763–64
child custody. *See* custody laws
  and protocols
child daycare centers (CDCC),
  Lithuania, 478
child deprivation protective
  systems, 949*t*, 950–53, 951*f*
child development, in India, 735
Child Development Index (CDI),
  771–72
child development model (South
  Korea), 319–20
child endangerment
  in Austria, 53–54
  in Germany, 197–98, 199*f*, 199–201,
    203–8, 206*t*

child exploitation protective
  systems, 949*t*, 950–52, 951*f*
"Child Exposed to Domestic
  Violence Is an Abused Child"
  report (Belgium), 71
child flourishing index, 8, 10*f*
child focused orientation
  compared to other typologies,
    945, 946*t*
  in Russia, 878–79, 893–96
"Child Friendly Districts/Cities"
  (KLA), Indonesia, 766–67
Child Guardianship Act
  (Lithuania), 471
Child Guidance Centres (OGCs),
  Japan, 288–89
childhood, legal definitions of
  in global typology, 949*t*,
    960–61
  in India, 725–26
  in Iran, 773–74
  in Lebanon, 798*t*
  overview, 4
  in Sweden, 158
  in Uganda, 904
Childhood and Adolescence Code
  (CAC), Ecuador, 669–70
Childhood and Youth Courts
  (Brazil), 614–15
Childhood Trauma Questionnaire
  (CTQ), 196
child inequality (Norway and
  Denmark), 129–30, 129*t*
child in need (England), 137–38,
  148
child labor
  in Canada, 95–96
  in Egypt, 693
  in Ghana, 711, 715
  in India, 727–28, 731, 744–45
  in Iran, 781
  in Lebanon, 799, 804
  in Nigeria, 834–35, 836–37, 844
  in Philippines, 856
  in Uganda, 902
Child Labour Act (India), 731
Child Labour in Africa conference
  (Nigeria), 834
Childline (England), 146–47
child maltreatment
  in Australia, 28
  in Belgium, 68–71, 72–74
  in Brazil, 610–11, 616–17
  in Canada, 91*f*, 91–93, 92*f*
  in China, 626, 636
  in Colombia, 650–51, 653–54
  in Czech Republic, 437–40

definitions of, 68–71, 323–24,
  347, 383–84, 565, 861
  in Egypt, 691–92
  in England, 143*t*, 149
  in France, 180–82
  in Germany, 195–96
  in Ghana, 710–11
  in India, 728–29, 742–43
  in Indonesia, 749–51, 759
  in Iran, 774–76, 781–83
  in Israel, 241–42, 241*t*
  in Italy, 267, 268*t*
  in Japan, 287
  in Lebanon, 799–800, 809–11
  in Lithuania, 469, 475–76
  in Mexico, 815–17, 816*t*, 821–26
  in Netherlands, 294–95, 295*t*
  in New Zealand, 37–39
  in Nigeria, 834, 836–40, 847*t*
  in Philippines, 854–57, 861
  in Poland, 488–95
  in Portugal, 507–8
  poverty and, 6
  right to protection from, 2–4
  in Slovak Republic, 530–31,
    531*f*, 532*t*
  in South Africa, 545, 551–52,
    556–58
  in South Korea, 318–19, 320,
    323, 324–25
  in Spain, 347–49, 348*t*, 349*t*
  in Switzerland, 357–60, 358*t*,
    359*t*
  in Uganda, 901–4
  in United States, 381–84
  in Uruguay, 565, 566–69
child maltreatment protective
  systems, 949*t*, 950–52, 951*f*,
  953–54
child marriage, 6
  in Egypt, 697–98
  in Ghana, 711
  in India, 727, 731, 744
  in Indonesia, 749, 751–52
  in Nigeria, 838–39
  in Uganda, 902, 905
  in Zimbabwe, 935–36
childminders (Nigeria), 834–35
child mortality
  in Brazil, 609–10
  in Colombia, 653
child-parent centers (Israel),
  250–51
child participation
  in Austria, 51
  in global typology, 949*t*, 962–63
  in Israel, 243, 255–56

in Netherlands, 308–9
in Norway and Denmark,
  124–25
in Slovak Republic, 539
in Switzerland, 369
Child Physical and Psychological
  Maltreatment (CPPM), 324
Child Protection (CP) plan,
  England, 147–48, 149
Child Protection Act (Estonia),
  450–51, 452, 453, 462
Child Protection Act (Norway),
  114–15, 116, 117, 124
*Child Protection and Welfare
  Strategy 2017–2022* (Ireland),
  224–25
Child Protection Committees
  (CPCs), Zimbabwe, 934
child protection conferences
  (England), 147–48
Child Protection Fund (CPF),
  931–32
Child Protection Income
  Management (Australia), 30
Child Protection Law (Argentina),
  592–93
Child Protection Network
  (Philippines), 866
Child Protection Officers (CPOs),
  Israel, 242–43, 244–46, 256
child protection orientation
  in Chile, 401
  compared to other typologies,
    639–40, 639*t*, 944–45, 945*t*,
    946*t*
  in Estonia and Latvia, 461–62
  in Russia, 878–79, 893–94
  in United States, 381–82
Child Protection Policy against
  Injury (Poland), 499–500
child protection processes
  in Australia, 28–29
  in Italy, 265–67
  in New Zealand, 37–39
Child Protection Program for
  Children in Emergency
  (Nigeria), 844–45
Child Protection Protocol
  Investigation (New Zealand),
  38–39
child protection service (CPS)
  agencies, South Korea, 317,
  322, 326–28
child protection systems. *See also
  specific countries*
  comparative analyses, 14–15
  definitions of, 904

child protection systems (*cont.*)
 global typology of, 19
 intrusive interventions by state,
  10–11
 out-of-home care and adoption
  rates by country, 12*t*
 overview, 3–5, 135–36
 primary orientations to, 18
 public confidence in
  governments, impact on view
  of, 16*f*, 16–17
 regulation of child protection,
  8–10
 social-cultural differences,
  impact on view of, 17–18
 stages of development, 4–5
 stages of institutional
  development, 19–20
Child Protection Teams
 (Switzerland), 367
child-rearing practices (South
 Korea), 320, 324
Children (Northern Ireland)
 Order 1995, 226–27
Children, Young Persons and
 Their Families Act 1989 (New
 Zealand), 26–27, 35, 36
Children Act (England), 135–38
Children and Family Care Centers
 (CAIF), Uruguay, 575, 579
Children and Family Court
 Advisory and Support Service
 (Cafcass), England, 144
Children and Social Work Act
 (England), 145
Children and Youth Protection
 Act (Iran), 775–76, 777–78,
 781, 782
Children and Youth Protection
 Commission (CPCJ),
 Portugal, 508, 509, 515*f*
Children First Act (Ireland),
 225–26
*Children First: National Guidelines
 for the Protection and Welfare
 of Children* policy (Ireland),
 223
children in conflict with the law
 in Czech Republic, 433–35
 in Estonia and Latvia, 458–61
 in India, 726–27, 730–31,
  736–37
 in Indonesia, 763–64
 in Lebanon, 809–10, 811
 in Uganda, 913–15
children in contact with the law
 in Indonesia, 763–64
 in Uganda, 913–15

Children of the People (*Los Chicos
 del Pueblo*), 591–92
Children's Act (Ghana), 707, 708*t*,
 710, 713–14
Children's Act (Uganda), 905–6,
 910
Children's Act (Zimbabwe),
 926–28
Children's Act 38 (South Africa),
 546–52, 553–54, 556
Children's Aid Society (CAS),
 Canada, 96, 99–100
Children's and Young People's
 Well-being Act 1989 (New
 Zealand), 26–27
children's courts
 in Australia, 29
 in South Africa, 549, 550–51
Children's Forum (Indonesia),
 766–67
children's judges (Lebanon), 811,
 812–13
children's rights orientation,
 955–56, 957
Children's Rights Protection
 Agencies (CRPA), Lithuania,
 470, 471
children's service agencies,
 Switzerland, 366–67, 375, 377
Children's Teams (New Zealand),
 39–40
Children's Universal Monetary
 Transfer (AUH), Argentina,
 594
Children's Welfare Program
 (Lithuania), 474
children with disabilities
 in Chile, 412
 in Czech Republic, 429–30
 in Ghana, 716
 in Greece, 276
 in India, 735
 on island of Ireland, 221–22
 in Lebanon, 800
 in Nigeria, 839–40
 in Russia, 883, 891
 in Uganda, 903
child rights. *See* rights of children
Child Rights Act (CRA), Nigeria,
 836
Child Rights International
 Network (CRIN), 129–30
child rights protective systems,
 949*t*, 950–52, 951*f*, 954–55
Child Rights Regulations (Ghana),
 708*t*
"child saving" movement
 (Canada), 95–96

Child Support Grant (CSG), South
 Africa, 545–46, 552, 553–54
child survival, in India, 734, 742
child trafficking
 in Egypt, 691
 in France, 191
 in Ghana, 711–12, 715
 in India, 728–29, 731
 in Indonesia, 749
 in Iran, 781
 in Lebanon, 799–800
 in Mexico, 822
 in Nigeria, 837, 844
 in Philippines, 857
 in Uganda, 902, 906
Child Welfare Act (Canada), 96
Child Welfare Act (Finland),
 157–58, 162
Child Welfare Act (Japan), 288,
 289, 291–92
Child Welfare Act (South Korea),
 317, 322, 323–24
child welfare assessment. *See*
 assessments of child welfare
Child Welfare Committees
 (CWCs), 742–43
Child Welfare Department
 (China), 636
Child Welfare Law (South Korea),
 321, 326
Child Welfare Services (CWS), in
 Austria
 child endangerment
  investigation, 53–54
 child welfare legislation, 49–52
 financing of, 60–61
 mandatory reporting, 52–53
 methods for delivery of
  provisions in, 59–60
 overview, 47–48
 reforms and criticism of, 61–64
 statistics on, 55–59, 55*t*, 57*t*
 support measures, 54–55
Child Welfare Services Law
 (Austria), 50–53
child well-being protective systems,
 949*t*, 950–52, 951*f*, 954
child witchcraft branding, in
 Nigeria, 840
Child Youth and Family (CYF)
 department, New Zealand,
 35–36, 37–38
Chile
 adoption in, 414, 415*t*
 alternative care services in,
  408–11
 bases of social allocations in,
  408

developments in social care from 1970–1990, 401–4

nature of social provisions in, 408

out-of-home care in, 12*t*, 403, 408–11, 410*t*

overview, 399

policy context in, 400–1

policy trends in, 406–7

protection services and assessment in, 412–14

review of policies and programs in, 414–19

rights orientation in, 956–58

rights perspective from 1990 on, 404–6

China

challenges for child protection in, 635–38

construction of future child protection system in, 639–41

cross-departmental collaboration in, 641–44, 642*f*

development of current policy in, 628–35

evolution of child protection policy in, 626–28

out-of-home care in, 12*t*, 637–38

overview, 625–26

rights orientation in, 956

Chrastava correctional institution, Czech Republic, 434–35

Christchurch Health and Development Study (New Zealand), 42–43

Christian communities in Lebanon, legal traditions of, 811–13

CHRT (Canadian Human Rights Tribunal), 102, 104

CIS (Canadian Incidence Study of Reported Child Abuse and Neglect), 91–93

Civil Code of the Islamic Republic of Iran, 778

Civil Federal Code (Mexico), 821

civil registration and vital statistics (CRVS), Indonesia, 750

civil society organizations

in Austria, 60

in Ghana, 719, 720

in India, 741

in Lebanon, 805

in Philippines, 852, 866–67

in Uganda, 918–19

client participation. *See* child participation; parent participation

CNCDH (*Commission nationale consultative des droits de l'homme*), France, 191

CNPCJR (National Commission for the Promotion of the Rights and Protection of Children and Youth), Portugal, 512–13

Code for Marriage and Family (Estonia), 446

Code of Children and Adolescents (Colombia), 656–57

Code of the Minor (Colombia), 654–55

coerced adoption, in England, 150–51

collective care (Soviet Union), 880–81

collectivism, 946–48, 947*t*

Colombia

administrative process of restoration of rights, 657–62

analysis of protection model in, 662–63

armed conflict in, 649–50, 654

children and adolescents in, 651–52

out-of-home care and adoption in, 12*t*

out-of-home care in, 659–61, 660*t*

overview, 648–51

protection of children and restoration of violated rights, 654–57

situations of non-observance and violation of rights in, 653–54

state response to cultural and religious diversity in, 961–62

colonial influence

in Brazil, 612

in Canada, 97–99

in Philippines, 852, 859

Commission for the Guardianship of Minors (CTM), Spain, 342–43, 344*f*

Commission nationale consultative des droits de l'homme (CNCDH), France, 191

Commission to Stop All Types of Violence Against Children (Mexico), 823

Committee for the Special Protection of Children (Philippines), 863

Community Based Integrated Child Protection (PATBM) programs, Indonesia, 766–67

community-based justice systems, 914–15

community-based organizations (CBOs), United States, 392–93

community-based services

in Belgium, 77–83

in England, 152

in Greece, 275

in Indonesia, 764–67

in Israel, 241*t*, 249–52, 251*f*

in Italy, 266

in Philippines, 860–61, 867–69, 870–71

in Russia, 886

in Slovak Republic, 539

in Uganda, 917, 919

in Uruguay, 577

in Zimbabwe, 938

Community-Based Services Department (Uganda), 916

community-based volunteers (Uganda), 919

community reporting (South Africa), 548–49

community services for juvenile offenders (Czech Republic), 433–35

comparative analyses of child protection systems, 944–48

competencies-oriented family work (Switzerland), 372

Comprehensive Programme on Child Protection 2012–2016 (CPCP), Philippines, 863, 864

Comprehensive System for the Protection of Children and Adolescents against Violence (SIPIAV), Uruguay, 568

definitions of violence and maltreatment, 565

levels of care, 572–77

overview, 564–65

principles of operation of, 566

Concept of Child Welfare State Policy (Lithuania), 471

Concept of Family Policy (Lithuania), 471

confidence in governments, 16*f*, 16–17

Confidential Centers of Child Abuse and Neglect (CCCAN), Belgium, 70, 72–73, 73*t*, 80–82, 85–86

Conflict Tactics Scale (CTS), 196

Confucianism, influence of

in China, 625–27

family rights orientation, 956

in South Korea, 320

congregate care (United States), 388

Connolly, M., 945–48

consensus-based risk assessment tools, 384–85

consent, in Sweden, 161–62, 165

conservative women's movement (Indonesia), 752–53

Consolidation Act on Social Services (CASS), Denmark, 114–15, 117, 124–25

Constitution of Ecuador, 670–71

Constitution of India, 729–30

Constitution of Lebanon, 797

Constitution of Slovak Republic, 8–9

Constitution of the Islamic Republic of Iran, 778

Constitution of Uganda, 905

contact family/contact person, 162–63

context of child violence, in global typology, 949*t*, 959–60

continuum of childcare (Uganda), 910–13

Convention on the Rights of Persons with Disabilities, 114–15

Coordination Commissions on Assistance to Victims of Child Abuse (Belgium), 77–78

Coordination of Child Protection against Violence guidebook (Slovak Republic), 529–30

corporal punishment, 17
in Canada, 101
in China, 637
in Czech Republic, 437–40
in Egypt, 691
in Finland and Sweden, 157
in global typology, 949*t*, 959–60
in Iran, 788–89
in Lebanon, 799, 803
in Lithuania, 475
in Mexico, 815, 818
in Philippines, 855–56
in Poland, 487–89, 492–94
in Portugal, 507
in South Africa, 556–57
in South Korea, 320, 324
in Switzerland, 358, 363–64
in Uruguay, 566–67, 569

Correa, R., 670

correctional institutions
in Czech Republic, 433
in Estonia and Latvia, 459–60

in Ghana, 712–13
in Lebanon, 807–9

Council for the Welfare of Children (CWC), Philippines, 862–63, 864

Council of Europe's European Committee of Social Rights, 189

counseling services
in Austria, 54, 59
in Germany, 208
in Greece, 272–73
in Italy, 266
in South Korea, 326–27, 328–29
in Switzerland, 372

County Board for Child Protection and Social Affairs (Norway), 121–22

Courage Protocol (Belgium), 78–79

CP (Child Protection) plan, England, 147–48, 149

CPCJ (Children and Youth Protection Commission), Portugal, 508, 509, 515*f*

CPCP (Comprehensive Programme on Child Protection 2012–2016), Philippines, 863, 864

CPCs (Child Protection Committees), Zimbabwe, 934

CPF (Child Protection Fund), 931–32

CPOs (Child Protection Officers), Israel, 242–43, 244–46, 256

CPPM (Child Physical and Psychological Maltreatment), 324

CPS (child protection service) agencies, South Korea, 317, 322, 326–28

CRA (Child Rights Act), Nigeria, 836

CRAS (Reference Centers of Social Assistance), Brazil, 617

CREAS (Specialized Reference Center for Social Welfare), Brazil, 618

Criminal Code (Canada), 101

Criminal Code (Ghana), 708*t*

Criminal Procedure Law (Iran), 782

criminal prosecution
in Belgium, 74–76
in Germany, 202–3
in Iran, 782

in Netherlands, 298, 303
in Poland, 499
in Switzerland, 363–64

criminal responsibility, age of (Iran), 773–74

CRIN (Child Rights International Network), 129–30

CRIP (*Cellule de recueil des informations préoccupantes*), France, 178–79

crisis center placements (Austria), 53–54

crisis counselling (Austria), 54

cross-departmental collaboration, in China, 641–44, 642*f*

CRPA (Children's Rights Protection Agencies), Lithuania, 470, 471

CRVS (civil registration and vital statistics), Indonesia, 750

CSG (Child Support Grant), South Africa, 545–46, 552, 553–54

CTM (Commission for the Guardianship of Minors), Spain, 342–43, 344*f*

CTQ (Childhood Trauma Questionnaire), 196

CTS (Conflict Tactics Scale), 196

CTSPC (Parent-Child Conflict Tactics Scale) method, 566

cultural context
in China, 626–27, 640–41
in Indonesia, 751–52, 754–55
in South Korea, 316, 318–21

cultural diversity, state response to, 949*t*, 961–62

custody laws and protocols
in China, 630–31
in Ecuador, 674
in Iran, 779–80
in Lebanon, 797–98, 812

CWC (Council for the Welfare of Children), Philippines, 862–63, 864

CWCs (Child Welfare Committees), 742–43

CWS (Austria). *See* Child Welfare Services, Austria

cyberbullying, 231, 232, 817

cyber security for children, 231–32

CYCCs (child and youth care centers), South Africa, 554–56, 559

CY-Committee (Child and Youth Committee), Denmark, 121–22

CYF (Child Youth and Family)
department, New Zealand,
35–36, 37–38
CYPA (Care of Young People Act),
Sweden, 157–58, 160, 165
Czech Republic
democratic legitimacy in,
425–28
domestic violence in, 437–40
family empowerment in, 435–37
juvenile justice in, 433–35
out-of-home care in, 12t, 424,
428–37, 430f
protection of children under 3
years of age in, 431–33
socialist legacy in, 423–25
substitute family care in, 428–31

D

damage reparation (Uruguay), 574
danger, types of, 180–82
data collection
in England, 148–49
in France, 180–82, 190–91
in Greece, 274
in Indonesia, 755
in Israel, 257
in Slovak Republic, 538
in Spain, 346, 347
in Switzerland, 358–59, 373–74
in Uganda, 918
in Zimbabwe, 937
daycare programs
in Israel, 251–52
in Netherlands, 297, 311
day centers (Lebanon), 806
DCPUs (District Child Protection
Units), India, 737, 740f
DCS (Director of Children's
Services), England, 144–45
decentralization of government
in Ecuador, 668, 673–74
in Greece, 272
in Indonesia, 756–58
in Philippines, 858–59, 864–65
in Uganda, 916–17
decision-making processes
in Finland and Sweden, 164–66
in Iran, 783–84
in Israel, 244–46
in Norway and Denmark,
121–22
in Switzerland, 370
Decree on Assistance to Victims
of Child Maltreatment in the
Wallonia-Brussels Federation,
70–71

Decree on Integral Youth Care
(IYC), Belgium, 70, 79–80
de-familialisation, 16–17
Defensorías ("defense offices"),
Argentina, 590
deinstitutionalization of residential
care
in Brazil, 613–14
in Czech Republic, 428–37
in Estonia and Latvia, 455–58
in Russia, 882–84
delivery of provisions
in Argentina, 594–603, 596t, 598t
in Australia, 32–33
in Austria, 59–60
in Brazil, 620
in Canada, 99–100
in Ghana, 718–20
in Israel, 252–55
in Lebanon, 807–11
in Netherlands, 307–9
in South Africa, 556–58
in South Korea, 327–28
in Switzerland, 375–76
in Uganda, 915–19
in United States, 392–93
Delta methodology, 305
democratic legitimacy, in Czech
Republic, 425–28
Denmark
adoption in, 12t, 966–67
child and parent participation
in, 124–25
decision-making bodies in,
121–22
family-service-oriented systems
in, 113–16
in international context, 129–30,
129t
intervention threshold in,
963–64
involuntary interventions in,
121–22
living standards in, 5
mandatory reporting in, 117
municipalities, role of, 117–18
out-of-home care in, 12t, 14t,
116, 119t, 121–24
overview, 112–13
policy development in, 125–29
regulation of child protection
in, 8–9
rights orientation in, 957–58
statistics on child protection in,
118, 119t
départements (France)
ASE interventions, 176–78

challenge of unaccompanied
children in, 187–89
funding services at local level,
179–80
local disparities in care, 184–85
local procedures and priorities
in, 178–79
role in child protection, 174
social and territorial inequalities
in, 176
Department of Children, Equality,
Disability, Integration and
Youth (Ireland), 223
Department of Family Therapy
(Uruguay), 577
Department of Juvenile Rights
Protection and Guardianship
(Lithuania), 470
Department of Social
Development (DSD), South
Africa, 551, 554, 559
Department of Social
Development (Zimbabwe),
926–28, 929–30
Department of Social Welfare
(DSW) (Australia), 35
Department of Social Welfare
(DSW) (Ghana), 713, 718–19
Department of Social Welfare
and Development (DSWD),
Philippines, 863, 865, 867
Departments of Social Services
(DSS), Israel, 244–46, 250–52,
253
deputyship (Switzerland), 361,
362t, 367
designated child protection services
(South Africa), 547–48
Development Support of Social
Work in the Client's Family
Environment in Social Work
and Family Area (2015—
2020), Slovak Republic, 530
digitalization of welfare services,
128–29
Directive Principles of State Policy
(DPSP), India, 729–30
Directorate for Child, Youth, and
Family Affairs (Norway),
127–28
Director of Children's Services
(DCS), England, 144–45
Dirty War (Argentina), 589–90
discipline, physical. See corporal
punishment
disproportionality in child welfare
(United States), 384, 390–91

District Child Protection Units
(DCPUs), India, 737, 740*f*
diversionary justice, 763–64
Doctrine of Social Irregularity,
401, 402–3
domestic violence
in Argentina, 594, 595*t*
in Belgium, 74*t*, 75*t*
in Brazil, 610–11, 616–17
in China, 629–30
in Czech Republic, 437–40
in France, 181
in Ghana, 714–15
in global typology, 949*t*,
959–60
in Indonesia, 749
in Lebanon, 798
in Mexico, 815–16, 821–23
in Philippines, 855
in Poland, 487–88, 491,
495–99
in Portugal, 507
in Uruguay, 566–68, 571
Domestic Violence Act (Ghana),
708*t*, 714–15
Domestic Violence Prevention
Law (Israel), 243
DPSP (Directive Principles of
State Policy), India, 729–30
drug abuse
in Egypt, 696
in Nigeria, 839
DSD (Department of Social
Development), South Africa,
551, 554, 559
DSS (Departments of Social
Services), Israel, 244–46,
250–52, 253
DSW (Department of Social
Welfare), Australia, 35
DSW (Department of Social
Welfare), Ghana, 713, 718–19
DSWD (Department of Social
Welfare and Development),
Philippines, 863, 865, 867
Dunedin Multidisciplinary Health
and Development Study
(New Zealand), 42–43

E

Early Child Development Strategy,
2005–2010 (Egypt), 690
Early Childhood Care and
Development Policy
(Ghana), 708*t*
early childhood education
(Lebanon), 800

early intervention and family
support, in global typology,
949*t*, 964
early intervention programs
in Australia, 32–33
in England, 142–43
in Germany, 198, 208
in Netherlands, 297
in Northern Ireland, 227–28
in Russia, 886–87
Early Intervention Transformation
Programme (EITP),
Northern Ireland, 227–28
early marriage. *See* child marriage
Early Start program (New
Zealand), 40
EBP. *See* evidence-based practice
ECA (Child and Adolescent
Statute), Brazil, 611, 612,
613–14
economic context
in Chile, 400–1
in Ecuador, 666–67, 668–69
in Egypt, 684
in Iran, 772–73
in Philippines, 853–54
in South Africa, 545
in South Korea, 318–21
in Zimbabwe, 922–26, 937
Economic Structural Adjustment
Programme (ESAP),
Zimbabwe, 923
Ecuador
achievements in, 679–80
challenges for child protection
in, 680–81
child protection legislation in,
669–70
Constitutional framework in,
670–71
custody laws and protocols
in, 674
financing of services in, 678–79
juvenile offender protection in,
677–78
migrant protection in, 678
organizational framework in,
671–73
out-of-home care in, 12*t*, 675,
676–77
overview, 666–67
political and economic upheaval
in 1990s, 667–69
protection measures in, 674
protocols for decentralized
services in, 673–74
special protection in, 675–77

state response to cultural and
religious diversity in, 961–62
education
in Argentina, 605
in Brazil, 609
in Canada, 105
in Chile, 413
in Colombia, 653
in Ecuador, 679–80
in Estonia and Latvia, 459–60
in France, 175
in India, 731, 735, 742
in Iran, 772–73
in Italy, 266
in Lebanon, 800, 803
living standards, 5–8
in Mexico, 815
in Nigeria, 843–44
of refugee and migrant children,
282
in Slovak Republic, 541
in Zimbabwe, 923, 929
education centers (Portugal),
513–14
Education Sector Development
Plan (2010–2015), Lebanon,
803
educative assistance (France), 183
Egypt
child labor in, 693
Early Child Development
Strategy in, 690
early marriage in, 697–98
evaluation of social protection
for children, 700–3
female circumcision in, 696–97
health problems of children in,
693–94
homeless children program, 700
legal framework for child
protection, 684–88
National Council for
Childhood and Motherhood
in, 688–89
National Strategy for
Childhood and Motherhood
in, 689–90
Our Country Players program,
700
out-of-home care and adoption
rates in, 12*t*
overview, 683–84
poverty in, 692–93
reproductive health in, 694–95
services to children, 698–700
situation analysis of children in,
690–98

strategies relevant to child
protection, 689
street children in, 695–96
substance abuse in, 696
violence against children in,
691–92
EITP (Early Intervention
Transformation Programme),
Northern Ireland, 227–28
ELFE survey (France), 182
eligibility criteria
in Finland and Sweden, 159–60,
161–62
in Iran, 783–84
in Spain, 336–38, 337f
in United States, 382
emergency centers (Israel), 248–49
emergency orders, in Israel, 245
emergency placements
in Austria, 53–54
in Finland, 159, 162, 164
in Germany, 199, 206–8, 206t,
210
in South Africa, 550–51
in Sweden, 160, 164
emerging adulthood, 102
emerging stage of development,
19–20, 950
emotional abuse
in Australia, 28
in Austria, 48–49, 52
in Belgium, 74t, 75t
in England, 143t, 149
in Germany, 196
in Israel, 241–42, 241t
in Netherlands, 294–95, 295t
in Nigeria, 838
in Philippines, 855
in South Africa, 545
in South Korea, 324–25
in Spain, 349t
in Uganda, 902
England
adoption in, 12t, 966
child/parent participation in,
963
child protection legislation in,
137–38
financing of services in,
145–46
home and community services
and supports in, 152
out-of-home care in, 12t, 14t,
143t, 149–51, 150t
overview, 135–36
policy context 1991–2020,
138–45

referral and assistance processes
in, 146–48
statistics on child protection in,
148–49
ESAP (Economic Structural
Adjustment Programme),
Zimbabwe, 923
Estonia
child protection legislation in,
450–51
child protection system and
policies from 1940–1991,
446–50
child removal and substitute
care in, 455–56, 457t
Family Law Act 2015, 8–9
family support services in, 454
historical and socio-legal
context in, 445–46
juvenile justice in, 458–61
mandatory reporting in, 453
organization of child protection
work in, 451–53
out-of-home care in, 12t, 455–
58, 457t
overview, 444–45
Eurochild, 276
European Charter of the Rights of
the Child, 333
*European Committee for Home-
Based Priority Action for
the Child and the Family
(EUROCEF) v. France*, 189
European Committee of Social
Rights, Council of Europe,
189
European Convention on Human
Rights, 114–15
EVBGG (First National Survey
on the Prevalence of Gender-
based and Generational
Violence), Uruguay, 567
Every Child Matters Green Paper
(England), 138–39, 141
evidence-based practice (EBP)
in Australia, 33–34
in Israel, 256
in New Zealand, 42–43
in Russia, 896
exceptional protection measures
(Argentina), 598t, 600
exits from out-of-home care
(United States), 386–90
ex lege guardianships (Spain), 338,
346, 346t
exploitation of children
in Chile, 413

in France, 191
in India, 727–28, 729
in Indonesia, 749
in Iran, 781
on island of Ireland, 231
in Lebanon, 799–800
in Mexico, 822
in Netherlands, 296
in Philippines, 854–57
in Slovak Republic, 532t
extrafamilial child maltreatment,
69, 75–76
extreme poverty
in Brazil, 609
in Chile, 400
in Egypt, 692–93
in Spain, 352
in Uganda, 908t
in Zimbabwe, 928

F

familialization, in global typology,
949t, 958–59
familiarized regime, 401
families, participation of. *See*
parent participation
Family Act (Slovak Republic), 8–9,
528, 531
family and child support
orientation, in global
typology, 964
Family and Guardianship Code
(Poland), 487–88
family-based care (Japan), 291–92
family-based payments (Portugal),
519–20
family care (Iran), 784, 786t, 789–90
family coaching (Austria), 59–60
Family Code (Russia), 881, 885
Family Commissaries (Colombia),
655, 657, 663
family courts
in Argentina, 590–91
in Chile, 405–6, 407, 418
in Colombia, 656
in Germany, 201, 210–11, 211t
in Nigeria, 841
Family Defenders (Colombia),
654, 655, 657
Family Development Response
(FDR), 100
family empowerment
in Brazil, 622
in Czech Republic, 435–37
Family First Prevention Services
Act (FFPSA), United States,
392

Family Group Conferences
(FGCs), 35–36, 39, 42
family guardianship (Netherlands),
303–5, 304*t*
family home foster care (Japan),
291
family hosting (Portugal), 522
Family Intervention Projects
(England), 142
Family Justice Centers (Belgium),
79
Family Law Act (Estonia), 8–9
family preservation
in South Korea, 316, 319
in Uganda, 910–13
in United States, 385–86
Family Protection Law (Iran), 780
family reunification
in Czech Republic, 431*f*, 431–32,
435–37
in Greece, 281
in Spain, 338
in United States, 389
family rights orientation, 955–57
family separation, 16–18
family service orientation, 18
in Chile, 401
in China, 640–41
compared to other typologies,
639–40, 639*t*, 944–45, 945*t*,
946*t*
in Germany, 198, 202
in Israel, 240, 255
in Italy, 270–71
in Norway and Denmark,
113–16
in Russia, 878–79, 893–94
in Slovak Republic, 540
in United States, 381–82
family-style care (Russia), 878,
883–84, 890–91, 893–94
family support services
in Australia, 30, 32–33
in Austria, 59–60
in Brazil, 617–19
in China, 638, 643
in Colombia, 659, 660*t*
in England, 137–38, 139–40, 142
in Estonia and Latvia, 454–55
in France, 182–83, 184
in Germany, 198–99, 206–9,
206*t*
in Greece, 272–73
in Indonesia, 755, 760–61
in Israel, 249–50
in Italy, 266, 270–71
in Japan, 289

in Netherlands, 297, 305–7,
306*t*, 309–10
in New Zealand, 39–40
in South Africa, 550
in South Korea, 326–27, 328–29
in Spain, 339–41
in Switzerland, 370–73, 372*f*
family violence
in global typology, 949*t*, 959–60
in Mexico, 821–23
in Philippines, 855
family/whānau placements (New
Zealand), 39, 40–41
family work (Finland), 162–63
FDR (Family Development
Response), 100
Federal Child Protection Act
(Germany), 212
Federal Children and Youth
Welfare Act (Austria), 61
Federal Council for Childhood,
Adolescence, and Family
(Argentina), 593–94
Federal Criminal Code (Mexico),
822–23
federalism, in Switzerland, 356–57,
360
female genital mutilation/cutting
(FGM/C)
in Egypt, 696–97
in Ghana, 710, 711, 714
in Nigeria, 838–39
in Uganda, 905
female suppression (Nigeria), 835
Fenninger-Buchner, D., 51–52
Ferreira, J. M. L., 519
FFPSA (Family First Prevention
Services Act), United States, 392
FGC (foster care grant), South
Africa, 552–54
FGCs (Family Group
Conferences), 35–36, 39, 42
financial crisis, impact on child
protection system
in Greece, 274–75
in Italy, 262
in Zimbabwe, 924
financing of child protection
services
in Argentina, 603–4, 605–6
in Australia, 32
in Austria, 60–61
in Brazil, 620
in Canada, 99
in Chile, 408, 410, 411, 418–19
in Ecuador, 678–79
in England, 141–42, 145–46

in Estonia and Latvia, 450
in Finland and Sweden, 166–68
in France, 175, 176, 179–80
in Ghana, 720–21
in Indonesia, 757–58, 765
in Israel, 252–55
in Italy, 268–69
in Lithuania, 467–68
in Mexico, 826
in Netherlands, 307–8
in New Zealand, 42
in Philippines, 869–70
in Russia, 891–92
in South Africa, 559–61
in South Korea, 317, 319–20,
328–29
in Spain, 343–45
in Switzerland, 375–76
in Uganda, 920
in United States, 392–93
in Uruguay, 579–81
in Zimbabwe, 935, 936
Finland
aftercare services in, 164
care orders in, 163–64
decision making in, 164–66
eligibility criteria in, 159–60,
161–62
emergency placements in, 164
history of child protection
policy in, 644
in-home services in, 162–63
main principles for services in,
157–58
mandatory reporting in, 158–59
organization and financing of
service provision in, 166–68
outcomes of child welfare
services in, 168–69
out-of-home care in, 12*t*, 14*t*,
160–61, 163–64
overview, 156–57
requests for services in, 158–59
First Information System (SIPI),
Uruguay, 568
First National Survey on the
Prevalence of Gender-based
and Generational Violence
(EVBGG), Uruguay, 567
First Nations Child and Family
Services (FNCFS), 103
First Nations communities
(Canada)
emerging practices for, 107
federally funded services, 102
history of child welfare services
for, 97–99

Jordan's Principle, 103–4
overrepresentation of, 94–95, 95f
structure of child welfare, 102–4
five-year plans (India), 731–33
Flanders, Belgium
  child welfare services in, 79–82, 86
  Coordination Commissions on Assistance to Victims of Child Abuse, 77–78
  extent of child maltreatment in, 72–73, 73t, 74t, 85–86
  Family Justice Centers, 79
  Flemish Forum of Child Abuse, 78
  Flemish Step-by-step Plan to Address Child Maltreatment, 78
  judicial treatment of abuse and neglect, 76
  out-of-home care in, 84t
Flemish Forum of Child Abuse (Belgium), 78
Flemish Step-by-step Plan to Address Child Maltreatment (Belgium), 78
FNCFS (First Nations Child and Family Services), 103
for-profit organizations
  in England, 146
  in Finland and Sweden, 166–67
  in Switzerland, 375
foster care
  in Argentina, 598t, 602
  in Australia, 31
  in Austria, 53–54, 55t, 56–57, 57t
  in Belgium, 84t
  in Brazil, 619–20
  in Canada, 93, 98–99
  in Chile, 408–11, 416–19
  in China, 630, 637–38
  in Colombia, 659–61, 660t
  in Czech Republic, 429–30, 431f
  in Ecuador, 675, 676–77
  in England, 146, 149–51, 150t
  in Estonia and Latvia, 456–58, 457t
  in Finland and Sweden, 163–64, 167
  in France, 183, 185
  in Germany, 209–10
  in Greece, 276–77
  in Indonesia, 762
  in Iran, 784, 786t
  on island of Ireland, 220–22, 221t

in Israel, 241t, 247–48, 254
in Italy, 266–67, 268t
in Japan, 289, 291–92
in Mexico, 825–26
in Netherlands, 305–7, 306t
in New Zealand, 40–41
in Norway and Denmark, 122
in Philippines, 867
in Portugal, 508–9, 522
in Russia, 888–89, 891–92
in Slovak Republic, 533, 534t
in South Africa, 552–54
in South Korea, 327, 328–29
in Spain, 347
in Switzerland, 373
in Uganda, 910–13
in United States, 386–90, 392
in Uruguay, 578
Foster Care Families' Service (Israel), 247
foster care grant (FGC), South Africa, 552–54
Foster Families Law 2016 (Israel), 248
Fostering Connections to Success and Increasing Adoptions Act, United States, 392
fragmentation of services
  in Chile, 418
  in Indonesia, 758–64
France
  assessments of child welfare in, 185–86
  best practices in, 186–87
  challenges for child protection in, 189–90
  funding services at local level, 179–80
  inter-sectoral collaboration in, 176–78
  local procedures and priorities in, 178–79
  observational blind spots in, 190–91
  out-of-home care in, 12t, 177, 183–85
  overview, 173–74
  state response to cultural and religious diversity in, 962
  types of danger and principles of intervention, 180–82
  types of interventions and local disparities in, 182–85
  unaccompanied foreign minors in, 187–89
  welfare system in, 174–76
Free Tuition Program (Canada), 106

Friedman, M., 1
Fukuoka city, Japan, 292
full care provision (Austria), 55–56, 55t, 58–59
funding of child protection services. See financing of child protection services

G

GAL (guardian ad litem), United States, 386–87
Gale, C., 416
GDP (Gross Domestic Product), 7f, 7–8
gender-based violence
  in Colombia, 653–54
  in Ghana, 710–11
  in Indonesia, 749
  in Nigeria, 838–39
General Health Law (Mexico), 824
General Law for Children and Adolescents (LGDNNA), Mexico, 823–24
General Law of the Rights of Children and Adolescents (Mexico), 820
German Community (Belgium), 67
Germany
  child and youth welfare offices in, 198–201
  child maltreatment in, 195–96
  core procedures and standards in, 203–8
  family courts in, 201, 210–11, 211t
  health system in, role in child protection, 201–2
  legal regulations regarding parental rights in, 197–98
  out-of-home care in, 12t, 14t, 206–8, 206t, 209–10
  overview, 195
  prosecuting authorities in, role in child protection, 202–3
  schools in, role in child protection, 203
  trends and forthcoming issues, 212
  types and development of interventions, 208–12
Ghana
  adoption in, 12t, 966
  bases of social allocations, 713–16
  child labor legislation, 715
  child/parent participation in, 962–63

Ghana (*cont.*)
children in vulnerable
circumstances in, 707–13
children with disabilities in, 716
Domestic Violence Act, 714–15
financing of child protection
services in, 720–21
history of child protection
policy enactment in, 706–7
Human Trafficking Act, 715
intervention threshold in, 963–64
Juvenile Justice Act, 715
legal protections for children's
rights, 713–14
methods for delivery of
provisions, 718–20
nature of social provisions in,
716–17
out-of-home care in, 12*t*, 712
overview, 706
rights orientation in, 956
state response to cultural and
religious diversity in, 961
traditional cultural practices, 17
Ghana NGOs Coalition on
the Rights of the Child
(GNCRC), 719
global child protection typology
characteristics of, 949*t*
child deprivation protective
systems, 949*t*, 950–53, 951*f*
child exploitation protective
systems, 949*t*, 950–52, 951*f*
child maltreatment protective
systems, 949*t*, 950–52, 951*f*,
953–54
child rights protective systems,
949*t*, 950–52, 951*f*, 954–55
child well-being protective
systems, 949*t*, 950–52, 951*f*,
954
comparative analyses of child
protection systems, 944–48
inductive approach to
developing, 948–55
overview, 19, 943–44
protective system characteristics,
962–67
social, political, and cultural
contexts of states, 955–62
global south, child protection
systems in, 860–61
GNCRC (Ghana NGOs
Coalition on the Rights of
the Child), 719
Gove Inquiry into Child Protection
in BC, Canada, 96–97

Government of National Unity
(GNU), Zimbabwe, 925
governments, public confidence
in, 16*f*, 16–17
Gray, M., 30
Greece
challenges for child protection
in, 276–78
child protection good practices,
278
child protection system in,
272–74
financial crisis, impact on child
protection system in, 274–75
foster care in, 276–77
legislative framework for child
abuse in, 277–78
out-of-home care in, 12*t*,
276–77
overview, 271
residential care in, 276
socio-economic framework,
271–72
unaccompanied children,
challenge of, 279–83
Grijns, M., 752
grooming of children by adults
(Ireland), 231
Gross Domestic Product (GDP),
7*f*, 7–8
Group Homes for teenagers
(Japan), 290
Group on Development of
Children for the Eleventh
Five Year Plan (2007–2012),
726
group rights orientation, 956
Growing Up in Australia
(Australia), 34
Growing Up in New Zealand
(New Zealand), 42–43
guardian ad litem (GAL), United
States, 386–87
Guardian Council Act (Norway), 10
guardianship care
in Indonesia, 762
in Iran, 779–80
in Lithuania, 471, 474–75,
479–80
in Netherlands, 303–5, 304*t*
in Philippines, 867
in Russia, 888*f*, 888
in Slovak Republic, 534*t*
in Spain, 338*f*, 338, 342–43, 346,
346*t*
Guardianship of Minors Act
(Zimbabwe), 926–28

Gugus Tugas TPPPO (Task
Force for the Prevention
and Handling of Crimes
of Human Trafficking),
Indonesia, 766–67

H
Hague Convention on the
Protection of Children and
Intercountry Adoption,
900–1
Hallett, C., 425
Hamogelotou Paidiou (Smile of
the Child), 273
HAQ–Centre for Child Rights,
741–42
Harmonized Social Cash Transfers
(HSCT), Zimbabwe, 930,
931–32, 933, 934, 935*t*
Harm to a Minor or a Helpless
Person (Penal) Law, Israel,
243
Haruv Institute, 252
Hasenfeld, Y., 751
HCC (Higher Council for
Childhood), 795–97, 807
HDI (Human Development
Index), 772–73, 853–54
Health and Social Care Trusts
(Northern Ireland), 218, 227
health care
in France, 175, 176
in Germany, 201–2
in Iran, 772–73
in Lebanon, 810–11
living standards, 5–8
helplines. *See* hotlines
Higher Council for Childhood
(HCC), 795–97, 807
HIV/AIDS epidemic
in Nigeria, 841–42
in Uganda, 901, 903–4
in Zimbabwe, 923, 928, 930, 930–31
home-based services
in England, 152
in Netherlands, 305–6, 306*t*,
309–10
Home for Life placement (New
Zealand), 41
Homeless Children Program
(Egypt), 700
homicides
in Brazil, 610
in Mexico, 817
in Nigeria, 838
in Philippines, 857
Horii, H., 752

hotlines
  in Belgium, 72–73, 79–80
  in China, 643
  in Egypt, 692
  in England, 146–47
  in Estonia and Latvia, 453
  in France, 178, 182
  in Indonesia, 760
  in Iran, 787
  in Japan, 288
  in Portugal, 517
  in United States, 382
House Home (Colombia), 659–
  60, 660t
Howlett, M., 30
HSCT (Harmonized Social Cash
  Transfers), Zimbabwe, 930,
  931–32, 933, 934, 935t
Human Development Index
  (HDI), 772–73, 853–54
human rights, in Brazil, 612
Human Rights Act (Norway), 114–15
human trafficking. *See* child
  trafficking
Human Trafficking Act (Ghana),
  708t, 715
Hunter, B., 30
hyperinflation, in Zimbabwe,
  924, 926

I

ICBF (Instituto Colombiano de
  bienestar familiar), 650–51,
  654, 655
ICPS (Integrated Child Protection
  Services), India, 736–37, 738t
IMLSASS (Israeli Ministry of
  Labor and Social Affairs
  and Services), 244, 247–49,
  253–54, 257
immigrant children, protection of
  in Ecuador, 678, 681
  in France, 187–90
  on island of Ireland, 232–33
  in Israel, 239–40
  in Italy and Greece, 278, 279–83
inappropriate caregivers (Iran),
  774–75, 779, 780–81, 789–90
INAU (Institute for Children and
  Adolescents of Uruguay),
  564–65, 576–79
incarceration of juveniles
  (Mexico), 817
INCC (Israel National Council for
  the Child), 252
Incredible Years program
  (Estonia), 454

Incredible Years program (New
  Zealand), 40
independent social workers,
  145–46
India
  age-based definitions for child
    in, 725–26
  case studies from, 744–45
  challenges for child protection
    in, 726–29
  child abuse legislation in,
    742–44
  Integrated Child Protection
    Services in, 736–37, 738t
  legal framework for child
    protection in, 729–31
  living standards in, 5
  NGOs in, 740–42
  out-of-home care and adoption
    in, 12t
  overview, 724–25
  policy framework for child
    protection in, 731–35
Indian Act (Canada), 98
Indigenous children
  in Australia, 25–26, 29, 30,
    31–32
  in Brazil, 609–10
  in Canada, 94–95, 95f, 97–99,
    102–4, 107
  in Colombia, 661–62
  in Ecuador, 666–67, 668–69
  in New Zealand, 25–26, 34–35,
    37–38, 40–42
  in United States, 390–91
indirect child protection measures
  (Portugal), 521–22
individualism, 946–48, 947t
Indonesia
  decentralization in, 756–58
  from fragmentation to
    integration in, 758–64
  institutional environment in,
    750–56
  intermediary structures in, 764–67
  interrelated issues in child
    protection in, 748–50
  out-of-home care and adoption
    in, 12t
  overview, 747–48
  traditional cultural practices, 17
Indonesia Child Help Line
  (TePSA), 760
Indonesian Child Protection
  Commission (KPAI), 759
inductive approach to developing
  global typology, 948–55

industrialism, 95–96, 316–17
infanticide, in Nigeria, 838
infant institutions (Japan), 290
infant protection (Czech
  Republic), 431–33
Infant Protection Law (Portugal),
  510
inflation
  in Egypt, 684
  in Zimbabwe, 924, 926, 937
informal systems
  in South Africa, 561
  in Uganda, 914–15
  in Zimbabwe, 938
inheritance laws (Lebanon), 798
in-home services
  in Austria, 59–60
  in Chile, 410t
  in Finland and Sweden, 159,
    162–63
  in France, 177, 182–83, 184
  in Germany, 198–99, 208–9
  in Norway and Denmark, 116
  in South Korea, 326–27, 328–29
  in Switzerland, 372, 373–74
  in United States, 385–86
Innovative Model of Family
  Preservation Management
  (Slovak Republic), 536–37
Insertion Social Income (RSI
  measure), Portugal, 521
Institute for Children and
  Adolescents of Uruguay
  (INAU), 564–65, 576–79
institutional care. *See* residential
  care
institutional care centers
  (Ecuador), 676–77
institutionalization (Mexico),
  817, 818t
institutionalization of rights
  (Argentina), 588, 591
institutionalized organizations,
  750–51
institutionalized stage of
  development, 19–20, 950
institutional reordering (Brazil),
  619–20
Instituto Colombiano de bienestar
  familiar (ICBF), 650–51,
  654, 655
integral protection
  in Argentina, 597–600, 598t
  in Brazil, 611–16
  in Colombia, 648–49
Integral Protection System
  (Argentina), 592–93, 603

integral specialized intervention programs (Chile), 412

Integrated Child Protection Services (ICPS), India, 736–37, 738*t*

Integrated Child Welfare Service Model (PKSAI), Indonesia, 760–61, 765–66

Integrated National System of Care (SNIC), Uruguay, 580–81

Integrated Service Delivery (ISD), Canada, 106

integration of services (Indonesia), 758–64

inter-agency councils (Philippines), 863

interdisciplinary teams (Poland), 501–2

intermediary structures (Indonesia), 764–67

internet technologies, impact on child welfare, 230–32

inter-sectoral collaboration (France), 176–78

intervention threshold, in global typology, 949*t*, 963–64

intrafamilial child maltreatment. *See* domestic violence

intrusive interventions by state, 10–11, 16–18

Inuit communities (Canada), 94–95, 97–99

investigation of maltreatment
in Australia, 27
in Colombia, 658
in England, 138
in Israel, 241*t*, 244–46
in Japan, 288
in Lebanon, 809–10
in Mexico, 825
in Netherlands, 299–302, 300*f*
in South Korea, 326
in United States, 382–83

Investing in Children Programme (New Zealand), 37

involuntary interventions
in Germany, 197–98, 201
in Norway and Denmark, 116, 121–22
in Sweden, 160

Iran
age-based definitions for child in, 773–74
at-risk children in, 774–76
challenges for child protection in, 788–90
monitoring and evaluation strategies, 785

out-of-home care in, 12*t*, 784, 786*t*
overview, 771–72
policies and legislation in, 777–85
responsible bodies and agencies in, 776–77
review of policies and programs in, 785–88
social welfare system in, 772–73
statistics on child protection in, 786*t*
types of care in, 784–85

Ireland
Brexit, impact on child safety, 228–30
child protection in Northern Ireland versus, 217–19
history of child protection in, 219–22
out-of-home care in, 12*t*, 14*t*, 220–22, 221*t*
overview, 216–17
policies and programs in, 222–26
protection of migrant children in, 232–33
technology and child welfare in, 230–32

ISD (Integrated Service Delivery), Canada, 106

Islam
in Indonesia, 751–52
in Iran, 788–89
in Lebanon, 797–800, 811–13

Israel
child maltreatment in, 241–42, 241*t*
child/parent participation in, 963
child protection legislation in, 242–44
community-based services in, 249–52, 251*f*
financing of child protection services, 252–55
investigation, substantiation, and decision-making processes in, 244–46
methods of provision, 252–55
out-of-home care in, 12*t*, 241*t*, 246, 247–49, 251*f*
overview, 239–41
trends and challenges in, 255–57

Israeli Ministry of Labor and Social Affairs and Services (IMLSASS), 244, 247–49, 253–54, 257

Israel National Council for the Child (INCC), 252

Italy
bases of social allocations in, 264–66
best practices, 269–71
child protection measures in, 266–67
child protection system in, 263–64
financing of child protection services in, 268–69
organizational settings in, 267–68
out-of-home care in, 12*t*, 14*t*, 266–67
overview, 261
social-demographic data, 262–63
statistics on child protection in, 267
unaccompanied children, challenge of, 279–83

IYC (Decree on Integral Youth Care), Belgium, 70, 79–80

J

Japan
adoption in, 12*t*, 966–67
Child Guidance Centres, 289
child maltreatment in, 287
child protection legislation in, 288
issues facing child protection in, 293
out-of-home care in, 12*t*, 289–91
overview, 287
referral and investigation processes in, 288
shift from institutional to family-based care in, 291–92

JLOS (Justice Law and Order Sector), Uganda, 914, 918

Jogaité, B., 478

joint-task force (JTF), Nigeria, 845–46

Jordan's Principle, 103–4

judicial representation program (Chile), 412

judicial system, role of
in Belgium, 74–77
in Chile, 418
in Ecuador, 673, 674
in France, 177–78
in Iran, 777, 782
in Italy, 264–65, 266*f*
in Lebanon, 807–9, 811, 812–13
in Mexico, 820–21
in Nigeria, 841
in Portugal, 509–11
in South Africa, 549, 550–51

Juez de Menores ("Judge of
    Minors"), Argentina, 589, 590
Justice Law and Order Sector
    (JLOS), Uganda, 914, 918
Juvenile (Care and Supervision)
    Law, Israel, 240, 242, 245
juvenile courts
    in Belgium, 76–77, 83
    in Chile, 406
    in Israel, 242–43
    in Italy, 264
    in Netherlands, 298, 301, 302,
        303–5, 304*t*
juvenile delinquency (India),
    726–27, 730–31
juvenile justice
    in Argentina, 603–4
    in Czech Republic, 433–35
    in Ecuador, 677–78
    in Estonia, 458–61
    in Ghana, 712–13, 715
    in India, 730–31
    in Indonesia, 763–64
    in Iran, 773–74
    in Latvia, 458–59
    in Lebanon, 809–10
    in Lithuania, 471–72
    in Mexico, 817
    in Netherlands, 297
    in Slovak Republic, 540
    in Uganda, 906, 913–15, 918
Juvenile Justice Act (Ghana),
    708*t*, 715
Juvenile Justice Act (India), 724–25,
    730–31, 742–43

K

Kemensos (Ministry of Social
    Affairs), Indonesia, 753–54,
    757–59, 760
Key Assets Japan, 292
kidnapping, in Argentina, 589–90
Kids Rights Index (KRI), 7–8, 9*f*,
    129–30, 129*t*
Kilkenny Incest Investigation
    (Ireland), 223
kinship care, 15
    in Australia, 31–32
    in Canada, 93–94
    in Chile, 410–11
    in England, 149–51, 150*t*
    in Finland and Sweden, 164
    in France, 183
    in Germany, 209–10
    in Iran, 784, 786*t*, 789–90
    on island of Ireland, 220–22, 221*t*
    in Israel, 247–48
    in Japan, 291

in New Zealand, 40–41
in Norway and Denmark, 122
in Russia, 888, 889
in South Africa, 552–54
in Uganda, 910–13
in United States, 388, 389–90
KKG (Act on Cooperation
    and Information in Child
    Protection), Germany, 198,
    203, 205–7
KLA ("Child Friendly Districts/
    Cities"), Indonesia, 766–67
Kolya (film), 423–24
Koranic Mallams (Nigeria), 835
Korea. *See* South Korea
KPAI (Indonesian Child
    Protection Commission), 759
KPPPA (Ministry for Women's
    Empowerment and Child
    Protection), Indonesia, 753–54,
    757–59
KRI (Kids Rights Index), 7–8, 9*f*,
    129–30, 129*t*

L

Labor Act (Ghana), 708*t*
Labor Law of Iran, 781
Laming Report (England),
    138–40
Latvia
    child protection legislation in,
        450–51
    child removal and substitute
        care in, 455–58, 457*t*
    family support services in,
        454–55
    historical and socio-legal
        context in, 445–46
    juvenile justice in, 458–61
    mandatory reporting in, 453
    organization of child protection
        work in, 451–53
    out-of-home care in, 12*t*, 455–58,
        457*t*
    overview, 444–45
    system and policies from
        1940–1991, 446–50
Lauristin, M., 448–50
Law 1 (Spain), 333–34
Law 21 (Spain), 333–34
Law 422 (Lebanon), 805, 807–13
Law 6 (Spain), 335–36
Law 8 (Spain), 334
Law against Domestic Violence
    (China), 629–30, 634, 637
Law for the Protection for
    Children and Adolescents
    (Mexico), 819–20

Law of Educational Guardianship
    (Portugal), 513–14
Law of Protection for Children
    and Youths (Portugal), 518
Law of Social Assistance (Mexico),
    824
Law on Child Protection (Czech
    Republic), 429
Law on Combating Human
    Trafficking (Iran), 781
Law on Minor and Medium
    Supervision of the Republic
    of Lithuania, 474
Law on the Fundamentals of the
    Protection of the Rights of
    the Child (Lithuania), 471,
    476, 477–78
Law on the Prevention of Juvenile
    Delinquency (China), 627–28
Law on the Protection of Minors
    (China), 626, 627–28, 635
laws. *See* legislation, child protection;
    specific laws by name
laymen, decision-making role of, 165
LCPC (Local Councils for the
    Protection of Children),
    Philippines, 865
LEAP (Livelihood Empowerment
    Against Poverty) cash transfer
    program, Ghana, 716, 717
least intrusion, principle of, 115
Lebanon
    approach to social welfare in,
        794–95
    legal framework in, 797–800,
        798*t*, 807–11
    legal traditions of religious
        communities in, 811–13
    national coordination of
        children's issues in, 795–97
    out-of-home care in, 12*t*, 806
    overview, 794
    policies and strategies for child
        protection in, 800–4
    religious values, role in child
        care system, 17
    state response to cultural and
        religious diversity in, 961
    welfare services for families and
        children in, 804–6
left-behind children, in China,
    629, 632
legal counseling (Ecuador), 676
legal framework for child protection
    in India, 729–31
    in Italy, 264–65
    in Lebanon, 797–800, 798*t*,
        807–11

legality principle, 115
legal representation of children
  in Chile, 412
  in Switzerland, 369–70
legal status, claims for, 281
legal system (Austria), 48
legislation, child protection
  in Argentina, 592–94, 595*t*
  in Australia, 27
  in Austria, 48–52
  in Brazil, 611–16
  in Canada, 100–2
  in China, 627–28, 635
  in Ecuador, 669–70
  in Egypt, 684–88
  in England, 137–38
  in Estonia and Latvia, 450–51
  in Germany, 197–98
  in Ghana, 706–7, 708*t*, 713–16
  in Greece, 278
  in India, 729–31, 742–44
  in Indonesia, 753–54, 753*t*
  in Iran, 777–85
  in Israel, 240, 242–44
  in Italy, 264–65
  in Japan, 288
  in Lebanon, 797–800, 798*t*
  in Lithuania, 471
  in Mexico, 818–26
  in Nigeria, 836
  in Northern Ireland, 226–27
  in Norway and Denmark,
    114–16
  in Philippines, 861–62
  in Poland, 487
  in Portugal, 509–11, 515–18
  in Russia, 881–82
  in Slovak Republic, 527–30,
    531
  in South Africa, 546–52
  in South Korea, 317, 321–23
  in Spain, 333–36
  in Switzerland, 361–65, 377
  in Uganda, 904–9
  in United States, 391–92
  in Uruguay, 570–71
  in Zimbabwe, 926–28
Leviner, P., 161–62
LGDNNA (General Law for
  Children and Adolescents),
  Mexico, 823–24
Life Free of Violence (Mexico), 826
life skills of children, 755
lifeworld-orientation principle,
  208–9
Lithuania
  child protection reform in,
    474–78

effectiveness of child protection
  in, 478–82
EU Structural Funds, impact on
  policy in, 473–74
law and policy development
  from 1990–2004, 470–72
out-of-home care and adoption
  in, 12*t*
overview, 467–70
Livelihood Empowerment Against
  Poverty (LEAP) cash transfer
  program, Ghana, 716, 717
living standards, 5–8
Local Councils for the Protection
  of Children (LCPC),
  Philippines, 865
"local diagram" (*schéma
  départemental*), France, 179
local observatory of child
  protection (ODPE), France,
  179, 186
local rights protection offices
  (Chile), 407
Local Safeguarding Children
  Board, England, 144–45
local teams (Netherlands), 297,
  305, 306, 306*t*, 307
looked-after children, placement
  of, 289–91
Los Chicos del Pueblo (Children of
  the People), 591–92
Loughton, T., 140–41

M

Madrid, Autonomous
  Community of
  legislation in, 335–36
  local provisions in, 339–41
  out-of-home care in, 347
  social provisions provided by,
    341–43, 342*f*
maintenance provisions for
  children, in Lebanon, 797–98
malnutrition
  in Brazil, 609–10
  in Colombia, 653
  in Egypt, 691, 693–94
  in India, 742
  in Mexico, 814–15
  in Zimbabwe, 923–24
maltreatment, child. *See* child
  maltreatment
maltreatment and sexual abuse
  protection programs (Chile),
  412
mandated services (Belgium), 80
mandatory reporting
  in Australia, 27

in Austria, 52–53
in Belgium, 71–72
in Canada, 100–1
in China, 629–30, 637, 643
in Denmark, 117
in England, 146–48
in Estonia and Latvia, 453
in Finland and Sweden, 158–59
in Germany, 201–2
in Ireland, 225–26
in Israel, 243
in Japan, 288
in Netherlands, 298
in New Zealand, 38–39
in Norway, 117
in South Africa, 548–51
in South Korea, 322–23, 325
in Switzerland, 363, 368
in United States, 382
*Manual of Organization and
  Operation for the National
  System of Integral Protection
  for Children and Adolescents*
  (Mexico), 826
Māori children, 25–26, 34–35, 37–38,
  40–42
marriage, child. *See* child
  marriage
maternal and child living support
  facility (Japan), 290
maternal health, in India, 734, 742
MCFIA (Ministry of Children
  and Family and Integration
  Affairs), Latvia, 452
MCLSW (Ministry of
  Cooperatives, Labor and
  Social Welfare), Iran, 776–77
Meitheal model (Ireland), 225–26
Melilla, Spain, 351, 352
mental health services
  in Ecuador, 676
  in Finland and Sweden, 169
  in Greece, 271–72, 273, 275
  in Japan, 290
  in South Korea, 325
MERP (Millennium Economic
  Recovery Programme),
  Zimbabwe, 924
methods for delivery of provisions.
  See delivery of provisions
Métis communities (Canada),
  94–95, 97–99
Mexico
  issues faced by children in, 814–18
  out-of-home care in, 12*t*, 825–26
  overview, 814
  policies and laws aimed at child
    abuse in, 823–26

policies and laws protecting rights of children in, 818–23
rights orientation in, 956–57
MGLSD (Ministry of Gender, Labour, and Social Development), Uganda, 915–16, 920
MICS (Multiple Indicator Cluster Survey), 566–67
middle-out approach to child protection (Philippines), 860–61, 864–67
MIES (Ministry of Economic and Social Inclusion), Ecuador, 672, 673–74, 675, 677
migrant children, protection of. See immigrant children, protection of
Millennium Economic Recovery Programme (MERP), Zimbabwe, 924
Minayo, M. C. S., 613–14
Ministries, Municipal, and District Assemblies (MMDAs), Ghana, 718–19, 720–21
Ministry for Women's Empowerment and Child Protection (KPPPA), Indonesia, 753–54, 757–59
Ministry of Children and Family and Integration Affairs (MCFIA), Latvia, 452
Ministry of Cooperatives, Labor and Social Welfare (MCLSW), Iran, 776–77
Ministry of Economic and Social Inclusion (MIES), Ecuador, 672, 673–74, 675, 677
Ministry of Education and Higher Education (Lebanon), 803
Ministry of Gender, Labour, and Social Development (MGLSD), Uganda, 915–16, 920
Ministry of Justice (Lebanon), 802–3, 807
Ministry of Labor (Lebanon), 804
Ministry of Public Health (Lebanon), 803–4
Ministry of Public Service, Labour, and Social Welfare (MPSLSW), Zimbabwe, 926–28, 929–30
Ministry of Social Affairs (Kemensos), Indonesia, 753–54, 757–59, 760
Ministry of Social Affairs (MOSA), Lebanon, 801–2, 804–5, 807

Ministry of Social Solidarity (Egypt), 698–700
Ministry of Solidarity and Social Security (Portugal), 516
Ministry of Women and Child Development (MWCD), India, 737
minor in need, defined, 242
Minors Code (Brazil), 612–13
minor trafficking. See child trafficking
missing children, in India, 729
mixed rights orientation, 955–56, 957
MMDAs (Ministries, Municipal, and District Assemblies), Ghana, 718–19, 720–21
MNMMR (National Movement of Street Boys and Girls), Brazil, 613
mobile teams (Lithuania), 477–78
Modernising Child, Youth and Family Expert Panel (New Zealand), 36–38, 39, 43
modernization, 1–2
modestly inclusive welfare system (China), 628–29
moral corruption of parents (Iran), 774–75, 779
MOSA (Ministry of Social Affairs), Lebanon, 801–2, 804–5, 807
MPSLSW (Ministry of Public Service, Labour, and Social Welfare), Zimbabwe, 926–28, 929–30
multidimensional family therapy (Estonia), 454
Multiple Indicator Cluster Survey (MICS), 566–67
municipalities, role in child protection
  in Estonia, 454
  in Finland and Sweden, 165, 166–67
  in Israel, 244–46, 250–52
  in Italy, 264, 267–68
  in Latvia, 454–55
  in Lithuania, 472
  in Netherlands, 297, 307
  in Norway and Denmark, 117–18, 127
  in Philippines, 864–67
  in Spain, 339f, 339–41
  in Switzerland, 356–57, 375
Muñoz-Guzmán, C., 414–15
Munro, E., 140–41
Munro report (England), 140–41

Munro Review of Child Protection (England), 139
MWCD (Ministry of Women and Child Development), India, 737
Myers-JDC-Brookdale Institute, 252

N

NAP1, II, III (National Action Plans for Children), Zimbabwe, 930–34, 936
nascent stage of development, 19–20, 948–50
National Action Plan for Children for 2013–2017 (Slovak Republic), 529
National Action Plan for the Prevention and Protection of Children from all Forms of Violence and Neglect (Lebanon), 801–2
National Action Plans for Children (NAP1, II, III), Zimbabwe, 930–34, 936
National Agency of Investigation and Innovation (ANII), Uruguay, 581
National Association of Welfare Organisations and Non-Governmental Organisations (NAWONGO), South Africa, 559–60
National Board of Social Services (Denmark), 127–28
National Case Management System (NCMS), Zimbabwe, 929, 932–33
National Center for Social Solidarity (Greece), 272–73
National Child Protection Agency (NCPA), South Korea, 317, 322, 327, 328
National Child Protection Register (NCPR), South Africa, 551–52
National Commission for the Promotion of the Rights and Protection of Children and Youth (CNPCJR). Portugal, 512–13
National Council for Intergenerational Equality (NCIE), Ecuador, 670–72, 678
National Council for Motherhood and Childhood (NCCM), Egypt, 685, 688–89
National Decentralized Comprehensive Child Protection System (Ecuador), 671–73, 678

National Development Plan 2013–2018 (Mexico), 820

National Disability Act (Ghana), 708t, 716

National Economic Development Priority Programme (NEDPP), Zimbabwe, 924–25

National Economic Revival Programme (NERP), Zimbabwe, 924

National Education Law (Argentina), 605

National Framework for Protecting Australia's Children, 26–27, 33

National Gender and Children's Policy (Ghana), 708t

National Guidelines to and Practice on Orphans and Vulnerable Children (Nigeria), 842–43

National Health Insurance Scheme (NHIS), Ghana, 716, 717

National Joint Taskforce for the Prevention of Child Sexual Abuse, Violence and Neglect (Nigeria), 845–46

National Law of "*Patronato de Menores*" (Argentina), 589

National Medium Term Development Plan (RPJMN), Indonesia, 754

National Movement of Street Boys and Girls (MNMMR), Brazil, 613

national observatory of child protection (ONPE), France, 179, 186

National Orphans Vulnerable Children Policy (Uganda), 906

National Outcomes Matrix (NOM) framework, 104–5

National Plan for Early Childhood, Childhood and Adolescence 2016– 2020, Uruguay, 580–81

National Plan for Good Living (Ecuador), 671

National Plan of Action for Children (NPAC), 2005, India, 734–35

National Plan of Action for Orphans and Vulnerable Children (Ghana), 708t

National Plan of Action for the Elimination of the Worst

Forms of Child Labor (Ghana), 708t

National Policy for Children, 2013 (India), 733–34

National Policy on Child Labor (Nigeria), 844

National Policy on Protection and Assistance to Trafficked Persons in Nigeria, 844

National Program for Child Development in China (2011–2020), China, 628

National Program for Counteracting Domestic Violence (Poland), 495–96

National Program to Combat Female Circumcision (Egypt), 697

National Public Education Administration (ANEP), Uruguay, 565

National Secretariat for Children's Rights (SENAF), Argentina, 593

National Service for Minors (SENAME), Chile institutions involved with, 407 model implemented by, 402–3 nature of social provisions, 408 review of policies and programs, 414–19

National Social Appeals Board (Denmark), 121, 122

National Social Development Strategy (NSDS), Lebanon, 794–95, 795t, 801

National Social Security System (SJSN), Indonesia, 764–65

National Society for Prevention of Cruelty to Children (NSPCC), 146–47

national solidarity, in France, 174–75, 187

National Standard for Improving the Quality of Life of Vulnerable Children in Nigeria, 842

National Strategic Programme Plan of Interventions for orphans and other vulnerable children (NSPPI), Uganda, 915

National Strategy for Childhood and Motherhood, 2017–2022 (Egypt), 689–90

National Strategy for Elimination of Violence Against Children 2016–2020 (STRANAS

PKTA 2016–2020), Indonesia, 754–56

National Strategy to Promote the Interests of Children in 2012–2017 (Russia), 882

National System of Family Welfare (Colombia), 654

National System of Integral Protection for Children (SPINNA), 821

National System of Integral Protection of the Family (Mexico), 824

Nationwide Diagnosis of the Problem of Violence Against Children (Poland), 493

natural family environment, principle of preference of, 531

nature of social provisions in Australia, 29–30 in Brazil, 617–20 in Chile, 408 in Ghana, 716–17 in New Zealand, 39–42 in Uganda, 909–15 in Uruguay, 572–77

NAWONGO (National Association of Welfare Organisations and Non-Governmental Organisations), South Africa, 559–60

NCCM (National Council for Motherhood and Childhood), Egypt, 685, 688–89

NCIE (National Council for Intergenerational Equality), Ecuador, 670–72, 678

NCMS (National Case Management System), Zimbabwe, 929, 932–33

NCPA (National Child Protection Agency), South Korea, 317, 322, 327, 328

NCPR (National Child Protection Register), South Africa, 551–52

NEDPP (National Economic Development Priority Programme), Zimbabwe, 924–25

neglect in Australia, 28 in Austria, 52 in Belgium, 68–71, 72–77, 74t, 75t

in Brazil, 611, 617
in China, 626, 636
in Colombia, 653–54
in England, 143*t*, 149
in France, 181–82
in Germany, 196
in Israel, 241–42, 241*t*
in Italy, 267, 268*t*
in Lithuania, 476, 481–82
in Netherlands, 294–95, 295*t*
in New Zealand, 37–39
in Nigeria, 836–40
in Philippines, 856
in Poland, 489–90
in Portugal, 507
in Slovak Republic, 532*t*
in South Korea, 324–25
in Spain, 337*f*, 337–38, 338*f*, 349*t*
in Switzerland, 358–59, 358*t*, 359*t*
in United States, 384
neoliberalism, 667–68
NERP (National Economic
    Revival Programme),
    Zimbabwe, 924
Netherlands
    AMHK, 298–99
    arrangements for delivery of
        services, 307–9
    assessment and referral in, 298
    certified agencies in, 302
    Child Care and Protection
        Board, 299–302
    child protection measures in,
        297, 303–5
    child protection system in,
        overview of, 301*f*
    Juvenile Court in, 302
    outcomes of child welfare
        services in, 309–10
    out-of-home care in, 12*t*, 14*t*,
        305–7, 306*t*, 309, 310
    overview, 294–96
    police and Public Prosecution
        Department in, 302–3
    principles of child protection
        in, 296–97
    reporting in, 298
    services for maltreated children
        and their families in, 305–7
network care
    in Italy, 268
    in Norway and Denmark, 122
Newpin, 33
New Zealand
    bases of social allocations in,
        34–37
    child/parent participation in,
        963

child protection processes in,
    37–39
evidence-based practice in,
    42–43
family and child support
    orientation in, 964
family support services in,
    39–40
financing of child protection
    services in, 42
nature of social provisions in,
    39–42
out-of-home care in, 12*t*, 40–42
overview, 25–27
state response to cultural and
    religious diversity in, 961–62
NGOs. *See* non-governmental
    organizations
NHIS (National Health Insurance
    Scheme), Ghana, 716, 717
Nigeria
    child maltreatment in, 834
    child protection post-1986
        conference, 835–36
    child protection pre-1986
        conference, 834–35
    child protection system, 840–41
    common forms of child abuse
        and neglect in, 836–40
    evaluation of existing policies
        in, 845–46, 847*t*
    historical overview of programs
        and policies in, 841–45
    out-of-home care in, 12*t*, 843
    overview, 832–33
    state response to cultural and
        religious diversity in, 961
NOM (National Outcomes
    Matrix) framework, 104–5
No More Blame Game (England),
    140–41
non-governmental organizations
    (NGOs)
    in Argentina, 591
    in Australia, 32–33
    in Colombia, 656
    in Germany, 198, 205
    in Ghana, 719, 720
    in Greece, 273
    in India, 740–42
    in Israel, 252–55
    in Lithuania, 470–71
    in New Zealand, 40
    in Nigeria, 832–33
    in Norway and Denmark,
        117–18
    in Philippines, 857–58, 866–67
    in Russia, 892–93

in South Africa, 559
in Zimbabwe, 930–31
non-profit organizations
    in China, 632–34
    in England, 143–44
    in Italy, 268
    in South Africa, 559–61
    in South Korea, 327–28
    in Switzerland, 375
Nordic countries. *See specific*
    countries
Northern Ireland
    Brexit, impact on child safety,
        228–30
    child protection in Ireland
        versus, 217–19
    history of child protection in,
        219–22
    out-of-home care and adoption
        rates in, 12*t*
    overview, 216–17
    policies and programs in,
        226–28
    protection of migrant children
        in, 232–33
    technology, impact on child
        welfare in, 230–32
Norway
    confidence in government, effect
        on out-of-home care, 16–17
    Czech criticism of child
        protection in, 427–28
    decision-making bodies and
        involuntary interventions in,
        121–22
    family-service-oriented systems
        in, 113–16
    Guardian Council Act, 10
    in international context, 129–30,
        129*t*
    involvement of children and
        families in, 124–25
    living standards in, 5
    mandatory reporting in, 117
    municipalities, role of, 117–18
    out-of-home care in, 12*t*, 14*t*,
        116, 119*t*, 121–24
    overview, 112–13
    policy development in, 125–29
    rights orientation in, 957–58
    statistics on child protection in,
        118, 119*t*
Norwegian Center for Child
    Behavioral Development
    (NUBU), 128
NPAC (National Plan of Action
    for Children), 2005, India,
    734–35

NSDS (National Social
Development Strategy),
Lebanon, 794–95, 795*t*, 801
NSPCC (National Society for
Prevention of Cruelty to
Children), 146–47
NSPPI (National Strategic
Programme Plan of
Interventions for orphans
and other vulnerable
children), Uganda, 915
NUBU (Norwegian Center
for Child Behavioral
Development), 128

O

objectivity principle, 115
observational blind spots, in
France, 190–91
ODPE (local observatory of child
protection), France, 179, 186
Office for Standards in Education,
Children's Services and Skills
(OFSTED), England, 141–42,
144
OGCs (Child Guidance Centres),
Japan, 288–89
OICGCYP (Orphaned and with
Inappropriate Care Givers
Children and Youth Protection
Act), Iran, 780–81, 790
old age pension, South Africa, 545–46
O'Leary, P. J., 765
123 hotline (Iran), 787
online child sexual exploitation,
857
ONPE (national observatory of
child protection), France,
179, 186
ONPE/CREAI ARA assessment
method, 186
opeka departments (Russia), 884–85
open setting interventions
(France), 182–83, 184
Oranga Tamariki Act 1989 (New
Zealand), 26–27, 38, 39
Oranga Tamariki—Ministry for
Children (New Zealand),
37–39, 42
Organization for Child Protection
(ALI), 252
Organization of the Guardianship
of Minors (OTM), Portugal,
509–10
Orphaned and with Inappropriate
Care Givers Children
and Youth Protection Act
(OICGCYP), Iran, 780–81, 790

Orphan's and Custody Court
(Latvia), 452–53
orphans and vulnerable children
(OVC)
in Ghana, 716
in Iran, 780–81
in Nigeria, 842–43
in Russia, 877, 879, 880–81
in South Africa, 553, 554
in Uganda, 906–7, 908*t*
in Zimbabwe, 926–28, 930–34
Ostwald, K., 757
OTM (Organization of the
Guardianship of Minors),
Portugal, 509–10
Our Country Players program
(Egypt), 700
out-of-home care
in Argentina, 598*t*, 602
in Australia, 31–32
in Austria, 56, 57*t*, 63–64
in Belgium, 84–85, 86–87
in Brazil, 619–20
in Canada, 93–94, 105–6
care settings, in global typology,
949*t*, 965–66
in child protection versus family
service orientations, 944–45,
945*t*
in Chile, 403, 408–11, 410*t*
in China, 637–38
in Colombia, 659–61, 660*t*
cultural differences, effect on,
16–18
in Czech Republic, 424, 428–37,
430*f*
in Denmark, 116, 119*t*, 121–24
in Ecuador, 675, 676–77
in England, 143*t*, 149–51, 150*t*
in Estonia and Latvia, 455–58, 457*t*
in Finland and Sweden, 160–61,
163–64
in France, 177, 183–85
in Germany, 206–8, 206*t*,
209–10
in Ghana, 712
in Greece, 276–77
in Iran, 784, 786*t*
on island of Ireland, 220–22,
221*t*
in Israel, 241*t*, 246, 247–49, 251*f*
in Italy, 266–67
in Japan, 289–91
in Lebanon, 806
in Mexico, 825–26
national rates, 11, 12*t*, 14–15, 14*t*
in Netherlands, 305–7, 306*t*,
309, 310

in New Zealand, 40–42
in Nigeria, 843
in Norway, 116, 119*t*, 121–24
in Philippines, 867
in Portugal, 508–9
in Russia, 878–80, 880*f*, 884–85,
887–92, 888*f*
in Slovak Republic, 531–36, 534*t*,
535*t*
in South Korea, 327
in Spain, 346–47, 350*f*
in Switzerland, 373–74
in Uganda, 910–13
in United States, 386–90
outsourcing of service provision
in England, 143–44
in Italy, 269
in Lebanon, 805
OVC. *See* orphans and vulnerable
children

P

P2TP2A (Center of Integrated
Services for Empowering
Women and Children),
Indonesia, 760–61
PAEFI (Protection and Specialized
Care Service for Families and
Individuals), Brazil, 618
PAFAC (Project for Support to
the Family and to Children),
Portugal, 517
PAIF (Service of Protection and
Integral Care to the Family),
Brazil, 617–18
Palacios, J., 967
PARD (Administrative Procedure
of Restoration of Rights),
Colombia, 656, 657–62
parental rights
in Chile, 408
in China, 630–31
in Czech Republic, 435–37,
436*f*
in Ecuador, 674
in Germany, 197–98
in Italy, 264
in Netherlands, 304–5, 304*t*
in Norway and Denmark,
122–23, 124–25
in Russia, 885–86
parent/child as active agents, in
global typology, 949*t*, 962–63
Parent-Child Conflict Tactics Scale
(CTSPC) method, 566
Parenting, Prevention and Family
Support (PPFS) program,
Ireland, 223–24, 225–26

parent participation
  in Austria, 51
  in global typology, 949*t*, 962–63
  in Netherlands, 308–9
  in Norway and Denmark, 124–25
  in Switzerland, 369
parents, 1. *See also* corporal
    punishment; family support
    services; parental rights
  family empowerment, 435–37, 622
  inappropriate caregivers, Iran,
    774–75, 779, 780–81
  separation from children,
    reasons for, 5–6
  support measures in Austria, 54
  withdrawal of responsibility in
    Switzerland, 361–62, 362*t*
parents' rights orientation, 955–56,
    957
participation in decision making.
    See child participation;
    parent participation
Particular Institutions of Social
    Solidarity (Portugal), 517
Partnered Response pathway (New
    Zealand), 39
PATBM (Community Based
    Integrated Child Protection)
    programs, Indonesia, 766–67
paternalistic function of
    government, 1, 402, 446,
    450–51
Pathways of Care study
    (Australia), 34
patronage families (Russia), 888,
    889
Penal (Harm to a Minor or a
    Helpless Person) Law, Israel,
    243
penal code (Belgium), 69–70
perception of maltreatment, in
    Uruguay, 569
Pereirinha, J. A., 518–19
permanent care and guardianship
    orders, 32
Permanent Conference on Child
    Abuse (Belgium), 78
Permissive Collectivism, 946–48,
    947*t*
Permissive Individualism, 946–48,
    947*t*
Philippines
  bottom-up approaches in,
    867–69
  challenges for child protection
    in, 869–71
  child maltreatment and
    exploitation in, 854–57

conceptualizing child protection
    systems in global south,
    860–61
  governance and social policy in,
    857–60
  middle-out approaches in,
    864–67
  out-of-home care in, 12*t*, 867
  overview, 851–52
  situation analysis of children in,
    852–54
  strengthening child protection
    system in, 869–71
  top-down approaches in,
    861–64
physical abuse
  in Austria, 52
  in Belgium, 74*t*, 75*t*
  in Brazil, 610–11, 616
  in Chile, 412
  in China, 626
  in Czech Republic, 437–40
  in Egypt, 691–92
  in England, 143*t*, 149
  in France, 181–82
  in Germany, 196
  in India, 742–43
  in Indonesia, 749
  in Israel, 241–42, 241*t*
  in Italy, 267
  in Japan, 288
  in Lebanon, 799
  in Lithuania, 475
  in Mexico, 815–17, 823
  in Netherlands, 294–95, 295*t*
  in Nigeria, 834, 838, 847*t*
  in Philippines, 855–56
  in Poland, 488–89, 491–94
  in Portugal, 507–8
  of refugee and migrant children,
    282
  in Slovak Republic, 532*t*
  in South Africa, 545, 556–57
  in South Korea, 324–25
  in Spain, 349*t*
  in Switzerland, 358–59, 358*t*,
    359*t*
  in Uganda, 902
  in United States, 384
  in Uruguay, 566–69
physical health of children
  in Brazil, 609–10
  in Colombia, 653
  in Egypt, 691, 693–94
  in India, 734, 742
  in Mexico, 814–15
  in Nigeria, 841–42
  in Zimbabwe, 923–24

physical punishment. *See* corporal
    punishment
PIEC (planning, intervention, and
    evaluation committee), Israel,
    246, 256
pilot programs (China), 631–32
Pilotti, F., 401
PJJ (*protection judiciaire de la
    jeunesse*), France, 177
PKSAI (Integrated Child Welfare
    Service Model), Indonesia,
    760–61, 765–66
Plan Ceibal (Uruguay), 572
planning, intervention, and
    evaluation committee
    (PIEC), Israel, 246, 256
Plan of Action (Lebanon), 802
POCSO (Protection of Children
    from Sexual Offences) Act,
    India, 731, 742–44
Poland
  child/parent participation in,
    963
  definitions of violence against
    children, 488–90
  interdisciplinary teams and
    special support centers in,
    501–4
  out-of-home care and adoption
    in, 12*t*
  overview, 486–87
  scope of violence against
    children in, 490–95
  social provisions in, 495–501
police, role of
  in Chile, 407
  in Germany, 202–3
  in Lebanon, 809–10
  in Netherlands, 302–3
  in Nigeria, 840–41
  in South Africa, 549
Police Service, England, 144–45
policy framework of child
    protection
  in Chile, 400–7
  in China, 628–35
  in Denmark, 125–29
  in England, 138–45
  in India, 731–35
  in Lithuania, 470–74
  in Norway, 125–29
  in South Korea, 318–21
  in United States, 391–92
Political Constitution of the
    United Mexican States, 819
political context
  in Indonesia, 752–53
  in Iran, 771

political context (*cont.*)
  in Philippines, 852
  in Switzerland, 356–57
Pollitt, C., 218–19
pornography, child
  in Lebanon, 799
  in Mexico, 822
  in Philippines, 857
Portugal
  evolution of child welfare
    system in, 515–18
  indirect child protection
    measures in, 521–22
  juridical framework in, 509–11
  out-of-home care in, 12*t*, 508–9
  overview, 506–8
  reform of child welfare system
    in, 512–15
  social policies in, 518–20
  social responses in, 522–24
  social welfare and assistance
    in, 508–9
PoS (Programme of Support),
  Zimbabwe, 930–31
poverty
  in Argentina, 591–92, 601, 603–4
  in Belgium, 85–86
  in Brazil, 609
  in Canada, 95–96
  in Chile, 400–1
  in Colombia, 651–53, 655–56
  in Ecuador, 666–69
  in Egypt, 692–93
  in France, 175
  in Greece, 271–72, 274
  in Indonesia, 748–49
  in Italy, 262
  in Latvia, 449
  in Lithuania, 467–68
  living standards, 5–8
  in Mexico, 814–15
  in Norway and Denmark, 129–30,
    129*t*
  in Philippines, 853–54, 856
  in South Africa, 545
  in South Korea, 318, 325
  in Spain, 352–53
  in Uganda, 907, 908*t*
  in Uruguay, 569–70
  in Zimbabwe, 922–26, 928
PPFS (Parenting, Prevention and
  Family Support) program,
  Ireland, 223–24, 225–26
predictive risk modeling (PRM), 385
prevention programs
  in Chile, 412
  in Greece, 278
  in Netherlands, 297

  in Philippines, 866
  in Portugal, 522–23
  in Russia, 886–88, 894–95
  in Uruguay, 572
primary versus secondary
  prevention (Russia), 886–87
principles of child protection
  in Chile, 405
  in Finland and Sweden, 157–58
  in France, 180–82
  in Germany, 197–98
  in Indonesia, 755–56
  in Netherlands, 296–97
  in Norway and Denmark, 115
  in Slovak Republic, 531
private provision of child
  protection services
  in Finland and Sweden,
    166–67
  in Israel, 252–55, 257
  in Norway and Denmark,
    117–18
  in Philippines, 866–67
privatization
  in Chile, 400
  in Ecuador, 667–68
PRM (predictive risk modeling),
  385
probation and mediation
  programs (Czech Republic),
  433–34
Procurator of Protection (Mexico),
  824–25
professional parenthood (Slovak
  Republic), 533
professional training
  in Brazil, 622
  in China, 638, 643–44
  in Ecuador, 680–81
Program 3 Online (Portugal),
  523–24
programmatic child protection
  services, in Uganda, 909, 915
Programme of Support (PoS),
  Zimbabwe, 930–31
Prohibition of Child Marriage Act
  (India), 731
Prohibition of Female Genital
  Mutilation Act (Uganda),
  8–9
Project for Support to the Family
  and to Children (PAFAC),
  Portugal, 517
projet pour l'enfant (PPE), France,
  185
PRONAPINNA (Protection
  System for the Rights of
  Children), Mexico, 821

proportionality principle, 115,
  197–98, 201
prosecution
  in Belgium, 74–76
  in Germany, 202–3
  in Greece, 277–78
  in Netherlands, 298, 303
prostitution of children, 799, 857
Protection and Specialized Care
  Service for Families and
  Individuals (PAEFI), Brazil,
  618
protection judiciaire de la jeunesse
  (PJJ), France, 177
protection of at-risk children
  (Lebanon), 807–9
Protection of Children and Youths
  in Danger Law (Portugal),
  512
Protection of Children from
  Sexual Offences (POCSO)
  Act, India, 731, 742–44
Protection of Headless Women
  and Orphaned Children Act
  (Iran), 780
Protection of the Rights of the
  Child Law (Latvia), 450–51,
  453, 462
Protection System for the
  Rights of Children
  (PRONAPINNA), Mexico,
  821
protective system characteristics,
  949*t*, 962–67
Protocol for the Management of
  Child Abuse and Neglect
  Cases (Greece), 278
psychiatric services. *See* mental
  health services
psychological abuse
  in Brazil, 611, 616
  in Japan, 288
  in Lithuania, 476
  in Mexico, 823
  in Philippines, 855
  in Poland, 488, 491–94
  in Slovak Republic, 532*t*
  in South Korea, 324–25
  in Switzerland, 358–59, 358*t*,
    359*t*
Puao-Te-Ata-Tu (Daybreak) report
  (Australia), 35
public confidence in governments,
  16*f*, 16–17
public policies, in Portugal, 518–
  19, 521–22
Public Prosecution Department
  (Netherlands), 302–3

public prosecutor's office
(Belgium), 74–75, 83
punishment, corporal. *See* corporal
punishment

Q

Quebec Incidence Studies (QIS),
92
queen mothers (Ghana), 719

R

racial disproportionality in child
welfare (United States), 384,
390–91
RAF (Regulation, Assessment,
and Follow-up) method,
254–55
Rape Crisis Centers (Israel), 252
reception systems for refugee and
migrant children, 281–82
recurrence of maltreatment, 104–5,
211–12
Reference Centers of Social
Assistance (CRAS), Brazil,
617
referrals to services
in England, 137–38, 142–43,
143*t*, 146–48
in Germany, 203–8
on island of Ireland, 219–20,
220*t*, 222
in Israel, 244–45
in Japan, 288
in Netherlands, 298
refugees. *See* immigrant children,
protection of
regional variability in services
in Argentina, 602–3
in Russia, 878
registry of violence, Uruguay,
566–68
Regulation, Assessment, and
Follow-up (RAF) method,
254–55
rehabilitation of at-risk children
(Lebanon), 807–9
religion, 17
in Indonesia, 751–52
in Iran, 788–89
in Lebanon, 797–800, 811–13
in Nigeria, 835
state response to religious
diversity, 949*t*, 961–62
relocation of refugee and migrant
children, 281
removal of children by state, 10–11.
See also out-of-home care
in Australia, 30–32

in Estonia and Latvia, 455–58,
457*t*
in Mexico, 825–26
in Slovak Republic, 534
in South Africa, 550–51
reordering, institutional (Brazil),
619–20
reporting
in Australia, 27
in Belgium, 71–72
in China, 629–30, 637, 643
in Mexico, 824–25, 828
in Netherlands, 298
in Philippines, 869
in South Africa, 548–51, 556–58
in Switzerland, 368
in United States, 382
Reporting Code (Netherlands),
298, 311
Republic Act (Philippines), 861
requests for services, in Finland
and Sweden, 158–59
research on child protection
services
in Australia, 33–34
in New Zealand, 42–43
residential care
in Argentina, 598*t*, 602
in Australia, 31
in Austria, 55*t*, 56, 57*t*, 61–62
in Belgium, 84*t*
in Brazil, 619–20
in Canada, 93
in Chile, 403, 408–10, 414–19
in China, 637–38
in Colombia, 659–61, 660*t*
in Czech Republic, 424, 428–37,
430*f*
in Ecuador, 675, 676–77
in England, 146, 149–51, 150*t*
in Estonia and Latvia, 455–58,
457*t*
in Finland and Sweden, 166–67
in France, 183, 185
in Germany, 209–10
in Ghana, 712
in Greece, 276
in Iran, 784, 786*t*
on island of Ireland, 220–22,
221*t*
in Israel, 241*t*, 247–49
in Italy, 266, 267, 268*t*
in Japan, 291–92
in Lebanon, 806
in Lithuania, 474–75, 480
in Netherlands, 305–7, 306*t*
in Nigeria, 843
in Norway and Denmark, 122

in Philippines, 867
in Portugal, 508–9
in Russia, 882–84, 887–88, 888*f*,
890–91, 892
in Slovak Republic, 531–36,
534*t*, 535*t*
in South Africa, 554–56
in South Korea, 327
in Soviet Union, 447–48, 880–81
in Spain, 347, 351–52
in Switzerland, 373
in Uganda, 910–13
residential schools
in Canada, 97–98
in Japan, 290
residual welfare system (China),
628–29
resocialization programs (Czech
Republic), 433–34
response models (Canada), 100
restoration of rights, in Colombia,
654–62
restorative justice
in Czech Republic, 433–35
in Estonia and Latvia, 461
in Indonesia, 763–64
reunification, family. *See* family
reunification
revictimization prevention
(Brazil), 615–16
rights of children, 1–3
in Argentina, 597–600
in Brazil, 613–14
in Chile, 404–6
in Colombia, 650, 656–57
in Ecuador, 668
in France, 174
in Ghana, 713–14
in India, 729–30, 734–35
in Ireland, 225, 226
Kids Rights Index, 7–8, 9*f*
in Latvia, 450–51
in Mexico, 818–23
in Norway and Denmark, 114–15,
124–25, 126
in Philippines, 861–62
in Uganda, 905
rights of parents. *See* parental rights
rights orientation, in global
typology, 949*t*, 955–58
rights perspective (Chile), 404–6
Rights Protection Department
(RPD), Chile, 406–7
Right to Education Act (India), 731
risk assessment
in Australia, 27
in Austria, 51, 53–54
in Ecuador, 675–76

risk assessment (*cont.*)
  in Germany, 205
  in New Zealand, 38–39
  in United States, 384–85
  in Uruguay, 574
risk interventions (Spain), 337*f*,
  337–38, 338*f*
risk-oriented child protection
  system, 18, 113–14
Roma children, 426–28, 432, 541
Rotlevi Committee (Israel), 244,
  246, 255–56
RPD (Rights Protection
  Department), Chile, 406–7
RPJMN (National Medium
  Term Development Plan),
  Indonesia, 754
RSI measure (Insertion Social
  Income) (Portugal), 521
RUMI database (Spain), 347
Russia
  alternative care in, 12*t*, 878–80,
    880*f*, 884–85, 887–92, 888*f*
  authority on alternative care
    placements, 884–85
  community-based early support
    in, 886
  deinstitutionalization reform
    in, 882–84
  financing of child protection
    services in, 891–92
  limitation or termination of
    parental rights in, 885–86
  NGOs in, 892–93
  ongoing policy reforms in, 893–97
  overview, 877–79
  postsocialist-era conventions,
    laws, and policies in, 881–82
  primary versus secondary
    prevention, 886–87
  Soviet model of collective and
    residential care in, 880–81
  state agencies in, 891
Russia without Orphans program,
  884

S
Safeguarding Board for Northern
  Ireland, 228
Safe Touches program, 278
Satgas PPA (Women's and
  Children's Protection Task
  Force), Indonesia, 766–67
SCC (Swiss Civil Code), 360–63,
  362*t*
SCFV (Service of Coexistence and
  Strengthening of Bonds),
  Brazil, 617, 618

schéma départemental ("local
  diagram"), France, 179
Schmidt Committee (Israel), 249–50
Schönbucher, V., 357
Schone, R., 199*f*, 199–201
School Feeding Programme
  (Ghana), 716, 717
school harassment, in Mexico,
  816–17
schools
  in Chile, 413
  in Estonia and Latvia, 459–60
  in Germany, 203
  in Greece, 278
  in Japan, 290
  in Switzerland, 372
Scott, W. R., 751
SCrC (Swiss Criminal Code),
  363–64
SCYC (Support Center Youth
  Care), Belgium, 80–82
SDCs (Social Development
  Centers), Lebanon, 804–5
SDGs (sustainable development
  goals), 129–30, 129*t*
sector-responsibility principle, 118
SENAF (National Secretariat
  for Children's Rights),
  Argentina, 593
SENAME (Chile). *See* National
  Service for Minors, Chile
SEP (Social Emergency Plan),
  Iran, 785–87
Service of Coexistence and
  Strengthening of Bonds
  (SCFV), Brazil, 617, 618
Service of Protection and Integral
  Care to the Family (PAIF),
  Brazil, 617–18
sex offender registry (South
  Africa), 551–52
sexual abuse
  in Austria, 52
  in Belgium, 74*t*, 75*t*
  in Brazil, 610–11, 616–17
  in Chile, 412, 413
  in China, 626
  in Colombia, 653–54
  in England, 143*t*, 149
  in France, 181–82, 191
  in Germany, 196
  in Ghana, 710–11
  in Greece, 278
  in India, 728, 731, 743–44
  in Indonesia, 749
  in Iran, 781
  in Israel, 241–42, 241*t*
  in Italy, 267

  in Japan, 288
  in Lebanon, 799, 810
  in Lithuania, 476
  in Mexico, 822
  in Netherlands, 294–95, 295*t*
  in New Zealand, 37–39
  in Nigeria, 834, 836, 838–39,
    847*t*
  in Philippines, 856, 862
  in Poland, 490, 494–95
  in Slovak Republic, 532*t*
  in South Africa, 545, 557–58
  in South Korea, 324–25
  in Spain, 349*t*, 352–53
  in Switzerland, 357, 358–59, 358*t*,
    359*t*, 363–64
  in Uganda, 901, 902, 906
  in United States, 384
SFC (Survivor Friendly Clinics),
  Zimbabwe, 934
SGB VIII (social code book 8),
  Germany, 198–200, 203
Short-Term Economic Recovery
  Programme (STERP),
  Zimbabwe, 925–26
Signs of Safety (SoS), 224–25
Silman Committee report, 248
single registry system, in
  Zimbabwe, 937
Sino-Finnish Center for Child
  Protection Research, Fudan
  University (China), 634–35
SIPI (First Information System),
  Uruguay, 568
SIPIAV (Uruguay). *See*
  Comprehensive System for
  the Protection of Children
  and Adolescents against
  Violence, Uruguay
Situation Analysis of Child
  Poverty and Deprivation in
  Uganda (2014), 907
Sixties Scoop (Canada), 98–99
SJSN (National Social Security
  System), Indonesia, 764–65
slavery of children, 799–800, 837
Slovak Republic
  assessment in, 536–37
  child maltreatment in, 530–31,
    532*t*
  child/parent participation in,
    963
  child protection legislation in,
    527–28
  examples of good practice in,
    537–38
  issues in child welfare system
    in, 538–40

legal and policy changes in, 529–30

out-of-home care in, 12*t*, 531–36, 534*t*, 535*t*

overview, 527

regulation of child protection in, 8–9

substitute family care in, 531–36, 534*t*, 535*t*

SLPC&SG Act (Social-legal Protection of Children and Social Guardianship Act), Slovak Republic, 528, 529, 537–38, 540

smart phones, impact on child welfare (Ireland), 230–32

Smile of the Child (Hamogelotou Paidiou), 273

SMS text messages, 572

SNIC (Integrated National System of Care), Uruguay, 580–81

social, political, and cultural contexts of states, 949*t*, 955–62

social action, 179–80

social assistance
in Ghana, 716
in Mexico, 824

social code book 8 (SGB VIII), Germany, 198–200, 203

social conflict, 337–38

social-cultural differences, 17–18

social democratic welfare-state model, 112–13, 114, 156–57

social-demographic data (Italy), 262–63

Social Development Centers (SDCs), Lebanon, 804–5

social emergency centers (Iran), 787

Social Emergency Plan (SEP), Iran, 785–87

social exclusion, in Greece, 271–72, 274

social exigency, 80

social inequalities, in France, 176

social insurance (Ghana), 716

Social Insurance Boards Child Protection Department (Estonia), 451–52

socialist legacy
in Czech Republic, 423–25
in Estonia and Latvia, 444, 445–48
in Lithuania, 470

socialization of youth care (Belgium), 79–80

Social-legal Protection of Children and Social Guardianship Act (SLPC&SG Act), Slovak Republic, 528, 529, 537–38, 540

socially unsafe situations (Russia), 884, 886–87

social media, impact on child welfare (Ireland), 230–32

social mobilization (Nigeria), 841

Social Network (Portugal), 523

social orphans (Russia), 877, 879, 886

social pedagogical services
in Germany, 198–99, 208–9
in Switzerland, 372

social policy
in Philippines, 857–60
in Portugal, 518–20

Social Protection of Children Act (Slovak Republic), 8–9

social service agencies, Switzerland, 366–67, 375, 377

Social Services Act (SSA), Sweden, 157–58, 161–62

Social Welfare Act (Finland), 162

social welfare boards (Sweden), 165

Social Work Act (Slovak Republic), 8–9, 528

social workers
in China, 634–35, 638
in Ecuador, 675–76
in England, 145–46, 152
in Finland and Sweden, 164, 168–69
in Germany, 203–5
in Greece, 275
in Portugal, 509, 510–11
in South Africa, 547–48, 550
in Uganda, 919
in Zimbabwe, 936–37

socioeconomic context
in Argentina, 603–5
in Ecuador, 666–67
in Estonia and Latvia, 445–46
in Greece, 271–72
in Philippines, 853–54
in Zimbabwe, 922–26, 937

SoS (Signs of Safety), 224–25

SOS Baby Home (Greece), 278

SOS children's villages (SOS CV), 455

SOS Children Teams (SOS-CT), Belgium, 82–83, 85–86

South Africa
bases of social allocations in, 546–52
child abuse in, 545
financing of child protection services in, 559–61
foster care and kinship care in, 552–54

methods for delivery of provisions, 556–58

National Child Protection Register, 551–52

out-of-home care and adoption in, 12*t*

overview, 544–46

reporting in, 548–51

residential care in, 554–56

Southern European model, 507

South Korea
bases of social allocations, 323–26
child protection legislation in, 321–23
delivery of services in, 327–28
economic, policy, and cultural context in, 318–21
financing of services in, 328–29
out-of-home care in, 12*t*, 17, 327
overview, 316–18
rights orientation in, 956
Special Act on the Punishment of Child Abuse, 8–9, 317, 322–23, 326
types of interventions in, 326–27

Soviet Union, 445–48, 470, 880–81

Spain
autonomous communities, social provisions provided by, 341–43
bases of social allocations in, 336–38
best interest of the child principle in, 349–51
child abuse in, 347–49, 348*t*, 349*t*
child protection legislation in, 333–36
eligibility criteria in, 336–38, 337*f*
extreme poverty and violence in, 352–53
financing of services in, 343–45
local social provisions, 339–41
out-of-home care in, 12*t*, 14*t*, 346–47, 350*f*
overview, 332–33
statistics on child protection in, 346–47
unaccompanied minors in, 351–52

spanking. *See* corporal punishment

Special Act on the Punishment of Child Abuse (South Korea), 8–9, 317, 322–23, 326

special educational facilities (Soviet Union), 447–48

special foster carers (Japan), 291

special hearings (Brazil), 615–16

special institute professional
parenthood (Slovak
Republic), 533
specialized care
in Ecuador, 675–77
in Lebanon, 805–6
in Netherlands, 297, 306–7
in Spain, 339–41
Specialized Children Police Unit
(Nigeria), 840–41
specialized professionals and
caregivers (Chile), 417
Specialized Reference Center for
Social Welfare (CREAS),
Brazil, 618
Special Protection of Children
Against Abuse, Exploitation
and Discrimination Act
(Philippines), 862
Special Social Protection (SSP),
Brazil, 618–19
special support centers (Poland),
502–4
SPHPN (Women's Health and
Life Experiences Survey),
Indonesia, 749
SPINNA (National System of
Integral Protection for
Children), 821
SPPA (Child Criminal Justice
System), Indonesia, 763–64
SRO-approach (Austria), 60
SSA (Social Services Act), Sweden,
157–58, 161–62
SSP (Special Social Protection),
Brazil, 618–19
stages of institutional
development, 19–20
standardized practice responses,
223–24
State Audit Report (Lithuania), 479
State Child Protection and
Adoption Service
(Lithuania), 476–77
State Inspectorate for the
Protection of Children's
Rights (Latvia), 452
state response to cultural and
religious diversity, in global
typology, 949t, 961–62
state role in child protection, 1,
10–11
state social care centers (Latvia),
456
State Welfare Organization (SWO),
Iran, 773, 776–77, 783–88
statutory intervention
in New Zealand, 38–39

in Switzerland, 374
in Uganda, 909–15
STERP (Short-Term Economic
Recovery Programme),
Zimbabwe, 925–26
stigmatization of biological
families (Chile), 417
Stop Bullying: Intervention
Program for Elementary
Schools (Greece), 278
STRANAS PKTA 2016–2020
(National Strategy for
Elimination of Violence
Against Children 2016–2020),
Indonesia, 754–56
Strategy of Preventing Violence
Against Children for
2008–2018 (Czech Republic),
438–39
street children
in Brazil, 613
in Chile, 412–13
in Egypt, 695–96
in Ghana, 712
in Lebanon, 800
in Nigeria, 836–37
in South Africa, 555
in Uganda, 903
Strengthening Families program
(New Zealand), 40
structural conditions (Philippines),
853–54
structured non-institutional care
programs (Finland), 162–63
SUAS (Unified Social Welfare
System), Brazil, 617
subsidiarity, 117–18, 356–57, 360
Subsidization Law of 2005 (Chile),
405–6
subsidy payments (Portugal),
519–20
substance abuse (Egypt), 696
substantiation
in Israel, 244–46
in United States, 383
substitute family care
in Czech Republic, 428–31
in Estonia and Latvia, 455–58, 457t
in Slovak Republic, 531–36,
534t, 535t
substitute homes (Colombia),
659–60, 660t
supervised freedom for at-risk
children (Lebanon), 807–9
supervised visitation centers
(Israel), 251
supervision orders (Netherlands),
303–5, 304t

Support Center to Families (CAF),
Spain, 339–41
Support Center Youth Care
(SCYC), Belgium, 80–82
Support of Deinstitualization of
Substitute Family Care (2007–
2013), Slovak Republic, 530
Sure Start family centers
(England), 138–39
surrogate care system (China),
630, 637–38
surrogate mothers (Uruguay), 578
survival skills of children, 755
Survivor Friendly Clinics (SFC),
Zimbabwe, 934
sustainable development goals
(SDGs), 129–30, 129t
Sweden
adoption in, 966
aftercare services in, 164
care orders in, 163–64
confidence in government, effect
on out-of-home care, 16–17
decision making in, 164–66
eligibility criteria in, 159–60,
161–62
emergency placements in, 164
in-home services in, 162–63
mandatory reporting in, 158–59
organization and financing of
service provision in, 166–68
outcomes of child welfare
services in, 168–69
out-of-home care in, 12t, 14t,
160–61, 163–64
overview, 156–57
principles for services in, 157–58
regulation of child protection,
8–9
requests for services in, 158–59
Swiss Civil Code (SCC), 360–63, 362t
Swiss Criminal Code (SCrC), 363–64
Switzerland
cantonal legislation in, 364–65
challenges for child protection
in, 376–77
child maltreatment in, 357–60,
358t, 359t
core procedures and standards
in, 367–70
federal legislation in, 361–64
financing and delivery of
services in, 375–76
in-home services and alternative
care in, 373–74
institutional framework, 365–67
out-of-home care in, 12t, 14t,
373–74

overview, 356–57
services for children and
families in, 370–73, 372f
SWO (State Welfare
Organization), Iran, 773,
776–77, 783–88

T

Tamutienė, I., 478
Task Force for the Prevention
and Handling of Crimes of
Human Trafficking (Gugus
Tugas TPPPO), Indonesia,
766–67
taxation. *See* financing of child
protection services
Technical Implementation Unit
(UPT), Indonesia, 759–61
teen pregnancies, 818, 902
temporary care
in China, 638
in Colombia, 659, 660t
in Russia, 887–88
in South Korea, 326–27
TePSA (Indonesia Child Help
Line), 760
theoretical typology, 945–48,
947t
therapeutic abuse, 839
therapeutic services
in Germany, 201–2
in Italy, 266
in Uruguay, 574, 576
third-party permanency orders, 32
threatened children (Lebanon),
807
360°—National Program for
Children and Youth at Risk
(Israel), 250
threshold of endangerment, 199f,
199–201
Title IV-E funding (United
States), 393
top-down approach to child
protection (Philippines),
860–64
Toronto Humane Society, 96
traditional cultural practices, 17
traditional rulers (Ghana), 719
Trafficking in Persons Act
(Uganda), 8–9, 906
transition to adulthood, 102, 184,
293
Triple P program (New Zealand),
40
trokosi slaves (Ghana), 710–11, 714
Troubled Families Programme
(England), 142–43

Tuition Waiver program (Canada),
106
Tusla, Child and Family Agency
(Ireland), 218, 223–26
tutelage (Spain), 338f, 342–43,
346, 346t
24-hour intervention programs
(Chile), 413
tympanic perforation, in Nigeria,
838

U

Uganda
bases of social allocation in,
904–9
child maltreatment in, 901–4
financing of services in, 920
methods for delivery of
provisions in, 915–19
nature and scope of social
provisions in, 909–15
out-of-home care in, 12t, 910–13
overview, 900–1
regulation of child protection,
8–9
rights orientation in, 956
unaccompanied foreign minors
(UAM)
in France, 187–89
in Italy and Greece, 279–83
in Spain, 351–52
Unified Social Welfare System
(SUAS), Brazil, 617
UN/ILO Convention on the
Worst Forms of Child Labor,
708t, 715
Union for the Protection of
Children in Lebanon
(UPEL), 805, 809
United Nations Committee on the
Rights of the Child (2016), 181
Slovak Republic report, 538–40
South Africa report, 544–45
United Nations Committee on the
Rights of the Child (2018),
345, 351
United Nations Convention on
the Rights of the Child
(UNCRC), 1–3, 190–91
in Argentina, 587–88, 589–92
in Austria, 48–49
child protection defined in, 904
in Chile, 404, 405
definition of child maltreatment
in, 347
in Ecuador, 666
in Egypt, 685
in Estonia and Latvia, 450–51

in Finland and Sweden, 158
in Ghana, 706–7
in India, 730
in Iran, 773, 777–78
in Ireland, 225
in Israel, 243–44
in Italy, 263
in Mexico, 818–19
in Norway and Denmark,
114–15
in Poland, 486–87
in South Korea, 322
in Spain, 333
in Uganda, 900–1
in Zimbabwe, 928
United Nations International
Children's Emergency Fund
(UNICEF), 6
child inequality index, 129–30,
129t
poverty index, 129t
poverty in Greece, 274
report on Brazil, 611
study on Chilean child
protection, 414
study on violence in Uruguay,
566–67
sustainable development goals
index, 129–30, 129t
well-being index, 129–30, 129t
United States
adoption in, 966
child maltreatment in, 381–84
child welfare system responses
in, 384–90
disproportionality in child
welfare in, 390–91
history of child protection
policy in, 644
intervention threshold in,
963–64
out-of-home care in, 12t, 14t, 15,
386–90
overview, 381
policy context in, 391–92
rights orientation in, 957
service delivery and financing
in, 392–93
state response to cultural and
religious diversity in, 961–62
universal services, 157
universal welfare-system, 262
UPEL (Union for the Protection
of Children in Lebanon),
805, 809
UPT (Technical Implementation
Unit), Indonesia, 759–61
urbanization, 95–96

Uruguay
bases of social allocations in, 564–71
challenges for child protection in, 581–82
child maltreatment in, 566–68
child protection system in, 564–65
definitions of violence and maltreatment in, 565
family and child support orientation in, 964
financing of child protection services in, 579–81
legal framework in, 570–71
nature of social provisions in, 572–77
out-of-home care and adoption in, 12t
overview, 561–62
perception of maltreatment in, 569
poverty in, 569–70
principles of operation of SIPIAV, 566
services offered by INAU in, 577–79

V

Vaudreuil, M., 96–97
Victim Friendly System (VFS), Zimbabwe, 934
victimization studies (France), 181–82
Victims Assistance Act (VAA), Switzerland, 358, 364
victim support (Germany), 202–3
violation of rights, in Colombia
administrative process of restoration of rights, 657–62
restoration of violated rights, 654–57
situations of, 653–54
violence against children. *See also* child maltreatment
in Austria, 48–49
in Brazil, 610–11
in Egypt, 691–92
in Lithuania, 475–76
in Mexico, 815–17, 816t
in Poland, 488–95
in Spain, 352–53
in Uganda, 901–2
in Uruguay, 565
Violence and Accident Surveillance System (VIVA), Brazil, 610

VIRAGE survey (France), 182
volatile substance misuse (VSM), 696
voluntary participation and consent
in Finland, 162
in Sweden, 157–58, 161–62, 165
in Switzerland, 374
voluntary reporting (South Africa), 548–49
vulnerability of children
in China, 628–29, 632
in Uganda, 906–7, 908t
Vulnerable Children Act 2014 (New Zealand), 36

W

Wallonia-Brussels Federation (WBF)
child welfare services in, 82–83, 86
Coordination Commissions on Assistance to Victims of Child Abuse, 77–78
Decree on Assistance to Victims of Child Maltreatment in, 70–71
extent of child maltreatment in, 73–74, 73t, 74t, 75t, 85–86
judicial treatment of abuse and neglect, 76–77
out-of-home care in, 84t
overview, 67
Permanent Conference on Child Abuse, 78
wards of the state (France), 183–84
WCPUs (Women and Children Protection Units), Philippines, 866
welfare states, 16–17, 401, 587–88
welfare system
in Australia, 29–30
in France, 174–76
in Greece, 271
in South Korea, 319
well-being of children, 5–8
in Austrian child welfare legislation, 48–50
in Norway and Denmark, 129–30, 129t
in Philippines, 853–54
whangai system (New Zealand), 34
WHO (World Health Organization), 565, 861
WHO-UNICEF Lancet commission report, 129–30, 129t
witchcraft branding, in Nigeria, 840

withdrawal of parental responsibility (Switzerland), 361–62, 362t
Women and Children Protection Units (WCPUs), Philippines, 866
Women's and Children's Protection Task Force (Satgas PPA), Indonesia, 766–67
Women's Health and Life Experiences Survey (SPHPN), Indonesia, 749
Working Together to Safeguard Children (England), 135–36, 139, 141, 146–47
World Health Organization (WHO), 565, 861

X

X institution (China), 633–34

Y

Youth and Family Centers (Netherlands), 297, 305
Youth Centers (Uruguay), 579
youth crime prevention (Denmark), 125
Youth Protection Schools Act (Canada), 96
Youth Welfare Act of 1989 (Austria), 61

Z

0–24 cooperation (Norway), 128–29
Zimbabwe
challenges for child protection in, 936–37
child protection issues in, 935–36
child protection systems in, 926–34
financing of services in, 935
out-of-home care and adoption in, 12t
recommendations for child protection in, 937–38
socioeconomic context in, 922–26, 927f
Zimbabwe Agenda for Sustainable Socio-Economic Transformation (Zim-Asset), Zimbabwe, 925–26
Zimbabwe Programme for Economic and Social Transformation (ZIMPREST), Zimbabwe, 924